Canadian Health Law and Policy

THIRD EDITION

General Editors

Jocelyn Downie, B.A., LL.B., M.A., M.Litt., LL.M., S.J.D.
Canada Research Chair in Health Law and Policy
Professor, Faculties of Law and Medicine
Dalhousie University

Timothy Caulfield, B.Sc., LL.B., LL.M.
Canada Research Chair in Health Law and Policy
Research Director, Health Law Institute
Professor, Faculty of Law,
Faculty of Medicine and Dentistry
University of Alberta

Colleen M. Flood, B.A., LL.B. (Honours), LL.M., S.J.D.
Canada Research Chair in Health Law and Policy
Faculty of Law, Department of Health Policy,
Management and Evaluation
University of Toronto
Scientific Director of the CIHR Institute of Health Services
and Policy Research

LexisNexis®

Canadian Health Law and Policy, Third Edition
© LexisNexis Canada Inc. 2007
July 2007

Members of the LexisNexis Group worldwide

Canada	LexisNexis Canada Inc, 123 Commerce Valley Dr. E. Suite 700, MARKHAM, Ontario
Argentina	Abeledo Perrot, Jurisprudencia Argentina and Depalma, BUENOS AIRES
Australia	Butterworths, a Division of Reed International Books Australia Pry Ltd, CHATSWOOD, New South Wales
Austria	ARD Betriebsdienst and Verlag Orac, VIENNA
Chile	Publitecsa and Conosur Ltda, SANTIAGO DE CHILE
Czech Republic	Orac, sro, PRAGUE
France	Éditions du Juris-Classeur SA, PARIS
Hong Kong	Butterworths Asia (Hong Kong), HONG KONG
Hungary	Hvg Orac, BUDAPEST
India	Butterworths India, NEW DELHI
Ireland	Butterworths (Ireland) Ltd, DUBLIN
Italy	Giuffré, MILAN
Malaysia	Malayan Law Journal Sdn Bhd, KUALA LUMPUR
New Zealand	Butterworths of New Zealand, WELLINGTON
Poland	Wydawnictwa Prawnicze PWN, WARSAW
Singapore	Butterworths Asia, SINGAPORE
South Africa	Butterworth Publishers (Pty) Ltd, DURBAN
Switzerland	Stämpfli Verlag AG, BERNE
United Kingdom	Butterworths Tolley, a Division of Reed Elsevier (UK), LONDON, WC2A
USA	LexisNexis, DAYTON, Ohio

Library and Archives Canada Cataloguing in Publication

Canadian health law and policy / general editors: Jocelyn Downie, Timothy Caulfield, Colleen M. Flood. — 3rd ed.

Includes index.
ISBN 978-0-433-45221-8

1. Medical laws and legislation—Canada. 2. Medical policy—Canada. I. Downie, Jocelyn Grant, 1962- II. Caulfield, Timothy A., 1963- III. Flood, Colleen M. (Colleen Marion), 1966-

KE3646.C343 2007	344.7104'1	C2007-903088-2
KF3821.C36 2007		

Printed and bound in Canada.

FOREWORD

Health care, we are told, is the number one issue on the minds of Canadians. We have an array of studies, commissions, books and reports that reflect the extent of the debate.

This third edition of *Canadian Health Law and Policy* is a little different because it reflects not only the policy debates that have surrounded us all, but speaks as well to the reality that whatever "system" is in place, a number of core legal issues will always be with us: what are the legal responsibilities of practitioners, and the rights of patients, dealing with the most difficult and emotional questions surrounding informed consent, negligence and decision-making about death itself? These are questions that need to be analyzed. They will, necessarily, lend themselves not to "the answers", but to a range of further questions and debates.

All of us need to be wiser on these questions, and wisdom will come only from the kind of informed discussion that is to be found in these pages. With new technologies come even more difficult issues, that is, those that the political process has notoriously been reluctant to deal with: reproductive questions and issues around genetics, stem cell therapies and other new technologies. These pose the fundamental moral dilemmas, which of necessity will lead to political and policy debates and eventually legislation.

It is crucial that policy, and legislation, reflect the complexity of this debate. While lawyers are often accused of making things more complicated and troubled than they really are, there is no avoiding the details of this debate. Some might like a return to the easy certainties of another time, but it is clear to any thoughtful person that this is not possible. The clients of the health care system rightly demand more information, more choices and more options; the old world of "doctor knows best" is gone forever. At the same time, physicians and other professionals are wrestling with the dilemmas of how to offer the best possible care when they see governments and other insurers more preoccupied with money than with health. These issues pose legal as well as personal and political challenges.

We are constantly testing what is known as "law's empire", to borrow Ronald Dworkin's well-known phrase. It is clear that the *Canadian Charter of Rights and Freedoms*, whose 25th anniversary we celebrated this year, has extended the boundaries of the justiciable. It is equally clear that a profound change in public attitudes and expectations, as well as revolutions in technology, make a return to a simple past impossible.

The papers in this book are a vital contribution to a debate that can only become more critical and complex. There is no more room for snap judgments. Health care is too important to be left to the bumper sticker, and it is only right that rigorous legal analysis will be brought to bear on these vital questions.

The Right Honourable Bob Rae
May 2007

ACKNOWLEDGMENTS

Once again, our first and greatest debt is owed to the contributors to this collection for all their hard work. We thank them for their excellent and innovative contributions to health law and policy scholarship. They have made this an invaluable and enriching experience, and this is reflected in the scholarship found in the pages of this book.

We would like to thank all of the research assistants who helped with all three editions of the book. In particular, we would like to thank Greig Hinds and Sujith Xavier at the Faculty of Law, University of Toronto, who have done the lion's share of administrative work in putting this new edition together. We would also like to thank all of our Faculty and Institute colleagues who provide us with stimulating and supportive intellectual homes, our wonderful and hardworking administrative staff, and finally our students, who represent the bright future of health law and policy in Canada. Finally, we would like to thank our families, who make it possible for us to pursue our dreams.

CONTRIBUTORS

RON BOUCHARD

Ron Bouchard, Ph.D., LL.B., LL.M., was called to the Bar in 2000. Prior to graduate work he practised intellectual property law, with an emphasis on biotechnology and pharmaceutical patents. He has been involved in the prosecution, acquisition, financing, distribution and litigation of intellectual property rights, appearing before the Federal Court of Canada on both trial and appeal matters, and the Supreme Court of Canada.

Before entering law, Ron completed a Ph.D. and Post-Doctoral Fellowship in the area of ion channel biophysics and intracellular ion imaging. He worked for several years as a scientist, and has consulted extensively over the years on matters pertaining to technology commercialization, intellectual property and other policy issues relevant to government and the life sciences industry.

He is currently in the S.J.D. program at the University of Toronto studying drug regulation and innovation from the perspective of systems dynamics and complex adaptive systems theory. He is an External Reference Group Member for Health Canada's new Progressive Licensing Framework for drug approval and for the CIHR's Public Private Partnership initiative.

PETER CARVER

Peter Carver, B.A. (U.B.C.), M.A. (Toronto), LL.B. (McGill), LL.M. (U.B.C.), is an Associate Professor at the Faculty of Law, University of Alberta. He teaches in the area of Canadian public law, including constitutional, administrative, immigration and mental health law. Professor Carver has a joint appointment with the Faculty of Rehabilitation Medicine, which reflects his interests in health law and disability studies. Prior to joining the University of Alberta, Professor Carver practised law in Vancouver, worked with the Office of the Ombudsman of British Columbia, and served as a Member of the Immigration and Refugee Board.

TIMOTHY CAULFIELD

Timothy Caulfield has been Research Director of the Health Law Institute at the University of Alberta since 1993. In 2002 he received a Canada Research Chair in Health Law and Policy. He is also a Professor in the Faculty of Law and the School of Public Health. His research has focussed on two general areas: biotechnology, ethics and the law; and the legal implications of health care reform in Canada. He has published over 100 academic articles and book chapters and often writes for the popular press. He is an Alberta Heritage Foundation for Medical Research Senior Scholar and the Principal Investigator for several large interdisciplinary research initiatives. He has been a visiting scholar at the Hasting Center for Bioethics in New York, at the University of Houston's Health

Law and Policy Institute, and at Stanford University's Program in Genomics, Ethics and Society. In 2000, he was awarded the University of Alberta's Martha Cook Piper Research Prize, in 2002 received the Alumni Horizon Award and in 2004 received the University's Media Relations award. In 2006 he became a member of the Canadian Academy of Health Sciences.

BERNARD DICKENS

Bernard Dickens is the Professor Emeritus of Health Law and Policy at the Faculty of Law, cross-appointed to the Faculty of Medicine and Joint Centre for Bioethics. After qualifying at the English Bar, completing a Ph.D. degree in Law at the University of London and coming to the University of Toronto in 1974, he earned a higher doctorate (LL.D. degree) in Medical Jurisprudence. He has over 380 publications, primarily in medical law and bioethics, and many international collaborations. In 1990-91 he was president of the American Society of Law, Medicine and Ethics, and is currently a vice-president of the World Association for Medical Law. He has worked on several World Health Organization projects, particularly on human experimentation and organ transplantation.

TRACEY EPPS

Tracey Epps has an LL.B./B.A.(Hons.) from the University of Auckland, and an LL.M. and S.J.D. from the University of Toronto. Prior to undertaking doctoral studies, she worked as a solicitor with Cairns Slane and Buddle Findlay in Auckland, and as a consultant with IBM Business Consulting in Toronto. She is an active member of the International Economic Interest Law Group of the American Society for International Law and a lecturer at the University of Otago, New Zealand.

ELAINE GIBSON

Elaine Gibson is the Associate Director, Research and Education of the Health Law Institute and Associate Professor of Law, Dalhousie University. She is cross-appointed to the Faculty of Health Professions. She has an LL.B. with distinction from the University of Saskatchewan and an LL.M. from the University of Toronto. She is a member of the Barristers' Societies of Nova Scotia and Saskatchewan. Her areas of expertise include health law, privacy and negligence. Her research focuses on legal issues surrounding electronic health information and confidentiality, public health, medical malpractice, and mental health law.

JOAN GILMOUR

Joan Gilmour, B.A., LL.B. (Toronto), J.S.M., J.S.D. (Stanford), of the Bars of Ontario and British Columbia, joined Osgoode Hall Law School's faculty in 1990, after practising civil litigation and administrative law. She teaches Health Law, Legal Governance of Health Care, Torts and Disability and the Law in the LL.B. program. She developed and is Director of Osgoode's part-time Master's

Program specializing in Health Law, and teaches graduate courses on Professional Governance, and Legal Frameworks of the Healthcare System. She is past Director of Osgoode's Institute for Feminist Legal Studies, and past Associate and Acting Director of York University's Centre for Health Studies.

Professor Gilmour's research and publications in health law span some of the most debated issues in contemporary society. She recently completed a major study on the effects of tort law on efforts to improve patient safety and reduce medical error. Current research projects include an examination of legal and ethical issues in decision-making about health care for children, and a study of the interrelationship of disability, gender, law and inequality. She has acted as a consultant to Health Canada, and completed a study for the Ontario Law Reform Commission on assisted suicide, euthanasia and foregoing life-sustaining treatment. She has also completed studies on health care restructuring and privatization, professional regulation of complementary and alternative medicine, and the interrelation of poverty, health and access to justice.

MICHAEL HADSKIS

Michael Hadskis is an Assistant Professor in the Faculty of Law, Dalhousie University, and is the Acting Associate Director, Research and Education, Health Law Institute. He is also the Kermesse Scholar of the IWK Health Centre Auxiliary and in that role provides policy advice to the IWK Research Ethics Board and serves as a member of the Board. Michael also sits on the Dalhousie University Health Sciences Research Ethics Board. Dalhousie recently awarded Michael the Health Sciences Research Ethics Board Distinguished Service Award. He teaches health law courses at the Law School, and oversees and delivers teaching in the Faculty of Medicine at the M.D. and post-graduate levels. Additionally, he oversees the health law curriculum in the Faculties of Dentistry and Health Professions. His research interests include neuroethics and the regulation of biomedical research.

IAN KERR

Ian Kerr holds the Canada Research Chair in Ethics, Law and Technology at the University of Ottawa, Faculty of Law, with cross-appointments to the Faculty of Medicine and the Department of Philosophy. In addition to his work on emerging health technologies, bioethics and the human-machine merger, Dr. Kerr has published books and articles on numerous topics at the intersection of ethics, law and technology and is currently engaged in two large research projects: (i) On the Identity Trail, supported by one of the largest ever grants from the Social Sciences and Humanities Research Council, examining the impact of information and authentication technologies on our identity and our ability to be anonymous; and (ii) An Examination of Digital Copyright, supported by a large grant from Bell Canada and the Ontario Research Network in Electronic Commerce, examining various aspects of the current effort to reform Canadian copyright legislation. His devotion to teaching has earned him six awards and citations, including the Bank of Nova Scotia Award of Excellence in Under-

graduate Teaching, the University of Western Ontario's Faculty of Graduate
Studies' Award of Teaching Excellence, and the University of Ottawa's
AEECLSS Teaching Excellence Award. Dr. Kerr sits as a member on numerous
editorial and advisory boards and is co-author of *Managing the Law: The Legal
Aspects of Doing Business*, a business law text published by Prentice Hall and
used by thousands of students each year at universities across Canada.

ROBERT P. KOURI

Robert P. Kouri is Professor of Law at the Faculté de droit of the Université de
Sherbrooke, where he also served as Associate Dean of Law-Research and Director of the graduate programs in Health Law and Policy. After having obtained a licentiate in law, he went on to complete a Master's degree and a
doctorate at McGill University. In addition to being co-author of three volumes
on health law, *La responsabilité civile médicale* with Professor Alain Bernardot,
L'intégrité de la personne et le consentement aux soins with Professor Suzanne
Philips-Nootens and *Éléments de responsabilité civile médicale* with Professor
Suzanne Philips-Nootens and Dr. Pauline Lesage, he has published several articles in the fields of civil and health law. He has acted as consultant to the Department of Justice Canada, the Minister of Justice of Quebec, the Civil Code
Revision Office and the Law Reform Commission of Canada. He is also a
member of the Research Ethics Board of Health Canada.

WILLIAM LAHEY

William Lahey is an Assistant Professor, Faculty of Law, Dalhousie University.
From June 1, 2004, he has been Deputy Minister for the Nova Scotia Department of Environment and Labour. As of September 1, 2007, he will be Director
of the Health Law Institute, Dalhousie University.

TRUDO LEMMENS

Trudo Lemmens is Associate Professor at the Faculties of Law and Medicine of
the University of Toronto. He is associated with the Joint Centre for Bioethics
and the Centre for Innovation Law and Policy. He holds law degrees from the
Katholieke Universiteit Leuven (K.U.Leuven) (Cand.Jur., Lic.Jur.) and from
McGill University (LL.M. bioethics; Doctorate in Civil Law). Prior to his appointment in the Faculty of Law, he worked as a bioethicist at the Centre for
Addiction and Mental Health in Toronto and as a researcher at McGill University, the Université de Montréal, and the K.U.Leuven. He has been a member of
the Institute for Advanced Studies in Princeton (2003-2004), a visiting fellow of
the Royal Flemish Academy of Belgium for Science and the Arts (2006-2007),
and a visiting professor at the K.U.Leuven and the University of Otago (New
Zealand) (both in 2006-2007).

   Trudo Lemmens' research currently focuses on how law and regulation
contribute to the promotion of ethics standards in the context of medical
research and biotechnological innovations. With Duff R. Waring, he recently
published *Law and Ethics in Biomedical Research: Regulation, Conflict of*

Interest, and Liability (Toronto: University of Toronto Press, 2006). In addition
to various chapters in books on health law and bioethics, his articles appeared in
the *University of Toronto Law Journal*; the *McGill Law Journal*; the *Hastings
Center Report*; the *Journal of Law, Medicine and Ethics*; *Social Science and
Medicine*; the *Canadian Medical Association Journal*; *Perspectives in Biology
and Medicine*; *PLoS Medicine*; and other law, ethics and science journals. He
teaches courses on Medical Law; Research Regulation; Public Health Law;
Privacy, Property and the Human Body; Research Ethics; and Legal Ethics and
Professionalism.

ERIN L. NELSON

Erin Nelson is a graduate of the University of Alberta. She completed her
B.Sc.P.T. in 1991 and her LL.B. in 1995. After clerking for Mr. Justice John
Sopinka of the Supreme Court of Canada, she completed her articles at Witten
Binder in Edmonton. She then spent two years as Project Manager at the Health
Law Institute in the Faculty of Law before leaving for Columbia University to
pursue graduate work in health law. She joined the Faculty of Law in 2000, after
obtaining her LL.M. from Columbia University, and has since also obtained her
J.S.D. from Columbia (2007). Professor Nelson teaches tort law, health care
ethics and the law, and health law and policy. Her research interests include: the
interface of health care law and ethics, women's health, issues in reproductive
health, and feminist legal theory. She has published articles and book chapters
on a number of health law related topics.

PATRICIA PEPPIN

Patricia Peppin, B.A. (Hons.), M.A., LL.B. (Queen's University) was a researcher in political studies and a political advisor before studying law. After
being called to the Bar of Ontario in 1982, she worked in the Ontario Government in policy and administration in the areas of disability, guardianship and
rights. Since 1987 she has taught health law, tort law and drug and biotechnology law in the Faculty of Law at Queen's University and has been Director of
the Law program in the School of Medicine and cross-appointed to the Department of Family Medicine. Her research and publications have focused on the
construction of perceptions through drug advertising, inequalities in health research, liability and regulation of the pharmaceutical industry, and feminist
analyses of law. She is currently working with Australian and Canadian researchers on gender equity in clinical trials and is writing about the creation of
knowledge about antidepressants.

SUZANNE PHILIPS-NOOTENS

Suzanne Philips-Nootens is a physician trained in anaesthesiology and is a
graduate of the Université de Louvain (Belgium). She also pursued legal studies
at the Université de Sherbrooke and McGill University. Upon completing her
baccalaureate and Master's degree in law, she commenced teaching at the Université de Sherbrooke, where she is presently Professor of Law and director of

the Master's program in Health Law and Policy. Her research and publications deal with medical liability as well as various issues of modern medicine. She is co-author of two monographs, *Éléments de responsabilité civile médicale* (3rd edition) with Dr. P. Lesage-Jarjoura and Professor R. Kouri, *L'intégrité de la personne et le consentement aux soins* (2nd edition) with Professor R. Kouri, and co-editor of *La recherche en génétique et en génomique: droits et responsabilités* with B. Godard, B.M. Knoppers and M.-H. Régnier.

NOLA RIES

Nola M. Ries, B.A.(Hons.) (Alberta), LL.B. (Victoria), M.P.A. (Victoria), LL.M. (Alberta), is Adjunct Professor, University of Victoria, and Research Associate, Health Law Institute, University of Alberta. She teaches and consults in the areas of health law and health information and privacy. Her research work addresses public health law, legal issues in health system reform and regulation of genetics and biotechnology. She is co-editor of and contributor to *Canadian Public Health Law and Policy*, serves on the editorial board of the Canadian HIV/AIDS Law and Policy Review and presents and publishes on a wide range of health law topics. Professor Ries is a member of the Bar of British Columbia and has practised constitutional, administrative and human rights law.

BARBARA VON TIGERSTROM

Barbara von Tigerstrom is Assistant Professor at the University of Saskatchewan College of Law. She holds an LL.B. from the University of Toronto and a Ph.D. in law from the University of Cambridge, and has worked at the Supreme Court of Canada, the University of Alberta Health Law Institute, and the University of Canterbury. Barbara's teaching and research are in the areas of health law, public health law and policy, human rights, public international law and international trade law. She is the author of the chapter on tobacco control in *Public Health Law and Policy in Canada* and has recently published articles on the International Health Regulations, public health jurisprudence in Canada, and regulation of complementary and alternative medicine. Her current research projects focus on chronic disease prevention, therapeutic products regulation, and global disease surveillance and control.

TABLE OF CONTENTS

TABLE OF CASES

INTRODUCTION

Colleen M. Flood, Timothy Caulfield and Jocelyn Downie

As editors we are thrilled to present to you this third edition of *Canadian Health Law and Policy*. New editions often involve authors dusting off their old chapters and revising them to reflect more current developments. We have taken a totally different approach, including the addition of four new chapters and new authors on all but one existing chapters, and asking all carry-over authors to write on completely new topics. The result is a fresh new look at Canadian health law and policy by both leading and upcoming outstanding scholars in the field.

I. HEALTH LAW AND POLICY: CONTEXT

What is increasingly evident today, five years after the publication of the second edition of *Canadian Health Law and Policy*, is that health law, once the obscure component of tort law, has become very popular among students, academics and practitioners. Reflecting this, Canadian law schools are offering more and more health-law related courses. In addition to basic medical jurisprudence courses, many schools are now offering courses on health systems law and policy, health care ethics, mental disability law, reproductive and sexual health law, biotechnology law, conflict resolution in health care law, and other topics. In addition, there is an increasing popularity of health law within other disciplines, evidenced by the burgeoning of health law courses being taught in other disciplines, for example, in dentistry, nursing, pharmacy, medicine and management.

Health law literature has experienced a similar evolution. There are now entire journals and monographs devoted to the area of health law, while journals for a wide variety of health professions include articles on health law topics on a regular basis. The University of Alberta, for example, publishes the *Health Law Journal* (a formal law review publication aimed largely at academics and practitioners) and the *Health Law Review* (a less formal publication with shorter pieces aimed at a broader audience including health care professionals). McGill University has recently launched an online journal, the *McGill Health Law Publication*, an interdisciplinary project consisting of peer-reviewed scholarly contributions by academics and practitioners alongside an organic online database — a resource of recent developments in the field of health law.

The rise in prominence and popularity of health law is perhaps most visible in legal practice. With the onslaught of cases coming before the Canadian courts, there are increasing numbers of lawyers specializing in health law and many larger firms now have entire departments devoted to health law. It is also possible to practise solely within the area of health law. Given changing scientific knowledge, patients' demand for the latest treatments, technologies and drugs (which are frequently of high cost and questionable benefit), and increased awareness of the system's apparent shortcomings in terms of timely treatment and safety issues, legal practitioners are being called on to challenge the long-established legal rules of Canadian Medicare. Legal practitioners are also increasingly called on to examine (and challenge) government resource allocation decisions and governance decisions on the part of health authorities and hospitals. Furthermore, they are often consulted for legal advice by hospitals, governmental agencies and other health care organizations, or hired full-time to focus on the development and assessment of health policy. The SARS crisis, the West Nile Virus and the tainted blood scandal have also all raised issues of the governance and safety of our public health and health care systems, generating commission reports, inquiries, mass tort claims and sometimes criminal actions.

Law reform (broadly understood) has also been caught up in the health law revolution. One need only look to the legal challenges in front of the courts at the moment to realize the intensity of this trend. At the time of writing, there are three different legal challenges in three different provincial courts dealing with access to health care issues,[1] along with a challenge to federal regulation of direct-to-consumer-advertising on the part of drug companies[2] and a further challenge to federal regulation of advertising on the part of tobacco companies.[3] These challenges, coupled with *Morgentaler*, *Rodriguez* and *Arndt*,[4] for example, indicate the complexities and nuances involved in the health law reform that is taking place through the courts. In addition to all of this are the legal and policy repercussions of the 2005 Supreme Court decision in *Chaoulli*[5] where the province of Quebec has been required to revamp regulations preventing the growth of private health insurance. This is having a ripple effect in other provinces. This decision also resurrects the thorny question of whether section 7 of the *Canadian Charter of Rights and Freedoms* should include positive rights (to health care and other governmental services) as opposed to rights to be free from governmental intrusion in private markets.

We often tell our students that health law is a field that touches most people's lives. Most people know someone who has had a first-hand interaction with the health care system in which such issues as access to timely services, informed consent, malpractice, safety or allocation of resources were confronted. Think of an elderly woman needing a hip replacement, a cancer patient needing life-prolonging drugs not covered by her provincial government, or a friend deciding to have a test to determine whether he has the gene for Huntington's disease.

---

[1] *Flora v. Ontario (Health Insurance Plan, General Manager)*, [2005] O.J. No. 5482, 207 O.A.C. 330 (Ont. S.C.J.); *William Murray v. R.*, Action No. 0601-09319; *Cilinger v. Centre hospitalier de Chicoutimi*, [2004] J.Q. no 2058, [2004] R.J.Q. 3083 (Que. S.C.).

[2] *CanWest Media Works Inc. v. Canada (Attorney General)*, [2006] O.J. No. 4403 (Ont. S.C.J.).

[3] *J.T.I. Macdonald Corp. v. Canada (Attorney General)*, [2005] Q.J. no 10915 (Que. C.A.).

[4] *R. v. Morgentaler*, [1993] S.C.J. No. 95, 107 D.L.R. (4th) 537 (S.C.C); *Rodriguez v. British Colombia (Attorney General)*, [1993] S.C.J. No. 94, [1993] 3 S.C.R. 519 (S.C.C.); *Arndt v. Smith*, [1994] B.C.J. No. 1137, [1994] 8 W.W.R. 568 (B.C.S.C.), revd on other grounds [1995] B.C.J. No. 1416, 126 D.L.R. (4th) 705 (B.C.C.A.), revd on other grounds [1997] S.C.J. No. 65 (S.C.C.).

[5] *Chaoulli v. Quebec (Attorney General)*, [2005] S.C.J. No. 33, [2005] 1 S.C.R. 791 (S.C.C.).

Indeed, we all interact with the health care system and, in doing so, are touched by health law.

Health law is also a part of our everyday lives, as evidenced by the plethora of health-related stories in the media. The sustainability of Medicare, privatization and other issues central to health care reform; the genetics revolution; the debates over stem cell research, HPV vaccination of all young girls, assisted suicide, the legal status of the fetus, biotechnology, human cloning, and privacy and information technology; the health of First Nations communities; and the obesity epidemic that is sweeping Canada — these are all topics which have recently engaged the Canadian public through articles in newspapers and magazines, and stories on television and radio.

From this brief contextualization of health law it is evident that this is a dynamic field, spurred by scientific, social, economic, philosophical and political forces. Below we touch on a number of these in an illustrative, but not exhaustive, overview of some of the key forces shaping the field.

First, over the past decade virtually every province has had to re-evaluate how its health care system is organized and financed. In the 1990s, the system experienced significant financial shocks with a sharp decline in growth of public spending on health care in the first half of the decade, followed by a subsequent re-injection of public funding in the latter half.[6] Reduction in public spending was achieved through significant cuts to the hospital sector and reductions in the number of physicians, nursing and other medical professionals that were trained. The result has been an increased reliance on home care, drug therapies, and other forms of care that fall outside the protection of the *Canada Health Act*[7] and therefore involve more private financing. Reduction in medical manpower has put great strain on the health care system, resulting in increasing concerns about lengthening wait times and arguments that access-related problems can be cured only by further privatization. Although since the mid-1990s there have been significant government reinvestments in the health care system, we have not seen public confidence rebound.

Financial merry-go-rounds have strained relationships between all relevant stakeholders (*e.g.*, providers, the federal and provincial governments, industry, patients and citizens). They have also raised many health law-related issues. Have cutbacks in public funding eroded the legal standard of care? What information must be disclosed to patients about health care reform initiatives? What legal mechanisms can patients use to protect access to safe and timely public health care services? What processes or frameworks should be employed to ensure fair decision-making in terms of what is publicly funded and what is left to the private sector? What challenges to these processes should be allowed? As the privately financed sector grows in Canada, how should it be regulated to ensure that its growth does not unduly harm the quality, equity and sustainability values that have traditionally underpinned the Canadian health care system?

---

[6]   Carolyn Hughes Tuohy, Colleen M. Flood & Mark Stabile, "How Does Private Finance Affect Public Health Care Systems?: Marshalling the Evidence from OECD Nations" (2004) 29 J. Health Pol. 359.

[7]   R.S.C. 1985, c. C-6.

Second, although Canada has not experienced a "malpractice crisis" to the same extent as the United States, over the past few years the number of lawsuits and the size of individual settlements awarded by the courts have increased markedly. In addition, there has arguably been an increase in the number of high-profile negligence and malpractice cases — for example, class action suits against medical device manufacturers and wrongful life lawsuits where a parent sues a health care professional for the birth of a disabled child. More recently, in Quebec, a class action has been lodged by breast cancer patients claiming negligence on the part of hospitals (and on the part of the Quebec government — although the court would not certify this part of the claim) for failure to provide timely treatment. Is this increased litigiousness a progressive trend? How should the law respond to it? Should the law develop, for example, to allow more frequent class actions against governments *vis-à-vis* their decision-making in health care to improve accountability for the public health care system?

Third, science and technology continue to be dominant forces shaping Canadian society. For example, genetics research is moving forward at an incredible pace. This genetics revolution has already provided us with a greater understanding of human biology and disease, a growing set of clinical genetics services, an increasing number of genetically derived pharmaceuticals, and even the hope of gene therapies. Our children will know more about their genetic selves than any generation in history. Moreover, the biotechnology industry, which is largely fuelled by the recent advances in molecular genetics, is currently one of the fastest-growing sectors of the Canadian economy. However, despite the promise of tremendous scientific and medical benefits, deep ethical concerns about the ultimate implications of genetic technology remain (*e.g.*, concern over genetic discrimination, stigmatization and the emergence of a "new eugenics"). Can our governing legal and regulatory institutions keep pace with these technological advances and harness science in pursuit of the public good?

Fourth, there have been rapid advances in information technology. There is now the potential, for instance, to have all personal health information stored as an electronic health record. The hope is that this will allow complete patient information to be accessed almost instantaneously, improving patient care and reducing system costs. The data that exist in electronic health records will also be tremendously valuable to researchers and will undoubtedly be used to respond to the increasing interest in evidence-based medicine, public health issues and the broad socio-economic determinants of health. However, new information technologies have also created and will create further privacy and confidentiality concerns. Health information is among the most sensitive information that can be gathered about a person. Will the law be able to provide the necessary protection for individuals while still allowing the advantages of information technology to be realized? How should this balance be struck?

Fifth, the field of bioethics is rapidly evolving in response, in part, to the increasing influence of new perspectives. Feminist bioethics, for example, has challenged the traditional approach taken to many issues in bioethics. The laws that are grounded in traditions, such as our deep reverence for the ethical principle of autonomy, are implicated in these challenges and lawmakers and law reformers are listening and responding to these new voices. For example, in the area of stem cell research, feminist concerns about the treatment of women needed to produce the eggs necessary for stem cell research appear to have influenced lawmakers.

As these and other forces continue to shape contemporary health law, it will remain a fascinating, vibrant, intellectually and emotionally challenging field of study. This book seeks to introduce its readers to this field, to provide a strong foundation for further study, and to convey our sense of the excitement and enthusiasm about the future of Canadian health law and policy.

II. ABOUT THE BOOK — WHAT'S NEW?

This third edition of *Canadian Health Law and Policy* presents a completely new and fresh outlook on perennial issues of interest in health law and emerging new spheres of study. The new edition brings together current and emerging perspectives from across Canada and incorporates the latest developments in the legislation, case law, and ethical and policy analysis.

The new edition contains four broad thematic areas: Professionals; Regulation of Services; Specific Areas in Health Law; and Future Concerns. Chapters in the second edition on Children and Adolescents and Genetics have been eliminated, while the chapters on Consent and Reproduction have been collapsed into single units, allowing for the addition of four new chapters. We realize that readers will still find those earlier chapters of value but refer them to the second edition (keep it on your shelves!). The four new chapters in this third edition are: Regulation of Pharmaceuticals in Canada (Chapter 8), Public Health (Chapter 12), Emerging Health Technologies (Chapter 13) and Charter Challenges (Chapter 14).

In addition to adding four new chapters we have also taken the novel approach of asking that almost all existing authors write on new topics. For example, Bernard Dickens authored the chapter on Informed Consent in the second edition, and this time around, he is dealing with medical negligence. Similarly, Trudo Lemmens is co-authoring a chapter with Ron Bouchard on Regulation of Pharmaceuticals in Canada whereas before he co-authored a chapter on research involving humans. Joan Gilmour, Erin Nelson and Barbara von Tigerstrom are returning authors and they are also writing on different topics. Robert Kouri and Suzanne Philips-Nootens are the only authors writing on the same topic (Quebec regulation) and this is because the Quebec chapter was only introduced in the second edition and all of the other authors had previously had an opportunity to write a chapter for the first edition and then revise and update their chapter for the second.

The book opens with William Lahey, who provides an overview in Chapter 1 of the laws and policies that establish and maintain Canadian Medicare. The central question he considers is how the system, as legally constructed, both addresses and fails to address the critical issue of access to health care services and treatments. He looks at how the design and operation of the system addresses (or raises) concerns about the cost of health care, the ongoing financial viability of the system and the availability of resources for society's other priorities. He also explores the demand for greater transparency, procedural inclusiveness and accountability at all levels of the system, including decision-making that defines the boundaries between public and private health care. The fourth major theme he addresses is the relationship of the single-payer system to basic Canadian values of equality and liberty, particularly in light of the growing involvement of the courts and the centrality of these values not only to Medicare, but also to the rights and freedoms that are protected under the *Canadian Charter of Rights and Freedoms*.

Chapter 2, authored by Tracey Epps, examines the regulation of health care professionals and, in particular, how regulation is delegated from the provincial governments to the professional associations. The chapter analyzes the implications of the policy choices in decisions to delegate.

Bernard Dickens deals with medical negligence in Chapter 3, outlining the legal landscape of medical negligence and highlighting all of the important aspects of this still-critical area of health care law.

In Chapter 4, Robert Kouri and Suzanne Philips-Nootens examine the contours of health law in Quebec under the civil law system. The chapter describes the state of the law in Quebec relating to medical liability and provides a number of illustrations of the legal reasoning, which may or may not be analogous to solutions proposed under the common law but which are consonant with the spirit of the civil law. They also explore the major obligations inherent in civil law in the physician-patient relationship (the duty to be informed and the duty to treat).

In Chapter 5, Patricia Peppin takes the reader through the legal landscape of informed consent. She situates the issue within the current case law and uses these cases to extract the relevant and important doctrines that lay the foundations of this area of the law.

Health information, issues of confidentiality and access are dealt with in Chapter 6 by Elaine Gibson. She starts the chapter with a discussion of confidentiality and then examines ownership, custodianship and the right of access to one's own information. The *Canadian Charter of Rights and Freedoms* is noted as having a strong influence in this area, particularly with respect to criminal law. Next she examines consensual and non-consensual collection, use and disclosure of health information.

In Chapter 7, Michael Hadskis examines the regulation of biomedical research in Canada and, in particular, the challenges of distinguishing clinical practice from biomedical research. From this point, Michael goes on to examine the legal and extra-legal instruments that directly or indirectly regulate the biomedical field in Canada.

Trudo Lemmens and Ron Bouchard deal with the regulation of pharmaceuticals in Canada in Chapter 8. They review the regulatory framework within which drugs are approved in Canada, outline the steps that manufacturers must undertake to obtain approval of their products, and trace the changing roles of public and private actors in drug development. They also highlight how the domestic drug regime is formulated and influenced by the international regimes while at the time highlighting relevant policy concerns.

In Chapter 9, Erin Nelson looks at how reproduction is regulated and provides an overview of reproductive law and policy in Canada. She highlights contemporary issues and controversies by looking at public law concerns of contraception, abortion and non-consensual sterilization, while in private law she examines wrongful births, wrongful conception claims and tort duties owed by women to their fetuses.

In Chapter 10, Peter Carver succinctly and adroitly contextualizes the issues of mental health law in Canada by exploring the legal frameworks currently in place and discussing the challenges and conflicts that continually emerge in this area.

Chapter 11, by Joan Gilmour, looks at the legal issues surrounding end of life care. This chapter explains the law governing refusal of treatment by patients who are able to make their own decisions about health care, and the legal principles applicable to decision-making about life-sustaining treatment when patients are not competent to make such decisions. It reviews the criminal prohibitions on assisted suicide and euthanasia, and examines how those laws have been applied. It highlights areas where the law is unclear or contentious, and indicates issues requiring additional clarification or reform.

In Chapter 12, Barbara von Tigerstrom looks at the law on public health. Public health law focuses on governmental powers and responsibilities in times of emergency and how regulatory frameworks are exercised. In addition to focusing on these aspects, von Tigerstrom pays particular attention to restrictions on personal freedoms, the role of governments and collective decision-making in confronting the risks of contemporary society.

In Chapter 13, Ian Kerr and Timothy Caulfield examine emerging health technologies (subsuming in this the chapter on genetics that appeared in the second edition). They focus on areas such as the Human Genome Project, Radio Frequency Identification and stem cell research, and nanotechnology. They also highlight how, through commercialization, issues associated with science and technology are transferred from a science-based milieu to the general public.

The final chapter, by Nola Ries, discusses ways in which the *Canadian Charter of Rights and Freedoms* may be used to challenge various aspects of health care delivery and regulation in Canada. The Charter is relevant to a wide range of health law topics — reproduction, mental health, public health and end of life decisions, to name just a few — and may be used to challenge various laws or government powers that impact individual rights and freedoms. Indeed, many laws that aim to achieve some health goal have been challenged under the Charter, and examples of the types of laws that may implicate Charter rights include: mental health laws and public health laws that authorize involuntary treatment of patients; laws restricting the activities of health care professionals; and laws that regulate foods, drugs and tobacco. Many of these topics are discussed in detail elsewhere in this book, so Chapter 14 focuses primarily on the use of Charter challenges to influence the allocation of health care resources and the structure of our publicly insured health care system.

From this brief summary of the chapters included in this third edition, it is evident that we have brought together some of the strongest academic voices within the field of health law. Regrettably, we have not been able to include all of the leading scholars in health law and policy in Canada — there are simply too few chapters to go around. Rest assured, however, that they will (re)appear in later editions. We were also not able to cover all areas of interest to health law and policy scholars; however, we have been able to identify and shed light on some of the most critical and important issues in health law facing us in 2007 and likely into the second decade of this new millennium. The editors have not sought to standardize the contributions. The diversity of topics discussed in the chapters illustrates the variety of styles and perspectives. Some chapters are quite doctrinal in approach, while others are policy oriented. The diversity of styles, views expressed and topics covered in this edition reflects health law's diversity as such and its tendency to grow and expand without restrictions.

III. CONCLUSION

It has been an enormous privilege and pleasure to work with our colleagues across the country on this third edition. We thank them for their scholarly contributions and their willingness to put their time and energy into this text. We hope that this edition, with fresh perspectives on core topics and the identification of new areas of scholarly pursuit, will not only be useful to instructors as a text for health law courses, but will also serve as a valuable guide to readers navigating the muddy waters of this still relatively new and constantly evolving field. We also hope that this book may inspire new scholars to take up health law and policy as an area of research and that these scholars will join us to tackle, debate, theorize and advance understanding in this exciting, challenging and rewarding field.

Chapter 1

MEDICARE AND THE LAW:
CONTOURS OF AN EVOLVING RELATIONSHIP*

William Lahey

I. INTRODUCTION

This chapter is about the role of law in the creation and operation of the Canadian health care system and the possible role of law in the evolution of that system. It is particularly about the relationship between law and the quasi-national program of public health insurance known as Medicare.[1] Accordingly, it

---

* This chapter is a revised version of a chapter previously published as "Chapter 2: The Legal Foundations of Canada's Health Care System", in Jocelyn Downie, Karen McEwen & William MacInnis, eds., *Dental Law in Canada* (Markham, ON: LexisNexis Butterworths, 2004), 29-90. The views expressed are solely those of the author. The research assistance of Scott Nesbitt and Mary-Elizabeth Walker and the helpful editing of Colleen Flood are gratefully acknowledged. Thank you Jocelyn Downie and Peter Oliver for your helpful comments.

[1] Readers who wish to pursue the topic more broadly will find valuable context in the extensive literature that is available on Canadian Medicare. This literature includes M.B. Decter, *Four Strong Winds: Understanding the Growing Challenges to Health Care* (Toronto: Stoddart, 2000); Nuala P. Kenny, *What Good is Health Care? Reflections on the Canadian Experience* (Ottawa: CHA Press, 2002); Lawrie McFarlane & Carlos Prado, *The Best Laid Plans: Health Care's Problems and Prospects* (Montreal & Kingston: McGill-Queen's University Press, 2002); and C. Tuohy, *Accidental Logics: The Dynamics of Change in the Health Care Arena in the United States, Britain and Canada* (New York: Oxford University Press, 1999). It also includes the reports produced by two recent national reviews of Canadian Medicare, one by the Royal Commission that was carried out by Roy Romanow, Q.C., and the other by a Senate committee chaired by Senator Michael Kirby: see Commission on the Future of Health Care in Canada, *Building on Values: The Future of Health Care in Canada — Final Report* (Ottawa: Commission on the Future of Health Care in Canada, 2002), online: <http://www.hc-sc.gc.ca/english/care/romanow/hcc0086.html>, and see, Senate Standing Committee on Social Affairs, Science and Technology, *The Health of Canadians — The Federal Role — Volume Six — Recommendations for Reform* (Ottawa: Senate Standing Committee on Social Affairs, Science and Technology, 2002), online: <http://www.parl.gc.ca/37/2/parlbus/commbus/senate/com-e/SOCI-E/rep-e/repoct02vol6-e.htm>. There is a growing literature on the role of the courts in shaping Canadian health system policy: see, for example, various of the chapters in Colleen M. Flood, ed., *Just Medicare: What's In, What's Out, How We Decide* (Toronto: University of Toronto Press, 2006) and in Colleen M. Flood, Kent Roach & Lorne Sossin, eds., *Access to*

is about the branches of Canadian law that answer the basic questions of how the provision of health care services is financed and how the delivery of those services is organized, managed, regulated and governed.

In Canada, these questions lead directly to a discussion of the *Canada Health Act*.[2] Along with the laws, policies and administrative systems of the provinces and territories that operationalize its general principles, this legislation is the legal foundation for the distinguishing characteristic of the Canadian health care system. This is the single-payer system through which all Canadians are promised uniform and universal access to a comprehensive range of physician and hospital services at public expense.

The study of the single-payer system by legal scholars is no longer in its infancy. Yet, health system law is still a relatively new branch of academic health law, probably because it has not been extensively litigated. It has been law for politicians, bureaucrats and administrators, rather than for lawyers and judges. As a result, it has been somewhat customary for those who write on the system from a legal perspective to explain the relevance and importance of law and of legal analysis to the broad issues of public policy that arise when Medicare is under discussion.[3] It is no longer necessary to begin this kind of chapter with that kind of explanation. On June 9, 2005, the Supreme Court of Canada dropped a bombshell into Canada's ongoing debate on the future of Medicare. In *Chaoulli v. Quebec*,[4] it ruled by a 4:3 majority that a Quebec law that prohibited contracts of private insurance applying to services available through public insurance, was unconstitutional. Media and others jumped to the conclusion that the court had sided with those who advocate privatization to solve Medicare's difficulties, particularly the problem of waiting times.[5] For some, it seemed that the court was not only saying that privatization was constitutionally permissible. It was saying that greater privatization was constitutionally mandatory.

Some experts in constitutional law have been able to say that they saw this clash between the courts and Medicare coming ever since Canada adopted an entrenched bill of rights in 1982.[6] But most experts would have to admit that the

---

Care, Access to Justice: The Legal Debate Over Private Health Insurance in Canada (Toronto: University of Toronto Press, 2005).

[2] *Canada Health Act*, R.S.C. 1985, c. C-6.

[3] Canadian Bar Association Task Force on Health Care, *What's Law Got to Do With It? Health Reform in Canada* (Ottawa: Canadian Bar Association, 1994); and Colleen M. Flood, "Chapter 1: The Anatomy of Medicare" in Jocelyn Downie, Timothy Caulfield & Colleen M. Flood, eds., *Canadian Health Law and Policy*, 2nd ed. (Markham, ON: LexisNexis Butterworths, 2002), 1 at 1-2.

[4] *Chaoulli v. Quebec (Attorney General)*, [2005] S.C.J. No. 33, [2005] 1 S.C.R. 791 (S.C.C.).

[5] See, for example, Gregory P. Marchildon, "The Chaoulli case: A Two-Tier Magna Carta?" (2005) 8:4 Healthcare Quarterly 49, and Lawrie McFarlane, "Supreme Court slaps for-sale sign on Medicare" (2005) 173 C.M.A.J. 269.

[6] *Canadian Charter of Rights and Freedoms*, Part I of the *Constitution Act, 1982*, being Schedule B to the *Canada Act 1982* (U.K.), 1982, c. 11. Although much of the commentary on *Chaoulli* is focused on the reliance by three of the majority judges on the Canadian Charter, the case was actually decided under Quebec's *Charter of Human Rights and Freedoms*, R.S.Q., c. C-12. See Allan C. Hutchinson, "'Condition Critical': The Constitution and Health Care", and Andrew

result in *Chaoulli* came as a surprise. Dr. Chaoulli and his co-plaintiff, Mr. Zeliotis, had lost in the Quebec Court of Appeal and at trial.[7] Their claim called upon the court to strike a blow against the single-payer system, a distinctive principle of Canada's most cherished social program. This seemed strongly against the grain of the court's tendency to be deferential to governments in matters of complex social policy, particularly in the design and delivery of large social programs where judicially imposed changes can carry wide-ranging implications.[8] Judicial intervention into the highly contentious debate over health care privatization seemed especially unlikely, given the iconic status of Medicare and of the *Canada Health Act*.

In defying these expectations, the majority judges used non-deferential language in criticizing Canadian governments for their management of Medicare. Whatever *Chaoulli* means for Medicare's future, it is clear that the law will matter, possibly a great deal, to the shape of that future. It will increasingly matter in different ways than it has in the past. No longer will law be primarily limited to an instrumental role, being the vehicle through which government decisions that are made on policy and political grounds are implemented. Particularly but not only through the lens of constitutional law, law will be an increasingly important influence and constraint on that decision-making. Likewise, it seems likely that in future the relevance of law to the organization of the health care system may not be as limited as it has been to establishing Medicare's general framework, with the details left to be fleshed out through political, administrative and clinical decision-making processes that are enabled by statute law. Instead, *Chaoulli* sends the message that law from outside the health care system will increasingly have system-wide impact through judicial intervention at the patient level, where decisions on the general design and functioning of Medicare have their impact on the lives of Canadians and their families. We can therefore expect to see the influence that legislative law has always had on Medicare from above supplemented and challenged by the growing influence of judicial law operating from below.

Thus, it is now clearer than it has ever been that health system law is not only an outcome of the political and policy processes that have produced and maintained Medicare. It is becoming an input into those processes of growing significance. Health law scholarship must embrace health system law just as it embraces more traditional subjects, such as medical malpractice law or professional regulation law. Equally, it is clear that health policy scholars must increasingly incorporate the significance of law and of the courts into their analysis and prescriptions for policy-making in Canadian health care. Conversely, if courts are to become increasingly active in health system issues, it is vitally

---

Petter, "Wealthcare: The Politics of the Charter Re-visited", in Colleen M. Flood, Kent Roach & Lorne Sossin, eds., *Access to Care, Access to Justice: The Legal Debate Over Private Health Insurance in Canada* (Toronto: University of Toronto Press, 2005) at 101 and 116, respectively.

[7] *Chaoulli c. Québec (Procureur général)*, [2000] J.Q. no. 479 (Que. S.C.), affd [2002] J.Q. no. 759 (Que. C.A.). Copies of these lower court decisions and of briefs and related materials are available at: <http://www.utoronto.ca/healthlaw/>.

[8] Numerous examples could be cited but one that most stands out in contrast to *Chaoulli* is *Gosselin v. Quebec (Attorney General)*, [2002] S.C.J. No. 85, [2002] 4 S.C.R. 429 (S.C.C.).

important for health system lawyers to be conversant with other disciplines, including economics, political science and health services administration.

This chapter will develop some broader themes as a means to understanding and evaluating the influence that law, particularly through adjudicative processes, is having and may come to have on Medicare's future. One of these is how the system, as legally constructed, both addresses and fails to address the central question of the access of Canadians to health care services and treatments. Another is the question of how the design and operation of the system addresses (or raises) concerns about the cost of health care, the ongoing financial viability of the system and the availability of resources for society's other priorities. A third revolves around the demand for greater transparency, procedural inclusiveness and accountability at all levels of the system, including on decision-making that defines the boundaries between public and private health care. A fourth is the relationship of the single-payer system to basic Canadian values of equality and liberty, particularly in light of the growing involvement of the courts and the centrality of these values not only to Medicare but also to the rights and freedoms that are protected under the *Canadian Charter of Rights and Freedoms*.

The balance of this chapter is divided into four parts. Part I aims to put the single-payer system into context. It does so by providing basic information that is critical to understanding the adoption of the single-payer system and to evaluating its continuing rationale and viability. Canadian health care spending, the health status of Canadians, some key aspects of the performance of the Canadian health care system, the basic organizational features of the systems that deliver service and the basic concepts and dynamics of health care insurance are each discussed.

With this background in place, Part II turns to the main concern of the chapter, the creation, operation and enforcement of the single-payer system. It begins with discussions of the role played by Canada's federal constitution in the design of the *Canada Health Act* and of the process of historical development that culminated in the Act's adoption and that continues to evolve through the dynamics of the federal-provincial process. It then focuses on unpacking the requirements that the Act places on the provinces in exchange for their eligibility for federal health funding. Part II then considers the implementation and enforcement of the *Canada Health Act* by overviewing the provincial laws and administrative systems that deliver public health insurance to Canadians, by outlining the extent of provincial compliance and of non-compliance with its requirements, and by then contrasting the lacklustre response of the federal government with the growing willingness of Canadians to use the courts both to protect, to extend and to challenge the essential premises of Medicare.

This leads to a discussion in Part III of programs of reform proposed in the various reports recently completed at both the provincial and federal levels, as well as in other forums. Part IV then offers some brief concluding remarks.

II. GETTING ORIENTED: SOME BASIC FACTS AND CONCEPTS

A. WHAT AND WHO IT COSTS — HEALTH CARE SPENDING IN CANADA

Total annual health care spending in Canada is now roughly $140 billion.[9] This represents 10.4 per cent of Gross Domestic Product (GDP) and equates to $4,411 per Canadian, putting Canada near the top in international comparisons of health care spending.[10] It is significantly behind the United States (which spends the most by far) and also behind countries such as Germany, Switzerland, and Norway. But Canada spends more than most other countries, though it spends roughly in the middle of the range between the highest and lowest spending OECD countries.[11]

Spending on health care is not the same across the country — in fact, it varies significantly. In 2005, it ranged at the low end from $3,900 per person in Quebec and $4,100 per person in Prince Edward Island to $4,800 per person at the high end in Alberta and Manitoba. Per capita differences in public funding follow the same pattern, with lower rates of spending in the east than prevail in the rest of the country.

Roughly 70 per cent of all Canadian spending on health care is public spending, with the balance obviously coming from private sources, mostly through private insurance. Through most of the 1990s, the percentage of private spending was growing due to the increased importance of services (including home care and prescription drugs) that are outside Medicare, and due also to the policy of financial restraint that all provincial governments followed through

---

[9] Canadian Institute for Health Information, *Health Care in Canada, 2006* (Ottawa: Canadian Institute for Health Information, 2006) at 5, online: <http://secure.cihi.ca/cihiweb/products/hcic2006_e.pdf>. The number given by CIHI for the year 2000 was $95 billion: see Canadian Institute for Health Information, *Health Care in Canada 2001* (Ottawa: Canadian Institute for Health Information, 2001) at xiv.

[10] Canadian Institute for Health Information, *Health Care in Canada, 2006* (Ottawa: Canadian Institute for Health Information, 2006), at 5. See also, Commission on the Future of Health Care in Canada, *Building on Values: The Future of Health Care in Canada — Final Report* (Ottawa: Commission on the Future of Health Care in Canada, 2002), online: <http://www.hc-sc.gc.ca/english/care/romanow/hcc0086.html>, and Canadian Institute for Health Information, *Health Care in Canada 2001* (Ottawa: Canadian Institute for Health Information, 2001) at xiv.

[11] The information in this and in the following paragraphs is taken from the following sources: Commission on the Future of Health Care in Canada, *Building on Values: The Future of Health Care in Canada — Final Report* (Ottawa: Commission on the Future of Health Care in Canada, 2002) at 4-6, 24-27, and 32-43; Senate Standing Committee on Social Affairs, Science and Technology, *The Health of Canadians — The Federal Role — Interim Report: Volume One — The Story So Far* (Ottawa: Senate Standing Committee on Social Affairs, Science and Technology, 2001) at 63-69, and 94, online: <http://www.parl.gc.ca/37/1/parlbus/commbus/senate/com-e/soci-e/rep-e/repintmar01-e.htm>; and Canadian Institute for Health Information, *Health Care in Canada, 2006* (Ottawa: Canadian Institute for Health Information, 2006) at 5. See also, Canadian Institute for Health Information, *National Health Expenditures Trends, 1975-2001* (Ottawa: Canadian Institute for Health Information, 2001).

most of that decade. In more recent years however, governments have reinvested in health care in an effort to restore stability and confidence in a system that was traumatized by the earlier restraint. In percentage terms, public spending has regained the ground lost to private sources.

The programs and services included in Medicare (hospital and physician services) account for over 40 per cent of total health care spending, and for more than half of all public spending. Virtually the total cost of these services is paid for in Canada by government. But Canadian governments also spend $26 billion on other health care services, a figure equating to roughly 25 per cent of total spending. A large proportion of this non-medicare spending is for home care, long-term care and prescription drugs. Spending in each of these other areas (overall and by governments) has increased steeply over the past decade or more.[12] Thus, whereas spending on Medicare represented 77 per cent of total provincial health spending in 1975, it represented 63 per cent of total provincial health spending in 2001.

The overall rate of growth in health care spending is often described as an existing or impending crisis, particularly when the aging of the population is taken into account. The Commission on the Future of Health Care in Canada (the Romanow Commission) found that since Medicare's national implementation in the early 1970s, health care spending in Canada has grown at an average rate that is 2.5 per cent higher than the growth rate of the Canadian economy. While this rate of growth is fairly comparable to what has been experienced by other health care systems in the developed world, the rate of growth in health care spending in the United States, which relies primarily on private insurance financing, has been significantly higher during the same time period. Before Canada's adoption of medicare, it had a rate of spending growth that more closely tracked the American one. Also important is the fact that total health care spending as a percentage of GDP is now just above its previous peak of 10.2 per cent in 1992. Facts such as these led the Standing Senate Committee on Social Affairs, Science and Technology (the Kirby Committee) to conclude that one of the myths about the Canadian system was that growth in spending was out of control.[13]

Yet, spending growth that is 2.5 per cent higher than economic growth poses a significant fiscal challenge for Canadians and their governments, particularly for provincial and territorial governments. Adjusting for inflation, per capita provincial spending on health care rose from $1,200 to $2,100 between 1975 and 2001. Health care spending that accounted for 28 per cent of provincial spending in the period 1974 to 1978, accounted for 35.4 per cent of provincial

---

[12]   Romanow reported prescription drug costs as rising from 6 per cent of health care spending in 1975 to 12 per cent in 2001 and noted that provincial spending on home care has gone from $26 million in 1975 to $2.7 billion in 2001, that provincial spending on nursing homes has gone from $800 million to $6.8 billion and that provincial spending on non-physician professional health care services has gone from $120 million to $800 million.

[13]   Writing in 2001, the committee stated that "... Canada has been successful in controlling total health care costs over the last decade": Senate Standing Committee on Social Affairs, Science and Technology, *The Health of Canadians — The Federal Role — Volume One — The Story So Far* (Ottawa: Standing Committee on Social Affairs, Science and Technology, 2001) at 94.

spending in 1999/2000.[14] These trends have raised the concern that spending on health care threatens spending in many other important areas of social and economic policy, including in areas that may be as vital to health as the delivery of health care services.[15] Skepticism often greets these worries, coming as they sometimes do from governments that are ideologically more committed to tax cuts than to program spending.[16] Nevertheless, in the absence of a significant shift in support for higher taxes, it is difficult to deny the significance of the risk that growing health care spending represents to the ability of governments to fund other priorities.

B. WHAT IT BUYS — THE HEALTH OF CANADIANS AND OF THEIR HEALTH CARE SYSTEM

Canada is, in relative and general terms, a country of healthy people.[17] In 1999, Canadians had a life expectancy at birth that ranked fifth among Organisation for Economic Co-operation and Development (OECD) countries. Among the same countries, Canada ranked eighth in the avoidance of preventable deaths and ninth in disability-free years of life. While these indicators obviously point to room for improvement, they show that Canadians enjoy an enviable level of general health.

There are however, causes for concern. Although infant mortality has gone from 27.3 deaths per 1,000 births in 1960 to 5.3 deaths per 1,000 births in 2000 (significantly lower than the U.S. rate), Canada rates only 17th among OECD countries on this indicator. In addition, the general healthiness of Canadians conceals large inequalities in health status among Canadians. The Kirby Committee described population health among Aboriginal Canadians as a "national disgrace", while Romanow described it as "simply unacceptable".[18]

---

[14] Canadian Institute for Health Information, *Preliminary Provincial and Territorial Government Health Expenditure Estimates: 1974-1975 to 2006-2007* (Ottawa: Canadian Institute for Health Information, 2006), suggesting (at 21) that 45 per cent of Ontario's program spending was in health care in 2004-2005, with three other provinces (Nova Scotia, Manitoba and British Columbia) above 40 per cent.

[15] Premier's Advisory Council on Health for Alberta, *A Framework for Reform: Report of the Premier's Advisory Council on Health* (December 2001), online: <http://www.health.gov.ab.ca/resources/publications/PACH_report_final.pdf>.

[16] See, for example, Steven Lewis & Colleen Maxwell, "Decoding Mazankowski: A Symphony in Three Movements" (2002) 2:4 HealthcarePapers 20.

[17] See the overview given in Commission on the Future of Health Care in Canada, *Building on Values: The Future of Health Care in Canada — Final Report* (Ottawa: Commission on the Future of Health Care in Canada, 2002) at 9-20, which these paragraphs draw upon. See also the discussion in Senate Standing Committee on Social Affairs, Science and Technology, *The Health of Canadians — The Federal Role — Interim Report: Volume One — The Story So Far* (Ottawa: Senate Standing Committee on Social Affairs, Science and Technology, 2001) at 73-80.

[18] Senate Standing Committee on Social Affairs, Science and Technology, *The Health of Canadians — The Federal Role: Volume Four — Issues and Options* (Ottawa: Senate Standing Committee on Social Affairs, Science and Technology, 2001) at 130, online: <http://www.parl.gc.ca/37/1/parlbus/commbus/senate/com-e/soci-e/rep-e/repintsep01-e.htm>. Romanow's characterization of the situation is found at 211 of *Building on Values* and a broader discussion about Aboriginal health status commences at 220. See also K. Bruce Newbold, "Problems in Search of

Chronic disease, the suicide rate, the death and injury rate from accidents, and the rate of substance addiction, are all much higher among First Nation communities than among Canadians generally.[19] The Romanow Commission also brought new attention to the lower health status that prevails among northern and Atlantic Canadian populations, as well as in rural areas across the country.[20]

Such disparities reflect deeper disparities in socio-economic conditions. In the health care policy literature, this raises the question of whether the health of Canadians might be better served by more spending in housing, nutrition, employment, economic development and social services rather than by higher (or even maintained) spending on the delivery of health care services.[21] This "determinants of health" perspective dovetails with the skepticism of many economists as to the benefits to be obtained from spending on health care services.[22] Such skepticism rests on the unavailability of evidence for the efficacy of many treatments,[23] on the positive evidence that exists of variation in treatment without discernable clinical justification or differing outcomes[24] and

Solutions: Health and Canadian Aboriginals" (1998) 23:1 J. of Community Health 59, and Constance MacIntosh, "Jurisdictional Roulette: Constitutional and Structural Barriers to Aboriginal Access to Health", in Colleen M. Flood, ed., *Just Medicare: What's In, What's Out, How We Decide* (Toronto: University of Toronto Press, 2006) at 193.

[19] The Senate Standing Committee found that heart problems, hypertension, and diabetes are three times higher in Aboriginal populations and that the rate of death due to injury and poisoning is 6.5 times higher. It found the rate of suicide among Aboriginal youth to be five to six times higher than the suicide rate for the general Canadian youth population; see *The Health of Canadians — The Federal Role: Volume Four — Issues and Options* (Ottawa: Senate Standing Committee on Social Affairs, Science and Technology, 2001) at 130. The Royal Commission on Aboriginal Peoples had documented that infant mortality was twice as high for Indian people and three times as high for the Inuit as for other Canadians: Royal Commission on Aboriginal Peoples, *Report of the Royal Commission on Aboriginal Peoples*, Volume 3 (Ottawa: Supply & Services Canada, 1996) at 127.

[20] Commission on the Future of Health Care in Canada, *Building on Values: The Future of Health Care in Canada — Final Report* (Ottawa: Commission on the Future of Health Care in Canada, 2002) at 16-20.

[21] S. Mhatre & R. Deber, "From Equal Access to Health Care to Equitable Access to Health: A Review of Canadian Provincial Health Commissions Reports" (1992) 22 Int'l J. of Health Services 645; M.G. Marmot & R.G. Wilkinson, *Social Determinants of Health* (Oxford: Oxford University Press, 1999).

[22] R.G. Evans & G.L. Stoddard, "Producing Health, Consuming Health Care", in R.G. Evans *et al.*, eds., *Why are Some People Healthy and Others Not? The Determinants of Health of Populations* (New York: Aldine De Gruyter, 1994). For a critique of this amazingly influential article that is sympathetic to a determinants of health model, see B. Poland *et al.*, "Wealth, Equity and Health Care: A Critique of a 'Population Health' Perspective on the Determinants of Health" (1998) 46 Soc. Sci. Med. 785. For a still broader critique, see Tee L. Guidotti, "Commentary: 'Why Are Some People Healthy and Others Not?' A Critique of the Population – Health Model" (1997) 30:4 Annals of the Royal Society of Physicians and Surgeons 203.

[23] G.L. Stoddard, M.L. Barer, R.G. Evans & V. Bhatia, *Why Not User Charges? The Real Issues — A Discussion Paper* (Ontario: The Premier's Council on Health, Well-being and Social Justice, 1996) at 6.

[24] As examples, see N.P. Roos & L.L. Roos, "Small Area Variations, Practice Style, and Quality of Care" in R.G. Evans *et al.*, eds., *Why are Some People Healthy and Others Not? The*

on the *prima facie* plausibility, especially with fee-for-service compensation, that provider economic self-interest will strongly influence the volume of delivered treatment.[25] Together, the determinants of health perspective and the skepticism of economists have helped to justify the determination of governments to control the growth in health care spending, whether or not they have followed through with more spending on the other determinants.

Canadians may be convinced of the need for more action on health determinants, especially after events such as the Walkerton E. coli disaster, but they are not convinced that this should be financed by less focus on the delivery of medical and hospital services to individuals.[26] Canadians want higher spending on health care, and they want it focused on maintaining or improving access to medical treatment. In short, they want more spending on health care services for sick people, ahead of spending that might mean fewer sick people.[27] They are supported by the lack of evidence for the efficacy of some preventative or promotional measures and also by the common sense observation that the paucity of evidence for the connection between the availability of health care treatment and health outcomes does not prove the non-existence of such a connection.[28] But the importance of the determinants of health (as opposed to our ability to affect them with public programs) and the skepticism of the economist cannot be ignored. At a minimum, they establish the need for better monitoring of the efficacy of health services and for more precise targeting of available resources on treatments and preventive programs that are supported by

---

Determinants of Health of Populations (New York: Aldine De Gruyter, 1994) 231, and J.V. Tu, C.L. Pashos C.D. Naylor *et al.*, "Use of Cardiac Procedures and Outcomes in Elderly Patients with Myocardial Infarction in the United States and Canada" (1997) 336: New Eng. J. Med. 1501.

[25] R.G. Evans, *Strained Mercy: The Economics of Canadian Health Care* (Toronto: Butterworths, 1984).

[26] The Walkerton Inquiry (The Honourable Dennis R. O'Connor, Commissioner), *Report of the Walkerton Inquiry, Part 1: The Events of May 2000 and Related Issues* (Toronto: Queen's Printer for Ontario, 2002).

[27] Commission on the Future of Health Care in Canada, *Building on Values: The Future of Health Care in Canada — Final Report* (Ottawa: Commission on the Future of Health Care in Canada, 2002) at 4, 31. The Kirby Committee reviewed a number of national polls on the attitudes of Canadians to health care and concluded, "When asked about spending priorities in health care, Canadians show a strong preference for 'bricks and mortar' infrastructure and research activities. Community-based activities are considered secondary, and activities that are seen as remote from front-line care are assigned the lowest priority for new health care funding"; Senate Standing Committee on Social Affairs, Science and Technology, *The Health of Canadians — The Federal Role — Interim Report: Volume One — The Story So Far* (Ottawa: Senate Standing Committee on Social Affairs, Science and Technology, 2001) at 50.

[28] On the first point especially (that the evidence for the effectiveness of action on the broader determinants is also not good), see C.M. Flood, "Moving Medicare Home: The Forces Shifting Care Out of Hospitals and Into Homes", in T.A. Caulfield & B. von Tigerstrom, eds., *Health Care Reform and the Law in Canada — Meeting the Challenge* (Edmonton: University of Alberta Press, 2002) 131 at 139. On the second point (that spending on the delivery of health care services has a positive impact on general population health), see P.-Y. Cremieux, P. Ouellette and C. Pilon, "Health Care Spending as Determinants of Health Outcomes" (1999) 8 Health Economics 627.

evidence of effectiveness. This is a leading theme of all of the official studies of the health care system that have been recently completed, including the reports of the Kirby Committee and of the Romanow Commission.

Both of these studies recommended retention and even expansion of Canada's system of publicly financed health care. But they also recommended many changes and improvements. This is understandable, given that the system is alleged to be not as healthy as the Canadians it serves. For example, in 2000, the World Health Organization ranked Canada in 30th position among all nations in health system performance.[29] This put Canada behind many countries that spend less on health and that allow a greater range of hospital and physician services to be privately purchased. But, like Canada, all of these countries have a public policy commitment to ensuring all citizens have at least basic health insurance coverage. This distinguishes them (and Canada) from the system in the United States (which ranked 37), where between 14 and 16 per cent of the population has no health insurance.

Canadian public opinion runs strongly toward the view that the system has deteriorated significantly and that Canada is in a perpetual health care crisis that now rivals its perpetual national unity crisis.[30] This view has its roots in the regular media coverage and the widespread personal experience of lengthy waits in emergency rooms, of doctor or nursing shortages that are serious enough to require the temporary closure of facilities or the permanent closure of programs, of aging equipment that cannot be replaced, and of intolerably long, uncertain and inconsistent waiting times for diagnostic and surgical procedures. Without a doubt, while governments and experts often seem most concerned with what it all is costing, Canadians seem consistently most concerned with the availability of dependable and timely access to necessary as well as desired health care services.

The issues of waiting lists and waiting times dominate this concern.[31] The Romanow Commission concluded that the public's perception that waiting lists and waiting periods are a serious problem was reason enough for action. Regarding the bottleneck in diagnostic services as the most immediate issue, it

---

[29] World Health Organization, *The World Health Report 2000: Health Systems — Improving Performance* (Geneva: World Health Organization, 2000), particularly at 200. The implications of this ranking for Canadian health care system reform, particularly relative to the first place ranking of France, is drawn out in Sholom Glouberman & Brenda Zimmerman, *Discussion Paper No. 8: Complicated and Complex Systems: What Would Successful Reform of Medicare Look Like?* (Ottawa: Commission on the Future of Health Care in Canada, 2002). The ranking is challenged by Raisa Deber, "Why Did the World Health Organization Rate Canada's Health System as 30th? Some Thoughts on League Tables" (2004) 2:1 Longwoods Review 2-7.

[30] This fundamental change in the attitude of Canadians is set out by C.H. Tuohy, "The Costs of Constraint and Prospects for Health Care Reform in Canada" (2002) 21:3 Health Affairs 32. Tuohy points out that Canadians have gone from being generally satisfied with their health care system to being as displeased with it as people in other countries are with their systems. She argues the atmosphere of crisis created by government restraint has created the first widespread openness to fundamental change since the founding of Medicare.

[31] In response, better information is finally being gathered as to the true nature and extent of the issue: see Canadian Institute for Health Information, *Waiting for Health Care in Canada: What We Know and What We Don't Know* (Ottawa: Canadian Institute for Health Information, 2006).

recommended a large and federally supported provincial investment into new diagnostic capacity within Medicare. Other reviews of the system have recommended more drastic measures. The Kirby Committee, while also supporting increased spending on medical equipment, also recommended a health care guarantee that would obligate provincial and territorial governments to fund necessary services in another jurisdiction whenever they were unable to provide them within medically acceptable wait times.[32] More dramatically, Alberta has twice seemed poised to experiment with a large scale program of privatization that would both require Albertans to pay for some services currently provided by Medicare and give them the option of paying privately for some of the services that would continue to be available through Alberta's public system.[33] The stated objectives have been to diversify health care's revenue stream, to harness the efficiency generated by competitive forces, to expand citizen choice and to move demand from the public system by focusing it more tightly on essential service that it would therefore be able to more quickly provide.

Another area of system performance that is receiving growing attention is patient safety. Estimates are that as many as 7.5 per cent of those who are treated in Canadian acute care hospitals experience an "adverse result" — an unintended injury or complication that is caused by health care management rather than by the underlying disease and that leads to death, disability or prolonged hospital stays.[34] Almost 40 per cent of these events were judged to have been highly preventable, suggesting that between 9,250 and 23,750 deaths could have been prevented in the year 2000. These numbers are lower but comparable to the alarming rates of adverse events reported for other countries.[35]

---

[32] On the health care guarantee, see Senate Standing Committee on Social Affairs, Science and Technology, *The Health of Canadians — The Federal Role — Volume Six: Recommendations for Reform* (Ottawa: Senate Standing Committee on Social Affairs, Science and Technology, 2002) at 11. On the need for additional diagnostic and medical equipment, see Senate Standing Committee on Social Affairs, Science and Technology, *The Health of Canadians — The Federal Role — Volume Five: Principles and Recommendations for Reform* (Ottawa: Senate Standing Committee on Social Affairs, Science and Technology, 2002) at 69-72.

[33] Premier's Advisory Council on Health for Alberta, *A Framework for Reform: Report of the Premier's Advisory Council on Health* (December 2001) and, more recently, Alberta Health, *Getting on With Better Health Care* (Edmonton: Alberta Minister of Health, 2006), online: <http://www.health.gov.ab.ca/key/reform_getting.html>. The latter document proposed that people be allowed to purchase enhanced medical goods beyond what doctors decide is medically necessary — for example, "a special kind of hip replacement", at 8. It also suggested a government commitment to "reasonable access to medically necessary, basic medicare services", leaving the others to private or not-for-private insurance, at 9. After consulting with Albertans, this "policy framework" has been reformulated in much more conventional directions. See Alberta Health, *Health Policy Framework — What We Heard from Albertans during March 2006* (Edmonton: Alberta Minister of Health, 2006), online: <http://www.health.gov.ab.ca/healthrenewal/renewal_heard.pdf>, as well as Alberta Health, *Getting on With Better Health Care — Health Policy Framework* (Edmonton: Alberta Minister of Health, 2006), online: <http://www.health.gov.ab.ca/healthrenewal/GettingBetterHealthcare.pdf>.

[34] G. Ross Baker *et al.*, "The Canadian Adverse Events Study: the incidence of adverse events among hospital patients in Canada" (2004) 170 C.M.A.J., 1678, online: <http://www.cmaj.ca/cgi/reprint/170/11/1678>.

[35] See G. Ross Baker & Peter G. Norton, "Adverse events and patient safety in Canadian health

It is therefore disconcerting that tackling the problem has, at least until recently, been less of a policy priority in Canada than in other countries, despite the occurrence in Canada of the sort of major events that have triggered wide-ranging reforms elsewhere.[36] The significant changes that have been implemented in other countries but not (with some exceptions) in Canada include the mandatory tracking and public reporting of incidents by individual hospitals and/or physicians, and the creation of centralized complaints processes that take the investigation of complaints out of the hands of the self-regulating professions and of the self-governing institutions against whom the complaints are likely to be made.[37] More broadly, other countries have done more than Canada has to frame the problem of patient safety as not only an issue of clinical practice and of individual or institutional responsibility but also of system governance.[38]

As these examples show, law can be one of the instruments that governments can use to address concerns about patient safety.[39] It must however, be used with prudence. Much of the very best work on medical error emphasizes the need for a shift from the culture of naming and blaming to one that emphasizes prevention and correction through the proactive identification, acknowledgement and discussion of error and its systemic roots.[40] Existing malpractice law and professional regulation law, with their heavy emphasis on individual responsibility and proximate causes, can be barriers to this shift. Additional law that simply accentuated these influences would be unhelpful. But it is certain that improvements in patient safety will involve changes in law and legal processes. In

---

care" (2006) 48:7 B.C. Medical Journal 326-28, which compares the Canadian numbers to those of other countries. Available online: <http://www.bcma.org/public/bc_medical_journal/bcmj/2006/sept_2006/adverse_events.pdf>.

[36] U.K., The Bristol Royal Infirmary Inquiry, *The Report of the Public Inquiry into Children's Heart Surgery at the Bristol Infirmary 1984-1995: Learning from Bristol* (Norwich: The Stationery Office Ltd. 2001); Manitoba Pediatric Cardiac Surgery Inquest, *The Report of the Manitoba Pediatric Surgery Inquest: An Inquiry into Twelve Deaths at the Winnipeg Health Sciences Centre in 1994* (Winnipeg Provinical Court of Manitoba, 2000). For overviews of what the Bristol Inquiry led to in the U.K., see A.C.L. Davies, "Don't Trust Me, I'm a Doctor — Medical Regulation and the 1999 NHS Reforms" (2000) 20 Oxford J. Legal Stud. 437, and C. Newdick, "NHS Governance After *Bristol*: Holding On, or Letting Go" (2002) 10 Med. L. Rev. 111.

[37] E. Bonney & G. Baker, "Current Strategies to Improve Patient Safety in Canada: An Overview of Federal and Provincial Initiatives" (2004) 7:2 Healthc. Q. 36; D. Briscoe, "New Zealand's Health Practitioner's Competence Assurance Act" (2004) 180:1 Med. J. Aust. 4; A. Davies, "Don't Trust Me I'm a Doctor: Medical Regulation and the 1999 N.H.S. Reforms" (2000) 20:3 Oxford J. Legal Stud. 437; B. Keogh *et al.*, "The Legacy of Bristol: Public Disclosure of Individual Surgeons' Results" (2004) 329: 7463 B.M.J. 450; and C. Zhan, "Assessing Patient Safety in the United States: Challenges and Opportunities" (2005) 43:3 Suppl. Med. Care 42-7.

[38] J. Braithwaite, J. Healy & K. Dwan, *The Governance of Health Safety and Quality: A Discussion Paper* (Canberra: Commonwealth of Australia, 2005); Michelle M. Mello, Cathy N. Kelly & Troyen A. Brennan, "Fostering Rational Regulation of Patient Safety" (2005) 30 J. Health Pol. 375.

[39] Tracey M. Bailey & Nola M. Ries, "Legal Issues in Patient Safety: The Example of Nosocomial Infection" (2005) 8 Healthcare Q. (Special Issue) 140.

[40] G.P. Baker & P. Norton, "Making Patients Safer! Reducing Error in Canadian Healthcare" (2001) 2:1 HealthcarePapers 10.

helping to identify what these changes should be, it might be useful for patient safety to be conceived less as an issue within specific areas of law (such as malpractice or professional regulation) and more as an issue of system governance that is impacted by a multitude of areas of law (including coronial inquiries statutes, employment law regimes and privilege laws) that have a cumulative impact on the issue that remains largely unexplored.[41]

C. HOW IT IS DELIVERED — BASIC ORGANIZATION FEATURES OF THE CANADIAN SYSTEM

Canadian Medicare is not socialized medicine.[42] The vast majority of health care services in Canada are received from care providers who work either as independent professionals in private practice or as the employees of health care institutions or firms that are controlled and operated by independent corporate bodies, by partnerships or by sole proprietors. Doctors are obviously the leading examples of the former, while hospitals that are public but not government institutions are leading examples of the latter. Other examples of privately owned institutions or firms that employ care providers are nursing homes, various other kinds of continuing care organizations and private clinics.

The independence of doctors needs to be stressed. Not only are they not government employees, they are usually not the employees of hospitals or of other clinical institutions. Instead, the doctor relationship with hospitals is based on admitting privileges (held in accordance with hospital by-laws) and with the related membership in a medical staff that is essentially a distinct self-governing entity within the hospital.[43] Canadians benefit from this physician autonomy. They can be sure that they are treated according to physician skill and judgment, not managerial direction.[44] On the other hand, this independence complicates

---

[41] See Jocelyn Downie *et al.*, *Patient Safety Law: From Silos to Systems: Final Report* (Halifax: Dalhousie Health Law Institute, 2006), online: <http://www.patientsafetylaw.ca/index.cfm? method=pub_documents.act_getFile&num_langPref=1&getObj=12>.

[42] See C.H. Tuohy, *Accidental Logics: The Dynamics of Change in the Health Care Arena in the United States, Britain and Canada* (New York: Oxford University Press, 1999) at 27-34 (where the Canadian collegial or accommodation model is distinguished from the American free market model and the British statist or hierarchical model) and at 203-37 (where the essential accommodation between the Canadian state and the medical profession that shaped Medicare is described as one of exclusive state responsibility for financing in exchange for physician retention of clinical and entrepreneurial independence via the fee-for-service compensation system). See also R.B. Deber, "Getting What We Pay For: Myths and Realities About Financing Canada's Health Care System" (2000) 21:2 Health L. Can. 9 at 12-13; and Colleen M. Flood, "Chapter 1: The Anatomy of Medicare" in Jocelyn Downie, Timothy Caulfield & Colleen M. Flood, eds., *Canadian Health Law and Policy*, 2nd ed. (Markham, ON: LexisNexis Butterworths, 2002) 1, at 3, 35-38 (as regards physicians) and at 40-42 (as regards hospitals).

[43] J.J. Morris, *Law for Canadian Health Care Administrators* (Toronto & Vancouver: Butterworths, 1996), and CCH, *Canadian Health Facilities Law Guide* (North York ON: CCH Canadian Ltd., 1998).

[44] The contrasting situation under managed care in the United States is illustrated dramatically by *Pegram v. Herdich*, 530 U.S. 211, 120 S.Ct. 2143 (2000).

management of the system in multiple ways. It may, for example, make a systemic approach to systemic challenges, such as patient safety, more illusive than it might otherwise be.

The separateness of the delivery system from government is illustrated in *Stoffman v. Vancouver General Hospital*,[45] where doctors challenged a mandatory retirement policy under section 15 of the Charter, which prohibits age discrimination.[46] Having first ruled in another case[47] that the Charter only applied to government or institutions controlled by government, the Supreme Court of Canada ruled that the Charter was not applicable in this case because the government of British Columbia could not be said to control the Vancouver General Hospital.

The functions that government does perform, in Canada and in other countries, can be divided into three categories. First, provincial governments are responsible for regulating the quality of health care services, whether or not it funds them.[48] For many health care professions, they do this through delegation of that responsibility to the profession itself. For institutional providers, provincial governments do the regulating directly.[49] For example, all provinces have a Hospitals Act that regulates public not-for-profit hospitals and one or more pieces of legislation that regulate nursing homes and other kinds of long term care facilities. Some of the provinces also have legislation that regulates the establishment and operation of private clinics, including those that operate on a for-profit basis.[50]

Second, governments fund the delivery of health care services. As discussed in more detail below, this is a function that in Canada is shared by the federal and provincial governments. For "medically necessary" hospital and physician services, government funding is largely exclusive. For other services, including home care, long-term care and prescription drugs, as well as dental care, the extent of government funding varies from province to province. Government funding for these non-medicare services can be subject to means testing, to co-payment and to deductibles that are not applied in any province to Medicare services. Some health care services are not funded in any provinces. Across the country, private insurance starts, for those who can afford it and who are not otherwise excluded, where government funding ends.

---

[45] [1990] S.C.J. No. 125, [1990] 3 S.C.R. 483 (S.C.C.).

[46] Section 15 of the Charter reads: "Every individual is equal before and under the law and has the right to the equal protection and equal benefit of the law without discrimination and, in particular, without discrimination based on race, national or ethnic origin, colour, religion, sex, age or mental or physical disability".

[47] *McKinney v. University of Guelph*, [1990] S.C.J. No. 122, [1990] 3 S.C.R. 229 (S.C.C.).

[48] See, for example, Marjorie A. Hickey & M. Michelle Higgins, "Chapter 6: Regulation of Dental Professionals" in Jocelyn Downie, Karen McEwen & William MacInnis, eds., *Dental Law in Canada* (Markham, ON: LexisNexis Butterworths, 2004) 161.

[49] J.J. Morris, *Law for Canadian Health Care Administrators* (Toronto & Vancouver: Butterworths, 1996), and CCH, *Canadian Health Facilities Law Guide* (North York, ON: CCH Canadian Ltd., 1998).

[50] See, for example, Ontario's *Independent Health Facilities Act*, R.S.O. 1990, c. I.3, and Saskatchewan's *Health Facilities Licensing Act*, S.S. 1996, c. H-0.02, as amended.

The third function that government performs is more difficult to precisely label, but could be broadly characterized as system governance or stewardship. Whatever it is called, it includes responsibility for establishing the general objectives of the system, for monitoring and evaluating the system's success against those objectives, for ensuring coordination and continuity between the different parts of the system and for ensuring reasonable access to health care services either through public funding or other means.[51] In short, it is the general state responsibility of ensuring that there is a functioning health care system in place, capable of delivering to citizens the level of health care that most would agree should be, and that international law says must be, available to all people.[52] In Canada, Medicare is the core of the state's response to these obligations but it does not exhaust them, since the obligations extend to the services beyond Medicare, as well as to the relationship between the two.

The decision of the Supreme Court of Canada in *Eldridge v. British Columbia*[53] aligns with this wider view of government's accountability for health care. The court applied section 15 of the Charter to a decision of B.C. hospitals not to fund interpreter services for hearing impaired patients, despite the earlier finding in *Stoffman*[54] that the Charter did not apply to B.C.'s hospitals because they were not controlled by British Columbia's government. The reason was that the decision on interpreter services (unlike the mandatory retirement policy) was a decision about access to services within Medicare, a government program that the hospitals provided on behalf of the British Columbia government.

An example of the manifestation of the ultimate responsibility of government for the design and functioning of the system as a whole can be seen in the creation in four provinces of a common legislative framework that applies to all regulated health care professions, in addition to the legislation that applies specifically to each one.[55] It can be seen as a Canadian example of a wider

---

[51] See D. Longley, *Health Care Constitutions* (London: Cavendish Publishing, 1996), especially Chapter 1, "Core Principles", where the health care system is spoken of as a "social enterprise" that is legally constructed in ways that define the "immutable core principles" around which decisions about law, policies and structures get made.

[52] The reference to international law is to art. 12 of the *International Covenant on Economic, Social and Cultural Rights*, December 16, 1966, 933 U.N.T.S. 3, Can. T.S. 1976 No. 46. It provides that State parties "recognize the right of everyone to the enjoyment of the highest attainable standard of physical and mental health", and commit themselves to "[t]he creation of conditions which would assure to all medical service and medical attention in the event of sickness". See Barbara von Tigerstrom, "Human Rights and Health Care Reform", in T.A. Caulfield & B. von Tigerstrom, eds., *Health Care Reform and the Law in Canada — Meeting the Challenge* (Edmonton: University of Alberta Press, 2002) 157.

[53] [1997] S.C.J. No. 86, [1997] 3 S.C.R. 624 (S.C.C.).

[54] *Stoffman v. Vancouver General Hospital*, [1990] S.C.J. No. 125, [1990] 3 S.C.R. 483 (S.C.C.).

[55] See, for example, *Regulated Health Professions Act, 1991*, S.O. 1991, c. 18. This type of "umbrella legislation" was first developed in Ontario in the 1980s: see *Striking a New Balance: A Blueprint for the Regulation of Ontario's Health Professions — Recommendations of the Health Professions Legislation Review* (Toronto: Queen's Printer, 1989). A subsequent review concluded that the new legislative framework had been so successful that it required only minor adjustments after 10 years of operation: see Ontario, Health Professions Advisory Council, *Adjusting the Balance: A Review of the Regulated Health Professions Act* (Toronto: Health Professions Regulatory Council, 2001). The opportunities that this type of legislative framework

international trend towards the "regulation of the regulators", by which a secondary layer of regulatory law is used to ensure that regulatory authority is not misappropriated to the interests of those to whom it has been given, as well as to ensure greater coordination and collaboration among regulatory actors.[56]

More dramatically, the ultimate responsibility of government for the system as a whole is illustrated through the process of regionalization that has been implemented in every province and territory.[57] Through this legislatively defined process, governance and management responsibility has been transferred from individual hospitals to regional boards of governance having responsibility for all (or most) of the hospitals in their legislatively defined regions.[58] Broader responsibility for the creation, governance and oversight of a broader and more integrated continuum of care that encompasses non-hospital services, such as public health, long-term care and home care, has also been devolved to these regional boards.[59] The provinces have also, to varying degrees, devolved many health care planning and policy functions formerly exercised provincially to the new regionalized structures.

Regionalization has been accomplished with great turmoil in the system. There is debate and uncertainty as to whether corresponding benefits have been achieved.[60] Ironically, given the decentralization that was intended,

---

could create for the fostering of more collaborative approaches to practice across professional boundaries are considered in William Lahey & Robert Currie, "Regulatory and Medico-legal Barriers to Interprofessional Practice" (2005) 19 J. of Interprofessional Care 197 (Supp).

[56] J. Braithwaite, J. Healy & K. Dwan, *The Governance of Health Safety and Quality: A Discussion Paper* (Canberra: Commonwealth of Australia, 2005).

[57] Ontario is in the final stages of establishing "Local Health Integration Networks", that will be structured and have comparable responsibilities to what other provinces (outside Quebec) call regional or district health boards. These are being established under the *Local Health System Integration Act, 2006*, S.O. 2006, c. 4. The process is explained in a series of information bulletins published by the Ministry of Health and Long Term Care; see Bulletin No. 1 — October 6, 2004 (setting out the vision and rationale) and Bulletin No. 22 — April 26, 2004 (transferring responsibility from the LHIN project team to LHINs), both available online: <http://www.health.gov.on.ca>.

[58] Prior to the current move to Local Health Integration Networks, Ontario pursued some of the rationalization objections of regionalization through a significant hospital consolidation process that saw many hospitals closed or merged into larger entities: see Health Services Restructuring Commission, *Looking Back, Looking Forward: The Ontario Health Services Restructuring Commission (1996-2000): A Legacy Report* (Ontario: Health Services Restructuring Commission, 2000). See also Colleen M. Flood, Duncan Sinclair & Joanna Erdman, "Steering and Rowing in Health Care: The Devolution Options" (2004) 30:1 Queen's L.J. 156-204.

[59] Regional health boards exercise this authority either through contractual relations with the public and private providers of these other services or by assuming direct responsibility for the delivery of these services, or through some combination of the two approaches; see, for example, *Regional Health Authorities Act*, C.C.S.M. c. R34, ss. 28, 29, 34, 36 and 44.1-44.6; *Nursing Home Act*, R.S.A. 2000, c. N-7, s. 2; *Health and Community Services Act*, S.N.L. 1995, c. P-37.1, s. 4.

[60] Government commissioned reviews of the system universally favour at least the retention of regionalization, and most have favoured a strengthening of it: see (in Nova Scotia) Minister's Task Force on Regionalized Health Care in Nova Scotia, *Final Report and Recommendations* (Halifax: Nova Scotia Department of Health, 1999); (in Saskatchewan) Commission on Medicare, *Caring for Medicare: Sustaining a Quality System* (Regina: The Commission on

regionalization has involved a definite loss of local autonomy, as local hospital boards and administrative structures have been displaced to make way for larger regionalized ones. It is similarly ironic that regionalization has been implemented through an assertion of government control of the system. It has meant government imposing a comprehensive and centrally planned organizational structure on a system that previously had been more or less indigenously organized in local communities. This has perhaps served to emphasize rather than to downplay government's ultimate accountability for the system. Regionalization legislation has tended to reinforce the implication of greater government control, by emphasizing the regionalized system's accountability to ministers of health and by stating ministerial responsibilities and powers more expansively and explicitly than had been the case in predecessor legislation.[61] The legislation gives ministers of health a role that is managerial as much as it is regulatory.

On the other hand, it has to be stressed that regionalization has not given legal control of hospitals to government but instead given it to regional boards that are as legally distinct from government as hospitals boards were previously. Further, regionalization has not affected the legal or practical independence of doctors, who continue to have essentially the same relationship with regional health boards as they had previously with hospitals, although the substance of that relationship (as opposed to its legal form) has been altered and complicated

---

Medicare, 2001) at 55-60; (in Quebec) Commission d'étude sur les services de santé et les services sociaux, *Emerging Solutions: Report and Recommendations* (Quebec City: Commission d'étude sur les services de santé sur les services sociaux, 2001) at 21-103; (in Alberta) Premier's Advisory Council on Health For Alberta, *A Framework for Reform: Report of the Premier's Advisory Council on Health* (December 2001) at 18-25; (and at the national level) Senate Standing Committee on Social Affairs, Science and Technology, *The Health of Canadians — The Federal Role — Volume Six: Recommendations for Reform — Highlights* (Ottawa: Standing Senate Committee on Social Affairs, Science and Technology, 2002) at 8, and Commission on the Future of Health Care in Canada, *Building on Values: The Future of Health Care in Canada — Final Report* (Ottawa: Commission on the Future of Health Care in Canada, 2002) at 6. In contrast, academic commentators are divided: compare Colleen M. Flood, "Chapter 1: The Anatomy of Medicare" in Jocelyn Downie, Timothy Caulfield & Colleen M. Flood, eds., *Canadian Health Law and Policy*, 2nd ed. (Markham, ON: LexisNexis Butterworths, 2002) at 45 and Colleen Flood, Duncan Sinclair & Joanna Erdman, "Steering and Rowing in Health Care: The Devolution Option" (2004) 30 Queen's L.J. 156 (both favourable), to Lawrie McFarlane & Carlos Prado, *The Best Laid Plans: Health Care's Problems and Prospects* (Montreal & Kingston: McGill-Queen's University Press, 2002) at 107; J. Church & P. Barker, "Regionalization of Health Services in Canada: a Critical Perspective" (1998) 28 Int'l J. of Health Services 467; and S. Glouberman & H. Mintzberg, "Managing the Care of Health and the Cure of Disease — Part I: Differentiation", (2001) 26 Health Care Management Rev. 56, all of whom are more skeptical. See also the papers in (2004) 5:1 HealthcarePapers, which is dedicated to the topic of regionalization and which is generally positive.

[61] See, for example, Nova Scotia's *Health Authorities Act*, S.N.S. 2000, c. 6. Such accountability may have also applied to the independent hospital boards that pre-dated the regionalized structures, but it was not expressed so explicitly in legislation. As in other provinces, the process of regionalization in Nova Scotia can be traced to a royal commission or equivalent report of the late 1980s or early 1990s; see Royal Commission on Health Care, *The Report of the Royal Commission on Health Care: Towards a New Strategy* (Halifax: Nova Scotia Royal Commission on Health Care, 1989).

in many ways by the transfer of authority from hospital sites to regional "headquarters".

Understanding the organization of the health care system has always been challenging and regionalization has not made it less so. The boundaries that divide government's attributed authority and accountability from those of regionalized health authorities are shaped by perception and behaviour as much as by statutory law. They are fluid and subject to constant renegotiation. This may explain why some can describe the system as a command and control monopoly that is organized, funded, and evaluated by government, and others can dismiss this description as nonsense that is completely at odds with the continuing clinical independence of doctors, the autonomy of the boards and of the administrators who run hospitals and the freedom of choice among doctors that is enjoyed by Canadians.[62]

D. HEALTH CARE AND INSURANCE

To understand any legal framework for health care financing, it is helpful to have an understanding of the economics that any such framework must address.[63] The starting point is to recognize that access to health care demands access to third party health care insurance. Health care is expensive and needed unpredictably, putting comprehensive self-insurance beyond the capacity of all but the very wealthy. The shifting of the immediate cost of treatment to a third party, whether a private or public insurer, introduces cost escalation concerns. This might be thought self-evident, as we might expect insured patients to be less cost-conscious than uninsured patients, at least for services (like many diagnostic services) that are not unpleasant or dangerous. In the language of economics, this is a "moral hazard", where a user of a service has become indifferent to the cost of their utilization of that service because the cost accrues to others. In health care, the moral hazard implicates the physician or other provider, as well as the patient. The information asymmetry that exists between doctors and their patients means that utilization is often a consequence of decisions made by doctors on behalf of patients. It is the indifference of doctors to the cost of services and treatments, rather than the indifference of their patients, that is the true moral hazard.

---

[62]   The view that Canadian health care is a government monopoly is accepted in *A Framework for Reform: Report of the Premier's Advisory Council on Health* (December 2001) (the so-called Mazankowski report), and is argued for in Brian Crowley and David Zitner, *Public Health, State Secret* (Halifax: Atlantic Institute for Market Studies, 2002). The alternative view is stated succinctly in Stephen Lewis & Colleen Maxwell, "Decoding Mazankowski: A Symphony in Three Movements" (2002) 2:4 Healthcare Papers 20 at 25. See also Stanley Hartt, "Arbitrariness, Randomness and the Principles of Fundamental Justice", in Colleen M. Flood, Kent Roach & Lorne Sossin, eds., *Access to Care, Access to Justice: The Legal Debate Over Private Health Insurance in Canada* (Toronto: University of Toronto Press, 2005) 505.

[63]   The discussion in this section draws throughout upon C.M. Flood, *International Health Care Reform: A Legal, Economic and Political Analysis* (London: Routledge, 2000), and especially on Chapter 2, "Arguments in Economics and Justice for Government Intervention in Health Insurance and Health Service Markets", at 15-40. Both quotes are from p. 21.

The potential for cost escalation is reinforced by fee-for-service compensation, since it creates an incentive for physicians to provide more rather than less units of their services in order to increase their incomes. Together, moral hazard, information asymmetry and fee-for-service compensation create a strong pressure for cost escalation. The consequences of these interactions extend beyond the cost of services provided directly by physicians, since the cost of other services (particularly the cost of hospital services and prescription drugs) is largely a function of physician decision-making.

Many influences discourage physician-generated demand. The moral and ethical obligations of the profession require exclusive attention to the best interest of each patient. This precludes harmful or unnecessary treatment. But these and other counteracting influences still leave physicians with wide discretion to choose between courses of treatment and to choose ones that are more income beneficial, even if only of marginal clinical value. The real or perceived fear of malpractice allegations and of liability can push doctors towards providing more rather than less, especially of diagnostic services and prescription drugs. One estimate that is often cited is that physician-generated demand may be as high as between 30 and 40 per cent of total utilization.[64] Even if that figure is high, there are many studies that have documented wide variations in the use of particular treatments between populations that cannot be explained by differences in population need or justified by different outcomes.

Finding ways of eliminating or at least reducing unnecessary utilization is a leading preoccupation of health care policy. In Canada, the reintroduction of user fees for medical services (or their retention for other services) is invariably mentioned, even though the evidence is that they disproportionably discourage utilization by the poor (who may need more service) and may increase spending in the long run by discouraging preventive care. The other approach that has been applied on a massive scale is to simply reduce and then to limit budgets and therefore the resources that doctors are able to utilize, thus ostensibly forcing concentration on the delivery of truly necessary services. This has contributed to the waiting list phenomenon discussed above. In the United States, managed care has been the policy instrument of choice. It either uses rules to limit the circumstances in which various treatments can be provided or financial incentives that encourage physicians to withhold rather than to provide care in particular circumstances, or some combination of the two.[65]

As this discussion indicates, the combined effect of information asymmetry, moral hazard and fee-for-service payment are problems for private as well as for public insurance systems. There are several other considerations that go more directly to the choice between public and private insurance. All flow from the

---

[64]   G.L. Stoddard, M.L. Barer, R.G. Evans & V. Bhatia, *Why Not User Charges? The Real Issues —
A Discussion Paper* (Ontario: The Premier's Council on Health, Well-Being and Social Justice,
1996) at 6. For a review of more recent studies that put the figure at a lower level, see Michel
Grignon *et al.*, *Discussion Paper No. 35 — Influence of Physician Payment Methods on the
Efficiency of the Health Care System* (Ottawa: Commission on the Future of Health Care in
Canada, November, 2002).

[65]   A succinct history and description of managed care can be found in R. Adams Dudley & Harold
S. Luft, "Managed Care in Transition" (2001) 344 New Eng. J. Med. 1087.

fact that private insurance is profit-driven, with the profit level being a function of the difference between, on the one hand, premiums collected and, on the other hand, administrative costs and claims paid. Absent state intervention, this will mean that the highest risk individuals are charged premiums that are unaffordable or affordable only at financially debilitating cost or that they will be more directly denied coverage through explicit exclusionary rules. If insurers do not engage in perfect risk segregation, and either deliberatively or inadvertently pool relatively low risk individuals with higher risk individuals, then "adverse selection" may occur. This is where individuals who can afford insurance nevertheless go without due to premiums that they regard as more expensive than is warranted by the likelihood of their need for insurance. Finally, independently of exclusions that are generated by risk selecting and risk pooling by insurers, private insurance will not reach people who cannot afford to pay any insurance premium.

The final concept to be considered is that of administrative and transaction costs. Private insurance systems obviously have multiple insurance companies that compete with one another to attract subscribers by providing good coverage at reasonable rates. They do this by paying careful attention to who they insure (risk selecting), by adjusting premiums to match likely claim experience (risk rating) and by managing claims to avoid unnecessary costs. All this is labour intensive work that adds to the administrative cost of the health care system as a whole. These costs are also driven up by the additional burden that is imposed on providers if they are required to apply the different procedures and rules of different insurers.

The Canadian single-payer system responds to these challenges by making universal insurance under non-profit public administration available on uniform terms and conditions to all residents of each province. Together, universality and the prohibition on profit taking eliminate risk selection and risk rating, and the associated administrative overhead. In consequence, administrative costs are thought to be much lower in the Canadian than in the American system and Canada does not have a population of people without any health insurance. To the extent that the Canadian system is funded by a generally progressive income tax system, it redistributes the financial burden of illness from the lower to the upper rungs of the socio-economic ladder and therefore, in general, from the less to the more healthy. Neither happens in an efficiently operating private insurance market.

E. FINANCING AND ACCESSING SERVICES OUTSIDE THE SINGLE-PAYER SYSTEM

Part of the context for the more detailed discussion of the single-payer system that follows in Part II is an understanding of how access to health care services is financed in Canada where the single-payer system is not applicable. It is not necessary to refer to the experience of the United States, where roughly 16 per cent of the population has no health insurance, to demonstrate the outcomes that are produced when reliance is placed primarily on private insurance in health care markets. The same outcomes can be demonstrated by looking at the example of non-Medicare services in Canada.

Dentistry is a good example. One of the recommendations of the famous Hall Commission, which was adopted, was that Medicare should from its inception cover dental surgical services that needed to be performed in a hospital. However, to date, no province has extended the single-payer system to the rest of dental services and they are not required to do so by the *Canada Health Act*. If they do establish programs of public insurance, they are not required to establish programs of universal coverage and in fact, none has done so. Indeed, the public financing of dental care is the exception rather than the rule.[66] Whereas almost 100 per cent of Canadian spending on Medicare services is public spending, 94 per cent of spending on dental services is private spending.[67] Access to dental care is therefore significantly a function of access to private dental health insurance, usually through employment benefits packages. As of the late 1990s, these plans applied to less than 50 per cent of Canadians, indicating that some of the dynamics that create the large body of Americans that are uninsured for medical and hospital services also operate in Canadian dentistry.[68] Not surprisingly, Canadians are significantly more likely to have visited a dentist in a given year if they have private insurance. It is also not surprising, given the positive correlation between income level and insurance coverage, to find a significant negative correlation between income level and the accessing of dental treatment. Whereas low income Canadians are as likely as other Canadians to have visited a physician in any 12-month period, those above 15 are roughly only half as likely to have visited a dentist as are high income Canadians.

The situation is similar when it comes to prescription drugs, one of the fastest growing costs in Canadian health care.[69] The *Canada Health Act* covers these costs only if the drugs are taken on an in-patient basis. All provinces have programs that provide substantial public funding for prescription drugs taken outside of hospitals. But funding is not based on the *Canada Health Act* principles of universality and comprehensiveness. Instead, publicly funded coverage is limited to certain groups (such as senior citizens or social assistance recipients), is subject to deductibles and/or co-payment requirements, or to a

---

[66] For a summary of provincial dental programs, see William Lahey, "Chapter 2: The Legal Foundations of Canada's Health Care System", in J. Downie, Karen McEwen & William MacInnis, eds., *Dental Law in Canada* (Markham, ON: LexisNexis Butterworths, 2004) 29 at 46-51. For arguments on the importance of oral health and of public dental coverage, particularly for children, see L.M. Kopelman, "On Duties to Provide Basic Health and Dental Care to Children" (2001) 26 J. Med. & Phil. 193; L.M. Kopelman & W.E. Mouradian, "Do Children Get Their Fair Share of Health and Dental Care" (2001) 26 J. Med. & Phil. 127; and H.P. Lawrence & J.L. Leake, "The U.S. Surgeon General's Report on Oral Health in America: A Canadian Perspective" (2001) 67 J. Can. Dent. Assoc. 587.

[67] Commission on the Future of Health Care in Canada, *Building on Values: The Future of Health Care in Canada — Final Report* (Ottawa: Commission on the Future of Health Care in Canada, 2002) at 24-26; Canadian Institute for Health Information, *Exploring the 70/30 Split: How Canada's Health Care System is Financed* (Ottawa: Canadian Institute for Health Information, 2005) at 75-82.

[68] A.I. Ismail, "Dental Care in Canada", in B.A. Burt & S.A. Eklund, *Dentistry, Dental Practice, and the Community*, 5th ed. (Philadelphia: W.B. Saunders Co., 1999) 134 at 140-41.

[69] Canadian Institute for Health Information, *Drug Expenditure in Canada: 1985-2005* (Ottawa: Canadian Institute for Health Information, 2006).

combination of the two.[70] This creates categories of Canadians who are not covered or not adequately covered by public programs. The result is that some Canadians (10 per cent by some estimates) are left without prescription drug insurance because they do not qualify for public insurance and the dynamics that work in private insurance markets prevent them from getting insurance from that direction. Another 10 per cent are thought to be underinsured.

Moreover, as decisions about prescription drug coverage are made provincially there is interprovincial variation in prescription drug programs.[71] This means that poorer Canadians have differential levels of access to prescription drugs depending on their province of residence. Thus, while there is a national uninsured rate of 10 per cent, the rate of uninsured in Newfoundland is 35 per cent, in Nova Scotia 24 per cent, in Prince Edward Island 27 per cent and in New Brunswick 33 per cent.[72] Particularly troubling is intraprovincial variation in the extent of government coverage for those suffering from high-cost chronic diseases. Drug therapy in such cases would, for most people, fit almost any definition of medical necessity.

As with dentistry and prescription drugs, there is variation across provinces and territories in the level of public funding for home care, where funding tends to be capped, status based or subject to co-payments and for funding across the country with respect to continuing care services, ambulance services and aspects of mental health services.[73]

The point here is not the simple one of saying that prescription drugs, home care and other services should be fully funded under Medicare. Nor is it to simplistically suggest that the provinces and territories are not spending enough

---

[70]   In British Columbia, Alberta, Saskatchewan and Manitoba, the government either makes coverage available to all residents or (in Alberta) makes the purchase of coverage through the province an option available to all residents. Coverage is however subject to significant deductibles. For example, in British Columbia, this deductible was $800 per year in 2003. In Ontario, the Ontario Drug Benefits Plan applies to senior citizens, to residents in continuing care and to persons receiving professional services in Ontario's home care program. Income adjusted co-payments apply, as does a $100 deductible for higher income seniors. In Quebec, a government agency makes prescription drug coverage available to all residents who are not covered by an employer-sponsored plan. In the Atlantic provinces, coverage is generally limited to senior citizens and subject to deductibles and co-payments. See Canadian Institute for Health Information, *Drug Expenditure in Canada, 1985-2005* (Ottawa: Canadian Institute for Health Information, 2006) at 3-26 and A-1 to A-15.

[71]   Canadian Institute for Health Information, "Chapter 6: Retail Drug Sales", in *Exploring the 70/30 Split: How Canada's Health Care System is Financed* (Ottawa: Canadian Institute for Health Information, 2005), 61-71; Lisa Priest, "The killing cost of drug treatment", *The Globe and Mail* (November 20, 2006) A1.

[72]   Senate Standing Committee on Social Affairs, Science and Technology, *The Health of Canadians — The Federal Role: Volume Four — Issues and Options* (Ottawa: Senate Standing Committee on Social Affairs, Science and Technology, 2001) at 75.

[73]   Colleen M. Flood, "Moving Medicare Home: The Forces Shifting Care out of Hospitals and into Homes", in Timothy A. Caulfield & Barbara von Tigerstrom, eds., *Health Care Reform and the Law in Canada: Meeting the Challenge* (Edmonton: University of Alberta Press, 2002) 131. For models categorizing the different approaches to the finding taken in developed countries, see C.H. Tuohy, C.M. Flood & M. Stabile, "How Does Private Finance Affect Public Health Care Systems? Marshalling the Evidence from OECD Nations" (2004) 29 J. Health Pol. 359.

money on public financing of services in these areas, due to the non-applicability of the *Canada Health Act*.[74] The point instead is to emphasize that, in the absence of a universal program of public financing that provides comprehensive coverage, the result is clearly differential access based on ability to pay. The result is differential exposure to the kind of potential for financial distress that Medicare was explicitly intended to guard Canadians against. Given the disparate capacity, circumstances and choices of Canada's provinces and territories, the lack of national approaches to the financing of these services of growing importance means that Canadians in some communities and regions are more exposed to these risks and burdens than are Canadians living elsewhere.

Wherever they live, all Canadians are affected by the passive privatization that is enabled by the limitation of the single payer model to hospital and physician services. This is the process whereby changes in medical science allow more treatment to be delivered on an extramural basis beyond the confines of the hospital or the doctor's office. For example, much of the growth in spending on prescription drugs and on home care is spending on health care needs that would have been addressed (though not as well) within the scope of Medicare at an earlier time. What has changed is the capacity of medicine to treat a multitude of conditions through drug therapies, often with the benefit of eliminating or reducing the length of stay needed in hospital. The rapid growth of home care is both an enabler of these developments and a response to them.

Passive privatization has reduced the effectiveness of Medicare in meeting some of its key objectives. It addition to reducing protection against the financial burden of illness, it has also reduced the scope of the health benefit that is delivered through Medicare. In the health care system of the 1960s, the inclusion of hospital services meant there would be reasonably comprehensive coverage not only for physician services but also for the services through which the full benefit of physician expertise was obtained. It is the latter element of the Medicare deal that is being eroded by the occupational and locational limitations of the *Canada Health Act*. There has been corresponding erosion in the commitment of Canadian health care policy to the key rationale for Medicare, namely, that access to the full benefit of modern medicine should be based only on need and not on the ability to pay.

This has happened without there being any structural change in the single payer system and without any amendment to the *Canada Health Act* or to the provincial and territorial laws that create and govern the programs of universal and comprehensive public health insurance that the *Canada Health Act* mandates. It has taken place, not as deliberated public policy, but through acceptance and encouragement of incremental changes and the operation of impersonal system dynamics. Across the country, provincial and territorial governments have responded by increasing funding and programming in a host of areas, including pharmacare, home care, respite care, adult day care and long-

---

[74] Between 1975 and 2001, total provincial spending on home care went from $26 million to $2.7 billion dollars. Between the same dates, nursing home spending went from $800 million to $6.8 billion. Prescription drug spending by the provinces has doubled since 1975; Commission on the Future of Health Care in Canada, *Building on Values: The Future of Health Care in Canada — Final Report* (Ottawa: Commission on the Future of Health Care in Canada, 2002) at 34.

term care. Nevertheless, both the Romanow Commission and the Kirby Committee (and the National Health Forum before them) advocated a uniform national response with two elements: a national program to support Canadians facing catastrophic drug expenses and extension of the principles of the *Canada Health Act* into the acute care portion of home care.[75]

III. THE SINGLE-PAYER SYSTEM

A. CONSTITUTIONAL FOUNDATIONS

Canadians associate Medicare with the *Canada Health Act*. This makes sense, even though this law is not legally applicable to the provinces, the level of government that actually pays the doctors and funds hospitals and hospital-based providers who provide the care. Instead, it applies only to the federal government, authorizing it (through the federal Minister of Health) to make grants to the provinces upon being satisfied that they have met the criteria of eligibility spelled out in the Act. And yet, notwithstanding the Act's limited legal effect, it is more important to the access that Canadians have to health care than any provincial statute. Moreover, Canadians identify with the Act in much the same way as they identify with the *Canadian Charter of Rights and Freedoms*, as a document that defines and protects fundamental aspects of Canadian citizenship. Like the Charter, the Act is thought of as defining what it is to be Canadian. To understand how legislation that is so limited in its legal effect has come to have such a broad and fundamental effect on Canadian policy and identity, it is necessary to understand how the Canadian Constitution divides legislative power over health between the federal and provincial governments.[76]

---

[75] Commissioner Romanow described home care as "The Next Essential Service" and recommended that home care services in three "priority" areas be brought under the umbrella of the *Canada Health Act*: mental health case management and intervention services, post-acute home care and palliative care. He also recommended action designed to bring relief to family care givers (including through employment insurance) whose services go largely unfunded in all parts of the country. On prescription drugs, he recommended the establishment of a federal "catastrophic drug transfer" that would operate outside the *Canada Health Act* and that would ensure consistent coverage across the country for the potentially catastrophic impact of high costs drugs; see Commission on the Future of Health Care in Canada, *Building on Values: The Future of Health Care in Canada — Final Report* (Ottawa: Commission on the Future of Health Care in Canada, 2002) at xxxi-xxxii. The recommendations of the Kirby Committee were similar, calling for a national plan that would operate outside the *Canada Health Act* to subsidize coverage for catastrophically expensive drug requirements and a national post-acute and palliative home care program to be funded 50/50 by the provinces and the federal government. The Committee also recommended extending employment insurance to those providing palliative home care; see Senate Standing Committee on Social Affairs, Science and Technology, *The Health of Canadians — The Federal Role — Volume Six: Recommendations for Reform* (Ottawa: Senate Standing Committee on Social Affairs, Science and Technology, 2002) at 12-16.

[76] For broader discussions, see M. Jackman, "The Constitutional Basis for Federal Regulation of Health" (1996) 5:2 Health L. Rev. 3 and, by the same author, "Constitutional Jurisdiction Over Health in Canada" (2000) 8 Health L.J. 95. Recently, the Romanow Commission commissioned a number of discussion papers on federalism and health care, including one by Andre Braën,

As explained in Part I, the delivery of health care services lies primarily with the provinces. Partly this is because the *Constitution Act, 1867*[77] gives to the provinces the exclusive authority to make (and administer) laws for the "establishment, maintenance, and management of hospitals, asylums, charities and eleemosynary institutions".[78] More broadly, it is because the more general provincial power to make laws on "property and civil rights" has been interpreted broadly by the courts to encompass most professional services and indeed, the buying and selling of most kinds of goods and services.[79] Thus, the provinces have authority to regulate the professional activities of doctors, nurses, dentists and physiotherapists on the same basis that they have authority to regulate lawyers, accountants and engineers.

The jurisdiction to finance the delivery of health care services is a divided one. The provinces have the direct authority to make and administer laws that deal with financing under their more general authority over all programs of public insurance against social and economic hardship. This broad authority to deal with programs of social insurance, and the understanding that it includes health insurance, dates from court rulings in the 1930s that unemployment insurance (later allocated to the federal level by constitutional amendment) was a provincial rather than a federal responsibility.[80] However, the same rulings recognized what has become known as the federal government's "spending power". It allows the federal government to indirectly fund programs of social insurance by making financial grants to the provinces that the provinces can then use to pay for the programs. It also allows the federal government to attach conditions to such grants, and thereby to exert influence over the provinces in the design and administration of the programs.

The legal correctness of the spending power is questioned by provinces and sometimes doubted by academics because it has no explicit foundation in constitutional text and only uncertain support in judicial rulings.[81] But practically, the federal spending power has played a vital role in the development of Canadian federalism. It has allowed the federal government to play a role in ensuring some consistency across the country in provincial social programs and therefore in how Canadian social citizenship is defined. More

---

Discussion Paper No. 2: Health and the Distribution of Powers in Canada (July 2002), and one by Howard Leeson, *Discussion Paper No. 12: Constitutional Jurisdiction Over Health and Health Care Services in Canada* (August 2002).

[77] *Constitution Act, 1867* (U.K.), 30 & 31 Vict., c. 3, reprinted in R.S.C. 1985, App. II, No. 5.

[78] *Ibid.*, s. 92(7).

[79] *Ibid.*, s. 92(13).

[80] See *Canada (Attorney General) v. Ontario (Attorney General)*; *Reference re Employment and Social Insurance Act*, [1936] S.C.J. No. 30, [1936] S.C.R. 427 (S.C.C.), and *Canada (Attorney General) v. Ontario (Attorney General)*; *Reference re Employment and Social Insurance Act*, [1937] A.C. 355 (J.C.P.C.) (affirming Supreme Court of Canada). The amendment of the Constitution that reversed these rulings as regards the specific issue of unemployment insurance (but not the general holding that schemes of social insurance were provincial) came in 1940, through (U.K.) 3-4 Geo. VI, c. 36, which added s. 91(2A), "Unemployment Insurance", to enumerated federal powers.

[81] For example, see A. Petter, "Federalism and the Myth of the Federal Spending Power" (1989) 68 Can. Bar Rev. 448.

broadly, the spending power has counteracted the imbalance that Canada's late 19th century Constitution creates by giving many of the governance responsibilities to the provinces and control of a large proportion of the resources to the federal government.

The *Canada Health Act* is the prime example of how the spending power allows the federal government to do indirectly what it cannot do directly. Federal attempts to establish a national health insurance plan (without provincial consent) would almost certainly be unconstitutional. But through the spending power and the *Canada Health Act*, the federal government has acted to ensure that each province establishes a health insurance plan that conforms to the criteria and conditions that, taken together, define the single-payer model. As discussed below, such a plan complies with the general principles of public administration, portability, universality, comprehensiveness and accessibility and with the specific conditions that user fees and extra billing be banned.

Before leaving the Constitution, it is worth noting that the federal role includes several direct service delivery responsibilities of tremendous and growing significance. The first is that the federal government is directly responsible for ensuring the delivery of health care services to Canada's First Nation communities.[82] The importance of this responsibility is obvious from the deplorable health status that is prevalent among these communities.[83] The second federal responsibility worth special mention here is the responsibility that the federal government shares with the provinces for the protection and promotion of public health.[84] As demonstrated dramatically by the experience of Ontario in 2003 with SARS, public health is becoming increasingly dependent on Canada's ability to deal with and respond to threats that have no regard for international or provincial boundaries. This is leading to greater reliance by all Canadians and by all Canadian governments on a robust, expanding and direct federal engagement with the health of Canadians.[85]

---

[82]   *Constitution Act, 1867*, s. 91(24).

[83]   Auditor General of Canada, "Status Report of the Auditor General of Canada — May 2006, Chapter 5: Management of Programs for First Nations" (Ottawa: Auditor General of Canada, 2006) at 141, online: <http://www.oag.bvg.gc.ca/domino/reports.nsf/html/20060505ce.html>.

[84]   Partly under the specific federal power to legislate on "Quarantine and the Establishment and Maintenance of Marine Hospitals", found at s. 91(11), and partly and more broadly under the more general federal power over criminal law, found at s. 91(27), and the general federal power to make laws for the "peace, order and good government of Canada", found in the preamble of s. 91. The latter power allows the federal government to deal with situations of national emergency or crisis and with other matters deemed to be of national dimensions or concern.

[85]   See the report of the National Advisory Committee on SARS and Public Health (the Naylor Committee), *Learning from SARS: Renewal of Public Health in Canada* (Ottawa: Health Canada, 2003), online: <http://www.phac-aspc.gc.ca/publicat/sars-sras/naylor/index.html>. In response to this report, the federal government adopted a public health strategy with three components: (1) a new federal Public Health Agency; (2) a Chief Public Health Officer for Canada and (3) a pan-Canadian public health network. See online: <http://www.phac-aspc.gc.ca/about_apropos/federal_strategy_e.html>. Following discussions with the provinces and territories, the Public Health Agency of Canada was created in 2004. See online: <http://www.phac-aspc.gc.ca/about_apropos/index.html>. In addition to being responsible for areas of direct federal responsibility in public health, the Agency plays a role of leadership in the formation of a public health system that includes the public health responsibilities of the

B. HISTORICAL DEVELOPMENT

Although public health care insurance has a Canadian history dating back at least to 1919, the story of Medicare can be said to start in 1944.[86] In that year, the Commonwealth Co-operative Federation, (the CCF) was elected into office in Saskatchewan under the charismatic leadership of Tommy Douglas. In 1947, it introduced universal hospital insurance. Alberta and British Columbia quickly followed and Newfoundland brought a similar program into Confederation in 1949. In 1957, the Liberal government of St. Laurent offered 50/50 federal cost-sharing to these provinces and to any other province that adopted a comparable program through the *Hospital Insurance and Diagnostic Services Act.*[87] By the end of 1961, all provinces were participating.

The question then became whether physician services should be similarly financed. Organized medicine was opposed to universal access, arguing instead for limited state intervention and for publicly funded insurance only for those who were unable to purchase it for themselves. With provincial support, "voluntariness" became organized medicine's theme, which it contrasted with "socialized medicine". In 1960, the Canadian Medical Association asked for the appointment of a royal commission to study health care reform, expecting it to endorse public insurance only for those with low incomes. Within weeks, Conservative Prime Minister John Diefenbaker announced the creation of such a commission, eventually appointing Emmett Hall, then Chief Justice of Saskatchewan, as Chair.

The CCF then moved again in Saskatchewan. In November of 1961, it introduced legislation creating a system of universal and comprehensive public insurance for physician services. The province's doctors responded with a three-week strike in July 1962 that ended with a mediated settlement that preserved the right of physicians to charge fees to patients in addition to those to be received under the new public plan and that gave physicians the options of partial and of non-participation in that plan.

---

provinces and territories. A more detailed discussion of the law of public health in Canada is available in N.M. Ries, "Chapter 1: Legal Foundations of Public Health in Canada", in Tracey Bailey *et al.*, eds., *Public Health Law and Policy in Canada* (Markham, ON: LexisNexis Butterworths, 2005).

[86] Full accounts are available in M. Taylor, *Health Insurance and Canadian Public Policy: The Seven Decisions That Created the Canadian Health Insurance System and Their Outcomes,* 2nd ed. (Montreal: McGill-Queen's University Press, 1987); M.Taylor, *Insuring National Health Care: The Canadian Experience* (Chapel Hill, NC: University of North Carolina Press, 1990); and C.D. Naylor, *Private Practice, Public Payment: Canadian Medicine and the Politics of Health Insurance, 1911-1966* (Montreal: McGill-Queen's University Press, 1986). A version that pays particular attention to the interaction of federalism and party politics is Antonia Maioni, *Parting at the Crossroads: The Emergence of Health Insurance in the United States and Canada* (Princeton: Princeton University Press, 1998). A shorter and very accessible version that pays special attention to the position taken through the process by the organized medical profession can be found in Nuala P. Kenny, *What Good is Health Care? Reflections on the Canadian Experience* (Ottawa: CHA Press, 2002) at 46-59.

[87] S.C. 1957, c. 28.

These events set the stage for Hall's report, delivered in 1964.[88] It came down squarely on the side of national adoption of the Saskatchewan model. The rationale was equal parts social justice and sound financial management. On the one hand, Hall argued that access to needed medical attention should depend solely on need and be entirely independent of ability to pay. On the other hand, he argued that public insurance that covered everyone and all medical services on uniform terms and conditions would cost less (primarily because of lower administrative costs) than a mixed system with diverse and competing private insurers. The Hall Commission also followed Saskatchewan's example in recommending that public insurance be limited for the time being to hospital and physician services, with the expectation of future expansion to cover other services, including home care, out-of-hospital drugs and dental care.

In 1966, Lester Pearson's minority Liberal government largely adopted Hall's recommendations and embodied them in the *Medical Care Act*.[89] It offered 50/50 sharing of the cost of physician services to every province that made such services accessible to all by establishing a scheme of publicly administered insurance that ensured universal, portable and comprehensive coverage. By the end of 1971, all provinces had adopted a qualifying plan, despite stiff initial resistance to the federal legislation from Ontario, Alberta and British Columbia.[90] The essential elements of Medicare as we know it today were in place. It had prevailed for many reasons, not least of which was the strength of the Hall recommendations. But many other factors, including the politics of the situation and the atmosphere of the times, played a vital role.[91]

The optimism that inspired the creation of Medicare dissipated quickly, once the bills started rolling in under the 50/50 cost-sharing arrangement. In 1977, the federal government of Pierre Trudeau ended its open-ended exposure by abandoning 50/50 cost-sharing of actual provincial expenditures and replacing it with a system of block grants (the Established Program Financing, or EPF grant system).[92] These block grants put federal contributions for health and higher education together and acknowledged the right of each province to use its grant in whatever way it saw fit. The EPF system also replaced 100 per cent annual cash transfers with a system consisting partly of annual cash transfers and partly of "tax points" that the federal government permanently relinquished to the provinces. Since the value of these tax points would change with the size of each provincial economy, the cash portion of the grants became residual, in the sense

---

[88]   Canada, *Royal Commission on Health Services*, Volumes I and II (Ottawa: Queen's Printer, 1964-65) (the Hall Report).

[89]   S.C. 1966-67, c. 64.

[90]   See Greg Marchildon, "Private Insurance for Medicare: Policy History and Trajectory in the Four Western Provinces", in Colleen M. Flood, Kent Roach & Lorne Sossin, eds., *Access to Care, Access to Justice: The Legal Debate Over Private Health Insurance in Canada* (Toronto: University of Toronto Press, 2005) 429.

[91]   Pearson's minority government was vulnerable in Parliament and electorally to the New Democratic Party, the successor to the national CCF, which was led in 1966 by Tommy Douglas; see Antonia Maioni, *Parting at the Crossroads: The Emergence of Health Insurance in the United States and Canada* (Princeton: Princeton University Press, 1998).

[92]   *Federal-Provincial Fiscal Arrangements and Established Programs Financing Act, 1977*, S.C. 1976-77, c. 10.

that the cash payment made to each province was determined by first establishing the size of the general grant and then deducting from it the current value of the transferred tax points. Finally, EPF included an escalator, at first applicable only to the cash portion of provincial grants but then to the entire grant. As the national economy grew, this escalator ensured corresponding increases in the size of EPF funding.

Around the same time, provincial governments began to rely increasingly on user fees as a means of protecting their own treasuries, partly to discourage what was believed to be widespread abuse of a "free" service. In accordance with the settlement that had ended the Saskatchewan strike of 1962 and that had not been disturbed in the design of the national program, many doctors throughout Canada continued to "extra bill" their patients for services that were covered under Medicare. These provincial trends led to the reappointment of Hall as a one-person committee of review by the Trudeau government and to the adoption in 1984 of the *Canada Health Act*, which combined the two earlier pieces of legislation into one comprehensive statute. It responded to growing concerns with physician extra billing and hospital user fees by stipulating dollar-for-dollar reductions from the federal transfer that would otherwise be payable to any province in which extra billing or user fees were charged. The Act also placed Medicare within the framework of the wider public policy of protecting, promoting and restoring "the physical and mental well-being of residents of Canada". Optically at least, the legislation was about ends (health) and not merely means (doctor and hospital services). The replacement of the technocratic legislative nomenclature of 1957 and of 1969 with the bold *Canada Health Act* of 1984 symbolized how universal health insurance had become, in only 15 years, a defining part of the Canadian identity that fell within the protection of the federal government. At this symbolic level, the Act aligned closely with Trudeau's earlier success in having Canada's constitution repatriated with the enshrined *Canadian Charter of Rights and Freedoms*.

The later history of Medicare as a national program has been one of further federal fiscal retrenchment and of federal-provincial bickering over the extent of that retrenchment.[93] The EPF escalator was reduced in 1986 and then eliminated in 1990, essentially freezing federal grants while provincial spending continued to grow at a rate that was higher than the general rate of inflation. In 1995, the Chretien government replaced the EPF with the Canada Health and Social

---

[93] This account of more recent developments in federal-provincial fiscal arrangements draws on the following sources: Jocelyn Downie, Timothy Caulfield & Colleen M. Flood, eds., *Canadian Health Law and Policy*, 2nd ed. (Markham, ON: LexisNexis Butterworths, 2002) at 28-31; R.B. Deber, "Getting What We Pay For: Myths and Realities About Financing Canada's Health Care System", (2000) 21:2 Health L. Can. 9 at 25-28 and 37; Sujit Choudhry, "Bill 11, the Canada Health Act and the Social Union: The Need for Institutions", in T.A. Caulfield & B. von Tigerstrom, eds., *Health Care Reform and the Law in Canada: Meeting the Challenge* (Edmonton: University of Alberta Press, 2002), 37 at 62-63; Commission on the Future of Health Care in Canada, *Building on Values: The Future of Health Care in Canada — Final Report* (Ottawa: Commission on the Future of Health Care in Canada, 2002) at 35-40; and F. Rocher and M. Smith, *Discussion Paper No. 18: Federalism and Health Care: The Impact of Political-Institutional Dynamics on the Canadian Health Care System* (Ottawa: Commission on the Future of Health Care in Canada, 2002).

Transfer (the CHST), which combined federal funding for health and higher education (until then under EPF) with federal social assistance program funding. Simultaneously, staged reductions in the cash portion of this funding were initiated. Between 1995-96 and 1998-99 it fell from $18.5 to $12.5 billion. These decreases in cash were off-set to some extent by continuing growth in the value of the tax points, but it can also be said that the growth in the tax points would have happened anyway and that the cuts in the cash contributions were therefore real cuts in the total federal contribution. Here, it needs to be emphasized that the federal government's enforcement leverage depends entirely on the cash portion of CHST funding. The only penalty that it can impose on provinces is to withhold some or all (depending on the breach) of the cash grant that would otherwise be made. It cannot reclaim, prevent or restrict the use of the tax points. Thus, there is concern that unless the cash portion of the federal contribution continues to be large enough to be meaningful to all provinces, the ability of the federal government to insist on national compliance with the *Canada Health Act* may be compromised.

C. RECENT DEVELOPMENTS

Starting in 2000, intergovernmental conferences have resulted in three health accords, each of which has resulted in more federal money being put into the CHST (now the CHT), with some going to the base as a permanent upward adjustment and some going in as a temporary adjustment.[94] The context for these accords included the provincial claim that, by 1998-99, the federal contribution to Medicare had dropped to as little as 16 per cent and the usual federal response (to the bewilderment of almost everyone), that this ignored the value of the tax points and the fact that the provinces were comparing federal spending as a percentage of the historic cost of Medicare to federal spending as a percentage of all current provincial spending on health. Such complexities led Romanow to observe that they made, "the value of the federal contribution to health care extremely obscure to even those most informed".[95] Partly to bring greater

---

[94]   Health Accords were reached in 2000, 2003 and 2004. For the 2000 Accord, see First Ministers' Meeting, "First Ministers' Meeting Communique on Health, September 11, 2000", Doc. 800-038/004 (Ottawa: September 11, 2000), online: <http://www.scics.gc.ca/cinfo00/800038004_e.html>. See also the associated news releases: First Ministers' Meeting, "Funding Commitment of the Government of Canada, September 11, 2000", Doc. 800-038/006 (Ottawa: September 9-11, 2000), online: <http://www.scics.gc.ca/cinfo00/80003806_e.html>, and "New Federal Investments to Accompany the Agreements on Health Renewal and Early Childhood Developments" (Ottawa: September 9-11, 2000), online: <http://www.scics.gc.ca/cinfo00/80003807_e.html>. For the 2003 Accord, see First Minister's Meeting, "2003 First Ministers' Accord on Health Care Renewal, February 5, 2003", Doc. 800-039 (Ottawa: February 4-5, 2003), online: <http://www.scics.gc.ca/pdf/800039004_e.pdf>. For the 2004 Accord, see First Ministers' Meeting, "A 10-Year Plan to Strengthen Health Care, September 16, 2004", Doc. 800-042 (Ottawa: September 13-16, 2004), online: <http://www.scics.gc.ca/cinfo04/800042005_e.pdf>.

[95]   Commission on the Future of Health Care in Canada, *Building on Values: The Future of Health Care in Canada — Final Report* (Ottawa: Commission on the Future of Health Care in Canada, 2002) at 38.

transparency and accountability to intergovernmental dynamics, Commissioner Romanow (and the Kirby Committee) recommended a national health council with a mandate to oversee and report upon health system performance.[96]

The opaqueness of intergovernmental fiscal arrangements is beyond the scope of this chapter. The more general highlights of the accords include the separation of health transfers from those for education and social services: as of 2004, the CHST has become the CHT and the CST. More broadly, the accords mean significant increases in the dollar value of federal health transfers to the provinces and territories. Through the accords, the federal cash contribution to health is brought from roughly $9.61 billion in 2000 to $16.5 in 2005/06 and to a projected level of $24 billion by 2009-10.[97] Clearly, a cash contribution increase of over 130 per cent over 10 years is significant. With the growing value of the previously transferred tax points, the increased cash contribution means that the total federal contribution in 2005/06 is roughly $30.6 billion, representing approximately 22 per cent of the $140 billion currently being spent on health care in Canada, and roughly 32 per cent of the total public spending of just under $100 billion. This does not include the amount spent directly by the federal government on health care services, including in providing health services to Aboriginal Canadians and public health programs to all Canadians, or in providing additional and targeted funding to the provinces and territories.

Still, as large as the cash transfer increases are in total dollars, they do not resolve the funding challenges faced by the provinces and territories. At most, they restore and maintain the relative value and credibility of the federal contribution. The 2000 and 2003 Accords took modest steps in this direction, committing the federal government only to increases of specific dollar amounts, leaving further increases (if any) in subsequent years entirely to the discretion of the federal government. In 2004, the much larger step of agreeing to a specific escalator of 6 per cent per year was taken, applying to the cash portion of the CHT transfer from 2006 onwards.[98] This has been a key provincial demand since unilateral federal elimination of the EPF escalator in 1990.

On the other side of each of the three accords are the commitments given by the provinces and territories for reforms that will improve system performance and health outcomes, particularly regarding access. In both the 2003 and 2004 documents, Canadian governments agreed to take action to give Canadians greater access to reformed primary care, to acute home care and to catastrophic drug coverage. They also agreed to address the growing problem of wait times. How all this was to be accomplished was left largely to the provinces and territories. To encourage action at that level, the federal government agreed in the 2003 Accord to create a Health Reform Fund worth $16 billion over five

[96] Commission on the Future of Health Care in Canada, *Building on Values: The Future of Health Care in Canada — Final Report* (Ottawa: Commission on the Future of Health Care in Canada, 2002), at 52-59.
[97] These figures are from the press release that accompanied the release of the 2004 Accord.
[98] Provincial and territorial expenditures are expected to increase by 3.8 per cent, adjusted for inflation, in 2006-2007: Canadian Institute for Health Information, *Preliminary Provincial and Territorial Government Health Expenditure Estimates: 1974-1975 to 2006-2007* (Ottawa: Canadian Institute for Health Information, 2006) at 3.

years. In the 2004 Accord, it agreed to a Wait Times Reduction Fund, worth $4.5 billion over six years. Both are to support initiatives that are launched at the provincial level, reflecting provincial circumstances and priorities, subject only to consistency with the broad objectives for an improved system that are laid out in the accords.

This avoidance of specific intergovernmental agreements to specific obligations reflects the pervasive influence of federal-provincial dynamics: first, Canada's decentralized federalism and the underlying theme of respect for jurisdictional boundaries that is the point of departure for each accord; second, the reinforcing influence of the history of decades of federal fiscal retrenchment from the equal financial partnership that ushered Medicare into existence; and third, the always delicate politics of national unity. But even with these influences at work, the 2004 Accord was more directive on system performance improvements. It committed governments to the development of a national pharmaceuticals strategy, with a report on progress by June 30, 2006.[99] It also committed governments to first dollar coverage of certain home care services, again by 2006. Most ambitiously, it committed governments to the development of common evidence based benchmarks for medically acceptable wait times in four priority areas by December 31, 2005 and to multi-year targets for achieving those benchmarks by December 31, 2007.[100]

Promising specific actions by specific dates strengthens the theme of enhanced accountability that runs running through each of the accords. Each accord contains an accountability commitment by governments — though importantly, the commitment is to their own constituents, not to the other level of government. In 2003, provincial and territorial governments committed to reporting to their own citizens on their use of health care dollars, on the operation of their programs and services, on health outcomes and status and on the actions being taken to increase the availability of diagnostic and other medical equipment. To reinforce these commitments, the 2003 Accord established an almost national version of the health council (called the Health Council of Canada) that had been recommended by Romanow and by the Kirby Committee. It was given the mandate of reviewing and reporting to Canadians on the implementation of the Accord.[101] In 2004, the mandate of the Health

---

[99]   The Federal/Provincial/Territorial Ministers Task Force on the National Pharmaceuticals Strategy issued an update and progress report in June 2006: see *National Pharmaceuticals Strategy Progress Report – Federal/Provincial/Territorial Ministerial Task Force, June, 2006*, available online: <http://www.hc-sc.gc.ca/hcs-sss/alt_formats/hpb-dgps/pdf/pubs/2006-nps-snpp/2006-nps-snpp_e.pdf>. As of May 22, 2007, little further seems to have been achieved.

[100] This more ambitious effort now seems to have been displaced by a series of bilateral agreements between the federal government and individual provinces and territories, whereby the federal government provides funding for the establishment of wait time guarantees that relate to specific services chosen by each province or territory. On this approach, the only consistency that has been achieved is the creation of *some* wait time guarantee in each province. There is no consistency achieved in terms of the services that have been made subject to a guarantee: see "There's nothing to these waiting-times guarantees", *Globe and Mail* (April 6, 2007), at A12.

[101] Quebec established its own version of a national health council, called the Quebec Council on Health and Welfare. Like Alberta, Quebec is not a "participating jurisdiction" in the Health Council of Canada.

Council of Canada was expanded to include monitoring progress in achieving improvements in wait times and in access to home care and reformed primary care. An element of conditionality and therefore of intergovernmental accountability was also added, with the proviso that all funding arrangements required compliance with these reporting commitments.

A final area worth separate mention is that of national institutional development. In addition to creating the Health Council of Canada, the 2003 Accord called for the establishment of the Canadian Patient Safety Institute and promised the completion of the Canada Health Infoway, initiated by Ottawa in the late 1990s. The 2004 Accord gave specific responsibilities to report on wait times to the previously established Canadian Institute for Health Information. It also "formalized" the process for avoiding and resolving disputes under the *Canada Health Act* that was originally established by an exchange of letters between Ministers of Health in 2002.[102] This calls for dispute avoidance through discussions, information exchange and "advance assessments", and allows either government to a dispute to initiate a process of resolution that moves from fact-finding and formal negotiations to an advisory opinion from a jointly appointed third party panel. It leaves final authority for decision-making to the federal Minister of Health and makes no provision for citizen initiated disputes. While collectively modest compared to the institutional development that some have advocated, these developments are nevertheless significant in moving Canada's "system of systems" closer to a national approach to at least core areas of difficulty and opportunity.[103]

The perceived need for three national health accords in four years is telling: clearly, political leaders recognized that public confidence in Canadian health care needed to be restored. Whether these types of accords can do this is an open question, given the generality of the language, the reliance on loosely coordinated effort across 14 independent jurisdictions instead of one united effort, and the fact that the accords are political rather than legal agreements. The early reports of the Health Council of Canada are encouraging but only mildly so: they are optimistic in tone and complimentary of many innovative initiatives that are going on, but point out there is a heavy reliance on pilot projects as the vehicle for change.[104] In addition, the Council has noted the

---

[102] The Health Canada description of the process, as well as the letter that was sent to provincial ministers of health by the federal minister in 2002, can be found online: <http://www.hc-sc.gc.ca/hcs-sss/medi-assur/avoid-prevent/index_e.html>. The Province of Quebec is not a party to this dispute resolution process.

[103] See Colleen M. Flood & Sujit Choudhry, *Discussion Paper No. 13: Strengthening the Foundations: Modernizing the Canada Health Act* (Ottawa: Commission on the Future of Health Care in Canada, 2002), online: <http://www.hc-sc.gc.ca/english/care/romanow/hcc0377.html>. See also Sujit Choudhry, "Bill 11, the Canada Health Act and the Social Union: The Need for Institutions", in T.A. Caulfield & B. von Tigerstrom, eds., *Health Care Reform and the Law in Canada: Meeting the Challenge* (Edmonton: University of Alberta Press, 2002).

[104] Health Council of Canada, *Health Care Renewal in Canada: Accelerating Change* (Toronto: Health Council of Canada, 2005), online: <http://www.healthcouncilcanada.ca/docs/rpts/2005/Accelerating_Change_HCC_2005.pdf>. Health Council of Canada, *Health Care Renewal in Canada: Clearing the Road to Quality — Executive Summary* (Toronto: Health Council of Canada, 2006), online: <http://www.healthcouncilcanada.ca/docs/rpts/2006/ExecSumEnglish2006.pdf>.

continuing inconsistency across Canada in how information, including on system performance, is gathered, tracked and reported.

Still, Canada now has the Health Council of Canada, as well as a Patient Safety Institute and a very active health information institute. All this is progress. It is positive also that the monitoring that will now go on through the Council (as well as through CIHI) will be in reinforcement to the greater reporting and (in some provinces) third party monitoring that is now going on at the provincial level across the country.[105] By carrying out its mandate, the Council may invest the accords with some of the normative weight that they lack as generally drafted non-binding political agreements. And finally, it has to be acknowledged that the accords are not without their own normative weight: the commitments made in the 2004 Accord as to wait times, primary care, home care and pharmaceutical coverage are, by the standards set by the earlier accords, quite specific and quite substantial. More encouragingly still, thus far at least, these commitments are being acted upon.[106] There is reason therefore, for optimism.[107]

D. THE FIVE CRITERIA OF THE CANADA HEALTH ACT

The stated objective of the *Canada Health Act* is to "establish criteria and conditions in respect of insured health services and extended health care services provided under provincial law that must be met before a full cash contribution may be made".[108] In reality, the Act has little impact on the funding or delivery of "extended health care services" and so, these will not be discussed further.[109]

---

[105] See, for example, the various reports issued or initiatives undertaken by Saskatchewan's Health Quality Council or by the Manitoba Centre for Health Policy.

[106] On December 12, 2005, provincial and territorial Ministers of Health announced the first ever nationally agreed upon benchmarks for maximum wait times in cancer treatment, cardiac surgery, vision care and orthopedics. The benchmarks included radiation therapy (within four weeks); hip and knee replacements (within 26 weeks); cataract removal (within 16 weeks for high-risk patients); breast cancer screening (every two years) and cardiac bypass surgery (within two weeks for Level 1 patients). The ministers promised more benchmarks "as new evidence is produced" and recommitted their jurisdictions to establishing multi-year by the end of 2007 for achieving their benchmarks. The press release and backgrounder is available online: <http://www.newswire.ca/en/releases/archive/December2005/12/c5919.html>.

[107] On the other hand, concerns are also being raised about whether promised actions are being taken: see Lisa Priest, "Vow broken on cancer wait times", *The Globe and Mail* (November 21, 2006) A1, and Lisa Priest *et al.*, "Creation of drug program imperative: Romanow", *The Globe and Mail* (November 21, 2006) A1; and Andre Picard, "Bickering stalls national drug plan to cover catastrophes", The Globe and Mail (October 5, 2006) A15.

[108] *Canada Health Act*, R.S.C. 1985, c. C-6, s. 4.

[109] Section 2 of the *Canada Health Act* defines "extended health care services" to mean nursing home intermediate care, adult residential care, home care and ambulatory care, subject to further definition through regulation. Section 4 speaks of the purpose of the Act as being the establishment "of criteria and conditions in respect of insured health services and extended health services provided under provincial law that must be met before a full cash contribution may be made" from the federal government to any province. The reality, however, is that the criteria and conditions that are established by the Act apply only to the obligations of the province to fund and restrict user charges and extra billing in respect of insured health services.

Instead, the focus here will be on how the Act affects the funding and delivery of "insured health services", that is, medically necessary hospital services, medically required physician services and dental-surgical services that must be performed in a hospital.[110]

The standards that the Act imposes on the provinces in respect of these services include the five criteria of public administration, universality, portability, comprehensiveness and accessibility. I will deal with the first three of these together and then separately with each of comprehensiveness and accessibility.

In addition to the five criteria, the Act also deals specifically with extra billing and user fees, mandating deductions from the federal contribution to the extent any province allows either, or both, to occur. These specific provisions (called "conditions" rather than criteria in the Act) are essentially specifications of the "accessibility" criteria, and they will be discussed as elements of accessibility, rather than as distinct pre-conditions to provincial receipt of federal contributions.

1. Public Administration, Universality and Portability

Public administration is satisfied if the health care insurance plan of a province is administered and operated on a non-profit basis by a public authority that is appointed or designated by the government of the province.[111] In most provinces at most times, the public authority has been the Department of Health. But subsection 8(1) makes it clear that this is not the only arrangement that is acceptable. It clearly authorizes the utilization of an entity that is distinct from but accountable to the government of a province. Accordingly, the administration of provincial health insurance plans either has been or is entrusted in different provinces to arm's-length commissions. Subsection 8(2) contemplates that the public authority (be it the government itself or a commission) may be given the authority to designate another agency to receive payments on its behalf or to "carry out on its behalf any responsibility in connection with the receipt or payment of accounts rendered for insured health services". This second level delegation would therefore appear to be valid only if limited to certain functions rather than to a complete transfer of overall responsibility for plan administration.

The public administration requirement serves a number of functions. One is to maintain accountability through the political process for the administration of a health insurance plan that is to be operated in accordance with the other criteria. Another is to avoid unnecessary operating costs, whether in the guise of profit-taking, the additional operating overhead that comes with multiple and competing providers of physician and hospital insurance, or the cost of

---

This means that provincial eligibility to a full cash contribution from the federal government is in no way dependent on provincial establishment of a comprehensive and universal scheme of publicly administered insurance that provides access to extended health care services. In other words, the *Canada Health Act* does not extend the single payer model to extended health care services.

[110] *Canada Health Act*, R.S.C. 1985, c. C-6, s. 2.

[111] *Ibid.*, s. 8(1).

regulating private providers to deal with such dynamics as adverse selection or prohibitive premiums for high risk persons. Paying attention to the limited scope of these objectives is important — this criterion demands non-profit public administration of *health insurance*, not in *health care services delivery*. On the question of who can deliver service, neither this criterion nor any other provision of the *Canada Health Act* has any direct application, although, as seen below, arguments can be made that delivery arrangements that jeopardize equal access based on need conflict with the spirit if not the letter of the universality and accessibility criteria.

On universality, the *Canada Health Act* says that each province must insure all of its "insured persons ... on uniform terms and conditions".[112] The Act defines insured persons as all residents of a province with the exception of members of the Canadian Forces, members of the R.C.M.P., inmates in federal penitentiaries and persons who have not completed a minimum residency requirement that is not in excess of three months.[113] A separate definition of "resident" allows provinces to exclude tourists, transients or visitors but also makes clear that public insurance is to apply to everyone lawfully in Canada who makes a province his or her home. It is noteworthy that the standard that is adopted is actually a provincial one. The requirement is for universal coverage on terms and conditions that are uniform as between the residents of the insuring province. Variation between provinces seems to be acknowledged. In this way, the construction of the Act recognizes both the legal reality that constitutional authority over health care is largely provincial and (perhaps) the practical reality that different provinces may choose or be required to define uniformity differently.

The universality requirement exemplifies the difference between insuring health care services on social rather than on market principles. Unlike free market systems of private insurance, the provincial administrators of Medicare cannot reduce their costs by directly or indirectly excluding from coverage those who are high risk due, for example, to pre-existing conditions, medical history, age, occupation or personal choices (such as whether or not they smoke or eat or drink excessively). At the same time, universality ensures participation in the plan of higher income people whose higher premiums (in the form of taxes) subsidizes the funding of health care for lower income people who are likely to require more of it. In this way, it eliminates the "risk pooling" that inhibits such subsidization in a purely private market regime.

The leading challenge to the universality criterion is the increasing availability in Canada of private clinics that allow Canadians to purchase diagnostic services and thereby circumvent waiting lists for obtaining the same service from publicly financed hospitals or clinics. Viewed narrowly, this advantageous access does not engage the universality criterion as long as access within the public system is inclusive and on uniform terms and conditions. But on a broader view, it is obvious that earlier diagnosis will mean early and therefore preferential access to treatment, including when that treatment is

---

[112] *Ibid.*, s. 10.
[113] *Ibid.*, s. 2.

required from the publicly funded system. To deal with this problem, Romanow has recommended an amendment to the Act to clarify that it does apply to medically necessary diagnostic services, and the creation of dedicated federal funding to increase the diagnostic capacity of the publicly funded system.[114]

On portability, the Act says that qualifying health care insurance plans must not impose minimum residency requirements of more than three months on anyone moving into that province from elsewhere in Canada.[115] Conversely, each provincial plan is required to continue to cover its residents who move to another province during the receiving province's qualifying period. The Act also says that the health insurance plan of a province must provide for the payment of the cost of insured services provided to its residents when they are travelling in another province at the rate that is approved by the plan of the service-providing province. In contrast, if services are provided outside Canada, the health insurance plan of the province of residence must (subject to some flexibility) pay for the services at the rates that would have applied if the work had been done in that province. Given the cost of medical treatment in the United States, this means that Canadians who receive treatment in that country can be left with substantial costs even after recovery of expenses in accordance with the Act.

2. Comprehensiveness

The comprehensiveness criteria requires provinces to insure (that is, to fund 100 per cent of the cost of) "all insured health services" provided by hospitals, medical practitioners and dentists.[116] As mentioned previously, "insured health services" are defined as hospital services, physician services and (if they must be provided in a hospital) surgical-dental services. "Hospital services" are defined to be any item on a list of services when determined to be "medically necessary for the purpose of maintaining health, preventing disease or diagnosing or treating an injury, illness or disability".[117] "Physician services" are defined as "medically required services rendered by medical practitioners".

No definition is given for the governing concepts of "medical necessity" and "medically required". It may be that a general and definitive definition is simply

---

[114] Commission on the Future of Health Care in Canada, *Building on Values: The Future of Health Care in Canada — Final Report* (Ottawa: Commission on the Future of Health Care in Canada, 2002) at xxv, xxix, 64-65 and 139-141.

[115] The portability requirements are found in s. 11 of the *Canada Health Act*, R.S.C. 1985, c. C-6.

[116] *Canada Health Act*, R.S.C. 1985, c. C-6, s. 9.

[117] Section 2 of the Act provides that "'hospital services' means any of the following services provided to in-patients or outpatients at a hospital, if the services are medically necessary for the purpose of maintaining health, preventing disease or diagnosing or treating an injury, illness or disability, namely, (a) accommodation and meals at the standard or public ward level and preferred accommodation if medcially necessary, (b) nursing service, (c) laboratory, radiological and other diagnostic procedures, together with the necessary interpretations, (d) drugs, biologicals, and related preparations when administered in the hospital, (e) use of operating room, case room and anaesthetic facilities, including necessary equipment and supplies, (f) medical and surgical equipment and supplies, (g) use of radiotherapy facilities, (h) use of physiotherapy facilities, and (i) services provided by persons who receive remuneration therefore from the hospital, but does not include services that are excluded by the regulations".

not possible, or it may be that the Act's silence on the meaning of these critical concepts was necessary to physician cooperation with Medicare.[118] Whatever the reason for it, the absence of legislative definition means that the meaning of these terms has been largely left to doctors. Medically necessary hospital services are those ordered by doctors and medically required physician services are those provided by physicians. This lightness of the legislative hand assumes an essentially passive role for governments and a largely reactive role for the governors and administrators of hospitals. Medicare gave to government the role of funding the services that doctors either provided directly or that doctors decided needed to be provided by hospitals. It gave to hospitals the role of having in place (also largely through government funding) the staff, equipment, programs and support services needed to provide the clinical services that doctors decided were clinically indicated.

This understanding of comprehensiveness is, however, subject to important qualification. First, provinces are required to insure only services that are provided because they are determined to be either medically necessary or required. Thus, in the case of hospitals, provinces must insure ward accommodation but are not required to insure semi-private or private accommodation, except where such accommodation is determined to be medically necessary. Second, decisions made at the provincial level place practical limits on the ability of physicians and their patients to access specific courses of treatment. These decisions include those relating to the acquisition and distribution of medical equipment and those relating to the addition of new drugs to the formulary that determines hospital eligibility for reimbursement.[119]

Third, the latitude that the *Canada Health Act* appears to leave with each treating physician to determine the meaning of medical necessity has been in every province limited by the processes that are used to determine the physician services that are assigned a fee code within the tariff of fees that allows physician to bill for their services. Across the country, this process involves a form of negotiation between the provincial government and the provincial medical association. For the most part, this process has resulted in steady expansion in the list of physician services that are covered under Medicare: as new services or new ways of providing service have emerged from technical and clinical developments they have been added to the fee code in most provinces. But there has been some "de-listing" of services from the tariff of fees in the various provinces as a budget reduction or control mechanism. Examples of services that have been de-listed are stomach stapling, wart removal, circumcision of newborns, tubal ligations, vasectomies and mamoplasty. In addition, various provinces have decided against providing full or any coverage for some new procedures. An example of this is the exclusion from coverage of certain procedures for the treatment of infertility, namely *in vitro* fertilization and intracytoplasmic sperm injection (ICSI).

---

[118] T. Caulfield, "Wishful Thinking: Defining 'Medically Necessary' in Canada" (1996) 4 Health L.J. 63. See also T.R. Marmor, "Medical Care and Public Policy: The Benefits and Burdens of Asking Fundamental Questions" (1999) 49 Health Policy 27.

[119] See Ontario Ministry of Health and Long Term Care, "Ontario Drug Benefit: How Drugs are Approved", online: <http://www.health.gov.on.ca/english/public/pub/drugs/approved.html>.

Thus, decisions made at a system level result in Medicare having a more constrained scope than the statutory reliance on the open-ended concept of medical necessity might suggest. As these decisions are made provincially, it becomes possible for comprehensiveness and therefore Medicare to mean something more in one province than another. This introduces access variation between provinces and between people within provinces based on ability to pay. It is questionable whether this makes sense, given that the underlying criteria is medical necessity, and given that federal acceptance of different answers to the question of what is medically necessary would seem to mean either the application of a variable standard across provinces or the consistent application of a lowest common denominator that is not mentioned in the Act (or in regulations made under the Act).

The process that has been used to make decisions about comprehensiveness raises other sorts of questions. As mentioned, for physician services, it is a negotiating process that is constructed on collective bargaining lines.[120] Indeed, the *Canada Health Act* contemplates this.[121] Like other collective bargaining processes, this one has been conducted largely behind closed doors. It has been said that the process derives political legitimacy from the participation of governments and clinical legitimacy from the participation of medical associations.[122] But these sources of legitimacy are likely to be undermined by the primary focus of the process on physician incomes and by the pervasive concern of governments for cost-containment as an overriding policy objective.

Decisions about what is covered by Medicare are at the heart of the system. A truly public system of health insurance would be one that includes the public in decisions of such fundamental importance. The question is how to do this while addressing the concern that a more open process would be unlikely to make the tough decisions that are and will be needed to ensure the ongoing sustainability of the system. It is possible to believe, as others argue, that greater openness and transparency are part of the answer to this question, either because they will lead either to greater acceptance of the need for tough decisions that limit the list of insured services to match available resources, or because they will lead to greater acceptance of the higher taxes needed to increase Medicare's capacity to fund a longer list of insured services.[123] A worry however, is the past tendency of the system to be better at adding new programs and services than it has been at removing old ones, even when the new was intended to replace the old. Another concern is the difficulty the system has had in achieving true engagement and

---

[120] For example, see Nova Scotia's *Medical Society Act*, S.N.S. 1995-96, c. 12, ss. 7, 8 and 9 and its *Health Services and Insurance Act*, R.S.N.S. 1989, c. 197, ss. 13, 13A and 13B.

[121] Clause 12(1)(c) of the Act requires each province to pay "reasonable compensation for all insured health services rendered by medical practitioners or dentists". Subsection 12(2) then says that this requirement is satisfied if the province commits itself to negotiating physician compensation with "provincial organizations" that represent doctors and accepts the resolution of disputes through conciliation or binding arbitration.

[122] C. Tuohy, *Accidental Logics: The Dynamics of Change in the Health Care Arena in the United States, Britain and Canada* (New York: Oxford University Press, 1999) at 260.

[123] Colleen M. Flood, Mark Stabile & Carolyn Tuohy, "What Is In and Out of Medicare? Who Decides?", in Colleen M. Flood, ed., *Just Medicare: What's In, What's Out, How We Decide* (Toronto: University of Toronto Press, 2006) 15 at 23.

participation by the general public, as opposed to the organizations who purport to represent them. A third worry is the risk that decisions on the scope of Medicare will not be connected to decisions on rates of taxation made through the electoral process. A casualty could be funding for other social programs, without the powerful constituency that health care holds.

Those who advocate for process reform are likely to face considerable skepticism because of the failure or mixed success of other attempts to elevate the definition of medical necessity into one of deliberated public policy. In Alberta for example, the task was given to an expert independent panel, in accordance with recommendations made in a report from the Premier's Advisory Council on Health for Alberta (the Mazankowski report).[124] This mandate was part of a broader policy of restricting the scope of Medicare and of licensing private surgical facilities to provide a broader range of surgical procedures.[125] Soon afterwards however, the panel reported that it was unable to reach any consensus on where the line between essential (or necessary) and non-essential services should be drawn. As with other comparable experiments, it is important to recognize that the panel was given the very difficult if not impossible task of developing lists of essential and non-essential services through an extraordinary intervention that was designed to supersede rather than to reform the normal decision-making process. Failure in such Herculean undertakings, especially when designed to achieve controversial preconceived outcomes, does not make a convincing argument against reforming the processes that more modestly grapple on a continuing basis with the opportunities and challenges that are presented by constantly evolving health needs and the rapidly changing world of medical technology and health care delivery practice.

Reform along these more modest lines can be seen in the creation of administrative tribunals in Ontario, Alberta, British Columbia and Quebec that are mandated to hear appeals where health insurance administrators decide not to fund out-of-country treatment where the treatment in question is not available

---

[124] One of the more well-known attempts at defining the list of services that would be funded under public insurance is the so-called Oregon Plan, in which the State of Oregon initiated a process of public deliberation that was intended to lead to a limited list of services that would be provided under the state's Medicaid program to low-income persons and to a ranking of these services for the purpose of resource allocation; see L. Jacobs, T. Marmor & J. Oberlander, "The Oregon Health Plan and the Political Paradox of Rationing: What Advocates and Critics Have Claimed and What Oregon Did" (1999) 24 J. Health Pol. 161, where the authors argue that the outcome was actually expanded access for health care services for Medicaid recipients. For a broader empirical study of how different countries decide the health care services that are and are not to be publicly funded, see C.M. Flood, M. Stabile & C.H. Tuohy, "The Borders of Solidarity: How Countries Determine the Public/Private Mix in Spending and the Impact on Health Care" (2002) 12 Health Matrix 297. There is also a very large philosophical literature on the question of what should be contained within a publicly funded health care system. For example, see D. Callaghan, "What is a Reasonable Demand on Health Care Resources: Designing a Basic Package of Benefits" (1992) 8 J. Contemp. Health L. & Pol'y 1. Finally, for a critique of de-listing as a cost-containment strategy, see M. Rachlis, "Defining Basic Services and De-Insuring the Rest: The Wrong Diagnosis and the Wrong Prescription" (1995) 152 C.M.A.J. 1401.

[125] *Health Care Protection Act*, R.S.A. 2000, c. H-1.

in Canada.[126] Whereas Quebec's tribunal is a general administrative appeal tribunal that hears appeals on decisions from across government, the tribunals in Ontario, Alberta and British Columbia are more specialized bodies that focus on the issue of out-of-country treatment or (in the case of Ontario) a broader range of health system issues. The Ontario tribunal (called the Ontario Health Services Appeal and Review Board) is the most elaborate of these, differentiated from the others by its independence from government and the formality of its proceedings. It has however, attracted criticism for the narrowness of its mandate, its dependency on the opinion of physicians, its slowness and its inaccessibility.[127]

Even with their limitations, the availability of such avenues of review enhance the legitimacy of the overall process by which decisions on comprehensiveness are made, solely by making those decisions subject to review by a known and established process.[128] In other provinces, a similar review may be available through an ombudsmen's office, but such offices do not have the authority to issue binding rulings. Another option may be a complaint under human rights law, but only where the decision not to fund is aligned with a prohibited ground of discrimination. This may be more difficult to establish in the wake of the decision of the Supreme Court of Canada in *Auton v. British Columbia*,[129] discussed below and in Chapter 14 in this volume. Finally, whether or not decisions to fund out-of-country treatments are subject to an administrative review, they are open to review by the courts under administrative law principles, as the decision in *Stein v. Quebec (Régie de l'Assurance-Maladie)*,[130] discussed below, illustrates.

The limited scope for recourse that is available through this range of nationally available mechanisms highlights the importance of the step that has been taken in the four largest provinces to establish more specialized administrative review processes. But even where such processes are put in place, they do not fully address the underlying problem, which is that the decisions that *de facto* define comprehensiveness are often initially taken out of the public eye, within health care bureaucracies and in physician negotiations, without much clarity either as to the criteria or the evidence on which they are based.

---

[126] Caroline Pitfield & Colleen M. Flood, "Section 7 'Safety Valves': Appealing Wait Times Witihin a One-Tier System", in Colleen M. Flood, Kent Roach & Lorne Sossin, eds., *Access to Care, Access to Justice: The Legal Debate Over Private Health Insurance in Canada* (Toronto: University of Toronto Press, 2005) 477.

[127] *Ibid.*, at 485-88, 490-96. The legislative framework for Ontario's Board consists of the following Acts and regulations: *Ministry of Health Appeal and Review Boards Act, 1998*, S.O. 1998, c. 18, Sched.; *Health Insurance Act*, R.S.O. 1990, c. H.6, s. 21(1) and R.R.O. 1990, Reg. 552, s. 28.4.

[128] Colleen M. Flood, Mark Stabile & Carolyn Tuohy, "What Is In and Out of Medicare? Who Decides?", in Colleen M. Flood, ed., *Just Medicare: What's In, What's Out, How We Decide* (Toronto: University of Toronto Press, 2006) 15; Caroline Pitfield & Colleen M. Flood, "Section 7 'Safety Valves': Appealing Wait Times Within a One-Tier System", in Colleen M. Flood, Kent Roach & Lorne Sossin, eds., *Access to Care, Access to Justice: The Legal Debate Over Private Health Insurance in Canada* (Toronto: University of Toronto Press, 2005), 477.

[129] *Auton (Guardian ad litem of) v. British Columbia (Attorney General)*, [2004] S.C.J. No. 71, [2004] 3 S.C.R. 657 (S.C.C.).

[130] [1999] Q.J. No. 2724, [1999] R.J.Q. 2416 (Que. C.A.).

An improved process would be one built differently from the ground up, where decisions on the scope of Medicare are initially made. It would establish a greater separation between the questions of what services should be covered and the question of what fees should be paid to doctors for providing those services. It would be one that, with or without this separation, was flexibly guided by criteria that would be defined in advance of their application to specific facts but that would be subject to revision in the course of the decision-making process. Opportunities for participation would extend into the application of the criteria to specific cases. Decisions would include not only the outcome, but also the rationale that explained the outcome. Finally, an improved process would reduce the institutionalized advantage that services already on the list might have over new services yet to be added. It would be more than a gatekeeper process, limited to reviewing new treatments or new ways of doing established things. It would have the broader responsibility of ensuring that the list of funded services generally included the services, both new and old, that meet the criteria for inclusion.

The objective of reforms along these lines would not be to convert the current process into an adjudicative one. Indeed, avoiding this conversion would be one of the challenges. The objective instead would be to make the process into a more open and transparent version of the policy-making process that it already is. This would be to preserve and enhance responsiveness and efficiency and to avoid undue segregation of decisions on particular treatments from the overall task of achieving a list of covered services that generally includes what belongs on the list and that generally excludes what does not. At the same time however, the process must not be so technically driven and utilitarian that other values, including compassion and respect for human rights, are excluded. Nevertheless, the emphasis on defined criteria and a rigorous commitment to evidence-based decision-making would be critical, in part to address the concern that a more open and inclusive process will lack the capacity to give negative as well as positive answers.

3. Accessibility

In discussions about the current status and the reform of the Canadian health care system, concerns about access invariably figure prominently. The relevant provisions are section 12 (dealing with the accessibility criteria) and sections 18 and 19 (dealing respectively with user charges and extra billing). Working together, these provisions deal with accessibility on two levels. First, they create a general and open-ended requirement of accessibility. Second, they deal specifically with two elements of accessibility, one being the compensation of physicians and the funding of hospitals and the other being point of services charges (banning user charges and extra billing).

The first and broader requirement says that a provincial plan "must provide for insured health services on uniform terms and conditions and on a basis that does not impede or preclude, either directly or indirectly, whether by charges made to insured persons or otherwise, reasonable access to those services by insured persons".[131] In the *Canada Health Act*, "reasonableness" means that the Act can be applied with sensitivity to the particular circumstances and factors of relevance to the standard of access that is needed, possible or desired in each province. Such flexibility was and is important in achieving and maintaining provincial participation in Medicare as a quasi-national program.

Having said that, the requirement for reasonable access implies an objective standard that must be capable of accomplishing the Act's larger objectives — protecting, promoting and restoring the physical and mental well-being of residents of Canada. The accessibility requirement therefore demands more than accessibility on terms and conditions that are uniform. It demands access on terms and conditions that ensure the general adequacy of access, as measured against these objectives.

What adequacy means will depend on many complex questions about (for example) what is a health care need, the ranking of needs, the efficacy of alternative courses of treatment, and the priority that should be given to health over other social goods. The *Canada Health Act* does not purport to answer these questions. But it does seem to contemplate that they will be asked. In doing so, the Act demands more of the provinces than the creation of a system of public funding that covers all medically necessary hospital and physician services. It demands that the provinces ensure a level of access to these services that is consistent with the objectives spelled out in the Act.

One implication is that funding must not just be public but adequate when measured against the need for service. But the implications go farther, since access can be affected by many other factors in the organization and operation of the health care system, including the allocation of funding among providers. There is nothing in the language of the *Canada Health Act* that establishes the irrelevance of these other factors. Clause 12(1)(*a*) does specify a concern with financial barriers, but it also goes beyond financial barriers. It speaks of barriers that impede or preclude reasonable access, "either directly or indirectly whether by charges made to insured persons *or otherwise*" (emphasis added).

In this aspect, the accessibility criterion demands a deeper level of interest by provincial and territorial governments in the delivery of services than is called for by the other criteria. Conversely, the accessibility criterion can be seen as authorizing the federal government to find provinces in non-compliance where reasonable access is "impeded or precluded" by the level of funding that a province provides to its health care system or by the choices the province makes in organizing, managing and regulating its health care system.

For example, the problem of waiting lists and of waiting times would seem to be one that could obviously bring a province into violation of the accessibility criteria, whether the cause of the problem was the inadequacy of public funding, sub-optimal allocation of funding or the failure to manage waiting lists and waiting times in a coordinated and coherent fashion. More ambitiously, it has been argued the accessibility criterion could potentially be engaged by a provincial plan (such as that considered in Alberta) to allow the private purchasing of a greater range of surgical services from for-profit clinics. This

---

[131] *Canada Health Act*, R.S.C. 1985, c. C-6, s. 12(1)(*a*).

would occur on a showing that the implementation of the plan was diverting physicians, nurses and other human and non-human resources from the public system, thereby reducing access to the services that continue to be publicly funded.[132]

As with comprehensiveness, accessibility can be enhanced by adjudicative mechanisms that are empowered to review the decisions of health systems officials who have the responsibility to deal with accessibility issues. In Ontario and Quebec, as in other provinces, bureaucrats are called upon to make decisions on requests for funding for out-of-country care where treatments that are part of Medicare cannot be made available on a timely basis to particular patients in-province. In both provinces, appeals from these decisions can be taken to the same tribunals that hear appeals from decisions about funding where the request is to receive funding to obtain a treatment outside Canada that is not included within Medicare. Such review mechanisms are referred to as "safety valves" in the literature.[133] In *Chaoulli*, the dissenting judges suggested that their availability weighed in favour of judicial deference to legislative decisions such as the decision of Quebec (and of other provinces) to protect public health care by banning private insurance for medical services available through Medicare. This deference is certain to be contingent however. It is not, for example, likely to be forthcoming where the administrative review process lacks independence from government, does not observe the principles of procedural fairness and does not have the authority to give such remedies as are demanded by the merits of the case.

The specific accessibility requirements of the *Canada Health Act* can be quickly dealt with. Clause 12(1)(*b*) requires payments to physicians for the delivery of insured health services, "in accordance with a tariff or system of payment authorized by the law of the province". The reference to a "tariff" indicates the underlying assumption that fee-for-service arrangements (with the incentive structure that they imply) would continue to be the standard method of physician compensation. In this line, it is interesting that the Act requires each province to pay reasonable compensation for all insured services rendered by doctors (as well as those rendered by dentists).[134] In contrast, it simply requires that payments be made to hospitals, "in respect of the cost of insured health services".[135] Thus, while it is a condition of federal funding that doctors be paid "reasonable compensation", all that is by implication required in the funding of

---

[132] Sujit Choudhry, "Bill 11, the Canada Health Act and the Social Union: The Need for Institutions", in T.A. Caulfield & B. von Tigerstrom, eds., *Health Care Reform and the Law in Canada: Meeting the Challenge* (Edmonton: University of Alberta Press, 2002) 37 at 68-72.

[133] There is much discussion of the "safety valve" concept in the wake of *Chaoulli v. Quebec (Attorney General)*, [2005] S.C.J. No. 33, [2005] 1 S.C.R. 791 (S.C.C.), where the dissenting judges portrayed the availability of such mechanisms as a rationale for non-intervention under the *Canadian Charter of Rights and Freedoms*. See Caroline Pitfield & Colleen M. Flood, "Section 7 'Safety Valves': Appealing Wait Times Within a One-Tier System", in Colleen M. Flood, Kent Roach & Lorne Sossin, eds., *Access to Care, Access to Justice: The Legal Debate Over Private Health Insurance in Canada* (Toronto: University of Toronto Press, 2005) 477.

[134] *Canada Health Act*, R.S.C. 1985, c. C-6, s. 12(1)(*c*).

[135] *Ibid.*, s. 12(1)(*d*).

hospitals is that they receive payments in consideration for the services they provide.

Finally, a discussion of accessibility under the *Canada Health Act* must include the section 18 requirement that deductions must be made from the federal contribution to any province to the extent that it allows extra billing to occur, and section 19, which specifies the same consequence for any province that allows the levying of user charges. These provisions are what set Canada's health care system apart from all others. No other system goes so far in making the state the exclusive source of financing for medical services. These prohibitions are often criticized based on the assumption that such charges could deter inappropriate utilization of services that are regarded as "free". As mentioned above, this critique rests on highly debatable premises.[136]

E. THE IMPLEMENTATION AND ENFORCEMENT OF THE CANADA HEALTH ACT

We now have a picture of what the *Canada Health Act* requires of the provinces. In this section, the question is whether the health care systems of the provinces satisfy these requirements. We look first at the legislation, administrative frameworks and policies through which the provinces establish and operate the scheme of publicly administered health insurance that is mandated by the *Canada Health Act*. We will then consider the enforcement of the Act in situations where the provincial reality arguably has departed from the ideal that is envisaged in the *Canada Health Act*.

1. Provincial Implementation

As mentioned above, only the provinces can enact public health insurance for the general population. It follows that for the single payer model to be a functioning reality for the residents of any province, the laws of that province must translate the general principles of the *Canada Health Act* into operating reality. Every province (and each of the territories) has in place a framework of laws that do exactly this by establishing a scheme of public health insurance that encompasses most physician and hospital services. In contrast to the almost breathtaking brevity of the *Canada Health Act*, these provincial frameworks are quite detailed, technical and complex. Moreover, although their basic objectives are very consistent, they differ considerably in how they go about achieving those objectives.

Thankfully, we do not have to deal with all this complexity. What is important to know is what is accomplished by the legislation of each of the provinces, no matter how differently organized, structured or written. In all provinces, health insurance legislation establishes a plan for the funding of doctor and hospital services; delegates the responsibility for administering that plan to a minister of health, government official or government agency; defines

---

[136] For a relatively current empirical perspective on these issues, see Noralou P. Roos *et al.*, "Does universal comprehensive insurance encourage unnecessary use? Evidence from Manitoba says 'no'" (2004) 170 C.M.A.J. 209.

insured services in such a way as to generally encompass the services that doctors and hospitals provide; gives all residents of the province a right to receive these services on uniform terms and conditions and (in compliance with the prohibitions on user fees and extra billing) without being charged any fee; and entitles doctors to compensation and hospitals to funding in place of the charges that each would otherwise levy to patients or their private insurers. In all these essential respects, all of the provinces have in place the legislative framework that the *Canada Health Act* mandates.

In fact, provincial legislation goes beyond what is required by the *Canada Health Act*. It has not only ensured the availability of publicly funded medical care, but also made the alternative of privately funded care largely unavailable within Canada, thereby greatly reinforcing the single-payer model.[137] In Quebec and several other provinces, private insurance for services that are included within the public scheme have been prohibited, but of course, this is the provision of Quebec law struck down in *Chaoulli v. Quebec (Attorney General)*.[138] More indirect, but effective mechanisms are relied upon in other provinces, as well as in Quebec and in the other provinces that have taken the further step of making private insurance unlawful. For example, in some jurisdictions physicians are required to elect between delivering service under the public scheme or outside of it. The consequence of an election to offer service privately is to make the cost of the service the full responsibility of the patient (or of his or her private insurer). In some provinces, doctors are also prohibited from charging more in private for providing a medical service than they would receive for providing the same service under Medicare. Essentially, this extends the *Canada Health Act* prohibition against extra billing to the provision of services outside Medicare.

For much of the history of Medicare, these types of restrictions have helped to make the private delivery and purchase of medical services an unattractive business proposition for doctors and patients, except in limited circumstances. The rationale for this relatively absolute approach is threefold: first, to prevent the private ability to pay from becoming a determinant of relative access to treatment; second, to prevent taxpayer subsidization of a parallel private system (and the preferential access it may provide); and third, to prevent the diversion of human and other resources from the public to the private system.

It is also worth noting that the principles of the *Canada Health Act* have significant influence beyond the making and administration of laws by provincial governments. Implicitly, they can be seen at work in many of the ways in which the delivery of care is organized and managed at the clinical and institutional level. It has been argued, for example, that the time spent on Ontario's waiting list for bypass surgery is directly correlated to acuity because of the internalization of the principles of the *Canada Health Act* into clinical and administrative processes.[139]

---

[137] C.M. Flood & T. Archibald, "The Illegality of Private Health Care in Canada" (2001) 164 C.M.A.J. 825.

[138] [2005] S.C.J. No. 33, [2005] 1 S.C.R. 791 (S.C.C.).

[139] Lawrie McFarlane & Carlos Prado, *The Best Laid Plans: Health Care's Problems and Prospects* (Montreal & Kingston: McGill-Queen's University Press, 2002) at 126.

But there are also many examples of clear or potential violations of the *Canada Health Act* being caused or tolerated by the provinces. Those that can be said to be clear violations relate to the more specific requirements of the Act. For example, the refusal of governments in Atlantic Canada to cover the "facility fees" for abortion services provided via private clinics where the service was otherwise funded publicly and the decision of an Alberta clinic to directly charge patients from other provinces for cataract surgery, both run contrary to the stipulation that user fees and extra billing should not be allowed. The refusal of Quebec to reimburse other provinces (except Ontario) at the rates of the other province for services provided to Quebec residents, the decision of Quebec, Ontario, Alberta and British Columbia to reimburse residents who receive service in the United States at rates that are below the rates that apply to the service if received in province, and the decision of Alberta to refuse to give dialysis to visitors from other provinces, all seem obviously contrary to the portability requirements.

The decisions, policies or situations that are more debatably in violation of the Act have to do with the broader requirements, and particularly with comprehensiveness and accessibility. For example, accessibility was arguably at issue when the wait for hip replacement surgery was at 60 weeks in Manitoba, when the wait for cataract surgery was 30 weeks in Saskatchewan and when the wait list was at 1,460 patients for hernia surgery in Quebec and at 1,200 patients for bypass surgery in Ontario. It seems even more clearly to have been in issue when staff shortages prompted Montreal hospitals to urge patients to stay away unless they had life-threatening injuries and when Toronto hospitals asked patients to sign waivers that showed they accepted the risk of long waits for cancer treatments as opposed to travelling to Buffalo for privately funded treatments.

2. Federal Enforcement

The enforcement mechanism provided to the federal government by the Canada *Health Act* is financial penalization of the offending province. If the violation is of one of the five criteria, the federal government is given the discretion to decide for or against penalization and a further discretion to decide on the amount of the penalty. In contrast, if the violation is of the prohibitions on user fees or extra billing, the Act stipulates dollar-for-dollar reductions in the cash transfer that would otherwise go to the offending province. The Act also stipulates the payment of the withheld amount once the charging of user fees or the extra billing ceases. In addition, since 1991, other federal legislation has authorized the federal government to enforce the *Canada Health Act* by withholding or reducing payments due to the offending province under any other federal statute, program or federal-provincial arrangement.[140]

The most important point is that the federal government has never exercised its discretionary power to financially penalize a province for breach of any of the general criteria. The only enforcement action that has ever been taken is in

---

[140] *Budget Implementation Act, 1991*, S.C. 1991, c. 51, s. 4, amending *Federal-Provincial Fiscal Arrangements Act*, R.S.C. 1985, c. F-8, s. 23.2.

respect of user fees and extra billing, where the *Canada Health Act* obligates matching reductions in the federal transfers. Initial provincial (and physician) resistance to the *Canada Health Act* (particularly to the bans on user fees and extra billing) resulted in a total amount of approximately $245 million being withheld from seven provinces between 1984 and 1987, all of which was later paid once the user charges or extra billing had been ended. Between November of 1995 and 1999, a total of approximately $6 million dollars had been withheld from four provinces that had permitted (or rather, had refused to pay for) a so-called "facility fee" at clinics that provided insured physician services.

The larger story is the federal inaction on possible violations of the five criteria, including on rather straightforward violations of the portability requirement. The lack of any federal action on the accessibility front in the face of prevalent concern about waiting times and waiting lists is particularly noteworthy, given the breadth of the concern for accessibility that is displayed in the drafting of the *Canada Health Act*. On the other hand, it is clear that waiting lists and waiting times are complex phenomena that are caused by many factors, many of which are not easily influenced by the kinds of tools that government has at its disposal.[141] This complexity encompasses the basic structural features of the system, including the independence of hospitals and of other health care institutions and the autonomy of physicians both within hospitals and from governments. In these circumstances, it is hard to see how the blunt instrument of financial penalization could be applied with sufficient sensitivity to cause and effect as to improve matters. Conversely, it is easy to see how it could make matters worse wherever funding was either a contributing cause to the waiting times or a necessary ingredient in their improvement. For these reasons, it is probably better for both levels of government to work together on the collaborative development and implementation of collaborative waiting time reduction strategies, such as those called for in the Health Accords of 2003 and 2004. Federal investments into national accountability infrastructure, including the Health Council of Canada and the Canadian Institute of Health Information, can perhaps do more to encourage diligence in the implementation of these strategies than can the imposition of financial penalties.

Still, the difficulties and practical implications of enforcement do not justify the failure of the federal government to conduct assessments of waiting times, whether nationally or provincially, for their consistency with the accessibility criteria. According to the Auditor General, the federal government does not even gather the kind of information that would be necessary for this kind of assessment, but instead relies on "field reports" from Health Canada staffers and on very general reports from the provinces.[142] These concentrate on describing the formal elements of health insurance legislation and administration, but include little or no detail on the actual operation of each provincial health care

---

[141] S. Lewis, M.L. Barer, C. Sanmartin, S. Ships, S.E.D. Short & P.W. MacDonald, "Ending Waiting-List Mismanagement: Principles and Practice" (2000) 162 C.M.A.J. 1297. New see, Health Canada, *Final Report of the Federal Advisor on Wait Times by Brian Postl, M.D.* (Ottawa: Minister of Health, 2006).

[142] Office of the Auditor General of Canada, *Report of the Auditor General of Canada to the House of Commons* (Ottawa: Auditor General's Office, 1999), c. 29, at 29-14 to 29-20, inclusive.

system. Although the *Canada Health Act* authorizes regulations that would require more detailed and operational reports from the provinces, no such regulations have been adopted.[143]

Why the federal passiveness? The prominence of the national unity file has undoubtedly been a factor with violations attributed to Quebec. It seems equally obvious that the federal cuts in cash transfers that took place in the 1990s and the ensuing argument about whether or not the federal government was doing its share did not create ideal conditions for assertions of federal power, especially on what might be regarded as debatable interpretations of the *Canada Health Act*. The growth in waiting lists and waiting times that has occurred in the provinces followed cuts in provincial levels of funding to hospitals (both for operations and equipment), which in turn paralleled the cuts that the federal government imposed on the provinces. It seems likely that the federal government has not been very anxious to point fingers for fear that its own contribution to the problems become more obvious. If so, federal non-enforcement supports the analysis of some commentators, more commonly based on the relationship between provincial governments and regional health authorities, that the interests of government as funding agent conflict with its responsibilities as the guarantor of performance and quality.[144] For some, this would fit with their characterization of the Canadian health care system as an "unregulated monopoly" that must be broken up through greater marketization of both funding and delivery. For others, it points to the need for independent institutions, such as a national health council, that can monitor the performance of the system with credibility and that have the mandate to report not only to governments but directly to Canadians.

Finally, it is important for lawyers to recognize that the influence of the federal government continues to be substantial despite the absence of an aggressive enforcement posture. The best evidence of this is the continuing adherence of all provinces and territories to the core design principles of the single payer system. While it can be said that this reflects the influence of provincial and territorial voters more than it does the direct influence of the federal government, it has to be acknowledged that the federal government plays an important role every time it is called upon to speak publicly about the consistency of provincial reform proposals with the *Canada Health Act*. In recent years, it has been required to do this most frequently with respect to proposals put forward by Alberta. The emphasis that Alberta has put on intergovernmental dispute resolution mechanisms even though federal action has never gone beyond the expression of ministerial opinion, would suggest that Ottawa carries a fairly large stick when it comes to protecting Medicare even though it has wielded it sparingly.

---

[143] *Canada Health Act*, R.S.C. 1985, c. C-6, s. 22(1)(c).

[144] Brian Crowley & David Zitner, *Public Health, State Secret* (Halifax: Atlantic Institute for Market Studies, 2002).

F. MEDICARE AND THE COURTS

Against this background of limited federal enforcement of the *Canada Health Act*, the question that arises in law is the extent to which Canadians can take matters into their own hands by seeking redress from the courts when Medicare fails to deliver reasonable access to necessary physician and hospital services. In considering this question, it is useful to distinguish on the one hand between direct judicial enforcement of the *Canada Health Act* and, on the other hand, judicial scrutiny of the financing, governing and managing of health care delivery under the provincial and territorial laws that implement the single payer system in each of the provinces and territories.

The prospects for success in proceedings that seek direct enforcement of the *Canada Health Act* by the courts are quite limited. As explained above, a province or territory cannot be taken to court for violating the *Canada Health Act*. This is because the Act does not in strict law even apply to the provinces, but only to the federal government in the exercise of its spending power.

There are however, two other routes for judicial enforcement of the Act, or at least of the criteria and conditions established by the Act. The first is an action against the federal government alleging a failure to penalize a province or provinces for their failure to abide by the Act.[145] Such an action would be heard as an administrative law case, where the question for the court is essentially whether the actions taken by an administrative authority (here, the Minister of Health) is authorized by the governing statute. If successful, such an action could result in the court directing the Minister of Health to take a specific action, such as deducting certain amounts from the payments being made to certain provinces. But that kind of outcome would be highly unlikely. In administrative law cases, the more usual outcome is a quashing of the reviewed decision and its referral back to the administrative authority for reconsideration in accordance with the applicable statute and with the benefit of whatever the court has said on the interpretation of the statute or on the procedures that should be followed in the administration of the statute. More importantly, such a proceeding is unlikely to be successful in the first place. The *Canada Health Act* places a broad discretion into the hands of the federal Minister of Health, a political decision-maker. The courts are generally reluctant to interfere with the exercise of such powers by government ministers, particularly where the decisions being made are of a broad policy nature affecting the interests of many as opposed to the specific rights of specific individuals.[146]

The second possibility (only available in some provinces) is for an action against provincial authorities where the *Canada Health Act* criteria have been written directly into provincial law, as they have been in British Columbia.[147] In

---

[145] Sujit Choudhry, "The Enforcement of the Canada Health Act" (1996) 41 McGill L.J. 461. See also Canadian Bar Association Task Force on Health Care, *What's Law Got To Do With It? Health Care Reform in Canada* (Ottawa: Canadian Bar Association, 1994).

[146] For a review of the jurisprudence, see William Lahey & Diana Ginn, "After the Revolution: Being Pragmatic and Functional in Canada's Trial Courts and Courts of Appeal" (2002) 25 Dal. L.J. 259.

[147] *Medicare Protection Act*, R.S.B.C. 1996, c. 286. This Act delegates the provincial government's

these provinces, individuals can ask the courts to review provincial government decisions or policies for consistency with the criteria as adopted in provincial law and, in that way, challenge provincial actions under the substance if not the letter of the *Canada Health Act*. Such legislation makes provincial compliance with the criteria legally mandatory and this gives the courts the ability to strike down provincial decisions that are in violation of the criteria, again, on administrative law principles. Thus, although the hurdle of establishing that a violation has occurred remains, the additional hurdle that exists in litigation against the federal government of convincing a court that it should interfere with the exercise of discretionary powers is either avoided or minimized, depending on how the provincial legislation is structured. This litigation, where available, opens avenues for greater individual enforcement of the principles of the single-payer system through the courts. It is interesting however that the leading example of a successful claim of this sort is the case of *Waldman v. British Columbia (Medical Services Commission).*[148] There doctors successfully argued that a provincial policy that limited the compensation of physicians relocating to British Columbia to 50 per cent of their billings unless they located in underserviced areas violated the part of the accessibility criterion that requires payment of "reasonable compensation" to physicians. It therefore dealt more directly with doctor rights than it did with patient rights to treatment, although it is easy to see how the former can have implications for the latter.

Broader judicial scrutiny of the financing, governing and managing of the delivery of health care services under provincial and territorial laws can take place under several branches of law. For example, where decisions about the level and distribution of funding cause harm or loss to a patient by constraining the system's capacity to provide quality services on a timely basis, liability in negligence could extend beyond the doctors, nurses and other providers who treated the patient to those (including government) who made the financing and allocation decisions. The law of negligence is discussed extensively elsewhere in this volume and will therefore not be further considered here. It suffices to say that while such liability is a possibility, establishing it in particular cases will face significant barriers, including the difficulties of proving causation and the general limits that the law places on liability when governments act in a policy-making capacity.[149]

The other branch of law that is potentially applicable is administrative law, whether or not *Canada Health Act* criteria have been written into provincial law.

---

responsibility to operate a plan of health insurance that accords with the *Canada Health Act* to the Medical Services Commission. Section 2 defines the purpose of the Act to be the preservation of "a publicly managed and fiscally sustainable health care system for British Columbia in which access to necessary medical care is based on need and not an individual's ability to pay". More importantly, s. 5(1) lays out the responsibilities and powers of the Commission and then says (in s. 5(2)), "The commission must not act under subsection (1) in a manner that does not satisfy the criteria described in section 7 of the *Canada Health Act* (Canada)." See also the *Regional Health Authorities Act*, C.C.S.M. c. R34, s. 2(2).
[148] [1999] B.C.J. No. 2014, 177 D.L.R. (4th) 321 (B.C.C.A.).
[149] Timothy A. Caulfield, "Malpractice in the Age of Health Care Reform" in T.A. Caulfield & B. von Tigerstrom, eds., *Health Care Reform and the Law in Canada: Meeting the Challenge* (Edmonton: University of Alberta Press, 2002) 11.

Here again, a large part of the story is the challenges that plaintiffs are likely to face in obtaining judicial intervention, due to the deference that the courts usually extend to administrative decisions that have significant policy element. An example of this deference is the refusal of the courts to review the decisions of the Health Services Restructuring Commission that was mandated to review the hospital and nursing homes sectors in Ontario in the 1990s and that ordered the closure and reorganization of a number of hospitals.[150]

But a Quebec case shows that there are limits to this deference, particularly as the decision-making becomes specific to individual and identifiable patients. The case is *Stein v. Québec (Régie de l'Assurance-maladie).*[151] Stein had colon cancer, which metastasized to his liver and required complex surgical intervention and chemotherapy treatment. He became frustrated with waiting his turn to receive this treatment in Quebec and proceeded to have it done in the United States. His subsequent application to the Quebec Regie de l'Assurance-maladie du Quebec (the RAMQ) for reimbursement was refused. Stein challenged this refusal in court as being administratively unreasonable and was successful. The Quebec Superior Court ordered the RAMQ to reimburse Stein.

So applied, administrative law gets at compliance with the principles of the *Canada Health Act*, especially as regards access, from the bottom up. It engages at the level of decisions that are made in particular cases, where the general principles are applied to specific patients, rather than at the level of decision-making about the general design, structure or capacity of a province's health care system. At the former level, as *Stein* demonstrates, judicial intervention is more likely. And equally importantly, such interventions can drive systemic responses from governments and their officials.

The *Stein* case will be read by lawyers as a case in administrative law, having to do with the court's finding that the decision to deny funding to Stein was "patently unreasonable" and therefore unauthorized by statute. For others, *Stein* can be read simply as an example of how the frustration, anxiety and anger over the inaccessibility of publicly insured services can make its way into court. It shows the question of waiting lists being transformed from a technocratic question about the management and organization of structures, processes, and systems into a question about the consequences for an individual Canadian of the movement of these broader and somewhat impersonal forces. With the question so transformed, *Stein* also shows at least one judge willing, against the grain of traditional judicial deference to government allocation activities, to impose standards of individual fairness and justice on a decision-making process that is all too likely to focus primarily on aggregate outcomes. To put it another way, it might be said that *Stein* indicates an emerging willingness in the courts to demand that health care policy-makers more tightly connect their decisions to an understanding (and a justification) of the consequences of those decisions for real flesh and blood citizens.

[150] *Pembroke Civic Hospital v. Ontario (Health Services Restructuring Commission)*, [1997] O.J. No. 3142, 36 O.R. (3d) 41 (Ont. Div. Ct.).
[151] [1999] Q.J. No. 2724, [1999] R.J.Q. 2416 (Que. S.C.). This case is analyzed in M.A. Somerville, "The Ethics and Law of Access to New Cancer Treatments" (1999) 6:3 Current Oncology 161.

The final area of law that needs to be mentioned is human rights law, particularly in the form of the *Canadian Charter of Rights and Freedoms*. This topic is the subject of Chapter 14 in this volume. Readers who want a detailed and more comprehensive discussion of the application of the Charter should refer to that chapter. Here, the focus is on the policy implications of trends in recent Charter decisions, and particularly of *Auton (Guardian ad litem of) v. British Columbia (Attorney General)* and of *Chaoulli v. Quebec*, both decided in 2005.[152]

Each of these cases concerned one of the two Charter provisions that are likely to have the greatest potential significance for Medicare. The *Auton* case dealt with section 15 (the equality guarantee) in the context of a challenge of the decision of the British Columbia government not to fund a form of applied behavioural therapy for children with autism (Lovaas therapy) that is generally provided by non-physician therapists. The *Chaoulli* case dealt with section 7 of the Charter (which guarantees life, liberty and security of the person) in the context of a challenge to Quebec's ban on contracts of private insurance covering physician and hospital services available under the Quebec version of Medicare. At this broad level, each case can be seen to have dealt with a Charter right that has significant alignment with the objectives and fundamental values of Medicare. This is most obviously true with the guarantee of equality, since equality of access is at the core of the single payer model. But it is also true of the section 7 guarantees, since Medicare was intended not only to ensure equality of access but to give Canadians access to a level and quality of medical care that would be effective in saving lives, preserving health and advancing well-being, all while protecting them from the financial hardship that they would otherwise face due to the high cost of health care. It was designed to achieve these objectives while preserving the independence of the medical profession and the autonomy of the patient-physician relationship.

At the same time, obvious tensions are observable between Medicare and sections 15 and 7. Medicare's commitment to equality is defined in terms of physician and hospital services. Where health depends on access to other kinds of health care services, Medicare can be said to extend differential levels of benefit. With respect to section 7, the growth of waiting lists and waiting times has meant that the capacity of Medicare to protect life and security of the person by ensuring dependable access to effective medical care has come into doubt.

In *Auton*, the Supreme Court of Canada unanimously ruled that British Columbia did not violate section 15 in deciding not to fund Lovaas therapy. It ruled, in effect, that the scope of Medicare was a matter for governments and legislatures, not for the courts, provided that governments maintained equality of access to the services that it does decide to include in Medicare.[153] Cutting through the technicalities of the constitutional analysis, this reflected the court's

---

[152] *Auton (Guardian ad litem of) v. British Columbia (Attorney General)*, [2004] S.C.J. No. 71, [2004] 3 S.C.R. 657 (S.C.C.). The decision of the British Columbia Court of Appeal, which found for Auton, can be found at [2002] B.C.J. No. 2258, 220 D.L.R. (4th) 411 (B.C.C.A.), affg [2001] B.C.J. No. 215, 197 D.L.R. (4th) 165 (B.C.S.C.). *Chaoulli v. Quebec (Attorney General)*, [2005] S.C.J. No. 33, [2005] 1 S.C.R. 791 (S.C.C.).

[153] *Eldridge v. British Columbia (Attorney General)*, [1997] S.C.J. No. 86, [1997] 3 S.C.R. 624.

desire to leave responsibility for allocating limited resources with governments and legislatures. In *Chaoulli*, a bitterly divided court ruled 4:3 that Quebec's ban on private insurance was, in light of the waiting lines that existed in the public system, a violation of the provision of the Quebec *Charter of Human Rights and Freedoms*[154] that parallels section 7 of the Canadian Charter. Three judges, including Chief Justice McLachlin, were prepared to reach the same conclusion on a national basis under section 7. Under both Charters, the underlying reasoning was the same: that waiting times in Quebec had become so dangerous to physical health and to psychological integrity as to make it constitutionally impermissible for Quebec to continue to deny Quebecers the option of seeking access through the alternative of private insurance. In effect, the majority seemed to be telling Canadian governments that they could not prevent Canadians from buying medical care privately if they were not providing acceptable access through the public system.

The activism of *Chaoulli* stands in marked contrast to the deference of *Auton*. An obvious interpretation is that the judges empathized more readily with patients waiting for potentially life-saving medical procedures (assumed to be at issue in *Chaoulli*) than they did with autistic children seeking access to a controversial therapy of uncertain efficacy. It is also possible to conclude that the difference reveals a more fundamental issue: the priority that the Charter gives to individual freedom — the right to be left alone by government — over the interests of those who stand to benefit from positive state action to address social and economic inequality.[155] This interpretation rests on more than the difference in outcome in the two cases. It rests more substantially on the failure of the *Chaoulli* majority to recognize that the interests of those who would have no alternative to the public system were deeply implicated in the constitutionality of legislative efforts to control the growth of privately financed medicine. But this assumes that the *Chaoulli* majority understood that an expanded private system would threaten the public system, particularly by attracting away scarce human resources. In fact, the majority dismissed this concern out of hand, despite the availability of plenty of supporting evidence and the conclusions of almost all of the independent studies that have been completed of the Canadian health care system. In this, *Chaoulli* raises serious questions about the capacity of the courts to adjudicate questions of health system design.[156]

Still, it is very important from a policy-making perspective to keep a sense of proportion in reacting to *Chaoulli*, as the Government of Quebec has arguably

---

[154] R.S.Q., c. C-12.

[155] See Allan C. Hutchinson, "'Condition Critical': The Constitution and Health Care", and Andrew Petter, "Wealthcare: The politics of the *Charter* Revisited", in Colleen M. Flood, Kent Roach & Lorne Sossin, eds., *Access to Care, Access to Justice: The Legal Debate Over Private Health Insurance in Canada* (Toronto: University of Toronto Press, 2005) at 101 and 116 respectively.

[156] Sujit Choudhry, "Worse than *Lochner*?" in Colleen M. Flood, Kent Roach & Lorne Sossin, eds., *Access to Care, Access to Justice: The Legal Debate Over Private Health Insurance in Canada* (Toronto: University of Toronto Press, 2005) 75. In Lawrie McFarlane, "Supreme Court slaps for-sale sign on Medicare" (2005) 173 C.M.A.J. 269, *Chaoulli* is compared to the *Dred Scott* decision.

done.[157] The ruling is now part of the policy-making landscape. It is critical that the policy response take the case seriously because it is virtually certain that the outcome in future cases will partly depend on what governments do — or do not do — in response to *Chaoulli*. The court's adjudication of future cases could depend on whether it comes to understand (as some of the judges seemed not to understand) that the elimination of all waiting is probably not a reasonable or desirable objective. The credibility with which governments can provide this education to the court will partly depend on the success they can demonstrate in documenting and eliminating the truly unreasonable wait times that undoubtedly do exist.

But it is equally important to guard against overreaction to the ruling for the simple reason that the objective of health care policy must continue to be an improved health care system, not compliance with a highly problematic judicial understanding of what that system would look like, or of the actions that could or should be taken to bring it about. A measured and calibrated response is partly warranted by the fact that *Chaoulli* is a decision that applies only in Quebec and that has a very uncertain future, independently of what governments do in response. This is not only due to the narrowness of Chaoulli's victory by a 4-3 majority, and the impact that changing membership of the court may have on that division. It is due to the number of points of constitutional doctrine on which *Chaoulli* arguably departs from earlier case law or takes section 7 and Charter analysis more generally in new and expansive directions, both within and beyond health care.[158]

A measured response to *Chaoulli* is also warranted by a careful analysis of what the case does and does not decide on the issue before it — the constitutionality of a prohibition of private insurance for services covered by Medicare.[159] The ruling does not express a preference for free market medicine,

---

[157] Minister of Health and Social Services, *Guaranteeing Access: Meeting the challenges of equity, efficiency and quality — Consultation document* (Quebec: Minister of Health and Social Services, 2006).

[158] In addition to the chapters of critique available in *Access to Care, Access to Justice*, the articles written thus far on *Chaoulli* include: François Béland, "The Chaoulli Judgment or How to Sell Off a Public Right" (2005) 1:1 Healthcare Policy 40, online: <http://longwoods.com/product. php?productid=17666&cat=392&page=1>; Philip Bryden, "Section 7 Outside the Criminal Context" (2005) 38 U.B.C. L. Rev. 507; Robert G. Evans, "Baneful Legacy: Medicare and Mr. Trudeau" (2005) 1:1 Healthcare Policy 20; Colleen M. Flood, "Just Medicare: The Role of Canadian Courts in Determining Health Care Rights and Access" (2005) 33:4 J. L. Med. & Ethics 669; David Hadorn, "The *Chaoulli* challenge: getting a grip on waiting lists" (2005) 173 C.M.A.J. 271; Gregory R. Hagen, "Personal Inviolability and Public Health Care: *Chaoulli v. Quebec*" (2005) 14:2 Health L. Rev. 34; Jeff A. King, "Constitutional Rights and Social Welfare: A Comment on the Canadian *Chaoulli* Health Care Decision" (2006) 69 Mod. L. Rev. 631; Martha Jackman, "Misdiagnosis or Cure? *Charter* Review of the Health Care System", in Colleen M. Flood, ed., *Just Medicare: What's In, What's Out, How We Decide* (Toronto: University of Toronto Press, 2006) at 58; and Antonia Maioni & Christopher Manfredi, "When the Charter Trumps Health Care — A Collision of Canadian Icons" (2005) 26:7 Policy Options 52.

[159] See Peter Russell, "*Chaoulli*: The Political versus the Legal Life of a Judicial Decision" and Bernard Dickens, "The *Chaoulli* Decision: Less than Meets the Eye — or More?" in Colleen M. Flood, Kent Roach & Lorne Sossin, eds., *Access to Care, Access to Justice: The Legal Debate*

despite the hints of this in the opinion authored by Chief Justice McLachlin and Justice Major. The stinging criticism that they direct at government is that it has done too little to manage the delivery of health care services, not that it has overreached or done too much. At any rate, their opinion is not the majority opinion, except to the extent that it overlaps with that of Justice Deschamps, who decided the case entirely under the Quebec Charter. On that common ground, the case only decides that governments cannot prohibit private insurance when they are not providing adequate access through the public system. The right in question is the right to health care services on a timely basis, not the right to service through the private marketplace. The access to private insurance ordered by the court is the remedy given for Quebec's failure to otherwise provide this right, not the right itself. It is possible that the remedy in another case might be an order prescribing the level and quality of access required in the public system.[160]

A related point is that *Chaoulli* does not decide that Canadian governments cannot act to protect the public health care system by using law to discourage or even block the development of a competing private system. Again, it is true that the opinion of Chief Justice McLachlin and Justice Major suggests otherwise. But this is only the opinion of three judges of a nine-member court. What is important is what is said in the swing opinion of Justice Deschamps. Her ruling that the prohibition on private insurance was not a justified infringement of individual rights was based on her conclusion that other options for guarding the public system, including a legislative cap on the fees that could be charged in the private system, were available to Quebec. It was clearly premised on the legitimacy of state action to protect the integrity of the public system by controlling the growth of a competing private system. It therefore seems very likely that in future cases, where the challenge may be to these other measures, Justice Deschamps would join the dissenting justices (Justices Binnie, Lebel and Fish) in upholding them. In fact, her *Chaoulli* opinion suggests that she would, like them, be more likely to uphold these measures the stronger the evidence of their effectiveness in preventing the growth of a parallel private system.

But even if *Chaoulli* does indeed put all legislative restraints on private medicine at risk, this does not necessarily spell the end of Canadian Medicare. Private medicine has never been illegal in Canada. The most that the law has done is to discourage its growth by making it difficult, uncertain or uneconomic. It may be true that the historically slow pace at which private medicine has grown shows that these soft limitations have been very effective.[161] But there is no way to tell. It seems equally plausible that the real explanation for the limited

---

Over Private Health Insurance in Canada (Toronto: University of Toronto Press, 2005) at 5 and 19 respectively.

[160] Lorne Sossin, "Towards a Two-Tier Constitution? The Poverty of Health Rights" and Kent Roach, "The Courts and Medicare: Too Much or Too Little Judicial Activism?", both in Colleen M. Flood, Kent Roach & Lorne Sossin, eds., *Access to Care, Access to Justice: The Legal Debate Over Private Health Insurance in Canada* (Toronto: University of Toronto Press, 2005), at 161 and 184 respectively.

[161] C.M. Flood & T. Archibald, "The Illegality of Private Health Care in Canada" (2001) 164 C.M.A.J. 825.

growth of private medicine has been that Medicare has, for most of its history, offered a deal to Canadians (and to Canadian doctors) that private medicine could not match. The early history of Medicare would seem to support this explanation.[162] Even when governments were forced (as in Saskatchewan) to tolerate or tried mightily (as in the other western provinces) to preserve room for a parallel private system, that private alternative soon withered due to its inability to compete.

Thus, if *Chaoulli* is an attack on Medicare, it is an attack on an ancillary element, not the essential core. Accordingly, a proportionate response, like the original response to the original resistance to Medicare, would focus primarily on restoration of the capacity of the public system to provide Canadians with consistently dependable access within reasonable time frames to quality care. As to whether or not governments can pull this off, the key question is probably not going to be whether or not they will be prevented from doing so by judicial intermeddling. Instead, the question is more likely to be whether governments have the capacity to make Medicare as successful in the 21st century as it was for most of the late 20th century, when public funds were perceived to be more unlimited, medicine was more simple and expectations were more modest.

Having said all that, *Chaoulli* is surely a milestone in the involvement of law and our judiciary in the ongoing development of our health care system. It establishes that, in the age of the Charter, health care policy is no more immune than is any other areas of public policy from the pervasive influence of Canada's shift from a constitutional order based unequivocally on legislative supremacy to one based on entrenched individual rights. In consequence, the right of Canadians to health care is in process of transitioning from a right that is defined by governments through their legislative and administrative processes to a right that Canadians will be able, to some still uncertain extent, demand from governments through the adjudicative process. Whatever else this may mean, it certainly means a new kind of accountability that requires governments to explain the rationale for their legislative and policy choices to the overseeing courts.

Accountability is also at issue in *Auton*. The difficulty is possibly that the case does not go far enough in reinforcing the accountability on governments and legislatures to base their decisions on sound evidence and on equal concern for the health and well-being of all citizens. From a policy perspective, the outcome in *Auton* respects the difficulty governments face in funding a health care system characterized by escalating costs while preserving fiscal capacity to address other public policy priorities. For some, it is an outcome that might also be supported by the lack of evidence for the efficacy of the particular autism treatment that was in issue in *Auton*. This argument, heavily relied upon by British Columbia, was very influential with the court, which grouped Lovaas therapy together with other "novel" therapies that were "emergent and only

---

[162] Greg Marchildon, "Private Insurance for Medicare: Policy History and Trajectory in the Four Western Provinces" in Colleen M. Flood, Kent Roach & Lorne Sossin, eds., *Access to Care, Access to Justice: The Legal Debate Over Private Health Insurance in Canada* (Toronto: University of Toronto Press, 2005) 429.

recently becoming recognized as medically required".[163] On this view, the facts of *Auton* demonstrate why questions about the scope of Medicare need to be decided within Medicare where clinical criteria can be appropriately evaluated and applied.

Skepticism about Lovaas treatment may be valid. But it needs to be remembered that similar criticism can be directed at various of the services that are provided by doctors and hospitals. Yet, law requires those services to be publicly funded largely because they are offered by physicians or in hospitals. In contrast, British Columbia, and every other province, deals on a more individualized basis with health care services provided outside hospitals by other providers (including the therapists who provide Lovaas treatment). Some are funded and some are not, depending on relatively objective factors such as the availability of resources, the supporting therapeutic evidence and the understood nature of the need, but also on more subjective factors such as the perceived credibility of the providers or therapy and the nature and extent of power (or of powerlessness) of the requesting group. Either way, the decision for or against funding is likely to have a certain "black box" quality. The decision would not, as it appears not to have in *Auton*, flow from a decision-making process that is laid out in law. Instead, as in *Auton*, such decisions are often made within and between bureaucracies, with uneven and uncertain participation by affected and interested persons.

Even if the final outcome in *Auton* is the right one because it leaves policy questions to governments and legislatures, the sheer breadth of the latitude that is left to governments (not only in health care but more broadly) is questionable. More demanding scrutiny under section 15 would impose a higher standard of accountability on government to at least validate that the denial of funding was indeed (for example) based on genuine concerns about clinical efficacy. This would provide greater protection for people such as those living with autism against the risk of having their needs ignored due to the institutionalized priority that is given to the needs of those who (for the most part) only require periodic attention during episodic periods of illness. Instead, what *Auton* arguably does is to extend this institutionalized preference from the *Canada Health Act* and parallel provincial statutes into constitutional law.

The point here is not to suggest that physician and hospital services should not be funded under a general policy. Instead, it is simply to illustrate through *Auton* how the legal compartmentalization of our health care system obscures

---

[163] Donna Greschner & Steven Lewis, " *Auton* and Evidence-Based Decision-Making: Medicare in the Courts" (2003) 82 Can. Bar Rev. 501-34. See also Donna Greschner, "*Charter* Challenges and Evidence-Based Decision-Making in the Health Care System: Towards a Symbiotic Relationship", in Colleen M. Flood, ed., *Just Medicare: What's In, What's Out, How We Decide* (Toronto: University of Toronto Press, 2006) at 42. For a broader consideration of the role of courts as health system policy-makers, see Christopher P. Manfredi & Antonia Maioni, "Courts and Health Policy: Judicial Policy Making and Publicly Funded Health Care in Canada" (2002) 27 J. Health Pol. 213, and Christopher P. Manfredi, "Déjà vu All Over Again: *Chaoulli* and the Limits of Judicial Policy-making", in Colleen M. Flood, Kent Roach & Lorne Sossin, eds., *Access to Care, Access to Justice: The Legal Debate Over Private Health Insurance in Canada* (Toronto: University of Toronto Press, 2005) 139.

the nature of the premises and assumptions on which we implicitly rely when we make choices about (for example) funding for treatments that are outside the scope of Medicare. These include a premise that medicine is generally superior to other responses to illness, suffering and disability, that curing is more important than caring (as well as prevention), that dealing with the episodic illness of the healthy is more important than dealing with chronic illness and disability, and that physical health takes priority over other dimensions of health, including mental health. Seen in this broader light, the *Auton* case is a manifestation of a decision-making dynamic that cuts across the Canadian health care system. As with Lovaas therapy, the question of public funding for drugs taken outside hospitals, for care received in the home, for long-term care, for palliative and hospice care and for various forms of established and emerging therapy, is decided individually in each province and outside the constraining influence of national standards or principles. In contrast, the funding of physician and hospital services is largely treated as decided by virtue of their status as "insured services" that fall under the protective framework of the *Canada Health Act*. This institutionalized asymmetry largely prevents the efficacy of medical services from being weighed against that of other types of care.

There is a legitimate concern that judicially imposed accountability will unavoidably focus attention on specific circumstances instead of general conditions and give more importance to the rights of individuals than to collective interests. The handling of the *Chaoulli* appeal gives considerable weight to these concerns. But on the other hand, given the tendency to "black box" decision-making in Canadian health care, an accountability that is unavoidable and that focuses attention on the impact on individual citizens of macro-level decision-making cannot be altogether bad.

IV. PROGRAMS OF REFORM

Five major studies of the Canadian system, two of national and three of provincial scope, have been completed in recent years. All pinned large hopes on primary care reform, the Holy Grail of Canadian health care policy and of its attachment to the determinants of health philosophy.[164] All recommended the retention of regionalization and most included specific recommendations on making it an even stronger component of the system. Two (Kirby and Fyke) recommended the transfer of the responsibility for the funding of physician services to the regional level. All recommended large investments in health information systems, including a system of comprehensive and portable electronic patient information cards. All viewed these investments as enablers of evidence-based decision-making that would lead to the wider and faster adoption of clinical, policy and administrative best practices, to the more

---

[164] The importance that has been placed on the reform of primary care can be traced to the well-known "Lalonde Report"; Hon. Marc Lalonde, *A New Perspective on the Health of Canadians: A Working Document* (Ottawa: Information Canada, 1974).

informed and precise allocation of resources and to the better monitoring of system performance. All stressed the theme of enhanced accountability. To achieve it, four of the studies recommended a new institution that would, independently of government, monitor system performance and report regularly to the public, to the system and to government on what was working and what was not and on why.[165]

There was also agreement, if only barely, on the central question of whether or not Canada should continue to rely on the single-payer system. Three of the reports (Romanow, Kirby and Fyke) strongly adopted that position. Quebec's Clair Report was more equivocal, saying on the one hand that the system should continue to be mainly funded from tax revenues but advising against ideological opposition to supplementary revenues from other sources in future years.[166] Alberta's Mazankowski Report was bolder. It recommended the exclusion from Medicare of non-essential medical services. This was not, by itself, a departure from Medicare's current limitation to medically necessary services. But the accompanying description of a system that was in crisis because it is an unregulated monopoly, that pretended to offer all things to all people and that therefore forced rationing, implied a significant rather than a marginal scaling back in the scope of Medicare. All this linked with the Report's strong support for revenue diversification, perhaps to include the use of Medical Savings Accounts that would reward healthy living and reduce the overall demand for health care consumption. The Report also envisaged a larger role for the private sector in the delivery of health care services, including those that would continue to be part of Medicare. Alberta law now contemplates this, even though Albertans remain significantly opposed.[167]

---

[165] Commissioner Fyke of Saskatchewan proposed the creation of a new institution to be called the Saskatchewan "Quality Council", which has been established: see *Health Quality Council Act*, S.S. 2002, c. H-0.04, as amended by S.S. 2002, c. R-8.2. In *A Framework for Reform: Report of the Premier's Advisory Council on Health* (Mazankowwki Report) (December 2001), the Premier's Advisory Council on Health Care for Alberta proposed a similarly mandated organization for Alberta to be called the "Outcomes Commission". Alberta now has established the Health Quality Council of Alberta: see <http://www.hqca.ca>. Meanwhile, in *Building on Values: The Future of Health Care in Canada — Final Report* (Ottawa: Commission on the Future of Health Care in Canada, 2002), Commissioner Romanow recommended the creation of the "Canada Health Council", and similarly, in *The Health of Canadians — The Federal Role — Volume Six: Recommendations for Reform* (Ottawa: Senate Standing Committee on Social Affairs, Science and Technology, 2002) the Senate Standing Committee on Social Affairs, Science and Technology recommended the appointment of a "National Health Care Commissioner" and the creation of a "National Health Care Council". As discussed in Part II, a version of the Romanow recommendation for a Canada Health Council (also consistent with the recommendations of the Senate Standing Committee) has now been created as part of the 2003 Health Accord. On the agenda and prospects for the council, see Michael B. Decter, "The Health Council of Canada: A Speculation on a Constructive Agenda" (2003) 6:4 Hospital Quarterly 30.

[166] Commission of Study on Health and Social Services, *Report and Recommendations: Emerging Solutions* (Quebec City: Commission of Study on Health and Social Services, 2001), online: <http://www.iigr.ca/pdf/documents/759_Quebec_Emerging_Solution.pdf>.

[167] Alberta, *Getting on with Better Health Care: Health Policy Framework, August, 2006* (Edmonton: Alberta Health and Wellness, 2006), online: <http://www.health.gov.ab.ca/healthrenewal/GettingBetterHealthcare.pdf>.

This direction was rejected categorically by Romanow but also (in large measure) by the other studies. Romanow rejected increased private financing primarily out of the concern that it would divert resources rather than burden from the public system, thereby further undermining the dependability and responsiveness of the public system, setting the stage for further privatization. Indeed, a central thrust of the Romanow Report was that the public system had to reclaim ground already lost to private delivery, especially in diagnostic services. The recommendations for an amendment of the *Canada Health Act* confirming its applicability to these services and for a significant and immediate increase (through targeted federal funding) in the capacity of the public system to provide them, were centerpieces of the Report.[168] They ran in the same direction as the Romanow vision of a future *Canada Health Act* that applied to prescription drugs and "priority" home care services.

In a nutshell, the core of the Mazankowski solution lay in some undefined level of privatization (both of financing and of delivery), while the core of the Romanow solution lay in expanding and increasing the delivery capacity of the public system as a means of halting and of reversing privatization. Where Mazankowski advocated a fundamental restructuring, including a diversification of money flows and a broadening of delivery options, Romanow was, in large measure, about increased, stabilized and protected federal funding, both for particular priorities and for ongoing operations.

Deciding between these directions calls less for legal than for other kinds of analysis. But several observations of value to that broader analysis do arise from the earlier discussion of the law and in particular, from the attention that has been paid to questions of process, particularly on decisions affecting access to services. One is to recognize that the implementation of solutions that follow the thinking of Mazankowski may create conditions that would violate the current requirements of the *Canada Health Act*, specifically universality, comprehensiveness and accessibility. Universality could be violated if the availability of private payment options allowed for circumvention of waiting lists in the public system. Comprehensiveness could be violated by a differentiation between covered (essential) and uncovered (non-essential) services that puts medically necessary services into the latter and excluded category. Accessibility could be violated if a parallel private system, even if limited to medically unnecessary services, became large enough to draw sufficient resources from the public system to adversely affect accessibility to medically necessary services within the public system. On each of these possibilities there would, of course, be competing arguments to be made. Much would depend on how a more pluralistic system was designed and implemented, including the protections that were put in place to protect the public system. And so, the point is not that reforms that follow the Mazankowski template are contrary to the *Canada Health Act*, but rather, that they could create conditions that *might* be contrary to the Act. What matters is that the question of consistency with the Act be addressed. This calls for robust national institutions

---

[168] Interestingly, however, the further recommendation, that private delivery of medicare services be prohibited, was not made.

that have a mandate to make sure these questions are asked and that the answers are acted upon. Canada still does not have these institutions in place, notwithstanding the encouraging institutional development that has happened in recent years.

With the Romanow solution (or variations thereof), the concern is the ability of a system predicated on strengthened commitment to the principles of the *Canada Health Act* to deliver dependable, timely and quality services at a sustainable level of public spending. The question, in particular, is whether a system that is publicly funded, regulated and governed can be depended upon to use increased capacity to address the problems of access, including those of waiting lists and waiting times that so concern Canadians. The Mazankowski analysis is that increased capacity is not enough, simply because the players in the system, particularly governments, have insufficient incentive to operate efficiently and responsively in accordance with patient requirements rather than with provider (or funder) requirements. The Kirby and Claire Reports shared some of the Mazankowski skepticism. Both stressed the importance of mechanisms that would drive change by putting in place incentives that would change behaviour by rewarding success and punishing failure, thus ensuring improved accountability and productivity. Thus Kirby followed Mazankowski in recommending a "care guarantee" that would entitle patients to treatment within clinically acceptable time frames and to receive it at public expense outside of their region, province or the country whenever their local system proved unable to do so.

The idea of care guarantees, rejected by Romanow, now has momentum. It was endorsed by both major parties in the 2006 federal election. The idea is now official government policy at the federal level. Supporters include the Canadian Medical Association and a growing constituency within the community of health policy experts. Care guarantees have a prominent place in Quebec's response to *Chaoulli* and they were, of course, already supported in Alberta, where they were first promoted. The depth of this growing consensus is still an open question, since it is a consensus on the concept, not the structural and operational details that are yet to be developed. It is therefore a consensus that encompasses a broad spectrum of difference. For example, whereas the current federal government seems to equate guarantees to the benchmarks that are under development, provinces and others see guarantees as a step beyond benchmarks. More fundamentally, whereas the Mazankowski and the Kirby vision was of a quasi legal rights, the Quebec model seems much more administrative, under which care within the guaranteed time-frame is part of the service that the system provides to the patient. In broad terms, this difference appears to reflect a more fundamental difference: the Mazankowski and Kirby formula has health care policy borrowing from the adjudicative paradigm associated with the *Canadian Charter of Rights and Freedoms* (and markets), whereas Quebec's approach seems to come more heavily from a social democratic paradigm. But even with these fundamental differences, the breadth of the growing policy consensus in favour of care guarantees powerfully demonstrates the extent to which health system policy thinking is now shaped by law and legal ideas and, more broadly, by a public policy culture that is now heavily oriented towards "rights thinking".

Romanow did not recommend care guarantees in part because he did not think the system was ready to ensure that they could be based on evidence, either as to their feasibility or their medical necessity. He was also concerned that they would introduce inflexibility into a system that is already difficult to manage because of rigid structures. But more fundamentally, the Romanow analysis was that care guarantees were an unnecessary risk. This reflects his fundamental confidence that clinicians, administrators, governors and governments would make the right decisions if they were given the right information, if the barriers to implementation of those decisions were removed and if sufficient and stable funding were made available to them. On this view, reform means adding to the present system the institutions and processes that will ensure the availability of information and demand accountability for using it or for deciding not to use it. There is no need, on this view, for the introduction of uncertain experiments (such as care guarantees or Medical Savings Accounts) in the name of aligning personal and institutional incentives with system objectives.

The confidence of Romanow that the desired level of system performance could be achieved through the creation of the enabling conditions depends on the validity of the report's basic premises. One of these premises, of course, is that the single-payer model is fundamentally sound. The second premise is that this soundness is due to the continuing priority given by Canadians to the values that underlie the single-payer system, particularly solidarity and equity, and to the clear superiority of the single-payer model to all others when considered against these values. A third premise is that the commitment of Canadians to these values drives the operation of the Canadian health care system and will ensure its sustainability and dependability, at least if the system is made and kept accountable to Canadians. The final premise, and perhaps the most speculative of the four, is the continuing presence throughout the Canadian system of a critical mass of care providers, administrators, volunteers, governors, public servants and engaged citizens who take much of their motivational and behavioural guidance from these same values. The alignment of the values of the system with the values of the people who make the system work is ultimately the reason for the Romanow confidence in a set of solutions that would continue Canada essentially on the path that it started down with Tommy Douglas and Emmett Hall more than 40 years ago. These premises are clearly consistent with the values of the single-payer system that are enshrined in the *Canada Health Act*. The question is whether they will, if implemented, produce the individualized results, particularly as regards access, that Canadians want, and that perhaps that the courts will increasingly demand.

V. CONCLUDING THOUGHTS

This overview of the Canadian health care system has concentrated on the design and functioning of the legal framework that created and that governs the single-payer system. It has tried to develop several larger themes that can provide the basis for the critical evaluation of the system's current structure and performance and of the various programs of reform that are discussed above and the growing role of the courts as producers of health system policy.

One of these themes is the role of law, legal institutions and legal ideas in shaping the uneven success of the system in delivering access to quality health care services. The chapter has tried to show how federal and provincial law work together to provide all Canadians with access to most doctor and hospital services with "no questions asked", without regard to their ability to pay and with minimal intrusion into the physician-patient relationship. This happens against the backdrop of the division of responsibilities that are created by the 1867 Constitution and by the interpretations that have been given to it by the courts. The federal-provincial bickering that is produced by this division of responsibilities gets most of the attention, for understandable reasons. But a more balanced picture would include the positive impact that Canada's federalism has had and continues to have on the Canadian health care system. This includes the very existence of Medicare and the continuing potential of a "system of systems" to generate innovation and experimentation that might not be possible in a more monolithic public system. Emerging national institutions, such as the Health Council for Canada and the Canadian Patient Safety Institute, can be regarded as limited by the restrictive parameters of Canada's federalism. Alternatively, they can be regarded as designed and mandated to exploit and to encourage this potential for innovation.

At the same time, this chapter has explored how access is not addressed by the laws that define and govern the single-payer system. For example, the law does not provide Canadians with options for ensuring accountability from governments for effective and robust implementation of the *Canada Health Act* through government-to-government mechanisms. It does not provide much scope for citizen-initiated enforcement as an alternative mechanism for ensuring that system level action is taken to address systemic barriers to access. Canadian law provides only limited "safety valve" protection that would allow Canadians to take personal access difficulties to independent and accountable decision-makers who have the authority to implement case-specific solutions. Importantly, administrative tribunals that provide this kind of personalized redress have been established in some provinces, but there is room for improvement in their structure, resourcing, processes and mandate. In other provinces, Canadians are unduly dependent on bureaucratically internalized processes that lack transparency, accountability and independence of action.

This theme of the need for institutional development at virtually all levels of the system also emerges from the discussion of the access of Canadians to services that are not covered by the single-payer system. Canadians do not have adequate opportunities for participation in the fundamentally important decisions that are made about what physician and hospital services are in and out of the public system of universal health insurance. But the larger story is perhaps that they also do not have adequate opportunities for involvement with the decisions that are made about the extent and terms of public funding that is provided to address health needs that are better addressed in other ways. These Canadians overwhelmingly belong to vulnerable groups who obviously benefit from Medicare as it is currently structured and legally protected. At the same time, one of the factors that contributes to the constrained resources that are available to meet their more specific needs is the comprehensiveness of the legal protection that is provided to access for everyone to physician and hospital. In this regard, the chapter has suggested that the asymmetry of Canada's single-payer system can produce consequences that are inconsistent with the broader objective of the *Canada Health Act*, "to protect, promote and restore the physical and mental well-being of residents of Canada". This calls for an intensified attention to the question of essentiality, not only in relation to physician and hospital services but more broadly. Broadened public engagement in these deliberative processes is called for by the values that underlie Medicare and by the values that infuse Canadian public law.

This need for procedural and institutional enhancement applies at all levels of the system. It might be summarized by saying that the persistent interest in what decisions have and should be made needs to be complemented by equal concern for the question of how decisions have and should be made. Considering the emphasis that is placed on the public quality of Canada's health care system, decision-making in health care in Canada's publicly financed and publicly governed health care system has been remarkably opaque and remote from the Canadian public.

Another theme to emerge is the closely related one of the extent and nature of government's involvement in and responsibility for the system and its performance. This chapter has suggested that the role of government in the Canadian system is in a period of transition. The implication to be drawn from the overall direction in Canadian health system governance, including from the imposed process of regionalization, is that provincial governments in particular are no longer playing the essentially passive funding role that was characteristic of the first three decades of Medicare. Instead, they have assumed more direct responsibility for the system's organizational configuration, for mandating priorities and objectives, for monitoring and evaluating performance and for establishing system-wide initiatives and institutions to deal with specific diseases (such as cancer) or more pervasive problems (such as patient safety). The growing involvement of governments in the management of waiting lists, as illustrated by Quebec's recent response to the *Chaoulli* decision, is an example of this. This trend and its apparent reinforcement by *Chaoulli* is somewhat ironic, given the tendency to think of *Chaoulli* as a threat to public health care.

At the same time however, physician autonomy both from government and from regional authorities has remained intact. One consequence is that the allocation of resources and thus the priorities of the system continue to be determined largely by physicians, notwithstanding all the talk of community empowerment through regional health authorities. From one direction, the concern is that this leaves the tendencies to cost-escalation that are produced under fee-for-service compensation undisturbed. From another direction, it causes concern that the system continues to emphasize the interests of particular patients in curative procedures and therapies over the broader interest of the community in preventive care. These dynamics push toward the rationale for greater management of physician clinical practice, whether through clinical practice guidelines, the adoption of other elements of managed care strategies, new systems of capitation funding or more drastic compensation system changes that "pay physicians to do less". But this invites a counter-response that physician autonomy is as much a pillar of the Canadian system as is government's responsibility for the costs, and not only because this is, and has been, good for physicians. It is also because it gives freedom of choice to the patient and reassurance to the patient that medical advice is at least that, whatever else its deficiencies. The power of this feature of Canadian Medicare is perhaps reflected in how little is said in any of the recent reports on potential physician responsibility for cost escalation or even on the responsibility of practice patterns for poor quality, notwithstanding the large literature on both topics. The point that is perhaps most important is that Canadians should appreciate that there may be a cost to be paid for preserving this traditional level of physician autonomy. It may be a price worth paying, but it is one caused by how we have structured our publicly funded and publicly governed system, not by the decision to have a publicly funded and publicly governed system.[169]

Finally, the chapter has explored how unresolved issues and the consequences of policy decisions are creating openings for the broader engagement of the courts with health care policy, guided primarily but not exclusively by the *Canadian Charter of Rights and Freedoms*. It is far too early in this process to confidently predict how far the courts will go or in what ways their intervention will change the system. Nevertheless, it does seem reasonable to regard recent cases as harbingers.

Whether one thinks this is a good or a bad thing will depend on many factors, including one's general opinions about what are and are not appropriate matters for the courts and one's level of confidence in the capacity of governments and other health systems actors to do what needs to be done to make Medicare effective and sustainable. It will depend on one's reading of *Auton* and of *Chaoulli* and of the response of governments to both decisions but especially to the latter. While neither decision is satisfactory, the larger concern is with *Chaoulli*. The remedy given by the majority in that case is a remedy that could only make sense as one that would give wealthier Canadians preferential access to medical care. This seems to rank individual liberty over collective equality, contrary to Canada's historic health care commitment to equal access based on need alone. Thus, Canadians are confronted with an apparent tension between the judicial understanding of Canadian values as manifested through the *Canadian Charter of Rights and Freedoms* and what has been the understanding of those values that most Canadians would associate with the *Canada Health Act*. In some commentary, this is portrayed as a collision between the Charter and Canadian values as represented by Medicare. But the reality of the situation is more complex than that, for the attachment that Canadians have continuously expressed to the *Canada Health Act* as a symbol of their citizenship is more or less equally matched by the attachment they have demonstrated for the same reason to the *Canadian Charter of Rights and Freedoms*. What is at stake then is potentially something even larger than Canada's commitment to public health

---

[169] Physician autonomy and organizational separateness may contribute to Canada's relatively weak showing in a recent international survey of primary care physicians: see The Commonwealth Fund, "New International Survey of Primary Care Physicians: Most U.S. Doctors Unable to Provide Patients Access to After-Hours Care; Half Lack Access to Drug Safety Alert Systems" (November 2, 2006), available online: <http://www.commonwealthfund.org/usr_doc/Press_Release3.pdf?section=4056>.

care. At stake is the understanding of collective values and of their relationship to one another that makes such a commitment possible and truly sustainable.

But as argued above, *Chaoulli* actually decides very little. If it does represent a threat to Medicare, the extent of that threat will only become apparent through later cases. Governments and other actors will have considerable opportunities to influence the direction that the courts take in those cases, through what they argue in court and through what they do (or do not do) before going to court.

One of the variables that may prove important is the extent to which Canadian judges see the single-payer system as not only concerned with the value of equality but also as a sophisticated mechanism for balancing equality with the individual autonomy and choice that is also a fundamental element of any humane health care system.

In the meantime, *Chaoulli* has helped to catalyze action on the waiting time situation, as national reports by eminent Canadians and national health accords did not. With *Auton*, the situation is different, given the wide latitude it gives to governments to decide what equality means in the health care funding context. From this perspective, *Chaoulli*, whatever its faults, has at least strengthened some of the accountability that all reviewers of the Canadian health care system have said is the fundamental reform that is necessary to the success of all the others.[170]

---

[170] See the argument by Lorraine Weinrib, "Charter Perspectives on Chaoulli — The Body and the Body Politic", in Colleen M. Flood, Kent Roach & Lorne Sossin, eds., *Access to Care, Access to Justice: The Legal Debate Over Private Health Insurance in Canada* (Toronto: University of Toronto Press, 2005) 56.

Chapter 2

REGULATION OF
HEALTH CARE PROFESSIONALS

Tracey Epps

I. INTRODUCTION

In Canada, provincial and territorial governments delegate a large measure of responsibility for governance of health professionals to the professions themselves. This chapter explores how these self-regulatory regimes operate, and analyzes the implications of the policy choice to delegate professional governance to members of the professions themselves. Section Two provides a general overview of regulation as a tool in the health care sector. Section Three examines the types of regulation that operate to govern health professionals, drawing a distinction between *input* regulation (focus on who may be admitted to the profession) and *output* regulation (focus on performance by those in the profession). Section Four looks at sources of regulation, paying particular attention to the predominant source of regulation in Canada, namely, self-regulation. Section Five provides an overview of regulation of health professionals in Canada, focusing on input and output regulation, as well as mechanisms for accountability and transparency. Finally, Section Six provides a brief discussion of some emerging issues for regulatory policy in this area.

II. OVERVIEW OF REGULATION

The term "regulation" has been described as "any process or set of processes by which norms are established, the behaviour of those subject to the norms monitored or fed back into the regime, and for which there are mechanisms for holding the behaviour of regulated actors within the acceptable limits of the regime (whether by enforcement action or by some other mechanism)".[1] In the health sector, regulation is a tool which allows policy-makers to establish norms

---

[1] C. Scott, "Analysing Regulatory Space: Fragmented Resources and Institutional Design" [2001] P. L. 329 at 331, cited in Bettina Lange, "Regulatory Spaces and Interactions: An Introduction" (2003) 12 Social and Legal Studies 411 at 411.

to which health professionals must adhere. For example, regulations may specify the scope of practice of a certain profession, and establish standards of practice. Through regulation, legislators may also hold health professionals accountable for adhering to norms through mechanisms such as complaints and discipline procedures.

Regulation effectively limits the freedom of both individuals and organizations by placing limits on activities and behaviour. For this reason, democratic norms demand that regulation be justified on principled grounds. The key justification for regulatory intervention in the health sector is that it is necessary to correct market failure arising from imperfect information and information asymmetries.[2] Health care markets are characterized by imperfect information due largely to uncertainty concerning the incidence of disease and the efficacy of treatment.[3] Information asymmetries arise between consumers and health professionals because consumers typically do not have the information needed to evaluate the competence of medical professionals; and the complexity of medical practice means that consumers are often unable to understand information they do have.[4]

Given that the consequences of error in the practice of medicine may be high and are potentially irreversible, regulatory intervention is considered necessary to protect the public by helping them to make knowledgeable choices,[5] and ensuring that professionals have the necessary qualifications to practice their profession.[6] In some cases, certification provides consumers with enough information about the educational or practice background of the professional to help them make an informed choice. In other areas, however, consumers will be unable to evaluate information about the service or products and the risks associated with an error may be high, and in these cases information disclosure alone is not sufficient means of consumer protection. This is where it is necessary to take stricter measures such as limiting entry to those practitioners who meet a minimum threshold of education and experience qualification.[7]

In addition to market failure justifications, the professions have long recognized that they themselves receive benefits from regulation and have supported legislation accordingly. In the U.S., for example, the American

---

[2]   See, generally, K.J. Arrow, "Uncertainty and the Welfare Economics of Medical Care" (1963) 53 American Economic Review 941 (making the presumption that health care markets will not reach a competitive equilibrium without non-market intervention).

[3]   *Ibid.*, at 941.

[4]   Margot Priest, "The Privatization of Regulation: Five Models of Self-Regulation" (1997-98) 29 Ottawa L. Rev. 233 at 253.

[5]   *Ibid.*

[6]   Tim Jost, ed., *Regulation of Healthcare Professions* (Chicago: Health Administration Press, 1997) at 2. See also J. Lieberman, *The Tyranny of the Experts* (New York: Walker & Co., 1970) at 246. (Lieberman argues that "performance of some occupations without due regard for professional standards of technical competence could result in death, serious bodily injury, catastrophic destruction or deprivation of legal rights".) See also D. Irvine, "The performance of doctors: the new professionalism" (1999) 353 The Lancet 1174, and A. Donabedian, "Evaluating Physician Competence" (2000) 78 Bulletin of the World Health Organization 857.

[7]   Margot Priest, "The Privatization of Regulation: Five Models of Self-Regulation" (1997-98) 29 Ottawa L. Rev. 233 at 253.

Medical Association and its constituent state societies were proactive in the development of professional licensure through which they hoped to eliminate competition from "unorthodox" schools of medicine.[8] Early supporters of licensure for the professions were also concerned with protecting trained medical practitioners from graduates of substandard medical institutions or from untrained lay healers.[9] As Jost notes, regulation of health professionals has in this manner served to maintain professional identity and orthodoxy, economic power, and social and educational elitism.[10]

Like any regulatory activity, the regulation of health professionals may be subjected to a positive analysis in order to explain the behaviour of, among others, legislators and bureaucrats. Among positive theories of regulation, a broad distinction can be made between "public" and "private" theories. These theories offer a useful perspective with which to consider regulation of health professionals. Public interest theories have as their central premise the idea that regulation is developed in order to further the "public interest"; while private interest theories find that regulation is not driven by pursuit of the public interest, but by the demand of private interests.[11] Public interest theories of regulation have been attacked on various grounds, including the inherent difficulties in giving normative content to the idea of the "public interest" which result in it being vulnerable to capture by those who exercise power in society.[12] This criticism is compounded by doubts concerning the expertise, objectiveness, efficiency, and competency of regulators;[13] arguments that such theories understate the degree to which economic and political influence has an impact on regulation;[14] as well as observed cases of regulatory failure.[15]

Private theories of regulation rely on the assumption that individuals act to advance their self-interest and do so rationally.[16] In a seminal 1971 article, Stigler finds that, as a rule, regulation is acquired by industry and is designed

---

[8] J.G. Burrow, *Organized Medicine in the Progressive Era: The Move Toward Monopoly* (Baltimore, MD: Johns Hopkins University Press, 1977), cited in Tim Jost, ed., *Regulation of Healthcare Professions* (Chicago: Health Administration Press, 1997) at 2.

[9] *Ibid.*

[10] Tim Jost, ed., *Regulation of Healthcare Professions* (Chicago: Health Administration Press, 1997).

[11] Robert Baldwin & Martin Cave, *Understanding Regulation: Theory, Strategy, and Practice* (New York: Oxford University Press, 1999) at 21.

[12] Mike Feintuck, *'The Public Interest' in Regulation* (New York: Oxford University Press, 2004) at 33.

[13] Robert Baldwin & Martin Cave, *Understanding Regulation: Theory, Strategy, and Practice* (New York: Oxford University Press, 1999) at 20. See also M.J. Trebilcock *et al.*, *The Choice of Governing Instrument (A study prepared for the Economic Council of Canada)* (Ottawa: Canadian Government Pub. Centre, 1982).

[14] Robert Baldwin & Martin Cave, *Understanding Regulation: Theory, Strategy, and Practice* (New York: Oxford University Press, 1999) at 20.

[15] Don Dewees, David Duff & Michael J. Trebilcock, *Exploring the Domain of Accident Law* (New York: Oxford University Press, 1996) at 215. The authors cite in this regard, Richard Braddock, *Product Liability: Economic Impacts* (Canberra: Law Reform Commission of Australia, 1989).

[16] Richard A. Posner, "Theories of Economic Regulation" (1974) 5 The Bell Journal of Economics and Management Science 335 at 337.

and operated primarily for its benefit.[17] In other words, industry "captures" the regulatory agency and uses regulation to prevent competition. In the context of regulation of health professionals, this tendency can be seen in the example given above of the medical professions in the U.S. seeking to eliminate competition from "unorthodox" schools of medicine, as well as more recent cases of professions seeking to maintain control over their practice areas.[18] For example, the American Society for Gastrointestinal Endoscopy and the American College of Gastroenterology undertook a national campaign in the early 1990s to convince hospitals that allowing family practitioners to perform endoscopies would be tantamount to condoning malpractice.[19] In Canada, dentists in Ontario have opposed efforts by dental hygienists to obtain the right to practise independently. As Adams writes, this situation is explicable by the fact that dental hygienists cannot attain greater professional status and autonomy, except at the expense of the dental profession's own claims to status and jurisdiction.[20]

It is widely accepted in Canada that legislative intent is for regulation of health professionals to be primarily a matter of the public interest.[21] In Ontario, for example, a report prepared prior to the 1991 implementation of the *Regulated Health Professions Act, 1991* ("RHPA")[22] recommended that:

> The important principle underlying each of the criteria [for regulation] is that the sole purpose of professional regulation is to advance and protect the public interest. The public is the intended beneficiary of regulation, not the members of the profession. Thus the purpose of granting self-regulation to a profession is not to enhance its status or to increase the earning power of its members by giving the profession a monopoly over the delivery of particular health services. Indeed, although these are common results of traditional regulatory models, they are undesirable results, and the model of regulation we recommend [the RHPA] aims to minimize them.[23]

Following these recommendations, the Ontario legislation was designed to advance the "public interest" in four ways: (i) protecting the public, to the extent

---

[17] George J. Stigler, "The Theory of Economic Regulation" (1971) 1 Bell Journal of Economics 3 at 3.

[18] See generally Frederic W. Hafferty & Donald W. Light, "Professional Dynamics and the Changing Nature of Medical Work" (1995) 35 Journal of Health and Social Behaviour 132. S. Clark, *State and Status* (Montreal and Kingston: McGill-Queen's University Press, 1995).

[19] Frederic W. Hafferty & Donald W. Light, "Professional Dynamics and the Changing Nature of Medical Work" (1995) 35 Journal of Health and Social Behaviour 132 at 136.

[20] Tracey L. Adams, "Inter-professional conflict and professionalization: dentistry and dental hygiene in Ontario" (2004) 58 Social Science and Medicine 2243 at 2243.

[21] Douglas Alderson & Deanne Montesano, *Regulating, De-Regulating, and Changing Scopes of Practice in the Health Professions — A Jurisdictional Review* (A Report Prepared for the Health Professions Regulatory Advisory Council, Ottawa, 2003) at 4. Although in some provinces it is acknowledged that regulations also exist to protect the integrity of the health profession and its professionals. See, for example, the statement by the Yukon Government, "Omnibus Act Proposed for Health Professions", Yukon Government Press Release #03-203, September 25, 2003.

[22] S.O. 1991, c. 18.

[23] Health Professions Legislation Review, *Striking a New Balance: A Blueprint for the Regulation of Ontario's Health Professions* (Toronto: Queen's Printer, 1989) at 9.

possible, from unqualified, incompetent and unfit health care providers; (ii) developing mechanisms to encourage the provision of high quality care; (iii) permitting the public to exercise freedom of choice of health care provider within a range of safe options; and (iv) promoting evolution in the roles played by individual professions and flexibility in how individual professions can be utilized, so that health services are delivered with maximum efficiency.[24]

The RHPA imposes a duty on the Minister of Health and Long-Term Care to, *inter alia*, "ensure that the health professions are regulated and co-ordinated in the public interest . . ."(s. 3). In addition, s. 3(2) of the Health Professions Procedure Code[25] expressly states that the regulatory Colleges, in carrying out their corporate objects, have a "duty to serve and protect the public interest". While the RHPA does not actually provide a definition of the term "public interest", Alderson and Montesano suggest that the legislation reveals six public interest principles, namely: protection from harm; quality of care; accountability; accessibility; equity; and equality.[26] They argue that the meaning of public interest is to protect the public from harm and that other public interest principles fall within, and must be understood within the context of, the guiding principle of protection from harm. Such a principle is admirable from a quality and safety perspective but care must be taken that other objectives are not compromised. For example, a policy that the highest qualified professional should provide certain treatments (*e.g.*, a physician) when a lesser qualified individual (*e.g.*, a nurse) could do the same job would potentially jeopardize access and efficiency.

Similar public interest legislative objectives are also found in other Canadian jurisdictions.[27] To what extent then, do private theories of regulation provide a useful lens through which to view self-regulation of health professionals? On the one hand, self-regulation may be seen as based on a "social contract" between the profession and the public.[28] That is, in exchange for a grant of authority to self-regulate, professionals are expected to maintain high standards of competence and moral responsibility.[29] The social contract rests upon the concept of professionalism, whereby it is understood that professionals will devote themselves to serving others rather than themselves.[30] In other words, there is an argument that professional bodies are motivated not simply by private interests, but also by ideals, principles, and values.

Self-interest undoubtedly exists among health professions. The concept of professionalism carries with it an inherent conflict of interest as professionals have a biased interest in the outcome of regulation and consequent motivation to

---

[24] *Ibid.*, at 2.

[25] Schedule 2 of the RHPA.

[26] Douglas Alderson & Deanne Montesano, *Regulating, De-Regulating, and Changing Scopes of Practice in the Health Professions — A Jurisdictional Review* (A Report Prepared for the Health Professions Regulatory Advisory Council, Ottawa, 2003) at 7.

[27] See, for example, British Columbia, *Health Professions Act*, R.S.B.C. 1996, c. 183, at s. 10(1) and (2); and Alberta, *Health Professions Act*, R.S.A. 2000, c. H-7, at s. 26(1).

[28] William M. Sullivan, "Medicine under threat: professionalism and professional identity" (2000) 162 C.M.A.J. 673 at 673.

[29] *Ibid.*

[30] Margaret Somerville, ed., *Do We Care? Renewing Canada's Commitment to Health* (Montreal: McGill-Queen's University Press, 1999) at 34.

enact policies that promote the professions' own goals rather than those that serve the interests of the public. In other words, self-regulatory regimes embody contrary tendencies — the push of self-serving economic (or political) interests and the pull of moral aspirations.[31]

It is not apparent that Canadian regulatory regimes result in the public interest mandate being fulfilled in the optimal manner. There are numerous instances of self-interest in self-regulatory schemes. Alderson notes the following criticisms of regulation of health professionals in Canada: (1) the continuing "turf" battles that are waged between various professions; (2) the monopolistic implications and impact of regulation, including the creation of artificial barriers to entry to practice, reduced competition, and restricted access to services; (3) lack of co-ordination between health professions; (4) regulatory regimes that are unable to adapt to changing technological/scientific innovations and advancements which in turn impact upon the efficient and effective delivery of health care services; (5) economic/political self-interest of the professions and regulators which are supported and encouraged though regulation; and (6) insufficient integration and/or coordination with other public and private consumer protection processes such as criminal or civil remedies.[32]

It is helpful to heed the advice of Gunningham and Rees who argue that the opposing tendencies of self-regulated bodies ought to put us on guard against analyzing institutions in terms only of self-interest or only normative expectations. Rather than choosing one perspective over the other, they suggest that we ought to ask about the different circumstances under which each is true. That is, when does self-regulation tend to result in self-serving standards and under what conditions might it become a real force for moral constraint and aspiration?[33]

III. TYPES OF REGULATION

Regulatory controls on health professionals belong to one of two broad catego-ries: input regulation or output regulation.[34] Input regulation focuses on who is entitled to provide health services while output regulation focuses on the quality of the services provided. The key distinction between the two forms of regula-tion is that input regulation is proactive, while output regulation is reactive in

---

[31]   Neil Gunningham & Joseph Rees, "Industry Self-Regulation: An Institutional Perspective" (1997) 19 Law and Pol'y 363 at 372.

[32]   Douglas Alderson & Deanne Montesano, *Regulating, De-Regulating, and Changing Scopes of Practice in the Health Professions — A Jurisdictional Review* (A Report Prepared for the Health Professions Regulatory Advisory Council, Ottawa, 2003) at 5.

[33]   Neil Gunningham & Joseph Rees, "Industry Self-Regulation: An Institutional Perspective" (1997) 19 Law and Pol'y 363 at 373.

[34]   A.D. Wolfson, M.J. Trebilcock & C.J. Tuohy, "Regulating the Professions: A Theoretical Framework" in S. Rottenberg, ed., *Occupational Licensure and Regulation* (Washington, D.C.: American Enterprise for Public Policy Research, 1980) 180 at 180.

nature.[35] However, both forms of regulation share the broad common goal of protecting the public.[36]

A. OUTPUT REGULATION

Output regulation has traditionally taken two key forms. First, civil liability; and second, monitoring and discipline of professionals in accordance with professional standards. More recently, a third form of regulation is increasingly being used which involves external assessment of health care services. While used more in the context of assessing institutions, there are indications, as discussed below, that this method of regulation may also be used in the case of individual health professionals in the future.

Civil liability is widely used in Canada as a mechanism to ensure quality of health services.[37] Civil liability may act as a constraint on health professionals and may be perceived as more objective than disciplinary action by the professions themselves. It has the advantage of imposing penalties to compensate consumers and deterring incompetent and unethical practice. In addition, it is relatively flexible and capable of evolution to reflect changing practices and norms. However, civil liability also has significant drawbacks as a means of ensuring quality of care and protecting the public. Litigation is expensive and beyond the means of many Canadians. The Canadian practice that costs follow the event means that an unsuccessful plaintiff must pay a proportion of the defendant's costs. It is therefore not profitable to pursue a claim if there is only a small likelihood of success. Studies have shown that it is often difficult for plaintiffs to prove their cases and they will therefore often require expert assistance, which is likely to be expensive. Another drawback of civil liability is what Trebilcock refers to as "claim consciousness".[38] That is, many consumers are ignorant of their legal rights and are unaware that they have a legal claim. Given the complexities of medical practice, it may also be difficult for consumers to detect instances of malpractice. Emotional barriers may also exist to adopting an adversarial position towards physicians to whom they have entrusted their care. It has been argued that physicians fear malpractice suits because they are both a professional threat and a personal ordeal.[39] However, the available evidence suggests that only a small proportion of negligently injured patients initiate malpractice claims. A study in New York in 1991, for example, found that only

[35] M.J. Trebilcock, C.J. Tuohy & A.D. Wolfson, *Professional Regulation: A Staff Study of Accountancy, Engineering and Law in Ontario: Prepared for the Professional Organization Committee* (Toronto: Ministry of the Attorney General, 1979) at 69.

[36] *Ibid.*, at 66.

[37] Between 1971 and 1990 the number of medical malpractice claims filed per 100 Canadian doctors increased from 0.55 to 1.7. M.J. Trebilcock, D. Dewees, & D. Duff, *Exploring the Domain of Accident Law: Taking the Facts Seriously* (New York: Oxford University Press, 1996) at 96.

[38] M.J. Trebilcock, D. Dewees, & D. Duff, *ibid.*, at 120.

[39] F.P. Grad, Book Review of *Medical Malpractice and the American Jury: Confronting the Myths about Jury Incompetence, Deep Pockets and Outrageous Damage Awards* by N. Vidmar (1996) 335 New Eng. J. of Med. 139. See also J. Rafuse, "Physicians' fear of legal action becoming 'pervasive', lawyer tells Ontario conference" (1995) 152 C.M.A.J. 573.

two per cent of patients who were negligently injured in that state initiated malpractice claims.[40] A more recent study found that of patients negligently injured in Utah and Colorado, only three per cent initiated claims.[41] Further, the Utah/Colorado study found that the tort system is unequal in its protection of patients, with the poor and the elderly being found particularly likely to suffer negligent injury and not sue.

The other main form of output regulation in professional markets is referred to as "professional monitoring" or discipline. In general, the advantages and disadvantages of discipline are similar as those for civil liability. Unlike civil liability, the disciplinary process is administered by the professional's peers.[42] This lends credibility to the process from the profession's perspective and may assist in promoting compliance with standards. It may arguably also lead to fewer errors in adjudication than in the civil liability system.[43]

However, because the process is administered by the profession itself, it is prone to being managed in a self-serving manner and may not be trusted by the public.[44] Like civil liability, the system is activated largely based on victim complaints which may prevent a barrier to hearing of complaints. Further, the professional discipline process does not provide compensation for victims, resulting in a lack of economic incentive for victims to pursue their complaints.

Recent years have seen an increase in a third form of output regulation where governments are focusing on quality of outcomes by using external assessment of health care services. This form of regulation has tended to concentrate on assessment of institutions rather than individual professionals, however, there is scope for it to be used more in the case of individual professionals. For example, the Health Quality Council of Saskatchewan was created in 2002 and has a legislative mandate to measure and report on the quality of care and to promote quality improvement.[45] The Council is responsible for developing quality indicators and publishes results of evaluations in its own publications as well as in peer-reviewed journals. The Council has initiated a number of projects to improve health outcomes, including to improve chronic disease management,

---

[40] A.R. Localio, A.G. Lawthers & T.A. Brennan, "Relation between malpractice claims and adverse events due to negligence: results of the Harvard Medical Practice Study III" (1991) 325 New Eng. J. Med. 245.

[41] D.M. Studdert *et al.*, "Negligent care and malpractice claiming behavior in Utah and Colorado" (2000) 38:3 Medical Care 250.

[42] See M.J. Trebilcock, "Regulating Service Quality in Professional Markets" in D.N. Dewees, ed., *The Regulation of Quality: Products, Services, Workplaces and the Environment* (Toronto: Butterworths, 1983) at 90-91; and M.J. Trebilcock, C.J. Tuohy & A.D. Wolfson, *Professional Regulation: A Staff Study of Accountancy, Engineering and Law in Ontario: Prepared for the Professional Organizations Committee* (Toronto: Ministry of the Attorney General, 1979) at 71.

[43] M.J. Trebilcock, "Regulating Service Quality in Professional Markets", *ibid.*, at 91. M.J. Trebilcock, C.J. Tuohy & A.D. Wolfson, *Professional Regulation: A Staff Study of Accountancy, Engineering and Law in Ontario: Prepared for the Professional Organizations Committee*, *ibid.*, at 69 and 77.

[44] M.J. Trebilcock, C.J. Tuohy & A.D. Wolfson, *Professional Regulation: A Staff Study of Accountancy, Engineering and Law in Ontario: Prepared for the Professional Organizations Committee*, *ibid.*, at 71-72.

[45] See the *Health Quality Council Act*, S.S. 2002, c. H-0.04.

asthma care, cancer care, as well as patient care and safety in Intensive Care Units. These types of projects may have potential to make recommendations regarding the practice of individual professionals.[46] Saskatchewan was the first province in Canada to create such an agency and it has been followed by other provinces including Alberta whose Health Quality Council has a mandate to promote patient safety and health service quality.[47]

Another recent initiative is that of hospital reports and performance agreements. In Ontario, the Ontario Hospital Association participates in a program which engages hospitals in performance measurement and management activities. The program produces publicly available performance measurement reports which cover a range of sectors including acute care, emergency departments, complex continuing care, and rehabilitation. Also, recent legislation requires Ontario hospitals to enter into a performance agreement with the Minister of Health and Long-Term Care.[48] Among other targets, the agreements set out performance standards. From 2007, legislated penalties will be imposed for failure to meet the standards, which may include fines on the CEO. Like the activities of the provincial councils discussed above, these performance agreements and hospital reporting initiatives have potential to be expanded to include measurement of individual performance.

B. INPUT REGULATION

Three main modes of regulation fall under the heading of input regulation. First, *licensure* gives a profession a monopoly on the activity regulated. This may be done through profession-specific practice legislation where licensed practitioners gain an exclusive right to deliver certain services. The impact of licensure is that licensed professionals are limited to performing certain types of procedures. In most cases, licensing regimes are controlled by a regulatory body with the delegated power to control entry into the profession. For example, in Nova Scotia a physician cannot practise unless he or she is licensed by the College of Physicians and Surgeons of Nova Scotia, while a nurse must be a member of the College of Registered Nurses of Nova Scotia. Under a licensing regime, there are usually strict admission requirements, often with competency tests and educational qualifications attached. Professional licensing systems have been criticized for their tendency to be captured by those with the greatest interest in limiting access to the regulated professions. The economist Milton Friedman was strongly critical of this aspect of licensing systems. He wrote that professional licensing boards are the contemporary equivalent of medieval guilds, arguing that "the considerations taken into account in determining who shall get a license often involve matters that, so far as a layman can see, have no relation whatsoever to professional competence".[49]

Second, *certification* is less restrictive than licensing and involves giving designated recognition to individuals who have met predetermined qualifications

---

[46] See Health Quality Council of Saskatchewan, online: <http://www.hqc.sk.ca>.
[47] Health Quality Council of Alberta, online: <http://www.hqca.ca>.
[48] *Commitment to the Future of Medicare Act, 2004*, S.O. 2004, c. 5.
[49] Milton Friedman, *Capitalism and Freedom* (Chicago: University of Chicago Press, 1962) at 141.

set by a regulatory agency or professional body. Non-certified individuals may still offer services but they may not use the term "certified" or the designated title. Certification is not as strict as licensing in the sense of creating a monopoly over the occupation as a whole. It may also be referred to as "title restriction" or "title reservation" and is a form of shorthand or credentialing signal for the public, indicating a certain background or educational level.[50] For example, in Manitoba, while massage therapists are not a regulated profession, they may only use the term "certified" if they have met certain educational requirements stipulated by the Canadian Massage Therapist Alliance.[51]

Third, *registration* is the least restrictive mode of input regulation and simply requires an individual to register their particulars with a designated agency.[52] All members of an occupational group who register may offer their services to the public; for example, in Kansas, the Board of Healing Arts maintains a register of individuals who are "physicians' assistants".[53] Cagle notes that registration is limited in the protection it can provide against incompetence, suggesting that all it has to offer is providing the identity of the practitioner so that an aggrieved patient can pursue legal redress.[54]

IV. SOURCES OF REGULATION

Regulatory regimes are best seen as occupying a continuum, with pure forms of government regulation and self-regulation at opposite ends.[55] Where there is direct state control over regulation of health professionals (classic "command and control" regulation), the state is responsible for all aspects of regulation and administration; however, this form of regulation is rarely used in the context of health professionals. Combinations of government and self-regulation are possible where a profession has authority to govern itself but relies on a state agency to carry out certain functions such as administration and adjudication of complaints. Such regimes would fall in the middle of the continuum. Self-regulation describes a situation where at least 51 per cent of the governing entity comprises of members of the profession. The governing entity is responsible for all decisions both administrative and profession-specific, such as clinical standard setting, ethical, investigative, and disciplinary matters. This is the predominant mechanism used to regulate health professionals in Canada.

---

[50]	Margot Priest, "The Privatization of Regulation: Five Models of Self-Regulation" (1997-98) 29 Ottawa L. Rev. 233 at 252.

[51]	See Canadian Massage Therapist Alliance, online: <http://www.cmta.ca/>.

[52]	Douglas Alderson & Deanne Montesano, *Regulating, De-Regulating, and Changing Scopes of Practice in the Health Professions — A Jurisdictional Review* (A Report Prepared for the Health Professions Regulatory Advisory Council, Ottawa, 2003) at 12.

[53]	*Ibid.*

[54]	M. Christine Cagle, J. Michael Martinez & William D. Richardson, "Privatizing Professional Licensing Boards: Self-Governance or Self-Interest?" (1999) 30 Administration and Society 734 at 737.

[55]	Neil Gunningham & Joseph Rees, "Industry Self-Regulation: An Institutional Perspective" (1997) 19 Law and Pol'y 363 at 366.

Even when a profession is self-regulated, the regime will usually, at some level, acknowledge the legislature's and executive's ultimate authority. Priest argues that self-regulation works best when it operates "in the shadow" of government intervention, receiving its impetus from the prospect of government action.[56] Similarly, Gunningham and Rees suggest that self-regulatory mechanisms underpinned by some form of state intervention are more resilient and effective than self-regulation in isolation.[57]

While self-regulatory schemes usually grant a large degree of autonomy to professional bodies to regulate their members (through rulemaking, monitoring, enforcement, and sanctions), government control is usually found in the structuring of the statute that delegates power to the body, and is often found in the power to approve regulations or bylaws established by the body.[58] An example of the executive's ultimate authority can be seen in Ontario's RHPA which in section 5(1) vests the Minister of Health and Long-Term Care with the power to require that a regulatory College inquire into the state of practice of a health profession in a particular locality or institution. Self-regulatory bodies are also subject to judicial review,[59] and may be subject to the *Canadian Charter of Rights and Freedoms*.[60]

A. GROUNDS FOR SELF-REGULATION

Several advantages are commonly claimed for self-regulation. First, it is argued that self-regulatory bodies have a greater degree of expertise and technical knowledge of practices in their particular area than independent agencies. In 1933, Durkheim wrote that professional groups have a distinctive capacity for becoming "agencies of moral education", an advantage conferred by their special knowledge and influence.[61] She argued that such groups are well-positioned to promote shared ethical practices within industry, because "occupational activity can be efficaciously regulated only by a group intimate enough with it to know its functions" and also because they are "near enough to the individuals to attract them strongly in their spheres of action".[62]

---

[56] Margot Priest, "The Privatization of Regulation: Five Models of Self-Regulation" (1997-98) 29 Ottawa L. Rev. 233 at 238.

[57] Neil Gunningham & Joseph Rees, "Industry Self-Regulation: An Institutional Perspective" (1997) 19 Law and Pol'y 363 at 366.

[58] Margot Priest, "The Privatization of Regulation: Five Models of Self-Regulation" (1997-98) 29 Ottawa L. Rev. 233 at 252.

[59] *Khan v. College of Physicians and Surgeons of Ontario*, [1992] O.J. No. 1725, 94 D.L.R. (4th) 193, 9 O.R. (3d) 641 (Ont. C.A.).

[60] Part I of the *Constitution Act, 1982*, being Schedule B of the *Canada Act, 1982* (U.K.) 1982, c. 11. See *Knutson v. Saskatchewan Registered Nurses Assn.*, [1990] S.J. No. 603, [1991] 2 W.W.R. 327, 75 D.L.R. (4th) 723 (Sask. C.A.).

[61] Emile Durkheim, *The Division of Labour in Society* (New York: MacMillan, 1933) at 5, cited in Neil Gunningham & Joseph Rees, "Industry Self-Regulation: An Institutional Perspective" (1997) 19 Law and Pol'y 363 at 371.

[62] Emile Durkheim, *The Division of Labour in Society* (New York: MacMillan, 1933) at 5 and 28, cited *ibid.*

Durkheim's statement alludes to several benefits which arguably flow from the expertise found within self-regulatory bodies. First, it is argued that the involvement of a professional's peers in the disciplinary process will assist in *promoting compliance* with standards and thus lead to fewer errors in adjudication than in tort law. That is, self-regulation utilizes peer pressure and internalizes responsibility for compliance. As Justice Cory stated in *Milstein v. Ontario College of Pharmacy*: "The peers of the professional person are deemed to have and, indeed, they must have special knowledge, training and skill that particularly adapts them to formulate their own professional standards and to judge the conduct of a member of their profession. No other body could appreciate as well the problems and frustrations that beset a fellow member."[63] Peer pressure is also arguably a benefit of professional self-regulation as professionals feel pressure to adhere to the standards set by their profession. Priest refers to "psychological buy-in" to regulation that individuals have had a hand in developing and for which they are responsible.[64]

Second, the expertise of self-regulating bodies arguably results in *lower costs* with respect to the formulation and interpretation of standards, as well as monitoring and enforcement. Also, administrative costs tend to be internalized in the profession rather than being passed directly on to taxpayers.[65] Whether or not the self-regulatory system is supervised by government, the costs to government are argued to be less than they would be if government took on the majority of the regulatory responsibilities.[66]

Third, it is argued that self-regulatory regimes benefit from *greater flexibility* due to the use of less formal rules and processes. Rules can be quickly and easily adjusted to meet changing circumstances as opposed to the time-consuming process of legislative reform.[67] Self-regulatory bodies also have the advantage of being able to hire staff as needed and pay competitive salaries to retain expertise.

Finally, it is argued that because self-regulation contemplates *ethical standards* of conduct which extend beyond the letter of the law, it may significantly raise standards of behaviour.[68]

---

[63] [1976] O.J. No. 2277 at para. 42, 13 O.R. (2d) 700 (Ont. Div. Ct.), vard [1978] O.J. No. 3434, 20 O.R. (2d) 283 (Ont. C.A.).

[64] Margot Priest, "The Privatization of Regulation: Five Models of Self-Regulation" (1997-98) 29 Ottawa L. Rev. 233 at 270, citing also E. Bardach & R.A. Kagan, *Going by the Book: The Problem of Regulatory Unreasonableness* (Philadelphia: Temple University Press, 1982) at 65-66; and J. Braithwaite, "Enforced Self-Regulation: A New Strategy for Corporate Crime Control" (1982) 80 Mich. L. Rev. 1466.

[65] Anthony Ogus, "Rethinking Self-Regulation" (1995) 15 Oxford J. Legal Stud. 97 at 98. It is arguable, however, that taxpayers are being charged indirectly through higher prices.

[66] Margot Priest, "The Privatization of Regulation: Five Models of Self-Regulation" (1997-98) 29 Ottawa L. Rev. 233 at 270.

[67] *Ibid.*, at 269.

[68] Neil Gunningham & Joseph Rees, "Industry Self-Regulation: An Institutional Perspective" (1997) 19 Law and Pol'y 363 at 366.

B. CRITICISMS OF SELF-REGULATION

Self-regulation of health professionals is subject to several criticisms. Most notably, it has been criticized for failing to ensure professional competence and to protect patients. Some commentators in Canada have argued that public confidence in physicians is waning, in part because of a high frequency of adverse events, of reports of hospital and professional mismanagement such as the pediatric cardiac surgery deaths in Winnipeg, and of professional malfeasance.[69] Critics charge that self-regulatory standards are usually weak, enforcement is ineffective, and punishment is secret and mild. These failures can be related back to the tension inherent in self-regulatory regimes between on the one hand, the public interest, and on the other, private interests that would otherwise be threatened by regulation.[70] Where regulatory powers are delegated to the professions, the members of those professions no longer have to seek to influence regulators to serve their interests but are in an optimal position to profit from rent-seeking. Priest argues that self-regulation is the ultimate form of regulatory agency capture and is incapable of being impartial and fair. She describes it as tantamount to "putting the fox to guard the henhouse".[71] Self-interest may result in "under-regulation" due to lack of enthusiasm on the part of members of the group. To use the fox/chicken analogy, "foxes may be more interested in the chickens than they are in controlling the other foxes".

Self-regulatory regimes are also vulnerable to "over-regulation" where the organization becomes similar to a government bureaucracy with rigid hierarchies, desire to expand territory, and placement of the interests of the organization before its mandate.[72] The resulting over-regulation, especially the artificial inflation of entry requirements, can result in an overall reduction in access to or increase in the cost of services available to the public. Prices might be increased where self-regulatory bodies create professionals "cartels" and block the substitution of lower-cost for higher-cost services of equivalent quality.[73] When the number of practitioners is reduced or the price increased, some consumers will do without the service, obtain it from unqualified practitioners, or do it themselves.[74] One U.S. newspaper, for example, cited a person attempting to perform a root canal themselves rather than going to an expensive dentist.[75]

---

[69] Editorial, "Can physicians regulate themselves?" (2005) 172 C.M.A.J. 717.

[70] Neil Gunningham & Joseph Rees, "Industry Self-Regulation: An Institutional Perspective" (1997) 19 Law and Pol'y 363 at 370.

[71] Margot Priest, "The Privatization of Regulation: Five Models of Self-Regulation" (1997-98) 29 Ottawa L. Rev. 233 at 271, citing M.G. Cochrane, "Buyer beware: the new regulatory reality in Canada", *Law Times* (September 1996).

[72] Margot Priest, "The Privatization of Regulation: Five Models of Self-Regulation" (1997-98) 29 Ottawa L. Rev. 233 at 273.

[73] Tim Jost, ed., *Regulation of Healthcare Professions* (Chicago: Health Administration Press, 1997) at 3.

[74] Manitoba Law Reform Commission, *Discussion Paper: The Future of Occupational Regulation in Manitoba* (Winnipeg: Law Reform Commission, 1993). Margot Priest, "The Privatization of Regulation: Five Models of Self-Regulation" (1997-98) 29 Ottawa L. Rev. 233 at 273.

[75] Tom Rademacher, "Don't Try This At Home" (*The Ann Arbor News* (February 9, 1997) at A11.

Over-regulation may also be to the detriment of those wanting to enter the profession. Jost argues that self-regulated health professions have tended to block entry into the professions by minorities and foreign trained professionals, and also that they have sought to restrict the development of alternative forms of medicine.[76] In Prince Edward Island, for example, physicians recently opposed the integration of nurse practitioners into the health care system, arguing that they were not qualified to practice and effectively shutting down a pilot project that would have enabled nurse practitioners to make certain services more accessible to the public.[77]

Self-regulation is also criticized for lacking many of the advantages of conventional government regulation "in terms of visibility, credibility, accountability, compulsory application to all ... greater likelihood of rigorous standards being developed, cost spreading ... and availability of a range of sanctions".[78] There may also be a breach of the separation of powers doctrine where the self-regulated profession has control over policy formulation, interpretation of the rules, adjudication and enforcement as well as rule-making.[79]

Finally, the flexibility inherent in self-regulatory regimes may be heralded as an advantage, but it is also a contributor to criticisms of self-regulation as it may result in the sacrifice of consumer representation or consultation. It may also imply vagueness or the exercise of discretion that can favour certain interests.[80]

In conclusion, self-regulation of health professionals has both positive and negative aspects. In Canada, governments have considered the positives sufficient to outweigh the negatives and self-regulation is the primary means of regulating health professionals. However, in reality, actions taken by self-regulatory bodies are often guided more by self-interest than the public interest and there is a thus a critical need for legislatures to provide checks and balances to guard against self-interested action, and ensure adequate accountability and transparency.[81]

---

[76] Tim Jost, ed., *Regulation of Healthcare Professions* (Chicago: Health Administration Press, 1997) at 3.

[77] C. Morris, "Nurse Practitioners Say They Face Barrier" October 11, 2005 (Nurse Practitioners Canada), online at Nurse Practitioners Canada: <http://www.npcanada.ca/portal>. Bickford notes that there has also been recent conflict in British Columbia where physicians have opposed the suggestion that nurse practitioners could perform some aspects of their job. Celeste Bickford, "Introducing Nurse Practitioners to British Columbia" (Simon Fraser University Undergraduate Seminar in Dialogue, 2005), available online: <http://www.sfu.ca/dialog/undergrad/projects.htm>.

[78] Kernaghan Webb & Andrew Morrison, "The Legal Aspects of Voluntary Codes" (Paper presented to Voluntary Codes Symposium, Office of Consumer Affairs, Industry Canada and Regulatory Affairs, Treasury Board 1996), cited in Neil Gunningham & Joseph Rees, "Industry Self-Regulation: An Institutional Perspective" (1997) 19 Law and Pol'y 363 at 370. See also Margot Priest, "The Privatization of Regulation: Five Models of Self-Regulation" (1997-98) 29 Ottawa L. Rev. 233 at 273 (arguing that accountability and transparency can get lost in the self-regulatory process).

[79] Anthony Ogus, "Rethinking Self-Regulation" (1995) 15 Oxford J. of Legal Stud. 97 at 99.

[80] Margot Priest, "The Privatization of Regulation: Five Models of Self-Regulation" (1997-98) 29 Ottawa L. Rev. 233 at 274.

[81] Andrew Green & Roy Hrab, *Self-Regulation and the Protection of the Public Interest*, Paper Prepared for the Panel on the Role of the Government (Toronto: University of Toronto, 2003) at 4. See also discussion below.

V. REGULATION OF HEALTH PROFESSIONALS IN CANADA

Regulation of health professionals in Canada dates back to 1778 when British-governed Quebec passed an Act which allowed British-educated "scientific" practitioners to set and pass licensing requirements.[82] However, it was not until the mid-19th century that the state set up a blueprint for professional licensing which allowed the health professions to select and govern their own members as well as prosecute those outside the profession who attempted to work within the exclusive area of the profession.

The regulation of occupations and professions in Canada is a provincial responsibility under s. 92(13) of the *Constitution Act, 1867.*[83] This section will first discuss input regulation (focusing on licensure); followed by output regulation (focusing on discipline and monitoring).

A. INPUT REGULATION: LICENSURE, CERTIFICATION AND REGISTRATION

Provincial and territorial legislation delegates competence, with varying degrees of discretion, for input regulation to self-governing professional bodies. Legislation principally sets out qualifications for (compulsory) membership in colleges and outlines required standards of practice. There are two main approaches in use across Canada. The first is a "framework" or "umbrella" legislative approach. The provinces and territories that use this approach have one piece of legislation that provides a regulatory framework for all self-governing health professions at the same time, and then enumerates professions to which these are applicable. In addition, profession-specific statutes may contain additional rules for each group. This can be interpreted as the more modern approach and is in part a response to criticism that arose during the 1990s that traditional systems of occupational regulation in the health professions are fragmented, complex and inconsistent.[84] The second approach is the more traditional one where individual statutes deal with each profession separately.

Provinces and territories adopting a framework approach include Ontario, British Columbia, Alberta, and the Yukon. Ontario's *Regulated Health*

---

[82]   This Act, along with others which followed in Upper Canada, were either inconsistently applied, repealed, never enforced, or flaunted by those they had excluded. The first licensing board in Upper Canada was not appointed until 1818. See Patricia O'Reilly, *Health Care Practitioners: An Ontario Case Study in Policy Making* (Toronto: University of Toronto Press, 2000) at 15 and footnote 3.

[83]   (U.K.) 1867, 30 & 31 Vict., c. 3, reprinted in R.S.C. 1985, App. II, No. 5.

[84]   See, for example, British Columbia Royal Commission on Health Care and Costs, *Closer to Home: The Report of the British Columbia Royal Commission on Health Care and Costs,* vol. 2 (Victoria: The Commission, 1991) at D-30; Alberta Workforce Rebalancing Committee, *New Directions for Legislation Regulating the Health Professions in Alberta: A Discussion Paper* (August 19, 1994) at 6; and Manitoba Law Reform Commission, *Discussion Paper: The Future of Occupational Regulation in Manitoba* (Winnipeg: Law Reform Commission, 1993) at 6.

Professions Act, 1991[85] (RHPA) regulates the scope of practice of 23 health professions in Ontario, which are covered by 21 respective regulatory Colleges.[86] As part of the RHPA, there is a procedural Code for all the regulated health professions. There are also profession-specific Acts which set matters such as the permitted scope of practice for members of the profession and specific provisions for election of Council members.

British Columbia has taken a similar approach with the enactment of the *Health Professions Act* in 1996.[87] Likewise, in Alberta, while most health professions are still regulated by their own statutes, the *Health Professions Act*[88] will eventually regulate 30 self-governing health professions in the province.

A key characteristic of framework legislation as implemented by Ontario, Alberta, and British Columbia is that the legislation outlines the manner in which the Colleges operate. In Ontario, the RHPA contains a Health Professions Procedural Code which establishes the structure of the Colleges which regulate the various professions.[89] The Procedural Code gives the Colleges responsibility for, *inter alia*, regulating the practice of the relevant health profession; developing and maintaining standards of qualification for those who apply for certificates of registration; and developing and maintaining standards of professional practice, knowledge, skill and professional ethics for their members.[90] It also sets out procedures for registration, complaints, discipline, reporting of health professionals, quality assurance, and the like. The Code is deemed to be part of each of the individual specific health profession Acts.[91] In this manner, it ensures that procedures are uniform across the regulated health professions. Similarly, in Alberta, the *Health Professions Act* requires all health professional Colleges to follow common rules to investigate complaints and to set educational and practice standards for registered members. Alberta is different from the other provinces in that its legislation grants the professional Colleges less discretion. While the Colleges administer licensure and registration, the legislation sets out detailed provisions as to the qualifications required for each profession.

Where framework legislation is employed, professional associations must apply for designation as a profession. For example, under the British Columbia *Health Professions Act*, where an application is made and it is considered to be in the public interest to do so, the Lieutenant Governor in Council may, by regulation, designate a health profession, in which he or she can prescribe various matters for a profession such as the scope of service.[92] At the time of

---

[85]   *Regulated Health Professions Act, 1991*, S.O. 1991, c. 18.
[86]   These colleges cover the following professions: audiologists; speech-language pathologists; chiropodists; podiatrists; chiropractors; dental hygienists; dental surgeons; dental technologists; denturists; dieticians; medical radiation technologists; medical laboratory technologists; massage therapists; midwives; nurses; optometrists; occupational therapists; opticians; pharmacists; physicians and surgeons; physiotherapists; psychologists; and respiratory therapists.
[87]   R.S.B.C. 1996, c. 183.
[88]   R.S.A. 2000, c. H-7.
[89]   Schedule 2 of the RHPA.
[90]   Section 3 of the Health Professions Procedural Code.
[91]   Section 4 of the RHPA.
[92]   Section 12.

writing, this legislation was in the process of implementation. A number of professions had been designated (including registered nurses, midwives, and traditional Chinese medical practitioners and acupuncturists), while regulations had been proposed for a number of others (including audiology and speech-language pathology). For other professions, applications for designation are still in the process of consideration. For example, the British Columbia Association of Clinical Counsellors is seeking designation of counselling therapists as a health profession and the creation of a College of Counselling Therapists under the *Health Professions Act.*[93] Regulations for individual professions set out scope of practice statements which describe what the profession does. In addition, lists of reserved actions set out higher risk, invasive activities that may be performed while providing the services described in their respective scope of practice statements. The same reserved actions may be granted to more than one profession. This represents a departure from the traditional practice whereby each profession had exclusivity in respect of certain services or procedures. It is intended to promote enhanced multidisciplinary practice and consumer choice.[94]

In provinces that take a more traditional approach, each health profession is regulated by an independent and separate piece of legislation. For example, in Saskatchewan, there are 21 statutes regulating different health professions. Each of these statutes grant the respective professional body self-governing competence. Other provinces and territories including Manitoba and the Maritime provinces also regulate health professions through profession-specific legislation, although there appears to be interest in some provinces in moving towards a framework approach. The Nova Scotia government, for example, has indicated that it intends to enact new legislation to provide a uniform framework for all professions.[95]

Quebec takes a slightly different approach from the other provinces and territories. It has a *Professional Code* which entrusts 45 "professional orders" with the right and responsibility to supervise and administer their professions.[96] Health professions are included along with other professions such as accountants, social workers, architects, and engineers. There are two types of professions: those with reserved titles only; and professions with reserved titles *and* an exclusive right to practise. A number of health professions are included in each category, for example, physicians and nurses.

The professional orders are responsible for ensuring professional competence which they do by establishing standards regarding admission to practise. They are responsible for controlling the title and the right to practise a profession; verifying the competence and integrity of candidates to the profession; ensuring that competence and integrity are maintained throughout the member's professional life; and punishing offences against the Professional Code, specific

---

[93] See British Columbia Association of Clinical Counsellors, online: <http://www.bc-counsellors.org/college.htm>.

[94] Ministry of Health, Government of British Columbia, "Health Professions Regulatory Reform in British Columbia", online: <http://www.healthservices.gov.bc.ca/leg/regulatoryreform.html>.

[95] See Nova Scotia Department of Health, "Health Professions Regulation: Proposal for Legislative Change" (Halifax: Department of Health, 2004).

[96] R.S.Q., c. C-26.

laws and related regulations.[97] In this manner, self-regulated bodies in Quebec seem to have more discretion with regard to licensure and standard setting than similar bodies in other provinces and territories.

B. OUTPUT REGULATION: MONITORING AND DISCIPLINING HEALTH PROFESSIONALS

1. Monitoring Standards and Ongoing Competence

Across the provinces and territories, self-regulated bodies are responsible for various activities which fall under the rubric of monitoring and disciplining health professionals. Where provinces have adopted framework legislation, the provisions for monitoring and disciplining will be the same for all professions covered by the legislation. For example, in Ontario, the *Health Professions Procedural Code* sets out procedures for monitoring and discipline that cover all 23 professions regulated under the RHPA.[98] Likewise, in Alberta, the *Health Professions Act* provides for those professions which it regulates. In provinces where each profession is subject to specific legislation, that legislation governs issues concerning monitoring and discipline. Again, the disadvantage of this approach compared to the framework approach is a lack of consistency across the health professions, resulting in confusion for both the public and professionals themselves.

The primary monitoring activity carried out by self-regulated professional bodies is the discipline of members who do not meet the standards set by the profession. Discipline is the means by which health professions enforce their standards, and its goal is to prevent actions which threaten the well-being of the public.[99] Professional bodies generally sanction, or discipline, three types of unacceptable behaviour on the part of their members: misconduct, incompetence and conduct unbecoming a member of the profession.[100] In general, "professional misconduct" refers to unacceptable conduct within the scope of the professional's practice. "Conduct unbecoming a member" usually relates to conduct outside the professional's practice which may bring the profession into disrepute. "Incompetence" describes conduct or a pattern of practice which falls below a generally accepted minimum level.[101] Incompetence may arise from incapacity (such as that caused by addiction or illness), and licensing bodies generally have

---

[97] The Quebec Professional System (Quebec Interprofessional Council, January 2007), Para. 5.2 (Control of the practice of a profession). Online: <http://www.professions-quebec.org/publications.html>.

[98] Schedule 2 to the *Regulated Health Professions Act, 1991*, S.O. 1991, c. 18.

[99] Manitoba Law Reform Commission, *Discussion Paper: The Future of Occupational Regulation in Manitoba* (Winnipeg: Law Reform Commission, 1993) at 51.

[100] Linette McNamara, Erin Nelson & Brent Windwick, "Regulation of Health Care Professionals" in J. Downie, T. Caulfield & C.M. Flood, eds., *Canadian Health Law and Policy*, 2nd ed. (Markham, ON: Butterworths Canada, 2002) 55 at 77.

[101] Linette McNamara, Erin Nelson & Brent Windwick, "Regulation of Health Care Professionals" in Jocelyn Downie, Timothy Caulfield & Colleen M. Flood, eds., *Canadian Health Law and Policy*, 2nd ed. (Markham, ON: LexisNexis Butterworths, 2002) 55 at 77, citing K.R. Hamilton, *Self-governing Professions: Digests of Court Decisions* (Aurora, ON: Canada Law Book, 1995) at 11-1.

the power to sanction a practitioner who is incapacitated, even though there have been no complaints or acts of misconduct.[102]

Various kinds of behaviour have been found to constitute unbecoming or unprofessional behaviour. For the most part, the definition of these terms has been left to disciplinary bodies and the courts, although some statutes provide guidance. For example, in section 46 of the *Medical Profession Act, 1981*, Saskatchewan provides examples of behaviour that is considered "unbecoming, improper, unprofessional, or discreditable conduct", including betraying a professional secret, alcohol addiction, employing an assistant not registered to provide the services being provided, and performing a service that is not justifiable on reasonable grounds.[103] A variety of behaviour has been found to constitute professional misconduct, including a physician's fraudulent overbilling of a provincial health plan,[104] sexual misconduct between professionals and their patients,[105] incompetent practice,[106] breaching patient confidentiality,[107] and in one case, intermixing Scientology and medical practice.[108]

Another key aspect of monitoring is to ensure continuing competence of regulated health professionals. In some cases, there are mandatory requirements for continuing education although it has also been argued that this does not significantly alter the actual performance of professionals.[109] Another mechanism widely used is a committee structure which allows inspection of health practices in order to ensure competence. For example, in Alberta, section 50 of the *Health Professions Act* provides that each college must establish a "continuing competence program" in order to maintain competence and enhance the

---

[102] Linette McNamara, Erin Nelson & Brent Windwick, "Regulation of Health Care Professionals" in Jocelyn Downie, Timothy Caulfield & Colleen M. Flood, eds., *Canadian Health Law and Policy*, 2nd ed. (Markham, ON: LexisNexis Butterworths, 2002) 55 at 77.

[103] S.S. 1980-81, c. M-10.1.

[104] *Moosa v. College of Physicians and Surgeons (Alberta)*, [1986] A.J. No. 1014, 68 A.R. 9 (Alta. C.A.). See also *Golomb v. College of Physicians and Surgeons (Ontario)*, [1976] O.J. No. 1707, 68 D.L.R. (3d) 25 (Ont. Div. Ct.).

[105] See, generally, James T. Casey, *The Regulation of Professions in Canada* (Toronto: Thomson Carswell, 2005 – Release 2). See for example, *Boodoosingh v. College of Physicians and Surgeons of Ontario*, [1990] O.J. No. 921, 73 O.R. (2d) 478 (Ont. Div. Ct.), affd [1993] O.J. No. 859, 12 O.R. (3d) 707*n* (Ont. C.A.), leave to appeal to S.C.C. refused [1993] S.C.C.A. No. 273, 69 O.A.C. 159*n* (S.C.C.); and *McKee v. College of Psychologists of British Columbia*, [1992] B.C.J. No. 207, [1992] 4 W.W.R. 197 (B.C.S.C.), revd on other grounds [1994] B.C.J. No. 1778, 116 D.L.R. (4th) 555, [1994] 9 W.W.R. 374 (B.C.C.A.).

[106] See, for example, *Green v. College of Physicians and Surgeons of Saskatchewan*, [1986] S.J. No. 723, 51 Sask. R. 241 at 258-59 (Sask. C.A.): "The medical profession has been granted a status which gives the public the right to expect that it will take reasonable measure to assure that reasonable skills will be exhibited by a doctor who is held out by the profession through the College as possessing the ability to practise medicine".

[107] *Shulman v. College of Physicians and Surgeons of Ontario*, [1980] O.J. No. 3627, 111 D.L.R. (3d) 689 (Ont. Div. Ct.).

[108] *Taams v. College of Physicians and Surgeons of British Columbia* (1977), 79 D.L.R. (3d) 377 (B.C.S.C.).

[109] See, for example, Health Professions Council, *Safe Choices: A New Model for Regulating Health Professions in British Columbia* (Vancouver: Government of British Columbia, Ministry of Health, 2001) at para 3.1.

provision of professional services.[110] The program may allow for practice visits by members of a competence committee, who may make a referral to the complaints director for various reasons including if, on the basis of information obtained from a practice visit or continuing competence program, they are of the opinion that a regulated member displays a lack of competence in the provision of professional services that has not been remedied by participating in the continuing competence program; the regulated member may be incapacitated, or that the conduct of the regulated member constitutes unprofessional conduct that cannot be readily remedied by means of the continuing competence program.[111]

In Saskatchewan, the *Medical Profession Act, 1981* provides that where the council or executive committee has reasonable grounds to believe a practitioner may not have adequate skill and knowledge to practise, they may appoint a competency committee to investigate.[112] Likewise, Manitoba provides for a standards committee with the power to require members to undergo retraining after reviewing their practice either on its own initiative or on a direction from the council.[113]

Ontario pays specific attention to the issue of sexual abuse. Its legislation establishes a patient relations program which includes measures for preventing sexual abuse of patients. The program is required to include education for members, guidelines for the conduct of members with their patients, training for the College's staff, and the provision of information to the public.[114] It also requires Colleges to fund therapy and counselling for patients who have been sexually abused.[115]

One issue that has arisen in provincial reviews of health professionals regulation is the desirability of separating the discipline and fitness to practice/competency functions of self-regulatory bodies. A recent report of the Ontario Health Professions Regulatory Advisory Council suggests that separation is necessary so that when professionals are involved in College quality improvement processes, they have confidence that when changes are identified as necessary in their practice, that there is no link to the disciplinary process but to the goals of enhanced competence and continuing improvement.[116]

[110] R.S.A. 2000, c. H-7.
[111] *Ibid.*, s. 51.
[112] S.S. 1980-81, c. M-10.1, s. 45.
[113] *Medical Act*, C.C.S.M., c. M90, s. 38.
[114] *Health Professions Procedural Code,* Sched. 2, RHPA, at s. 84.
[115] *Ibid.*, at s. 85.7. Prince Edward Island also has a similar provision in its *Medical Act*, R.S.P.E.I. 1988, c. M-5, at s. 38.4.
[116] Health Professions Regulatory Advisory Council, *Regulation of Health Professionals in Ontario: New Directions* (Ottawa: Health Professions Regulatory Advisory Council, 2006) at 22.

2. The Discipline Process

Discipline processes usually consist of four stages: detection, investigation, hearing, and appeal.[117] The most common way of detecting a problem which warrants investigation is through consumer complaints. This has been criticized because consumers may not always be in a position to recognize that a situation warrants a complaint and may feel uncomfortable in complaining about a health professional to whom they had entrusted their care.[118]

Some provinces require members to report situations where an inquiry may be warranted. For example, in British Columbia, the *Health Professions Act* requires that a registered member report to the registrar any member believed to be not competent to practise the designated health profession, or suffering from a physical or mental ailment, emotional disturbance, or addiction to alcohol or drugs that impairs his or her ability to practise the designated health profession if they believe that the continued practice of the designated health profession might constitute a danger to the public.[119] Similarly, Manitoba's *Medical Act* requires members to report to the registrar if they believe that another member has a mental or physical disorder that may affect his or her fitness to practise yet continues to practise when counselled not to do so.[120] A similar provision exists in British Columbia where one member suspects that another has engaged in sexual misconduct.[121] In addition, some provinces afford discretion to college registrars or the like to instigate investigations. In Alberta, the *Health Professions Act* provides that where the complaints director[122] has reasonable grounds to believe that the conduct of a regulated member constitutes unprofessional conduct, they may treat the information or non-compliance as a complaint and act on it pursuant to section 55 which allows them to take a number of actions including conducting an investigation.[123] In Manitoba, the *Medical Act* allows the investigations committee to receive referrals directly from the registrar or executive committee.[124]

Once a problem has been detected, an investigation is initiated. Investigations are generally mandatory, and the powers of investigators generally are established statutorily.[125] The purpose of investigations is to eliminate or resolve

---

[117] See *Stephen v. College of Physicians and Surgeons of Saskatchewan*, [1990] S.J. No. 536, 89 Sask. R. 25 (Sask. Q.B.); and *Khosla v. Alberta*, [1993] A.J. No. 640, 12 Alta. L.R. (3d) 325 (Alta. Q.B.).

[118] Linette McNamara, Erin Nelson & Brent Windwick, "Regulation of Health Care Professionals" in Jocelyn Downie, Timothy Caulfield & Colleen M. Flood, eds., *Canadian Health Law and Policy*, 2nd ed. (Markham, ON: LexisNexis Butterworths, 2002) 55 at 78.

[119] R.S.B.C. 1996, c. 285, s. 32.

[120] R.S.M. 1987, c. M50, s. 39.

[121] *Health Professions Act*, R.S.B.C. 1996, c. 183, s. 32.4.

[122] "Complaints director" means the complaints director of the relevant college.

[123] R.S.A. 2000, c. H-7, s. 56.

[124] R.S.M. 1987, c. M50, s. 45(1)(*b*).

[125] Relying on complaints is problematic for a few reasons. Consumers may not know when rules have been broken, may not have enough confidence to report improprieties, or may make unfounded complaints because of lack of understanding; Manitoba Law Reform Commission, *Discussion Paper: The Future of Occupational Regulation in Manitoba* (Winnipeg: Law Reform

some charges as quickly as possible, and to gather evidence about charges which will be proceeding to the next stage of the process.

If an investigation determines that a complaint has merit, typically the complaint will proceed to a hearing, where a panel will hear evidence and decide whether or not the professional's conduct was inappropriate and deserves sanction. Hearings tend to be strongly adversarial in nature, with parties represented by lawyers. At the conclusion of the hearing, the panel will determine what (if any) penalty should be imposed, for example, reprimand, suspension, loss of licence, conditions on a licence, mandatory remedial education, a fine, costs or a combination of these options. A right of appeal from the decision may be explicit or implicit in a professional statute.

Governing bodies have a legal duty to act fairly and observe the principles of "nature justice" in their investigation and prosecution of a complaint.[126] What will be considered a fair and satisfactory process in each case will depend on the process spelled out in the particular statutes governing each profession in each province, other provincial statutes that apply (for example, those concerning evidence), and on general administrative law principles.[127]

A number of provinces encourage mediation and settlement as an alternative to a formal hearing process. For example, section 57 of Nova Scotia's *Medical Act* provides that after a matter is referred to a hearing committee, the member complained of may tender a settlement agreement that includes admission of a violation and the member's consent to a specified disposition.[128] Prince Edward Island's *Medical Act* states that wherever it is appropriate, the complaint should be referred to mediation, thus eliminating the need for either an investigation or disciplinary action.[129] Other provinces also provide for alternative dispute resolution, for example, in British Columbia, several health profession statutes contain provisions for various forms of alternative dispute resolution while some professions engage in alternative dispute resolution as a matter of practice.[130] An informal process such as mediation may be preferable to the adversarial nature

---

Commission, 1993) at 53. Also recall the discussion above regarding the drawbacks of relying on civil liability and discipline as regulatory mechanisms.

[126] K.R. Hamilton, *Self-Governing Professions: Digests of Court Decisions* (Aurora, ON: Canada Law Book Co., 1995) at 5. See also G. Sharpe, *The Law and Medicine in Canada*, 2nd ed. (Toronto: Butterworths, 1987) at 243. J.J. Morris, *Law for Canadian Health Care Administrators* (Toronto: Butterworths, 1996) at 55.

[127] A full discussion of what constitutes fairness at all of the stages of the process is beyond the scope of this chapter. For a general discussion of how administrative law principles have been applied to physicians, nurses, and other health care professionals, see G. Sharpe, *The Law and Medicine in Canada*, 2nd ed., *ibid.*, at 234; J.J. Morris, *Law for Canadian Health Care Administrators*, *ibid.*, at 67. For a general discussion of the principles of administrative law which would apply to the discipline process, see D.P. Jones & A.S. de Villars, *Principles of Administrative Law*, 2nd ed. (Toronto: Carswell, 1994).

[128] S.N.S. 1995-96, c. 10.

[129] R.S.P.E.I. 1988, c. M-5, s. 32.6.

[130] Health Professions Council, *Safe Choices: A New Model for Regulating Health Professions in British Columbia* (Vancouver: Government of British Columbia, Ministry of Health, 2001) at para 3.5.

of disciplinary hearings, particularly as it allows both the complainant patient and the respondent physician to have an input into the final outcome.

C. ACCOUNTABILITY AND TRANSPARENCY

Recent years have seen increasing public demands for accountability and transparency in regulation of health professionals.[131] These demands are being addressed by provincial governments through various mechanisms including maintenance of some government control over the self-regulating professions, increased levels of public representation on the governing councils of professional colleges, and the introduction of public discipline hearings. While these are welcome moves, questions remain as to their effectiveness. Moreover, there appears to be little in the way of regular evaluation of the performance of self-regulatory bodies in monitoring and disciplining professionals, suggesting a key area for further development.

In some cases, professional legislation requires government approval of rules or bylaws. For example, in British Columbia, section 19(3) of the *Health Professions Act*[132] provides that a regulatory body's bylaws do not take effect until they are approved by the Lieutenant Governor in Council. This may be compared to the now repealed *Nurses (Registered) Act* in the same province which gave the Registered Nurses Association of British Columbia broad, unfettered rule-making power.[133] This Association argued in favour of such a power that "requiring government control over every substantive structural or process decision is the antithesis of self governance and undermines the concept of professional responsibility and accountability which is at the heart of any profession ... a government's role must be limited to ensuring that the professions meet minimum standards of accountability, but that does not include 'second guessing' every decision of the profession relating to its processes and standards of practice and ethics, in respect of which government has no particular expertise".[134]

In British Columbia, the medical profession has expressed its dissatisfaction with a requirement in the *Health Professions Act* which permits the minister to request a board to amend or repeal an existing bylaw for its college or to make a new bylaw. Further, where a board does not comply with such a request, the Lieutenant Governor in Council may amend or repeal the existing bylaw or make the new bylaw.[135] The medical profession has argued that this unilateral right to impose a rule weakens the independence of professions and the credibility of self-governing bodies. It argues that requirements for public

---

[131] See, for example, Health Professions Regulatory Advisory Council, *Regulation of Health Professionals in Ontario: New Directions* (Ottawa: Health Professions Regulatory Advisory Council, 2006) at 13.

[132] R.S.B.C. 1996, c. 183.

[133] R.S.B.C. 1996, c. 335.

[134] Health Professions Council, *Safe Choices: A New Model for Regulating Health Professions in British Columbia* (Vancouver: Government of British Columbia, Ministry of Health, 2001).

[135] R.S.B.C. 1996, c. 183, s. 19(6).

representation on governing bodies, annual reports, and a provision that rules be approved by the Lieutenant Governor are adequate to ensure accountability.[136]

Ontario has a similar provision in its legislation.[137] However, in the 1995 case of *Szmuilowicz v. Ontario (Minister of Health)*,[138] the court ruled that the Lieutenant Governor in Council's power is not unfettered but must be exercised with due regard for the purpose and intent of the statute. The court found that "when the Minister sees fit to override a determination made by a self-governing body of professionals authorized by the legislature to determine such issues, the views of the self-governing body of the profession should be taken into consideration by the court in determining whether the Minister pushed the definition of "professional misconduct" beyond permissible limits, given that the term is peculiarly defined by the standards of the profession".[139]

A number of provinces have requirements for public appointees on councils of professional colleges. In Ontario, for example, most profession-specific legislation prescribes the number of public appointees required on professional councils. A recent study by the Health Professions Advisory Council found that slightly less than 50 per cent of council members are public appointees.[140] The Lieutenant Governor in Council appoints the public members. Quebec and Alberta also require public representation on professional self-regulatory bodies. In Quebec, the professional orders are managed by a Bureau which must include "a few" directors appointed to represent the public.[141] In Alberta, the Physician Performance Committee which is charged with conducting a general assessment of professional performance and practitioners, is required to include one non-physician public member out of a total of five to nine members.[142] In British Columbia, prior to recent amendment, the *Health Professions Act* provided that the registration, discipline, inquiry, quality assurance and patient relations committees must have at least one-third public membership.[143] A review of the legislation in 2001 noted that most professions objected to this provision on the basis that the issues under consideration are best judged by a panel of peers and that delays may occur in finding public members for panels.[144] However, a review of the legislation concluded that public membership is an important public accountability measure and is therefore appropriate.[145] It is not clear what

---

[136] Health Professions Council, *Safe Choices: A New Model for Regulating Health Professions in British Columbia* (Vancouver: Government of British Columbia, Ministry of Health, 2001) at para E.1.

[137] Section 5(1)(c) *Regulated Health Professions Act, 1991*, S.O. 1991, c. 18. See also s. 95, which contains a list of a regulatory body's rule-making powers which are subject to Cabinet approval.

[138] [1995] O.J. No. 1699, 24 O.R. (3d) 204 (Ont. Div. Ct.).

[139] *Ibid.*, at para. 48.

[140] Health Professions Regulatory Advisory Council, *Regulation of Health Professionals in Ontario: New Directions* (Ottawa: Health Professions Regulatory Advisory Council, 2006) at 77.

[141] Paragraph 6.2.

[142] *Medical Profession Act*, R.S.A. 2000, c. M-11, s. 39.

[143] See R.S.B.C. 1996, c. 183, ss. 14(2), 15(2), 16(2), 17(2), 18(2), and 19(1).

[144] Health Professions Council, *Safe Choices: A New Model for Regulating Health Professions in British Columbia* (Vancouver: Government of British Columbia, Ministry of Health, 2001) at para F.3.

[145] *Ibid.*

approach the amended legislation takes; while it provides for regulations to set out rules governing the composition of committee membership, such regulations have not yet been enacted.

A number of provinces also require disciplinary hearings to be public, although there tend to be exceptions for certain cases. For example, the British Columbia *Health Professions Act* provides an exception where the complainant or the respondent requests that the hearing be held in private, and the discipline committee is satisfied that a private hearing would be appropriate in the circumstances.[146] In contrast, other provinces do not require disciplinary hearings to be made public at all, for example, Saskatchewan.

There is as yet inadequate research to determine how successful public representation requirements have been in Canada. However, the U.S. experience would suggest that results are likely to be mixed. Studies there have found that simply placing citizen members on self-regulatory bodies does not ensure that the public interest is protected, although improved protection is one possible outcome.[147] Unfortunately, another possible outcome is that the public member might feel accountable to the professional group rather than to the "public interest".[148] As Graddy and Nichols argue, health professionals "enjoy a certain mystique and can intimidate those not in their profession".[149] One study which found favourable outcomes from a public interest perspective was that carried out by Broscheid who found that the presence of public members on licensing boards leads to an emphasis on licensing requirements that can be better justified with quality control arguments. That is, strong consumer interests increase education-related licensing requirements, while professional interests are associated with licensing requirements whose purpose does not seem to go beyond entry restriction.[150] In a recent report, the Ontario Health Professions Regulatory Advisory Council noted that public appointees to professional councils receive only a small honorarium for their work. Compared to professional members, the report found that public appointees may have the impression of being second-class members. The report recommended restoring equilibrium in order that public appointees engage in the governance process fully.[151] This issue was noted by the Ontario College of Physicians and Surgeons which was recently forced to postpone a disciplinary hearing because there were no public members available to serve on a scheduled panel. The College suggested several steps that could be taken to improve the situation, including increasing the *per diem* rate paid to public members, providing public

---

[146] Section 38(3).

[147] M. Christine Cagle, J. Michael Martinez & William D. Richardson, "Privatizing Professional Licensing Boards: Self-Governance or Self-Interest?" (1999) 30 Administration and Society 734 at 759.

[148] *Ibid.*

[149] Elizabeth Graddy & Michael E. Nichol, "Public Members on Occupational Licensing Boards: Effects on Legislative Regulatory Reforms" (1989) 55:3 Southern Economic Journal 610.

[150] Andreas Broscheid & Paul E. Teske, "Public members on medical licensing boards and the choice of entry barriers" (2003) 114 Public Choice 445 at 456.

[151] Health Professions Regulatory Advisory Council, *Regulation of Health Professionals in Ontario: New Directions* (Ottawa: Health Professions Regulatory Advisory Council, 2006) at 75.

appointees with a strong and effective orientation program, and giving public members the ability to participate fully in every component of the regulatory process.[152]

VI. EMERGING ISSUES IN REGULATION OF HEALTH PROFESSIONALS

A key success factor for regulatory regimes will be the extent to which they remain relevant to the health sector as it evolves. The past decade or so has seen significant changes in the sector. In terms of medical practice, there have been rapid technological and medical advances that have changed the way in which services are delivered, consumed, and managed.[153] Of particular interest is the increasing use of telehealth for both diagnosis and treatment, as well as the increased use of multidisciplinary and collaborative care, and popularity of complementary and alternative medicine. A key systemic change is the increasing interest in privately funded and/or delivered health care services as provinces look to ways to ensure the future sustainability of the health care system. This section discusses briefly some of the issues that arise for regulation of health professionals from these developments.

A. MULTIDISCIPLINARY AND COLLABORATIVE CARE

Multidisciplinary and collaborative care requires a regulatory system that allows experimentation and innovative approaches in human resources utilization and management.[154] In some cases, legislation makes it difficult to do so; for example, by forbidding registered members of a college to practise in association with a non-member. As well, some legislation prohibits professionals from being affiliated with or establishing a partnership with non-registrants. In British Columbia, section 93(1) of the *Medical Practitioners Act* makes it an offence to practise medicine in partnership with a non-member unless the written consent of the Executive Committee of the College of Physicians and Surgeons of British Columbia (CPSBC) is obtained.[155] Such provisions have the potential to create unnecessary barriers to interdisciplinary practice. Other barriers to interdisciplinary practice may take the form of restrictions on dual licensure such as in British Columbia where chiropractors are restricted from practising physical therapy in addition to chiropody.[156]

---

[152] College of Physicians and Surgeons of Ontario, Pre-Budget Submissions to the Standing Committee on Finance and Economic Affairs (February 2, 2006).

[153] Health Professions Regulatory Advisory Council, *Regulation of Health Professionals in Ontario: New Directions* (Ottawa: Health Professions Regulatory Advisory Council, 2006) at 10.

[154] *Ibid.*, at 11.

[155] R.S.B.C. 1996, c. 285.

[156] *Chiropractors Act*, R.S.B.C. 1996, c. 48, s. 21(1).

B. TELEHEALTH

The terms "telehealth", "telemedicine", and "e-health" are used interchangeably and may be broadly defined as "the use of communications and information technologies to overcome geographic distances between health care practitioners or between practitioners and service users for the purposes of diagnosis, treatment, consultation, education and health information transfer".[157] Telehealth encompasses Internet or Web-based "e-health" solutions, as well as video-based applications. There are many telehealth initiatives in place across Canada, covering a wide range of areas from the provision of health information and advice via telephone to diagnostic services utilizing electronic technologies and robotic surgery from a distance.[158]

Telehealth raises a number of issues with respect to regulation and licensure where health professionals provide services to patients located outside of the professional's jurisdiction. Two aspects of input regulation are particularly important; qualification and locus of accountability. Regarding qualification, if different provinces impose divergent requirements for entry into practice, it may be difficult for physicians in one province to get permission to practise in another province. Regarding the locus of accountability, this is key to determining which jurisdiction has the authority to investigate and discipline health professionals providing telehealth services.

There are essentially two options for determining the locus of accountability. First, it may be stipulated as being the physician's location. Where this happens, the patient is "virtually transported" to the physician's location and the physician does not need any additional licences to treat the patient.[159] It has been argued that this approach does not afford out-of-province/territory patients sufficient protection. This argument is based on the belief that the agency best able to ensure protection of patients is the regulatory agency in the patient's home province. As well, there may be practical problems involved in investigating complaints where the physician providing services is regulated in a jurisdiction different from that of the patient. For example, a patient may have difficulty participating in discipline proceedings in another province.[160]

The second option is to take a patient-centric approach where the locus of accountability is the patient's location. With this approach, the physician providing the service must be authorized to practise in the jurisdiction where the patient is located.[161] Advantages cited for this approach are (i) that provinces ought to have the most control possible over the health care services received by

---

[157] R.W. Pong & J.C. Hogenbirk, "Licensing Physicians for Telehealth Practice: Issues and Policy Options" (1999) 8 Health Law Review 3 at 3.

[158] *Ibid.*

[159] Sabrina Hasham, Rajen Akalu & Peter G. Rossos, *Medico-Legal Implications of Telehealth in Canada* (Toronto: University of Toronto, 2003) at 12. They note that the G-8 Global Healthcare Applications Subproject recommends establishing the locus of accountability as the physician's location to reduce licensure obstacles.

[160] Raymond W. Pong & John C. Hogenbirk, "Licensing Physicians for Telehealth Practice: Issues and Policy Options" (1999) 8 Health Law Review 3 at 8.

[161] Sabrina Hasham, Rajen Akalu & Peter G. Rossos, *Medico-Legal Implications of Telehealth in Canada* (Toronto: University of Toronto, 2003) at 12.

their residents; and (ii) that it will help to both ensure higher practice standards and control the behaviour of health professionals through the threat of licence suspension or revocation.[162] However, there are also serious downsides. On a practical level, it will be difficult to develop a process for telehealth practitioners to obtain dual or multiple licences. With regards to access to health care services, the scenario of having physicians obtain licences on a province-by-province basis may constrain the growth of telehealth.

The Federation of Medical Regulatory Authorities of Canada (FMRAC) has developed broad guidelines on telehealth and has suggested that provincial licensing authorities develop specific telehealth regulations. It recommends a patient-centric approach and that a physician providing treatment to a patient via telehealth must be licensed to practise in the jurisdiction of the patient's residence.[163] In the absence of a national licensing scheme or mutual recognition arrangements whereby provincial regulatory agencies recognize each other's licensure policies, such a scheme would seem only to benefit FMRAC members who would receive multiple licensing fees. It also has the potential to constrain the development of telehealth services given extra administrative requirements and monetary costs placed on physicians wishing to provide such services.

As Hasham *et al.* note, provincial Colleges have been slow to adopt policies that will further interprovincial telehealth.[164] In Alberta, the College of Physicians and Surgeons has largely adopted FMRAC's recommendations in its bylaws by requiring that a health professional wishing to provide telehealth services to a patient within Alberta must be specifically licensed to do so and must submit to the jurisdiction of the College concerning any matters arising from their practice of telemedicine in Alberta.[165] Such an approach protects the College's jurisdiction and exclusivity, arguably to the detriment of the development of telehealth.

Hasham *et al.* find that of all the provincial Colleges, the Collège des Médecins du Quebec appears to have the most comprehensive policy framework on telehealth.[166] It is also an approach that arguably supports the growth of telehealth. Contrary to FMRAC recommendations and to the practice in Alberta, Quebec deems the location of the telehealth treatment to be where the physician practises. The Collège justifies this position on the grounds that it is necessary to protect patients by ensuring that physicians licensed by the province are accountable for their acts to the authorities governing them, regardless of where their patients are located.[167] Physicians registered in Quebec who practise remote

---

162 Raymond W. Pong & John C. Hogenbirk, "Licensing Physicians for Telehealth Practice: Issues and Policy Options" (1999) 8 Health Law Review 3 at 8.

163 Federation of Medical Licensing Authorities of Canada, *Policy Statements and Guidelines — Telemedicine* (1999).

164 Sabrina Hasham, Rajen Akalu & Peter G. Rossos, *Medico-Legal Implications of Telehealth in Canada* (Centre for Innovation Law and Policy, University of Toronto, 2003).

165 Alberta, *Bylaws of the College of Physicians and Surgeons of Alberta* (January 3, 2003) s. 107.

166 Collège des Médecins du Quebec, Background Paper, "Telemedicine" (Quebec, May 2000).

167 The Collège cites the decision of *Paquette v. Committee on Discipline of the Corporation professionnelle des médecins du Quebec* (February 10, 1995), Montreal 500-09-000060-913 (Que. C.A.).

medicine will be subject to the regulations of the Collège, whereas physicians from outside Quebec are accountable for their competence and their acts to the authorities governing them.

C. COMPLEMENTARY AND ALTERNATIVE MEDICINE

While there is no exclusive list of what constitutes complementary and alternative (CAM) therapies, a well-accepted starting definition finds that CAM is a broad domain of healing resources that encompasses all health systems, modalities, and practices and their accompanying theories and beliefs, other than those intrinsic to the politically dominant health system of a particular society or culture in a given historical period. CAM includes all such practices and ideas self-defined by their users as preventing or treating illness or promoting health and well-being. Boundaries within CAM and between the CAM domain and the domain of the dominant system are not always sharp or fixed.[168]

Recent years have seen an increase in the demand for CAM.[169] As such, there has been an increase in the number of CAM practitioners, as well as the use of alternative therapies by mainstream medical practitioners.[170] Increasingly, CAM practitioners have sought to engage in a process of "professionalization" in order to gain greater legitimacy as well as benefits such as enhanced income, status, and power.[171] The term "professionalization" refers to the transition from "occupation" to self-regulated "profession".[172] A key aspect of this process is achieving a position of professional dominance such that the government will grant statutory self-regulatory status. Given that mainstream physicians benefit from a restrictive regulatory regime that does not recognize the status of CAM

---

[168] Linette McNamara, Erin Nelson & Brent Windwick, "Regulation of Health Care Professionals" in Jocelyn Downie, Timothy Caulfield & Colleen M. Flood, eds., *Canadian Health Law and Policy*, 2nd ed. (Markham, ON: LexisNexis Butterworths, 2002) 55 at 86, citing, among other sources, Theodore de Bruyn, "Taking Stock: Policy Issues Associated with Complementary and Alternative Health Care" in *Perspectives on Complementary and Alternative Health Care: A Collection of Papers Prepared for Health Canada* (Ottawa: Public Works and Government Services Canada, 2001) at II.18; and N.I.H. Panel on Definition and Description, "Defining and Describing Complementary and Alternative Medicine" (1997) 3:2 Alternative Therapies 49.

[169] See, for example, Linda Buske, "Popularity of alternative health care providers continues to grow" (2002) 166 C.M.A.J. 366.

[170] In Ontario at least, a key reason for this increase is demographic change as consumers and practitioners of CAM therapies arrive from countries where these approaches are accepted parts of health care. Health Professions Regulatory Advisory Council, *Regulation of Health Professionals in Ontario: New Directions* (Ottawa: Health Professions Regulatory Advisory Council, 2006).

[171] Sandy Welsh et al., "Moving Forward? Complementary and alternative practitioners seeking self-regulation" (2004) 26:2 Sociology of Health and Illness 216 at 221.

[172] Sandy Welsh et al., ibid., at 217, citing A. Abbott, *The System of Professions: An Essay on the Division of Expert Labor* (Chicago: The University of Chicago Press, 1988); S. Cant & U. Sharma, "Demarcation and transformation within homeopathic knowledge: A strategy of professionalisation" (1996) 42 Social Science and Medicine 579; M. Saks, *Professions and the Public Interest: Medical Power, Altruism and Alternative Medicine* (London: Routledge, 1995).

practitioners, they have traditionally opposed granting of such status. Despite this, a number of provinces across Canada are moving towards granting self-regulation to CAM practitioners. For example, in British Columbia under the *Health Professions Act*, there is a regulation relating to traditional Chinese medicine practitioners and acupuncturists.[173] Ontario became the second province to grant self-regulation to traditional Chinese medicine when it passed the *Traditional Chinese Medicine Act* in 2005.

In a recent study of naturopaths, traditional Chinese medicine practitioners, and acupuncturists and homeopaths, Welsh *et al.* found that these groups are using a variety of strategies, based on claims to knowledge of medical science, to demarcate which groups should receive statutory regulation.[174] In other words, CAM practitioners are seeking to create boundaries around who is considered a practitioner with a credible knowledge base, and who is not.

In addition to obtaining self-regulatory status, in some provinces, professions allow non-traditional medicine to be practised without fear of reprimand. For example, in Ontario, the *Medicine Act, 1991* states that a member is not guilty of professional misconduct or incompetence "solely on the basis that the member practises a therapy that is non-traditional or that departs from the prevailing medical practice unless there is evidence that proves that the therapy poses a greater risk to a patient's health than the traditional or prevailing practice".[175]

D. PRIVATE HEALTH CARE

Recent years have seen an increase in the numbers of privately owned, for-profit independent health facilities that operate both within and outside the public health care system.[176] Such facilities, which offer services such as physiotherapy and laboratory testing, rely largely on physician referrals for patients. Choudhry *et al.* suggest that this fact raises two serious issues. First, the facilities may compensate physicians for referrals (a kickback), a practice that can potentially distort clinical judgments. Second, physicians can make referrals to facilities that they themselves own (self-referral), raising similar concerns.[177] Choudhry *et al.* examine the rules established by self-regulatory bodies in Canada governing financial relationships between physicians and private for-profit clinics. They find that eight provinces explicitly regulate kickbacks; in those that do not, the general prohibition on professional misconduct could potentially be interpreted to prohibit kickbacks.[178] The provisions against kickbacks vary in their scope, with seven provinces invoking a blanket prohibition on any kickback, while

---

[173] Traditional Chinese Medicine Practitioners and Acupuncturists Regulation (B.C. Reg. 385/2000).
[174] Sandy Welsh *et al.*, "Moving Forward? Complementary and alternative practitioners seeking self-regulation" (2004) 26:2 Sociology of Health and Illness 216 at 217.
[175] S.O. 1990, c. 30, s. 5.1.
[176] Sujit Choudhry, Niteesh K. Choudhry & Adalsteinn D. Brown, "Unregulated private markets for health care in Canada? Rules of professional misconduct, physician kickbacks and physician self-referral" (2004) 170 C.M.A.J. 1115 at 1115.
[177] *Ibid.*
[178] *Ibid.*, at 1116.

Quebec only prohibits kickbacks if it would jeopardize the "professional independence of a physician".[179] Seven provinces regulate self-referral to facilities in which physicians have personally invested while four provinces regulate referrals to facilities in which "immediate" family members have invested. The regulations vary, with some provinces only requiring disclosure of investment interests and others prohibiting self-referrals completely.[180]

Choudhry *et al.* argue that while some provinces have rules governing kickbacks and self-referrals, these rules are often inadequate and require reform. For example, only five provinces prohibit physicians from paying or offering to pay kickbacks, an action which represents a conflict of interest by seeking to induce referrals regardless of patient health status. And with respect to self-referrals, they find that regulation is often inadequate, particularly where restrictions only relate to investments held by immediate family (given the ease of circumventing the restrictions by placing investments in the name of extended family members), and where only disclosure is required.[181] Saver sounds a cautionary note with respect to Choudhry *et al.*'s call for stricter regulation against kickbacks and self-referrals. While acknowledging the problems that these practices pose for Canadian health care, he argues that introducing overly broad bans could result in unintended consequences. In particular, he suggests that such an approach could crowd out health care finance and delivery innovations such as gainsharing programs (a reward and participation system where organizations and workers share the financial gains arising through reforms such as increased productivity, quality enhancement and cost reduction).[182] It is critical that doors not be closed to potential reforms such as gainsharing programs that might assist hospitals and other organizations to implement operational reform that would in turn improve service levels.

VII. CONCLUSION

Regulation of health professionals is complicated by competing public and provider interests.[183] Public interest dictates that the regulatory system protect the public from harm by ensuring that professionals are suitably qualified to perform services and that those services are of an appropriate quality. Professional interests, on the other hand, suggest that those being regulated will seek to advance their own economic welfare.

---

[179] See, *e.g.*, *General Regulation — Medicine Act*, O. Reg. 114/94, ss. 15 and 16.
[180] For a detailed discussion, see Sujit Choudhry, Niteesh K. Choudhry & Adalsteinn D. Brown, "Unregulated private markets for health care in Canada? Rules of professional misconduct, physician kickbacks and physician self-referral" (2004) 170 C.M.A.J. 1115 at 1116.
[181] *Ibid.* See also Moe Litman, "Self-Referral and Kickbacks: Fiduciary Law and the Regulation of 'Trafficking in Patients'" (2004) 170 C.M.A.J. 1119 at 1119-20.
[182] Richard S. Saver, "The Costs of Avoiding Physician Conflicts of Interest: A Cautionary Tale of Gainsharing Regulation" in C.M. Flood, ed., *Just Medicare: What's In, What's Out, How We Decide* (Toronto: Toronto University Press, 2006) 281 at 282.
[183] Andreas Broscheid & Paul E. Teske, "Public members on medical licensing boards and the choice of entry barriers" (2003) 114 Public Choice 445 at 447.

Tension arises between public and self-interest in all aspects of Canada's regulatory system. On the input side, self-interest of professionals leads to efforts to restrict entry to their profession in order to maintain exclusivity and increase rents. They may also attempt to restrict designation of other professions (for example, physicians resisting the designation of nurse practitioners). On the other hand, the public are interested in ensuring that entry restriction is based on factors relevant only to qualification, so as to ensure affordability and quality of care. The case of a person attempting a root canal at home represents the perverse results from a public interest perspective when professions are able to restrict entry such that prices rise and services are rendered inaccessible to many members of the public. In Canada, the tendency for self-interest to dominate has been visible in the case of dentists and physicians seeking to restrict independent practice by dental hygienists and nurse practitioners respectively.

Tension also arises in the realm of output regulation, where self-interest leads to a tendency for health professionals to protect their colleagues in disciplinary matters. Public interest, on the other hand, dictates that individuals have a right to have their complaints heard and to seek appropriate redress. Often in Canada, professional bodies have been accused of failing to enforce standards of professional conduct or rendering inappropriate disciplinary action against physicians guilty of incompetence. These tensions — and the ability of professional groups to capture the regulatory system to advance their interests — have been recognized by provincial legislators who have taken steps to increase transparency and public accountability of self-regulating bodies. Increasingly, there are requirements for public representatives on the councils of self-regulating bodies, and for disciplinary hearings to be open to the public. Reforms such as those in Ontario to develop an umbrella approach to regulation of professions have sought to enhance consistency of regulation across professions. These developments are welcome but must be evaluated and strengthened to ensure achievement of the goal of protecting the public. Introduction of a legislated process to independently evaluate the performance of regulated bodies in their duties is an idea that warrants investigation.

This chapter concluded with a discussion of several recent and ongoing changes in the way in which health care services are delivered, and highlighted some of the regulatory issues that accompany these developments. In these areas, as well as in the more traditional areas of regulation, provincial legislatures must be proactive in reviewing regulatory mechanisms and institutional designs in order to ensure that regulation serves its intended purpose of public protection and is an enabler of progress in the health care sector. Given the tendency of individuals and groups to advance their own self-interest, it should not be taken for granted that professionals will pursue such goals unless incentives are in place to ensure such an outcome.

Chapter 3

MEDICAL NEGLIGENCE

Bernard Dickens*

I. INTRODUCTION

The area of legal study once modestly described as Law and Medicine or Medical Law, approached as a specialized division of tort law addressing battery and negligence, has evolved as Health Law, and its historic and prospective contexts are addressed by linkage with health policy. As now understood, health law and policy embrace not only the human lifespan but such areas as medical research, genetics, drug development, artificially assisted reproduction and biotechnology. The pedagogical constraint to contain the potential range of health law and policy within a teaching curriculum often requires that public health law and policy be addressed separately, because legal principles apply differently. For instance, the emphasis on individual consent characteristic of clinical health care may be replaced by democratic or legislative consent, sometimes at the sacrifice of individual liberties and preferences.[1]

Despite its mature richness, however, health law and policy continue to be centred on medical negligence. The exclusion or minimization of medical negligence may be crucial to patients' health, enjoyment of life, and very survival. Not every medical error is avoidable or a result of negligence (see III.B.2 below), but many errors are negligent. The volume of medical errors justifies concern about the proportion of errors that are due to medical negligence. Canadians can take no comfort from the conclusion reached in 2000 by the U.S. Institute of Medicine that each year at least 44,000 and perhaps as many as 98,000 Americans die in hospitals due to avoidable medical errors.[2] These figures do not include deaths due to errors in outpatient care or home care, but even at the lower estimate, deaths due to preventable medical errors

* I am indebted to Professor Gerald Robertson, Q.C., for his preparation of this topic in the first and second editions of this book. Much of his scholarship and research are reflected in this chapter.

[1] T.M. Bailey, T. Caulfield & N.M. Ries, *Public Health Law and Policy in Canada* (Markham, ON: LexisNexis Butterworths, 2005).

[2] L.T. Kohn, J.M. Corrigan & M.S. Donaldson, eds., *To Err Is Human: Building a Safer Health System* (Washington D.C.: National Academy Press, 2000).

exceed deaths attributable to motor vehicle accidents, breast cancer, or HIV/AIDS.

The crude Canadian rule of thumb of taking 10 per cent of U.S. statistics does not necessarily apply to health care, because a higher percentage of Canadian than of U.S. residents enjoys health care insurance coverage due to the universality provision of the *Canada Health Act*, and access to hospital and other health services also differs. It has been estimated that in fiscal year 2000, from 9,250 to 23,750 Canadians admitted to acute care hospitals died as a result of preventable adverse events.[3] A further contrast with the U.S. is how likely, and able, Canadian residents are to react to dissatisfaction with their medical care by suing their doctors.[4] It is apparent, however, that the avoidance of and the response to negligent errors in medical care warrant critical legal attention, and that the law of medical negligence remains a core issue in the study of Canadian health law and policy.

II. NEGLIGENCE AND MALPRACTICE

It is common to treat "medical negligence" and "malpractice" as synonymous terms, or to regard negligence as a major form of malpractice. However, legislation and regulations may distinguish negligence from malpractice. For instance in Ontario, when the limitation period under section 17 of the former *Health Disciplines Act* was superseded by the *Regulated Health Professions Act*, section 89(1) of the Health Professions Procedural Code retained the historical provision regarding any action arising out of "negligence or malpractice".[5] This raises the question of what forms of medical conduct can constitute actionable malpractice without regard to negligence.

Touching a person without appropriate consent or other legal authorization constitutes a battery in tort law, and may be an assault in criminal law. If a health care provider has battered or assaulted a patient, it is no defence that the battery or assault was done carefully. The Supreme Court of Canada has held, however, that treating a patient with consent that is not adequately informed (see Chapter 5) is actionable not in battery, since even inadequately informed consent negates battery, but only in negligence if legal requirements, such as damage, are satisfied.[6]

When there is a contract between a health care provider and a patient, an action for breach of contract may be brought separately from or in the alternative to an action for negligence and/or battery. Surgery performed for

[3] G.R. Baker *et al.*, "The Canadian Adverse Events Study: The Incidence of Adverse Events Among Hospital Patients in Canada" (2004) 170 C.M.A.J. 1678; see also S.B. McIver, *Medical Nightmares: The Human Face of Errors* (Toronto: Chestnut Publishing, 2001).
[4] See J.R.S. Prichard, *Liability and Compensation Issues in Health Care: A Report to the Conference of Deputy Ministers of Health of the Federal/Provincial/Territorial Review on Liability and Compensation Issues in Health Care* (Toronto: University of Toronto Press, 1990).
[5] *Regulated Health Professions Act, 1991*, S.O. 1991, c. 18, Sched. 2, s. 89(1) now superseded by the *Limitations Act, 2002*, S.O. 2002, c. 24, Sched. B, s. 4.
[6] *Reibl v. Hughes*, [1980] S.C.J. No. 105, 114 D.L.R. (3d) 1 (S.C.C.).

instance by reading an X-ray plate the wrong way round, or on the wrong limb or organ,[7] may be actionable on all three grounds. Breach of fiduciary duty may found an equitable claim against a physician, whether or not a relationship with a patient is contractual. This may arise not only when a physician acts unconscionably or takes advantage of a patient,[8] such as by succumbing to a conflict of interest, but also when disregarding a patient's interests.[9] Courts may be disposed to develop jurisprudence on fiduciary duties as physicians move towards a salaried and away from a fee-for-service basis of remuneration that in the past would have afforded contractual remedies.

Malpractice liability may also arise for false arrest and imprisonment, such as through negligent or otherwise improper employment of powers of involuntary detention under mental health legislation,[10] and for other torts including defamation, such as by writing libellous reports regarding patients, or for instance making slanderous statements about them, or about colleagues. However, legislation may afford protection when reports or statements are made in good faith and without gross negligence, such as in reporting child abuse or neglect.

III. THE ELEMENTS OF NEGLIGENCE

At common law, the customary elements of tort liability for negligence are that the plaintiff must show, on a balance of probability that:

(a) the defendant owed the plaintiff a legal duty of care;
(b) the defendant breached that duty of care;
(c) the plaintiff suffered legally recognized damage; and
(d) the damage was caused by the defendant's breach of the duty of care.

A. DUTY OF CARE

1. Duty to Patients

Much legal initiative goes into plaintiffs' attempts to show that those they select to sue for negligence owed them legal duties of care, as opposed to mere moral or conscientious duties, but it is rarely contested that physicians owe legal duties of care to their patients. It may be contested that those suing physicians actually were their patients. Since physicians usually may decline accept persons as their patients, in the ordinary course of practice, no one has a general right to be the patient of any particular physician. If physicians discriminate against persons who want to be their patients on grounds of race, age or other prohibited

---

[7] *Urbansky v. Patel*, [1978] M.J. No. 211, 84 D.L.R. (3d) 650 (Man. Q.B.).
[8] *Norberg v. Wynrib*, [1992] S.C.J. No. 60, 92 D.L.R. (4th) 449 (S.C.C.).
[9] *McInerney v. MacDonald*, [1992] S.C.J. No. 57, 93 D.L.R. (4th) 415 (S.C.C.).
[10] *Mullins v. Levy*, [2005] B.C.J. No. 1878, 258 D.L.R. (4th) 460 (B.C.S.C.), application for reconsideration granted in part [2006] B.C.J. No. 1065, 267 D.L.R. (4th) 31 (B.C.S.C.).

grounds, they may violate provincial human rights laws,[11] but for instance pediatricians can decline to accept adults as patients, and geriatricians can decline to accept younger patients.

Emergency instances may constitute an exception to this rule. In Quebec, the provincial *Charter of Human Rights and Freedoms* requires physicians and others to attempt within reason to rescue those in peril[12] and jurisprudence in common law provinces is showing some sympathy for the same duty, of reasonable medical rescue.[13] The *Code of Ethics* of the Canadian Medical Association (CMA)[14] directs a physician in section 18 to "[p]rovide whatever appropriate assistance you can to any person with an urgent need for medical care". Courts may be willing to convert this professional ethical duty into a legal duty of care, if physicians are seen less as independent professionals than as a public resource.[15]

In some circumstances, physicians may have a duty of care not to treat their patients, but promptly to refer them to colleagues whose skills are more suited to the patients' needs.[16] That is, physicians have no duty, outside emergency cases, to undertake treatment they know or reasonably should know to be beyond their capacities, but should propose appropriate referrals. The duty to refer also applies regarding procedures in which physicians conscientiously object to participate.[17] Physicians are not responsible for negligence of those to whom they properly refer their patients, but they are responsible for negligent acts by those whose treatment of their patients they supervise, if supervision falls short of legally required standards.

Once the physician-patient relationship is established, the physician cannot terminate it arbitrarily, because abandonment of patients is a form of negligence.[18] This common law and fiduciary duty is embodied in section 19 of the CMA *Code of Ethics*, which directs a physician that "[h]aving accepted professional responsibility for a patient, [you should] continue to provide services until they are no longer required or wanted; until another suitable physician has assumed responsibility for the patient; or until the patient has been given reasonable notice that you intend to terminate the relationship". This

---

[11]   *Korn v. Potter*, [1996] B.C.J. No. 692, 134 D.L.R. (4th) 437 (B.C.S.C.).

[12]   L.R.Q., c. C-12, art. 2; see S. Rodgers-Magnet, "The Right to Emergency Medical Assistance in the Province of Quebec" (1980) 40 R. du B. 373.

[13]   *Egedebo v. Windermere District Hospital Assn.*, [1993] B.C.J. No. 298, 78 B.C.L.R. (2d) 63 (B.C.C.A.), leave to appeal to S.C.C. refused [1993] S.C.C.A. No. 149 (S.C.C.).

[14]   Canadian Medical Association, *Code of Ethics* (Ottawa: CMA, 2004) (CMA *Code of Ethics*).

[15]   However, in *Terra Energy v. Kilborn Engineering Alberta Ltd.*, [1999] A.J. No. 221, 170 D.L.R. (4th) 405 (Alta. C.A.), leave to appeal to S.C.C. refused [1999] S.C.C.A. No. 316 (S.C.C.), the Alberta Court of Appeal held that compliance with a professional engineer's code of professional ethical conduct was not an implied term of a contract for services, but was a matter for the governing body of the profession.

[16]   *Jaglowska v. Kreml*, [2002] M.J. No. 344, 167 Man. R. (2d) 71 (Man. Q.B.), revd [2003] M.J. No. 333, 177 Man. R. (2d) 280 (Man. C.A.).

[17]   See *Zimmer v. Ringrose*, [1981] A.J. No. 596, 124 D.L.R. (3d) 215 (Alta. C.A.), leave to appeal to S.C.C. refused [1981] S.C.C.A. No. 200 (S.C.C.), on the duty to refer in cases where practitioners are obliged to decline to perform services; see also CMA *Code of Ethics*, ss. 12, 19.

[18]   *Zimmer v. Ringrose*, *ibid.*

applies for instance to retirement from practice, office relocation, conscientious objection, change of practice pattern such as to concentrate in a specialty, and ending professional responsibility for a refractory patient.

As private corporations, hospitals *per se* are not licensed to practise medicine, but they bear both direct corporate and often vicarious liability for the medical and other care they accommodate and facilitate (see V.A below).[19] Perhaps more than physicians, they are subject to the "holding out" principle of tort law, in that they hold themselves out, either expressly or impliedly, as being willing and capable to provide assistance.

In *Bateman v. Doiron* it was noted that:

> A hospital has an obligation to meet standards reasonably expected by the community it serves in the provision of competent personnel and adequate facilities and equipment and also with respect to the competence of physicians to whom it grants privileges to provide medical treatment. It is not responsible for negligence of physicians who practice in the hospital, but it is responsible to ensure that doctors or staff are reasonably qualified to do the work they might be expected to perform.[20]

By operating emergency care departments, hospitals induce their relevant communities to rely upon them, and they assume a duty of care to provide adequate personnel, equipment and resources to manage reasonably anticipated emergencies. There may be limits to the non-delegable duty of care they owe for the negligent acts of their staff, such as physicians who are not salaried staff members but who practise only within their facilities by billing health services insurers or patients on a fee-for-service basis,[21] but hospitals' direct and vicarious liability must be addressed when negligence within their scope of operation causes injury. If hospitals intend to close or limit opening hours of emergency departments, for instance, they must give adequate prior notice to their appropriate communities and ambulance services, and indicate to which other facilities emergency cases should go.[22]

2. Duty to Non-Patients

In treating their patients negligently, physicians may incur liability not only to the patients but also to third parties foreseeably at risk of suffering injury. For instance, negligent treatment of a patient's infection may create liability to family members and partners to whom the patient may transmit the infection. A physician who failed to disclose to a husband that he may have contracted HIV infection from a blood transfusion, for instance, was held liable when the man

---

[19] See E. Picard & G. Robertson, *Legal Liability of Doctors and Hospitals in Canada*, 3rd ed. (Toronto: Carswell, 1996).

[20] *Bateman v. Doiron*, [1991] N.B.J. No. 714, 8 C.C.L.T. (2d) 284 at 290 (N.B.Q.B.), affd [1993] N.B.J. No. 598, 18 C.C.L.T (2d) 1 (N.B.C.A.).

[21] *Yepremian v. Scarborough General Hospital*, [1980] O.J. No. 3592, 110 D.L.R. (3d) 513 (Ont. C.A.); but see *Jaman Estate v. Hussain*, [2002] M.J. No. 283, 166 Man. R. (2d) 51 (Man. C.A.), finding the Ontario Court of Appeal decision unpersuasive.

[22] *Baynham v. Robertson*, [1993] O.J. No. 2838, 18 C.C.L.T. (2d) 15 (Ont. Gen. Div.).

subsequently infected his wife.[23] Similarly, a surgeon who negligently removed a patient's only healthy kidney was held liable to her father who donated one of his kidneys to aid her survival, because it was held foreseeable that a parent would donate in these circumstances.[24]

Courts are increasingly hearing claims on behalf of children born with disabilities attributed to negligent medical care of their mothers. Physicians' liability to women patients' subsequently born children relates to what physicians should know and disclose about the effects that treatment options may have on such patients' children. Women do not bear legal liability for the choices they make that affect their own unborn children.[25] If physicians disclose risks to fetuses[26] that women patients give informed consent to take, physicians bear no legal liability to the patients' children born with consequent injuries. However, if physicians do not recognize or disclose risks to fetuses that are later born alive with injuries the children would have been spared with physicians' due anticipation and disclosure, liability may arise to the parents, and also to the children themselves. Mothers, unlike the children, may even succeed on the claim that physicians' failure to disclose denied them the opportunity to abort their pregnancies.[27]

Injured children's rights to sue for negligent care of their mothers while they were *in utero* are not recognition of "fetal rights" or of their pre-born status as "fetal patients". Canada adheres to the historical common law "born alive" rule. Therefore, individuals' rights accrue only upon their live birth,[28] meaning that fetuses are no longer fetuses but have become what the law recognizes as "human beings" or "persons".[29] Once live births occur, however, the born persons may bring claims on the basis that negligent genetic or other diagnosis of their parents before they were born or even conceived denied them therapeutic care *in utero*, such as maternal dietary management or fetal surgery.

It is interesting to speculate on whether Canadian courts would follow an Illinois court that awarded damages to a child born severely disabled eight years after its mother was transfused with negligently mislabelled blood.[30] The jaundice and related disabilities affecting the child became actionable only on the child's live birth, but the case may be seen as the negligent mislabelling and transfusion creating a continuing wrong. This became apparent only when, in pre-natal monitoring of the former patient, fetal blood incompatibility with the mother's blood was traced back to the negligent mislabelling of the transfused blood, resulting in the born child's impairments. The analogy would be with the

---

[23]   *Pittman Estate v. Bain*, [1994] O.J. No. 463, 112 D.L.R. (4th) 257 (Ont. Gen. Div.).

[24]   See *Urbansky v. Patel*, [1978] M. J. No. 211, 84 D.L.R. (3d) 650 (Man. Q.B.).

[25]   *Dobson (Litigation Guardian of) v. Dobson*, [1999] S.C.J. No. 41, 174 D.L.R. (4th) 1 (S.C.C.); see also *Winnipeg Child and Family Services (Northwest Area) v. G. (D.F.)*, [1997] S.C.J. No. 96, 152 D.L.R. (4th) 193 (S.C.C.).

[26]   Meaning products of human conception at any time before live birth, *i.e.*, including embryos.

[27]   See the discussion in *Arndt v. Smith*, [1997] S.C.J. No. 65, 148 D.L.R. (4th) 48 (S.C.C.).

[28]   *Winnipeg Child and Family Services (Northwest Area) v. G. (D.F.)*, [1997] S.C.J No. 96, 152 D.L.R. (4th) 193 (S.C.C.); compare *R. v. Sullivan*, [1991] S.C.J. No. 20, 63 C.C.C. (3d) 97 (S.C.C.) on criminal negligence.

[29]   *Winnipeg Child and Family Services (Northwest Area) v. G. (D.F.)*, *ibid.*

[30]   *Renslow v. Mennonite Hospital*, 367 N.E.2d 1250 (Ill. S.C. 1977).

foreseeability of a negligently designed or constructed wall standing for 10 years, and collapsing onto a two-year-old child.

A further area of physicians' potential liability to third parties concerns the duty to protect them, such as by warning them or others of possible sources of harm. For instance, plaintiffs who were injured in motor vehicle accidents have succeeded in claims against physicians who failed to discharge their duty to warn vehicle-licensing authorities of their patient's unfitness to drive.[31] This is a variant of the widely discussed *Tarasoff* case in California,[32] in which a campus clinic, through its psychotherapist and supervising psychiatrist, failed to act protectively when a student was found liable to kill or injure a young woman he knew. The student arranged to share accommodation with her brother, and killed her when she returned to town. His conviction for second degree murder was set aside on the ground that he suffered from mental disorder. Her family sued the university on the claim that it owed her a duty of care, such as to warn her or them of the danger its clinic personnel foresaw. The claim succeeded, on the basis of the principle of tort law that when, in a special relationship, a person anticipates or reasonably should anticipate that a third party is in peril, the person is obliged to take reasonable protective action.

In this case, the psychotherapist-patient relationship was found to be special, and the protective duty could be discharged by warning the potential victim or those guarding her interests if known[33] or, if unknown, such as in the case of unfitness to drive, of warning police or comparable authorities whose vigilance would be liable to prevent the harm. Prevention would not only spare victims' injuries, but would also prevent patients from causing injuries and so becoming offenders. This duty does not arise, however, when both patients and third parties are joint victims of a predisposition to suffer harm, such as from common genetic inheritance.

B. BREACH OF DUTY — THE STANDARD OF CARE

1. General Principles

The general principle governing the standard of care that medical practitioners are legally required to observe was expressed by the Ontario Court of Appeal, and affirmed by the Supreme Court of Canada, in 1956. Written in the gendered language of its time, it provides that:

> Every medical practitioner must bring to his task a reasonable degree of skill and knowledge and must exercise a reasonable degree of care. He is bound to exercise that degree of care and skill which could reasonably be expected of a normal, prudent practitioner of the same experience and standing, and if he holds himself out as a specialist, a higher degree of skill is required of him than of one who does not profess to be so qualified by special training and ability.[34]

---

[31] *Toms v. Foster*, [1994] O.J. No. 1413, 7 M.V.R. (3d) 34 (Ont. C.A.); *Spillane v. Wasserman*, [1998] O.J. No. 2470, 41 C.C.L.T. (2d) 292 (Ont. C.A.).

[32] *Tarasoff v. Regents of the University of California*, 551 P.2d 334 (Cal. S.C. 1976) (*Tarasoff*).

[33] See Chapter 6 on confidentiality and privacy aspects.

[34] *Crits v. Sylvester*, [1956] O.J. No. 526, 1 D.L.R. (2d) 502 at 508 (Ont. C.A.), *per* Schroeder J.A.,

It does not follow from this proposition that the medical profession can itself set the standards to which its members are legally required to perform. If the profession could set the standard failure to satisfy which would constitute negligence, the profession might succumb to a self-serving temptation to set low standards. Standards are judicially set as a matter of law, under judicial powers and duties to separate tortious from non-tortious conduct and, for instance, to interpret and apply the usually implied terms of contracts for delivery of medical care. The Supreme Court of Canada has noted that:

> [W]hile conformity with common practice will generally exonerate physicians of any complaint of negligence, there are certain situations where the standard practice itself may be found to be negligent. However, this will only be where the standard practice is "fraught with obvious risks" such that anyone is capable of finding it negligent, without the necessity of judging matters requiring diagnostic or clinical expertise.[35]

The principle that specialists are held to the standard of specialists has some refinements. Under the "holding out" rule, those who hold themselves out as possessing specialist skills, although they have no specialist qualification or training, will be held to the standard they profess.[36] Psychiatrists who practise by psychoanalysis will, however, be held only to standards of psychoanalytical practice, not to those of psychiatrists whose practice is based on psychopharmacology.

In both general and specialist medical practice, there may be more than a single standard. Under the "respected minority" rule, a practitioner may be found to have complied with a legally acceptable standard even if the practice in issue is not followed by the mainstream of practitioners, but only by a respected minority of them. This rule accommodates evolution in professional practice. When more recently qualified practitioners may conform to more modern techniques and convictions, some may retain the style of practice of former times. They cannot pursue discredited or obscure methodologies, but may adhere to traditional practices and conventional remedies. Similarly, pioneering practice may be accepted as it becomes established on the basis of modern research and scientific study. For instance, the findings of evidence-based medicine may be introduced into clinical care before they are widely adopted by the profession, and new genetic understanding may be applied in advance of its widespread adoption. This does not accommodate eccentric, maverick or unproven practice, but permits both traditional and more innovative practitioners' defences against negligence claims based on their non-mainstream practice. Expert witnesses will be called to testify as to whether a minority style of practice is adequately respected.

Limitation Acts require plaintiffs to initiate complaints within a given time from when they actually knew or reasonably should have known that they have a cause of action.[37] Limitation periods may also be suspended during plaintiffs'

affd [1956] S.C.J. No. 71, [1956] S.C.R. 991 (S.C.C.).
[35] *ter Neuzen v. Korn*, [1995] S.C.J. No. 79, 127 D.L.R. (4th) 577 (S.C.C.) at para. 41.
[36] *Poole v. Morgan*, [1987] A.J. No. 1414, [1987] 3 W.W.R. 217 (Alta. Q.B.).
[37] *Patterson v. Anderson*, [2004] O.J. No. 3619, 72 O.R. (3d) 330 (Ont. S.C.J.).

disability.[38] Action may therefore be initiated some time after the procedure complained of was performed. Further, the process of litigation may be prolonged, so that a case is presented at trial several years after the allegedly negligent procedure was undertaken. Justice requires, as Sopinka J. observed in the Supreme Court of Canada, that "the conduct of physicians must be judged in the light of the knowledge that ought to have been reasonably possessed at the time of the alleged act of negligence".[39] Accordingly, findings of fault based on knowledge only subsequently available cannot stand.[40]

Historically, Canadian law applied the so-called "locality rule", by which a physician's conduct was measured against the standard of like practitioners in the area. The Supreme Court of Canada adopted this rule, observing in *Wilson v. Swanson* that "the medical man must possess and use, that reasonable degree of learning and skill ordinarily possessed by practitioners in similar communities in similar cases".[41] This rule was adopted from the United States, where the practice of rural medicine was and to an extent remains something of a medical specialty. However, in Canada, the locality rule has become discredited.[42] With the development of Canadian Medicare[43] funded by taxpayers' close to equal liability to pay, and support under the *Canada Health Act*[44] for everyone's reasonable access to medically necessary care, it appears inequitable that residents of one locality may have less entitlement to a given standard of care than residents of other localities in the same province.[45] The rule was also objectionable even in earlier times for insulating pockets of substandard practice.

Accepting everyone's entitlement to the same minimum standard of care unavoidably raises the Orwellian spectre among equals that some are more equal than others. Residents in the catchment area of university-affiliated medical centres and centres of medical excellence may indeed receive a higher standard of care than residents of more remote areas, certainly for treatment of conditions whose sufferers cannot practicably be referred or transported to such centres. Despite the demise of the locality rule, the standard of care must be applied realistically with regard to the resources and facilities available to physicians and patients. Physicians cannot be legally faulted for not using equipment or resources where none is available.[46] This applies not only to high-technology

---

[38] See *E. (D.) (Guardian ad litem of) v. British Columbia*, [2005] B.C.J. No. 492, 252 D.L.R. (4th) 689 (B.C.C.A.).

[39] *ter Neuzen v. Korn*, [1995] S.C.J. No. 79, 127 D.L.R. (4th) 577 at 589 (S.C.C.).

[40] *Grass (Litigation Guardian of) v. Women's College Hospital*, [2005] O.J. No. 1403, 75 O.R. (3d) 85 (Ont. C.A.), leave to appeal to S.C.C. refused [2005] S.C.C.A. No. 310 (S.C.C.).

[41] *Wilson v. Swanson*, [1956] S.C.J. No. 58, 5 D.L.R. (2d) 113 at 124 (S.C.C.), *per* Abbott J.

[42] See *Sunnucks (Litigation Guardian of) v. Tobique Valley Hospital*, [1999] N.B.J. No. 344, 216 N.B.R. (2d) 201 (N.B.Q.B.).

[43] See Chapter 1 on the Canadian health system.

[44] R.S.C. 1985, c. C-6.

[45] For the example of Quebec, see the discussion in *Chaoulli v. Quebec (Attorney General)*, [2005] S.C.J. No. 33, [2005] 1 S.C.R. 791 (S.C.C.).

[46] *Rodych v. Krasey*, [1971] M.J. No. 106, [1971] 4 W.W.R. 358 (Man. Q.B.) recognized the constraints on a physician examining a patient at a remote roadside on a cold December morning.

equipment that requires services of skilled medical technicians, but also to delivery of basic care by skilled nursing and related personnel. The standard of care may accordingly be higher in urban than rural localities for treatment of some emergency and routine conditions, and higher in urban localities with medical schools than in urban localities without schools.

Physicians' dilemmas in use of available but scarce resources are aggravated by pressures of cost-containment.[47] Their ethical and legal duties may be in conflict, since the CMA *Code of Ethics*, on "Responsibilities to Society", requires practitioners to "[r]ecognize the responsibility of physicians to promote equitable access to health care resources", and to "[u]se health care resources prudently",[48] by applying scarce public resources to most equitable and beneficial effect, while the law requires each practitioner to serve fiduciary and perhaps implied contractual obligations to each individual patient. The dilemma was brought into focus in *Law Estate v. Simice*,[49] where a patient died following the physician's decision not to order an available diagnostic CT scan due to pressure from hospital and provincial medical association authorities to be economic in use of this costly tool. Allowing the family's negligence claim, the trial judge, later upheld by the provincial Court of Appeal, observed that:

> [I]f it comes to a choice between a physician's responsibility to his or her individual patient and his or her responsibility to the medicare system overall, the former must take precedence in a case such as this. The severity of the harm that may occur to the patient who is permitted to go undiagnosed is far greater than the financial harm that will occur to the medicare system if one more CT scan procedure only shows the patient is not suffering from a serious medical condition.[50]

Hospital authorities may limit each physician's power to order "one more CT scan procedure" for each of their patients whose diagnosis a scan may assist by denying physicians the choice, immunizing them from legal liability for negligence, at the cost of making the hospital itself a defendant in litigation.[51]

A physician's lack of resources, like a lack of specialist or other skill, may trigger the legal duty to refer a patient to a more suitably equipped practitioner or facility. It may be negligent to fail to refer, since physicians are expected to be aware of the limits of their own skills, and to recognize the general limits of the facilities in which they practice, although not necessarily on a case-by-case basis. For instance, they should recognize when they should refer their patients to specialists, and refer them promptly, such as when diagnosis shows the need of specialist referral or when a patient fails to respond to treatment the physician

---

[47] See T.A. Caulfield, "Malpractice in the Age of Health Care Reform" in T.A. Caulfield & B. von Tigerstrom, eds., *Health Law Reform and the Law in Canada: Meeting the Challenge* (Edmonton: University of Alberta Press, 2002), at 11-36.

[48] CMA *Code of Ethics*, ss. 43-44.

[49] *Law Estate v. Simice*, [1994] B.C.J. No. 979, 21 C.C.L.T. (2d) 228 (B.C.S.C.), affd [1996] B.C.J. No. 2596, [1996] 4 W.W.R. 672 (B.C.C.A.).

[50] *Ibid.*, at 228 C.C.L.T. (B.C.S.C.).

[51] See *Bateman v. Doiron*, [1991] N.B.J. No. 714, 8 C.C.L.T. (2d) 284 (N.B.Q.B.), affd [1993] N.B.J. No. 598, 18 C.C.L.T. (2d) 1 (N.B.C.A.).

was legally entitled to initiate. For life-threatening conditions, even a short delay in referral can constitute negligence.[52]

It is not clear how far the duty to refer may extend, since a particular patient's circumstances may have to be considered. Referral to another conveniently accessible practitioner or hospital may be expected, but a patient's access to a more distant source of care may not be practically feasible. A single parent with young dependent children, for instance, may not be able to take a day or more to travel. Patients should not be tantalized with information of treatments that are beyond their reach. In contrast, patients with the capacity and resources to travel might have to be informed of where they may access services from which they may benefit in other towns, provinces, or countries. Although provincial residents should not have to travel out of their locality or province for timely access to the care indicated for their medical conditions,[53] physicians may have at least to inquire whether travel for care is an option. For services not covered by provincial health insurance plans, for instance, such as resort to reproductive technologies, Canadian specialist practitioners may be expected to be aware of resources available in the United States and perhaps elsewhere. Indeed for some conditions, such as HIV/AIDS, patients may expect to be informed of where they may enter research studies of new but unproven products or combinations of products.[54]

An aspect of measuring physicians' compliance with the legally required standard of care is to assess whether treatment conformed to medically approved practice or professionally set guidelines. Proven departure from such practice or guidelines may leave a practitioner vulnerable to liability for negligence, unless, for instance, a deliberate departure can be shown to fall under the "respected minority" rule. The burden of proof of this is liable to fall on the defendant practitioner. On the other hand, conformity to the approved practice or guideline will not necessarily constitute a sound defence. It has been seen that, in general, when a physician acts according to recognized and respected professional practice, negligence will not be found, but that standards are set as a matter of law, and professional practice that is "fraught with obvious risks" will not be legally approved.[55] Further, where non-technical matters are concerned that do not require the assessment of medical specialists, triers of fact, whether judges or juries, may determine whether physicians acted reasonably or were negligent.

2. Error of Judgment

Lawyers are perhaps more familiar than physicians with recognizing that many matters cannot be determined accurately, but call for determination by an exercise of judgment; legal officers who are required to resolve conflicting evidence are accordingly named "judges". Any exercise of judgment is liable to prove incorrect. Trial judgments are liable to be reversed on appeal, and appeal courts may decide by slender majorities, since differences of opinion are

---

[52] See *Dillon v. LeRoux*, [1994] B.C.J. No. 795, [1994] 6 W.W.R. 280 (B.C.C.A.).
[53] See *Chaoulli v. Quebec (Attorney General)*, [2005] S.C.J. No. 33, [2005] 1 S.C.R. 791 (S.C.C.).
[54] See Chapter 7 on research.
[55] *ter Neuzen v. Korn*, [1995] S.C.J. No. 79, 127 D.L.R. (4th) 577 (S.C.C.).

common. Reversed or dissenting judgments are not necessarily "wrong", even though they do not prevail. Similarly with an exercise of medical judgment, it is not necessarily flawed or negligent even though it may prove erroneous. That is, liability to be erroneous is often inherent in an exercise of judgment.[56]

Physicians sometimes claim that the legal requirement that they make decisions, for instance about patients' capacity to understand information, about offer of optimal care to patients and, for instance, about appropriate use of scarce resources, is impossible to satisfy, because they cannot be certain to be right. The legal response is that physicians are not legally required to make correct decisions, but only to make decisions correctly. That is, they should take account of all factors properly to be considered, and exclude factors that should have no bearing. In the *Law Estate* case,[57] for instance, the requirement of economy in use of resources was not a matter the physician was legally entitled to consider. In the U.S. *Tarasoff* case,[58] although the prediction that the patient would kill proved tragically correct, the defence was that psychotherapists and psychiatrists cannot predict dangerousness accurately, and so cannot ensure protection. The judicial response was that professionals are not legally required to make correct predictions, but are required to act appropriately in light of the predictions they actually make.

The law distinguishes between negligence and error of judgment. A proven mistake does not in itself prove negligence. It must also be shown that a reasonable physician, in the same material circumstances, would not have made this mistake. The principle has been stated in the Supreme Court of Canada that:

> An error in judgment has long been distinguished from an act of unskillfulness or carelessness or due to lack of knowledge. Although universally accepted procedures must be observed, they furnish little or no assistance in resolving such a predicament as faced the surgeon here. In such a situation a decision must be made without delay based on limited known and unknown factors; and the honest and intelligent exercise of judgment has long been recognized as satisfying the professional obligation.[59]

Error of judgment is most often apparent in misdiagnosis. Illustrations of non-negligent misdiagnoses are diagnosing infant meningitis as chicken pox,[60] and bowel obstruction as gastroenteritis,[61] failure to diagnose acute vascular insufficiency,[62] and causing a lung collapse injury (pneumothorax) when performing a fine needle aspiration on a breast lump.[63] Initial diagnostic error

---

[56] A. Merry & R.A. McCall Smith, *Errors, Medicine and the Law* (Cambridge: Cambridge University Press, 2001); see also O. Quick, "Outing Medical Errors: Questions of Trust and Responsibility" (2006) 14 Med. L. Rev. 22.

[57] *Law Estate v. Simice*, [1994] B.C.J. No. 979, 21 C.C.L.T. (2d) 228 at 240 (B.C.S.C.), affd [1996] B.C.J. No. 2596, [1996] 4 W.W.R. 672 (B.C.C.A.) (*Law Estate*).

[58] *Tarasoff v. Regents of the University of California*, 551 P.2d 334 (Cal. S.C. 1976) (*Tarasoff*).

[59] *Wilson v. Swanson*, [1956] S.C.J. No. 58, 5 D.L.R. (2d) 113 at 120 (S.C.C.) *per* Abbott J.

[60] *Siddle (Guardian ad litem of) v. Poole*, [1990] B.C.J. No. 2691 (B.C.C.A.).

[61] *Davies v. Gabel Estate*, [1994] S.J. No. 605, [1995] 2 W.W.R. 35 (Sask. Q.B.), affd [1997] S.J. No. 138, [1997] 6 W.W.R. 459 (Sask. C.A.).

[62] *Smith v. Aggarwal*, [1991] A.J. No. 221, 114 A.R. 361 (Alta. Q.B.).

[63] *Comeau v. Fenzl*, [2000] N.B.J. No. 254 (N.B.Q.B.).

may be non-negligent when it is reasonable in light of the patient's presenting symptoms, but the patient's failure to respond to treatment based on that diagnosis may create a legal duty to reconsider the diagnosis, and rediagnose the patient. Failure to reconsider the initial diagnosis may violate the required standard of care, and constitute a negligent breach of that standard. For instance, when a patient suffered a ruptured appendix, she was misdiagnosed as having pelvic inflammation. When she failed to respond to treatment for that condition and steadily deteriorated, the physicians did not reconsider their diagnosis. After four days in hospital, she died of the ruptured appendix. The physicians were held negligent not for their original error of judgment, but for not appropriately reviewing whether that diagnosis was erroneous.[64]

Although neither a physician nor a hospital may be legally liable for an error of judgment, an individual practitioner should review the basis of an erroneous decision and learn from the experience. Hospitals and the medical profession should attempt to dispel the atmosphere of fault, blame and shame that has often surrounded recognition of error, and pursue its origins openly, in order to reduce the risk of repetition and advance the education of practising members of the profession. Medical journals are publishing case studies of errors,[65] and more are being opened to discussion at medical Grand Rounds. Audit of practitioners' practice should identify abnormally high levels of error, not for purposes of discipline but as a feature of institutional quality assurance. Identification of origins of error can result in improved procedures, such as by information sharing among medical team members responsible for care of the same patient, clear labelling with perhaps colour-coding of drugs delivered in similar packaging, and double-checking of prescribed dosage levels of drugs. Further, errors attributable to hospital staff work exhaustion can be addressed by regulation of work hours and mandatory rest periods.

Hospitals that fail to monitor the incidence of physicians' and other staff members' errors, including both negligent and non-negligent errors, may themselves be liable to be held negligent. Courts may reinforce institutional vigilance by their disposition to find hospitals negligent that do not monitor and introduce strategies to reduce rates of error, much as courts enforced instrument and sponge counts before completion of invasive surgery by holding surgeons and hospitals inescapably negligent in their absences, if instruments or sponges were left inside patients. Reciprocating judicial requirements of hospital inquiry into origins of error is the privilege and inadmissibility in evidence of reports of such inquiries, so that hospitals that compel staff members' disclosure of error and analyze the causes will not furnish ammunition to be available in litigation brought against them or their staff members.

Judicial protection of hospitals' self-scrutiny may be opposed by plaintiffs' lawyers, who resist physicians' and hospitals' claims of privilege, but may be consistent with evolutions in concepts of institutional management practice. This accepts that, consistent though it is with the historical focus of medical training on individual performance, errors often result principally from failures of

---

[64] *Bergen Estate v. Sturgeon General Hospita District No. 100*, [1984] A.J. No. 2575, 52 A.R. 161 (Alta. Q.B.).

[65] See The Lancet, "Uses of Error", named contribution in each number.

institutional and wider systems. Studies in cognitive psychology and human-factors engineering indicate that safety often requires more than reliance on individual carefulness.

The concept of "latent" errors has been developed,[66] meaning deficiencies in the design, organization, maintenance, training, and management of systems, such as institutional health care systems, that create conditions in which individuals are more likely to make errors.[67] Management decisions that create excessive workloads,[68] for instance, or that designate tasks to improperly trained or equipped personnel, make errors more likely, such as emergency room physicians or nurses not having time to check that they are administering the right drugs or dosages. Correcting systemic defects in institutional management may offer the most effective way to reduce human error,[69] and may be the most relevant focus of preventive strategies. Litigation against individual physicians, though understandable from a patient's perspective, may systemically be a distraction.

When a physician and/or hospital recognizes that an error has occurred, the issue arises of whether there is a legal duty to disclose this to the patient.[70] Guidance may be found in the jurisprudence on disclosure for informed consent, where the Supreme Court of Canada requires disclosure of material risks to patients.[71] Accordingly, errors that do not affect patients or their care may not have to be disclosed. For instance, if a surgeon or surgical team member drops an instrument on the floor, which then has to be inspected for damage and re-sterilized, and the surgery is prolonged by no more than a few minutes or a less suitable instrument is effectively used, it is not clear that, on recovery, the patient needs to be informed. How instruments are handled and exchanged during surgery may have to be reviewed for avoidance of repetition, but, since the outcome and risks of the surgery were not affected, and no injury to the patient resulted, no disclosure may be required, even under fiduciary duties. Similarly, if a decimal point is erroneously misplaced in a prescription, but prescription double-checking exposed and corrected the risk of the patient receiving one-tenth or 10 times the intended dosage, the self-correcting procedure has worked and the patient need not be informed of the initial error, even if it presented a "near miss".

The focus of the professional ethical duty is on harm. The CMA *Code of Ethics*[72] provides in section 14 that an ethical physician shall "[t]ake all reasonable steps to prevent harm to patients; should harm occur, disclose it to the patient". Further, several provincial Colleges of Physicians and Surgeons

---

[66]   J.T. Reason, *Human Error* (Cambridge: Cambridge University Press, 1990).

[67]   See L. Leape & A.M. Epstein, "A Series on Patient Safety" (2002) 347 New Eng. J. Med. 1272.

[68]   See D.M. Gaba & S.K. Howard, "Fatigue among Clinicians and the Safety of Patients" (2002) 347 New Eng. J. Med. 1249.

[69]   J.T. Reason, *Managing the Risks of Organizational Accidents* (Aldershot, U.K.: Ashgate, 1997).

[70]   M. Waite, "To Tell the Truth: The Ethical and Legal Implications of Disclosure of Medical Error" (2005) 13 Health L.J. 1.

[71]   See *Reibl v. Hughes*, [1980] S.C.J. No. 105, 114 D.L.R. (3d) 1 (S.C.C); and Chapter 5 on Informed Consent.

[72]   CMA, *Code of Ethics*.

require similar disclosure, as do practices in many hospitals. Failure to observe such requirements is a disciplinary offence.[73] The ethical duty relates more to fiduciary duties than to negligence law.

Perhaps the earliest Canadian judgment acknowledging the duty of disclosure was *Stamos v. Davies*,[74] in which a surgeon punctured the plaintiff's spleen in attempting a lung biopsy. As a result of the error, the spleen had to be removed by subsequent surgery. The lung biopsy was unsuccessful, and had to be repeated at the same time. The physician failed to inform the patient of the erroneous puncture, but advised the patient only that the biopsy had not been successful and had to be repeated, which was true. The court applied informed consent law, and found breach of the legal duty to disclose the error. However, since the repeat surgery was necessary in any event, the court found that the patient had suffered no additional injury occasioned by the error, and awarded no damages for the breach of disclosure. While this finding applies principles of negligence law, the court did not address fiduciary duty or punitive damages, nor, since with due disclosure the patient might have declined to allow this physician to undertake the repeat surgery, possible liability for battery. If none of these alternative bases of claim was pleaded, of course, the judge would have been justified in not addressing them.

If a court finds an error of judgment not to have been negligent, failure to disclose it to the patient it harmed may still be actionable for breach of fiduciary duty. If the error was negligent, however, and was deliberately concealed, an action may succeed for negligence, and attract punitive damages. For instance, in *Gerula v. Flores*,[75] the defendant surgeon operated on the wrong disc in the patient's back, and later altered the hospital record to conceal the error before undertaking further surgery on the disc that should have been operated on initially. The Court of Appeal held that $40,000 in punitive damages should be paid because of the physician's dishonesty. The English Court of Appeal has indicated that a hospital is also obliged to disclose negligent errors,[76] but there seems to be no Canadian authority on the point.

Due disclosure of harmful errors, and giving apologies, may be deterred by the fear that, since error and apology are associated with wrongdoing, they will increase the chances of patients bringing legal actions. This intuitive apprehension has little if any empirical support, however, and evidence exists that physicians' honesty, apology, and sincere expressions of regret for the patients' discomfort and inconvenience may disincline patients from litigation.[77]

---

[73] See Chapter 2 on the health professions.

[74] *Stamos v. Davies*, [1985] O.J. No. 2625, 52 O.R. (2d) 10 (Ont. H.C.J.); see also *Kueper v. McMullin*, [1986] N.B.J. No. 89, 30 D.L.R. (4th) 408 (N.B.C.A.); and *Kiley-Nikkel v. Danais*, [1992] J.Q. no. 1836, 16 C.C.L.T. (2d) 290 (Que. S.C.).

[75] [1995] O.J. No. 2300, 126 D.L.R. (4th) 506 (Ont. C.A.).

[76] *Lee v. South West Thames Regional Health Authority*, [1985] 2 All E.R. 385 (C.A.).

[77] See M. Waite, "To Tell the Truth: The Ethical and Legal Implications of Disclosure of Medical Error" (2005) 13 Health L.J. 27.

C. DAMAGE

Unlike the tort of, for instance, battery, which is actionable *per se*, negligence is actionable only when the plaintiff has suffered damage, or injury. In most cases, the injury is obvious, such as organ or tissue damage, the pain and inconvenience of repetition of medical procedures,[78] adverse consequences of use of pharmaceutical products or medical devices, or of failures to undertake indicated interventions that prolong patients' pain, discomfort and suffering. Beyond physical injuries are equally demonstrable losses of, for instance, employment income and business opportunities. Courts are also able to quantify future losses, such as rehabilitation costs, and costs of future care, such as in the *Yepremian* case where, in an agreed structured settlement, the court determined annuity payments dependent on the severely disabled plaintiff's years of survival.[79] Similarly, estimated forfeited years of life, and lost enjoyment of companionship and family life or opportunities, or *solatium*, can be financially assessed, as can lost means of family financial support, both support children may have received from their parents, and that aged parents may have received from their adult children.

For instance in *Bowlby v. Oosterhuis*,[80] the plaintiff, the mother of a child, had her family physician insert an intrauterine device (I.U.D.) for contraceptive purposes. He recommended replacement in two years' time, and she therefore returned to him for replacement. On examining her, the physician could not find the I.U.D. inserted before, and may have supposed its spontaneous expulsion. He inserted a second I.U.D. The plaintiff suffered significant pain and bleeding. She had another physician remove the second I.U.D., and in the following 10 or so years unsuccessfully tried to have another child, but eventually stopped trying and decided to have tubal ligation for contraceptive purposes. Four years later, it was found that the first I.U.D. inserted had remained in her body. When the family physician was held negligent in failing to trace the first I.U.D., damages were awarded for her pain. Further, she and her husband received assessed compensation for the emotional suffering of involuntary infertility, on the finding that the first I.U.D. was the proximate cause of her failure to conceive.

In some cases, however, there is a legal issue whether what is claimed as an injury can be judicially recognized as such. The historical instance concerned mental suffering or psychological pain and suffering. Courts were skeptical of such claims unless they were shown to follow from physical injury. According to the "impact rule", courts would be willing to recognize a head of claim for mental suffering only as an adjunct to a claim for physical injury. They were fearful, however, that, in the absence of demonstrable physical injury, mental suffering would be simulated for self-serving purposes, such as to gain compensation or to support vexatious litigation brought by angry, resentful, humiliated, or jealous litigants. In a historical concession perhaps to social stratification, however, persons of social or professional status could succeed in

---

[78]   See for instance *Bonfoco v. Dowd*, [2000] O.J. No. 3799, 136 O.A.C. 339 (Ont. C.A.).

[79]   *Yepremian v. Scarborough General Hospital (No. 2)*, [1981] O.J. No. 2889, 120 D.L.R. (3d) 341 (Ont. H.C.J.) (*Yepremian*).

[80]   [2003] O.J. No. 1130, 63 O.R. (3d) 748 (Ont. S.C.J.).

defamation actions for loss of reputation and for being lowered in the estimation of right-thinking members of their communities.[81]

The impact of medical negligence can have material, psychological and other dimensions. For instance in *Udeschini v. Juma*,[82] the plaintiff was negligently misdiagnosed by a cardiologist as suffering from a generalized, progressive incurable heart disease, and followed the cardiologist's advice to take early retirement. The plaintiff did not learn that the diagnosis was erroneous for 10 years. The defendant was held liable in negligence for the plaintiff's loss of income due to his early retirement, but also for the severe depression he suffered due to worry about his heart condition. It may be questioned whether, had the plaintiff continued in his employment despite his concern about a heart condition, his depression alone would have founded a successful negligence claim.

Courts are becoming increasingly disposed to moderate the severity of the "impact rule", with growing recognition that injury to a loved one can be a cause of compensable injury for distress, and that even a "near miss" may cause mental anxiety, if a stranger was injured when it well might have been the complainant, such as a passenger in a public transit vehicle where another was killed or severely injured due to an operator's negligence. In these cases, however, there is impact on another, whether someone to whom the complainant is emotionally or physically close. If the "near miss" resulted in no actual injury at all, it is not clear that distress that injury might have occurred, to someone else or a complainant, would be legally actionable. This is consistent with the basic proposition of negligence law that legally recognized damage must be shown. If such damage was caused, unusual emotional injury is compensable, under the "eggshell skull" rule that wrongdoers take their victims as they find them, whether physically or emotionally fragile. However, if no legal wrong was done, such as in making a non-negligent error, a person's emotional susceptibility does not become actionable in itself, or make an actor a wrongdoer and a susceptible person a legal victim.

A matter on which modern law remains unclear concerns claims for what is described, somewhat unevenly, as "wrongful birth" and "wrongful life". The former arises when parents sue for the births of children they intended not to conceive or to carry to term, due for instance to negligently conducted genetic counselling, contraceptive care or sterilization procedures, or to negligent prenatal diagnosis. The latter arises when action is taken by or on behalf of children claiming that, had their parents been treated without negligence, they would not have been conceived, or if conceived, would not have been born. The law is more clear that "wrongful conception" is actionable, such as when negligently conducted tubal ligation or vasectomy results in unplanned pregnancy that ends in induced or spontaneous abortion.

However, when a child is born, even of an unwanted and negligently induced pregnancy, the historical attitude that it is a "blessing" that transcends all detriments can be found to persist in some judicial rulings. The "blessing"

---

[81] See S.M. Waddams, *The Law of Damages*, looseleaf (Aurora, ON: Canada Law Book), at 4.10 to 4.220.

[82] [1998] O.J. No. 580, 52 O.T.C. 343 (Ont. Gen. Div).

approach is supported by religiosity such as is seen in a 2004 report of the U.S. President's Council on Bioethics, which urges that all children be received in submissive gratitude as "gifts".[83] Two contemporaneous 1978 trial judgments show the contrast. In *Doiron v. Orr*,[84] where in fact a sterilization procedure was found not to have been negligently performed, the Ontario trial judge considered it "grotesque" that parents should seek compensation for a child's birth. However, in *Cataford v. Moreau*,[85] a Quebec trial judge considered the claim routine, and assessed damages, as reduced by the off-setting financial benefits to the parents of the provincial child-support policy.

In *Kealey v. Berezowski*[86] in 1996, the Ontario trial court noted the change in approach since 1978, and proposed a structure to determine the quantum of damages. In her analysis to clarify the law, however, the judge observed that:

> Courts have struggled with the novel question at issue in this case [damages for wrongful birth claims] because, in the absence of legislative guidelines for assessing damages of this kind, they are driven back on standard principles of negligence law or public policy. Both may be inadequate for the task.[87]

In a scholarly judgment reviewing, comparing and contrasting Canadian, British and U.S. jurisprudence, the judge distinguished different approaches and bases of claim. On the facts of the case, a married woman with two boys requested contraceptive sterilization, which the court found was performed negligently. She gave birth to a healthy daughter, and stated that her family was quite happy with this, and could afford the costs of childcare. The court accordingly assessed damages to cover costs only of confinement and delivery, and those associated with repetition of a sterilization procedure.

However, the court added that had sterilization been requested to prevent birth of a handicapped child, and negligence resulted in birth of such a child, damages would include the additional costs of caring for the child's needs due to the handicap, during the years when parents are legally obliged to supply their children's necessaries of life, which include medically indicated care.[88] Further, had sterilization been requested because the family could not afford the costs of child rearing, and those costs had arisen due to medical negligence, whether the child was handicapped or healthy, damages would include childcare costs.

In a British case in the House of Lords, involving birth of a healthy child, the Law Lords considered *Kealey*, and rejected it,[89] apparently reversing earlier jurisprudence.[90] However, the House of Lords subsequently approved modest damages for care of a healthy child because the mother was visually impaired.[91] Accordingly, as in Canada, the jurisprudence appears unsettled, some judges and

[83] President's Council on Bioethics, *Beyond Therapy: Biotechnology and the Pursuit of Happiness* (New York: Harper Collins, 2003) at 70.
[84] [1978] O.J. No. 3388, 86 D.L.R. (3d) 719 (Ont. H.C.J.).
[85] *Cataford v. Moreau* (1978), 114 D.L.R. (3d) 585 (Que. S.C.).
[86] [1996] O.J. No. 2460, 136 D.L.R. (4th) 708 (Ont. Gen. Div.) (*Kealey*).
[87] *Ibid.*, at 731 D.L.R., *per* Lax J.
[88] *R. v. Brooks* (1902), 5 C.C.C. 372 (B.C.S.C.); *R. v. Lewis* (1903), 7 C.C.C. 261 (Ont. C.A.).
[89] *McFarlane v. Tayside Health Board*, [1999] H.L.J. No. 50, [2000] 2 A.C. 59 (H.L.).
[90] See *Udale v. Bloomsbury Area Health Authority*, [1983] 1 W.L.R. 1098 (Q.B.D.).
[91] *Rees v. Darlington Memorial Hospital N.H.S. Trust*, [2003] 4 All E.R. 987 (H.L.).

courts applying a "blessing" approach, other invoking perceptions of public policy ranging from policy opposition to physicians becoming responsible for costs of families rearing their children, to opposition to immunizing medical negligence if it results in birth of a possibly severely handicapped child. Similarly, some judges and courts reject a distinction between healthy and handicapped children, because of fear of stigmatizing the latter, and between affluent and impoverished families, on the grounds of everyone's equality under the law.

In the U.S., the courts were seen to "bust the blessing balloon"[92] in a 1971 Michigan case. A pharmacist negligently misread a woman's prescription for a contraceptive drug (Norinyl) and instead provided her with a tranquilizer (Nardil), resulting in birth of her eighth child. Her claim for negligence required proof of damage, but the trial judge followed precedent to rule that a child's birth could not be regarded in law as a species of damage. The Michigan Court of Appeals reversed this judgment, invoking a democratic perception of public sentiment. It observed that:

> To say that for reasons of public policy contraceptive failure can result in no damage as a matter of law ignores the fact that tens of millions of persons use contraceptives daily to avoid the very result which the defendant would have us say is always a benefit, never a detriment. Those tens of millions of persons, by their conduct, express the sense of the community.[93]

The court accordingly awarded damages to the woman, and modest amounts to her husband and existing seven children, recognizing that the latter would have less of their mother's time and attention.

United States law remains generally sympathetic to this approach, although judicial idiosyncrasy remains, as in Canada and the U.K., on determination of damages for childcare costs. In the U.S., the issue has inevitably been colonized, as much else, by abortion policy and politics. Instrumental anti-abortion reasoning, however, proves inconclusive. Some abortion opponents oppose damage awards against physicians whose wrongful conduct has resulted in childbirth, on the ground that their potential liability gives them an incentive to recommend and to perform or facilitate abortion. Others support parental powers of recovery, however, on the ground that barring their compensation gives them an incentive to pursue and achieve abortion. There is widespread agreement, however, in the U.S., Canada and beyond, that the general legal duty of plaintiffs to mitigate their damages should not disentitle plaintiffs to recovery of damages because they declined to abort an unplanned pregnancy, or on birth to surrender a child for adoption.[94] This is consistent with "eggshell skull" reasoning that, if physicians have wronged their patients, they cannot claim relief from paying compensation because the patients are the sort of people who reject abortion or adoption.

---

[92] J.S. Ranous & J.J. Sherrin, "Busting the Blessing Balloon: Liability for the Birth of an Unplanned Child" (1975) 39 Alb. L. Rev. 221.

[93] *Troppi v. Scarf*, 187 N.W.R.2d 511 at 517 (Mich. C.A. 1971).

[94] See the discussion in *McFarlane v. Tayside Health Board*, [1999] H.L.J. No. 50, [2000] 2 A.C. 59 (H.L.).

Highly objectionable, not only to religiously based opponents of abortion, may be the very description given to so-called "wrongful life" claims, brought by or on behalf of disabled children. The description arose as a dismissive parody of the Fatal Accident Acts, which founded claims for "wrongful death". The concept that a child's life is an injury to the child itself may induce a visceral rejection. It was in this spirit of denial in 1967 that the New Jersey Supreme Court, a leading U.S. court on matters of medical law, dismissed one of the earliest claims for negligent sterilization damages brought not only by the parents but also on behalf of the child.[95] The court dismissed both claims, and on the latter, the court addressed the goal of compensatory damages. It observed that their purpose is to place negligently injured plaintiffs in the positions in which they would have been had the negligence not occurred.

Thus, so far as money is able, such plaintiffs are to be restored to how they would have been if they had remained uninjured. The disabled would, by financial compensation, be made as capable as if they had not become injured. This measure of damages was found impossible to apply to children's claims that, without negligent care of their parents, they would not have been conceived or born, since, while courts can measure and compensate the difference between illness or disability and normal health and ability, they cannot measure a child's actual condition against "the utter void of nonexistence".[96] Further, "even if such alleged damages were cognizable, a claim for them would be precluded by the countervailing public policy supporting the preciousness of human life".[97]

Canadian jurisprudence tends to echo this basis of rejection of wrongful life claims,[98] and children's lawyers try to frame litigation on their behalf in terms that avoid the wrongful life description.[99] Some courts have allowed claims so described to proceed,[100] but the prevailing opinion appears to be that claims by disabled children that their injuries are legally attributable to negligence that resulted in their parents conceiving them, or to their mothers gestating them to birth, can be successfully resisted by characterizing them as wrongful life claims.

This is generally the position in U.S. jurisdictions, although in 1980 Californian courts found children's disabilities shown in wrongful life claims to be compensable,[101] on the grounds that the bases of damage awards in tort are not confined to restoration of conditions had injuries not occurred, and that the philosophical difficulty can be overcome by plaintiffs' lawyers' resourcefulness and judicial responsiveness. Indeed, in 2000, the New Jersey Supreme Court

[95] *Gleitman v. Cosgrove*, 227 A.2d 689 (N.J.S.C. 1967).
[96] *Ibid.*, at 692.
[97] *Ibid.*, at 693.
[98] See *Arndt v. Smith*, [1995] B.C.J. No. 1416, 126 D.L.R. (4th) 705 (B.C.C.A.), revd on other grounds [1997] S.C.J. No. 65, 148 D.L.R. (4th) 48 (S.C.C.).
[99] See *McDonald-Wright (Litigation Guardian of) v. O'Herlihy*, [2005] O.J. No. 1636, 75 O.R. (3d) 261 (Ont. S.C.J.), affd [2007] O.J. No. 478 (Ont. C.A.).
[100] *Cherry (Guardian ad litem) v. Borsman*, [1992] B.C.J. No. 1687, 94 D.L.R. (4th) 487 (B.C.C.A.), leave to appeal to S.C.C. refused [1992] S.C.C.A. No. 472, 99 D.L.R. (4th) vii (S.C.C.); *Bartok v. Shoakeir*, [1998] S.J. No. 645 (Sask. C.A.).
[101] *Curlender v. Bio-Science Laboratories*, 106 Cal. App.3d 811 (Cal. C.A. 1980); see also *Harbeson v. Parke-Davis*, 656 P.2d 483 (Wash. S.C. 1983).

reversed its 1967 decision and admitted wrongful life actions.[102] Canadian courts have approved token compensation for a plaintiff who suffered a battery without which she might have died, when a Jehovah's Witness was wrongly given a blood transfusion,[103] and the award of $20,000 is now commonly accepted as appropriate when no scales exist for compensation assessment.

If a child that would otherwise have been born in good health is born with disability, due to medical negligence in its mother's prenatal care or counselling, it is not contested that it is entitled to recover damages. Whether it offends public policy that it should recover because negligence denied its parents the choice not to conceive, or to conceive a different child in better circumstances, or to terminate the pregnancy, is a matter on which judgment or guidance of the Supreme Court of Canada is still to be provided. The judges might refer to the jurisprudence of the U.K., U.S. and, for instance Australia,[104] as well as to the evolution of Canadian court decisions, to resolve an issue that many find beyond their direct interests, but at the centre of important values.

D. CAUSATION

A plaintiff cannot succeed in a negligence claim simply by showing that the defendant owed the plaintiff a legal duty of care, was negligent in failing to satisfy the legal standard of care, and that the plaintiff suffered a legally recognized injury. Success requires the plaintiff also to show, on a balance of probability, that the defendant's negligence caused the injury. The usual test of causation is the "but for" test, meaning that the plaintiff must show that, but for the defendant's negligence, the plaintiff would not have suffered the injury.

The Supreme Court of Canada, in a leading judgment, confirmed the "traditional principles in the law of torts that the plaintiff must prove on a balance of probabilities [*sic*] that, but for the tortious conduct of the defendant, the plaintiff would not have sustained the injury complained of".[105] An illustrative scenario is life-saving emergency surgery on a patient at high risk of death. When, following surgery, the patient dies, it may be shown on behalf of dependants or the patient's estate, or admitted by the defendant, that negligent errors occurred in the conduct of the surgery or in after-care. The negligence claim will not succeed, however, unless the plaintiff can show that, but for the negligence, it was more likely than not that the patient would have survived. If there is a high mortality rate associated with the patient's condition, which explained why the surgery was attempted, the plaintiff may be unable to discharge the burden of proof.

For instance, in a case in which a patient in his thirties died from colon cancer, his estate sued two physicians, Dr. O and Dr. H, for negligence. The defendants denied negligence, but argued in the alternative that the cancer was highly unusual and aggressive, rapidly evolving into a lethal form. The action was allowed against Dr. O in negligence and breach of contract, but dismissed

---

[102] *Procanik v. Cillo*, 478 A.2d 755 (N.J.S.C. 1984).

[103] *Malette v. Shulman*, [1990] O.J. No. 450, 67 D.L.R. (4th) 321 (Ont. C.A.).

[104] *Cattanach v. Melchior* (2003), 77 A.L.J.R. 1312 (H.C.A.).

[105] *Snell v. Farrell*, [1990] S.C.J. No. 73, 72 D.L.R. (4th) 289 at 293-94 (S.C.C.).

against Dr. H on the ground that, although that physician's professional negligence was established, the patient's cancer was so advanced that, even with Dr. H's management of the patient's treatment that met the standard of care, he would not have survived.[106]

Similarly, in the *Yepremian* case,[107] a physician standing in for a family physician conducted an insufficient examination of a patient, whose family later took him to a local hospital emergency department when his condition deteriorated. He was admitted to hospital and seen the next morning by an endocrinologist, who initially missed his symptoms of diabetic coma, and then over-prescribed medication. The family physician's replacement was held not liable because, although providing substandard care, no injury would have resulted had the endocrinologist acted appropriately. That is, the replacement physician's negligence did not cause the injury the patient suffered. The acts of the endocrinologist were new intervening acts that broke the chain of causation between the first physician's conduct and the injury.

Since *Reibl v. Hughes*,[108] many negligence claims allege negligent (non)disclosure of material information that caused plaintiffs to make choices of care that they would not have made if adequately informed. Unlike claims that involve complex physiological, biological or, for instance, pharmaceutical evidence of causation presented by expert witnesses, these cases turn on understanding of human psychology and disposition, and may be tried by juries. The claim is that, even if procedures undertaken complied with the standard of care and the plaintiff was exposed to no more than the irreducible minimum risk inherent in a particular form of treatment, had due disclosure been made, the plaintiff would have chosen a different treatment option, and so not been exposed to that risk; that is, that but for the negligent (non)disclosure, the plaintiff would not have accepted to run that risk.

Plaintiffs must satisfy the double test of showing that, with due disclosure, they would not have consented to the treatments they received, and also that a prudent or reasonable person in their circumstances would not have consented. For instance, a patient convinced a court that, with due disclosure of the risks of the sterilization procedure she underwent, she would have not proceeded. She was a sincere Roman Catholic, and was troubled about the procedure because it was contrary to her religion. Due disclosure of risks of the procedure might well have persuaded her not to proceed. She failed in her claim, however, because many prudent, reasonable women in her circumstances, properly informed, consented to that procedure.[109]

In contrast, in *Arndt v. Smith*,[110] a woman who went to considerable medical lengths to achieve the pregnancy she keenly wanted, was exposed to rubella (German measles). She asked her physician if this presented any risk to the

---

[106] *Lindahl Estate v. Olsen*, [2004] A.J. No. 967, 360 A.R. 310 (Alta. Q.B.).

[107] *Yepremian v. Scarborough General Hospital*, [1980] O.J. No. 3592, 110 D.L.R. (3d) 513 (Ont. C.A.); but see *Jaman Estate v. Hussain*, [2002] M.J. No. 283, 166 Man. R. (2d) 51 (Man. C.A.), finding the Ontario Court of Appeal decision unpersuasive.

[108] [1980] S.C.J. No. 105, 114 D.L.R. (3d) 1 (S.C.C.).

[109] *Videto v. Kennedy*, [1981] O.J. No. 3054, 125 D.L.R. (3d) 127 (Ont. C.A.).

[110] [1997] S.C.J. No. 65, 148 D.L.R. (4th) 48 (S.C.C.).

pregnancy, and was incorrectly told that it did not, although the physician should have informed her that it posed a low risk of causing severe fetal damage. She sued for negligence when she gave birth to a child that suffered from such damage, claiming that, if properly informed, she would have terminated the pregnancy. Evidence showed that many pregnant women exposed to rubella choose abortion. She failed in her action, however, because she was unable to show that, if properly informed, she would have made that choice. She had a history of discounting medical information, and had pursued her chance of achieving pregnancy with determination, so she could not show that she would more likely than not have terminated the pregnancy.

Causation includes failure to prevent a reasonably foreseeable consequence that there is a duty of care to anticipate and prevent. In a case in which a father of two children underwent a vasectomy, he later fathered a healthy third child. He and his wife sued the physician for negligent misrepresentation due to the physician's misreading of the urologist's report. The report disclosed that, following the procedure, the plaintiff continued to have motile sperm, but the defendant physician advised the plaintiff that his sperm count was zero. He and his wife then discontinued contraceptive precautions. It was held that the physician's misreading was negligent, and that this negligence was the legal cause of the third child's birth.[111]

Some earlier jurisprudence suggested that medical negligence cases differ from other negligence claims in that, once a plaintiff has shown an association between the defendant's breach of the standard of care and an injury, the evidentiary burden shifts to the defendant, usually a medical specialist with particular understanding of physiological, biological or other scientific knowledge of cause-and-effect relationships, to disprove causation. The Supreme Court of Canada has now rejected a shift to defendants of the burden of proof, but not necessarily to plaintiffs' disadvantage.

In the leading case on causation, *Snell v. Farrell*,[112] the patient lost the sight of an eye following an operation performed by the defendant, an ophthalmic surgeon. He was held negligent in continuing the surgery after noticing a haemorrhage in the eye. The issue the Supreme Court of Canada addressed was whether the surgeon's negligence caused the patient's partial blindness. The trial judge applied the House of Lord's decision in *McGhee v. National Coal Board*,[113] and found causation established if the defendant's negligence was shown to have "materially increased the risk" of the injury. The Supreme Court rejected this reasoning, holding that *McGhee* does not support the proposition that a material increase in risk of injury is in itself proof of causation, nor does it result in the onus of proof shifting to the defendant.[114]

However, the Supreme Court emphasized that trial judges, particularly in medical negligence cases, should not be reluctant to adopt a "robust and

---

[111] *Bevilacqua v. Altenkirk*, [2004] B.C.J. No. 1473, 242 D.L.R. (4th) 338 (B.C.S.C.).

[112] [1990] S.C.J. No. 73, 72 D.L.R. (4th) 289 (S.C.C.).

[113] [1972] 3 All E.R. 1008 (H.L.) (*McGhee*).

[114] Nevertheless, *McGhee* has retained an impact in Canadian medical malpractice cases; see *Webster v. Chapman*, [1997] M.J. No. 646, [1998] 4 W.W.R. 335 (Man. C.A.), leave to appeal to S.C.C. refused [1998] S.C.C.A. No. 45, [1998] 227 N.R. 395*n*.

pragmatic approach", and may draw an inference of causation from the evidence presented. As Sopinka J. said for the court:

> The legal or ultimate burden remains with the plaintiff, but in the absence of evidence to the contrary adduced by the defendant, an inference of causation may be drawn, although positive or scientific proof of causation has not been adduced.[115]

If some evidence to the contrary is adduced by the defendant, the trial judge is entitled to take a robust and pragmatic approach to it. Sopinka J. added, however, that:

> It is not, therefore, essential that the medical experts provide a firm opinion supporting the plaintiff's theory of causation. Medical experts ordinarily determine causation in terms of certainties whereas a lesser standard is demanded by the law.[116]

That is, while certainty in medical science and expertise approaches a 100 per cent standard, "reasonable" certainty in civil law need be only at a 51 per cent standard. The language of Sopinka J. has been applied in numerous cases, with the effect that plaintiffs in medical negligence cases have not been held to fastidious standards of proof that medical defendants' negligence was the cause of patients' injuries.

A claim of loss of a chance of cure or relief is measured by this standard of proof. For a plaintiff to show that denial or delay of a treatment option caused injury, the plaintiff must show that, had the chance of that treatment been taken, it is more likely than not that the injury would not have occurred. For instance, a plaintiff who suffered from diabetes for many years developed a sore between toes of her left foot. The defendant physician did not examine her but promised to make an appointment for her to see a skin specialist. He failed to do this, and gave her no further instructions or warnings. The sore became infected and gangrene set in, resulting in below the knee amputation.

At trial for negligence, both the plaintiff's and defendant's expert witnesses testified that, had the plaintiff received an aggressive form of treatment, her leg might have been saved. However, in light of her pre-existing medical condition, of severe atherosclerosis, no witness was prepared to say that it was more likely than not that with proper treatment amputation would have been unnecessary. The trial judge found for the plaintiff because the defendant had denied her a "window of opportunity" to save her leg. However, the Ontario Court of Appeal allowed an appeal and reversed this finding.[117] The plaintiff had failed to show that, on a balance of probability, but for the loss of the chance of treatment, she would have avoided amputation. She established no more than the loss of a less than 50 per cent chance of saving her leg had the defendant not been negligent.[118]

---

[115] *Snell v. Farrell*, [1990] S.C.J. No. 73, 72 D.L.R. (4th) 289 at 301 (S.C.C.).

[116] *Ibid.*

[117] *Cottrelle v. Gerrard*, [2003] O.J. No. 4194, 67 O.R. (3d) 737 (Ont. C.A.), leave to appeal to S.C.C. refused [2003] S.C.C.A. No. 549 (S.C.C.).

[118] Compare *Gregg v. Scott*, [2005] U.K.H.L. 2, [2005] 2 A.C. 176; see V. Black, "Ghost of a Chance: *Gregg v. Scott* in the House of Lords" (2005) 14 Health L. Rev. 38; and contrast *Chester v. Afshar*, [2005] 1 A.C. 134 (H.L.).

IV. DEFENCES

The overwhelming majority of physicians practising in Canada, and perhaps all, including those who have retired, are members of the Canadian Medical Protective Association (CMPA).[119] Many hospitals require physicians' membership as a condition of appointing them to their staffs, and of allowing physicians privileges to practice under their auspices. Indeed, a hospital may even contribute to physicians' membership fees, which in high risk specialties, such as neurosurgery and obstetrics and gynecology, in more litigious provinces, can be several tens of thousands of dollars annually.[120] Hospitals require membership because, should hospitals incur legal liability due to physicians' misconduct, which can run into millions of dollars,[121] they want to ensure that they can claim indemnities against physicians that can be met, if necessary through the resources of the CMPA.

The CMPA is not an insurance company, but a professional self-defence organization. Commercial insurance companies may assess each claim to determine whether it is cheaper to settle than to fight. The CMPA in contrast considers the impact of each case on the overall interests of the medical profession. It does not waste resources defending claims its own medical personnel and consultants find indefensible, but will pursue contentious claims and matters of principle to the highest possible level, including taking matters of principle to the Supreme Court of Canada even when plaintiffs discontinue their involvement.[122] Accordingly, claims for medical negligence are liable to be vigorously defended when the CMPA considers a defence feasible on the facts, or on a matter of legal principle important to the profession.

The most common defence is that the claim has been brought out of time. Limitation Acts may vary from province to province, setting times within which a writ must be issued, such as two years[123] or less,[124] and sometimes depending on whether the defendant is a physician, a hospital or other health care professional.[125] Further, time begins to run from different starting points, including from when the plaintiff actually knew, or reasonably should have known, a cause of action may exist, or from when professional services terminated in respect of the matter about which the complaint arose, whether or not the plaintiff knew or reasonably could have known of the cause of action.

---

[119] See Canadian Medical Protection Association (CMPA) online: <http://www.cmpa.org>.

[120] For instance in Ontario for 2006, membership fees for obstetricians exceeded $78,000. General practitioners' fees outside Ontario and Quebec in contrast were $1,644 if no obstetrics, anesthesia, emergency care or surgery are undertaken.

[121] See *Yepremian v. Scarborough General Hospital (No. 2)*, [1981] O.J. No. 2889, 120 D.L.R. (3d) 341 (Ont. H.C.J.).

[122] See for instance *McInerney v. MacDonald*, [1992] S.C.J. No. 57, 93 D.L.R. (4th) 415 (S.C.C.), where the plaintiff took no further action in the case following discovery of documents, but the CMPA, for the defendant physician, took the case to trial, and provincial and federal appeal courts.

[123] See for instance Alberta's *Limitations Act*, R.S.A. 2000, c. L-12, s. 2.

[124] See for instance, six months, P.E.I.'s *Dental Profession Act*, R.S.P.E.I. 1988, c. D-6, s. 11(2).

[125] Contrast two years under P.E.I.'s *Medical Act*, R.S.P.E.I. 1988, c. M-5, s. 49.

With the increasing sophistication of medical interventions and, for instance, long-term adverse effects of use of interventions, drugs and medical devices, it appears oppressive and unjust that patients may be time-barred before they can be aware that they have been negligently treated, or negligently informed.[126] The Supreme Court of Canada has explained what is known as the "discoverability rule", according to which the limitation period does not start to run until the plaintiff discovers, or ought to have discovered, the material facts on which the cause of action is based.[127] However, Courts of Appeal in some provinces, notably Alberta,[128] Manitoba,[129] and Newfoundland and Labrador,[130] have held the discoverability rule inapplicable in medical malpractice actions. In such provinces, negligently injured patients and related plaintiffs may lose their claims to compensation if evidence of negligence and the injury it caused failed to materialize within the limitation period. Further, some legislation sets absolute limits, such as 10 years in Alberta.[131] However, fraudulent concealment of negligence or injury will suspend running of the limitation period until the fraud becomes apparent. In a case where a physician deceived family members as to the treatment program in which a patient died, for instance, and created a false set of notes to conceal details of the care delivered, the strict wording of the limitation legislation was held inapplicable. The court held that an unscrupulous defendant who stood in a special relationship with the injured party could not be allowed to use a limitation provision as an instrument of fraud.[132]

A more complicated case arose when, following her treatment of injuries suffered in a vehicle accident, a patient received written reports from her family practitioner and treating physician that she would fully recover. When treatment involving the family physician to overcome injury-related infertility failed, she sued both physicians for negligent advice. The Alberta *Limitation of Actions Act* provided a limitation period for physicians of one year from the termination of services, but the plaintiff commenced her action over two years after she received the medical reports. The trial judge found both physicians liable for negligent misrepresentation. The Court of Appeal allowed the surgeon's appeal, since action was taken out of time. However, the action against the family

[126] See G. Robertson, "*Scott v. Birdsell*: Limitation Periods in Medical Malpractice cases" (1994) 32 Alta. L. Rev. 181.

[127] *Kamloops (City) v. Nielsen*, [1984] S.C.J. No. 29, [1984] 2 S.C.R. 2 (S.C.C.); *Central Trust Co. v. Rafuse*, [1986] S.C.J. No. 52, [1986] 2 S.C.R. 147, vard [1988] S.C.J. No. 104 (S.C.C.); *M. (K.) v. M. (H.)*, [1992] S.C.J. No. 85, [1992] 3 S.C.R. 6 (S.C.C.); *Murphy v. Welsh*, [1993] S.C.J. No. 83, [1993] 2 S.C.R. 1069 (S.C.C.); *Peixeiro v. Haberman*, [1997] S.C.J. No. 31, [1997] 3 S.C.R. 549 (S.C.C.).

[128] *Langenhahn v. Czyz*, [1998] A.J. No. 432, [1998] 10 W.W.R. 235 (Alta. C.A.), leave to appeal to S.C.C. refused [1998] S.C.C.A. No. 293 (S.C.C.).

[129] *Fehr v. Jacob*, [1993] M.J. No. 135, [1993] 5 W.W.R. 1 (Man. C.A.); *J. (A.) v. Cairnie Estate*, [1993] M.J. No. 351, [1993] 6 W.W.R. 305, supplementary reasons [1993] M.J. No. 433 (Man. C.A.).

[130] *Snow (Guardian ad litem of) v. Kashyap*, [1995] N.J. No. 15, 125 Nfld. & P.E.I.R. 182 (Nfld. C.A.).

[131] *Limitations Act*, R.S.A. 2000, c. L-12, s. 3(1)(b).

[132] *Giroux Estate v. Trillium Health Care*, [2005] O.J. No. 226, 249 D.L.R. (4th) 662 (Ont. C.A.).

practitioner was not statute-barred, because it was commenced within one year of that practitioner attempting to treat the patient's inability to conceive.[133]

Under general principles, Limitation Acts do not apply their limitation periods during a potential plaintiff's incapacity, due for instance to minority age or mental disability. If injury is claimed to have arisen before or at birth, therefore, and the prevailing age of majority is, for instance, 18 years, action may be taken within the limitation period after majority age is reached. Taking account of how long a case may take to reach trial, judgment may not be delivered until over two decades after a negligent incident. Damages awarded at a rate of compound interest from the date of injury may be significant. The chance of liability being found, or even of litigation being commenced, so long after an alleged negligent incident encourages retired physicians to maintain membership in the CMPA, although under the membership contract the CMPA may be liable to consider defence of a claim dating back to a physician's earlier period of membership even though membership has not been retained.

An uncommon but complete basis of defence is that the plaintiff waived the right to sue for medical negligence. In *Hobbs v. Robertson*,[134] a hospital requested a Jehovah's Witness patient asking for a hysterectomy to sign a refusal of blood document that stated that she accepted the consequences of refusing a blood transfusion that might become medically indicated in the course of surgery. There was no discussion of whether she would be treated if she refused to sign. Against the operating physician's advice, she opted for a method of procedure that entailed greater risk of bleeding, despite receiving information that if excessive bleeding occurred, she might die. She signed a release document that provided that the hospital, its agents and personnel and the attending doctors, were released "from any responsibility whatsoever for unfavourable reactions or complications or any untoward results" due to her refusal of blood or its derivatives.

The patient suffered excessive bleeding, was not transfused, and died. Her husband and children sued, alleging negligent conduct of the surgery, and that the release covered only the usual risk inherent in the surgery when properly performed, not negligent performance. However, the judge ruled that, had negligence caused the excessive bleeding, it would have been remedied by blood transfusion, but for the patient's informed refusal. The plaintiffs accepted that blood transfusion would have saved the patient's life. Referring to *Malette v. Shulman*,[135] where damages were awarded for battery for transfusing a Jehovah's Witness who carried evidence of refusal of blood, the judge found that the patient accepted every risk of excessive bleeding, and that "her death was 'due to' her refusal to permit the administration of blood products".[136] This afforded a

---
[133] *Kelly v. Lundgard*, [2001] A.J. No. 906, 202 D.L.R. (4th) 385 (Alta. C.A.).
[134] [2004] B.C.J. No. 1689, 243 D.L.R. (4th) 700 (B.C.S.C.). Note [2006] B.C.J. No. 266, 265 D.L.R. (4th) 537 (B.C.C.A.), where the B.C. Court of Appeal ordered retrial, on issues of contract law, *volenti* and Charter rights, so that the hospital's position could be clarified.
[135] [1990] O.J. No. 450, 67 D.L.R. (4th) 321 (Ont. C.A.).
[136] *Hobbs v. Robertson*, [2004] B.C.J. No. 1689, 243 D.L.R. (4th) 700 at 716 (B.C.S.C.); see also [2004] B.C.J. No. 2402, 246 D.L.R. (4th) 380 (B.C.S.C.), revd [2006] B.C.J. No. 266, 265 D.L.R. (4th) 537 (B.C.C.A.) holding that a request to sign a waiver is not a violation of freedom

physician proven to have been negligent a full defence if there would have been no injury to a patient who received a blood transfusion.

A defence that may reduce rather than eliminate a negligent defendant's liability to pay compensation is contributory (sometimes called "comparative") negligence, meaning that a patient's own negligence contributed to the damage suffered. For instance, a patient who failed to use crutches following a bone biopsy, and fell and broke her leg, was held to be 20 per cent responsible for her injury.[137] A common form of patients' contributory negligence is that they fail to arrange, or to keep, follow-up appointments. A patient has been held 25 per cent liable for failing to revisit her doctor when she suffered continuing chest pains,[138] and in a wrongful birth case the patient was found 100 per cent at fault for failing to attend a follow-up appointment for an ultrasound examination, resulting in birth of a child with *spina bifida*.[139]

If physicians warn patients that, following medical procedures, they should not drink alcohol or, for instance, smoke tobacco[140] or drive vehicles, and their failure to follow such warnings aggravates injuries they suffer due to medical negligence, courts will take their own negligence into account in assessing defendants' financial responsibility for injuries they suffer. Courts are looking more critically at patients' own responsibility for the extent of injuries they suffer due to medical negligence. This is a counterpoint to the greater autonomy patients have achieved in recent decades. As Picard and Robertson have observed:

> As patients strive for (and achieve) a more equal role in their medical care and in the doctor-patient relationship, it is predictable and just that there will be more patients found to be contributorily negligent, with a consequential reduction in the compensation awarded.[141]

That is, if patients want to achieve more responsibility for their medical care, they must take more responsibility for their own behaviour that aggravates any injuries caused by the negligence of their health care providers.

V. INSTITUTIONAL NEGLIGENCE

A. HOSPITALS[142]

It has been seen that, though individual health service providers are often the named defendants in Canadian medical negligence litigation, the circumstances conditioning errors are often to be found in failures of institutional manage-

---

of religion, contrary to the *Canadian Charter of Rights and Freedoms*, s. 2(a), 7 or 15(1).

[137] *Brushett v. Cowan*, [1990] N.J. No. 145, 69 D.L.R. (4th) 743 (Nfld. C.A.).

[138] *Anderson (Litigation guardian of) v. Nowaczynski*, [1999] O.J. No. 4485 (Ont. S.C.J.).

[139] *Patmore (Guardian ad litem of) v. Weatherston*, [1999] B.C.J. No. 650 (B.C.S.C.).

[140] *Dumais v. Hamilton*, [1998] A.J. No. 761, 219 A.R. 63 (Alta. C.A.).

[141] E. Picard & G. Robertson, *Legal Liability of Doctors and Hospitals in Canada*, 3rd ed. (Toronto: Carswell, 1996) at 284.

[142] See generally, Picard and Robertson, *ibid.*

ment.[143] Accordingly, suing hospitals instead of or in addition to doctors who practise in their facilities is sometimes an appropriate strategy for plaintiffs. Indeed in the U.K., hospital-based physicians enjoy a Crown immunity in some circumstances, and negligence litigation involving National Health Service (NHS) hospitals and health authorities is handled by the NHS Litigation Authority.[144]

An important legal distinction concerns the tort liability that hospitals bear for their own institutional negligence, that is, their direct liability, and their vicarious liability for acts of their personnel arising as a matter of legal policy. There can at times be uncertainty about whether a potential claim is better pursued as direct or vicarious liability, and each may be alleged in the alternative. When hospitals bear vicarious liability, they may be disposed to seek indemnities against those for whose acts they are held so liable. If plaintiffs elect to sue hospitals rather than their employees, the defendant hospitals may initiate third party proceedings against their employees to bring them into the litigation. For this reason, hospitals may be unable to represent their employees in litigation, and may for instance require those eligible to join the CMPA for representation and ability to satisfy hospitals' indemnity claims.

Hospitals and their medical staff members are not necessarily in an adversarial relationship, however, and may collaborate in agreement with such agencies as the CMPA. Further, though hospitals frequently have the legal status of private corporations, their infrastructure is almost invariably strongly if not entirely financially supported by provincial Ministries of Health, under global budgetary arrangements and sometimes supplementary funding. Because provincial health authorities depend on hospitals for discharge of their responsibilities,[145] they cannot passively allow hospital corporations to become insolvent or bankrupt, and are usually obliged to ensure their financial viability. In the out-of-court settlement of the *Yepremian* case,[146] for instance, the Ontario Ministry of Health and the CMPA contributed to payment, the latter perhaps to obviate the hospital's third-party or indemnity claim against the responsible physician, whom the plaintiff had not sued.

1. Vicarious Liability

Hospitals are governed by the general rule of tort law that employers are vicariously liable for the torts of their employees committed in the course of employment. If a hospital employee, such as a nurse or radiology technician is negligent and causes injury to the hospital's patient, the hospital will be held legally liable. The patient is not required to prove that the hospital itself was at

---

[143] J.T. Reason, *Managing the Risks of Organizational Accidents* (Aldershot, U.K.: Ashgate, 1997).

[144] See J.K. Mason & G.T. Laurie, *Law and Medical Ethics*, 7th ed. (Oxford: Oxford University Press: 2006), at 303-5.

[145] *Eldridge v. British Columbia (Attorney General)*, [1997] S.C.J. No. 86, 151 D.L.R. (4th) 577 (S.C.C.).

[146] *Yepremian v. Scarborough General Hospital (No. 2)*, [1981] O.J. No. 2889, 120 D.L.R. (3d) 341 (Ont. H.C.J.).

fault in any way, such as in recruiting, training or equipping the employee. Vicarious liability arises automatically from the employer-employee relationship, based on the negligence of the employee alone. The negligent act must have been undertaken, however, in the course of employment. For instance, a hospital will not be vicariously liable if an employee with no record of previous misconduct takes advantage of a vulnerable patient to commit sexual abuse, although a health care clinic has been held vicariously liable for the sexually abusive acts of an employee that were sufficiently related to authorized conduct to justify the imposition of liability. The clinic significantly increased the risk of harm from sexual abuse by putting the employee in his position and requiring him to perform assigned tasks in the course of which the abuse occurred.[147]

Arguably the key legal principle in this context is that, as a general rule, doctors who work in hospitals, whether on a full-time or a part-time basis, are not employees of the hospital, but only independent contractors. The hospital is accordingly not vicariously liable for their negligent acts.[148] The typical physician-hospital relationship is that physicians are given hospital privileges, usually for 12-month renewable periods, which entitle them to admit and treat patients. They are paid not by the hospital, but by billing the provincial health insurance plan on a contractual fee-for-service basis. In contrast to their status as independent contractors, is the status of physicians salaried as hospital staff members, interns and residents, who are regarded as hospital employees and for whose negligent acts the hospitals may be vicariously liable.

An evolving tendency is for physicians to move towards salaried employment by hospitals, being paid by provincial governments or by regional health authorities. Provinces often prefer this system of pre-set annual funding to the open-ended principle of fee-for-service billing, in which physicians may, for instance, increase their incomes 50 per cent by requiring patients' follow-up visits at four-, eight- and 12-month intervals rather than at six- and 12-month intervals. Salaried employment also allows physicians to undertake teaching responsibilities and unfunded research without loss of income derived from patient care. Legal implications are that the contractual relationship between patients and physicians no longer exists, perhaps encouraging courts to develop jurisprudence binding physicians to patients through fiduciary duties, and that hospitals may bear vicarious liability for salaried physicians' negligence.

2. Direct Liability

In contrast to hospitals' no-fault vicarious liability is their direct liability for faults in patients' care and treatment attributable to them, usually through acts and omissions of their senior administrative officers, under principles of corporate responsibility. The duties that hospitals owe their patients in particular and their communities in general include the duties to:

(i)   select and maintain competent, adequate staff;

---

[147] *Weingerl v. Seo*, [2005] O.J. No. 2467, 256 D.L.R. (4th) 1 (Ont. C.A.).

[148] See the full discussions in *Yepremian v. Scarborough General Hospital*, [1978] O.J. No. 3457, 88 D.L.R. (3d) 161 (Ont. H.C.J.), vard [1980] O.J. No. 3592, 110 D.L.R. (3d) 513 (Ont. C.A.).

(ii) provide proper instruction and supervision of staff;

(iii) provide and maintain proper and adequate equipment and facilities for patients and staff; and

(iv) establish systems necessary for the safe operation of the hospital.

Instances in which hospitals have been found in breach of their own duty of care include failure to have a proper system to ensure that an X-ray report from a radiology department was sent to the emergency room physician in time, which resulted in a patient's fracture being misdiagnosed,[149] misdirection in receipt of pap test results causing harmful delay in diagnosis of cervical cancer,[150] and failure to have a necessary drug in an emergency room to save the life of a patient suffering an asthma attack.[151]

Whether a hospital's level of staffing and equipment is reasonable is increasingly measured against a determination of "community expectations". It has been judicially observed that a hospital "has an obligation to meet standards reasonably expected by the community it serves in the provision of competent personnel and adequate facilities and equipment".[152] By this criterion of reasonable community expectations, a Moncton, New Brunswick hospital was found not negligent in staffing its emergency department with part-time family physicians rather than with experienced emergency room physicians. The judge observed that:

> [T]o suggest that the defendant Moncton Hospital might be reasonably expected by the community to staff its emergency department with physicians qualified as expert in the management of critically ill patients does not meet the test of reality, nor is it a reasonably expected community standard. The non-availability of trained and experienced personnel, to say nothing of the problems of collateral resource allocation, simply makes this standard unrealistic, albeit desirable.[153]

As provinces face growing needs for economy in expenditure on health care services, but also pressure to reduce waiting times for necessary care, the concept of community expectations may be developed by courts adjudicating hospitals' claims that less than ideal provision of care nevertheless satisfies community standards, and patients' claims that they are reasonably entitled to expect more than hospitals have been able to provide.

B. Governments and Quasi-Governmental Agencies

The *Chaoulli* case,[154] successfully challenging the legal basis of governmental limits on private provision of health care insurance and services,[155] shows how

---

[149]　*Osburn v. Mohindra*, [1980] N.B.J. No. 63, 29 N.B.R. (2d) 340 (N.B.Q.B.).

[150]　*Braun Estate v. Vaughan*, [2000] M.J. No. 63, [2000] 3 W.W.R. 465 (Man. C.A.).

[151]　*Lahey Estate v. St. Joseph's Hospital*, [1993] N.B.J. No. 617, 137 N.B.R. (2d) 366 (N.B.C.A.), leave to appeal to S.C.C. refused [1993] S.C.C.A. No. 459 (S.C.C.).

[152]　*Bateman v. Doiron*, [1991] N.B.J. No. 714, 8 C.C.L.T. (2d) 284 at 290 (N.B.Q.B.), affd [1993] N.B.J. No. 598, 18 C.C.L.T. (2d) 1 (N.B.C.A.).

[153]　*Ibid.*, at 292 (N.B.Q.B.).

[154]　*Chaoulli v. Quebec (Attorney General)*, [2005] S.C.J. No. 33, [2005] 1 S.C.R. 791 (S.C.C.) (*Chaoulli*).

[155]　See C.M. Flood, K. Roach & L. Sossin, eds., *Access to Care, Access to Justice: The Legal Debate over Private Health Insurance in Canada* (Toronto: University of Toronto Press, 2005).

governmental policies and practices have become targets of patients' litigation based on complaints of inadequate and negligent medical services. In this case, the Supreme Court of Canada reversed provincial courts' rejection of claims expressing dissatisfaction with governmental services, but some lower courts have allowed negligence claims to proceed to trial. In *Mitchell (Litigation Administrator of) v. Ontario*,[156] an infant died in a health centre emergency department. The plaintiffs alleged that delayed care and overcrowding causing death were attributable to government funding reductions and health facility restructuring decisions, and sued the province in contract, for Charter violation, in negligence and for breach of fiduciary duty. The motions judge allowed the negligence claim to proceed, but was reversed by the Divisional Court because the province was held to owe no private law duty of care.

The outbreak of severe acute respiratory syndrome (SARS) in Toronto in 2003 triggered several claims against governmental authorities. In *Williams v. Canada (Attorney General)*,[157] a class action alleged operational negligence against the federal Crown, the provincial Crown, and the City of Toronto. Motions brought by the federal Crown and the City of Toronto to strike out the claim were granted, but the motion by the provincial Crown was dismissed. Neither the federal Crown nor the City of Toronto were found to owe a private law duty of care to the plaintiff class. However, Cullity J. allowed claims to go to trial alleging negligence of the provincial government in premature lifting of SARS emergency measures, and in advice to hospitals to ease their infection control procedures, which were claimed to have exposed some class members to preventable infection.

The same judge also allowed claims for negligence brought by infected nurses against the provincial government to proceed to trial,[158] and by family members of a nurse who died from SARS infection and had infected them.[159] The judge made no findings of liability on these claims, but found only that they warranted trial based on a full record of the facts, because it was not plain and obvious on the governmental motions to dismiss them that they had no prospect of success. Accordingly, the principles of provincial governmental liability for medically related negligence remain to be resolved.

Provincial governments have delegated or devolved many of their responsibilities for health care to quasi-governmental agencies, such as regional health authorities and health professional licensing authorities. Even when agencies to which governments have delegated their responsibilities, such as hospitals, are not bound by the *Canadian Charter of Rights and Freedoms* in their day-to-day administration, for instance in hiring staff and contracting for supplies,[160] they are required to comply with Charter provisions in exercise of their delegated functions.[161] Accordingly, when, for instance, regional health

---

[156] [2004] O.J. No. 3084, 242 D.L.R. (4th) 560 (Ont. Div. Ct.).

[157] [2005] O.J. No. 3508, 257 D.L.R. (4th) 704 (Ont. S.C.J.).

[158] *Abarquez v. Ontario*, [2005] O.J. No. 3504, 257 D.L.R. (4th) 745 (Ont. S.C.J.).

[159] *Laroza v. Ontario*, [2005] O.J. No. 3507, 257 D.L.R. (4th) 761 (Ont. S.C.J.).

[160] *Stoffman v. Vancouver General Hospital*, [1990] S.C.J. No. 125, 76 D.L.R. (4th) 700 (S.C.C.).

[161] *Eldridge v. British Columbia (Attorney General)*, [1997] S.C.J. No. 86, 151 D.L.R. (4th) 577 (S.C.C.).

authorities, which exist in every Canadian jurisdiction except Nunavut, Ontario and Yukon, make decisions on resource allocation that patients or prospective patients find disadvantageous, such individuals acting alone or in class action suits, may sue. They may claim on grounds of negligence and, for instance, under section 15(1) of the Charter, alleging "discrimination based on ... religion, sex, age or mental or physical disability".

An increasing willingness of courts to allow negligence claims against governments to proceed to trial[162] may indicate an equal or greater willingness to find regional health authorities bound by a legal duty of care, because they are created to be closer, more responsive and more accountable than province-wide ministries to their community members in setting priorities for resource management. Whether they are liable for inadequate health system design and/or negligent provision of care, such as in causing delays in access to treatment, may depend on how, or whether, courts distinguish between their policy and operational decisions.

The Supreme Court of Canada has recognized that governmental authorities should not necessarily be held accountable in negligence law in the same way as private individuals and bodies, because in matters of policy, they bear democratic rather than judicial accountability. The court recognized that the executive branch of government, acting within constitutional limits,

> ... must be free to govern and make true policy decisions without becoming subject to tort liability as a result of those decisions. On the other hand, complete Crown immunity should not be restored by having every government decision designated as one of policy. Thus, the dilemma giving rise to the continuing judicial struggle to differentiate between policy and operation ....

> The dividing line between "policy" and "operation" is difficult to fix, yet it is essential that it be done.[163]

Accordingly, while policy decisions are open to judicial scrutiny to ensure compliance with constitutional, including Charter, values, they will not be measured according to the standards of negligence law. In contrast, methods of implementation of policy choices may be subject to observance of a standard of care.

In 1984, the Supreme Court of Canada addressed the contrast between public law and private law relevant to governmental duties to private persons and bodies. It proposed that:

> ... in order to decide whether or not a private law duty of care existed, two questions must be asked:

> (1) is there a sufficiently close relationship between the parties ... so that, in the reasonable contemplation of the [governmental] authority, carelessness on its part might cause damage to that person? If so,

---

[162] *Decock v. Alberta*, [2000] A.J. No. 419, 186 D.L.R. (4th) 265 (Alta. C.A.); contrast *Mitchell (Litigation Administrator of) v. Ontario*, [2004] O.J. No. 3084, 71 O.R. (3d) 571 (Ont. Div. Ct.).
[163] *Just v. British Columbia*, [1989] S.C.J. No. 121, 64 D.L.R. (4th) 689 at 704 (S.C.C.). The court cited with approval Mason J. in *Sutherland Shire Council v. Heyman* (1985), 60 A.L.R. 1 (H.C.A.).

(2) are there any considerations which ought to negative or limit (a) the scope of the duty and (b) the class of persons to whom it is owed or (c) the damages to which a breach of it may give rise?[164]

If a decision is operational rather than of policy[165] it therefore is credible although not authoritative to claim that regional health authorities are liable to patients for negligent breach of a duty of care that is owed to them, in the same way that a police authority has been held liable to individuals injured through its failure to conduct proper inquiries and enforce police discipline.[166]

Regional health authorities are not empowered to control conduct of physicians, since provincial governments have delegated that responsibility to Colleges of Physicians and Surgeons. In *McClelland v. Stewart*,[167] plaintiffs who were sexually assaulted by a treating physician sued the provincial College for negligence and misfeasance in public office in failing to investigate their allegations. The motions judge allowed a motion to strike out the latter claim, but dismissed a motion to strike out the negligence claim. On the College's appeal of the decision to permit the negligence claim to proceed, the Court of Appeal relied upon a Supreme Court of Canada decision under the Quebec *Civil Code*[168] to find that, at common law too, regulatory bodies might bear the private law liability to individuals claimed by the plaintiffs. The College's appeal was therefore dismissed, and the action allowed to proceed on its merits.

[164] *Kamloops (City) v. Nielsen*, [1984] S.C.J. No. 29, 10 D.L.R. (4th) 641 at 662-63 (S.C.C.).
[165] The policy/operational distinction has more recently been rejected by the highest courts in the U.K. and U.S.A. and doubted in Australia. Its effectiveness and reliability were also questioned by Sopinka J. in *Brown v. British Columbia (Minister of Transportation and Highways)*, [1994] S.C.J. No. 420, 112 D.L.R. (4th) 1 at 3-4 (S.C.C.).
[166] *Odhavji Estate v. Woodhouse*, [2003] S.C.J. No. 74, 233 D.L.R. (4th) 193 (S.C.C).
[167] [2004] B.C.J. No. 1852, 245 D.L.R. (4th) 162 (B.C.C.A.), leave to appeal to S.C.C. refused [2004] S.C.C.A. No. 492 (S.C.C.).
[168] *Finney v. Barreau du Québec*, [2004] S.C.J. No. 31, 240 D.L.R. (4th) 410 (S.C.C.) (*sub nom. McCullock-Finney v. Barreau du Québec*).

Chapter 4

CIVIL LIABILITY OF PHYSICIANS UNDER QUEBEC LAW

Robert Kouri
Suzanne Philips-Nootens

I. INTRODUCTION

The law is a reflection of the history, language, mores, and economy of a people. Although drawing inspiration from another jurisdiction can enrich the law, ill-considered borrowings between legal systems can disturb the philosophical cohesion of a body of law. In this regard, one cannot gloss over the fundamental dichotomy between the common law, where jurisprudence is the primary source of law, and the civil law, based upon Roman law, in which the judge applies the law rather than creates it.

Quebec civil law has on occasion adopted certain principles from the common law. The Supreme Court "trilogy"[1] on the evaluation of damages for personal injury serves as a perfect example. Yet in the area of medical liability, even William Campbell James Meredith, a Quebec writer who was far from adverse to looking to the common law for possible solutions, felt constrained to write:

> It must be emphasized, however, that common law decisions should be applied in Quebec civil law only when the principles underlying the particular subject matter are the same under both systems. Even then they should be treated merely as "persuasive" precedents and not as binding authorities.[2]

But Professor Paul-André Crépeau, writing the same year as Meredith (1956), set in motion forces which are still strongly felt today in Quebec medical malpractice law. Crépeau argued that problems must be resolved only according to civil law principles, contrary to what had been, up to then, a far from

---

[1] *Andrews v. Grand & Toy Alberta Ltd.*, [1978] S.C.J. No. 6, [1978] 2 S.C.R. 229 (S.C.C.); *Thornton (Next friend of) v. Prince George School District No. 57*, [1978] S.C.J. No. 7, [1978] 2 S.C.R. 267 (S.C.C.); *Arnold v. Teno*, [1978] S.C.J. No. 8, [1978] 2 S.C.R. 287 (S.C.C.).

[2] William Campbell James Meredith, *Malpractice Liability of Doctors and Hospitals* (Toronto: Carswell, 1956) at xi of the introduction.

exceptional practice.[3] In the following chapter we will describe the state of the law in Quebec relating to medical liability[4] and provide several illustrations of legal reasoning which may or may not be analogous to solutions proposed under the common law, but which are, we submit, consonant with the spirit of the civil law.

First we will review the general principles of civil liability, and then describe the major obligations inherent in the physician-patient relationship, namely, the duty to obtain informed consent, and the duty to treat, which includes the related obligations to attend and to respect professional secrecy.

II. BRIEF OVERVIEW OF THE GENERAL PRINCIPLES GOVERNING CIVIL LIABILITY

Medical liability is not afforded special treatment by the *Civil Code of Quebec* even though since 1994, several articles of Book One of the Code — generally under Title Two dealing with Certain Personality Rights — establish rights devoted to the integrity of the person, to medical care, to psychiatric evaluations, and to confinement in an establishment.[5] The liability of a physician arising from his or her relationship with a patient is thus governed by the general principles of civil responsibility as set out in the Third Chapter of Book Five dealing with Obligations.[6] The liability of hospitals, which will be alluded to in the course of this discussion but not otherwise dealt with, also falls under these general principles.

A. BASIC CONDITIONS OF CIVIL LIABILITY

From an etymological point of view, "to be liable" is to be bound to answer for one's actions or to be held to make reparation for the injury caused to another. The obligation to indemnify does not arise unless the person has committed a fault that actually caused the injury complained of by the victim. These fundamental conditions must be met whether the juridical relationship between the parties is contractual or extracontractual. Despite many attempts to add to the legal burden assumed by physicians,[7] the courts have generally refused to go

---

[3]   Paul-André Crépeau, *La responsabilité civile du médecin et de l'établissement hospitalier* (Montreal: Wilson & Lafleur Ltée, 1956) at 249.

[4]   Jean-Louis Baudouin & Patrice Deslauriers, *La responsabilité civile*, 6th ed. (Cowansville, QC: Éditions Yvon Blais, 2003) at 109ff & 138ff. Alain Bernardot & Robert P. Kouri, *La responsabilité civile médicale* (Sherbrooke: Éditions Revue de Droit Université de Sherbrooke, 1980) at 9 n. 15.

[5]   The *Civil Code of Quebec*, S.Q. 1991, c. 64, arts. 26 to 31 (hereafter sometimes refered to as the Code or C.C.Q.).

[6]   Arts. 1457 to 1481 C.C.Q.

[7]   Notably through presumptions or through the "loss of a chance". The ongoing debate whether victims of medical error should be indemnified under a no-fault system similar to the auto insurance scheme in Quebec resurges periodically in the literature, see generally Thierry Bourgoignie, ed., *Accidents thérapeutiques et protection du consommateur: vers une responsabilité médicale sans faute au Québec?* (Cowansville, QC: Éditions Yvon Blais, 2006)

down this road, feeling that any fundamental changes should more properly be effected by legislation rather than by judicial activism.

1. Fault

In law, a fault can be defined as the failure to fulfil a duty or the violation of an obligation.[8] The duty in question may be imposed by law (for example, specific rules or standards relating to safety), it can result from a personal undertaking (within the framework of a contract), and it may also be inherent in a general duty of abiding by the rules of conduct so as not to cause harm to others. The celebrated French jurist, Demogue introduced the concept of the intensity of obligations, a distinction which determines the scope of an undertaking, whether voluntarily assumed or imposed by law.[9] Under Quebec law, an obligation involves one of three levels of intensity. In the case of an *obligation of means* or *of diligence*, the debtor must do all that is in his or her power, given the circumstances and the means available, to attain the desired result. Therefore, an individual will have a defence to an action if there exists factors or risks beyond one's control resulting in the failure of a particular act or intervention. An *obligation of result* presupposes that a specific anticipated outcome lies within the debtor's control, and thus the failure *per se* to attain the result promised constitutes a fault. Although this type of obligation is more frequently encountered in contractual relationships, it can also occur in an extracontractual context because of certain presumptions of liability of legislative origin.[10] For its part, an *obligation of warranty* imposes a duty to assume, under all circumstances including superior force, the legal consequences of non-performance. This type of obligation can be found in certain types of contracts as well as in particular cases of extracontractual liability, such as the responsibility of principals for injury caused by the fault of servants or employees in the performance of their duties.[11]

In Quebec law the distinction between these different types of obligations determines the burden of proof imposed upon plaintiffs and the means of exoneration available to defendants depend upon this classification. In the case of an obligation of means, the plaintiff must prove by a preponderance of the evidence that the debtor was at fault and thus the debtor may seek exoneration

---

and more particularly the chapter written by Robert Tétrault, "Esquisse d'un régime québécois d'indemnisation des victimes d'accidents thérapeutiques" at 251.

[8] Jean-Louis Baudouin & Patrice Deslauriers, *La responsabilité civile*, 6th ed. (Cowansville, QC: Éditions Yvon Blais, 2003) at 109ff nn. 138ff.; Alain Bernardot & Robert P. Kouri, *La responsabilité civile médicale* (Sherbrooke, QC: Éditions Revue de Droit Université de Sherbrooke, 1980) at 9 n. 15.

[9] Paul-André Crépeau, *L'intensité de l'obligation juridique ou des obligations de diligence, de résultat et de garantie*, Centre de Recherche en Droit Privé et Comparé du Québec (Cowansville, QC: Éditions Yvon Blais, 1989); Jean-Louis Baudouin, Pierre-Gabriel Jobin & Nathalie Vézina, *Les obligations*, 6th ed. (Cowansville, QC: Éditions Yvon Blais, 2005) at 36 n.33.

[10] For example, the liability of the custodian of an animal, art. 1466 C.C.Q.

[11] Art. 1463 C.C.Q. See also Paul-André Crépeau, *L'intensité de l'obligation juridique ou des obligations de diligence, de résultat et de garantie*, Centre de Recherche en Droit Privé et Comparé du Québec (Cowansville, QC: Éditions Yvon Blais, 1989) at 59 n. 104.

by proving an absence of fault on his or her part. In the case of obligation of result, the plaintiff's burden is much easier to fulfill since fault resides in the mere fact of not having attained the result promised. In this situation, the only means of avoiding liability is by proving that non-fulfillment of the obligation results from superior force.[12] As for obligations of warranty, once the plaintiff has established non-performance of the undertaking, the right to indemnification is virtually ensured, since even superior force cannot obviate the defendant's liability.[13]

Generally speaking, most duties inherent in medical practice are viewed as obligations of means.[14] Jurisprudence and doctrine are unanimous in this regard.[15] This being the case, how must one proceed in order to determine whether a physician has acted in conformity with the standards of conduct expected of a member of the medical profession? On this point also there is unanimity in that "the criterion applicable is that of a normally prudent and competent practitioner"[16] acting in conformity with current standards of medical science. An *in abstracto* or objective approach is thus retained.[17] Accordingly, in the evaluation of a person's conduct, one must take into account certain circumstances relative to the individual, which normally include the level of training or specialization. "It would be abnormal that a medical specialist, performing an act falling within his or her field of specialization, be compared to that which a general practitioner would have done under similar circumstances".[18] One thus compares a generalist to a generalist and a specialist to a specialist.

---

off

[12] Art. 1470 C.C.Q.

[13] *Ibid.*

[14] Unless the physician was reckless enough to guarantee a result, in which case liability would lie if the result was not attained: *Fiset v. St-Hilaire*, [1976] C.S. 994 (Que. S.C.). A promise of this nature is contrary to the *Code of Ethics of Physicians*, R.R.Q., c. M-9, r. 4.1, s. 83: "A physician must refrain from guaranteeing, explicitly or implicitly, the effectiveness of an examination, investigation or treatment, or the cure of a disease."

[15] See the doctrine and cases cited by Pauline Lesage-Jarjoura & Suzanne Philips-Nootens, *Éléments de responsabilité civile médicale — le droit dans le quotidien de la médecine*, 2nd ed. (Cowansville, QC: Éditions Yvon Blais, 2001) at 41 n. 55 and note 24, at 244-246 nn. 290-292 and footnotes 4 to 8.

[16] *Cloutier v. Hôpital le Centre Hospitalier de l'Université Laval*, [1990] J.Q. No. 294, [1990] R.J.Q. 717 at 721 (Que. C.A.) (our translation). Pauline Lesage-Jarjoura & Suzanne Philips-Nootens, *Éléments de responsabilité civile médicale — le droit dans le quotidien de la médecine*, 2nd ed. (Cowansville, QC: Éditions Yvon Blais, 2001) at 41 n. 55, at 244-246 nn. 290-292 and notes 4 to 8.

[17] Jean-Louis Baudouin & Patrice Deslauriers, *La responsabilité civile*, 6th ed. (Cowansville, QC: Éditions Yvon Blais, 2003) at 128 n. 170; Pauline Lesage-Jarjoura & Suzanne Philips-Nootens, *Éléments de responsabilité civile médicale — le droit dans le quotidien de la médecine*, 2nd ed. (Cowansville, QC: Éditions Yvon Blais, 2001) at 46-49 nn. 62-66. *Gordon v. Weiswall*, [1998] J.Q. No. 7, [1998] R.R.A. 31 (Que. C.A.).

[18] Alain Bernardot & Robert P. Kouri, *La responsabilité civile médicale* (Sherbrooke, QC: Éditions Revue de Droit Université de Sherbrooke, 1980) at 13 n 22 (our translation). The Supreme Court of Canada expressed its approval of this approach in the case of *ter Neuzen v. Korn*, [1995] S.C.J. No. 79, [1995] 3 S.C.R. 674 (S.C.C.) (case originating in British Columbia).

One must also take into account the external circumstances under which the medical acts in question are performed. Is the physician working in a large city or close to a university medical centre where he or she can easily consult with specialists and have recourse to sophisticated diagnostic procedures, or is his or her practice situated in a remote area and with limited resources? Although the courts will likely be more frequently faced with these issues due to growing demands on the health system, as matters stand there would appear to be no clear position adopted in the jurisprudence.[19]

The burden of proof, in medical liability cases as elsewhere, rests upon the plaintiff and unless this standard is met, the defendant will be exonerated.[20] In a field as complex as medicine, the testimony of experts is generally indispensable for determining fault.[21]

A physician is not expected to be infallible. Provided the standard of a reasonable professional has been met, a physician who makes an error in diagnosis or in treatment will not be held liable even though an injury is sustained. As the Quebec Court of Appeal pointed out in *Blanchette v. Léveillé*, a case involving maxillofacial surgery, "[in] the absence of proof [that current standards of medical practice have not been met], one cannot infer that appellant is liable by the mere fact that abnormalities appeared a few days after the intervention, performed under the circumstances described".[22] The Supreme Court has also formally acknowledged this principle.[23]

Under certain circumstances, direct proof of fault may not be available, in which case legislation provides for the possibility of establishing fault by invoking presumptions of fact,[24] an indirect means of proof having a certain resemblance to the common law notion of *res ipsa loquitur*. Presumptions of fact are conclusions that can be drawn by the court provided they are "serious, precise and concordant".[25] They must not to be confused with legal presumptions or presumptions created by legislation.[26] In offering proof by presumption of

---

[19]   See section IV.A below, the duty to treat.

[20]   Art. 2803 C.C.Q.

[21]   The depth of knowledge and the qualifications of an expert obviously play a major role in establishing his or her credibility before the courts. See *Ratelle v. Hôpital Cité de la Santé de Laval*, [2000] R.R.A. 697 (Que. S.C.), affd B.E. 2005BE-17 (Que. C.A.): expert congratulated by the court for his objectivity. *Contra, F. (L.) v. Villeneuve*, [1999] J.Q. No. 6498, [1999] R.R.A. 854 (Que. S.C.), affd [2002] J.Q. No. 1057, [2002] R.R.A. 296 (Que. C.A.): expert severely criticized by the court for excessive partiality towards the party that retained his services.

[22]   [1998] J.Q. No. 1257 at para. 28, [1998] R.R.A. 385 at 390 (Que. C.A.) (our translation).

[23]   *St-Jean v. Mercier*, [2002] S.C.J. No. 17 at para. 53, [2002] 1 S.C.R. 491 at 511 (S.C.C.), affg [1999] J.Q. No. 2584, [1999] R.J.Q. 1658 (Que. C.A.) and [1998] J.Q. No. 234 (Que. S.C.); *Lapointe v. Hôpital Le Gardeur*, [1992] S.C.J. No. 11 at para. 31, [1992] 1 S.C.R. 351 at 363 (S.C.C.). See also, *inter alia, Vigneault v. Mathieu*, [1991] J.Q. No. 1079, [1991] R.J.Q. 1607 (Que. C.A.); *Tremblay v. Claveau*, [1990] J.Q. No. 278, [1990] R.R.A. 268 (Que. C.A.).

[24]   Art. 2846 C.C.Q. states: "A presumption is an inference established by law or the court from a known fact to an unknown fact."

[25]   Art. 2849 C.C.Q.

[26]   Art. 2847 C.C.Q.: "A legal presumption is one that is especially attached by law to certain facts; it exempts the person in whose favour it exists from making any other proof". Thus it suffices to establish that the conditions giving rise to the presumption are met in order for the presumption to take effect.

fact, the plaintiff must convince the trier of fact that only through an inference of fault on the part of the defendant can the injury to the victim be explained. According to the Quebec Court of Appeal, the conditions to be met for applying presumptions of fact "allow for a significant measure of judicial discretion".[27] In order to avoid altering the fundamental nature of an obligation of means, one must not confuse proof of fault by presumptions of fact with failure to attain the anticipated results of a medical act. A lack of success in treatment does not necessarily imply medical fault. Only through a thorough analysis of all pertinent elements and circumstances can an inference of fault can drawn.[28]

2. Injury

The establishment of harm or injury is intrinsic to medical liability since, as already pointed out, the notion of liability relates to the duty of indemnifying the victim. The injury suffered may be "bodily, moral or material" according to art. 1607 of the *Civil Code of Quebec*. Any injury, whether present or future, must be certain[29] (as opposed to being merely hypothetical or eventual). It must also be an immediate and direct consequence of the defendant's fault. Bodily or mental injury usually includes patrimonial (*e.g.*, temporary or permanent inability to work, costs of present and future care) and extrapatrimonial (*e.g.*, loss of physical integrity, pain and suffering, loss of enjoyment of life) aspects. While a discussion of the means of evaluating injury and the payment of damages goes beyond the scope of this chapter,[30] we do note that an injury resulting from a medical fault can be of a purely moral nature.[31]

In addition, the Quebec *Charter of Human Rights and Freedoms* provides for awarding punitive damages in cases of unlawful and intentional interference with a fundamental right or freedom[32] which includes, *inter alia*, the right of inviolability of the person. The *Civil Code of Quebec* also alludes to this type of damages.[33] However, the Supreme Court has set out a stringent intent requirement: the person must have "... a desire or intent to cause the consequences of his or her wrongful ..." conduct, or act "with full knowledge of the immediate and natural or at least extremely probable consequences that his

---

[27] *Chabot v. Roy*, [1997] J.Q. No. 3096 at para. 53, [1997] R.R.A. 920 at 929 (Que. C.A.) (our translation).

[28] See more particularly *Vigneault v. Mathieu*, [1991] J.Q. No. 1079, [1991] R.J.Q. 1607 (Que. C.A.); *Liberman v. Tabah*, [1990] J.Q. No. 802, [1990] R.J.Q. 1230 (Que. C.A.).

[29] Art. 1611 C.C.Q.

[30] See the detailed analysis of Jean-Louis Baudouin & Patrice Deslauriers, *La responsabilité civile*, 6th ed. (Cowansville, QC: Éditions Yvon Blais, 2003) at 336ff nn. 422ff and jurisprudence cited; see arts. 1614 to 1620 C.C.Q.

[31] *Massinon v. Ghys*, [1996] R.J.Q. 2258 (Que. S.C.): breast cancer undetected by a specialist in the field.

[32] *Charter of Human Rights and Freedoms*, R.S.Q., c. C-12, s. 49.

[33] Art. 1621 C.C.Q.

or her conduct will cause".[34] Consequently, the awarding of punitive damages in medical liability cases is, in fact, very rare.[35]

3. Causal Relationship Between Fault and Injury

In the words of Baudouin J., the injury suffered must be the "logical, direct and immediate consequence of fault",[36] a determination which the courts treat as a question of fact left entirely to the appreciation of the trial judge.[37] The trier of fact must be convinced of the existence of a direct relationship between the defendant's fault and the victim's situation. However, a review of the jurisprudence reveals that the issue of causation is rarely discussed unless it lies at the very heart of the dispute, usually involving contradictory expert testimony, difficulties of proof of causation or defences based on a lack of causation. As is also the case in proving fault, the plaintiff may seek to establish causation indirectly through presumptions of fact.[38] For instance, although the Supreme Court in *Morin v. Blais*[39] concluded that a presumption of causation existed due to the particular circumstances of the case, this presumption was, by the very nature of these circumstances, one of fact and not of law since it was based solely on inference.[40] In medical liability cases in general, many decisions have

---

[34] *Québec (Public Curator) v. Syndicat National des Employés de l'hôpital St-Ferdinand*, [1996] S.C.J. No. 90 at para. 121, [1996] 3 S.C.R. 211 at 262 (S.C.C.).

[35] One could add that as a general rule, in the few cases where punitive damages were awarded, they tended to be fairly modest. See, *e.g.*, *Bédard v. Gauthier*, [1996] R.R.A. 860 (Que. S.C.), where an orthopaedic surgeon on call who refused to attend a patient was condemned to pay $2,000 as compensatory and punitive damages for the physical, psychological and moral harm caused. In *Jagura-Parent v. Dvorkin*, B.E. 99BE-442 (C.Q.) plaintiff was awarded punitive damages to the amount of $5,000 because a physician refused to correct an erroneous medical report which stated that the patient was epileptic and thus should not be allowed to drive a motor vehicle. On the other hand, in *Soccio v. Leduc*, [2004] J.Q. No. 2485, [2004] R.J.Q. 1254 (Que. S.C.), revd [2007] J.Q. No. 1137 (Que. C.A.), the Superior Court granted $100,000 as punitive damages in addition to compensatory damages because the defendant psychiatrist had drafted a supplementary report in conformity with an employer's wishes in order to facilitate discharging an employee. The Court of Appeal reversed this decision, stating that the trial judge's finding of fact was erroneous.

[36] Jean-Louis Baudouin & Patrice Deslauriers, *La responsabilité civile*, 6th ed. (Cowansville, QC: Éditions Yvon Blais, 2003) at 460 n. 584 (our translation).

[37] In *St-Jean v. Mercier*, [2002] S.C.J. No. 17 at para. 104, [2002] 1 S.C.R. 491 at 528 (S.C.C.), Gonthier J. wrote: "In contrast, in the determination of causation one is inquiring into whether something happened between the fault and the damage suffered so as to link the two. That link must be legally significant in an evidentiary sense, but it is rendered no less a question of fact". This point of view was followed in *Labonté v. Tanguay*, [2003] J.Q. No. 6539 at para. 19, [2003] R.R.A. 774 at 775 (Que. C.A.), affg [2002] R.R.A. 62 (Que. S.C.).

[38] Alain Bernardot & Robert P. Kouri, *La responsabilité civile médicale* (Sherbrooke, QC: Éditions Revue de Droit Université de Sherbrooke, 1980) at 77 n. 115; Jean-Louis Baudouin & Patrice Deslauriers, *La responsabilité civile*, 6th ed. (Cowansville, QC: Éditions Yvon Blais, 2003) at 472 n. 605.

[39] [1977] S.C.J. No. 128, [1977] 1 S.C.R. 570 (S.C.C.).

[40] Robert P. Kouri, "From Presumptions of Fact to Presumptions of Causation: Reflections on the Perils of Judge-Made Rules in Quebec Medical Malpractice Law" (2001) 32 R.D.U.S. 213.

clearly reaffirmed that no legal presumptions against physicians exist.[41] One must therefore be very wary when certain judges make overly generalized statements seemingly to the contrary, if the affirmations are not explicitly supported by the facts.[42]

A physician whose fault is established can attempt to seek exoneration by proving a lack of causation. The defendant can do this by arguing that what occurred was an "unforeseeable and irresistible event",[43] in other words, a case of superior force over which, due to its very nature, he or she had no control — or that it resulted from the act or fault of either the victim or of a third person. Each of these elements constitutes a *novus actus interveniens* which interrupts the causal connection between the physician's fault and the victim's injuries, provided, according to the courts, that its gravity or importance is at least equal, if not superior to, the fault committed by the physician.[44] In other circumstances, several faults may cause the harm, in which case the court will apportion liability, including that of the victim if the situation so indicates, in proportion to the seriousness of the fault of each person involved.[45]

A victim may be faced with a complex situation in which each of several persons (for example, a team of physicians and nurses) committed a fault capable of causing the injury, only one fault caused the injury, and it cannot be established with a sufficient degree of certainty which person actually caused the harm.

In order to avoid the inequity involved in depriving the patient of his or her recourse, art. 1480 of the *Civil Code of Quebec* provides a solution of jurisprudential origin: all persons who have committed a fault which may have caused the injury are to be held solidarily liable unless they can discharge a reverse onus of proof that there was no causal connection between each individual fault and the injury.

An obvious and simple means of defence available to the defendant in appropriate circumstances is that of extinctive prescription, according to which

---

[41] For example, *Camden-Bourgault v. Brochu*, [1996] J.Q. No. 4586, [1996] R.R.A. 809 (Que. S.C.), affd [2001] J.Q. No. 1327, [2001] R.R.A. 295 (Que. C.A.), leave to appeal to S.C.C. refused [2001] C.S.C.R. no. 279; *Zanchettin v. Demontigny*, [1994] J.Q. No. 1163, [1995] R.R.A. 87 (Que. S.C.), affd [2000] J.Q. No. 2640, [2000] R.R.A. 298 (Que. C.A), leave to appeal to S.C.C. refused, [2000] C.S.C.R. no. 418, [2002] 1 S.C.R. xi; *Bérubé v. Cloutier*, [2000] J.Q. No. 1452, [2000] R.R.A. 484 (Que. S.C.), affd [2003] J.Q. No. 3068, [2003] R.R.A. 374 (Que. C.A.).

[42] See, *e.g.*, in *St-Jean v. Mercier*, [1999] J.Q. No. 2584, [1999] R.J.Q. 1658 (Que. C.A.), affd [2002] S.C.J. No. 17, [2002] 1 S.C.R. 491 (S.C.C.): "the court may thus presume the existence of a causal link" (at 1666 (C.A.)) (our translation).

[43] Art. 1470 C.C.Q.

[44] More particularly *Liberman v. Tabah*, [1990] J.Q. No. 802, [1990] R.J.Q. 1230 (Que. C.A.): fault of the nursing staff and of an intern following a thyroidectomy; *Boulet v. Léveillé*, [1990] R.R.A. 412 (Que. S.C.): fault of members of the family and of another hospital. In order to constitute a *novus actus interveniens*, there must also be an interval or time lag between the first and second fault: see Jean-Louis Baudouin & Patrice Deslauriers, *La responsabilité civile*, 6th ed. (Cowansville, QC: Éditions Yvon Blais, 2003) at 467 n. 593. See also *Chouinard v. Robbins*, [2001] J.Q. No. 6081 at para. 32, [2002] R.J.Q. 60 at 65 (Que. C.A.).

[45] Art. 1478 C.C.Q.

an action in damages for bodily injury must be brought within three years.[46] Sometimes, the appearance of injury resulting from a medical fault will not materialize instantaneously as, for instance, when a compress is forgotten in an abdominal cavity[47] or when there has been only a partial removal of an organ.[48] In such situations, the prescriptive period will run from the day the damage appears for the first time.[49]

B. NATURE OF THE PHYSICIAN-PATIENT RELATIONSHIP

The basis of this relationship, whether contractual or extracontractual, in fact has relatively little influence on the physician's obligations and consequently on his or her liability, except in regard to civil liability for the act of another. The differences which *do* exist play a role on a more technical level relating to modalities of the recourse in damages.

1. Contractual Relationship

The notion that an *intuitu personae* contract exists between the physician and his or her patient has formed part of Quebec law since the end of the 1950s.[50] Despite the importance of access to medical services in our society, a physician does not have to enter into a contractual relationship with all those who would wish to do so. He or she enjoys the right not to contract under the *Act Respecting Health Services and Social Services*[51] and, in deference to his or her religious or moral sensibilities, can refuse to treat for reason of conscience according to the *Code of Ethics of Physicians.*[52] This right of refusal is not without certain limitations. For example, the refusal to contract cannot be based on discrimination prohibited by the *Charter of Human Rights and Freedoms*[53]

---

[46]   Art. 2925 C.C.Q. Whether the regime is contractual or extracontractual.
[47]   *Thomassin v. Hôpital de Chicoutimi*, [1990] J.Q. No. 1247, [1990] R.J.Q. 2275 (Que. S.C.), affd [1997] J.Q. No. 2748, [1997] R.J.Q. 2121 (Que. C.A.).
[48]   *Drolet v. Côté*, [1983] C.S. 719 (Que. S.C.), but revd on the issue of liability, [1986] J.Q. No. 206, [1986] R.R.A. 11 (Que. C.A.).
[49]   Art. 2926 C.C.Q. It is difficult to demand of the victim that he or she act before even knowing the condition from which he or she is suffering. To decide otherwise would be contrary to common sense.
[50]   *X. v. Mellen*, [1957] B.R. 389 (Que. C.A.). Paul-André Crépeau, *La responsabilité civile du médecin et de l'établissement hospitalier* (Montreal: Wilson & Lafleur Ltée, 1956). Although the therapeutic relationship is based on confidence, one cannot help but notice that due to various modern phenomena such as changes in the manner of practising medicine (*e.g.*, the growing popularity of group practice and walk-in clinics), the lack of medical personnel, the multiplication of specialties, and the exponential growth of medical technology, this particular aspect of the medical contract, regrettably, is being constantly eroded. See Alain Bernardot & Robert P. Kouri, *La responsabilité civile médicale* (Sherbrooke, QC: Éditions Revue de Droit Université de Sherbrooke, 1980) at 166 n. 246. See also *Code of Ethics of Physicians*, R.R.Q., c. M-9, r. 4.1, s. 18.
[51]   R.S.Q., c. S-4.2, s. 6.
[52]   *Code of Ethics of Physicians*, R.R.Q., c. M-9, r. 4.1, s. 24.
[53]   R.S.Q., c. C-12, s. 10: race, sexual orientation or handicap. *Hamel v. Malaxos*, [1993] J.Q. No. 2114, [1994] R.J.Q. 173 (C.Q.): dentist who refused to continue treating a patient who was HIV-

and by the *Code of Ethics of Physicians.*[54] The refusal cannot arise out of a certain sentiment of vengeance,[55] nor can it violate a legal obligation such as the duty of coming to the assistance of a person whose life is in danger, as set out in the Quebec *Charter of Human Rights and Freedoms,*[56] the *Act Respecting Health Services and Social Services,*[57] the *Act Respecting Medical Laboratories, Organ, Tissue, Gamete and Embryo Conservation, and the Disposal of Human Bodies*[58] and the *Code of Ethics of Physicians.*[59] It is open to debate whether certain innovative ways of organizing health care in Quebec, such as the regrouping of family physicians to serve a particular segment of the population, will still afford physicians some latitude in the enrolment of patients they wish to serve.[60]

A contractual relationship gives rise to certain reciprocal rights and obligations. Over and above the four facets of the doctor-patient relationship alluded to in the introduction lies the principle that a treating physician undertakes to personally care for the patient. He or she cannot delegate fulfilment of these duties to someone else without the express or tacit consent of the person being treated. The following case illustrates this rule. A surgeon convinced a young woman of the importance of undergoing surgery to correct a patent *ductus arteriosus* (a fetal blood vessel connecting the left pulmonary artery to the aorta) which failed to close at birth. In the course of the operation, the surgeon decided to have his surgical resident perform the actual surgery under his direct supervision. Serious complications occurred and a malpractice action was brought. The decision to delegate a key part of the operation to an assistant was severely criticized by the court, which held that the patient had the right to expect that the physician whose services she retained would actually perform the surgery.[61]

As for the patient, his or her principal obligation is to collaborate with the physician in order to contribute as much as possible to a successful treatment outcome. Accordingly, the patient must provide all pertinent information necessary in order to facilitate an accurate diagnosis, respect all directives and recommendations made by the physician,[62] and accept, if indicated, recourse to

---

positive.

[54]   *Code of Ethics of Physicians*, R.R.Q., c. M-9, r. 4.1, s. 23: the nature of the illness or for moral reasons, modification added to the Code in 1994.

[55]   *Comité-médecins-2*, [1988] D.D.C.P. 160, [1990] D.D.C.P. 334 (T.P.): refusal to treat a patient and her family by all physicians of a clinic for reasons of resentment.

[56]   R.S.Q., c. C-12, s. 2. This duty is imposed on all citizens. *Zuk v. Mihaly*, [1989] R.R.A. 737 (Que. S.C.).

[57]   R.S.Q., c. S-4.2, s. 7.

[58]   R.S.Q., c. L-0.2, s. 43.

[59]   R.R.Q., c. M-9, r. 4.1, s. 38.

[60]   Pauline Lesage-Jarjoura & Suzanne Philips-Nootens, *Éléments de responsabilité civile médicale — le droit dans le quotidien de la médecine*, 2nd ed. (Cowansville, QC: Éditions Yvon Blais, 2001) at 18 n. 21.

[61]   *Currie v. Blundell*, [1992] J.Q. No. 331, [1992] R.J.Q. 764 (Que. S.C.).

[62]   *St-Cyr v. Fisch*, [2003] J.Q. No. 4707 at para. 34, [2003] R.J.Q. 1582 at 1591 (Que. S.C.), affd on this point: [2005] J.Q. No. 9876 at para. 94, [2005] R.J.Q. 1944 at 1956 (Que. C.A.), leave to appeal to S.C.C. granted [2005] C.S.C.R. no. 430 (S.C.C.), notice of discontinuance filed September 1, 2006.

consultants or a transfer of his or her case to another doctor. The patient must also keep the physician informed of all developments and undertake appropriate initiatives indicated by circumstance and by common sense. As other scholars note, this duty of compliance imposed upon the patient devolves from that patient's right of autonomy.[63] In one instance, a 43-year-old pregnant woman refused to undergo genetic screening by amniocentesis as recommended by her physician and subsequently gave birth to a child with Down's Syndrome. In her suit, the patient was unable to prove that her obstetrician failed to properly advise her of this precaution. Indeed, the facts established quite the contrary. As a result, she had to assume, in the words of the court, the dramatic consequences of her own decision.[64] In cases of this nature, the suit is usually dismissed due to the fault of the "victim", provided of course that the physician has indeed been sufficiently clear and precise in fulfilling the duty to inform.

2. Extracontractual Relationship

Various circumstances can prevent a patient from contracting for medical care, such as unconsciousness following an accident, a preexisting state of incapacity, or sudden incapacity due to illness. Notwithstanding the absence of a contractual relationship, physicians on call and those who provide care in emergency situations do not have the right to withdraw from a case and must provide care even though no contractual relationship has been entered into.

If a capable patient, without having previously retained the services of a particular physician with admitting privileges, goes to a hospital to receive care, the patient is deemed to have contracted with the institution itself and not with any physician, nor indeed with the other members of staff who are called upon, under the terms of their employment, to actually provide the services offered by the hospital.[65] In such a case, the hospital would be obliged not only to provide

---

[63] Alain Bernardot & Robert P. Kouri, *La responsabilité civile médicale* (Sherbrooke, QC: Éditions Revue de Droit Université de Sherbrooke, 1980) at 221 n. 325.

[64] *Bouchard v. Villeneuve*, [1996] J.Q. No. 2288, [1996] R.J.Q. 1920 (Que. S.C.) (appeal rejected on motion). To the same effect, *Bergeron v. Faubert*, [1996] J.Q. No. 5469, [1996] R.R.A. 820 (Que. S.C.), affd [2000] J.Q. No. 6184 (Que. C.A.): a veterinarian who had surgery in both hands and who refused to follow orders concerning restrictions on the use of his hands.

[65] The so-called "hospital contract" in Quebec has undergone an evolution similar to that of the medical contract. See Paul-André Crépeau, *La responsabilité civile du médecin et de l'établissement hospitalier* (Montreal: Wilson & Lafleur Ltée, 1956); Paul-André Crépeau, "La responsabilité médicale et hospitalière dans la jurisprudence québécoise récente" (1960) 20 R. du B. 433; Jean-Louis Baudouin & Patrice Deslauriers, *La responsabilité civile*, 6th ed. (Cowansville, QC: Éditions Yvon Blais, 2003) at 998 and 999, nn. 1449-1450, at 1041 and 1043 n. 1514-1515. Certain writers have gone so far as to suggest that the obligations of a hospital can only be extracontractual in nature since hospitals cannot refuse to treat patients. See Andrée Lajoie, Patrick A. Molinari & Jean-Louis Baudouin, "Le droit aux services de santé: légal ou contractuel?" (1983) 43 R. du B. 675. *Contra*, Suzanne Nootens, "La remise en cause du contrat hospitalier" (1984) 44 R. du B. 625. Indeed, the ascendancy of the state over hospitals has increased dramatically and their autonomous status has in fact become somewhat more illusory. Formally, however, they remain distinct legal entities and as such are free to enter into contractual relationships with persons requiring their services, according to an opinion generally held until recently by the Quebec Court of Appeal. See *Houde v. Côté*, [1987] J.Q. No. 282,

hospital services but also medical care.[66] Should the patient suffer injury in the course of treatment, the hospital would be contractually liable for the fault of another, namely for those members of its staff who have been designated to fulfil its obligations.[67]

A fairly recent judgment of the Quebec Court of Appeal appears to dispute this approach. Justice Rochon held that a hospital could not undertake to provide actual medical services on the grounds that the administration of medical care, as opposed to hospital care, is the exclusive prerogative of health professionals.[68] A finding of this nature is very difficult if not impossible to justify, since the exclusion of the hospital's liability for errors in treatment would logically encompass *all* specialized professional acts (nursing, radiology, hemodynamics, physical therapy, *etc.*) performed within its walls.[69] It is hoped that the Court of Appeal will soon have occasion to reconsider its position on this point.

When a patient, due to his or her incapacity, is not able to actually contract with the hospital, the traditional approach to extracontractual responsibility would make the institution liable only for those persons considered its agents and servants according to art. 1463 of the *Civil Code of Quebec*. The requirement that there exist a master-servant relationship between the person at fault and the hospital renders somewhat problematic the potential liability of institutions for physicians practising within its walls, due precisely to the absence of a relationship of subordination or dependency between the hospital and doctors with hospital privileges in the exercise of their profession.[70] This difference in remedies afforded victims, which results from the distinction between contractual and extracontractual hospital liability, has caused some debate in legal writing.[71] Like others,[72] we are inclined to believe that the very

---

[1987] R.J.Q. 723 (Que. C.A.); *Lapointe v. Hôpital Le Gardeur*, [1989] J.Q. No. 1660, [1989] R.J.Q. 2619 (Que. C.A.). The Supreme Court did not express any opinion on this point since it decided there was no fault on the part of the physician: *Lapointe v. Hôpital Le Gardeur*, [1992] S.C.J. No. 11, [1992] S.C.R. 351 (S.C.C.). See also François Tôth, "Contrat hospitalier moderne et ressources limitées: conséquences sur la responsabilité civile" (1990) 20 R.D.U.S. 313.

[66]   In which case the physician-patient relationship is extracontractual. Pauline Lesage-Jarjoura & Suzanne Philips-Nootens, *Éléments de responsabilité civile médicale — le droit dans le quotidien de la médecine*, 2nd ed. (Cowansville, QC: Éditions Yvon Blais, 2001) at 31-32 n. 43-44.

[67]   Art. 1458 C.C.Q.

[68]   *Hôpital de l'Enfant-Jésus v. Camden-Bourgault*, [1996] J.Q. No. 4586, [1996] R.R.A. 809 (Que. S.C.), affd [2001] J.Q. No. 1325, [2001] R.J.Q. 832 (Que. C.A.). For a critique of this position see Robert P. Kouri, "L'arrêt Hôpit al de l'Enfant-Jésus c. Camden-Bourgault et le contrat hospitalier occulté: aventurisme ou évolution?" (2004) 35 R.D.U.S. 307.

[69]   François Tôth, "Contrat hospitalier moderne et ressources limitées: conséquences sur la responsabilité civile" (1990) 20 R.D.U.S. 313.

[70]   *Act Respecting Health Services and Social Services*, R.S.Q., c. S-4.2, s. 236, "A physician, dentist or midwife other than a member of the managerial staff of the instititution is deemed not to be a member of the staff of the institution".

[71]   See on this point Pauline Lesage-Jarjoura & Suzanne Philips-Nootens, *Éléments de responsabilité civile médicale — le droit dans le quotidien de la médecine*, 2nd ed. (Cowansville, QC: Éditions Yvon Blais, 2001) at 33 n. 44 and the authorities cited in footnote 121 of their text.

[72]   François Tôth, "Contrat hospitalier moderne et ressources limitées: conséquences sur la responsabilité civile" (1990) 20 R.D.U.S. 313. To the same effect: Jean-Louis Baudouin &

existence of a recourse in damages must not be subject to the vagaries of the juridical relationship binding the parties. Since hospitals have the legal obligation to provide health care, they must be held liable to the patient for the non-fulfilment of this duty through application of the *qui agit per alium agit per se* rule,[73] which does not rely on a master-servant relationship.

C. LIABILITY FOR THE ACT OF ANOTHER AND FOR THE MATERIAL UTILIZED

A physician may be held liable not only for his or her own fault but also for the acts of medical auxiliaries and for the material utilized. With regard to medical auxiliaries, two elements must be considered, namely the nature of the acts performed as well as the nature of the relationship between the physician and the patient. Nursing care and other so-called "hospital acts" fall under the authority of the institution. Medical acts, as defined in the *Medical Act*,[74] are reserved to physicians, although certain of them may be delegated under specific conditions to other care providers on staff.[75]

Medical residents, trainees, and interns are also viewed as agents or servants of the institution.[76] However, if they perform a medical act under the supervision or direction of a physician, the physician becomes liable to the patient for the acts so performed. In cases where there is a medical contract, it becomes a question of contractual liability for the act of another. A physician may have certain of his or her professional obligations fulfilled by another[77] (which often happens in a university hospital setting) provided of course certain precautions are taken. But the physician will consequently assume the risks resulting from the non-fulfillment of these obligations,[78] as occurred when a particular manipulation performed by a resident under supervision in order to close a *ductus arteriosus* ended disastrously.[79] In the absence of a contract with the patient, in order to apply art. 1463 of the *Civil Code of Quebec*, which establishes an absolute

---

Patrice Deslauriers, *La responsabilité civile*, 6th ed. (Cowansville: Éditions Yvon Blais, 2003) at 1043 n. 1516.

[73] Albert Mayrand, *Dictionnaire des maximes et locutions latines utilisées en droit*, 3rd ed. (Cowansville, QC: Éditions Yvon Blais, 1994) at 421: "He who acts through another acts for himself" (our translation). Paul-André Crépeau, "La responsabilité civile de l'établissement hospitalier en droit civil canadien" (1981) 26 McGill L.J. 673 at 733-734.

[74] R.S.Q., c. M-9, s. 31.

[75] *Regulation Respecting the Activities Contemplated in Section 31 of the Medical Act which May [Be] Engaged in by Classes of Persons Other than Physicians*, R.R.Q., c. M-9, r. 1.3.

[76] *Act Respecting Health Services and Social Services*, R.S.Q., c. S-4.2, s. 236. Jean-Pierre Ménard & Denise Martin, *La responsabilité médicale pour la faute d'autrui* (Cowansville, QC: Éditions Yvon Blais, 1992) at 85.

[77] *Murray-Vaillancourt v. Clairoux*, [1989] J.Q. No. 2524, [1989] R.R.A. 762 at 771 (Que. S.C.).

[78] Art. 1458 C.C.Q. Alain Bernardot & Robert P. Kouri, *La responsabilité civile médicale* (Sherbrooke, QC: Éditions Revue de Droit Université de Sherbrooke, 1980) at 342 and 344, notes 521 and 526; Suzanne Nootens, "La responsabilité civile du médecin anesthésiste", Part 2 (1989) 19 R.D.U.S. 317 at 373.

[79] *Currie v. Blundell*, [1992] J.Q. No. 331, [1992] R.J.Q. 764 (Que. S.C.). In this case, there was fault resulting from the decision to delegate itself.

presumption of liability against the principal for injury caused by an agent or servant in the performance of his or her duties, the medical auxiliary must indeed be under the physician's control. Control in this context implies the power to give orders and instructions on the manner of fulfilling the work assigned.

The liability of a physician for the act of another does not apply to fellow physicians when they are acting on an equal footing. Each must assume responsibility for his or her own acts according to an agreed-upon division of tasks (as occurs for example, between a surgeon and an anaesthetist).[80] Otherwise when acting in concert, they may all be held liable since, in the presence of common obligations, liability is solidary.[81]

The Code does not specifically address liability resulting from harm caused by the material or products utilized in treatment and thus this is left to the general rules of contract. If there is no contract between the parties, art. 1465 C.C.Q. provides for the extracontractual liability of the person having custody of a thing for damages resulting from its autonomous act. In the hospital environment, the institution is generally responsible for the condition and the good working order of appliances and devices. The physician may, however, be answerable for harm resulting from the inadequate supervision or improper operation of certain equipment. In private clinics on the other hand, the physicians assume full liability for any injury caused by their equipment.[82]

Having reviewed the general rules governing civil liability, we now turn to the principal duties of physicians.

III. THE DUTY TO INFORM AND TO OBTAIN CONSENT

The fundamental goal of the duty to inform is to ensure respect of the patient's right to autonomy, expressed through the patient's free and informed consent, always bearing in mind that consent is an ongoing process rather than a simple formality or a signature on a consent form. However, overwhelming the patient with a plethora of detail in the name of providing full information can be as inimical to patients' rights as untoward reticence. Ideally, the information provided must suffice in order to enable a person to make the best decision possible. In reality, it must provide the means for the patient to arrive at a decision which may or may not necessarily be reasonable, but will at least be enlightened.[83]

---

[80] Pauline Lesage-Jarjoura & Suzanne Philips-Nootens, *Éléments de responsabilité civile médicale, le droit dans le quotidien de la médecine*, 2nd ed. (Cowansville, QC: Éditions Yvon Blais, 2001) at 113 to 115 nn. 154 to 156.

[81] Art. 1523 C.C.Q. Jean-Louis Baudouin & Patrice Deslauriers, *La responsabilité civile*, 6th ed. (Cowansville, QC: Éditions Yvon Blais, 2003) at 912 n. 1362. In *Marcoux v. Bouchard*, both surgeons were exonerated: [2001] S.C.J. No. 51, [2001] 2 S.C.R. 726, affg [1999] J.Q. No. 3055, [1999] R.R.A. 447 (Que. C.A.), affg [1995] J.Q. No. 2325, [1995] R.R.A. 1149 (Que. S.C.).

[82] Pauline Lesage-Jarjoura & Suzanne Philips-Nootens, *Éléments de responsabilité civile médicale — le droit dans le quotidien de la médecine*, 2nd ed. (Cowansville, QC: Éditions Yvon Blais, 2001) at 121ff., nn. 167ff.

[83] Alain Bernardot & Robert P. Kouri, *La responsabilité civile médicale* (Sherbrooke: Éditions

Arriving at informed consent is a two-stage process: informing the patient and then getting consent.

A. THE DUTY TO INFORM

Generally speaking, the duty to inform exists towards the patient and not towards others unless, of course, they represent the patient or are authorized to decide on the patient's behalf. In other words, information is provided to the person to whom the treatment decision devolves. In practice, this means to a capable adult, or to a minor patient directly in the case of a minor 14 years of age or more when the care is required by the minor patient's state of health.[84] For adults incapable of giving consent, information is given to the lawfully appointed representative of the patient, who may be, under Quebec law, a mandatary, tutor or curator. If a patient lacks formal representation, information is provided to the married, civil union or *de facto* spouse, to a close relative or to a person who shows a special interest in the patient.[85] For minors under 14 years of age, the person having parental authority or the tutor must be informed.[86]

The Quebec *Code of Ethics of Physicians* specifically provides that a physician cannot reveal a serious prognosis to the family without the consent of the patient unless there is "just cause".[87] Consultation with the family is advised but is not a duty.[88] There is no obligation to arrive at a consensus amongst the relatives with regard to therapeutic choice.

The duty to inform rests upon the person who will carry out the diagnostic test or treatment.[89] The treating physician will be held liable for having failed to inform if he or she erroneously takes for granted that information was provided by someone else such as the referring physician, a nurse or an assistant. Nevertheless, the courts have held that a physician is not liable if the patient has indeed been adequately informed through some other source.[90]

In advising the patient, the physician must impart technical knowledge of a medical nature to a person often lacking a scientific background. For this reason, a reductionist approach usually becomes necessary; the information should be presented in simple and clear terms best adapted to the patient's level of comprehension[91] and not, we submit, to the standard of the reasonable

Revue de Droit Université de Sherbrooke, 1980) at 117 n. 172.

[84] Arts. 11 and 14 para. 2 C.C.Q. See also *Labbé v. Laroche*, [2000] J.Q. No. 5652, [2001] R.R.A. 184 (Que. S.C.), in which the information was provided to a minor aged 14 years and two months, as well as to the Youth Protection authorities who had custody of the minor.

[85] Art. 15 C.C.Q.

[86] Art. 14, para. 1 C.C.Q.

[87] *Code of Ethics of Physicians*, R.R.Q., c. M-9, r. 4.1, s. 20(5).

[88] Alain Bernardot & Robert P. Kouri, *La responsabilité civile médicale* (Sherbrooke, QC: Éditions Revue de Droit Université de Sherbrooke, 1980) at 132 n. 198.

[89] *Lamarre v. Hôpital du Sacré-Coeur*, [1996] J.Q. No. 663, [1996] R.R.A. 496 (Que. S.C.); *Chartier v. Sauvé*, [1997] J.Q. No. 258, [1997] R.R.A. 213 at 215 (Que. S.C.); *Currie v. Blundell*, [1992] J.Q. No. 331, [1992] R.J.Q. 764 at 775 (Que. S.C.).

[90] *Mainville v. Hôpital Général de Montréal*, [1992] R.R.A. 579 (Que. S.C.).

[91] *Morrow v. Royal Victoria Hospital*, [1972] C.S. 549 (Que. S.C.), affd [1989] J.Q. No. 2239, [1990] R.R.A. 41 (Que. C.A.); *Dunant v. Chong*, [1985] J.Q. No. 523, [1986] R.R.A. 2 (Que.

patient as proposed by the Supreme Court in *Reibl v. Hughes*[92] and *Hopp v. Lepp.*[93] Although physicians enjoy a certain latitude in communicating information, this flexibility relates to the terminology utilized and the mode of presentation rather than to the actual content. Indeed, language barriers[94] or a physical impairment such as deafness[95] could require adjustments in the manner of communicating information, but would not excuse dispensing with the duty to inform. As will be explained below, due to jurisprudence since *Reibl* and *Hopp*, the general tendency is toward offering more complete information in order to ensure respect for the patient's rights. The specific manner in which information is provided is left to the discretion of the physician although in most cases, it will be verbal. The use of information sheets, pamphlets, video cassettes or other such means, while valid, cannot, in all cases, suffice in fulfilling the duty to inform since the information to be imparted must be adapted to each particular patient and he or she must be afforded the opportunity to raise and obtain responses to questions. Moreover, the duty to inform goes beyond merely presenting information in an objective, dispassionate manner. The physician has an affirmative duty to advise or counsel[96] even though the Quebec *Code of Ethics of Physicians*[97] is silent on this point. Since the physician-patient relationship is based on confidence,[98] loyalty and trust,[99] advising the patient to opt for a particular alternative or expressing a bias in favour of a particular treatment choice is acceptable provided the physician is motivated solely by the patient's best interests.

1. Content of the Duty to Inform

The *Civil Code of Quebec* speaks of "care" in the broadest sense at art. 11; care includes "examinations, specimen taking, removal of tissue, treatment or any other act". It would appear that care encompasses not only situations where the care is absolutely necessary for the health of the person but also those cases where the care would be conducive to improving well-being, avoiding health deterioration or providing comfort and relief from pain and suffering. In establishing specific rules governing consent, certain nuances are, however,

C.A.).
[92] [1980] S.C.J. No. 105, [1980] 2 S.C.R. 880 (S.C.C.).
[93] [1980] S.C.J. No. 57, [1980] 2 S.C.R. 192 (S.C.C.). See *Dodds v. Schierz*, [1986] J.Q. No. 1801, [1986] R.J.Q. 2623 at 2630 (C.A.) (opinion of Monet J.); *Chouinard v. Landry*, [1987] J.Q. No. 1625 at paras. 97, 98, [1987] R.J.Q. 1954 at 1968, 1969 (Que. C.A.) (opinion of LeBel J.), leave to appeal to S.C.C. refused [1988] C.S.C.R. no. 15, [1988] 1 S.C.R. vii.
[94] *Ciarlariello v. Schacter*, [1993] S.C.J. No. 46 at para. 54, [1993] 2 S.C.R. 119 at 140 (S.C.C.).
[95] *Eldridge v. British Columbia (Attorney General)*, [1997] S.C.J. No. 86 at para. 55, [1997] 3 S.C.R. 624 at 677 (S.C.C.).
[96] *Bolduc v. Lessard*, [1989] J.Q. No. 737 at para. 85, [1989] R.R.A. 350 at 358 (Que. S.C.), affd [1993] J.Q. No. 605, [1993] R.R.A. 291 (Que. C.A.); *Lauzon v. Taillefer*, [1991] R.R.A. 62 at 72 (Que. S.C.).
[97] R.R.Q., c. M-9, r. 4.1.
[98] *Johnson v. Harris*, [1990] J.Q. No. 1467 at para. 75, [1990] R.R.A. 832 at 841 (Que. S.C.).
[99] *Bolduc v. Lessard*, [1989] J.Q. No. 737 at para. 88, [1989] R.R.A. 350 at 358 (Que. S.C.), affd [1993] J.Q. No. 605, [1993] R.R.A. 291 (Que. C.A.).

introduced by the *Civil Code of Quebec* in that it distinguishes "care required by the state of health" from "care not required by the state of health".[100]

This fundamental distinction set out in the *Civil Code of Quebec* has significant consequences for both the extent of the duty to inform and the capacity to consent.

(a) Care Required by One's State of Health

As a general rule, the following elements are relevant to fulfilling the duty to inform.

(i) The Diagnosis

Before being advised of the various therapeutic options available, the patient must be made aware of his or her affliction or illness. In order to arrive at a proper diagnosis, it may be necessary to perform certain invasive or risky diagnostic procedures. Each such procedure, which otherwise could constitute an infringement of one's integrity, has to be the object of specific consent based upon adequate information.

The failure to reveal a diagnosis can prevent a patient from pursuing appropriate treatment. In *Laferrière v. Lawson*,[101] the Supreme Court awarded damages resulting from a surgeon's failure to inform his patient that the lump he had removed from her breast was cancerous. Even though, according to expert testimony, the patient was unlikely to survive her illness, her estate was indemnified for the psychological distress suffered resulting from the fact that she was unaware of her true situation and thus deprived of the possibility of pursuing active treatment in the hope of obtaining a remission. However, the court refused to grant damages for the "loss of a chance" of recovery since the causal relationship between the physician's fault and the patient's death could not be established by a preponderance of the evidence.

(ii) The Nature of the Treatment Proposed and Its Chances of Success

The physician must reveal the type of treatment recommended, its necessity and its intended result. In order to be properly informed of the outcome of an intervention, the patient should be advised of the chances of success or failure,[102] and made aware of the repercussions of a negative outcome.[103] It is reasonable that the chances of success be revealed since only the individual concerned can truly decide whether the degree of risk of failure is worth authorizing an intrusion upon his or her integrity. When a physician glosses over the possibility of failure of a medical act or projects an exaggerated sense of optimism

---

[100] See, for example, arts. 13 to 18 C.C.Q.

[101] [1991] S.C.J. No. 18, [1991] 1 S.C.R. 541 (S.C.C.), modifying [1988] J.Q. No. 2245, [1989] R.J.Q. 27 (Que. C.A.).

[102] *Faucher-Grenier v. Laurence*, [1987] R.J.Q. 1109 at 1114 (Que. S.C.) (concerning the success rate of tubal ligations).

[103] Jean-Louis Baudouin & Patrice Deslauriers, *La responsabilité civile*, 6th ed. (Cowansville, QC: Éditions Yvon Blais, 2003) at 1014 n. 1471.

unrepresentative of the true situation, the risks which are normally borne by a sufficiently enlightened patient will be assumed by the health professional. Indeed, in *Fiset v. St-Hilaire*,[104] a surgeon who assured his patient suffering from Madelung's disease that surgery would certainly improve her condition, was held liable in damages even without proof of any fault in the performance of the surgery. Because the surgeon promised an improvement, his obligation of diligence or of means in treating the patient became an obligation of result.[105]

(iii) The Risks of Treatment

In *Hopp v. Lepp*[106] and *Reibl v. Hughes*,[107] the Supreme Court affirmed that one must disclose to the patient the gravity of the operation and any material, special and unusual risks attendant upon its performance. It also underlined in *Reibl*[108] that "... if a certain risk is a mere possibility which ordinarily need not be disclosed, yet if its occurrence carries serious consequences, as for example, paralysis or even death, it should be regarded as a material risk requiring disclosure".

On this question of risk, Baudouin J., concurring with the majority of the Court of Appeal panel in *Drolet v. Parenteau*,[109] expressed the opinion that one had to take into account two factors in evaluating the hazards of treatment: the probability of the hazard occurring, and the severity of the injury if it occurs.

In setting out a standard to be applied in relation to probability, one writer, M.A. Somerville, has proposed a fixed percentage:

> ... [It] is suggested that any risk greater than one percent probability of causing irreversible morbidity should be disclosed. Risks of death with a lesser probability of occurring should also be disclosed, but for this most serious risk, it is difficult to state a minimum level.[110]

At first glance, this approach appears not to have received the endorsement of the courts in Quebec and indeed, on occasion, has been formally disavowed. For example, Baudouin J. stated in *Drolet v. Parenteau*:[111]

> I do not think, however, that in a purely abstract, one could even say arbitrary manner, it is possible to decide mathematically and state for example that a risk of 1%, of 0.04% or of 0.001% is negligible and that its divulgation can be systematically avoided.[112]

---

[104] [1976] C.S. 994 (Que. S.C.).
[105] See also *Gingues v. Asselin*, [1990] J.Q. No. 731 at para. 52, [1990] R.R.A. 630 at 636 (Que. S.C.).
[106] [1980] S.C.J. No. 57, [1980] 2 S.C.R. 192 at 210 (S.C.C.).
[107] [1980] S.C.J. No. 105, [1980] 2 S.C.R. 880 at 884-85 (S.C.C.).
[108] *Ibid.*
[109] [1994] J.Q. No. 167, [1994] R.J.Q. 689 (C.A.), revg in part [1991] J.Q. No. 2583, [1991] R.J.Q. 2956 (Que. S.C.).
[110] Margaret A. Somerville, "Structuring the Issues in Informed Consent" (1981) 26 McGill L.J. 740 at 757.
[111] [1994] J.Q. No. 167, [1994] R.J.Q. 689 (Que. C.A.), revg in part [1991] R.J.Q. 2956 (Que. S.C.).
[112] *Drolet v. Parenteau*, [1994] J.Q. No. 167 at para. 71, [1994] R.J.Q. 689 at 706 (Que. C.A.) (our translation).

However, notwithstanding Baudouin J.'s rejection of a single standard, an examination of Quebec jurisprudence indicates a clear inclination on the part of the courts to retain one per cent of probability of risk as a benchmark, at least in cases of therapeutic treatment.[113]

It is worth noting that the duty to inform relates not only to "... immediate risks linked to the intervention itself, but also to potential consequences which may manifest themselves during the post-operative phase or even beyond".[114] In addition, the extent of the duty to inform will vary according to the nature of care required by the patient's state of health.

An intervention or treatment can also affect certain functions such as a person's mobility, ability to pursue various activities, and even comfort. The importance or gravity of this type of risk will vary according to the particular circumstances of each patient.[115]

(iv) Therapeutic Alternatives

When there exists a choice between various therapeutic approaches, the physician must indicate the alternatives available and set out the risks and advantages of each.[116] In accordance with this principle, the Supreme Court in *McCormick v. Marcotte*[117] held a physician liable for failing to reveal the advantages and disadvantages of two methods for reducing a fracture, especially since he refused to utilize the method recommended by a specialist called in for consultation.[118]

The patient must also be informed of the consequences should the proposed treatments be refused, even when the patient is asymptomatic and the operation is not urgent.[119] Each individual is certainly free to decline treatment, but he or she must be apprised of all pertinent facts.

(v) Answer Questions

The duty of responding to specific questions raised by the patient has been upheld by the Supreme Court in *Hopp v. Lepp*.[120] A patient's questions can signify that he or she has misunderstood the information received, or that he or she would like additional information concerning certain aspects of treatment

---

[113] Robert P. Kouri & Suzanne Philips-Nootens, *L'intégrité de la personne et le consentement aux soins,* 2nd ed. (Cowansville, QC: Éditions Yvon Blais, 2005) at 292-93 n. 315 and cases cited.

[114] *Drolet v. Parenteau*, [1994] J.Q. No. 167 at para. 70, [1994] R.J.Q. 689 at 706 (Que. C.A.) (our translation).

[115] The case of *Binette v. Éthier*, J.E. 79-972 (Que. S.C.) is a striking example of this.

[116] *Chouinard v. Landry*, [1987] J.Q. No. 1625 at para. 101, [1987] R.J.Q. 1954 at 1969 (Que. C.A.) (LeBel J.), leave to appeal to S.C.C. refused [1988] C.S.C.R. No. 15, [1988] 1 S.C.R. vii (S.C.C.).

[117] [1972] S.C.J. No. 83, [1972] S.C.R. 18 (S.C.C.), affg [1969] B.R. 454 (Que. C.A.).

[118] See also *Tremblay v. Boyer*, [1977] C.S. 622 (Que. S.C.) (concerning treatment choice involving breast implants); *Sunne v. Shaw*, [1981] C.S. 609 (Que. S.C.) (failure to advise patient of a more conservative course of action to treat a malocclusion); *O'Shea v. McGovern*, [1989] R.R.A. 341 at 345-46 (Que. S.C.), affd [1994] Q.J. No. 601, [1994] R.R.A. 672 (Que. C.A.) (surgical removal of a portion of the colon rather than merely removing a rectal polyp).

[119] *Currie v. Blundell*, [1992] J.Q. No. 331, [1992] R.J.Q. 764 (Que. S.C.).

[120] [1980] S.C.J. No. 57, [1980] 2 S.C.R. 192 at 210 (S.C.C.).

which would not normally require revelation or elucidation. In the first case, a lack of comprehension could indicate a need for the physician to better adapt the description of particular aspects of the proposed intervention to the patient's powers of comprehension. In the second case, by expressing a greater need for information, the patient is in fact unilaterally extending or expanding the physician's duty to inform since the mere fact of raising a question creates a correlative duty to adequately respond to it.[121]

It should be noted that failing to raise questions or to query aspects of treatment which should have been revealed spontaneously by the physician does not constitute an implicit renunciation by the patient to the right to information regarding these points.

(vi) The Behaviour Expected of the Patient

The patient must often play an active role in his or her treatment. This may require performing specific acts or avoiding certain behaviours. The physician must take the initiative and indicate to the patient the manner in which he or she must collaborate during treatment and convalescence. The patient should also be made aware of certain signs or symptoms which may signal a complication or aggravation of the condition for which treatment has been administered.[122] The average patient cannot be presumed to possess this type of knowledge and must be advised accordingly.

Once he or she has been properly informed, the non-compliance of the patient can be then be raised as a defence to a malpractice action, as occurred in the case of *Dame Cimon v. Carbotte*.[123] Complaining of a mass in her breast, the patient was diagnosed as suffering from breast dysplasia. As a precaution, her physician taught the patient how to perform a breast self-examination and advised her to return immediately should she detect any change. About one year later, another physician discovered that the breast tumour was now cancerous, and a mastectomy had to be performed. In answer to her suit alleging an error in diagnosis, the defendant successfully argued that she had failed to follow his instructions to monitor the state of her breast and to advise him of any changes.

(b) Care Not Required by the Patient's State of Health

Although not intended to improve one's health or ensure one's comfort, the care to which reference is made under this heading nonetheless relates to treatment administered in the interest of the patient. Quebec jurisprudence appears to establish a significantly higher standard when the treatment is non-therapeutic and elective as opposed to therapeutically indicated. As Crépeau J. stated in *Kimmis-Patterson v. Rubinovich*,[124] in matters of non-therapeutic surgery, the duty of divulging risks is comprehensive whereas in cases of necessary surgery,

---

[121] Margaret A. Somerville, "Structuring the Issues in Informed Consent" (1981) 26 McGill L.J. 740 at 774.

[122] *Drolet v. Parenteau*, [1994] J.Q. No. 167 at para. 75, [1994] R.J.Q. 689 at 707 (Que. C.A.).

[123] [1971] C.S. 622 (Que. S.C.).

[124] [1996] J.Q. No. 5470, [1996] R.R.A. 1123 at 1129 (Que. S.C.), revd on other grounds [1999] J.Q. No. 5574, [2000] R.R.A. 26 (Que. C.A.).

only serious, normally foreseeable risks must be revealed to the patient. The most obvious examples include cosmetic surgery and sterilizations for purely contraceptive purposes.[125] The opinion of Rothman J. in *Hamelin-Hankins v. Papillon*,[126] involving dermabrasion to eliminate hyperpigmentation of the skin, accurately reflects the attitude of the courts in situations of this type:

> In cases of plastic surgery, however, where the decision to be made by the patient is more subjective and personal than therapeutic, I believe the doctor has a duty to be especially careful to disclose completely all material risks and, certainly, any special risks, as well as the consequences for the patient should such risks materialize. In matters of this kind, there is normally no urgency, the relevant problems can be explained to the patient, and the patient can weigh the medical risks against his own non-medical desires and priorities. Since there is no therapeutic need for the operation, a patient might well decide that he would prefer to live with a blemish rather than take the risk.[127]

Justice Vallerand in *Dulude v. Gaudette*[128] is even more categorical. In matters relating to plastic surgery, he feels that the physician has the duty to "reveal all risks inherent in this type of undertaking, without any reservations."[129]

The potential *sequelae* of treatment may be temporary or permanent and the patient must be so informed.[130] For instance, a physician was found liable when a young female patient was not informed that injections to treat alopecia carried a foreseeable risk of provoking the growth of facial hair.[131] Likewise in *Blais v. Dion*,[132] a surgeon performing a facelift failed to inform the patient that there could be scarring, and was obliged to pay damages when, in fact, scars remained.

2. Exceptions or Limitations to the Duty to Inform

A physician's duty to inform is attenuated when therapeutic privilege can be invoked or when, under certain circumstances, a state of emergency exists. The duty to inform is obviated when the patient renounces his or her right to information.

[125] *Stevens v. Ackman*, [1989] R.R.A. 109 at 110 (Que. S.C.) (dealing with the risks of a vasectomy). For the purposes of this discussion, we exclude altruistic medical acts such as the gift of organs and tissue for purposes of transplantation, as well as participation in experimentation as a research subject.
[126] [1980] C.S. 879 (Que. S.C.).
[127] *Hamelin-Hankins v. Papillon*, [1980] C.S. 879 at 881 (Que. S.C.).
[128] [1974] C.S. 618 at 621 (Que. S.C.).
[129] *Ibid.*
[130] Jean-Louis Baudouin & Patrice Deslauriers, *La responsabilité civile*, 6th ed. (Cowansville, QC: Éditions Yvon Blais, 2003) at 1015 n. 1472.
[131] *Binette v. Éthier*, J.E. 79-972 (Que. S.C.).
[132] J.E. 85-934 (Que. S.C.).

Canadian Health Law and Policy

(a) Therapeutic Privilege

In addition to the possibility of concealing "a fatal or grave prognosis" from a patient, as provided for by the Code of Ethics of Physicians,[133] Quebec jurisprudence[134] has generally recognized the right of a physician to downplay or even gloss over certain truths which, in the opinion of a reasonable physician, could have a significant adverse physical or psychological effect on the patient.

Despite these clear authorities acknowledging its acceptance, the principle of therapeutic privilege is not totally devoid of controversy. For instance, if the patient asked specific questions concerning risks which, under normal circumstances, a physician would be entitled to conceal, would the privilege lapse? The Court of Appeal in O'Hearn v. Estrada[135] appears to suggest that if a patient so requested, an obligation to be completely candid would exist and he or she would assume the consequences of being told the unvarnished truth.

(b) Emergency Situations

The Civil Code of Quebec provides that consent to medical care is not required in cases of emergency when it cannot be obtained in due time.[136] Consequently the duty to inform may be similarly set aside. In Boyer v. Grignon,[137] the surgeon was exonerated for having operated on a patient suffering from an aortic aneurism that was discovered during surgery originally intended to remove what was thought to be a benign tumour. Given the gravity of the situation, it was decided that since the patient's life was in danger, the surgeon was not bound to inform him of the risk of losing his voice as a result of the operation.

In different situations, and while not eliminating it entirely, an emergency may limit the extent of the duty to inform where certain constraints such as insufficient time do not allow all pertinent information to be provided to the patient.[138]

---

[133] R.R.Q., c. M-9, r. 4.1, s. 57.

[134] Brunelle v. Sirois, [1974] C.S. 105 (Que. S.C.), revd [1975] C.A. 779 (Que. C.A.), involved a patient having to undergo bilateral cerebral arteriography because of a suspected aneurysm. The patient was not advised of the risk of loss of vision which could result from the arteriography because this information would have increased his blood pressure, thus aggravating the risk of rupturing the aneurysm. In Dunant v. Chong, [1985] J.Q. No. 523, [1986] R.R.A. 2 (summary) (Que. C.A.), the patient became blind as a result of an operation for the removal of a brain tumour. The Court of Appeal approved the trial judge's finding that the surgeon had acted properly in not informing the patient of this risk since it would have provoked a state of anguish or distress which would have compromised the outcome of the operation. For a detailed description of the conditions for invoking therapeutic privilege, see Pauline Lesage-Jarjoura & Suzanne Philips-Nootens, Élements de responsabilité civile médicale — le droit dans le quotidien de la médecine, 2nd ed. (Cowansville, QC: Éditions Yvon Blais, 2001) at 156 n. 201.

[135] [1984] J.Q. No. 533, J.E. 84-449 at 16 (Que. C.A.).

[136] Art. 13 C.C.Q.

[137] [1988] J.Q. No. 327, [1988] R.J.Q. 829 (Que. S.C.).

[138] Jean-Louis Baudouin & Patrice Deslauriers, La responsabilité civile, 6th ed. (Cowansville, QC: Éditions Yvon Blais, 2003) at 1017 n. 1474.

(c) Renunciation of the Right to Information

It may occur that the patient will express a refusal to be informed of the particulars concerning treatment. In this eventuality, it is logical to state that obtaining a consent that is truly informed would be highly unlikely given the state of ignorance in which the patient has willingly placed himself or herself. This raises the question of whether a patient can indeed renounce so fundamental a right when the repercussions for one's integrity could be far from negligible. Would such a renunciation be contrary to public order?

In an *obiter* relating to therapeutic care, the Supreme Court in *Reibl v. Hughes*[139] affirmed that:

> It is, of course, possible that a particular patient may waive aside any question of risks and be quite prepared to submit to the surgery or treatment, whatever they be. Such a situation presents no difficulty.

In matters of care not required by the state of health,[140] opinions are not as clear; most writers favour that there can be no waiver of this right.[141] Unfortunately, these writers do not explain why one cannot renounce the right to information.

One should not lose sight of the fact that the rule of inviolability requires that any interference with a person's integrity must be authorized by law or consented to by the individual involved.[142] In all logic, there is no reason for the validity of a waiver of the right to information to depend on the purpose of the act to be performed; a renunciation is either valid or invalid. Obviously, consent to any medical act can be enlightened only if the person involved has been provided with or possesses adequate information. Yet while informing the patient is a duty imposed upon the physician, receiving the information is not an obligation on the part of the patient — it is a right intended for his or her protection. Why then could not the subject forgo this right? If the law permits a person to renounce his or her inviolability, it would seem coherent to conclude that the right to information should be governed by the same considerations.

B. THE DUTY TO OBTAIN CONSENT

According to the *Private Law Dictionary and Bilingual Lexicons — Obligations*,[143] consent is the "assent of a person to an act that another cannot accom-

---

[139] [1980] S.C.J. No. 105, [1980] 2 S.C.R. 880 at 895 (S.C.C.).

[140] This term, which is used in the *Civil Code of Quebec*, refers to non-therapeutic care and should not be confused with elective treatment or surgery. Elective treatment is not essential and is intended to correct a non life-threatening condition.

[141] Margaret A. Somerville, "Structuring the Issues in Informed Consent" (1981) 26 McGill L.J. 740 at 773; Pauline Lesage-Jarjoura & Suzanne Philips-Nootens, *Éléments de responsabilité civile médicale — le droit dans le quotidien de la médecine*, 2nd ed. (Cowansville, QC: Éditions Yvon Blais, 2001) at 155 n. 200; Louise Potvin, *L'obligation de renseignement du médecin* (Cowansville, QC: Éditions Yvon Blais, 1984) at 72.

[142] Art. 10 C.C.Q.

[143] *Private Law Dictionary and Bilingual Lexicons — Obligations* (Cowansville, QC: Éditions Yvon Blais, 2003) at 56.

plish without this formality". The requirement acknowledges the fact that a capable person remains the best judge of his or her interests.

As a matter of law, one must distinguish consent required for entering into a medical contract from consent which must be given prior to each medical act other than routine care in the context of a medical contract that has already been formed. The failure to consent to a contract of care places the question of liability within the realm of extracontractual responsibility. But once a medical contract has been validly entered into, any unauthorized medical intervention constitutes a violation of this contract and any resulting liability will lie in contract.

As to the modalities of consent, it may be given either expressly or tacitly. Except for anaesthesia, medical interventions and other treatment provided in an establishment governed by the *Act Respecting Health Services and Social Services*,[144] care not required by the patient's state of health, the alienation of a part of one's body, or participation in an experiment,[145] there is no formal requirement that consent be provided in writing. Although consent is often given verbally, there is no bar to consent by gesture or sign of assent. However, Quebec courts have held that the burden of proving lack of consent rests on the plaintiff.[146]

1. The Principle of Consent

Article 10 of the *Civil Code of Quebec* enunciates two principles, the first reiterating the rule of inviolability, and the second affirming that any interference with a person can take place only with the free and enlightened consent of that person unless otherwise authorized by law. In order to be valid, consent must be provided by an informed person having the capacity to act and who, in fact, is acting freely and without constraint.

The Code clearly distinguishes between incapacity as it relates to the legal status of a person requiring protection and the situation of an individual who is *de facto* incapable of providing consent. Capacity is a juridical notion which describes the faculty of enjoying and of exercising rights.[147] Inaptitude to consent may exist independently of the institution of protective supervision, just as a person under protective supervision due to insanity may be considered factually capable during an interval of lucidity.[148] As Baudouin J. has had occasion to

---

[144] R.S.Q., c. S-4.2. According to s. 79 of the legislation, these establishments would include local community service centres, hospital centres, child and youth protection centres, residential and long-term care centres, and rehabilitation centres.

[145] Art. 24 C.C.Q.

[146] *Chouinard v. Landry*, [1987] J.Q. No. 1625 at para. 49, [1987] R.J.Q. 1954 at 1962 (Que. C.A.); *Dulude v. Gaudette*, [1974] C.S. 618 at 622 (Que. S.C.).

[147] Jean Pineau, Danielle Burman & Serge Gaudet, *Théorie des obligations*, 4th ed. (Montreal: Éditions Thémis, 2001) at 228, n. 108.

[148] See the decision of LeBel J. in *Institut Philippe-Pinel de Montréal v. Blais*, [1991] R.J.Q. 1969 at 1973 (Que. S.C.): "Capacity to consent to or to refuse treatment is not evaluated in light of the situation of the individual but according to his or her decisional autonomy and capacity to comprehend and appreciate the issues involved" (our translation).

point out, "the mere fact that a person is under protective supervision does not create a presumption of inaptitude to consent to medical care".[149]

Quebec legislation does not define the notion of incapacity (in French "inaptitude"), nor does it set out criteria for determining whether a person is incapable of giving consent. Article 258 of the *Civil Code of Quebec* does, however, describe a number of situations in which inaptitude could be encountered, such as "illness, deficiency or debility due to age which impairs the person's mental faculties or physical ability to express his or her will".

Due to the silence of the law, Quebec courts have had to develop criteria to be applied in determining incompetency. In the case of *Institut Philippe-Pinel de Montréal v. Blais*[150] involving a mental patient's refusal of treatment, Le Bel J. proposed that due to their persuasiveness, the standards established by the *Hospitals Act*[151] of Nova Scotia be retained as guidelines.[152] This approach has since been confirmed by subsequent jurisprudence.[153]

In situations where the patient is incapable of giving or refusing consent to care, consent must be provided by someone authorized by law to act on his or her behalf.[154] When acting for another, the person so authorized "is bound to act in the sole interest of that person, taking into account, as far as possible, any wishes the latter may have expressed".[155] Moreover, if the person authorized indeed gives consent, he or she must "ensure that the care is beneficial notwithstanding the gravity and permanence of certain of its effects, that it is advisable in the circumstances and that the risks incurred are not disproportionate to the anticipated benefit".[156]

In keeping with the categories set out in the *Civil Code of Quebec*, our examination of the law of consent will deal first with care required by the state of health and second with non-therapeutic care,[157] examining in each case the situation of adults who are incapable of consenting and that of minors.

---

[149] *W. (J.M.) v. W. (S.C.)*, [1996] J.Q. No. 65 at para. 40, [1996] R.J.Q. 229 at 235 (Que. C.A.) (our translation).

[150] [1991] R.J.Q. 1969 (Que. S.C.).

[151] R.S.N.S. 1989, c. 208, s. 52(2).

[152] According to these criteria, one must determine whether the person "(a) understands the condition for which treatment is proposed; (b) understands the nature and purpose of the treatment; (c) understands the risks involved in undergoing the treatment; (d) understands the risks involved in not undergoing the treatment; and (e) whether or not his ability to consent is affected by his condition" (*Institut Philippe-Pinel de Montréal v. Blais*, [1991] R.J.Q. 1969 at 1974 (Que. S.C.)).

[153] *Hôpital Charles-Lemoyne v. Forcier*, [1992] R.D.F. 257 (Que. S.C.); *Institut Philippe-Pinel de Montréal v. G. (A.)*, [1994] J.Q. No. 837 at para. 72, [1994] R.J.Q. 2523 at 2534 (Que. C.A.).

[154] Art. 11 C.C.Q.

[155] Art. 12, para. 1 C.C.Q.

[156] Art. 12, para. 2 C.C.Q.

[157] We will not discuss experimentation nor the gift of organs and tissue since certain of these questions are dealt with in other parts of this book.

(a) Consent to Care Required by the State of Health of the Person

(i) Adults Incapable of Consenting

The incapable adult does not lose the enjoyment of his or her rights, but merely the exercise of them. A person's incapacity must not serve as a pretext to deny fundamental rights, which explains why legislation grants certain powers to legal representatives or, in specified cases, to persons in the patient's circle of friends or family to provide consent. For medical care in particular, the *Civil Code of Quebec* stipulates:

> [Consent] is given by his or her mandatary, tutor or curator. If the person of full age is not so represented, consent is given by his or her married, civil union or *de facto* spouse or, if the person has no spouse or his or her spouse is prevented from giving consent, it is given by a close relative or a person who shows a special interest in the person of full age.[158]

In the absence of a legal representative, one must follow the order set out in the Code. Although this hierarchy seems relatively simple, the reality of human relationships can complicate the choice of the person authorized to consent. It is surprising to note, for instance, the lack of specific rules of antecedence between the various close relatives or between close relatives and a person showing a special interest in the incapable person. Even the expression "special interest" remains fairly vague and would appear to include a close friend, a *de facto* custodian of the patient, an in-law, a spiritual advisor, *etc.*

In certain situations involving incapable adults, it may be necessary to have recourse to the court. Specifically provided for in art. 16 of the Code, three sets of circumstances render judicial intervention obligatory when the care involved is required by the person's state of health: when the person who may consent on behalf of the incapable adult is prevented from doing so, when he or she unjustifiably refuses to give consent, or when the patient "categorically refuses to receive care, except in the case of hygienic care or emergency".[159] Paradoxically, art. 23, para. 2 requires that the refusal of the person concerned be respected "unless the care is required by his state of health". Thus, recourse to the court in this type of situation must be viewed as a form of verification that the care is indeed required for the patient because once this condition is met, the authorization of the court must be given. In practice, authorizations of this nature have usually involved the administration of antipsychotic medication to mental patients.[160]

---

[158] Art. 15 C.C.Q.

[159] Art. 16 C.C.Q. In deciding whether or not to authorize treatment, the court must obtain the opinion of experts, of the mandatary, of the tutor or the curator and of the tutorship council. It may also obtain the opinion of any person who shows a special interest in the person concerned by the application (art. 23, para. 1 C.C.Q.).

[160] See for example, *Institut Philippe-Pinel de Montréal v. Blais*, [1991] R.J.Q. 1969 (Que. S.C.); *Hôpital Charles-Lemoyne v. Forcier*, [1992] R.D.F. 257 (Que. S.C.); *Cité de la Santé de Laval v. Lacombe*, [1992] R.J.Q. 58 (Que. S.C.); *Institut Philippe-Pinel de Montréal v. G. (A.)*, [1994] J.Q. No. 837, [1994] R.J.Q. 2523 (Que. C.A.). See also Robert P. Kouri & Suzanne Philips-Nootens, "Le majeur inapte et le refus catégorique de soins de santé: un concept pour le moins ambigu" (2003) 63 R. du B. 3 at 26-27.

(ii) Unemancipated Minors

For purposes of medical treatment, the *Civil Code of Quebec* distinguishes between minors 14 years of age and older and minors under 14 years of age. It should be pointed out that the age of 14 retained by legislation for consenting to medical care, does not necessarily take into account the maturity or even the discernment of the minor, which, as experience often indicates, is not always proportional to age.

According to art. 14, para. 2 of the Code, a minor 14 years of age or more may consent alone to care required by his or her state of health. Should the minor's condition necessitate hospitalization for over 12 hours, the person having parental authority[161] or the tutor shall merely be informed of that fact, without any other information being divulged. The intent of this legislation is to facilitate access to medical care for adolescents, including abortion services, treatment of sexually transmitted diseases and problems related to drug and alcohol abuse. As the law presently stands, it would appear that access to contraceptive services can only be provided for therapeutic reasons. Unless one is prepared to conclude that as a general principle, the tender age of a young girl is a contraindication for pregnancy, then any medical act intended to prevent conception should be viewed as care not required by the state of health of young women, and the conditions of art. 17 of the Code would then apply.[162] It seems counterintuitive however, to ban access to birth control products and services while authorizing abortion due to the youthfulness of a pregnant child.

Article 16, para. 2 C.C.Q. requires the authorization of the court in cases where the minor aged 14 or more refuses care except in cases of emergency where one's life is in danger or one's integrity is threatened. In this situation, the consent of the person having parental authority or of the tutor suffices. When the court is called upon to rule, art. 23 indicates that it would not be held to respect the minor's refusal.[163]

As regards consent to care required by the state of health of a minor less than 14 years old, the codal provisions are very clear: consent is given by the person having parental authority or by the tutor.[164] An unjustified refusal by the parents or tutor would give rise to recourse to the courts under art. 16.[165] Any consent or refusal on behalf of the minor would have to respect the criteria of art. 12.[166]

---

[161] Under art. 600 C.C.Q., the father and mother exercise parental authority together.

[162] "A minor fourteen years of age or over may give his consent alone to care not required by the state of his health; however, the consent of the person having parental authority or the tutor is required if the care entails a serious risk for the health of the minor and may cause him grave and permanent effects".

[163] *Protection de la Jeunesse — 884*, [1998] R.J.Q. 816 (Que. S.C.) (a child refused an operation on religious grounds, believing that her scoliosis would be corrected by prayer).

[164] Art. 14, para. 1 C.C.Q.

[165] *In Re Goyette: Centre de Services Sociaux du Montréal Métropolitain*, [1983] C.S. 429 (Que. S.C.); *Couture-Jacquet v. Montreal Children's Hospital*, [1986] Q.J. No. 258, [1986] R.J.Q. 1221 (Que. C.A.); *Protection de la Jeunesse — 332*, [1988] R.J.Q. 1666 (Que. S.C.).

[166] Article 12 reads in part as follows: "A person who gives his consent to or refuses care for another person is bound to act in the sole interest of that person, taking into account, as far as possible, any wishes the latter may have expressed". To which one must add the words of art. 33

(b) Consent to Care Not Required by the State of Health of the Person

A straightforward reading of the *Civil Code of Quebec* provisions governing care not required by the state of health of the person indicates that the rules pertaining to non-therapeutic care administered in the sole interest of the person (purely contraceptive sterilization, cosmetic surgery, *etc.*) differ from those relating to medical acts of an altruistic nature (organ donations, experimentation). We will limit our examination of the law of consent to care administered in the exclusive interest of the patient. Since no specific rules govern consent by capable adults to this type of care, other than requiring that it be provided in writing, our analysis will deal with incapable adults and with minors who, as vulnerable persons, are protected by additional safeguards.

(i) Incapable Adults

Article 18 of the *Civil Code of Quebec* states that consent to non-therapeutic care for incapable adults is provided by the mandatary, tutor or curator. In addition, the authorization of the court is necessary "if the care entails a serious risk for health or if it might cause grave and permanent effects".

Two aspects of art. 18 should be emphasized. Firstly, the law requires that the incapable adult be represented by a mandatary, tutor or curator. Since close relatives, spouses and others who have not otherwise been designated as representatives are excluded from the list,[167] it follows that non-therapeutic care cannot be administered to an incapable person unless he or she has designated a mandatary in anticipation of his or her incapacity,[168] or has been placed under a regime of protective supervision.[169]

Secondly, the representative's consent alone will suffice provided the care does not entail a serious risk for health or cause grave and permanent effects. The stringency of these conditions would appear to limit the representative's authority to authorizing only minor medical acts such as the elimination of a birthmark for aesthetic reasons, orthodontia or the prescription of certain forms of contraception, such as an intrauterine device. If, on the other hand, the care indeed involves a serious risk for health or grave and permanent effects, approval of the court becomes necessary. Since the care in question is not required by the patient's state of health, his or her refusal will constitute an absolute bar to any such authorization.[170] The inconsistency inherent in this situation is that if the patient is so incapable as to be unable to express an opinion for or against the intervention, the patient's power to refuse disappears.

C.C.Q., which include factors such as "the moral, intellectual, emotional and material needs of the child, ... the child's age, health, personality and family environment and to the other aspects of his situation".

[167] In contradistinction to art. 15 C.C.Q. concerning therapeutic care which allows relatives, spouses and others who are not representatives, to consent to care required by the state of health.

[168] Art. 2166 C.C.Q.

[169] Art. 256 C.C.Q.

[170] Art. 23, para. 2 C.C.Q. states: "The court is also bound to obtain the opinion of the person concerned unless that is impossible, and to respect his refusal unless the care is required by his state of health".

Obviously, the most controversial intervention which falls within the purview of art. 18 is the non-therapeutic sterilization of mentally challenged women. While the risks inherent in this type of surgery are fairly minimal, by its very nature, the operation will produce "grave and permanent effects" for the individual.

In the Supreme Court of Canada case of *E. (Mrs.) v. Eve*,[171] a widow sought court authorization to have her daughter sterilized, fearing the negative emotional impact of a pregnancy for her daughter, as well as the inability of her daughter to care for a child, who would then become Mrs. E.'s responsibility. Speaking on behalf of the Supreme Court panel, La Forest J. felt that the courts exercising their *parens patriae* powers could authorize only those acts which were necessary for the person under protection. Since Eve's mother failed to establish the advantages of surgery for Eve herself as opposed to the convenience of others, the court declined the requested authorization. At first blush, La Forest J. appears to have issued a blanket condemnation of sterilization for the mentally incompetent:

> The grave intrusion on a person's rights and the certain physical damage that ensues from non-therapeutic sterilization without consent, when compared to the highly questionable advantages that can result from it, have persuaded me that it can never safely be determined that such a procedure is for the benefit of that person. Accordingly, the procedure should never be authorized for non-therapeutic purposes under the *parens patriae* jurisdiction.[172]

Further on however, he writes:

> If sterilization of the mentally incompetent is to be adopted as desirable for general social purposes, the legislature is the appropriate body to do so. It is in a position to inform itself and it is attuned to the feelings of the public in making policy in this sensitive area.[173]

Even though this type of operation is not specifically mentioned in the *Civil Code of Quebec*, arguably the Code provisions meet the standard set out by La Forest J., as the patient's representative must consent, and the patient, the tutorship council and experts must be consulted before the court can authorize any sterilization.[174] It should also be noted that unlike the conditions for enabling the courts to act under their *parens patriae* powers, the Code requires that any act must be undertaken in the "sole interest of that person".[175] Refusing a mentally incompetent person access to certain birth control methods available to the general population, all in the name of "protecting" her rights, can be as morally blameworthy as sterilization for the convenience of those close to the mentally challenged person. Nevertheless, due to the potential for abuse, we feel that the Code provisions would permit the sterilization of incompetents only in highly exceptional circumstances.

---

[171] [1986] S.C.J. No. 60, [1986] 2 S.C.R. 388 (S.C.C.).
[172] *Ibid.*, at para. 86 S.C.J., at 431 S.C.R.
[173] *Ibid.*, at para. 88 S.C.J., at 431 S.C.R.
[174] Art. 23 C.C.Q.
[175] Art. 12 C.C.Q.

(ii) Minors

As is the case with therapeutic care, the *Civil Code* distinguishes between minors 14 years of age or more and those less than 14 in matters relating to consent to non-therapeutic care. Article 17 states the principle that "[a] minor 14 years of age or over may give his consent alone to care not required by the state of his health". But it places restrictions on the exercise of this capacity:

> [The] consent of the person having parental authority or of the tutor is required if the care entails a serious risk for the health of the minor and may cause him grave and permanent effects.

Contrary to one's initial impression, the limitations placed by art. 17 on the minor's powers of consent do not unduly restrict his or her autonomy since the conditions imposed by the Code are cumulative and as such, would not concern acts that a minor would likely wish to undertake alone. For example, as the law stands, a minor can consent to non-surgical forms of contraception,[176] to an early abortion for non-therapeutic reasons, or to being provided with the "morning after" pill.

When the minor is less than 14 years of age, art. 18 stipulates that the person having parental authority or the tutor may consent alone provided there is no serious risk for health nor any grave and permanent effects. If the intervention proposed indeed involves a serious risk for health or grave and permanent effects, authorization of the court becomes necessary. In this situation, the minor child has a right to be consulted. If he or she expresses a refusal, then the court is bound to respect this refusal since the care is not required by the patient's state of health.[177]

2. Corollary: The Right to Refuse Treatment

It is generally admitted in Quebec law that a capable patient has the right to refuse treatment even at the risk of putting his or her life in danger.[178] An important issue which remains to be resolved in this regard is whether this refusal of treatment must be informed.

In two cases of common law origin, the Supreme Court appears to have posited a symmetrical approach to both consent and refusal: both must be informed. In *Hollis v. Dow Corning Corp.*,[179] La Forest J., speaking for the court, stated:

> The doctrine of "informed consent" dictates that every individual has a right to know what risks are involved in undergoing or foregoing medical treatment and a concomitant right to make meaningful decisions based on a full understanding of those risks.

---

[176] Pauline Lesage-Jarjoura & Suzanne Philips-Nootens, *Éléments de responsabilité civile médicale — le droit dans le quotidien de la médecine*, 2nd ed. (Cowansville, QC: Éditions Yvon Blais, 2001) at 222 n. 277.

[177] Art. 23, para. 2 C.C.Q.

[178] *B. (N.) v. Hôtel-Dieu de Québec*, [1992] J.Q. No. 1, [1992] R.J.Q. 361 (Que. S.C.); *Manoir de la Pointe Bleue (1978) Inc. v. Corbeil*, [1992] J.Q. No. 98, [1992] R.J.Q. 712 (Que. S.C.).

[179] [1995] S.C.J. No. 104 at para. 24, [1995] 4 S.C.R. 634 at 656 (S.C.C.).

In *Reibl v. Hughes*,[180] Laskin C.J.C. affirmed that the fundamental issue relating to consent involves the "patient's right to know what risks are involved in undergoing or foregoing certain surgical or other treatment".[181]

A right to be informed does not include a duty or obligation to be informed. If a capable patient refuses to be informed, he or she must assume the consequences of this refusal. Nonetheless, the physician must offer to provide the relevant information.

Even if consent to care is given prior to a medical intervention, it remains an ongoing process.[182] The patient is free to authorize an interference with his or her integrity, and the patient is just as free to withdraw this authorization at any time. Indeed, it may occur that during treatment, fear, pain or discomfort will provoke a reaction that could be interpreted as a withdrawal of consent. In order to distinguish an involuntary reaction to pain or discomfort from an actual refusal of further treatment, one's only recourse is to rely on the standard of a reasonable person's appreciation of the event. If, in the eyes of a reasonable person, the patient's protestations are more likely the manifestation of discomfort than an actual refusal, the medical act can be continued. However, since the patient's right to autonomy and inviolability are involved, the burden of proof in this type of situation will have to be assumed by the physician. In *Courtemanche v. Potvin*[183] for instance, a patient undergoing a myelogram claimed to have begged the neurologist to stop the procedure. The court rejected the plaintiff's action in damages, taking into consideration the exceptionally low tolerance to discomfort of the patient in question who suffered from hypochondria. It was felt that his protestations were cries of pain.

As a general rule, when consent has been withdrawn, the physician must interrupt treatment, subject to the *caveat* put forward by Cory J. in *Ciarlariello v. Schacter*:[184]

> Thus, if it is found that the consent is effectively withdrawn during the course of the proceeding then it must be terminated. This must be the result except in the circumstances where the medical evidence suggests that to terminate the process would be either life threatening or pose immediate and serious problems to the health of the patient.

3. The Emergency Exception to the Requirement of Consent

An emergency situation constitutes more than a simple means of exoneration for having proceeded with treatment without authorization; it in fact replaces consent. According to art. 13, para. 1 of the *Civil Code of Quebec*: "Consent to medical care is not required in case of emergency if the life of the person is in

---

[180] [1980] S.C.J. No. 105, [1980] 2 S.C.R. 880 (S.C.C.).
[181] *Ibid.*, at 895 S.C.R.
[182] Pauline Lesage-Jarjoura & Suzanne Philips-Nootens, *Éléments de responsabilité civile médicale — le droit dans le quotidien de la médecine*, 2nd ed. (Cowansville, QC: Éditions Yvon Blais, 2001) at 170 n. 215.
[183] [1996] R.R.A. 829 (Que. S.C.).
[184] *Ciarlariello v. Schacter*, [1993] S.C.J. No. 46 at para. 42, [1993] 2 S.C.R. 119 at 136 (S.C.C.).

danger or his integrity is threatened and his consent cannot be obtained in due time."

As a result, in order to justify an intrusion upon one's inviolability without the consent of the person or of a third party authorized to consent on his or her behalf, the patient or the third party must in fact be incapable of being informed, of expressing consent and the situation must be of such a gravity that the patient's life or integrity is in peril. It should be noted that this exception to the requirement of consent cannot be invoked in cases where "the care is unusual or has become useless or where its consequences could be intolerable for the person".[185] There are thus three exceptions to the emergency exception!

The first exception deals with unusual treatment: physicians cannot impose extraordinary or experimental interventions on patients (such as artificial heart implants).[186] The second exception states that treatment cannot have become useless; in other words, heroic or futile treatment cannot be imposed upon a terminally ill patient. As for the third exception involving the consequences of care which could be intolerable for the person, it would appear to apply to those who, for philosophical or religious reasons, would not have consented to care had they been able to express an opinion.[187]

C. VIOLATION OF THE DUTY TO INFORM AND CAUSATION

A patient inadequately informed as to the risks, advantages and disadvantages of medical treatment and who, on the basis of this lack of information, has authorized a medical act which gives rise to injury, may claim damages provided, of course, the physician's failure to advise actually caused the harm. Must the patient prove that had he or she known the truth, consent to treatment would not have been forthcoming (the "subjective standard"), or must the patient go further and establish that had a reasonable person in the patient's situation been aware of the truth, treatment would have been refused (the "modified objective standard")?

Traditionally, the issue of causation in cases of violation of the duty to inform was not a source of controversy in Quebec law, since the courts have tended to rely on a subjective standard of appreciation. The case of *Dulude v. Gaudette*,[188] in which a plastic surgeon was sued for not having advised his patient of the risks of augmentation mammoplasty surgery, is a classic example of this approach. While finding that the surgeon had indeed inadequately advised his patient, Vallerand J. nonetheless rejected the claim on the basis of a lack of causal relationship between the physician's fault and the plaintiff's injuries:

---

[185] Art. 13, para. 2 C.C.Q.

[186] A hypothesis actually raised during parliamentary commission hearings by Dr. Augustin Roy, president of the Corporation Professionnelle des Médecins du Québec, Journal des Débats: Commissions Parlementaires, 4e session, 32e législature, p. B-1661.

[187] The Ontario case of *Malette v. Shulman*, [1987] O.J. No. 1180, 47 D.L.R. (4th) 18 (Ont. H.C.J.), affd [1990] O.J. No. 450, 67 D.L.R. (4th) 321 (Ont. C.A.), would likely have had the same outcome in Quebec.

[188] [1974] C.S. 618 (Que. S.C.).

Plaintiff avers that had she known of the slightest possibility of that which took place actually occurring, she would never have undergone the operation. I do not have any doubt as to her sincerity coloured by hindsight. I must, however, point out that as a pretty and coquettish young woman anxious to remain such, she preferred corrective surgery to a fur coat offered by her husband.

I cannot believe that evoking the highly unlikely possibility of the complications from which she eventually suffered, would have deterred her from pursuing her plan.[189]

However, following the Supreme Court decision in the Ontario case of *Reibl v. Hughes*[190] proposing a "modified objective criterion",[191] the courts in Quebec began to adapt this standard.[192] But then, the Court of Appeal entered the fray and became divided on this particular question,[193] which inevitably led to a certain amount of confusion in the courts of first instance.[194]

At this point, a compromise of sorts between the modified objective and subjective standard was broached at the appellate level. In *Pelletier v. Roberge*,[195] the Court of Appeal employed the expressions "rational subjectivity" and "subjective reasonableness" for the first time apparently in order to bridge the gulf. Speaking on behalf of the panel, Brossard J. introduced this new approach in the following terms:

> Appellant rightly submits that Quebec jurisprudence has not retained the strictly objective test laid down by the Supreme Court in the case of *Reibl v. Hughes*. This, however, is only partially true. In effect, our jurisprudence is made up of a duality of opinions on this subject, and it is only in our last three decisions ... that this Court has settled on a test that one could describe as based on "rational subjectivity" or "subjective reasonableness," which consists of determining and appreciating, in light of the nature of the risk and the evidence, what would have been the reasonable probable response of that particular patient, as opposed to the

---

[189]   *Ibid.*, at 622 (our translation).

[190]   [1980] S.C.J. No. 105, [1980] 2 S.C.R. 880 (S.C.C.).

[191]   *Ibid.*, at 898-900 S.C.R. At 899-900, Laskin C.J.C. writes: "In saying that the test is based on the decision that a reasonable person in the patient's position would have made, I should make it clear that the patient's particular concerns must also be reasonably based; otherwise, there would be more subjectivity than would be warranted under an objective test".

[192]   See, *e.g.*, *Barette v. Lajoie*, J.E. 85-853 (Que. S.C.); *Dionne v. Ferenczi*, [1987] R.R.A. 420 (Que. S.C.).

[193]   *O'Hearn v. Estrada*, [1984] J.Q. No. 533, J.E. 84-449 (Que. C.A.); *Dunant v. Chong*, [1985] J.Q. No. 523, [1986] R.R.A. 2 (summary) (Que. C.A.); *Chouinard v. Landry*, [1987] J.Q. No. 1625, [1987] R.J.Q. 1954 (Que. C.A.), leave to appeal to S.C.C. refused, [1988] C.S.C.R. No. 15, [1988] 1 S.C.R. vii (S.C.C.).

[194]   *Weiss v. Solomon*, [1989] J.Q. No. 312, [1989] R.J.Q. 731 (Que. S.C.); *Stevens v. Ackman*, [1989] R.R.A. 109 (Que. S.C.); *O'Shea v. McGovern*, [1989] R.R.A. 341 (Que. S.C.); *Masson v. De Koos*, [1990] R.R.A. 818 (Que. S.C.); *Lacharité v. Waddell*, [1998] J.Q. No. 4753, [1998] R.R.A. 459 (Que. S.C.). However, in *Rafferty v. Kulcycky*, [1989] Q.J. No. 1708, [1989] R.R.A. 582 (Que. S.C.) and in *Murray-Vaillancourt v. Clairoux*, [1989] J.Q. No. 2524, [1989] R.R.A. 762 (Que. S.C.), the objective standard was applied.

[195]   [1991] J.Q. No. 1624, [1991] R.R.A. 726 (Que. C.A.).

response of a reasonable person in the abstract sense as set out in *Reibl v. Hughes.*[196]

Justice Baudouin further elucidated the parameters of this test in *Drolet v. Parenteau*:[197]

> The civil liability of a physician is not however automatically engaged by the mere fact of having wrongfully fulfilled the duty of informing. According to our jurisprudence, one must apply a test which, in our opinion, is essentially a subjective test and consists of evaluating if the patient, in the circumstances in question, would still have consented to the intervention if he or she had been adequately informed. This appreciation is usually made in light of the patient's testimony. Obviously, this testimony must be evaluated with care and other factors must be considered. It is for this reason that often, the courts ask themselves what a normally prudent and diligent person would have decided in that particular case, a so-called "objective" test, but one which, in my opinion, relates essentially to the credibility of this testimony. This objective test does not replace the subjective test. It merely completes it.[198]

It is undeniable that the modified objective test, the subjective test and the "rational subjectivity" or "subjective reasonableness" test each present certain advantages and shortcomings. The challenge is to adopt the test most in keeping with the fundamental principles of the civil law. In our opinion, both the modified objective test and the standard of "subjective reasonableness" fail to respect the genius of Quebec liability law.

Without question, the greatest merit inherent in the modified objective test is to discount testimony based on bitterness and hindsight. Yet, in the guise of substantive law, its role is essentially evidentiary[199] and would appear to circumscribe the trier of fact's function in evaluating testimony. In at least two cases on appeal from Quebec in matters unrelated to medical law, the Supreme Court reaffirmed the trial judge's sovereign powers of appreciation of the evidence. Reasserting a principle previously acknowledged in *W.T. Rawleigh v. Dumoulin*,[200] Lamont J. wrote in *Montreal Tramways Co. v. Léveillé*,[201] a celebrated case involving proof through testimony of a causal relationship between harm caused to a child born with club feet and a fall suffered by her mother during pregnancy:

> It was urged that to so hold would open wide the door to extravagance of testimony and lead, in all probability, to perjury and fraud. I am not apprehensive on this point for, although in certain cases special care will be required on the part of the judge ... I feel quite confident that the rules of evidence are adequate to require satisfactory proof of responsibility and that the determination of the

---

[196] *Ibid.*, at 734 R.R.A. (our translation).
[197] [1994] J.Q. No. 167, [1994] R.J.Q. 689 (Que. C.A.).
[198] *Ibid.*, at para. 78 J.Q., at 707 R.J.Q. (our translation).
[199] Ellen I. Picard & Gerald B. Robertson, *Legal Liability of Doctors and Hospitals in Canada*, 3rd ed. (Scarborough, ON: Carswell, 1996) at 167.
[200] [1926] S.C.J. No. 35, [1926] S.C.R. 551 (S.C.C.).
[201] [1933] S.C.J. No. 40, [1933] S.C.R. 456 (S.C.C.).

relation of cause and effect will not involve the court in any greater difficulty than now exists in many of our cases.[202]

There are many other reservations regarding the adoption of the modified objective test. For instance, in the exercise of fundamental rights under the Quebec *Charter of Human Rights and Freedoms*,[203] including the right to inviolability and freedom,[204] a person has the right to refuse care even if this refusal is not in his or her best interests and could not, by any stretch of the imagination, be considered reasonable according to an objective standard. This being the case, then how can anyone presume to judge one's personal choice in light of what a reasonable person in the plaintiff's situation would have decided?[205] Moreover, in cases of therapeutic privilege, how can this exception to the duty of fully informing, based on the sensibilities or the precarious state of health of a particular patient — a subjective appreciation — be reconciled with the notion that the presumed reaction of this patient would necessarily conform to that of a reasonable person in similar circumstances?

The most telling objection to the *Reibl* test of causation occurs when the proposed intervention does not have a therapeutic purpose, as in the case of cosmetic surgery. How can one compare the reaction of a particular individual to that of a reasonable person since in this type of situation, most reasonable people would arguably forgo the risks of surgery under general anaesthesia just to correct a minor or imagined imperfection? In *Dulude v. Gaudette*,[206] did not Vallerand J. find that given the choice by her husband, the plaintiff nonetheless expressed a preference for risky breast enhancement surgery rather than receive the gift of a fur coat? Likewise in *Johnson v. Harris*[207] involving cosmetic surgery to remove an abdominal scar, Macerola J. felt impelled to write:

> This is a case involving purely elective plastic surgery. All depends upon the patient's choice. In effect, the circumstances would lead one to believe that an ordinary person would prefer to live with an aesthetic imperfection than run the risk of physical harm as a result of an operation.[208]

In proposing a so-called "rational subjectivity" test, the Quebec Court of Appeal has undoubtedly sought to reaffirm the principles of the civil law while protecting health professionals from "retrospective analysis and bitterness".[209] In addition, this criterion would at least appear to be an expression of deference towards the moral and persuasive authority of the Supreme Court by appearing to incorporate objective elements in the evaluation of testimony. As a compromise between the modified objective and subjective tests however, this proposed solution suffers from one major weakness in that it fails to distinguish

---

[202] *Ibid.*, at 465 S.C.R.

[203] R.S.Q., c. C-12.

[204] *Charter of Human Rights and Freedoms*, R.S.Q., c. C-12, s. 1.

[205] *Reibl v. Hughes*, [1980] S.C.J. No. 105, [1980] 2 S.C.R. 880 at 899-900 (S.C.C.).

[206] [1974] C.S. 618 (Que. S.C.).

[207] [1990] J.Q. No. 1467, [1990] R.R.A. 832 (Que. S.C.).

[208] *Johnson v. Harris*, [1990] J.Q. No. 1467 at para. 77, [1990] R.R.A. 832 at 841 (Que. S.C.) (our translation).

[209] *Reibl v. Hughes*, [1980] S.C.J. No. 105, [1980] 2 S.C.R. 880 at 898 (S.C.C.).

the fundamental difference between substantive and adjective law. In deciding *Reibl*, the Supreme Court intended to restructure the law governing consent in medical malpractice,[210] an aspect of substantive tort law, whereas through "rational subjectivity" or "subjective reasonableness", the Quebec Court of Appeal appears to be proposing criteria relating exclusively to proof. This nuance is far from academic because as a general rule, in appreciating the evidence and more particularly evidence adduced through testimony, the Court of Appeal must avoid substituting its opinion on the credibility of witnesses for that of the trier of fact.[211] But when the issue involves application of a substantive rule, the revisionary powers of an appellate court take full effect. One must also avoid confusing actual corroboration of the plaintiff's testimony with a determination of what a reasonable person would have decided in similar circumstances. The testimony of a person corroborated by the factual circumstances of the case will invariably be closer to the truth than the application of an objective standard which must, by its very nature, remain conjectural. Even if one were to favour application of the "rational subjectivity" or "subjective reasonableness" criterion as a rule of prudence in matters of proof, one would have to do so with much circumspection in order to avoid imposing upon the trier of fact, directives which could hinder his or her appreciation of the victim's testimony.

IV. THE DUTY TO TREAT AND CORRELATIVE OBLIGATIONS

While the duty to treat the patient is at the very heart of the physician-patient relationship, the duty to attend the patient in light of the evolution of the illness or condition becomes a natural extension of the more fundamental duty to provide care. The greatest number of suits against physicians have generally arisen from violations of these two obligations. The general principles of civil liability having been set out in the first part of this chapter, that which follows deals essentially with the determination of fault with respect to the duties to treat and to attend. We will then turn to duties of professional secrecy and confidentiality of medical records.

A. THE DUTY TO TREAT

As has already been pointed out, the duty to treat is considered an obligation of diligence or of means; the physician must utilize all means at his or her disposal to ensure proper diagnosis, treatment or relief for the patient. Due to the risks inherent in this type of activity, the physician cannot be held to an obligation of result. In their approach to this fundamental distinction, the courts have tended

---

[210] Ellen I. Picard & Gerald B. Robertson, *Legal Liability of Doctors and Hospitals in Canada*, 3rd ed. (Scarborough, ON: Carswell, 1996) at 116.

[211] *Beaudoin-Daigneault v. Richard*, [1984] S.C.J. No. 2, [1984] 1 S.C.R. 2 at 8-9 (S.C.C.); *Lapointe v. Hôpital Le Gardeur*, [1992] S.C.J. No. 11 at para. 15, [1992] 1 S.C.R. 351 at 358 (S.C.C.).

to differentiate the realization of risks inherent in medical practice from actual
civil fault resulting from negligence or imprudence.

1. Extent of the Duty to Treat

In the words of the Quebec Court of Appeal in a landmark 1957 decision, the
physician must "provide his patient with conscientious, attentive care in conformity with accepted standards of medical science".[212] In applying this standard, a
physician's professional conduct is compared to that which a prudent, diligent,
competent colleague enjoying similar training and placed in the same circumstances would have done. The assessment is thus *in abstracto*, according to
objective criteria.

Fault may occur at any stage of the duty to treat, whether in the course of
diagnosis or during treatment itself. The best way to illustrate this is through the
presentation of actual illustrations drawn from jurisprudence.

(a) Conscientious and Attentive Care

It is important that a physician listen to the patient and take into account his or her
complaints in order to arrive at an accurate diagnosis. Thus a physician who
concluded that a patient was suffering from cataracts whereas the presence of pain
would have tended to indicate glaucoma, was held liable for his failure to properly
diagnose the condition.[213] Moreover, a physical examination, an examination of
the back of the eye and the measurement of ocular pressure, all of which was
indicated in cases of this nature, would have enabled the physician to properly
diagnose the illness.[214] In another decision, an intern discharged a patient who,
following an accident, still had a metal particle under the eyelid. The resulting
infection caused the loss of the eye. The court criticized the intern, *inter alia*, for
having failed to conform to the most basic of precautions.[215] In yet another, older
case, an anaesthetist forgot to ensure that the pipes or tubing to his medical
apparatus were properly connected and consequently deprived the patient of
oxygen. The patient emerged from surgery in a neurovegetative state and died
months later. The physician was found to have acted "without due thought in
preparing for the intervention, omitting a fundamental precaution and lacking
vigilance in the administration of the anaesthesia itself".[216]

The failure to have recourse to certain specific procedures can also become a
source of liability if it leads to an inaccurate diagnosis, as for example when a
fracture has not been detected because an X-ray examination was not
performed.[217] Similarly, good medical practice would require that a spermogram

---

[212] *X. v. Mellen*, [1957] B.R. 389 at 416 (Que. C.A.) (our translation).
[213] *Lauzon v. Taillefer*, [1991] R.R.A. 62 (Que. S.C.).
[214] *Ibid.*
[215] *Boies v. Hôtel-Dieu de Québec*, [1980] C.S. 596 at 603 (Que. S.C.), vard [1985] J.Q. No. 537, J.E. 85-976 (Que. C.A.).
[216] *Covet v. Jewish General Hospital*, [1976] C.S. 1390 at 1393-94 (Que. S.C.).
[217] *Laurent v. Hôpital Notre-Dame de l'Espérance*, [1974] C.A. 543 (Que. C.A.), vard [1977] S.C.J. No. 66, [1978] 1 S.C.R. 605 (S.C.C.).

be performed in order to verify the success of a vasectomy,[218] that renal and auditory functions be verified when certain antibiotics are prescribed,[219] and that the pathologist's report be consulted following a tubal ligation.[220] A physician who fails to inform a patient that a breast biopsy established the presence of cancer must answer for damages resulting from having prevented the patient from pursuing active treatment for several years.[221]

On the other hand, an error in diagnosis will not give rise to liability if the physician has acted, given the circumstances, in a competent, diligent fashion. For example, a child diagnosed by the treating physician with having a viral infection following vaccination was in reality suffering from meningitis. In this case, two other physicians had arrived at the same conclusion. As a result, the treating physician was exonerated.[222] A similar finding occurred in the case of *Gendron v. Leduc*, where the physician, relying on the patient's statement that she had already undergone a hysterectomy, performed surgery for a cervical polyp and discovered in the course of the operation, an intact but atrophied uterus.[223]

When an error occurs, a conscientious physician must so inform the patient as soon as possible so that the diagnosis or treatment can be revised and physical or psychological harm can be avoided.[224]

It has been previously pointed out that fault is determined by taking into account the actual circumstances, including those of time and place, in which the physician is providing care. An immediate danger for the patient's life — an emergency in the strictest sense — may justify acts or omissions which, under different circumstances, would be totally unacceptable. This is illustrated in a case involving a patient in severe respiratory distress due to an asthma attack who had to be intubated in order to be saved. The perforation of the esophagus which resulted from the intubation did not lead to liability.[225]

---

[218] *Engstrom v. Courteau*, [1986] R.J.Q. 3048 (Que. S.C.).

[219] *Gburek v. Cohen*, [1988] J.Q. No. 1693, [1988] R.J.Q. 2424 (Que. C.A.).

[220] *Cooke v. Suite*, [1995] J.Q. No. 696, [1995] R.J.Q. 2765 (Que. C.A.).

[221] *Laferrière v. Lawson*, [1991] S.C.J. No. 18, [1991] 1 S.C.R. 541 (S.C.C.). The physician was held liable for the injury resulting from the moral suffering of the patient when she learned the truth, but not for her death since there was no proof that on a balance of probabilities his error had caused her death.

[222] *Tremblay v. Claveau*, [1990] J.Q. No. 278, [1990] R.R.A. 268 (Que. C.A.).

[223] *Gendron v. Leduc*, [1989] J.Q. No. 304, [1989] R.R.A. 245 (Que. C.A.). See also other cases cited by Pauline Lesage-Jarjoura & Suzanne Philips-Nootens, *Éléments de responsabilité civile médicale — le droit dans le quotidien de la médecine*, 2nd ed. (Cowansville, QC: Éditions Yvon Blais, 2001) at 43, para. 57, nn. 32-33 of their text.

[224] *Kiley-Nikkel v. Danais*, [1992] J.Q. No. 1836, [1992] R.J.Q. 2820 (Que. S.C.): a woman underwent a mastectomy following the pathologist's error in diagnosis. The surgeon never told her the truth and she not only underwent unnecessary surgery, she also suffered the anguish of thinking she had cancer. Indeed, there is a duty to report any incident, accident or complication which may have a significant impact on the patient's state of health. See *Code of Ethics of Physicians*, R.R.Q., c. M-9, r. 4.1, s. 56. See also *Health Services and Social Services Act*, R.S.Q., c. S-4.2, s. 8.

[225] But there would be liability for having failed to attend the patient: *Harewood-Green v. Spanier*, [1995] J.Q. No. 2825, [1995] R.R.A. 147 (Que. S.C.), affd [2000] J.Q. No. 4500, [2000] R.R.A. 864 (Que. C.A.).

Work in an emergency room has its own set of difficulties, including and most notably, unfamiliarity with the patients. The courts take this fact into account, as illustrated in the case of *Bouchard v. Bergeron* in which it was readily acknowledged that: "The emergency room physician does not know the patient who seeks out his services; ... . He is not familiar with his habits, his character."[226] Yet the fact of practising in a university setting "... with all the investigative equipment necessary, [a] hospital where there can be found physicians of all specialities"[227] will tend to impose a higher standard regarding the quality of care provided.

(b) Care in Keeping with Current Standards

The *Code of Ethics of Physicians* is clear: "A physician must practise his profession in accordance with the highest possible current medical standards; to this end, he must, in particular, develop, perfect and keep his knowledge and skills up to date."[228]

A surgeon practised a cholecystectomy on a female patient and later had occasion to reoperate on the patient in order to correct some adhesions. Following the second operation, the patient suffered an arterial thrombosis which left her hemiplegic. Not only was she a smoker, she was also on anovulants and the surgeon failed to advise her to stop smoking and taking the pill before the operation. A special committee created by the Government of Canada to study vascular complications linked to birth control pills had recommended that anovulants be discontinued prior to major surgery and this report had been distributed to all physicians. The defendant surgeon was thus unable to plead ignorance of its existence and was held liable for failing to have met current medical standards of practice.[229]

In another tragic case, a physician specialized in the screening and treatment of breast cancer tended to utilize diagnostic techniques qualified as experimental such as "diaphanoscopy" and "thermography". In addition, he erroneously interpreted not only the standard tests to which he had recourse but also the more obvious clinical signs indicative of the presence of cancer. When his patient, who demanded a closer follow-up due to her fears regarding this particular type of cancer, finally decided to consult another surgeon, it was too

---

[226] *Bouchard v. Bergeron*, [1994] R.R.A. 967 at 979 (Que. S.C.). The physician did not recognize a rare neurological condition due especially to problems of communication with the patient.

[227] *Harewood-Green v. Spanier*, [1995] J.Q. No. 2825 at para. 159, [1995] R.R.A. 147 at 167 (Que. S.C.) (our translation), affd [2000] J.Q. No. 4500, [2000] R.R.A. 864 (Que. C.A.). The physicians were liable for having failed to diagnose a perforation of the esophagus since they did not go further in the pursuit of a diagnosis. In *St-Jean v. Mercier*, [1999] J.Q. No. 2584, [1999] R.J.Q. 1658 (Que. C.A.), affd [2002] S.C.J. No. 17, [2002] 1 S.C.R. 491 (S.C.C.), an orthopedist did not act in a conscientious manner when he neglected to perform a proper examination of a patient suffering from a spinal fracture. It is only due to a lack of causation that the physician was exonerated because the damage had already been suffered as a result of an accident.

[228] *Code of Ethics of Physicians*, R.R.Q., c. M-9, r. 4.1, s. 44.

[229] *Poulin v. Prat*, [1995] J.Q. No. 1665, [1995] R.J.Q. 2923 (Que. S.C.), affd on the question of liability, [1997] J.Q. No. 3125, [1997] R.J.Q. 2669 (Que. C.A.).

late since her cancer was by then inoperable. For obvious reasons, her original physician was held liable.[230]

A physician is not required to systematically employ the most modern examinations or advanced treatment techniques. Only those which are considered part of standard practice at the time of the events in question are to have been applied. A gynaecologist who failed to propose that the patient undergo an alpha-fetoprotein test then considered experimental, was exonerated from all liability when her baby was born suffering from the same congenital defects (*hydrocephalus* and *meningocele*) as an older sibling.[231]

A physician, however, cannot rely on the defence of customary practice. A case in point involved a dentist who, like the majority of this profession at the time,[232] did not utilize a dental dam and thus failed to prevent the patient from accidentally swallowing a needle during surgery. He was found liable in damages due to this oversight. Thus a court may decide that an existing practice within a profession is not sufficiently secure.

There may exist a lack of unanimity within the medical profession regarding what constitutes best practice when several alternative approaches are available. In order to be recognized, the method adopted by the physician must be accepted by a significant proportion of the medical profession. As normally occurs in situations of this nature, courts must rely upon expert opinion. If the experts called are all credible but unable to reach a consensus, then the physician defendant will normally not be found liable as the plaintiff has failed to meet the burden of proof by a preponderance of the evidence.[233] The courts' role does not extend to resolving purely scientific controversies.

It is interesting to note that while very few decisions have actually found physicians liable for a simple lack of knowledge, the courts have instead tended to impute civil responsibility on the basis of negligence resulting from inadequate knowledge. In this regard, the issue of professional incompetence *per se* seems to figure more often in disciplinary proceedings brought by the College of Physicians.[234]

---

[230] *Massinon v. Ghys*, [1996] R.J.Q. 2258 (Que. S.C.).

[231] *Bérard-Guillette v. Maheux*, [1989] J.Q. No. 841, [1989] R.J.Q. 1758 (Que. C.A.), leave to appeal to S.C.C. refused [1989] C.S.C.R. no. 344 (S.C.C.).

[232] *Boudreau-Gingras v. Gilbert*, J.E. 82-446 (Que. S.C.): 57 per cent of the practitioners do not install them, 43 per cent do.

[233] Alain Bernardot & Robert P. Kouri, *La responsabilité civile médicale* (Sherbrooke, QC: Éditions Revue de Droit Université de Sherbrooke, 1980) at 198 n. 290; Pauline Lesage-Jarjoura & Suzanne Philips-Nootens, *Éléments de responsabilité civile médicale — le droit dans le quotidien de la médecine*, 2nd ed. (Cowansville, QC: Édition Yvon Blais, 2001) at 51 nn. 69-70ff at 259 n. 304 and cases cited.

[234] Pauline Lesage-Jarjoura & Suzanne Philips-Nootens, *Éléments de responsabilité civile médicale — le droit dans le quotidien de la médecine, ibid.*, at 254 n. 303 and examples cited.

(c) Care Provided within the Physician's Area of Competence

(i) The General Rule

The *Code of Ethics of Physicians* states:

> A physician must, in the practice of his profession, take into account his capacities, limitations and the means at his disposal. He must, if the interest of his patient requires it, consult a colleague, another professional or any competent person, or direct him to one of these persons.[235]

Since patients are entitled to receive the best care possible under the circumstances, a physician must not undertake treatment or interventions which exceed his or her personal qualifications or skills relative to the setting in which he or she is practising. Generally, the courts will compare a generalist to a generalist in light of current medical practice.[236] But if a general practitioner were to go beyond his or her field of practice, there is a strong possibility that he or she would be compared to a specialist to whom the patient should normally have been referred. In one case, a general practitioner, in attempting to treat a leg fracture, utilized an outdated technique contrary to the advice of a specialist called in for consultation. The court refused to accept his plea that he was unfamiliar with the technique recommended.[237] Likewise, when a dentist undertook to provide treatments which obviously exceeded his level of competence, the court evaluated his professional behaviour in light of the standard expected of a specialist.[238] For their part, specialists sued in malpractice must prove that they possess the level of skill consonant with specialty practice and indeed, patients who consult specialists are entitled to expect a higher standard of competence. This point is emphasized in jurisprudence, particularly in the cases of *Rouillier v. Chesney*[239] and *Gordon v. Weiswall*.[240]

(ii) Consultations

A physician may simply wish to benefit from another doctor's insight in order to receive guidance in a situation presenting certain difficulties, or a patient may desire the reassurance of a second opinion. In Quebec, it is unacceptable for a treating physician to refuse the patient's request. If a greater level of expertise than that possessed by the primary physician is required, or if the treating physician lacks the investigative tools necessary (radiology, gastroscopy, catheterization, *etc.*), there would have to be a consultation with a more competent or experienced colleague. By failing to do so or by refusing to

---

[235] *Code of Ethics of Physicians*, R.R.Q., c. M-9, r. 4.1, s. 42.

[236] This point of view is changing over time since the custom of quickly referring patients to specialists has given way to a tendency of extending the scope of activities of general practitioners.

[237] *McCormick v. Marcotte*, [1972] S.C.J. No. 83, [1972] S.C.R. 18 (S.C.C.). Alain Bernardot & Robert P. Kouri, *La responsabilité civile médicale* (Sherbrooke, QC: Éditions Revue de Droit Université de Sherbrooke, 1980) at 179 n. 265.

[238] *Silver v. Baker*, [1998] J.Q. No. 808, [1998] R.R.A. 321 (Que. C.A.).

[239] [1993] R.R.A. 528 (Que. S.C.).

[240] [1992] R.R.A. 815 (Que. S.C.).

transfer the patient to someone more qualified to provide the requisite care, the treating physician risks being held liable should complications arise.

The decision in *Camden-Bourgault v. Brochu*[241] is illustrative. After having fallen from a ladder, a male patient with a history of diabetes and vascular problems was taken to emergency. Despite suffering severe pain and being unable to put weight on his legs, the patient, diagnosed as having suffered a torn muscle, was provided with analgesics and then discharged. Two days later, the appearance of tissue necrosis led to the eventual amputation of both feet. The emergency physician was held to blame, not for an initial error in diagnosis but for having failed to consult specialists present in the hospital who were familiar with the patient, and for having inadequately provided for patient follow-up, given the circumstances. In another case, liability was attached to a defendant-physician who insisted on treating a patient with severe headache as a case of migraine, instead of immediately transferring the case to neurology, where the patient was eventually diagnosed as suffering from an aneurysm.[242]

In determining the liability of the parties involved, how should one analyze the relationship between the treating physician and the consultant? Obviously, it is important that there be a clear understanding between them not only so that their respective roles can be properly fulfilled but also in order to determine who will actually be in charge of the patient. Unless a patient has entered into a special agreement with the consultant, it is generally held that the physician of record will assume the duty to treat and to attend the patient.[243] Since the treating physician ultimately decides whether or not to follow the recommendations of the consultant, traditional doctrine posits that the physician of record alone will assume liability for errors committed by the consultant.[244] Some argue, however, that this point of view must be qualified in light of current medical practices characterized by an information explosion and by the development of very advanced fields of specialization. How can one expect a treating physician who consults a more competent colleague, precisely in order to benefit from his or her greater knowledge, to be in a position to evaluate the opinion advanced by the specialist? Could it not be argued that each physician enjoys a certain

---

[241] [1996] J.Q. No. 4586, [1996] R.R.A. 809 (Que. S.C.), affd [2001] J.Q. No. 1327, [2001] R.R.A. 295 (Que. C.A.), leave to appeal to S.C.C. refused [2001] C.S.C.R. no. 279 (S.C.C.).

[242] *Montpetit v. Léger*, [2000] J.Q. No. 3119, [2000] R.J.Q. 2582 (Que. S.C.). To the same effect: *Chouinard v. Robbins*, [1998] J.Q. No. 3507, [1999] R.R.A. 65 (Que. S.C.), revd on other grounds [2001] J.Q. No. 6081, [2002] R.J.Q. 60 (Que. C.A.) (diagnosis that the patient was psychotic but failure to refer the case to a psychiatrist). Other physicians have been sanctioned by the disciplinary committee of the College of Physicians of Quebec; see more particularly the cases cited in Pauline Lesage-Jarjoura & Suzanne Philips-Nootens, *Éléments de responsabilité civile médicale — le droit dans le quotidien de la médecine*, 2nd ed. (Cowansville, QC: Éditions Yvon Blais, 2001) at 269 n. 322.

[243] The mere fact of authorizing an interference with one's right of inviolability when permission is granted to a consultant to examine the patient does not *per se* constitute the conclusion of a new contract.

[244] Alain Bernardot & Robert P. Kouri, *La responsabilité civile médicale* (Sherbrooke, QC: Éditions Revue de Droit Université de Sherbrooke, 1980) at 179 n. 265; Jean-Pierre Ménard & Denise Martin, *La responsabilité médicale pour la faute d'autrui* (Cowansville, QC: Éditions Yvon Blais, 1992) at 40.

independence within his or her own sphere of activity and would logically assume liability only for medical acts performed within that realm? According to this point of view, the physician of record would be liable for coordinating the care provided by himself or herself in light of the recommendations of the consultant, whereas each consultant would answer only for examinations or treatments personally administered[245] or for treatment recommendations expressed to the treating physician. Beyond being responsible for his or her own acts, the physician of record would also be liable, along with the specialist, for any error which could have been detected by both of them such as an improperly taken X-ray, or a grossly erroneous medication dosage.

In cases of disagreement between the treating physician and the consultant, the physician of record is free to follow or to disregard the recommendations of the physician called in for consultation, but would do so at his or her own risk since no part of blame could be passed on to the consultant.[246] If need be, in case of uncertainty as to treatment options, nothing would prevent seeking an additional opinion from, for example, an *ad hoc* medical committee struck for this purpose.[247]

The courts have not yet had occasion to express an opinion on the division of tasks and of liability between the treating physician and the consultant. As can be seen from the jurisprudence cited above, the decided cases appear to deal mainly with issues such as the failure to consult, of not following the opinion of the consultant or of failure to provide adequate follow-up.

The traditional physician-patient relationship may undergo certain trans-formations resulting from the fact that diagnosis and treatment may be provided by a person who is not physically present. We refer, of course, to telemedicine.

2. A New Way of Practising: Telemedicine

As a new phenomenon, telemedicine is assuming greater importance in medical practice and is undoubtedly changing the traditional manner of providing care.[248] Due to its various applications, this notion can be defined in several ways. Telehealth in general is said to apply to all diagnostic, therapeutic and consulta-tive medical services provided from a distance through modern technology.[249] The European Commission defines it as:

---

[245] See *Therrien v. Launay*, [2005] J.Q. No. 5303 at para. 466, [2005] R.R.A. 349 at 403 (Que. S.C.), affd [2005] J.Q. No. 9043, J.E. 2005-1345 (Que. C.A.), leave to appeal to S.C.C. refused [2005] C.S.C.R. no. 427 (S.C.C.).

[246] Jean-Pierre Ménard & Denise Martin, *La responsabilité médicale pour la faute d'autrui* (Cowansville, QC: Éditions Yvon Blais, 1992) at 45; Pauline Lesage-Jarjoura & Suzanne Philips-Nootens, *Éléments de responsabilité civile médicale — le droit dans le quotidien de la médecine*, 2nd ed. (Cowansville, QC: Éditions Yvon Blais, 2001) at 275 n. 331.

[247] *Tremblay v. Claveau*, [1990] J.Q. No. 278, [1990] R.R.A. 268 (Que. C.A.).

[248] Agency for Health Services and Technology Assessment, *Télésanté et télémédecine au Québec — état de la question* (Montréal: CÉTS, 1998).

[249] The College of Physicians of Quebec refers to means of telecommunication: Position du Collège des médecins du Québec sur la Télémédecine, online: <http://www.cmq.org/DocumentLibrary/UploadedContents/CmsDocuments/positiontelemedecinefr00.pdf>.

Rapid access to shared and remote expertise by means of telecommunications and information technologies, no matter where the patient or the relevant information is located ...[250]

The Commission's definition thus emphasizes an important aspect of telemedicine, which one may call the "delocalization" of medical practice. The physician and the patient are not in the same physical location. This occurs for instance in cases of telesurgery,[251] or when the treating physician consults a specialist in another location through transmission of radiological images or other data for interpretation. There can also be telesurveillance or telemonitoring of a patient at home or elsewhere, or "telementoring" by an experienced surgeon of a less experienced colleague, *etc.* Since the rules governing civil liability[252] are usually determined by the place where the injurious act occurred, where in reality would each medical act be deemed to have been performed in cases such as these? There is a disquieting lack of unanimity on this question.[253] Certain American states have decided that the act will be considered as having been performed where the patient is located. This opinion, while being held by the Federation of Medical Regulatory Authorities of Canada, is not generally adhered to in all provinces. Indeed, in the Province of Quebec, the *Act Respecting Health Services and Social Services* stipulates that "telehealth services are considered provided at the place where the health or social services professional who was consulted practises".[254] We feel however that since medical acts necessarily have only one focal point, namely the patient, the patient's location should have been retained as determinant.

Issues concerning the *situs* of the act notwithstanding, the specific standards established for each branch of telemedicine must also be taken into consideration in establishing fault. In his or her utilization of this new medical tool, has the physician acted in conformity with standard practices? Moreover, given the opportunities afforded by telemedicine, it could even be possible to fault a physician for not having had recourse to these tools if the required equipment were indeed available and if he or she possessed the skills and training to benefit therefrom.[255]

Teleconsultations are presently the most often utilized forms of telemedicine. We have already described the nature of the relationship between the treating

---

[250] European Commission, DG XIII, Telehealth, Report on Question 6/2, 1998. See also Jim Grisby, "Current Status of Domestic Telemedicine" (1995) 19 J. Med. Syst. 19; L. Belochi, F. Loeurng & M. Fitzgerald, "The Use of Telecommunications for Medical Diagnosis and Patient Care" in *Telemedicine Glossary: Glossary of Standards, Concepts, Technologies and Users*, Version 1.3 (Brussels: P. Fatelnig, 1999).

[251] In one case recently reported involving the United States and France, the surgeon in one country remotely controlled the robot "performing" the surgery in the other.

[252] As well as permits to practise and all related aspects such as hospital privileges, *etc.*

[253] See, generally, Robert P. Kouri & Sophie Brisson, "Les incertitudes juridictionnelles en télémédecine, où est posé l'acte médical?" (2005) 35 R.D.U.S. 521.

[254] *Act Respecting Health Services and Social Services*, R.S.Q. c. S-4.2, s. 108.2.

[255] College of Physicians of Quebec, Position du Collège des médecins du Québec sur la Télémédecine, online: <http://www.cmq.org/DocumentLibrary/UploadedContents/CmsDocuments/positiontelemedecinefr00.pdf>.

physician and the consultant under normal circumstances, but in consultations through telecommunication, the process is not quite the same since the consultant does not actually meet the patient but can, on occasion, ask him or her questions. The necessity of providing the consultant with all pertinent information in the possession of the physician of record assumes greater importance, as does the decision to follow or disregard the recommendations of the consultant. For his or her part, the consultant must decline to offer an opinion if there are insufficient elements necessary to make a proper evaluation of the case. Otherwise, the consultant could be deemed to have acted negligently and thus held liable. In attributing fault, one would have to analyze the nature of the acts performed by each participant according to the type of consultation. An act falling within the specialty of the consultant (radiology or tissue analysis, for example) would engage only his or her liability, unless, here also, there was negligence on the part of the treating physician in communicating information or in taking certain decisions following the consultation. While Quebec courts have not yet been called upon to decide these issues, several writers and study groups are working to provide a complete overview of the legal issues involved.[256]

What would occur if the equipment used proved defective? In matters of teleconsultation, the equipment itself cannot directly cause harm to the patient since it serves only as a means of exchanging information between two or more physicians. These physicians must thus refrain from issuing opinions on the basis of images or data of inferior quality. On the other hand, in cases such as surgical operations performed from a distance, or home-surveillance, should a device injure the patient, liability for the act of a thing could come into play.[257]

Obviously, the whole field of telemedicine requires the elaboration of specific rules in order to answer these and similar questions, especially with regard to international or cross-border practices.

B. THE DUTY TO ATTEND

1. Nature of the Duty

The duty to attend falls within the purview of the duty to treat. Section 5 of the *Act Respecting Health Services and Social Services*[258] establishes the right to

---

[256] See more particularly: Nancy Robb, "Telemedicine May Help Change the Face of Medical Care in Eastern Canada" (1997) 156 C.M.A.J. 1009; John D. Blum, "Telemedicine Poses New Challenge for the Law" (1999) 20 Health L. Can. 115; Centre de Recherche en Droit Public (CRDP), Pierre Trudel & Mylène Beaupré, *Bilan préliminaire des questions de droit soulevées par la pratique de la télémédecine de consultation*, rapport préparé pour le département d'administration de la santé de l'Université de Montréal, Montréal, 1997; Mo Watanabe, "Report on Telehealth" (Canadian Society of Telehealth, 5th International Conference on Medical Aspects of Telemedicine, Montreal, October 1-4, 2000); Sabrina Hasham, Rajen Akalu, Peter G. Rossos, "Medico-Legal Implications of Telehealth in Canada", a paper prepared by the Centre for Innovation Law and Policy of the University of Toronto, published online September 25, 2003: <http://www.innovationlaw.org/userfiles/page_attachments/library/1/working_Medico_Legal_622910.pdf>.

[257] Art. 1465 C.C.Q.

[258] R.S.Q., c. S-4.2, s. 5: "Every person is entitled to receive, with continuity and in a personalized and safe manner, health services and social services which are scientifically, humanly and

continuity in the provision of services. Likewise the *Code of Ethics of Physicians* states:

> A physician who can no longer provide the required medical follow-up of a patient must, before ceasing to do so, ensure that the patient can continue to receive the required care and contribute thereto to the extent necessary.[259]

In essence, this obligation is founded upon the duty not to abandon the patient once treatment has been initiated, whether the duty to treat results from contract or by sole operation of law in the absence of a contractual relationship. A number of disciplinary decisions have sanctioned physicians for failing to respect this fundamental obligation.[260] Emergency practice, the custodial role of institutions, a proliferation in the number of consultations requested and the shortening of hospital stays have all produced a need to pay greater attention to this aspect of the doctor-patient relationship. Is it acceptable for a hospitalized patient to be unable to identify his or her treating physician?

As in the case of the duty to treat, the duty to attend must, as a rule, be assumed personally by the treating physician. Yet it is a well-known common practice in university settings that post-operative follow-up, for example, is generally provided by the surgical residents who remain under the control and responsibility of the surgeon having actually performed the operation. Since it is the surgeon's duty that is being fulfilled by others, this calls into play the principles of liability for the act of another to which we have alluded above. The same general rule applies to developments occurring in the course of treatment: the physician must respond to calls from medical personnel or from residents who feel that the treating physician's intervention is required. The same principle applies to specialists on call who must be available to provide support to general practitioners or emergency physicians who are in need of assistance.[261]

Ensuring an attentive follow-up implies that the physician must provide the patient, or those within the patient's entourage, sufficient indication of what is expected of them such as, for example, the medication to be taken or the signs and symptoms which could signal a complication or deterioration. The particular complaints and anxieties of the patient must also be given serious consideration,

---

socially appropriate". For a striking illustration of a violation of this duty in a hospital setting, see *Lacombe v. Hôpital Maisonneuve-Rosemont*, [2004] J.Q. No. 423 at para. 36, [2004] R.R.A. 138 at 142 (Que. S.C.) (an elderly woman suffering respiratory problems was left unattended on a stretcher in a hospital corridor for four hours during the night).

[259] R.R.Q., c. M-9, r. 4.1, s. 35.

[260] *Girard v. Ordre professionnel des médecins*, [1995] D.T.P.Q. no. 106, [1995] D.D.O.P. 259 (T.P.): a detainee in a police station deemed a malingerer by the physician who refused to administer treatment even though the patient was in shock; *Blitte v. Ordre professionnel des médecins*, [1998] D.T.P.Q. no. 154, [1998] D.D.O.P. 321 (T.P.): a cardiologist leaves for two months, merely leaving a message on his answering machine; *Ordre professionnel des médecins v. Pelletier*, [2005] D.D.O.P. 160 (C.D. Méd.): a rheumatologist who agreed to provide a patient with a written evaluation failed to do so despite promises to this effect and who also failed to keep numerous appointments. Fortunately, these are rare examples.

[261] The sanctions imposed in these cases are most often disciplinary, dealt with at a local level in the institution. See nevertheless *Bédard v. Gauthier*, [1996] R.R.A. 860 (C.Q.), in which a specialist, pleading fatigue, refused to answer calls from his colleagues.

as is illustrated in the case of *Drolet v. Parenteau.*[262] A female patient lost the sight in one eye following plastic surgery on her eyelids (bilateral blepharoplasty). The surgeon disregarded certain symptoms which presented in the hours and days following surgery and thus overlooked the incipient indications of a rare but serious and well-known complication. Moreover, due to the insufficiency of instructions given to those close to the patient who were physicians in their own right, they failed to react in time.[263] In another case, a woman called the attention of her gynaecologist to a birthmark on her right buttock but he did not attach any importance to the presence of this lesion. She died three years later as a result of a generalized melanoma for which her gynaecologist was held liable, the court refusing to lend credence to his argument that it was the duty of his patient to have reminded him of her problem![264]

Because it is impossible to be available at all times, physicians tend to practise as a group. In this type of situation, even if the patient has a regular physician, he or she could, at any time, be attended by another member of the group who would have access to the medical record and to all other pertinent information relating to that patient. Arrangements of this kind greatly facilitate the organization and division of work and thus provide a greater sense of security to the client. On the other hand, should complications arise in the course of treatment, group practice may make it more difficult to establish the liability of those involved when the patient has in fact been seen by various members of the group. In order to establish solidary liability under these circumstances, each debtor of the duty to care for the patient must have committed a prejudicial fault[265] or, more clearly stated, must actually have been involved in administering treatment.[266] Under art. 1525, para. 3 of the *Civil Code of Quebec*, the exploitation of a group practice clinic constitutes the carrying on of "an organized economic activity" and on this basis legal solidarity exists between its members. Since the summer of 2001, the Quebec government has adopted a policy of actively encouraging family practitioners to engage in group practice as one of its priorities within a more general approach to reforming the health care system.[267]

Walk-in clinics established through private initiative also constitute an alternative means of offering health services. They enable persons suffering

[262] [1994] J.Q. No. 167, [1994] R.J.Q. 689 (Que. C.A.), revg in part [1991] J.Q. No. 2583, [1991] R.J.Q. 2956 (Que. S.C.): found liable only for having failed to attend and not for any fault in treatment.

[263] Que. C.A., *ibid.*, at 701 R.J.Q.

[264] *Stunell v. Pelletier*, [1999] J.Q. No. 4992, [1999] R.J.Q. 2863 (Que. S.C.).

[265] Art. 1523 C.C.Q.; Pauline Lesage-Jarjoura & Suzanne Philips-Nootens, *Éléments de responsabilité civile médicale — le droit dans le quotidien de la médecine*, 2nd ed. (Cowansville, QC: Éditions Yvon Blais, 2001) at 322 n.395.

[266] Pauline Lesage-Jarjoura & Suzanne Philips-Nootens, *Éléments de responsabilité civile médicale — le droit dans le quotidien de la médecine*, 2nd ed. (Cowansville, QC: Éditions Yvon Blais, 2001) at 322 n. 395.

[267] Quebec, Commission of Study on Health and Social Services, *Emerging Solutions — Report and Recommendations* (Québec: Ministère de la Santé et des Services Sociaux, Direction des Communications, December 18, 2000) (Clair Report).

from less serious conditions to avoid having to attend hospital emergency rooms. However, by their very nature, they raise certain legal dilemmas including the determination of who is the actual treating physician and who will ensure adequate follow-up of the patient. If the physician practising in this type of setting is responsible for the medical acts performed, he or she is working in conditions quite analogous to that of an emergency room physician since in both settings, neither usually knows the patient. It is felt that the courts will tend to take these circumstances under consideration in order to determine whether or not a medical fault has occurred.[268]

Another recent phenomenon in relation to the provision of health services — the development of home care — involves opportunities resulting from advances in technology and a concomitant desire on the part of the government to reduce the costs of these services. It is obviously more comforting for a patient to be treated in his or her home provided this environment is conducive to adequate care and does not impose an excessive burden on the family. The system of follow-up must ensure that given the situation of the patient and his or her entourage, adequate care can be provided.[269] This type of determination concerns not only the physician; nursing, social services, and local community health centres must also be involved. In cases of injury in the home care setting, one must prove the fault of one or several of these persons as well as a causal link with the injury in order to establish liability.

2. Suspension and Termination of the Duty to Attend

A physician cannot always be at the beck and call of a patient. He or she is entitled to a personal and family life, to enjoy holidays and even to be indisposed on occasion. Consequently, there must be a system established in order to ensure adequate coverage of patients. Under certain circumstances, it may become necessary to transfer the patient to the care of a more specialized practitioner or to a physician who is in a better position to provide proper treatment. Greater specialization in medicine, various modalities of practice in the hospital setting and walk-in clinics all give rise to situations where the replacement of physicians or the transfer of patients may occur.

(a) Temporary Replacement

When the replacement of a physician is only temporary, the physician who is replaced normally reassumes responsibility for the patient upon his or her return. The patient must be properly informed of the fact that the treating physician will be temporarily replaced, the duration of this replacement, the identity and qualifications of the replacing physician and the possibility of retaining the services of another physician if the patient so desires. In the context of individ-

---

[268] See section IV.A.1.(a) "Conscientious and Attentive Care", which was discussed earlier.

[269] See more particularly Jean-Pierre Ménard, "Virage ambulatoire et responsabilité médicale et hospitalière" in Service de la Formation Permanente du Barreau du Québec, *Développements récents en responsabilité médicale et hospitalière (1999)* (Cowansville, QC: Éditions Yvon Blais, 1999) at 109.

ual practice, the physician must be diligent in the choice of a replacement so that in his or her absence, the patient will receive uninterrupted adequate care. The physician must provide the replacement with all necessary information in order that the latter can properly fulfil his or her tasks. In this regard, the medical record must be clear and complete. As for the replacing physician or *locum tenens*, he or she assumes all the duties of the physician replaced and must ensure continuity of care in a diligent and competent manner. The replacement must refrain from undertaking new initiatives unless the condition of the patient so requires since it is not for him or her to unduly interfere with treatment already initiated unless an obvious error has been discovered. When the period of replacement has come to an end, the replacing physician must in turn provide the original physician with all pertinent information arising from his or her attendance upon the patient.

There are very few cases dealing with replacement *per se*. A less recent Quebec decision found that a physician was liable for the injury caused to a patient as a result of his replacement's failure to respond to a patient's calls.[270] Certain writers have sought to justify this point of view[271] whereas other have raised doubts as to its validity, arguing that each physician involved should be answerable only for his or her own fault because the contract existing between the treating physician and the patient should be deemed suspended during the interval of replacement. Interestingly enough, this approach has received some measure of support. In the case of *De Bogyay v. Royal Victoria Hospital*,[272] for example, the Court of Appeal held that the replacing physician, and not the treating physician who was on vacation, would be liable for the suicide of a patient. This decision even held that a second contract had been concluded between the patient and the physician acting as a replacement.

(b) Permanent Transfer

There can be no possible doubt in the case of a permanent transfer that the relationship between the treating physician and the patient is terminated and a new legal relationship is entered into with the physician to whom the patient is transferred, provided of course the second physician is willing to assume responsibility for this patient. A simple request for a transfer in itself is insufficient; the doctor approached must agree to take on the patient:

> A physician who wishes to refer a patient to another physician must assume responsibility for that patient until the new physician takes responsibility for the latter.[273]

All pertinent information must be provided to the new physician in order that he or she can properly treat the patient and ensure continuity of care. One must be

---

[270] *Bergstrom v. G.*, [1967] C.S. 513 (Que. S.C.).

[271] Alain Bernardot & Robert P. Kouri, *La responsabilité civile médicale* (Sherbrooke, QC: Éditions Revue de Droit Université de Sherbrooke, 1980) at 186 n. 276.

[272] [1987] J.Q. No. 1413, [1987] R.R.A. 613 (Que. C.A.). See also *Drapeau-Gourd v. Power*, J.E. 82-424 (Que. S.C.).

[273] *Code of Ethics of Physicians*, R.R.Q., c. M-9, r. 4.1, s. 33.

particularly careful in cases where the actual transfer poses risks for the patient in light of his or her health status. For example, one must ensure that the patient can be transported safely. The case of *Lapointe v. Hôpital Le Gardeur* is very eloquent in this connection. A four-year-old child suffered an injury to her arm and was bleeding profusely. She was transported to a first hospital, Le Gardeur, where the physician on call administered first aid and decided to transfer the patient to a pediatric hospital because of a lack of resources necessary to perform the required surgery. A certain amount of confusion arose during the actual transfer. The child suffered a cardio-respiratory arrest, was resuscitated but sustained significant permanent *sequelae*. The Supreme Court of Canada overturned the Court of Appeal and re-established the decision of the trial judge exonerating the first physician since he was found not to have committed any fault under the circumstances.[274]

C. PROFESSIONAL SECRECY AND MEDICAL RECORDS

We will allude briefly to these two elements inherent in the physician-patient relationship for purposes of information only since no exceptional rules of civil liability are involved.

1. Professional Secrecy

Professional secrecy has always been a cornerstone of medical deontology. As the present *Code of Ethics* provides: A physician "must keep confidential the information obtained in the practice of his profession".[275] As a corollary to the right of privacy and respect of human dignity, this duty is specifically recognized by the Quebec *Charter of Human Rights and Freedoms*,[276] and as such is considered a fundamental right. Its scope is extensive, encompassing all information having come to the physician's knowledge in the course of his or her professional activities.

Since the right to secrecy is vested in the patient, he or she has the right to expressly or tacitly allow certain confidential information to be released. For instance, a patient may request that the physician communicate pertinent information to a colleague for purposes of consultation or for effecting a transfer. Similarly, the information can be included in a medical certificate or report intended for an employer or an insurance company in furtherance of a claim. A tacit renunciation to confidentiality in favour of close family members may be inferred from their presence during consultation or treatment, unless, of course, the patient objects. One cannot, however, presuppose a tacit renunciation by the mere fact that the patient is obliged to provide information to clerical staff

---

[274] *Lapointe v. Hôpital Le Gardeur*, [1992] S.C.J. No. 11, [1992] 1 S.C.R. 351 (S.C.C.). Likewise: *Green v. Surchin*, [1993] Q.J. No. 1865, [1993] R.R.A. 821 (Que. S.C.), affd [1997] Q.J. No. 198, [1997] R.R.A. 39 (Que. C.A.), leave to appeal to S.C.C. refused [1997] C.S.C.R. No. 122 (S.C.C.).

[275] *Code of Ethics of Physicians*, R.R.Q., c. M-9, r. 4.1, s. 20(1).

[276] R.S.Q., c. C-12, s. 9.

at a reception desk within the hearing of others in facilities poorly designed to ensure privacy.

Certain situations, by their very nature, allow for the divulgation of confidential information without the patient's authorization. Indeed, several laws provide for this possibility.[277] Likewise, by the mere fact of initiating a malpractice suit against a physician, pertinent medical information may be revealed since everyone has the right to a full defence. The trial judge enjoys, in this regard, broad discretionary powers concerning the admissibility of information normally protected.[278] On the other hand, when a physician is summoned to testify in judicial proceedings other than in a malpractice suit brought by his or her patient, the legal situation remains far from clear. Certain judgments have held that the decision to breach confidentiality falls within the sole discretion of the physician. We feel that the better approach would be for the judge to decide what information is essential for the proper administration of justice within the framework of the litigation pending before the court.[279]

The *Code of Ethics of Physicians* itself provides that in addition to the reasons alluded to above, it is not possible to reveal confidential information "except when the patient or the law authorizes him to do so, or when there are compelling and just grounds related to the health or safety of the patient or of others".[280] Since the *Code of Ethics* specifically states "may reveal", this implies that the decision to reveal is left to the physician's discretion in certain cases where, for example, there may be a need to ensure proper surveillance by the family of a depressive patient or of a patient requiring special monitoring following surgery. Moreover, legislation undoubtedly inspired by the Supreme Court's decision in *Smith v. Jones*[281] allows professionals governed by the *Professional Code*[282] to "communicate information protected by professional secrecy, in order to prevent an act of violence, including suicide, where... there is an imminent danger of death or serious bodily injury to a person or to an identifiable group of persons". The question is much more difficult when it becomes necessary to go against the wishes of a non-violent patient who represents nonetheless a risk for persons close to him or her due to a particular medical condition such as a sexually transmitted disease or HIV. A physician could be faced with the choice of either actually warning third parties and being exposed to a suit by a patient whose right to secrecy has been violated, or else remaining silent and being sued by those close to the patient who may have

---

[277] See, for example, *Youth Protection Act*, R.S.Q., c. P-34.1; *Public Health Act*, R.S.Q., c. S-2.2; *Highway Safety Code*, R.S.Q., c. C-24.2.

[278] *Goulet v. Lussier*, [1989] J.Q. No. 1204, [1989] R.J.Q. 2085 (Que. C.A.).

[279] Pauline Lesage-Jarjoura & Suzanne Philips-Nootens, *Éléments de responsabilité civile médicale — le droit dans le quotidien de la médecine*, 2nd ed. (Cowansville, QC: Éditions Yvon Blais, 2001) at 348-49 nn. 420-421; *Société d'habitation du Québec v. Hébert*, [2004] J.Q. No. 3192, [2004] R.R.A. 446 (Que. S.C.).

[280] *Code of Ethics of Physicians*, R.R.Q., c. M-9, r. 4.1, s. 20(5). See also s. 21.

[281] [1999] S.C.J. No. 15, [1999] 1 S.C.R. 455 (S.C.C.), involving the issue whether a psychiatrist retained by defendant's counsel in order to assist in preparing an accused's defence, would be allowed to reveal the fact that the individual was a sexual sadist likely to commit future offences of a violent nature.

[282] R.S.Q. c. C-26, s. 60.4.

suffered harm due to the physician's failure to warn. We feel that as the better of two alternatives, doctors should choose in favour of protecting the life and health of others.[283]

2. The Medical Record

As an indispensable component of good medical practice as well as a means of evaluating the quality of care, physicians are obliged to keep accurate records in accordance with several statutory and regulatory provisions which deal with the drafting and maintaining of medical records. These provisions include the *Act Respecting Health Services and Social Services*[284] and its regulations, the *Act Respecting Access to Documents Held by Public Bodies and the Protection of Personal Information*[285] and the *Act Respecting the Protection of Personal Information in the Private Sector.*[286] Quebec has, in effect, tended to focus on the need to safeguard privacy in its approach to legislation in this regard.

The question of ownership of medical records has been the subject of some debate in the past, but the Supreme Court of Canada appears to have resolved this issue in *McInerney v. MacDonald*[287] by deciding that while medical records, as repositories of information for purposes of treatment, should belong to the physician, the clinic, or the hospital establishment, the patient has a vital interest in and a right of access to the information contained therein. As beneficiary of the right to confidentiality, the patient can waive this right and allow others to take cognizance of the medical file. At first glance, the Supreme Court of Canada, in *Frenette v. Metropolitan Life Insurance Co.*,[288] appears to have broadly interpreted authorizations of this kind in favour of insurance companies.[289] However, in its more recent decision in *Glegg v. Smith & Nephew Inc.*,[290] the court narrowed the ambit of this holding. It held that by initiating a malpractice action involving issues of pain and suffering, shock and nervousness, the patient had granted an implied waiver of confidentiality regarding production of her psychiatric record. According to LeBel J.:

> [*Frenette v. Metropolitain Life Insurance Co.*] did not establish a principle that an express or implied waiver would authorize unlimited and uncontrolled access to a

---

[283] See, more particularly, Donald G. Casswell, "Disclosure by a Physician of AIDS-Related Patient Information: An Ethical and Legal Dilemma" (1989) 68 Can. Bar Rev. 225.

[284] R.S.Q., c. S-4.2.

[285] R.S.Q., c. A-2.1.

[286] R.S.Q., c. P-39.1.

[287] [1992] S.C.J. No. 57, [1992] 2 S.C.R. 138 (S.C.C.).

[288] [1992] S.C.J. No. 24, [1992] 1 S.C.R. 647 (S.C.C.).

[289] According to L'Heureux-Dubé J., writing on behalf of the court: "A patient's right to the confidentiality of his medical records is a relative right which a patient may waive without restriction as to scope or time", [1992] S.C.J. No. 24 at para. 76, [1992] 1 S.C.R. 647 at 695. In addition, when a clear waiver has been given, "the holder of the right has, of his own accord, put aside his privacy [... and therefore] no balancing of interests in necessary", [1992] S.C.J. No. 24 at para. 50, [1992] 1 S.C.R. 647 at 678 (S.C.C.).

[290] [2005] S.C.J. No. 29, [2005] 1 S.C.R. 724 (S.C.C.).

patient's medical record. On the contrary, the limits on secrecy are reflected in the principle of relevance, which applies at all stages of a civil action.[291]

Accordingly, the pertinence of the information to which access is requested, in light of the specific purposes for which it is intended, shall determine the extent to which access will in fact be provided, notwithstanding the generality of the terms in which the authorization is couched. The issue is thus reduced to one of ensuring, as much as possible given the circumstances, the protection of a fundamental right, while favouring a just outcome between the parties.

V. CONCLUSION

The liability of physicians is governed by the general rules of civil responsibility as set out by the *Civil Code of Quebec* and its interpretation by jurisprudence and doctrine. Certain trends have emerged, transforming the physician-patient relationship, and making doctors more conscious of patient's rights. The development of the notion of informed consent by the courts is a case in point. By its nature, the medical contract will always remain an association built essentially on trust.

Despite a readily discernible tendency to treat the patient as an active participant in what has become a collaborative and egalitarian relationship, successfully suing a hospital or physician remains a very expensive and a highly unpredictable undertaking. Certain simplistic solutions such as attenuating the burden of proof in medical malpractice cases or imposing a much higher standard of conduct on the members of one of the most extensively regulated occupations in Canada would be highly inequitable. It is undeniable that pressures are building in Quebec to institute a no-fault system of indemnification for victims of medical misadventure. For the moment, the economic burden of such a system would appear to be the primary obstacle to its implementation.

---

[291] *Ibid.*, at para. 21 S.C.J., at 736 S.C.R.

Chapter 5

INFORMED CONSENT

Patricia Peppin[*]

I. INTRODUCTION

The legal doctrine of informed consent protects patients' interests in bodily integrity and asserts the right of patients to decide about medical treatments based on knowledge of the relative advantages and disadvantages. Justice La Forest, for the majority of the Supreme Court of Canada in *Hollis v. Dow Corning Corp.*, stated:

> The doctrine of "informed consent" dictates that every individual has a right to know what risks are involved in undergoing or foregoing medical treatment and a concomitant right to make meaningful decisions based on a full understanding of those risks ... The doctrine of 'informed consent' was developed as a judicial attempt to redress the inequality of information that characterizes a doctor-patient relationship.[1]

In *Malette v. Shulman*, Robins J.A., for the Ontario Court of Appeal, expressed the principle in this way:

> The doctrine of informed consent has developed in the law as the primary means of protecting a patient's right to control his or her medical treatment ... The right of self-determination, which underlies the doctrine of informed consent, also obviously encompasses the right to refuse medical treatment ... The doctrine of informed consent is plainly intended to ensure the freedom of individuals to make choices concerning their medical care. For this freedom to be meaningful, people must have the right to make choices that accord with their own values, regardless of how unwise or foolish those choices may appear to others.[2]

Participation in decision-making provides the opportunity to exercise choice according to one's own values and beliefs and protects patients from

---

[*] I would like to thank the Lederman Law Library Head Librarian Nancy McCormack, and researchers Samantha Irvine, Jonathan Burton-MacLeod, Dan McKeown and Gary Chui for their assistance.
[1] [1995] S.C.J. No. 104, [1995] 4 S.C.R. 634 (S.C.C.) at paras. 24-25.
[2] *Malette v. Shulman*, [1990] O.J. No. 450, 72 O.R. (2d) 417 at 423-24 (Ont. C.A.), affg [1987] O.J. No. 1180, 64 O.R. (2d) 243 (Ont. H.C.J.).

paternalistic imposition of treatment decisions. The doctrine of informed consent changed radically in 1980 when the Supreme Court of Canada decided *Hopp v. Lepp* and *Reibl v. Hughes*.[3] As these decisions have been implemented, a shift to greater patient involvement in decision-making has been discernible. At the same time, courts, including the Supreme Court itself, have engaged in critical assessment of the doctrine, and particularly of the modified test of causation. These doctrines are analyzed in Parts II and III of this chapter. Some legislatures have taken steps to codify and expand the frameworks applying to consent to treatment, while others have confined their reforms to advance directives. These developments are examined briefly in Part IV. Since 1980, profound changes in the provision of health care and availability of knowledge have had an impact on implementation of the doctrines in practice, affecting disclosure of information and patients' abilities to participate in decision-making. The context within which medical treatment decisions are made has altered radically in the intervening decades as practice has shifted to collaborative care provided by a range of health practitioners, patients have been deinstitutionalized to community settings, the range of treatment alternatives has expanded, bringing both benefits and risks, and spiralling costs accompanied by planning lag have led to delays in access to care. The final section critically assesses the extent to which the law has promoted the achievement of greater equality in the doctor-patient relationship, understanding of health information and participation in decision-making.

II. INFORMED CONSENT IN BATTERY

The early common law doctrine of trespass *vi et armis* which protected the interest in freedom from direct and forcible bodily intrusions[4] evolved into the action in battery, which requires an intentional act of touching without consent. Intent is inferred from the knowledge or substantial certainty that such an invasion of bodily integrity will result from the intentional act, as the bullet hitting the body results from pulling the trigger. Intent is distinguishable from motive, as the well-intentioned manager found when he manipulated the arm of the protesting woman injured by a fall at the New Dreamland Roller Skating Rink.[5] Significantly, the battery action requires no proof of actual injury to the plaintiff apart from the harm inherent in the invasion of the bodily integrity and as a result the damages reflect the injury to the dignitary interest of the individual.

---

[3]   *Hopp v. Lepp*, [1980] S.C.J. No. 57, [1980] 2 S.C.R. 192 (S.C.C.); *Reibl v. Hughes*, [1980] S.C.J. No. 105, [1980] 2 S.C.R. 880 (S.C.C.).
[4]   John G. Fleming, *The Law of Torts*, 7th ed. (Sydney: The Law Book Company, 1987) at 23-24.
[5]   Clayton v. New Dreamland Roller Skating Rink, 82 A.2d 458 (Sup. Ct. N.J. 1951).

A. ELEMENTS OF CONSENT IN BATTERY

Consent must meet certain requirements be valid.[6] It must be informed, capable and voluntary. The information required is the nature and quality of the act. Capacity refers to the mental ability to make the decision in addition to any legal capacity established by statute or common law. Consent must be given by a capable person or by a person legally entitled to decide on behalf of an incapable person. Voluntary acts are those free of coercion or duress. Fraud or misrepresentation vitiates consent. The doctrine of unconscionability, an exploitation of the power imbalance between the parties, is another possible basis for undermining consent.[7]

Consent may be expressed, orally or in writing, or may be implied from behaviour. Express consent must refer clearly to the act to be performed and the actor. Implied consent may be given clearly where the behaviour indicates it, as when a person offers his or her limb for treatment. In an 1891 Massachusetts case of mass smallpox vaccination that was mandatory for entry into the United States, a woman arriving on board ship who discussed with the doctor whether she needed it and then lifted her arm, was found to have implied her consent: "In determining whether she consented, he could be guided only by her overt acts and the manifestations of her feelings".[8] Documents such as hospital forms may be created for other purposes such as hospital management or protection from liability. These documents are evidence and must be examined to determine whether they accurately reflect what transpired between the parties, the true basis for consent. In *Tremblay v. McLauchlan*, the patient had signed a consent form without reading it. The court found that the form did not preclude his legal action since the form was only as good as the material disclosure.[9]

Consent is a defence provable by the defendant rather than an element of the tort requiring proof by the plaintiff. The Supreme Court of Canada affirmed this view in the four judge majority judgment by McLachlin J. in *Non-Marine Underwriters, Lloyd's of London v. Scalera.*[10] The three minority judges, concurring in the result, took a position dramatically at odds with battery's goal of protecting autonomy, dignity and bodily integrity, in positing that the plaintiff had the onus of proving the harmful or offensive nature of the contact by proving that the defendant knew that she was not consenting or that a reasonable person in the defendant's position would have known that the plaintiff was not consenting. In contrast, in *Toews (Guardian ad litem of) v. Weisner*, the

---

[6]   These requirements have been incorporated into statutes in some of the provinces and territories, as discussed in Part V below.

[7]   In *Norberg v. Wynrib*, [1992] S.C.J. No. 60, [1992] 2 S.C.R. 226 (S.C.C.), additional reasons at [1992] S.C.J. No. 109, 2 S.C.R. 318 (S.C.C.), three judges in the plurality found for the plaintiff on the basis of battery because of the unconscionable behaviour of the defendant, Dr. Wynrib, of obtaining sexual acts in return for prescriptions for the barbiturate to which Laura Norberg was addicted. The other three judges found that she had consented to the sexual acts. Two judges found a breach of fiduciary duty and one found for her in negligence. Five of six judges found for the plaintiff on the basis of inequality analysis.

[8]   *O'Brien v. Cunard S.S. Co.*, 28 N.E. 266 (Mass. 1891).

[9]   [2001] B.C.J. No. 1403 (B.C.C.A.) at para. 28.

[10] [2000] S.C.J. No. 26, [2001] 1 S.C.R. 551 (S.C.C.). The disposition of the case was unanimous.

vaccination of a minor without the consent of the parents was held to be a battery even though Weisner, the community health nurse, held an honest belief that the students' parents had consented.[11] Further, although as a general principle consent may be implied based on the plaintiff's or substitute decision-maker's behaviour, it was not reasonable to draw such an inference based on the erroneous belief.[12]

B. NATURE OF CONSENT

Consent refers to a specific act by a specific person. Different procedures, acts on other body parts and acts carried out by others all indicate an absence of consent. Following the Supreme Court of Canada's decision in *Reibl v. Hughes*, battery continues to be the appropriate action in situations where there is no consent at all or where the act exceeds the consent, apart from emergencies.[13] Negligence law applies in other circumstances, where disclosure is inadequate. Situations where there is no consent at all include those where one of the requirements for valid consent is missing, because the consent is not informed or not made with capacity or is not voluntary; where the consent has been vitiated; where a procedure has been performed on the wrong body part; where another person has performed the procedure; where the act has been refused; or where consent has been given to one procedure and another non-emergency procedure has been performed.[14] The specific nature of consent creates a boundary around the consent that excludes collateral matters. For example, in *Halkyard v. Mathew*, a case involving the physician's non-disclosure of his epilepsy, the trial judge found no fraud or misrepresentation, no evidence that the physician was covering up in order to obtain consent to the surgery, no obligation to disclose, no materiality of the risk and no battery, since the patient consented to the surgery she received.[15]

Fraud or misrepresentation as to the consequences of having sex with someone with a sexually transmitted disease (STD) has been found not to undermine the consent since the woman in this case consented to the act itself, even if she did not agree to the collateral matter of the STD.[16] The Supreme

---

[11] [2001] B.C.J. No. 30 (B.C.S.C.).

[12] *Allan v. New Mount Sinai Hospital* (1980), 28 O.R. (2d) 356 (Ont. H.C.J.), revd [1981] O.J. No. 2874, 33 O.R. (2d) 603 (Ont. C.A.), applied in *Toews (Guardian ad litem of) v. Weisner*, [2001] B.C.J. No. 30 (B.C.S.C.) at para. 20.

[13] [1980] S.C.J. No. 105, [1980] 2 S.C.R. 880 (S.C.C.).

[14] For example, in class certification proceedings in *Rideout v. Health Labrador Corp.*, [2005] N.J. No. 228 (Nfld. S.C. (T.D.)), class certification for battery was denied because the patients had consented to have examinations performed with the medical instruments while other parts of the action were certified based on the alleged improper sterilization of the instruments. Other examples are consenting to toe surgery and having a spinal fusion (*Schweizer v. Central Hospital*, [1974] O.J. No. 2205 (Ont. H.C.J.)) and wrong limb surgery, a common enough problem that quality assurance programs now require the correct part to be marked with a magic marker and initialled by the surgeon.

[15] [1998] A.J. No. 986 (Alta. Q.B.), affd [2001] A.J. No. 293 (Alta. C.A.).

[16] *Hegarty v. Shine* (1878), 4 L.R. Ir. 288 (C.A.). The *ex turpi causa* doctrine barred recovery since the plaintiff had participated in the "illegal or immoral act" of having sex outside marriage.

Court of Canada revisited the *Criminal Code* sexual assault provision whose fraud definition had been amended to remove mention of the nature and quality of the act in *R. v. Cuerrier*, a case involving non-disclosure of the defendant's HIV-positive status.[17] Justice Cory, with three judges concurring, declined to find the defence of consent successful where the defendant had concealed his status, and effectively expanded the boundaries of consent to include the consequences of the act. Consent is vitiated by fraud under this section if the failure to disclose is dishonest and results in deprivation by putting the complainant at risk of suffering serious bodily harm. This formulation imports the risk analysis of negligence to the intentional area. Justice L'Heureux-Dubé stated that fraud occurs when a dishonest act induces another to consent, regardless of the risk or danger posed by the act. Justices Gonthier and McLachlin confined fraud to the nature of the act or identity of the partner but considered sexually transmitted diseases an exception so that inducing consent on this basis would vitiate consent. Since the law of tort and criminal law are related areas, the action in battery may expand its conceptual boundaries in a similar fashion. Alternatively, the act itself could be recast to include the STD, to acknowledge that consent to sex with an STD differs from consent to sex without one.

In an emergency situation, it is permissible at common law to provide treatment without consent to "save the life or preserve the health" of the person.[18] The basis for the emergency exception has been debated but the better opinion finds its foundation not in an imagined implied consent but in a loose notion of necessity.[19] In *Ciarlariello v. Schacter*, the Court also protected the right of individuals to withdraw their consent during a procedure unless stopping it would endanger the patient's life or threaten immediate and serious health problems.[20] Beginning the analysis with the patient's right to decide what is done to his or her own body, including the right to be free of procedures to which consent has not been given, Cory J. found that this right must include the right to stop a procedure.[21] The onus to determine whether consent has been withdrawn falls on the doctor. Once consent has been withdrawn, consent must be given again before the procedure continues, with disclosure of material changes in the risks if circumstances have changed but without repeated disclosure if circumstances have not altered. The scope of the original consent becomes relevant in these cases, as in *McNeil v. Yamamoto*, where the patient's consent to excision of a vaginal nodule was held to extend to a larger nodule than expected

---

[17] [1998] S.C.J. No. 64 (S.C.C.); *Criminal Code*, R.S.C. 1985, c. C-46.

[18] *Marshall v. Curry (No. 2)*, [1933] 3 D.L.R. 198 (N.S.C.A.). The criteria for emergencies have been expanded in some provincial consent statutes.

[19] Lord Goff in *In re F. (Mental Patient: Sterilisation)*, [1989] 2 W.L.R. 1021 at 1084-85 (H.L. (E.)) characterized it as a third category of necessity cases, in addition to public and private necessity, concerned with actions in necessity taken "to preserve the life, health or well-being of another who is unable to consent to it. This necessity principle is broader than emergencies, applying to situations where it is not possible to communicate with the person, as in cases of mental incapacity". Canadian substitute decision-making legislation would govern the mental incapacity situation.

[20] [1993] S.C.J. No. 46, [1993] 2 S.C.R. 119 (S.C.C.).

[21] *Ibid.*, at para. 42.

whose excision required penetration of the vaginal wall.[22] Exceptions to informed consent are also found in legislation, such as public health statutes.[23] The role of age and capacity in determining when minors may consent to treatment is discussed in Chapter 11, section II.A.b.

C. REFUSAL BY PRIOR CAPABLE WISH

The right to refuse a treatment is a corollary of the right to decide what is done with one's body. Refusal is not usually considered controversial for capable persons making current decisions. More complex are those situations in which individuals unable to participate in decision-making due to their incapacity have expressed prior capable wishes to refuse treatment. A situation of this type arose in the case of *Malette v. Shulman*, in which the Ontario Court of Appeal affirmed the trial judge's finding of battery in an emergency situation involving a blood transfusion to an unconscious woman who had expressed a prior wish to refuse blood.[24] Dr. Shulman provided a blood transfusion to save the life of the unconscious Mme. Malette, although he had been made aware of a signed printed card in her wallet stating her refusal to accept blood or blood products based on her Jehovah's Witness belief. This case raised the issue of the effectiveness of a prior capable wish to refuse an emergency treatment necessary to save a life. The Ontario Court of Appeal found the signed card a valid expression of her wish. They considered four state interests — in the protection of life, the prevention of suicide, the prevention of harm to innocent third parties such as minor children and the preservation of the ethical integrity of the medical profession. These were first set out as "countervailing" interests in the end-of-life case of an incapable intellectually disabled man, *Supt. of Belchertown State School v. Saikewicz*, and were subsequently considered in guardianship and end-of-life cases.[25] These puzzling interests appeared without constitutional analysis and were offered as a trump card in cases in which the very issue before the court was a fundamental individual right. The Ontario Court of Appeal found that the state's interest in the protection of life would not override the individual's autonomy interest and in reaching this conclusion, they strongly affirmed the individual's right to express, and have respected, prior capable wishes about treatment.

The Ontario Court of Appeal considered and rejected several other lines of argument raised by the defence. One argument relied on the emergency exception to the requirement of informed consent. Since the emergency

---

[22] [2004] M.J. No. 457 (Man. Q.B.).

[23] Ellen I. Picard and Gerald B. Robertson, *Legal Liability of Doctors and Hospitals in Canada*, 3rd ed. (Toronto: Carswell, 1996) at 49-54.

[24] [1990] O.J. No. 450, 72 O.R. (2d) 417 (Ont. C.A.), affg [1987] O.J. No. 1180, 63 O.R. (2d) 243 (Ont. H.C.J.).

[25] 373 Mass. 728, 370 N.E.2d 417 (1977). See *Brody v. New England Sinai Hospital, Inc.*, 398 Mass. 417, 497 N.E.2d 626 (1986); *Cruzan v. Director, Missouri Department of Health*, 110 S. Ct. 2841 (1990). See also Barry R. Furrow, Sandra H. Johnson, Timothy S. Jost & Robert L. Schwartz, *Health Law: Cases, Materials and Problems*, 2nd ed. (St. Paul, Minn.: West Publ. Co., 1991) at 1099-1102. See also *Rodriguez v. British Columbia (Attorney General)*, [1993] S.C.J. No. 94, [1993] 3 S.C.R. 579 (S.C.C.).

exception applies in the absence of a patient's decision, and the Court had recognized an express refusal in finding that the card was a valid expression of her prior capable wish, the emergency exception did not apply. Another line of argument was based on the obligation to disclose information and ensure that patients comprehend it. This requirement is considered in Part III as part of the duty of disclosure in negligence. The defence argued that a parallel "informed refusal" requirement must exist and that the requirement would not have been met where it was impossible to disclose the information and ensure that she had understood it. The Court rejected this argument, commenting on the fact that no prior relationship existed. Where no prior doctor-patient relationship exists, as in an emergency situation where the doctor and patient have no opportunity to discuss such issues in advance, refusal would never be possible. It could also be argued that the defence argument reflects an understanding of informed decision-making that exists only in negligence. Since battery requires only disclosure of the nature of the act of touching, and validity rests on that information and not comprehension of consequences, such a defence to a battery action should fail.

The defence also argued that the card was invalid. Mme. Malette's card was a printed card prepared by her church, the Jehovah's Witnesses, stating that blood substitutes were acceptable but that blood and blood products were not acceptable in any circumstances. The card had been signed but had not been dated or witnessed. After a nurse found the card and informed Dr. Shulman, he gave the blood transfusion, and he continued to do so when her daughter arrived later and confirmed her mother's belief in refusing blood. The Court found that the daughter's statement was not relevant to the issue.[26] Dr. Shulman raised questions about relying on the card's validity in the absence of witnesses to affirm it or a date to indicate current adherence to its views. No evidence that the act was involuntary was present in this case and the Court rejected these speculative positions and found that the fact that she was carrying it in her wallet indicated that it reflected her views. Providing a sense of certainty for health practitioners about the existence of prior capable wishes is important particularly when decisions with profound consequences are being made without time to examine the issues in depth. As discussed in Part IV, some provincial/territorial legislatures have codified the common law and have set out with greater clarity the legal requirements in particular circumstances. This case is a strong affirmation of the individual's right to autonomy and to an entitlement to respect for their prior capable wishes.

Subsequently, in *Fleming v. Reid*, the Ontario Court of Appeal reached the same conclusion with respect to prior capable wishes to refuse treatment with neuroleptic drugs in a psychiatric facility to which the appellants, Reid and Gallagher, had been involuntarily confined under a Lieutenant Governor's Warrant.[27] They struck down the Ontario *Mental Health Act* provision authorizing the area review board to override an involuntarily committed individual's wish if the Board decided treatment was in the person's best

---

[26] At this time, provisions to transfer authority to substitute decision-makers were poorly defined, apart from guardianship proceedings.
[27] [1991] O.J. No. 1083, 4 O.R. (3d) 74 (Ont. C.A.).

interests.[28] Justice Robins relied on the *Malette v. Shulman* case for the statement of the common law principle of informed consent affirming that the patient's right is paramount to any societal interest and found that the individual's common law right to decide what may be done to his or her body was "co-extensive" with the constitutional right to security of the person, "both of which are founded on the belief in the dignity and autonomy of each individual".[29] The section 7 Charter right to security of the person had been infringed by the statutory provision, the infringement was not in accordance with the principles of fundamental justice because of the absence of a hearing, and it was not saved by section 1. The Ontario Court of Appeal declared the provision of no force or effect.[30]

A recent case involved a member of the Jehovah's Witness faith, Daphine Hobbs, who had signed a hospital form in which she refused blood and absolved the hospital and any attending doctors from responsibility for any effects, including death, from the refusal of blood. The British Columbia Court of Appeal has ordered a retrial because they found the facts insufficient given the case's far-reaching implications, which include public policy and Charter questions.[31] At trial, Dr. Robertson was found to have performed a hysterectomy using a vaginal method assisted by laporoscopy and to have delayed switching to the abdominal method for almost an hour after he should have when Ms. Hobbs began to bleed critically. No transfusion was administered since she had refused it and her husband also refused on her behalf when told of her critical situation. Ms. Hobbs died as a result. The defendant admitted to negligence in performing the surgery and to the negligence causing her death.[32] The trial judge found that Ms. Hobbs assumed the risks associated with blood loss through her refusal and found for the defendant.[33] On appeal the Court pointed to the particular need for evidence about whether the hospital would have denied admission if she had declined to sign the form, as part of a determination of whether such a document would be contrary to public policy. A further important issue raised by the plaintiffs is whether a refusal and release can insulate a doctor from responsibility for the very negligence that led to the need for the blood transfusion.

---

[28] *Mental Health Act*, R.S.O. 1980, c. 262, as am. 1987, c. 37, s. 12.

[29] [1990] O.J. No. 45, 72 O.R. (2d) 417 (Ont. C.A.), affg [1987] O.J. No. 1180, 63 O.R. (2d) 243 (Ont. H.C.J.).

[30] *Canadian Charter of Rights and Freedoms*, Part I of the *Constitution Act, 1982*, being Schedule B to the *Canada Act 1982* (U.K.), 1982, c. 11, s. 7. *R. v. Parker*, [2000] O.J. No. 2787 (Ont. C.A.) upheld the stay of charges for medical marijuana use, declaring the provision of no force or effect under the Charter, finding a broad criminal prohibition preventing access to necessary treatment inconsistent with the principles of fundamental justice and citing Robins J.A. in *Fleming v. Reid*, [1991] O.J. No. 1083, 4 O.R. (3d) 74 (Ont. C.A.) on the principle of informed consent as "fundamental and deserving of the highest order of protection" (at para. 102) and finding informed consent doctrine the "closest analogue", in the right to self-determination, to the entitlement to drug therapy (at para. 135).

[31] *Hobbs v. Robertson*, [2006] B.C.J. No. 266 (B.C.C.A.) at para. 34, sending for retrial [2004] B.C.J. No. 1689 (B.C.S.C.).

[32] *Ibid.*, at para. 2 (C.A.).

[33] *Hobbs v. Robertson*, [2004] B.C.J. No. 1689 (B.C.S.C.) at para. 93.

Throughout the period before 1980, the battery action provided the legal basis for patients to sue doctors for failure to provide treatment information and it is the current basis for action when there is no consent at all or the procedure exceeds the consent. From a tactical point of view, the action in battery has significant advantages for the plaintiff. The defendant has the onus of proving informed consent. Causation is not an element of the tort. Battery requires no proof of harm and so damages are available to compensate for the infringement of the plaintiff's bodily integrity. Fraud, misrepresentation and unconscionability may all be available to vitiate the consent.

III. INFORMED DECISION-MAKING IN NEGLIGENCE

Since the 1980 Supreme Court decisions in *Hopp v. Lepp* and *Reibl v. Hughes*, most actions for failure to inform patients have been litigated in negligence.[34] These negligence actions focus on inadequate disclosure in a situation where the health professional owes a duty of care, as opposed to the lack of disclosure of the nature and quality of the act that characterizes the battery action. As in all negligence actions, the plaintiff must prove the elements of the action — a duty of care owed by the health practitioner to the patient, a breach of the standard of care, factual causation linking the defendant's negligence to the plaintiff's harm, remoteness, and actual harm to the plaintiff.

A. DUTY OF DISCLOSURE

In declaring that a doctor had a duty to disclose information about a proposed procedure, the Supreme Court of Canada took a significant step in the direction of patient participation in decision-making. The *Hopp v. Lepp* case, the first 1980 decision, arose out of spinal surgery that required a second neurosurgeon to operate to remove extruded disc material that would not have been apparent in the first operation, a procedure that resulted in nerve damage that caused permanent disabilities.[35] Chief Justice Laskin stated that the underlying principle is the right of patients to decide what if anything should be done with their bodies and found that the doctor owed a duty of disclosure to the patient.[36] He stated the duty as follows:

> In summary, the decided cases appear to indicate that, in obtaining the consent of a patient for the performance upon him of a surgical operation, a surgeon, generally, should answer any specific questions posed by the patient as to the risks involved and should, without being questioned, disclose to him the nature of the proposed operation, its gravity, any material risks and any special or unusual risks attendant upon the performance of the operation. However, having said that, it should be added that the scope of the duty of disclosure and whether or not it has been

---

[34] *Hopp v. Lepp*, [1980] S.C.J. No. 57, [1980] 2 S.C.R. 192 (S.C.C.); *Reibl v. Hughes*, [1980] S.C.J. No. 105, [1980] 2 S.C.R. 880 (S.C.C.).

[35] *Hopp v. Lepp*, *ibid.*

[36] *Ibid.*, at 196.

breached are matters which must be decided in relation to the circumstances of each particular case.[37]

Further, "even if a certain risk is a mere possibility which ordinarily need not be disclosed, yet if its occurrence carries serious consequences, as for example, paralysis or even death, it should be regarded as a material risk requiring disclosure".[38] The Court clearly established a broad standard of disclosure based on patients' need to know and rejected the alternative professional disclosure standard based on customary disclosure of the profession. The Supreme Court of Canada found medical evidence important but "at most" only one factor to be considered since it is a particular patient and particular treatment that are at issue in the decision.[39] "Materiality connotes an objective test, according to what would reasonably be regarded as influencing a patient's consent", they decided.[40] Probable risks need to be disclosed and possible risks with grave consequences may well be material.[41] Scope and breach "are matters which must be decided in relation to the circumstances of each particular case".[42] Significantly, the Supreme Court required that informed decision-making be assessed in an individualized way by taking account of the context.[43] Finding that there was nothing in the record to indicate that there were possible risks beyond those in any operation, to which Mr. Lepp had consented, the Court found no breach of the duty of disclosure. As a result, there was no need to proceed to the causation analysis.

In *Reibl v. Hughes*, John Reibl was diagnosed with hyptertension and a specialist, Dr. Hughes, recommended a carotid endarterectomy to surgically remove a blockage in his left carotid artery.[44] As a result of the "very poor communication"[45] by Dr. Hughes, Mr. Reibl mistakenly believed that his headaches would be cured and did not understand the risks of the procedure, including the risk of non-fatal stroke, which could occur in 10 per cent of cases, and death from stroke of under 4 per cent, for a cumulative risk of 14 per cent.[46] The Supreme Court noted that Mr. Reibl's first language was Hungarian but that he was intelligent and capable of understanding the information. A risk of having a stroke would also have existed if he had postponed the surgery but it

---

[37] *Ibid.*, at 210.
[38] *Reibl v. Hughes*, [1980] S.C.J. No. 105, [1980] 2 S.C.R. 880 at 884-85 (S.C.C.), summarizing their earlier position.
[39] *Hopp v. Lepp*, [1980] S.C.J. No. 57, [1980] 2 S.C.R. 192 at 209 (S.C.C.).
[40] *Ibid.*
[41] *Ibid.*
[42] *Ibid.*, at 210.
[43] In considering the definition of material risks, Laskin C.J.C. made reference to the standard adopted in *Canterbury v. Spence*, 464 F.2d 772 (D.C.Cir. 1972), cert. denied, 409 U.S. 1064*n*, which found materiality when a reasonable person in what the doctor knew or should know to be the patient's position would likely attach significance to the risk in deciding whether to proceed with the proposed treatment.
[44] [1977] O.J. No. 2289 (Ont. H.C.J.) at paras. 5-6, revd [1978] O.J. No. 3502, 21 O.R. (2d) 14 (Ont. C.A.), affd [1980] S.C.J. No. 105, [1980] 2 S.C.R. 880 (S.C.C.).
[45] Ellen I. Picard, *Legal Liability of Doctors and Hospitals in Canada*, 1st ed. (Toronto: Carswell, 1977) at 71-72.
[46] *Reibl v. Hughes*, [1977] O.J. No. 2289 (Ont. H.C.J.) at paras. 12, 21.

would have been postponed and was indeterminate, unlike the surgical risk. Mr. Reibl suffered a massive stroke as a result of the surgery and became paralyzed on one side and impotent.

The standard of care for disclosure includes the nature of the treatment and its gravity; the material risks, including probability and gravity, grave consequences even if they have a low probability, and what the doctor knows or should know the patient deems relevant; special or unusual risks; the alternatives and their risks, including the risk of not proceeding with the treatment; and the answers to any questions asked by the patient.[47] The elements, apart from questions, are what reasonable patients would want to know about these factors. The measure of material risk involves not only a risk-benefit calculation. In addition, they found, "What the doctor knows or should know that the particular patient deems relevant to a decision whether to undergo prescribed treatment goes equally to his duty of disclosure as do the material risks recognized as a matter of required medical knowledge".[48] Doctors and other health practitioners are not aware of all the personal circumstances that might be relevant to the patient's decision but disclosure of the risks should either trigger a discussion of those factors by the patient or enable the patient to make the decision without discussion.

Alternatives must also be disclosed. Chief Justice Laskin considered the issue of alternatives to the proposed treatment in a passage referring to *Canterbury v. Spence* indicating that disclosure included "alternative means of treatment and their risks".[49] Later courts have considered the requirement in a variety of circumstances. In *Van Mol (Guardian ad litem of) v. Ashmore*, the British Columbia Court of Appeal found that the full range of alternatives, including the alternative methods of carrying out the cardiac surgery, should have been disclosed to the 16-year-old patient.[50] The Ontario Court of Appeal has considered these cases recently in *Van Dyke v. Grey Bruce Regional Health Centre* and concluded that it is the patient's decision and so the doctor must equip the patient with the information necessary to make an informed choice. Where there is more than one medically reasonable treatment and the risk/benefit analysis engaged by the alternatives involves different considerations, a reasonable person would want to know about the alternatives and would want the assistance of the doctor's risk/benefit analysis of the various possible treatments before deciding whether to proceed with a specific treatment.[51]

---

[47] Chief Justice Howland provided a useful — and often-quoted — summary of the Supreme Court's conclusions in *Videto v. Kennedy*, [1981] O.J. No. 3054 (Ont. C.A.).

[48] *Reibl v. Hughes*, [1980] S.C.J. No. 105, [1980] 2 S.C.R. 880 at 894 (S.C.C.).

[49] *Ibid.*, at 895; *Canterbury v. Spence*, 464 F.2d 772 (D.C. Cir. 1972), cert. denied, 409 U.S. 1064*n*. Krever J. noted later in *Ferguson v. Hamilton Civic Hospitals* that the obligation to disclose alternatives to the procedure and its risks was "implicit" in the quotation. *Ferguson v. Hamilton Civic Hospitals*, [1983] O.J. No. 2497, 40 O.R. (2d) 577 (Ont. H.C.J.), affd [1985] O.J. No. 2538 (Ont. C.A.).

[50] [1999] B.C.J. No. 31 (B.C.C.A.), leave to appeal refused [1999] S.C.C.A. No. 117 (S.C.C.).

[51] [2005] O.J. No. 2219 (Ont. C.A.) at para. 67, leave to appeal refused [2005] S.C.C.A. No. 335 (S.C.C.).

Although some cases have indicated that where a divergence of views exists in the medical profession and the physician disagrees with an option, the physician needs only to disclose those alternatives thought to be advantageous to the patient, Picard and Robertson considered that the duty to disclose alternatives should extend beyond this to alternatives considered inappropriate by the doctor, who should provide an explanation of this opinion.[52] The existence of alternatives outside the scope of the profession, for instance in the area of complementary medicine or other health professions, poses a particular problem of expertise and it seems unlikely that a court would find an obligation to disclose those alternatives considered not to meet the standard of care or to require expertise beyond the scope of practice of the health practitioner. Caulfield and Feasby have commented about complementary and alternative medicine that the expansive disclosure obligations in Canada indicate that physicians are likely to be required to disclose known risks, to counsel about the existence of risks, to discuss efficacy and to consider the possible application of the broader research standard of disclosure.[53] The requirement to disclose alternatives should be held to the standard of care of the profession to protect patients from untested therapies until they are able to meet the standard of care. Hunter Prillaman commented that, "Under such a standard, a physician could avoid the danger of having to describe the theories of quacks or to explain treatments too new to have a track record, but could still be held to have a duty to keep up with the relevant literature and other sources of information, and to inform patients of new treatments as they met the criteria of acceptance".[54]

Bernard Dickens made a powerful argument in favour of disclosure of certain kinds of information when physicians disagree with a procedure based on their own values or conscientious beliefs.[55] As he noted, participation in such procedures is not normally expected but still a duty exists to their own patients and to those likely to seek their care to tell them which procedures they are unwilling to provide and to give reasonable advice on available services of these types along with access to it. Emergency contraception, which must be provided within 72 hours, provides an important instance of these principles. Dickens noted that failure to disclose the option to those to whom the duty is owed may lead to civil liability, breach of fiduciary duty, negligence for failure to refer, breach of contract for fraudulent misrepresentation, criminal liability for criminal negligence causing bodily harm and contravention of a provincial human rights code provision, since non-disclosure may be seen as discrimination against women and as inhuman and degrading treatment. Some

---

[52]   Ellen I. Picard & Gerald B. Robertson, *Legal Liability of Doctors and Hospitals in Canada*, 3rd ed. (Toronto: Carswell, 1996) at 129.

[53]   Timothy Caulfield & Colin Feasby, "Potions, Promises and Paradoxes: Complementary Medicine and Alternative Medicine and Malpractice Law in Canada" (2001) 9 Health L.J. 183 at paras. 18-21.

[54]   Hunter L. Prillaman, "A Physician's Duty to Inform of Newly Developed Therapy" (1990) 6 J. Contemp. Health Law & Pol'y 43 at 58.

[55]   Bernard Dickens, "Informed Consent" in Jocelyn Downie, Timothy Caulfield & Colleen Flood, eds., *Canadian Health Law and Policy*, 2nd ed. (Markham, ON: LexisNexis Butterworths, 2002) at 148-49.

refusals may also contravene provisions in international documents. He concluded, "Accordingly, the right to object to perform or immediately to participate in medical procedures on grounds of conscience carries no parallel right to refuse to inform those eligible to receive these procedures where or how they are practically accessible".[56] This issue has become highly politicized in the United States, where half the states have pending bills containing conscience clauses and some have already enacted legislation to permit a pharmacist to refuse to dispense emergency contraception or, in one state, to require pharmacists to dispense contraception approved by the Food and Drug Administration.[57]

The disclosure obligation is intended to create a degree of understanding sufficient for the patient to make an informed choice. For example, the Supreme Court stated that because of Mr. Reibl's language difficulties, Dr. Hughes should have ensured that he comprehended the information, and similarly in *Ciarlariello v. Schacter* stated this duty broadly by requiring that the burden rest on the doctor to show the patient's comprehension.[58] Picard and Robertson have expressed reservations about this level of responsibility, finding it too onerous and impractical for the physician, and instead suggesting that reasonable steps be taken to ensure understanding.[59] In *Byciuk v. Hollingsworth*, McMahon J. found that the physician must take reasonable steps to determine whether the patient understood, agreeing with the Picard and Robertson critique, but also found that if the physician discloses remotely, as with videos and pamphlets about gastroplasty and the brief office visit in this case, then there is a higher burden to ensure understanding.[60] Justice McMahon usefully noted the factors of deference and intimidation that can confound interaction between doctor and patient. With the understanding of the power imbalance between doctors and patients reflected in the Supreme Court's decisions in *Hollis v. Dow Corning Corp.* and *Norberg v. Wynrib*, it would be surprising if the Court were to retrench from its position that understanding, and not simply describing, lies at the core of informed decision-making.[61]

Elective procedures require a different and higher standard of disclosure. In *White v. Turner*, a case that raised the issue in the context of reconstructive breast surgery, Linden J. found that it was necessary to disclose even the minimal risks of reconstructive breast surgery, including box-like appearance and asymmetrical nipples, and the nature of the scarring with mammoplasty, which were found to be special or unusual risks:[62] "Where an operation is elective, as this one was, even minimal risks must be disclosed to patients, since

---

[56]   *Ibid.*, at 149.
[57]   Michelle Oberman & Lisa Ikemoto, Case Study, Health Law Teachers Conference (Baltimore: June 2006).
[58]   *Reibl v. Hughes*, [1980] S.C.J. No. 105, [1980] 2 S.C.R. 880 at 895 (S.C.C.); *Ciarlariello v. Schacter*, [1993] S.C.J. No. 46, [1993] 2 S.C.R. 119 at 140 (S.C.C.).
[59]   Ellen I. Picard & Gerald B. Robertson, *Legal Liability of Doctors and Hospitals in Canada*, 3rd ed. (Toronto: Carswell, 1996) at 136.
[60]   [2004] A.J. No. 620 (Alta. Q.B.).
[61]   *Hollis v. Dow Corning Corp.*, [1995] S.C.J. No. 104, [1995] 4 S.C.R. 634 (S.C.C.); *Norberg v. Wynrib*, [1992] S.C.J. No. 60, [1992] 2 S.C.R. 226 (S.C.C.), additional reasons at [1992] S.C.J. No. 60, [1992] 2 S.C.R. 318 (S.C.C.).
[62]   (1981), 31 O.R. (2d) 773 (Ont. H.C.J.), affd [1982] O.J. No. 3097 (Ont. C.A.).

'the frequency of the risk becomes much less material when the operation is unnecessary for his medical welfare'".[63] The disclosure duty applies broadly, not only to material risks but also to other aspects of the procedure about which the reasonable patient would want information.[64] For instance, in *Skeels Estate v. Iwashkiw*, the physician should have disclosed the safety limitations of the particular facility that the doctor had promoted as a safe place to have the patient's baby, as well as the risk of shoulder dystocia that required a higher level of care than could be provided there during the delivery.[65] This case also illustrated the higher standard of disclosure required for elective procedures where the Court commented that since it was an elective decision concerning where to have the delivery, the "information component must be very high as the patient had other viable and easily exercisable options".[66]

The duty to disclose is a continuing duty that applies to risks discovered after treatment has begun. Although the act of disclosure is often delegated to others, the non-delegable nature of the obligation requires the treating physician to determine that the standard of care is met. As collaborative care becomes more common, responsibilities among team members will need to be carefully delineated. Courts have found it necessary to disclose medical errors such as leaving a drill bit inside a patient's mouth after a dental procedure.[67] Operating on the wrong vertebrae, and then concealing the error and attempting to remedy it by redoing the back surgery led to successful battery claims for the first surgery on the wrong body part which included liability for all the consequences, and for the second surgery, consent for which was undermined by the breach of fiduciary duty.[68]

The duty to disclose has not been extended to personal characteristics of the physician, such as the HIV status in *Halkyard v. Mathew*, or the fact that it was his first such surgery after certification as a fully qualified specialist in *Hopp v. Lepp*.[69] The question of whether disclosure is required for procedures that are unavailable due to funding shortfalls has received some attention. Courts have also found that the risk that should have been disclosed was the one that arose, and not simply that the procedure would have been avoided if proper disclosure had been made. This issue arose in *Brito (Litigation Guardian of) v. Woolley*, where the risk of cord compression and the alternative of a Cesarean section

---

63   *Ibid.*, at para. 69 (H.C.J.), quoting Grange J. in *Videto v. Kennedy*, [1980] O.J. No. 3538 (Ont. H.C.J.) at para. 25.

64   Ellen I. Picard & Gerald B. Robertson, *Legal Liability of Doctors and Hospitals in Canada*, 3rd ed. (Toronto: Carswell, 1996).

65   [2006] A.J. No. 666 (Alta. Q.B.) at para. 149.

66   *Ibid.*, at para. 161.

67   *Kueper v. McMullin*, [1986] N.B.J. No. 89 (N.B.C.A.), finding that the duty arose after the drill bit broke and that the alternatives should have been discussed, although the plaintiff lost on causation.

68   *Gerula v. Flores*, [1995] O.J. No. 2300 (Ont. S.C.J.).

69   *Halkyard v. Matthew*, [1998] A.J. No. 986 (Alta. Q.B.), affd [2001] A.J. No. 293 (Alta. C.A.); *Hopp v. Lepp*, [1980] S.C.J. No. 57, [1980] 2 S.C.R. 192 (S.C.C.). See also Barry R. Furrow, "Must Physicians Reveal Their Wounds?" (1996) 5 Cambridge Q. of Healthcare Ethics 204; Brenda J. Johnson, "Recent Decisions: Must Doctors Disclose Their Own Personal Risk Factors? *Halkyard v. Mathew*" (2001) 10 Health L. Rev. 18.

were not disclosed and one twin was injured by cord compression during a vaginal delivery.[70]

In analyzing the materiality of risks, Laskin C.J.C. considered several exceptions to the duty to disclose.[71] Waiver is the right to forego something to which one would otherwise be entitled and in this case the entitlement is to information. In considering the *volenti* defence to an action resulting from a mogul hill inner tube race designed to promote a ski resort where participants were served copious amounts of alcohol, the Supreme Court of Canada stated that voluntary assumption of risk includes assumption of both the physical risks and the legal risks, and that a waiver signed without knowledge and intent does not support the voluntary assumption of risk defence or act as a contractual defence.[72] In the context of disclosure, waiver is problematic since it leaves a capable patient without information to make the decision and exposes a doctor to a conflict of roles if the doctor assumes the role of the patient. It is clearly impossible for a health practitioner to ensure comprehension of information that the patient has declined to receive. A decision must made by the patient or an authorized person before it is legally appropriate for a health practitioner to proceed with the provision of care, and failure to determine that the patient has consented to a procedure exposes a physician to a battery action. Solving this problem could lead to the involvement of other family members, with the consent of the patient, or to an explanation of the respective roles of doctor and patient in decision-making along with encouragement to decide, and may call for particular sensitivity to cultural differences. A further dimension of the issue arises in situations where the patient declines to participate and defers to family members' decisions. It has been suggested that simply broadening the view of autonomy is mistaken unless it takes account of the possibility of injustice and that autonomous choices must be authentic "in the sense of being free of coercive formative influences".[73]

Therapeutic privilege is based on the idea that it is better in some circumstances for the patient not to know the information. As Howland C.J.C. phrased it in *Videto v. Kennedy* in summarizing the duty to disclose: "The emotional condition of the patient and the patient's apprehension and reluctance to undergo the operation may in certain cases justify the surgeon in withholding or generalizing information as to which he would otherwise be required to be more specific."[74] Such an exception is in direct opposition to the principles of autonomy and physical inviolability and, as Caulfield and Feasby have argued, therapeutic privilege should be limited to serious mental distress cases.[75] It has been mentioned or applied in only a few cases and generally

[70] [2003] B.C.J. No. 1539 (B.C.C.A.) at paras. 23-25, leave to appeal refused [2003] S.C.C.A. No. 418 (S.C.C.).
[71] *Reibl v. Hughes*, [1980] S.C.J. No. 105, [1980] 2 S.C.R. 880 at 895 (S.C.C.).
[72] *Crocker v. Sundance Northwest Resorts Ltd.*, [1988] S.C.J. No. 60, [1988] 1 S.C.R. 1186 at 1201-03 (S.C.C.).
[73] Insoo Hyun, "Waiver of informed consent, cultural sensitivity, and the problem of unjust families and traditions" (Sept./Oct. 2002) 32(5) Hastings Center R. 14 at 15.
[74] [1981] O.J. No. 3054 (Ont. C.A.) at para. 11.
[75] Timothy Caulfield & Colin Feasby, "Potions, Promises and Paradoxes: Complementary

given a narrow scope, and it has been excluded in one, *Meyer Estate v. Rogers*, which found that no such therapeutic privilege existed because of its potentially erosive effect on informed consent.[76] For example, in *Pittman Estate v. Bain*,[77] Lang J. found that such a privilege existed when a patient is unwilling to hear bad news or where their health is precarious enough that the news would trigger unnecessary harm but that it did not apply to absolve Dr. Bain of failing to disclose that Mr. Pittman might be HIV-positive as a result of a transfusion. Dr. Bain had not investigated sufficiently Pittman's emotional state or considered the risk to him and others in relation to the disadvantages of disclosure.[78] Therapeutic privilege has not been included as an exception to the disclosure requirement in any of the consent legislation enacted in Canada, discussed in Part IV below, arguably removing the exception through legislative occupation of the disclosure field; waiver has been included as an exception in Prince Edward Island.

Common risks are considered to be exceptions to disclosure obligations owed by manufacturers and retailers regarding risks of which people would generally be aware. For example, the extremely small — one in a million — risk of Streptococcus A infection and even lower risk of necrotizing fasciitis, did not need to be disclosed to a kidney donor because it was within the public domain and general knowledge about infections.[79] Determining the level of common knowledge may be problematic.

B. CAUSATION

The second major element in a negligence action is causation. Several questions of causation exist simultaneously in negligent disclosure actions. First, the plaintiff must prove factual causation between the procedure and the harm, by applying the but-for test and those alternatives, such as the material contribution test, that supplement it. For example, Mr. Reibl's surgery led to the stroke that caused his physical harm. In the medical and scientific field, causation may be particularly difficult to prove. As Sopinka J. found for the Court in *Snell v. Farrell*, legal proof is distinguishable from scientific proof and an inference of causation may be drawn where positive or scientific proof has not been made, in

Medicine and Alternative Medicine and Malpractice Law in Canada" (2001) 9 Health L.J. 183 at para. 23.

76 [1991] O.J. No. 139 (Ont. Gen. Div.).

77 [1994] O.J. No. 463 (Ont. Gen. Div.) at paras. 700-713, suppl. reasons at [1994] O.J. No. 3410 (Ont. (Gen. Div.)).

78 As Picard and Robertson have noted, therapeutic privilege has been acknowledged by the Supreme Court in the analogous situation of access to patient's records in *McInerney v. MacDonald*, [1992] S.C.J. No. 57 (S.C.C.) at paras. 28-31: Ellen I. Picard & Gerald B. Robertson, *Legal Liability of Doctors and Hospitals in Canada*, 3rd ed. (Toronto: Carswell, 1996) at 148n.

79 *Kovacich v. St. Joseph's Hospital*, [2004] O.J. No. 4471 (Ont. S.C.J.) at paras. 144-47. The trial judge also thought that a reasonable person with his characteristics would not be deterred from the treatment. A similar conclusion was reached in another necrotizing fasciitis case, *Best v. Hoskins*, [2006] A.J. No. 48 (Alta. Q.B.).

the absence of rebuttal evidence by the defendant.[80] Uncertainty is particularly troublesome where multiple actors engage in conduct that may or may not contribute to the harm, additively or in combination with the other factors. Courts have responded to this dilemma by relying on a variety of alternative tests.[81]

Second, it is necessary to prove decision causation, to connect the inadequate disclosure to the harm.[82] This application of the but-for test requires examining whether the harm would have been avoided if adequate disclosure had been made. The test employed by the Supreme Court added a further step to this analysis by requiring an objective element. The plaintiff has the onus of proving that if the health practitioner had disclosed adequately, the reasonable patient in the position of the plaintiff would have declined the procedure that the plaintiff accepted. This "modified objective" test of causation was adopted by the Court instead of a subjective test of causation because of its concern about the "hindsight and bitterness" they thought that plaintiffs would inevitably bring to court in the aftermath of injury, that would make it problematic for judges to separate what they would have done from what they say they would have done.[83] The reasonable person in Mr. Reibl's shoes, the Court decided, would have postponed the procedure, based in large part on the fact that in just over a year and a half Mr. Reibl would have been entitled to disability benefits through a work-based pension. They also considered the determinate risks of surgery as opposed to the risk of postponing the surgery to an indeterminate time. Although the Court was unanimous in its decision, the modified objective test has provoked concern among commentators and, more recently, among the minority members of the Supreme Court itself in *Arndt v. Smith*,[84] discussed below.

C. CRITIQUE

The modified objective test can be criticized on multiple dimensions. Although the but-for test of causation determines whether the negligence makes a difference by comparing what happened with the negligence and what would have happened "but-for" the negligence, the modified objective test requires more. Its hypothetical comparison is combined with the need to prove what a hypothetical reasonable patient in the patient's circumstances would have done. As Gerald Robertson noted, this combination of the hypothetical and the

---

[80]   [1990] S.C.J. No. 73, [1990] 2 S.C.R. 311 (S.C.C.).

[81]   *Bonnington Castings Ltd. v. Wardlaw*, [1956] 1 All E.R. 615 (H.L.); *McGhee v. National Coal Board*, [1972] 3 All E.R. 1008 (H.L.); *Athey v. Leonati*, [1996] S.C.J. No. 102 (S.C.C.); *Webster v. Chapman*, [1997] M.J. No. 646 (Man. C.A.), leave to appeal refused [1998] S.C.C.A. No. 45 (S.C.C.); *Fairchild v. Glenhaven Funeral Services Ltd.*, [2002] 3 W.L.R. 89 (H.L.); and *Resurfice Corp. v. Hanke*, [2007] S.C.J. No. 7 (S.C.C.).

[82]   Alan Meisel & Lisa D. Kabnick, "Informed Consent to Medical Treatment: An Analysis of Recent Legislation" (1980) 41 U. Pitt. L. Rev. 407 at 438-39 used the terms "injury causation" and "decision causation".

[83]   Laskin C.J.C. in *Reibl v. Hughes*, [1980] S.C.J. No. 105, [1980] 2 S.C.R. 880 at 897-99 (S.C.C.), quoted a Comment "Informed Consent — A Proposed Standard for Medical Disclosure" (1973) 48 N.Y.U.L. Rev. 548 at 550.

[84]   [1997] S.C.J. No. 65 (S.C.C.).

negative makes it difficult for the plaintiff to prove causation in general and creates an impossible situation for the onus-bearing plaintiff in situations where it is equally reasonable both to proceed and to decline.[85]

Second, the reasonableness standard has been subject to the criticism of bias. Feminist scholars have criticized the "reasonable man" standard in tort law for its normative bias.[86] Far from being a neutral and universally applicable standard, the reasonableness standard hides a gendered and class-ridden notion of appropriate behaviour that fails to take account of others' experiences and views. Only the man on the Clapham omnibus can meet the standard. Twerski and Cohen have made another argument — that the psychological literature has indicated that most decisions are illogical.[87] If there is no such thing as a reasonable person, or only one version that only some people can meet, then the plaintiff should not be required to meet that standard.

Third, another problem lies in demonstrating that the reasonable patient would have declined the treatment proposed by the doctor, which is likely to have been a reasonable proposal. Chief Justice Laskin considered this problem but thought that the particular situation and the balance of subjective and objective factors would reduce its force. Having said that, however, he thought that the patient's particular concerns must be reasonably based so that fears unrelated to the treatment would not be causative but economic considerations could be.[88] Another formulation of this thought is that reasonable patients do what their doctors recommend. The mistrust of patient's reports may more properly be seen as an evidentiary concern that could be addressed through close assessment of credibility. The Supreme Court itself recognized this later in the manufacturer-consumer relationship in *Hollis v. Dow Corning Corp.*, where it stated that the problem could be handled through cross-examination and the trial judge's weighing of the testimony; however, the Court did not disturb the modified objective test for the doctor-patient relationship and set out differences between the manufacturer-consumer and doctor-patient relationship that would justify using a subjective test in the pharmaceutical company disclosure situation.[89]

Fourth, and most fundamentally, the test does not protect autonomy. The imposition of the reasonableness standard requires that the decision be reasonable. Autonomy does not require reasonable decisions. On the contrary, the principle of autonomy supports a patient's right to make decisions based on whatever values and beliefs and idiosyncratic ideas the patient holds.

Fifth, a subjective standard would fit the logic of causation analysis more clearly since it would connect the fault of the defendant to the harm experienced

---

[85]   Gerald B. Robertson, "Overcoming the Causation Hurdle in Informed Consent Cases: The Principle in *McGhee v. N.C.B.*" (1984) 22 Univ. W. Ont. L. Rev. 75.

[86]   Leslie Bender, "Changing the Values in Tort Law" (1990) 25 Tulsa L.J. 759; Lucinda Finley, "A Break in the Silence: Including Women's Issues in a Torts Course" (1989) 1 Yale J. L. & Feminism 41.

[87]   Aaron D. Twerski & Neil B. Cohen, "Informed Decision Making and the Law of Torts: The Myth of Justiciable Causation" (1988) 3 U. Ill. L. Rev. 607.

[88]   *Reibl v. Hughes*, [1980] S.C.J. No. 105, [1980] 2 S.C.R. 880 at 899-900 (S.C.C.).

[89]   [1995] S.C.J. No. 104, [1995] 4 S.C.R. 634 (S.C.C.) at para. 46.

by the plaintiff without the distracting and unjust embellishment of a reasonable patient. A modified test of causation may be unjust to both parties in certain circumstances. Consider a variation in which the real patient, unlike the reasonable patient in the patient's shoes, would have proceeded. The plaintiff still wins. This result — where the patient who would have acted just the same regardless of the doctor's disclosure wins the action — seems unjust to the doctor. In the reverse situation, where the reasonable patient would have proceeded with the treatment, but the actual patient would have declined the procedure and avoided the injury as a result, the plaintiff loses and the resulting lack of compensation seems unjust to the patient. In both cases, the tort requirement that the defendant's fault be connected to the actual plaintiff's harm through the medium of causation is unmet.[90] Only when the behaviour of both the reasonable and subjective patients is consonant is the required connection made, and then the reasonable patient is superfluous.

The dissonance problem would be resolved if a subjective test were applied in addition to the reasonable patient test. The injustice to the doctor would be removed, but only when both the hypothetical reasonable patient and the actual patient would decline the procedure that the patient had accepted would the plaintiff win. The possibility of both tests applying was considered in the American case of *Truman v. Thomas*.[91] This 4:3 decision supported the action of Mrs. Thomas' children for wrongful death in a case involving a physician's failure to warn of the material risks of *not* consenting to a recommended pap smear and expanding the duty of disclosure to include the risks of not undergoing the procedure. The majority found that the fiduciary duty in the doctor-patient relationship meant that the patient should have been given all the information material to her decision, including not only the risks of the procedure but also the risks of not undergoing it and the probability of a successful outcome. The majority noted that the reasonable person test of causation is necessary but not sufficient, stating: "If the jury were to reasonably conclude that Mrs. Truman would have unreasonably refused a pap smear in the face of adequate disclosure, there could be no finding of proximate cause".[92]

The proposition that causation requires a dual test has not been decided in a Canadian court, although several courts have given the matter consideration. Justice Lambert referred to statements by Linden J. in *White v. Turner* and Robins J.A. in *Buchan v. Ortho Pharmaceutical (Canada) Ltd.*, to the effect that the Court had required not merely the subjective test but also the reasonableness test, as indicating that they thought both tests needed to be met, but their statements are equally consistent with an interpretation that the *Reibl* test was simply more onerous in adding the element of reasonableness.[93] In *Baksh-White*

---

90 Ernest Weinrib, "A Step Forward in Factual Causation" (1975) 38 Mod. L. Rev. 518.

91 611 P.2d 902 (Cal. 1980).

92 *Ibid.*, at 907.

93 *Arndt v. Smith*, [1995] B.C.J. No. 1416 at paras. 34-42 (B.C.C.A.); *White v. Turner*, [1981] O.J. No. 2512, 31 O.R. (2d) 773 (Ont. H.C.J.) at paras. 58, 67-69; *Buchan v. Ortho Pharmaceutical (Canada) Ltd.*, [1986] O.J. No. 2331, 54 O.R. (2d) 92 (Ont. C.A.) at para. 69; *Reibl v. Hughes*, [1980] S.C.J. No. 105, [1980] 2 S.C.R. 880 (S.C.C.). He referred as well to Southin J.A.'s comment in *Hollis v. Dow Corning Corp.*, [1993] B.C.J. No. 1363, 16 C.C.L.T. (2d) 140 at 177

v. Cochen, Snowie J. applied a subjective test, finding that if she had been informed of the material risk of bowel perforation — material in part because she had an increased risk because of three previous surgeries — the plaintiff would have proceeded with the hysterectomy, because she had a self-directed and focused approach to having the procedure, had research knowledge and was a nurse.[94] Because of the finding on subjective causation, Snowie J. decided that it was unnecessary to consider what the reasonable person in her shoes would have done. The analysis in *Reibl v. Hughes*[95] does not support a two-tiered test since the court conceptualized and chose between dichotomous options.[96] It remains to be seen what will be decided when the risk-taking plaintiff is paired with the prudent reasonable person in the patient's shoes.[97]

D. ARNDT V. SMITH

The *Arndt v. Smith* case provided the Supreme Court of Canada with the opportunity to revisit the causation test.[98] Carole Arndt sued Dr. Margaret Smith for breach of the duty of disclosure, arguing that if she had been adequately warned of the risk of chronic varicella syndrome during her pregnancy, she would have had an abortion. Ms. Arndt became ill with chicken pox and asked her family physician, Dr. Smith, about the risks to the fetus during the 12th week of her pregnancy. Dr. Smith said she would find the answers and, after doing research, Dr. Smith told her in the 14th week of some risks but not the risk of chronic varicella syndrome. The probability of chronic varicella syndrome was 0.23 per cent, about a quarter of one per cent, but if it arises, it causes seriously disabling results. The trial judge, Hutchison J., found that Dr. Smith did not disclose this risk because it was a very low risk statistically, she did not want Ms. Arndt to worry about this risk, and she thought that abortion would not have been medically defensible. At the time these events took place in 1986, the

---

(B.C.C.A.) about the separate issue of what would happen if the reasonable person would opt against the treatment while the patient would opt for it.

94   [2001] O.J. No. 3397 (Ont. S.C.J.).

95   *Reibl v. Hughes*, [1980] S.C.J. No. 105, [1980] 2 S.C.R. 880 at 895 (S.C.C.).

96   Justice Lambert reached this conclusion, agreeing with Southin J.A., that it does not give "a considered answer to that question" and that the "general tenor" of the analysis eliminates the subjective question: *Arndt v. Smith*, [1995] B.C.J. No. 1416 (B.C.C.A.) at para. 39.

97   This problem is distinguishable from the evidentiary issue posed in *Jaskiewicz v. Humber River Regional Hospital*, [2001] O.J. No. 6 (Ont. S.C.J.). The trial judge applied the modified objective test but commented *obiter* on the absence of connecting evidence because of the plaintiff's lack of testimony on what she would have done, saying that it was an essential part of the process since the modified objective test acts as a test of credibility of the subjective statement. In *Hartjes v. Carman*, [2003] O.J. No. 3344 (Ont. S.C.J.) at para. 23, affd [2004] O.J. No. 5597 (Ont. Div. Ct.), a breast uplift surgery case in which the plaintiff was not asked whether she would have proceeded, the trial judge confined *Jaskiewicz* to its own facts and found it unnecessary to ask the self-serving question. Affirming the decision, the Divisional Court respectfully disagreed with disentitling a plaintiff for failing to testify that she would not have had the procedure if warned, and stated that a trial judge may determine the causal connection on other evidence.

98   [1997] S.C.J. No. 65 (S.C.C.).

Morgentaler case had not been decided and Ms. Arndt would have had to apply to a Therapeutic Abortion Committee to obtain permission for an abortion; in addition, she would have been at increasing risk during the second trimester.[99] Her daughter Miranda was born with chronic varicella syndrome, which caused brain damage requiring tube feeding for her lifetime, surgery for breathing difficulties and severely diminished quality of life.[100]

At trial, Hutchison J. found negligence in disclosure but no causation. The trial judge took into account two main points: Ms. Arndt's strong desire for a child and her skepticism of mainstream medicine, based on wanting a midwife along with the doctor and the fact that they did not want to have an ultrasound. The last factor was considered to indicate "less concern with risks in foresight than in hindsight" and, based on the two factors of her desire and her mistrust, the trial judge concluded that she would have carried the pregnancy to term if she had been informed.[101] Whether the trial judge applied a subjective or an objective test of causation was a matter of dispute in the higher courts. The British Columbia Court of Appeal found that the trial judge had applied the wrong test and ordered a new trial.[102] These judgments raised important issues about the modified objective test and threw the matter wide open for Supreme Court consideration.

The Supreme Court of Canada decided on a 6:3 basis to retain the modified objective test of causation. In doing so, however, the majority judgment by Cory J. stated that the court must take into account any "particular concerns" and "any special considerations" of the patient and that the reasonable patient must be taken to have the patient's reasonable beliefs, fears, desires and expectations.[103] A purely subjective fear unrelated to material risks should not be considered.[104] By highlighting the *Reibl* subjective elements as the bases for these points, Cory J. has provided them with further legitimacy today and given direction in a situation in which competing interpretations have flourished.[105] Chief Justice Laskin had stated that the patient's concerns in the modified objective test must be reasonably based. As examples, he cited matters that would affect causation — fears related to undisclosed risks or economic concerns that relate to an undisclosed risk.[106] It posed a relatively easy case in which to identify the "in the shoes of" elements, since the pension and the indeterminacy of the risk are factors clearly within the context of the plaintiff's life.

In contrast, the list that Justice Cory outlined — of beliefs, fears, desires and expectations — consists of factors that are clearly internal values and beliefs and are much more clearly identifiable as matters relevant to autonomous decision-making.[107] If these factors, which must still be reasonable, are to be based on the

---

[99] *R. v. Morgentaler*, [1988] S.C.J. No. 1, [1988] 1 S.C.R. 30 (S.C.C.).
[100] *Arndt v. Smith*, [1995] B.C.J. No. 1416 (B.C.C.A.) at para. 6.
[101] *Arndt v. Smith*, [1994] B.C.J. No. 1137 (B.C.S.C.) at paras. 59-60.
[102] *Arndt v. Smith*, [1995] B.C.J. No. 1416 (B.C.C.A.) at para. 105.
[103] *Arndt v. Smith*, [1997] S.C.J. No. 65 (S.C.C.) at para. 9.
[104] *Ibid.*, at paras. 12, 14.
[105] For example, McLachlin J. noted at para. 64 that it has been read in different ways.
[106] *Reibl v. Hughes*, [1980] S.C.J. No. 105, [1980] 2 S.C.R. 880 at 899-900 (S.C.C.).
[107] In *Felde v. Vein and Laser Medical Centre*, [2003] O.J. No. 4654 (Ont. C.A.), Moldaver J.A.

individual rather than drawn from a hypothetical reasonable person, then the test has clearly become more subjective and the "shoes" have gone inside. A more subjective test of this sort may reduce to some extent the potential for norm-based and biased analysis, but the continued constraint of unreasonable beliefs indicates that the loss of fully autonomous decision-making is not being compensated and that the belief in logical decision-making remains strong. As well, Cory J. remained concerned about the evidentiary problem. Justice Cory's judgment, for Lamer C.J.C., and La Forest, L'Heureux-Dubé, Gonthier and Major JJ., concluded that there was no causation since the reasonable person in Ms. Arndt's shoes would not have had an abortion, taking into account the same factors as the lower courts, and restoring the trial judgment.

The minority judges all supported use of the subjective test of causation. Justice McLachlin, finding that the trial judge correctly applied the subjective test, concurred in the dismissal of the appeal based on the finding of no causation. She reasoned that the subjective test is preferable since it fits negligence principles better than the modified objective test, it is fair to both plaintiff and defendant, and it:

> takes into account the plaintiff's right of choice, rather than presuming that choice on the basis of a hypothetical reasonable person. And it permits serious consideration of the plaintiff's evidence as to what that choice would have been ... At the same time, it is fair to the physician, who may introduce evidence of what the reasonable patient would have done as it bears on the choice the particular patient at bar would have made.[108]

She also thought that the subjective test could accommodate cases of two equally reasonable choices since it focuses on the choice that the plaintiff would have made, determined on the balance of probabilities and based on an examination of all the evidence. In contrast, the objective test "depreciates the plaintiff's personal choice in such situations and deprives her testimony of any weight".[109]

She rejected the theory advanced by Lambert J.A. in the Court of Appeal that the plaintiff had lost the opportunity to decide, and that the loss of choice should itself be compensable, stating that Laskin C.J.C. had rejected this battery theory.[110] For the same reason, she rejected the fiduciary obligation argument, stating that recovery becomes "virtually automatic" on proof of breach of disclosure and that she saw no reason to depart from the existing law in negligence.[111] As Philip Osborne noted in his 1995 annotation to *Arndt v. Smith*, Justice Lambert used fiduciary duty analysis, which has been a developing area

---

found that the timing of the surgical procedure may or may not be a significant factor in assessing the modified objective test and it was significant in this case, and Borins J.A., concurring, found it "significant that both Reibl and Arndt recognize that 'special considerations affecting the particular patient' may play a significant role in the causation analysis" (at para. 29).

[108] *Arndt v. Smith*, [1997] S.C.J. No. 65 (S.C.C.) at para. 66.
[109] *Ibid.*, at para. 67.
[110] *Ibid.*, at para. 37.
[111] *Ibid.*, at para. 38.

in Canadian medical law, to alter the causation analysis.[112] The theories are similar in that both do away with the requirement of causation and compensate the lost right itself. Justice Lambert would have chosen the fiduciary obligation only after applying the modified objective test to determine whether "some reasonable patients in the plaintiff's position would have taken a different course than the uninformed plaintiff actually took", regardless of whether another group of people would have decided the same way as the uninformed plaintiff.[113] This approach would remove the onus problem in the equally reasonable alternative situation, apply a lower standard to the number of reasonable people necessary to trigger an alternative test, and avoid the measurement problem for the plaintiff in trying to prove that "a reasonable person" equivalent to a majority of people would have decided otherwise than the plaintiff, although it continues to place weight on what others would do and requires them to be reasonable.

The fact that six of nine judges upheld the modified objective test of causation is significant in that it requires adherence to a test that has been resoundingly criticized and has now been supported by three of nine judges.[114] At the same time, the majority judges have made the test somewhat more subjective both in emphasizing the *Reibl* elements of subjectivity and in making the "in the shoes of" test a more interior and particularized one. When put to the test in this most subjective of situations, however, the weight was given to the reasonable person. The dissenting judges, Sopinka and Iacobucci JJ., expressed a concern that Ms. Arndt's own statement that she would have had an abortion was not considered adequately. It is possible to view her skepticism about mainstream medicine and opposition to ultrasound as a concern to protect her fetus in the face of new technologies and it is not apparent how care to avoid injury automatically translates into a desire to carry a potentially injured fetus to term. Erin Nelson and Timothy Caulfield have commented that, "It could be argued that the Court allowed an idiosyncratic concern (distrust of mainstream medicine) to outweigh an objectively reasonable fear (fear of the potential impact of chicken pox on the fetus)".[115] As Wood J.A. stated in the British Columbia Court of Appeal: "The fact that a woman prefers a natural form of childbirth, with a minimum of medical intervention and the assistance of a midwife, cannot by itself reasonably support the inference that she would knowingly disregard or take lightly the risk of serious birth defect resulting from an illness contracted during her pregnancy".[116] Determining risk-bearing behaviour is a difficult enterprise at any time since people vary widely in their assessments of risk and in their willingness to assume them. Determining the choice that an abstract reasonable person would make about such a personal and difficult matter as terminating a pregnancy seems like an illegitimate exercise.

---

[112] Philip H. Osborne, "Annotation to *Arndt v. Smith*" (1995) 25 C.C.L.T. (2d) 264.
[113] *Arndt v. Smith*, [1995] B.C.J. No. 1416 (B.C.C.A.) at para. 49, where Lambert J.A. set out four options.
[114] Erin Nelson & Timothy Caulfield, "You Can't Get There From Here: A Case Comment on *Arndt v. Smith*" (1999) 32 U.B.C. L. Rev. 353.
[115] *Ibid.*, at 359.
[116] *Arndt v. Smith*, [1995] B.C.J. No. 1416 (B.C.C.A.) at para. 87.

Reproductive matters, involving ethical and personal questions of an intimate nature, are particularly difficult to second-guess through a requirement of objectivity. Do judicial views on pregnancy and its termination have a place in such an intimate and far-reaching decision? Justice Wood stated that:

> As Mr. Justice Lambert has pointed out, the rule in *Reibl v. Hughes* is inadequate to the point where injustice can surely result from its application. That is particularly so in cases such as this, where any treatment decision involves a delicate balancing of overlapping personal, ethical, and medical considerations which can lead to more than one 'reasonable' choice.[117]

In *Buchan v. Ortho Pharmaceutical (Canada) Ltd.*, the Ontario Court of Appeal rejected the modified objective test for the test of causation for the manufacturer's failure to disclose action. Justice Robins said that where the manufacturer had failed to warn physicians of the risks of stroke in taking birth control pills and the patient would not have proceeded:

> [w]hether a so-called reasonable woman in the plaintiff's position would have done likewise is beside the point. The selection of a method of preventing unwanted pregnancy in the case of a healthy woman is a matter, not of medical treatment, but of personal choice ... So long as the court is satisfied that the plaintiff herself would not have used the drug if properly informed of the risks, this causation issue should be concluded in her favour regardless of what other women might have done.[118]

This position sustains the argument in favour of a subjective test, particularly in situations involving wide ranges of choice that are highly dependent on patients' own — possibly unreasonable — values and beliefs.[119]

IV. STATUTES GOVERNING INFORMED CONSENT

A. STATUTES

Some provinces and territories have enacted fully developed health care consent legislation while others have legislated in the personal directives area and regarding some aspects of consent to treatment. Legislation grew out of the need to provide methods to transfer treatment decision-making authority to substitute decision-makers in short-term circumstances in which guardianship legislation would be inadequate. The *Canadian Charter of Rights and Freedoms* provided

---

[117] *Ibid.*, at para. 91 (B.C.C.A.).

[118] [1986] O.J. No. 2331, 54 O.R. (2d) 92 (Ont. C.A.) at para. 77.

[119] The Supreme Court of Canada, in the leading case of *Hollis v. Dow Corning Corp.*, [1995] S.C.J. No. 104, [1995] 4 S.C.R. 634 (S.C.C.), adopted the subjective test of causation for the manufacturer. Justice La Forest found that the manufacturer had a greater likelihood of devaluing risk and overvaluing benefit than the doctor and found much in the inequality of information and resources between manufacturer and patient to counter such a modification. Although the Court retained the modified objective test for the doctor-patient relationship, his concern for lack of information extended to that relationship and might have provided a basis for such a modification to a subjective test of causation.

an impetus for change in the area of guardianship for mentally incompetent persons.[120] Some reforms involved guardianship and delegation of authority through advance directives or powers of attorney for personal care. As a general matter, comprehensive consent legislation provides a framework for disclosure of information to meet informed consent standards; establishes processes for capacity determination in circumstances such as treatment, admission to care facilities and everyday care where long-term guardianship would be unnecessary or cumbersome; sets out standards to determine who should make a substitute decision for an incapable person; establishes the standards to be applied in making a substitute decision; and provides legal processes for reviews and procedures to deal with specific circumstances. Such comprehensive statutes have been enacted in Ontario, British Columbia, Prince Edward Island and Yukon.[121] Provisions for proxy decision-making and/or advance directives have also been specified in legislation in Alberta, Manitoba, Newfoundland and Labrador, the Northwest Territories, Nova Scotia, Nunavut and Saskatchewan.[122]

B. LITIGATION

Litigation concerning the Ontario legislation has resulted in several important precedents.[123] *Re Koch* was an early case involving evaluations of incapacity after allegations of incapacity by one marital partner against the other while they were engaged in a separation dispute.[124] Justice Quinn identified the "formidable" power of the incapacity determination, noted that persons are entitled to be unreasonable in their decision-making as long as the decision is reasoned, and found that the evaluators of incapacity should have been alert to the compromising impact of the separation and should have protected her process rights. The right knowingly to be foolish is not unimportant; the right to voluntarily assume

---

[120] *Canadian Charter of Rights and Freedoms*, Part I of the *Constitution Act, 1982*, being Schedule B to the *Canada Act 1982* (U.K.), 1982, c. 11, s. 7.

[121] British Columbia: *Health Care (Consent) and Care Facility (Admission) Act*, R.S.B.C. 1996, c. 181. Unproclaimed portions of this Act were repealed in 2006 by the *Supplements Repeal Act*, S.B.C. 2006, c. 33, s. 1 in force May 18, 2006, ss. 2, 4-18 not in force. This statute affects or will affect the *Adult Guardianship Act*, R.S.B.C. 1996, c. 6; *Representation Agreement Act*, R.S.B.C. 1996, c. 405; *Public Guardian and Trustee Act*, R.S.B.C. 1996, c. 383. Ontario: *Health Care Consent Act, 1996*, S.O. 1996, c. 2, Sch. A; *Substitute Decisions Act, 1992*, S.O. 1992, c. 30. Prince Edward Island: *Consent to Treatment and Health Care Directives Act*, R.S.P.E.I. 1988, c. C-17.2. Yukon: *Adult Protection and Decision-Making Act*, S.Y. 2003, c. 21, Sched. A; *Care Consent Act*, S.Y. 2003, c. 21, Sched. B; *Public Guardian and Trustee Act*, S.Y. 2003, c. 21, Sched. C.

[122] *Personal Directives Act*, R.S.A. 2000, c. P-6; *Health Care Directives Act*, S.M. 1992, c. 33; *Infirm Persons Act*, R.S.N.B. 1973, c. I-8; *Advance Health Care Directives Act*, S.N.L. 1995, c. A-4.1; *Personal Directives Act*, S.N.W.T. 2005, c. 16; *Medical Consent Act*, R.S.N.S. 1989, c. 279; *Hospitals Act*, R.S.N.S. 1989, c. 208; *Involuntary Psychiatric Treatment Act*, S.N.S. 2005, c. 42; *Powers of Attorney Act*, S.Nu. 2005, c. 9; *Adult Guardianship and Co-decision-making Act*, S.S. 2000, c. A-5.3; *Health Care Directives and Substitute Health Care Decision Makers Act*, S.S. 1997, c. H-0.001.

[123] *Health Care Consent Act, 1996*, S.O. 1996, c. 2, Sch. A; *Substitute Decisions Act, 1992*, S.O. 1992, c. 30.

[124] [1997] O.J. No. 1487, 33 O.R. (3d) 485 (Ont. Gen. Div.).

risks is to be respected. The State has no business meddling with either. The dignity of the individual is at stake.[125]

A.M. v. Benes was a case in which a constitutional argument was made about the amount of information provided to substitute decision-makers about the nature of their responsibilities under the Act.[126] Substitute decision-makers (SDMs) must decide on the basis of prior capable wishes expressed when at least 16 years of age, or, if no such wish exists, on the basis of the best interests, as defined in the *Health Care Consent Act*.[127] If the health practitioner determines that the substitute decision-maker has failed to decide according to this requirement, the matter may be sent to the Consent and Capacity Board, to give directions to the SDM or make the decision on its own.[128] The Ontario Court of Appeal found that this provision did not contravene the section 7 Charter rights of the incapable person in failing to give substitute decision-makers notice of their responsibilities.[129] Instead the Court found a statutory obligation to ensure that they understood their responsibilities in the provision that no treatment shall be given unless the health practitioner has formed the opinion that the person is incapable and the substitute decision-maker has consented "in accordance with" the Act.[130] This decision is highly significant since it fills a gap created when advocates and rights advisers were removed from the system apart from mental health facilities. It is important to ensure that health practitioners are able to carry out this responsibility, through educating them about their roles and responsibilities under the statute. Further, it adds another dimension to the duty to ensure comprehension discussed in Part III.

In *Starson v. Swayze*, a case involving an appeal of a mental incapacity finding, the Supreme Court of Canada reached a 6:3 decision that the reviewing judge had correctly determined the standard on review to be reasonableness and had correctly applied it in finding the Board unreasonable.[131] The Board's decision on capacity had been based on their view that Starson denied his mental disorder and failed to appreciate the consequences of his decision, but these views were not founded on evidence. Second, the Board incorrectly applied the definition of capacity, which requires a finding that the person lacks the *ability* to understand the information and appreciate the consequences of the decision and not simply a finding that the person does not understand the information or appreciate the consequences. Further, their view of the patient's best interests was irrelevant to their mandate to decide the capacity issue. The dissenting judges, in a decision written by McLachlin C.J.C., considered the Board's decision to have been within the range of reasonable conclusions and the conclusions amply based on the evidence. The majority protects individuals

---

[125] *Ibid.*, at 521, cited with approval in *Starson v. Swayze*, [2003] S.C.J. No. 33, [2003] 1 S.C.R. 722 (S.C.C.) at para. 76.

[126] [1999] O.J. No. 4236 (Ont. C.A.).

[127] *Health Care Consent Act, 1996*, S.O. 1996, c. 2, Sched. A, s. 21.

[128] *Ibid.*, s. 37.

[129] *Canadian Charter of Rights and Freedoms*, Part I of *the Constitution Act, 1982*, being Schedule B to the *Canada Act 1982* (U.K.), 1982, c. 11, s. 7.

[130] *Health Care Consent Act, 1996*, S.O. 1996, c. 2, Sched. A, s. 10(1)(b).

[131] [2003] S.C.J. No. 33, [2003] 1 S.C.R. 722 (S.C.C.).

from Board actions that rely more on Board members' views about treatment need than on the range of individuality that autonomy is supposed to protect.

Legislative requirements for informed consent in Ontario, B.C., P.E.I. and Yukon combine both the criteria for valid consent in battery and the criteria for disclosure in negligence. Since negligence imposes a duty, it is not much of a stretch to find that consent without fulfilment of the duty would be invalid, but negligence law operates on different principles. Gerald Robertson concluded that this requirement of negligence disclosure to make consent valid as informed is an effective repudiation of Laskin C.J.C.'s separation of battery and negligence in *Reibl v. Hughes* and, hopefully, that proceeding in battery again would remove the obstacles posed by the modified objective test of causation.[132] The provisions have not yet led to such a revolutionary result, although they continue to be anomalous. The Ontario Court of Appeal commented recently that the Ontario statutory definition of informed consent, which was not in force when the case before them began, contains "many of the same principles found in the common law of informed consent. The extent, if any, to which the statute departs from the common law will have to be addressed if and when that issue arises".[133]

V. IMPLICATIONS OF THE COMMON LAW CONSENT DOCTRINE

A. ACHIEVING THE PURPOSE OF INFORMED CONSENT

The Supreme Court of Canada established a duty of disclosure that required physicians to provide the information necessary for patients to act as autonomous decision-makers. The decision reflected the concerns from the consumer and feminist movements for a greater role for patients in their own health care decisions and a desire to move away from the paternalistic approach that had previously characterized the doctor-patient relationship. In his classic book, *The Silent World of Doctor and Patient*, Jay Katz analyzed how patient participation in decision-making was "an idea alien to the ethos of medicine", reflecting deeply held views about the role of silence in creating trust.[134] This trust, he argued, was unidirectional, and needed to be replaced by mutual trust. Resistance among physicians existed during the period following the decision, but by 2000, the duty appeared so well-established — through attrition, generational change and acceptance — as to be uncontroversial.

Empowerment of patients through disclosure was the foundation of the Supreme Court's decision and its most enduring accomplishment. To the extent that patients possess information as the basis of their choices about treatment, they may act as autonomous individuals. The patient needs sufficient

---

[132] Gerald B. Robertson, "Ontario's New Informed Consent Law: Codification or Radical Change?" (1994) 2 Health L.J. 88; *Reibl v. Hughes*, [1980] S.C.J. No. 105, [1980] 2 S.C.R. 880 at 891-92 (S.C.C.).

[133] *Van Dyke v. Grey Bruce Regional Health Centre*, [2005] O.J. No. 2219 (Ont. C.A.) at para. 63, leave to appeal refused [2005] S.C.C.A. No. 335 (S.C.C.).

[134] Jay Katz, *The Silent World of Doctor and Patient* (London: The Free Press, 1984).

understanding to be able to assess the proposed treatment in light of the patient's values, beliefs, goals and circumstances — all of which may or may not be disclosed to the doctor.

The Supreme Court counter-balanced the power given to patients at the duty stage by providing doctrinal protection to physicians through adoption of the "reasonable patient in the position of the patient" test of causation. As Cory J. expressed it in *Arndt v. Smith*:

> ... its modified objective test for causation ensures that our medical system will have some protection in the face of liability claims from patients influenced by unreasonable fears and beliefs, while still accommodating all the reasonable individual concerns and circumstances of plaintiffs.[135]

This doctrine undermines the autonomy of the patient by preventing unreasonable and idiosyncratic views from being actionable. It is not clear how many claims would have been won if a subjective test of causation had been in place. In his review of litigation at the 20-year mark, Professor Robertson found that plaintiffs were still losing on causation, as they had been 10 years after the 1980 decisions but, surprisingly, a shift on the part of some judges to a more subjective application made it even harder for plaintiffs to win.[136] *Brito (Guardian ad litem of) v. Woolley* illustrates such a loss in a case finding breach of the disclosure of a low risk/grave consequences Cesarean section alternative to vaginal delivery that deprived a women of important health information, but which the Court of Appeal found she would not have chosen because her doctors would have recommended against it and she trusted her physicians.[137] Professor Robertson concluded that, in part, this results from contradictory reasoning about the same factors in different courts and questionable inferences drawn from other risk-taking behaviours.[138] His most encouraging conclusion relates to an increased level of disclosure: patients still lose badly on causation "but increasingly because the required information has in fact been disclosed by the physician, which may be an indication that the legal standard is having a positive impact on medical practice."[139] The most important legacy of the 1980 cases may be the enhancement of patient participation in decision-making. Compensation for this failure to reveal needed information remains an unrequited loss. The right to make choices that are considered unreasonable is not compensable under the negligence action.

---

[135] [1997] S.C.J. No. 65 (S.C.C.) at para. 15.
[136] Gerald B. Robertson, "Informed Consent 20 Years Later" (2003) Health L.J. Special Edition 153 at 157-59.
[137] [2003] B.C.J. No. 1539 (B.C.C.A.) at paras. 40-47, leave to appeal refused [2003] S.C.C.A. No. 418 (S.C.C.).
[138] Gerald B. Robertson, "Informed Consent 20 Years Later" (2003) Health L.J. Special Edition 153 at 158.
[139] *Ibid.*, at 159.

B. DOCTRINAL IMPLICATIONS

The causation test prevents recovery in many circumstances. Twerski and Cohen argued that what we know about decision-making is that it is in fact illogical rather than reasonable, that it depends on presentation of the information, and that it is affected by prior idiosyncratic information. The uncertainties created by these factors undermine the credibility of the legal analysis.[140] The literature on semiotics provides support for their view on presentation, as it indicates how meaning is constructed based on the viewer's values and beliefs, which are anticipated and called upon by presentation in forms such as advertising. The creation of knowledge about diseases, treatments and patients for physicians and patients affects the acceptance of certain treatments. Power and profits are secured through presentation of information, and medical judgments capture these perceptions and values.

As an alternative to the negligence action, recovery could be given for the failure to disclose *per se* in the absence of any proof of resulting harm. As Marjorie Maguire Schultz has argued, informed consent doctrine "embeds the protection of patient choice within the interest in physical well-being" and out of fear of false claims, diminishes protection for the patient's right to choose.[141] If choice were protected as an independent interest, the "factual cause issue would be narrower and simpler — whether the patient's right to choose had been encroached upon as a result of a doctor's failure to disclose".[142] This approach appears to have been forestalled — at least temporarily — by the division between battery and negligence actions and by McLaughlin J.'s rejection, and the other judges' implicit rejection, of the Lambert J.A. approach in *Arndt v. Smith*.[143] As noted in Part II, the battery approach has advantages for plaintiffs although the dignitary tort approach or valuation of lost choice approach produces lower damage awards than the negligence action.

Short of this solution, better protection would be provided to the plaintiff if the court were to presume the reasonableness of the plaintiff's position and reverse the onus to require the defendant health practitioner to rebut this presumption, as has happened in the products liability failure to warn cases. Justice Robins for the Ontario Court of Appeal in *Buchan v. Ortho Pharmaceutical (Canada) Ltd.* created a rebuttable presumption that the doctor would have disclosed the risks to the patient if the manufacturer had disclosed the product risks to the doctor and La Forest J. in *Hollis v. Dow Corning Corp.* declined to require proof by the plaintiff of the hypothetical and denied access to the learned intermediary defence to non-disclosing manufacturers, since both Courts found a fundamental lack of fairness in requiring proof of such an element.[144] Justice La Forest, drawing a "close analogy" to *Cook v. Lewis*, stated

---

[140] Aaron D. Twerski & Neil B. Cohen, "Informed Decision Making and the Law of Torts: The Myth of Justiciable Causation" (1988) 3 U. Ill. L. Rev. 607.

[141] Marjorie Maguire Shultz, "From Informed Consent to Patient Choice: A New Protected Interest" (1985) 95 Yale L. J. 219.

[142] *Ibid.*

[143] [1997] S.C.J. No. 65 (S.C.C.).

[144] *Buchan v. Ortho Pharmaceutical (Canada) Ltd.*, [1986] O.J. No. 2331, 54 O.R. (2d) 92 (Ont.

that the plaintiff's power of proof, if not destroyed, had been seriously undermined by the hypothetical proof requirement and because of her "position of great information inequality" in relation to both manufacturer and doctor, she was uninvolved in the causal chain.[145] Similarly, a doctor who has destroyed the patient's possibility of proof could appropriately be required to rebut the presumption of causation.

As another partial remedy, the negligence action could compensate a loss by valuing elements other than the purely physical loss experienced by the plaintiff. The model for this valuation would be the Supreme Court of Canada's analysis in *Laferrière v. Lawson* of the losses arising out of Dr. Lawson's failure to disclose to Mme. Fortier-Dupuis for five years that she had breast cancer.[146] The action failed to prove that timely disclosure would have made a difference to her life expectancy and no liability was imposed for loss of the chance of living, with La Forest J. dissenting on this point. The Court fashioned a different remedy and awarded damages for the psychological harm experienced during the period after discovering her diagnosis and the deprivation caused by the denied benefit of earlier treatment, which would likely have improved her condition. These losses had clearly been caused by the defendant's negligence sufficiently to ground injury causation. This method provides a helpful way to avoid problems in finding injury causation where survival cannot be proven on the balance of probabilities and where a court is reluctant to compensate for loss of a chance. By changing the way the harm is conceptualized, the decision causation test will also be subtly altered to a test of whether the contextualized reasonable patient, if adequately informed of the risk of the reconceptualized loss, would have gone ahead. Because the loss is valued differently, the nature of disclosure changes, and with it, the nature of the decision that would have been made. For example, if the loss is conceptualized as the lost opportunity to be injury-free for a longer period of time in *Reibl*, or the lost opportunity to make a decision whether to take care of a child with a disability in *Arndt*, then the decision itself may be seen differently, even from a reasonable point of view.[147]

C.A.) at paras. 59, 63-66; *Hollis v. Dow Corning Corp.*, [1995] 4 S.C.R. 634, [1995] S.C.J. No. 104 (S.C.C.) at paras. 60-61. Justice La Forest saw only one situation where the manufacturer could be absolved, "in cases where some extraneous conduct by the doctor would have made the failure to give adequate warning irrelevant" (at para. 59).

[145] *Cook v. Lewis*, [1951] S.C.J. No. 28, [1951] S.C.R. 830 (S.C.C.), *per* Rand J.; *Hollis v. Dow Corning Corp.*, [1995] S.C.J. No. 104, [1995] 4 S.C.R. 634 (S.C.C.), at paras. 57-60. See Bernard J. Garbutt III & Melinda E. Hofmann, "Recent Developments in Pharmaceutical Products Liability Law: Failure to Warn, the Learned Intermediary Defense, and Other Issues in the New Millennium" (2003) 58 Food & Drug L.J. 269 for discussion of recent U.S. developments.

[146] [1991] S.C.J. No. 18, [1991] 1 S.C.R. 541 (S.C.C.).

[147] Sanda Rodgers made a similar argument with respect to valuing the real losses experienced by women, including care for the child and the home, in wrongful birth actions where the reproductive injury results in the birth of a child and also suggested that the loss of reproductive autonomy itself should be compensable. Sanda Rodgers, "Taking Care of Baby: Denying Legal Recovery for the Birth of a Child" (1999-2000) 1 J. Women's Health & L. 235.

In the related product liability disclosure action, Berger and Twerski have suggested compensating the deprivation of informed choice without proof of injury causation in those toxic tort cases involving lifestyle drugs where the causal link between product and harm is problematic and unresolved when litigation commences, where information about the alleged link was known or could have been revealed through testing, and where the information has not been disclosed to patients.[148] In cases such as these involving non-therapeutic lifestyle drugs, decision causation would be resolved in favour of the plaintiff since the lifestyle enhancement would be clearly outweighed by the material risk.[149] They recommended that the emotional distress of the lost choice be the basis for the damage award. Such a protection for negligent infliction of emotional distress would be consistent with the Supreme Court's view in *R. v. Morgentaler* that infringements of security of the person include psychological stress.[150]

C. INFORMED CONSENT IN PRACTICE

Has informed consent doctrine succeeded in enabling patients to participate in decision-making? Cathy Jones was a participant observer in a hospital for six months while she studied these interactions.[151] She identified four features that doctors cited in the late 1980s as objections to informed consent: (1) "Patients neither understand nor remember what they're told"; (2) "Testing patients' understanding is too resource intensive"; (3) "Patients want physicians to make decisions for them"; and (4) "Physicians can convince almost any patient to do what the physician believes is best for the patient".[152] After making suggestions to deal with these objections, she concluded that shifting the power balance was necessary to achieve informed consent. Patients need to trust themselves more and this self-trust comes through others trusting them more.[153] Vulnerable patients are not autonomous and more power produces less vulnerability but also a position of not having to take responsibility. Cathy Jones argued that if we are serious about patient autonomy and decision-making, we must render a patient's shifting of responsibility to the physician unacceptable, and we must insist that patients take primary responsibility for making decisions relating to their health care.[154]

The question remains whether the current system is able to provide an environment in which patients' desires for the doctor-patient relationship — such as mutual trust, listening skills, truthfulness in disclosure, openness, respect, discussion of uncertainties and confidentiality — can be achieved.

---

[148] Margaret A. Berger & Aaron D. Twerski, "Uncertainty and Informed Choice: Unmasking *Daubert*" (2005) 104 Mich. L. Rev. 257.

[149] *Ibid.*, at 149*n*.

[150] [1988] S.C.J. No. 1, [1988] 1 S.C.R. 30 (S.C.C.).

[151] Cathy J. Jones, "Decision-Making: Toward a New Self-Fulfilling Prophecy" (1990) 47 Wash. & Lee L. Rev. 379.

[152] *Ibid.*, at 409-25.

[153] *Ibid.*, at 427.

[154] *Ibid.*, at 421.

Today medicine is practised in a way that differs significantly even from its 1980 counterpart, in the involvement of a bigger range of health practitioners, the increasing acceptance of collaborative care, shorter periods of hospitalization, the wide availability of sophisticated technology for diagnostics and treatment, dramatically increased prescription drug usage and rapid information-processing. From the perspective of patients, much more information is available. Internet access, media coverage, consumer groups (some funded by the pharmaceutical industry) and direct-to-consumer advertising provide information in forms that vary greatly in their degree of reliability. The doctor-patient dyad is no longer the sole, or even perhaps primary, source of patient information, as it had been in the period leading up to the 1980 decisions when medicine had achieved primacy over other health care providers and family members and when technology continued to promise progress in care. At the same time the economics of patient care have changed dramatically, so that timely access can no longer be guaranteed. Because the service system is fragmented, higher degrees of sophistication are required for patients to make their way effectively to the needed care. Because there are few patient advocates available to counsel patients about services or legal rights, health practitioners often advise patients and their families about these issues, sometimes as a legal requirement. Unless health professionals are educated in legal issues early in their education and are supported in continuing education in this area, they will lack the expertise to put into effect their own responsibilities and to ensure that patients' rights are respected in the decision-making process.

Through this period, the pharmaceutical industry has vastly expanded its influence over the sources of information available to physicians, controlling to a greater extent the structuring of information that reaches physicians and then patients. They have done this by increasing the percentage of research funded by industry, by expanding their ties to medical journals, government regulators and physician assessors, and by increasing the funding allocated to promotional activities such as advertising to consumers directly, in whatever form is permitted, and to physicians through detailers, print advertising and educational seminars.[155] Preparation of articles by industry representatives and researchers with ties to industry permits the industry to sell their products and construct product knowledge under the guise of peer-reviewed authorship. Unless independent and reliable sources of information are available to physicians, they will be unable to exercise professional judgment about proposed treatment alternatives and unable to convey knowledge to patients. Informed consent rests on the premise that the information is adequate. This expectation is undermined by biases that exist throughout the process of knowledge construction.

Empowerment of patients depends as well on contextual elements such as race, age, gender and class. These social factors form part of the inquiry into dominance and equality in the health practitioner-patient relationship. For

---

[155] Jerry Avorn, *Powerful Medicine: The Benefits, Risks, and Costs of Prescription Drugs* (New York and Toronto: Vintage Books, 2005); John Abramson, *Overdosed America: The Broken Promise of American Medicine* (New York: HarperCollins, 2004); Jerome P. Kassirer, *On The Take: How Medicine's Complicity With Big Business Can Endanger Your Health* (New York: Oxford University Press, 2005).

example, individuals vary in the degree to which they can access and evaluate internet information, depending on a range of factors including literacy, geography, poverty, availability of resources, level of education and critical awareness of sources. These power relationships among the participants need to be taken into account in the attempt to secure participation in decision-making. As Susan Sherwin argued, creating personal control over health care requires an examination of context that includes medical structures themselves as sources of power and status that have contributed to women's inequality.[156] The myth of autonomy incorrectly perceives patients as empowered to act when they are not, and understanding this requires us to take account of the medicalization of women's bodies and sexist, racist and paternalistic norms.[157] Jennifer Nedelsky has pointed out that a liberal notion of autonomy focuses on atomistic individuals and fails to reflect "the inherently social nature of human beings", beings whose social context is "literally constitutive of us".[158] She suggested that autonomy consists not only of self-determination but also probably of "comprehension, confidence, dignity, efficacy, respect, and some degree of peace and security from oppressive power".[159] Autonomy is enabled by relationships that provide experience and guidance in autonomy. The doctrine of informed decision-making can encourage the capacity to be autonomous through enhancing the individual's power in the relationship.

Participation in decision-making is critical to achieving autonomy and respect for individuals' values and beliefs. In global health it is increasingly recognized that such human rights interact with health so that improving the rights of citizens to make decisions about themselves and their dependent family members is a means to achieve better health status. Improving access to accurate information and educating people so that they can understand and assess the information are vital steps to the achievement of autonomy and empowerment.

---

[156] Susan Sherwin, "Feminist and Medical Ethics: Two Different Approaches to Contextual Ethics" (1989) 4 Hypatia 57.

[157] Erin Nelson, "Reconceiving Pregnancy: Expressive Choice and Legal Reasoning" (2004) 49 McGill L.J. 593 at 614.

[158] Jennifer Nedelsky, "Reconceiving Autonomy: Sources, Thoughts and Possibilities" (1989) 1 Yale J. L. & Feminism 7 at 8.

[159] *Ibid.*, at 9.

Chapter 6

HEALTH INFORMATION: CONFIDENTIALITY AND ACCESS

Elaine Gibson

I. INTRODUCTION

The prototype for health information is physician notes, recorded on paper in the course of or following a face-to-face interaction with a patient, and stored in cardboard files in large metal filing cabinets. The body of jurisprudence and legislation developed over time for such a circumstance was, if not straightforward, at least reasonably coherent. But the health information world has changed dramatically over the past 50 years. Not only is the physician-patient model no longer the dominant model, it has been eclipsed by such developments as multiplication of types of health professions, team-based practice, digitized billing records, electronic health records, telehealth, telerobotics and telesurgery, tissue samples rich in genetic information, commercial practice and research. Each of these developments presents challenges for the law to grapple with. As we shall see in this chapter, sometimes laws are more successful than at other times in coping with the brave new world of modern health information.

Most of the legal protections for health information are based in statute. There are, however, some significant areas carved out in common law.

This chapter commences with a discussion of confidentiality, and then of ownership, custodianship and the right of access to one's own information. The *Canadian Charter of Rights and Freedoms*[1] has had a strong influence on law in this area, particularly in the area of criminal law. A discussion of the Charter is followed by an overview of the types of legislation, both federal and provincial, as well as jurisdictional issues in the areas of health and of information.

Next I examine consensual and non-consensual collection, use and disclosure of health information. A number of exceptions to confidentiality have been carved out to satisfy the apparent requirements of various sectors of society such as child protection and legal proceedings. In some circumstances there is a duty to disclose and in others, disclosure is permitted but not mandated.

---

[1] Part I of the *Constitution Act, 1982*, being Schedule B to the *Canada Act 1982* (U.K.), 1982, c. 11 (Charter).

The last part of the chapter covers a couple of areas within health wherein specialized demands for health information are being made, such as electronic health records and globalization and public health. These areas push the limits in terms of our traditional conceptions of health information, and give rise to questions as to whether particular uses are legitimate, often without the consent of the sources of such information.

II. CONFIDENTIALITY

The duty of confidentiality in the context of provision of health care services has a long and venerable history in ethics and in law. In 1928 the Supreme Court of Canada in *Halls v. Mitchell* incorporated into common law the essence of the Hippocratic Oath, ruling in the context of physician-patient relations that:

> Nobody would dispute that a secret [acquired in the course of a medical practitioner's practice] is the secret of the patient and, normally, is under his control, and not under that of the doctor. *Prima facie*, the patient has the right to require that the secret shall not be divulged; and that right is absolute, unless there is some paramount reason which overrides it.[2]

Specifically, the Hippocratic Oath states that "whatsoever I shall see or hear in the course of my profession ... if it be what should not be published abroad, I will never divulge".[3] Thus, in the case of personal information garnered in the course of physician practice, one commences with the premise that this information is to be kept confidential.[4] The principle underlying this practice was discussed in *Halls v. Mitchell* as follows:

> It is, perhaps, not easy to exaggerate the value attached by the community as a whole to the existence of a competently trained and honourable medical profession; and it is just as important that patients, in consulting a physician, shall feel that they may disclose the facts touching their bodily health, without fear that their confidence may be abused to their disadvantage.[5]

The same logic underlying this principle applies to personal information acquired not just by physicians but throughout the health care system, in that trust that one's information will not be broadcast indiscriminately is

---

[2]   [1928] S.C.R. 125 (S.C.C.) at para. 17. Note that, despite the strong language, the majority finds that the information at issue was not in fact confidential, having been conveyed to an official in order to obtain official information. The reference to confidentiality of personal health information was being used in contrast and therefore is *obiter*.

[3]   *Hippocrates*, W.H. Jones, trans. (Cambridge: Harvard University Press, 1923). Cited in M. Marshall & B. von Tigerstrom, "Health Information", in Jocelyn Downie, Timothy Caulfield & Colleen Flood, eds., *Canadian Health Law and Policy*, 2nd ed. (Markham, ON: LexisNexis Butterworths, 2002) at 190.

[4]   Confidentiality is the obligation of the third party holder of information to respect its secrecy. Privacy is more difficult to define in that it is nuanced and subject to multiple interpretations, but it is generally agreed that it focuses on the individual or group and not on a third party.

[5]   [1928] S.C.R. 125 (S.C.C.) at para. 21.

fundamental to patients feeling comfortable in revealing deeply personal and private facts and beliefs to their health care providers.

Legal and ethical duties of confidentiality operate in rough parallel. A health professional practices under a Code of Ethics[6] which may in turn be incorporated under her or his professional governing legislation.[7] Thus, in the case of a self-governing profession, breach of an ethics code provides grounds for discipline by the governing body, for example, the College of Physicians and Surgeons.

The Quebec *Charter of Human Rights and Freedoms* protects confidential information as follows:

> Every person has a right to non-disclosure of confidential information. No person bound to professional secrecy by law and no priest or other minister of religion may, even in judicial proceedings, disclose confidential information revealed to him by reason of his position or profession, unless he is authorized to do so by the person who confided such information to him or by an express provision of law. The tribunal must, *ex officio*, ensure that professional secrecy is respected.[8]

Information does not lose its confidential nature by virtue of the fact that someone has broadcast it to third parties. In *Calgary Regional Health Authority v. United Western Communications Ltd.*,[9] a nurse supplied the *Alberta Report* magazine editor with copies of internal hospital documents discussing the performance of late-term abortions, including the names of some of the doctors and nurses participating. At a hearing an injunction was sought restraining the magazine from publishing an article containing information internal to the hospital. One of the arguments of the editor was that they had already distributed these documents to others and so the interlocutory injunction being sought should not be granted. Justice Hawko for the Alberta Court of Queen's Bench disagreed, stating:

> The fact that the defendants, or some other person, have already sent this information on to others does not make it knowledge in the public domain. The defendants cannot by their actions take something which is confidential and turn it into something which is not. It still retains its protection.[10]

Confidentiality is, however, never considered so sacrosanct that competing forces may not be seen to override it. In fact, as we shall see, most of the

---

[6] See Canadian Medical Association, *CMA Code of Ethics* (update 2004) at ss. 31-37, online: Canadian Medical Association <http://www.cma.ca/index.cfm/ci_id/2419/la_id/1.htm>; Canadian Nurses Association, *Code of Ethics for Registered Nurses*, online: Canadian Nurses Association http://www.cna-nurses.ca/cna/documents/pdf/publications/CodeofEthics 2002_e.pdf at 14; National Association of Pharmacy Regulatory Authorities, *The Model Standards of Practice for Canadian Pharmacists* (2003), online: National Association of Pharmacy Regulatory Authorities <http://www.napra.org/pdfs/practice/model_std_practice/MSPCP-Nov2005.pdf>; Canadian Dental Association, *CDA Code of Ethics* at Art. 9, online: Canadian Dental Association <http://www.cda-adc.ca/en/cda/about_cda/code_of_ethics/index.asp>.

[7] Quebec *Code of Ethics of Dentists*, R.R.Q. 1981, c. D-3, r. 4, s. 3.06.01; Nova Scotia *Code of Ethics Regulations*, N.S. Reg. 119/97, s. 1.

[8] Quebec *Charter of Human Rights and Freedoms*, R.S.Q., c. C-12, art. 9. Article 5 of the Quebec Charter also provides the right to respect for one's private life.

[9] [1999] A.J. No. 805, 75 Alta. L.R. (3d) 326 (Alta. Q.B.).

[10] *Ibid.*, at para. 18.

discussion in law and in this chapter consists of the numerous circumstances in which it has been deemed appropriate to set aside the duty of confidentiality in favour of some other, apparently compelling, cause.

III. CUSTODIANSHIP, OWNERSHIP, AND ENTITLEMENT TO ACCESS

Both common law and statute have adopted the concept of custodianship or trusteeship when a patient's health information is being held by another party, whether health care provider, hospital, long-term care facility, research centre or department of health. The property or ownership model has been considered at common law and ultimately rejected by the Supreme Court of Canada. Interestingly, we have recently seen its resurgence in the form of a claim by an Aboriginal organization of ownership over health information of Aboriginal people,[11] but no court has substantiated this claim as of yet. The patient's entitlement to access this information may be seen as corollary to questions of ownership or custodianship.

The Supreme Court of Canada weighed into the matter of ownership and custodianship of health information in its 1992 judgment in *McInerney v. MacDonald*,[12] a case involving a patient's right to access her own health information. This case was decided in the absence of New Brunswick legislation speaking to the issue of access. Mrs. MacDonald sought from her family physician Dr. McInerney not only copies of the health records drafted and tests ordered by Dr. McInerney, but also those that had been compiled from previous treating physicians. Dr. McInerney was willing to provide copies of the records she had drafted but took the position that Mrs. MacDonald would need to approach the other physicians for copies of those records. All three levels of court found in favour of Mrs. MacDonald, albeit for different reasons. Justice Turnbull for the New Brunswick trial court ruled that patients have a proprietary interest in their own information. A majority of the Court of Appeal decided that the question was not ownership, but that there was an implied contract between physician and patient for information ancillary to treatment. Part of this contract was an entitlement to access that information.

A unanimous Supreme Court of Canada ruled that neither of these approaches — proprietary or contractual — was necessary for the disposition of the case. The Court found that the physical file belonged to the physician but that the patient was entitled to access the file contents, barring unusual circumstances that would make it inappropriate or dangerous. Justice LaForest indicated that, while the information contained therein "remains, in a fundamental sense, one's own",[13] it is not necessary to "reify"[14] this to a property

---

[11]   Valerie Gideon, "Understanding OCAP (Ownership, Control, Access, Possession) and its Ties to Privacy" (2002) *NAHO Network News* at 4, online: NAHO <http://www.naho.ca/english/pdf/summer2002.pdf>.

[12]   [1992] S.C.J. No. 57, [1992] 2 S.C.R. 138 (S.C.C.).

[13]   *Ibid.*, at para. 18.

[14]   *Ibid.*, at para. 25.

interest. Rather, a trust-like relationship in the nature of a fiduciary duty develops when a patient imparts information to a physician.[15]

Health information legislation is constructed around the concept of a "health information custodian"[16] or "trustee",[17] which may include a multitude of organizations, corporations, and facilities as well as health care practitioners. In Ontario, anyone whose primary function is to provide health care services in exchange for payment, whether or not such services are publicly funded, is included in the definition of health care practitioner, although interestingly, Aboriginal healers and midwives are excluded along with faith healers.[18] Agents of the custodian, providers of information technology services, and persons who receive personal health information from a custodian are all assigned responsibilities pursuant to the statute. It would appear that insurance companies that receive information such as prescription claims directly from individuals as opposed to from custodians are excluded from the Ontario legislation, as they do not fall within the definition of a custodian.[19] This is a curious exception given the quantity and sensitivity of personal health information these companies handle.

IV. THE CANADIAN CHARTER OF RIGHTS AND FREEDOMS

Is there a right to informational privacy under the *Canadian Charter of Rights and Freedoms*? The answer is an unequivocal "yes" in the area of criminal law. In other areas of law, however, the answer is less clear.

One of the first cases decided by the Supreme Court of Canada under the Charter, *Hunter v. Southam Inc.*,[20] involved a documents search authorized by a warrant issued under authority of the *Combines Investigation Act*. The Court found the procedures for issuance of a warrant violated Charter section 8, protection against unreasonable search and seizure, in that the person authorized to issue the warrant was not an impartial arbiter and the statute failed to set an appropriate standard for such issuance, given the privacy interest engaged.

A string of cases have followed in which bodily substances were taken or turned over to the police without consent. In *R. v. Dyment*,[21] a blood sample taken for medical purposes was handed over to the police at their request and

---

[15] Note that the Australian High Court in *Julie Breen v. Cholmondeley W Williams* (1996) 186 CLR 71 ruled otherwise — *i.e.*, that the patient does not have a right to access her or his health information — and was highly critical of the Supreme Court of Canada judgment in *McInerney v. MacDonald*, denying that the physician/patient relationship gives rise to a fiduciary duty, and finding that the records belong to the physician.

[16] *Personal Health Information Protection Act, 2004*, S.O. 2004, c. 3, Sch. A, s. 3.

[17] *Personal Health Information Act*, C.C.S.M. c. P33.5, s. 1(1); *Health Information Protection Act*, S.S. 1999, c. H-0.021, s. 2(*t*).

[18] *Personal Health Information Protection Act, 2004*, S.O. 2004, c. 3, Sch. A, s. 3(4).

[19] Ann Cavoukian, Information and Privacy Commissioner of Ontario, "A Guide to the Personal Health Information Protection Act" (Toronto: IPC, 2004), online: <http://www.ipc.on.ca/images/Resources/hguide-e.pdf> at 11.

[20] [1984] S.C.J. No. 36, [1984] 2 S.C.R. 145 (S.C.C.).

[21] [1988] S.C.J. No. 82, [1988] 2 S.C.R. 417 (S.C.C.).

resulted in a conviction for driving while intoxicated. Justice La Forest, writing for the majority, stated:

> [T]he sense of privacy transcends the physical. The dignity of the human being is equally seriously violated when use is made of bodily substances taken by others for medical purposes in a manner that does not respect that limitation. In my view, the trust and confidence of the public in the administration of medical facilities would be seriously taxed if an easy and informal flow of information, and particularly of bodily substances from hospitals to the police, were allowed. [22]

The fact that a warrant was not sought was found to be "a flagrant breach of personal privacy"[23] in violation of section 8 of the Charter and not salvageable under section 24(2) as the admission of the evidence in these circumstances "would bring the administration of justice into disrepute".[24]

In *R. v. Dersch*,[25] the treating physician took a blood sample from the unconscious accused despite his earlier refusal, and in turn provided the test results to the police in response to their warrantless request. The conduct of the police was found to constitute unreasonable search and seizure, again not admissible due to section 24(2).[26]

R. v. S.A.B.[27] involved a pregnant 14-year-old who indicated she was a victim of sexual assault by the accused. Fetal tissue was seized following her abortion, and a blood sample was taken from the accused pursuant to a warrant granted *ex parte* in accordance with sections 487.04 to 487.09 of the *Criminal Code*. The DNA matched and the accused claimed a violation of his Charter rights in the taking of the sample. The Supreme Court of Canada upheld the impugned sections under section 8 in that they require a warrant, at which point the interest in law enforcement is balanced against privacy interests, and they limit the issuance of DNA warrants to designated offences.

A presentencing report by a psychologist in *R. v. Shoker*[28] recommended that the accused be subjected to random urinalysis, blood or breathalyzer tests as part of his conditions for probation, and the sentencing judge so ordered. This order was struck down by the Supreme Court of Canada as violating section 8 of the Charter in the absence of a governing regulatory or statutory framework.

In the recent case of *R. v. Rodgers*,[29] the Crown applied *ex parte* under *Criminal Code* section 487.055(1)(c) for authorization for the taking of a blood sample from the accused for entry into the national DNA data bank. A majority of the Supreme Court of Canada upheld the constitutionality of the section, finding as follows:

---

[22] *Ibid.*, at para. 38.
[23] *Ibid.*
[24] *Ibid.*, Charter, s. 24(2).
[25] [1993] S.C.J. No. 116, [1993] 3 S.C.R. 768 (S.C.C.).
[26] But see *R. v. Colarusso*, [1994] S.C.J. No. 2, [1994] 1 S.C.R. 20 (S.C.C.), in which a majority of the court found on similar facts a violation of s. 8 but upheld the seizure under s. 24(2).
[27] [2003] S.C.J. No. 61, [2003] 2 S.C.R. 678 (S.C.C.); R.S.C. 1985, c. C-46.
[28] [2006] S.C.J. No. 44 (S.C.C.).
[29] [2006] S.C.J. No. 15 (S.C.C.).

Society's interest in using this powerful new technology to assist law enforcement agencies in the identification of offenders is beyond dispute. The resulting impact on the physical integrity of the targeted offenders is minimal. The potential invasive impact on the right to privacy has carefully been circumscribed by legislative safeguards that restrict the use of the DNA data bank as an identification tool only. As convicted offenders still under sentence, the persons targeted by s. 487.055 have a much reduced expectation of privacy. Further, by reason of their crimes, they have lost any reasonable expectation that their identity will remain secret from law enforcement authorities.[30]

The above cases all revolved around section 8 of the Charter. Section 7 has also been examined concerning privacy of health information, primarily concerning the special circumstance wherein persons accused of sexual assault seek access to their victims' counselling records. For a period of time this was so routine that L'Heureux-Dubé J. was moved to state that "[f]rom a quick perusal of lower court judgments, it would appear as if a request for therapeutic records in cases of sexual assault is becoming virtually automatic, with little regard to the actual relevancy of the documents".[31] In response to the striking down of previous *Criminal Code* provisions, sections 278.1 to 278.91 were enacted and have been upheld by a majority of the Supreme Court of Canada in *R. v. Mills*. The victim's security was found to be engaged in the circumstances:

> This Court has on several occasions recognized that security of the person is violated by state action interfering with an individual's mental integrity … Therefore, in cases where a therapeutic relationship is threatened by the disclosure of private records, security of the person and not just privacy is implicated.[32]

In balancing the accused's right to make full answer and defence against the victim's right against unreasonable search and seizure, the Court stated:

> The values protected by privacy rights will be most directly at stake where the confidential information contained in a record concerns aspects of one's individual identity or where the maintenance of confidentiality is crucial to a therapeutic, or other trust-like, relationship.[33]

The section 7 right to liberty also covers aspects of privacy; indeed, La Forest J. has commented that "privacy is at the heart of liberty in a modern state".[34] And in *R. v. O'Connor*, L' Heureux-Dubé J. stated that when one's personal information is exposed to others against one's wishes, "it is an invasion of the dignity and self-worth of the individual, who enjoys the right to privacy as an essential aspect of … liberty in a free and democratic society".[35]

---

[30] *Ibid.*, at para. 5.

[31] [1997] 1 S.C.R. 80 (S.C.C.) at para. 147 in dissent. In this case the therapeutic records had been destroyed by the sexual assault crisis centre to prevent their use in judicial proceedings, leading a majority of the Supreme Court of Canada to order a stay of proceedings as the accused's right to make full answer and defence had been compromised.

[32] *R. v. Mills*, [1999] S.C.J. No. 68, [1999] 3 S.C.R. 668 (S.C.C.) at para. 85.

[33] *Ibid.*, at para. 89.

[34] *R. v. Dyment*, [1988] S.C.J. No. 82, [1988] 2 S.C.R. 417 (S.C.C.) at para. 17, drawing on the work of Alan Westin.

[35] [1995] S.C.J. No. 98, [1995] 4 S.C.R. 411 (S.C.C.) at para. 119.

Finally, section 15 is implicated in balancing sexual assault victims' right to privacy in their counselling records against the rights of the accused:

> Equality concerns must also inform the contextual circumstances in which the rights of full answer and defence and privacy will come into play. In this respect, an appreciation of myths and stereotypes in the context of sexual violence is essential to delineate properly the boundaries of full answer and defence ... The accused is not permitted to "whack the complainant" through the use of stereotypes regarding victims of sexual assault.[36]

Note that all of the above cases have arisen in the criminal law context. There has been considerably less discussion of a Charter right to privacy of information in civil law. In *Canadian AIDS Society v. Ontario*,[37] the plaintiffs argued that notification of blood donors of their HIV-positive status many years after the blood had been collected and without any indication to the donors that such testing would be done constituted a violation of their section 7 and section 8 rights. Justice Wilson for the Ontario Court of Justice (General Division) found that the right to security of the person would indeed be violated by such notification, as the donors' psychological integrity would be shaken, but that there was no violation of the principles of fundamental justice. The claim under section 8 was that the "seizure" of the donated blood for testing, which had been conducted in order to notify recipients of their possible receipt of tainted blood, was unreasonable. The court disagreed, finding the seizure reasonable in light of the public health imperative at stake.

Thus, there is at least one decision outside the criminal context that has found section 7 to be relevant *vis-à-vis* personal health information. The Supreme Court of Canada has not, however, made such a finding. Its most recent pronouncement on the matter of section 7 protection of information privacy appears to have been in *Ruby v. Canada (Solicitor General)*.[38] The appellant argued that his right to access information held by the government was corollary to the right to privacy under section 7 and was violated by provisions of the *Privacy Act*. The Court chose not to rule on this argument, and decided that even if such a violation was present, the provisions were in accordance with principles of fundamental justice.[39]

V. OVERVIEW OF LEGISLATIVE LANDSCAPE

Laws governing health information might politely be described as smorgasbord in nature. Some protections have developed in common law, for instance, the entitlement in certain circumstances to access records for purposes of judicial

---

[36] *R. v. Mills*, [1999] S.C.J. No. 68, [1999] 3 S.C.R. 668 (S.C.C.) at para. 90.

[37] [1995] O.J. No. 2361 (Ont. Gen. Div.), affd [1996] O.J. No. 4184, 31 O.R. (3d) 798 (Ont. C.A.), leave to appeal to S.C.C. refused [1997] S.C.C.A. No. 33 (S.C.C.).

[38] [2002] S.C.J. No. 73, [2002] 4 S.C.R. 3 (S.C.C.).

[39] For expanded discussion of Charter s. 7 in the civil law context, see von Tigerstrom *et al.*, "Alberta's Health Information Act and the Charter: A Discussion Paper" (2001) 9 Health L. Rev. 2 at paras. 21-29. *Privacy Act*, R.S.C. 1985, c. P-21.

proceedings. The great majority, however, have been legislated due to lacunae in development of the common law. This section commences with a brief discussion of the constitutional division of powers in the areas of health and of information. The lion's share of legislation is provincial/territorial, leading to significant differences in coverage depending on one's jurisdiction. For instance, the Atlantic provinces and northern territories are at present the only jurisdictions without provincial legislation governing information in the private sector. Not all is provincial; for example, since 1983 there has been federal legislation governing personal information held by government and its agencies. And the federal government has stepped into the scene in major fashion in recent years with its enactment of the *Personal Information Protection and Electronic Documents Act* (PIPEDA).[40] This section introduces the various major pieces of legislation, both federal and provincial, and discusses their scope. Details of the legislation regarding permitted collection, use and disclosure, as well as remedial provisions, will be covered in later sections of this chapter.

A. CONSTITUTIONAL DIVISION OF POWERS

Jurisdiction is divided for both matters of health and matters of information, with the provinces/territories responsible for the lion's share of each. The *Constitution Act, 1867* allocated marine hospitals and quarantine to the federal government,[41] whereas the provinces were assigned power over "the Establishment, Maintenance, and Management of Hospitals, Asylums, Charities, and Eleemosynary Institutions in and for the Province, other than Marine Hospitals".[42] Most health matters were assumed by the provinces pursuant to this power over hospitals as well as power over property and civil rights and matters of a local or private nature. To this day this division exists, with federal jurisdiction over quarantine being interpreted to apply only to ingress and egress into and out of Canada.[43] The *Canada Health Act*[44] was not an assertion of federal jurisdiction over health matters; rather, it invoked federal spending power to gain the participation of the provinces/territories in a program of Medicare for hospitals and medically necessary physician services.[45]

As to information, the federal government was granted jurisdiction over census and statistics.[46] However, the topic of information *per se* was not likely in the minds of the drafters of the *Constitution Act, 1867*, and certainly was not mentioned in the document. As information has become a commodity of considerable import in recent years, it has been interpreted to fall primarily under the provincial power over property and civil rights[47] and matters of a local

---

[40] S.C. 2000, c. 5 (PIPEDA).
[41] *Ibid.*, 30 & 31 Vict., c. 3 (U.K.) at s. 91(11).
[42] *Ibid.*, at s. 92(7).
[43] See, *e.g.*, *Quarantine Act*, S.C. 2005, c. 20.
[44] *Canada Health Act*, R.S.C. 1985, c. C-6.
[45] For more extensive discussion see Chapter 14.
[46] *Constitution Act, 1867*, 30 & 31 Vict., c. 3 (U.K.), s. 91(6).
[47] *Ibid.*, s. 92(13).

or private nature.[48] However, the fact that jurisdiction over both health and information rests primarily with the provincial governments has not deterred the federal government from enacting legislation governing information management, including health information, most notably PIPEDA.[49] Because the legislation only applies to information collected, used or disclosed in the course of commercial activity, the government has relied on its trade and commerce power in asserting its constitutionality.[50]

A challenge to the constitutionality of PIPEDA has been brought before the Court of Appeal by the Attorney General for Quebec.[51] The claim is that PIPEDA trenches on Quebec's constitutional competence with respect to property and civil rights, and that a provision in the statute giving the federal government the right to review a provincial statute to ensure substantial similarity is incompatible with principles of federalism. The scope of the federal trade and commerce power, scrutinized by the Supreme Court of Canada in *General Motors of Canada Ltd. v. City National Leasing Ltd.*,[52] will be under close scrutiny, and some consider the stakes enormous.[53]

B. FEDERAL LEGISLATION

1. *Personal Information Protection and Electronic Documents Act*

The *Personal Information Protection and Electronic Documents Act*[54] was brought into force in a number of stages between 2001 and 2004.[55] Since January 1, 2004, it has been in force both for information crossing provincial boundaries and also intra-provincially in provinces that do not have legislation declared by the Governor in Council to be "substantially similar"[56] to PIPEDA in providing information protection. In other words, in provinces with legislation declared "substantially similar", PIPEDA applies only to information going into and out of the province and to information collected, used or disclosed in connection with the operation of a federal work, undertaking or business, but not to information being kept within the province. The Ontario *Personal Health*

48 *Ibid.*, s. 92(16).
49 Additional federal legislation that touches on health information includes the *Food and Drugs Act*, R.S.C. 1985, c. F-27, *Controlled Drugs and Substances Act*, S.C. 1996, c. 19, *Quarantine Act*, S.C. 2005, c. 20.
50 *Constitution Act, 1867*, 30 & 31 Vict., c. 3 (U.K.), s. 91(2).
51 Reference to the Court of Appeal relating to the Law on the protection of the personal information and electronic documents (L.C. 2000, c. 5), O.I.C. 1368-2003, G.O.Q. 2003.II.184.
52 [1989] S.C.J. No. 28, 1 S.C.R. 641 (S.C.C.).
53 See, *e.g.*, Simon Chester, "Privacy Act imperils provinces' ability to make local business laws" *Financial Post* (January 6, 2004).
54 S.C. 2000, c. 5.
55 PIPEDA came into force in three stages: January 2001 for interprovincial transfers of information, with the exception of health information, and for the operations of federal works, undertakings and businesses; January 2002 for interprovincial transfers of health information; and January 2004 for the former plus intraprovincial transfers of information.
56 PIPEDA, S.C. 2000, c. 5, s. 26(2)(*b*).

Information Protection Act[57] is the first health information-specific legislation to have been declared substantially similar.[58] General private sector information legislation in Quebec,[59] British Columbia[60] and Alberta[61] has been declared substantially similar.[62] Alberta is in a unique and curious position in that only its health information legislation is not substantially similar. Thus, information in the private sector within Alberta is subject to PIPEDA only if it is health information; it is subject also to the *Health Information Act* so long as it is collected, used, held or disclosed by a health care services provider who is publicly funded.[63] In all provinces, PIPEDA still applies to information that crosses provincial/territorial or federal borders.

PIPEDA covers solely personal information, defined as "information about an identifiable individual, but does not include the name, title or business address or telephone number of an employee of an organization".[64] Thus, information pursuant to which there is no reasonable potential for identification of an individual appears to fall outside its mandate. However, there is also a lengthy and detailed definition of personal health information, as follows:

"personal health information", with respect to an individual, whether living or deceased, means

(a) information concerning the physical or mental health of the individual;

(b) information concerning any health service provided to the individual;

(c) information concerning the donation by the individual of any body part or any bodily substance of the individual or information derived from the testing or examination of a body part or bodily substance of the individual;

(d) information that is collected in the course of providing health services to the individual; or

(e) information that is collected incidentally to the provision of health services to the individual.[65]

---

[57] *Personal Health Information Protection Act, 2004*, S.O. 2004, c. 3, Sch. A.

[58] Health Information Custodians in the Province of Ontario, P.C. 2005-2224, November 28, 2005 SOR/2005-399, Canada Gazette Vol. 139, No. 25, December 14, 2005, online: Government of Canada <http://canadagazette.gc.ca/partII/2005/20051214/html/sor399-e.html>.

[59] *An Act Respecting the Protection of Personal Information in the Private Sector*, R.S.Q. c. P-39.1.

[60] *Personal Information Protection Act*, S.B.C. 2003, c. 63.

[61] *Personal Information Protection Act*, S.A. 2003, c. P-6.5.

[62] Organizations in the Province of British Columbia Exemption Order, P.C. 2004-1164 12 October, 2004 SOR/2004-220, *Canada Gazette* Vol. 138, No. 22 (November 3, 2004), online: Government of Canada <http://canadagazette.gc.ca/partII/2004/20041103/html/sor220-e.html>; Organizations in the Province of Alberta Exemption Order, P.C. 2004-1163 (October 12, 2004), SOR/2004-219, *Canada Gazette* Vol. 138, No. 2 (November 3, 2004), online: Government of Canada <http://canadagazette.gc.ca/partII/2004/20041103/html/sor219-e.html>.

[63] *Health Information Act*, R.S.A. 2000, c. H-5, s. 1(1)(*o*).

[64] PIPEDA, S.C. 2000, c. 5, s. 2(1).

[65] PIPEDA, S.C. 2000, c. 5, s. 2(1).

Note the breadth, which at times could be seen to contradict the definition of personal information. For example, "information collected in the course of providing health services to an individual" could include non-individually identifiable items of information, yet they would appear to be covered. Note also that the definition of personal health information is broad enough to include information regarding a deceased individual, and information as to body parts or substances, but does not include the samples themselves.[66]

PIPEDA only applies to personal information collected, used or disclosed "in the course of commercial activity", which is "[a]ny particular transaction, act or conduct or any regular course of conduct that is of a commercial character, including the selling, bartering or leasing of donor, membership or other fundraising lists."[67] This rather tautological definition has been at least mildly elucidated in *Rodgers v. Calvert*,[68] in which the court found that the profit or non-profit character of an organization is not conclusive as to whether or not PIPEDA applies, and that the mere exchange of consideration in providing personal information and a membership fee in exchange for membership in an organization does not in and of itself constitute commercial activity. Likewise, the court found that the production of a membership list by an organization, short of trading or selling such a list, does not constitute a commercial activity.[69]

Is the provision of health care services a commercial activity? The most substantial guidance to date on this topic has been a document produced by Industry Canada[70] which addresses various issues surrounding PIPEDA's applicability to the health care services community. Industry Canada suggests that PIPEDA does apply to the activities of pharmacies, laboratories and health care providers in private practice. On the other hand, in its view, PIPEDA does not apply to provincially funded hospitals as "their core activities are not commercial in nature".[71] Engaging in some activity such as charging a fee for a cast or for a private room does not bring PIPEDA into play, in its view, as this only happens in connection with the hospital's core activity, which is non-commercial. This interpretation is dubious, as the phrase "core activity" is found nowhere in PIPEDA itself; nor, arguably, is the concept. Also, this interpretation contradicts the fact that the Act focuses on a specific activity and not on the nature of an organization. Further, the application of a "preponderant purpose"

---

[66] For a *contra* view, *i.e.*, arguing that tissues, bodily substances and samples are included in the definition, see L. Rozovsky & N. Inions, *Canadian Health Information*, 3rd ed. (Markham, ON: LexisNexis Butterworths, 2002) at 19.

[67] PIPEDA, S.C. 2000, c. 5, s. 2(1).

[68] *Ibid.*, s. 2(1); *Rodgers v. Calvert*, [2004] O.J. No. 3653 (Ont. S.C.J.). For further discussion of the meaning of "commercial activity" see *Ferenczy v. MCI Medical Clinics*, [2005] O.J. No. 2076 (Ont. C.A.).

[69] *Rodgers v. Calvert, ibid.*, at para. 56.

[70] Industry Canada, not the Office of the Privacy Commissioner nor Health Canada, is the federal Department under whose auspices PIPEDA falls, since its aim is commerce and not health care services *per se*.

[71] Industry Canada, "PIPEDA Awareness Raising Tools (PARTs) Initiative for the Health Sector: Questions and Answers", online: Industry Canada <http://strategis.ic.gc.ca/epic/site/ecic-ceac.nsf/en/gv00235e.html> at 7.

test has already been rejected by the Ontario Superior Court in its interpretation of "commercial activity" under PIPEDA.[72] This "preponderant purpose" test, under which one looks to whether the main purpose of an activity is the making of profit, had been adopted by the Supreme Court of Canada in the context of whether an activity constitutes a business for the purpose of taxation under the *Assessment Act*.[73] However, the Ontario Superior Court ruled that this test is not applicable to PIPEDA, given the different purposes of the two statutes. Clearly there is much analysis of the scope of the commercial activity provision yet to come, given the relative infancy of this statute.

Where PIPEDA applies, then, what does it actually do? It lays out a number of principles for the handling of personal information, including the following: collecting,[74] using,[75] disclosing[76] and retaining only the minimum information necessary for the purpose;[77] identifying this purpose[78] and, subject to a number of exceptions, obtaining the consent of the information source individual;[79] and seeking further consent if the information is to be used or disclosed for other purposes.[80] The legislation also provides the individual with a right of access, and to have incorrect information amended.[81] Other rules attempt to ensure transparency,[82] accuracy,[83] accountability[84] and the safeguarding of information being held.[85] Details of these provisions will be examined in later sections of this chapter.

2. *Privacy Act* and *Access to Information Act*

The *Privacy Act*,[86] and its companion *Access to Information Act*,[87] apply to personal information collected, used, retained or disclosed by the federal public sector. Personal information is defined as "information about an identifiable individual that is recorded in any form". It is widely acknowledged that there is a need for review and updating, in particular because electronic and digital forms of information were not but should now be explicitly included in their

---

[72] *Rodgers v. Calvert*, [2004] O.J. No. 3653 (Ont. S.C.J.) at para. 50.

[73] *Ontario (R.A.C.) v. Caisse Populaire de Hearst Ltée*, [1983] S.C.J. No. 8 [1983] 1 S.C.R. 57 (S.C.C.).

[74] PIPEDA, S.C. 2000, c. 5, Sch. 1, s. 4.4.

[75] *Ibid.*, Sch. 1, s. 4.3.

[76] *Ibid.*, s. 5(3).

[77] *Ibid.*, Sch. 1, s. 4.4.

[78] *Ibid.*, Sch. 1, ss. 4.2, 4.2.5.

[79] *Ibid.*, Sch. 1, s. 4.3.

[80] *Ibid.*, Sch. 1, s. 4.3.1.

[81] *Ibid.*, Sch. 1, s. 4.9.

[82] *Ibid.*, Sch. 1, s. 4.8.

[83] *Ibid.*, Sch. 1, s. 4.6.

[84] *Ibid.*, Sch. 1, s. 4.1.

[85] *Ibid.*, Sch. 1, s. 4.7.

[86] *Privacy Act*, R.S.C. 1985, c. P-21.

[87] *Access to Information Act*, R.S.C. 1985, c. A-1.

purview, and also because of the need to reconcile these statutes with other federal legislation.[88]

3. Other Federal Legislation

In addition to PIPEDA and the *Privacy Act* and *Access to Information Act*, there are a number of other federal statutes relevant to the handling of personal information. The *Statistics Act* authorizes the collection of information "to collect, compile, analyse, abstract and publish statistical information relating to the commercial, industrial, financial, social, economic and general activities and condition of the people".[89] Health information is included in its purview.

The *Controlled Drugs and Substances Act* provides for the collection of personal information regarding controlled drug prescriptions to attempt to stop "double doctoring" or attending on more than one health care provider to obtain multiple prescriptions for a controlled drug within 30 days.[90] The *Criminal Code*[91] contains numerous provisions regarding personal information, some of which are discussed in the Charter and judicial proceedings sections of this chapter. The *Quarantine Act* authorizes the collection of personal information regarding travellers from the person in charge of a conveyance,[92] and places a duty on travellers to provide any information reasonably required by a screening or quarantine officer.[93]

C. PROVINCIAL AND TERRITORIAL LEGISLATION

There are a number of different kinds of provincial/territorial legislation impacting directly on health information. Some provinces have enacted health-information-specific legislation. Others have legislation that covers personal information in the private sector, including health information. All have legislation governing information in the public sector, which may include hospitals and extended care facilities.

Another kind of legislation enacted by a number of provinces creates a statutory form of redress specifically for violations of privacy, which may include the misuse of personal health information. There are also multiple pieces of legislation aimed at the governance of members of the health professions, as well as hospitals, nursing homes and extended care facilities, which include provisions on confidentiality and disclosure of information. Finally (but not

---

[88]   See, *e.g.*, Jennifer Stoddart, Privacy Commissioner of Canada, "Privacy Today and Tomorrow — Priorities for the Next Seven Years" (Address given at the Canadian Access and Privacy Association Annual General Meeting, November 23, 2004) online: <http://www.privcom. gc.ca/speech/2004/sp-d_041123_e.asp>;   Heather Black, Assistant Privacy Commissioner of Canada, "Privacy Law Reform: Responding to a Networked World" (Address given as part of the McCarthy Tétrault Speaker Series, Halifax, Nova Scotia, February 3, 2005) online: <http://www.privcom.gc.ca/speech/2005/sp-d_050203_e.asp>.
[89]   *Statistics Act*, R.S.C. 1985, c. S-19, s. 3(*a*).
[90]   *Controlled Drugs and Substances Act*, S.C. 1996, c. 19.
[91]   *Criminal Code*, R.S.C. 1985, c. C-46.
[92]   *Quarantine Act*, S.C. 2005, c. 20, ss. 34 and 38.
[93]   *Ibid.*, s. 15(1).

exhaustively), there are statutes aimed at protection of vulnerable individuals, such as children and disabled adults. Each will be introduced in this section, and elaborated upon in subsequent discussion.

1. Health-Information-Specific Legislation

A number of provinces have enacted legislation that deals exclusively with health information, in the belief that the area is both complex and worthy of specific and focused protection. In ascending order of recency of legislation in force, these provinces are Manitoba, Alberta, Saskatchewan and Ontario.[94] The Ontario legislation is the most lengthy and arguably the most complex, as the government was able to draw upon lessons from its previous abortive attempts to legislate in this area[95] and on the experience of other provinces with health information legislation already in place.

The primary aim of these statutes is to provide for the protection of personal health information being collected, used, stored or disclosed by an entity other than the individual who is the information source. Personal health information or, in the case of Alberta, individually identifying information, is defined in various ways in the legislation. Basically, the legislation tends to provide wide scope to the types of information that fall under its rubric. Thus, it may include information with respect to the donation of body parts or body substances;[96] health card number;[97] genetic information;[98] payment information;[99] family health history;[100] and an individual's substitute decision-maker.[101] The Manitoba definition includes only recorded information, whereas Ontario's includes information in oral form.[102] In Ontario, Alberta and Saskatchewan, the personal health information of a deceased individual is protected;[103] in Manitoba it is protected for the first 30 years after death.[104]

---

[94] *Personal Health Information Act,* C.C.S.M. c. P33.5; *Health Information Act,* R.S.A. 2000, c. H-5; *Health Information Protection Act,* S.S. 1999, c. H-0.021; *Personal Health Information Protection Act, 2004,* S.O. 2004, c. 3, Sch. A.

[95] *Personal Health Information Protection Act, 1997*; Bill 159, *Personal Health Information Privacy Act,* 2000, 1st Sess., 37th Legis., Ontario, 2000 (First Reading December 7, 2000, referred to the Standing Committee on General Government December 11, 2000).

[96] *Health Information Protection Act,* S.S. 1999, c. H-0.021, s. 2(*m*)(iii); *Personal Health Information Protection Act, 2004,* S.O. 2004, c. 3, Sch. A, s. 4(1)(*e*).

[97] *Personal Health Information Protection Act, ibid.,* s. 34(2).

[98] *Personal Health Information Act,* C.C.S.M. c. P33.5, s. 1(1).

[99] *Health Information Act,* R.S.A. 2000, c. H-5, s. 27(1)(*g*); *Personal Health Information Act,* C.C.S.M. c. P33.5, s. 1(1); *Personal Health Information Protection Act, 2004,* S.O. 2004, c. 3 Sch. A, s. 4(1)(*d*).

[100] *Personal Health Information Protection Act, 2004,* s. 4(1)(*g*).

[101] *Ibid.*

[102] *Personal Health Information Act,* C.C.S.M. c. P33.5, s. 1(1); *Personal Health Information Protection Act, ibid.,* s. 4(1).

[103] *Personal Health Information Protection Act, ibid.,* s. 2. *Health Information Act,* R.S.A. 2000, c. H-5; *Health Information Protection Act,* S.S. 1999, c. H-0.021, s. 2(*m*) — the definition of "personal health information" includes an individual living or deceased.

[104] *Personal Health Information Act,* C.C.S.M. c. P33.5, s. 3(2).

(a) Non-Directly-Identifying Information

One of the interesting aspects of scope of coverage relates to information that is not directly identifying but may in combination with other information provide identification of an individual. Manitoba excludes from the statute information that, when combined with other information available to the holder, does not permit individuals to be identified.[105] Ontario and Saskatchewan similarly acknowledge the risk of identification through combining non-directly identifying information, but add a reasonableness component — for example, in the case of Saskatchewan, the information is protected under the statute if it can *reasonably* be expected to permit identification.[106] Ontario defines identifying information as "information that identifies an individual or for which it is reasonably foreseeable in the circumstances that it could be utilized, either alone or with other information, to identify an individual".[107]

The Alberta legislation takes a very different approach. It does not exclude non-identifying information but permits its collection, use and disclosure, the latter subject to minor conditions. Its definition of non-identifying health information is problematically over-broad, in that it "means that the identity of the individual who is the subject of the information cannot be readily ascertained from the information".[108] "Ready ascertainment" is a much more lax standard than that of "reasonable expectation". Also, while the legislation does discuss "data matching", the protections against data matching do not apply unless two or more electronic databases are being merged. By deduction, then, other pieces of individually non-identifying information, so long as they are not electronic, may be merged to provide identification but will not be subject to statutory protection in Alberta.[109]

(b) Non-Individually-Identifying Information

Another striking feature of the Alberta *Health Information Act* (HIA) is that, along with individuals' personal health information, protection is granted for health services provider information.[110] This form of protection came under scrutiny when physicians in Alberta protested the passing of information by pharmacists to IMS Health which identified physicians' prescribing habits, to be used by pharmaceutical corporations for targeted individual marketing purposes.[111] A similar case under PIPEDA had failed in that prescribing patterns were found to be a work product and hence not to fall under the definition of personal information.[112] However, the explicit inclusion of health services

---

[105] *Ibid.*, s. 3.
[106] *Health Information Protection Act*, S.S. 1999, c. H-0.021, s. 3(2).
[107] *Personal Health Information Protection Act, 2004*, S.O. 2004, c. 3, Sch. A, s. 4(2).
[108] *Health Information Act*, R.S.A. 2000, c. H-5, s. 1(1)(*p*).
[109] For more thorough discussion of this point, see Barbara von Tigerstrom, "Alberta's *Health Information Act* and the *Charter*: A Discussion Paper" (2000) 9:2 Health L.R. 3-21.
[110] *Health Information Act*, R.S.A. 2000, c. H-5, s. 1(1)(*k*).
[111] *IMS Health Canada, Ltd. v. Information and Privacy Commissioner*, [2005] A.J. No.1293 (Alta. C.A.).
[112] *Finding #15*, 2001 CanLII 21546 (P.C.C.).

provider information in the definition of personal information in the HIA resulted in a finding by the Alberta Information and Privacy Commissioner that this practice violated the statute.[113]

With health care budgets exploding, more and more the delivery of health care services has come under scrutiny for efficiency and cost-savings purposes. This scrutiny has meant the identification and comparison of the outcomes ratings of specific practitioners, departments, institutions and regional health authorities. This in turn has led to concerns being raised about the privacy rights of these individuals and groups. The Alberta legislation exemplifies respect for the privacy of professionals and health care organizations. At the other end of the spectrum, the government of Manitoba has established a physician profile website which identifies any practice restrictions or terms or conditions on registration, final disciplinary actions by the College of Physicians and Surgeons, medical malpractice judgments and criminal convictions against the physician.[114] Its potentially strong effects are weakened by the fact that it is based primarily on self-reporting, and only final disciplinary actions, judgments and convictions are reportable. Nevertheless, it is an interesting development in Canadian health law and policy, as historically, a physician's record of practice has been in a practical sense off-limits to the general public. The facilitation of access to physician profiles was one of the measures recommended by Sinclair J. in the report of an inquiry following the deaths of infants at the pediatric cardiac surgery unit of the Winnipeg Health Sciences Centre.[115]

2. Private Sector Personal Information Legislation

Quebec,[116] British Columbia[117] and Alberta[118] have enacted legislation that protects personal information in the private sector. The Alberta *Personal Information Protection Act* does not apply to "health information as defined in the Alberta *Health Information Act* to which that Act applies".[119] The definition of personal information in this legislation is less encompassing than in health information-specific legislation, referring to "information about an identifiable

---

[113] Judicial review underway. See Alberta, Office of the Information and Privacy Commissioner, "Alberta Pharmacists and Pharmacies" Order H2002-003, File No. H0036 (March 19, 2003), online: OIPC <http://www.oipc.ab.ca/ims/client/upload/H2002-003.pdf>.

[114] Bill 31, *The Medical Amendment (Physician Profiles and Miscellaneous Amendments) Act*, 3rd Sess., 37th Leg., Manitoba, 2002 (assented to August 9, 2002); *Medical Act*, C.C.S.M. c. M90.

[115] Judge Murray Sinclair, Provincial Court of Manitoba, *The Report of the Manitoba Pediatric Cardiac Surgery Inquest: An Inquiry into Twelve Deaths at the Winnipeg Health Sciences Centre in 1994* (2001), online: Government of Manitoba <http://www.pediatriccardiacinquest. mb.ca>. For further discussion of this issue see M. Marshall & B. von Tigerstrom, "Health Information", in Jocelyn Downie, Timothy Caulfield & Colleen Flood, eds., *Canadian Health Law and Policy*, 2nd ed. (Markham, ON: LexisNexis Butterworths, 2002) at 174-76.

[116] *An Act Respecting the Protection of Personal Information in the Private Sector*, R.S.Q. c. P-31.1.

[117] *Personal Information Protection Act*, S.B.C. 2003, c. 63.

[118] *Personal Information Protection Act*, S.A. 2003, c. P-6.5.

[119] *Ibid.*, s. 4(3)(f).

individual"[120] or that "allows the person to be identified"[121] without acknowledgment of issues regarding indirect identifiers.

3. Public Sector Personal Information Legislation

Every province and territory in Canada has legislation that aims to protect
personal information held by governments and other public sector bodies.
Unlike in all other jurisdictions, the New Brunswick *Protection of Personal
Information Act*[122] deals solely with protection and not with access to information held by or under the care and control of the government. Newfoundland and
Labrador has the opposite: its government passed legislation covering both
protection of personal information and access, but the former provisions have
not yet been declared in force.[123] This type of legislation is of foremost importance in provinces and territories without other forms of information legislation
in that often hospitals and other health care facilities fall under its rubric.[124]

4. Provincial Privacy Acts

The provinces of British Columbia, Manitoba, Newfoundland and Labrador, and
Saskatchewan have enacted legislation purporting to protect individuals against
invasions of privacy, including informational privacy.[125] Their scope is seriously
limited in that the actions of the defendant must have been wilful or, in the case
of Manitoba, the violation of privacy must have been committed "substantially,
unreasonably and without claim of right".[126] Indeed, despite the egregious nature
of the violation in *Peters-Brown v. Regina District Health Board*,[127] there was
found to be no violation of the Saskatchewan Privacy Act. This case concerned
Ms. Peters-Brown, an employee of a correctional institution who had been
successfully treated for Hepatitis B. Five years later a list of names of individuals for whom bodily fluid precautions should be taken, which included the name
of Ms. Peters-Brown, was circulated at her workplace and caused her considerable distress. While the court found that the hospital had been negligent in its
management of the list such that it could fall into the hands of employees of the
correctional institution, no violation of the *Privacy Act* was found in that the

---

[120] *Personal Information Protection Act*, S.B.C. 2003, c. 63, s. 1; *Personal Information Protection Act*, S.A. 2003, c. P-6.5, s. 1(*k*).

[121] *An Act Respecting the Protection of Personal Information in the Private Sector*, R.S.Q. c. P-31.1, s. 2.

[122] *Protection of Personal Information Act*, S.N.B. 1998, c. P-19.1.

[123] *Access to Information and Protection of Privacy Act*, S.N.L. 2002, c. A-1.1.

[124] *Access to Information and Protection of Privacy Act*, S.N.W.T. 1994, c. 20; *Freedom of Information and Protection of Privacy Act*, S.N.S. 1993, c. 5.

[125] *Privacy Act*, R.S.B.C. 1996, c. 373; *Privacy Act*, C.C.S.M. c. P125; *Privacy Act*, R.S.N. 1990, c. P-22; *Privacy Act*, R.S.S. 1978, c. P-24.

[126] *Privacy Act*, C.C.S.M., c. P125, s. 2(1).

[127] [1996] S.J. No. 609, [1996] 1 W.W.R. 337, 136 Sask. R. 126 (Sask. Q.B.), affd [1996] S.J. No. 761, [1997] 1 W.W.R. 638, 148 Sask. R. 248 (Sask. C.A.). The hospital was found liable for negligence and breach of contract.

violation had not been not "wilful". There was no evidence before the court as to how the list had made its way from the hospital to the correctional facility.

On the other hand, a British Columbia court has indicated that it would have found a violation of their *Privacy Act vis-à-vis* health information in the context of the videotaping and television airing of baldness correction surgery.[128] The reporter was falsely advised by a contractor with the clinic that the subject had consented to use of the videotape, which showed the plaintiff's face. Default judgment was issued, but the court also indicated it would have found that there was a violation of the *Privacy Act*.

5. Other Provincial Legislation

Provincial legislation governing specific aspects of health care services, such as hospitals, nursing homes and mental health services, often include provisions regarding the handling of personal health information.[129] Public health legislation addresses disclosure of health information.[130] Some jurisdictions have legislation establishing a cancer registry.[131] Every province has legislation making mandatory the reporting of child abuse,[132] and some also have mandatory reporting of adult abuse.[133]

VI. CONSENSUAL COLLECTION, USE AND DISCLOSURE

The health information statutes as well as PIPEDA operate on the basic model of consent to collection of information, and use and disclosure are also premised on consent, but with multiple exceptions. What constitutes consent, however, differs from statute to statute; so too do the circumstances wherein consent may be waived.

PIPEDA permits different forms of consent, depending on the sensitivity of the type of information being collected. However, it also indicates that medical records would almost always be considered sensitive, implying that explicit consent is likely required.[134] Under Ontario's *Personal Health Information Protection Act, 2004* (PHIPA), consent must be knowledgeable, which is inferred "… if it is reasonable in the circumstances to believe that the individual knows: (*a*) the purposes of the collection, use or disclosure, as the case may be;

---

[128] *Hollinsworth v. BCTV*, [1996] B.C.J. No. 2638 (B.C.S.C.), affd [1998] B.C.J. No. 2451, 59 B.C.L.R. (3d) 121 (B.C.C.A.). Appeal dismissed and British Columbia Court of Appeal found no liability on the part of BCTV.

[129] See, *e.g.*, *Hospitals Act*, R.S.N.S. 1989, c. 208, s. 71 (confidentiality of hospital records); *Continuing Care Act*, R.S.B.C. 1996, c. 70, s. 11 (confidentiality of client information).

[130] For more detail see Elaine Gibson, "Public Health Information Privacy and Confidentiality", in Timothy Caulfield & Nola Ries, eds., *Public Health Law in Canada* (Markham, ON: LexisNexis Butterworths, 2005) at 89.

[131] See, for example, the *Cancer Programs Act*, R.S.A. 2000, c. C-2.

[132] *Child and Family Services Act*, C.C.S.M. c. C80, s. 18.

[133] *Adult Protection Act*, R.S.N.S. 1989, c. 2, s. 5(1).

[134] *Personal Information Protection and Electronic Documents Act*, S.C. 2000, c. 5, Sch. 1, s. 4.3.4.

and (*b*) that the individual may give or withhold consent".[135] Note that the individual therefore, by implication, need not necessarily be aware of the actual content of the information in order to proffer a knowledgeable consent.

Saskatchewan's *Health Information Protection Act* (HIPA), similarly to other jurisdictions, provides a list of exceptions to the need for collection directly from the subject individual. Following are the most salient:

(*a*) the individual consents to collection of the information by other methods;
(*b*) the individual is unable to provide the information;
(*c*) the trustee believes, on reasonable grounds, that collection directly from the subject individual would prejudice the mental or physical health or the safety of the subject individual or another individual;
(*d*) the information is collected, and is necessary, for the purpose of:

(i) determining the eligibility of the individual to participate in a program of the trustee or receive a product or service from the trustee ... or
(ii) verifying the eligibility of the individual who is participating in a program of the trustee or receiving a product or service from the trustee;

(*e*) the information is available to the public ...[136]

The only information that is to be collected is that reasonably necessary for the purpose for which it is being collected,[137] and the source individual is to be notified of that purpose.[138] For other uses and disclosures, consent of the individual is to be obtained unless the circumstance falls within one of the many exceptions permitted by statute.[139]

Under the Ontario legislation, consent may be inferred where the sharing of information is to another custodian for health care purposes, unless the individual has expressly indicated a lack of consent.[140] In the circumstance wherein the custodian is disclosing personal health information for a health care purpose, and believes that the absence of consent means that he or she is not disclosing all the information considered reasonably necessary for the purpose, the custodian is required to inform the person to whom the information is being conveyed of this limitation.[141]

VII. NON-CONSENSUAL USE AND DISCLOSURE

The reader will recall that in the initial quote from *Halls v. Mitchell*, the right of confidentiality is referred to as absolute in the absence of a paramount reason to

[135] *Personal Health Information Protection Act, 2004*, S.O. 2004, c. 3, Sch. A, s. 18(5).
[136] *Health Information Protection Act*, S.S. 1999, c. H-0.021, s. 25(1).
[137] *Personal Health Information Act*, C.C.S.M. c. P33.5, s. 13(2).
[138] *Personal Information Protection and Electronic Documents Act*, S.C. 2000, c. 5, Sch. 1, s. 4.2.3; *Health Information Act*, R.S.A. 2000, c. H-5, s. 33(3).
[139] *Health Information Protection Act*, S.S. 1999, c. H-0.021, ss. 26, 27.
[140] *Personal Health Information Protection Act, 2004*, S.O. 2004, c. 3, Sch. A, s. 20(2).
[141] *Ibid.*, s. 38(2).

set it aside. What could constitute such a reason? Further guidance is provided in the following quote:

> Such reasons may arise, no doubt, from the existence of facts which bring into play overpowering considerations connected with public justice; and there may be cases in which reasons connected with the safety of individuals or of the public, physical or moral, would be sufficiently cogent to supersede or qualify the obligations *prima facie* imposed by the confidential relation.[142]

The requirement of consent to use and disclosure of personal health information is subject to a number of exceptions. These may include the provision of health care services, disclosure to relatives and other interested parties, warning third parties of risk of serious harm, protection from abuse, judicial and quality review proceedings, public health, governmental purposes, and the conduct of research. Following is discussion of these exceptions.

A. PROVISION OF HEALTH CARE SERVICES

There is a general presumption that information may be shared among health care services providers, referred to by Industry Canada as the "circle of care". This occurs under the umbrella of "implied consent".[143] The provinces of Ontario and Manitoba allow for an opting out of this implied consent, sometimes referred to as a "lock box". Manitoba's legislation incorporates this concept as follows:

> A trustee may disclose personal health information without the consent of the individual the information is about if the disclosure is
>
> (a) to a person who is providing or has provided health care to the individual, to the extent necessary to provide health care to the individual, unless the individual has instructed the trustee not to make the disclosure ...[144]

Ontario's PHIPA states that a custodian may disclose personal health information to another health information custodian where reasonably necessary for the provision of health care and where the individual's consent cannot be obtained in a timely manner. However, this is not to occur if the individual objects to such disclosure.[145] In this circumstance, if the custodian or trustee believes that not all the information is being conveyed that is necessary for the provision of health care to the individual, he or she must advise the recipient of this fact.[146] The Manitoba legislation contains no such requirement.

---

[142] *Halls v. Mitchell*, [1928] S.C.R. 125 (S.C.C.) at para. 17.

[143] Industry Canada, "PIPEDA Awareness Raising Tools (PARTs) Initiative for the Health Sector: Questions and Answers," online: Industry Canada <http://strategis.ic.gc.ca/epic/site/ecic-ceac.nsf/en/gv00235e.html> at 3, 6.

[144] *Personal Health Information Act*, C.C.S.M. c. P33.5, s. 22(2).

[145] *Personal Health Information Protection Act, 2004*, S.O. 2004, c. 3, Sch. A, s. 38(1)(a).

[146] *Ibid.*, s. 38(2).

B. Disclosure to Relatives and Other Interested Parties

Personal health information may be disclosed under Ontario legislation in order to contact a relative, friend or other potential substitute decision-maker to seek consent on behalf of an incapacitated individual.[147] Saskatchewan permits disclosure regarding current health services to next-of-kin and others with whom the individual has a close personal relationship provided that the individual has not expressed a contrary wish regarding such disclosure.[148] In Ontario, a facility may disclose that an individual is a patient or resident, the individual's general health status in broad terms, and the location of the individual within the facility, unless the individual objects to such disclosure.[149]

Disclosure may be made about a deceased individual for identification purposes and also for informing any person "it is reasonable to inform in the circumstances" that the individual is deceased,[150] "to a relative of a deceased individual if the trustee reasonably believes that disclosure is not an unreasonable invasion of the deceased's privacy"[151] and of the circumstances of death where appropriate.[152] Also, in Ontario, the individual's spouse, partner, sibling or child may receive information concerning the deceased reasonably that would impact on their own or their children's health care.[153] Of special note is the fact that this could occur even if the individual had indicated, prior to death, that he or she did not wish family members to have access to his or her health information.

C. Duty or Right to Warn Third Parties

An appreciation of a potential duty to warn has developed in Canada based on principles outlined by the Supreme Court of California in *Tarasoff v. Regents of the University of California.*[154] In this case a man told his psychologist that he was planning to kill his former girlfriend. The psychologist advised campus police but did not warn the woman, who was indeed subsequently murdered by Mr. Tarasoff. The California courts ruled that the psychiatrist, in the circumstances of an imminent plausible threat to the life of an identifiable individual or group of individuals, had a duty to try to prevent the occurrence of harm. This duty had not been met by notifying the police; rather, it extended on the facts of the case to taking other measures, which might have included contacting the woman herself.

While not yet squarely adopted by Canadian courts, several courts have cited *Tarasoff* with approval. Most notable is the Supreme Court of Canada case of *Smith v. Jones.*[155] A psychiatrist hired by the defence to perform an assessment

---

[147] *Ibid.*, s. 38(1)(c).

[148] *Health Information Protection Act*, S.S. 1999, c. H-0.021, s. 27(2)(c)(2).

[149] *Personal Health Information Protection Act, 2004*, S.O. 2004, c. 3, Sch. A, s. 38(3).

[150] *Personal Health Information Act*, C.C.S.M. c. P33.5, s. 22(2)(c).

[151] *Ibid.*, s. 22(2)(d).

[152] *Personal Health Information Protection Act, 2004*, S.O. 2004, c. 3, Sch. A, s. 38(4).

[153] *Ibid.*, s. 38(4)(c).

[154] 131 Cal. Rptr. 14 (Cal. 1976).

[155] [1999] S.C.J. No. 15, [1999] 1 S.C.R. 455 (S.C.C.).

of the accused came to the view that the accused had developed an intricate plan to murder prostitutes in Vancouver and, if released, was likely to actualize this plan. The psychiatrist sought judicial guidance as to whether he was entitled to warn the prosecution and the court of this plan, thereby potentially influencing whether or not the accused would be released. A majority of the Supreme Court of Canada ruled that solicitor-client privilege could be set aside in favour of warning the court of this clear, serious and imminent threat. Note, however, that unlike in *Tarasoff*, the Court did not identify a *duty* to warn in these circumstances; rather, it was left to the discretion of the psychiatrist. Since solicitor-client privilege is the strongest privilege in Canadian law, the confidentiality of health information obtained in a trust relationship would reasonably fall under such an exception also. However, it is not accurate to call it an obligation or duty to warn, but rather a permission on the part of the health care provider to do so in law.

Each of the health information statutes has included this developing common law right to warn third parties.[156] Manitoba's PHIA states that disclosure may be made without consent if the disclosure is:

(b) to any person if the trustee reasonably believes that the disclosure is necessary to prevent or lessen a serious and immediate threat to

   (i) the health or safety of the individual the information is about or another individual, or

   (ii) public health or public safety;[157]

In Ontario, where a custodian believes on reasonable grounds that a disclosure "is necessary for the purpose of eliminating or reducing a significant risk of serious bodily harm to a person or group of persons",[158] he or she may disclose personal health information without consent. Note that this provision applies regardless of whether the individual has explicitly indicated the information is not to be disclosed.

D. PROTECTION FROM ABUSE

Every province and territory in Canada has legislation that aims to protect children in case of abuse. There rests an obligation on professionals, and in some cases on all individuals, to report suspected or known child abuse.[159]

In addition, some provinces have mandatory reporting in case of adult abuse, if a person is subjected to physical or sexual abuse or inadequate care and is

---

[156] *Health Information Act*, R.S.A. 2000, c. H-5, s. 35(1)(*m*); *Health Information Protection Act*, S.S. 1999, c. H-0.021, s. 27(4)(*a*).

[157] C.C.S.M. c. P33.5, s. 22(2).

[158] *Personal Health Information Protection Act, 2004*, S.O. 2004, c. 3, s. 40(1).

[159] The Nova Scotia *Children and Family Services Act*, S.N.S. 1990, c. 5, for example, contains two standards for reporting, a higher standard that applies to professionals and officials (s. 24) and a standard that applies to everyone (s. 32(1)).

incapable of protecting her or himself from such abuse due to a physical or mental disability.[160]

E. JUDICIAL AND QUALITY REVIEW PROCEEDINGS

The sensitivity of much personal health information has resulted in a fair amount of review by both courts and legislatures to establish proper circumstances for its disclosure for purposes of judicial proceedings, whether civil or criminal. There has also been much discussion regarding the obtaining of bodily substances, such as blood and tissue samples, for testing for alcohol levels and DNA matching in light of the *Canadian Charter of Rights and Freedoms*. And internal incident reviews by hospitals and other health care institutions have become increasingly important in response to concerns regarding patient safety, meriting their own sets of rules. Each of these matters will be discussed in turn.

1. Civil

Are health records admissible in civil proceedings? The short answer is yes, in some circumstances. It will depend in large part on whether a class privilege attaches to the records, or whether privilege is to be sought on a case-by-case basis, and on whether the person who is the subject of the information contained in the records has either explicitly or implicitly waived his or her right to confidentiality.

The hearsay rule prevents statements made by persons other than the witness before the court from being introduced as evidence of the truth of the information contained therein, but it is subject to a series of exceptions. The Supreme Court of Canada decided in 1970 that hospital records were indeed one of these exceptions, provided they were "made contemporaneously by someone having a personal knowledge of the matters then being recorded and under a duty to make the entry of record".[161] This means that patient charts may be introduced as *prima facie* proof of their contents, but may be challenged for accuracy. A number of provinces also have provisions to this effect in their Evidence Acts.[162]

But there remains the question of whether patient records should be introduced in a given proceeding because of their confidential nature. The Supreme Court of Canada affirmed in 1997 in *A.M. v. Ryan*[163] that, generally

---

[160] *Adult Protection Act*, R.S.N.S. 1989, c. 2; *Protection for Persons in Care Act*, R.S.A. 2000, c. P-29.

[161] *Ares v. Venner*, [1970] S.C.J. No. 26, [1970] S.C.R. 608 (S.C.C.).

[162] L. Rozovsky & N. Inions, *Canadian Health Information*, 3rd ed. (Markham, ON: LexisNexis Butterworths, 2002) at 54.

[163] [1997] S.C.J. No. 13, [1997] 1 S.C.R. 157 (S.C.C.). Class privilege in the form of solicitor-client privilege did apply in the case of *Smith v. Jones*, [1999] S.C.J. No. 15, [1999] 1 S.C.R. 455 (S.C.C.). A psychiatrist examined the accused in preparation of a pre-sentencing report on behalf of the accused. The report was found to be covered by solicitor-client privilege, but an exception was made in the circumstances. For further discussion see section VII.C, Duty to Warn, of this chapter. Class privilege also applied to protect the names of police informants in *Canada (Solicitor General) v. Ontario (Royal Commission of Inquiry into the Confidentiality of Health Records*,

speaking, there is no class privilege in the case of records held by a health professional on behalf of a patient.[164] Privilege must therefore be argued on a case-by-case basis under the Wigmore principles.[165] Thus, it is up to the party seeking to prevent disclosure to establish that the communication originated in confidence, that it is essential to the relationship that this confidence be protected, that the protection of this relationship is in the public interest, and that the privacy interest outweighs the probative value of the information. The onus is still on the party seeking production to establish the relevance of the information contained therein, as per the applicable rules of court.

In *Frenette v. Metropolitan Life Insurance Co.*,[166] the insurer of the deceased paid the basic indemnity for death but refused to pay the additional accidental death benefit, believing that death was caused by suicide and therefore excluded. The deceased, when applying for insurance, had signed a statement authorizing access to his records by the insurer "for the purposes of risk assessment and loss analysis".[167] When the hospital which had treated the deceased two days prior to his death refused to share his hospital record with the insurer, the insurer launched a lawsuit to receive the record. The Supreme Court of Canada ruled that the agreement by the insured to have his records reviewed for purposes of loss analysis constituted an explicit waiver, thus entitling the insurance company to his entire record held by the hospital.

Waiver of one's right to confidentiality may also be implicit. In *Glegg v. Smith & Nephew*,[168] the plaintiff suffered an allergic reaction to an implant following fracture of her femur. She had the implant removed and sued the manufacturer and attending physicians. The defendants sought access to medical records held by a psychiatrist she had consulted following the first surgery, but access was denied due to confidentiality. A unanimous Supreme Court of Canada ruled that by bringing a civil action claiming physical and psychiatric injury due to the actions of the manufacturer and physicians, the plaintiff in effect placed her medical history directly on trial. Thus, she had implicitly waived her right to have her information kept confidential by her psychiatrist.

2. Criminal

The Crown is obliged to reveal to the accused all relevant information in its possession unless the information is privileged.[169] If the accused wishes to access third party information not in the hands of the Crown, he or she may apply for issuance of a subpoena. In light of the particular sensitivity of sexual assault

---

[1981] S.C.J. No. 95, [1981] 2 S.C.R. 494 (S.C.C.) regardless of the fact that the physicians and hospital employees concerned were in breach of their duty of confidentiality in passing patient information on to the police.

[164] Interestingly, the U.S.S.C. decided earlier in the same year that class privilege does indeed attach in the context of psychotherapist-patient communications: *Jaffee v. Redmond*, 518 U.S. 1 (1996).

[165] *A.M. v. Ryan*, [1997] S.C.J. No. 13, [1997] 1 S.C.R. 157 (S.C.C.) at para. 20.

[166] [1992] S.C.J. No. 24, [1992] 1 S.C.R. 647 (S.C.C.).

[167] *Ibid.*, at para. 18.

[168] [2005] S.C.J. No. 29, [2005] 1 S.C.R. 724 (S.C.C.).

[169] *R. v. Stinchcombe*, [1991] S.C.J. No. 83, 3 S.C.R. 326 (S.C.C.) as cited in *R. v. O'Connor*, [1995] S.C.J. No. 98 (S.C.C.) at para. 4.

victim records, the *Criminal Code* now contains a detailed three-step procedure which determines whether such records will be provided to the accused.[170] The first question is whether the record is likely relevant to an issue at trial or to the competence of a witness to testify. Second, without having actually viewed the record, the judge is to balance the accused's ability to make full answer and defence against the complainant's right to privacy and equality. If the scale is in favour of the accused, the judge then reviews the record in light of a number of factors to determine whether it is appropriate to provide them to the accused. These provisions have been upheld by the Supreme Court of Canada in *R. v. Mills*.[171]

If the Crown wishes to gain access to patient records for purposes of prosecution, it may apply for a search warrant under *Criminal Code* section 487(1)(*b*).[172] Where the justice hearing the application is satisfied on reasonable grounds that evidence regarding the commission of an offence will be acquired, a warrant is issued authorizing the police to undertake a search and seizure.[173] A warrantless search is *prima facie* a violation of section 8 of the *Canadian Charter of Rights and Freedoms*, the right to be protected against unreasonable search and seizure.[174] If section 8 is violated, the court turns to section 24(2) of the Charter to determine whether use of the information gained through the illegal search would bring the administration of justice into disrepute; if so, the evidence is not permitted to be used at trial.[175]

The trial court in *R. v. Serendip Physiotherapy Clinic*[176] ruled that at common law, the high degree of confidentiality of patient records required that section 487 of the *Criminal Code* have read into it a number of additional protections similar to those for sexual assault victim records. The trial decision was overturned by the Ontario Court of Appeal and leave to appeal to the Supreme Court of Canada was denied.[177]

3. Obtaining of Bodily Substances

The taking of blood or tissue samples for purposes of testing for intoxication or DNA banking and matching is authorized by a number of sections of the *Criminal Code*.[178] However, it is recognized as highly invasive of one's privacy and bodily integrity. Major cases involving a violation of the Charter have been discussed in section IV of this chapter, "*Canadian Charter of Rights and Freedoms*". The case of *R. v. R.C.*,[179] however, did not involve the Charter. In

---

[170] *Criminal Code*, R.S.C. 1985, c. C-46, ss. 278.1 to 278.91.

[171] [1999] S.C.J. No. 68, 3 S.C.R. 668 (S.C.C.).

[172] *Criminal Code*, R.S.C. 1985, c. C-46, s. 487(1)(*b*).

[173] *Canadian Broadcasting Corp. v. New Brunswick (Attorney General)*, [1991] S.C.J. No. 88 (S.C.C.).

[174] *Hunter v. Southam Inc.*, [1984] S.C.J. No. 36, [1984] 2 S.C.R. 145 (S.C.C.).

[175] *R. v. Collins*, [1987] S.C.J. No. 15, [1987] 1 S.C.R. 265 (S.C.C.) at para. 19.

[176] [2004] O.J. No. 4653, 73 O.R. (3d) 241 (Ont. C.A.), leave to appeal refused, [2004] S.C.C.A. No. 585 (S.C.C.).

[177] *Ibid.*

[178] *Criminal Code*, R.S.C. 1985, c. C-46, ss. 487.051(2), 487.052.

[179] [2005] S.C.J. No. 62, [2005] 3 S.C.R. 99 (S.C.C.).

this case a 13-year-old boy stabbed his mother in the foot with a pen and struck her in the face. The young offender pleaded guilty to assault with a weapon, which is a designated offence, and breach of an undertaking. Section 487.051(2) of the *Criminal Code* requires that the court order the taking of a DNA sample if a person is convicted of a designated offence unless the effect of such an order be "grossly disproportionate to the public interest". The Supreme Court of Canada restored the finding of the trial judge that given these facts, including the age of the accused, the taking and retention of a DNA sample was not sufficiently in the public interest to warrant the serious intrusion on the accused's personal and informational privacy.

4. Quality/Incident Review

Patient safety has become a major focus both in Canada and internationally. This has led to an increasing focus on risk management, peer review, incident review and quality assurance, both to allay concerns regarding patient safety and to reduce costs of litigation. Patients seek access to review documents, while health care institutions attempt to keep such documents out of the hands of prospective plaintiffs. Governments at present appear to empathize with institutions, accepting the argument that health care providers will be more willing to openly disclose information regarding adverse events and near-misses if they do not fear that legal proceedings will result therefrom. In turn, greater openness is intended to lead to prevention of subsequent adverse incidents. Thus, legislated protection for disclosure of such reviews may be found in various types of legislation, the most recent of which, the *Quality of Care Information Protection Act, 2004*[180] of Ontario, is stand-alone legislation protecting against all but criminal and other federal proceedings.

A number of provinces have addressed this issue in either their Evidence Act[181] or their Medical Act.[182] In Nova Scotia, additional protection for health professionals has been provided through an addition to the *Freedom of Information and Protection of Privacy Act*, which reads as follows:

> The head of a local public body that is a hospital may refuse to disclose to an applicant a record of any report, statement, memorandum, recommendation, document or information that is used in the course of, or arising out of, any study, research or program carried on by or for the local public body or any committee of the local public body for the purpose of education or improvement in medical care or practice.[183]

Medical and hospital records pertaining to the patient are excluded;[184] in other words, patients are still entitled to access such records.

The health information statutes of Alberta, Manitoba and Saskatchewan have addressed this topic in differing ways. In each case, disclosure of personal information to a review committee may be without consent of the individual. In

---

[180] S.O. 2004, c. 3, Sch. B.
[181] See, for example, *Evidence Act*, R.S.N.S. 1989, c. 154, ss. 60-61.
[182] *Medical Act*, R.S.P.E.I. 1988, c. M-5.
[183] *Freedom of Information and Protection of Privacy Act*, S.N.S. 1993, c. 5, s. 19D(1).
[184] *Ibid.*, s. 19D(2).

Alberta, the custodian must refuse to disclose the findings of a review committee to the individual; in Manitoba and Saskatchewan, the trustee is entitled but not mandated to refuse disclosure.

In conjunction with its new *Personal Health Information Protection Act, 2004,* the province of Ontario has chosen to enact stand-alone legislation to protect this type of information from judicial scrutiny. The *Quality of Care Information Protection Act, 2004*[185] is designed to protect quality of care information prepared by or for a quality of care committee. It is intended to facilitate disclosure to a committee reviewing the quality of services delivered by an organization by rendering the information not subject to disclosure for other purposes, especially legal proceedings.[186] However, criminal proceedings or other matters under federal jurisdiction are not included in the exemption — in other words, disclosures to the quality of care committee are not protected from production for criminal matters. This Act overrides PHIPA in that it permits any person to disclose personal health information to a quality of care committee, even if it would otherwise be a violation of PHIPA.[187] Information that is "contained in a record that is maintained for the purpose of providing health care to an individual" — in other words, what we would normally describe as a patient record — is excluded from protection under the *Quality of Care Information Protection Act, 2004.*[188] Interestingly, it also excludes "facts contained in a record of an incident involving the provision of health care to an individual", unless these facts are also fully included in the patient record.[189] Thus, the individual is entitled to disclosure of all facts concerning his or her care that are revealed before the quality of care committee. The Act also contains an exception where disclosure of quality of care information is required to reduce the significant risk of serious bodily harm to one or more persons.[190] The Information and Privacy Commissioner is not granted jurisdiction over the Act.

F. PUBLIC HEALTH

Each province and territory has legislation dealing with public health matters, and the federal government has passed *An Act respecting the establishment of the Public Health Agency of Canada.*[191] Provincial legislation differs greatly in its content. All, however, cover aspects of duty on individuals to self-report, mandatory reporting by third parties, duty of confidentiality of public health authorities, contact notification, public notification, surveillance, epidemiology and research.[192] Not all cover information sharing outside the province. Ontario's

---

[185] S.O. 2004, c. 3, Sch. B, s. 5.

[186] *Ibid.*

[187] *Ibid.,* s. 3.

[188] *Ibid.,* s. 1.

[189] *Ibid.,* s. 1.

[190] *Ibid.,* s. 4(4).

[191] *An Act respecting the establishment of the Public Health Agency of Canada,* S.C. 2006, c. 5 (in force December 15, 2006).

[192] For further details see Elaine Gibson, "Public Health Information Privacy and Confidentiality" in

new PHIPA has addressed this topic, allowing for disclosure to medical officers of health within Ontario and to public health authorities throughout Canada, including at the federal level, to facilitate health protection and promotion.[193]

G. GOVERNMENT

As explained in the section on freedom of information and protection of privacy legislation, these statutes outline the conditions under which governments may collect, use, and disclose information. Health information legislation also contains provisions for custodians or trustees to share personal health information with government. Generally these include for purposes of determining eligibility for funding, funding services, auditing, planning and management, and keeping a registry of disease or body parts or fluids. In Ontario, at the request of the Minister of Health and Long-Term Care, disclosure for monitoring or verifying claims for payment for publicly funded health care goods and services is mandatory.[194]

PHIPA contains detailed provisions creating and governing an intermediate body referred to as a "health data institute"[195] for analysis of the health system on behalf of the Minister of Health. Such institutes are to be reviewed on a periodic basis by the Access and Privacy Commissioner to ensure that information is being de-identified and confidentiality is being protected.[196]

H. RESEARCH

The Tri-Council Policy Statement[197] is an agreement between the three major federal research funding agencies — the Medical Research Council (now Canadian Institutes of Health Research), the Social Sciences and Humanities Research Council, and the National Sciences and Engineering Research Council — to a set of rules that must be followed by institutions receiving funding from these agencies. Its provisions on confidentiality and research uses of health

---

Timothy Caulfield & Nola Ries, eds., *Public Health Law in Canada* (Markham, ON: LexisNexis Butterworths, 2005).

[193] *Personal Health Information Protection Act, 2004*, S.O. 2004, c. 3, s. 39(2). Justice Archie Campbell in his Second Interim Report on SARS and Public Health Legislation has criticized this section for its lack of clarity and, in particular, for not making mandatory such information sharing: see Justice Archie Campbell, "Second Interim Report: SARS and Public Health Legislation" (2005), online: SARS Commission <http://www.sarscommission.ca/report/ Interim_Report_2.pdf>.

[194] *Personal Health Information Protection Act, 2004, ibid.*, s. 46(1).

[195] *Ibid.*, s. 47. The Institute for Clinical Evaluative Sciences has been approved under these provisions.

[196] *Ibid.*, s. 47(10).

[197] Canadian Institutes of Health Research, Natural Sciences and Engineering Research Council of Canada, Social Sciences and Humanities Research Council of Canada, *Tri-Council Policy Statement: Ethical Conduct for Research Involving Humans*, 1998 (with amendments 2000, 2002, 2005), online: Government of Canada <http://www.pre.ethics.gc.ca/english/ policystatement/policystatement.cfm>.

information are frustratingly vague.[198] Factors to be considered when proposing to utilize identifiable personal information include:

(a)   The type of data to be collected;

(b)   The purpose for which the data will be used;

(c)   Limits on the use, disclosure and retention of the data;

(d)   Appropriate safeguards for security and confidentiality;

(e)   Any modes of observation (*e.g.*, photographs or videos) or access to information (*e.g.*, sound recordings) in the research that allow identification of particular subjects;

(f)   Any anticipated secondary uses of identifiable data from the research;

(g)   Any anticipated linkage of data gathered in the research with other data about subjects, whether those data are contained in public or personal records; and

(h)   Provisions for confidentiality of data resulting from the research.[199]

While these are identified as factors to be considered, there is not a great deal of specific guidance as to the weighting of the various factors. Thus, each of the provinces with health information legislation has included further guidance for the conduct of research utilizing identifiable personal information.[200] Manitoba's PHIA establishes a health information privacy committee, which is tasked with the review of health research project proposals seeking to utilize information held by government and its agencies.[201] One-fourth of the composition of the committee is to be persons who are not health professionals, researchers or government employees.[202] The committee is authorized to approve projects that require access to personal health information in identifiable form without the consent of individuals if it is not practical to obtain consent, it is necessary to use identifiers, and sufficient confidentiality safeguards are in place such that the benefits of the research outweigh the risks. Where a research proposal requires direct contact with individuals, the trustee is permitted to release names and addresses to the researcher without consent; for release of any further information, the trustee requires the consent of the individual.[203]

---

[198]   In response to this vagueness, the Canadian Institutes of Health Research has developed a series of recommendations intended to aid "by offering additional detail and practicality": Canadian Institutes of Health Research, "CIHR Best Practices for Protecting Privacy in Health Research" (Ottawa: Public Works and Government Services Canada, 2005) at 4.

[199]   Canadian Institutes of Health Research, Natural Sciences and Engineering Research Council of Canada, Social Sciences and Humanities Research Council of Canada, *Tri-Council Policy Statement: Ethical Conduct for Research Involving Humans*, 1998 (with amendments 2000, 2002, 2005), online: Government of Canada <http://www.pre.ethics.gc.ca/english/policystatement/policystatement.cfm> at art. 3.2(*a*)-(*h*).

[200]   *Health Information Act*, R.S.A. 2000, c. H-5, ss. 48-56; *Personal Health Information Act*, C.C.S.M. c. P33.5, ss. 24, 59; *Personal Health Information Protection Act, 2004*, S.O. 2004, c. 3, s. 44; *Health Information Protection Act*, S.S. 1999, c. H-0.021, s. 29.

[201]   *Personal Health Information Act*, C.C.S.M. c. P33.5, ss. 24, 59.

[202]   *Ibid.*, s. 59(2).

[203]   *Ibid.*, s. 24(5).

Ontario's PHIPA contains detailed provisions regarding the disclosure of health information pursuant to the conduct of research: the researchers must submit a completed application, a research plan and the documented approval of a research ethics board. Interestingly, the research ethics board must be somewhat differently constituted than what is required by the Tri-Council Policy Statement[204] in that it requires a member knowledgeable in privacy issues.[205] The research plan must identify the affiliation of all persons involved in the research,[206] the reason individual consent is not being sought, the necessity for any planned linkage of databases, and a description of all persons who will have access to the information.[207] Finally, the researcher must enter an agreement with the custodian that attempts to ensure that information is kept confidential,[208] including commitments not to publish identifying information, not to contact the individual except through the custodian, and to notify the custodian of any breach.[209]

VIII. OVERSIGHT

Federal and provincial privacy commissioners generally are not vested with authority to make binding decisions. There are, however, exceptions: the British Columbia Information and Privacy Commissioner's orders are enforceable,[210] and both the Alberta and Ontario Commissioners make binding orders under their health information legislation.[211] Commissioners are empowered to investigate pursuant to a complaint, and may also launch an investigation where there are reasonable grounds to believe there has been a contravention of the statute. There are provisions for mediation and alternate dispute resolution.

Under PIPEDA, decisions of the federal Privacy Commissioner are non-binding, but a dissatisfied complainant may seek a binding judgment in Federal Court.[212] Recourse in the provinces is to Superior Court; in Ontario, for instance, even though the order of the Commissioner is binding, where damages are sought, the individual must proceed to the Superior Court of Justice. It is

---

[204] Canadian Institutes of Health Research, Natural Sciences and Engineering Research Council of Canada, Social Sciences and Humanities Research Council of Canada, Tri-Council Policy Statement: Ethical Conduct for Research Involving Humans, 1998 (with amendments 2000, 2002, 2005), online: Government of Canada <http://www.pre.ethics.gc.ca/english/policystatement/policy statement.cfm>.

[205] O. Reg. 329/04, s. 15(1).

[206] *Personal Health Information Protection Act, 2004*, S.O. 2004, c. 3, s. 44(2).

[207] O. Reg. 329/04, s. 16.

[208] *Personal Health Information Protection Act, 2004*, S.O. 2004, c. 3, Sch. A, s. 44(5).

[209] *Ibid.*, s. 44(6).

[210] *Freedom of Information and Protection of Privacy Act*, R.S.B.C. 1996, c. 165, s. 59; *Personal Information Protection Act*, S.B.C. 2003, c. 63, s. 53.

[211] *Health Information Act*, R.S.A. 2000, c. H-5, s. 81; *Personal Health Information Protection Act, 2004*, S.O. 2004, c. 3, s. 61.

[212] *Personal Information Protection and Electronic Documents Act*, S.C. 2000, c. 5, s. 14(1).

necessary at this stage that the applicant establish "actual harm", which may include an award of up to $10,000 for mental anguish.[213]

IX. ELECTRONIC HEALTH INFORMATION

One of the areas providing the greatest challenge to our notions of health information is the electronicization of health information. Commissioner Romanow dedicated a chapter of the final report of the Commission on the Future of Health Care in Canada to this topic,[214] and developments continue apace, with Alberta rolling out the first province-wide integrated electronic health record.[215] Once records are in electronic form, their potential for various uses, including research, public health, accounting, quality assessment and even law enforcement makes them a valuable asset. And when different databases, for example, social assistance and health, are merged, their value for such uses increases dramatically. However, control is required so that personal health information is not indiscriminately made available to multiple users without consent of the source individual.[216]

The provinces of Alberta and Ontario have responded to the challenge with provisions in their health information legislation. The Alberta HIA contains extensive provisions on "data matching", defined as "the creation of individually identifying health information by combining individually identifying or non-identifying health information or other information from two or more electronic databases", [217] and permits such matching without consent under certain conditions.[218] Ontario has developed by regulation a set of standards:

> ... with which a health information custodian is required to comply when using electronic means to collect, use, modify, disclose, retain or dispose of personal health information, including standards for transactions, data elements for transactions, code sets for data elements and procedures for the transmission and authentication of electronic signatures.[219]

---

[213] *Ibid.*, s. 65(2), (3).

[214] For critique of the Romanow recommendations regarding electronic health records, see E. Gibson, "Jewel in the Crown? The Romanow Commission Proposal to Develop a National Electronic Health Record System" (2003) 66 Sask. L. Rev. 647.

[215] Alberta, Alberta Netcare, "Welcome to the Alberta Netcare Site", online: Government of Alberta <http://www.albertanetcare.ca>.

[216] For extensive discussion of issues concerning longitudinal research databases, and especially the thorny issue of consent, see Timothy Caulfield & Nola Ries, "Consent, Privacy and Confidentiality in Longitudinal, Population Health Research: Canadian Legal Context" (2004) Health L.J. Supplement 1-65.

[217] *Health Information Act*, R.S.A. 2000, c. H-5, s. 1(1)(g).

[218] *Ibid.*, ss. 68-72.

[219] *Personal Health Information Protection Act, 2004*, S.O. 2004, c. 3, Sch. A, s. 73(1)(h).; O. Reg. 329/04, s. 6.

X. GLOBALIZATION

Pressures of globalization are revealed in our economic, social, and cultural systems, and information flow is a not insignificant part of these systems. Indeed, PIPEDA was enacted in response to an edict by the European Union (EU) that specified EU countries would discontinue the trade of information for commercial purposes with countries that could not promise similar levels of protection of personal information as that in force within the EU. The Canadian government drafted legislation framed around a voluntary code of Fair Information Practices that had been developed by the Canadian Standards Association. This resulted in a peculiar piece of legislation in that the code is attached to the legislation as a "Schedule", yet much of the substance is contained in this schedule. It is also rather unique in legislative circles in that it contains phrases such as "should" rather than the mandatory "shall".[220]

Another development has been the adoption by the World Health Organization of new *International Health Regulations* (IHRs),[221] which aim to facilitate international trade and travel while minimizing the risk of the spread of infectious diseases. Canada is highly likely to be a signatory to the IHRs, yet presently lacks the ability to compel provinces and territories to provide the information needed to comply. This was noted to be a serious problem during SARS, with the federal government not receiving the information it needed to report in turn to the World Health Organization.[222] Discussion is underway to develop information sharing agreements between the provinces and territories and the federal government, in part to attempt to circumvent this problem.

XI. CONCLUSION

This chapter has covered a number of salient aspects of protection of health information at common law and in legislation as well as under the *Canadian Charter of Rights and Freedoms*. It has highlighted a couple of emerging issues, in particular electronicization of health records and globalization. Other major issues *vis-à-vis* information collection, use, storage and disclosure include genetics, Aboriginal health, employees, mental health, and HIV/AIDS, to name but a few. The ultimate pressure faced by legislators and courts is to affirm privacy, autonomy and freedom of choice while facilitating low-risk and high-value uses of health information, as well as other interests such as criminal law prosecution and protection of the public. Needless to say, the answers are not clear and this topic will continue to present challenges in the foreseeable future.

---

[220] See, *e.g.*, *Personal Health Information Protection Act, 2004*, S.O. 2004, c. 3, Sch. 1, s. 4.2.3, 4.2.5, 4.5.2.

[221] World Health Assembly, *International Health Regulations* (2005), 58th World Health Assembly, WHA58.3, online: WHO <http://www.who.int/csr/ihr/en/>.

[222] Health Canada, "Learning From SARS: Renewal of Public Health in Canada" (October 2003), online: Health Canada <http://www.phac-aspc.gc.ca/publicat/sars-sras/pdf/sars-e.pdf> at 39.

Chapter 7

THE REGULATION OF HUMAN BIOMEDICAL RESEARCH IN CANADA

Michael Hadskis[*]

I. INTRODUCTION

On September 13, 1999, researchers at the University of Pennsylvania Institute for Human Gene Therapy injected a gene enclosed in a dose of attenuated cold virus[1] into 18-year-old Jesse Gelsinger's hepatic artery.[2] Four days later, Jesse died as a result of a severe immune reaction to the injected agent.[3] Jesse's estate later commenced a lawsuit against the researchers, their institutions, and the boards within these institutions that reviewed and approved the study in which Jesse had enrolled. A pretrial settlement was struck between the parties within weeks.[4]

Prior to Jesse's involvement in the gene-therapy study, he had experienced a life-long struggle with a partial ornithine transcarbamylase deficiency. This inherited disorder causes toxic levels of ammonia to build up in a person's body. Although the condition is chronic, for some individuals it can be managed by controlling ammonia levels through drug therapy and dietary regimes.[5] This was so for Jesse. He made the decision to enroll in the research project knowing that, even if the genes worked, the positive effects would last a maximum of six weeks. Jesse's participation was motivated by his desire to assist with the development of a treatment for others who might acquire the disorder in the

---

[*]   The author would like thank Mary-Elizabeth Walker (2008 LL.B. candidate) for her truly expert research assistance.
[1]   An attenuated virus is a virus that has been weakened or made less virulent.
[2]   This artery distributes blood into a person's liver.
[3]   Barbara Sibbald, "Death But One Unintended Consequence of Gene-Therapy Trial" (2001) 164 C.M.A.J. 1612.
[4]   Paul L. Gelsinger, "Uninformed Consent: The Case of Jesse Gelsinger" in Trudo Lemmens & Duff R. Waring, eds., *Law and Ethics in Biomedical Research: Regulation, Conflict of Interest and Liability* (Toronto: University of Toronto Press, 2006) 12 at 30.
[5]   See emedicine, "Ornithine Transcarbamylase Deficiency", online: <http://www.emedicine.com/PED/topic2744.htm>.

future. However, before deciding to participate, he had not been made aware of serious (but nonfatal) adverse events experienced by prior research participants or of adverse reactions encountered during preclinical testing on animals.[6] Also, financial conflicts of interest involving the principal researcher had not been disclosed — he held patents covering aspects of the technology as well as stock in Genovo, a biotechnology company that was collaborating in the research.[7] There were other shortcomings with the research. At the time Jesse received the viral vector, his ammonia levels exceeded the predetermined safe baseline limit for the study. The researchers had also not fulfilled their obligations to report adverse events to the United States Food and Drug Administration and other oversight bodies.[8]

The Gelsinger case is by no means the only human biomedical research scandal that has shaken the research community and raised public concern over the conduct of research. Notorious scandals such as the studies conducted under the Nazi regime, the Tuskegee Syphilis Study, and the Tudor (Monster) Study constitute only some of the other research atrocities that have occurred in Europe and the United States.[9] Canada has not been immune from controversial research, as exemplified by the mind-altering studies in the 1950s carried out by Dr. Ewen Cameron at Montreal's Allen Memorial Hospital, research involving the administration of LSD to inmates at Kingston's Prison for Women, and the death of James Dent during his participation in gene transfer research in Toronto.[10] Though it is not difficult to identify instances of research scandal, the many benefits of biomedical research can also be recited with ease. Better understanding of disease processes, the development of new or improved diagnostic devices and tests, and the creation of effective therapies have all sprung from biomedical research. This research is also increasingly being used to confirm whether therapies already in use are actually efficacious.[11] In view of

---

[6]   Paul L. Gelsinger, "Uninformed Consent: The Case of Jesse Gelsinger" in Trudo Lemmens & Duff R. Waring, eds., *Law and Ethics in Biomedical Research: Regulation, Conflict of Interest and Liability* (Toronto: University of Toronto Press, 2006) 12 at 28.

[7]   Julian Savulescu, "Harm, Ethics Committees and the Gene Therapy Death" (2001) 27 J. Med. Ethics 148.

[8]   Paul L. Gelsinger, "Uninformed Consent: The Case of Jesse Gelsinger" in Trudo Lemmens & Duff R. Waring, eds., *Law and Ethics in Biomedical Research: Regulation, Conflict of Interest and Liability* (Toronto: University of Toronto Press, 2006) 12 at 28.

[9]   These studies are described in Jocelyn Downie, "Contemporary Health Research: A Cautionary Tale" (2003) Health L.J. (Special Edition) 1 at 3-5. See also: H.K. Beecher, "Ethics and Clinical Research" (1966) 274 New Eng. J. Med. 1354; Simon Verdun-Jones & David N. Weisstub, "The Regulation of Biomedical Research Experimentation in Canada: Developing An Effective Apparatus for the Implementation of Ethical Principles in a Scientific Milieu" (1996-1997) 28 Ottawa L. Rev. 297 at 307-308; R. Levine, *Ethics and Regulation of Clinical Research*, 2nd ed. (New Haven, CT: Yale University Press, 1988) at 69-72.

[10] Kathleen Cranley Glass, "Questions and Challenges in the Governance of Research Involving Humans: A Canadian Perspective" in Trudo Lemmens & Duff R. Waring, eds., *Law and Ethics in Biomedical Research: Regulation, Conflict of Interest and Liability* (Toronto: University of Toronto Press, 2006) 35 at 36-37.

[11] Jocelyn Downie, "Contemporary Health Research: A Cautionary Tale" (2003) Health L.J. (Special Edition) 1 at 1-2.

the substantial potential benefits and risks that attend human biomedical research, the mechanisms that shape or control this critical human endeavour warrant scrutiny.

This chapter will examine the regulation of human biomedical research in Canada. Part II discusses the importance of distinguishing clinical practice from human biomedical research. Part III outlines the legal and extra-legal instruments that directly or indirectly regulate Canadian biomedical research. With that as a backdrop, the procedural and substantive aspects of the research ethics review mechanisms established by the key regulatory instruments are addressed in Part IV. Part V explores the prospect of legal liability for the main actors in biomedical research when research participants sustain research-related injuries. The chapter concludes, under Part VI, with some general remarks about the need to reform Canada's current regulatory framework for biomedical research.

II. DISTINGUISHING HUMAN BIOMEDICAL RESEARCH FROM CLINICAL PRACTICE

Much has been written about the distinction between clinical practice and human biomedical research and the murky border that divides the two. In 1979, the United States National Commission for the Protection of Human Subjects of Biomedical and Behavioral Research Practice issued a report, *The Belmont Report: Ethical Principles and Guidelines for the Protection of Human Subjects of Research*,[12] that in part addressed the boundaries between practice and research. The report defined clinical practice as "interventions that are designed solely to enhance the well-being of an individual patient or client and that have a reasonable expectation of success" and research as "an activity designed to test an hypothesis, permit conclusions to be drawn, and thereby to develop or contribute to generalizable knowledge (expressed, for example, in theories, principles, and statements of relationships)". Simply put, the gaze of health professionals engaged in the former activity is to be fixed on diagnosing and treating individual patients' health conditions, while those embarking on biomedical research aim to advance scientific knowledge and develop methods to diagnose and treat future patients.[13]

The release of *The Belmont Report* did little to put an end to the struggle to meaningfully clarify the complex interplay that often exists between the delivery of medical care and the conduct of research.[14] A major contributor to this

---

[12]   National Commission for the Protection of Human Subjects of Biomedical and Behavioral Research, *The Belmont Report: Ethical Principles and Guidelines for the Protection of Human Subjects of Research* (1979), online: <http://ohsr.od.nih.gov/guidelines/belmont.html>.

[13]   Kathleen Cranley Glass, "Questions and Challenges in the Governance of Research Involving Humans: A Canadian Perspective" in Trudo Lemmens & Duff R. Waring, eds., *Law and Ethics in Biomedical Research: Regulation, Conflict of Interest and Liability* (Toronto: University of Toronto Press, 2006) 35.

[14]   Margaret A. Somerville, "Clarifying the Concepts of Research Ethics: A Second Filtration"

struggle is the reality that research and clinical practice frequently occur in conjunction since many medical interventions are delivered by physician-researchers and form the subject of formal research projects into the interventions' safety and efficacy. Real or apprehended conflicts may exist between physician-researchers' distinct commitments to their patients and to answering the research questions they have posed. The trend toward evidence-based therapies is likely to see a significant rise in this type of research. Interventions considered new or innovative in the sense that they deviate from standard medical practice have also been fodder for the clinical practice versus research debate, particularly with respect to surgical innovation.[15] Confusion in this area has been fostered by the imprudent use of the word "experimental" to describe this activity. As *The Belmont Report* clarifies: "The fact that a procedure is 'experimental,' in the sense of new, untested or different, does not automatically place it in the category of research."[16] In other words, the innovative nature of the activity is not a necessary or sufficient condition to be labelled research. As will become apparent further on in this chapter, the application or non-application of regulatory instruments can turn on whether an activity is considered clinical practice or research. Therefore, the need for clarity around the use of the word "research" is more than an academic interest.

In the context of this chapter, research will be defined as "a systematic investigation to establish facts, principles or generalizable knowledge" — this definition is being adopted for reasons of expediency since it is employed by the *Tri-Council Policy Statement on the Ethical Conduct of Research Involving Humans* (TCPS), a document that plays a central role in the regulation of biomedical research in Canada.[17] It is, however, not the hallmark of clarity or precision, thus leaving uncertainty about what activities are caught in its grasp.[18]

(1981) 29 Clinical Research 101; Benjamin Freedman, Abraham Fuks & Charles Weijer, "Demarcating Research and Treatment: A Systematic Approach for the Analysis of the Ethics of Clinical Research" (1992) 40 Clinical Research 653; Simon Verdun-Jones & David N. Weisstub, "Consent to Human Experimentation in Québec: The Application of the Civil Law Principles of Personal Inviolability to Protect Special Populations" (1995) 18 Int'l J. L. & Psychiatry 163 at 178-179; Bernard M. Dickens, "What is a Medical Experiment?" (1975) 113 C.M.A.J. 635.

[15] For example, see: M. McKneally & D. Abdallah, "Introducing New Technologies: Protecting Subjects of Surgical Innovation and Research" (2003) 27 World Journal of Surgery 930; S. Strasberg & P. Ludbrook, "Who Oversees Innovative Practice? Is There a Structure That Meets the Monitoring Needs of New Techniques?" (2003) 196 Journal of the American College of Surgeons 938; and G. Agich, "Ethics and Innovation in Medicine" (2001) 27 J. Med. Ethics 295.

[16] National Commission for the Protection of Human Subjects of Biomedical and Behavioral Research, *The Belmont Report: Ethical Principles and Guidelines for the Protection of Human Subjects of Research* (1979), online: <http://ohsr.od.nih.gov/guidelines/belmont.html>.

[17] TCPS, commentary under article 1.1. Online: <pre-ethics.gc.ca/English/policystatement/policystatement.cfm>.

[18] For instance, see Michael Yeo, *Biobank Research: The Conflict Between Privacy and Access Made Explicit*, prepared for The Canadian Biotechnology Advisory Council (February 10, 2004), online: <http://www.cbac-cccb.ca/epic/internet/incbac-cccb.nsf/en/ah00514e.html>, where this issue is addressed in the health information context. Yeo asks at footnote 17: "Where does one draw a line between research and health surveillance or monitoring? At what point does quality

For this and other reasons the definition is under review by the body charged with the stewardship of the TCPS.[19] As well, other definitions of research are beginning to emerge in Canada, particularly in the context of health information legislation.[20]

III. THE REGULATORY LANDSCAPE

The Canadian regulatory landscape for biomedical research involving humans consists of a complex patchwork of diverse forms of regulatory instruments. It has been characterized by some commentators as a "confusing" and "complex, decentralized, and multi-sourced arrangement for regulating research".[21] Others have remarked that its unwieldy nature stems from the reality that the law "applies almost inadvertently to the enterprise of biomedical research"[22] and that "the Canadian regulatory approach to research involving humans … is an incomplete mosaic of rules that range from formal legal regulations, to administrative policies and voluntary guidelines".[23] The confusing nature of the regulatory landscape may, at least in part, explain the results of Health Canada's

---

assurance or even health system management end and research begin? What distinguishes a disease registry from a research database? How does one distinguish a patient from a research subject in the context of a health information network? At what point does the patient or the research subject vanish into bits or bytes or pieces or strands such that one no longer speaks of research involving human subjects? How do we differentiate clinical care and research in the context of drug utilization and feedback systems? At what point does a collection of information become a database, and at what point does a database become a business, or the activity of research a commercial activity?" See also: Subgroup on Procedural Issues for the TCPS (ProGroup), *Refinements to the Proportionate Approach to Research Ethics Review in the TCPS*, prepared for The Interagency Advisory Panel on Research Ethics (PRE) (December 2005), online: <http://www.pre.ethics.gc.ca/english/workgroups/progroup/Consultation.cfm>, which provides the following additional examples: interviews with experts or public figures; evaluation of therapy and non-validated practices; audits; monitoring of quality of service; program evaluation; records review; quality assurance; resource utilization and cost-benefit analysis.

[19] PRE is the body that has been given this mandate. Some of the problematic aspects of the TCPS definition of research are set out in PRE's public consultation document: Subgroup on Procedural Issues for the TCPS (ProGroup), *Refinements to the Proportionate Approach to Research Ethics Review in the TCPS*, prepared for The Interagency Advisory Panel on Research Ethics (PRE) (December 2005), online: <http://www.pre.ethics.gc.ca/english/workgroups/progroup/Consultation.cfm> (date accessed: 4 July 2006).

[20] For example, see *Personal Health Information Protection Act, 2004*, S.O. 2004, c. 3, Sched. A, s. 2, where "research" is defined as "a systematic investigation designed to develop or establish principles, facts or generalizable knowledge, or any combination of them, and includes the development, testing and evaluation of research".

[21] Jocelyn Downie & Fiona McDonald, "Revisioning the Oversight of Research Involving Humans in Canada" (2004) 12 Health L.J. 159 at 174.

[22] B. Dickens, "Governance Relations in Biomedical Research" in M. McDonald, ed., *The Governance of Health Research Involving Human Subjects* (Ottawa: Law Commission of Canada, 2000) 93 at 93.

[23] M. Hirtle, "The Governance of Research Involving Human Participants in Canada" (2003) 11 Health L.J. 137 at 139-40.

2003-2004 inspections of 45 clinical drug trials, which revealed 292 deviations from regulatory requirements.[24] The outline of the chief regulatory instruments which follows is intended to assist the reader in navigating Canada's research governance framework.

A. OVERVIEW OF THE PRINCIPAL REGULATORY INSTRUMENTS

1. Tri-Council Policy Statement on the Ethical Conduct of Research Involving Humans (TCPS)

In 1998, the Medical Research Council (now the Canadian Institutes for Health Research (CIHR)), the National Sciences and Engineering Research Council (NSERC), and the Social Sciences and Humanities Research Council (SSHRC), hereinafter "the Tri-Agencies", issued the TCPS. This document establishes an ethical framework for the conduct of human participant research, including studies involving human remains, cadavers, tissues, biological fluids, embryos or fetuses;[25] some naturalistic observation;[26] research involving identifiable personal information collected from participants through interviews, question-naires, observation, access to private records, and other means;[27] and secondary use of data when the data can be linked to individuals.[28] The TCPS relies on multidisciplinary, local research ethics boards (REBs) to approve, require modifications in, or reject proposed studies. REBs may also require ongoing studies to be altered or terminated. REB decision-making is to be informed by the national norms set out in the TCPS on such issues as participant consent, conflicts of interest, the protection of participants' privacy and confidentiality, and ensuring that the potential harms of research do not outweigh the potential benefits.

Determining when a particular activity is captured by the TCPS is not always a straightforward matter. An important preliminary question to answer is whether the relevant activity meets the TCPS definition of "research" that was discussed in the previous section. If not, the TCPS does not apply to it. However, even if the activity constitutes research under that definition, it does not necessarily follow that the TCPS will apply. Being a policy statement, the TCPS lacks the inherent legal authority of a legislative instrument. Instead, the scope and extent of its regulatory impact rests on other factors. One such factor is that the Tri-Agencies will only consider funding or continuing to fund researchers and research institutions that adhere to the TCPS. Indeed, as a condition of receiving funding, institutions must enter into a formal "Memorandum of Understanding" with these agencies, the terms of which

---

[24] Health Products and Food Branch Inspectorate, *Summary Report of the Inspections of Clinical Trials Conducted in 2003/2004*, Report to Health Canada (December 14, 2004), online: <http://www.hc-sc.gc.ca/dhp-mps/compli-conform/clini-pract-prat/report-rapport/2003-2004_tc-tm_e.html>.

[25] TCPS, art. 1.1(b).

[26] Naturalistic observation is the study of human behaviour in a natural environment.

[27] TCPS, commentary under art. 3.2. See also art. 3.1 and its corresponding commentary.

[28] TCPS, art. 3.3.

expressly require compliance with the provisions of the TCPS.[29] As well, the Tri-Agencies' grant applications require applicant researchers to certify compliance with all of the agencies' policies regarding the ethical conduct of research, including the TCPS, if the research will involve human participants. In 2004, CIHR published a document, *CIHR Procedure for Addressing Allegations of Non-Compliance with Research Policies*,[30] which enumerates the sanctions that can be imposed on institutions and researchers for breaching TCPS requirements. In addition to the possibility of researchers and institutions being ineligible for continued funding, CIHR may require researchers to refund all or part of the funds already paid under the grant, whether the non-compliance is deliberate or inadvertent. Other funding bodies, both federal[31] and provincial,[32] also require compliance with the TCPS as a condition for the receipt of research funds.

The regulatory impact of the TCPS is not necessarily dependent on the presence of public funding for research. Members of some professional organizations may be required to seek ethics review from a TCPS-compliant REB before conducting human research or risk being subject to disciplinary action by their regulatory bodies. For instance, the College of Physicians and Surgeons of Alberta requires physicians to seek the approval of its own TCPS-compliant REB (the Research Ethics Review Committee) unless the project is otherwise subject to the authority of another research ethics review agency that the College deems appropriate.[33]

In addition to the circumstances already outlined, other factors may serve to promote compliance with the TCPS. Ethics review of the kind provided for in the TCPS is often a condition of publication in peer-reviewed journals.[34] Additionally, as discussed below, courts may invoke non-legal instruments such as the TCPS when determining the liability of researchers, REB members, and research institutions in tort actions arising from personal injuries or some other

---

[29] The Memorandum of Understanding is available online: <http://www.nserc-crsng.gc.ca/institution/mou_e.htm>.

[30] Canadian Institutes of Health Research, *CIHR Procedure for Addressing Allegations of Non-Compliance with Research Policies* (Updated December 2006), online: <http://www.cihr-irsc.gc.ca/e/25178.html>.

[31] For example, National Research Council, *NRC Policy for Research Involving Human Subjects* (last modified December 15, 2005), online: <http://www.nrc-cnrc.gc.ca/randd/ethics/policy_e.html>.

[32] For example, the Nova Scotia Health Research Foundation (see *2006/07 Nova Scotia Health Research Foundation Competition Guidelines*, online: <http://www.nshrf.ca/AbsPage.aspx?siteid=1&lang=1&id=1182>) and the Manitoba Health Research Council (see *2006 Manitoba Health Research Council Competition Guidelines*, online: <http://mhrc.mb.ca/funding/competition.asp>).

[33] Michael Hadskis & Peter Carver, "The Long Arm of Administrative Law: Applying Administrative Law Principles to Research Ethics Boards" (2005) 13:2&3 Health L.R. 19 at 23.

[34] Jocelyn Downie & Fiona McDonald, "Revisioning the Oversight of Research Involving Humans in Canada" (2004) 12 Health L.J. 159 at 163. See also: International Committee of Medical Journal Editors, *Uniform Requirements for Manuscripts Submitted to Biomedical Journals: Writing and Editing for Biomedical Publication* (updated February 2006), online: <http://www.icmje.org/>.

actionable harm sustained by research participants as a result of their participation in research. Of course, the impact of this factor on promoting compliance very much depends on researchers appreciating how these instruments may be used by the courts.

2. Clinical Trial Regulations under the *Food and Drugs Act* and the Good Clinical Practice: Consolidated Guidelines

The regulation of drug research in Canada is canvassed in considerable detail in Chapter 8, Regulation of Pharmaceuticals in Canada. This section is merely intended to provide a thumbnail sketch of two of the key instruments that regulate this research: Part C, Division 5 of the *Food and Drug Regulations*[35] (*Clinical Trial Regulations*), and the *Good Clinical Practice: Consolidated Guidelines*[36] (*GCP Guidelines*). The *Clinical Trial Regulations*, passed pursuant to the federal *Food and Drugs Act*,[37] establish legal requirements concerning the conduct of "clinical trials". A clinical trial is defined in the regulations as an investigation regarding a drug for use in humans that involves human participants and that is intended to: "discover or verify the clinical, pharmacological or pharmacodynamic effects of the drug, identify any adverse events in respect of the drug, study the absorption, distribution, metabolism and excretion of the drug, or ascertain the safety or efficacy of the drug".[38] The *Clinical Trial Regulations* apply to all clinical trials in Canada, irrespective of how this research is being funded.

The *Clinical Trial Regulations* require trial sponsors to apply to Health Canada for authorization to sell or import a drug for the purposes of conducting a clinical trial.[39] Typically, trials are sponsored by pharmaceutical companies, although the regulations also govern trials that do not have commercial sponsorship. Clinical trial applications must include, among other items, a copy of the trial protocol (*i.e.*, a document describing "the objectives, design, methodology, statistical considerations and organization"[40] of the trial) and the name of the researcher responsible to the sponsor for the conduct of the clinical trial at each clinical site. In order to secure Health Canada's authorization to sell or import a drug for the purposes of a clinical trial, the sponsor must satisfy a number of conditions, one of which requires the sponsor to obtain approval of the REB at each clinical trial site.[41] The REB must attest, in writing, that it reviewed and approved the protocol and informed consent forms and that it carries out its functions in a manner consistent with "good clinical practices",[42]

---

[35] *Food and Drug Regulations*, C.R.C., c. 870, Part C, Division 5: *Drugs for Clinical Trials Involving Human Subjects* (*Clinical Trial Regulations*).
[36] This is documented on Health Canada's website. See: <http://www.hc-sc.gc.ca/dhp-mps/prodpharma/applic-demande/guide-ld/ich/efficac/e6_e.html>.
[37] *Food and Drugs Act*, R.S.C. 1985, c. F-27, s. 30.
[38] *Clinical Trial Regulations*, s. C.05.001.
[39] *Ibid.*, s. C.05.003.
[40] *Ibid.*, s. C.05.001.
[41] *Ibid.*, ss. C.05.006(c) and C.05.010(d).
[42] *Ibid.*, s. C.05.012(h).

which are defined as "generally accepted clinical practices that are designed to ensure the protection of the rights, safety and well-being of clinical trial subjects and other persons, and the good clinical practices referred to in section C.05.010".[43] Section C.05.010 lists, in very general terms, a variety of the sponsor's obligations including, among others, ensuring that the trial is scientifically sound and clearly described in the protocol, that the trial is conducted in accordance with the protocol and regulations, that individuals involved in the conduct of the trial are appropriately qualified, and that the written informed consent of participants is obtained.

The lack of specificity in the *Clinical Trial Regulations* around what represents good clinical practices is somewhat ameliorated through Health Canada's "endorsement"[44]/ "adoption"[45] of the principles and practices provided for in the *GCP Guidelines*, an international guideline developed by the International Conference on Harmonization of Technical Requirements for Registration of Pharmaceuticals for Human Use. The *GCP Guidelines* provide greater detail than the *Clinical Trial Regulations* respecting the duties and responsibilities of REBs,[46] investigators, and sponsors,[47] and to some degree reflects the substantive and procedural norms in the TCPS. While Health Canada has taken the position that the *GCP Guidelines* are meant to assist investigators and sponsors in how to comply with the *Clinical Trial Regulations* and has noted that they do not have the force of law,[48] it is critical to note that it has relied on the *GCP Guidelines* to interpret section C.05.010 when carrying out its inspections and investigations to assess compliance with these regulations[49] pursuant to the *Food and Drugs Act*.[50]

Health Canada has implemented a *Compliance and Enforcement Policy*[51] that addresses the measures it may take in response to contraventions of the *Food and Drugs Act* and *Clinical Trial Regulations*. Examples of the types of actions that may be pursued are warning letters, suspension or cancellation of an

---

[43] *Ibid.*, s. C.05.001.
[44] See Health Canada's website: <http://www.hc-sc.gc.ca/dhp-mps/prodpharma/applic-demande/guide-ld/ich/efficac/e6_e.html>.
[45] *Ibid.*
[46] The *GCP Guidelines* do not actually refer to Research Ethics Boards. Instead, they use the terms "Institutional Review Boards" or "Independent Ethics Committees", which mean the same thing.
[47] *GCP Guidelines*, ss. 3-5.
[48] This is documented on Health Canada's website. See: <http://www.hc-sc.gc.ca/dhp-mps/prodpharma/applic-demande/guide-ld/ich/efficac/e6_e.html>.
[49] See Health Products and Food Branch Inspectorate, *Summary Report of the Inspections of Clinical Trials Conducted in 2003/2004*, Report to Health Canada (December 14, 2004), online: <http://www.hc-sc.gc.ca/dhp-mps/compli-conform/clini-pract-prat/report-rapport/2003-2004_tc-tm_e.html>.
[50] A reasonable argument can be made that Health Canada is enforcing the *GCP Guidelines* by way of its inspections. See Trudo Lemmens, "Federal Regulation of REB Review of Clinical Trials: A Modest But Easy Step Towards an Accountable REB Review Structure in Canada" (2005) 13:2&3 Health L. Rev. 39 at 44.
[51] Health Products and Food Branch Inspectorate, *Compliance and Enforcement Policy*, Policy-0001, Health Canada (May 31, 2005), online: <http://www.hc-sc.gc.ca/dhp-mps/alt_formats/hpfb-dgpsa/pdf/compli-conform/pol_1_e.pdf>.

authorization to sell or import a drug for the purposes of a clinical trial, injunctions, and criminal prosecutions.[52]

3. Quebec Instruments

The *Civil Code of Québec*[53] provides specific legislative direction in several important areas of human research. It deals with the risk-benefit ratio to which competent adults may be exposed,[54] clarifies that "innovative care required by the state of health of the person concerned does not constitute [research]",[55] establishes requirements for the use of human organs and other tissue in research,[56] and sets conditions precedent for the participation of minors and incompetent adults in research, including the requirement for such research to be approved and monitored by an REB formed by the Minister of Health and Social Services or another REB designated by the Minister.[57] The Fonds de la recherche en santé du Québec (FRSQ) is tasked with supporting health research in Quebec and plays a critical role in regulating human participant research in the province. All research involving humans that takes place in Quebec's public institutions requires approval and monitoring by an REB.[58] REBs affiliated with institutions that host FRSQ-funded research must comply with FRSQ's regulatory framework and standards[59] which mandate, among other things, adherence to the TCPS.[60] In 1994, the Department of Health and Social Services established an REB (known as the "Central Ethics Committee") that reports to the department and falls under FRSQ's administrative management. That REB is responsible for ensuring that research involving incompetent minors and adults is in compliance with the *Civil Code of Québec* and all applicable ethical standards before it is allowed to commence. It is also charged with monitoring ongoing studies of this nature.[61]

---

[52]   *Ibid.*

[53]   *Civil Code of Québec*, S.Q. 1991, c. 64.

[54]   *Ibid.*, art. 20.

[55]   *Ibid.*, art. 21.

[56]   *Ibid.*, arts. 22-24.

[57]   *Ibid.*, art. 21.

[58]   Fonds de la recherche en santé du Québec (FRSQ), "The FRSQ reassures Québecers: Québec keeps close watch" (FRSQ Press Release, January 23, 2003), online: <http://www.muhc.ca/files/research/fiches_media_english.pdf>.

[59]   *Ibid.*

[60]   Fonds de la recherche en santé du Québec, *Guide d'éthique et d'intégrité scientifique de la recherche (Research Ethics and Scientific Integrity Guidelines)*, 2nd ed. (Montreal: FRSQ, 2003) at 35. Also, FRSQ research funding contracts stipulate compliance with the TCPS (Personal Communication, Johane de Champlain, FRSQ Ethics Coordinator, to Mary-Elizabeth Walker, Research Assistant, June 30, 2006).

[61]   Fonds de la recherche en santé du Québec (FRSQ), "The FRSQ reassures Québecers: Québec keeps close watch" (FRSQ Press Release, January 23, 2003), online: <http://www.muhc.ca/files/research/fiches_media_english.pdf>.

4. International Instruments

(a) United States

The growing involvement of Canadian researchers in multi-national health research requires these researchers to familiarize themselves with the relevant regulatory frameworks adopted by other countries. The United States is one such country. There, Title 45, Part 46 of its *Code of Federal Regulations* prescribes legal standards for the protection of human research participants that apply to research funded by the United States Department of Health and Human Services (DHHS), which includes the National Institutes of Health, or research that is conducted in an institution that receives federal (U.S.) funding for research. Subpart A of the regulations provides the basic rules for the protection of human participants. Other subparts of the regulations set out additional protections for: pregnant women, human fetuses, and neonates,[62] prisoners,[63] and children.[64] Under these regulations, Institutional Review Boards (the United States equivalent of Canadian REBs) must review research involving humans according to norms that broadly resemble those found in the TCPS.

Other American instruments also regulate research. For instance, Parts 40 and 56 of Title 21 of the *Code of Federal Regulations*,[65] which fall under the auspices of the United States Food and Drug Administration, apply to human research that uses drugs, medical devices, and biological products, regardless of whether the research is federally funded. A multitude of other federal and state laws may also be relevant depending on the research activities being pursued.[66]

Canadian researchers who carry out research supported by DHHS funding must comply with the *Code of Federal Regulations*, even if the research is conducted outside the United States. Canadian institutions that host such research are required to file an "assurance" of compliance with these regulations with the United States Office for Human Research Protections.[67]

(b) The Nuremberg Code and the Declaration of Helsinki

Two international documents, the *Nuremberg Code* and the *Declaration of Helsinki*, have played an important role in the evolution of Canadian regulatory

---

[62] Title 45 *Code of Federal Regulations*, Part 46, Subpart B.
[63] *Ibid.*, Subpart C.
[64] *Ibid.*, Subpart D.
[65] Title 21 *Code of Federal Regulations*, Parts 40 and 56.
[66] For an overview of the United States regulatory regime for research involving humans, see Richard M. Wagner, "Ethical Review of Research Involving Human Subjects: When and Why is IRB Review Necessary?" (2003) 28 Muscle & Nerve 27; Also, Ken Gatter, "Fixing Cracks: A Discourse Norm to Repair the Crumbling Regulatory Structure Supporting Clinical Research and Protecting Human Subjects" (2005) 73 U.M.K.C. Law Review 581 at 587-89.
[67] Title 45 *Code of Federal Regulations*, § 46.103(a). For a discussion of the application of United States laws and policy to research conducted outside the United States, see: National Institutes of Health, United States Department of Health and Human Services, *Human Participant Protections Education for Research Teams*, National Cancer Institute (2002), online: <http://cme.cancer.gov/clinicaltrials/learning/humanparticipant-protections.asp>.

instruments for the protection of human research participants. The *Nuremberg Code*, which was introduced to the international community in 1948, sets out standards for physicians to follow when carrying out experiments on human participants. It was developed in response to the Military War Crimes Tribunal's condemnation of the atrocities committed by Nazi physicians on concentration camp prisoners in the name of human experimentation.[68] The *Declaration of Helsinki*, developed by the World Health Association and adopted by the 18th World Medical Assembly in Helsinki in 1964, also establishes guidelines regarding human biomedical research.[69]

These international instruments continue to influence the regulation of research in Canada. For example, the *GCP Guidelines* expressly provide that clinical trials "should be conducted in accordance with the ethical principles that have their origin in the Declaration of Helsinki, and that are consistent with the [*GCP Guidelines*] and the applicable regulatory requirement(s)".[70] Additionally, in part relying on the principles set out in the *Declaration*, in 1989, a Canadian court found a physician liable for not adequately disclosing the risks involved in taking part in a biomedical research project to a participant who had died as a result of his participation in the project.[71] Also noteworthy is FRSQ's statement that it "subscribes to the principles" contained in the *Nuremberg Code* and the *Declaration of Helsinki*.[72]

5. Other Canadian Regulatory Instruments

The instruments described above are by no means the only instruments that impact the conduct of health research activities in Canada. Medical codes of ethics, judge-made law on matters such as informed consent[73], provincial/territorial legislation on *post-mortem* gifts of bodies or body parts for research,[74] and legislation restricting research involving psychiatric patients,[75] can also exert direct or indirect regulatory control.[76] Researchers and REBs must

---

[68]   G. Annas & M. Grodin, "Introduction" in G. Annas & M. Grodin, eds., *The Nazi Doctors and the Nuremberg Code* (New York: Oxford University Press, 1992) 3 at 3-4.

[69]   M. Munden, "Ethical Conduct of Human Research Part 1: The Declaration of Helsinki" (2004) 4:5 Clinical Researcher 2.

[70]   *GCP Guidelines*, s. 2.1.

[71]   *Weiss v. Solomon*, [1989] J.Q. No. 312, [1989] R.J.Q. 731, 48 C.C.L.T. 280 (Que. S.C.). This case is discussed more fully later in the chapter.

[72]   Fonds de la recherche en santé du Québec (FRSQ), "The FRSQ reassures Québecers: Québec keeps close watch" (FRSQ Press Release, January 23, 2003), online at: <http://www.muhc.ca/files/research/fiches_media_english.pdf>.

[73]   See *Halushka v. University of Saskatchewan* (1965), 53 D.L.R. (2d) 436 (Sask. C.A.) and *Weiss v. Solomon*, [1989] J.Q. No. 312, [1989] R.J.Q. 731, 48 C.C.L.T. 280 (Que. S.C.). Both cases are discussed later in the chapter.

[74]   For example, see: *Human Tissue Gift Act*, R.S.N.S. 1989, c. 215, s. 6(2); *Human Tissue Donation Act*, R.S.P.E.I. 1988, c. H-12-1, ss. 5(1), 12(1); *Human Tissue Gift Act*, R.S.Y. 2002, c. 117, s. 5(1).

[75]   For example, see: *Mental Health Act*, C.C.S.M. c. M110; *Mental Health Act*, R.S.N.W.T. 1988, c. M-10.

[76]   Bartha Knoppers, "Ethics and Human Research: Complexity or Confusion?" in Michael

also be aware of provincial/territorial[77] and federal[78] legislation relating to personal information that may have enormous implications for the collection, use, and disclosure of personal health information in the research context.

Other instruments can also exert control. The *Assisted Human Reproduction Act,*[79] discussed in Chapter 9: Regulating Reproduction, plays a critical role in regulating assisted human reproduction-related research (*e.g.*, the use of embryos). There is also the *Criminal Code*[80] (*e.g.*, the provisions respecting assault[81] and criminal negligence[82]), and the *Medical Devices Regulations*[83] passed under the *Food and Drugs Act* which regulate the use of unlicensed medical devices in clinical investigations and the use of already licensed devices outside the terms of their respective licences.

B. REGULATORY GAPS

The patchwork nature of Canada's regulatory framework for biomedical research falls short of offering a comprehensive research oversight system. As Downie and McDonald observe, "excepting clinical trials, research conducted in private physician's offices, community-based organizations, charitable organizations, industry, and [some] government departments ... is largely free of regulation".[84] While there is an absence of empirical data to precisely define the size of the regulatory gap, the gap is estimated to be a "significant problem".[85] This is disconcerting for several reasons, the most significant of which is that research participants are exposed to increased risk of harm since the checks and balances that are available through the application of research ethics review mechanisms are absent. Another concern relates to the need to develop and maintain public trust and confidence in the research governance system. If the public perceives that adequate safeguards are missing for the protection of the rights, safety, and wellbeing of participants, whatever public confidence presently exists will swiftly erode. Loss of public support for research funding

---

McDonald, ed., *The Governance of Health Research Involving Human Subjects* (Ottawa: Law Commission of Canada, 2000) 109.

[77] For example, see *Health Information Act,* R.S.A. 2000, c. H-5, s. 49; *Personal Health Information Protection Act, 2004,* S.O. 2004, c. 3, Sch. A. Also see Chapter 6, Health Information: Confidentiality and Access.

[78] *Personal Information Protection and Electronic Documents Act,* S.C. 2000, c. 5.

[79] *Assisted Human Reproduction Act,* S.C. 2004, c. 2.

[80] R.S.C. 1985, c. C-46.

[81] *Ibid.,* s. 265.

[82] *Ibid.,* s. 219.

[83] *Medical Devices Regulations,* SOR/98-282.

[84] Jocelyn Downie & Fiona McDonald, "Revisioning the Oversight of Research Involving Humans in Canada" (2004) 12 Health L.J. 159 at 164.

[85] *Ibid.,* at 165. Kathleen Cranley Glass, "Questions and Challenges in the Governance of Research Involving Humans: A Canadian Perspective" in Trudo Lemmens and Duff R. Waring, eds., *Law and Ethics in Biomedical Research: Regulation, Conflict of Interest and Liability* (Toronto: University of Toronto Press, 2006) 35 at 43, also expresses concern regarding the fact that ethics review is not mandatory for all research conducted in Canada.

initiatives and difficulty recruiting participants are just two of the reasonably foreseeable byproducts of such erosion.[86]

IV. RESEARCH REVIEW

It is clear from the preceding discussion that the main regulatory instruments governing biomedical research involving humans have established REBs[87] as the workhorses of the governance regime. REBs are charged with a number of roles and responsibilities in relation to the reviews they conduct. The *Clinical Trial Regulations* define the principal mandate of REBs as being "to approve the initiation of, and conduct periodic reviews of, biomedical research involving human subjects in order to ensure the protection of their rights, safety and well-being".[88] Curiously, the TCPS does not contain a clear statement respecting the primary role of REBs, although it is widely accepted that their chief mandate is the protection of research participants.[89]

Some have argued that the maintenance of scientific integrity forms a secondary aim of REB review, as evidenced by the requirement that REBs satisfy themselves that proposed research possesses sufficient scientific rigour before approval is granted.[90] Support for this view is found in the TCPS, where "scholarly review" is deemed to be one of the substantive elements of research ethics review.[91] Yet another role assigned to TCPS-compliant REBs is to serve as a consultative body on research ethics for the research community.[92] It has

---

[86] Jocelyn Downie & Fiona McDonald, *ibid.*, at 165-66.

[87] This chapter will concentrate on REBs affiliated with public research institutions such as public hospitals and universities. While not specifically addressed here, the reader should be aware of the presence of private (for profit) REBs that can be retained to review human research being carried out by private sector organizations, typically pharmaceutical companies. For a discussion about private REBs, see T. Lemmens & A. Thompson, "Non-institutional Commercial Review Boards in North America: A Critical Appraisal and Comparison with IRBs" (2001) 13:2 IRB: A Review of Human Subjects Research 1.

[88] *Clinical Trial Regulations*, s. C.05.001.

[89] Marie Hirtle, Trudo Lemmens & Dominique Sprumont, "A Comparative Analysis of Research Ethics Review Mechanisms and the ICH Good Clinical Practice Guideline" (2000) 7 Eur. J. Health L. 265 at 271; Charles Weijer, "Continuing review of clinical research Canadian-style" (Jun 2002) 25:3 Clinical and Investigative Medicine 92 at 92; Jocelyn Downie & Fiona McDonald, "Revisioning the Oversight of Research Involving Humans in Canada" (2004) 12 Health L.J. 159 at 159.

[90] Kathleen Cranley Glass & Trudo Lemmens, "Conflict of Interest and Commecialization of Biomedical Research: What is the Role of Research Ethics Review?" in Timothy Caulfield and Bryn Williams-Jones, eds., *The Commericalization of Genetic Research: Ethical, Legal, and Policy Issues* (New York: Kluwer Academic/Plenum Publishers, 1999) 79 at 85; Eric M. Meslin, "Ethical Issues in the Substantive and Procedural Aspects of Research Ethics Review" (1993) 13 Health L. Can. 179 at 179.

[91] TCPS, art. 1.5 and corresponding commentary. Specifically, the commentary notes that the "primary tests to be used by REBs should be ethical probity and high scientific and scholarly standards".

[92] TCPS, commentary under art. 1.1.

also been suggested that REBs serve to protect their host institutions against liability by ensuring that unlawful or unethical research does not commence or continue.[93]

Part IV is divided into two sections. The first will focus on procedural features of research ethics review and the second will examine some of the substantive aspects of the review. Procedural matters include "the process or mechanism of research review, including the way in which the REB functions as a committee and how protocols make their way from the investigator's hands through"[94] the review process, whereas substantive matters concern "the content of research ethics review, particularly the principles or criteria used by REBs to assess the ethical acceptability of research protocols".[95]

A. PROCEDURAL ASPECTS OF RESEARCH ETHICS REVIEW

Much of the attention that has been given to the regulation of biomedical research has concentrated on the substantive aspects of research ethics review. While such rules are of doubtless importance, no less crucial are the procedures that are employed throughout the REB decision-making process. Decision outcomes, parties' perceptions about whether they have been treated fairly, and public confidence in the research governance regime are all potentially affected by the procedures REBs follow. As will be seen, the regulatory instruments establish inconsistent procedures, there are procedural gaps, and some of the procedural norms may not be optimized to achieve the primary objective of research ethics review.

1. Research Ethics Board Composition

The regulatory instruments typically set parameters around the number of members that REBs must have as well as the kinds of backgrounds and expertise that the REB membership needs to collectively possess. Article 1.3 of the TCPS requires that, for biomedical research, an REB must consist of at least five members, including both men and women, of whom at least two members possess "broad expertise in the methods or in the areas of research" covered by the REB, at least one member who is "knowledgeable in ethics", another who is "knowledgeable in the relevant law", and at least one member who has "no affiliation with the institution, but is recruited from the community served by the institution". The stated rationale for this membership requirement is to "ensure the expertise, multidisciplinarity and independence essential to competent research ethics review by REBs".[96] The mixture of expertise in relevant subject matters, the diversity of perspectives among the various experts, and the

---

[93] Eric M. Meslin, "Ethical Issues in the Substantive and Procedural Aspects of Research Ethics Review" (1993) 13(3) Health L. Can. 179 at 179.

[94] *Ibid.*

[95] *Ibid.*

[96] TCPS, commentary under art. 1.3.

community perspective is intended to promote sound decision-making on the part of the REB.

Variability in REB membership requirements exists among the instruments. The *Clinical Trial Regulations* and *GCP Guidelines*, although not in direct conflict with the TCPS, contain somewhat different membership requirements. The *Clinical Trial Regulations* require the majority of the REB to be Canadian citizens or permanent residents[97] and there must be one member whose primary experience and expertise is in a non-scientific discipline.[98] These requirements are not expressly stated in the TCPS. Even the *Clinical Trial Regulations* and *GCP Guidelines* are not entirely consistent; for instance, the former instrument provides that there must be a member knowledgeable in Canadian laws relevant to the biomedical research to be approved[99] and the latter is silent on the matter of legal expertise on the REB. In Quebec, the composition of REBs established under Article 21 of the *Civil Code of Québec* is set out under Part 1 of the *Gazette officielle du Québec*[100] and essentially mirrors the TCPS membership requirements.

Research participant representation on REBs is not mandated under the TCPS or any of the other regulatory instruments. The TCPS does stress the importance of community representation by declaring it "essential to help broaden the perspective and value base of the REB beyond the institution, and thus advances dialogue with, and accountability to, local communities".[101] Nevertheless, knowledge of the local community and the absence of institutional affiliation (where this actually exists[102]) does not equate to competence in providing insight into the interests and perspectives of research participants. On this score, a 2000 Law Commission of Canada study concluded that although "there are supposed to be 'lay' or 'community' representatives on many REBs, there is no requirement that lay representatives be knowledgeable about research subjects, let alone have been involved in research as subjects or as parts of groups that are often studied".[103] It bears stressing that the TCPS contains a mechanism that allows for research participant representation "in the event that the REB is

---

[97]   *Clinical Trial Regulations*, s. C.05.001.

[98]   *Ibid.*, s. C.05.001; *GCP Guidelines*, s. 3.2.1.

[99]   *Ibid.*, s. C.05.001.

[100] Conditions d'exercice des comités d'éthique de la recherche désignés ou institués, *Gazette officielle du Québec*, 29 août 1998.I.no35.1039.

[101] TCPS, commentary under art. 1.3.

[102] The extent to which research boards actually recruit persons without an institutional affiliation has been questioned. A 1990 report authored by Paul M. McNeill and others on Australian REBs (in that country, such boards are termed "Institutional Ethics Committees") revealed that, "in the main", appointments of lay and non-institutional member to IECs stemmed "from recommendations given by other committee members or by staff within the institution". See Paul M. McNeill, *The Ethics and Politics of Human Experimentation* (New York: Cambridge University Press, 1993) at 90. Although this study concerned IECs and is dated, it seems reasonable to assume that such selection methods are not uncommon in Canada.

[103] Michael McDonald, "Conclusions and Recommendations" in Michael McDonald, ed., *The Governance of Health Research Involving Human Subjects* (Ottawa: Law Commission of Canada, 2000) 293 at 304.

reviewing a project that requires ... research subject representation", in which case the REB "should nominate appropriate *ad hoc* members for the duration of the review" or actually modify the membership "should this occur regularly".[104] However, the TCPS' position on this issue is noteworthy for several reasons. First, the framers of the TCPS did not consider that research participant representation would, as a general rule, be required during the ethics review process or they would have included such representatives in the basic membership requirements under Article 1.3. Second, even where a particular project "requires" research participant representation, their inclusion on the REB is not mandatory. Third, where these representatives are nominated as "*ad hoc* members", they do not have voting rights.[105] Some commentators have not only called for mandatory research participant representation on REBs, but have also argued in favour of requiring equal numbers of science and participant members.[106]

2. The Application of Administrative Law to Research Ethics Boards

Before discussing some of the specific processes REBs follow in discharging their decision-making role, it is appropriate to first address whether REBs must conduct this function in accordance with administrative law precepts. This is an issue of considerable significance given the direct impact this body of law can have on the decision-making process and the resultant effects on the interests of those who hold a stake in the outcome of REB decisions. REB members and researchers have a particular interest in the application of administrative law to the REB decision-making process. Resort can be had to this body of law to clarify ambiguous or vague procedural requirements in the relevant regulatory instruments, or to obtain guidance where these instruments are entirely silent on a procedural matter. Moreover, legal recourse (in the form of judicial review proceedings) for researchers who are aggrieved by an REB decision would be made possible by virtue of the application of administrative law.

The TCPS states that REBs need "to act, and be seen to be acting, fairly and reasonably",[107] that they need to "function impartially"[108] and "provide a fair hearing to those involved",[109] and that these boards must "be guided by principles of natural and procedural justice in their decision making".[110] These statements appear to be overt gestures toward the importance of REBs' adherence to basic administrative law principles when exercising their decision-

---

[104] TCPS, commentary under art. 1.3.
[105] See PRE, *Interpreting the TCPS* (last modified June 1, 2006), online: <http://www.pre.ethics.gc.ca/english/policyinitiatives/interpretations/interpretation005.cfm>.
[106] Paul M. McNeill, *The Ethics and Politics of Human Experimentation* (New York: Cambridge University Press, 1993) at 207-236, and Duff Waring & Trudo Lemmens, "Integrating Values in Risk Analysis of Biomedical Research: The Case for Regulatory and Law Reform" in Law Commission of Canada, *Law and Risk* (Vancouver: U.B.C. Press, 2006).
[107] TCPS, commentary under art. 1.8.
[108] TCPS, art. 1.9.
[109] *Ibid.*
[110] TCPS, commentary under art. 1.10.

making functions. In any event, it has been argued that university and hospital-based REBs may fall within the purview of administrative law given that "they derive their authority from parent statutes [*i.e.*, the legislative instruments relating to the establishment and operation of universities and hospitals] which permit university and hospital boards to create internal bodies with mandatory powers; they operate at least indirectly under government control, through research-funding arrangements; and they serve important public purposes within a statutory context".[111] Additionally, the express mandates given to REBs in the context of the statutory regimes relating to clinical drug trials,[112] personal health information,[113] research involving minors or incompetent adults,[114] and the regulation of physicians, might very well attract administrative law obligations.[115] Other commentators have also raised the prospect of REBs being subject to administrative law.[116] As of the writing of this chapter, there have been no reported cases of administrative law remedies being sought from a Canadian court in respect of an REB decision. Thus, definitive guidance on the applicability of administrative law to REB decision-making in Canada is lacking. In the United States[117] and England,[118] there are reported cases involving judicial review of decisions made by the equivalent decision-making bodies in those countries, and legal commentators in New Zealand have opined that New Zealand courts may well be open to such proceedings, although this has yet to be tested.[119]

---

[111] Michael Hadskis & Peter Carver, "The Long Arm of Administrative Law: Applying Administrative Law Principles to Research Ethics Boards" (2005) 13:2&3 Health L. Rev. 19 at 20.

[112] That is, the *Clinical Trial Regulations*.

[113] For example, the *Health Information Act*, R.S.A. 2000, c. H-5, s. 49, and *Personal Health Information Act, 2004*, S.O. 2004, c. 3, Sch. A., s. 44.

[114] *Civil Code of Québec*, S.Q. 1991, c. 64, art. 21.

[115] Michael Hadskis & Peter Carver, "The Long Arm of Administrative Law: Applying Administrative Law Principles to Research Ethics Boards" (2005) 13:2&3 Health L. Rev. 19 at 20.

[116] Sana Halwani, "Her Majesty's Research Subjects: Liability of the Crown in Research Involving Humans" in Trudo Lemmens and Duff R. Waring, eds., *Law and Ethics in Biomedical Research: Regulation, Conflict of Interest and Liability* (Toronto: University of Toronto Press, 2006) 228 at 235-36.

[117] For example, see *Halikas v. University of Minnesota*, 856 F.Supp. 1331 (D. Minn. 1994). Also see Lars Noah, "Deputizing Institutional Review Boards to Police (Audit?) Biomedical Research" (2004) 25(3) Journal of Legal Medicine 267 for a discussion about the possibility of administrative law remedies only being available in respect of Institutional Review Boards (the U.S. equivalent of REBs) that operate within public institutions.

[118] For example, see *R. v. Ethical Committee of St. Mary's Hospital, ex parte Harriott*, [1988] 1 FLR 512, where judicial review was sought in regards to the decision of an infertility services ethical committee of a hospital.

[119] John Dawson, Mary Foley & Nicola Peart, "Research Ethics Committees" in John Dawson and Nicola Peart, eds., *The Law of Research: A Guide* (Dunedin NZ: University of Otago Press, 2003) 47 at 57-58.

3. Initiating Research Ethics Board Review

In those instances where the proposed activities require REB review, the researcher will need to identify the REB or REBs from which he or she will need to seek approval. In the past, research was typically carried out at only one institution; now it is commonplace for research to be conducted at multiple centres within and between provinces as well as in centres in different countries.[120] According to the TCPS, "[e]ach institution is accountable for the research carried out in its own jurisdiction or under its auspices." However, institutions can, through the use of inter-institutional (reciprocity) agreements, authorize their REBs "to accept the review of other REBs constituted under the [TCPS]."[121] Despite the availability of such arrangements, REBs and their affiliated institutions have been indisposed to entering into these agreements due to the potential liability they think they might be exposed to should the other REB(s) fail to meet applicable standards.[122] In the absence of such an arrangement, researchers who are conducting multi-centred research must seek ethics approval from each relevant REB, which carries with it the possibility of variance in review outcomes between REBs; for example, a consent form acceptable to one may not be so to another because of differing interpretations of the applicable disclosure requirements. There is also the potential for gross inefficiency as starkly demonstrated by a national epidemiological study in the United Kingdom that required ethics approval from 176 REBs. By the end of this laborious process, 50 hours of photocopying time had been used to copy 60,000 sheets of paper.[123]

The application or submission materials that researchers must provide to REBs can vary according to the specific demands of the relevant REB and the particular type of research being proposed. The required documentation can include research summaries that must follow the format adopted by the REB(s); consent forms; participant recruitment tools (*e.g.*, draft advertisements, letters of invitation/introduction, and telephone scripts); questionnaires; interview guidelines; contracts entered into with sponsors (including confidentiality agreements); and the researchers' *curriculum vitae*. Although the TCPS does not detail the documents that must be reviewed by an REB, the *GCP Guidelines* do.[124]

---

[120] Jocelyn Downie & Fiona McDonald, "Revisioning the Oversight of Research Involving Humans in Canada" (2004) 12 Health L.J. 159 at 175.

[121] TCPS, commentary under art. 1.2.

[122] Kathleen Cranley Glass, "Questions and Challenges in the Governance of Research Involving Humans: A Canadian Perspective" in Trudo Lemmens and Duff R. Waring, eds., *Law and Ethics in Biomedical Research: Regulation, Conflict of Interest and Liability* (Toronto: University of Toronto Press, 2006) 35 at 41.

[123] Jocelyn Downie & Fiona McDonald, "Revisioning the Oversight of Research Involving Humans in Canada" (2004) 12 Health L.J. 159 at 176.

[124] *GCP Guidelines*, ss. 3.1.2 and 3.1.3.

4. Types of Research Ethics Board Review

The TCPS puts forward two types of REB review: full and expedited. Full review is the "default requirement" under the TCPS.[125] That is, unless it is appropriate to proceed by way of expedited review, a full review is necessary. Before setting out the basis for deciding whether to hold an expedited or full review, each form of review will be described.

Under the TCPS, full reviews involve regularly scheduled,[126] face-to-face REB meetings[127] during which each research project before the REB is discussed with the aim of reaching a decision as to whether to "approve, reject, propose modifications to, or to terminate any proposed or ongoing research ... using the considerations set forth in [the TCPS] as the minimum standard".[128] The REB must "provide a fair hearing"[129] to researchers and must "accommodate reasonable requests from researchers to participate in discussions about their proposals"[130] before reaching a decision; however, researchers cannot be present at the meeting when the REB deliberates on their proposals.[131] In terms of quorum requirements for full review meetings, the TCPS states that when "there is less than full attendance, decisions requiring full review should be adopted only if the members attending the meeting possess the range of background and expertise stipulated in Article 1.3".[132] Simply complying with the minimum quorum requirements set out in Article 1.3 may not, in all instances, be sufficient for an adequate review of some research proposals. In addition to maintaining the proper proportion of community members, an REB may also need to add members based on the nature of the proposals before it.[133] This can occur where the expertise necessary to review a particular protocol is absent from the REB's regular membership. For example, when the proposed study concerns a new form of cancer treatment for children, the addition of an experienced pediatric oncologist may be required (assuming such an expert does not already sit on the REB). The *GCP Guidelines* also provide for a mechanism to obtain expert input when such is needed.[134]

On completing its discussion of a research proposal, the REB must reach a reasoned, well-documented decision.[135] If consensus among the members attending the meeting cannot be reached, the decision outcome is determined

---

[125] TCPS, art. 1.9 and commentary under art. 1.6.
[126] *Ibid.*, art. 1.7.
[127] The commentary under TCPS, art. 1.7 states, "Face-to-face meetings are essential for adequate discussion of research proposals and for the collective education of the REB".
[128] TCPS, art. 1.2.
[129] *Ibid.*, art. 1.9.
[130] *Ibid.*, article 1.9; *GCP Guidelines*, s. 3.2.5.
[131] *Ibid.*, article 1.9; *GCP Guidelines*, s. 3.2.5.
[132] *Ibid.*, commentary under art. 1.7.
[133] *Ibid.*, commentary under art. 1.3.
[134] *GCP Guidelines*, s. 3.2.6.
[135] TCPS, art. 1.8 and commentary under art. 1.9.

according to the procedural rules mandated by the institution (*e.g.*, a simple majority or some greater majority).[136]

Expedited review often takes the form of a designated REB member (often the REB Chair) or a small subcommittee of the REB having the power to carry out the review on behalf of the full REB. In practice, this may well mean that those conducting the expedited review will not possess the full range of expertise and experience that exists within the REB as a whole. As well, fewer people will pore over the research documentation submitted to the REB. Approvals granted through an expedited REB review process must nonetheless be reported to the full REB, thus permitting the entire REB "to maintain surveillance over the decisions made on its behalf",[137] however, such reporting is often not done or is merely cursory.

Pursuant to the TCPS, decisions about the level of REB review required for a particular study are to be made in accordance with the concept of "proportionate review", which holds that the care taken in assessing the research should be directly proportionate to the potential harms associated with it.[138] A proportionate approach "starts with an assessment, primarily from the viewpoint of the potential subjects, of the character, magnitude and probability of potential harms inherent in the research".[139] Foundational to the proportionate approach is the TCPS conception of "minimal risk". If the research involves no more than minimal risk, it may qualify for expedited review.[140] As will be seen later in the chapter, the application of the minimal risk standard extends beyond its use in determining what type of REB review is to be held.[141] Minimal risk exists if "potential subjects can reasonably be expected to regard the probability and magnitude of possible harms implied by participation in the research to be no greater than those encountered by the subject in those aspects of his or her everyday life that relate to the research".[142] In the context of biomedical research, any risk of harm that participants would have been exposed to as a consequence of undergoing medical treatment irrespective of their participation in the study, is not considered in the minimal risk calculus. However, those interventions that serve only the needs of the study are included.

Further to this concept, possible harms are to be assessed according to the chance that they will unfold (the probability variable) and the gravity of the consequences should the harm come to pass (the magnitude variable). There are several potential categories of harm that need to be considered in terms of their

---

[136] *Ibid.*, commentary under art. 1.9.
[137] *Ibid.*, commentary under art. 1.6.
[138] *Ibid.*, art. 1.6.
[139] *Ibid.*, commentary under art. 1.6.
[140] *Ibid.*, commentary under art. 1.6.
[141] The minimal risk standard is also used in determining: whether informed consent requirements can be waived or altered (art. 2.1(c)); who should provide participants with explanations about scientific or scholarly aspects of the research (commentary under art. 2.4); whether incompetent persons can be enrolled in research (art. 2.5); whether informed consent is needed for secondary use of data involving identifying information (commentary under art. 3.4); and the type of continuing review process that research is to be subjected to (commentary under art. 1.13).
[142] TCPS, s. 1.C1.

probability and magnitude: physical; psychological; social (*e.g.*, stigmatization, insurability, and employability); financial; legal (exposure to civil or criminal liability); and intrusion on privacy.[143] If the aggregate risks of harm associated with the research interventions[144] exceed the "everyday life" risks threshold, the research does not meet the minimal risk definition and should not proceed by way of expedited review.

The minimal risk standard has sparked vigorous debate in Canada and the United States, which has adopted a similar standard.[145] Some claim that the shifting everyday life threshold is impractical and unjust. It is claimed that individuals and communities vary widely regarding the risks they encounter in the ordinary course of a day and that it would be morally wrong for the minimal risk standard to be more likely met for research involving sick people or persons living in high crime, low income communities (*e.g.*, some inner cities) than healthy people or persons living in safer, more affluent areas.[146] Moreover, at the research approval stage, how are REBs going to prospectively evaluate individuals' everyday risks when they have yet to be recruited?[147] Even if the potential participants are known, how are REBs going to go about the task of quantifying the risks?[148] In defence of the minimal risk standard, others claim that the standard "provides a sound normative basis for the assessment of nontherapeutic research risk".[149] They argue that the standard refers to risks common to us all (*e.g.*, driving a car and crossing the street) not just specific individuals or communities and, regarding the quantification problem, they assert that it can be averted by relying on qualitative/ categorical determinations.[150] Nonetheless, other difficulties may persist, such

---

[143] See David B. Resnik, "Eliminating the Daily Life Risks Standard from the Definition of Minimal Risk" (2005) 31 J. Med. Ethics 35 at 35, and Subgroup on Procedural Issues for the TCPS (ProGroup), *Refinements to the Proportionate Approach to Research Ethics Review in the TCPS*, prepared for PRE (December 2005), online: <http://www.pre.ethics.gc.ca/english/workgroups/progroup/Consultation.cfm>.

[144] As distinct from the risks connected with the therapeutic interventions to which the patient would otherwise be exposed.

[145] The TCPS minimal risk standard is similar, but not identical, to its counterpart in the relevant American instrument: Title 45 *Code of Federal Regulations*, §46.102(i). However, its use of the "everyday life" threshold (or the equivalent "daily life" threshold in the United States) lends it to the same criticisms lodged against the American instrument.

[146] Loretta Kopelman, "Estimating Risk in Human Research" (1981) 29 Clinical Research 1, and Loretta Kopelman, "Moral Problems in Assessing Research Risk" (2000) 22:5 I.R.B. 3.

[147] This is a concern attributed to Chris Levy in James A. Anderson & Charles Weijer, "Minimal Risk and its Implications" (2001) 11:1 N.C.E.H.R. Communique 15 at 19.

[148] Loretta Kopelman, "Estimating Risk in Human Research" (1981) 29 Clinical Research 1, and Loretta Kopelman, "Moral Prolems in Assessing Research Risk" (2000) 22:5 I.R.B. 3.

[149] Paul Miller & Charles Weijer, "Moral Solutions in Assessing Research Risk" (2000) 22:5 I.R.B. 6 at 6.

[150] Benjamin Freedman, Abraham Fuks & Charles Weijer, "*In Loco Parentis*: Minimal Risk as an Ethical Threshold for Research upon Children" (1993) 23:2 Hastings Center Report 13; Charles Weijer, "The Ethical Analysis of Risk" (2000) 28 J. L. Med. & Ethics 344; Charles Weijer, "The Analysis of Risks and Potential Benefits in Research" (1999) 9:2 N.C.E.H.R. Communique 16; James A. Anderson & Charles Weijer, "Minimal Risk and its Implications" (2001) 11:1

as inconsistent determinations by REBs due to nebulous qualitative criteria.[151] To resolve the debate, one author proposes the elimination of the everyday life threshold; instead, research should be found to pose no more than minimal risk where "the probability and magnitude of the harm or discomfort anticipated in research are no greater than those encountered during the performance of routine physical or psychological examinations or tests".[152] This too may be problematic since it would likely invite endless debate and inconsistent decisions about what counts as a routine test.

The minimal risk standard is the only criterion set out in the TCPS for REB decision-making concerning whether to proceed by way of expedited or full review.[153] This is a substantial shortcoming since some minimal risk research should undergo full review.[154] An example of this would be a minimal risk research project involving long-term care facility residents with Alzheimer's disease that is being conducted by facility caregivers. Ethical concerns about the recruitment of participants who may be highly dependent on their caregivers and about how competency assessments will be conducted would render expedited review inappropriate. Quebec has addressed this problem, at least for certain persons who may be vulnerable. In that province, expedited reviews cannot be held in relation to research involving incompetent minors and adults, even if it presents only minimal risks.[155] Some research institutions in common law Canada have developed policies requiring that research involving incompetent persons must undergo full review.[156] The Interagency Advisory Panel on Research Ethics (PRE) has recently proposed that the potential vulnerability of participants be an explicit criterion for assessments respecting the appropriate level of REB review.[157] The proportionate review scheme that it has recommended would replace expedited reviews with a "delegated review

---

N.C.E.H.R. Communique 15.

[151] David B. Resnik, "Eliminating the Daily Life Risks Standard from the Definition of Minimal Risk" (2005) 31 J. Med. Ethics 35 at 35.

[152] *Ibid.*, at 37-38.

[153] However, commentary under TCPS, art. 1.6 does provide examples of research that may qualify for expedited review. These include: "Annual renewals of approved projects in which there has been little or no change in the ongoing research"; "Research involving review of patient records by hospital personnel"; and "Affirmations [from researchers] that conditions laid down by the REB as a condition of approval have been met".

[154] Charles Weijer, "The Ethical Analysis of Risk" (2000) 28 J. L. Med. & Ethics 344 at 358.

[155] Québec, Fonds de la recherche en santé du Québec, *Guide d'éthique et d'intégrité scientifique de la recherche (Research Ethics and Scientific Integrity Guidelines)*, 2nd ed. (Montreal: FRSQ, 2003) at 57.

[156] For example, see Section 7.2 of McMaster University's "Research Ethics Guidelines and Researcher's Handbook", available online: <http://www.mcmaster.ca/ors/ethics/faculty_guide lines_handbook.htm#7>.

[157] PRE, "Refinements to the Proportionate Approach to Research Ethics Review in the TCPS", available online: <http://www.pre.ethics.gc.ca/english/workgroups/progroup/Consultation. cfm>. According to PRE, vulnerability "exists along a continuum and is influenced by many factors including (but not limited to): Subject capacity (mental, emotional), Age, Wellness or health status, Institutionalization, Power relationships, Gender and gender identity, Setting and recruitment, Dependency."

process" (which is similar to the expedited review process described above) and would rely on the "interaction of vulnerability and risk of harm" to determine what type of review ought to be conducted.[158]

Expedited reviews have a very limited role in clinical drug trials. The *GCP Guidelines* state that REBs should have written procedures that provide for expedited reviews for "minor change(s) in ongoing trials", but this is noted to be subject to "applicable regulatory requirements".[159] The *Clinical Trial Regulations* do not speak to the use of expedited review mechanisms. Assuming this void can be filled by the *GCP Guidelines*, it would seem that expedited reviews of proposed drug trials cannot be undertaken and, with respect to ongoing trials, such reviews can only be conducted in the context of minor changes in the trials. No guidance is provided regarding what counts as a minor change.

5. Impartiality and Independence

The integrity of the ethics review system and the maintenance of the public's confidence in it rests on REBs and their individual members being unencumbered by extraneous influences during the decision-making process. The imperative for impartial decision-makers and independent decision-making bodies is a longstanding element of natural justice[160] and is partially voiced in some of the relevant regulatory instruments for biomedical research. The policy that underscores this imperative is reflected in the frequently rehearsed legal maxim: "Justice must not only be done, but must manifestly and undoubtedly be seen to be done."[161] This maxim should have no less purchase in the context of REB decision-making.

As a matter of administrative law, individual decision-makers can be disqualified on the basis of actual bias or a reasonable apprehension of bias, the latter form of bias may be found "where a reasonable person, knowing the facts concerning the member, would suspect that the member may be influenced, albeit unintentionally, by improper considerations to favour one side in the matter to be decided".[162] Similarly, the TCPS indicates that in order to "maintain the independence and integrity of ethics review, it is of the highest importance that members of the REB avoid real or apparent conflicts of interest".[163] Although the TCPS uses the term "conflict of interest", for all intents and purposes, the existence of a conflict of interest constitutes "bias" in the decision-making context. The TCPS does not contain a general test for determining whether an apparent conflict of interest exists on the part of REB members.[164]

---

[158] Subgroup on Procedural Issues for the TCPS (ProGroup), *Refinements to the Proportionate Approach to Research Ethics Review in the TCPS*, prepared for PRE (December 2005), online: <http://www.pre.ethics.gc.ca/english/workgroups/progroup/Consultation.cfm>.

[159] *GCP Guidelines*, s. 3.3.5.

[160] David Phillip Jones & Anne S. De Villars, *Principles of Administrative Law*, 4th ed. (Scarborough, ON: Carswell, 2004) at 366.

[161] *Ibid.*, at 366.

[162] Sara Blake, *Administrative Law in Canada*, 3rd ed. (Markham, ON: Butterworths, 2001) at 94.

[163] TCPS, s. 4B.

[164] In contrast, as will be discussed later in this chapter, the TCPS does set a general test for

Nonetheless, this instrument contains more direction on the issue of conflicts of interest than the *Clinical Trial Regulations*, which are entirely silent on the matter, or the *GCP Guidelines*, which provide only scant direction.[165] If administrative law applies to REBs, it can fill the void by furnishing the judicial definition of a reasonable apprehension of bias and a rich body of case law interpreting the rule against bias in a variety of decision-making contexts.

Administrative law is rife with examples of situations where courts have found a reasonable apprehension of bias. Such findings have been made where familial, personal, employment, or business relationships prevail between the decision-maker and a party to the proceeding.[166] A financial interest in the outcome of the proceeding is another common example.[167] Given that REB members are largely drawn from the staff and professionals (many of whom are biomedical researchers themselves) from the host institution, strong potential exists for the research ethics review process to be tainted by bias. The TCPS indirectly acknowledges this through the following examples of situations where a "clear"[168] conflict exists: the member's own research project is being reviewed;[169] the member otherwise "has a personal interest in the research under review (*e.g.*, as a researcher or as an entrepreneur)";[170] or where the member has "been in direct academic conflict or collaboration with the researcher whose proposal is under review".[171] Two points are noteworthy here. First, with respect to the last-mentioned situation, it is likely that REB members from many research institutions, particularly those of modest size, will have engaged in academic collaboration with the researchers whose studies are under review. Second, other unaddressed situations may be alive in a given case, such as the direct or indirect pressure some REB members may feel to approve a research project due to the financial implications of the study for their institution or situations where members take part in reviewing research proposals submitted to the REB by their superiors or close colleagues.[172] Indeed, some members who work at the host institution may feel that their prospects for tenure and promotion would be damaged if they are considered responsible for mounting barriers to the productivity of the institution's research program.

---

apparent conflicts of interest on the part of researchers.

[165] The direction under the *GCP Guidelines* consists of one sentence in s. 3.2.1 advising that only those REB members "who are independent of the investigator and the sponsor of the trial should vote/provide opinion on a trial-related matter".

[166] David Mullan, *Administrative Law*, 3rd ed. (Toronto: Carswell, 1996) at 295.

[167] David Phillip Jones & Anne S. De Villars, *Principles of Administrative Law*, 4th ed. (Scarborough, ON: Carswell, 2004) at 373.

[168] TCPS, s. 4B "Conflicts of Interest by REB Members".

[169] *Ibid.*

[170] *Ibid.*, art. 1.12.

[171] *Ibid.*, commentary under art. 4.1.

[172] Kathleen Cranley Glass & Trudo Lemmens, "Conflict of Interest and Commercialization of Biomedical Research: What is the Role of Research Ethics Review?" in Timothy Caulfield and Bryn Williams-Jones, eds., *The Commercialization of Genetic Research: Ethical, Legal and Policy Issues* (New York: Kluwer Academic/Plenum Publishers, 1999) 79 at 90.

A conflict of interest may come to the REB's attention by virtue of self-disclosure by a member (as mandated by the TCPS[173]) or by way of a researcher's allegation of bias stemming from, for example, personal animosity or professional rivalry between the member and the researcher. On being presented with a possible conflict of interest, the REB needs to gather information relevant to the matter and then make a ruling before proceeding with the review. This may be relatively straightforward when dealing with one of the so-called clear conflict of interest situations outlined in the TCPS. In other instances, such as the case where a superior's project is the subject of the review, REBs should apply the facts to the legal test outlined above. The absence of any reported Canadian jurisprudence respecting judicial proceedings being brought against REBs makes it difficult to predict how stringently this test should be applied. It bears highlighting that "the standard of scrutiny of an adjudication by a 'domestic' tribunal may be somewhat less intense than in other contexts",[174] as has been seen in litigation involving allegations of bias against members of university tenure committees and like peer review bodies.[175] On the other hand, the imposition of a less exacting standard in the REB context may well be inappropriate since REB decisions may have profound adverse consequences for the rights, safety, and well-being of research participants, who do not have an effective voice in the review process.

Where a conflict of interest is found to exist, the REB member concerned must absent him or herself from the meeting venue while the REB conducts its review of the relevant research project and must not have any further involvement in the matter. The TCPS requires that such action be taken[176] and administrative law precepts also demand the adoption of this approach.[177] Parenthetically, it should be noted that the review of the relevant project must be postponed until an appropriate replacement member is obtained in those instances where the removal of the member possessing the conflict would result in a loss of quorum.

In addition to the requirement that individual REB members be impartial, the structure and operation of a particular REB must not give rise to a reasonable apprehension of bias. Again, the law demands this of administrative adjudicators[178] and this requirement finds expression in Section 4C of the TCPS, which states that "the public trust and integrity of the research process require that the REB maintain an arm's-length relationship with the parent organization and avoid and manage real or apparent conflicts of interest".

---

[173] TCPS, art. 4.1.

[174] David Mullan, *Administrative Law*, 3rd ed. (Toronto: Carswell, 1996) at 303.

[175] For example, see *Paine v. University of Toronto*, [1981] O.J. No. 3187, 131 D.L.R. (3d) 325 (Ont. C.A.), leave to appeal to S.C.C. refused [1982] S.C.C.A. No. 239 (S.C.C.).

[176] TCPS, art. 1.12 and s. 4A "Conflicts of Interest by REB Members".

[177] Sara Blake, *Administrative Law in Canada*, 3rd ed. (Markham, ON: Butterworths, 2001) at 107.

[178] David Phillip Jones & Anne S. De Villars, *Principles of Administrative Law*, 4th ed. (Scarborough, ON: Carswell, 2004) at 387.

6. Review of Ongoing Research

Once a research project has received REB approval and is underway, there is a continuing need to safeguard research participants. Regarding the importance of ongoing ethics review, one author observes: "Continuing review of approved research is essential to ensure that research is conducted as planned, that research subjects comprehend the information given to them in the consent process, and that the potential benefits and risks of the study participation remain acceptable."[179] Others have identified the purposes of continuing review as including education of research staff, quality assurance, and prevention of misconduct on the part of researchers and their staff.[180] These reasons provide strong support for the implementation of appropriate oversight and review mechanisms.

The key regulatory instruments impose some ongoing review obligations. The TCPS states that continuing ethics review is a collective responsibility involving a number of actors, including REBs and researchers.[181] While continuing ethics review is mandatory, the TCPS allows for a considerable degree of latitude respecting the nature and timing of these reviews. Pursuant to the TCPS, the review should, at a minimum, consist of a "succinct" annual status report to the REB. Beyond this, the rigour of the review is to be determined according to the "proportionate approach", with minimal risk studies requiring only a "minimal review process".[182] The review of research exceeding this threshold can, in addition to the submission of an annual status report, include: random audits of the consent process; review of reports of adverse events; review of patients' charts; and the provision of progress reports, at predetermined intervals, containing "an assessment of how closely the researcher and the research team have complied with the ethical safeguards initially proposed".[183]

The TCPS also indicates that safety monitoring committees (also referred to as "Data Safety Monitoring Boards") can be established. Biostatisticians, scientists, bioethicists, and clinicians knowledgeable about the relevant research project usually sit on these committees.[184] They are most commonly used in the context of clinical drug trials, where the possibility that trial participants may experience adverse drug reactions is often a concern. These committees typically analyze adverse events with the goal of determining the likelihood that a relationship exists between an adverse occurrence in the health of a participant and his or her participation in the research. They may also perform interim analyses of clinical outcome data to determine if there is sufficient "evidence

---

[179] C. Weijer, "Continuing Review of Research Approved by Canadian Research Ethics Boards" (2001) 164 C.M.A.J. 1305 at 1305.

[180] J. McCusker *et al.*, "Monitoring Clinical Research: Report of One Hospital's Experience" (2001) 164 C.M.A.J. 1321 at 1321.

[181] TCPS, art. 1.13 and corresponding commentary.

[182] *Ibid.*, art. 1.13(a) and corresponding commentary.

[183] *Ibid.*, art. 1.13 and corresponding commentary.

[184] A. Slutsky & J. Lavery, "Data Safety and Monitoring Boards" (2004) 350 New Eng. J. Med. 1143 at 1143.

that one treatment has greater efficacy or causes greater harm than another".[185] As well, a safety monitoring committee may request additional information from researchers, require revisions to research documentation (*e.g.*, informed consent forms), or recommend the early termination of the research.[186] The specific regulatory requirements under the *Clinical Trial Regulations* respecting adverse effects monitoring and reporting are discussed in Chapter 8, Regulation of Pharmaceuticals in Canada.

Despite the existence of regulatory requirements for ongoing monitoring, there is overwhelming evidence that REBs are investing the vast majority of their resources in the ethics approval phase,[187] leaving their monitoring responsibilities largely unfulfilled.[188] Senator Michael Kirby's 2002 report, *The Health of Canadians — The Federal Role*, remarks that "few [REBs] monitor the conduct of research once a research protocol has been approved [and therefore] … often have limited knowledge of what happens after they have approved a research protocol".[189] This is not surprising in light of REBs' substantial research approval workloads and the finite limited resources (financial and human) at their disposal.[190] Nonetheless, with no or limited knowledge of what happens to participants after they are enrolled in studies, how much confidence can reasonably be placed in the research ethics review process?

---

[185] *Ibid.*, at 1143.

[186] *Ibid.*

[187] Michael McDonald, "Ethics and Governance" in Michael McDonald, ed., *The Governance of Health Research Involving Human Subjects* (Ottawa: Law Commission of Canada, 2000) 19 at 61.

[188] Jocelyn Downie & Fiona McDonald, "Revisioning the Oversight of Research Involving Humans in Canada" (2004) 12 Health L.J. 159 at 177-78; Charles Weijer, "Continuing Review of Research Approved by Canadian Research Ethics Boards" (2001) 164 C.M.A.J. 1305 at 1305-1306; Charles Weijer, "Continuing Review of Clinical Research Canadian-Style" (2002) 25:3 Clinical and Investigative Medicine 92 at 92-93; Charles Weijer, Stanley Shapiro, Abraham Fuks, Kathleen Cranley Glass & Myriam Skrutkowska, "Monitoring Clinical Research: An Obligation Unfulfilled" (1995) 152 C.M.A.J. 1973; Eric M. Meslin, "Ethical Issues in the Substantive and Procedural Aspects of Research Ethics Review" (1993) 13:3 Health L. Can. 179 at 185-86; Marie Hirtle, "The Governance of Research Involving Human Participants in Canada" (2003) 11 Health L.J. 137 at 144; Catherine Miller, "Protection of Human Subjects of Research in Canada" (1995) 4:1 Health L. Rev. 8 at 10; Michael McDonald, "Canadian Governance of Health Research Involving Human Subjects: Is Anybody Minding the Store?" (2001) 9 Health L.J. 1 at 10-11; and Jane McCusker, Zita Kruszewski, Belaine Lacey & Benjamin Schiff, "Monitoring clinical research: report of one hospital's experience" (2001) 164(9) C.M.A.J. 1321.

[189] The Standing Senate Committee on Social Affairs, Science and Technology, *The Health of Canadians — The Federal Role*, vol. 6, Final Report (Ottawa: The Senate, 2002) (Kirby Report) at s. 12.7.2, available online: <http://www.parl.gc.ca/37/2/parlbus/commbus/senate/com-e/SOCI-E/rep-e/repoct02vol6part4-e.htm#CHAPTER%20TWELVE>.

[190] Jocelyn Downie & Fiona McDonald, "Revisioning the Oversight of Research Involving Humans in Canada" (2004) 12 Health L.J. 159 at 180; and Abbyann Lynch, "Research Ethics Boards — Operational Issues I" (1999) 9:2 & 10:1 N.C.E.H.R. Communique 9 at 12-13.

B. SUBSTANTIVE ASPECTS OF RESEARCH ETHICS REVIEW

After being presented with the information pertaining to a particular research project through the ethics review process, TCPS-compliant REBs must deliberate on a number of substantive issues. Regarding applications for approval of a proposed study, these issues include: whether there is a "favourable" harms-benefits balance;[191] whether risks to participants have been minimized; whether "net benefits" of the research (*e.g.*, benefits for participants and other individuals, benefits for society as a whole, and the advancement of knowledge) have been maximized; whether participant selection criteria are fair and equitable; whether the recruitment process is appropriate; whether the proposed consent process is ethically and legally valid; whether vulnerable persons will be respected; whether the privacy of participants and the confidentiality of identifiable personal information being collected for research purposes are properly protected;[192] whether an actual, perceived, or potential conflict of interest exists on the part of the researchers and, if so, how it should be dealt with;[193] and whether the research is meritorious and meets scholarly standards.[194] Where ongoing research is under review, REBs most often entertain issues concerning whether the harms-benefits balance has remained unchanged and, if it has changed, what action needs to be taken (*e.g.*, consent form amendments or the immediate termination of the study).

The *GCP Guidelines* also set out substantive norms that are to inform REB decision-making. In addition to the requirement that they comply with the ethical principles in the *Declaration of Helsinki*,[195] REBs are to: weigh foreseeable risks and inconveniences against anticipated benefits for individual trial participants and society;[196] evaluate the scientific "soundness" of the protocol;[197] ensure "freely given informed consent" is obtained from participants;[198] ensure compliance with applicable privacy and confidentiality rules;[199] and pay "special attention" to trials that include "vulnerable subjects".[200] The *GCP Guidelines*, on the whole, offer less guidance than the TCPS on many of these substantive norms.

Substantive issues related to consent, privacy and confidentiality, and conflicts of interest on the part of researchers, have received the greatest

---

[191] The TCPS explains that this means that "the foreseeable harms should not outweigh anticipated benefits" (at I6).

[192] TCPS, s. 3.

[193] *Ibid.*, art. 4.1 and corresponding commentary.

[194] *Ibid.*, art. 1.5 and corresponding commentary. This may involve evaluating a study's objectives and the degree to which it might further the understanding of a phenomenon (merit); the research design and methodology; the justification given for the proposed sample size; and the proposed statistical analysis.

[195] *GCP Guidelines*, s. 2.1.

[196] *Ibid.*, s. 2.2.

[197] *Ibid.*, s. 2.5.

[198] *Ibid.*, s. 2.9.

[199] *Ibid.*, s. 2.11.

[200] *Ibid.*, s. 3.1.1. The term "vulnerable subjects" is defined in s. 1.61.

attention by legal commentators, research ethicists, and policy-makers. They
will form the focus of this section of the chapter.

1. Consent

In order for consent to participate in research to be legally and ethically valid,
three conditions must be satisfied: the consent must be informed; the consent
must be voluntarily given; and the person giving consent must be mentally
competent. Each of these conditions is discussed below.

(a) Consent to Participate in Research Must Be Informed

In the medical treatment context, the Supreme Court of Canada[201] has on
multiple occasions expressed its view that commitments to dignity and autonomy require that individuals have the right to determine whether and to what
extent they will accept medical interventions. As detailed in Chapter 5, Informed
Consent, a robust body of law on the issue of informed consent exists in Canada.
Comparatively, reported case law expounding on the doctrine of informed
consent in the area of human biomedical research is limited. For the most part,
researchers and REB members have relied on extra-legal documents to obtain
direction on the matter of informed consent. This section will address the
modest body of case law on informed consent in the research context and will
then outline the relevant norms found in the TCPS, *Clinical Trial Regulations*
and *GCP Guidelines*.

The 1965 Saskatchewan Court of Appeal case of *Halushka v. University of
Saskatchewan*[202] is one of two seminal judicial decisions in Canada on the issue
of informed consent in biomedical research. In this case, a University of
Saskatchewan student was offered $50 to participate in a study that was intended
to investigate individuals' circulatory response while under general anaesthesia.
The study was being conducted by medical researchers employed by the
University of Saskatchewan. During the consent process, the student participant
was verbally instructed that his participation would involve having a catheter or
tube inserted into a vein in his left arm and that he would receive a "new"
anaesthetic agent. He was also told that this was a "safe test and there was
nothing to worry about". The participant signed a brief consent form containing
a clause releasing the researchers and others from liability for "any untoward
effects or accidents" arising from his participation.

The next day, he underwent the research interventions that had been
explained to him, with the exception that after inserting the catheter into the vein
in his left arm, the researchers advanced it toward his heart. At this point, the
participant experienced discomfort and the anaesthetic agent was administered.
The catheter was then put through the chambers of his heart. Concerned that the
anaesthesia level was too light, the researchers increased the amount of the

---

[201] For example, see *Ciarlariello v. Schacter*, [1993] S.C.J. No. 46, [1993] 2 S.C.R. 119, 100 D.L.R.
(4th) 609 (S.C.C.); and *Starson v. Swayze*, [2003] S.C.J. No. 33, [2003] 1 S.C.R. 722, 225
D.L.R. (4th) 385 (S.C.C.).
[202] (1965), 53 D.L.R. (2d) 436, 52 W.W.R. 608 (Sask. C.A.).

anaesthetic agent and the participant experienced complete cardiac arrest that was caused by the agent. Although successfully resuscitated, he had sustained damage and brought a tort action against the researchers. A central issue in the case was whether the consent given by the participant was adequately informed. Finding against the researchers, the court determined that they had failed to inform the participant about, among other things, the risks associated with the use of an anaesthetic and the fact that the catheter would be advanced through his heart.

Several important common law principles arise from the decision. In terms of the researchers' disclosure obligation, the court opined that "... the duty imposed upon those engaged in medical research ... to those who offer themselves as subjects for experimentation ... is at least as great as, if not greater than, the duty owed by the ordinary physician or surgeon to his patient".[203] The court also noted that a subject "is entitled to a full and frank disclosure of all the facts, probabilities and opinions which a reasonable man might be expected to consider before giving his consent".[204] Even putting aside the court's regrettable use of equivocal language respecting the differences between the disclosure standards for medical treatment and research, this case provides limited guidance on defining the contemporary disclosure standard in research. This is largely due to the fact that it was decided 15 years before the Supreme Court of Canada, in *Hopp v. Lepp*[205] and *Reibl v. Hughes*,[206] established the so-called modified objective patient test for disclosure in the context of medical treatment. That test requires disclosure of information a reasonable person *in the patient's position* would require to make an informed decision. The *Reibl* standard is higher than that which existed for medical treatment when *Halushka* was decided[207] (*i.e.*, according to the *Halushka* court, patients were merely entitled to a reasonably clear explanation of the treatment and of the natural and expected outcome of it).

Therefore, subject to the below remarks about therapeutic privilege, it would be difficult to sustain a claim that *Halushka* provides definitive judicial support for a higher standard in research than the medical treatment standard established in *Reibl*. While it may be argued that the *Halushka* court intended to make a general claim that, whatever the treatment standard might be from time to time, the research standard will always be higher, it could also reasonably be contended that the court's decision was inextricably linked to the relatively low disclosure standard for treatment that existed in 1965. In any event, the rationale behind the genesis of the modified objective patient test should have equal purchase in the medical research realm, thus the *unmodified* objective participant standard in *Halushka* is unlikely to be applied in the future.

---

[203] *Ibid.*, at 443-44.
[204] *Ibid.*, at 444.
[205] [1980] S.C.J. No. 57, [1980] 2 S.C.R. 192, 112 D.L.R. (3d) 67 (S.C.C.).
[206] [1980] S.C.J. No. 105, [1980] 2 S.C.R. 880, 114 D.L.R. (3d) 1 (S.C.C.) (*Reibl*).
[207] The elevated standard flowing from *Reibl* is acknowledged in Ellen Picard and Gerald Robertson, *Legal Liability of Doctors and Hospitals in Canada*, 3rd ed. (Scarborough, ON: Carswell, 1996) at 150.

Importantly, the court found that the failure to inform subjects about a relevant aspect of the study is actionable, even if this information does not relate to the ultimate cause of the damage, provided that the participant would have decided not to participate if it had been disclosed during the consent process. Therefore, it mattered not in *Halushka* that advancing the catheter through the participant's heart did not contribute to the damage he sustained, because the court had found that he may well have refused to participate if such an intervention had been disclosed by the researchers. A final point of significance arising from *Halushka* is the court's pronouncement that there "can be no exceptions to the ordinary requirements of disclosure in the case of research as there may well be in ordinary medical practice", including the therapeutic privilege exception.[208] This is because researchers do "not have to balance the probable effect of lack of treatment against the risk involved in the treatment itself."[209]

The second seminal decision in Canada, *Weiss v. Solomon*,[210] was issued in 1989, some 24 years after *Halushka*. In *Weiss*, the Quebec Superior Court was called upon to decide whether a recruiting physician, a physician-researcher, the hospital in which the two worked, and the hospital's REB bore legal liability in connection with the death of a research participant (Weiss) during an eye drops study. After undergoing cataract surgery, Weiss was approached by his surgeon about participating in a research study being conducted by a physician-researcher concerning the effectiveness of certain eye drops at reducing a particular negative side effect of cataract surgery. Weiss was told that he would receive no therapeutic benefit through his participation. Information about the eye drops (including its side effects) was also provided, and he was further informed that fluorescein angiography would be performed in order to verify the impact of the drops. Weiss signed a consent form containing the following statement respecting the fluorescein agent: "Some patients may develop a minor allergic reaction to this injection, but the majority of patients have no side effects."[211] Above his signature, the form read: "I have been told of the possible side effects and unfavourable reactions that can happen and what my alternatives are. I have had a chance to ask questions to the doctor and have received acceptable answers".[212] Soon after receiving the fluorescein injection, Weiss, who had a pre-existing asymptomatic heart condition (hypertrophic cardiomyopathy), suffered cardiac failure and died. Weiss' family commenced an action based, in part, on their allegation that Weiss had not been informed about the risk of heart failure from fluorescein injection.

---

[208] *Halushka v. University of Saskatchewan* (1965), 53 D.L.R. (2d) 436 at 444, 52 W.W.R. 608 (Sask. C.A.). Therapeutic privilege is discussed in Chapter 5, Informed Consent.

[209] *Ibid.*

[210] [1989] J.Q. No. 312, [1989] R.J.Q. 731, 48 C.C.L.T. 280 (Que. S.C.).

[211] This passage from the consent form is set out in Benjamin Freedman & Kathleen Cranley Glass, "*Weiss v. Solomon*: A Case Study in Institutional Responsibility for Clinical Research" (1990) 18 Law Med. Health Care 395 at 395-96.

[212] See Benjamin Freedman & Kathleen Cranley Glass, *ibid.*, at 396.

The Quebec Superior Court found that Weiss' cardiac failure was an adverse reaction to the fluorescein injection, that his heart condition was a contraindication to fluorescein angiography, that he had not been informed of the slight risk of cardiac arrest from such injections, and that he likely would have declined to participate in the study had he been so informed. The hospital (through its REB) and the researcher were held liable in negligence for the failure to properly inform Weiss. On the road to making this determination, the court relied on *Halushka*, *Reibl v. Hughes*,[213] the *Civil Code of Québec*, the *Declaration of Helsinki*, and other authorities. According to this case, "the duty to inform in [research involving no anticipated therapeutic benefits to participants] is the most exacting possible. All risks must be disclosed, even those which are rare or remote, especially if they entail serious consequences."[214] The extent of the disclosure obligation by researchers was not qualified by an objective participant construct, modified or unmodified, and thus this case would seemingly support the presence of differing disclosure standards for research and treatment. The court also found that the defendants could not seek shelter under the clause in the consent form inviting Weiss to ask clarifying questions. In the court's opinion, all of the risks had to be disclosed, with or without prompting by participants.

It bears highlighting that *Halushka* and *Weiss* dealt with research presenting no anticipated therapeutic benefits for the participants. There are no reported cases in Canada that discuss the applicable disclosure standard for research with anticipated therapeutic benefits for participants where the research had undergone an ethics or peer review process.[215] It therefore remains unresolved whether the *Reibl* standard for medical therapy or a more rigorous one would be imposed by a court in such instances. A caveat is also in order for research possessing no anticipated benefits for participants. *Weiss* has not received relevant judicial consideration in Quebec or elsewhere in Canada; consequently, it remains to be seen whether the case will be followed in the common law provinces or even by a higher court in Quebec.

Some of the regulatory instruments already referenced in this chapter also establish disclosure standards. For example, the TCPS provides that researchers "shall provide, to prospective subjects or authorized third parties, full and frank disclosure of all information relevant to free and informed consent".[216] The *Clinical Trial Regulations* indicate that consent must be "given in accordance with the applicable laws governing consent", which would embrace relevant common law and legislative requirements. The regulations further stipulate that a clinical drug trial participant must be informed of "the risks and anticipated

---

[213] [1980] S.C.J. No. 105, [1980] 2 S.C.R. 880, 114 D.L.R. (3d) 1 (S.C.C.).

[214] Ellen Picard & Gerald Robertson, *Legal Liability of Doctors and Hospitals in Canada*, 3rd ed. (Scarborough, ON: Carswell, 1996) at 150.

[215] Benjamin Freedman & Kathleen Cranley Glass, "*Weiss v. Solomon*: A Case Study in Institutional Responsibility for Clinical Research" (1990) 18 Law Med. Health Care 395, note that there are Canadian cases dealing with "experimental" treatment (*i.e.*, treatment that deviates from the standard of care for the medical intervention in question) but they "do not deal with instances of research in the sense of a formal protocol that sets forth an objective and a set of procedures designed to reach that objective, as in the *Weiss* case" (at 397).

[216] TCPS, art. 2.4.

benefits to his or her health arising from participation in the clinical trial, and all other aspects of the clinical trial that are necessary for that person to make the decision to participate".[217] Pursuant to the *GCP Guidelines*, subjects are to be "informed of all aspects of the trial that are relevant to the subject's decision to participate".[218] Similar to *Weiss*, none of these instruments expressly require the employment of a modified or unmodified objective participant standard when determining the specific research-related information falling within the scope of their disclosure requirements. However, the TCPS and *GCP Guidelines* list, in some detail, the sort of information beyond the reasonably foreseeable risks/harms[219] that must be disclosed by researchers. Included in this information are the research purpose and procedures,[220] the benefits that may arise from participation,[221] a person's right not to participate or to withdraw from the research,[222] the presence of a conflict of interest on the part of the researcher, and how participants' confidentiality will be protected and any limits regarding such protections.[223]

The TCPS and *GCP Guidelines* offer additional direction on the subject of informed consent. The TCPS allows REBs to approve research projects that waive or alter the informed consent requirements contained in that document if certain conditions are met[224] and although it is exceedingly unlikely that research involving medical interventions would satisfy these conditions. Understandably, the *GCP Guidelines* do not allow for the possibility that its informed consent requirements can be waived or altered given the significant risks associated with drug trials. As well, the TCPS requires consent to be evidenced in writing unless there are "good reasons"[225] for not doing so.[226] In the case of drug trials, the *GCP Guidelines* state that an informed consent form must be signed by participants or

---

[217] *Clinical Trial Regulations*, s. C.05.010 (h).

[218] *GCP Guidelines*, s. 1.28.

[219] The TCPS, art. 2.4(c), states that a "comprehensible description of reasonably foreseeable harms … that may arise from research participation" must be provided. Somewhat more expansively, the *GCP Guidelines*, s. 4.8.10(g), indicate that the "reasonably foreseeable risks or inconveniences to the subject and, when applicable, to an embryo, fetus, or nursing infant" are to be disclosed.

[220] TCPS, art. 2.4(b); *GCP Guidelines*, s. 4.8.10(b) and (d).

[221] TCPS, art. 2.4(c); *GCP Guidelines*, s. 4.8.10(h).

[222] TCPS, art. 2.4(d); *GCP Guidelines*, s. 4.8.10(m).

[223] TCPS, commentary under art. 2.4 and the preamble to art. 3.1; *GCP Guidelines*, s. 4.8.10 (n) and (o).

[224] TCPS, art. 2.1(c), allows for such waivers or alterations where: "The research involves no more than minimal risk to the subjects"; "The waiver or alteration is unlikely to adversely affect the rights and welfare of the subjects"; "The research could not practicably be carried out without the waiver or alteration"; "When ever possible and appropriate, the subjects will be provided with additional pertinent information after participation" and "The waivered or altered consent does not involve a therapeutic intervention."

[225] Such reasons could include, among others, situations where it is culturally unacceptable to seek written consent: see TCPS, art. 2.1(b) and corresponding commentary.

[226] TCPS, art. 2.1(b).

their substitute decision-makers[227] and special procedures are specified for persons who are unable to read the consent form.[228]

Before leaving the topic of informed consent, it warrants emphasizing that researchers' obligations extend beyond merely disclosing information to participants and/or their substitute decision-makers; they must also ensure the person giving consent understands and appreciates the information provided. Picard and Robertson take the position that the researcher's duty in this regard should be at least as demanding as that for therapeutic interventions.[229] Accordingly, "the researcher must take reasonable steps to ensure that the subject actually understands the information presented, and must be sensitive to any signs or circumstances suggesting a lack of understanding".[230] Reports that between 20 and 40 per cent of persons possessing decisional-capacity do not understand one or more important aspects of research participation (*e.g.*, the attendant risks and the right to withdraw)[231] suggest that researchers are not taking such steps.

The informed consent process must not be rushed or treated as "perfunctory routine".[232] Potential participants must be given ample time[233] and opportunity to ask questions and contemplate whether they want to participate.[234] Furthermore, the language used during the process, both oral and written, should be straightforward, devoid of technical jargon,[235] and fixed at an appropriate comprehension level for the particular participant. This is something that many researchers fail to achieve.[236] The time devoted to this process can depend on many variables such as the potential participant's emotional state, the

---

[227] *GCP Guidelines*, s. 4.8.8. Similarly, s. C.05.010(h) of the *Clinical Trial Regulations* provides that a written informed consent must be obtained.

[228] *GCP Guidelines*, s. 4.8.9.

[229] Ellen Picard & Gerald Robertson, *Legal Liability of Doctors and Hospitals in Canada*, 3rd ed. (Scarborough, ON: Carswell, 1996) at 151.

[230] *Ibid.*

[231] David Wendler, "Can We Ensure That All Research Subjects Give Valid Consent?" (2004) 164 Archives of Internal Medicine 2201 at 2202.

[232] TCPS, commentary under art. 2.4.

[233] See David N. Weisstub & Simon N. Verdun-Jones, "Biomedical Experimentation Involving Elderly Subjects: The Need to Balance Limited, Benevolent Protection with Recognition of a Long History of Autonomous Decision-Making (Part I)" (1998) 18:3 Health L. Can. 95 at 100, where the authors note that the elderly need more time to process complex information and, therefore, research involving this population should use "information sessions tailored to suit the time requirements of the prospective participant" so as to maximize "the ability of individuals to engage meaningfully in the decision to participate in research".

[234] TCPS, art. 2.4; *GCP Guidelines*, s. 4.8.7.

[235] *GCP Guidelines*, s. 4.8.6.

[236] See Alan R. Tait, Terri Voepel-Lewis, Shobha Malviya & Sandra J. Philipson, "Improving the Readability and Processability of a Pediatric Informed Consent Document" (2005) 159 Archives of Pediatrics & Adolescent Medicine 347 at 347; J. Flory & E. Emanuel, "Interventions to Improve Research Participants' Understanding in Informed Consent for Research: A Systemic Review" (2004) 292 J.A.M.A. 1593 at 1599; James R.P. Ogloff & Randy K. Otto, "Are Research Participants Truly Informed? Readability of Informed Consent Forms Used in Research" (1991) 1:4 Ethics & Behavior 239 at 241-42.

environment where the information is provided (*e.g.*, an individual's home versus the researcher's office), and the participant's maturity level.[237]

(b) Consent to Participate Must Be Voluntary

The TCPS and the *GCP Guidelines* highlight the need for informed consent to participate in research to be given by a free agent.[238] The "free" and "informed" elements of consent should not be conflated. That is, individuals can be informed of all relevant information about a study and fully understand and appreciate this information, yet their agreement to participate may be ethically and legally invalid because it was not freely given. Under both instruments, consent cannot be considered free (*i.e.*, "voluntary"[239]) if it was "coerced" or "unduly influenced".[240] These critical terms are not defined in either instrument. *The Belmont Report* defines coercion as "an overt threat of harm [that] is intentionally presented by one person to another in order to obtain compliance" and describes the conceptually distinct term[241] of undue influence as "an offer of an excessive, unwarranted, inappropriate or improper reward or other overture in order to obtain compliance".[242]

Much attention has been dedicated to undue influence and the various forms it can take. Monetary payments and the presence of power relationships (*e.g.*, the imbalance of power between physicians and patients) are two commonly cited examples. The *GCP Guidelines* are silent on the issue of monetary payments and the TCPS merely directs REBs to be sensitive to the "possibility" of undue influence where these payments would "lead subjects to undertake actions that they would not ordinarily accept" and that, in so doing, they are to "pay attention to issues such as the economic circumstances of those in the pool of prospective subjects, and the magnitude and probability of harms".[243] Elsewhere, it notes that: "As an offer of payment in relation to research participation exceeds the normal range of benefits open to the research subject, it is increasingly likely to amount to an undue incentive for participation."[244] This guidance begs more questions than it answers: Is payment in excess of reimbursement for out-of-pocket expenses ever acceptable?[245] If it is permissible to compensate participants for such things as inconvenience[246] and assumption of

---

[237] TCPS, commentary under art. 2.4.

[238] TCPS, art. 2.1(a); *GCP Guidelines*, s. 2.9.

[239] The TCPS uses the terms "free" and "voluntary" interchangeably.

[240] TCPS, art. 2.2; *GCP Guidelines*, s. 4.8.3.

[241] For a discussion about what constitutes undue inducement (influence) and the distinction between undue inducement and coercion, see Ezekiel J. Emanuel, "Ending Concerns About Undue Inducement" (2004) 32 J. L. Med. & Ethics 100-105.

[242] National Commission for the Protection of Human Subjects of Biomedical and Behavioral Research, *The Belmont Report: Ethical Principles and Guidelines for the Protection of Human Subjects of Research* (1979), online at: <http://ohsr.od.nih.gov/guidelines/belmont.html>.

[243] TCPS, commentary under art. 2.4.

[244] *Ibid.*, s. 1.C1.

[245] Leah E. Hutt, "Paying Research Subjects: Historical Considerations" (2003) 12:1 Health L. Rev. 16 at 18.

[246] This question has been answered for the province of Quebec. Under article 25 of the *Civil Code*

risk, then how can the compensation for each be properly calibrated so as to not lead participants to undertake actions they would otherwise avoid? In order to take into account relative economic circumstances, should wealthier people receive higher payments than people of lesser financial means for their participation in the same study?[247] As a practical matter, how are REB members going to apprise themselves of the financial wherewithal of all individuals within economically diverse pools of potential participants? Some authors have argued that these perplexing issues could be resolved if research participation by healthy individuals were characterized as a kind of labour relation thereby warranting labour-type legislation.[248]

Contextual factors in addition to individuals' financial circumstances require researchers and REBs to be attentive to the issue of voluntariness. For instance, elderly patients in long-term care facilities can be extremely dependent on caregivers for fulfillment of their basic physical, social, and emotional needs, which tends to promote passivity and unquestioned compliance with instructions and can threaten "the psychological ability of older persons to contradict someone, such as a physician, upon whom they are dependent".[249] Prisoners[250] and civilly committed persons[251] are also markedly dependent on persons in authority within the custodial institution and, therefore, are ripe for being unduly influenced to participate in research. Moreover, voluntary choice can be influenced by other power imbalances that can reside in relationships between employers and employees, and instructors and students.[252] Concerns about voluntariness are extremely acute when the consent of desperately ill patients is being sought in relation to studies (usually drug trials) that hold the last hope of rescue.[253]

(c) Consent to Participate Must Be Given by Competent Persons

Ethical obligations of researchers and REB members must be at their highest when persons with diminished decisional capacity are involved in research.

---

of Québec, participants can be paid "an indemnity as compensation for the loss and inconvenience suffered" through their participation in research. No other "financial reward" can be given.

[247] Trudo Lemmens & Carl Elliott, "Justice for the Professional Guinea Pig" (2001) 1:2 American Journal of Bioethics 51 at 52.

[248] *Ibid.*

[249] Kathleen Cranley Glass, "Informed Decision-Making and Vulnerable Persons: Meeting the Needs of the Competent Elderly Patient or Research Subject" (1993) 18 Queen's L.J. 191 at 208 & 231.

[250] Julio Arboleda-Florez, "The Ethics of Biomedical Research on Prisoners" (2005) 18 Current Opinion in Psychiatry 514.

[251] Julio Arboleda-Florez & David N. Weisstub, "Ethical Research with the Mentally Disordered" (1997) 42 Can. J. Psychiatry 485 at 486-87.

[252] TCPS, commentary under art. 2.2.

[253] For a discussion of such research, see Charles L. Bosk, "Obtaining Voluntary Consent for Research in Desperately Ill Patients" (2002) 40:9 Medical Care V64; and Sarah Hewlett, "Consent to Clinical Research — Adequately Voluntary or Substantially Influenced?" (1996) 22 J. Med. Ethics 232 at 234.

Diminished capacity may owe to the incomplete cognitive development that exists during various phases of childhood, the impact of mind-altering substances, or the presence of a disorder that results in temporary or permanent cognitive impairment. Enormous care must be exercised in the proper conduct of capacity determinations since erroneous findings of incompetence can seriously infringe a participant's right to self-determination. This may occur if researchers assume persons with mental disabilities lack capacity.[254] At the same time, a mistaken finding of capacity may foreclose the engagement of safeguards for the protection of persons who are vulnerable by reason of their diminished capacity.

The capacity test for participation in research set out in the TCPS applies to all individuals regardless of their age. This test is similar to many provincial/territorial statutory and common law tests for determining whether a patient is competent to consent to medical treatment, though the TCPS[255] rightly cautions that the law on competence can vary between jurisdictions[256] thus making it "difficult to pin down the notion of what is considered *legally competent*".[257] According to the TCPS, individuals must possess two distinct competencies: the ability to *understand* the information that is relevant to making a decision about participating in the specific study[258] and the ability to appreciate the consequences of making a decision to participate in the study.[259] The first competency involves the cognitive ability of participants to process and retain information about matters relevant to participation such as the potential harms and benefits that might be occasioned if they are enrolled in the study. That is, they must understand the relevant facts concerning the study.[260] The second calls for the ability to evaluate the information about the study that they have acquired. This demands the ability to apply the relevant information to a person's individual circumstances and to weigh the consequences of participating or not participating.[261] Capacity determinations must hinge only

---

[254] Julio Arboleda-Florez & David N. Weisstub, "Ethical Research with the Mentally Disordered" (1997) 42 Can. J. Psychiatry 485 at 488; Paddi O'Hara & Ineke Neutel, "A Shadow of Doubt: Ethical Issues in the Use of Proxy Consent in Research. Part I: When are Proxies Needed and How Do They Make Their Decisions?" (2004) 9:1 Canadian Bioethics Society Newsletter 7 at 7.

[255] TCPS, s. 2E.

[256] See Chapter 5, Informed Consent, and Chapter 11, Death, Dying and Decision-making about End of Life Care.

[257] Paddi O'Hara & Ineke Neutel, "A Shadow of Doubt: Ethical Issues in the Use of Proxy Consent in Research. Part II: Competence and Proxy Consent in Terms of Guidelines and Regulations" (2004) 9:2 Canadian Bioethics Society Newsletter 7 at 8.

[258] See TCPS, s. 2E, and *Starson v. Swayze*, [2003] S.C.J. No. 33, [2003] 1 S.C.R. 722, 225 D.L.R. (4th) 385 (S.C.C.).

[259] *Ibid.*

[260] This statement is made on the basis of a broad application of the legal principles from *Starson v. Swayze, ibid.*, to the research realm.

[261] This statement is made on the basis of a broad application of the legal principles from *Starson v. Swayze, ibid.*, to the research realm.

on the application of the relevant test, not the researcher's conception of whether participation is in the person's best interests.[262] It should also be noted that competence is not global or static.[263] An individual may have the capacity to consent to participate in one study (*e.g.*, the completion of a questionnaire that solicits non-sensitive information) but not another (*e.g.*, a clinical trial involving a new chemotherapy agent). Moreover, a particular person's ability to consent to participate in a study may fluctuate, even over short time intervals.[264]

The TCPS expressly states that researchers must comply with all relevant legal requirements respecting competency.[265] Chapter 10, Mental Health Law in Canada, and Chapter 11, Death, Dying and Decision-making About End of Life Care, discuss the legal presumption of capacity that exists for adults in Canada and for some minors in some provinces. The implications of finding a person competent or incompetent are also discussed. Suffice it to say here that competent adults can consent to participate in research, irrespective of whether it holds any potential benefits for them. As has been canvassed in Chapter 11, minors who satisfy the common law capacity test are considered "mature minors" and can consent to medical treatment, although this may be subject to the possible application of the "welfare principle" which holds that mature minors can only consent to beneficial or therapeutic medical interventions.[266] Although there is a lack of clarity in the law regarding whether the mature minor doctrine applies to minors' participation in research because no court has been asked to rule on the matter,[267] the courts may well hold that it does, at least for research with anticipated benefits to the participants.[268]

Significant ethical and legal issues arise when considering whether persons lacking capacity can be enrolled in a specific study. Including only competent participants in research can unfairly exclude certain groups, such

---

[262] See David N. Weisstub & Simon N. Verdum-Jones, "Biomedical Experimentation Involving Elderly Subjects: The Need to Balance Limited, Benevolent Protection with Recognition of a Long History of Autonomous Decision-Making (Part II)" (1998) 18:4 Health L. Can. 105 at 107-108.

[263] TCPS, s. 2E. See also Julio Arboleda-Florez & David N. Weisstub, "Ethical Research with the Mentally Disordered" (1997) 42 Can. J. Psychiatry 485 at 486.

[264] See Paddi O'Hara & Ineke Neutel, "A Shadow of Doubt: Ethical Issues in the Use of Proxy Consent in Research. Part I: When are Proxies Needed and How Do They Make Their Decisions?" (2004) 9:1 Canadian Bioethics Society Newsletter 7. The authors comment that some persons with Alzheimer's tend to be less able to make decisions in the evening (a phenomenon known as "sundown").

[265] TCPS, section 2E.

[266] This principle is reflected in consent legislation in some jurisdictions. See Chapter 11, Death, Dying and Decision-making About End of Life Care.

[267] Francoise Baylis, Jocelyn Downie & Nuala Kenny, "Children and Decision-making in Health Research" (2000) 8:2 Health L. Rev. 3 at 4.

[268] Erin L. Nelson, "Legal and Ethical Issues in ART 'Outcomes' Research" (2005) 13 Health L.J. 165 at 182; and Claire Bernard & Bartha Maria Knoppers, "Legal Aspects of Research Involving Children in Canada" in Bartha Maria Knoppers, ed., *Canadian Child Health Law* (Toronto: Thompson Educational Publishing Inc., 1992) 259 at 299.

as children and persons with mental disabilities, from the benefits of research. Thus, "automatic exclusion of prospective research subjects based on mental disability, or diagnosis per se, is not consistent with the TCPS" [269] or conceptions of distributive justice, inclusiveness, and equality. However, there are ethical and legal restrictions on the inclusion of persons lacking capacity in research. The balance of this section is devoted to outlining these limitations.

The TCPS and *GCP Guidelines* state that legally incompetent persons, regardless of the reasons for their incompetence, cannot be enrolled in research unless three conditions are met. First, the research question can only be addressed by enrolling persons who are incapacitated.[270] For example, this may be met where it cannot be presumed that a particular treatment will be safe and efficacious for children purely on the basis of research outcomes regarding adult populations. History has shown that dangerous consequences can result from erroneous assumptions respecting the generalizability of adult data.[271] However, if competent persons would make equally fitting participants for a given study, incompetent persons cannot be enrolled.

Second, consent must be sought from the incompetent person's legally authorized representative.[272] Where minors are involved, the legally appropriate substitute decision-makers are the minors' parents or guardians[273] but, as addressed below, their powers are substantially constrained. The situation is less clear with incompetent adults, as it is doubtful that the person's next-of-kin can lawfully consent to medical interventions (whether the intervention is undertaken for therapeutic or research purposes) unless this is authorized by a court, a legislative instrument, or an advance directive.[274] Alarmingly, evidence suggests that researchers and REB members lack knowledge of who is legally authorized to consent to research on behalf of an incompetent adult participant.[275]

Third, the research cannot expose the incompetent person to more than minimal risks without the potential for direct benefits for them.[276] This

---

[269] See PRE, *Interpreting the TCPS* (last modified June 1, 2006), online at: <http://www.pre.ethics. gc.ca/english/policyinitiatives/interpretations/interpretation009.cfm> and the TCPS, article 5.3.

[270] TCPS, art. 2.5(a); *GCP Guidelines* s. 4.8.14(a). See also Christy Simpson, "Children and Research Participation: Who Makes What Decisions" (2003) 11:2 Health L. Rev. 20 at 22; See Paddi O'Hara & Ineke Neutel, "A Shadow of Doubt: Ethical Issues in the Use of Proxy Consent in Research. Part I: When are Proxies Needed and How Do They Make Their Decisions?" (2004) 9:1 Canadian Bioethics Society Newsletter 7 at 8.

[271] Some examples are provided in Paul B. Miller & Nuala P. Kenny, "Walking the Moral Tightrope: Respecting and Protecting Children in Health-Related Research" (2002) 11 Cambridge Quarterly of Healthcare Ethics 217 at 218.

[272] TCPS, art. 2.5(b); *GCP Guidelines* s. 4.8.14.

[273] Erin L. Nelson, "Legal and Ethical Issues in ART 'Outcomes' Research" (2005) 13 Health L.J. 165 at 176.

[274] Lorne E. Rozovsky, *The Canadian Law of Consent to Treatment*, 3rd ed. (Markham, ON: LexisNexis Butterworths, 2003) at 73.

[275] G. Bravo, M. Paquet & M.-F. Dubois, "Knowledge of the Legislation Governing Proxy Consent to Treatment and Research" (2003) 29 J. Med. Ethics 44-50.

[276] TCPS, art. 2.5(c). More precisely, the *GCP Guidelines*, s. 4.8.14(b) and (c), state that the

criterion's apparent authorization of non-beneficial minimal risk research involving incompetent individuals may run afoul of the common law as well as relevant legislative prohibitions that exist in some provinces. Regarding the common law, the Supreme Court of Canada's decision in *Eve v. E. (Mrs.)*[277] has been interpreted by some to be relevant to this issue. In *Eve*, the Supreme Court of Canada dealt with an application that had been brought by "Mrs. E." for court approval (under its *parens patriae* jurisdiction) to give her consent to sterilize "Eve", her incompetent adult daughter, because of a concern that if Eve became pregnant Mrs. E. would have to assume sole responsibility for the care of her daughter's child. The court denied Mrs. E.'s application on the basis that a court's *parens patriae* jurisdiction can only be exercised for the protection and benefit of the person with the disability. In the court's view, the sterilization was being sought for the benefit of Mrs. E., not Eve. While the case did not involve biomedical research, Dickens[278] and others[279] have argued that, in the absence of constitutionally valid legislative authority, its principles can reasonably be extended to impede substitute decision-makers from being able to lawfully consent to the inclusion of incompetent persons in medical research that poses any risks if there is no immediate medical benefit to the incompetent individual. It has been contended that this would mean that parents cannot even consent to interventions such as heel or finger-prick blood testing of their children that is being conducted for research purposes alone.[280] It is immaterial that the research might benefit other children.[281] Taking a less restrictive slant on *Eve*, other commentators have argued that the decision can be read as indicating that parents can authorize research with no direct medical benefit, provided there is potential for other benefits, such as psychological, social, and religious benefit.[282] It has been speculated that the uncertainty around how future courts may interpret *Eve* "has probably had a chilling effect on research involving children in Canada."[283] If the more restrictive interpretation is ultimately judicially embraced, it is feared that important research will not involve

---

foreseeable risks to the participants must be low and the negative impact on the participant's well-being must be minimized and low.

[277] [1986] S.C.J. No. 60, [1986] 2 S.C.R. 388, 31 D.L.R. (4th) 1 (S.C.C.).

[278] Bernard M. Dickens, "The Legal Challenge of Health Research Involving Children" (1998) 6 Health L.J. 131-148.

[279] Erin L. Nelson, "Legal and Ethical Issues in ART 'Outcomes' Research" (2005) 13 Health L.J. 165 at 177; Julio Arboleda-Florez & David N. Weisstub, "Ethical Research with the Mentally Disordered" (1997) 42 Can. J. Psychiatry 485 at 488; Robert S. Williams, "Pediatric Research and the Parens Patriae Jurisdiction in Canada and England" (1999) 18 Medicine & Law 525-46; Sonja Grover, "On the Limits of Parental Proxy Consent: Children's Right to Non-Participation in Non-Therapeutic Research" (2003) 1 Journal of Academic Ethics 349 at 371.

[280] Bernard M. Dickens, "The Legal Challenge of Health Research Involving Children" (1998) 6 Health L.J. 131 at 135.

[281] *Ibid.*, at 133-34.

[282] This alternative interpretation of *Eve* is canvassed in Francoise Baylis, Jocelyn Downie & Nuala Kenny, "Children and Decision-making in Health Research" 2000 8:2 Health L. Rev. 3 at 7-8.

[283] *Ibid.*, at 8.

incompetent persons and the groups to which they belong will be deprived the benefits of medical advancements, thus becoming "therapeutic orphans".[284]

As previously alluded to, a province/territory can attempt[285] to legislatively authorize substitute consent for the participation of incompetent persons in research. Quebec has done so under article 21 of its *Civil Code of Québec*. Pursuant to that provision, substitute consent can be given for the participation of incompetent minors and adults in research that exposes them to risk of harm without the potential to benefit them, but there are important limitations. Consent cannot be given if the incompetent person will be exposed to "serious risk" to his or her health or where he or she understands the nature and consequences of the experiment and objects to participation. As well, if the incompetent person is the only subject of the research, it must have "the potential to produce benefit to the person's health or only if, in the case of [research] on a group, it has the potential to produce results capable of conferring benefit to other persons in the same category or having the same disease or handicap". However, such research must be approved and monitored by an REB formed or designated by the Minister of Health and Social Services.[286]

It has been suggested that advance directives are a viable means of avoiding the legal and ethical quagmire concerning the involvement of incompetent persons in research.[287] Specifically, it has been put forward that presently competent individuals whose cognitive capacity is decreasing or fluctuating could issue a directive specifying their wishes to consent to or refuse future participation in non-therapeutic research.[288] Several Canadian jurisdictions have advance health care directives legislation that addresses the power of a substitute decision-maker to consent to the participation of the maker of the directive (the "director") in medical research. For example, such instruments

---

[284] Francoise Baylis & Jocelyn Downie, "An Ethical and Criminal Law Framework for Research Involving Children in Canada" (1993) 1 Health L.J. 39. See also: David N. Weisstub & Simon N. Verdun-Jones, "Biomedical Experimentation Involving Elderly Subjects: The Need to Balance Limited, Benevolent Protection with Recognition of a Long History of Autonomous Decision-Making (Part I)" (1998) 18:3 Health L. Can. 95 at 99.

[285] This can be attempted, but the legislative instrument could be challenged under the *Canadian Charter of Rights and Freedoms*, Part I of the *Constitution Act, 1982*, being Sched. B to the *Canada Act 1982* (U.K.), 1982, c. 11. See Bernard M. Dickens, "The Legal Challenge of Health Research Involving Children" (1998) 6 Health L.J. 131 at 145-46.

[286] A detailed explanation of art. 21 of the *Civil Code of Québec* is set out in Simon Verdun-Jones & David N. Weisstub, "Consent to Human Experimentation in Québec: The Application of the Civil Law Principles of Personal Inviolability to Protect Special Populations" (1995) 18 Int'l J. L. & Psychiatry 163 at 176-79.

[287] George F. Tomossy & David N. Weisstub, "The Reform of Adult Guardianship Laws: The Case of Non-Therapeutic Experimentation" (1997) 20(1) Int'l J. L. & Psychiatry 113.

[288] This would require detailed instructions regarding critical details, such as the type of research that the makers of these directives wished to participate in, as well as the research interventions and levels of risk of harm that would be acceptable to them. See George F. Tomossy & David N. Weisstub, "The Reform of Adult Guardianship Laws: The Case of Non-Therapeutic Experimentation" (1997) 20 Int'l J. L. & Psychiatry 113 at 131.

in Newfoundland and Labrador[289] and Manitoba[290] prohibit a proxy appointed under an advance directive from consenting to "medical treatment for the primary purpose of research" unless express authorization for this is given in the directive. Prince Edward Island[291] allows substitute consent for medical research in the absence of express authorization in the directive if the research is likely to benefit the director. In Alberta, without clear instructions in the directive, substitute consent is barred if the participation in the research "offers little or no potential benefit to the maker" of the directive.[292] Other provinces also have relevant legislation.[293]

It does not necessarily follow from a determination of incapacity that the incompetent person cannot take part in the decision to participate in research. Article 2.7 of the TCPS requires researchers to "seek to ascertain the wishes" of the "legally incompetent" individual if that person "understands the nature and consequences of the research". If such a person "dissents", his or her participation is precluded. This article has been criticized by a number of commentators. If the prospective participant understands the nature and consequences of the research, it is not immediately apparent why Article 2.7 describes that person as being legally incompetent.[294] Moreover, when the prospective participant is a child, allowing his or her "dissent to function as the moral equivalent of a refusal by a person with decision making capacity, without first having determined that the child has decisional capacity, is to seriously undermine parental responsibility for promoting children's interests".[295] The only province that has provided direct guidance on the legal implications of assent/dissent in research is Quebec. Article 21 of the *Civil Code of Québec* states that a minor or adult who is incapable of giving consent cannot be enrolled in research if he or she "objects".

2. Privacy and Confidentiality

Recall that the general regulatory framework for human research has widely been characterized as a complex, confusing patchwork of legal and extra-legal instruments. This description is also apt for those aspects of the framework that establish privacy and confidentiality norms regarding the collection, use, and

---

[289] *Advance Health Care Directives Act*, S.N.L. 1995, c. A-4.1, s. 5(3).

[290] *Health Care Directive Act*, C.C.S.M. c. H27, s. 14(a).

[291] *Consent to Treatment and Health Care Directives Act*, R.S.P.E.I. 1998, c. C-17.2, s. 12.

[292] *Personal Directive Act*, R.S.A. 2000, c. P-6, s. 15(d).

[293] For British Columbia, see the *Health Care (Consent) and Care Facility (Admission) Act*, R.S.B.C. 1996, c. 181, s. 18(1) and the *Representation Agreement Act*, R.S.B.C. 1996, c. 405, s. 9. For the Northwest Territories (including Nunavut), see the *Health Care Regulations*, N.W.T. Reg. 050-97, s. 1 under the *Guardianship and Trusteeship Act*, S.N.W.T. 1994, c. 29. For New Brunswick, see the *Nursing Homes Act*, S.N.B. 1982, c. N-11, s. 13.

[294] Erin L. Nelson, "Legal and Ethical Issues in ART 'Outcomes' Research" (2005) 13 Health L.J. 165 at 180.

[295] Francoise Baylis, Jocelyn Downie & Nuala Kenny, "Children and Decision-making in Health Research" (2000) 8:2 Health L. Rev. 3 at 4. See also: David C. Flagel, "Children as Research Subjects: New Guidelines for Canadian REBs" (2000) 22:5 I.R.B. 1 at 3.

disclosure of personal information for health research. This particular "unwieldy hodgepodge of laws and regulations"[296] reflects history's piecemeal treatment of privacy and confidentiality issues in the health sector generally.[297] Chapter 6, Health Information: Confidentiality and Access, has addressed the panoply of instruments of which researchers and REBs must take heed when discharging their legal and ethical responsibilities and will not be further explained in any detail here. As demonstrated in that chapter, the applicability of such instruments to the proposed research may depend on many factors, some of which include: the type of personal information to be collected, used, or disclosed in the research; the nature of the research institution involved in the research (*e.g.*, public or private); the presence of research funding from certain granting agencies (*e.g.*, CIHR); whether the research constitutes a commercial activity; and the geographic location where the research is being carried out.

The TCPS[298] and the *GCP Guidelines*[299] include respect for privacy and confidentiality in their guiding principles. The latter instrument directs that applicable regulatory requirements regarding privacy and confidentiality are to be met but provides scant guidance on how these interests are to be protected. In contrast, the TCPS has a section on privacy and confidentiality[300] that addresses matters such as the use of "identifiable personal information"[301] in records collected for a purpose other than the research at issue (*i.e.*, secondary use of data)[302] and data linkage studies[303] that are now blossoming as society becomes ensconced in the electronic era. Additionally, several other parts of the TCPS are sprinkled with relevant substantive rules such as the sections dealing with genetic research[304] (including banking of human genetic material[305]) and the use of human tissue more broadly.[306]

In 2005, CIHR released a document entitled *CIHR Best Practices for Protecting Privacy in Health Research*[307] ("Best Practices") that was intended to provide guidance for health researchers and REBs on substantive matters relating to research involving personal information. According to CIHR, this document is "intended as voluntary guidance for the health research

---

[296] Patricia Kosseim, "The Landscape of Rules Governing Access to Personal Information for Health Research: A View from Afar" (2003) Health L.J. (Special Edition) 113 at 115.
[297] *Ibid.*
[298] TCPS, Introduction, at i5.
[299] *GCP Guidelines*, s. 2.11.
[300] TCPS, s. 3.
[301] This term is defined as "information relating to a reasonably identifiable person who has a reasonable expectation of privacy" and includes "information about personal characteristics such as culture, age, religion and social status, as well as their life experience and educational, medical or employment histories" (Section 3 at 3.2).
[302] TCPS, arts. 3.3, 3.4, and 3.5.
[303] *Ibid.*, art. 3.6.
[304] *Ibid.*, s. 8.
[305] *Ibid.*, art. 8.6 and corresponding commentary.
[306] *Ibid.*, s. 10.
[307] CIHR, *CIHR Best Practices for Protecting Privacy in Health Research* (Ottawa: Public Works and Government Services Canada, 2005).

community",[308] yet it also indicates that the practices "are based on and are consistent with the TCPS, and they are designed to assist in the interpretation of the TCPS by offering additional detail and practicality".[309] If the document is to be used to determine what various TCPS provisions actually mean, it is difficult to grasp how compliance could be viewed as voluntary for those members of the research community who are obligated to adhere to the TCPS by virtue of having entered into a contractual agreement with CIHR (or some other funding body) that requires compliance with the TCPS.

The Best Practices are organized around 10 elements:

1. determining the research objectives and justifying the data needed to fulfill these objectives;
2. limiting the collection of personal data;
3. determining if consent from individuals is required;
4. managing and documenting consent;
5. informing prospective research subjects about the research;
6. recruiting prospective research subjects;
7. safeguarding personal data;
8. controlling access and disclosure of personal data;
9. setting reasonable limits on retention of personal data; and
10. ensuring accountability and transparency in the management of personal data.

Importantly, the Best Practices delineate researchers' and REBs' privacy-related responsibilities. For researchers, these responsibilities include, among other things, "being aware of all applicable policies and laws in the jurisdictions in which the research is conducted and conducting their research in accordance with such requirements".[310] REBs' responsibilities involve, but are not limited to, "reviewing any proposed and ongoing research involving humans in accordance with the TCPS and its principles, as well as other applicable laws and policies, including: ... federal, provincial and territorial legislation; and relevant laws, regulations, policies and/or research contexts of other countries, when research is to be conducted in those countries".[311] The sheer breadth and complexity of the potentially relevant regulatory instruments outlined in Chapter 6, Health Information: Confidentiality and Access, gives some idea of how tall an order this really is, particularly for already resource-strapped REBs. While REBs may find some assistance in the REB member "knowledgeable in the relevant law",[312] it is critical to remember that this person's role is merely to "alert REBs to legal issues and their implications, not to provide formal legal opinions nor to serve as legal counsel for the REB".[313] So, for example, she may inform her fellow REB members that there is an issue surrounding the possible application of the federal

---

[308] *Ibid.*, at 18.
[309] *Ibid.*, at 18.
[310] *Ibid.*, at 88.
[311] *Ibid.*, at 89.
[312] TCPS, art. 1.3(c).
[313] *Ibid.*, commentary under art. 1.3.

Personal Information Protection and Electronic Documents Act[314] to the research project at hand and that, if it applies, there is some issue regarding whether the research proposal is consistent with the Act's consent provisions. However, it is beyond the scope of her responsibilities to actually resolve these and like issues.

Although the Best Practices document can aid in the interpretation of the TCPS, it is of limited value in traversing the maze of privacy law. This is because adherence to the document does not necessarily ensure compliance with other relevant regulatory instruments. On this point, the document states in boldface type: "These Privacy Best Practices do not replace existing laws, policies and professional codes of conduct that apply to certain types of personal information, designated organizations and/or specific kinds of activity. Researchers, REBs and institutions should be aware of, and continue to comply with, the relevant laws, policies and codes, including the TCPS, that govern research in their respective jurisdictions."[315] Tables of concordance containing references to some Canadian privacy legislation are appended to the document;[316] however, CIHR notes that they are to "only be used as preliminary guidance"[317] and then advises: "The application of the legal provisions in the tables to a particular research project must be determined in consultation with a legal advisor."[318] It remains to be seen whether REBs and researchers will take it upon themselves to seek independent legal advice respecting such issues.

3. Conflicts of Interest Involving Researchers

The presence of a conflict of interest in the research setting can severely compromise the integrity and effectiveness of the Canadian governance regime by undermining the trust relationship between researchers and research participants, research sponsors, research institutions, and the public. Although the existence of such conflicts is not confined to biomedical research, "the special value placed on health, and the special trust placed in universities make health care centres and universities particularly vulnerable to public scrutiny and accountability".[319] Thompson defines a conflict of interest as "a set of conditions in which professional judgment concerning a primary interest (such as a patient's welfare or the validity of research) tends to be unduly influenced by a secondary interest (such as financial gain)".[320] As discussed in Part II, the

---

[314] *Personal Information Protection and Electronic Documents Act*, S.C. 2000, c. 5.

[315] CIHR, *CIHR Best Practices for Protecting Privacy in Health Research* (Ottawa: Public Works and Government Services Canada, 2005), at 18.

[316] *Ibid.*, Appendix A-7 at 114.

[317] *Ibid.*, at 21.

[318] *Ibid.*

[319] Kathleen Cranley Glass & Trudo Lemmens, "Conflict of Interest and Commercialization of Biomedical Research: What is the Role of Research Ethics Review?" in Timothy Caulfield & Bryn Williams-Jones, eds., *The Commercialization of Genetic Research: Ethical, Legal and Policy Issues* (New York: Kluwer Academic/Plenum Publishers, 1999) 79 at 79.

[320] Dennis F. Thompson, "Understanding Financial Conflicts of Interest" (1993) 329 New Eng. J. Med. 573 at 573. This definition has been quoted with approval by numerous authors. For

primary interest of all researchers "should be valid answers to research questions, since scientific progress which contributes to improved health care is the final goal of research".[321] Where the researchers "are also treating physicians, the well-being of individual patients is a concurrent primary interest."[322] Secondary interests of researchers may include, among others: career advancement through the publication of study results in reputable journals; peer recognition; pleasing research sponsors; financial gain arising from funding acquisition, honoraria, subsidized overhead, and patents; satisfaction of intellectual curiosity; and scientific development.[323]

The interests of research participants and researchers can coincide or conflict.[324] The expanding body of literature devoted to exposing the negative impacts of the commercialization of biomedical research on researchers' design and conduct of studies as well as study results, offers a bountiful supply of examples of clashing interests.[325] In order to meet the demand for participants for clinical drug trials, sponsoring companies have used participant recruitment strategies such as the payment of handsome recruitment fees to researchers, researcher recruitment bonuses, competitive enrolment schemes, and completion fees for retaining participants in the study. These practices have been criticized for encouraging researchers not to strictly apply inclusion and exclusion criteria, for causing them to put pressure on people to agree to participate and not to withdraw from the study, and for encouraging them to deviate from informed consent standards.[326]

---

examples, see: Kathleen Cranley Glass & Trudo Lemmens, *ibid.*, at 83; Sheldon Krimsky, "The Ethical and Legal Foundations of Scientific 'Conflict of Interest'" in Trudo Lemmens & Duff R. Waring, eds., *Law and Ethics in Biomedical Research: Regulation, Conflict of Interest and Liability* (Toronto: University of Toronto Press, 2006) 63 at 63; Lorraine E. Ferris & C. David Naylor, "Promoting Integrity in Industry-Sponsored Clinical Drug Trials: Conflict of Interest Issues for Canadian Health Sciences Centres" in Trudo Lemmens and Duff R. Waring, eds., *Law and Ethics in Biomedical Research: Regulation, Conflict of Interest and Liability* (Toronto: University of Toronto Press, 2006) 95 at 96.

[321] Kathleen Cranley Glass & Trudo Lemmens, *ibid.*, at 86.

[322] *Ibid.*

[323] *Ibid.*, at 86-87.

[324] Gerald S. Schatz, "Are the Rationale and Regulatory System for Protecting Human Subjects of Biomedical and Behavioral Research Obsolete and Unworkable, or Ethically Important but Inconvenient and Inadequately Enforced?" (2003-2004) 20 Journal of Contemporary Health Law and Policy 1 at 17. The potential for conflicting interests is well described in Kathleen Cranley Glass & Trudo Lemmens, *ibid.*

[325] See Jonathan Kimmelman, Francoise Baylis & Kathleen Cranley Glass, "Stem Cell Trials: Lessons from Gene Transfer Research" (2006) 36:1 Hastings Center Report 23-26, and Kathleen Cranley Glass & Trudo Lemmens, *ibid.*

[326] Timothy Caulfield, "Legal and Ethical Issues Associated with Patient Recruitment in Clinical Trials: The Case of Competitive Enrolment" (2005) 13:2&3 Health L. Rev. 58-61; Lorraine E. Ferris & C. David Naylor, "Promoting Integrity in Industry-Sponsored Clinical Drug Trials: Conflict of Interest Issues for Canadian Health Sciences Centres" in Trudo Lemmens and Duff R. Waring, eds., *Law and Ethics in Biomedical Research: Regulation, Conflict of Interest and Liability* (Toronto: University of Toronto Press, 2006) 95 at 96; Trudo Lemmens & Paul B. Miller, "The Human Subjects Trade: Ethical and Legal Issues Surrounding Recruitment Incentives" (2003) 31 J. L. Med. & Ethics 398; Timothy Caulfield & Glenn Griener, "Conflicts

The circumstances in which Dr. Nancy Olivieri found herself illustrate how conflicts of interest problems can creep into research projects.[327] During the course of a clinical trial that was being conducted by Olivieri and others in order to evaluate the use of a drug in treating persons with a blood disorder, Olivieri became concerned about evidence that, in her opinion, pointed to the toxicity of the study drug and to its loss of efficacy. She told the commercial sponsor (Apotex Research Inc.) and the REB affiliated with her hospital about these issues. The REB instructed Olivieri to, among other things, inform participants about these concerns but Apotex, who disagreed with the validity of Olivieri's concerns, responded by terminating the trial at Olivieri's study site and by threatening to vigorously pursue all legal remedies against her if she breached a confidentiality agreement she had entered into with the sponsor.[328] Although Olivieri ultimately decided to disclose her concerns to the participants, the powerful interest she had in complying with the confidentiality agreement (and not being mired in a protracted, costly legal battle) plainly conflicted with the safety and well-being of the participants.[329]

Canada does not have a legislative scheme to deal with conflicts of interests involving biomedical researchers. The *Clinical Trial Regulations*[330] (and the *GCP Guidelines*[331]) are almost entirely silent on the issue of conflicts of interest. REBs and researchers that govern their affairs according to the TCPS are given some direction on this issue. Section 4 of the TCPS is committed to the topic of conflicts of interest. Article 4.1 requires researchers to "disclose actual, perceived or potential conflicts of interest to the REB" and advises REBs to

---

of Interest in Clinical Research: Addressing the Issue of Physician Remuneration" (2002) 30 J. L. Med. & Ethics 305; and P. Saradhi Puttagunta, Timothy A. Caulfield & Glenn Griener, "Conflicts of Interest in Clinical Research: Direct Payment to the Investigators for Finding Human Subjects and Health Information" (2002) 10:2 Health L. Rev. 30.

[327] For a thorough description and an excellent analysis of the Olivieri case, see Jocelyn Downie, Patricia Baird & Jon Thompson, "Industry and the Academy: Conflicts of Interest in Contemporary Health Research (2002) 10 Health L.J. 103.

[328] A letter to Olivieri from Dr. Michael Spino, Vice President of Scientific Affairs, Apotex Research Inc., reads in part:

As you now [*sic*], paragraph 7 of the [research contract] provides that all information whether written or not, obtained or generated by you during the term of the [contract] and for a period of three years thereafter, shall be and remain secret and confidential and shall not be disclosed in any manner to any third party except with the prior written consent of Apotex. Please be aware that Apotex will take all possible steps to ensure that these obligations of confidentiality are met and will vigorously pursue all legal remedies in the event that there is any breach of these obligations.

This excerpt is set out in Robert A. Phillips & John Hoey, "Constraints of interest: lessons at the Hospital for Sick Children" (1998) 159 C.M.A.J. 955 at 955.

[329] Jon Thompson, Patricia Baird & Jocelyn Downie, *The Olivieri Report: The Complete Text of the Report of the Independent Inquiry Commissioned by the Canadian Association of University Teachers* (Toronto: James Lorimer & Co., 2001).

[330] *Clinical Trial Regulations*, s. C.05.001.

[331] *GCP Guidelines*, s. 3.2.1.

develop mechanisms to "address and resolve" such conflicts.[332] Commentary
under the article "suggests" that the presence or absence of a conflict of interest
can be determined by asking "whether an outside observer would question the
ability of the individual to make a proper decision despite possible considerations
of private or personal interests"[333] or alternatively, "whether the public would
believe that the trust relationship between the relevant parties could reasonably
be maintained if they had accurate information on the potential sources of
conflict of interest".[334]

An REB, in conducting its ethics review of proposed or ongoing research, is
required to assess whether the researcher has a conflict of interest and, if so, to
decide what action, if any, is needed to address the situation. In order to properly
discharge this responsibility, the REB must acquire adequate knowledge about
the research project. The information that will often be required includes, among
other things, details about the nature of any financial or other relationship
between the sponsor and the researcher (*e.g.*, the existence of *per capita*
payments[335]) details about the research budget, the presence of any potential
commercial interests of the researcher,[336] and the nature of the relationship
between the researcher and the research participants. Only if it is in possession
of this type of information can the REB properly decide whether a potential
concern exists.

If the REB concludes that a conflict exists, the REB will next need to decide
how to deal with this situation. Once again, the TCPS relies on the "proportionate
approach" to set out a number of possible REB dispositions, including requiring
the researcher to disclose this conflict to prospective participants during the free
and informed consent process if the conflict is "significant",[337] or compelling the
researcher to abandon one of the conflicting interests if the conflict "is so
pervasive that it is not enough merely to disclose it to the research subjects" and
others.[338] The REB may also do nothing where the conflict does not warrant
specific action.[339] Regrettably, the TCPS provides little guidance on when a
conflict can be regarded as significant or when it is sufficiently insignificant to
justify doing nothing. At least one author contends that the concept of autonomy
and legal disclosure standards demand complete disclosure of a conflict of
interest in every case.[340]

[332] TCPS, art. 4.1.
[333] *Ibid.*, s. 4A.
[334] *Ibid.*
[335] These are fixed sum payments researchers may receive from the research sponsor for the recruitment of each research participant. *Per capita* payments are addressed in the commentary under arts. 7.2 and 7.3 of the TCPS.
[336] TCPS, s. 4A.
[337] *Ibid.* As well, art. 2.4(e) also directly speaks to the disclosure obligation in the context of conflict of interests.
[338] *Ibid.*, s. 4A.
[339] *Ibid.*
[340] David T. Marshall, *The Law of Human Experimentation* (Markham, ON: Butterworths, 2000) at 106.

V. CIVIL LIABILITY FOR PERSONAL INJURIES SUSTAINED BY RESEARCH PARTICIPANTS

Researchers, REBs, research institutions, and others[341] may be exposed to legal liability for personal injuries sustained by individuals as a result of their participation in research studies. Thomson, a preeminent Canadian practitioner in pharmaceutical and health law, has recently predicted an increased likelihood of litigation in Canada in connection with adverse events from clinical trials and other research activities.[342] Legal actions are most likely to sound in the torts of negligence and/or battery, although other causes of action may be pleaded.[343] The elements of a negligence action have been detailed in Chapter 3, Medical Negligence. In sum, a negligence action is made out by a plaintiff on establishing that the defendant owed them a legal duty of care, that the defendant breached the duty by not meeting the requisite standard of care, and that the defendant's failure to meet the standard of care caused the plaintiff to suffer legally recognized damage. A battery action involves a "direct, intentional, and physical interference with the person of another that is either harmful or offensive to a reasonable person".[344]

There is little doubt that researchers owe a duty of care to the individuals that they enroll in their studies.[345] Their liability in negligence will most likely hinge on whether they met the applicable standard of care, which would likely require researchers to exercise the care and skill of a "reasonable researcher" under similar circumstances[346] in designing and conducting the study, including the provision of proper care during any medical intervention. Additionally, respecting informed consent, researchers must meet the applicable disclosure standard as discussed earlier in this chapter or risk being held negligent if the "court is satisfied that a reasonable person in the research subject's position would probably not have agreed to participate in the research if full disclosure of information had been made"[347] (*i.e.*, the causal element of a negligence action). As previously stated, it is

---

[341] Others that may be included in such lawsuits include research staff that are employed by researchers and research sponsors, including the Crown. For a detailed examination of Crown liability, see Sana Halwani, "Her Majesty's Research Subjects: Liability of the Crown in Research Involving Humans" in Trudo Lemmens and Duff R. Waring, eds., *Law and Ethics in Biomedical Research: Regulation, Conflict of Interest and Liability* (Toronto: University of Toronto Press, 2006) 228. A discussion of liability of sponsors in general can be found in Mary M. Thomson, "Bringing Research into Therapy: Liability Anyone?" in Trudo Lemmens and Duff R. Waring, eds., *Law and Ethics in Biomedical Research: Regulation, Conflict of Interest and Liability* (Toronto: University of Toronto Press, 2006) 183 at 195-96.

[342] Mary M. Thomson, *ibid.*, at 185.

[343] Such actions include breach of contract. See Mary M. Thomson, *ibid.*, at 185.

[344] Philip H. Osborne, *The Law of Torts*, 2nd ed. (Toronto: Irwin Law, 2003) at 226.

[345] Susan Zimmerman, "Translating Ethics into Law: Duties of Care in Health Research Involving Humans" (2005) 13:283 Health L. Rev. 13 at 15.

[346] David T. Marshall, *The Law of Human Experimentation* (Markham, ON: Butterworths, 2000) at 46; and Medical Research Council of Canada ("MRC"), *Report of the Working Group on Liability* (Ottawa: MRC, undated) at 7.

[347] Gerald B. Robertson, "Report on Liability in Research" (Ottawa: MRC, 2000) at 17.

generally accepted that extra-legal documents that speak to ethical research norms such as the TCPS, *GCP Guidelines*, or *Declaration of Helsinki*,[348] though not binding on the courts, may well be used in negligence actions to define the legal standards against which researchers will be measured.[349]

Weiss is illustrative of the care and skill that must be exercised in the design and conduct of a study. The court in that case determined that the participant's heart condition (hypertrophic cardiomyopathy) should have excluded his involvement in the study, or at least required careful monitoring if he were permitted to participate. This obligated the researchers to screen prospective participants for the presence of the condition, which they failed to do. Interestingly, in making this finding, the court did not reference any standard of the profession on the issue of screening for cardiac disease.[350]

Researchers could also be exposed to a battery action if they undertake a medical intervention on a participant on the basis of a consent that is legally vitiated because it was not given voluntarily or the person lacked decisional capacity.[351] A researcher's reliance on a non-mature minor's consent to a blood draw for the purpose of a genetic study is an example of the latter situation. The former is exemplified by a situation where a researcher/treating physician coerced a competent adult's consent to a blood draw by implying that the person would not receive the medical care they would otherwise be entitled to if they did not agree to participate in the genetic study.

Researchers may be tempted to shield themselves from lawsuits by seeking liability waivers from participants. However, the TCPS and the *GCP Guidelines* specify that the consent process cannot contain oral or written statements to the effect that participants are waiving any legal rights[352] or are releasing the researcher or others from liability for negligence.[353]

REB members can also be held directly liable for damage sustained by research participants. Since the REB itself does not have legal personality,[354] plaintiffs would be required to commence proceedings against each of its

---

[348] Recall the earlier discussion regarding the *Weiss* court's use of this instrument when establishing the applicable disclosure standard. See section IV.B.1.a of this chapter.

[349] Angela Campbell & Kathleen Cranley Glass, "The Legal Status of Clinical and Ethics Policies, Codes, and Guidelines in Medical Practice and Research" (2001) 46 McGill L.J. 473 at 480; Mary M. Thomson, "Bringing Research into Therapy: Liability Anyone?" in Trudo Lemmens and Duff R. Waring, eds., *Law and Ethics in Biomedical Research: Regulation, Conflict of Interest and Liability* (Toronto: University of Toronto Press, 2006) 183 at 187; Medical Research Council of Canada ("MRC"), *Report of the Working Group on Liability* (Ottawa: MRC, undated) at 7; Susan Zimmerman, "Translating Ethics into Law: Duties of Care in Health Research Involving Humans" (2005) 13:2&3 Health L. Rev. 13 at 17.

[350] Kathleen Cranley Glass & Benjamin Freedman, "Legal Liability for Injury to Research Subjects" (1991) 14 Clinical and Investigative Medicine 176 at 178.

[351] This is in contrast to an action based on a lack of informed consent, which according to the law must be framed in negligence not battery. See *Ciarlariello v. Schacter*, [1993] S.C.J. No. 46, [1993] 2 S.C.R. 119 at 132, 100 D.L.R. (4th) 609 (S.C.C.), and *Reibl v. Hughes*, [1980] S.C.J. No. 105, [1980] 2 S.C.R. 880, 114 D.L.R. (3d) 1 at 11 (S.C.C.).

[352] TCPS, commentary under article 2.4.

[353] *GCP Guidelines*, section 4.8.4.

[354] Gerald B. Robertson, "Report on Liability in Research" (Ottawa: MRC, 2000) at 30.

individual members and not the board as a collective. Legal action is likely to be cast in terms of the negligent performance of their mandate as members of the REB. Since REB members are charged with protecting the rights, safety, and well-being of research participants, the existence of a duty of care would unquestionably follow.[355] Individuals serving on the REB are likely to be held to the standard of care of a "reasonable REB member" holding the same expertise, thereby allowing for the possibility that members possessing greater expertise in a relevant area (*e.g.*, law, ethics, and medicine) will be held to a higher standard than other board members (*e.g.*, community members).[356] A breach of the standard of care might be alleged to have occurred if, for example, the REB member approves an informed consent form that does not adequately inform participants of a risk of harm[357] or approves a protocol that does not provide for adequate safeguards during the research,[358] including screening mechanisms for possible contraindications to their participation.[359] As outlined above, under the TCPS, REBs are responsible for ensuring that ongoing research studies have an appropriate continuing ethics review process, the rigour of which is to be proportionate to the risk of harm that attends the study. In view of the limited amount of ethics oversight that is taking place for ongoing research, this may be another area in which REB members are at legal peril.[360] The TCPS would be just as relevant in defining the legal standard of care for REB members as it would for researchers,[361] a daunting prospect given the myriad of obligations it rests on REB members' shoulders.

Research institutions, including universities and hospitals, may be directly or vicariously liable for a research participant's injuries. Direct liability may be occasioned where the institution has itself acted negligently. As is the case for researchers and REB members, it is accepted that research institutions owe a duty of care to participants and that, in connection with establishing the standard of care, the "reasonable research institution" yardstick would be utilized by the courts. To meet this standard, research institutions would, at a minimum, need "to take reasonable care to hire competent researchers, to have adequate research

---

[355] Mary M. Thomson, "Bringing Research into Therapy: Liability Anyone?" in Trudo Lemmens and Duff R. Waring, eds., *Law and Ethics in Biomedical Research: Regulation, Conflict of Interest and Liability* (Toronto: University of Toronto Press, 2006) 183 at 198.

[356] Linda M. Bordas, "Tort Liability of Institutional Review Boards" (1984-85) 87 W. Va. L. Rev. 137 at 148; and B. Robertson, "Report on Liability in Research" (Ottawa: MRC, 2000) at 30.

[357] Linda M. Bordas, *ibid.*, at 143; Jennifer L. Gold, "Watching the Watchdogs: Negligence, Liability, and Research Ethics Boards" (2003) 11 Health L.J. 153 at 161-71; and Ruth Scheuer, "Research in the Hospital Setting on Human Subjects: Protecting the Patient and the Institution" (1993) 60 Mount Sinai J. Med. 391 at 394.

[358] Ruth Scheuer, *ibid.*

[359] Jennifer L. Gold, "Watching the Watchdogs: Negligence, Liability, and Research Ethics Boards" (2003) 11 Health L.J. 153 at 161-71.

[360] Mary M. Thomson, "Bringing Research into Therapy: Liability Anyone?" in Trudo Lemmens and Duff R. Waring, eds., *Law and Ethics in Biomedical Research: Regulation, Conflict of Interest and Liability* (Toronto: University of Toronto Press, 2006) 183 at 199; and Linda M. Bordas, "Tort Liability of Institutional Review Boards" (1984-85) 87 W. Va. L. Rev. 137 at 146.

[361] Gerald B. Robertson, "Report on Liability in Research" (Ottawa: MRC, 2000) at 34.

facilities, to appoint competent people to its REB, and (through its REB) to conduct protocol reviews according to Canadian and international codes and guidelines governing such research".[362] In *Weiss*, the defendant hospital was liable, through its REB,[363] for the inadequate review of the ophthalmic drops research protocol and consent forms and for not having a defibrillator on hand. Research institutions could also be held vicariously liable for tortuous acts or omissions of researchers, despite not having engaged in any wrongdoing itself. The nature of the employment relationship for many university faculty members and hospital staff will satisfy the test for vicarious liability, thus making their institutions potentially liable for injuries sustained by participants in their studies. Although the situation is less clear with physician-researchers who have merely been granted privileges by their host hospitals because they are generally considered to be independent contractors and not employees of the hospital, one commentator has opined that hospitals may nonetheless be vicariously liable for physicians conducting research within the hospital.[364]

VI. CONCLUSION

Canada's regulatory framework for human biomedical research is marred by complexity and inefficiency. As this chapter has demonstrated, what, if any, regulatory instruments apply to a given study depends on a great many variables: the particular country or countries, province or provinces, and institution or institutions that will host the research; the type of research being conducted; the professional and institutional affiliations of the researchers; the age and mental status of the participants; the type of information and material collected from or about the participants; and the funding sources for the research. The confusion and frustration biomedical research stakeholders experience when attempting to navigate the current regulatory regime is not difficult to appreciate. REB members find the multiplicity of regulatory instruments to be "extremely confusing"[365] and, worse yet, others are simply unaware of all the major standards.[366] There is certainly no reason to assume researchers are faring any

---

[362] *Ibid.*, at 33.

[363] The court did not discuss the specific rational for holding the hospital liable for the actions of the REB. There are speculations that it was because the REB members were appointed by the hospital in furtherance of its legislative obligation regarding research. See Kathleen Cranley Glass & Benjamin Freedman, "Legal Liability for Injury to Research Subjects" (1991) 14 Clinical and Investigative Medicine 176 at 179.

[364] Gerald B. Robertson, "Report on Liability in Research" (Ottawa: MRC, 2000) at 33; Medical Research Council of Canada ("MRC"), *Report of the Working Group on Liability* (Ottawa: MRC, undated) at 28.

[365] Brenda Beagan, "Ethics Review for Human Subjects Research: Interviews With Members of Research Ethics Boards and National Organizations" in M. McDonald, ed., *The Governance of Health Research Involving Human Subjects* (Ottawa: Law Commission of Canada, 2000) 173 at 229.

[366] Jocelyn Downie & Fiona McDonald, "Revisioning the Oversight of Research Involving Humans in Canada" (2004) 12 Health L.J. 159.

better. This state of affairs is particularly troublesome given that the rights and wellbeing of research participants and the credibility of the research governance system hang in the balance. Observing that much would be gained from the revision and harmonization of the current system, commentators are increasingly calling for an effective, efficient, accountable, and fair national[367] or provincial[368] regulatory framework that encompasses all health research involving humans.

[367] Jocelyn Downie, "The Canadian Agency for the Oversight of Research Involving Humans: A Reform Proposal" (2006) 13 Accountability in Research 75; Jocelyn Downie, "Contemporary Health Research: A Cautionary Tale" (2003) Health L.J. (Special Edition) 1 at 8; and Kathleen Cranley Glass, "Questions and Challenges in the Governance of Research Involving Humans: A Canadian Perspective" in Trudo Lemmens and Duff R. Waring, eds., *Law and Ethics in Biomedical Research: Regulation, Conflict of Interest and Liability* (Toronto: University of Toronto Press, 2006) 35 at 44.

[368] Daryl Pullman, "Research Governance, Bio-politics and Political Will: Recent Lessons from Newfoundland and Labrador" (2005) 13:2&3 Health L. Rev. 75-79.

Chapter 8

REGULATION OF PHARMACEUTICALS IN CANADA

Trudo Lemmens and Ron A. Bouchard*

I. INTRODUCTION

Pharmaceutical products occupy an increasingly important place in the provision of health care, particularly in an industrialized country such as Canada. More than 22,000 pharmaceutical products are currently available on the Canadian market,[1] and the number continues to grow. In 2005, for example, 63 new drugs were submitted for evaluation to Health Canada, in addition to 227 new uses or new formulations and 139 new generic drugs.[2] Consumption of pharmaceuticals has increased exponentially. Although many pharmaceutical products are an essential component of patient care for a multitude of diseases and conditions, this increased consumption raises concerns with respect to increased costs as well as potential public health implications.

Even though the provincial health care plans in Canada only provide limited coverage[3] for pharmaceuticals, public spending on drug products has risen

* Research for this chapter was funded by Genome Canada through the Ontario Genomics Institute, by Génome Québec, the Ministère du Développement Économique et Régional et de la Recherche du Québec and the Ontario Cancer Research Network, as part of the ARCTIC project. Ron A. Bouchard was also funded by a CIHR Health Law & Policy Program grant and by the Lupina Foundation Comparative Program in Health & Society at the Munk Centre for International Studies in Toronto. During the writing of this chapter, Trudo Lemmens was a fellow of the Royal Flemish Academy of Belgium for Science and the Arts and a visiting Professor at the K.U. Leuven. We thank Leigh Harrison-Wilson for invaluable assistance with footnotes and tracking down sources under a substantial time constraint, and Professor Joel Lexchin for providing comments on an earlier draft.

[1] Health Canada, "Access to Therapeutic Products: The Regulatory Process in Canada", online: <http://www.hc-sc.gc.ca/ahc-asc/pubs/hpfb-dgpsa/access-therapeutic_acces-therapeutique_e.html> at 3.

[2] *Ibid.*, at 12.

[3] The percentage of coverage has risen from 15 to 39 per cent in Canada over the past 25 years. See Robyn Tamblyn, "Evidence-Based Utilization of Prescription Drugs: Challenges and Directions for the Future in Canada", online: <http://www.irpp.org/events/archive/sep02/tamblyn.pdf>.

enormously. As a result, whether and to what extent pharmaceuticals ought to be covered by private and public health plans has become a primary concern in Canadian health care policy debates. Indeed, the fastest rising component of total health care spending in Canada is represented by prescription drugs. Total drug expenditures were $4 billion, $10 billion and $18 billion in 1985, 1995 and 2002.[4] *Per capita* drug expenditures were $150, $350 and $600 for the same fiscal years. In the period between June 2004 and June 2005 a total of 378 million prescriptions were filled in Canada.[5] Expenditures on pharmaceutical products are increasing faster and more substantially than all other expenses within the Canadian health care system,[6] with an average growth rate of 9.7 per cent during the period 1985–2002 compared with 6.4 per cent for total health spending. According to OECD data,[7] by 2002 Canada ranked third in the world in *per capita* drug expenditures, behind only the United States and France. A similar pattern emerges in the United States,[8] where just under 50 per cent of Americans use at least one drug prescription drug *daily* and carry on average 11 different prescriptions per year. In 2001 alone, Americans held 3.1 billion prescriptions worth an estimated U.S. $132 billion. The projected cost of prescription drugs is estimated to be approximately U.S. $415 billion by 2014. Thus, the market for pharmaceuticals in North America is substantial and growing.[9]

Increased consumption of pharmaceutical products is associated with a high number of adverse events. A recent study of the cause of emergency department visits in 67 representative US hospitals came to the conclusion that adverse drug

[4] Canadian Institute for Health Information, "Drug Expenditure in Canada", Canadian Institute for Health Information, online: <http://secure.cihi.ca/cihiweb/dispPage.jsp?cw_page=AR_80_E>.
[5] Government of Canada, "The Canadian Pharmaceutical Industry: April 2002 Innovation Profile", Innovation in Canada, online: <http://innovation.gc.ca/gol/innovation/site.nsf/en/in02587.html>: Industry Canada, "Canadian Pharmceutical Industry Profile", Health Care in Canada online: <http://strategis.ic.gc.ca/epic/internet/inlsg-pdsv.nsf/vwapj/pharmaprofile.pdf/$FILE/pharmaprofile.pdf>; IMS Health, Canadian Drug Stores and Hospitals Purchase Audit 2004; Canadian Institutes of Health Information; IMS Health Compuscript Report 2004.
[6] Canadian Institute for Health Information, "Drug Expenditure in Canada", Canadian Institute for Health Information, online at: <http://secure.cihi.ca/cihiweb/dispPage.jsp?cw_page=AR_80_E>.
[7] *OECD Health Data 2004* (Paris: Organisation for Economic Cooperation and Development and IRDES, 2004).
[8] G. Crister, "One Nation, Under Pills: They can have our meds when they pry them out of our cold, dead hands", *LA Times*, December, 15, 2002.
[9] A recent survey of Fortune 500 firms (*Public Citizen*, "Pharmaceutical Industry Ranks As Most Profitable Industry—Again: Drug Companies Top All Three Measures of Profits in New Fortune 500 Report", April 18, 2002, *Public Citizen*, online: <http://www.citizen.org/pressroom/release.cfm?ID=1088> demonstrated that the return on capital in the pharmaceutical industry has far exceeded that for an index of all Fortune 500 firms since 1970. Median profits as a percent revenue for all firms were approximately 4, 5, 4, and 4 per cent for FYs 1970, 1980, 1990 and 2000 respectively whereas those in the pharmaceutical sector were approximately 9, 10, 14 and 18 per cent for the same years, notwithstanding a potential reduction in research and development times required for drug development from 109 to 71 months (>3 yrs) from FY 1986 to FY 2000: European Generic Medicines Association, "A bitter pill to swallow: myths and realities of the pharmaceutical industry", European Generic Medicines Association Report 2003, online: <http://www.egagenerics.com/doc/ega_myths-reality.pdf>.

events accounted for 2.5 per cent of emergency department visits for all unintentional injuries. The authors of the study estimated that more than 700,000 people per year are treated in an emergency room due to adverse drug effects, or 2.4 individuals per 1,000 population.[10] Similarly, a 1998 meta-analysis of 39 studies of drug-induced side effects concluded that these have become the sixth leading cause of mortality in hospitalized patients.[11] Although many of these deaths are associated with errors in prescription and provision, and notwithstanding the difficulties of interpreting the results of these studies,[12] it is clear that drug consumption comes with significant risks.[13]

Moreover, concerns have been voiced about the influence of financial interests of the pharmaceutical industry on the development, promotion and sale of pharmaceutical products. Industry has increasingly gained control over the various stages between the creation and sale of pharmaceutical products. A host of recent books and scholarly articles sketch a troubling picture of how these interests often negatively impact on medical research, drug development and drug consumption.[14] Several controversies, often involving tragic results for vulnerable populations such as children and adolescents,[15] suggest that private interests have affected the reliability of scientific evidence that is used in the drug approval process and in health care decision-making. They also seem to have led to a downplaying or even hiding of potential safety problems with drug products. Particular concerns have further been expressed over how financial interests contribute to the shaping of diagnostic criteria for various diseases, consumer demand for drug products, and even in the creation of new disease categories.[16]

---

[10] Daniel S. Budnitz, Daniel A. Pollock, Kelly N. Weidenbach *et al.*, "National Surveillance of Emergency Department Visits for Outpatient Adverse Drug Events" (2006) 296 J.A.M.A. 1858.

[11] See J. Lazarou, B.H. Pomeranz & P.N. Corey, "Incidence of Adverse Drug Reactions in Hospitalized Patients: A Meta-Analysis of Prospective Studies" (1998) 279 J.A.M.A. 1200.

[12] See William M. Tierney, "Adverse Outpatient Drug Events — A Problem and an Opportunity" (2003) 348 New Engl. J. Med. 1587.

[13] See for example, Thomas Moore, Bruce Psaty & Curt Furberg, "Time to Act on Drug Safety" (1998) 279 J.A.M.A. 1571.

[14] See United Kingdom, House of Commons Health Committee, *The Influence Of The Pharmaceutical Industry. Fourth Report of Session 2004-2005*, vol. 1, online: <http://www.publications.parliament.uk/pa/cm200405/cmselect/cmhealth/42/42.pdf>; Ray Moynihan & Alan Cassels, *Selling Sickness: How the World's Biggest Pharmaceutical Companies Are Turning Us All Into Patients* (Vancouver: GrayStone Books, 2005); Marcia Angell, *The Truth About the Drug Companies: How They Deceive Us and What To Do About It* (New York: Random House, 2004); Jerome Kassirer, *On the Take: How Medicine's Complicity with Big Business Can Endanger Your Health* (New York: Oxford University Press, 2004); John Abramson, *Overdo$ed America: The Broken Promise of American Medicine* (New York: Harper Collins, 2004); Jay S. Cohen, *Overdose: The Case Against the Drug Companies* (New York: Penguin, 2001); Charles Medawar, *Medicines Out of Control?: Antidepressants and the Conspiracy of Goodwill* (Amsterdam: Aksant Academic Publishers, 2004); Trudo Lemmens, "Leopards in the Temple: Restoring Scientific Integrity to the Commercialized Research Scene" (Winter 2004) 32 J.L. Med. & Ethics 641.

[15] See discussion in section V.A, *infra*.

[16] See the special issues on Disease Mongering in PLoS Medicine 2006: PloS Medicine, "A Collection of Articles on Disease Mongering", Public Library of Science, online: <http://collections.plos.org/plosmedicine/diseasemongering-2006.php>.

As a result, many commentators have called for reform of drug regulation.[17] The growing public-private partnerships in research and drug development and their impact on the regulatory control of pharmaceuticals are in this context the target of much criticism. Ensuring the safety and efficacy of pharmaceuticals in continuously changing health care, research and economic environments has been an increasingly significant challenge for public health. In this chapter, we seek to give a critical overview of various components of this important public health topic. We review the general regulatory framework in which drugs are approved in Canada. We outline the steps required to be taken by pharmaceutical manufacturers to obtain regulatory approval and trace the changing roles of public and private actors in the drug development cycle, using several recent controversies related to pharmaceutical products to illustrate this point. We also describe how drug regulation in Canada is connected to other domestic and international regulatory regimes that relate to various aspects of pharmaceutical product development, medical research and health care. Finally, we review several important new developments involving federal policies that underpin pharmaceutical regulation in Canada, with particular emphasis on the increasing partnership between Canadian policy-makers and corporate interests. Indeed, the larger regulatory landscape surrounding pharmaceuticals is undergoing significant change at this time and it is important to situate this development in the context of the current regulatory regime. In order to appreciate the nature of these policy changes, and to facilitate a critical assessment of their potential impact, we will first give a brief overview of the history of drug regulation. A sketch of the historical context helps to understand the rationale behind drug regulation and to appreciate the important role for regulatory oversight of pharmaceutical product development and marketing.

II. HISTORY OF DRUG REGULATION IN CANADA: THE BIG PICTURE

Concerns about potential side effects and lack of efficacy of pharmaceuticals are nothing new. Since the early days of drug manufacturing, controversies have erupted over the safety and efficacy of drug products. In fact, many of the early drugs were not well regarded by the medical profession. In the late 19th century,

---

[17] For critical analyses of serious safety problems associated with popular drugs, see, *e.g.*, John Abramson, *Overdo$ed America: The Broken Promise of American Medicine* (New York: Harper Collins, 2004); Jay S. Cohen, *Overdose: The Case Against the Drug Companies* (New York: Penguin, 2001). Cohen mentions a list of 10 popular pharmaceuticals that were withdrawn from the market between 1997 and 2001 for safety reasons. Cohen and Abramson also discuss other drugs which raise significant (and not always sufficiently acknowledged) safety concerns for some patients, including popular drugs such as Viagra, cholesterol-lowering drugs and antihypertensive drugs. See Cohen, in particular at 66-128; and Abramson, at 23-38 and 55-71. See also Marcia Angell, *The Truth About the Drug Companies: How They Deceive Us and What To Do About It* (New York: Random House, 2004); Jerome Kassirer, *On the Take: How Medicine's Complicity with Big Business Can Endanger Your Health* (New York: Oxford University Press, 2004).

the dean of Harvard Medical School, Oliver Wendell Holmes, stated bluntly that if all available drugs "could be sunk to the bottom of the sea, it would be all the better for mankind, and the worse for the fishes".[18] The first national statutes enacted at the end of the 19th and the beginning of the 20th century imposed minimum standards for the production of food and drugs in reaction to serious scandals involving public exposure to harmful drug products.[19] The early drug laws of Canada and the United States were inspired by the 1862 United Kingdom *Bill for Preventing Adulteration of Articles of Food and* Drink, which was promulgated following the poisoning of several hundred people after a pharmacist included arsenic in peppermint lozenges.[20] Analogous legislation was enacted in Canada as part of the 1875 *Inland Revenue Act* and the 1884 *Adulteration Act*, the latter of which set standards for strength, quality and purity and rendered the sale or manufacturing of adulterated drugs a criminal offence. The ambit of these early statutes was very limited and focused on the purity of the ingredients. The requirement that ingredients be non-lethal, for example, was only added in the United States in 1937, after more than 100 patients died as a result of taking a sulfanalimide-containing product which had been manufactured with a toxic solvent.[21] At the time, there was no regulatory evaluation of risks and benefits.

It is only with the development of more industrial drug production and when pharmaceuticals started to play a more prominent role in health care that initiatives emerged to organize an independent and systematic analysis of drug safety and efficacy. Due to its larger population, pharmaceutical industrial base and lobbying sector, the United States quickly became the focal point for much discussion of food and drugs regulation. Efforts to independently evaluate pharmaceuticals were first undertaken in the United States by the medical profession. The American Medical Association (AMA) played an important role as an independent evaluator of drug products. The organization set up its own laboratory and only permitted drug advertisements in the Journal of the American Medical Association of products that obtained its seal of approval.[22] Particularly after the Second World War, the AMA conducted detailed analyses

---

[18]   Quoted in Jerry Avorn, *Powerful Medicines: The Benefits, Risks, and Costs of Prescription Drugs* (New York: Alfred A. Knopf, 2004) at 40.

[19]   See, *e.g.*, Jerry Avorn, *ibid.*, at 43-44. See also Philip J. Hilts, *Protecting America's Health: The FDA, Business, and One Hundred Years of Regulation* (New York: Alfred Knopf, 2003), particularly Chapters 3-7; Stephen Ceccoli, "Divergent Paths to Drug Regulation in the United States and the United Kingdom" (2002) 14:2, J. Pol. History 135; and Patricia I. Carter, "Federal Regulation of Pharmaceuticals in the United States and Canada" (1999) 21 Loy. L.A. Int'l & Comp. L. Rev. 215.

[20]   See Patricia I. Carter, *ibid.*, at 216-220. See also Robert E. Curran, *Canada's Food and Drug Laws* (Chicago: Commerce Clearing House, 1953) at 143-45; William Wassenaar, "Drug Regulation in Canada" (1978) 2 L. Med. Q. 209.

[21]   Jerry Avorn, *Powerful Medicines: The Benefits, Risks, and Costs of Prescription Drugs* (New York: Alfred A. Knopf, 2004) at 43.

[22]   See Stephen Ceccoli, "Divergent Paths to Drug Regulation in the United States and the United Kingdom" (2002) 14:2 J. Pol. History 135 at 149; and Philip J. Hilts, *Protecting America's Health: The FDA, Business, and One Hundred Years of Regulation* (New York: Alfred Knopf, 2003).

of drug products and production processes and published report cards in its journal. It is perhaps a forshadowing of later developments in the control of safety and efficacy of pharmaceuticals that the AMA abolished this program in the 1950s because of concerns about losing an increasingly important source of advertising revenue for its journal.[23]

It took yet another major controversy to shake governmental agencies and legislators into more serious action. The impetus for direct governmental control of pharmaceuticals is clearly associated with the Thalidomide disaster, which resulted in the birth of thousands of severely deformed babies in the late 1950s and early 1960s.[24] Thalidomide was introduced in several European countries since 1957 as a sedative and to treat morning sickness in first-stage pregnancy. It was sold for years before the medical community and health agencies realized it was directly related to severe congenital deformations in newborns. In the United States, introduction of the drug had been held up by a medical officer at the Food and Drug Administration who was concerned about the lack of good safety data for the drug.[25] The contrast between the devastating impact of the swift introduction of Thalidomide in Europe, and the beneficial results of delay of its launch in the United States as a result of administrative action by an attentive government official, may very well have been the most important determinant of change to the landscape of drug regulation.[26] The idea of stringent control of pharmaceuticals by a governmental agency came to be seen as a core component of the state's obligation to protect citizens against harm. The United States Congress passed a bill imposing not only safety but also efficacy requirements on new pharmaceuticals.[27] The 1962 Kefauver-Harris amendments to the *Food, Drug, and Cosmetic Act* of 1938[28] had a major impact also in other countries. For the first time, regulatory agencies received the authority to screen out not only lethal but also ineffective drug products. The first monumental task of the drug regulatory agencies was to evaluate drugs already on the market, which took the Food and Drug Administration in the United States more than two decades.[29] It is telling that more than 2,000 products disappeared from the market after this evaluation process, and many others were

---

[23]   Philip J. Hilts, *ibid.*, at 127.

[24]   For a discussion of the impact of Thalidomide on drug regulation, see Jerry Avorn, *Powerful Medicines: The Benefits, Risks, and Costs of Prescription Drugs* (New York: Alfred A. Knopf, 2004) at 43-44; Philip J. Hilts, *ibid.*, at 144-65; Tracey Whitehead, "Pharmacopolitics: Drug Regulation in the United States and Germany" (2005) 18:2 Social History of Medicine 334; Stephen Ceccoli, "Divergent Paths to Drug Regulation in the United States and the United Kingdom" (2002) 14:2 J. Pol. History 135, particularly at 140-41.

[25]   See Stephen Ceccoli, *ibid.*, at 168 footnote 60.

[26]   Jerry Avorn, *Powerful Medicines: The Benefits, Risks, and Costs of Prescription Drugs* (New York: Alfred A. Knopf, 2004) at 44.

[27]   *Ibid.*

[28]   The amendments were passed to ensure drug efficacy and greater drug safety. Drug manufacturers were required for the first time to prove to the USFDA the effectiveness of their products before marketing: Food and Drug Administration, "Milestones in U.S. Food and Drug Law History", FDA Backgrounder, online: <http://www.cfsan.fda.gov/mileston.html>.

[29]   Jerry Avorn, *Powerful Medicines: The Benefits, Risks, and Costs of Prescription Drugs* (New York: Alfred A. Knopf, 2004) at 45.

withdrawn in subsequent years. Similar changes to the Canadian *Food and Drug Act* were made in response to Thalidomide in 1963.[30]

The Thalidomide tragedy highlighted the importance not only of the prior evaluation of the safety and efficacy of a drug, but also of a reporting and registration system for adverse events. The regulatory systems introduced in response understandably focused on preventing market entry of pharmaceutical products in the absence of sufficient evidence of safety and efficacy, as well as on better coordinating the gathering of information on safety and efficacy once a drug was approved and marketed. Industry now had to conduct detailed clinical trials to obtain regulatory approval. The review of clinical trial data and of the product itself by the regulatory agencies was a crucial aspect of the new control system. The barriers to entry thus created led to reasonably lengthy evaluation periods. Delays in the approval of pharmaceutical products were not well received by industry, particularly by brand-name drug companies, because they shortened the most lucrative period for sale. It is not surprising that the pharmaceutical industry pushed hard to obtain shorter review times and decreased administrative requirements for drug approval.[31] Notwithstanding that the purpose of the regulatory approval process was to protect consumers, pressure to shorten the review period grew over time from patient advocacy groups, particularly in the context of the HIV/AIDS crisis.[32] As new medications offered a last hope in the face of the severe and debilitating symptoms of HIV/AIDS, vocal and efficient activism from HIV/AIDS and other patient advocacy groups created additional pressure to create a faster and more "flexible" review system for approval of pharmaceuticals.

This combination of industry lobbying and patient advocacy led to several significant changes in the regulatory system in the 1990s. Most significantly, review times were shortened. The move towards shorter review times was accompanied in North America by a shift in the financial structure of the drug review system. Industry agreed to pay a substantial fee for the review of new pharmaceutical products in exchange for a commitment by the regulatory agencies to meet drug-review performance goals,[33] thereby obtaining significant

---

[30] Patricia I. Carter, "Federal Regulation of Pharmaceuticals in the United States and Canada" (1999) 21 Loy. L.A. Int'l & Comp. L. Rev. 215 at 220.

[31] J. Lexchin, "Transparency in Drug Regulation: Mirage or Oasis", Canadian Centre for Policy Alternatives, online: <http://policyalternatives.ca/index.cfm?act=news&do=Article&call=913&pA =9471C2A&type-57 at 9. See Marcia Angell, *The Truth About the Drug Companies: How They Deceive Us and What To Do About It* (New York: Random House, 2004).

[32] For a discussion of the impact of HIV/AIDS on drug regulation and the organization of clinical trials, see Panel on Monitoring the Social Impact of the AIDS Epidemic, National Research Council, *The Social Impact of AIDS in the United States* (Washington DC: National Academies Press, 1993), particularly Chapter 4, at 80-114. See also Philip J. Hilts, *Protecting America's Health: The FDA, Business, and One Hundred Years of Regulation* (New York: Alfred Knopf, 2003) at 246. For an interesting discussion of the increasingly significant role of the more than 3,000 interest groups in the context of drug regulation, and the impact of patient advocacy on drug regulation, see Daniel P. Carpenter, "The Political Economy of FDA Drug Review: Processing, Politics, and Lessons for Policy" (2004) 23:1 Health Affairs 52.

[33] Philip J. Hilts, *Protecting America's Health: The FDA, Business, and One Hundred Years of Regulation* (New York: Alfred Knopf, 2003) at 280. The Food and Drug Administration

influence over allocation of new resources. As discussed below, a substantial part of the funding for drug review in Canada and the United States now comes from so-called "user fees".[34]

In addition, accelerated review times were introduced for novel drugs that show promise in the treatment of serious and life-threatening diseases. Special or expanded access programs were also established, under which drugs already on the market in other countries can be imported into the country even if national regulatory review has not been finalized.[35] Similarly, efforts were undertaken at the international level to streamline various approval processes and avoid costly and time-consuming differences in standards associated with clinical trials and drug approval, particularly through the International Conference on Harmonization of Good Clinical Practice (ICH-GCP).[36] The ICH-GCP is an international network established by the drug regulatory agencies of Europe, Japan and the United States, in collaboration with pharmaceutical manufacturers' associations.[37] Canada has observer status in this network. Harmonized regulatory guidelines were developed, which were integrated in various regulatory structures. The United States Food and Drug Administration[38] and Health Canada[39] introduced the ICH-GCP as guidance documents in 1997.

---

explicitly recognizes the influence industry has on the allocation of the user fees. See Food and Drug Administration, "White Paper Prescription Drug User Fee Act (PDUFA): Adding Resources and Improving Performance in FDA Review of New Drug Applications", FDA, online: <http://www.fda.gov/oc/pdufa/PDUFAWhitePaper.pdf>; Patricia I. Carter, "Federal Regulation of Pharmaceuticals in the United States and Canada" (1999) 21 Loy. L.A. Int'l & Comp. L. Rev. 215.

[34] In a recent publication, J. Lexchin suggests that up to 70 per cent of the budget for drug review recently came from user fees. See J. Lexchin, "Transparency in Drug Regulation: Mirage or Oasis", Canadian Centre for Policy Alternatives, online: <http://policyalternatives.ca/index.cfm?act=news&do=Article&call=913&pA=94761C2A&type=5>. This figure would, however, now be closer to 45-50 per cent: J. Lexchin, personal communication (October 22, 2006). In the United States, the contribution of user fees to the overall budget for drug review increased from 7 per cent in 1993 to 53 per cent in 2004. See Anna W. Matthews, "Drug Firms Use Financial Clout to Push Industry Agenda at FDA", *Wall Street Journal*, September 1, 2006 at A1.

[35] See section IV, *infra*, for a more detailed discussion.

[36] The ICH was conceived in 1989 at the WHO Conference of Drug Regulatory Authorities (ICDRA) in Paris, at which time the International Federation of Pharmaceutical Manufacturers and Associations (IFPMA) was approached to discuss a joint regulatory-industry initiative on international harmonization, online: <http://www.ich.org/cache/compo/276-254-1.html>.

[37] The governing body of the ICH is known as the steering committee. It has 14 members. The three sponsors (U.S., EU and Japan) have two committee members each from their respective regulatory authorities and two from industry (*i.e.*, the European Federation of Pharmaceutical Industries Association, the Japanese Pharmaceutical Manufacturers Association, and the Pharmaceutical Research and Manufacturers of America). The ICH secretariat is the International Federation of Pharmaceutical Manufacturers Associations, which also has two members on the committee: For review, see: ICH, "Official web site for ICH", online: <www.ich.org>.

[38] (1997) 62 Federal Register 25691.

[39] Health Products and Food Branch, "ICH Guidance E6: Guideline for Good Clinical Practice: Consolidated Guideline", Health Canada, online: <http://www.hc-sc.gc.ca/dhp-mps/prodpharma/applic-demande/guide-ld/ich/efficac/e6_e.html>.

In addition to faster review times, industry also obtained substantial governmental concessions associated with concerns over the impact of regulatory review on patent protection.[40] Various regulatory initiatives were introduced that created linkages between the drug approval process and patent legislation,[41] ensuring, *inter alia*, that the time lost during review could be compensated through patent term extension and other periods of non-patent market exclusivity.

III. FEDERAL, PROVINCIAL, TERRITORIAL RESPONSIBILITIES

A. FEDERAL RESPONSIBILITIES

Pursuant to the *Constitution Act, 1867*,[42] the federal government has jurisdiction over all matters pertaining to intellectual property, drug approval, manufacturing, labelling and pricing, post-market safety and effectiveness, and market competitiveness.[43] Health Canada's Health Products and Foods Branch (HPFB) regulates clinical trials and grants market authorization based on an assessment of the safety, efficacy and quality of drug products. The Therapeutic Products Directorate (TPD) applies the *Food and Drugs Regulations*[44] (FDR) under the authority of the *Food and Drugs Act*[45] (FDA) to ensure pharmaceuticals sold in Canada are safe and effective. In addition to approval of new drugs, the federal government also regulates drug pricing through the Patented Medicines Prices Review Board (PMPRB). Industry Canada is responsible for administering the *Patent Act*[46] and the *Patented Medicines (Notice of Compliance) Regulations*[47] (*NOC Regulations*). The *NOC Regulations* belong to a class of legal instruments referred to as "linkage regulations", which tie patent protection for marketed pharmaceuticals to the domestic drug approval process. As such, the *Patent Act* and *NOC Regulations* control entry of generic drugs into the market and thus access by Canadians to affordably priced medication. Notably, this access is regulated by Industry Canada even though regulatory approval for all drugs is granted by Health Canada.

---

[40] See section VI.F, *infra*, for a more detailed discussion.

[41] Regulatory Impact Analysis Statement, SOR/93-133, C. Gaz. 1993. II. vol. 127, No. 6. 1388.

[42] (U.K.), 30 & 31 Vict., c. 3, online: <http://lois.justice.gc.ca/en/const/index.html>. For review of Canadian and United States food and drugs legislation, see Patricia I. Carter, "Federal Regulation of Pharmaceuticals in the United States and Canada" (1999) 21 Loy. L.A. Int'l & Comp. L. Rev. 215.

[43] Federal/Provincial/Territorial Ministerial Task Force, "National Pharmaceuticals Strategy: Progress Report", Health Canada, online: <http://www.hc-sc.gc.ca/hcs-sss/pubs/care-soins/2006-nps-snpp/index_e.html> at 17; Aslam H. Anis, "Pharmaceutical policies in Canada: another example of federal-provincial discord" (2000) 162:4 C.M.A.J. 523.

[44] C.R.C., c. 870.

[45] R.S.C. 1985, c. F-27.

[46] R.S.C. 1985, c. P-4.

[47] SOR/93-133.

B. PROVINCIAL/TERRITORIAL RESPONSIBILITIES

Regulatory approval does not equate to payment for drugs by provincial payers, as prescriptions for drugs outside of those in hospital are not covered under the *Canada Health Act*.[48] These decisions are made by governments of individual provinces and territories, which have the constitutional responsibility for funding health care services. Each provincial or territorial drug plan sets specific price and other cost-containment guidelines, including mandating cost-effectiveness analyses of new drugs in relation to existing drug products. It has been noted that significant tension between federal and provincial/territorial jurisdictions arises out of the constitutional division of powers as it relates to pharmaceuticals.[49] While the federal government is responsible for regulatory approval of drugs, intellectual property rights pertaining to drugs, market competitiveness, and the policies underpinning these issues, it is primarily the provinces that cover pharmaceutical costs not directly borne by consumers.

IV. REGULATORY APPROVAL OF PHARMACEUTICALS IN CANADA

A. INTRODUCTION

Health Canada is responsible for promoting and preserving the health, safety and well-being of Canadians. Its mission is to prevent and reduce risks to individual health, promote health, ensure high-quality health services that are efficient and accessible, reduce health inequalities and provide health information to help Canadians make informed decisions.[50] Regulatory approval of pharmaceuticals is done under the umbrella of the FDA, FDR, *NOC Regulations* and the *Patent Act*, which together govern the safety, effectiveness, quality and availability of brand-name and generic pharmaceuticals in Canada. The FDA has been held to be *intra vires* the Parliament of Canada[51] under the criminal law and public safety provisions of section 91 of the *Constitution Act, 1867* and under Parliament's residual power to makes laws for the peace, order and good government of Canada. The FDA and FDR are administered by the Therapeutic Products Directorate (TPD) of the HPFB of Health Canada. The *NOC Regulations* and *Patent Act* are administered by Industry Canada. The TPD is the equivalent of the Centre for Drug Evaluation and Research (CDER) of the United States Food and Drug Administration and is responsible for assessing the safety, efficacy and quality of pharmaceuticals and medical devices in a timely manner.

---

48 R.S.C. 1985, c. C-6.

49 Aslam H. Anis, "Pharmaceutical policies in Canada: another example of federal-provincial discord" (2000) 162:4 C.M.A.J. 523.

50 Health Canada, "Mission, Values, Activities", About Health Canada, online: <http://www.hc-sc.gc.ca/ahc-asc/activit/about-apropos/index_e.html>.

51 *Standard Sausage Co. v. Lee*, [1934] 1 D.L.R. 706 (B.C.C.A.); *C.E. Jamieson & Co. (Dominion) Ltd. v. Canada (Attorney General)*, [1987] F.C.J. No. 826, 12 F.T.R. 167 (F.C.T.D.).

The new drug approval process in Canada parallels that in the United States, after which it was modelled.[52] The process in both jurisdictions is divided into four phases: Preclinical Studies, Clinical Trials, New Drug Submission and Marketing. Under section 2 of the FDA, a "drug" is "any substance or mixture of substances manufactured, sold or represented for use in (a) the diagnosis, treatment, mitigation or prevention of a disease, disorder or abnormal physical state, or its symptoms, in human beings or animals, (b) restoring, correcting or modifying organic functions in human beings or animals, or (c) disinfection in premises in which food is manufactured, prepared or kept". Substances regulated by Health Canada as drugs include prescription, non-prescription, brand-name and generic pharmaceuticals, vaccine, recombinant and blood-related biologics, radio-pharmaceuticals, homeopathic, traditional and herbal natural health products, disinfectants and veterinary medications.

B. PRECLINICAL STUDIES

The drug development cycle begins with preclinical studies. Preclinical studies are not regulated by the government. It is up to the applicant manufacturer, or "sponsor", to gather and submit all necessary and sufficient preclinical data to indicate that it is safe to conduct clinical trials on humans. This includes all *in vitro*, *in vivo* and animal model experiments, including animal and/or disease model validation studies, required to verify the safety of a potential drug candidate, its potential therapeutic uses, and, to a limited degree, the existence and extent of its toxic effects in animals.

C. CLINICAL TRIALS

Based on data from preclinical studies, a sponsor makes an application to the TPD for approval to conduct clinical trials in humans. This is done through a Clinical Trial Application[53] (CTA), whereby the applicant manufacturer must satisfy requirements specified under the FDR related to safety, dosage and effectiveness of the drug candidate. The specific requirements for a CTA are defined in Division 5 of the FDR, which prescribes a 30-day default review period for applications. A CTA must be filed prior to the initiation of a clinical trial in Canada. HPFB must review the application and notify the sponsor within 30 days if the application is found to be deficient or else the sponsor may proceed. Sponsors may request a pre-CTA consultation meeting, often in cases involving new active substances or applications entailing complex issues new to Health Canada. Pre-CTA consultations typically involve presentation by the sponsor of relevant data, discussions of concerns regarding drug development and requests for guidance on the acceptability of the proposed clinical trial.

---

[52] Patricia I. Carter, "Federal Regulation of Pharmaceuticals in the United States and Canada" (1999) 21 Loy. L.A. Int'l & Comp. L. Rev. 215 at 230; Robert E Curran, "Canadian regulation of food drugs, cosmetics and devices: An overview" (1975) 30 Food Drug Cosm. L.J. 644 at 648.

[53] Health Canada, "Guidance for Clinical Trial Sponsors: Clinical Trial Applications", online: <http://www.hc-sc.gc.ca/dhp-mps/prodpharma/applic-demande/guide-ld/clini/ctdcta_ctddec_e.html#3>.

Sponsors must file a CTA prior to undertaking any clinical trial that is part of the drug development process. This includes clinical trials involving drug products already marketed where the proposed use of the product is outside the parameters of the approved NOC or Drug Identification Number (DIN), *e.g.*, under conditions where the indication and clinical use, target patient population, route of administration, or dosage regimen differs from the previously approved product. Under the FDR,[54] clinical trials are divided into four categories depending on their size and purpose.[55]

Phase I trials are usually conducted on a small number of healthy volunteers (20 to 80) and are generally the first studies of a new drug in humans. They aim at exploring the general pharmacological and pharmacokinetic properties of a drug: whether the drug is safe overall, what the acute side effects are, and how the drug is absorbed, metabolized and eliminated by the body. About 70 per cent of new drugs pass this first phase. Phase II trials generally involve 100 to 300 patients who suffer from the disease for which the drug under study has been developed. They aim at evaluating the efficacy of the drug in these patients and at determining its common short-term side effects. About one in three compounds of all those that start the process move on to a Phase III trial, which is generally a randomized double blind controlled trial, in which a large number of patients (1,000 to 5,000) receive the drug over a period of up to several years.[56] In this phase, more precise measurements are made of the drug's efficacy and its side effects, including long-term side effects. In this phase, the drug may be studied on specific patient-populations and also be compared to available alternatives to assess its comparative efficacy. Of all drugs entering into Phase III, 70 to 90 per cent are finally approved.

The term Phase IV trial is used for various types of studies performed once a drug has been approved. Phase IV trials can aim at assessing long-term efficacy and safety of the drug, at different ways of administering the drug, and at comparing a drug with other drugs from the same class. Phase IV trials are particularly important to assess the long-term safety of new drugs, particularly classes of new chemical entities that have not been previously tested for long-

---

[54] Health Canada, "Guidance for Clinical Trial Sponsors: Clinical Trial Applications", *ibid.* See also *Regulations Amending the Food and Drug Act Regulations (1024 — Clinical Trials)*, SOR/2001-203; Health Products and Food Branch, "ICH Guidance E6: Guideline for Good Clinical Practice: Consolidated Guideline", Health Canada, online: <http://www.hc-sc.gc.ca/dhp-mps/prodpharma/applic-demande/guide-ld/ich/efficac/e6_e.html>; Health Products and Food Branch, "Guidance for Industry: General Considerations for Clinical Trials, ICH Topic E8", Health Canada, online: <http://www.hc-sc.gc.ca/dhp-mps/prodpharma/applic-demande/guide-ld/ich/efficac/e8_e.html>.

[55] Useful background information on clinical trials can be found at: Carol Rados, "Inside Clinical Trials: Testing Medical Products in People" (2003) 37:5, FDA Consumer Magazine, online: <http://www.fda.gov/fdac/features/2003/503_trial.html>; ClinialTrials.gov, "An Introduction to Clinical Trials", online: <http://www.clinicaltrials.gov/ct/info/resources#Intro>; Thomson CenterWatch, "Background Information on Clinical Research", Patient Resources, online: <http://www.centerwatch.com/patient/backgrnd.html>.

[56] In a double-blinded randomized controlled trial, research subjects are randomly assigned to either a treatment or a control arm (other drug or placebo), whereby neither the patient nor the researcher knows who is distributed to what arm of the trial.

term safety. Unfortunately, some Phase IV studies are merely used as a means to introduce new drugs to a large number of physicians and patients, thus blurring the line between post-approval marketing and research.[57]

Drug approval is based on data from Phases I–III trials. Under section C.05.010 of the FDR, all clinical trials in Canada must be conducted in accordance with the International Conference on Harmonisation Good Clinical Practices (GCP), an international standard for clinical trial practices which aims at implementing ethical principles outlined in the World Medical Association Declaration of Helsinki.[58] Prior to commencement of a Clinical Trial sponsors are required to submit a Clinical Trial Site Information Form.[59]

Under section C.01.016 of the FDR, a sponsor is required to notify Health Canada of any serious, unexpected adverse drug reaction that occurs inside or outside Canada during a clinical trial within 15 days after becoming aware of the information where such reaction is neither fatal nor life-threatening. Where an adverse reaction is fatal or life-threatening, Health Canada must be notified immediately, where possible, or otherwise within seven days after becoming aware of the information. Adverse drug reactions during clinical trials that are both serious and unexpected are subject to expedited reporting to Health Canada. Expedited reporting is not required where reactions are serious but expected or where reactions are deemed unrelated to the study product, even if expected.[60]

Prior to initiation of a clinical trial, the proposed trial protocol and informed consent must be reviewed and approved by a Research Ethics Board (REB). Under the provisions of sections C.05.005 to C.05.012 of the FDR, the sponsor must submit the name of the REB that approved the trial prior to the commencement of the trial and retain a copy of a signed Research Ethics Board Attestation to the effect that the REB carried out its functions in a manner consistent with GCP. The sponsor is also required to submit information pertaining to a refusal of any portion of the proposed protocol by an REB.

The Attestation Form contains only limited information. It basically confirms that the protocol has been reviewed by an REB and informs the regulatory

---

[57] See "Commercialized Medical Research and the Need for Regulatory Reform" in C.M. Flood, ed., *Just Medicare: What's In, What's Out, How We Decide* (Toronto: University of Toronto Press, 2006) at 396.

[58] For the text of the ICH-GCP, see <http://www.hc-sc.gc.ca/dhp-mps/prodpharma/applic-demande/guide-ld/ich/efficac/e6_e.html>; for the Declaration of Helsinki see: <http://www.wma.net/e/policy/b3.htm>.

[59] Health Canada, "Clinical Trial Site Information Form", Drugs and Health Products, online: <http://www.hc-sc.gc.ca/dhp-mps/prodpharma/applic-demande/form/ctsif_dldcf_e.html>.

[60] Each ADR which is subject to expedited reporting should be reported individually in accordance with the data element(s) specified in Health Canada/ICH, "Guidance Document E2A: Clinical Safety Data Management: Definitions and Standards for Expedited Reporting", Drugs and Health Products, online: <http://www.hc-sc.gc.ca/dhp-mps/prodpharma/applic-demande/guide-ld/ich/efficac/e2a_e.html>. Further definitions and standards for expedited reporting of adverse drug reactions are described in Health Canada/ICH, "Guidance Document E2A: Clinical Safety Data Management: Definitions and Standards for Expedited Reporting", Drugs and Health Products, *ibid.*

agency whether the protocol had previously been rejected. There seems to be significant regulatory confidence in the work of the Canadian REBs. While REB review has thus been firmly integrated as a crucial requirement of drug approval, it is surprising that there is no firm regulatory structure surrounding REBs.[61] Indeed, there are no formal federal or provincial regulations governing REBs, including procedural requirements for REB review, establishment of REBs, or rules determining REB jurisdiction. The latter seems particularly problematic, as there are no rules preventing "REB shopping" in Canada. Sponsors are free to submit clinical trials to the REB of their choice and can also turn to another REB where the threshold for review is seen to be too onerous. The ICH-GCP guideline, which is integrated in Canada as a guidance document,[62] contains formal rules regarding REB review, but the ICH-GCP themselves rely on the existence of more detailed national rules.[63] Health Canada has explicitly stated that the ICH-CGP document is not binding, leaving considerable room for interpretive flexibility.[64] Health Canada could probably intervene under the authority of the FDA[65] when the ICH-GCP rules are not respected, by either clinical investigators, sponsors or an REB, and could ultimately suspend a clinical trial.[66]

Compliance and enforcement with the provisions of the FDA and FDR are conducted by the HPFB Inspectorate, which is responsible for inspections, investigations, establishment licensing and related laboratory functions. Under section 22 of the FDA, the HPFB has the authority to conduct inspections of clinical trial facilities and protocols. This does not occur often (two per cent of clinical trials[67]), and may be initiated following registry of a complaint or concern about a particular clinical trial with HPFB. Inspectors have the authority to enter and inspect manufacturing and storage locations to monitor compliance with the FDA and FDR at any reasonable time. An inspector may, on reasonable grounds, in the absence of a search warrant before entering the premises, seize

---

[61] Trudo Lemmens, "Federal Regulation of REB Review of Clinical Trials: A Modest But Easy Step Towards An Accountable REB Review Structure in Canada" (2005) 13:2-3 Health L. Rev. 39, particularly at 43-45.

[62] See Health Products and Food Branch, "ICH Guidance E6: Guideline for Good Clinical Practice: Consolidated Guideline", Health Canada, online: <http://www.hc-sc.gc.ca/dhp-mps/prodpharma/applic-demande/guide-ld/ich/efficac/e6_e.html>.

[63] See Marie Hirtle, Trudo Lemmens & Dominique Sprumont, "A Comparative Analysis of Research Ethics Review Mechanisms and the ICH Good Clinical Practice Guideline" (2000) 7 Eur. J. Health L. 265 at 268.

[64] "Guidance documents are administrative instruments not having force of law and, as such, allow for flexibility in approach. Alternate approaches to the principles and practices described in this document may be acceptable provided they are supported by adequate scientific justification." Health Products and Food Branch, "ICH Guidance E6: Guideline for Good Clinical Practice: Consolidated Guideline", Health Canada, online: <http://www.hc-sc.gc.ca/dhp-mps/prodpharma/applic-demande/guide-ld/ich/efficac/e6_e.html>.

[65] *Standard Sausage Co. v. Lee*, [1934] 1 D.L.R. 706 (B.C.C.A.); *C.E. Jamieson & Co. (Dominion) Ltd. v. Canada (Attorney General)*, [1987] F.C.J. No. 826, 12 F.T.R. 167 (F.C.T.D.).

[66] Anne Tomalin, "New Clinical Trial Legislation in Canada" (September 2001) Regulatory Affairs Focus 1 at 2.

[67] Health Canada, "Access to Therapeutic Products: The Regulatory Process in Canada", online: <http://www.hc-sc.gc.ca/ahc-asc/pubs/hpfb-dgpsa/access-therapeutic_acces-therapeutique_e.html>.

and detain any article in contravention of the FDA.[68] The HPFB has recently begun using its authority to inspect REBs involved in the evaluation of the clinical trials.[69]

D. REGULATORY SUBMISSIONS

Under circumstances where a sponsor has completed all necessary clinical trials it may submit a New Drug Submission (NDS) to the TPD in compliance with sections C.08.002, C.08.003, and C.08.005.1 of Part C, Division 8 of the FDR. An NDS is filed where data from clinical trials show a new drug has potential therapeutic value outweighing its risks (adverse events, toxicity). The NDS comprises four "volumes",[70] containing data on drug safety, efficacy and quality, including data from all relevant preclinical studies and clinical trials pertaining to drug manufacturing, packaging, labelling, claimed therapeutic value, conditions for use and side effects. The NDS does not have to contain the raw data, but only summaries of those data. Sponsors have to make the raw data available to the regulatory agency on request.[71] The "Comprehensive Summary" volume is pivotal in the review process, as it contains factual, concise descriptions of the methodology, results, conclusions, and evaluation of each relevant investigational and clinical study. It contains separate discussions and evaluations of the significance of each area of study and an integrated appraisal of the overall content of available information as it pertains to the safety and effectiveness of the product under the proposed conditions of use. Sponsors are encouraged to structure submissions in the Common Technical Document (CTD) format, which is a common format for the preparation of pharmaceutical submissions described in the ICH guidance on the *Common Technical Document for Registration of Pharmaceuticals for Human Use*.[72]

Other types of regulatory submissions may be made as well. Under section C.08.002.1 of the FDR, a generic sponsor may submit a document referred to as an Abbreviated New Drug Submission (ANDS). Rather than

---

[68] *C.E. Jamieson & Co. (Dominion) Ltd. v. Canada (Attorney General)*, [1987] F.C.J. No. 826, 12 F.T.R. 167 at 172 (F.C.T.D.).

[69] HPFB's *Summary Report of Inspections of Clinical Trials in 2003-2004* indicates that it visited five REBs which had approved the 45 clinical trials which the agency inspected in that period: Health Products and Food Branch, "Summary Report of Inspections of Clinical Trials in 2003-2004", Health Canada, online: <http://www.hc-sc.gc.ca/hpfb-dgpsa/inspectorate/gcp_inspection_sum_rep_2003-2004_e.pdf>.

[70] For details, see Health Protection Branch, "Preparation of Human New Drug Submissions. Therapeutic Products Programme Guideline", Health Canada, online: <http://www.hc-sc.gc.ca/dhp-mps/prodpharma/applic-demande/guide-ld/newdrug-drognouv/prephum_e.html>.

[71] J. Lexchin, personal communication (October 22, 2006).

[72] "International Conference on Harmonisation of Technical Requirements for Registration of Pharmaceuticals for Human Use (ICH)", Official web site for ICH, online: <http://www.ich.org/cache/compo/276-254-1.html>. Further information pertaining to Canadian drug review requirements, at Health Canada, "Notice: Common Technical Document ICH-M4", online at: <http://www.hc-sc.gc.ca/dhp-mps/prodpharma/applic-demande/guide-ld/ich/multidisciplin/ctd_m4_notice_e.html>.

focusing on preclinical and clinical trial data, however, the focus of the ANDS is on bioequivalence, safety, efficacy, drug manufacturing, packaging and labelling. To satisfy the ANDS requirements, a generic drug must be "equivalent" to the reference brand-name product (referred to as a Canadian reference product, or CRP). For this to occur, a generic version must be the pharmaceutical equivalent and "bioequivalent" to the CRP, have the same route of administration as the CRP and its conditions of use fall must be within those of the CRP. Bioequivalence means that the generic drug product must have the same systemic effects (therapeutic and adverse) as the CRP when administered to patients under the same conditions as the CRP. According to the *NOC Regulations*, bioequivalence may be based on assessment of pharmaceutical characteristics, bioavailability studies, pharmacodynamic studies or clinical trials. In most cases, however, it is based on bioavailability studies. Where the generic version is deemed safe and efficacious and meets the same chemistry and manufacturing requirements as the CRP it will be deemed bioequivalent under section C.08.004(4) of the FDR. An NOC is issued only where the federal review indicates equivalence of the generic to the CRP and all patent issues have been addressed under the *NOC Regulations*.

In addition, a Supplemental New Drug Submission (SNDS) may be granted under sections C.08.003 and C.08.003.1 of the FDR, to a sponsor, typically brand-name manufacturers, for changes to an already-marketed drug. Typically, an SNDS application is made for changes to the dosage form, strength, formulation, method of manufacture, labelling, or recommended route of administration of the drug product, or if the manufacturer wants to expand the indications (claims or conditions of use). Under section C.08.002.1 of the FDR, a generic sponsor may also make a parallel supplemental abbreviated submission (SANDS).

E. REVIEW OF REGULATORY SUBMISSIONS

HPFB reviews NDS, ANDS, SNDS and SANDS submissions to assess the safety, efficacy and quality of the drug candidates, and potential risks and benefits of the product, including product monographs, product labels and other information the manufacturer intends to provide to practitioners and consumers. Different classes of therapeutic products have different target screening and review times.[73] Drug submission performance times are reported quarterly by Health Canada and posted on its website.[74]

---

[73] For review, see Health Canada, "Access to Therapeutic Products: The Regulatory Process in Canada", online: <http://www.hc-sc.gc.ca/ahc-asc/pubs/hpfb-dgpsa/access-therapeutic_acces-therapeutique_e.html>.

[74] Health Canada, "Drug Submission Performance Reports", online: <http://www.hc-sc.gc.ca/dhp-mps/prodpharma/applic-demande/docs/perform-rendement/index_e.html>.

Current review times[75] are reasonably in line with those of other jurisdictions with similar legislation, procedures and review processes. Historically, however, drug approval times in Canada have not been as fast as other nations. In 1993 review times reached a zenith of 34 months, one of the slowest in the world.[76] At that time, the federal government repealed Canada's compulsory licensing regime, replaced it with the *NOC Regulations* and instituted pricing controls monitored by the PMPRB. It also cut the budget for the TPD, forcing it to turn to cost recovery measures in order to survive.[77] In 1996, the TPD announced fast-tracking of eligible NDS and SNDS submissions intended for the treatment, prevention or diagnosis of serious, life-threatening or severely debilitating illnesses or conditions.[78] In return for user fees, the pharmaceutical industry specifically requested improvements in the speed of regulatory approval.[79] By 1999 the pharmaceutical industry was contributing about 70 per cent of TPD's budget,[80] and approval times had decreased rapidly and substantially.[81] Implementation of government-wide user fees in Canada was formalized in the

---

[75] Current target times for review of priority, NOCc, standard and ANDS applications are 180, 200, 300 and 180 days, respectively. For review, see Health Canada, "Access to Therapeutic Products: The Regulatory Process in Canada", online: <http://www.hc-sc.gc.ca/ahc-asc/pubs/hpfb-dgpsa/access-therapeutic_acces-therapeutique_e.html> at 11-13 and Health Canada, "Overview of the Canadian federal drug review process", online: <http://www.hc-sc.gc.ca/ahc-asc/pubs/hpfb-dgpsa/overview-apercu_drug-med_rev_pro_03_07_e.html> at 19-20; Information on performance can also be found at Health Canada, "Regulatory Review of Pharmaceuticals, Biologics and Medical Devices", online: <http://www.hc-sc.gc.ca/ahc-asc/pubs/hpfb-dgpsa/performance_rendement_2004_e.html>.

[76] Patricia I. Carter, "Federal Regulation of Pharmaceuticals in the United States and Canada" (1999) 21 Loy. L.A. Int'l & Comp. L. Rev. 215 at 235.

[77] J. Lexchin, "Transparency in Drug Regulation: Mirage or Oasis", Canadian Centre for Policy Alternatives, online: <http://policyalternatives.ca/index.cfm?act=news&do=Article&call=913&pA=94761C2A&type=5>.

[78] Health Products and Food Branch, "Guidance for Industry: Priority Review of Drug Submissions", Health Canada, online: <http://www.hc-sc.gc.ca/dhp-mps/prodpharma/applic-demande/guide-ld/priorit/priordr_2006_e.html>.

[79] J. Lexchin, "Transparency in Drug Regulation: Mirage or Oasis", Canadian Centre for Policy Alternatives, online: <http://policyalternatives.ca/index.cfm?act=news&do=Article&call=913&pA=94761C2A&type=5>.

[80] J. Lexchin, "Drug withdrawals from the Canadian market for safety reasons 1963–2004" (2005) 172 C.M.A.J. 765.

[81] According to Lexchin (J. Lexchin, "Drug withdrawals from the Canadian market for safety reasons 1963–2004" (2005) 172 C.M.A.J. 765), approval times for new molecular entities decreased from 27 months in 1993 to 19 months by 2001. Under Health Canada's Therapeutic Access Strategy, by 2005 88 per cent, 91 per cent and 100 per cent of the regulatory review backlog for brand-name, generic and over-the-counter drugs was cleared. For review of how this was accomplished, see Health Canada, "Therapeutic Products Directorate. Business Transformation: Annual Progress Report 2004-2005", online: <http://hc-sc.gc.ca/dhp-mps/alt_formats/hpfb-dgpsa/pdf/prodpharma/bt_rep_to_rap_2004_05_e.pdf>. These reductions are not insignificant in light of the fact that between 2001 and 2005 the numbers of NDS, ANDS, SNDS and SANDS submissions increased by 232, 19 and 540 per cent, respectively: Health Products and Food Branch, "Annual Drug Submission. Performance Report – Part I. Therapeutic Products Directorate (TPD) 2005", Health Canada, online: <http://hc-sc.gc.ca/dhp-mps/alt_formats/hpfb-dgpsa/pdf/prodpharma/tpd_dpt_annual_annuel_05_e.pdf>.

2004 *User Fees Act.*[82] Some have suggested that user fees result in a significant reduction in the standard for review and a concomitant increase in risk for the drug-consuming public,[83] while others have vigorously denied this.[84] There is no question of the stakes for faster review times for pharmaceutical firms, as it is well known that substantial profits can be made by moving through the drug development cycle quickly. One recent study in the United States indicated that in 2000–2005, the five fastest drug developers gained an average of U.S. $1.1 billion each in incremental prescription revenue and saved U.S. $30 million in out-of-pocket costs when directly compared with those of the slowest companies. This was due in part to a savings of 17 months in the development and regulatory cycle.[85] Possibly in order to allay such concerns, in Budget 2003, $190 million was provided to the TPD over five years under Health Canada's new Therapeutic Access Strategy[86] (TAS) aimed at improving "the timeliness of Health Canada's regulatory process with respect to human drugs while preserving the principle that safety is of paramount concern".

There are different review times for different types of regulatory submissions. Special consideration relating to drug submissions qualifying under sections C.08.010 or C.08.011 of the FDR for special access purposes may be warranted. "Priority review" may be granted in this context,[87] but only where new products are intended for treatment, prevention or diagnosis of "serious, life-threatening or severely debilitating disease or condition". Moreover, no product can currently be marketed for that disease or condition and the new product must entail a "significant increase in efficacy or decrease in risk" over existing drugs. The same safety, efficacy and quality conditions apply during the review process. The main difference is presumably the accelerated review time.

---

[82] *User Fees Act*, S.C. 2004, c. 6. For guidance documents pertaining to the regulatory approval process, see online: <http://www.hc-sc.gc.ca/dhp-mps/prodpharma/applic-demande/guide-ld/costs-couts/index_e.html>.

[83] Mary E. Wiktorowicz, "Emergent Patterns in the Regulation of Pharmaceuticals: Institutions and Interests in the United States, Canada, Britain and France" (2003) 28:4 J. Health, Pol. 615; L. Eggertson, "Drug approval system questioned in US and Canada" (2005) 172:3 C.M.A.J. 317; J. Lexchin, "Drug withdrawals from the Canadian market for safety reasons, 1963–2004" (2005) 172 C.M.A.J. 765.

[84] J. Graham, "Approving New Medicines in Canada: Health Canada Needs a Dose of Competition" (June 2005) Fraser Forum 9.

[85] Tufts Centre for the Study of Drug Development Impact, "Fastest drug developers consistently best peers on key performance metrics" (2006) 8:5 Tufts Centre for the Study of Drug Development Impact Report.

[86] Health Canada, "Regulation and Beyond: Progress on Health Canada's Therapeutics Access Strategy", online: <http://www.hc-sc.gc.ca/hcs-sss/pubs/care-soins/2005-therap-strateg/index_e.html>.

[87] Health Products and Food Branch, "Guidance for Industry: Priority Review of Drug Submissions", Health Canada, online: <http://www.hc-sc.gc.ca/dhp-mps/prodpharma/applic-demande/guide-ld/priorit/priordr_2006_e.html>.

F. NOTICE OF COMPLIANCE

Once all regulatory requirements pertaining to safety, effectiveness and quality have been met, the sponsor is issued a Notice of Compliance (NOC). A NOC[88] is a notification, issued pursuant to paragraph C.08.004(1)(a) of the FDR, indicating that a manufacturer has complied with sections C.08.002, C.08.002.1 or C.08.003 and C.08.005.1 of the regulations. A NOC is given where benefits of a drug outweigh its risks and risks can be managed. If the drug fails its NDS, a Notice of Non-Compliance (NON) is issued, requesting more information from the sponsor. Sponsors may appeal decisions by the HPFB. Both brand-name and generic manufacturers obtain NOCs for their respective drug products. While brand-name sponsors obtain theirs under the auspices of the FDA and regulations, generic sponsors obtain their NOCs under the *NOC Regulations*. Health Canada maintains a public database[89] containing searchable information on drugs that have been authorized for use in Canada. Information in the database includes brand name, DIN, manufacturer, medicinal ingredient(s), submission class, therapeutic class, product type and NOC date.

Under section C.08.004 or section C.08.005 of the FDR, the TPD may grant a sponsor a NOC with conditions (NOCc) where sufficient preliminary evidence of safety and effectiveness is available.[90] A NOCc is granted to expedite patient access to potentially life-saving drugs under circumstances of dire illness. Under Health Canada policy,[91] eligibility for a NOCc is restricted to drug products "intended for the treatment, prevention or diagnosis of serious, life-threatening or severely debilitating illnesses or conditions for which (a) there is no alternative therapy available on the Canadian market or, (b) where the new product represents a significant improvement in the benefit/risk profile over existing products". The program was initiated in May 1998, partially in response to requests by patient advocacy groups for experimental treatments.[92] The NOCc allows the sponsor to manufacture and market a drug in Canada on the condition that it undertakes additional studies to confirm the alleged benefit. In order to

---

[88] Health Canada, "Guidance for Industry: Notice of Compliance", online: <http://www.hc-sc.gc.ca/dhp-mps/prodpharma/notices-avis/index_e.html>.

[89] *Ibid.*

[90] Guidance for Industry: Notice of Compliance with Conditions (NOC/c), online: <http://www.hc-sc.gc.ca/dhp-mps/prodpharma/applic-demande/guide-ld/compli-conform/noccg_accd_2006_e.html>.

[91] Health Canada, Notice of Compliance with Conditions -NOC/c (Therapeutic Products), online: <http://www.hc-sc.gc.ca/dhp-mps/prodpharma/notices-avis/conditions/noccfs_accfd_2005_e.html>.

[92] *Ibid.* Initial data available in such circumstances may be limited due to the small number of patients eligible for participation in clinical trials. Even with larger sample sizes, data on final outcomes such as morbidity and mortality may be lacking and only data which measure the drug's effect on surrogate markers may be available (surrogate markers are parameters that when measured directly are reasonably likely, based on available evidence, to predict an effect of a drug on recognized clinical outcomes such as morbidity and mortality). In instances warranting an NOCc, sufficient testing has been done to substantiate that an effect on a surrogate marker is predictive of clinical benefit. Even so, TPD's position is that until surrogate markers can be validated, evidence of the effect of a drug on non-validated surrogate markers cannot replace data that demonstrate an effect on recognized clinical endpoints. In such instances, TPD may request additional confirmatory studies to further verify the clinical benefit of the drug.

ensure this occurs, the FDR provides the HPFB with jurisdiction to monitor the safety and effectiveness of the drug candidate through post-market surveillance. A Special Access Program (SAP) allows health care professionals limited access to drugs not yet approved for sale in Canada where emergencies exist, and conventional therapies have failed or are unavailable. Decisions are made on a case-by-case basis. If a special access request is approved a Letter of Authorization is sent to the requesting physician and sponsor and it is up to the sponsor whether or not to provide the drug to the patient and, if so, under what conditions. As mentioned earlier, special review procedures and special access programs have been deemed by government regulators, patient advocacy groups and industry to be important tools to avoid delays in access to promising new therapies for patients suffering from serious and life-threatening diseases, including, among others, HIV/AIDS, ALS (Lou Gehrig's disease) and certain forms of advanced cancer.

G. DRUG IDENTIFICATION NUMBER

Under section C.01.014 of the FDR, no manufacturer shall sell a drug in dosage form unless a drug identification number (DIN) has been assigned for that drug and the assignment of the number has not been cancelled pursuant to section C.01.014.6.[93] In the case of a new drug, a new drug submission filed pursuant to Division 8 of the *Food and Drug Regulations* is regarded as an application for a DIN. When a product is not subject to Division 8, the application is called a DIN submission. This includes new chemical entities and drugs that are not new chemical entities. The latter get a DIN provided that the drug has been previously approved and sold in Canada. Exceptions to the current DIN requirements include radiopharmaceuticals, blood and blood products. The DIN requirement has survived constitutional attack and has been declared *intra vires* the Parliament of Canada.[94]

H. LABELLING INFORMATION AND DRUG MONOGRAPH

Once a NOC and a DIN are obtained, the drug product must be packaged and distributed with information to assist consumers in making informed decisions. Under Parts C, D and G of the FRD, such information includes literature accompanying the drug product, product monograph, product package label and the label on the product container.[95] Since October 2004, drug product monographs must include consumer information clearly outlining the purpose of the drug, how to use it and any potential side effects and information for health care professionals needed to treat and counsel patients. Under section C.05.011 of the

---

[93]   Health Canada, "Guideline on Preparation of DIN Submissions", Drugs and Health Products, online: <http://www.hc-sc.gc.ca/dhp-mps/prodpharma/applic-demande/guide-ld/din/pre_din_ind_e.html>.

[94]   *C.E. Jamieson & Co. (Dominion) Ltd. v. Canada (Attorney General)*, [1987] F.C.J. No. 826 12 F.T.R. 167 (F.C.T.D.).

[95]   Health Canada, "Notice. Product Monograph", Drugs and Health Products, online: <http://www.hc-sc.gc.ca/dhp-mps/prodpharma/applic-demande/guide-ld/monograph/pm_mp_e.html>.

FDR, the drug product bears a label indicating, *inter alia*, the name of the drug, adequate directions for use, a quantitative list of the active ingredients, expiration date, potency of the drug, method of administration and the DIN. Under section C.08.006, if the label contains any false or misleading information, the sponsor's NOC can be revoked.

I. ADVERSE EFFECTS MONITORING AND REPORTING

Under the FDA, drug manufacturers have the legal onus to monitor the safety of their products following market entry, including reporting serious side effects, failure of the product to "produce the desired effect" and studies providing new safety information.[96] Under the provisions of section C.01.016 of the FDR, no manufacturer shall sell a drug unless the manufacturer, with respect to any adverse drug reaction or any serious adverse drug reaction known to the manufacturer that occurs after this section comes into force, furnishes to Health Canada a report of all information in respect of any serious adverse drug reaction that has occurred inside or outside of Canada with respect to the drug, within 15 days after receiving the information.[97] Under section C.05.012 of the regulations, manufacturers have an obligation to keep records respecting all adverse events in respect of the drug that have occurred inside or outside Canada, including information that specifies the indication for use and the dosage form of the drug at the time of the adverse event. However, reporting requirements for lack of safety only apply to "new drugs" as defined under Division 8 of the FDR.[98] The Marketed Health Products Directorate (MHPD) is responsible for all post-market assessment and surveillance of pharmaceuticals in Canada as well as biologics, medical devices, natural health products and radio-pharmaceuticals. The HPFB oversees all adverse reaction reports. The MHPD administers a Canadian Adverse Drug Reaction Monitoring Program, which has one central and seven regional reporting centres.[99] ADR reports are gathered in the Canadian Adverse Drug Reaction Information System. Since 2005, an Online Query and Data Extract database provides the public with

---

[96] For a good overview of the post-market surveillance system in Canada and recommendations to improve it, see Sasha Kontic, *Assessing the Effectiveness of the Prescription Drug Post-Market Surveillance System in Canada: The Need for a More Active Regulatory Role* (LL.M. Thesis) (Toronto: University of Toronto, Faculty of Law, 2005).

[97] Health Canada, "Guidelines for Reporting Adverse Reactions to Marketed Drugs: Guidelines for the Canadian Pharmaceutical Industry on Reporting Adverse Reactions to Marketed Drugs (Vaccines Excluded)", Drugs and Health Products, online: <http://www.hc-sc.gc.ca/dhp-mps/medeff/report-declaration/guide/guide-ldir_indust_e.html>; Public Health Agency of Canada, "Guidelines for Reporting Adverse Events Associated with Vaccine Products", Canada Communicable Disease Report, online: <http://www.phac-aspc.gc.ca/publicat/ccdr-rmtc/00vol26/26s1/index.html>.

[98] Health Canada, "Access to Therapeutic Products: The Regulatory Process in Canada", online: <http://www.hc-sc.gc.ca/ahc-asc/pubs/hpfb-dgpsa/access-therapeutic_acces-therapeutique_e.html>.

[99] Health Canada, "Drugs and Drug Products" online: <http://www.hc-sc.gc.ca/dhp-mps/medeff/databasdon/index_e.html>. For a list of the centres: Health Canada, "List of Regional Adverse Reaction (AR) Centres", online: <http://www.hc-sc.gc.ca/hpfb-dgpsa/tpd-dpt/adr_regions_e.html>.

information on suspected adverse reactions. According to Health Canada, the database contains 170,000 records, dating back to 1965.[100]

J. DIRECT-TO-CONSUMER ADVERTISING

Under section 3 of the FDA, no person shall advertise any drug to the general public as a treatment, preventative or cure for diseases, disorders or abnormal physical states listed in Schedule A to the FDA, which contains most diseases for which sponsors would desire to advertise their products. Section 9(1) provides no person shall advertise any drug in a manner that is false, misleading or deceptive or is likely to create an erroneous impression regarding its character, value, quantity, composition, merit or safety. Section 30 gives the Governor in Council authority to make regulations respecting the labelling and packaging and the offering, exposing and advertising for sale of food, drugs, cosmetics and devices. Under sections C.01.027 and C.01.044 of the FDR where a person advertises to the general public a drug for human use, the person shall not make any representation other than with respect to the brand name, proper name, common name, price and quantity of the drug. Under section C.08.002, no person shall advertise a new drug unless the manufacturer of the new drug has filed with the Minister an NDS or ANDS, has received a NOC, and has submitted specimens of the final version of any labels, including package inserts, product brochures and file cards, intended for use in connection with the advertised drug.

From the provisions of the FDA reviewed above it is clear that advertising pharmaceuticals to the general public as a "treatment, preventative or cure for diseases, disorders or abnormal physical states" is *per se* illegal in Canada, thus precluding direct-to-consumer advertising (DTCA). The United States and New Zealand are currently the only jurisdictions permitting such advertising.[101] In the United States, Congress allowed DTCA in 1985 following its protection under the First Amendment free speech doctrine[102] and in more liberal form in 1997 through legislative amendment.[103] By 2004 sponsors were spending approximately U.S. $4.5 billion per year on DTCA.[104] In Canada, consultations

---

[100] See "Canadian Adverse Drug Reaction Monitoring Program (CADRMP) Online Query and Data Extracts," online: <http://www.hc-sc.gc.ca/dhp-mps/medeff/databasdon/database-basedon_annou -annon_e.html>.

[101] David M Gardner, Barbara Mintzes & Alex Ostry, "Direct-to-consumer prescription drug advertising in Canada: Permission by default?" (2003) 169 C.M.A.J. 425. See also B. Mintzes, "Direct-to-consumer advertising of prescription drugs in Canada", Health Council of Canada Report, online: <http://www.healthcouncilcanada.ca/docs/papers/2006/hcc_dtc-advertising_200601 _e_v6.pdf>; Health Canada, "Direct to Consumer Advertising (DCTA) of Prescription Drugs", Legislative Renewal Issue Paper, online: <http://hc-sc.gc.ca/ahc-asc/pubs/legren/consumer- consommateur_e.html>.

[102] *Virginia State Board of Pharmacy v. Virginia Citizens Consumer Council Inc.*, 425 U.S. 748 (1976).

[103] *Food and Drug Administration Modernization Act of 1997*, P.L. 105-115, 111 Stat. 2296, November 21, 1997.

[104] A. Bernstein & J. Bernstein, "The Information Prescription for Drug Regulation", NYLS Legal Studies Research Paper No. 05/06-27, Social Science Research Network, online: <http://papers.ssrn.com/sol3/papers.cfm?abstract_id=902160>.

between industry and the federal government on this issue have been ongoing since 1996, and a momentum seems to have been created in favour of adopting some form of legal DTCA.[105] Recently, the CanWest corporation has challenged the constitutionality of the provisions under the FDA and FDR forbidding DTCA, claiming they contravene s. 2(*b*) of the *Canadian Charter of Rights and Freedoms* guaranteeing freedom of expression.[106]

Of the three types of DTCA (product claim, reminder and help-seeking), the most significant concerns have been expressed over product claim advertisements.[107] These have been demonstrated to significantly affect the behaviour of both consumers and prescribing physicians.[108] Yet, the United States Food and Drug Administration does not verify advertisements before they are aired or published. While it can send a letter to reprimand a company for providing misleading information to the public, the letters are not associated with any significant penalties.[109] Interestingly, while DTCA has increased in the last couple of years and criticism grows over inaccurate DTCA, the number of letters issued by the Food and Drug Administration has decreased.[110] Control of

---

[105] Health Canada, "Direct to consumer advertising (DCTA) of prescription drugs", Legislative Renewal Issue Paper, online: <http://hc-sc.gc.ca/ahc-asc/pubs/legren/consumer-consommateur_e.html>, particularly section 3.3. In an interview with the CBC a Health Canada official indicated in 2002 that it was time for DTCA, stating that if regulated effectively, advertising can be a good means of conveying high-quality information to consumers, essentially echoing the words of Rx&D, the brand-name pharmaceutical manufacturers association: Erica Johnson, "Direct-to-consumer advertising", CBC news, online: <http://www.cbc.ca/consumers/market/files/health/directads/>.

[106] Court File 05-W-303001 PD2; *CanWest MediaWorks Inc. v. Attorney General Canada*. Statement of Claim issued by the Ontario Superior Court on December 23, 2005.

[107] See, *e.g.*, Advertising Campaigns of Branded and Unbranded Messages — Policy Statement. Ottawa: Health Canada, Therapeutic Products Directorate. 2000, online: <http://www.hc-sc.gc.ca/dhp-mps/advert-publicit/pol/advert-pub_camp_e.html>.

[108] David M Gardner, Barbara Mintzes and Alex Ostry. "*Direct-to-consumer prescription drug advertising in Canada: Permission by default?*" (2003) 169 C.M.A.J. 425. See also B. Mintzes, "Direct-to-consumer advertising of prescription drugs in Canada", Health Council of Canada Report, online: <http://www.healthcouncilcanada.ca/docs/papers/2006/hcc_dtc-advertising_200601_e_v6.pdf>; Health Canada, "Direct to consumer advertising (DCTA) of prescription drugs", Legislative Renewal Issue Paper, online: <http://hc-sc.gc.ca/ahc-asc/pubs/legren/consumer-consommateur_e.html>. There is some evidence to suggest that the influence on physician prescription has more to do with express requests by patients than with whether the drug was advertised or not. Not surprisingly, industry is increasingly targeting consumers, because they influence physician prescribing behaviour. See B. Mintzes *et al.*, "Influence of direct to consumer pharmaceutical advertising and patient's requests on prescribing decisions: two site cross sectional survey" (2002) 324 B.M.J. 278.

[109] See Jay S. Cohen, *Overdose: The Case Against the Drug Companies* (New York: Penguin, 2001) at 157.

[110] John Abramson discusses how oversight of DTCA by the United States FDA has decreased in the last couple of years. He points out that the number of letters citing drug companies for advertising violations dropped to 24 in 2002, compared to an average of 95 letters in 1999 and 2000. Considering the significant increase in DTCA and the many examples of problematic advertising, some of which he discusses, this is unlikely caused by an increase in the integrity of DTCA. See John Abramson, *Overdo$ed America: The Broken Promise of American Medicine* (New York: Harper Collins, 2004) at 149-67.

advertisements is very much left within the hands of industry, which cannot be expected to safeguard public health interests. Even though substantial doubts have been expressed regarding all of the grounds offered by the pharmaceutical sector (educating public, earlier diagnosis, improved patient compliance, and greater patient autonomy) in support of DTCA,[111] it currently takes place without considerable and more fiduciary regulatory oversight.[112]

It is worth mentioning that misleading advertisement for pharmaceuticals is already a concern in Canada.[113] Drug companies have made repeated attempts to stretch the boundaries of what the law permits under the FDA. Indeed, viewers of both television and film have been exposed to suggestive and often misleading advertisements for recognizable pharmaceutical products for years, yet, no significant sanctions have been enacted against such practices. The publicity for Zyban[114] is a case in point. It was advertised for four full months as a product claim advertisement without sanction by Health Canada. The fact that enforcement of the current more stringent regime is already difficult in Canada amounts to a clear warning sign for what may transpire should DTCA be allowed.

V. REGULATORY CHALLENGES

A. RECENT CONTROVERSIES AND THE LIMITS OF THE CURRENT DRUG REGULATORY PROCESS

The regulatory approval process for pharmaceuticals in Canada has prevented unsafe pharmaceutical products from entering the market. It has also allowed regulatory agencies to remove products from the market when evidence became available that they created unacceptable risks which did not outweigh expected benefits. Health Canada has used its jurisdiction and mandate to protect public health also by issuing warnings and restricting the use of certain products. Even so, a growing number of controversies have also exposed the weaknesses and

---

[111] For review, see David M Gardner, Barbara Mintzes and Alex Ostry, "Direct-to-consumer prescription drug advertising in Canada: Permission by default?" (2003) 169 C.M.A.J. 425. See also B. Mintzes, "Direct-to-consumer advertising of prescription drugs in Canada", Health Council of Canada Report, online: <http://www.healthcouncilcanada.ca/docs/papers/2006/hcc_dtc-advertising_200601_e_v6.pdf>.

[112] For some examples of problematic advertisements in the United States, see Jay S. Cohen, *Overdose: The Case Against the Drug Companies* (New York: Penguin, 2001) at 156-57; and John Abramson, *Overdo$ed America: The Broken Promise of American Medicine* (New York: Harper Collins, 2004) at 152-67, who also discusses some of the problems associated with such advertisements.

[113] See B. Mintzes, "Direct-to-consumer advertising of prescription drugs in Canada", Health Council of Canada Report, online: <http://www.healthcouncilcanada.ca/docs/papers/2006/hcc_dtc-advertising_200601_e_v6.pdf>.

[114] David M Gardner, Barbara Mintzes & Alex Ostry, "Direct-to-consumer prescription drug advertising in Canada: Permission by default?" (2003) 169 C.M.A.J. 425. See also B. Mintzes, "Direct-to-consumer advertising of prescription drugs in Canada", *ibid.*

serious limitations of the current system. The controversies involve drugs that have been massively prescribed, often over an extended period of time and to patient populations well beyond those studied in formal clinical trials, which highlights how the "safety and efficacy" of pharmaceutical products is a serious public health concern. While a thorough review of such controversies is beyond the scope of this chapter, two recent examples highlight some of the serious limitations of the current drug regulatory regime.

Several controversies surround serotonin reuptake inhibitors (SSRIs), which have been prescribed to millions of people around the world for a host of conditions even though serious questions remain as to their efficacy and safety. SSRIs were originally developed to treat depression, but their producers have relentlessly tried to expand the scope of allowable uses to include a wide variety of related and unrelated ailments, including anxiety, post-traumatic stress disorder, "pre-menstrual dysphoric disorder", urinary incontinence, and so on.[115] For a long time, concerns were expressed about the potential side effects of these drugs.[116] Shortly after the first SSRI (fluoxetine, or Prozac) was introduced on the market, the United States Food and Drug Administration held hearings to determine whether the drug caused an increased risk for agitation, suicidal ideation and suicidal thinking in some patients. It concluded at that time that there was insufficient evidence to establish a causal link but recommended that further studies be undertaken to determine long-term safety and efficacy. These studies were never undertaken.[117]

The same issue came up again more recently, in the context of the use of SSRIs for the treatment of children and adolescents. Even though SSRIs did not have regulatory approval for this use, they were extensively prescribed in an "off-label" manner (outside of the ambit of regulatory approval for a drug). This time, the controversies culminated in a lawsuit by the Attorney General of New York against GlaxoSmithKline (GSK), one of the producers of SSRIs, for "repeated and persistent fraud by misrepresentation, concealing and otherwise failing to disclose to physicians information in its control concerning the safety and effectiveness of its antidepressant medication paroxetine" in treating children and adolescents suffering from depression.[118] The Attorney General accused GSK of hiding important clinical trials data and of using a highly selective set of data to promote off-label prescription of the drug to treat children and adolescents. While the lawsuit was settled out of court, evidence that became available raised troubling questions about the ability of

---

[115] See Carl Elliott, *Better than Well: American Medicine Meets the American Dream* (New York: Norton, 2003) at 124; Edward Shorter, *A History of Psychiatry: From the Era of the Asylum to the Age of Prozac* (New York: John Wiley and Sons, 1997) at 29. See also in general: Ray Moynihan & Alan Cassels, *Selling Sickness: How the World's Biggest Pharmacetuical Companies Are Turning Us All Into Patients* (Vancouver: Greystone Books, 2005); and Charles Medawar, *Medicines Out of Control?: Anti-depressants and the Conspiracy of Goodwill* (Amsterdam: Aksant Academic Publishers, 2004).
[116] See in general, David Healy, *Let Them Eat Prozac* (Toronto: James Lorimer, 2003).
[117] *Ibid.*
[118] *AG New York v. GlaxoSmithKline*, June 2, 2004 at para 38. See the discussion in Trudo Lemmens, "Leopards in the Temple: Restoring Scientific Integrity to the Commercialized Research Scene" (2004) 32 J. L. Med. Ethics 641.

pharmaceutical companies to control and manipulate medical research. It appeared that GSK conducted several clinical trials which raised serious concerns about the safety and efficacy of the drug in children and adolescents. Nevertheless, the company managed to get a selection of positive results from one trial published in a leading psychiatric journal with some of America's most prominent psychiatrists as authors. Offprints of the study were subsequently distributed by the company's sales agents, to promote off-label prescription of the drug. An editorial in the *Lancet* referred to the controversies surrounding SSRIs as a "disaster" for evidence-based medicine.[119]

Another controversy is centred around the osteoarthritis drug rofecoxib, better known as Vioxx. Critics have pointed out that tens of thousands of people[120] may have suffered myocardial infarct or stroke as a result of taking Vioxx, turning this into "an enormous public health issue".[121] Although MerckFrosst, the producer of Vioxx, pulled the drug from the market in 2004, there were calls for further research into adverse effects as early as 2001 and such calls had allegedly been ignored and on the contrary countered by aggressive marketing.[122] There was also very severe criticism on the lack of intervention by the regulatory agencies in the United States[123] and Canada. An editorial in the *Canadian Medical Association Journal* stated that in the Vioxx case, "[b]oth the FDA and Health Canada have failed miserably in carrying out … their public mandates".[124] Even medical journals were tarnished in this controversy: the *New England Journal of Medicine* was accused of inappropriately delaying the publication of a correction in its journal.[125]

What do these and other controversies tell us? First, they confirm that the current regulatory process focuses too much on short-term efficacy and safety of drug products. The approval process outlined in section IV, *supra*, creates an initial hurdle, but there is little control on what happens after a drug is approved. Once a drug is on the market, it can be widely prescribed to patient populations for which the drug was never approved nor tested, even though off-label

[119] "Depressing Research" (editorial) (2004) 363(9418), The Lancet 1341.

[120] Eric J. Topol indicates that the drug was being taken by 80 million people when it was pulled from the market. According to his extrapolations from the studies that discovered the risk, 160,000 out of 10 million people may have suffered from an infarctus or stroke. See "Failing the Public Health — Rofecoxib, Merck, and the FDA" (2004) 351 N. Eng. J. Med. 1707 at 1708.

[121] Eric J. Topol, *ibid.*, at 1707.

[122] *Ibid.*

[123] In the United States, criticism even came from whistleblowers within the Food and Drug Administration. See Mark Greener, "Drug Safety on Trial" (2005) 6 EMBO Reports 202; G. Harris, "F.D.A., Strong Drug Ties and Less Monitoring", *New York Times*, December 6, 2004 at A1.

[124] "Vioxx: lessons for Health Canada and the FDA" (editorial) (2005) 172 C.M.A.J. 5.

[125] See Richard Smith, "Lapses at the New England Journal of Medicine" (2006) 99 J. Royal Soc. Med. 380. Smith points out that the journal had made significant profits from the sale of reprints of the original study in which positive claims about Vioxx were made. Merck had bought 900,000 reprints of the 2000 article for an amount estimated at around U.S. $750,000. Even though it had been informed of problems with the study in 2001, the journal waited until 2005 to publish a correction.

prescription cannot be directly promoted. Some companies allegedly used scientific publications to promote such off-label prescriptions.

The controversies also highlight the importance of and the need for better long-term safety monitoring. While drug regulatory agencies request reporting of adverse events, there appears to be no regulatory basis for imposing systematic long-term safety studies. In the context of SSRIs and Vioxx, critics have pointed out that the importance of further safety studies were raised by medical researchers, and in the case of SSRIs even regulatory agencies, but that such studies were never implemented.[126] Indeed, drug regulatory agencies can recommend long-term safety studies and are sometimes involved in funding such studies themselves.[127] They seem unable, however, to legally enforce this as a requirement. In 2006, in the wake of the Vioxx debacle, the United States Congress asked the Government Accountability Office (GAO) to investigate the problems associated with post-marketing control. The GAO concluded that the "FDA lacks a clear and effective process for making decisions about, and providing management oversight of, postmarket drug safety issues" and that it "lacks authority to require certain studies and has resource limitations for obtaining data".[128] Pharmaceutical companies have no financial interest in conducting such studies and may in fact have an interest to avoid them. Since long-term follow-up studies are expensive and public funding for large clinical drug trials scarce, it may take a long time before sufficient serious adverse events are detected and move the regulatory agencies into action. Probationary regulatory approval contingent on post-marketing studies may help rectify this problem, as proposed by Health Canada in its recent "Blueprint for Renewal" discussion paper.[129]

Within Canadian and United States drug regulatory agencies, most of the increases in resources of the last decades have gone to ensuring an efficient and fast regulatory approval process.[130] Industry has gained significant influence within the drug regulatory system through its user-fee contributions and uses this influence to request a disproportionate distribution of funding towards fast drug approval, rather than long-term safety monitoring.[131] The

---

[126] For Vioxx, see Eric J. Topol, "Failing the Public Health — Rofecoxib, Merck, and the FDA" (2004) 351 N. Eng. J. Med. 1707; for SSRIs, see David Healy, *Let Them Eat Prozac* (Toronto: James Lorimer, 2003).

[127] Fran Hawthorne, *Inside the FDA: The Business and Politics Behind the Drugs We Take and the Food We Eat* (Hoboken N.J.: John Wiley, 2005) at 158.

[128] United States Government Accountability Office, *Report to Congressional Requesters. Drug Safety: Improvement Needed in FDA's Post-Market Decision and Oversight Process*, GAO-06-402 (Washington DC: March 2006) at 5.

[129] Health Products and Food Branch, "Blueprint for Renewal: Transforming Canada's Approach to Regulating Health Products and Food", Health Canada, online: <http://www.hc-sc.gc.ca/ahc-asc/branch-dirgen/hpfb-dgpsa/blueprint-plan/index_e.html> at 7, 9, 17 and 21.

[130] See S. Pomper, "Drug Rush: Why the Prescription Drug Market is Unsafe at High Speeds", Washington Monthly, online: <http://www.washingtonmonthly.com/features/2000/0005.pomper.html>.

[131] For a good discussion of the influence of industry on the United States Food and Drug Administration, particularly the impact of the user fee system, see Fran Hawthorne, *Inside the FDA: The Business and Politics Behind the Drugs We Take and the Food We Eat* (Hoboken, N.J.: John Wiley, 2005) at 143-77.

controversies show how thousands of people can be seriously harmed by premature introduction of pharmaceutical products. Promoting fast review becomes particularly problematic when it is not accompanied by significant improvements to post-marketing review and monitoring of side-effects of products that are already on the market. In the wake of some of the controversies, more resources have been allocated to such monitoring, but it is questionable whether they are sufficient.[132]

A major and underappreciated problem is that the requirements imposed by drug regulation only provide limited assurance about a drug's safety and efficacy. Regulatory agencies currently require that two pivotal clinical trials show that a drug has relative efficacy in a vaguely defined population.[133] A drug can be approved even if many more trials have failed to show efficacy.[134] The positive trials may show that a drug works only in a small number of patients, without providing details on the profile of these patients and without guidance about who could be harmed by the product.[135] Critics have pointed out, and some of the controversies confirm how problematic this can be, that the trials do not aim at evaluating whether drugs offer any comparable advantage over existing drug or other therapies. Once the drug is approved, marketing strategies can lead to the indiscriminate promotion of a product that is potentially much inferior to other products and that may result in significant harm to some patients.

These controversies also highlight how pharmaceutical companies are able to control the process by which scientific evidence is generated, as well as the preparation of publications and the integration of these publications in marketing strategies.[136] David Healy and Dinah Cattell demonstrated in a 2003 article how one particular medical communications company (Current Medical Directions) coordinated the scientific publication strategy of the popular SSRI sertraline (Zoloft).[137] The company, which was involved in organizing the clinical trials, gathering the data and writing up the results, strategically used academic authors

---

[132] For a proposal of financing post-marketing drug safety studies through the imposition of different user fees, see Daniel Carpenter, "A Proposal for Financing Postmarketing Drug Safety Studies by Augmenting FDA User Fees" Health Affairs, Web Exclusive, October 18, 2005, 24 Supp. 3 W5-469. See also Marcia Angell, *The Truth About the Drug Companies: How They Deceive Us and What To Do About It* (New York: Random House, 2004) at 112; David Healy, *Let Them Eat Prozac* (Toronto: James Lorimer, 2003) at 85.

[133] See Thomas A. Ban, "Towards a clinical methodology for neuropsychopharmacological research" (forthcoming) at 5 (paper in possession of authors).

[134] Marcia Angell, *The Truth About the Drug Companies: How They Deceive Us and What To Do About It* (New York: Random House, 2004) at 112. See also David Healy, *Let Them Eat Prozac* (Toronto: James Lorimer, 2003) at 85.

[135] Thomas A. Ban, "Towards a clinical methodology for neuropsychopharmacological research" (forthcoming) at 5; and Thomas A. Ban, "Academic psychiatry and the pharmaceutical industry" (2006) 30 Progress in Neuro-Psychopharmacology and Biological Psychiatry 429.

[136] For a more detailed discussion see Trudo Lemmens, "Piercing the Veil of Corporate Secrecy About Clinical Trials" (2004) 34:5 Hastings Center Report 14, and Trudo Lemmens, "Leopards in the Temple: Restoring Integrity to the Commercialized Research Scene" (2005) 32:4 J. L. Med. & Ethics 641.

[137] David Healy & Dinah Cattell, "Interface Between Authorship, Industry and Science in the Domain of Therapeutics" (2003) 183 Br. J. Psychiatry 22-27.

to get scientific publications in leading medical journals. Up to 64 per cent of the scientific publications on Zoloft were coordinated by Current Medical Directions. This and related reports raise troubling questions about ghost-authorship and the full-fledged integration of scientific publications in marketing strategies.[138] The ability to manipulate and control research creates a significant challenge for a system which relies very much on self-reporting and leaves much of the regulatory initiative in the hands of those who have significant financial interests in the outcome of research, which can be used as a powerful tool to boost drug sales. It seems reasonable therefore to conclude that the transparency[139] and integrity[140] of medical research have become "the foremost medical research issue of our age".

When a drug is approved, the United States Food and Drug Administration at one time released a "Summary Basis of Approval", which included the reviews of pharmacological, toxicological data and the comments of the Food and Drug Administration reviewers but not all the detailed reports submitted to the agency.[141] It now provides access to edited reports of reviewers.[142] Health Canada, on the other hand, provided access only to the official product monograph, which contains much less information than what is made available in the United States.[143] The TPD announced in 2004 it would disclose a

---

[138] See also Annette Flanagin *et al.*, "Prevalence of Articles with Honorary Authors and Ghost Authors in Peer-Reviewed Medical Journals" (1998) 280 J.A.M.A. 222; and Thomas Bodenheimer, "Uneasy Alliance — Clinical Investigators and the Pharmaceutical Industry" (2000) 342 N. Engl. J. Med. 1539.

[139] Calls for more transparency are not new. As far back as 1996, the International Working Group of Health Action International released a "Statement on Transparency and Accountability in Drug Regulation" calling for transparency of drug information: see International Working Group on Transparency and Accountability in Drug Regulation, "Statement of International Working Group on Transparency and Accountability in Drug Regulation", online: <http://www.haiweb.org/pubs/sec-sta.html>. See also J. Lexchin, "Secrecy and the Health Protection Branch" (1998) 159 C.M.A.J. 481 at 482-83. Lexchin describes there how his own request for information about the clinical trials supporting Health Canada's approval of a pediatric treatment that had been disapproved by the World Health Organization were never answered. Transparency in Canadian drug regulation was highlighted as a major issue in the February 2000 report of Health Canada's Science Advisory Board Committee on the Drug Review Process (Report of the Committee on the Drug Review Process of the Science Advisory Board to Health Canada: see Health Canada Science Advisory Board, "Report of the Committee on the Drug Review Process", Health Canada, online: <http://www.hc-sc.gc.ca/sr-sr/pubs/advice-avis/sab-css/rep-rap/drp-pdm_e.html>. See also a more recent April 2004 report: House of Commons Standing Committee on Health, "Opening the Medicine Cabinet: First Report on Health Aspects of Prescription Drugs. Report of the Standing Committee on Health", House of Commons Canada, online: <http://cmte.parl.gc.ca/cmte/CommitteePublication.aspx?COM=8791&Lang=1&SourceId=76297>.

[140] Shane Neilson, "Healy and Goliath: The Creation of Psychopharmacology" (2004) 170 C.M.A.J. 501 at 501.

[141] M. Baram, "Making Clinical Trials Safer for Human Subjects" (2001) 27 Am. J. L. & Med. 253 at 262.

[142] J. Lexchin, personal communication (October 22, 2006).

[143] See J. Lexchin, "Secrecy and the Health Protection Branch" (1998) 159 C.M.A.J. 481 at 482-83. Lexchin's own request for information about the clinical trials supporting Health Canada's approval of a pediatric treatment that had been disapproved by the World Health Organization

Summary Basis of Decisions document.[144] The SBD document contains "regulatory, safety, efficacy and quality (chemistry and manufacturing) considerations" relating to market approval by the TPD. Critics have argued that the information released by TPD is insufficient to enable medical professionals to properly assess the safety and efficacy of medications.[145] Lexchin and colleagues cite several examples in which SBD disclosures would not have circumvented problems arising from discrepancies between data submitted to regulators and that found in the published literature. They point out that disclosure processes used by the United States Food and Drug Administration would have identified such problems before serious harm occurred.

In Canada, data submitted by pharmaceutical companies is deemed to be "commercially sensitive" and as such constitutes confidential information under the federal *Access to Information Act*[146] (AIA). Under section 20(6) of this act, disclosure can be made where it is in the public interest as it relates to public health and safety. Nevertheless, the TPD will not release information where public interest in disclosure is outweighed by financial loss or prejudice to the competitive position of the disclosing party. This approach is related to the obligations created by Article 1711 of the 1994 North American Free Trade Agreement (NAFTA) and Article 39 of World Trade Organization's Agreement on Trade Related aspects of Intellectual Property (TRIPS), pertaining to data and market exclusivity. These require commercially sensitive information to be kept confidential. The AIA has never been successfully employed in order to force disclosure even under circumstances where harm to the public has occurred.[147]

In both countries, no clinical trial or other data is made available if a drug is not approved. This is also the case when a pharmaceutical company applies for approval of a new use for a drug that is already on the market. In addition, when a pharmaceutical company conducts further clinical trials of a marketed product, it has to report safety data to the regulatory agencies, but there is no obligation to disclose the data publicly. Thus, even clinical trial data indicating serious risks of an already approved drug can remain hidden. As Jeanne Lenzer points out: "The use of trade-secret laws to conceal deaths and serious side effects linked to drugs has the obvious flaw of putting profits before public health."[148]

---

was never answered.

[144] Health Canada, "Summary Basis of Decision", Drugs and Health Products, online: <http://www.hc-sc.gc.ca/dhp-mps/prodpharma/sbd-smd/index_e.html>.

[145] J. Lexchin, "Transparency in drug regulation: Mirage or Oasis", Canadian Centre for Policy Alternatives, online: <http://www.policyalternatives.ca/index.cfm?act=news&do=Article&call= 913&pA=ecd96aa2&type=5>; J. Lexchin & B. Mintzes, "Transparency in drug regulation: Mirage or oasis?" (2004) 171 C.M.A.J. 1363.

[146] *Access to Information Act*, R.S.C. 1985, c. A-1.

[147] J. Lexchin, "Transparency in Drug Regulation: Mirage or Oasis", Canadian Centre for Policy Alternatives, online: <http://www.policyalternatives.ca/>.

[148] Jeanne Lenzer, "Drug Secrets: What the FDA Isn't Telling", Slate, online: <http://www.slate.com/id/2126918/>. Ann Silversides also states bluntly that by keeping the results of clinical trials secret, "Health Canada is placing proprietary and commercial interests above those of the public". See Anne Silversides, "Transparency and the Drug Approval Process at Health Canada", Paper for Women and Health Protection (Fall 2005), online: <http://whp-apsf.ca/pdf/transparency.pdf> at 9.

Clearly, if there is no obligation to disclose important clinical trials data, and if reports in the scientific literature are unreliable or incomplete, it is difficult if not impossible to maintain that physicians actually engage in truly evidence-based medical practice.[149]

B. PROPOSALS FOR REGULATORY REFORM

One positive result of these controversies is that there is a groundswell of support for initiatives that aim at remedying some of the exposed problems. First of all, it is worth pointing out that drug regulatory agencies are trying, albeit prudently, to improve post-marketing review of safety of pharmaceutical products. In the United States, the budget for post-marketing evaluation was augmented for the fiscal years 2006 and 2007.[150] In 2006, the budget for drug safety increased by about U.S. $7 million, and by $5 million in 2007, a significant part of which went to better adverse event reporting, increasing the staff of CDER , and establishing a Drug Safety Oversight Board.[151]

As pointed out earlier, Health Canada has also improved post-marketing surveillance of pharmaceuticals. It changed its Canadian Adverse Drug Reaction Monitoring Program by introducing in May 2005 an Online Query and Data Extract database, which gives the public and physicians easier access to information about adverse drug reactions.[152] Former liberal Minister of Health Ujjal Dosanjh further announced in 2005 that a significant part of a $170 million five-year drug safety budget would be earmarked for post-marketing surveillance of adverse events. He also created a permanent advisory body on drug safety.[153] It should be noted that calls for improving adverse event reporting in Canada precede the Vioxx controversy. In 2001, a coroner's jury made 59 recommendations, many regarding post-marketing surveillance, following the tragic death of Vanessa Young, as a result of complications due to cisapride (Prepulsid) toxicity.[154] The jury expressly recommended mandatory reporting by

---

[149]   Raymond DeVries & Trudo Lemmens, "The Social and Cultural Shaping of Medical Evidence" (2006) 62 Soc. Sci. Med. 2694.

[150]   It should be noted, however, that the budget for post-marketing review remains minimal compared to the budget for new drug review, and that the increases for drug safety pale in comparison with increases for hot topic items such as pandemic preparedness and "war-on-terror"-related food safety issues. See Andrew C. von Eschenbach, Acting Commissioner of the Food and Drug Administration, "Statement before The House Agriculture, Rural Development, FDA and Related Agencies Appropriations Subcommittee, United States House of Representatives (February 16, 2006)", United States Food and Drug Administration, online: <http://www.fda.gov/ola/2006/budget_hearing0216.html>.

[151]   It is interesting to note that the 2007 budget sets aside U.S. $30.5 million for pandemic preparedness and U.S. $ 20 million for "food defense". See Andrew C. von Eschenbach, *ibid.*

[152]   See Health Canada, "Canadian Adverse Drug Reaction Monitoring Program (CADRMP) Online Query and Data Extracts", Drugs & Health Products, online: <http://www.hc-sc.gc.ca/dhp-mps/medeff/databasdon/database-basedon_annou-annon_e.html>.

[153]   See Laura Eggertson, "'New approach' as Health Canada seeks conditional licences for drugs, new pediatric office" (2005) 172 C.M.A.J. 864. It is unclear whether this resource allocation has been respected by the new government and whether the advisory board still exists.

[154]   Editorial, "Lessons from cisapride" (2001) 164 C.M.A.J. 1269.

physicians and pharmaceutical companies of all "serious" adverse reactions within 48 hours.[155] It further recommended that information pertaining to adverse effects provided to physicians and patients be updated to reflect such information and that all efforts should be made to maintain current written and electronic databases pertaining to adverse effects, including monthly bulletins for health care professionals and media coverage of important warnings.

Another measure to promote public accountability which is receiving increased attention is the introduction of mandatory clinical trial registration. Clinical trials registries are already integrated in some drug regulatory systems.[156] In the United States, a clinical trials databank for serious and life-threatening diseases was established under the 1997 *Food and Drug Administration Modernization Act*.[157] The registry, set up by the National Institutes of Health's National Library of Medicine, contains essential clinical trial information on both private and public trials involving such conditions and is publicly accessible.[158]

In the wake of the lawsuit against GlaxoSmithKline and other related controversies, the idea of mandatory registration of all clinical trials has received widespread support.[159] In 2004, a Ministerial Summit on Health Research in Mexico invited the WHO to take a leading role in the establishment of an

---

[155] The jury defined serious as "a noxious and unintended response to a drug that occurs at any dose and that requires inpatient hospitalization or prolongation of existing hospitalization, causes congenital malformation, results in persistent or significant disability or incapacity, is life-threatening or results in death".

[156] For discussion of the legal, ethical and intellectual property issues relating to registration, see Trudo Lemmens & Ron A. Bouchard, *Comments on the Legal, Regulatory and Ethical Aspects of the WHO Clinical Trial Registry Platform*. Submitted to the World Health Organization as part of the Formal Consultation on Disclosure Timing Policy. Geneva, April 26, 2006, online: <http://www.who.int/ictrp/011_Lemmens_Bouchard_5April06.pdf>.

[157] P.L. 105-115.

[158] See United States Department of Health and Human Services, Food and Drug Administration, Center for Drug Evaluation and Research (CDER), Center for Biologics Evaluation and Research (CBER), "Guidance for Industry Information Program on Clinical Trials for Serious or Life-Threatening Diseases and Conditions (March 2002)", U.S. Food and Drug Administration: Center for Drug Evaluation and Research, online: <http://www.fda.gov/cder/guidance/4856fnl.htm>. One recent study raises concern however, regarding compliance. The study looked at 127 cancer trials that fit the criteria for mandatory registration, and found that only 48 per cent of them had been registered. Study reported in Erick H. Turner, "A Taxpayer-Funded Clinical Trials Registry and Results Database: It already exists within the US Food and Drug Administration" (2004) 1(3) PLoS Medicine e60 at 180. Available online: <http://medicine.plosjournals.org/perlserv/?request=get-document&doi=10.1371/journal.pmed.0010060>; J. Derbis, T. Toigo, J. Woods, B. Evelyn & D. Banks, "FDAMA Section 113: Information program on clinical trials for serious and life-threatening diseases" (poster). Ninth Annual FDA Science Forum; April 24 2003, Washington, D.C., reported by Turner PloS Medicine 2004.

[159] See, *e.g.*, the Ottawa Declaration on Clinical Trials Registration, signed by more than 130 experts from five different continents, which called for the establishment of a legally enforceable clinical trials registration requirement. See Karmela Krleza-Jeric, A-W Chan, K. Dickersin *et al.*, "The Ottawa Statement, Part One: Principles for international registration of protocol information and results from human trials of health-related interventions" Ottawa Statement on Trial Registration: Cochrane/CIHR meeting, online: <http://ottawagroup.ohri.ca/statement.html>.

international clinical trials registry.[160] After extensive public consultation, and notwithstanding the fact that the pharmaceutical industry expressed its disagreement over the timing of public disclosure of many important clinical trials data,[161] the WHO recommended in May 2006 new standards for the registration of all clinical trials.[162] This initiative does not create a legally binding obligation to register clinical trials. However, in combination with other initiatives, particularly that of the International Committee of Medical Journal Articles,[163] the WHO initiative is setting a new standard for clinical trials. It will likely be followed by many national regulatory initiatives. Health Canada has already organized a consultation process to consult with various parties and the public about a mandatory clinical trials registration system in Canada.[164]

Mandatory clinical trials registration would be an important step in the promotion of transparency of clinical trials. It will help avoid the situation where results from a clinical trial can remain behind a veil of corporate secrecy. However, it will clearly not remediate all of the problems highlighted by the recent controversies, such as those associated with the increasing control of industry over the design of studies, the gathering and analysis of data, and the writing up of results. In theory, the accuracy and reliability of clinical trials can be verified by independent researchers, when information about these trials is made publicly available through trial registration. But the sheer number of clinical trials undertaken by industry makes it very hard to conduct a detailed evaluation of all trials. Some organizations, such as the Cochrane Collaborative,[165] have taken it as their mission to assess available medical evidence in

---

[160] For information on the WHO initiative, see World Health Organization, "International Clinical Trials Registry Platform", online: <http://www.who.int/ictrp/en/>. Information on the Summit can be found on that web site at World Health Organization, "Ministerial Summit on Health Research", Research Policy and Cooperation, online: <http://www.who.int/rpc/summit/en/>. In 2004, the World Health Organization (WHO) had already set up a registry for all of the research it supports. See Fiona Fleck, "WHO and Science Publishers Team Up on Online Register of Trials" (2004) 328 B.M.J. 854.

[161] See Karmela Krleža-Jeric, "Clinical Trial Registration: The Differing Views of Industry, the WHO, and the Ottawa Group" (2005) 2(11), PLoS Medicine e378, online: <medicine.plosjournals.org/perlserv/?request=get-document&doi=10.1371/journal.pmed.0020378>.

[162] See World Health Organization, News Release, "The World Health Organization announces new standards for registration of all human medical research", online: <http://www.who.int/mediacentre/news/releases/2006/pr25/en/index.html>.

[163] The International Committee of Medical Journal Editors (ICMJE) is a committee that includes 12 of the most prestigious medical journals. It announced in 2004 a new editorial policy, imposing registration of a clinical trial prior to commencing human subject recruitment as a condition for publication of the results of the study in their journals. See Catherine De Angelis, Jeffrey M. Drazen, Frank A. Frizelle *et al.*, "Clinical Trial Registration: A Statement from the International Committee of Medical Journal Editors" (2004) 351 N. Engl. J. Med. 1250. See also: <http://www.icmje.org/>.

[164] See Health Canada website on clinical trial registration: Health Canada, "Registration and Disclosure of Clinical Trial Information", Drugs and Health Products, online: <http://www.hc-sc.gc.ca/dhp-mps/prodpharma/activit/proj/enreg-clini-info/index_e.html>.

[165] P.J. White, "Evidence-based medicine for consumers: a role for the Cochrane Collaboration" (2002) 90 J. Med. Libr. Assoc. 218; J. Volmink *et al.*, "Research synthesis and dissemination as a bridge to knowledge management: the Cochrane Collaboration" (2004) Oct 82 Bull. World

a given area, and have become reputable and reliable evaluators of the integrity of available data. But their resources remain very limited compared to industry budgets for clinical trials. More importantly, the registry still relies on accurate gathering of information and accurate reporting by those with a financial interest in the outcome of the research, which has been a serious concern in the context of some of the controversies described earlier. Adverse events in clinical trials can be described inaccurately, for example, or research subjects can be preselected in order to skew the results of the trial. It has also become difficult to find truly independent investigators, with no financial ties to industry. This is also why there is an increased recognition of the need for stricter conflict of interest guidelines within academia,[166] and for increased governmental funding for independent health research.[167]

The fact that industry remains in control of the research under a clinical trial registration system may explain the relatively weak resistance against registration initiatives. Consequently, many recent calls for reform have in common that they try to separate the interests of those who design, review and conduct clinical trials from those with financial interests in the end-results.[168] More radical proposals include the establishment of a new independent national

---

Health Organ. 778.

[166] Association of American Medical Colleges. Task force on financial conflicts of interest in clinical research. *Protecting subjects, preserving trust, promoting progress: policy and guidelines for the oversight of individual financial conflict of interest in human subjects research* (2001), online: <http://www.aamc.org/research/coi/start.htm>; Association of American Medical Colleges. Task force on financial conflicts of interest in clinical research. *Protecting subjects, preserving trust, promoting progress II – principles and recommendations for oversight of an institution's financial interests in human subjects research* (2002), online: <http://www.aamc.org/research/coi/start.htm>; Institute of Medicine, *Integrity in Scientific Research: Creating an Environment that Promotes Responsible Conduct* (Washington D.C.: National Academies Press, 2002). For a discussion of various approaches to conflicts of interests, see Trudo Lemmens, "Conflict of Interest in Medical Research: Historical Developments" in Ezekiel E. Emanuel *et al.*, eds., *The Oxford Textbook of Clinical Research Ethics* (New York: Oxford University Press, 2006) and Trudo Lemmens & Lori Luther, "Conflicts of Interest of Clinician-Researchers" in Peter S. Singer & Adrian Viens, eds., *Cambridge Textbook of Bioethics* (Cambridge: Cambridge University Press, forthcoming 2007) and references there.

[167] See James R. Brown, "Self-Censorship" in Trudo Lemmens & Duff R. Waring, *Law and Ethics in Biomedical Research: Regulation, Conflict of Interest, and Liability* (Toronto: University of Toronto Press, 2006); Jocelyn Downie, "Grasping the Nettle: Confronting the Issue of Competing Interests and Obligation in Health Research Policy" in Colleen M. Flood, ed., *Just Medicare: What's In, What's Out, How We Decide* (Toronto: University of Toronto Press, 2006) 427; Trudo Lemmens, "Commercialized Medical Research and the Need for Regulatory Reform" in Colleen M. Flood, *ibid.*, at 396.

[168] See, for example, A.J.J. Wood, C.M. Stein & R. Woosley, "Making Medicines Safer: The Need for an Independent Drug Safety Board" (1998) 339 N. Engl. J. Med. 1851; Sheldon Krimsky, *Science in the Private Interest: Has the Lure of Profits Corrupted Biomedical Research* (Lanham MD: Rowman & Littlefield, 2003) at 229; Marcia Angell, *The Truth About the Drug Companies: How They Deceive Us and What To Do About It* (New York: Random House, 2004) at 244-47; Wayne A. Ray & C. Michael Stein, "Reform of Drug Regulation — Beyond an Independent Drug-Safety Board" (2006) 354 N. Eng. J. Med. 194; Jay S. Cohen, *Overdose: The Case Against the Drug Companies* (New York: Penguin, 2001) at 198-211.

institute for drug testing.[169] This new drug testing institute would assume control over all clinical drug trials, which are now organized by industry. A company wishing to apply for approval of a new drug would negotiate with this new institute an appropriate protocol. The institute would invite tenders from certified drug evaluation centers for conducting the trials. In this manner, academic research centers could replace much of their current corporate funding from clinical drug trials by participating in such independent system of drug evaluation. Clinical drug trials would thus be conducted and analyzed by people who have no financial stake in the outcome of the trial.

In a 2005 article in the *New England Journal of Medicine*, Wayne A. Ray and C. Michael Stein make a detailed proposal for the development of a new agency with three different branches.[170] Their proposal is interesting for the fact that it not only deals with problems associated with drug approval and post-marketing surveillance, but also with the potential manipulation of drug information in marketing. They recommend the establishment of a Center for Drug Approval, a Center for Post-Marketing Studies, and a Center for Drug Information. The three Centers would each be independent but part of a unified Drug Agency which would be funded by a tax on pharmaceutical sales. The Center for Drug Approval would be in charge of initial licensing of new drugs. The release of some new drugs could be "phased", *i.e.*, restricted pending the completion of post-marketing studies.[171] These studies would be organized through the Center for Post-Marketing Studies, which would itself select the independent investigators who would receive a contract to conduct the studies.[172] The Center for Drug Information would play a very active role in communicating information on pharmaceuticals to physicians and to the public. It would be in charge of designing more effective labels and would also establish direct communication channels with physicians. As the authors state, "effective communication of information should become a central responsibility of regulators".[173]

---

[169] See, for example, Sheldon Krimsky, *Science in the Private Interest: Has the Lure of Profit Corrupted Biomedical Research?* (Lanham MD: Rowman & Littlefield, 2003) at 229; Marcia Angell, *The Truth About the Drug Companies: How They Deceive Us and What To Do About It* (New York: Random House, 2004) at 244-47.

[170] Wayne A. Ray & C. Michael Stein, "Reform of Drug Regulation — Beyond an Independent Drug-Safety Board" (2006) 354 N. Eng. J. Med. 194.

[171] Others refer to the need to introduce "conditional approval" pending further post-marketing studies. See also Health Products and Food Branch, "Blueprint for Renewal: Transforming Canada's Approach to Regulating Health Products and Food", Health Canada, online: <http://www.hc-sc.gc.ca/ahc-asc/alt_formats/hpfb-dgpsa/pdf/hpfb-dgpsa/blueprint-plan_e.pdf>, at 7, 9, 17 and 21.

[172] Less radical proposals also underscore the importance of obtaining post-marketing data from independent sources. Jerry Avorn, for example, suggests that the federal authorities in the United States should be more actively involved in promoting independent postmarketing research. They should either provide the full funding, or work with health insurance companies and academic medical centers to organize independent clinical trials, evaluating the long-term safety and efficacy of pharmaceutical products: Jerry Avorn, *Powerful Medicines: The Benefits, Risks, and Costs of Prescription Drugs* (New York: Alfred A. Knopf, 2004) at 383-87. His proposal also involves an initial differentiation of new drugs into different categories, depending on their expected value. See *ibid.*, at 381-82.

[173] Wayne A. Ray & C. Michael Stein, "Reform of Drug Regulation — Beyond an Independent

Finally, in the wake of several recent large and unexpected drug withdrawals, commentators have pointed out that it would be better to separate the task of drug approval from the task of investigating serious post-marketing problems.[174] This seems even more important in light of the growing interdependence of the Canadian and United States drug regulatory agencies on the pharmaceutical industry. As pointed out earlier[175] the drug regulatory process is focusing on fast and efficient drug approval, under pressure from industry, which provides an increasingly important proportion of the drug regulatory agencies' budget and has become, so to speak, the agencies' client. Although it is unavoidable that some side effects become apparent only after a drug is marketed, the massive withdrawals over the last couple of years can be seen as a failure of the approval process. The agency that has approved the drug seems to have an institutional conflict of interest, when it has to investigate a product it approved and decide whether or not to withdraw it from the market.[176]

VI. NEW GOVERNMENT POLICIES RELATING TO PHARMACEUTICALS

A. Balancing Public and Private Interests in Canada: The National Pharmaceuticals Strategy

The regulatory approval and safety assessment of pharmaceuticals is in Canada an integral part of a much wider pharmaceutical policy. According to the Government of Canada there are five "pillars" of federal pharmaceutical policy: (1) intellectual property, (2) pharmaceutical research and development, (3) international trade policy, (4) health care and (5) consumer protection.[177] With this five-prong policy, the government attempts to balance the rights and interests of public and private parties in the funding, commercialization and regulation of pharmaceuticals in Canada.[178] In June 2006, government outlined

---

Drug-Safety Board" (2006) 354 N. Eng. J. Med. 194 at 199.

[174] See Jerry Avorn, *Powerful Medicines: The Benefits, Risks, and Costs of Prescription Drugs* (New York: Alfred A. Knopf, 2004) at 373; A.J.J. Wood, C.M. Stein & R. Woosley, "Making Medicines Safer — The Need for an Independent Drug Safety Board" (1998) 339 N. Engl. J. Med. 1851.

[175] See section IV, *supra*.

[176] As several authors have pointed out, for other economic activities which entail risks (often with less risk of harm to members of the public) and for which governmental oversight exists, the governmental agencies that regulate the industry are separate from the agencies that investigate failures in the system. See A.J.J. Wood, C.M. Stein & R. Woosley, "Making Medicines Safer — the Need for an Independent Drug Safety Board" (1998) 339 N. Engl. J. Med. 1851; Jay S. Cohen, *Overdose: The Case Against the Drug Companies* (New York: Penguin, 2001) at 198 and 199-200; Jerry Avorn, *Powerful Medicines: The Benefits, Risks, and Costs of Prescription Drugs* (New York: Alfred A. Knopf, 2004) at 373.

[177] See Barbara Oullet, *Pharmaceutical Management and Price Control in Canada*. Presentation to the North American Pharmaceutical Summit, March 31, 2006, at 7.

[178] See Regulatory Impact Analysis Statement, SOR/93-133, C. Gaz. 2004. Vol. 138, No. 50; Federal/Provincial/Territorial Ministerial Task Force on the National Pharmaceuticals Strategy:

its plans for the future in the *National Pharmaceuticals Strategy Progress Report*[179] (NPS report). This report was prepared by provincial Health Ministers (save Quebec) and intended to assess key challenges and opportunities in the area of pharmaceutical management relating to the three broad themes of access to affordable health care; safety, efficacy and appropriate use of pharmaceuticals; and maintaining a sustainable health care system.[180] The NPS report identified drug safety, effectiveness and use as key challenges of the current Canadian drug regime. Adverse drug reactions were seen to be particularly problematic in this regard. The report claimed it was imperative to have "accurate, unbiased and up-to-date information about a drug's effectiveness", and it identified what it called a lack of information regarding "real world drug performance" as the main challenge. The report does not look, however, at increasing the transparency of pre- or post-marketing clinical trial reporting or regulatory approval.

According to the Ministerial Task Force,[181] issues of safety, effectiveness and use could be best addressed by leveraging "opportunities" to increase research *capacity* and by working with health care professionals to improve prescribing habits. Given recent events surrounding documented but unreported side effects

---

"National Pharmaceuticals Strategy: Progress Report", Health Canada, online: <http://www.hc-sc.gc.ca/hcs-sss/pubs/care-soins/2006-nps-snpp/index_e.html>; Treasury Board of Canada, *Smart Regulation. Report on Actions and Plans: Fall 2005 Update*, Library and Archives Canada, online: <www.regulation.gc.ca/docs/report1/rap_e.pdf>; Conference Board of Canada, "Six Quick Hits for Canadian Commercialization: Leaders' Roundtable on Commercialization", online: <http://www.conferenceboard.ca/documents.asp?rnext=1248>; Institute for Competitiveness and Prosperity, "Rebalancing priorities for Canada's prosperity. Report on Canada, March 2006", online: <http://www.competeprosper.ca/public/ott06.pdf>; Expert Panel on Commercialization, "People and Excellence: The Heart of Successful Commercialization: Vols 1 & 2", online: <http://strategis.ic.gc.ca/epic/internet/inepc-gdc.nsf/en/tq00016e.html>.

[179] Federal/Provincial/Territorial Ministerial Task Force on the National Pharmaceuticals Strategy, "National Pharmaceuticals Strategy Progress Report", *ibid.*

[180] Federal/Provincial/Territorial Ministerial Task Force on the National Pharmaceuticals Strategy, "National Pharmaceuticals Strategy Progress Report", *ibid.*, at 7. The NPS arose from a First Ministers meeting in September 2004. The Ministers deemed nine elements of the health care system to be fundamental to their *10-Year Plan to Strengthen Health Care*: Develop, assess and cost options for catastrophic pharmaceutical coverage; Establish a common National Drug Formulary for participating jurisdictions based on safety and cost effectiveness; Accelerate access to breakthrough drugs for unmet health needs through improvements to the drug approval process; Strengthen evaluation of real-world drug safety and effectiveness; Pursue purchasing strategies to obtain best prices for Canadians for drugs and vaccines; Enhance action to influence the prescribing behaviour of health care professionals so that drugs are used only when needed and the right drug is used for the right problem; Broaden the practice of e-prescribing through accelerated development and deployment of the Electronic Health Record; Accelerate access to non-patented drugs and achieve international parity on prices of non-patented drugs; and Enhance analysis of cost drivers and cost-effectiveness, including best practices in drug plan policies. (see Health Canada, "First Minister's Meeting on the Future of Health Care 2004", Health Systems, online: <http://www.hc-sc.gc.ca/hcs-sss/delivery-prestation/fptcollab/2004-fmm-rpm/index_e.html>). The Ministers requested that their respective health Ministers produce a national strategy by June 2006 based on these elements.

[181] Federal/Provincial/Territorial Ministerial Task Force on the National Pharmaceuticals Strategy, "National Pharmaceuticals Strategy Progress Report", *ibid.*, at 20.

associated with SSRI use in child, teenaged, and adult populations as well as
well cardiovascular problems associated with antiosteoarthritis drugs, one could
safely assume that increasing the transparency and breadth of clinical trial or
post-approval adverse effects reporting would greatly improve the safety and
efficacy profile of most drugs moving through the regulatory process. This
would accord with the stated Purpose and Objectives of the NPS to provide
better evidence for regulator and health professional decision-makers, safer and
more effective drug treatments, and more open and transparent processes for
regulatory approval and ethical resource allocation.[182]

Another important issue identified in the NPS report is that of access to
affordable generic medications. However, while the Ministers are clear in
articulating this goal, the means by which it is to be presumably achieved is
open to significant criticism. The report is fairly specific[183] in stipulating that
increased access to generic medication will be facilitated by amendments
currently being debated to the *NOC Regulations*, FDA and FDR.[184] However,
what is missing in the report is that these amendments are not aimed at
bolstering intellectual property or regulatory rights of generic manufacturers, or
curing obvious defects in the *NOC Regulations* that make them amenable to
abuse by brand-name pharmaceutical companies, or even to accelerate access to
generic medications. Rather, they are intended to extend non-patent market and
data exclusivity rights attaching to clinical trial and other regulatory data
submitted by brand-name manufacturers under TRIPS from five years to a
maximum of 8.5 years, notwithstanding Federal Court of Appeal jurisprudence[185]
to the effect that Canada does not need to undertake such measures to be TRIPS-
compliant. Previous amendments proposed in 2004[186] had the maximal period of
time at 11.5 years. The proposed "remedy" offered in the NPS report is therefore
more akin to supporting, rather than opposing, patent monopolies for brand-
name pharmaceutical companies, as is clear from statements in the report
underscoring the "crucial role the innovative pharmaceutical industry plays in
the development of breakthrough drugs" and that intellectual property protection
is "key to encouraging and supporting innovation".

A final element of the NPS report relevant to this discussion is its claim to
safeguard public health by developing measures to for "gathering, interpreting

[182] *Ibid.*, at 24.
[183] *Ibid.*, at 40.
[184] Regulatory Impact Analysis Statement. Regulations Amending the Food and Drug Regulations
      (Data Protection), C. Gaz. 2004. Vol. 138, No. 50; Regulatory Impact Analysis Statement.
      Regulations Amending the Patented Medicines (Notice of Compliance) Regulations, C. Gaz.,
      2004. Vol. 138, No. 50; Regulatory Impact Analysis Statement. Regulations Amending the Food
      and Drug Regulations (Data Protection), C. Gaz. 2006. Vol. 140, No. 24; Regulatory Impact
      Analysis Statement. Regulations Amending the Patented Medicines (Notice of Compliance)
      Regulations, C. Gaz. 2006. Vol. 140, No. 24.
[185] *Bayer, Inc. v. Canada*, [1999] F.C.J. No. 826, 243 N.R. 170 (F.C.A.), leave to appeal to S.C.C.
      refused [1999] S.C.C.A. No. 386 (S.C.C.).
[186] Regulatory Impact Analysis Statement. Regulations Amending the Food and Drug Regulations
      (Data Protection). C. Gaz. 2004. 2004 Vol. 138, No. 50; Regulatory Impact Analysis Statement.
      Regulations Amending the Patented Medicines (Notice of Compliance) Regulations, C. Gaz.
      2004. 2004 Vol. 138, No. 50

and applying" drug safety and effectiveness information.[187] To this end four strategies were enunciated, including creation of a national oversight body to assess "real world" drug safety and effectiveness, establishment of a network of pharmaceutical research "Centres of Excellence" and regional adverse effects reporting centres, encourage "front-line" reporting of adverse event data, and establishment of standards for "transparency of evidence" including public disclosure of medical evidence. However, while all four goals are welcome and laudable, the only recommendations tabled by the Ministers was to "engage stakeholders" on the four themes and work towards completion of a business plan for the pharmaceutical network. It remains to be seen whether government will act to ensure increased transparency in the approval process beyond the minimal level currently seen with the much criticized Summary Basis of Decision document,[188] particularly given current amendments to the *NOC Regulations*, FDA and FDR which extend, not reduce, data, market and pediatric exclusivity.

B. DRUG PRICING — THE PATENTED MEDICINES PRICES REVIEW BOARD (PMPRB)

The PMPRBwas created in 1987 and given expanded powers to investigate and regulate drug prices under Bill C-91 in 1993 when the compulsory licensing regime in Canada was abolished and the government of the day felt drug prices would need to be curtailed.[189] Attacks on the PMPRB following its creation by multinational pharmaceutical firms established that creation of the board was *intra vires* the Parliament of Canada as a proper exercise of its jurisdiction over patent protection for new drugs.[190] In *ICN v. Canada*, the Federal Court of Appeal held that the powers of the PMPRB are to be construed broadly in light of the fact that the legislative purpose of the PMPRB is to replace price controls mandated by the previous compulsory licensing regime, which itself had been broadly construed.

---

[187] Federal/Provincial/Territorial Ministerial Task Force on the National Pharmaceuticals Strategy, "National Pharmaceuticals Strategy Progress Report", Health Canada, online: <http://www.hc-sc.gc.ca/hcs-sss/pubs/care-soins/2006-nps-snpp/index_e.html>.

[188] J. Lexchin, "Transparency in Drug Regulation: Mirage or Oasis", Canadian Centre for Policy Alternatives, online: <http://policyalternatives.ca/index.cfm?act=news&do=Article&call=913&pA=94761C2A&type=5>; J. Lexchin & B. Mintzes, "Transparency in drug regulation: Mirage or oasis?" (2004) 171 C.M.A.J. 1363.

[189] Patricia I. Carter, *"Federal Regulation of Pharmaceuticals in the United States and Canada"* (1999) 21 Loy. L.A. Int'l & Comp. L. Rev. 215; See also Gunar K. Gaikis, "Pharmaceutical patents in Canada. An update on compulsory licensing" (1992) 42 Patent World 19; D.G. McFetridge, *Intellectual Property Rights and the Location of Innovative Activity: The Canadian Experience with Compulsory Licensing of Patented Pharmaceuticals* (Presented at the National Bureau of Economic Research (NBER) Summer Institute, Cambridge MA, July 29, 1997).

[190] *Manitoba Society of Seniors v. Canada (Attorney General)*, [1991] M.J. No. 22, 35 C.P.R. 3d 66 (Man. Q.B.); affd [1992] M.J. No. 482, 45 C.P.R. 3d 194 (Man. C.A.); *ICN Pharmaceuticals, Inc. v. Canada (Patented Medicine Prices Review Board)*, [1996] F.C.J. No. 1065, [1997] F.C. 32 (F.C.A.).

The purpose of the PMPRB is to ensure that prices of patented and non-patented medicines are not excessive.[191] To this effect it monitors and reports prices of non-patented drugs and publishes annual reports on its efforts. The PMPRB mandate does not include setting drug prices, analyzing relative cost-effectiveness or value of new drugs or taking an active role in formulary listing and reimbursement pricing. As noted elsewhere in this chapter, these responsibilities are assumed either by the provinces and territories under their constitutional jurisdiction or, to some degree, by the CDR. In order to determine whether the price for a given drug is "excessive", new drugs are labelled in one of three categories: Category 1 refers to line extensions of existing medicines. The price of a Category 1 drug is presumed excessive if it does not bear a reasonable relationship to the price of other medicines of the same strength sold by the patentee; Category 2 refers to breakthrough or substantial improvements over existing drugs. The price of a Category 2 drug is presumed excessive if it exceeds the prices of all the medicines in the same therapeutic class or the median of the prices in seven countries (France, Germany, Italy, Sweden, Switzerland, the United Kingdom and the United States). Category 3 refers to new chemical entities offering moderate, little or no therapeutic improvement. The price of a Category 3 drug is presumed excessive if it exceeds the prices of all the medicines in the same therapeutic class. The vast majority of drugs reviewed by the PMPRB and parallel agencies in other jurisdictions are line extensions rather than true innovative breakthrough products.[192]

The PMPRB also monitors the price of existing drugs, which is considered excessive if it exceeds the increase in the general Canadian Consumer Price Index. Following lobbying by industry and Parliamentary review, the PMPRB now monitors and reports prices of non-patented drug prices, using international median prices as a benchmark.[193] The PMPRB monitors and reports the prices of non-patented drugs even though provincial and territorial governments have

---

[191] Patented Medicines Prices Review Board, "Compendium of Guidelines, Polices and Procedures", online: <http://www.pmprb-cepmb.gc.ca/english/View.asp?x=654>.

[192] For example, the PMPRB found over a five-year term that of 455 new drugs, 204 (45 per cent) were line extensions, 226 (49.5 per cent) drugs were new products or new dosage forms of existing medicines that provided moderate, little or no improvement over existing medicines and only 25 (5.5 per cent of total) comprised a substantial therapeutic improvement or breakthrough product: *Patented Medicine Prices Review Board. Annual Report 2000.* Ottawa, 2001. A similar report assessed the innovative value of new drugs on the French market. It found that during a 21-year period 7 (0.25 per cent) of 2,693 new drugs marketed constituted a major therapeutic innovation in an area where no treatment was previously available, 73 (10 per cent) were important advances but with limitations and 1,780 (~91 per cent) were either superfluous new products or new indications for older drugs that did not add to the clinical possibilities offered by previously available products: "Drugs in 2001: A number of ruses unveiled" (2002) 11 Prescrire International 58. In the United States, the Food and Drug Administration has stated that only 15 per cent of new medications marketed between 1989 and 2000 were true innovative drugs: Song Hee Hong, Marvin D. Shepherd, David Scoones, & Thomas T.H. Wan, "Product-Line Extensions and Pricing Strategies of Brand-Name Drugs Facing Patent Expiration" (2005) 11 J. Manag. Care Pharm. 746.

[193] Federal/Provincial/Territorial Ministerial Task Force on the National Pharmaceuticals Strategy, "National Pharmaceuticals Strategy Progress Report", Health Canada, online: <http://www.hc-sc.gc.ca/hcs-sss/pubs/care-soins/2006-nps-snpp/index_e.html>.

jurisdiction for regulating the prices of such drugs under section 91(13) of the *Constitution Act, 1867*. When manufacturers set the price of a patented medicine too high, the PMPRB first attempts to have the manufacturer reduce the price voluntarily. Barring this, it can hold a public hearing into the price following which it can order the manufacturer to reduce the price withdraw the manufacturer's market authorization, or impose a fine equal to or double the amount of the excessive increase in price.[194]

C. INTELLECTUAL PROPERTY RIGHTS — PATENTS, NOC REGULATIONS AND TRIPS

There has been a substantial shift over the course of the last 15 years in the relationship between intellectual property rights for pharmaceuticals enshrined in the *Patent Act* and the requirements for regulatory approval of drugs found in the FDA and FDR. For a significant time prior to 1993, Canada had in place substantial provisions in the *Patent Act* allowing compulsory licensing under certain conditions.[195] As part of negotiations and obligations under NAFTA and TRIPS, Canada's compulsory licensing regime for pharmaceuticals was repealed in favour of "linkage regulations" referred to as the *NOC Regulations*. So-called linkage regulations tie patent protection for marketed pharmaceuticals to the drug approval process. As such they control both entry of generic drugs into the Canadian market and access by Canadians to affordable medication. Linkage regulations also create a dual role for governmental agencies:[196] on the one hand, they are charged with ensuring the safety and efficacy of pharmaceutical products while on the other they play an important role in protecting the competitive advantage of pharmaceutical companies as well as industrial development in Canada and abroad. This raises the concern that the regulatory approval system has become too reliant on industry self-regulation, and that the independence of the regulatory agencies has suffered as a result.[197]

---

[194] Meghan McMahon, Steve Morgan & Craig Mitton, "The Common Drug Review: A NICE start for Canada?" (2006) 77 Health Policy 339 at 346-47; See also Patented Medicines Prices Review Board, "Compendium of Guidelines, Polices and Procedures", online: <http://www.pmprb-cepmb.gc.ca/english/View.asp?x=654>.

[195] Gunar K. Gaikis, "Pharmaceutical patents in Canada. An update on compulsory licensing" (1992) 42 Patent World 19; D.G. McFetridge, *Intellectual Property Rights and the Location of Innovative Activity: The Canadian Experience with Compulsory Licensing of Patented Pharmaceuticals* (presented at the National Bureau of Economic Research (NBER) Summer Institute, Cambridge MA, July 29, 1997).

[196] R.S. Eisenberg, "Patents, product exclusivity, and information dissemination: how law directs biopharmaceutical research and development" (2003) 72 Fordham Law Rev. 477; R.A. Bouchard, "Should scientific research in the lead-up to invention vitiate obviousness under the Patented Medicines (Notice of Compliance) Regulations: To test or not to test?" (2007) 6(1) C.J.L.T. 1; R.A. Bouchard, "Living separate and apart is never easy: Inventive capacity of the PHOSITA as the tie that binds obviousness and inventiveness" (2007) 4(1) U.O.L.T.J. 1.

[197] R.S. Eisenberg, *ibid.* M. McBane, "Health Canada proposing to eviscerate the Food & Drugs Act" *The CCPA Monitor*, Vol. 10, No. 8, February 2004; J. Lexchin, "Intellectual property rights and the Canadian pharmaceutical marketplace: Where do we go from here?" (2005) 35 Int'l J. Health Services 237; B. Campbell & M. Lee, "Putting Canadians at Risk: How the federal

In addition to patent protection *per se*, new provisions were added to the FDA and FDR pertaining to data and market exclusivity. These terms refer to additional periods of time whereby pharmaceutical companies are granted market monopolies linked to test and other data submitted to Health Canada in the context of regulatory submissions. The substance and procedure of the *NOC Regulations* were based on analogous legislation and policy in the United States.[198] Prior to this point, patent protection and regulatory approval of pharmaceuticals were governed by two completely different sets of statutes as well as different policy goals and objectives.

Since its coming into force there has been long-standing and substantial criticism of the linkage regulation regime both in the U.S. and Canada, coming primarily from the generic drug industry[199] as well as public lobbying groups concerned about access to affordable medication.[200] Industry Canada, which oversees the *NOC Regulations*, has maintained that the regulations continue to be in the public interest even though the Supreme Court of Canada has gone so far as to call them "draconian" in its leading patent cases.[201] In addition, the *NOC Regulations* were heavily criticized in 2001 by the Romanow Commission on the Future of Health Care in Canada ("Romanow Commission"), which alleged that delays in market entry of cheaper generic medications have cost Canada's health care system hundreds of millions dollars by obliging consumers to pay for monopoly-priced versions for longer than warranted by Canada's traditional patent law.[202]

In particular, the Romanow Commission took aim at a practice allowed under the *NOC Regulations* called "evergreening". Evergreening refers to the use of

government's deregulation agenda threatens health and environmental standards", Canadian Centre for Policy Alternative Working Paper, online <www.policyalternatives.ca/documents/National_Office_Pubs/2006/Putting_Canadians_at_Risk_summary.pdf>; Anne Silversides, "Transparency and the Drug Approval Process at Health Canada", Paper for Women and Health Protection (Fall 2005), online: <http://whp-apsf.ca/pdf/transparency.pdf>.

[198] *Drug Price Competition and Patent Restoration Act 1984* (Pub. L. No. 98-417, 98 Stat. 1585, Codified as amended at 21 USC § 355 (2000)), commonly known as the *Hatch-Waxman Act.*

[199] See "Patently Absurd", Canadian Generic Pharmaceutical Association, online: <http://www.canadiangenerics.ca/en/issues/federal.shtml>.

[200] For example, National Union of Public and General Employees (NUPGE), Alliance of Seniors to Protect Canada's Social Programs, Canadian Health Coalition, Canadian Pensioners Concerned, Inc. (National), Congress of Union Retirees of Canada, Council of Senior Citizens' Organizations of British Columbia and National Pensioners and Senior Citizens Federation: National Union of Public and General Employees, "NUPGE continuesc campaign to halt 'evergreening'", online: <http://www.nupge.ca/news%5F2004/n18oc04a.htm>. For review of the United States landscape, see Andrew A. Caffrey & Jonathan M. Rotter, "Consumer protection, patents and procedure: Generic drug market entry and the need to reform *Hatch-Waxman Act*" (2004) 9 Virg. J. Law & Tech. 1.

[201] *Merck Frosst Canada Inc. v. Canada (Minister of National Health and Welfare)*, [1998] S.C.J. No. 58, [1998] 2 S.C.R. 193 (S.C.C.); *Bristol-Meyers Squibb Co. v. Canada (Attorney General)*, [2005] S.C.J. No. 26, [2005] 1 S.C.R. 533, 2005 SCC 26 (S.C.C.) at paras. 24 and 146; *AstraZeneca Canada Inc. v. Canada (Minister of Health)*, [2006] S.C.J. No. 49, [2006] 2 S.C.R. 560, 2006 SCC 40 (S.C.C.) at para. 17.

[202] Roy J. Romanow, Q.C., *Building on Values: The Future of Health Care in Canada* (Ottawa: Commission on the Future of Health Care in Canada, 2002) at 208.

multiple automatic stays of two years in length by brand-name pharmaceutical companies. These stays can be cumulated over potentially very long periods of time by way of strategic listing of patents on the patent register relative to litigation by generic pharmaceutical companies under the NOC Regulations.[203] These stays operate cumulatively with periods of market exclusivity arising from the patent monopoly. That no grounds need be proved by brand-name pharmaceutical companies other than merely *initiating* a defence to a generic brand-name pharmaceutical company's notice of allegation (of non-infringement or invalidity of a brand-name company's listed patent) is what led the Supreme Court to refer to the *NOC Regulations* as "draconian". Ironically, the United States has significantly diminished the capacity of brand-name pharmaceutical companies to engage in evergreening practices following lobbying by a multitude of interested parties which led to a detailed study by the United States Federal Trade Commission.[204] Unfortunately, the Canadian government continues, at least in its 2004 and 2006 Regulatory Impact Analysis Statements pertaining to the *NOC Regulations*,[205] to maintain that the interests of the public and those of the brand-name pharmaceutical industry are "balanced" when this seems clearly not the case.[206] As such, the *NOC Regulations* have had a significant impact not only on the standard of patentability in Canada, but also on the distribution of benefits derived from publicly funded biomedical research.[207] It is possible that this is related to the increasing project of Industry Canada to push its innovation and competitiveness agendas and how this has been "enabled" by the increasing public-private partnership of the federal government and industry in Canada compared to other jurisdictions such as the

---

[203] For a more detailed description, see R.A. Bouchard, "Should scientific research in the lead-up to invention vitiate obviousness under the Patented Medicines (Notice of Compliance) Regulations: To test or not to test?" (2007) 6(1) C.J.L.T. 1; R.A. Bouchard, "Living separate and apart is never easy: Inventive capacity of the PHOSITA as the tie that binds obviousness and inventiveness" (2007) 4(1) U.O.L.T.J. 1.

[204] United States Federal Trade Commission, "Generic Drug Entry Prior to Patent Expiration: An FTC Study", <http://www.ftc.gov/os/2002/07/genericdrugstudy.pdf>. For review of the history of this report, see Andrew A. Caffrey & Jonathan M. Rotter, "Consumer protection, patents and procedure: Generic drug market entry and the need to reform the *Hatch-Waxman Act*" (2004) 9(1) Virg. J. Law & Tech. 1.

[205] Regulatory Impact Analysis Statement. Regulations Amending the Food and Drug Regulations (Data Protection), C. Gaz. 2004. 2004 Vol. 138, No. 50; Regulatory Impact Analysis Statement. Regulations Amending the Patented Medicines (Notice of Compliance) Regulations, C. Gaz. 2004. 2004 Vol. 138, No. 50; and Regulatory Impact Analysis Statement. Regulations Amending the Food and Drug Regulations (Data Protection), C. Gaz. 2006. Vol. 140, No. 24; Regulatory Impact Analysis Statement. Regulations Amending the Patented Medicines (Notice of Compliance) Regulations, C. Gaz. 2006. Vol. 140, No. 24.

[206] R.A. Bouchard, "Should scientific research in the lead-up to invention vitiate obviousness under the Patented Medicines (Notice of Compliance) Regulations: To test or not to test?" (2007) 6(1) C.J.L.T. 1; R.A. Bouchard, "Living separate and apart is never easy: Inventive capacity of the PHOSITA as the tie that binds obviousness and inventiveness" (2007) 4(1) U.O.L.T.J. 1.

[207] Ron A. Bouchard, "Balancing public and private interests in commercialization of publicly funded biomedical technologies: Is there a role for compulsory government royalty fees?" (2007) 13(2) B.U.J. Sci. & Tech. L. 1; Ron A. Bouchard & Trudo Lemmens, "The Privatization of Medical Research: A third way" (2007) Nature Biotechnology (forthcoming).

United States, Britain and France.[208] More will be said about this in sections 6.4-
6.6, *infra.*

D. FRIEND OR FOE FOR THE "PUBLIC" INTEREST? SMART REGULATION

The Government of Canada's recent Smart Regulation[209] initiative is a substantial and potentially far-reaching federal government initiative[210] aimed at improving the regulatory performance of Canada and strengthening the policy, processes, and administrative tools required to enhance national competitiveness and prosperity in the global economic arena. The initiative is based on two reports commissioned in regard to regulatory reform: the 2002 report of the Organisation for Economic Development (OECD)[211] and the 2004 report of the External Advisory Commission on Smart Regulation.[212] It involves a series of programs intended to enshrine substantial cultural change within government civil service regarding, among other things, the degree of public-private partnership in federal policy-making. The stated principles of the initiative are: to protect the health and safety and Canadians, to reflect the values of Canadians, to learn from the best and use the best, and ensure ongoing coordination among government departments and branches.[213] The five themes of regulatory reform are a healthy Canada, environmental sustainability, safety and security, aboriginal prosperity and innovation, productivity and business environment. The Privy Council Office has recently indicated that to effect change in relation to these themes it plans to strengthen regulatory management by developing new policies, improve efficiency by facilitating coordination across different branches of government, and implement the principles enumerated above in policies directed to health care, business innovation and productivity.[214] From

[208] Patricia I. Carter, "Federal Regulation of Pharmaceuticals in the United States and Canada" (1999) 21 Loy. L.A. Int'l & Comp. L. Rev. 215; Mary E. Wiktorowicz, "Emergent Patterns in the Regulation of Pharmaceuticals: Institutions and Interests in the United States, Canada, Britain and France" (2003) 28 J. Health Pol. 615; B. Campbell & M. Lee, "Putting Canadians at Risk: How the federal government's deregulation agenda threatens health and environmental standards", Canadian Centre for Policy Alternative Working Paper, online: <www.policyalternatives.ca/documents/National_Office_Pubs/2006/Putting_Canadians_at_Risk _summary.pdf>.

[209] Specific, Measurable, Attainable, Realistic, Timely regulations.

[210] External Advisory Committee on Smart Regulation, "Smart Regulation: A Regulatory Strategy for Canada. Report to the Government of Canada", online: <http://www.pco-bcp.gc.ca/smartreg-regint/en/08/sum.html>.

[211] Organisation for Economic Cooperation and Development, "OECD Praises Canada's Regulatory Reforms and Encourages Sustained Momentum", Regulary Reform, online: <http://www.oecd.org/document/23/0,2340,en_2649_37421_1835224_1_1_1_1_37421,00.html>.

[212] External Advisory Committee on Smart Regulation, "Smart Regulation: A Regulatory Strategy for Canada. Report to the Government of Canada", online: <http://www.pco-bcp.gc.ca/smartreg-regint/en/08/sum.html>.

[213] Speech by Reg Alcock, "Government of Canada's Implementation Plan for Smart Regulations", Treasury Board of Canada Secretariat, online: <http://www.tbs-sct.gc.ca/media/ps-dp/2005/0324_e.asp>.

[214] *Ibid.*

this information, publicly disclosed to Canadians, it is clear the purpose of the Smart Regulation is to move Canada onto the new "global economic stage" while protecting the health, safety, security and values of Canadians. The question remains however, as to whose definitions of health, safety, security and values are to guide the government in constructing and implementing its reform project? This is a legitimate and important question given the increasing public-private partnership in the area of pharmaceutical regulation.[215] As noted by Janice Graham,[216] while the Smart Regulation initiative explicitly recognizes the importance of safeguarding public health and safety, it appears predominantly aimed at securing conditions for an innovative economy. Indeed, it takes a close reading of government press releases and reports in light of related and historical policy documents and commentary to arrive at this conclusion, a problem which has not escaped public notice.[217] The Smart Regulation initiative has been strongly criticized for the fact that it will undermine public scrutiny.[218] Typical of criticism is the statement that should the strategy become law, the "government risks no longer being a protector of public health but a cheerleader for economic growth" at the risk of public health.[219] Caution has been advised on several fronts,[220] including the assumption that Canadian policy must track American policy, risk assessment should be governed by cost-benefit analysis rather than the precautionary principle (otherwise, a standard of no evidence of harm will take precedence over a requirement for scientific evidence of safety and efficacy), undue optimism regarding the ability or desire of private parties to participate fully in the regulatory process, and lack of clarity on the issue of whether smart regulation equates to de-regulation.

---

[215] Patricia I. Carter, "Federal Regulation of pharmaceuticals in the United States and Canada" (1999) 21 Loy. L.A. Int'l & Comp. L. Rev. 215.

[216] Janice Graham, "Smart Regulation: Will the government's strategy work?" (2005) 173 C.M.A.J. 1469 at 1469.

[217] See *e.g.*, M. McBane, "Health Canada proposing to eviscerate the Food & Drugs Act", The CCPA Monitor, February 2004; B. Campbell & M. Lee, *Putting Canadians at Risk: How the federal government's deregulation agenda threatens health and environmental standards*, Canadian Centre for Policy Alternative Working Paper, September 2006 online: <policyalternatives.ca/documents/National_Office_Pubs/2006/Putting_Canadians_at_Risk_summary .pdf>; A. Silversides, *Transparency and the drug approval process at Health Canada*, Women and Health Protection Report, December 2005; Janice Graham, "Smart Regulation: Will the government's strategy work?" (2005) 173 C.M.A.J. 1469.

[218] See, *e.g.*, M. McBane, *ibid.*; B. Campbell & M. Lee, *ibid.*; Anne Silversides, "Transparency and the Drug Approval Process at Health Canada", Paper for Women and Health Protection (Fall 2005), online: <http://whp-apsf.ca/pdf/transparency.pdf>.

[219] Janice Graham, "Smart Regulation: Will the government's strategy work?" (2005) 173 C.M.A.J. 1469 at 1469.

[220] In his speech on the Smart Regulations dated March 24, 2005, President of the Treasury Board Reg Alcock specifically indicated the Prime Minister had committed Canada to a plan of regulatory cooperation with the United States: Speech by Reg Alcock, "Government of Canada's Implementation Plan for Smart Regulations", Treasury Board of Canada Secretariat, online: <http://www.tbs-sct.gc.ca/media/ps-dp/2005/0324_e.asp>. See also Janice Graham, "Smart Regulation: Will the government's strategy work?" (2005) 173 C.M.A.J. 1469.

One of the main themes arising out of speeches and documents from government sources pertaining to its Smart Regulation initiative is that of moving into a 21st-century geo-political context. There are certain words and phrases the government uses that are politically loaded in this regard. The main vector the government has chosen to get there is through the "economy". Its political goal is "productivity" and "prosperity" for Canadians and the buzzwords (or push mechanisms) are the twin drivers of "innovation and competitiveness". Many of the underlying reforms discussed in this chapter to the FDA, FDR, AIA, *NOC Regulations* and *Patent Act*, and Canada's level of voluntary compliance with international instruments such as NAFTA and TRIPS are in service of these goals and objectives. Importantly for Canadians, particularly insofar as it relates to the safety and efficacy of pharmaceuticals, this represents a sea change in priority-setting in terms of shifting the focus of government from a conscious and active "gatekeeping" or fiduciary function in balancing public and private interests to more of a tenuous, if not naïve, partnership with the private sector.

Public speeches and government press releases related to the Smart Regulation initiative highlight this very narrow focus on innovation, on creating a positive business environment, and on improving the competitiveness of the Canadian biotechnology industry. The current regulatory regime, governmental officials have publicly stated, frustrates economic and social goals. Smart Regulation, in contrast, is presented as a panacea that sets the stage for businesses to innovate and grow and provide opportunity and prosperity for Canadians.[221] In a press release accompanying the Expert Advisory Committee's comments on Smart Regulation, Gaetan Lussier, Chair of the Committee, states that Canada must be "more bold" in its use of regulations to achieve better competitiviness, productivity, investment, and growth of key industrial sectors, necessitating a major change in approach. Lussier also invoked that there is public support by Canadians for such a major policy shift. He argues that recent studies show how Canadians now see social and economic goals as intertwined, believe that there is an excessive compliance burden on business, and clearly accept that markets, trade and competition serve both public and private interests. This characterization of "public opinion" is at odds with the Auditor General of Canada's view, who in a 2000 report to Parliament reviewing federal health regulations noted that Health Canada itself reported that Canadians "strongly believe that the health and safety must take precedence over economic and other considerations".[222] In a somewhat debatable understatement, Lussier

---

[221] See, *e.g.*, the 2005 speech accompanying the launch of the government's Implementation Plan for Smart Regulation: Speech by Reg Alcock, "Government of Canada's Implementation Plan for Smart Regulations", Treasury Board of Canada Secretariat, online: <http://www.tbs-sct.gc.ca/media/ps-dp/2005/0324_e.asp>; see also University of Toronto Joint Centre for Bioethics, Genome Canada, IDRC, and NRC, "Energizing Canadian Foreign Policy Through Science & Technology Innovation: Vision, Benefits, And Policy Goals" (Working Paper), online: <http://www.utoronto.ca/jcb/genomics/documents/EnergizeCanFPWhitepaper.pdf>.

[222] B. Campbell & M. Lee, "Putting Canadians at Risk: How the federal government's deregulation agenda threatens health and environmental standards", Canadian Centre for Policy Alternative Working Paper, online: <http://www.policyalternatives.ca/documents/National_Office_Pubs/

notes that this revised profile of the Canadian public interest "represents an important change" from previous characterizations. Thus, it is not surprising that the Committee's vision and principles for Smart Regulation are (1) Trust, in Canadian products and services, markets and government institutions, (2) Innovation, in order to enhance market performance, competitiveness, entrepreneurship and investment in the Canadian economy, and (3) Protection, in so far as the regulatory system must safeguard human health, safety and the environment within the context of dynamic global markets. It comes as no surprise therefore to hear government officials and their consultants employ management jargon to the effect that its new Smart Regulations will allow Canada to "stay ahead of the curve" and "punch above its weight" in moving into the new global economic arena.[223]

It should be noted that debates of this nature are not new in Canada. Indeed, according to the OECD,[224] Canada has been a "pioneer and leader" in the area of regulatory reform, a process which began in the 1980s and continued into the 1990s with Bill C-62, the *Regulatory Efficiency Bill*.[225] Bill C-62 was meant to harmonize existing regulations with the goal of increasing regulatory efficiency and relieving the public, particularly the business community, of unnecessarily burdensome or costly regulations. It failed to pass due to concerns expressed by the Canadian Scrutiny Committee[226] that the reforms represented a major departure from the traditions of Canadian law and government and were inconsistent with constitutional values such as the principles of fairness and equity. In particular, the Committee noted that the initiative endowed the government with undue discretion to put aside regulations protecting the general public interest in favour of those supporting discrete business concerns that amounted in effect to "private agreements" between government and industry. It is noteworthy that this earlier regulatory initiative seems to parallel the spirit of the Smart Regulation.

　2006/Putting_Canadians_at_Risk_summary.pdf> at 22. See also Health Canada, "National Consultations Summary Report", online: <http://www.hc-sc.gc.ca/ahc-asc/pubs/legren/1998-legislation_e.html>.

[223] University of Toronto Joint Centre for Bioethics, Genome Canada, IDRC, and NRC, "Energizing Canadian Foreign Policy Through Science & Technology Innovation: Vision, Benefits, And Policy Goals" (Working Paper), online: <http://www.utoronto.ca/jcb/genomics/documents/EnergizeCanFPWhitepaper.pdf>.

[224] Organisation for Economic Cooperation and Development, "OECD Praises Canada's Regulatory Reforms and Encourages Sustained Momentum", Regulary Reform, online: <http://www.oecd.org/document/23/0,2340,en_2649_37421_1835224_1_1_1_1_37421,00.html>.

[225] For an informative discussion of Bill C-62 and it's failure owing to concerns expressed by the Canadian Standing Committee for the Scrutiny of Regulations, see the debate of same in the context of Australian policy reform: Parliament of Victoria Law Reform Committee, "Regulatory Efficiency Legislation", online: <http://www.parliament.vic.gov.au/lawreform/RegulatoryEfficiency/relr/contents.html>.

[226] Canada, Parliament, Standing Joint Committee for the Scrutiny of Regulations, "Report on Bill C-62", February 16, 1995.

E. WHAT IS THE BEST ROAD AHEAD FOR DRUG REGULATION? PRECAUTIONARY PRINCIPLE OR RISK-BENEFIT ANALYSIS?

One of the most significant health-related criticisms levelled at the Smart Regulation is that the government is attempting to vacate its traditional fiduciary or gatekeeper responsibility to protect public health with regard to the mechanism by which new drugs are evaluated by moving to a more risk analysis-dominated framework.[227] According to its Smart Regulation *Fall 2005 Update*,[228] the federal government is planning to implement a "risk-based drug licensing model that will support early access to promising new therapies", including amendments to the FDR. The first and second phases of amendments to cover first "highest and lowest-risk products" then "medium-risk" products are expected to be completed by December 2007 and 2008, respectively. Further, Health Canada has proposed as part of its Smart Regulation initiative to eliminate the FDA entirely, replacing it with a new *Health Protection Act*[229] which would formally vacate the precautionary principle in favour of a newer risk management approach, thus putting economic factors on par with health protection.[230] One advocacy group has charged that this amounts to a clear abrogation of the common law duty of care owed to the public by Health Canada.[231]

The current policy framework in which drug approval implicitly embedded is referred to as the precautionary principle. Consistent with Galen's injunction to "first, do no harm" (*Primum non nocere*[232]) the term refers to the notion that when an activity, such as drug approval, raises a threat of harm to human health, precautionary measures should be undertaken even if some aspects of the cause and effect relationships have not yet been scientifically established.[233] The precautionary principle is however not universally accepted in health policy circles, in part, because there are so many different definitions of the term in use.[234] Independent of the definition, the principle is widely agreed to comprise

---

[227] B. Campbell & M. Lee, "Putting Canadians at Risk: How the federal government's deregulation agenda threatens health and environmental standards", Canadian Centre for Policy Alternative Working Paper, online: <http://www.policyalternatives.ca/documents/National_Office_Pubs/2006/Putting_Canadians_at_Risk_summary.pdf>.

[228] Government of Canada, "Smart Regulation Report on Actions and Plans: Fall 2005 Update", online: <http://www.regulation.gc.ca/default.asp@language=e&page=report.htm>.

[229] Detailed Legislative Proposal — Health Protection Legislative Renewal: Canada Health Protection Act, online: <http://www.hc-sc.gc.ca/ahc-asc/pubs/legren/propos-a_e.html>.

[230] B. Campbell & M. Lee, "Putting Canadians at Risk: How the federal government's deregulation agenda threatens health and environmental standards", Canadian Centre for Policy Alternative Working Paper, online: <http://www.policyalternatives.ca/documents/National_Office_Pubs/2006/Putting_Canadians_at_Risk_summary.pdf> at 43.

[231] M. McBane, "Health Canada proposing to eviscerate the Food & Drugs Act", The CCPA Monitor, February 2004.

[232] Attributed to Claudius Galenus of Pergamum (131-201 CE).

[233] Pauline Barrieu & Bernard Sinclair-Desgagné, "On precautionary policies" (2006) 52 Management Science 1145 at 1147.

[234] Currently, there are between 14 and 19 different versions implemented globally: P. Sandin, "Dimensions of the Precautionary Principle" (1999) 5 Human Ecol. Risk Assess. 889; D.

three elements:[235] the presence of scientific uncertainty, a significant threat of harm, and a set of possible precautionary actions to avoid such harm. As noted by the Royal Society of Canada,[236] proponents view the principle as a proactive and anticipatory approach to human health while detractors see it more as an unscientific approach which impairs economic and technological development based on unfounded fears.

The focus of the policy debate over precautionary principle as it relates to drug approval in Canada is (1) how to balance scientific uncertainty with risk in the context of inherently dangerous products; and (2) who should have the burden of adducing evidence of safety. In so-called "strong" formulations of the principle, absolute proof of safety is necessary prior to allowing a certain activity. In this scenario, it is the pharmaceutical sponsor who carries the legal burden of proof to introduce necessary and sufficient evidence of drug safety. While consistent with a government gatekeeping function, however, this formulation clearly presents a problem for the drug approval process seen in the larger context. Binding of drug molecules to molecular targets, and the downstream effects of such binding are highly complicated and Phase I-III clinical trial populations comprise a small and narrowly circumscribed fraction of the total population of the drug consuming public. Front-loading the approval process to the approval stage will also tend to offend the so-called "rule of three" regarding adverse effects.[237] It also minimizes the role of "objective" scientific evidence in favour of a more non-evidentiary and cautionary stance. By contrast "weak" articulations of the principle allow activities to be undertaken in the absence of any scientific proof at all,[238] which presents obvious and serious risks to human health. Middle or more moderate articulations open the door to some type of cost-benefit analysis and avoid pitfalls associated with extremes of both positions. The burden of proof can fall on either party, depending on the articulation.

VanderZwaag, "The Precautionary Principle in environmental law and policy: Elusive rhetoric and first embraces" (1999) 8 J. Envtl. L. & Prac. 355; Pauline Barrieu & Bernard Sinclair-Desgagné, "On precautionary policies" (2006) 52 Management Science 1145 at 1147.

[235] C. Raffensperger & J. Tickner, eds., *Protecting Public Health and the Environment: Implementing the Precautionary Principle* (Washington, D.C.: Island Press, 1999).

[236] Royal Society of Canada Expert Panel Report on the Future of Food Biotechnology, "Elements of precaution: Recommendations for the regulation of food biotechnology in Canada" (2001) 64(1-2) J. Toxicol. Environ. Health A 1-210 at 194.

[237] J.A. Hanley & A. Lippman-Hand, "If nothing goes wrong, is everything all right? Interpreting zero numerators" (1983) 249 J.A.M.A. 1743. The rule of three holds that to capture at least one occurrence of adverse events at a frequency of 1:100 or greater at a 95 per cent confidence level, the appropriate size of the pre-approval study population would need to be at least 300. For more serious and infrequently observed adverse effects with a frequency of 1:1,000 the appropriate sample size would be 3,000. Given that the total Phase I-III clinical trial population assessed by Health Canada is typically between 3,000-5,000, strong statistical analyses of adverse effects distribution in various segments of the population are only possible in the post-approval stage where much larger and more diverse patients populations are exposed to new drugs.

[238] Kenneth R. Foster, Paolo Vecchia & Michael H. Repacholi, "Risk Management: Science and the Precautionary Principle" (2000) 288(5468) Science 979 at 979.

The moderate position has been advocated by the United States Institute of Medicine (IOM) in its detailed report, *The Future of Drug Safety*.[239] In making what appears to be a somewhat controversial statement to the effect regulatory approval "does not represent a lifetime guarantee of safety and efficacy", the IOM has taken a position which respects unavoidable uncertainties involved in scientific investigation *per se*,[240] and properly points out that even the best drug safety system in the world will not prevent serious adverse reactions to marketed pharmaceuticals due in part to their complex mechanisms of action (hence the denotation of pharmaceuticals in product liability actions as "inherently dangerous") and narrow clinical trial study populations compared with actual prescribing practices by physicians. Thus, as noted by the IOM, regulatory agencies must strike a delicate balance between judging the risks and benefits of a new drug, including whether the need for more study to increase certainty before approval outweighs delaying the release of the drug into the marketplace and into the hands of health care providers and their patients. An important distinction between the approach advocated by the federal government in its Smart Regulation initiative and that of the IOM is that while the latter has accepted a risk-based approval process, it is embedded in a "life-cycle approach" that continues to underscore evidence of safety and efficacy in both pre- and post-approval stages. It also places responsibility for effective regulation firmly on the United States Food and Drug Administration, the pharmaceutical sector *and* prescribing physicians. As such, the IOM's reform proposal appears to maintain the legal burden of proof for evidence of safety and efficacy on drug manufacturers while avoiding pitfalls associated with placing blame on just one party. It also recognizes that the legitimacy and credibility of regulatory agencies, the pharmaceutical industry and practising physicians have come to be intertwined in the public eye.[241]

---

[239] Board on Population Health and Public Health Practice, *The Future of Drug Safety: Promoting and Protecting the Health of the Public*, Institute of Medicine of the National Academies, online: <http://www.iom.edu/CMS/3793/26341/37329.aspx>.

[240] See, *e.g.*, Gunther S. Stent, *Paradoxes of Progress* (San Franciso: W.H. Freeman, 1978); John L. Casti, *Searching For Certainty: What Scientists Can Know About the Future* (New York: Morrow & Co. 1990); Paul W. Glimcher, *Decisions, Uncertainty and the Brain: The Science of Neuroeconomics* (Cambridge, MA: MIT Press, 2003).

[241] The Committee stated that its

> vision of a transformed drug safety system has at its core a lifecycle approach to drug risk and benefit — not a new concept, but one that has been implemented, at best, in a limited and fragmented manner. For FDA, attention to risk and benefit over a drug's lifecycle would require continuous availability of new data and ongoing, active reassessment of risk and benefit to drive regulatory action (responsive to the accumulating information about a given drug), and regulatory authority that is strong both before and after approval. For the industry, attention to risk and benefit over the lifecycle will require increased transparency toward FDA in the process of elucidating and communicating emerging information about a drug, and acceptance of changes intended to strengthen drug safety. Importantly, FDA's credibility is intertwined with that of the industry, and a more credible drug safety system is in everyone's best interest. For the health care delivery system, a lifecycle approach to risk and benefit implies the need to heed and follow FDA communication about drug safety matters and to exercise appropriate caution in drug-related decision making (from formularies to

It is clear from government statements, press releases and policy documents, that the federal government will take a *balancing* approach to its Smart Regulation risk-benefit framework as it applies to drug regulation.[242] The question remains as to how *balanced* the new approach will be, and how a move from a strong (100 per cent evidence of safety) to moderate (75 per cent or greater evidence of safety) precautionary principle to a risk-benefit analysis which expressly balances the public interest in health and safety with corporate cost considerations (*e.g.*, 50 per cent or less evidence of safety) will impact on public health under circumstances where many Canadians already suffer, and indeed die, from the adverse effects of new drugs every year.

F. TRANSFORMING PHARMACEUTICAL REGULATION IN CANADA: A BLUEPRINT FOR RENEWAL

Finally, in October 2006, Health Canada released a *Blueprint for Renewal: Transforming Canada's Approach to Regulating Health Products and Food.*[243] This discussion paper, released by the HPFB, encompasses many elements of the debates discussed thus far in section VI. It refers to placing a risk-benefit framework at the forefront of the regulatory approval process,[244] replacing the current FDA and regulations with new legislation[245] and underscoring the importance of measures to support the market position of brand-name pharmaceutical firms (innovation and commercialization agenda, "timely" market entry, intellectual property protection, data exclusivity) in a global economy where Canada's productivity is seen to be at risk.[246] The document also expresses a clear concern for patient safety,[247] with explicit references to controversies surrounding adverse effects surfacing in the post-approval phase and to the limimtations of the existing regulatory regime recognizing for example that "Health Canada lacks the authority to compel additional safety, efficacy and effectiveness studies as a condition of continued marketing or when additional

prescribing) in recognition of the limited information available at the time of drug approval. Also, the health care delivery system would benefit from consistently basing prescribing decisions on the science, and exercising caution in regard to the industry's influence on the practice of medicine.
Board on Population Health and Public Health Practice, *The Future of Drug Safety: Promoting and Protecting the Health of the Public*, Institute of Medicine of the National Academies, online: <http://www.iom.edu/CMS/3793/26341/37329.aspx>.

[242] B. Campbell & M. Lee, "Putting Canadians at Risk: How the federal government's deregulation agenda threatens health and environmental standards", Canadian Centre for Policy Alternative Working Paper, online: <http://www.policyalternatives.ca/documents/National_Office_Pubs/2006/Putting_Canadians_at_Risk_summary.pdf> at 7, 17, 22 and 43-48.
[243] Health Products and Food Branch, *Blueprint for Renewal: Transforming Canada's Approach to Regulating Health Products and Food*, Health Canada, online: <http://www.hc-sc.gc.ca/ahc-asc/alt_formats/hpfb-dgpsa/pdf/hpfb-dgpsa/blueprint-plan_e.pdf>.
[244] *Ibid.*, at 17, 27, 33, 34, and 39.
[245] *Ibid.*, at 26.
[246] *Ibid.*, at 7-9, 11, 20 and 38.
[247] *Ibid.*, at 7, 9, 21 and 27.

research suggests that additional research is warranted."[248] Mechanisms proposed to shore up patient safety include increased transparency in the regulatory approval process,[249] improved clinical trials registration,[250] better reporting of post-approval side effects,[251] and moving from a more discrete system of approval and post-approval monitoring to a "life-cycle" approach to regulatory approval.[252] Included in the reform basket for discussion are several welcome initiatives, including "probationary" regulatory approval contingent on post-marketing surveillance of adverse effects, a requirement for sponsors to submit pharmacovigilance plans as part of their regulatory submission packages, jurisdiction to require sponsors to conduct post-market studies (including head-to-head comparisons and large observational studies on drug effectiveness) and initiatives to address under-reporting of post-marketing adverse effects.[253]

The *Blueprint* differs in "pith" if not substance from the NPS, TAS, Smart Regulation and commentaries on all three from the Privy Council and Health Canada. In particular, it articulates a clear concern for patient safety in light of, and indeed specifically because of,[254] recent reports of serious adverse effects caused by new drug products. The issue of patient safety is the oft-repeated reason given for the potential reforms alluded to above and for the shift to a product "life-cycle" approach. The latter is given considerable play in the *Blueprint*, reminiscent of the IOM's Future of Drug Safety report.[255] Nevertheless, policy positions from each of the NPS, TAS, and Smart Regulation permeate the *Blueprint*, particularly the need to "balance" patient safety with Canada's obligations under TRIPS and the desire to facilitate scientific and technical innovation by ensuring a regime that protects intellectual property rights for pharmaceutical inventions. Rather than consumer protection being the focal point of the regulatory process, as is true currently,[256] the *Blueprint* posits that "many things have changed" since the FDA was brought into force in 1953, "including the view of citizens on the role of government in

---

[248] *Ibid.*, at 7.

[249] *Ibid.*, at 23, 24, 35 and 39. Note, however, that two of the four major references to "transparency" in the *Blueprint* document refer not to increasing access to information or facilitating informed decision-making by the public but rather to the need for a risk-assessment model. For example, at p. 39 it is stated: "Parliament has determined that regulatory decisions in the public interest require Health Canada to identify and assess safety and effectiveness issues to determine the level of acceptable risk of a health product when weighed against its benefits".

[250] *Ibid.*, at 14.

[251] *Ibid.*, at 7, 9, 17 and 21.

[252] *Ibid.*, at 16.

[253] *Ibid.*, at 9 and 21.

[254] *Ibid.*, at 7 and 11.

[255] *The Future of Drug Safety: Promoting and Protecting the Health of the Public*, Institute of Medicine of the National Academies, September 2006: Board on Population Health and Public Health Practice, "The Future of Drug Safety: Promoting and Protecting the Health of the Public", Institute of Medicine of the National Academies, online: <http://www.iom.edu/CMS/3793/26341/37329.aspx>.

[256] Health Products and Food Branch, *Blueprint for Renewal: Transforming Canada's Approach to Regulating Health Products and Food*, Health Canada, online: <http://www.hc-sc.gc.ca/ahc-asc/alt_formats/hpfb-dgpsa/pdf/hpfb-dgpsa/blueprint-plan_e.pdf> at 6.

regulation". It is not surprising therefore that there is no discussion of the precautionary principle in the *Blueprint*, nor any on the substance or procedures to be used to render risk-benefit decisions, what benchmarks for success will be used, which parties will be responsible for assessing and defining acceptable levels of risk in the absence of the "first, do no harm" approach, or that brand-name pharmaceutical companies have called the iniative a "step in the right direction".[257]

Some hints come from the *Blueprint* itself. According to the discussion document, Health Canada wants a "21st century toolkit" to assess the regulatory approval process. The proposed risk management and assessment activities will be "defined by the business processes" supporting "generation of new knowledge", which "enable rather than create obstacles" to commercialization of pharmaceuticals, and which focus on "internationally benchmarked" frameworks and instruments in the context of a "high-performance" organization that seeks "strategic ... regulatory cooperation" and "enhanced partnerships and stakeholder involvement."[258] From previous policy documents, it is likely that the international benchmark is that of the ICH-CGP, an organization comprising regulatory bodies and brand-name pharmaceutical associations. It is also likely that brand-name pharmaceutical manufacturers will comprise one of the largest and frequently consulted stakeholder groups during subsequent discussions over the mechanisms and implementation of the risk assessment model, as was true for repeal of Canada's compulsory licensing provisions and the replacement thereof with the current "linkage regulations" governing generic entry.[259] Indeed, the *Blueprint* is specific that the new regulatory model will focus not only on risk-benefit assessment, "but also elements of risk management, risk communication and market intervention" and that previous stakeholder consultations with the ICH on periodic safety reporting, pharmacovigilance planning, and expedited reporting are merely "awaiting new authorities to be fully implemented".[260]

At this stage, however, it is too early to know what model Canadians will end up with at the end of the current reform cycle. For example, there is no

---

[257] Smart Regulation: A Step in the Right Direction. Canada's Research-based Pharmaceutical Companies. Press release, online: <http://www.canadapharma.org/SmartRegulationMarch24 2005.pdf>.

[258] Health Products and Food Branch, *Blueprint for Renewal: Transforming Canada's Approach to Regulating Health Products and Food*, Health Canada, online: <http://www.hc-sc.gc.ca/ahc-asc/alt_formats/hpfb-dgpsa/pdf/hpfb-dgpsa/blueprint-plan_e.pdf> at 20 and 26-27.

[259] Gunar K. Gaikis, "*Pharmaceutical patents in Canada. An update on compulsory licensing*", (1992) 42 Patent World 19; D.G. McFetridge, *Intellectual Property Rights and the Location of Innovative Activity: The Canadian Experience with Compulsory Licensing of Patented Pharmaceuticals* (presented at the National Bureau of Economic Research (NBER) Summer Institute, Cambridge MA, July 29, 1997); Roy J. Romanow, Q.C., *Building on Values: The Future of Health Care in Canada* (Ottawa: Commission on the Future of Health Care in Canada, 2002).

[260] Health Products and Food Branch, *Blueprint for Renewal: Transforming Canada's Approach to Regulating Health Products and Food*, Health Canada, online: <http://www.hc-sc.gc.ca/ahc-asc/alt_formats/hpfb-dgpsa/pdf/hpfb-dgpsa/blueprint-plan_e.pdf> at 17.

indication in the *Blueprint* as to whether Health Canada's "life-cycle approach" will continue to underscore evidence of safety and efficacy from a consumer protection perspective, or whether pharmaceutical sponsors will continue to have the legal burden of proving their products are safe and effective or whether the standard of "no evidence of harm" will take precedence as recently discussed by Graham.[261] It is not clear whether consumer safety will be paramount in whatever risk assessment model is ultimately employed by Health Canada. It also falls to be seen whether resource-heavy proposals to be undertaken by pharmaceutical sponsors such as probationary regulatory approval, pharmacovigilance plans, mandatory post-market studies or clinical trials and up-to-date reporting of post-marketing adverse effects will survive numerous rounds of "stakeholder consultations" and industry lobbying. Finally, it is unclear whether Health Canada would, as has the IOM, recognize that the legitimacy and credibility of regulatory agencies, the pharmaceutical industry and practicing physicians are fundamentally intertwined. In our view, it is desirable, from a public health perspective, that furture regulatory initiates by HPFB emphasize consumer safety, in light of the various uncertainties involved in the drug development cycle.[262]

VII. CONCLUSION

In this chapter, we provided a general overview of the historical context in which the regulatory structure surrounding pharmaceuticals emerged and discussed how the strict emphasis on protection against premature introduction of pharmaceuticals has been gradually whittled away under pressure from both industry and patient advocacy groups. We then described the current regulatory structure, and illustrated how flexibility has been built into the system and how "timely review" of new drugs has become an important regulatory focus for Health Canada. In recent years this focus has been called into question in light of numerous controversies associated with severe and often fatal adverse effects in the post-approval stage. These tragedies highlight how serious public health concerns are associated with the introduction of potentially harmful drug products after a relatively circumscribed pre-approval process and reveal serious flaws in the current regulatory structure. They also point to the need for an improved and independent long-term safety monitoring of drugs, including "probationary" approval contingent on necessary and sufficient evidence of post-marketing safety and efficacy data. Various proposals were discussed, emphasizing the need for a strong and independent regulatory review system that can provide a counterbalance against well-described financial interests involved in drug development.

---

[261] Janice Graham, "Smart Regulation: Will the government's strategy work?" (2005) 173 C.M.A.J. 1469 at 1470.

[262] At the time of the submission of this chapter, HFBP is organizing further consultation with stakeholders on its *Blueprint*. See Consultation on Health Canada's *Blueprint for Renewal: Transforming Canada's Approach to Regulating Health Products and Food* online: <http://www.hc-sc.gc.ca/ahc-asc/public-consult/consultations/col/blue-bleu/index_e.html>.

Finally, we discussed various Canadian government policies associated with pharmaceuticals. We paid particular attention to the growing emphasis in Canadian policy circles on the need to combine laws and policies aimed at promotion of pharmaceutical innovation and national productivity with consumer protection, the latter of which has been a cornerstone of food and drugs regulation in Canada for nearly 100 years. By contrast, the newly proposed Smart Regulation initiative clearly fits an approach to drug regulation that is intended to balance public and private interests in the form of public-private partnerships. This approach reflects a profound reliance on the role of industry in conducting appropriate clinical studies and gathering and reporting data necessary to satisfy regulatory approval requirements and inform ongoing governmental policy initiatives. The move away from a more precautionary approach to drug regulation seems remarkable when viewed in the context of the latest controversies associated with pharmaceutical products. Indeed, as has been discussed throughout this chapter, the sheer volume and scope of these controversies, combined with massive drug withdrawals during the same period of time, has led to increased international calls for *more* stringent and independent drug regulatory review processes rather than the opposite. It is hard to reconcile the somewhat naïve promotion of increased public-private partnerships and the accompanying "flexible approach" towards drug regulation with calls for law reform that support a move away from a more self-regulatory system. Whether concerns of this nature (or the attendant risk for public health) will be mitigated or worsened by the federal government's *Blueprint* to replace the FDA and FDR with its new risk assessment-based legislation and "life-cycle" approach to drug regulation remains to be seen.

Chapter 9

REGULATING REPRODUCTION

Erin Nelson

I. INTRODUCTION

Reproductive decision making takes place in a web of overlapping public and private concerns — political and ideological, socio-economic, health and health care — all of which engage the public and involve strongly held opinions and attitudes about appropriate conduct on the part of individuals and the state. Decisions about reproducing are deeply meaningful to us as individuals and are of profound consequence to society. And, it is now possible to actively make decisions about childbearing in ways which would not have been open in the past. We now can make choices about aspects of the reproductive process that, in the past, were matters of chance; we routinely see evidence of the social concerns that these issues raise in the popular press[1] and popular culture.[2]

The shift from reproduction as a matter of chance to an opportunity for deliberate choice has led to greater state involvement in reproductive activity. The introduction of medical products and procedures to prevent conception, to terminate pregnancy and to initiate pregnancies *in vitro*, have yielded regulation aimed at consumer protection and quality control, much as is the case with other medications, medical devices and procedures. But the complexities introduced by increased choice in reproduction go beyond issues of safety and quality, in that they also introduce new policy challenges. Reproductive choices, controversial as they sometimes are, demand a carefully

---

[1] See, *e.g.*, Rob Stein, "A Boy for You, a Girl for Me: Technology Allows Choice: Embryo Screening Stirs Ethics Debate", *The Washington Post* (December 14, 2004) A01, online: <http://www.washingtonpost.com/wp-dyn/articles/A62067-2004Dec13.html>; Canadian Press, "Quebec challenges constitutionality of federal anti-cloning law" Canada.com (December 17, 2004), online: <http://www.mediresource.sympatico.ca/health_news_detail.asp?channel_id=16& menu_item_id=&news_id=5562>; Mark Henderson, "First 'designer baby' could save his brother", The Times Online (November 29, 2004), online: <http://www.timesonline. co.uk/article/0,,8122-1380616,00.html>.

[2] See, *e.g.*, *Godsend* (2004), a movie in which a fertility scientist clones the dead son of a grieving couple. The movie's website has a link to the "Godsend Institute", which purports to be an actual clinic that performs reproductive cloning (see online: <http://www.godsendinstitute.org/ home.html>).

balanced response from law and policy. This is particularly the case given that the history of reproductive regulation is a history of discounting women's needs and interests and burdening the exercise of their reproductive autonomy.

Women's role in reproduction demands that regulation be grounded in respect for women's reproductive autonomy and concern for women's reproductive health. But a tension exists between the need for state involvement to ensure access to reproductive health services and the need to ensure that women are free to make their own reproductive decisions. While a full discussion of the scope and meaning of reproductive autonomy cannot be undertaken here, it is a theme that underlies this discussion of reproductive regulation.

The aim of this chapter is to provide an overview of reproductive law and policy in Canada. It is not possible to address all of the issues in detail here, given the scope of the topic; instead, I will highlight issues of current importance and controversy. In the public law context, I will consider abortion, contraception, non-consensual sterilization, state intervention in the lives of pregnant women and the regulation of assisted reproductive technologies (ARTs). In the private law context, I will examine wrongful birth and wrongful conception claims, and tort duties owed by pregnant women to their fetuses.

II. ABORTION IN LAW AND POLICY

Abortion was criminalized in Canada in the 19th century.[3] In 1969, the abortion provisions in the *Criminal Code*[4] were modified to make it possible for women to obtain legal abortions; section 251 of the *Criminal Code* permitted therapeutic abortions where the woman received the approval of a hospital therapeutic abortion committee (made up of three physicians), on the basis that continuation of the pregnancy would endanger her life or health. While permitting abortion in some circumstances, the provisions instituted a rigid administrative structure which could impede a woman's ability to obtain abortion services. Pro-choice advocates therefore continued to lobby for legislative change.[5]

In 1988, section 251 of the *Criminal Code* was struck down by the Supreme Court of Canada in *R. v. Morgentaler*,[6] on the ground that it violated women's

---

[3] Prior to the 19th century, expertise around pregnancy and childbirth rested with midwives, usually women. In the 19th century, as part of the drive to wrest control over obstetrical care from midwives, physicians campaigned to criminalize abortion. See Reva Siegel, "Reasoning from the Body: a Historical Perspective on Abortion Regulation and Questions of Equal Protection" (1992) 44 Stan. L. Rev. 261; Janine Brodie, Shelley A.M. Gavigan & Jane Jenson, *The Politics of Abortion* (Toronto: Oxford University Press, 1992).

[4] R.S.C. 1985, c. C-46.

[5] See Sanda Rodgers, "The Legal Regulation of Women's Reproductive Capacity in Canada" in Jocelyn Downie, Timothy Caulfield & Colleen Flood, eds., *Canadian Health Law and Policy*, 2nd ed. (Markham, ON: LexisNexis Butterworths, 2002) at 334-35; see also Canada, Department of Justice, Committee on the Operation of the Abortion Law, *Report* (Ottawa: Minister of Supply and Services Canada, 1977) for an itemization of concerns with the operation of s. 251 of the *Criminal Code.*

[6] [1988] S.C.J. No. 1, [1988] 1 S.C.R. 30 (S.C.C.) [*Morgentaler*].

constitutionally enshrined right to security of the person. The section was found to violate section 7 of the *Canadian Charter of Rights and Freedoms*,[7] not because it prohibited abortion in all but limited circumstances, but because the administrative process that it put into place could deprive women of security of the person in a manner that did not accord with the principles of fundamental justice.[8] In other words, the Court struck down the law not because criminal prohibition of abortion is impermissible under the Charter, but because the law created an arbitrary and unfair decision-making process.[9]

One year after the *Morgentaler* decision, the federal government introduced a new restrictive abortion Bill.[10] The Bill was passed in the House of Commons, but was defeated by a vote of 44:43 in the Senate. Since then, no new federal law governing abortion has been introduced, although several provinces have enacted legislation or regulations purporting to govern the provision of abortion services.[11] The provincial statutes have generally either attempted to restrict

---

[7] Part I of the *Constitution Act, 1982*, being Schedule B to the *Canada Act 1982* (U.K.), 1982, c. 11 [Charter].

[8] *R. v. Morgentaler*, [1988] S.C.J. No. 1, [1988] 1 S.C.R. 30 (S.C.C.).

[9] For example, different committees took different approaches to the interpretation of what constituted a threat to a woman's health. Some hospitals did not have therapeutic abortion committees, which meant that some jurisdictions did not have any legal access to abortion. *R. v. Morgentaler, ibid.*

[10] Bill C-43 was introduced by Justice Minister Doug Lewis. The Bill recriminalized abortion, except in situations where a woman's doctor thought the woman's life or health was threatened. Health was defined to include mental, physical and psychological health. See Sanda Rodgers, "The Legal Regulation of Women's Reproductive Capacity in Canada" in Jocelyn Downie, Timothy Caulfield & Colleen Flood, eds., *Canadian Health Law and Policy*, 2nd ed. (Markham, ON: LexisNexis Butterworths, 2002) at 331.

[11] British Columbia passed a regulation pursuant to the *Medical Services Act*, R.S.B.C. 1979, c. 255; B.C. Reg. 54/88, which provided that the only insured abortion services were those provided in a hospital in cases where continuing the pregnancy posed a significant threat to a woman's life. The regulation was struck down as *ultra vires* the province: *British Columbia Civil Liberties Assn. v. British Columbia (Attorney General)*, [1988] B.C.J. No. 373, 24 B.C.L.R. (2d) 189 (B.C.S.C.). In Manitoba, a regulation excluding non-hospital abortions from the province's health insurance plan was also ruled *ultra vires*: see *Lexogest Inc. v. Manitoba (Attorney General)*, [1993] M.J. No. 54, 101 D.L.R. (4th) 523 (Man. C.A.). The province of New Brunswick amended its *Medical Act*, S.N.B. 1981, c. 87 to provide the penalty of licence suspension for any physician who performed (or was likely to perform) abortion services outside a hospital; this amendment was found to be *ultra vires* the province: *Morgentaler v. New Brunswick (Attorney General)*, [1995] N.B.J. No. 40, 121 D.L.R. (4th) 431 (N.B.C.A.). New Brunswick has since amended the legislation and regulations to remove the penalty of licence suspension for the performance of abortions in private clinics, but maintains the prohibition on paying for such abortions. Accordingly, Dr. Morgentaler is once again involved in litigation with the province of New Brunswick, this time arguing that the prohibition on funding for clinic abortions violates ss. 7 and 15 of the Charter, as well as the *Canada Health Act*, R.S.C. 1985, c. C-6. See *Morgentaler v. New Brunswick*, [2004] N.B.J. No. 130, 2004 NBQB 139, (N.B.Q.B.). Nova Scotia enacted legislation creating significant penal sanctions for anyone providing health care services outside a hospital; this, too, was struck down as *ultra vires*: *R. v. Morgentaler*, [1993] S.C.J. No. 95, 107 D.L.R. (4th) 537 (S.C.C.). Prince Edward Island enacted regulations under the *Health Services Payment Act*, R.S.P.E.I. 1988, c. H-2, that permitted coverage by the province's health care insurance plan for only those abortions performed in a

funding for abortion services to those provided in hospitals, or to preclude the provision of abortion outside a hospital setting; most of these statutes have been found to be *ultra vires* provincial jurisdiction (or beyond the scope of their parent legislation) and therefore unconstitutional.

Canada is the sole Western nation without any criminal (or direct governmental) control over the provision of abortion services. Under current Canadian law, a woman may have an abortion at any time, for any reason. The absence of a criminal prohibition against abortion, however, has not translated into readily accessible abortion services. Currently, pregnancy termination is governed in diverse ways across the country, with significant variations among jurisdictions. Timing, site and methods of pregnancy termination are generally governed by provincial physician regulatory bodies,[12] and provincial governments control access to and funding for abortion services pursuant to their jurisdiction over the delivery of health care.

The implication of this approach to regulation of abortion services is enormous variation in the accessibility of these services across the country. For example, only four provinces[13] cover the full cost of abortions performed in clinics[14] (as opposed to hospitals). A recent report by the Canadian Abortion

---

hospital, and only where a committee of five doctors authorized the abortion. The P.E.I. Court of Appeal upheld these regulations as being authorized by the *Health Services Payment Act* (*Morgentaler v. Prince Edward Island (Minister Health and Social Services)*, [1993] P.E.I.J. No. 75, 139 D.L.R. (4th) 603 (P.E.I.C.A.)). As Sanda Rodgers notes, the decision of the P.E.I.C.A. is anomalous and is arguably wrongly decided. See Sanda Rodgers, "The Legal Regulation of Women's Reproductive Capacity in Canada", *ibid.*, at 341. Between 1999 and 2005, the province of Quebec required women to pay for part of the cost of abortion procedures performed in private clinics. Recently, the Quebec Superior Court ordered the province to pay $13 million to reimburse these women: see *Association pour l'accès à l'avortement c. Québec (Procureur général)*, [2006] J.Q. No. 8654, 2006 QCCS 4694 (Que. C.S.). The government of Quebec has decided not to appeal the decision.

[12] See, for example, College of Physicians and Surgeons of Alberta, Policy: Termination of Pregnancy (rev. June 2000), online: CPSA, <http://www.cpsa.ab.ca/publicationsresources/attachments_policies/Termination%20of%20Pregnancy.pdf>; and College of Physicians and Surgeons of British Columbia Policy Manual (rev. Feb. 2000), online: CPSBC, <https://www.cpsbc.ca/cps/physician_resources/publications/resource_manual/abortion>.

[13] British Columbia, Alberta, Ontario, and Newfoundland and Labrador (see Laura Eggerston, "News: Abortion Services in Canada: A Patchwork Quilt with Many Holes" (2001) 164:6 CMAJ 847). In Manitoba, a class action has been initiated in an attempt to force the provincial government to pay for clinic abortions on the basis that the regulations that prohibit such payment contravene ss. 7 and 15 of the Charter. See *Jane Doe 1 v. Manitoba*, [2004] M.J. No. 456 (Man. Q.B.) (granting the applicants' motion for summary judgment and declaring the offending provision of the *Manitoba Health Services Insurance Act*, R.S.M. 1987, c. H35, s. 116(1)(h), 116(2), Manitoba Regulation 46/93, s. 2(28) of no force and effect), revd in part [2005] M.J. No. 335 (Man. C.A.); *Jane Doe 1 v. Manitoba*, [2005] M.J. No. 335 (Man. C.A.) (allowing the government's appeal from the summary judgment in favour of the plaintiffs; *Jane Doe 1 v. Manitoba*, [2005] S.C.C.A. No. 513 (dismissing the applicants' motion for leave to appeal to the Supreme Court of Canada). The *Jane Doe* case differs from *Lexogest Inc. v. Manitoba (Attorney General)*, [1993] M.J. No. 54, 101 D.L.R. (4th) 523 (Man. C.A.), in that the Charter issues were not decided in *Lexogest*.

[14] Which ranges from $300 to $900, depending upon the gestational age of the fetus and geographic location. See The Morgentaler Clinic, online: <http://www.morgentaler.ca> (each

Rights Action League (CARAL) notes that only 17.8 per cent of Canadian hospitals perform abortion services.[15] Other barriers to access noted in the CARAL study include: the need to travel outside one's community;[16] anti-choice physicians who refuse to refer women to those who provide abortion services; lack of availability of information about abortion services; long waiting periods; hospital gestational limits on abortion services; and anti-choice "counselling" centres.[17] The executive director of the CARAL has noted the significant implications of funding policy on the availability of abortion services: "Ironically, it seems to be getting worse rather than better since the Morgentaler decision in 1988. There are a number of barriers and the [number is increasing]".[18]

Medical abortion, although superior to surgical abortion in very early pregnancy (up to seven weeks gestation)[19] and a safe alternative up to 24 weeks gestation, is not readily available in Canada, because the medication involved — mifepristone — has not been approved for use in Canada. Where medical abortion is available, providers rely on an off-label use of methotrexate, a drug that is not recommended for inducing abortion because it poses a risk of fetal malformation if the pregnancy is not successfully terminated.[20] The Society of Obstetricians and Gynaecologists of Canada has urged Health Canada to work with industry and with professional organizations to ensure the availability of mifepristone in Canada, and notes that "[t]he use of such medication for terminating early pregnancy constitutes a significant medical and public health gain and has received medical acceptability in Europe and the USA".[21] The use of mifepristone and misoprostol "can make abortion earlier, more accessible, safer, less traumatic, less medicalised and less expensive".[22] Up to nine weeks

---

clinic location has a separate website which lists fees, and explains whether the provincial health care insurance plan covers the cost of abortion services).

[15] See Canadian Abortion Rights Action League, "Protecting Abortion Rights in Canada" (2003), online: <http://canadiansforchoice.ca/caralreport.pdf>.

[16] Laura Eggerston, "News: Abortion Services in Canada: A Patchwork Quilt with Many Holes" (2001) 164:6 C.M.A.J. 847. In both P.E.I. and Nunavut, women must travel outside their home jurisdiction in order to obtain abortion services. See Canadian Abortion Rights Action League, "Protecting Abortion Rights in Canada", *ibid.*

[17] Canadian Abortion Rights Action League, "Protecting Abortion Rights in Canada", *ibid.*

[18] As quoted in Laura Eggerston, "News: Abortion Services in Canada: A Patchwork Quilt with Many Holes" (2001) 164:6 C.M.A.J. 847 at 847.

[19] Marge Berer, "Medical Abortion: Issues of Choice and Acceptability" (2005) 13 Reproductive Health Matters 25 at 27. Medical abortion is superior at this early gestational stage because surgical abortion is often incomplete when attempted at this point in pregnancy. While it is likely often the case that women do not know they are pregnant at this very early stage, for those who are aware and who wish to terminate the pregnancy, the option of doing so immediately with a medical approach seems far superior to having to wait for some number of weeks for surgical abortion.

[20] In other words, if the abortion is incomplete or unsuccessful and the pregnancy continues, the use of methotrexate poses a risk to the health of the fetus. "Medical Abortion: A Fact Sheet" (2005) 13 Reproductive Health Matters 20 at 20.

[21] Society of Obstetricians and Gynaecologists of Canada, "SOGC Policy Statement: Mifepristone" (2003) 25(3) J. Obstet. Gynaecol. Can. 235.

[22] Marge Berer, "Medical Abortion: Issues of Choice and Acceptability" (2005) 13 Reproductive

gestation, medical abortion can take place at home if the woman prefers that option to waiting in the clinic, and need only involve two visits to the clinic.[23] Medical abortion may not be an option desired by a majority of women, but there is evidence of its safety, efficacy and acceptability as an alternative to surgical abortion, at least in the early part of pregnancy.[24]

Another barrier to access faced by women seeking abortion services relates to the availability of health care providers able and willing to perform the procedure. Concerns have been raised about the insufficiency of training in abortion procedures offered by medical schools,[25] as well as in relation to the scope of conscientious objection to the provision of abortion services.[26] From a Canadian legal perspective, the scope of conscientious objection to the provision of abortion services is unsettled.[27] There is no Canadian case law or legislation that clearly delineates the rights or responsibilities of providers who object to abortion for moral reasons, although it seems clear that the law of negligence demands that providers are at least obligated to refer their patients to providers who will discuss the option with them and help them to make arrangements.[28]

Health Matters 25 at 26.

[23] Janice Raymond has argued that medical abortion using mifepristone and misoprostol is highly medicalized, time consuming and painful: see Janice G. Raymond, "RU 486: Progress or Peril" in Joan C. Callahan, ed., *Reproduction, Ethics and the Law: Feminist Perspectives* (Indianapolis: Indiana University Press, 1995) at 286. As Marge Berer points out, however, it need not be so highly medicalized — as with surgical abortion, there need only be two clinic visits: one to prescribe the drug and give instructions on use as well as on complications, and one follow-up visit to ensure that the abortion is complete and that there are no complications. This is identical to the clinical schedule with surgical abortion. Berer also notes that most women who have experienced medical abortion have been satisfied with the procedure and would choose it again. See Marge Berer, "Medical Abortion: Issues of Choice and Acceptability", *ibid.*, at 26, 29).

[24] In the United States, concerns have been voiced about the safety of mifepristone, but the data indicates that medical abortion is a safe and effective option. See, *e.g.*, Association of Reproductive Health Professionals, "What You Need to Know: Mifepristone Safety Overview", online: Association of Reproductive Health Professionals <http://www.arhp.org/files/mifepristonefactsheet.pdf>; Jillian T. Henderson *et al.*, "Safety of mifepristone abortions in clinical use" (2005) 72(3) Contraception 175.

[25] See Laura Eggerston, "News: Abortion Services in Canada: A Patchwork Quilt with Many Holes" (2001) 164:6 C.M.A.J. 847 at 848; Laura Shanner, "Pregnancy Intervention and Models of Maternal-Fetal Relationship: Philosophical Reflections on the Winnipeg C.F.S. Dissent" (1998) 36 Alta. L. Rev. 751 at 764; Bonnie Steinbock, "Symposium: Opening Remarks" (1999) 62 Albany L. Rev. 805 at 806.

[26] See, *e.g.*, Bernard M. Dickens & Rebecca J. Cook, "The scope and limits of conscientious objection" (2000) 71 Int'l J. Gynecology & Obstetrics 71 at 73; Bernard M. Dickens, "Informed Consent" in Jocelyn Downie, Timothy Caulfield & Colleen Flood, eds., *Canadian Health Law and Policy*, 2nd ed. (Markham, ON: LexisNexis Butterworths, 2002) at 148.

[27] Indeed, the scope of conscientious objection is somewhat unclear in ethical and other legal contexts as well. See Julie Cantor & Ken Baum, "The Limits of Conscientious Objection — May Pharmacists Refuse to Fill Prescriptions for Emergency Contraception?" (2004) 351(19) New Eng. J. Med. 2008; R. Alta Charo, "The Celestial Fire of Conscience — Refusing to Deliver Medical Care" (2005) 352(24) New Eng. J. Med. 2471; Sanda Rodgers & Jocelyn Downie, "Abortion: Ensuring Access" (2006) 175(1) C.M.A.J. 9.

[28] See Bernard M. Dickens & Rebecca J. Cook, "The scope and limits of conscientious objection" (2000) 71 Int'l J. Gynecology & Obstetrics 71; Bernard M. Dickens, "Informed Consent" in

Ultimately, as Bernard Dickens points out, the "primary responsibility to ensure patients' reasonable access to medically indicated care falls on the provincial government[s]". It is therefore the state's responsibility to ensure that women have access to abortion services, and that women's reproductive autonomy is not held hostage to physicians' moral views.

III. CONTRACEPTION AND STERILIZATION

A. CONTRACEPTION

Contraceptive services were criminally prohibited in Canada between 1892 and 1969. Contraceptives are now generally available in Canada, but, as in the case of abortion services, barriers to access continue to exist. These barriers are largely financial and regulatory, but also encompass the issue of provider conscientious objection, especially in relation to emergency contraception (EC).

Financial barriers to contraceptive access pose a complex problem. Canada's health care system provides universal coverage of physician and hospital services, but most provincial health care plans do not include prescription drug coverage,[29] nor do they include non-prescription contraceptives such as condoms, spermicides, the contraceptive sponge and intra-uterine devices.[30] As a result of the organization and structure of the health care system around physician and hospital services, the most affordable contraceptive option may also be the most permanent — surgical sterilization.[31] While the provision of tubal ligation or vasectomy without charge[32] is clearly not coercive, it is nonetheless cause for concern. If women are led to choose sterilization even where it is not an optimal method of contraception in their particular circumstances (that is, they may wish to have more children in the future) because it is more affordable than non-permanent options, then the autonomous quality of the choice becomes questionable. Poor women who wish to avoid pregnancy in the short term may be led to the most permanent contraceptive

---

Jocelyn Downie, Timothy Caulfield & Colleen Flood, eds., *Canadian Health Law and Policy*, 2nd ed. (Markham, ON: LexisNexis Butterworths, 2002) at 148. Dickens notes that fiduciary law also protects patients from their physicians' failure to disclose options or to refer due to the provider's moral convictions.

[29] Some provinces have "pharmacare" programs which provide some prescription drug coverage. See, for example, Manitoba Health, Manitoba Pharmacare Program Information 2004-2005, online: <http://www.gov.mb.ca/health/pharmacare/index.html>; Government of British Columbia, Ministry of Health Services, Welcome to BC Pharmacare, online: <http://www. healthservices.gov.bc.ca/pharme/index.html>.

[30] Some contraceptive methods are available without charge to certain individuals (for example, those who attend sexual health or university health clinics) or in certain jurisdictions (where prescription drugs are covered), but availability is variable and unpredictable, depending on the specific contraceptive an individual seeks to use, and where the individual lives in Canada.

[31] Tubal ligation and vasectomy procedures are provided as insured services in most Canadian provinces. Intrauterine device insertion is also covered under health care insurance plans, but the devices themselves must be purchased from a pharmacy.

[32] Note that this is not the case in all Canadian jurisdictions.

option, due to the costs of other methods. The answer to this potential concern seems clear: the health care system should provide a wide range of contraceptive options as insured services. Not only would this approach lead to a better range of options for women, it would also help to reduce the incidence (and associated costs) of abortion and the social costs created by unwanted and mistimed pregnancies.

A significant non-financial barrier to access requires attention as well, and that is the Canadian regulatory environment. In a recent study comparing the availability of contraceptive methods in Canada to availability in other countries,[33] researchers found that Canadian women have access to a significantly smaller range of hormonal contraceptive products than women in the U.S., France, Sweden, Denmark and the U.K.[34] In relation to newer contraceptive products, Canadian women have access to the fewest options.[35] The study also points out that, while regulatory approval for new drug products in Canada tends to lag approximately six months behind the United States, as of January 1, 2004, Canada was 29.6 months behind for six contraceptive products seeking regulatory approval.[36] The authors conclude that:

> Canada appears to be lagging behind other countries with respect to the availability of hormonal contraceptive options. A wider choice of contraceptive options, including a variety of dosage forms, routes of administration and chemical entities, can improve access to effective contraception ... [and] reduce the number of unplanned and unwanted pregnancies.[37]

Emergency contraception has also been the subject of much recent concern in both Canada and the U.S.[38] When used within 72 hours after unprotected sexual

---

[33] D. Azzarello & J. Collins, "Canadian access to hormonal contraceptive drug choices" (2004) 26(5) J. Obstet. Gynaecol. Can. 489 at 490.

[34] Canadian women have access to 35 per cent of contraceptive products available worldwide, and 37 per cent of hormonal contraceptives. Figures for the other countries studied are as follows: U.S. 58 per cent and 59 per cent; U.K. 52 per cent and 54 per cent; France 44 per cent and 54 per cent; Sweden 44 per cent and 50 per cent. D. Azzarello & J. Collins, "Canadian access to hormonal contraceptive drug choices", *ibid.*, at 495-97.

[35] Canadian women have access to 22 per cent of available contraceptive products. Women in Denmark have the greatest number of options (67 per cent of available products). D. Azzarello & J. Collins, "Canadian access to hormonal contraceptive drug choices", *ibid.*, at 496. As the authors note, "[d]ifferent dose regimens and routes of hormonal contraceptive administration offer a range of efficacy, side-effect profiles and advantages and disadvantages that allow each woman to make an optimal choice". In addition, wider choice may improve compliance with drug regimens, leading to more effective use of hormonal contraceptives (at 496-97).

[36] D. Azzarello & J. Collins, "Canadian access to hormonal contraceptive drug choices", *ibid.*, at 495. The authors note that hormonal contraceptive products and hormone replacement therapy products all required longer review times than Viagra, a drug used in erectile dysfunction. The shortest approval time for an HRT product was 111 days longer than the approval time required for Viagra. It is unclear why this is the case, because information is not readily available due to restrictions in the *Access to Information Act*, R.S.C. 1985, c. A-1. See 495, 498.

[37] D. Azzarello & J. Collins, "Canadian access to hormonal contraceptive drug choices", *ibid.*, at 499.

[38] See, *e.g.*, Joanna N. Erdman & Rebecca J. Cook, "Protecting Fairness in Women's Health: The Case of Emergency Contraception" in Colleen M. Flood, ed., *Just Medicare: What's In, What's*

intercourse, EC[39] prevents 89 per cent of expected pregnancies. It is most effective when used within 24 hours of unprotected sex (when it prevents 95 per cent of expected pregnancies), and least effective when taken more than 49 hours post-intercourse (when it prevents 58 per cent of expected pregnancies).[40] It is abundantly clear that timely access to EC is essential. Until recently, EC was only available in most Canadian jurisdictions with a physician's prescription.[41] Women can now obtain EC by requesting it directly from pharmacists, meaning that the impediment to access created by the need for a prescription has been cleared away. But other potential obstacles have emerged. The first is increased cost for EC due to pharmacy charges for counselling related to its provision. As Joanna Erdman and Rebecca Cook note, the cost of a single dose of EC is approximately $18, but once pharmacists' consultation fees are added, the price increases to at least double the cost of the drug.[42]

The second obstacle relates to privacy concerns arising from the information collection practices of many pharmacists who dispense EC.[43] A form

---

Out, How We Decide (Toronto: University of Toronto Press, 2006) 137; Joanna N. Erdman & Rebecca J. Cook, "Morning after pill still faces hurdles" (May 21, 2004) *National Post*, A18. See also: Editorial, "Emergency contraception moves behind the counter" (2005) 172(7) CMAJ 845; and Laura Eggerston & Barbara Sibbald, "Privacy issues raised over Plan B: women asked for names, addresses, sexual history" (2005) 173(12) C.M.A.J. 1435; Alastair J.J. Wood, Jeffrey M. Drazen & Michael F. Greene, "A sad day for science at the FDA" (2005) 353 New Engl. J. Med. 1197 at 1198.

[39] There are two primary methods of EC. One uses a high dose of combination oral contraceptive pills containing both estrogen and progesterone/levonorgestrel (the Yuzpe method); the other is levonorgestrel alone, which is marketed under the brand name "Plan B". See, *e.g.*, Rebecca J. Cook, Bernard M. Dickens & Mahmoud F. Fathalla, *Reproductive Health and Human Rights: Integrating Medicine, Ethics, and Law* (Oxford: Oxford University Press, 2003) at 289. The efficacy rates given here are for levonorgestrel: see D.A. Grimes *et al.*, "Randomised controlled trial of levonorgestrel versus the Yuzpe regimen of combined oral contraceptives for emergency contraception" (1998) 352:9126 Lancet 428.

[40] Rebecca J. Cook, Bernard M. Dickens & Mahmoud F. Fathalla, *ibid.*, at 289.

[41] Prior to April 2006, EC was available without a prescription in Quebec, Saskatchewan and British Columbia. See Barbara Sibbald, "Nonprescription status for emergency contraception" (2005) 172(7) C.M.A.J. 861.

[42] See, *e.g.*, Joanna N. Erdman & Rebecca J. Cook, "Morning after pill still faces hurdles" (May 21, 2004) *National Post*, A18. See also: Editorial, "Emergency contraception moves behind the counter" (2005) 172(7) C.M.A.J. 845; and Laura Eggerston & Barbara Sibbald, "Privacy issues raised over Plan B: women asked for names, addresses, sexual history" (2005) 173(12) C.M.A.J. 1435, noting that the fee charged is approximately $20.

[43] See Laura Eggerston & Barbara Sibbald, "Privacy issues raised over Plan B: women asked for names, addresses, sexual history", *ibid.* In an especially interesting turn of events, these stories around Plan B played a part in the emergence of serious concerns over the editorial independence of the Canadian Medical Association Journal, Canada's well-respected generalist medical journal. See, *e.g.*, International Committee of Medical Journal Editors, "ICMJE Expresses Concern Over Firing of CMAJ Editors", online: <http://www.icmje.org/cmaj.htm> (accessed October 21, 2006); Helen Branswell, "Former Supreme Court head named to review embattled CMAJ governance structure", Canada.com, online: <http://www.canada.com/topics/news/national/story.html?id=e87e10da-6dc6-4176-aaaf-d2c7cfe4350c&k=66395>; CMAJ, Press Release: "CMAJ Acting Editor-in-Chief Accepts Editorial Board Resignations" (March 16, 2006), online: <www.cmaj.ca/misc/press/cmaj_release_mar16.pdf> (accessed October 21, 2006).

recommended for use by the Canadian Pharmacists Association (CPhA) asks for "personal data, including the woman's name, address, the date of her last menstrual period, when she had unprotected sex, and her customary method of birth control, [and] ... the reason for dispensing the medication".[44] If women are or could be deterred from seeking access to EC because of their fears around the collection and storage of sensitive information, then the practice itself creates an obstacle to access. Privacy commissioners in a number of Canadian jurisdictions have articulated concerns about the CPhA form, noting that personal information is not normally collected by pharmacists when they dispense Schedule II drugs.[45] Ontario pharmacists have now decided not to routinely collect personal information when dispensing EC, and privacy commissioners in two other provinces have raised the issue with local professional regulators.[46]

As noted, the other appreciable roadblock to access in the contraceptive context is conscientious objection to their provision by health care professionals.[47] Canadian pharmacists assert a right to conscientiously object to the provision of services (and to the provision of referrals to those who will furnish the requested service) that they find morally or religiously offensive.[48] The phenomenon of conscientious objection in Canada has not been thoroughly studied, meaning that it is difficult to ascertain the frequency with which it poses a problem for contraceptive access, but anecdotal accounts illustrate that it does occur.[49] Ideally, health care professionals should never be required to participate in procedures or services they find morally objectionable. But there must be limits to the protection of provider conscience where such protection threatens women's health and well-being. To date, no Canadian court has explicitly addressed the issue of provider obligations and the role of conscience,[50] meaning that it is left to policy makers to address the question of conscientious objection.

---

[44] Laura Eggerston & Barbara Sibbald, "Privacy issues raised over Plan B: women asked for names, addresses, sexual history", *ibid.*

[45] Laura Eggerston, "Ontario pharmacists drop Plan B screening form" (2006) 174(2) C.M.A.J. 149.

[46] *Ibid.*

[47] As has been noted by others, conscientious objection to the provision of hormonal contraceptives (including emergency contraception) can create significant barriers to access for women, particularly low-income women and those who live in rural areas. See Holly Teliksa, "Recent Development: Obstacles to Access: How Pharmacist Refusal Clauses Undermine the Basic Health Care Needs of Rural and Low-Income Women" (2005) 20 Berkeley J. Gender L. & Just. 229; Tania Khan & Megan Arvad McCoy, "Sixth Annual Review of Gender and Sexuality Law: VI. Healthcare Law Chapter: Access to Contraception" (2005) 6 Geo. J. Gender & L. 785.

[48] See Mike Mastromatteo, "Alberta pharmacist wins concessions in right-to-refuse case" (December 2003) *The Interim*, online: <www.theinterim.com/2003/dec/02alberta.html>. See also The Protection of Conscience Project, online: <www.consciencelaws.org/>.

[49] See, *e.g.*, Mike Mastromatteo, "Alberta pharmacist wins concessions in right-to-refuse case", *ibid.*; Barbara Sibbald, "Nonprescription status for emergency contraception" (2005) 172(7) C.M.A.J. 861.

[50] There are signals, though, that lead to the fairly safe conclusion that Canadian law requires physicians who object to participating in certain procedures for reasons of conscience to refer their patients to a provider who do not similarly object. See, *e.g.*, Rebecca J. Cook & Bernard M. Dickens, "Access to emergency contraception" (2003) 25(11) J. Obstet. Gynaecol. Can. 914. Cook & Dickens cite *Zimmer v. Ringrose*, [1981] A.J. No. 596, 124 D.L.R. (3d) 215 (Alta.

One solution that would remove both barriers to access to EC is to make it available without the need for pharmacist intervention at point of sale. As Erdman and Cook have argued, there is a persuasive case for permitting EC to be sold "over-the-counter" as opposed to "behind-the-counter".[51] Erdman and Cook argue that Health Canada's review of levonorgestrel indicates that the drug is safe for use as EC by virtually all women,[52] it has minimal side effects, there have been no reports of serious consequences due to acute overdose, and there are no contraindications to its use.[53] Ultimately, it is up to the National Drug Scheduling Advisory Committee (NDSAC)[54] of the National Association of Pharmacy Regulatory Authorities (NAPRA) to decide whether a drug is made available behind the counter or over the counter, and NAPRA is currently being urged to conduct a drug scheduling review of levonorgestrel.[55]

C.A.), where the Alberta Court of Appeal held that the physician's failure to refer his patient to a local physician who would facilitate an abortion amounted to negligence (for failure to provide appropriate follow-up care). While this case does not deal with a refusal to refer because of conscientious objection (indeed, the physician's reason for referring his patient to a U.S. practitioner rather than a local physician was to ensure the abortion took place as soon as possible), it does indicate that the courts are likely to see a failure to provide an appropriate referral as negligence tantamount to abandonment. Cook & Dickens also refer to *McInerney v. MacDonald*, [1992] S.C.J. No. 57, [1992] 2 S.C.R. 138 (S.C.C.), which holds that physicians owe fiduciary duties to their patients, and note that this surely requires that physicians must place their patients' well-being ahead of their own personal convictions.

[51] Joanna N. Erdman & Rebecca J. Cook, "Protecting Fairness in Women's Health: The Case of Emergency Contraception" in Colleen M. Flood, ed., *Just Medicare: What's In, What's Out, How We Decide* (Toronto: University of Toronto Press, 2006) at 137.

[52] A major issue in the U.S. with respect to non-prescription access to EC is safety, particularly safety for women aged 16 and younger. That this concern is specious is quite obvious when placed in context with the FDA's approach to other medications. As one group of authors explains:

... other over-the-counter drugs, such as acetaminophen and aspirin, can cause death when taken inappropriately. At a meeting of a similar FDA advisory committee, data were presented indicating that acetaminophen ingestion results in 56,680 emergency department visits, 26,256 hospitalizations and 458 deaths in the United States every year; a large number of these events affect persons younger than 17 years of age. The FDA has shown no inclination to restrict the availability of these drugs to young people by requiring them to have a prescription. Why not?

Alastair J.J. Wood, Jeffrey M. Drazen & Michael F. Greene, "A sad day for science at the FDA" (2005) 353 New Engl. J. Med. 1197 at 1198.

[53] Joanna N. Erdman & Rebecca J. Cook, "Protecting Fairness in Women's Health: The Case of Emergency Contraception" in Colleen M. Flood, ed., *Just Medicare: What's In, What's Out, How We Decide* (Toronto: University of Toronto Press, 2006) at 140-46.

[54] Once a drug is no longer under federal government control (as is now the case with levonorgestrel), it is up to provincial and territorial regulatory bodies to determine how the drug may be sold. Provincial and territorial regulatory authorities act on the basis of recommendations made by the NDSAC. See Joanna N. Erdman & Rebecca J. Cook, "Protecting Fairness in Women's Health: The Case of Emergency Contraception", *ibid.*, at 138-39.

[55] Marilou McPhedran, on behalf of Women & Health Protection, Canadian Women's Health Network, Society of Obstetricians & Gynaecologists of Canada, and the Canadian Federation for Sexual Health, *Public Interest Brief on Emergency Contraception* (2006) (copy on file with the author).

B. STERILIZATION

Sterilization is the most common form of contraception worldwide.[56] It is, for the most part, uncontroversial that sterilization should be available to those who would choose it as a method of contraception,[57] but its use in some contexts provides cause for significant concern.[58] Specifically of interest here is the issue of consent to sterilization by or on behalf of those who may, by reason of intellectual disability or mental illness, lack the immediate capacity to make such decisions.[59] Most commonly, this occurs when intellectually disabled or mentally ill women (or men) are sterilized without their consent.

Canadian law around non-consensual sterilization has been clear since the decision of the Supreme Court of Canada in *E. (Mrs.) v. Eve*:[60] a third party may not authorize the non-therapeutic sterilization of an individual who is incapable of consenting for him or herself, nor may the court do so under its *parens patriae* jurisdiction. The decision in *Eve* has been harshly criticized in both academic and judicial opinion,[61] and at least one author has raised questions about its continued persuasiveness.[62] Clearly, a balance needs to be struck

---

[56] Emily Jackson, *Regulating Reproduction: Law, Technology, Autonomy* (Oxford: Hart Publishing, 2000) at 19, Robert Blank, *Fertility Control: New Techniques, New Policy Issues* (New York: Greenwood Press, 1991).

[57] Recently, however, the board of a Catholic hospital in Saskatchewan modified its existing policy, deciding that sterilization procedures would no longer be available at the hospital. The policy change was made in order to improve compliance with the Catholic Health Care Ethics Guide. See Kiply Lukan Yaworski, "Catholic hospital wrestles with ethics of, stops tubal ligations", *Canadian Catholic News* (September 25, 2006), online: Catholic Online <http://www.catholic.org/international/international_story.php?id=21391>.

[58] For example, the "emergency" in India in the late 1970s, and involuntary sterilization of indigent women in Latin American countries (see, *e.g.*, Rebecca J. Cook, Bernard M. Dickens & Mahmoud F. Fathalla, *Reproductive Health and Human Rights: Integrating Medicine, Ethics, and Law* (Oxford: Oxford University Press, 2003) at 315-22).

[59] Mental health law and policy is a complex area of the law; a detailed discussion is beyond the scope of this chapter.

[60] *E. (Mrs.) v. Eve (Guardian ad litem)*, [1986] S.C.J. No. 60, [1986] 2 S.C.R. 388 (S.C.C.) [*Eve*].

[61] In *Re B (A Minor) (Wardship: Sterilisation)*, [1987] 2 All E.R. 206 (H.L.), the House of Lords authorized the sterilization of a mentally disabled 17-year-old girl, holding that the procedure was in her "best interests". Lord Hailsham refers to La Forest J.'s decision in *Eve* as follows (at 213):

> I find, with great respect, his conclusion ... that the procedure of sterilisation "should never (*sic*) be authorised for non-therapeutic purposes" totally unconvincing and in startling contradiction to the welfare principle which should be the first and paramount consideration in wardship cases. Moreover, for the purposes of the present appeal, I find the distinction he purports to draw between "therapeutic" and "non-therapeutic" purposes of this operation in relation to the facts of the present case above as totally meaningless and, if meaningful, quite irrelevant to the correct application of the welfare principle. To talk of the "basic right" to reproduce of an individual who is not capable of knowing the causal connection between intercourse and childbirth, the nature of pregnancy, what is involved in delivery, unable to form maternal instincts or to care for a child appears to me wholly to part company with reality.

[62] Dwight Newman, "An Examination of Saskatchewan Law on the Sterilization of Persons with Mental Disabilities" (1999) 62 Sask. L. Rev. 329-46 at para. 16: "When combined with the

between the potential advantages and disadvantages of the various methods of contraception and the desire to preserve an individual's fertility when there may be no real likelihood that it will ever matter to the individual whether or not he or she can bear children. However, given the fluidity of capacity,[63] the historical willingness of decision-makers to take a pessimistic view of the facts of these cases,[64] and "the grave intrusion on a person's rights and the certain physical damage"[65] occasioned by non-consensual sterilization, this restrictive approach seems preferable to one which might permit sterilization in anticipation of problems which might never materialize.[66] Such an approach seems particularly appropriate now, in light of the developments in reproductive technology such as long-acting injectable and implantable hormonal contraceptives, safer intrauterine devices, emergency contraception and medical abortion, and contraceptive pills that are intended to suppress menstruation as well as ovulation.[67]

IV. RECOVERY OF DAMAGES FOR CHILDBEARING AND CHILDREARING

As reproductive technology has become increasingly sophisticated, expectations about the level of control one has over one's reproductive capacity have shifted. Individuals now routinely seek to control the number and timing of their children, as well as the health and developmental attributes of the children they bear. When these aims are frustrated by medical negligence, parents may seek compensation for costs related to the pregnancy and birth, including costs of childrearing. These claims are variously referred to as wrongful conception, wrongful pregnancy and wrongful birth claims.[68] In general, the wrongful birth

---

criticism it faces in Canadian academic and law reform writing, the judgment is of rather uncertain persuasive force. While the case may articulate a rule, one might wonder to what extent this rule can stand in its present form when it has been the subject of such criticism".

[63] For a discussion of the evolving nature of children's capacity acknowledged in law and ethics, see generally, Joan M. Gilmour, "Children, Adolescents and Health Care" in Jocelyn Downie, Timothy Caulfield & Colleen Flood, eds., *Canadian Health Law and Policy*, 2nd ed. (Markham, ON: LexisNexis Butterworths, 2002) at 210-21; American Association of Pediatrics, Committee on Bioethics, "Informed Consent, Parental Permission and Assent in Pediatric Practice" (1995) 95(2) Pediatrics 314; Christine Harrison *et al.*, "Bioethics for Clinicians: 9. Involving Children in Medical Decisions" (1997) 156 C.M.A.J. 825-28.

[64] See, *e.g.*, Jonathan Montgomery, "Rhetoric and 'Welfare'" (1989) 9 Oxford J. Legal Stud. 395 at 397-99.

[65] [1986] S.C.J. No. 60, [1986] 2 S.C.R. 388 (S.C.C.) at para. 86.

[66] See Danny Sandor, "Sterilisation and Special Medical Procedures on Children and Young People: Blunt Instrument? Bad Medicine?" in I. Freckelton & Kerry Petersen, *Controversies in Health Law* (Sydney: Law Federation Press, 2000) at 16.

[67] See, for example, U.S. Food and Drug Administration, "FDA Talk Paper: FDA Approves Seasonale Oral Contraceptive" (September 5, 2003), online: <http://www.fda.gov/bbs/topics/ANSWERS/2003/ANS01251.html>.

[68] A related type of claim is the claim for wrongful life. This species of negligence claim is brought by a child born with disabilities seeking compensation for pain and suffering, claiming that but

claim involves a claim for the negligent failure of a physician to inform a pregnant woman of circumstances that might lead her to terminate the pregnancy. Such cases usually involve the birth of a child with illness or disability,[69] and the claim for damages reflects the increased costs of maintenance resulting from the child's illness or disability. Wrongful conception (or wrongful pregnancy) claims are brought where a provider is said to have been negligent in giving contraceptive advice or performing a sterilization procedure and, as a result, an unwanted pregnancy occurs. These categories are somewhat slippery — sometimes wrongful conception cases concern the birth of a child with disabilities — and the case law can justly be described as confused (and confusing). Recently, for example, two Alberta trial judges came to opposing conclusions on damages in factually similar cases.[70] What follows is an attempt to distill some general ideas about this species of negligence claim.

Initially, wrongful birth and wrongful conception claims met with reluctance on the part of Canadian judges, but they are now fairly well established in Canadian jurisdictions.[71] The courts have awarded damages for the "inconveniences" and any lost income caused by pregnancy and childbirth, but have been inconsistent when it comes to awarding the costs of childrearing.

---

for the physician's negligence, he or she would not have been born. Wrongful life claims will not be considered further here. See Ellen I. Picard & Gerald B. Robertson, *Legal Liability of Doctors and Hospitals in Canada*, 3rd ed. (Toronto: Carswell, 1996) at 213. In *Krangle (Guardian ad litem of) v. Brisco*, [1997] B.C.J. No. 2740, 154 D.L.R. (4th) 707 (B.C.S.C.), [2002] S.C.J. No. 8 (S.C.C.), the Court categorized the cases as follows:

- unwanted conception following a failed medical sterilization procedure performed on either parent;
- unwanted birth following a failed medical abortion;
- loss of opportunity to have an abortion following failure to be provided with necessary medical information or advice; and,
- physical damage to the fetus resulting from a medical procedure during pregnancy.

[69] This group of cases also includes unsuccessful abortion procedures, and late or missed diagnoses of pregnancy, where by the time pregnancy is discovered, termination is no longer an option.

[70] In *M.S. v. Baker*, [2001] A.J. No. 1579, 100 Alta. L.R. (3d) 124 (Alta. Q.B.), Moreau J. would have awarded damages for the costs of raising the unplanned child to age 18 (if she had found the defendant physician negligent), on the theory articulated in *Kealey v. Berezowski*, [1996] O.J. No. 2460, 136 D.L.R. 4th 708 (Ont. Gen. Div.) that the motivation for the sterilization governs the recovery of such damages. Justice Moreau concluded that financial circumstances were an important consideration in the plaintiffs' decision to proceed with sterilization, and therefore would have awarded damages for childrearing. In *M.Y. v. Boutros*, [2002] A.J. No. 480, 2 Alta. L.R. (4th) 153 (Alta. Q.B.), Rawlins J. would not have awarded childrearing costs, even if she had found the physician to be negligent. Justice Rawlins disagreed with the approach adopted in *Kealey* and *Baker*, and instead followed the ruling of the U.K. House of Lords in *McFarlane v. Tayside Health Board*, [2000] 2 A.C. 59 (H.L.), although it is not clear on what basis she did so. She found that the Law Lords were unanimous in declining to award the costs of raising a healthy child, although all five arrived at this result for different reasons. Justice Rawlins then went on to consider the "offset-benefits" approach to considering whether damages for childrearing should be awarded, and concluded that although this approach was not adopted in *McFarlane*, she "accept[ed] that the benefits a child brings to a family outweigh the costs of that child to a family".

[71] *Doiron v. Orr*, [1978] O.J. No. 3388, 86 D.L.R. (3d) 719 (Ont. H.C.J.); *Colp v. Ringrose* (1976), 3 Med. Q. 72 (Alta. T.D.); *Pozdzik (Next friend of) v. Wilson*, [2002] A.J. No. 450 (Alta. Q.B.).

Courts are loath to award the full costs of childrearing in wrongful conception cases, although they appear to be less so where the claim is for the additional costs of raising a child born with disabilities.[72]

Several approaches to damage assessment in wrongful conception cases have been considered by courts in Canada, the United States, the United Kingdom and Australia. Some courts have taken the position that, as the birth of a child is occasion for joy even where it is the result of provider negligence, no damages can be awarded to parents.[73] Others have taken the opposite approach, holding that a principled approach to tort law demands full recovery of all losses flowing from the pregnancy and birth, including the full costs of childrearing.[74] Still other courts have attempted to offset the benefits of the child's presence in the parents' lives against the costs of raising that child in arriving at an award of damages.[75] Finally, and most commonly, courts have awarded limited damages to compensate women for the pregnancy and childbirth, and both parents for "start-up" costs relevant to the newborn, but have stopped short of awarding any additional rearing costs.[76] Complete recovery for the costs of raising the child is rare,[77] meaning that parents are generally compensated for little if any of the actual costs that result from the provider's negligence.

---

[72] *Cherry (Guardian ad litem of) v. Borsman*, [1991] B.C.J. No. 315, 75 D.L.R. (4th) 668 (B.C.S.C.), vard [1992] B.C.J. No. 1687, 94 D.L.R. (4th) 487 (B.C.C.A.); *Joshi (Guardian ad litem of) v. Wooley*, [1995] B.C.J. No. 113, 4 B.C.L.R. (3d) 208 (B.C.S.C.).

[73] See *Roe v. Dabbs*, [2004] B.C.J. No. 1485, 2004 BCSC 957 (B.C.S.C.), at paras. 189-193, for a description of the various approaches taken to awarding damages in wrongful conception cases.

[74] This is the common law position in Australia (see *Cattanach v. Melchior*, [2003] H.C.A. 38, 215 C.L.R. 1). The common law has been overruled by statute in three jurisdictions. See *Civil Liability Act 2003* (Qld.), s. 49; *Civil Liability Act 2002*, (N.S.W.) s. 71; and *Civil Liability Act 1936*, (S.A.) s. 67.

[75] This is often referred to as the "offset-benefits" approach. See *Suite c. Cooke*, [1995] J.Q. No. 696, R.J.Q. 2765 (Que. C.A.), and *Chaffee v. Seslar*, 786 N.E.2d 705 (Ind. 2003) at 707-08, in which the Supreme Court of Indiana clearly and concisely explains the state of play in American jurisdictions. For cases adopting this approach, see *Univ. of Arizona Health Sciences Ctr. v. Superior Court*, 136 Ariz. 579, 667 P.2d 1294, 1299 (1983); *Ochs v. Borrelli*, 187 Conn. 253, 445 A.2d 883, 886 (1982); *Sherlock v. Stillwater Clinic*, 260 N.W.2d 169, 175-76 (Minn. 1977).

[76] *McFarlane v. Tayside Health Board*, [2000] A.C. 59 (H.L.); *Rees v. Darlington Memorial Hospital NHS Trust*, [2003] U.K.H.L. 52, [2003] All E.R. 987 (H.L.) (in which the majority of the House of Lords acknowledged the wrong to parents from violation of their reproductive autonomy and awarded a conventional sum of £15,000). Like the House of Lords in *Rees*, the British Columbia Supreme Court awarded non-pecuniary damages to the parents in *Bevilacqua v. Altenkirk*, [2004] B.C.J. No. 1473, 2004 BCSC 945 (B.C.S.C.) and *Roe v. Dabbs*, [2004] B.C.J. No. 1485, 2004 BCSC 957 (B.C.S.C.). In *Mummery v. Olsson*, [2001] O.J. No. 226 (Ont. S.C.J.); *M.Y. v. Boutros*, [2002] A.J. No. 480, 11 C.C.L.T. (3d) 271 (Alta. Q.B.), the courts refused to award any damages for childrearing, while in *Kealey v. Berezowski*, [1996] O.J. No. 2460, 136 D.L.R. (4th) 708 (Ont. Ct. Gen. Div.) and *M.S. v. Baker*, [2001] A.J. No. 1579, [2002] 4 W.W.R. 487 (Alta. Q.B.), the courts held that childrearing damages may be awarded where the motivation for sterilization is financial.

[77] See, *e.g.*, *Cattanach v. Melchior*, [2003] H.C.A. 38, 215 C.L.R. 1; *Custodio v. Bauer*, 251 Cal. App.2d 303, 59 Cal. Rptr. 463 (Cal. Ct. App. 1967); *Lovelace Med. Ctr. v. Mendez*, 111 N.M. 336, 805 P.2d 603 (N.M. 1991); *Zehr v. Haugen*, 318 Or. 647, 871 P.2d 1006 (1994); and *Marciniak v. Lundborg*, 153 Wis.2d 59, 450 N.W.2d 243 (1990).

Various policy arguments have been deployed in rationalizing the departure from principle marked by the refusal to award the full measure of damages to parents who have established provider negligence leading to the birth of an unwanted child. Most of these arguments boil down to essentially the same premise — that "it is morally offensive to regard a normal, healthy baby as more trouble and expense than it is worth".[78] Less troubling to courts is the reality that this approach leaves parents — especially women — who have been negligently deprived of their right to limit the size of their family without compensation for the most significant part of their loss.[79]

Women are generally the primary caregivers for their young children and, where couples choose to have one of them take time out of the labour force in order to raise children, it is almost exclusively the female member of the couple.[80] Thus, the impact of judicial policy favouring limited (or no) recovery for wrongful conception is largely borne by women. And physicians (and society) are told, in effect, that violating women's reproductive autonomy bears few consequences. Arguably, the effects of denying claims for childrearing damages in wrongful conception cases go well beyond the confines of tort law. The gendered impact of decisions to reject these claims undermines women's reproductive autonomy and hence their ability to participate fully in social, economic and political life.

Wrongful birth claims, in which parents are generally asking for costs of childrearing related to the child's disability, have been approached much more generously than have those related to the birth of a healthy child.[81] In the genetics context, the cases have dealt with negligence in failing to provide or to refer parents for genetic counselling, resulting in the birth of two children with Duchenne muscular dystrophy,[82] and negligence in failing to inform parents of the availability of prenatal genetic testing, resulting in the birth of a child with Down Syndrome.[83] Recently, the British Columbia Supreme Court decided a

---

[78]   Lord Millet in *McFarlane v. Tayside Health Board*, [2000] 2 A.C. 59 at 113 (H.L.).
[79]   See Elizabeth Adjin-Tettey, "Claims of Involuntary Parenthood: Why the Resistance?" (paper presented at Emerging Issues in Tort Law, University of Western Ontario, June 2006) (copy on file with the author); See Nicolette Priaulx, "Joy to the World! A (Healthy) Child is Born! Reconceptualizing 'Harm' in Wrongful Conception" (2004) 13(1) Social & Legal Studies 5; Ben Golder, "From *McFarlane* to *Melchior* and beyond: Love, Sex, Money and Commodification in the Anglo-Australian Law of Torts" (2004) 9 Torts Law Journal 1.
[80]   See, *e.g.*, Reva Siegel, "Reasoning from the Body: A Historical Perspective on Abortion Regulation and Questions of Equal Protection" (1992) 44 Stanford L. Rev. 261 at 375; Arlie Hochschild, *The Second Shift* (New York: London Books, 1989); Sylvia Ann Hewlett & Carolyn Buck Luce, "Off-Ramps and On-Ramps: Keeping Talented Women on the Road to Success" (2005) Harvard Bus. Rev. 43 at 44; and Sandra Fredman, *Women and the Law* (Oxford: Oxford University Press, 1997) at 180.
[81]   There are also "wrongful conception" cases where the child was born with disabilities and the additional costs of rearing attributable to the disabilities have been compensated: *Parkinson v. St James and Seacroft University Hospital NHS Trust*, [2001] 3 All E.R. 97; *Joshi (Guardian ad litem of) v. Wooley*, [1995] B.C.J. No. 113, 4 B.C.L.R. (3d) 208 (B.C.S.C.).
[82]   *H. (R.) v. Hunter*, [1996] O.J. No. 4477, 32 C.C.L.T. (2d) 44 (Ont. Gen. Div.).
[83]   *Krangle (Guardian ad litem of) v. Brisco*, [2002] S.C.J. No. 8, [2002] 1 S.C.R. 205; *Jones v. Rostvig*, [1999] B.C.J. No. 647, 44 C.C.L.T. (2d) 313 (B.C.S.C.).

case involving a claim for damages respecting a child who was born with spina bifida.[84] The child's mother claimed that her physician was negligent in failing to refer her for an ultrasound. In this case, the physician also successfully claimed contributory negligence on the part of the child's mother for failing to follow medical advice.[85] The physician did not order an ultrasound because the mother did not return to the physician's office for a second prenatal visit office until later in pregnancy than such testing would normally be offered.

Damages do not seem to pose the same moral difficulty in the wrongful birth context as in wrongful conception claims,[86] but wrongful birth claims do give rise to interesting causation problems. In *Arndt v. Smith*, the plaintiff contracted chicken pox in the twelfth week of her pregnancy with her daughter, Miranda, and was assured by her physician, Dr. Smith, that the risks to the fetus were minimal, including limb and skin abnormalities. Although Dr. Smith was aware of more serious risks, including mental retardation and cortical atrophy, she did not inform Ms. Arndt of these risks on the basis that she did not wish to "unduly worry an expectant mother about an improbable risk and one for which she would not advise therapeutic abortion".[87]

Miranda was born with congenital varicella syndrome, which led to multiple disabilities. After Miranda's birth, Ms. Arndt sued Dr. Smith, alleging failure to inform her of the risks of infection with chicken pox while pregnant and further alleging that, had she been properly informed of the risks, she would have terminated the pregnancy. The trial judge found that Dr. Smith had breached her duty to inform, but went on to conclude that even if she had been told of the

---

[84] *Patmore (Guardian ad litem of) v. Weatherston*, [1999] B.C.J. No. 650 (B.C.S.C.).

[85] *Ibid*. See also *Zhang v. Kan*, [2003] B.C.J. No. 164, 15 C.C.L.T. (3d) 1 (B.C.S.C.), where the British Columbia Supreme Court assessed the plaintiff's contributory negligence at 50 per cent. The plaintiff sought a referral for amniocentesis from the defendant physician; he informed her that it was too late in her pregnancy for amniocentesis, even though she was only 17 weeks pregnant at the time. The Court noted that the plaintiff doubted the defendant's advice, but did not seek a second opinion, or seek to have the test elsewhere.

[86] Some authors have noted the distinction being made on the basis of disability as a significant cause for concern. See, *e.g.*, *Cattanach v. Melchior*, [2003] H.C.A. 38 at para. 164, *per* Kirby J.: "Apart from the arbitrariness of this exception it has a further flaw. It reinforces views about disability and attitudes towards parents and children with physical or mental impairments that are contrary to contemporary Australian values reinforced by the law".

[87] *Arndt v. Smith*, [1994] B.C.J. No. 1137, 21 C.C.L.T. (2d) 66 at para. 54 (B.C.S.C.) affd [1997] S.C.J. No. 65 (S.C.C.). This concern around "unduly worrying" an expectant mother is actually something of a delicate issue. Obviously, a robust approach to reproductive autonomy would recognize the significance of the pregnant woman of having this information. Without it, she is not in a position to decide whether or not to continue the pregnancy and risk having a severely, multiply disabled child (which, in turn, will have immense significance for her own life). Yet it is not entirely clear that informing a pregnant woman that she runs a minimal risk of her child being born with multiple, severe disabilities and health issues is helpful to a woman's ability to make choices. See Barbara Katz Rothman, *The Tentative Pregnancy: Prenatal Diagnosis and the Future of Motherhood* (New York: Viking, 1986) at 180-81:

> The whole thing about the new technology they are offered is that it gives choice. That is what it is all about, after all, the opening up of new reproductive choices. But for most women the choices are all so dreadful that trying to find one she can live with is terribly hard. Taking the least awful choice is not experienced as "choosing"...

very small risk of serious deformities, Ms. Arndt would not have terminated the pregnancy. In other words, Ms. Arndt's action failed on the question of causation. The decision was appealed to the British Columbia Court of Appeal and to the Supreme Court of Canada, a majority of which ultimately upheld the trial judge's decision.[88]

V. TORT DUTIES OF PREGNANT WOMEN

To what extent is a pregnant woman's choice of activities circumscribed by the fact of her decision to reproduce? Is she free to engage in risky conduct while pregnant? Can a woman be sued by her child for conduct during pregnancy that results in her child being born with disabilities?[89] In *Dobson (Litigation Guardian of) v. Dobson,*[90] the Supreme Court of Canada held that she cannot.

The *Dobson* case involved a claim by a child against his mother (or, more accurately, his mother's insurer) for her allegedly negligent driving. Ms. Dobson was involved in a collision, and her fetus was delivered prematurely that same day. Ryan Dobson was born with permanent mental and physical impairments, including cerebral palsy. The case advanced to the Supreme Court of Canada on the preliminary question of whether a pregnant woman owes a tort law duty of care to her fetus.

The lower courts held that the narrow issue requiring consideration in this case was the potential liability of a pregnant woman for negligent driving

---

[88] This decision, as well as the decision in *Mickle v. Salvation Army Grace Hospital Windsor Ontario,* [1998] O.J. No. 4683, 166 D.L.R. (4th) 743 (Ont. Gen. Div.), illustrates one of the significant difficulties that courts have in wrongful birth cases — some reasonable women might choose to carry a pregnancy to term, in spite of warnings of possible fetal ill-health or disability; other reasonable women might choose to terminate the pregnancy under those circumstances. The test for causation in Canadian common law is whether a reasonable person in the position of the patient, having been properly informed of the risks, would have taken a different approach with respect to treatment. Given that two equally reasonable choices exist, the test seems unworkable in these circumstances. In its decision in *Arndt v. Smith,* the British Columbia Court of Appeal specifically invited the Supreme Court of Canada to deal with this point, but the decision of the Supreme Court does not address the issue. See Erin Nelson & Timothy Caulfield, "You Can't Get There From Here: A Case Comment on *Arndt v. Smith*" (1998) 32 U.B.C. L. Rev. 353.; see also Vaughn Black & Dennis Klimchuk, "Case Comment: *Hollis v. Dow Corning*" (1996) 75 Can. Bar Rev. 355 at 363 (explaining problems with the test for causation).

[89] In *Winnipeg Child and Family Services (Northwest Area) v. G. (D.F.),* [1997] S.C.J. No. 96, 152 D.L.R. (4th) 193 (S.C.C.) [*Winnipeg*], the Supreme Court of Canada considered the potential liability of a woman for her conduct during pregnancy, in the context of an application to detain (and treat) a pregnant woman who was addicted to sniffing glue. The purpose of the proceedings was to obtain authority to detain the woman so that she could receive treatment for her addiction. Therefore, the Court was not asked to determine whether a woman could be liable to her child for her conduct prior to the child's birth. The Court concluded that tort law does not permit the granting of such an order, with the aim of protecting the fetus from potential harm. The Court went on to hold that tort law should not be extended to allow a fetus to assert a claim against its mother, in part due to the implications of such a finding with respect to the ability of pregnant women to make autonomous lifestyle choices.

[90] [1999] S.C.J. No. 41, 174 D.L.R. (4th) 1 (S.C.C.) [*Dobson*].

causing injuries to her born alive child.[91] Therefore, any policy considerations that might arise in cases involving negligence in "lifestyle choices"[92] were, in the Courts' view, irrelevant.[93] The Court of Appeal concluded that the duty of a pregnant woman toward her unborn fetus in the context of driving a motor vehicle is a part of her "general duty to drive carefully", and that if a child suffers injury as a result of the mother's negligent driving during pregnancy, the child should be able to sue for compensation.[94] To hold otherwise would constitute a partial exception to a pregnant woman's general duty to drive with care.

A majority of the Supreme Court of Canada allowed Cynthia Dobson's appeal, holding that "[t]he public policy concerns raised in this case are of such a nature and magnitude that they clearly indicate that a legal duty of care cannot, and should not, be imposed by the courts upon a woman towards her foetus or subsequently born child".[95] The policy concerns articulated by the Court fall into two primary categories: those relating to the privacy and autonomy rights of women,[96] and the difficulties inherent in articulating a judicial standard of conduct for pregnant women. With respect to the privacy and autonomy rights of women, the court refused to impose a duty of care upon pregnant women, because "[t]o do so would result in very extensive and unacceptable intrusions into the bodily integrity, privacy and autonomy rights of women".[97]

---

[91]   [1997] N.B.J. No. 232, 148 D.L.R. (4th) 332 (N.B.C.A.) revd [1999] S.C.J. No. 41 (S.C.C.).

[92]   By this, Hoyt C.J.N.B. seems to have meant such things as cigarette smoking, consumption of alcohol and other legal or illegal substances, and the taking of or refusal to take medication.

[93]   The Court made reference to the fact that this distinction has been employed in legislation in the United Kingdom: the *Congenital Disabilities (Civil Liability) Act 1976* (U.K.), c. 28. The Act provides that mothers cannot be sued by their children for prenatal injuries, with the exception of injuries caused by motor vehicle accidents. The specific reason for this exception is the existence of a mandatory insurance regime with respect to motor vehicles; the U.K. Law Commission that recommended the enactment of this legislation was of the view that permitting recovery by the child (to the extent of the policy limits) in this situation would decrease the anxiety pregnant women feel in relation to driving: see Law Commission Report (Law Com. No. 60) on Injuries to Unborn Children, 1974, Cmnd. 5709.

[94]   The Court of Appeal found support for its decision in an Australian case (*Lynch v. Lynch (By Her Tutor Lynch)* (1991), 25 N.S.W.L.R. 411 (N.S.W.C.A.)) and in some of the U.S. jurisprudence. It should be noted, however, that there is no consistency among U.S. decisions as to whether a pregnant woman does owe a duty of care toward her fetus. In part, the development of the law on this point in the U.S. seems to have been confounded by the existence of what is known as the doctrine of "parental immunity".

[95]   *Dobson (Litigation Guardian of) v. Dobson*, [1999] S.C.J. No. 41, 174 D.L.R. (4th) 1 (S.C.C.) at para. 76.

[96]   *Ibid.*, at para. 78. While Cory J. refers at length in his decision to such "privacy and autonomy rights", which he refers to at one point as "fundamental rights" (para. 31), he does not explain the derivation or character of those rights.

[97]   *Ibid.*, at para. 23. Although the facts of the case related solely to the question of negligent driving during pregnancy, the Court was concerned about the broader implications of any decision they might make, given the common law process; as Cory J. noted at para. 28: "There is no rational and principled limit to the types of claims which may be brought if such a ... duty of care were imposed upon pregnant women".

In its reasons in *Dobson*, the Supreme Court invited legislative intervention in this area of private law, and at least one province has taken up that invitation.[98] In November 2005, the Alberta Legislature passed the *Maternal Tort Liability Act*,[99] which provides that:

> 4. A mother may be liable to her child for injuries suffered by her child on or after birth that were caused by the mother's use or operation of an automobile during her pregnancy if, at the time of that use or operation, the mother was insured under a contract of automobile insurance evidenced by a motor vehicle liability policy.

Section 5(1) of the Act provides that the liability created by section 4 is limited in quantum to the automobile insurance policy limits.

In introducing the Bill to the legislature, the government indicated that its intent was to create a limited exception to the common law position set out in *Dobson*.[100] According to the Bill's sponsor, "[t]he proposed provision relates only to motor vehicle accidents and does not change tort law in any way other than to provide a limited exception to the common law concept of maternal tort immunity".[101] Further, the government's stated objective in passing this legislation was to provide a means of accessing insurance funds to benefit the child, the mother and the family as a whole.[102] It remains to be seen whether the legislation will have only this narrow effect, or whether it will prove to be just the beginning of maternal liability for conduct during pregnancy.

---

[98] *Ibid.*, at para. 76: "However, unlike the courts, unlike the courts, the legislature may, as did the Parliament of the United Kingdom, enact legislation in this field, subject to the limits imposed by the *Canadian Charter of Rights and Freedoms*".

[99] S.A. 2005, c. M-7.5.

[100] *Dobson (Litigation Guardian of) v. Dobson*, [1999] S.C.J. No. 41, 174 D.L.R. (4th) 1 (S.C.C.).

[101] Alberta, Legislative Assembly, *Hansard* (November 16, 2005) at 1681 (*per* Mr. Oberle).

[102] Alberta, Legislative Assembly, *Hansard* (November 16, 2005) at 1681 (*per* Mr. Oberle). The government's reasons for proceeding with the *Maternal Tort Liability Act* are intriguing. In addressing the Bill, the government stated that situations requiring legislation of this nature arise infrequently. Why, then, did the government decide to pursue this route? In the Spring of 2004, a Private Bill was introduced to the Private Bills Committee of the Alberta Legislature in an attempt to create an exception to the applicability of the *Dobson* case for Brooklynn Rewega. Brooklyn was born blind and suffering from cerebral palsy allegedly as a result of a motor vehicle accident caused by her mother, who was five months pregnant with Brooklyn at the time (see Alberta, Legislative Assembly, Private Bills Committee Transcripts (April 20, 2004), available online: <isys.assembly.ab.ca:8080/isysadvmenu.html>). Before the Private Bills Committee made a determination about whether to introduce the Bill to the Legislature, an election was called and the Legislature dissolved. In November 2005, both the *Maternal Tort Liability Act* and the *Brooklynn Hannah George Rewega Right of Civil Action Act*, S.A. 2005, c. 51, were debated and passed by the Alberta Legislature. In his comments on the *Maternal Tort Liability Act*, the Minister of Justice and Attorney General of Alberta stated that the private bill relating to Brooklyn Rewega addressed an issue of public policy, and that a private bill was not the appropriate place to deal with issues of public policy (Alberta, Legislative Assembly, *Hansard*, (November 21, 2005) 1772 (*per* Mr. Stevens).

VI. COERCIVE TREATMENT OF PREGNANT WOMEN

In the previous section, issues of private law related to the behaviour of pregnant women were considered; here, I am concerned with state action that threatens the ability of pregnant women to act autonomously, and with state responses to reproduction by certain classes of women.[103]

The type of state action that is of concern here is the legal imposition of medical care or other treatment intended to protect the fetus from the actions or decisions of the pregnant woman. Where a pregnant woman refuses medically recommended care, state intervention can take the form of coercive medical treatment. In cases where the pregnant woman is addicted to substances alleged to be harmful to the fetus, state intervention is potentially wide-ranging and can include criminal prosecution, sentencing practices intended to restrict the woman's access to the substance she is addicted to, and the use of child welfare and/or mental health legislation to attempt to constrain the behaviour of pregnant addicts.

All forms of state intervention in pregnancy purportedly serve the same aim — to protect the fetus who may suffer harm as a result of the pregnant woman's behaviour, whether that consists in refusing recommended medical interventions or ingesting a potentially feto-toxic substance. Commendable though that objective may be, all of these interventions involve — to a greater or lesser degree — violations of the pregnant woman's bodily integrity and reproductive autonomy. If a woman is required to submit to a Cesarean section because, in her physician's opinion, the baby cannot be safely delivered otherwise, the violation is particularly profound. The same goes for detention in a health care facility or incarceration. But even in the case of less invasive measures, it must be borne in mind that the woman's bodily integrity is implicated. Respect for women's reproductive autonomy in this context thus requires that the state proceed with great caution.

There are few reported Canadian cases concerning coercive medical treatment in pregnancy (although similar issues were raised in *Winnipeg Child and Family Services (Northwest Area) v. G. (D.F.),* as will be discussed below),[104] but lower court decisions indicate that these matters have received

---

[103] Numerous commentators have noted that state intervention in the lives of pregnant women is almost exclusively directed at women who are addicted to drugs, poor women and women of colour. See, *e.g.*, Lynn M. Paltrow, "Punishment and Prejudice: Judging Drug Using Pregnant Women" in Julia E. Hanigsberg & Sara Ruddick, eds., *Mother Troubles: Rethinking Contemporary Maternal Dilemmas* (Boston: Beacon Press, 1999) at 59; Dorothy E. Roberts, "Racism and Patriarchy in the Meaning of Motherhood" (1993) 1 Am. U. J. Gender & L. 1; Dorothy E. Roberts, "Punishing Drug Addicts Who Have Babies: Women of Color, Equality and the Right of Privacy" (1991) 104 Harv. L. Rev. 1419; Sanda Rodgers, "The Legal Regulation of Women's Reproductive Capacity in Canada" in Jocelyn Downie, Timothy Caulfield & Colleen Flood, eds., *Canadian Health Law and Policy*, 2nd ed. (Markham, ON: LexisNexis Butterworths, 2002) at 331; and Françoise Baylis, "Dissenting with the Dissent: *Winnipeg Child and Family Services (Northwest Area) v. G. (D.F.)*" (1998) 36 Alta. L. Rev. 785.

[104] But see Rachel Roth, *Making Women Pay: The Hidden Costs of Fetal Rights* (Ithaca: Cornell University Press, 2000) at 94-95, who notes that it is not possible to ascertain the full extent of court-ordered medical intervention in pregnancy. Roth's work suggests that by no means all such

judicial consideration. In *Re Children's Aid Society of City of Belleville and T.*,[105] the Ontario Provincial Court held that a fetus can be a "child in need of protection" under the *Child and Family Services Act*[106] and, accordingly, granted an order making the "child" a ward of the Children's Aid Society for a period of three months. The Court also issued an order under the *Mental Health Act*,[107] for assessment of the pregnant woman by a physician, on the basis that her behaviour posed a danger to both herself and the "child".

In *Re Baby R.*, the Superintendent of Child and Family Services apprehended a fetus during labour after the pregnant woman refused to consent to delivery via Cesarean section. Ms. R. was never notified of the apprehension and, ultimately, consented to the surgery "practically at the door of the operating room".[108] The child was apprehended immediately following its birth, and the Provincial Court judge held that the apprehension was justified. On appeal by the mother, the British Columbia Supreme Court overturned the order of the Provincial Court, on the basis that the *Family and Child Service Act*[109] gave the Superintendent the power to apprehend only "living children that have been delivered".[110]

In *Re A*, the Children's Aid Society of Hamilton-Wentworth sought an order subjecting Mrs. A.'s fetus to the supervision of the Society, and requiring Mrs. A. to seek prenatal care from a physician whose name was to be provided to the Society. In addition, Society asked the court to order Mrs. A. to make "immediate plans" for a hospital birth, advise the Society of the name of the hospital, and to attend at the hospital for the child's birth.[111] The Society also requested that the order grant a further order "requiring P.A. to be detained in hospital until the birth of the child and to undergo all necessary medical procedures for the well-being of the unborn child", in the event that Mrs. A. refused to comply with the original order.[112] The order was sought on the basis of the Court's jurisdiction under the *Child and Family Services Act*,[113] or, in the alternative, its jurisdiction *parens patriae*. The Court concluded, albeit "reluctantly",[114] that it had no jurisdiction to make an order that would require the forcible confinement of the pregnant woman in order to protect the fetus.

In *Winnipeg*, the Supreme Court of Canada considered the broad question of whether there is any foundation in law to support the detention of a pregnant woman for the purpose of protecting her fetus. When Ms. G. was five months pregnant with her fourth child,[115] and addicted to sniffing glue, Winnipeg Child

---

cases are reported in law reports (or elsewhere, for that matter).

[105] [1987] O.J. No. 2606, 59 O.R. (2d) 204 (Ont. Prov. Ct.).

[106] S.O. 1984, c. 55, s. 37.

[107] R.S.O. 1980, c. 262, s. 10(1).

[108] *Re Baby R.*, [1988] B.C.J. No. 2986, 53 D.L.R. (4th) 69 at 73 (B.C.S.C.).

[109] S.B.C. 1979, c. 11.

[110] *Re Baby R.*, [1988] B.C.J. No. 2986, 53 D.L.R. (4th) 69 at 80 (B.C.S.C.).

[111] *Re A. (In Utero)*, [1990] O.J. No. 1347, 72 DLR (4th) 722 at 723-24 (Ont. U.F.C.).

[112] *Ibid.*, at 723-24.

[113] S.O. 1984, c. 55.

[114] *Re A. (In Utero)*, [1990] O.J. No. 1347, 72 DLR (4th) 722 at 728 (Ont. U.F.C.). The Court thus overruled *Re Children's Aid Society of Belleville and T.*, [1987] O.J. No. 2606, 59 O.R. (2d) 204 (Ont. Prov. Ct.).

[115] Her three children were all wards of the state.

and Family Services sought an order for mandatory detention so that Ms. G. could be kept at a place of safety (and required to undergo treatment for her addiction). The order was granted by the Manitoba Court of Queen's Bench, which held that both the *Mental Health Act*[116] and the court's inherent jurisdiction could be invoked in support of the order.[117] The Manitoba Court of Appeal struck down the order, holding that Ms. G. was not incompetent (as required before the issuance of an order under the *Mental Health Act*), and concluding that the lower court erred in relying on the *parens patriae* jurisdiction.[118] In spite of the invalidity of the court order, Ms. G. voluntarily remained at the Winnipeg Health Sciences Centre until her discharge a number of weeks later. Ultimately, Ms. G. gave birth to a healthy baby who remained in her custody.

The Supreme Court of Canada granted leave to appeal and, ultimately, concluded that an order of the type granted in this case could not be supported by statute, tort law or the court's inherent jurisdiction *parens patriae*. The Court noted the significant policy issues that arise in the context of contemplating the extension of the common law in this way[119] — in particular, the Court noted the dramatic impact on women's fundamental liberties that would result from extending the common law to permit an order for the detention and treatment of a pregnant woman to prevent harm to the fetus — as well as the ramifications of such a change for other areas of tort law.[120] As in the case of tort law duties of pregnant women, the Supreme Court took the view that "the changes to the law sought on this appeal are best left to the wisdom of the elected legislature".[121]

Other cases on point have dealt with the removal of a child after birth, based on the mother's conduct during pregnancy.[122] In *Re Children's Aid Society for the District of Kenora and JL*,[123] the child suffered from fetal alcohol syndrome resulting from the mother's alcohol abuse during her pregnancy. The Ontario Provincial Court held that a fetus was entitled to protection under the *Child Welfare Act*. In *British Columbia (Superintendent of Child and Family Services) v. M. (B.)*,[124] a baby born addicted to methadone (whose mother had been

---

[116] C.C.S.M., c. M110.

[117] *Winnipeg Child and Family Services (Northwest Area) v. G. (D.F.)*, [1996] M.J. No. 386, 138 D.L.R. (4th) 238 (Man. Q.B.).

[118] *Winnipeg Child and Family Services (Northwest Area) v. G. (D.F.)*, [1996] M.J. No. 398, 138 D.L.R. (4th) 254 (Man. C.A.).

[119] *Winnipeg Child and Family Services (Northwest Area) v. G. (D.F.)*, [1997] S.C.J. No. 96, 152 D.L.R. (4th) 193 (S.C.C.) at paras. 30-45.

[120] *Ibid.*, at paras. 18-57.

[121] *Ibid.*, at para. 59. Indeed, McLachlin J. refers repeatedly to the possibility of legislative action throughout her judgment.

[122] See also *Joe v. Director of Family and Children's Services for Yukon Territory*, [1986] Y.J. No. 40, 1 Y.R. 169 (Y.T.S.C.), striking down a provision of the Yukon *Children's Act*, R.S.Y. 1986, c. 22, s. 133 which permitted child welfare authorities "to apply to a judge for an order requiring [a pregnant] woman to participate in such reasonable supervision or counselling as the order specifies in respect of her use of addictive or intoxicating substances". The court found the provision to be unconstitutionally vague.

[123] (1981), 134 D.L.R. (3d) 249 (Ont. Prov. Ct.).

[124] [1982] B.C.J. No. 468, 135 D.L.R. (3d) 330 (B.C.C.A.).

advised by her physician to continue to take methadone during pregnancy) was apprehended, and an order of permanent custody was made in favour of the child welfare authorities. In upholding the order, Proudfoot J. stated that "it would be incredible to come to any other conclusion than that a drug-addicted baby is born abused".[125] Finally, in *Ackerman v. McGoldrick*,[126] a baby apprehended after her father absconded with her was returned to her mother's care, as there was no evidence that she was in need of protection. The baby's mother had ingested drugs on one or two occasions during her pregnancy, but at the time of the hearing, the baby was developing normally.

State intervention in the lives of pregnant women can take a variety of forms. Arguably, and depending heavily on what is meant by intervention, state intervention in the lives of pregnant women might sometimes be very desirable. If we take intervention to mean, for example, the positive involvement of the state in the lives of pregnant women in seeking out and helping those who need assistance with prenatal care, addiction treatment, nutrition, care of other children, or protection from a violent spouse, then there is clearly an important role for intervention. If, on the other hand, we take it to mean what it seems to mean now — forced obstetrical treatment, incarceration, detention or other forms of punishment — intervention in pregnancy is misguided and unlikely to further the alleged goal of healthy mothers and healthy children.[127]

In the case of medical treatment, respect for women's bodily integrity clearly requires that women's decisions about what medical treatment they will or will not accept must be deferred to, even where it appears that this decision might lead to a less than desirable outcome for the pregnant woman and/or the fetus. Health care providers may attempt to persuade a woman to change her mind about treatment, they may advise her about all of the concerns they have for her potential child should she refuse the treatment, but they may not coerce her to agree to the procedure, either physically or through the use of threats.

But what about the pregnant drug addict? Is she capable of exercising autonomy? If not, do her decisions deserve respect? The situation of substance-addicted pregnant women is complex. Clearly, addictions have great potential to interfere with autonomy.[128] But to treat addicts as being completely incapable of exercising autonomy is misguided. Take, for example, Ms. G,[129] the pregnant woman whose behaviour was at issue in the *Winnipeg* case. A social worker learned that Ms. G. was pregnant and was addicted to sniffing glue.[130] Ms. G. expressed an interest in getting help for her addiction, and agreed to enter a

---

125 *Ibid.*, at 335.

126 [1990] B.C.J. No. 2832 (B.C. Prov. Ct.).

127 See John Seymour, *Childbirth and the Law* (New York: Oxford University Press, 2000) at 230, 238; Sanda Rodgers, "The Legal Regulation of Women's Reproductive Capacity in Canada" in Jocelyn Downie, Timothy Caulfield & Colleen Flood, eds., *Canadian Health Law and Policy*, 2nd ed. (Markham, ON: LexisNexis Butterworths, 2002) at 354.

128 See, *e.g.*, Carolyn McLeod, "Women's Autonomy and the 'G' Case" (May 1998) 3(2) Canadian Bioethics Society Newsletter.

129 *Winnipeg Child and Family Services (Northwest Area) v. G. (D.F.)*, [1997] S.C.J. No. 96, 152 D.L.R. (4th) 193 (S.C.C.).

130 As noted earlier, Ms. G. had three children, all of whom were wards of the state. See *Winnipeg Child and Family Services (Northwest Area) v. G. (D.F.)*, *ibid.*

treatment facility. When the social worker returned to accompany Ms. G. to the treatment centre, Ms. G. was high and refused to go. Instead of waiting until Ms. G. was sober, Winnipeg Child and Family Services sought an order compelling Ms. G. to remain "in a place of safety", and requiring treatment for her addiction.[131]

These facts illustrate that, if not fully autonomous, Ms. G. was nonetheless capable of exercising autonomy, at least while not under the influence of the substance to which she was addicted. While her decision not to accompany the social worker to the treatment centre was not autonomous[132] and arguably need not be respected, seeking a court order to compel her to enter addiction treatment shows utter contempt for the minimal autonomy she was capable of exercising. Pregnant women who are addicted to harmful substances are not likely to be helped by mandatory treatment, given the "general consensus in the field of addiction treatment ... that many of the addict's beliefs and attitudes must change if she is to modify her behavior, and this change will not occur in treatment if she is there unwillingly".[133] In addition to being ineffective, mandatory treatment is likely to further undermine the limited autonomy these women can claim.[134]

VII. ASSISTED REPRODUCTIVE TECHNOLOGIES

The Canadian response to the flourishing science of assisted reproduction has a long and complex history, beginning with the appointment of the Royal Commission on New Reproductive Technologies in 1989.[135] The political discussion around regulating reproductive technologies in Canada has been ongoing since the Royal Commission's final report in 1993,[136] and continues despite the recent enactment of legislation aimed at comprehensively governing research and clinical applications of assisted reproductive technologies (ARTs).

---

[131] *Winnipeg Child and Family Services (Northwest Area) v. G. (D.F.), ibid.*

[132] This is borne out by her decision to remain in the addiction treatment program even after order of the Manitoba Court of Queen's Bench mandating treatment was stayed two days later, pending appeal. See *Winnipeg Child and Family Services (Northwest Area) v. G. (D.F.), ibid.*

[133] Carolyn McLeod & Susan Sherwin, "Relational Autonomy, Self-Trust and Health Care for Patients who are Oppressed" in Catriona Mackenzie & Natalie Stoljar, eds., *Relational Autonomy: Feminist Perspectives on Autonomy, Agency and the Social Self* (Oxford: Oxford University Press, 2000) at 271.

[134] McLeod & Sherwin are particularly concerned about addicted women who lack self-trust, since imposing treatment simply further diminishes their decision-making power. See *ibid.*, at 273-74.

[135] The Ontario Law Reform Commission and the Law Reform Commission of Canada also studied reproductive and genetic technologies: see Ontario Law Reform Commission, *Report on Human Artificial Reproduction and Related Matters* (Toronto: Ontario Law Reform Commission, 1985); Law Reform Commission of Canada, *Medically Assisted Procreation (Working Paper 65)* (Ottawa: Minister of Supply and Services Canada, 1992).

[136] Royal Commission on New Reproductive Technologies, *Proceed with Care: Final Report of the Royal Commission on New Reproductive Technologies* (Ottawa: Minister of Supply and Services Canada, 1993).

In 2004, after 11 years of debate, discussion[137] and failed attempts at legislating, the *Assisted Human Reproduction Act*[138] (AHR Act) received Royal Assent. The AHR Act creates categories of prohibited and controlled activities, regulates privacy and access to information, establishes the Assisted Human Reproduction Agency of Canada (AHRA), and sets out provisions relating to administration, inspection and enforcement of the provisions of the AHR Act and Regulations.[139] In short, the AHR Act designates ART-related activities as either prohibited or controlled; the majority of the AHR Act is devoted to the regulation of the controlled activities. Several sections of the AHR Act (those concerning prohibited and controlled activities)[140] are now in force, and the remainder of the Act (dealing with the regulatory framework) will be developed and implemented over a period of three years.[141] Because of this gradual implementation process, the regulatory situation will remain indeterminate for some time yet, but some general observations can be made about the structure and aims of the legislation.

Rather than setting out broad legislative goals in a preamble, the "overriding principles" of the Act are set out in a declaratory section.[142] These principles include the paramountcy of the health and well-being of children born through ART procedures, the acknowledgment of the fact that ART practice affects women more "directly and significantly" than it does men, and that measures

---

[137] See, *e.g.*, Timothy Caulfield, "Bill C-13: The Assisted Human Reproduction Act: Examining the Arguments Against a Regulatory Approach" (2002) 11 Health L. Rev. 20 [Bill C-13]; Timothy Caulfield, "Clones, Controversy and Criminal Law: A Comment on the Proposal for Legislation Governing Assisted Human Reproduction" (2001) 39 Alta. L. Rev. 335 ["Clones, Controversy and Criminal Law"]; Alison Harvison Young & Angela Wasunna, "Wrestling with the Limits of Law: Regulating New Reproductive Technologies" (1998) 6 Health L.J. 239; Francoise Baylis, "Human Cloning: Three Mistakes and an Alternative" (2002) 27:3 J. Med. & Philosophy 319.

[138] S.C. 2004, c. 2.

[139] According to s. 66 of the AHR Act, the Minister of Health must present proposed regulations to both the House of Commons and the Senate. The "relevant committees" of each House will then have an opportunity to consider and report on the regulations, and the Minister is to take into account these reports and, in the event that the regulation is not modified to incorporate recommendations of the committees, the Minister "shall lay before that House the reasons for not incorporating [them]". (s. 66(4)). The only exceptions to the requirement of presenting proposed regulations to Parliament are found in s. 67, and occur (i) where the changes made by the regulation to existing regulation are, in the opinion of the Minister, "so immaterial or insubstantial that s. 66 should not apply in the circumstances" (s. 67(1)(*a*)); and (ii) in situations where the regulation must be made immediately "to protect the health or safety of any person" (s. 67(1)(*b*)).

[140] Prior to the coming into force of the Act, a voluntary moratorium was in place to deal with concerns around the prohibited activities. See Health Canada, "News Release: Membership of Advisory Committee on Interim Moratorium on Reproductive Technologies announced" January 24, 1996, Health Canada online: <http://www.hc-sc.gc.ca/ahc-asc/media/nr-cp/1996/1996_09_e.html>.

[141] See Health Canada, Notice of Intent to Develop the Components of the Regulatory Framework under the Assisted Human Reproduction Act (October 5, 2004), online: <http://www.hc-sc.gc.ca/hl-vs/reprod/hc-sc/legislation/noi-ai_e.html>. No regulations have been adopted as of May 16, 2007.

[142] *AHR Act*, S.C. 2004, c. 2, s. 2.

must be taken to ensure the protection of women's health and well-being, reference to the importance of informed consent and non-discrimination in the provision of ART services, and identification of the fact that health and ethical concerns are raised by the commercialization of reproductive capacity.[143]

A number of ART-related clinical and research practices are prohibited by the AHR Act; maximum penalties for the commission of prohibited activities are a fine of $500,000 or a 10-year term of imprisonment, or both.[144] Prohibited activities include:

- cloning;[145]
- creating an embryo for research purposes (other than the narrow research purpose of improving or providing instruction in ART procedures);[146]
- creating an embryo from an embryo or fetus;[147]
- maintaining an embryo *in vitro* for more than 14 days;[148]
- sex selection for non-medical purposes;[149]
- commercial surrogacy;[150]
- purchase of gametes or embryos;[151] and
- use of reproductive material without consent.[152]

The AHR Act also creates a class of controlled activities — use of human gametes or embryos,[153] transgenic research in certain situations,[154] reimbursement of expenses incurred by gamete or embryo donors or surrogate mothers[155] and the use of premises to carry out controlled activities[156] — which may only be carried out in accordance with the regulations and a licence.

As noted above, the AHR Act also deals with privacy and access to information. Key provisions here include a section which requires the AHRA to maintain a personal health information registry about gamete and embryo donors, persons undergoing ART procedures, and those conceived through the

---

[143] The other governing principles relate to the need for measures to safeguard human health, safety, dignity and rights in the use of ARTs, and a reference to the importance of human diversity, individuality and the integrity of the human genome.

[144] AHR Act, S.C. 2004, c. 2, s. 60.

[145] *Ibid.*, s. 5(1)(*a*).

[146] *Ibid.*, s. 5(1)(*b*).

[147] *Ibid.*, s. 5(1)(*c*).

[148] *Ibid.*, s. 5(1)(*d*).

[149] *Ibid.*, s. 5(1)(*e*). Other prohibitions under section 5 are: germ line alteration (s. 5(1)(*f*)); transfer of non-human gametes, embryos or fetuses into a human being (s. 5(1)(*g*)); use (for reproductive purposes) of any human gametes reproductive material that is or was transplanted into a non-human animal (s. 5(1)(*h*)); creation of a chimera or hybrid (s. 5(1)(*i*)); and advertising (s. 5(2)) or paying (s. 5(3)) for the performance of prohibited activities.

[150] *Ibid.*, s. 6. This includes prohibitions on payment to the surrogate mother herself or an intermediary, and also prohibits the acceptance of payment by an intermediary.

[151] *Ibid.*, s. 7.

[152] *Ibid.*, s. 8 [not yet in force].

[153] *Ibid.*, s. 10.

[154] *Ibid.*, s. 11.

[155] *Ibid.*, s. 12 [not yet in force].

[156] *Ibid.*, s. 13.

use of such procedures.[157] In addition, the AHRA will be able to disclose, upon request by a person conceived by means of ART procedures, health reporting information relating to a gamete or embryo donor. Identifying information about the donor will not be disclosed without the consent of the donor.[158] Moreover, where two persons who have reason to believe that they may be related[159] submit a request in writing, the AHRA will inform them "whether it has information that they are genetically related and, if so, the nature of the relationship".[160]

Arguably, the most significant feature of the legislation is the creation of the regulatory body, the AHRA.[161] The AHRA will operate at arm's length from the federal government, but will be accountable to Parliament through the Minister of Health.[162] The objectives of the Agency are clearly spelled out in the legislation. They centre on the protection and promotion of the health, safety, human dignity and human rights of Canadians, and seek to foster the application of ethical principles in relation to ART practice.[163] The AHRA will be empowered to comprehensively regulate ART techniques used both in the clinical and research settings. Its mandate will comprehend powers in relation to licensing,[164] inspection and enforcement,[165] and the provision of advice to the Minister of Health on matters integral to the AHR Act.[166] The AHRA will also monitor and evaluate national and international developments in ART practice,[167] consult with persons and organizations both within and outside Canada,[168] and collect, analyze and maintain health reporting information relating to controlled activities.[169] Finally, the Agency will provide information to the public and relevant professions respecting ART practice and regulation and risk factors for infertility.[170] The Agency's Board of Directors will be made up of members reflecting "a range of backgrounds and disciplines relevant to the Agency's objectives",[171] and may not include a licensee or applicant for a licence, or a director, officer, shareholder or partner of a licensee or applicant.[172]

---

[157] *Ibid.*, s. 17 [not yet in force].
[158] *Ibid.*, s. 18(3) [not yet in force].
[159] Where one or both were conceived by means of an ART procedure involving human reproductive material from the same donor.
[160] AHR Act, S.C. 2004, c. 2, s. 18(4) [not yet in force].
[161] *Ibid.*, s. 21. For an in-depth discussion of the anticipated role and structure of the AHRA, see Erin L. Nelson, "Comparative Perspectives on the Regulation of Assisted Reproductive Technologies in the United Kingdom and Canada" (2006) 43 Alta. L. Rev. 1023-1048.
[162] Health Canada, "Backgrounder: The Assisted Human Reproduction Agency of Canada", online: Health Canada <http://www.hc-sc.gc.ca/hl-vs/reprod/hc-sc/legislation/agenc_e.html>.
[163] AHR Act, S.C. 2004, c. 2, s. 22.
[164] *Ibid.*, s. 24(1)(a) [not yet in force].
[165] *Ibid.*, s. 24(1)(g) [not yet in force].
[166] *Ibid.*, s. 24(1)(b).
[167] *Ibid.*, s. 24(1)(c).
[168] *Ibid.*, s. 24(1)(d).
[169] *Ibid.*, s. 24(1)(e) [not yet in force].
[170] *Ibid.*, s. 24(1)(f).
[171] *Ibid.*, s. 26(2).
[172] *Ibid.*, s. 26(8).

Because the regulatory sections of the AHR Act are not yet in force, it is necessary to consider as well the regulatory environment outside the scope of the legislation, in order to get a clear picture of the regulatory landscape in Canada. The current picture involves some regulation of ARTs, but regulation is neither comprehensive nor integrated, nor is it uniformly applied or enforced.[173]

A number of Canadian jurisdictions have legislation concerning the status of children born as a result of ARTs,[174] but in most provinces, the common law governs on this issue.[175] Processing, testing and distribution of semen for donor insemination[176] is governed by the *Food and Drugs Act*.[177] The Quebec *Act Respecting Medical Laboratories, Organ, Tissue, Gamete and Embryo Conservation, and the Disposal of Human Bodies* regulates centres which collect, conserve or distribute human gametes with a view to using them in medical or scientific procedures.[178] In addition, some provinces regulate the use of donor sperm, and all provinces have human tissue legislation.[179] There are also professional guidelines and policies in place to help guide medical practice involving some aspects of assisted human reproduction. In particular, the Society of Obstetricians and Gynecologists of Canada and the Canadian Fertility and Andrology Society have produced a joint policy statement on ethical issues in assisted reproduction,[180] which sets out ethical guidelines in relation to sperm sorting for non-medical reasons, preconception arrangements, oocyte donation, disposition of frozen embryos, research on human embryos, intra-cytoplasmic sperm injection (ICSI), preimplantation genetic diagnosis (PGD), social

---

[173] Even once the AHR Act is fully in force, issues remain that are not contemplated by the legislation, including the status of gametes and embryos. See, *e.g.*, Roxanne Mykitiuk & Albert Wallrap, "Regulating Reproductive Technologies in Canada" in Jocelyn Downie, Timothy Caulfield & Colleen Flood, eds., *Canadian Health Law and Policy*, 2nd ed. (Markham, ON: LexisNexis Butterworths, 2002) at 399-408. See also *Caufield v. Wong*, [2005] A.J. No. 428 (Alta. Q.B.), where Sanderman J. treats embryos and gametes as property.

[174] The legislation is not uniform. Alberta has passed a new *Family Law Act* (S.A. 2003, c. F-4.5, ss. 12 (surrogacy) and s. 13 (assisted conception)). In the Yukon Territory, the *Children's Act*, R.S.Y. 2002, c. 31, s. 13, provides for determination of paternity in the case of artificial insemination (as does the Newfoundland legislation: *Children's Law Act*, R.S.N.L. 1990, c. C-13, s. 12). In Manitoba, the *Vital Statistics Act*, C.C.S.M., c. V60, s. 3(6) speaks to birth registrations in cases involving artificial insemination.

[175] For a discussion of the case law on point, see Roxanne Mykitiuk, "Beyond Conception: Legal Determinations of Filiation in the Context of Assisted Reproductive Technologies" (2001) 39 Osgoode Hall L.J. 771 at 791-814; see also Simon R. Fodden, *Family Law* (Toronto: Irwin Law, 1999), c. 5, "6. A Note on Reproduction Technology".

[176] Processing and Distribution of Semen for Assisted Conception Regulations, SOR/96-254, as am.

[177] R.S.C. 1985, c. F-27.

[178] R.S.Q., c. L-0.2, ss.1(m.1) [not in force]. These centres are known as "gamete or embryo conservation centres".

[179] For example, *Human Tissue Gift Act*, R.S.A. 2000, c. H-15. A few such statutes, although they deal generally with organ transplantation, do not define "tissue" narrowly, and therefore could be involved in the regulation of some aspects of ARTs; see, *e.g.*, *Human Tissue Act*, R.S.N.W.T. 1988, c. H-6.

[180] Canadian Fertility and Andrology Society & Society of Obstetricians and Gynaecologists of Canada, "Joint Policy Statement: Ethical Issues in Assisted Reproduction" (1999) 21(1) J. Obstet. Gynaecol. Can. 1.

screening and participation in reproductive technologies, and medical and genetic screening of gamete and embryo donors.

Finally, research involving ARTs is governed by the *Tri-Council Policy Statement: Ethical Conduct for Research Involving Humans* (TCPS),[181] which has rules in place as to ethically appropriate uses of human genetic material, gametes, embryos and fetuses. Chapter 8 of the TCPS, which governs human genetic material, states that research involving germ line genetic alteration is not ethically acceptable.[182] Chapter 9, which considers ethical issues involving human gametes, embryos or fetuses indicates that use of commercially obtained gametes in research is not acceptable,[183] and it also precludes research into the creation of hybrid individuals,[184] the creation of a human embryo solely for research purposes[185] and research into cloning, ectogenesis, creation of animal/human hybrids, and transfer of embryos between humans and other species.[186]

Currently, only one Canadian jurisdiction provides funding for *in vitro* fertilization (IVF) treatment, and only in very limited circumstances[187] (although all cover related investigative and diagnostic procedures). It has been noted that Canada is one of the few jurisdictions with a publicly funded health care system

---

[181] Canadian Institutes of Health Research, Natural Sciences and Engineering Research Council of Canada & Social Sciences and Humanities Research Council of Canada, *Tri-Council Policy Statement: Ethical Conduct for Research Involving Humans* (Ottawa: Public Works and Government Services Canada, 1998) online: <http://www.pre.ethics.gc.ca/english/policy statement/policystatement.cfm> [*Tri-Council Policy Statement*].

[182] Tri-Council Policy Statement, Art. 8.5.

[183] *Ibid.*, Art. 9.2.

[184] *Ibid.*, Art. 9.3.

[185] The use of surplus embryos created for reproductive purposes is permitted, provided that the following conditions are met (see *ibid.*, Art. 9.4):
   (a)   The ova and sperm from which they were formed are obtained in accordance with Articles 9.1 and 9.2;
   (b)   The research does not involve the genetic alteration of human gametes or embryos;
   (c)   Embryos exposed to manipulations not directed specifically to their ongoing normal development will not be transferred for continuing pregnancy; and
   (d)   Research involving human embryos takes place only during the first 14 days after their formation by combination of the gametes.
   Article 9.1, referred to here, requires researchers to obtain the informed consent of persons whose gametes are sought to be used in research.

[186] *Ibid.*, Art. 9.5.

[187] The province of Ontario provides coverage for up to three cycles of IVF in cases where a woman's fallopian tubes are completely occluded. If a live birth is achieved after IVF treatment, another three cycles may be provided. See Edward G. Hughes & Mita Giacomini, "Funding in vitro fertilization treatment for persistent subfertility: the pain and the politics" (2001) 76(3) Fertility and Sterility 431; Sharon Ikonomidis & Bernard Dickens, "Ontario's decision to defund in vitro fertilization treatment except for women with bilateral fallopian tube damage" (1995) 21(3) Can. Public Policy 379. While not covering IVF treatment in the public healthcare system, since 2002, the province of Quebec has allowed persons undergoing IVF treatment to claim a 30 per cent refundable tax credit. See Beverly Hanck & Katharina Böcker, Letter from the Infertility Awareness Association of Canada, "Canada Reducing Multiple Births: A Strategy for Canada" (August 30, 2005), online: <http://www.icsi.ws/information/enewsletter/nov-05/letter_from_Canada>.

that excludes funding for IVF and related procedures.[188] One province's refusal
to cover infertility treatment under its health care insurance plan was the subject
of an unsuccessful Charter challenge.[189]

VIII. CONCLUSION

The time is long past when reproduction was chiefly a matter of chance — when
heterosexual intercourse was the only mode of conception, and when the
outcome of each pregnancy was unpredictable. The introduction of reproductive
technologies — including contraception, medical and surgical abortion, prenatal
and preimplantation diagnosis and assisted reproductive technologies — has
ushered in a new era in reproductive decision-making, an era of complex and
complicated choices. With these choices has come increasing state involvement
in reproduction.

Developing legal and policy strategies aimed at regulating reproduction is a
complex task that requires consideration of conflicting needs, rights and
interests. While reproductive law and policy have clear significance to men and
women alike, they have particular significance for women, not only because of
the unique role women play in the process of reproduction, but because of the
reality of the consequences of reproduction on all aspects of women's lives.
Decisions about whether, when and with whom to reproduce, about how many
children to have and about what kind of children to bear shape women's lives to
a much greater (and more specific) extent than they do men's lives. Women's

[188] Laura Shanner & Jeffrey Nisker, "Bioethics for clinicians: Assisted reproductive technologies"
(2001) 164(11) C.M.A.J. 1589 at 1591. See also Beverly Hanck & Katharina Böcker for the
Infertility Awareness Association of Canada, *Access to IVF with Reduced Multiple Birth Risks:
A Public Health Strategy for Assisted Reproduction in Canada*, ibid.

[189] *Cameron v. Nova Scotia (Attorney General)*, [1999] N.S.J. No. 297, 177 D.L.R. (4th) 611
(N.S.C.A.), leave to appeal denied [1999] S.C.C.A. No. 531 (S.C.C.). The denial of coverage for
ICSI and IVF was initially challenged on the basis of ss. 7 and 15 of the Charter. The trial judge
gave short shrift to the s. 7 claim, which was not pursued before the Court of Appeal. As to the
plaintiffs' s. 15 claim, the trial judge found that the government had not discriminated against the
plaintiffs as infertile persons in deciding not to cover infertility treatment services; he found it
unnecessary to consider whether infertility amounts to a disability (*Cameron v. Nova Scotia
(Attorney General)*, [1999] N.S.J. No. 33, 172 N.S.R. (2d) 227 (N.S.S.C.). In the Court of
Appeal, the plaintiffs were successful in their assertion that infertility is a physical disability and
that the province's failure to fund infertility treatment services drew a discriminatory distinction
between the infertile and the fertile (who receive full coverage for reproduction-related
healthcare needs). The Court concluded, however, that the exclusion of IVF and ICSI from
coverage was justified under s. 1 of the Charter, in that it was related (and proportional) to the
pressing objective of delivering the best possible healthcare coverage in the context of limited
financial resources. In its decision in *Auton (Guardian ad litem of) v. British Columbia (Attorney
General)*, [2004] S.C.J. No. 71 (S.C.C.), the Supreme Court of Canada held that the denial of a
"non-core" medically necessary service does not amount to discrimination under s. 15 of the
Charter, as "the legislative scheme does not promise that any Canadian will receive funding for
all medically required treatment"; rather, it leaves non-core services to the discretion of the
provinces. Taken together with the Court's refusal to hear the *Cameron* case, it seems that *Auton*
suggests that any future s. 15 claim to funding for infertility treatment will be an uphill battle.

career paths and, by implication, financial security may be determined by their ability to make reproductive decisions. Reproduction can have significant effects on women's health, both during and after pregnancy. And, women are frequently the primary caregivers of the children they bear.[190] Assisted reproductive technologies are currently a focal point for law, policy and public discussion but, as this chapter illustrates, there is work to be done in all areas of reproductive decision-making in order to ensure that law and policy respect women's reproductive autonomy and safeguard their reproductive health.

---

[190] See, *e.g.*, Joan Williams, *Unbending Gender: Why Family and Work Conflict and What to Do About It* (Oxford: Oxford University Press, 2000) at 48, 156-57.

Chapter 10

MENTAL HEALTH LAW IN CANADA

Peter J. Carver

I. INTRODUCTION

A. RECENT DEVELOPMENTS

The field of Canadian mental health law has experienced several important developments in the four years since the publication of the second edition of this book.[1] A Senate Committee released a comprehensive report on mental health services, "Out of the Shadows at Last".[2] Nova Scotia rewrote its mental health laws, expanding the criteria for involuntary hospitalization, and adopting "community treatment orders" as a mechanism to require persons with mental illness living in the community to comply with treatment programs.[3] The Supreme Court of Canada rendered judgment in a significant case concerning competency and the right to refuse psychiatric treatment.[4] Parliament amended Part XX.1 of the *Criminal Code*[5] dealing with "mental disorder", and shortly thereafter the Supreme Court had occasion to consider an important aspect of the forensic system.[6] And Canada's highest courts addressed the issue of whether

---

[1] See Archibald Kaiser, "Mental Disability Law" in T. Caulfield, J. Downie & C. Flood, eds., *Canadian Health Law and Policy* (Markham, ON: LexisNexis Butterworths, 2002) at 251-330. As the title suggests, that chapter provides a broad overview of mental disability, and includes excellent discussions of such issues as the legacy of abuse, poverty and institutionalization.

[2] *Out of the Shadows at Last: Transforming Mental Health, Mental Illness and Addiction Services in Canada*, Final Report of the Standing Committee on Social Affairs, Science and Technology (Ottawa: Senate of Canada, May 2006). See discussion in Part II of this chapter.

[3] *Involuntary Psychiatric Treatment Act*, S.N.S. 2005, c. 42. The community treatment order provisions commence at section 47 — see discussion in Part IV of this paper. The Act was proclaimed to come into force on July 3, 2007 by O.I.C. No. 238, April 24, 2007. Note that in late 2006, Newfoundland and Labrador also adopted a new statute, the *Mental Health Care and Treatment Act*, S.N.L. 2006, c. M-9.1, proclaimed to come into force October 7, 2007.

[4] *Starson v. Swayze*, [2003] S.C.J. No. 33, [2003] 1 S.C.R. 722 (S.C.C.). See discussion in Part IV of this chapter.

[5] *An Act to Amend the Criminal Code (Mental Disorder) and to Make Consequential Amendments to Other Acts*, S.C. 2005, c. 22; R.S.C. 1985, c. C-46. See discussion in Part V of this chapter.

[6] *Mazzei v. British Columbia (Director of Forensic Services)*, [2006] S.C.J. No. 7, [2006] 1 S.C.R. 326 (S.C.C.). See discussion in Part V of this chapter.

the constitutionally guaranteed equality rights of children with mental disabilities oblige governments to provide public funding to cover intensive behavioural intervention (IBI) services for children with autism.[7] This chapter uses these events as an informal organizing tool, with each receiving attention successively in Parts II through VI.

Before getting to the details of these developments and what they represent with respect to the direction of mental health law, it may be helpful to locate this area of legal concern within the broader contexts of social response to mental disability and of Canadian law.

B. MENTAL DISABILITY AND THE LAW

Why is mental disability a category of interest or attention in law?[8] After all, to describe and use the term seems to admit of a making of differences, a marginalizing, that seems inconsistent with general concepts of equality before the law. Can this differentiation be justified? Two possible justifications can be given. The first is that the phenomena captured by the term "mental disability" have significance with respect to several of the standard assumptions which underlie legal relationships in our society. One such assumption is that of the autonomous individual, conceived as a person capable of exercising legal rights and responsibilities by acting with intention, making agreements and giving consent to actions by other persons that affect him or her. On the basis of this assumption, we hold individuals responsible in law for their decisions and actions. We include in this the responsibility of individuals for their own well-being. To the extent that mental disability interferes with individual autonomy and responsibility, the law must respond with alternative solutions. We can identify five "dimensions" in which Canadian law has played a role in the social response to mental disability, and the laws most associated with them.

1. Public Safety Dimension

(a) The problem: the risk of harm to third persons posed by conduct of a person with a mental impairment for which they are not responsible, and which is viewed as not being amenable to the "deterrence" of penal law.
(b) Response: laws governing committal under the *Criminal Code* for persons found not criminally responsible by reason of mental disorder, and civil committal laws.

This dimension turns largely on making predictions of dangerousness based on diagnoses of mental condition. This is a famously difficult endeavour.[9]

---

[7]   *Auton v. British Columbia (Attorney General)*, [2004] S.C.J. No. 71, 3 S.C.R. 657 (S.C.C.), and *Wynberg v. Ontario; Deskin v. Ontario*, [2006] O.J. No. 2732 (Ont. C.A.). See discussion in Part VI of this chapter.
[8]   The best single reference dealing with the various different aspects of mental disability in Canadian law remains G. Robertson, *Mental Disability and the Law in Canada*, 2nd ed. (Toronto: Carswell, 1994).
[9]   A useful analysis and critique of predictions of dangerousness in the mental health field is given by Archibald Kaiser, "Mental Disability Law" in T. Caulfield, J. Downie & C. Flood, eds.,

2. Therapeutic Dimension

(a) The problem: the need to facilitate the providing of health care responsive to diagnosed mental disability, including overcoming barriers caused by interference with the individual's ability to seek out or consent to needed therapy;

(b) Response in law: civil mental health laws relating to treatment and consent; laws establishing therapeutic programs for persons seeking and qualifying for therapy.

3. Individual Autonomy Dimension

(a) The problem: interference with the individual's capacity or competence to make autonomous decisions with legal effect concerning one's property or person.

(b) Response: adult guardianship laws, and laws providing for appointment and guidance of substitute decision makers.

A second reason for law to take cognizance of mental disability has more to do with the historical socioeconomic experience of persons with mental disabilities in Canada. That reality was recognized by the Supreme Court in the 1991 case, *R. v. Swain*:

> The mentally ill have historically been the subjects of abuse, neglect and discrimination in our society. The stigma of mental illness can be very damaging. The intervener, [the Canadian Disability Rights Council], describes the historical treatment of the mentally ill as follows:
>
>> For centuries, persons with a mental disability have been systematically isolated, segregated from mainstream of society, devalued, ridiculed, and excluded from participation in ordinary social and political processes.
>
> The above description is, in my view, unfortunately accurate and appears to stem from an irrational fear of the mentally ill in our society.[10]

The response to that reality has given rise to two further encounters between law and mental disability, as follows.

4. Social Welfare Dimension

(a) The problem: social disadvantages in income and other social goods experienced by persons as a consequence of mental dysfunction or impairment, principally related to underemployment or unemployment.

(b) Response: laws establishing social benefits programs, turning in whole or in part on describing the "target" group(s) through eligibility criteria drawn in terms of functional impairments interfering with work performance. Such laws would include disability benefits programs, disability insurance plans, housing programs, *etc.*

Canadian Health Law and Policy (Markham, ON: LexisNexis Butterworths, 2002) at 251-330.
[10] [1991] S.C.J. No. 32, [1991] 1 S.C.R. 933 (S.C.C.) at para. 39, *per* Lamer C.J.C.

5. Human Rights Dimension

(a) The problem: to protect individuals with mental disabilities, or those perceived to have disabilities, from the harmful effects of stigma, disrespect, and exclusion from mainstream social goods and activities.

(b) Response: equality rights in section 15 of the *Canadian Charter of Rights and Freedoms*,[11] and provisions in federal and provincial human rights legislation against discrimination on grounds of mental disability.

"Mental disability" in the human rights context is understood in a broad and non-medical fashion, not associated with particular dysfunctions, but with disadvantage caused by social response to actual or perceived variations from cognitive or emotional norms. The Supreme Court has stated that "disability" can include a subjective component of being *perceived* as having a disability:

> Whatever the wording of the definitions used in human rights legislation, Canadian courts tend to consider not only the objective basis for certain exclusionary practices (i.e. the actual existence of functional limitations), but also the subjective and erroneous perceptions regarding the existence of such limitations. Thus, tribunals and courts have recognized that even though they do not result in functional limitations, various ailments such as congenital physical malformations, asthma, speech impediments, obesity, acne and, more recently, being HIV positive, may constitute grounds of discrimination.[12]

Like other provinces, Alberta has adopted a broad definition of "mental disability" in its *Human Rights, Citizenship and Multiculturalism Act*,[13] in keeping with the Court's approach: "'mental disability' means any mental disorder, developmental disorder or learning disorder, regardless of the cause or duration of the disorder". In this respect, Canada's equality rights law has departed markedly from the model adopted by the U.S. Supreme Court in interpreting the *Americans with Disabilities Act* (ADA).[14] Claimants qualify for that statute's protection only on the basis of proving that they have an impairment that substantially interferes with activities of daily living.[15]

In Canadian law, "mental disorder" has become the term most commonly used to describe what is generally understood as "mental illness". This is a narrower category than "mental disability", a subset of the latter term. Which of the five dimensions outlined above is viewed as most needing attention depends both on events occurring in Canadian society, and on the political perspectives that interested parties bring to the subject. In very general terms, Canadian law tended in the past to place emphasis on the dimensions above in order from

11 *Canadian Charter of Rights and Freedoms*, Part I of the *Constitution Act, 1982*, being Schedule B of the *Canada Act 1982* (U.K.), 1982, c. 11.
12 *Québec (Commission des droits de la personne et des droits de la jeunesse) v. Montreal (City)*, [2000] S.C.J. No. 24, [2000] 1 S.C.R. 665 (S.C.C.) at para. 48, *per* L'Heureux-Dubé J.
13 R.S.A. 2000, c. H-14, s. 44(1)(*h*).
14 42 U.S. 1210. For extensive discussion of the U.S. experience with the ADA and for comparative issues in mental disability and mental health law, see M.L. Perlin, A.S. Kanter, M.P. Treuthart, E. Snell & K. Gledhill, *International Human Rights and Comparative Mental Disability Law* (Durham, N.C.: Carolina Academic Press, 2006).
15 See *Sutton v. United Air Lines Inc.*, 527 U.S. 471 (U.S.S.C. 1999).

headings 1. to 5. This continues to be true for advocacy groups comprising families of persons with mental illness and the psychiatric community. Patients and patients' rights advocates have tended, by contrast, to emphasize legal recourses in the opposite order, from 5. to 1. Until the adoption of the Charter and for several years thereafter, Canadian law appeared to be moving in the same direction. It seems fair to suggest that in recent years, the pendulum has shifted back.

Most of this chapter concerns itself with mental health law, an area of law in which the dimensions of public safety, treatment and individual autonomy have predominated. Following that discussion, the chapter returns to a consideration of human rights issues involving mental disability.

C. THE STRUCTURE OF CANADIAN MENTAL HEALTH LAW

The principal characteristic of mental health law[16] is that it is a law based on legal compulsion or coercion. In this respect, Nova Scotia's new statute, the *Involuntary Psychiatric Treatment Act*, is aptly titled.[17] Common law principles governing health care assume a standard model in which patients seek treatment for illness, and enter into voluntary arrangements with clinicians. To the extent that persons with mental health problems seek assistance in the same fashion, those common law principles apply to the care they receive. The fact that the presenting problem manifests itself in psychological rather than physiological symptoms makes no difference, and would not itself necessitate a separate legal regime.

The two principal means of compulsory intervention have been involuntary committal to a psychiatric hospital facility, and the provision of psychiatric treatment in the absence of the individual patient's consent. These measures require statute law both to grant the authority to intervene in a coercive fashion, and to limit the scope of this authority. While provincial mental health statutes deal with various other matters in the delivery of mental health services, their *raison d'être* remains this framework of lawful coercion.

A striking fact about Canada's mental health "law" in the early 21st century is that Canada's provinces and territories have adopted quite different approaches to the issues of involuntary hospitalization and treatment. There are two reasons for the variation in mental health law across provinces and territories. The first is Canada's constitutional architecture, which places the greater part of health care within provincial jurisdiction. Consequently, there can be several answers at any one time to the question "how does mental health law operate in Canada?" Ultimately, there is no substitute for consulting the legislation of the particular jurisdiction with which one is concerned.[18]

---

[16] For overviews, and for differing perspectives, on the subject, see H. Savage & C. McKague, *Mental Health Law in Canada* (Toronto: Butterworths, 1987); and, J. Gray, M. Shone & P. Liddle, *Canadian Mental Health Law and Policy* (Markham, ON: LexisNexis Butterworths, 2000).

[17] S.N.S. 2005, c. 42.

[18] The 10 provincial and two territorial mental health statutes are the following: *Mental Health Act*, R.S.A. 2000, c. M-13; *Mental Health Act*, R.S.B.C. 1996, c. 288; *Mental Health Act*, C.C.S.M. c. M110; *Mental Health Services Act*, S.N.B. 1997, c. M-10.2; *Mental Health Act*,

Parliament and provincial legislatures both have jurisdiction in the area of mental health law under the Canadian Constitution. Provincial jurisdiction is broader, lying in the general authority of provinces over health care said to be based in jurisdiction over "matters of a local and private nature" in section 92(16) of the *Constitution Act, 1867*,[19] and over hospitals in section 92(7). The principal source of federal jurisdiction is located in its authority over criminal law in section 91(27). The rough division in mental health laws and services set out by the Constitution is between civil mental health, a matter of provincial jurisdiction, and the forensic system governing criminal conduct caused by mental disorder, a matter of federal jurisdiction.

More specifically, federal jurisdiction has been found to relate to laws directed at protecting public safety, while provincial jurisdiction relates to laws directed at treatment of illness. The two domains overlap. For example, provincial jurisdiction over health and the federal jurisdiction over public safety both support involuntary detention, but for different purposes. In *Schneider v. British Columbia*, the Supreme Court of Canada upheld provincial legislation that provided for the involuntary detention of heroin addicts for purposes of treatment.[20]

Similarly, both jurisdictions support laws governing treatment and consent to treatment. Federal power over the latter has to date been limited to requiring assessment and treatment of individuals found "not fit for trial due to mental disorder". Section 672.58 of the *Criminal Code* authorizes psychiatric treatment on an involuntary basis for unfit accused, for the limited purpose of restoring them to fitness.[21]

R.S.N.L. 1990, c. M-9; *Involuntary Psychiatric Treatment Act*, S.N.S. 2005, c. 42 and *Hospitals Act*, S.N.S. 1989, c. 208; *Mental Health Act*, R.S.O. 1990, c. M.7; *Mental Health Act*, R.S.P.E.I. 1988, c. M-6.1; *Civil Code of Quebec*, S.Q. 1991, c. 64, ss. 10-31, and *An Act Respecting the Protection of Persons Whose Mental State Presents Danger to Themselves or to Others*, R.S.Q., c. P-38.001; *Mental Health Services Act*, S.S. 1984-85-86, c. M-13.1; *Mental Health Act*, R.S.N.W.T. 1988, c. M-10 (Northwest Territories and Nunavut); *Mental Health Act*, R.S.Y. 2002, c. 150. Hereinafter, these statutes will frequently be referred to as "the statute" or "mental health statute" of the specified province(s).

[19]   (U.K.), 30 & 31 Vict., c. 3, reprinted in R.S.C. 1985, App. II, No. 5.

[20]   Referring to involuntary detention under B.C.'s *Heroin Treatment Act* (then S.B.C. 1978 c. 24), Dickson J. said:

> This intervention is necessarily provincial. The compulsory aspects of this intervention are incidental to the effectiveness of the treatment, narcotic addiction by its very nature being a compulsive condition over which the individual loses control. Although coercion will obviously play a significant role it seems to me that the dominant or most important characteristic of the *Heroin Treatment Act* is the treatment and not the coercion. The Legislature of British Columbia in my view has sought to treat persons found to be in a state of psychological or physical dependence on a narcotic as sick and not criminal. The Legislature is endeavouring to cure a medical condition, not to punish a criminal activity.

[1982] S.C.J. No. 64 at para. 51, [1982] 2 S.C.R. 112 (S.C.C.).

[21]   The Supreme Court of Canada recognized that Parliament's jurisdiction over criminal law, and specifically over the law of criminal procedure, extended to provisions governing persons deemed unfit to stand trial for a criminal offence in *R. v. Demers*, [2004] S.C.J. No. 43, [2004] 2 S.C.R. 489 (S.C.C.) (Lebel J. dissenting).

The second reason for variety is generational. Provinces have drafted and amended their mental health legislation at different times, and depending when this has been done, the laws have been influenced by different thinking about the appropriate balance between individual rights, public safety, and therapeutic interests. To sketch this history in broad strokes, we can see three "generations" of thinking at work. The first, running from the early 20th century to the late 1960s, emphasized public safety and institutionalization. From the late 1960s to approximately the mid-1990s, a shift in emphasis to greater protection of individual rights took place. This coincided with the introduction of the Charter in 1982, and a dramatic reduction in institutional populations. The third phase is ongoing. Since the mid-1990s, several provinces, including Saskatchewan, British Columbia, Ontario, and, most recently, Nova Scotia, have engaged in extensive revisions of their mental health statutes. This period has seen a lowering of the legal standards for involuntary admission to hospital, and an extending of the reach of compulsory treatment to community services. At the same time, procedures for assessing treatment competency of patients, and for facilitating substitute decision-making for incapable patients, have received considerable attention. These changes coincide with increased concern in society over the role of untreated mental illness in such issues as homelessness, and the growing strength of organizations representing families of persons with mental illness in political advocacy.

The Charter provides further constitutional context within which mental health laws operate. The Charter places limits on the powers of the state to intervene in individuals' lives. As such, the compulsory aspects of mental health law encounter several Charter rights and are subject to the limits they impose. The most significant Charter rights in this regard are sections 7 and 15(1). Section 7 protects rights of "liberty" and "security of the person", which are precisely the interests compromised by involuntary hospitalization and treatment without consent, respectively. Section 15(1), as noted, guarantees equality before and under the law and equal benefit and protection of the law without discrimination on several enumerated grounds, including "mental disability". Differential legislative treatment accorded persons with mental disorders should and does raise section 15(1) issues. Since the Charter and the standards it imposes apply both to federal and provincial laws, it is an interesting question why these have not had the effect of creating greater uniformity in mental health laws across Canada. This results in part from the leeway which the justification clause in section 1 allows with respect to "reasonable limits" that can be placed on Charter rights. It also reflects the difficulty patients face in trying to bring Charter issues before Canadian courts. In addition to problems with the lack of resources needed to pursue the difficult issues involved in Charter challenges, the very changeability of mental conditions and of individual patients' status under mental health law creates a further barrier. Many potential cases become "moot" before they can be raised in a formal setting. Even though relatively few Charter challenges to civil mental health laws have made their way to courts across the country, the Charter plays an important role in structuring mental health laws. Several Charter issues are discussed at some length in Parts III through VI of this chapter.

II. CONTEMPORARY UNDERSTANDING OF MENTAL DISORDER AND ITS TREATMENT

The May 2006 Report, *Out of the Shadows at Last*, by the Senate's Standing Committee on Social Affairs, Science and Technology, provides a good overview of current approaches to the treatment of mental illness. Building on several recent provincial reports on mental health service systems,[22] *Out of the Shadows at Last* summarizes much of the current Canadian and international thinking on the subject. The Report emphasizes the social determinants of mental illness,[23] and community-based treatment and support services. The Committee refers to its preferred approach as based on the idea of "Recovery", which it describes this way:

> Recovery is not the same thing as being cured. For many individuals, it is a way of living a satisfying, hopeful, and productive life even with limitations caused by the illness; for others, recovery means the reduction or complete remission of symptoms related to mental illness.[24]

The Committee's emphasis on community-based services and integration of persons with mental illness into the community indeed reflects the concerns of clients of the system, family and other caregivers, and ministry officials who have recognized the cost savings in moving care from hospital facilities to the community. In a sense, however, this emphasis avoids dealing with the precise issues that are the principal concerns of mental health law. It is doubtful that a distinct body of law is needed to facilitate delivering community mental health services. Indeed, the Committee's recommendations concerning law are quite limited. This is partly because health law falls largely within provincial jurisdiction. It is also likely due to the fact that the core of mental health law, its coercive aspects, play only a limited role in community-based services and supports.

This goes to another distinction within the field of mental health: that between serious mental disorders, and less serious disorders. The Committee recognizes this distinction in saying:

---

[22] See, for example, *Plan d'action en santé mentale 2005-2010 — La force des liens* (Quebec: Ministère de la santé et des services sociaux, 2005); *Community Mental Health Evaluation Initiative: Making a Difference* (Ontario, 2004).

[23] *Out of the Shadows at Last: Transforming Mental Health, Mental Illness and Addiction Services in Canada* (The Report), Final Report of the Standing Committee on Social Affairs, Science and Technology (Ottawa: Senate of Canada, May 2006), Section 3.1.3 at 41:

> In particular, the Committee believes it is extremely important to stress the significance of what are called the social determinants of health in understanding mental illness and in fostering recovery from it. The Committee was repeatedly told that factors such as income, access to adequate housing and employment, and participation in a social network of family and friends, play a much greater role in promoting mental health and recovery from mental illness than is the case with physical illness. As well, it is important to see that the direction of causality goes both ways, from the mental (psychological, emotional, etc.) to the physical (neurobiological) as well as from the physical to the mental.

[24] *Ibid.*, at 42.

Epidemiological data indicate that, each year, roughly 3% of the population will experience a serious mental illness, and that another 17% or so will experience mild to moderate illness. The full range of services must be available therefore to address the needs of both broad categories of people.[25]

Serious disorders, those which predominate among involuntarily hospitalized populations, generally include schizophrenia,[26] manic depression (bipolar disorder),[27] and severe depression. Estimates place the prevalence of schizophrenia among the Canadian population at 1 per cent. A common symptom of schizophrenia is the auditory hallucination, that is, the hearing of voices. Other common symptoms include believing that one's thoughts are broadcast to others, or that one's actions are under the control of another. Manic depressive illness, or bipolar disorder, also affects approximately 1 per cent of the population. In the manic phase, persons with bipolar disorder may also experience delusions. Persons with severe depression are at serious risk of suicide.

For contemporary psychiatry, the principal mode of treatment for schizophrenia is antipsychotic medication. This coincides with the growing acceptance of schizophrenia as having biological rather than social causes. Antipsychotics are generally divided into first-generation and second-generation drugs. First-generation drugs were introduced in the 1950s, and included chloropromazine and haloperidol. While many people with schizophrenia experience improvement when taking these medications, the medications also frequently cause potentially severe side effects, the most common of which is tardive dyskinesia,[28] whose symptoms include involuntary movements of the tongue and mouth. Other side effects of medication include sedation, dry mouth, blurred vision, stiffness, tremor and restlessness. The second generation of antipsychotic drugs was introduced in the 1990s. The most effective second-generation drug is clozapine. Second-generation drugs appear to cause fewer of these side effects than the first-generation drugs did, but have other side effects such as weight gain. There are newer drugs being introduced for schizophrenia, and of course there are many others for other mental illnesses.

The Senate Committee emphasizes that even for persons with serious mental illnesses, treatment and rehabilitation is best accomplished in the community, and not in institutional facilities. The Report acknowledges the success of programs such as Assertive Community Teams and Intensive Care Management in working closely and on an interdisciplinary basis with individuals with serious mental illness in maintaining their health in the community.[29] Three provinces — Ontario, Saskatchewan and Nova Scotia — have introduced

[25] *Ibid.*, 3.4 at 50.
[26] See E. Fuller Torrey, *Surviving Schizophrenia* (New York: Quill, 2001).
[27] See E. Fuller Torrey, *Surviving Manic Depression* (New York: Quill, 2002).
[28] For a description of tardive dyskinesia, and its causation by exposure over time to antipsychotic medications, see the website of the National Alliance on Mental Illness (NAMI), online: <http://www.nami.org/Content/ContentGroups/Helpline1/Tardive_Dyskinesia.htm>.
[29] *Out of the Shadows at Last: Transforming Mental Health, Mental Illness and Addiction Services in Canada*, Final Report of the Standing Committee on Social Affairs, Science and Technology (Ottawa: Senate of Canada, May 2006), at section 5.6.

"Community Treatment Orders" into their mental health laws to support interventions of this kind. Their utility is considered in Part IV, below.

III. INVOLUNTARY HOSPITALIZATION

Every Canadian province and territory has laws that provide for involuntary committal on grounds of mental disorder. Committal provides lawful authority to detain an individual in hospital premises. This includes the authority to employ security measures to prevent patients from leaving hospital without permission, and authority to issue warrants to apprehend and return an involuntary patient to hospital.

Civil committal has both procedural and substantive dimensions. The procedural dimension includes all the steps which must be taken to effect and continue committal, including identifying who may complete certificates stating an opinion concerning an individual's mental condition,[30] how many certificates are needed to effect committal, the period for which the certificates remain effective, and a review tribunal process by which patients may challenge certificates.

Substantive criteria for committal go to the facts which the law requires to be present in order to hospitalize an individual on an involuntary basis. Nova Scotia's newly enacted *Involuntary Psychiatric Treatment Act*[31] (IPTA) incorporates virtually all of the substantive criteria employed variously in the statutes of other provinces. This statute can therefore serve as a template to examine each of the substantive criteria. Section 17 of IPTA provides for involuntary hospitalization on the following bases stated as the opinion of a psychiatrist:

(a) the person has a mental disorder;
(b) the person is in need of the psychiatric treatment provided in a psychiatric facility;
(c) the person, as a result of the mental disorder,

(i) is threatening or attempting to cause serious harm to himself or herself or has recently done so, has recently caused serious harm to himself or herself, is seriously harming or is threatening serious harm towards another person or has recently done so, or
(ii) is likely to suffer serious physical impairment or serious mental deterioration, or both;

---

[30] All Canadian jurisdictions grant this authority to physicians, or in certain cases, to psychiatrists only (*e.g.*, Nova Scotia's *Involuntary Psychiatric Treatment Act*, S.N.S. 2005, c. 42. This approach can be contrasted with that of many U.S. states, in which committal orders are made by "mental health courts" (administrative tribunals), which conduct hearings, generally in psychiatric hospital facilities, within 72 hours of a patient's initial involuntary admission. For an overview of U.S. law on civil committal, see Paul S. Appelbaum, *Almost a Revolution: Mental Health Law and the Limits of Change* (New York: Oxford University Press, 1994) at 20.
[31] S.N.S. 2005, c. 42.

(d) the person requires psychiatric treatment in a psychiatric facility and is not suitable for inpatient admission as a voluntary patient; and

(e) as a result of the mental disorder, the person does not have the capacity to make admission and treatment decisions. The psychiatrist may admit the person as an involuntary patient by completing and filing with the chief executive officer a declaration of involuntary admission in the form prescribed by the regulations.

A. PRESENCE OF A MENTAL DISORDER

Terms and definitions of the underlying mental conditions supporting committal vary widely. Several provinces use the term "mental disorder". The Alberta statute reads:

> "[M]ental disorder" means a substantial disorder of thought, mood, perception, orientation or memory that grossly impairs
>
> (i) judgment,
> (ii) behaviour,
> (iii) capacity to recognize reality, or
> (iv) ability to meet the ordinary demands of life.[32]

Ontario defines "mental disorder" as "any disease or disability of the mind".[33] Both capture the major mental illnesses of schizophrenia and serious mood disorders, which comprise the great preponderance of diagnosed conditions among committed patients across Canada. They likely do not capture developmental disabilities. No province expressly lists intellectual disability as a basis for committal. British Columbia removed the phrase "mentally retarded" from its definition of "person with a mental disorder" in 1998. Prince Edward Island is the only province to cite mental disorder resulting from alcohol or drug abuse in its committal criteria.[34] IPTA defines "mental disorder" as a "substantial disorder of behaviour, thought, mood, perception, orientation or memory that severely impairs judgement, behaviour, capacity to recognize reality or the ability to meet the ordinary demands of life, *in respect of which psychiatric treatment is advisable*" (emphasis added). The latter phrase makes treatability part of the definition of mental disorder (see below).

Ontario authorities have used the open-ended definition of "mental disorder" in that province's statute to effect the committal of a pedophile nearing the end of a criminal sentence on the basis that he continued to pose a danger to the

---

[32] R.S.A. 2000, c. M-13, s. 1(*g*).

[33] R.S.O. 1990, c. M-7, s. 1.

[34] Section 1(*k*) of the P.E.I. Statute, R.S.P.E.I. 1988, c. M-6.1, reads:

> "mental disorder" means a substantial disorder of thought, mood, perception, orientation or memory that seriously impairs judgment, behaviour, capacity to recognize reality or ability to meet the ordinary demands of life and *includes a mental disorder resulting from alcohol or drug addiction or abuse*, but a mental handicap or learning disability does not, of itself, constitute mental disorder.

(emphasis added).

community.[35] Persons committed for disorders such as pedophilia will generally be competent to refuse treatment, raising a host of difficult issues (see "Treatment and Consent", Part IV, below).

B. NEED FOR PSYCHIATRIC TREATMENT

To the extent that treatment is a justification for the coercive features of mental health law, it would seem to follow that only persons who have disorders amenable to psychiatric treatment should be subject to committal. Like Nova Scotia, British Columbia makes treatability a requirement for committal:

> "[P]erson with a mental disorder" means a person who has a disorder of the mind that requires treatment and seriously impairs the person's ability
>
> (a)   to react appropriately to the person's environment, or
> (b)   to associate with others.

"Treatment" is then defined as "safe and effective psychiatric treatment".[36] A requirement of treatability implies that a mental condition for which no known treatment is available cannot serve as the basis for civil committal. Arguably, personality disorder of the nature of psychopathy falls in this category. Notoriously difficult to treat, and associated by many in the psychiatric community with disruptive conduct harmful to a therapeutic environment, the B.C. definition may serve to exclude this group from the civil system.

C. THE HARM CRITERIA

The degree of "harm" caused by mental disability needed to support civil committal is the most controversial issue in this area of legal concern. Every Canadian jurisdiction makes imminent, serious bodily harm directed to self or others a basis for committal. This certainly covers risks of non-trivial physical harm to third parties, and of suicidal and serious self-mutilating behaviour. This level of harm is often referred to as the "dangerousness" standard. Controversy continues to exist around how far beyond (that is, below) a dangerousness standard committal criteria should go, particularly to questions of self-harm. This goes largely to two sub-questions:

(a)   Nature of harm: should protection extend beyond serious physical harm?
(b)   Imminence of harm: should protection extend to harm that is not imminent, but will likely occur if no intervention occurs in the meantime?

At the "low" end of the scale would be criteria that permit involuntary hospitalization for risks of mental deterioration that may occur if a person is not treated. This is often referred to as a "wellbeing" or "welfare" standard,

---

[35]   *Starnaman v. Penetanguishene Mental Health Centre*, [1995] O.J. No. 2130, 24 O.R. (3d) 701 (Ont. C.A.).
[36]   R.S.B.C. 1996, c. 288, s. 1. Treatability also appears in the committal criteria, which state in s. 22(3)(c)(i) of the B.C. statute, that the person "requires care, supervision and control in or through a designated facility".

directed at intervention to protect the individual's well-being, irrespective of whether his or her condition poses an imminent physical risk to self or others. Where a particular jurisdiction lies along the spectrum from a dangerousness to a welfare standard depends both on the wording used in its mental health statute, and on judicial interpretation of that wording. Canadian courts have varied considerably in their interpretations. As a general matter, it can be said that no Canadian jurisdiction employs a strict dangerousness standard for civil committal.

Several jurisdictions use statutory criteria that specify that the requisite harm must be physical in nature. Prior to 2000, Ontario's statute used these criteria:

> [that the person] is suffering from a mental disorder of a nature or quality that likely will result in
>
> (d)   serious bodily harm to that person,
> (e)   serious bodily harm to another person, or
> (f)   imminent and serious bodily impairment of that person.[37]

While this phrasing appears to embody a dangerousness standard, Ontario courts interpreted the wording to support the continued committal of a patient because, if released, she would return to poor eating habits that might result in a stroke.[38] This is much closer to a welfare standard approach. In 2000, Ontario nevertheless removed the word "imminent" from this provision.[39]

Certain provincial statutes expressly use the words "danger" or "dangerous". The Alberta statute states that a physician may certify a person with a mental disorder who is "in a condition presenting [or likely to present] a danger to the person or others". In 1985, an Alberta court ruled that this phrase required that the danger be almost immediate, not merely a consequence of a deterioration in condition to a point of dangerousness likely to occur over several weeks.[40] The legislature then inserted the bracketed phrase. Subsequent Alberta decisions suggest that the predicted consequences of a patient's ceasing to take medications is sufficient for a finding of danger.[41]

Like Nova Scotia, several provinces have adopted an express welfare standard through use of the phrase "substantial mental or physical deterioration". The Ontario *Mental Health Act* goes further and creates a class of persons subject to civil commitment that might be termed the "treatable, chronically mentally ill". For members of this class, the history of their mental disorder and of its previous treatment serve as predictors of harm. This largely replaces the need for the observation of present harmful behaviour.[42]

---

[37]   *Mental Health Act*, R.S.O. 1990, c. M.7, s. 20(5) (am. 2000, c. 9, s. 7).

[38]   *B. (L.)* v. *O'Doherty*, 38 A.C.W.S. (2d) 152 (Ont. Dist. Ct.).

[39]   S.O. 2000, c. 9, s. 7(2).

[40]   *M.* v. *Alberta*, [1985] A.J. No. 915, 63 A.R. 14 (Alta. Q.B.).

[41]   See for example, *B.T.* v. *Alberta Hospital*, [1997] A.J. No. 894 (Alta. Q.B.).

[42]   The *Mental Health Act*, R.S.O. 1990, c. M.7, s. 20(1.1) reads:

> 20(1.1)   The attending physician shall complete a certificate of involuntary admission or a certificate of renewal if, after examining the patient, he or she is of the opinion that the patient,
>
> (*a*)   that has previously received treatment for mental disorder of an ongoing or

D. NOT SUITABLE FOR VOLUNTARY ADMISSION

This requirement appears to ensure that certification for involuntary hospitalization occurs only in the last resort, when an individual cannot be admitted to a
psychiatric facility on a voluntary basis. This may not necessarily mean that an
individual can avoid involuntary committal by agreeing to voluntary admission
to hospital. In certain provinces (see below), involuntary status permits treating
an individual without his or her consent. The perceived need to facilitate
treatment may serve as a basis for certification.

E. CAPACITY TO CONSENT TO TREATMENT

Nova Scotia and Saskatchewan alone require as part of a hospital committal that
the individual be incapable of giving or withholding consent to treatment.[43] This
means that only persons for whom substituted consent will be needed can be
subject of involuntary hospitalization. This approach avoids the kind of dilemma
posed by situations like that of Scott Starson in Ontario, (see Part IV, Consent to
Treatment, below): a hospitalized but treatment-capable individual who refuses
recommended psychiatric treatment. That situation, much criticized by the
psychiatric community, can result in housing an individual without providing
treatment. The Nova Scotia approach ensures that involuntary committal is
closely connected to active treatment of mental disorder. Of course, having such
a requirement means that committal will not be available for some persons
whose mental condition otherwise meets the requisite harm standard, including
dangerousness, but who have treatment capacity. It also permits involuntary
hospitalization of an individual who is presently incapable, but who expressed
prior capable wishes concerning treatment.

---

recurring nature that, when not treated, is of a nature or quality that likely will
result in serious bodily harm to the person or to another person or substantial
mental or physical deterioration of the person or serious physical impairment of
the person;

(*b*) has shown clinical improvement as a result of the treatment;

(*c*) is suffering from the same mental disorder as the one for which he or she
previously received treatment or from a mental disorder that is similar to the
previous one;

(*d*) given the person's history of mental disorder and current mental or physical
condition, is likely to cause serious bodily harm to himself or herself or to another
person or is likely to suffer substantial mental or physical deterioration or serious
physical impairment ...

[43] *Mental Health Services Act*, S.S. 1984-85-86, c. M-13.1, s. 24(2)(*a*):
[the physician] has probable cause to believe that ...
(ii) as a result of the mental disorder the person is unable to fully understand and to
make an informed decision regarding his need for treatment or care and
supervision.

F. COMMITTAL CRITERIA AND THE CANADIAN CHARTER OF RIGHTS AND FREEDOMS

Section 7 of the Charter reads:

> Every individual has the right to life, liberty and security of the person, and the right not to be deprived thereof except in accordance with the principles of fundamental justice.

Section 7 is the first of the Charter's "legal rights", which include the right to be free from "arbitrary detention" in section 9. These sections provide relevant constitutional protections against the interference by the state with individual liberty, including freedom of movement. This protection is understood to extend both to the procedure, or "due process", by which the state may take away an individual's liberty, and to the substantive criteria for doing so.[44]

Despite the fact that sections 7 and 9 of the Charter apply to civil committal and create constitutional boundaries within which these laws operate, only two significant Charter challenges on this issue have come before our courts. In *Thwaites,*[45] the Manitoba Court of Appeal struck down statutory criteria that stated a person could be certified when, in the opinion of a physician, he or she "should be confined as a patient in a psychiatric facility". The court ruled that by failing to establish objective criteria related to mental condition and risk of harm, this provision exposed individuals to arbitrary detention and so breached section 9 of the Charter. Justice Philp stated: "I do not think it can be said that, in the absence of a 'dangerousness' or like standard, the provisions impair as little as possible the right of a person 'not to be arbitrarily detained'".[46] The Manitoba Legislature then amended the statute to include the standard of a "likelihood of serious harm". This standard was subsequently upheld.[47]

The committal criteria in B.C.'s *Mental Health Act* were challenged in 1993 in *McCorkell v. Riverview Hospital.*[48] The petitioner argued that the statute violated sections 7 and 9 of the Charter by authorizing committal where a person "requires care, supervision and control in a Provincial mental health facility for his own protection or for the protection of others". He argued that only criteria based strictly on dangerousness could be justified under the Charter as the standard for restriction of an individual's liberty. Justice Donald of the British Columbia Supreme Court rejected this argument. In particular, he rejected the plaintiff's attempt to draw an analogy between criminal law, in which the state's power to restrict liberty is circumscribed by extensive substantive and procedural protections for accused persons, and mental health law:

> Statutes dealing with criminal law are penal in nature; incarceration is a punishment of culpable individuals and serves the objectives of public safety and

---

[44] *Reference re Motor Vehicle Act (British Columbia), Section 94(2)*, [1985] S.C.J. No. 73, 2 S.C.R. 486 (S.C.C.).

[45] *Thwaites v. Health Sciences Centre Psychiatric Facility*, [1988] M.J. No. 107, 40 C.R.R. 326 (Man. C.A.).

[46] *Ibid.*, at 332.

[47] *Bobbie v. Health Sciences Centre*, [1988] M.J. No. 485, 49 C.R.R. 376 (Man. Q.B.).

[48] [1993] B.C.J. No. 1518 (B.C.S.C.).

denunciation of crime. The *Mental Health Act* involuntarily detains people only for the purpose of treatment; the punitive element is wholly absent.[49]

Citing the Manitoba cases, Donald J. continued:

In the Manitoba legislation, "serious harm" is not qualified; it can include harms that relate to the social, family, vocational or financial life of the patient as well as to the patient's physical condition. The operative word in the British Columbia act is "protection" which necessarily involves the notion of harm.... The Manitoba cases dealt initially with a statute that had no criteria at all, then with an amended statute with criteria remarkably like British Columbia's act which passed a Charter examination.[50]

The decisions in *Thwaites* and *McCorkell* have binding force only in Manitoba and British Columbia, respectively. Taken together, and in the absence of other decisions, they describe the following situation: while mental health statutes must set out objective harm criteria for committal, and not leave this as a mere matter of medical judgment, considerable leeway exists with respect to the kinds of harm which will justify committal.

IV. CONSENT TO TREATMENT IN MENTAL HEALTH LAW

The question of whether competent involuntary patients should have the right in law to refuse psychiatric treatment is the most disputed issue in mental health law. Patients' rights advocates argue that the right to refuse treatment should be available to persons with mental illnesses on the same basis that it is for everyone with respect to non-psychiatric health care. Many family group advocates and psychiatrists believe that permitting involuntary patients to refuse psychiatric treatment not only imposes a barrier to restoring patients to health, but also results in having persons detained in hospital without being able to be treated.

In legal terms, the consent to treatment issue concerns this question: does statute law permit the state to override a *competent refusal* of psychiatric treatment? If an individual lacks capacity to give or withhold consent to treatment in the first place, then a process for substitute decision making is necessary and the individual will not himself or herself be able to refuse treatment. Much of the debate over the consent issue is really a disagreement over whether there is ever such a thing as a *competent* refusal by an involuntary patient. Many people who oppose recognition of a right to refuse treatment believe that major mental illness makes it impossible for an individual to understand that he or she is ill and in need of treatment. In their view, only a naive or shallow understanding of mental illness would suggest otherwise. Certainly, many persons who meet the criteria for involuntary admission to a psychiatric facility will lack treatment competence. Canadian law, however, rejects global assumptions about decision-making capacity. It views competence as a mutable quality that must be assessed with respect to the specific activity in

---

[49]   *Ibid.*, at para. 45.
[50]   *Ibid.*, at para. 58.

question. A person may be incompetent for one purpose, such as making a will, but competent with respect to another, such as health care. As a consequence, and as a matter of principle, competence to consent to treatment must be assessed independently from the issue of whether the individual otherwise meets statutory criteria for involuntary status. A further complicating factor related to the consent issue is that a person may, during a period of competence, express a wish to refuse psychiatric treatment should he or she later become incompetent. Several provinces have sought to encourage pre-planning for periods of incompetence with respect to health care decisions generally, through instruments such as personal directives[51] and representation agreements.[52] The status of pre-expressed refusals poses a particular challenge to law governing decision-making in mental health settings.[53] Given the episodic nature of much mental illness, the availability of legal techniques for pre-planning treatment choices has particular significance.

In Canada, four distinct approaches to the question of consent to treatment can be identified. Only one of these approaches, that employed in Ontario, recognizes a right to refuse treatment for involuntary patients that corresponds to the common law right to refuse medical treatment. The approaches are:
(a) a right to refuse treatment (Ontario);
(b) no right to refuse treatment (British Columbia);
(c) a right to refuse, subject to a "best interests" override (Alberta, Manitoba);
(d) excluding capable individuals from committal (Saskatchewan, Nova Scotia).

A. RIGHT TO REFUSE TREATMENT: ONTARIO

Ontario law on this question was established by the decision of the province's Court of Appeal in *Fleming v. Reid*,[54] a Charter case from 1991. This remains the only judicial decision in Canada that addresses the constitutional dimension of the issue. The *Fleming* case concerned a previously expressed competent refusal. An individual who had experienced several involuntary admissions in his life stated a wish to refuse medications should he be committed again. When this occurred, the treating psychiatrist proposed that the patient take medications covered by the refusal. The substitute decision-maker for the now incompetent patient was the Public Trustee. Acting under a statutory obligation to abide by the individual's previously expressed competent wish, the Public Trustee refused to consent to the treatment plan. The treating psychiatrist applied to the province's Review Board to override the refusal. The Board did so, on the basis that the *Mental Health Act* obliged the Board to make a treatment decision based

---

[51] *Personal Directives Act*, R.S.A. 2000, c. P-6.

[52] *Representation Agreement Act*, R.S.B.C. 1996, c. 405.

[53] For an example of the kind of complications that can follow from a pre-expressed wish to refuse treatment, see the litigation in *Conway v. Jacques*, [2002] O.J. No. 2333, 59 O.R. (3d) 737 (Ont. C.A.), in which the Ontario Court of Appeal found grounds for rejecting the patient's wishes due to changed circumstances, but three years later the issue of competency was still being disputed [2005] O.J. No. 400, 250 D.L.R. (4th) 178 (Ont. S.C.J.).

[54] [1991] O.J. No. 1083, 4 O.R. (3d) 74 (Ont. C.A.).

on the patient's best interests, not on his or her wishes. The Ontario Court of Appeal ruled this to be invalid as a violation of "security of the person" under section 7 of the Charter. The Court concluded that the statute denied the patient's right to refuse treatment by making it subject to a best interests test. Moreover, the statute did this without requiring that any hearing be held into whether the patient's competent wishes should be honoured, irrespective of what might be thought to be in his best interests.[55]

A narrow reading of *Fleming* might focus on this last point and suggest that a statutory scheme that balances a patient's competent wishes against his or her therapeutic best interests (without holding either to be determinative in every case) would be constitutional. However, the Court of Appeal's ruling implied a broader understanding of the individual's right to refuse treatment when it said of the issues relevant to a hearing into a previously expressed refusal of treatment:

> [T]here may be questions as to the clarity or currency of the wishes, their applicability to the patient's present circumstances, and whether they have been revoked or revised by subsequent wishes or a subsequently accepted treatment program. The resolution of questions of this nature is patently a matter for legislative action. But, in my respectful view, it is incumbent on the legislature to bear in mind that, as a general proposition, psychiatric patients are entitled to make competent decisions and exercise their right to self-determination in accordance with their own standards and values and not necessarily in the manner others may believe to be in the patients' best interests.[56]

Ontario statute law now incorporates the *Fleming* principles.[57] The Consent and Capacity Board, created after *Fleming* to replace the former Review Board, has no power to override a competent treatment refusal by an involuntary patient.

In 2001, the film *A Beautiful Mind* won the Academy Award for Best Picture. Based on true events, it told the story of Nobel Prize-winning mathematician John Nash, a person with schizophrenia who managed, not without difficulty, to maintain a long career at Princeton University despite successfully resisting pharmaceutical treatment for his condition. Just a year after the *A Beautiful Mind* was honoured at the Academy Awards, the Supreme Court of Canada rendered judgment in *Starson v. Swayze*,[58] a case with facts strikingly similar to the story of John Nash. The *Starson* case shows how the law established in *Fleming* operates in practice.

Scott Starson had been hospitalized involuntarily pursuant to the mental disorder provisions of the *Criminal Code*.[59] He was diagnosed with bipolar disorder. His psychiatrists recommended treatment involving various medications, including antipsychotics. Starson refused. He stated that his great

---

[55]   *Ibid.*, at paras. 51-56.

[56]   *Ibid.*, at para. 55.

[57]   Provisions on consent, the obligations of substitute decision-makers with respect to consent, and the applications which can be made to the Consent and Capacity Board are found in the *Health Care Consent Act, 1996*, S.O. 1996, c. 2, Sch. A.

[58]   [2003] S.C.J. No. 33, 1 S.C.R. 722 (S.C.C.).

[59]   See Part V. R.S.C. 1985, c. C-46, Part XX.1, s. 672.54(*c*).

and only passion in life was physics. While Starson had never been employed or affiliated with an educational institution, he had co-authored at least one paper with a leading physicist, and was recognized among physicists as a good and creative thinker. Starson said that he was familiar with the medications proposed for his treatment and with their side effects, which included the dulling of his thinking processes.

The principal issue before the Supreme Court was whether Starson had capacity to give or withhold consent to treatment. The Ontario *Health Care Consent Act, 1996* (HCCA) sets out the following test for competence in section 4(1):

> A person is capable with respect to a treatment, admission to a care facility or a personal assistance service if the person is able to understand the information that is relevant to making a decision about the treatment, admission or personal assistance service, as the case may be, and able to appreciate the reasonably foreseeable consequences of a decision or lack of decision.[60]

In Ontario, determinations of whether a person meets this test of capacity are made by the Consent and Capacity Board, a statutory tribunal empowered under the HCCA. Starson testified before the Board that while he understood he had mental "problems", he did not acknowledge the diagnosis of bipolar disorder. He said at one point that his work in physics would contribute to the building of spaceships. He rejected the idea that antipsychotic medications could ever resolve his "problems". He was not asked, and never said, whether he understood that if his condition did not change, he might continue to be detained in hospital indefinitely. The Board concluded that he lacked sufficient understanding and appreciation of his condition and the proposed treatment to be capable of making a treatment decision. A majority of six Supreme Court Justices disagreed. All nine Justices agreed that the test set out in the HCCA corresponds with the common law's understanding of capacity and requires an assessment of the individual's *ability* to understand and appreciate his or her circumstances, not merely of the individual's *actual* understanding of those circumstances. The majority concluded that the evidence before the Board failed to demonstrate that Starson lacked capacity in this sense. Writing for the majority, Major J. stated:

> In my view, the Board's reasons, as stated earlier, appear to be overly influenced by its conviction that medication was in Professor Starson's best interest. The Board arrived at its conclusion by failing to focus on the overriding consideration in this appeal, that is, whether that adult patient had the mental capacity to choose whether to accept or reject the medication prescribed. The enforced injection of mind-altering drugs against the respondent's will is highly offensive to his dignity and autonomy, and is to be avoided unless it is demonstrated that he lacked the capacity to make his own decision.[61]

---

[60] S.O. 1996, c. 2, Sch. A.
[61] *Starson v. Swayze*, [2003] S.C.J. No. 33, [2003] 1 S.C.R. 722 (S.C.C.) at para. 91. The majority acceded to Starson's request to be referred to as "Professor Starson" despite the fact that he had never been employed by a post-secondary institution in Canada or elsewhere.

Starson represents strong support for the principle of individual autonomy. Nevertheless, the case did not address any constitutional issues, and dealt only with interpretation of the Ontario statute on capacity. It was also highly dependent on its facts. These are all reasons to think that its implications are limited.

What is of some interest in *Starson* is what the Court implicitly says about the issue of whether legislatures may override competent refusals of psychiatric treatment. While the Supreme Court majority did not comment specifically on whether *Fleming* represents good law on the Charter status of the right to refuse treatment, it twice referred approvingly to the case in more general terms.[62]

B. NO RIGHT TO REFUSE TREATMENT: BRITISH COLUMBIA

British Columbia stands at the opposite end of the spectrum from Ontario on the issue of consent. The province maintains an approach that was long used in Canada: the directors of psychiatric facilities may authorize treatment for involuntarily committed patients without obtaining their consent. Section 31 of the B.C. statute states that "treatment authorized by the director is deemed to be given with the consent of the patient". Further, the *Health Care (Consent) and Care Facility (Admission) Act*, which essentially codifies the common law on consent to treatment, is expressly stated not to apply to involuntary patients in psychiatric hospitals.[63] This legislative distinction between psychiatric patients and all other individuals with respect to the right to consent would appear to raise an issue of discrimination under section 15(1) of the Charter. Such a claim would, of course, be subject to the government's seeking to justify the distinction under section 1, or even on the basis that it "corresponds to the needs" of psychiatric patients.[64]

---

[62] *Ibid.*, at para. 75, where Major J. said:
> The right to refuse unwanted medical treatment is fundamental to a person's dignity and autonomy. This right is equally important in the context of treatment for mental illness: see *Fleming v. Reid* (1991), 4 O.R. (3d) 74 (C.A.)...:
> > Few medical procedures can be more intrusive than the forcible injection of powerful mind-altering drugs which are often accompanied by severe and sometimes irreversible adverse side effects.
> Unwarranted findings of incapacity severely infringe upon a person's right to self-determination.

At para. 101, Major J. added:
> In *Fleming v. Reid* ... Robins J.A. observed ... that neuroleptic medication carries with it "significant, and often unpredictable, short term and long term risks of harmful side effects". Professor Starson clearly appreciated the extent of these risks. However, it was the intended purpose of the medication that he primarily objected to.
(emphasis omitted).

[63] R.S.B.C. 1996, c. 181, s. 2.

[64] In *Law v. Canada (Minister of Employment and Immigration)*, [1999] S.C.J. No. 12, 1 S.C.R. 497 (S.C.C.), "correspondence to need" is identified by the Court as one of four contextual issues that might show that a distinction in law is not, in fact, discriminatory for purposes of s. 15(1). See paras. 69-71.

Under this model, there is no requirement to assess an involuntary patient's treatment competency, nor is there any role for a substitute decision-maker to make treatment decisions on the patient's behalf. This does not mean, of course, that informal practices of assessing competence, respecting patients' treatment wishes, and working with family members cannot be employed.

This approach ensures that treatment can be provided to involuntary patients with a minimum of procedural delay. Given that it involves the clearest denial of a right to consent to treatment, it might seem the most vulnerable to Charter challenge on *Fleming*-like grounds. The decision in *McCorkell* dealing with committal criteria, which emphasized the therapeutic purposes of mental health law, may signal a different judicial view in B.C.

C. "BEST INTERESTS" OVERRIDE: ALBERTA AND MANITOBA

The mental health statutes of Alberta and Manitoba recognize the distinction between treatment competence and incompetence, and the right of a competent patient to refuse proposed treatment. However, in Alberta, the hospital board or attending physician may apply to the Review Panel for a review of the refusal. The Review Panel must act in what it believes to be the patient's best interests, and on that basis may override the refusal and order that the proposed treatment be administered.[65] This is quite similar to the pre-*Fleming* system in Ontario. In Manitoba, a similar override of a refusal is available, although only with respect to a refusal made on an incompetent patient's behalf by their substitute decision-maker.

These models involve significantly greater procedural rights for an involuntary patient around treatment decisions than is the case in British Columbia. Nevertheless, the Alberta statute in particular provides for overriding a competent refusal in the patient's best interests. This model is also potentially vulnerable to a Charter challenge on *Fleming*-type grounds.

D. TREATMENT INCAPABILITY: SASKATCHEWAN AND NOVA SCOTIA

As earlier stated, Saskatchewan and Nova Scotia include treatment incompetence in the substantive criteria for involuntary hospitalization. This effectively avoids the consent to treatment dilemma. That is, any person who is treatment competent cannot be involuntarily hospitalized. The question of respecting or overriding a competent refusal does not arise. This model would seem to satisfy any Charter concerns. It does mean that competent persons with mental disorders who present a danger to others will not be committable. Only should they become incompetent, or commit an offence which brings them under the *Criminal Code*, will it be possible to detain them. A potential ambiguity in the approach adopted by Saskatchewan and Nova Scotia exists with respect to an individual committed to hospital on the basis of current incompetence, but who is then discovered to have given a competent refusal of treatment at an earlier, pre-committal time.

---

[65] *Mental Health Act*, C.C.S.M., c. M110, s. 30, and *Mental Health Act*, R.S.A. 2000, c. M-13, s. 29.

E. NON-PSYCHIATRIC AND EXCEPTIONAL TREATMENTS

Statutory provisions that authorize treatment of involuntary patients without consent apply to treatment directed at mental disorder or its symptoms. Medical treatment for unrelated physiological matters, such as dental surgery, must be provided to an involuntary patient on the same basis as to any other person: with the patient's consent, or if the patient is incompetent, by consent of Substitute Decision-maker (SDM) or in an emergency. Should this limit not be expressly stated in the statute, it should follow from the fact that both detention and non-consensual treatment are premised on the existence of mental disorder and the need to facilitate its treatment.

Special prohibitions or protections may exist with respect to treatments that are more invasive or controversial than standard psychiatric therapy. These may prevent SDMs from consenting on a patient's behalf, or impose additional obligations in the authorizing process. For example, Alberta prohibits "psychosurgery" unless both the patient and the review panel agree to it.[66] Ontario's *Health Care Consent Act, 1996* excludes medical procedures done for research or tissue transplant purposes, and non-therapeutic sterilization, from its substitute decision-making provisions. Electro-convulsive therapy (ECT) is not singled out in provincial statutes for particular attention, but hospital and Ministry policy often imposes additional precautions, such as obtaining a second opinion.

F. COMMUNITY TREATMENT ORDERS

Saskatchewan, Ontario and Nova Scotia have incorporated "community treatment orders" (CTOs) into their mental health statutes.[67] Based on models in several U.S. states, where CTOs are generally referred to as "outpatient committal", this mechanism is intended to impose a duty to comply with psychiatric treatment on mentally ill individuals living in the community. The idea is to break the connection between involuntary hospitalization and non-consensual psychiatric treatment, and by addressing the problem of treatment non-compliance to keep persons healthy and in the community. It is worth asking, however, whether the extension of coercive mental health measures from the hospital into the community is either necessary, or consistent with the idea that the community represents a better alternative to institutional care, espoused by, among others, the Senate in *Out of the Shadows at Last*.

The CTO scheme has its own substantive "committal" criteria. The statutory criteria in Ontario require that in order to issue a CTO: (1) the subject of the CTO must have previous involvement with the mental health system; (2) the subject must meet substantive criteria for mental disorder and risk of harm; and (3) it must be possible to put a "community treatment plan" in place for the

---

[66] *Mental Health Act*, R.S.A. 2000, c. M-13, s. 29(5).
[67] Ontario *Mental Health Act*, R.S.O. 1990, c. M.7, s. 33; for Saskatchewan, see *Mental Health Services Amendment Act, 1993*, S.S. 1993, c. 59, as amended by *Mental Health Services Amendment Act, 1996*, S.S. 1996, c. 17; for Nova Scotia, see *Involuntary Psychiatric Treatment Act*, S.N.S. 2005, 42, s. 46.

subject. The target group for CTOs is the "revolving door" or chronic client. In order to be subject to a CTO, a person must have been hospitalized on at least two occasions or for 30 days or more within the preceding three years. The legislation does not limit the previous hospitalizations to involuntary committals. Therefore, individuals who voluntarily admit themselves to psychiatric facilities may make themselves eligible for later CTO committal.

The CTO must include a "community treatment plan". The issuing physician has several responsibilities with respect to the plan. The physician must develop the plan in consultation with the individual and any health practitioners intended to be involved in providing care in the community, ensure that the services set out in the plan are available in the community and assess the individual as being capable of complying with the treatment plan. Further, "the person or his or her substitute decision-maker [must consent] to the community treatment plan in accordance with the rules for consent under the *Health Care Consent Act 1996*".[68] Other provisions set out certain required elements of a community treatment plan. The issuing physician has several additional obligations, such as ensuring that the individual has consulted with a "rights adviser", and that copies of the CTO get to appropriate parties, including any health practitioners named in the plan. Further, the physician is made responsible for "general supervision" of the CTO.[69] The CTO expires after six months unless renewed.

The Saskatchewan and Nova Scotia schemes differ from Ontario's in the following respects. A person is eligible for CTO committal if he or she has been hospitalized in a psychiatric facility for a cumulative total of 60 days in the preceding two years. Only persons who are incompetent to consent to treatment can be the subject of a CTO, which is consistent with each province's criteria for civil committal. Saskatchewan, like Ontario, makes it a requirement that the issuing physician find the person able to comply with the CTO. In Saskatchewan, a CTO must be "validated" by a second physician. It remains in effect for three months, and is renewable. The differences between the provinces on the consent issue are important, and clearly relate to the general issue of consent to mental health treatment in each jurisdiction. As noted, in Ontario, a competent refusal of treatment cannot be overridden.

Patients' groups have consistently criticized CTOs as an unnecessary and intrusive mechanism that stigmatizes persons with mental illness as needing to be subject to state control, even in the community.[70] Apart from the argument over stigma, there are reasons for questioning whether the CTOs are capable of meeting the goals intended by proponents. The problem of non-compliance with psychiatric treatment by persons living in the community is a complex one, and it remains unclear whether the CTO can succeed in addressing it by compulsion.

---

[68] *Mental Health Act*, R.S.O. 1990, c. M.7, s. 33.1(4)(*f*).

[69] The attending physician is relieved of liability for any "default or neglect" of other persons providing treatment under the plan (*ibid.*, s. 33.6(1)). By implication, the physician appears not to be relieved of liability for default or neglect in his or her own responsibilities under the plan. Other health practitioners providing treatment under the plan "are responsible for implementing the plan to the extent indicated in it".

[70] See, for example, the website of the "No Force Coalition" formed in Ontario to oppose the introduction of CTOs in 2000, online: <http://www.qsos.ca/qspc/nfc/cto.html>.

For one thing, the CTO itself is not easily enforced. While it might be thought that non-compliance with a CTO would be sanctioned by involuntary committal to hospital, statutes do not go that far and for good reason. Hospital committal depends on a person's meeting substantive committal criteria related to mental condition and therapeutic need. Committal should not be available as penalty or punishment for failure to comply with an order.

The only sanction for non-compliance with a CTO is the physician's power to issue a form of warrant, authorizing police officers to convey the non-compliant person for purposes of a mental examination. This is not insignificant. A frequent complaint of family members of chronically mental ill persons is the difficulty they encounter in obtaining help, including from police, to get their unwilling relative to a physician or to hospital when symptoms of acute illness appear. Nevertheless, it is questionable to what degree this authority changes the dynamics of community mental health treatment.

The success of CTOs may largely depend on their being part of a comprehensive plan that puts in place significant treatment resources, including ready contact with and support from health care professionals. Planning and support of this kind appears to be intended by the legislation. If CTO schemes work only to the degree that the client is provided with comprehensive treatment and support services, however, it seems reasonable to ask whether similar results could be achieved without issuing a CTO.[71] The province of Ontario undertook a legislatively mandated[72] review of CTO effectiveness in 2004. Although it was completed in 2005, the Ministry of Health's report concerning this study has not yet been released.[73]

A different means of maintaining a person on a treatment program in the community is a leave of absence from hospital for involuntary patients. Several provinces, including Manitoba and British Columbia, have enhanced statutory leave provisions to permit psychiatric facilities to gradually reintroduce involuntary patients into the community while remaining subject to committal and the authority of the facility. Leaves of absence are granted on conditions, often including compliance with a treatment plan. If a patient ceases to comply, or starts to decompensate, he or she can be brought back to hospital under the continuing involuntary status.

The leave of absence approach has advantages over the more complex CTO. The starting place is hospital and in-patient treatment, rather than an effort to

---

[71]   For further discussion of the CTO, see the author's "A New Direction for Mental Health Law: *Brian's Law* and the Problematic Implications of Community Treatment Orders", in T. Caulfield & B. Von Tigerstrom, eds., *Health Care Reform and the Law in Canada: Meeting the Challenge* (Edmonton: University of Alberta Press, 2001), at 187-222; F. Boudreau & P. Lambert "Compulsory Community Treatment? Part I: Ontario Stakeholders' Response to 'Helping Those Who Won't Help Themselves'" (1993) 12 Canadian Journal of Community Mental Health 57, and Part II: The Collision of Views and Complexities Involved: Is It 'The Best Possible Alternative?'" (1993) 12 Canadian Journal of Canadian Mental Health 79, and Shelley Trueman, "Community Treatment Orders and Nova Scotia: the Least Restrictive Alternative?" (2003) 11 Health L.J. 1.

[72]   *Mental Health Act*, R.S.O. 1990, c. M.7, s. 33.1(9).

[73]   For information concerning the legislated review of continuing treatment orders in Ontario, see online: <http://www.ctoproject.ca>.

enforce compliance on an individual living in the community who may not meet standard committal criteria.

A concern from a civil liberties perspective about leaves of absence is that they might too easily be used as a means of retaining control over individuals who, in fact, no longer meet the criteria for involuntary committal. To date, however, Canadian courts have not been receptive to this argument. In an Alberta case, a patient with an extensive history of self-mutilation argued that repeated leaves which only required him to spend weeknights in hospital were inconsistent with his meeting Alberta's dangerousness criteria for committal. The court disagreed, finding no presumptive inconsistency between a leave of absence and continued certification. The judge commented:

> The granting of leaves of absence on a regular basis allows [the patient] a degree of freedom and human dignity, while at the same time decreasing the likelihood that he will harm himself.[74]

A similar ruling was made in an Ontario case in which a patient argued that because he had received repeated leaves, even though the statute permitted only one leave, he should be declared discharged from involuntary status. The judge described leaves of absence as "a win-win situation", the benefits of which should not be lost by too technical an interpretation of the statute.[75]

V. THE FORENSIC PSYCHIATRIC SYSTEM

A. PART XX.1 OF THE CRIMINAL CODE

The forensic psychiatric system deals with persons who commit criminal offences as a consequence of mental illness. Canada's forensic law was overhauled in 1992 following the Charter decision in *R. v. Swain*.[76] Prior to 1992, the *Criminal Code* provided for a plea of "not guilty by reason of insanity" (NGRI). If found NGRI, the accused individual was automatically and indefinitely detained in hospital on a "Lieutenant Governor's warrant", meaning that release from hospital was ultimately dependent on a decision of the provincial Cabinet.

In *Swain*, the Supreme Court of Canada ruled that the NGRI process violated sections 7 and 9 of the Charter. Parliament responded by introducing a new Part XX.1 to the *Criminal Code* to govern this area. The term "insanity" and the finding of NGRI were replaced by "not criminally responsible by reason of mental disorder" (NCRMD). The legal test is that the accused did not appreciate "the nature and quality of the [criminal] act or omission or [know] that it was wrong."[77] In addition to NCRMDs, Part XX.1 of the *Criminal Code* and forensic

---

[74] *Wurfel v. Alberta Hospital (Edmonton)*, [1999] A.J. No. 868 (Alta. Q.B.) at para. 67, *per* Lee J.
[75] *Lavallie v. Kingston Psychiatric Hospital*, [1999] O.J. No. 4306 (Ont. S.C.J.) at para. 29, *per* Belch J.
[76] [1991] S.C.J. No. 32, [1991] 1 S.C.R. 933 (S.C.C.).
[77] *Criminal Code*, R.S.C. 1985, c. C-46, s. 16(1).

psychiatric services also deal with individuals found unfit to stand trial due to mental illness.

A person found NCRMD is not subject to automatic detention in hospital. Rather, section 672.54 of the *Code* sets out several factors to be taken into consideration with respect to making a disposition of hospital custody, release on conditions or absolute discharge:

> Where a court or Review Board makes a disposition pursuant to subsection 672.45(2) or section 672.47 or 672.83, it shall, taking into consideration the need to protect the public from dangerous persons, the mental condition of the accused, the reintegration of the accused into society and the other needs of the accused, make one of the following dispositions that is the least onerous and least restrictive to the accused:
>
> > (a) where a verdict of not criminally responsible on account of mental disorder has been rendered in respect of the accused and, in the opinion of the court or Review Board, the accused is not a significant threat to the safety of the public, by order, direct that the accused be discharged absolutely;
> >
> > (b) by order, direct that the accused be discharged subject to such conditions as the court or Review Board considers appropriate; or
> >
> > (c) by order, direct that the accused be detained in custody in a hospital, subject to such conditions as the court or Review Board considers appropriate.

Following initial disposition, ongoing decision-making authority over the individual's continued detention lies with forensic Review Boards established in and by each province. Review Boards must conduct periodic hearings for each patient.

The Supreme Court considered the Charter status of this scheme in *Winko v. British Columbia*.[78] The Court ruled that "dangerousness", in terms of posing "a significant threat to public safety", is the appropriate basis for forensic committal. This standard corresponds to the federal government's constitutional jurisdiction over the criminal law. It has national application. The Court ruled that an NCRMD person is entitled to an absolute discharge from custody when he or she is determined to no longer pose a significant threat to public safety. Short of an absolute discharge, Review Boards may order conditional discharges from hospital detention, which permit a return to the community on conditions, such as working with a treatment team.

The *Criminal Code* provisions do not authorize psychiatric treatment of NCRMD persons. Therefore, the authority to treat, including any authority to treat where the individual is unable or unwilling to consent to psychiatric treatment, falls to be determined by the provincial mental health law in the province where the individual is detained. For this reason, forensic patients are often certified under mental health statutes as well as being detained pursuant to the *Criminal Code*. Forensic psychiatric facilities are provincially operated, either as free-standing hospitals or as forensic units in mental health hospitals.

---

[78]   *Winko v. British Columbia (Forensic Psychiatric Services)*, [1999] S.C.J. No. 31, [1991] 2 S.C.R. 625 (S.C.C.).

Winko also argued that as an NCRMD person, he remained subject to indefinite detention, and might well be detained beyond the maximum sentence he could have received had he been found guilty of the criminal offence. This, he claimed, constituted discrimination based on mental disability contrary to section 15 of the Charter. The Court ruled, however, that because the system is based on individualized assessment of the person's mental condition, it does not rely on stereotypes of mental illness and so is not discriminatory.

In 2005, Parliament amended various aspects of Part XX.1 of the *Criminal Code*. Most of the amendments were of a housekeeping nature. They included repealing the capping provision, and a dangerous offender sentencing provision linked to capping. Submissions to a Parliamentary committee had recommended extending the powers of Review Boards with respect to ordering psychiatric assessments of patients, and making more detailed orders concerning therapeutic matters. The Senate Committee made similar recommendations.[79] Parliament did not act on these recommendations. Nevertheless, a case concerning the interpretation of Review Board powers under section 672.54 came before the Supreme Court in 2006, and the Court effectively expanded Board authority in ways not unlike those proposed. The case, *Mazzei v. British Columbia (Director of Forensic Services)*,[80] contains an interesting discussion about the nature of psychiatric treatment, and the responsibility of an administrative tribunal charged with supervising treatment plans.

B. THE ROLE OF REVIEW BOARDS: MAZZEI V. BRITISH COLUMBIA

The issue of forensic Review Boards' powers to intervene in matters going to treatment, has arisen repeatedly in the jurisprudence emerging from Review Board decisions. The argument has generally aligned forensic hospitals and governments on one side, arguing for restricted Board jurisdiction, against Boards and patients on the other. That was true in two cases decided by the Supreme Court in late 2003: *Penetanguishene Mental Health Centre v. Ontario*[81] and *Pinet v. St. Thomas Psychiatric Hospital*.[82] In both instances, the principal issue concerned whether the duty placed on Review Boards by section 672.54 to ensure that its dispositions are "the least onerous and least restrictive to the accused" extends to the entirety of a Board's order, including any conditions placed on an accused's release into the community or hospital detention. In *Penetanguishene*, the Ontario Review Board ordered that the accused be detained in hospital, but added the conditions that he be held in a medium security rather than a maximum security facility, and that he have certain grounds privileges.

[79] *Out of the Shadows at Last: Transforming Mental Health, Mental Illness and Addiction Services in Canada*, Final Report of the Standing Committee on Social Affairs, Science and Technology (Ottawa: Senate of Canada, May 2006), Section 4.3, "The Mental Disorder Provisions of the *Criminal Code*".
[80] [2006] S.C.J. No. 7, [2006] 1 S.C.R. 326 (S.C.C.).
[81] [2003] S.C.J. No. 67, [2004] 1 S.C.R. 498 (S.C.C.).
[82] [2004] S.C.J. No. 66, [2004] 1 S.C.R. 528 (S.C.C.).

The government of Ontario appealed, arguing that the Board had erred in ordering the added conditions based on its understanding of what would be least restrictive of the accused's liberty, within the context of hospital detention. The government argued that the liberty interest pertained only to the Board's choice of "bare" disposition between an absolute discharge, a conditional discharge, and hospital detention. Once having made that decision, the Board was not obliged to take the accused's liberty interests into account.

An interesting feature of this case is that the Ontario and Nunavut Review Boards opposed the government's position, even though that position ostensibly argued for a broad, unfettered Board discretion. What was going on? In short, the Crown, on behalf of its forensic officials, was seeking to keep the Review Board out of "micro-managing" (its word) the in-hospital treatment program of an NCRMD accused in the interests of greater freedom of movement than the hospital might deem appropriate.

The Court unanimously rejected the government's interpretation of section 672.54. Justice Binnie stated:

> The heart of the Crown's argument is that a "least onerous and least restrictive" requirement may undermine treatment needs. The Crown argues the "least onerous and least restrictive" requirement would impose undue rigidity, whereas the "appropriateness" test guarantees flexibility. With respect, these arguments do not do justice to the wording of s. 672.54. Just as the Crown is wrong, I think, to try to detach the word "appropriate" from the factors listed in s. 672.54 in order to give Review Boards greater "flexibility", so, too, the Crown is wrong, with respect, to try to detach the "least onerous and least restrictive" requirement from its statutory context. Section 672.54 directs the Review Board to have regard to "the other needs of the accused". At the forefront of these "other needs" is the need for treatment.[83]
> (emphasis omitted).

This implies that Review Boards may include in their orders conditions that enter with some detail into the planning of the context within which forensic psychiatric treatment is provided to the NCRMD accused. That question arose again, but in a much more direct fashion, in *Mazzei v. British Columbia (Director of Forensic Services)*.

Vernon Mazzei had been a forensic patient in B.C. since 1986. Over the years, the B.C. Review Board granted Mazzei several conditional releases from the province's major forensic hospital facility. On every occasion Mazzei breached the terms of his release, and was returned to hospital custody. At a Board hearing in 2002, Mazzei's counsel argued that his client, an Aboriginal, wished to attend a First Nations residential rehabilitation program. The hospital treatment team merely sought renewal of the hospital custody order, without suggesting any new therapeutic options for Mazzei. Evidently frustrated at the treatment teams lack of imagination,[84] the Board issued an order concerning Mazzei's continued custodial status that included these three points:

---

[83]   [2003] S.C.J. No. 67, [2004] 1 S.C.R. 498 (S.C.C.) at para. 67.

[84]   "The Board expressed concern over the 'late' and inadequate information provided by Mazzei's case manager and treatment team; his supervising psychiatrist's absence at the hearing; and his case manager's inability to answer many of the Board's questions": [2006] S.C.J. No. 7, [2006] 1 S.C.R. 326, (S.C.C.) at para. 3.

8. THAT for the accused's next hearing the Director undertake a comprehensive global review of Mr. Mazzei's diagnostic formulations, medications and programs with a view to developing an integrated treatment approach which considers the current treatment impasse and the accused's reluctance to become an active participant in his rehabilitation;

9. THAT for his next hearing the Board be provided with an independent assessment of the accused's risk to the public in consideration of the above refocussed treatment plan;

10. THAT the Director undertake assertive efforts to enroll the accused in a culturally appropriate treatment program ... [85]

The Director of Forensic Services appealed from this order. He argued that a bright line should be drawn between the Board's power to make orders concerning an accused's custodial status, and the authority of forensic treatment personnel teams to make decisions concerning treatment matters. The Court agreed that section 672.54 does not grant Review Boards the power to order "a particular course of treatment". This would be inconsistent with the division of powers over health care between the federal and provincial governments. A federal statute such as the Code could not grant a power to make treatment decisions.[86] Nevertheless, the Court proceeded to distinguish between making treatment decisions, and supervising the overall treatment program of an accused. The Court described the latter as lying within the role of the Review Board. The Court elaborated on the distinction between these two roles in this way:

> In essence, conditions "regarding" medical treatment or its supervision are those conditions that Review Boards may impose to ensure that the NCR accused is provided with opportunities for appropriate and effective medical treatment, in order to help reduce the risk to public safety and to facilitate rehabilitation and community reintegration. The scope of this power would arguably include anything short of actually prescribing that treatment be carried out by hospital authorities. It would therefore include the power to require hospital authorities and staff to question and reconsider past or current treatment plans or diagnoses, and explore alternatives which might be more effective and appropriate.[87]

Only by fulfilling such a supervisory role "regarding" treatment can Review Boards properly serve the dual purposes of Part XX.1 — enhancing public safety, while protecting the liberty interests of the accused. To properly perform this role, the Board must be able to "form its own independent opinion of an accused's treatment plan and clinical progress, and ultimately of the accused's risk to public safety and prospects for rehabilitation and reintegration".[88] That is, the Board must be able to assess efficacy of past and proposed treatment plans independently of treating personnel. Its task is not merely to accept what it is told by them about treatment matters. To form an independent assessment, the Board requires adequate information:

[85] *Ibid.*, at para. 4.
[86] *Ibid.*, at para. 34.
[87] *Ibid.*, at para. 39.
[88] *Ibid.*, at para. 42.

These goals simply cannot be accomplished without accurate, independent, and up-to-date information on an accused's mental condition, treatment plan, clinical progress, and prospects for rehabilitation. This justifies a Board's power to supervise the medical treatment provided thus far, and to suggest or explore alternative approaches where necessary. Review Boards may therefore validly require hospital staff to re-examine a diagnosis or a treatment plan, and to consider alternatives which might be more effective or appropriate, — thus requiring hospital authorities to justify their position regarding any "treatment impasse".[89]

With respect to the order that the Director conduct a comprehensive review of Mazzei's diagnosis and current treatment, the Court found that this did not interfere with the medical services approved and implemented by the Director and hospital staff; nor does this condition interfere with the Director's ultimate discretion and authority with respect to the specific treatment provided... It does, however, represent a clear and acceptable limit on the Director's ability to act as the sole judge of the efficacy of a treatment approach, and as a valid exercise of the Board's supervisory powers over the provision of opportunities for appropriate medical treatment.[90]

The Supreme Court thereby made it clear that forensic Review Boards should play an active role in addressing problems arising from the therapeutic relationship between the forensic system and the individual patient.

VI. THE HUMAN RIGHTS DIMENSION OF MENTAL DISABILITY

A. EQUALITY RIGHTS AND MODELS OF DISABILITY

Persons with disabilities have emphasized the social dimension of disability, the degree to which disadvantage experienced as disability is not so much a consequence of biological impairment as of the design of mainstream activities and environments. By failing to take broad ranges of (dis)abilities into account, mainstream design effectively excludes and stigmatizes those who fall outside its narrow norms. This insight lies at the heart of the social model of disability that largely defines the equality rights project of the disability rights movement. Canadian law has largely embraced the social model of disability. This is the signal triumph of the disability rights movement in the quarter-century that has passed since the adoption of the *Canadian Charter of Rights and Freedoms* in 1982. The Supreme Court of Canada has approved this approach to understanding disability in the context of anti-discrimination law:[91]

---

[89] *Ibid.*

[90] *Ibid.*, at para. 57.

[91] The WHO classification reads:

    The World Health Organization (WHO) has adopted an International Classification of Functioning, Disability and Health (ICF) that breaks the phenomenon of disablement into three component dimensions:

    1. Impairment referring to the biological dimension or source of functional limitations;

The true focus of the s. 15(1) disability analysis is not on the impairment as such, nor even any associated functional limitations, but is on the problematic response of the state to either or both of these circumstances. It is the state action that stigmatizes the impairment, or which attributes false or exaggerated importance to the functional limitations (if any), or which fails to take into account the "large remedial component" ... [that] creates the legally relevant human rights dimension to what might otherwise be a straightforward biomedical condition.[92]

For the purposes of human rights law, this understanding and the social model generally leads to a broad understanding of the term "disability". Any biological/physiological impairment, whether real or merely perceived, can be disabling given the social response to it, including features of social design that exclude persons with that impairment from participation.

Therefore, anti-discrimination law in Canada employs a broad understanding of disability that provides protection to the whole spectrum of impairments, from the most serious to those not generally considered to be serious at all. This serves an important interest of equality by contributing to a sense that all people operate on a single continuum of abilities or (dis)abilities, rather than being divided into the able-bodied and the disabled.

B. SECTION 15 OF THE CANADIAN CHARTER OF RIGHTS AND FREEDOMS

The national advocacy organization representing persons with disabilities intervened in *Law Society of British Columbia v. Andrews*,[93] the first section 15 case to reach the Supreme Court. The case concerned a challenge by a non-citizen to a law that limited the practice of law to citizens. The interventions by disability and other groups into a case that might have appeared unrelated to their interests made a real difference: the Court issued a judgment that adopted an understanding of section 15 as promoting substantive rather than formal equality, that is, as seeking to ameliorate conditions of disadvantage in Canadian society.

Eight years later, the Supreme Court elaborated on its substantive understanding of constitutional equality in a case involving persons with disabilities. In *Eldridge v. British Columbia (Attorney General)*,[94] a deaf couple whose child was born prematurely and a deaf individual with various illnesses that required frequent medical attention challenged the failure of the province's

---

2. Activity limitation referring to the inability or difficulty in executing a task or action;

3. Participation restriction referring to limitations to participation resulting from social response and environment.

This model, which is intended to permit standard international classifications of disablement, reduces biology to only one aspect of the problem of disability. It permits recognition of different responses to that problem: biomedical and rehabilitative, social policy, and legal recourses. The legal response is conceived as being most important at the level of addressing participation barriers.

[92] *Granovsky v. Canada*, [2000] S.C.J. No. 29, [2000] 1 S.C.R. 703 (S.C.C.).

[93] [1989] S.C.J. No. 6, [1989] 1 S.C.R. 143 (S.C.C.).

[94] [1997] S.C.J. No. 86, [1997] 3 S.C.R. 624 (S.C.C.).

public health insurance plan and Vancouver General Hospital to cover the costs of sign language interpreters for patients. In a unanimous decision, the Court ruled that section 15 imposes such an obligation on government if needed to ensure that persons with disabilities receive the same benefits that other citizens receive under legislated schemes such as public health insurance. The Court identified the two main objectives of equality rights to be: (1) to prohibit the attribution of untrue characteristics based on stereotyping attitudes (for example, racist or sexist attitudes); and (2) to take into account true characteristics (for example, mobility or communication impairments) that act as barriers to the equal enjoyment of rights and benefits available to mainstream society. The latter objective is particularly important for persons with disabilities. It gives rise to a duty of accommodation. That is, where governments design schemes providing general benefits, they are under a duty to accommodate persons with disabilities so that they have equal enjoyment of those benefits. This duty may be subject to a limit of reasonableness, or undue hardship.[95]

The *Eldridge* reasoning strongly figured in the Supreme Court's 1999 reworking of its equality rights analysis in *Law v. Canada (Minister of Employment and Immigration).*[96] There, the Court reiterated that substantive equality, including the duty to accommodate, lies at the heart of its understanding of equality. It went on to state, however, that in order to succeed on section 15 claims, plaintiffs would need to show that impugned government action had offended their human dignity. This introduced a further step into equality analysis, putting claimants in the position of needing to identify a pejorative or stereotyping element in the state's treatment of their interests. Few section 15 claims based on physical or mental disability have succeeded before the Court since it developed the *Law* test.[97]

With respect to mental disability specifically, the Supreme Court has held claims can be made on the basis of differential treatment, or failure to accommodate, and can be based on a comparison with physical disability. This permitted a successful claim concerning a disability benefits plan that provided inferior benefits for employees with a mental disorder than for those with physical impairments.[98]

---

[95] In *Eldridge, ibid.,* at para. 95, the Court found that the cost of sign language interpreters in medical services would amount to a tiny fraction of the province's overall health insurance budget. It therefore ordered the government of British Columbia to administer its health insurance plans in "a manner consistent with the requirements of section 15(1)" — *i.e.,* to pay for interpretation service as part of health insurance.

[96] [1999] S.C.J. No. 12, [1999] 1 S.C.R. 497 (S.C.C.).

[97] The only successful challenge was *Martin v. Nova Scotia (Workers Compensation Board),* [2003] S.C.J. No. 54, [2003] 2 S.C.R. 504 (S.C.C.), which dealt with a denial of equal Workers Compensation Board benefits to persons with chronic pain syndrome. See discussion of the autism litigation in Section VIII.

[98] *Battlefords and District Co-operative Ltd. v. Gibbs,* [1996] S.C.J. No. 55, 3 S.C.R. 566 (S.C.C.). Benefits for mental disability lasted only so long as the individual was hospitalized, whereas benefits continued indefinitely for employees with physical disabilities.

C. HUMAN RIGHTS LEGISLATION

The *Canadian Charter of Rights and Freedoms* is part of the Constitution and as such applies to the laws of Canada (federal and provincial) and to government actors. The Charter is not, however, the only document protecting equality rights. Each province as well as the federal government has passed human rights statutes which extend rights protections into the most important areas of social activity, including services customarily available to the public (a phrase that incorporates most public and commercial activities), tenancy and employment.[99]

Human rights protections have succeeded in producing a mini-revolution in the way in which employers are required to respond to mental illness in the workplace. The key concept in bringing this revolution about is the duty of accommodation. In a 1999 case, *Meiorin*,[100] the Supreme Court elaborated a powerful understanding of the duty to accommodate in employment. In that case, a female forest firefighter challenged newly introduced standard qualifications as being discriminatory on the grounds of gender. The qualifications included a test of aerobic capacity that could be met by most men in good physical condition, but not by most women. The Court stated that where standard qualifications have the effect of denying employment to an individual on the basis of a protected characteristic, the onus shifts to the employer to establish that the impugned work rule is a *bona fide* work requirement. To do so, the employer must prove that the rule is reasonably necessary to work performance,[101] and that it is impossible to accommodate individual employees sharing the characteristics of the claimant without imposing undue hardship

---

[99] A typical statement governing employment is found in section 13 of the B.C. *Human Rights Code*, R.S.B.C. 1996, c. 210:

> 13(1) A person must not
> (a) refuse to employ or refuse to continue to employ a person, or
> (b) discriminate against a person regarding employment or any term or condition of employment ...
> because of the race, colour, ancestry,... physical or mental disability, sex, sexual orientation or age of that person.
> .....
> (4) Subsections (1) and (2) do not apply with respect to a refusal, limitation, specification or preference based on a bona fide occupational requirement.

[100] *British Columbia (Public Service Employee Relations Commission) v. British Columbia Government and Service Employees' Union (Meiorin)*, [1999] S.C.J. No. 46, [1999] 3 S.C.R. 3 (S.C.C.).

[101] The full three-step test set out by the Court in *Meiorin*, *ibid.*, is:

> 1. The employer adopted the rule for a reason rationally connected to job performance.
> 2. The employer adopted the rule in an honest and good faith belief that it was necessary to work performance.
> 3. The rule is reasonably necessary to work performance. To show this, it must be demonstrated that it is impossible to accommodate individual employees sharing the characteristics of the claimant without imposing undue hardship upon the employer.

In practice, the first two steps rarely emerge as issues, other than in those cases where it is alleged that an employer has acted in bad faith.

upon the employer.[102] There are relatively few circumstances in which individual accommodation is impossible without causing undue hardship.

This concept has been of extraordinary benefit to employees experiencing mental distress or illness. Employers have an obligation to accommodate the employee's illness to the point of undue hardship. This may mean providing leaves of absence, offering counselling programs, providing the opportunity to move to another position where symptoms, such as stress, may be alleviated, or reorganizing work responsibilities. Even if an employer had not previously been aware of an employee's mental health issue prior to becoming concerned about work performance, the duty to accommodate arises once the information is provided. Employers who believe or suspect that emotional or psychological problems lie behind an employee's poor performance or inappropriate conduct may have a duty to make inquiries and offer accommodation.

The defence that a particular accommodation may cause undue hardship to the employer is difficult to establish. Ontario's *Human Rights Code* describes hardships as including only costs incurred by the employer and health and safety reasons may be cited as hardships.[103] An employer may not establish undue hardship by showing that a particular accommodation will lower workplace morale, disturb customers, or interfere with rights set out in a collective agreement, such as seniority provisions.[104]

Most, if not all, collective agreements now either expressly or implicitly incorporate human rights protections into their terms. Therefore, disputes over particular accommodations, and undue hardship, have become routine matters in the grievance and arbitration world of the organized workplace. It is difficult to overstate how influential this push from the labour relations community is to the regularization of these ideas in Canadian society.[105] While unorganized workplaces may not provide the easy access to arbitration and grievance processes that is true of the unionized sector, the same human rights protections apply to both — recourse, however, must be sought through the human rights complaint, investigation and hearing process.

While these breakthroughs in legal protections of workers on the basis of mental disability have had a significant impact for persons already in the workforce, it is questionable how helpful they have been for persons who have little or no attachment to the workforce in the first place. This group includes, of course, individuals with serious mental illness. One explanation is that anti-discrimination laws most benefit those persons who are already employed over those seeking employment at the entry level. The argument for accommodating an existing employee to permit her to remain at work is generally strong. Employees will often have the resources of experienced union representatives,

---

[102] *British Columbia (Superintendent of Motor Vehicles) v. British Columbia (Council of Human Rights)*, [1999] S.C.J. No. 73, [1999] 3 S.C.R. 868 (S.C.C.).

[103] *Human Rights Code*, R.S.O. 1990, c. H.19, s. 17(2).

[104] For an overview of the duty to accommodate under the Ontario legislation, see "Policy and Guidelines on Disability and the Duty to Accommodate" (2000, Ontario Human Rights Commission), online: <http://www.ohrc.on.ca/en/resources/PolicyDisAccomz>.

[105] Michael Lynk, "Accommodating Disabilities in the Canadian Workplace" (1999) 7 Canadian Labour and Employment Law Journal 183.

employer consultants and arbitrators put at their disposal to work out solutions. This is a quite different situation than that faced by the individual who comes cold to an employment opportunity, asking for accommodations of individual needs, and whose only recourse is to pursue a human rights complaint.[106]

D. THE AUTISM SERVICES LITIGATION

The most significant Charter section 15 litigation concerning mental disability in the last several years is that concerning services for children with autism, or autism spectrum disorder (ASD). The litigation has been driven by the demand by parents for a particular treatment modality for their children: intensive behavioural intervention (IBI). Intensive behavioural intervention requires one-to-one behavioural work with an individual child for up to 40 hours each week, generally provided by non-physician health professionals. It can cost up to $60,000 per year. Proponents of IBI believe it to be the only currently known effective therapy that ameliorates the symptoms of autism.

In British Columbia, families of children with autism argued that IBI therapy should be provided as a "medically necessary service" under the province's public health insurance program. When the B.C. government refused, the parents proceeded to court, alleging that the refusal constituted discrimination against their children on the grounds of mental disability. The families succeeded before the B.C. Supreme Court and Court of Appeal. The Supreme Court of Canada overturned these decisions in *Auton v. British Columbia (Minister of Health)*.[107] In a unanimous judgment, the Court determined that Canada's publicly insured health care system does not extend coverage to all therapeutic measures, but only those which fall within the definition of "medically required services" in the *Canada Health Act*, that is, physician services and hospital services. Beyond those services, each provincial government retains the discretion to decide which treatments are sufficiently established and cost-effective to be brought under public coverage.[108] Since children with autism received core medical services equally with all other citizens, they were not the subject of discrimination.

The decision in *Auton* has been subject of extensive criticism by equality rights theorists[109] who find it to be an exercise in the kind of formal equality the

---

[106] For further discussion of this issue, and an empirical overview of disability cases before human rights tribunals in Canada, see J. Mosoff, "Is the Human Rights Paradigm 'Able' to Include Disability: Who's In? Who Wins? What? Why?" (2000) Queen's L. J. 225.
[107] [2004] S.C.J. No. 71, [2004] 3 S.C.R. 657 (S.C.C.).
[108] Chief Justice McLachlin described the benefit provided by Canada's health care system as follows (*ibid.*, at para. 35):
> In summary, the legislative scheme does not promise that any Canadian will receive funding for all medically required treatment. All that is conferred is core funding for services provided by medical practitioners, with funding for non-core services left to the Province's discretion. Thus, the benefit here claimed — funding for all medically required services — was not provided for by the law.
[109] See several essays in two recent collections dealing with s. 15 jurisprudence: S. McIntyre & S. Rogers, *Diminishing Returns: Inequality and the Canadian Charter of Rights and Freedoms* (Markham, ON: LexisNexis Butterworths, 2006), and F. Faraday, M. Denike & M.K.

Court had criticized in *Andrews* and *Eldridge*. The substantive equality issue in the case, going to whether children with ASD were discriminated against by being limited to the same core therapies as everyone else, was not broached by the Court. Instead, the Court found that IBI was an "experimental" therapy which provincial governments were entitled to fund or not fund in their discretion. In the Court's view, this distinguished the claim in *Auton* from that in *Eldridge*:

> *Eldridge* was concerned with unequal access to a benefit that the law conferred and with applying a benefit-granting law in a non-discriminatory fashion. By contrast, this case is concerned with access to a benefit that the law has not conferred. For this reason, *Eldridge* does not assist the petitioners.[110]

Equality rights is a comparative concept. Claimants are required to identify a "comparator group" which is advantaged with respect to the benefit or protection provided by the impugned law, *vis-à-vis* the claimant group. In *Auton* the parents argued that one relevant comparator group was that of "adults with mental illness". That is, they argued that children with ASD are disadvantaged in comparison with adults with mental illness with respect to having their most important therapeutic needs met by public health care. This was a rare occasion when adults with mental illness have been argued to be advantaged relative to another group in society. In actuality, as reflected in the Senate's *Out of the Shadows at Last* Report, many services sought by mental health consumers — such as psychologists' services — are not presently covered by public health care. Not surprisingly, perhaps, the Supreme Court found this comparison unconvincing.

While the *Auton* decision closed the door on constitutional claims to have IBI services provided as a medical service, other claims were made to obtain IBI through educational and social service systems. A series of claims was launched in Ontario against that government's policy of limiting IBI services to children under the age of six. In the *Wynberg v. Ontario* case, parents of autistic children challenged the policy under Charter section 15 as constituting discrimination on grounds both of mental disability and age.[111] Following a year-long trial in which several of North America's leading experts on ASD and IBI testified, Kiteley J. ruled in the parents' favour on both grounds. In July 2006, the Ontario Court of Appeal granted the government's appeal.[112] With respect to the disability discrimination claim, the Court of Appeal ruled that the claimants failed to establish that with respect to the statutory benefit of "special education services", children with autism were differently treated than other "exceptional students" who were eligible for special education. This was largely an evidentiary question that followed from the way in which the case had been structured before the trial court. Concerning the discrimination claim based on

---

Stephenson, *Making Equality Rights Real: Securing Substantive Equality Under the Charter* (Toronto: Irwin Law, 2006).

[110] [2004] S.C.J. No. 71, [2004] 3 S.C.R. 657 (S.C.C.) at para. 38.

[111] [2005] O.J. No. 1228, 252 D.L.R. (4th) 10 (Ont. S.C.J.).

[112] [2006] O.J. No. 2732, 269 D.L.R. (4th) 435 (Ont. C.A.), application for leave to appeal dismissed [2006] S.C.C.A. No. 441 (S.C.C.).

age, the Court of Appeal found that the cut-off at age six did not represent stereotyping of older autistic children as being "irredeemable", and further that the targeting of the IBI program to children under age six corresponded to the pre-school age identified by experts as the "window of opportunity" for IBI.[113]

The long-term impact of the autism litigation remains to be assessed. This may be one instance in which the legal outcome of litigation is less important than its role in mobilizing social forces. In the roughly five years that autism services were the subject of Charter claims in British Columbia and Ontario, IBI services for children with autism greatly expanded across Canada. Several provinces amended legislation in order to make the provision of services for children with developmental disabilities and special needs a more routine and fair process, including new levels of administrative appeal.

At the same time, the relationship of the claim in *Auton* to the social model of disability is problematic. One intervener in the case who identified herself as having autism, Michelle Dawson, opposed the petitioners' claim on the basis that IBI represents a therapy directed at ameliorating or curing the symptoms of autism through behavioural methods. Ms. Dawson opposed the idea underlying the litigation that to be a person with autism is to be faced with ineffable tragedy. Such an idea, she argued, is inconsistent with the social model and its emphasis on acceptance and accommodation of disability.

VII. CONCLUSION

This chapter might have been presented in reverse order. A signal achievement of disability rights movements in Canada and abroad in the past 30 years has been to refocus thinking about disability, including mental disability, in terms of human rights issues. This has involved questioning the significance of biology in disadvantaging persons with disabilities when compared with the impact of social determinants of disadvantage. However, the area of disability that has been least amenable to this kind of analysis is that of mental disorder. There, state interventions directed at treatment and public protection have continued to predominate. This corresponds to the contemporary understanding of mental disorder as having neurobiological causes calling for pharmacological treatment. This chapter has given pride of place and attention to the legal interventions that follow from and support this understanding. In future, legislation directed at mental disorder may come to place greater emphasis on social supports and

---

[113] *Ibid.*, at para. 53:

> Moreover, from its inception, the IEIP was targeted at the two to five age group. It was designed to take advantage of the window of opportunity that all experts agree these children present at that age. It was designed to meet their particular circumstances. The implementation of a program that is so centred on its target group carries no message that would worsen any mistaken preconception that, because of their age, autistic children age six and over are irredeemable compared to the younger group, even if such a pre-existing stereotype existed. In our view, because the focus of the program was entirely on helping the two to five age group, and because it is so tailored to their circumstances, it cannot be taken to say anything demeaning about older autistic children.

access to therapeutic programs sought out by clients themselves, not mandated by Canadian society.[114] We are not there yet.

---

[114] For one thought-provoking attempt to depict what such legislation might look like, see A. Kaiser, "Imagining an Equality Promoting Alternative to the Status Quo of Canadian Mental Health Law" (2003) Health Law J. 185-206.

Chapter 11

DEATH, DYING AND DECISION-MAKING ABOUT END OF LIFE CARE

Joan M. Gilmour*

I. INTRODUCTION

Legal issues involving decision-making at the end of life have long given rise to concern. The Law Reform Commission of Canada noted that when it designed the first in-depth Canadian study on euthanasia, aiding suicide and cessation of treatment in the mid-1970s, "the question of cessation of treatment and, more generally, that of euthanasia, was a constant and urgent concern among members of the medical profession, a number of lawyers and a large proportion of the Canadian public".[1] That observation remains accurate today. While the law has become more settled over the last 30 years, troubling questions still abound. Technological advances, our growing ability to sustain life in circumstances where doing so would have been an impossibility until recently, and new sensitivity to the discriminatory potential in determinations about end of life care mean that decision-making is becoming increasingly complex and difficult, making the need for authoritative guidance more pressing. Even in areas where the law is clear, such as the criminal prohibition on assisted suicide, deep divisions in values and judgment persist, evidenced by strong arguments that the law is failing Canadians and ought to be changed.[2] Other issues remain highly contentious as well. Yet despite numerous government and law commission reports and substantial academic commentary recommending reform, governments have been slow to respond.[3]

---
* I am grateful for the research assistance of Gabrielle Cohen and Paul Martin.
1 Law Reform Commission of Canada, "Euthanasia, Aiding Suicide and Cessation of Treatment", Working Paper 28 (Ottawa: Department of Supply and Services Canada, 1982) at 11.
2 See J. Downie, *Dying Justice: A Case for Decriminalizing Euthanasia and Assisted Suicide in Canada* (Toronto: University of Toronto Press, 2004); B. Sneiderman, "Latimer in the Supreme Court: Necessity, Compassionate Homicide, and Mandatory Sentencing" (2001) 64 Sask. L.R. 511.
3 See, *e.g.*, Law Reform Commission of Canada, *Euthanasia, Aiding Suicide and Cessation of Treatment* (Ottawa: Minister of Supply and Services Canada, 1983); Senate of Canada, *Of Life and Death, Special Senate Committee Report on Euthanasia and Assisted Suicide* (Ottawa:

Given the gravity and difficulty of these issues, and given that they routinely arise in decision-making about end of life care, it is surprising that they have seldom been the subject of legal consideration in Canada. For the most part, there has been little litigation and only limited legislative reform. At the federal level, despite extensive deliberation by a Special Committee of the Senate on euthanasia and assisted suicide, as well as an earlier working paper and report by the Law Reform Commission of Canada, the government has not acted to implement legislative change. Private Members' Bills introduced in the House of Commons over the years have not advanced beyond second reading or referral to committee.[4] Provinces and territories have been more active on the legislative front. Most have enacted legislation to govern substitute decision-making in the event of decisional incapacity; some have also codified requirements for obtaining consent to health care.[5] These initiatives are a welcome advance because they establish a legislatively sanctioned framework for decision-making about health care, including life-sustaining treatment. However, they still leave important questions unanswered.

Although there is a need to clarify and/or reform the law in some respects, it is important to emphasize that many decisions about end of life care are made every day in Canada, and that the great majority of them are absolutely unexceptional from the point of view of law: they are clearly legal. These decisions are already so difficult for all involved that they ought not be made still more fraught by unwarranted concern about what is and is not legally permissible. While there are issues that urgently require guidance, cases in which the law is unsettled are a minority.

This chapter explains the law governing refusal of treatment by patients who are able to make their own decisions about health care, and the legal principles applicable to decision-making about life-sustaining treatment when patients are not competent to do so. It reviews the criminal prohibitions on assisted suicide and euthanasia, and examines how those laws have been applied. It highlights

---

Minister of Supply and Services Canada, 1995), Senate of Canada, Special Subcommittee to Update "Of Life and Death", *Quality End-of-Life Care: The Right of Every Canadian* (Ottawa: Senate of Canada, 2000), online: <http://www.parl.gc.ca/36/2/parlbus/commbus/senate/com-e/upda-e/rep-e/repfinjun00-e.htm>; S. Carstairs, *Still Not There: Quality End-of-Life Care: A Progress Report* (June 2005), online: <http://www.sen.parl.gc.ca/scarstairs/PalliativeCare/Still%20Not%20There%20June%202005.pdf>; Manitoba Law Reform Commission, *Withholding or Withdrawing Life Sustaining Medical Treatment*, Report #109 (Winnipeg: Manitoba Law Reform Commission, 2003); J. Gilmour, *Study Paper on Assisted Suicide, Euthanasia and Foregoing Treatment* (with additional chapters by K. Capen, B. Sneiderman & M. Verhoef) (Toronto: Ontario Law Reform Commission, 1996); J. Downie, *ibid.*

[4] B. Curry, "Parliament's assisted-suicide debate expected to split parties", *Globe and Mail*, (October 14, 2005) at A4, reports on the most recent of these, Bill C-407, *An Act to Amend the Criminal Code (Right to Die with Dignity)*; see generally, *Of Life and Death, ibid.*, App. E, "Legislative Proposals Previously Introduced to Parliament" at A-33-A-34.

[5] See, *e.g.*, *Substitute Decisions Act, 1992*, S.O. 1992, c. 30. On advance directives in Canada, see generally S. Carstairs, *Still Not There: Quality End-of-Life Care: A Progress Report* (June 2005), online: <http://www.sen.parl.gc.ca/scarstairs/PalliativeCare/Still%20Not%20There%20June%202005.pdf> at 41-42, and Dalhousie University Health Law Institute End of Life Project, online: <http://www.as01.ucis.dal.ca/dhli/cmp_advdirectives_faq/default.cfm>.

areas where the law is unclear or contentious, and indicates issues requiring additional clarification or reform. Developments in other jurisdictions where similar issues have arisen, as well as relevant policies that may assist in decision-making are identified as well. This summary of the current state of the law and the controversies and debates that remain outstanding will delineate the legal parameters that govern decision-making, reinforce the standards that patients are entitled to expect as part of adequate end of life care (such as appropriate pain management), and guide decision-makers as new issues arise.

II. WITHHOLDING AND WITHDRAWING POTENTIALLY LIFE-SUSTAINING TREATMENT

A. DECISIONALLY CAPABLE PATIENTS

1. Adults

Health care providers must obtain legally valid consent before treating patients. This requirement is based on individuals' right to bodily integrity, and the respect for autonomy that is basic to the common law. Justice Cardozo's early pronouncement that: "Every human being of adult years and sound mind has the right to determine what shall be done with his own body" has become a guiding precept in decision-making in this area.[6] Competent individuals can decide about the treatment to which they will consent, but also the treatment they will refuse. In *Malette v. Shulman*, a physician who knew an unconscious patient carried a Jehovah's Witness card refusing blood under any circumstances was held liable for battery when he administered a blood transfusion needed to save her life.[7] As the Ontario Court of Appeal noted, the patient had chosen to make her refusal to consent to blood transfusions known in the only way she could, and in doing so, had validly restricted the treatment that could be provided. Her directions governed in a later period of incompetence. The court clearly identified the rights to self-determination and bodily integrity as the controlling values in the doctor-patient relationship: "the right to determine what shall be done with one's own body is a fundamental right in our society. The concepts inherent in this right are the bedrock upon which the principles of self-determination and individual autonomy are based".[8]

The right to consent to or refuse treatment has constitutional dimensions as well. In *Fleming v. Reid*, the Ontario Court of Appeal held that a statute depriving involuntary patients of any right to have prior competent decisions about medication taken into account during a later period of incompetence

---

[6] *Schloendorff v. Society of New York Hospital*, 105 N.E. 92 at 93 (N.Y. 1914), *per* Cardozo J.

[7] *Malette v. Shulman*, [1990] O.J. No. 450, 72 O.R. (2d) 417 (Ont. C.A.), affg [1987] O.J. No. 1180, 63 O.R. (2d) 243 (Ont. H.C.J.); see also *Hobbs v. Robertson*, [2004] B.C.J. No. 1689, 2004 BCSC 1099 (B.C.S.C.) (release executed by patient refusing blood products because of religious faith relieved physician of liability for death of patient resulting from negligently performed operation when effects of negligence could have been remedied by blood transfusion).

[8] *Malette, ibid.*, at para. 41.

breached their constitutionally protected right to security of the person. Writing for the court, Robins, J.A. stated that:

> The common law right to bodily integrity and personal autonomy is so entrenched in the traditions of our law to be ranked as fundamental and deserving of the highest order of protection. This right forms an essential part of an individual's security of the person and must be included in the liberty interests protected by s.7 [of the *Canadian Charter of Rights and Freedoms* [9]]. Indeed, in my view, the common law right to determine what shall be done with one's own body and the constitutional right to security of the person, both of which are founded on the belief in the dignity and autonomy of each individual, can be treated as co-extensive. [10]

A competent patient's refusal of treatment must be honoured by health care providers regardless of the individual's motive, and regardless of whether others consider it ill advised. [11]

Courts have affirmed that patients have the right to refuse treatment even when doing so will result in death. In *B. (N.) v. Hôtel-Dieu de Québec*, Nancy B., a decisionally capable young woman, sought an injunction requiring the hospital in which she was a patient, its staff and her physicians to refrain from administering treatment without her consent, and to stop treatment in progress at her request. [12] Since developing Guillain-Barré syndrome (a neurological disease) three years earlier, she had been permanently paralyzed and unable to breathe without assistance. She wanted to be removed from the ventilator that sustained her life, but was physically unable to do so herself. The suit was not contested, but the defendant hospital and her physician were concerned about their potential criminal liability. The Quebec Superior Court affirmed her right to refuse continued treatment, and made an order permitting her physician to stop respiratory support when she so requested, and to ask the hospital for any necessary assistance "so that everything takes place while respecting the dignity of the plaintiff". [13] Several weeks after this decision, Nancy B. requested that ventilator support be discontinued; she died shortly afterwards. [14] While the court based its decision on the Quebec *Civil Code*'s requirement of patient consent to treatment, the Supreme Court of Canada has confirmed that the judgment in *B.*

---

[9]   *Canadian Charter of Rights and Freedoms*, Part I of the *Constitution Act, 1982*, being Schedule B to the *Canada Act 1982* (U.K.), c. 11.

[10] *Fleming v. Reid*, [1991] O.J. No. 1083, 4 O.R. (3d) 74 (Ont. C.A.) at para. 39, *Conway v. Jacques*, [2002] O.J. No. 2333, 59 O.R. (3d) 735 (Ont. C.A.) at para. 28.

[11] *Fleming v. Reid*, *ibid.*, at paras. 30-36.

[12] [1992] Q.J. No. 1, 86 D.L.R. (4th) 385 (Que. S.C.); see also *Manoir de la Pointe Bleue (1978) Inc. c. Corbeil*, [1992] J.Q. No. 98, R.J.Q. 712 (Que. C.S.) (granting petition of a long-term care institution for a declaration that it must neither administer treatment nor transfer a patient elsewhere without consent when the patient, a 35-year-old man rendered quadriplegic in an accident, had executed a legal directive requesting that he be allowed to die by starvation).

[13] *B. (N.) v. Hôtel-Dieu de Québec*, *ibid.*, at 389-90.

[14] B. Sneiderman, "Decision-Making at the End of Life" in Jocelyn Downie, Timothy Caulfield & Colleen Flood, eds., *Canadian Health Law and Policy*, 2nd ed. (Markham, ON: LexisNexis Butterworths, 2002) at 504.

(N.) v. Hôtel-Dieu de Québec correctly states the law in common law provinces as well:

> Canadian courts have recognized a common law right of patients to refuse consent to medical treatment, or to demand that treatment, once commenced, be withdrawn or discontinued (*Ciarlariello v. Schachter* ...). This has been specifically recognized to exist even if the withdrawal or refusal of treatment may result in death (*Nancy B. v. Hotel Dieu de Quebec* ... and *Malette v. Shulman* ...). [15]
> [citations omitted]

In sum, decisionally capable patients can consent to or refuse even life-sustaining treatment, and once commenced, can withdraw consent and require that treatment be discontinued.[16]

2. Mature Minors

In order to consent to or refuse treatment, an individual must be decisionally capable. The law presumes decisional capacity, that is, that an individual has sufficient ability to understand and appreciate the nature and consequences of treatment and its alternatives to be able to make a decision about whether to proceed with it or not.[17] Obviously, young children cannot satisfy that test. However, many older minors are decisionally capable. Under the "mature minor rule" that is part of the common law, when a minor is able to understand the nature and consequences of a treatment decision, he or she can give legally valid consent to treatment, and physicians cannot rely on parental consent instead.[18] However, although a mature minor can consent to medically recommended treatment, it is not clear whether and to what extent he or she can either refuse such treatment, or consent to treatment that is not beneficial or therapeutic.[19] The argument that a minor can only consent to care that would be of benefit is sometimes referred to as "the welfare principle".[20] It suggests that a mature minor can only make those decisions about medical care that others would consider to be in his or her interests;[21] as such, it challenges the extent to which

---

[15] *Rodriguez v. British Columbia (Attorney General)*, [1993] S.C.J. No. 94, [1993] 3 S.C.R. 519 (S.C.C.) at para. 156.

[16] *Ciarlariello v. Schachter*, [1993] S.C.J. No. 46, [1993] 2 S.C.R. 119 (S.C.C.).

[17] *C. (J.S.) v. Wren*, [1986] A.J. No. 1166, [1987] 2 W.W.R. 669 (Alta. C.A.); *Starson v. Swayze*, [2003] S.C.J. No. 33, [2003] 1 S.C.R. 722 (S.C.C.).

[18] *Johnston v. Wellesley Hospital*, [1970] O.J. No. 1741, 17 D.L.R. (3d) 139 (Ont. H.C.J.); *C. (J.S.) v. Wren, ibid.*, *Van Mol (Guardian ad litem of) v. Ashmore*, [1999] B.C.J. No. 31, 168 D.L.R. (4th) 637 (B.C.C.A.), leave to appeal refused, [2000] B.C.J. No. 1474, 188 D.L.R. (4th) 327 (B.C.C.A.).

[19] See generally J. Gilmour, "Children, Adolescents and Health Care", in *Canadian Health Law and Policy*, 2nd ed. (Markham, ON: LexisNexis Butterworths, 2002), at 213-19; J. Costello, "If I Can Say Yes, Why Can't I Say No? Adolescents at Risk and the Right to Give or Withhold Consent to Health Care" in R.S. Humm, ed., *Child, Parent and State: Law and Policy Reader* (Philadelphia: Temple University Press, 1994), at 490-503.

[20] Manitoba Law Reform Commission, *Minors' Consent to Health Care* (Report No. 91) (Winnipeg: The Commission, 1995) at 5.

[21] B. Sneiderman, J. Irvine & P. Osborne, *Canadian Medical Law: An Introduction for Physicians, Nurses and Other Health Care Professionals*, 2nd ed. (Toronto: Carswell, 1995) at 48-49;

the law will be guided by a commitment to mature minors' interests in self-determination and autonomy, similar to that which prevails *vis-à-vis* adults. In some provinces, aspects of this question have been addressed by legislation. Statutory provisions may explicitly incorporate welfare principles into decision-making.[22] Other provinces provide that on reaching a specified age, minors are presumed capable of consenting to treatment.[23] Still others take the opposite approach and obviate the mature minor rule, at least when child welfare authorities are involved. In Alberta, for instance, courts have held that provincial child welfare legislation displaces the common law mature minor doctrine, such that child welfare authorities can be authorized to consent to treatment regardless of whether the minor is capable of making her own decisions about health care.[24] In those circumstances, the minor does not have the right to refuse treatment considered essential by the treating physicians and accepted as such by child welfare authorities. Child welfare legislation in British Columbia has been interpreted similarly. In *B. (S.J.) (Litigation Guardian of) v. British Columbia (Director of Child, Family and Community Services)*, the British Columbia Supreme Court authorized life-preserving blood transfusions on this basis for a decisionally capable 14-year-old girl suffering from cancer, who refused blood on the grounds of religious conscience as a Jehovah's Witness.[25]

Manitoba Law Reform Commission, *ibid.*, at 5-7.

[22] For instance, in Quebec the *Civil Code* provides that while a minor over 14 can consent to care, the consent of the person having parental authority is also necessary if the care sought is not medically required, entails a serious health risk, and may cause grave and permanent effects — art. 17; F. Campeau, "Children's Right to Health under Quebec Civil Law" in B. Knoppers, ed., *Canadian Child Health Law* (Toronto: Thomson Educational Publishing, 1992), at 209-58; see also R. Kouri & S. Philips-Nootens, "Civil Liability of Physicians Under Quebec Law" in Jocelyn Downie, Timothy Caulfield & Colleen Flood, *Canadian Health Law and Policy*, 2nd ed. (Markham, ON: LexisNexis Butterworths, 2002) at 556-66. In British Columbia, a minor's consent to treatment is effective if the health care provider is satisfied not only that the minor is decisionally capable, but also that the health care is in his or her best interests: *Infants Act*, R.S.B.C. 1996, c. 223, s. 17. New Brunswick has a similar legislative provision governing decisionally capable minors under the age of 16, who can validly consent to medical treatment, provided the medical practitioner or dentist is of the opinion that it is in the best interests of the minor and his or her continuing health and well-being: *Medical Consent of Minors Act*, S.N.B. 1976, c. M-6.1, s. 3.

[23] See, *e.g.*, *Child and Family Services* C.C.S.M. c. C80, s. 25(2).

[24] *Alberta (Director of Child Welfare) v. B.H.*, [2002] A.J. No. 518 (Alta. Q.B.); *C.U. v. McGonigle*, [2003] A.J. No. 238 (Alta. C.A.).

[25] [2005] B.C.J. No. 836, 42 B.C.L.R. (4th) 321 (B.C.S.C.), authorized blood transfusions and ordered that there be no obstruction of the administration of blood to her if needed as part of her cancer treatment. S.J.B. and her parents came to Ontario; B.C.'s Director of Child and Family Services obtained an interim custody order; Ontario courts directed its enforcement. In upholding an earlier order that S.J.B. return to B.C., Paisley J. suggested in *obiter* that even if she were a mature minor and decisionally capable, her refusal of treatment would only have to be followed under the *Health Care Consent Act, 1996*, S.O. 1996, c. 2, Sch. A, in Ontario if she were 16 (*British Columbia (Director of Child, Family and Community Services) v. S.J.B. (Litigation Guardian of)*, Ct. File No. 05-FA-013526 (May 3, 2005) (Ont. S.C.J.)). That statement is in my view incorrect. Justice Paisley relied on a provision in the Ontario legislation meant to ensure that the prior capable "wishes" of people who are decisionally *incapable* are followed; it is inapplicable to a current refusal of treatment by a decisionally capable individual. Justice

Where the issue has not been settled by legislation, questions remain about the applicability of the welfare principle and the extent to which the general regime governing consent to health care in a province or territory will apply to mature minors. The tension reflects an uneasiness with autonomy as the overriding value advanced by the law in this context, rather than protection of the minor's life and health, as the minor is seen as still being vulnerable. It is mitigated somewhat by judicial recognition that the degree of understanding and appreciation of the consequences of the treatment and its alternatives that is required for a finding of decisional capacity will vary with the gravity of the decision.[26] Refusing treatment that is necessary to preserve life legitimately requires a greater appreciation of the ramifications of the decision than refusing less serious treatment. This is not to say that a mature minor can never reject life-sustaining treatment, but that the minor must have sufficient judgment to do so, and that a conclusion the minor is decisionally capable to make such a choice should be subjected to closer scrutiny.

Decisions by mature minors to refuse life-sustaining treatment have been upheld by the courts in some instances, particularly when the refusal was grounded on religious belief. In *Walker v. Region 2 Hospital Corp.* and *Re Y. (A.)*, both of which involved 15-year-old boys with cancer who were Jehovah's Witnesses and refused blood needed in connection with chemotherapy, courts concluded that the boys were mature minors and decisionally capable, based on their thoughtful consideration of both their religious beliefs and their decisions about treatment, as well as their experience of living with the disease.[27] However, prognoses in both of these cases were very poor in any event, the treatment was onerous, and the boys' physicians advised that the treatment required their patients' support in order for it to have a chance of success.[28] In these circumstances, it would have been difficult to justify the treatment as being in their best interests.

The conjunction of being an adolescent with firmly held religious beliefs and a grave illness is not always sufficient to support a finding of decisional capacity, however. While religious faith is a positive and valued attribute, it cannot be equated with, and does not necessarily imply, a co-existing capacity to

Paisley's decision was reversed on appeal, on the basis that he had erred in refusing to hear *viva voce* evidence from the appellants: *British Columbia (Director of Child, Family and Community Services) v. Bahris*, [2006] O.J. No. 2652, 28 R.F.L. (6th) 9 (Ont. C.A.). The issue was moot by that time, however, since S.J.B. and her parents had returned to B.C., reached agreement with the Director allowing treatment in New York at a hospital experienced in treating members of the Jehovah's Witnesses without transfusions, and the B.C. order had been vacated. At the time the Ontario Court of Appeal released its judgment in June 2006, she was considered cancer-free: *ibid.*, at para. 7. In Manitoba, see *Manitoba (Director of Child and Family Services) v. A.C.*, [2007] M.J. No. 26 (Man. C.A.), to similar effect.

[26] See, *e.g.*, *Children's Aid Society of Metropolitan Toronto v. T.H.*, [1996] O.J. No. 2578, 138 D.L.R. (4th) 144 at 171 (Ont. Gen. Div.).

[27] *Walker (Litigation Guardian of) v. Region 2 Hospital Corp.*, [1994] N.B.J. No. 626, 150 N.B.R. (2d) 362 (N.B.C.A.), *Re Y. (A.)*, [1993] N.J. No. 197, 111 Nfld. & P.E.I.R. 91 (Nfld. U.F.C.); see also *Children's Aid Society of Metropolitan Toronto v. L.D.K.*, [1985] O.J. No. 803, 48 R.F.L. (2d) 164 (Ont. Prov. Ct.).

[28] *Walker, ibid.*, at 482; *Re Y. (A.), ibid.*, at 95, 96.

decide about treatment and comprehend the reasonably foreseeable consequences of such decisions.[29] A more positive prognosis may also affect a court's determination, or at least, its assessment of whether a minor actually comprehends what the treatment offers, and what refusing it means. In *B. (S.J.)*, in which the court relied on provincial child welfare legislation to order treatment over a mature minor's objections, the estimated survival rate with the treatment proposed (including the administration of blood) was 70 per cent.[30]

In order for consent to treatment to be valid, the person concerned must not only be able to understand the necessary information about treatments, alternatives, and consequences, but also able to make a choice that is voluntary. In *Re T.T.D.*, the court held that a 13-year-old boy suffering from osteosarcoma (bone cancer) who refused consent to medically recommended chemotherapy and amputation of his leg was not a mature minor. Justice Rothery concluded that the boy was so deeply influenced by his father (who had given him inaccurate information about his condition, the treatment proposed, and the likelihood that non-medical alternative therapies could be successful) that he did not understand and appreciate the result of refusing the treatment proposed, and further, that the structure and dynamics of his family were such that he could not make a voluntary decision about treatment in any event.[31]

A final issue that arises in this area concerns the relationship between the courts' *parens patriae* jurisdiction, which is to be exercised to protect those who are vulnerable, and both legislation extending the presumption of capacity to older minors, and the common law rights of a mature minor.[32] The tension between the sometimes contradictory underlying policies is evident, and authorities are few. In New Brunswick, the Court of Appeal suggested in *Walker* that once it had determined that a minor was mature and decisionally capable, its *parens patriae* jurisdiction was displaced; however, as noted previously, it had also concluded that blood transfusions were not in the minor's best interests in any event.[33] Courts in other provinces have reached the opposite conclusion, holding that in the context of decisions about health care, the common law *parens patriae* jurisdiction is not ousted by legislation, or that legislation has preserved *parens patriae* powers.[34] In that vein, in *B. (S.J.)*, the British Columbia

---

[29]   *Children's Aid Society of Metropolitan Toronto v. T.H.*, [1996] O.J. No. 2578 (Ont. Gen. Div.).

[30]   [2005] B.C.J. No. 836, 42 B.C.L.R. (4th) 321 (B.C.S.C.) at para. 8.

[31]   [1999] S.J. No. 143, 171 D.L.R. (4th) 761 (Sask. Q.B.). Shortly after the court released its decision, the boy's physicians discovered that the cancer had spread, and the proposed treatment could not help him. His parents tried alternative health therapies and other experimental treatment, but he died a few months later (see J. Gilmour, "Children, Adolescents and Health Care", in Jocelyn Downie, Timothy Caulfield & Colleen Flood, *Canadian Health Law and Policy*, 2nd ed. (Markham, ON: LexisNexis Butterworths, 2002), at 218).

[32]   In Manitoba, for instance, the *Child and Family Services Act*, C.C.S.M., c. C80, was amended to provide that child welfare authorities shall not authorize medical treatment for children apprehended under the Act who are 16 years or older without the consent of the child: S.M. 1995, c. 23, s. 2.

[33]   [1994] N.B.J. No. 626, 150 N.B.R. (2d) 362 (N.B.C.A.); *Kennett Estate v. Manitoba (Attorney General)*, [1998] M.J. No. 337, 129 Man. R. (2d) 244 (Man. C.A.).

[34]   *Ney v. Canada (Attorney General)*, [1993] B.C.J. No. 993, 79 B.C.L.R. (2d) 47 at 59 (B.C.S.C.), *B. (R.) v. Children's Aid Society of Metropolitan Toronto*, [1994] S.C.J. No. 24, [1995] 1 S.C.R.

Supreme Court concluded that child welfare legislation in that province was effective to protect the life of a mature minor endangered by her own refusal to accept necessary medical treatment, unconstrained by common law limits placed on the *parens patriae* powers of the court.[35] Taking these cases as a whole, it is apparent that legislation will seldom be held to have supplanted courts' *parens patriae* powers over minors entirely; rather, the two will co-exist and supplement each other.

3. Limitations

Obvious limitations on the right to consent to and refuse treatment are found in sections 14 and 241 of the *Criminal Code*, which vitiate the effect of consent to one's own death and prohibit aiding suicide.[36] In *Rodriguez v. British Columbia (Attorney General)*, an unsuccessful challenge to the constitutionality of the prohibition on assisted suicide, the Supreme Court of Canada held that, although Sue Rodriguez had the right to refuse even life- preserving treatment, she did not have a right to assistance in bringing about her own death, either at common law or under the *Canadian Charter of Rights and Freedoms*.[37] The Court maintained the distinction between refusing treatment, which is permissible even where death will result, and assisting in taking a life, which is unlawful. However, the difference between what constitutes assisting a patient to refuse treatment and assisting the patient to die is not always so clear in practice.[38] In the case of Nancy B., for instance, the actions of third persons removing her from the ventilator were characterized as assisting her to refuse continued treatment. They could equally well have been characterized as assisting her to die, since the result that would follow (and indeed, was intended) was obvious to all. Nonetheless, whether always logically defensible or not, the difference in legal consequences between the two is clear.

B. DECISIONALLY INCAPABLE PATIENTS

1. Patients with Advance Directives

Most Canadian provinces have passed legislation making provision for some form of advance directive. While referred to by different names (personal directive, health care directive, power of attorney for personal care, and others), they are meant to provide people who are decisionally capable with a means to retain some control over decisions about their treatment in the event of a later period of incompetence. The statutory regimes are not uniform, but the types of directives permitted fall into two basic categories. Advance directives may allow a decisionally capable individual either to designate someone to make decisions about health care on his or her behalf (proxy

---

315 (S.C.C.).

[35] [2005] B.C.J. No. 836, 42 B.C.L.R. (4th) 321 (B.C.S.C.) at para. 70.

[36] R.S.C. 1985, c. C-46.

[37] [1993] S.C.J. No. 94, [1993] 3 S.C.R. 519 (S.C.C.).

[38] B. Sneiderman, "The Rodriguez Case: Where Do We Go from Here?" (1999) 2 Health L.J. 1.

directive), or to specify types of treatment that he or she wants accepted or rejected, should the need arise (instructional directive). It may also be possible to combine the two. Since statutory regimes governing advance directives and consent to health care vary from province to province, the specific provisions in the jurisdiction in question should be reviewed to determine what is permitted.[39] Some provinces allow for reciprocity as well, such that advance directives executed in other jurisdictions can be honoured.[40] Where a patient has executed a legally valid advance directive that is applicable in the circumstances, then the patients' instructions (as to the treatment, decision-maker or both) must be followed. Substitute decision-makers' authority will be limited by applicable statutory provisions.[41]

---

[39]   Ontario: *Health Care Consent Act, 1996*, S.O. 1996, c. 2, Sch. A, *Substitute Decisions Act, 1992*, S.O. 1992, c. 30; British Columbia: *Representation Agreement Act*, R.S.B.C. 1996, c. 405, *Health Care (Consent) and Care Facility (Admission) Act*, R.S.B.C. 1996, c. 181; Alberta: *Personal Directives Act*, R.S.A. 2000, c. P-6; Saskatchewan: *Health Care Directives and Substitute Health Care Decision Makers Act*, S.S. 1997, c. H-0.001; Manitoba: *Health Care Directives Act*, C.C.S.M. c. H27, *Child and Family Services Act*, C.C.S.M. c. C80, s. 25; Quebec: *Civil Code of Québec*, S.Q. 1991, c. 64, arts. 10-25, 2130-2185; New Brunswick: *Infirm Persons Act*, R.S.N.B. 1973, c. I-8; Nova Scotia: *Medical Consent Act*, R.S.N.S. 1989, c. 279; Prince Edward Island: *Consent to Treatment and Health Care Directives Act*, R.S.P.E.I. 1988, c. C-17.2; Newfoundland and Labrador: *Advance Health Care Directives Act*, S.N.L. 1995, c. A-4.1; Yukon Territory: *Health Act*, R.S.Y. 2002, c. 106, *Adult Protection and Decision-Making Act*, S.Y. 2003, c. 21, Sch. A; Northwest Territories: no legislation, although the *Powers of Attorney Act*, S.N.W.T. 2001, c. 15 may support creation of a living will; Nunavut: no legislation. In British Columbia, the *Adult Guardianship and Personal Planning Statutes Amendment Act, 2006*, 2nd Sess., 38th Parl., would formalize the status of advance directives (instructional directives), in addition to representation agreements (proxy directives) which are already recognized (First reading April 27, 2006) online: <http://www.leg.bc.ca/38th2nd/1st_ read/gov32-1.htm>.

[40]   Carstairs, *Still Not There: Quality End-of-Life Care: A Progress Report* (June 2005) online: <http://www.sen.parl.gc.ca/scarstairs/PalliativeCare/Still%20Not%20There%20June%202005 .pdf>; British Columbia, Saskatchewan, Manitoba, Ontario and P.E.I. have provided for this type of reciprocity.

[41]   For instance, physicians owe an independent duty of care to the patient, not only at common law but pursuant to s. 215 of the *Criminal Code*, R.S.C. 1985, c. C-46: "Everyone is under a legal duty ... to provide necessaries of life to a person under his charge if that person is unable, by reason of ... illness ... to withdraw himself from that charge". If a physician had reason to believe the substitute decision-maker's instructions were not in keeping with the prior capable wishes or, failing that, best interests of the patient, the physician cannot simply comply with such instructions — see generally, B. Sneiderman, "Decision-Making at the End of Life" in Jocelyn Downie, Timothy Caulfield & Colleen Flood, eds., *Canadian Health Law and Policy*, 2nd ed. (Markham, ON: LexisNexis Butterworths, 2002) at 510. See also G. Godlovitch, I. Mitchell, C. Doig, "Discontinuing life support in comatose patients: an example from Canadian case law" (2005) 172(9) C.M.A.J. 1172, commenting on an Alberta decision, *In the Matter of Robert Kenneth Durksen, Dependent Adult* (September 16, 1999) Lethbridge/Macleod DA06-02070 (JCQBA) (Alta. Surr. Ct.), in which it was held that court approval was required before a public guardian could authorize discontinuation of ANH.

2. Patients without Advance Directives: Prior Capable Instructions or Wishes

In many respects, legislation governing advance directives, substitute decision-making and consent to health care has overtaken the common law. However, there are Canadian jurisdictions without legislation on the subject; even where legislation is in place, it may not apply to particular situations, or an individual may not have complied with the legislative requirements for a valid advance directive. In the absence of legislation, the common law will govern. Decisions such as *Malette v. Shulman* establish that at common law, an individual's instructions about future care or the identity of designated decision-makers should prevail in treatment decisions after the onset of incapacity.[42] Both *Malette v. Shulman* and *Fleming v. Reid* suggest that such directions need not have been expressed in any particular manner.[43] Judicial recognition of advance instructions in cases such as these is consistent with the very high value that the law places on self-determination.

In some jurisdictions, that approach is now mandated by legislation as well. In Ontario, for instance, the *Health Care Consent Act, 1996* directs the substitute decision-maker for a decisionally incapable person who has not executed a power of attorney for personal care (the term used to refer to advance directives in that province) to follow the individual's prior capable wishes about health care, if these are known and applicable in the circumstances.[44] "Wishes" need not be contained in a power of attorney to be binding; they can be expressed orally, in writing, or in any other manner.[45] Statutory regimes vary among provinces; regard should be had to the legislation that governs in the province in question.

3. Patients without Advance Directives: Best Interests

Most people have not executed an advance directive, and their wishes about treatment may not be known. Even existing advance directives may be inapplicable in the circumstances. Where a patient is decisionally incapable and the substitute decision maker does not know of a preference that applies to the situation and is sufficiently precise to guide treatment decisions, then both at common law and under applicable statutory regimes, determinations about treatment are to be made in the patient's best interests.[46]

---

[42] [1990] O.J. No. 450, 72 O.R. (2d) 417 (Ont. C.A.), affg [1987] O.J. No. 1180, 63 O.R. (2d) 243 (Ont. H.C.J.). The Canadian Medical Association, Canadian Nurses Association and Canadian Healthcare Association issued a "Joint Statement on Preventing and Resolving Ethical Conflicts Involving Health Care Providers and Persons Receiving Care" that recognizes as one of the principles of the therapeutic relationship that health care decisions should be consistent with the patient's known preferences, either found in an advance directive or communicated orally — 160(12) C.M.A.J. 1757, 1758 (June 15, 1999), online: <http://www.cha.ca/documents/joint.htm>.

[43] *Malette v. Shulman, ibid.*, at 431 (Ont. C.A.); *Fleming v. Reid*, [1991] O.J. No. 1083, 4 O.R. (3d) 74 at 85-86 (Ont. C.A.). *Malette* was cited with approval in *Rodriguez v. British Columbia (Attorney General)*, [1993] S.C.J. No. 94, [1993] 3 S.C.R. 519 at 598.

[44] S.O. 1996, c. 2, Sch. A, s. 21.

[45] *Ibid.*, s. 5.

[46] As to the common law, see *Eve v. Mrs. E.*, [1986] S.C.J. No. 60, 31 D.L.R. (4th) 2 (S.C.C.); for

Any assessment of an individual's best interests must be based on an underlying value system, a conception of what constitutes "the good", both for that person and generally. In the past, decisions about the treatment that would be in a patient's best interests have often neither articulated the underlying choice of values on which the determination was made, nor justified that choice over other possibilities. Legislation that identifies criteria to guide determinations about best interests makes the values and interests that are to be taken into consideration when making decisions about treatment on behalf of others much more explicit. In Ontario's *Health Care Consent Act, 1996* for example, substitute decision-makers are directed to consider *inter alia* consistency with the person's value system formed while capable, his or her preferences, the burdens and benefits of the treatment and alternatives, including non-treatment, and which alternative would be least restrictive or intrusive.[47] Clearly, if each of these factors were assessed individually, they might suggest different conclusions about whether to consent to or refuse treatment. It is not always clear how such conflicts should be resolved. However, substitute decision-makers are subject to oversight and intervention; when challenged in court or before a tribunal, their decisions are evaluated on a standard of correctness.[48] In contrast, tribunal decisions assessing a patient's best interests are generally reviewed using a standard of reasonableness.[49]

4. Types of Treatment Substitute Decision-makers Can Refuse

A substitute decision maker must decide about treatment in accordance with the decisionally incapable person's prior capable directions or wishes, or if none are known or applicable, based on his or her best interests. He or she must also comply with applicable legislative restrictions. This general framework for decision-making applies to decisions about life-sustaining treatment as well. Absent any statutory restrictions, a substitute decision-maker can legitimately conclude that it is not in an incapable person's best interests to consent to or continue treatment, even if that treatment is necessary to preserve life. There is no distinction drawn in law between withholding and withdrawing treatment. Concluding that a person's best interests lie in foregoing life-sustaining treatment can be an agonizing decision to make, and is not a decision that will

---

an example of a statutory best interests test, see the *Health Care Consent Act, 1996*, S.O. 1996, c. 2, Sch. A, s. 21; *Conway v. Jacques*, [2002] O.J. No. 2333, 59 O.R. (3d) 735 (Ont. C.A.) (when the patient's prior capable wish is not applicable to changed circumstances, the substitute decision-maker is to decide in the patient's best interests, and not try to determine what the patient would have decided in light of changed circumstances).
[47] *Health Care Consent Act, 1996, ibid.*; *Scardoni v. Hawryluck*, [2004] O.J. No. 300, 69 O.R. (3d) 700 (Ont. S.C.).
[48] *B. (R.) v. Children's Aid Society of Metropolitan Toronto*, [1994] S.C.J. No. 24, [1995] 1 S.C.R. 315 (S.C.C.); *A.M. v. Benes*, [1999] O.J. No. 4236, 46 O.R. (3d) 271 (Ont. C.A.); *Scardoni v. Hawryluck, ibid.*
[49] *T. (I.) v. L. (L.)*, [1999] O.J. No. 4237, 46 O.R. (3d) 284 (Ont. C.A.); *Conway v. Jacques*, [2002] O.J. No. 2333, 59 O.R. (3d) 735 (Ont. C.A.). However, when interpreting the law, the standard applied is one of correctness: *Starson v. Swayze*, [2003] S.C.J. No. 33, [2003] 1 S.C.R. 722 (S.C.C.) at para. 5, *per* McLachlin J.

be taken lightly. It requires careful consideration of the benefits and burdens of treatment, as well as the totality of the person's circumstances and welfare.

It is sometimes suggested that the provision of artificial nutrition and hydration (ANH) is in a different category, such that a substitute decision-maker cannot decline this form of treatment. Common bases for this claim are that medical therapies are invasive in ways that artificial nutrition is not, or that feeding is a form of care rather than treatment, or that foregoing artificial nutrition differs from refusing other forms of life-sustaining treatment because death will certainly result, or because of its special symbolic or emotional significance.[50] These arguments are not well-founded. Artificial nutrition and hydration are forms of medical treatment like other types of life-sustaining treatment that support or replace normal bodily functions, such as ventilators and dialysis.[51] Other than a few decisions involving decisionally capable individuals, Canadian courts have seldom addressed the issue of foregoing ANH.[52] However, courts in the United States and the United Kingdom have consistently held that artificial nutrition and hydration are forms of life-prolonging medical treatment like other types of life support.[53] Patients can refuse ANH, and unless prohibited or restricted by statute, substitute decision-makers can do so on behalf of decisionally incapable persons as well, either pursuant to their prior capable instructions or wishes, or failing that, when doing so is in the patient's best interests.

5. Disagreement Among Family Members

There are two aspects to decision-making about life-sustaining treatment when a patient is decisionally incapable. Consideration must be given not just to how to decide, but also who decides. Where a statutory framework is in place, it will include a means to identify the appropriate substitute decision-maker. Absent an appointed substitute or someone designated in an advance directive, the substitute decision-maker will be a family member willing and able to act, with priority being determined by the degree of their relation to the person con-

---

[50] See, *e.g.*, P. Derr, "Why Food and Fluids Can Never Be Denied" (1986) Hastings Center Rep. 28; *Of Life and Death, Special Senate Committee, Report on Euthanasia and Assisted Suicide* (Ottawa: Minister of Supply and Services Canada, 1995) at 42.

[51] The Special Senate Committee also concluded that artificial nutrition and hydration are types of treatment, and consequently, just as with other forms of life-sustaining treatment, can be withheld or withdrawn in appropriate circumstances — *Of Life and Death, Special Senate Committee Report on Euthanasia and Assisted Suicide, ibid.*, at 45. See also D. Casarett, J. Kapo & A. Caplan, "Appropriate Use of Artificial Nutrition and Hydration — Fundamental Principles and Recommendations" (2005) 353 N.E.J.M. 2607; S. Post, "Tube Feeding and Advanced Progressive Dementia" (2001) 31 Hastings Center Report 36.

[52] G. Godlovitch, I. Mitchell, C. Doig, "Discontinuing life support in comatose patients: an example from Canadian case law" (2005) 172(9) C.M.A.J. 1172-73.

[53] See, *e.g.*, *Airedale NHS Trust v. Bland*, [1993] 2 W.L.R. 359 (H.L.); A. Meisel, "Barriers to Foregoing Nutrition and Hydration in Nursing Homes" (1995) 21 Am. J. Law & Med. 334 at 353, listing the many American appellate decisions that have accepted that artificial nutrition and hydration are forms of life-prolonging treatment, and that decisions to cease ANH can be considered in the same way as other forms of such treatment.

cerned.[54] Legislation usually identifies a default decision maker such as the Public Trustee if no one in the family can or will take on the responsibility.[55] In jurisdictions without legislation governing consent to health care, Sneiderman explains that for incompetent patients without an advance directive, the physician "should be the central figure in the decision-making process" about life-sustaining treatment; provided the decision is medically reasonable, the law has "refrained from interfering".[56] The family will and should still be consulted, but absent legislated decision-making authority, its role is to facilitate but not control decision-making.

Conflict may arise not only between family members and health care providers, but also among family members. While in theory this should be resolved by either the terms of the patient's advance directive, if there is one, or if not, by the operation of the statutory framework that designates which family member(s) are authorized to act as substitute decision-maker, that is not always the case. Even when there is a designated substitute decision-maker, other family members may disagree vehemently with his or her decisions about the person's care, and especially, about continuing life-sustaining treatment. Again, there are no Canadian cases that address this issue.

The controversy surrounding the case of Terry Schiavo in the United States highlights the potential that such conflicts could arise in Canada as well. Terry Schiavo was a young woman who suffered a cardiac arrest in 1990 that left her in a coma, which evolved into a persistent vegetative state.[57] She was cared for in a nursing home, and although her husband and parents initially agreed on treatment plans, after a few years, disagreements ensued about what treatment to pursue. Her parents urged aggressive therapy, while her husband, who was her legal guardian, wanted basic care because her prognosis for neurological recovery was hopeless. Her parents began a 10-year series of legal challenges to her husband's guardianship and his attempts to refuse medical treatment. The courts concluded there was clear and convincing evidence of Terry's prior capable wishes that she did not want to be "kept alive on a machine".[58] When Terry's parents were unsuccessful in the courts, they turned to political intervention. In 2003, following a second, court-ordered removal of Terry's feeding tube, the Florida legislature passed what came to be known as "Terry's law", which gave the state governor the prerogative of re-inserting it, and required the appointment of a special guardian *ad litem* to review her case. Although that law was later deemed unconstitutional by the Florida Supreme

---

54   See, *e.g.*, *Health Care Consent Act, 1996*, S.O. 1996, c. 2, Sch. A, s. 20.
55   *Ibid.*
56   B. Sneiderman, "Decision-making at the End of Life" in Jocelyn Downie, Timothy Caufield & Colleen Flood, eds., *Canadian Health Law and Policy*, 2nd ed. (Markham, ON: LexisNexis Butterworths, 2002) at 511-13.
57   The description and chronology of events are described in R. Cranford, "Facts, Lies and Videotapes: The Permanent Vegetative State and the Sad Case of Terry Schiavo" (2005) 33 J.L.M.E. 363 at 364-70.
58   *In re Guardianship of Schiavo*, 780 So.2d 176 (Fla. 2d DCA 2001); *In re Schiavo*, 2002 WL 31817960 (Fla. Cir. Ct. Nov. 22, 2002); *In re Guardianship of Schiavo*, 800 So.2d 640 (Fla. 2d Dist. Ct. App. 2003); *Schiavo ex rel. Schindler v. Schiavo*, 2005 U.S. Dist. LEXIS 4265 (Fla. 2d Dist. Ct. 2005).

Court, the guardian *ad litem* did complete a comprehensive medical and legal summary of her care, concluding that the process and substance of proceedings had conformed with the guidelines in Florida law.[59] During the last week of her life, the U.S. Congress passed legislation to move the case from the Florida state courts to the federal court system, but the Florida District Court and the 11th Circuit Court of Appeals held that the evidence submitted by her parents was insufficient to justify a new trial or review.[60] The case sparked immense national and international interest. Media attention was intense and unrelenting during the last year of Terry's life. Right to life groups and disability rights activists staged sit-ins outside the nursing home, with Terry's parents and other members of her family pleading to save her life. Finally, after again being authorized by court order and pursuant to her husband's instructions, artificial nutrition and hydration were discontinued and Terry died in April 2005.

The *Schiavo* case gave rise to extensive debate and reflection in the United States. It called into question the basis on which decisions about end of life care are made in that country, highlighting concerns about the sufficiency of the evidence relied on in applying the substituted judgment standard typically used to guide substitute decision-making (which aims to identify the decision the patient would make if able to do so). It is not that the law could not respond to Terry Schiavo's situation — it did, repeatedly — but that its application gave rise to serious second thoughts about the framework that had been legislated. Some commentators have suggested that by demonstrating the shortcomings in living wills and substituted judgment, the case may have shattered the consensus about end of life care built up over years through a series of state laws and court decisions.[61] However, as Carl Schneider points out, even if Terry Schiavo had expressed her wishes more clearly, or had executed an advance directive, it would not have made a difference; her parents had indicated that "they would have fought to have it voided because they did not believe it was consistent with their and her beliefs".[62] Others argue that Schiavo will not lead to lasting changes in decision-making about end of life care, particularly given the courts' rulings and the well-established rights of incompetent patients.[63] While the framework that governs substitute decision-making in the United States is not identical to that in Canada, there are similarities, and developments in American case law on issues that arise in end of life care have informed many of our conclusions about what is and is not acceptable. The attempted political

---

[59] J. Wolfson, "Erring on the Side of Theresa Schiavo: Reflections of the Special Guardian ad Litem" (2005) 35 Hastings Center Report 16.

[60] *Schiavo ex re. Schindler v. Schiavo*, 358 F.Supp.2d 1161 (M.D. Fla. 2005), affd *Schiavo ex rel. Schindler v. Schiavo*, 403 F.3d 1298 (11th Cir. (Fla.) 2005), rehearing en banc denied *Schiavo ex rel. Schindler v. Schiavo*, 404 F.3d 1270 (11th Cir. (Fla.) 2005), rehearing denied *Schiavo ex rel. Schindler v. Schiavo*, 404 F.3d 1282 (11th Cir. (Fla.) 2005), stay denied *Schiavo ex rel. Schindler v. Schiavo*, 544 U.S. 957, 125 S.Ct. 1722 (2005).

[61] See, *e.g.*, R. Dresser, "Schiavo's Legacy: The Need for an Objective Standard" (2005) 35 Hastings Center Report 20.

[62] C. Schneider, "Hard Cases and the Politics of Righteousness" (2005) 35 Hastings Center Report 24, quoting Terry Schiavo's guardian *ad litem*, 358 F.Supp.2d 1161 (M.D. Fla. 2005).

[63] L. Hampson & E. Emmanuel, "The Prognosis for Change in End-of-Life Care After the Schiavo Case" (2005) 24 Health Affairs 972.

interventions by state and federal governments in Terry Schiavo's care are reflective of a very different political environment in the United States, and unlikely to find any counterpart in Canada. However, we are not immune to family disagreements. While Americans have been far more litigious about end of life care than Canadians, the same kind of conflict among family members could certainly occur here as well, and could result in litigation.

The controversy also brought evolving views about end of life care and disability to the fore. Commenting on the role of the disability community as events unfolded towards the end of Terry Schiavo's life, Adrienne Asch emphasized that:

> ... the apprehension in the disability community, apprehension about societal indifference and neglect, is more understandable after reviewing a few of the many instances in which law, medicine, bioethics and government programs failed to help traumatically disabled patients discover the financial, technological, social, and psychological resources that could sustain them and provide the opportunity for rewarding life. When people with relatively intact cognitive and emotional capacities are neglected, neglect is even more likely for those with greatly diminished cognitive and emotional function. [64]

She urges incorporation of a disability equality perspective into assessments of both family decision-making and patients' "supposedly autonomous" decisions about ending life-sustaining treatment, as well as increased support to enable people with disabilities to live their lives, rather than simply endorsing treatment withdrawal. However, as Martha Minow has noted, while one may undervalue the life of an individual who cannot speak for himself, on the other hand, "one may also in unconscious and well-meaning cruelty greatly underestimate the extent of the suffering and deprivations experienced".[65] There are occasions when it is in a person's best interests not to continue to fight death. In the United States, *Blouin, Administratrix of the Estate of Pouliot v. Spitzer* is a case in point.[66] It demonstrates the damage that can result when a surrogate's ability to avoid harmful treatment at the end of an incompetent patient's life is inappropriately limited. In that case, New York law precluded a surrogate from terminating life-sustaining treatment without clear proof of the incapacitated person's intent. Sheila Pouliot was a terminally ill and severely developmentally disabled 42-year-old woman who was admitted to hospital with gastrointestinal bleeding and pain, associated with what the examining physicians concluded was a terminal illness. They advised that further treatment would likely prolong her suffering. Her family, after meeting with her treating physicians, the hospital ethics committee and clergy, asked that treatment, including ANH, be withheld and only palliative treatment be provided. Even a guardian *ad litem* appointed at the instance of the hospital petitioned the court to terminate all nutrition and

---

[64] A. Asch, "Recognizing Death While Affirming Life: Can End of Life Reform Uphold a Disabled Person's Interest in Continued Life?" (2005) 35(6) Hastings Center Special Report S31-S36 at S32.

[65] "Beyond State Intervention in the Family: Baby Jane Doe" (1985) U. Mich. J.L. Reform 933 at 961.

[66] 356 F.3d 348 (2nd Cir. 2002); see also *In the Matter of Scott Matthews*, 225 A.D. 2d 142, 650 N.Y.S. 2d 373, 1996 N.Y. App. Div. LEXIS 12210 (N.Y.S.C. App. Div. 1996).

hydration. The state's insistence on continuing artificial nutrition and hydration against all medical advice and against the wishes of her family, until finally halted by court order after numerous court proceedings, demonstrated a misguided effort to avoid discriminating against a dying patient on the basis of disability. It resulted in a death that has been described as "torturous".[67] The governing legislation has since been amended to permit the guardian of a mentally retarded person to decide to withhold life-sustaining treatment, including ANH, where there is no reasonable hope of maintaining life, or it poses an extraordinary burden. While Asch raises the possibility of setting limits on the law's commitment to patient autonomy in end of life care to counteract the constant devaluation of the lives of people with disabilities, cases like that of Sheila Pouliot are a reminder that any proposal to do so must take real account of the potential that such measures could do great harm as well.

6. Minors

Parents are recognized as the substitute decision-makers for their decisionally incapable children at common law, and absent an express appointment of someone else, are also designated as such in provincial statutes governing consent to health care. Parents are under a legal duty to ensure their children are provided with needed medical care, and when making decisions about their child's health care, must act in his or her best interests.[68] However, they are not entirely free to choose or refuse medical treatment for their child in accordance with their own beliefs, no matter how conscientiously held.

Both at common law and under the *Canadian Charter of Rights and Freedoms,* protecting a child's life and promoting his or her well-being are recognized as important functions of the state; it will intervene when necessary to protect the child's life or health.[69] For instance, in *B. (R.) v. Children's Aid Society of Metropolitan Toronto,* the Supreme Court of Canada held that a temporary wardship order was appropriate to permit the Children's Aid Society to consent to treatment when Jehovah's Witness parents had refused consent to a blood transfusion needed to prevent serious injury to their daughter's health.[70] Thus, although parents are accorded a "protected sphere" of parental decision-making, their ability to depart from medical recommendations in determining what is in their child's best interests is circumscribed.

More difficult issues arise when the appropriate course of treatment is less clear, as is often the case when considering withholding or requiring other types of potentially life-prolonging treatment that are not as widely accepted, or that impose serious burdens on the recipient, or offer physically beneficial effects that are less apparent, or entail serious risk of other harmful effects. Courts reject basing decisions about withholding life-preserving treatment on

---

[67] A. Ouellette, "When Vitalism is Dead Wrong: The Discrimination Against and Torture of Incompetent Patients by Compulsory Life-Sustaining Treatment" (2004) 79 Indiana L.J. 1.

[68] *B. (R.) v. Children's Aid Society of Metropolitan Toronto,* [1994] S.C.J. No. 24, [1995] 1 S.C.R. 315 (S.C.C.).

[69] *Ibid.*

[70] *Ibid.*

judgments about the quality of an individual's life. In *British Columbia (Superintendent of Child and Family Services) v. Dawson*, the British Columbia Supreme Court reversed a Provincial Court decision and authorized surgical intervention to replace a shunt in an institutionalized child with severe disabilities over the opposition of his parents.[71] The surgery was medically recommended and would improve the child's condition. Non-treatment would have significant deleterious effects. The court concluded that no one could judge the quality of life of the child's life to be so low as not to be worth continuing; decisions about treatment could not be made on that basis.

This is not to say that life-sustaining treatment can never be withheld from a child; there have been instances where courts have upheld parents' decisions not to pursue aggressive treatment. In *Saskatchewan (Minister of Social Services) v. P. (F.)*, the Saskatchewan Provincial Court denied the government's application to have an infant declared in need of protection when his parents decided not to seek a liver transplant for him. [72] While the child's chances of survival with the transplant were good, and death was certain and imminent without it, the court noted that the child would always suffer serious side effects, some of which were themselves potentially life-threatening, that the decision necessarily involved not just medical considerations but important psychological, social and emotional components as well, and most significantly in the court's view, that the parents' decision was "made totally within the bounds of current medical practice", and "did not depart" from values that society expects from thoughtful, caring parents of a terminally ill child. While medical opinion is highly significant, it will not always be determinative. In *Couture-Jacquet v. Montreal Children's Hospital*, the court supported the family's decision not to have their young child undergo another course of chemotherapy, despite medical recommendations.[73] The burden the treatment would impose on her, the damage it would cause, and the very small chance of benefit, justified the decision to forego treatment.

To summarize, while the cases recognize a permitted sphere of parental decision-making about children's health care, their discretion is subject to boundaries, defined by the courts and by societal expectations of those charged with the care of those who are most vulnerable. It is not always clear from the limited jurisprudence when parental decision-making will cross the line, particularly when the treatment is risky and burdensome, and the benefits few or unlikely. Where the burden of continued treatment far exceeds the benefits, parents and the health care team may agree that it is appropriate to withdraw life-sustaining treatment, and there is no need for the involvement of child welfare authorities or courts. Withdrawing life-sustaining therapies is an accepted part of end of life care in Canadian hospitals, and proceeds in accordance with accepted medical practice and parental consent. It is where

---

71　[1983] B.C.J. No. 38, 145 D.L.R. (3d) 610 (B.C.S.C.), revg (*sub nom. Re D. (S.)*) [1983] B.C.J. No. 663, 42 B.C.L.R. 153 (B.C. Prov. Ct.). See also *New Brunswick (Minister of Health and Community Services) v. B. (R.)*, [1990] N.B.J. No. 404, 106 N.B.R. (2d) 206 (N.B.Q.B.), *Re Goyette: Centre de Services Sociaux de Montréal*, [1983] C.S. 429 (Que. C.S.).

72　[1990] S.J. No. 708, 69 D.L.R. (4th) 134 at 143 (Sask. Prov. Ct.).

73　[1986] Q.J. No. 258, 28 D.L.R. (4th) 22 (Que. C.A.).

there is disagreement over a proposed plan of treatment by parents or health care providers with serious consequences for the life or health of the child that courts may become involved. Given the law's strong orientation towards preserving life and protecting those who are vulnerable, especially children, in those situations courts will not often conclude that it is in a child's best interests that life support be withdrawn.

III. PAIN AND SYMPTOM CONTROL IN PALLIATIVE CARE

Palliative care is "care aimed at alleviating suffering — physical, emotional, psychosocial, or spiritual — rather than curing. It is concerned with the comfort of the suffering individual".[74] While still a relatively new field, it is widely acclaimed as a treatment option for patients with diseases that are not responsive to curative options. In its 1995 report, *Of Life and Death*, the Special Senate Committee on Euthanasia and Assisted Suicide found that access to palliative care was seriously inadequate. A decade later, Senator Sharon Carstairs concluded in her 2005 report on progress in providing quality end of life care, *Still Not There*, that serious deficiencies in access continued to prevail; estimates are that no more than 15 per cent of Canadians have access to palliative hospice care.[75] Significant disparities exist across the country not only in access, but also in quality of care and cost to the patient.

An important part of palliative care is the management of pain and disease symptoms. Although adequate pain control can be achieved for all but a minority of patients, reality often falls short. The Supreme Court of Canada has clearly accepted that the administration of drugs for pain control in dosages that the physician knows may hasten death where it is necessary to achieve the therapeutic purpose of relieving suffering is acceptable medical practice.[76] Yet as the Special Senate Committee noted in *Of Life and Death*, despite the medical profession's ability to control pain, physicians frequently do not administer the medication required because of misplaced concern about the possibility of addiction, or because of potentially life-shortening effects.[77] There are strong arguments that both the common law duty of care that health professionals owe to their patients and professional standards of practice require practitioners to provide patients with adequate pain management to relieve suffering.

---

[74] Senate of Canada, *Of Life and Death, Special Senate Committee Report on Euthanasia and Assisted Suicide* (Ottawa: Minister of Supply and Services Canada, 1995) at 14.

[75] Online: <http://www.sen.parl.gc.ca/scarstairs/PalliativeCare/Still%20Not%20There%20June%202005. pdf> at 1.

[76] *Rodriguez v. British Columbia (Attorney General)*, [1993] S.C.J. No. 94, [1993] 3 S.C.R. 519, 607 (S.C.C.).

[77] Senate of Canada, *Of Life and Death, Special Senate Committee Report on Euthanasia and Assisted Suicide* (Ottawa: Minister of Supply and Services Canada, 1995) at 28-29. See also D. Hoffman and A. Tarzian, "Dying in America — An Examination of Policies that Deter Adequate End-of-Life Care in Nursing Homes" (2005) 33 J. L. Med. Ethics 294.

Physicians' legal, ethical and professional obligations require them to ensure appropriate pain relief.

Palliative care may include the use of total sedation, that is, "the practice of rendering a person totally unconscious through the administration of drugs without potentially shortening life".[78] It is sometimes employed to support terminally ill patients suffering intolerable pain that cannot be relieved by other forms of treatment; patients with dyspnea (shortness of breath) and delirium with agitation may also require such sedation.[79] As the Senate Committee noted, "the legal status of this practice is clear. If the sedation is done with the informed consent of the patient or the patient's surrogate, it is legal".[80] Health professionals acknowledge that when the practice is extended to terminal sedation, it will have the effect of shortening life, although this is not the purpose for which it is provided. The justification for this practice is based on informed consent and the principle of double effect, that is, that the intent is to terminate the patient's symptoms, not the patient's life.[81]

IV. DENYING TREATMENT: THE FUTILITY DEBATES

Substitute decision-makers acting pursuant to the legislative framework or, if none is applicable, common law principles can decide that treatment should be withheld or withdrawn because it is futile.[82] More often, however, it is health care providers who want to end treatment while the family wants it continued; physicians may conclude that treatment is useless because the patient cannot benefit, while families urge that basic life functions can be maintained or restored, and that this patient's life, even if one of biologic existence only, should be preserved. Difficult decisions must be made about where decision-making power lies in these instances, and also about whether and how concerns about access to resources by this patient and others should be taken into account in decision-making. The issues are not just economic; health care providers raise legitimate concerns about the morality of being required to provide what they

---

[78] Senate of Canada, *Of Life and Death, Special Senate Committee Report on Euthanasia and Assisted Suicide, ibid.*, at 14.

[79] E. Latimer, "Euthanasia, Physician-Assisted Suicide and the Ethical Care of Dying Patients" (1994) 151 C.M.A.J. 1133 at 1134.

[80] Senate of Canada, *Of Life and Death, Special Senate Committee Report on Euthanasia and Assisted Suicide* (Ottawa: Minister of Supply and Services Canada, 1995) at 33.

[81] D. Sulmasy & E. Pellegrino, "The Rule of Double Effect: Clearing Up the Double Talk" (1999) 159(6) Arch. Intern. Medicine 545 (on ethical acceptability). But see *contra* H. Kuhse, "From Intention to Consent: Learning from Experience with Euthanasia", in M. Battin, R. Rhodes & A. Silvers, eds., *Physician Assisted Suicide: Expanding the Debate* (New York: Routledge, 1998), at 252, 258-59; and D. Orentlicher, "The Supreme Court and Terminal Sedation: An Ethically Inferior Alternative to Physician-Assisted Suicide", in M. Battin, R. Rhodes & A. Silvers, eds., *ibid.*, at 301.

[82] *London Health Sciences Centre v. K. (R.) (guardian ad litem of)*, [1997] O.J. No. 4128, 152 D.L.R. (4th) 724 at 735 (Ont. Gen. Div.).

consider ineffective and sometimes damaging therapy to a patient contrary to their own beliefs and those of the medical profession generally.[83]

A. DEVELOPMENTS IN THE UNITED STATES AND ENGLAND

The debate about futile treatment began in the early 1980s in the United States, sparked by studies demonstrating the ineffectiveness of cardiopulmonary resuscitation (CPR) for certain categories of patients.[84] Although the issue has been addressed in a number of lawsuits in the United States, it cannot be said there is a consensus on the issue comparable to the one recognizing a patient's right to refuse life-sustaining treatment. However, American courts have generally not been prepared to both go against family wishes and authorize a step that would result in a patient's life ending, at least in circumstances where it is apparent that family members are actively involved and trying conscientiously to determine the patient's best interests.[85] Further, a number of states have enacted legislation restricting circumstances in which life-sustaining treatment can be withheld from a decisionally incapable person at the instance of a substitute decision-maker, even if all involved in the patient's care agree that treatment is futile and ought not be continued.[86]

English courts have been both more deferential to medical opinion, and willing to acknowledge financial constraints on the health care system as a factor that can be taken into account by a health authority in decision-making.[87] Yet the issue of how decisions are to be made about futile treatment is not

---

[83]   See generally J. Gilmour, *Study Paper on Assisted Suicide, Euthanasia and Foregoing Treatment* (Toronto: Ontario Law Reform Commission, 1996) at 229-35; J. Gilmour, "Death and Dying", in M.J. Dykeman, J. Morris, L. Bayne & J. Barry, eds., *Canadian Health Law Practice Manual* (Markham, ON: LexisNexis Butterworths, 2000), at 8.34-8.43; *Scardoni v. Hawryluck,* [2004] O.J. No. 300, 69 O.R. (3d) 700 (Ont. S.C.).

[84]   J. Paris, "Pipes, Colanders and Leaky Buckets: Reflections on the Futility Debate" (1993) 2 Cambridge Q. Healthcare Ethics 147; M. Gordon, "Cardiopulmonary Resuscitation in the Elderly Long-Term Care Population: Time to Reconsider" (1994) 27 Ann. R.C.P.S.C. at 81-83.

[85]   The issue first came to the fore in ethical debate in the 1990s in the U.S., with the case of Helga Wanglie, an elderly woman in a persistent vegetative state who was dependent on a respirator. The hospital where she was a patient wished to remove her from the ventilator; her husband and family did not. Although the only issue before the court was determining who should act as substitute decision-maker (it settled on the husband), the question of futile treatment was clearly the subtext that prompted the hospital to commence the application in court. Helga Wanglie died three days after the court made its order, still on a ventilator: M. Angell, "The Case of Helga Wanglie: A New Kind of 'Right to Die' Case" (1991) 325 N.E.J.M. 511-12. See, *e.g., Baby K,* 382 F. Supp. 1022 (E.D. Va. 1993), affd, 16 F.3d 590 (4th Cir. 1994), cert. denied 115 S. Ct. 91 (1994), and generally, J. Gilmour, *Study Paper on Assisted Suicide, Euthanasia and Foregoing Treatment* (Toronto: Ontario Law Reform Commission, 1996) at 231, and references cited therein.

[86]   A. Ouellette, "When Vitalism is Dead Wrong: The Discrimination Against and Torture of Incompetent Patients by Compulsory Life-Sustaining Treatment" (2004) 79 Indiana L.J. 1.

[87]   *Airedale NHS Trust v. Bland,* [1993] W.L.R. 359 (H.L.); *R. v. Cambridge Health Authority, ex p. B.,* [1995] 2 All E.R. 129 (C.A.); *Re G.,* [1995] 2 F.C.R. 46 (Fam. Div.) (application by hospital to withdraw life support; patient's wife not opposed but patient's mother opposed — application granted).

settled in that country either, except to the extent that courts have confirmed a significant, ongoing role for the judiciary in decision-making.[88] Thus, in *An NHS Trust v. B.*, an application by a hospital seeking approval for the withdrawal of life support from an infant with a serious, disabling and fatal degenerative neuromuscular condition, the court held that, although both the views of the child's parents and the treating physicians about treatment required careful consideration in its deliberations, determining the child's "objective best interests" remained its responsibility.[89] It ordered that ventilator support must be continued, but did not require that CPR or antibiotic therapy be repeated. Despite the generally deferential attitude to medical judgment in England, courts have increasingly recognized that these decisions engage more than medical considerations.

Judges in England have also become more supportive of the rights of competent patients, not only to consent to or refuse treatment, but importantly, to require the provision of treatment necessary to preserve life. In *R. (Ex p. Burke) and the General Medical Council*, the claimant, a decisionally capable 44-year-old man, suffered from a degenerative neurological condition similar to multiple sclerosis that left him severely disabled; he would eventually require artificial nutrition and hydration (ANH).[90] The medical evidence was that he would retain his full cognitive faculties even during the end stages of the disease. He brought an application challenging the General Medical Council's guidelines, "Withholding and Withdrawing Life-prolonging Treatments: Good Practice in Decision-Making". Burke was concerned that the guidelines would permit a physician to withdraw ANH from him against his will, causing him acute physical and mental suffering and eventually, his death; he wanted to ensure that he would be provided with ANH until he died of natural causes, and that the decision remained his, rather than a physician's.[91] On appeal to the House of Lords, the court emphasized that the case did not engage concerns about either allocation of scarce resources or access to experimental therapy; rather, the treatment sought was "a routine staple" provided to many people with

---

[88] *R. (Ex. P. Burke) and the General Medical Council*, [2004] EWHC 1879 (Admin.), (2004) 79 B.M.L.R. 126, [2005] Q.B. 424, [2005] 2 W.L.R. 431 at paras. 195-211 (noting understanding in England that some medical procedures, while not unlawful in themselves, nonetheless require the prior sanction of the court).

[89] [2006] EWHC 507 (Fam.) (requiring continuation of ventilator support, but authorizing hospital and physicians to refrain from providing certain other forms of life support); see also *Wyatt v. Portsmouth Hospital NHS Trust*, [2005] EWCA Civ. 1181, [2005] 3 F.C.R. 263 (C.A.), 86 BMLR 173, for a similar analysis of the decision-making process. And see *An NHS Trust v. D.*, [2005] EWHC 2439 (Fam.); [2006] 1 F.L.R. 638, holding that it was not in the best interests of D., a 32-year-old woman suffering from a terminal genetic neurological illness who was in a vegetative state (likely with no awareness) and no prospect of improvement, to try to prolong her life. Accordingly, over the opposition of D.'s parents and relatives but with the support of the Official Solicitor acting on behalf of D., the court granted the NHS Trust's application for a declaration that it need not take invasive steps to treat her, should she contract a potentially life-threatening condition or her breathing fail.

[90] [2004] EWHC 1879 (Admin.), (2004) 79 B.M.L.R. 126, [2005] Q.B. 424, [2005] 2 W.L.R. 431.

[91] *Ibid.*, at para. 6.

a range of conditions, and without great expense.[92] The court accepted that, given the statutory mandate of the General Medical Council (the self-regulating body for physicians in the U.K.), it was appropriate for it to give advice on matters such as this. However, insofar as such advice asserts or assumes propositions of legal principle, it is amenable to judicial review in order to identify and correct any legal error.[93]

The court issued a declaration that the claimant's decision or valid advance directive indicating that he wanted to be provided with ANH would be determinative of his best interests, at least where death was not imminent and he was not comatose (when different considerations may prevail). Failure or refusal to comply by a hospital caring for him would breach his rights under the European Convention of Human Rights (and from the court's analysis, likely its common law duties of care as well).[94] It also held that prior judicial authorization is required before ANH can be withheld or withdrawn from a patient where there is any doubt or disagreement about the patient's competence, best interests, condition or prognosis with and without ANH, or where there is evidence that the patient resists or disputes withdrawing ANH (even if incompetent), or that the person when competent, or other persons with "a reasonable claim to have their views or evidence taken into account", such as family members, assert that withdrawing ANH contravenes the patient's wishes or is not in his or her best interests.[95] The House of Lords strongly affirmed the existence of a right to require life-preserving treatment. That right, shaped in part by the European Convention on Human Rights, is an important new consideration that will have to be taken into account in future decisions. It is not yet clear how it will be affected by considerations of access to scarce resources, or to experimental or innovative therapies; both these factors had been held to appropriately limit claims for treatment in earlier decisions.[96]

B. CANADA

In Canada, there are almost no cases that consider how to resolve disputes about whether continued treatment is futile.[97] In *Child and Family Services of Central Manitoba v. Lavallee*, an infant had been left in a persistent vegetative state following a savage attack three months after birth, and had been immediately taken into care by child welfare authorities. There was no hope that his condition would improve; it was only a matter of time until he contracted a life-threatening illness. His physician recommended a "Do Not Resuscitate" order be

---

[92] *Ibid.*, at paras. 27-29.
[93] *Ibid.*, at paras. 33, 215.
[94] *Ibid.*, at paras. 214-5, 225.
[95] *Ibid.*, at para. 214(*g*).
[96] *R. v. Cambridge Health Authority ex p. B.*, [1995] 2 All E.R. 129 (C.A.).
[97] *London Health Sciences Centre v. K. (R.) (guardian ad litem of)*, [1997] O.J. No. 4128, 152 D.L.R. (4th) 724 (Ont. Gen. Div.) began as an application by a hospital for a declaration that it could lawfully discontinue all life-support measures to a patient in a persistent vegetative state, despite his spouse's refusal to consent. However, since she did eventually consent during the course of the proceedings, it was not necessary for the court to determine that issue.

placed on the boy's chart; his parents refused consent.[98] The Manitoba Court of Appeal agreed that a DNR order was appropriate, but concluded that because a DNR order authorizes *non*-treatment, not treatment, neither parental nor judicial consent was required. It considered the decision to write such an order purely a matter of medical judgment. It approved of the order indirectly, however, noting that while it seemed counter-intuitive, the best interests of a child could lie in being permitted to die:

> it is in no one's interest to artificially maintain the life of a terminally-ill patient who is in an irreversible vegetative state. That is unless those responsible for the patient being in that state have an interest in prolonging life to avoid criminal responsibility for the death.[99]

The court's analysis of the meaning of "treatment" and the ambit of the physician's authority in *Lavallee* is troubling, and in my view, incorrect. Part of the difficulty arises from the convention that has developed with respect to CPR — that consent is presumed unless it has been specifically refused, leading to the expectation that that CPR will always be performed in the event of cardiac arrest even when inappropriate as a treatment modality.[100] It follows logically that in order not to administer CPR, consent is required to depart from the norm. This is not true of other treatments. The court's conclusion that "treatment" must refer to some positive intervention is not tenable in light of this background.[101] A DNR order is generally one part of a plan for treatment; a treatment plan cannot sensibly be accepted or rejected if an integral part of it is carved out by an

---

[98] *Child and Family Services of Central Manitoba v. Lavallee*, [1997] M.J. No. 568, 154 D.L.R. (4th) 409 (Man. C.A.). The *Child and Family Services Act*, C.C.S.M. c. C80, s. 25, provided that where a child has been apprehended by child welfare authorities and parents refuse to consent to recommended medical treatment, the agency can apply to the court for authorization to treat, a determination to be made in the best interests of the child.

[99] *Ibid.*, at para. 8.

[100] Canadian Medical Association, Canadian Nurses Association, Canadian Healthcare Association, Catholic Health Association of Canada, "Joint Statement on Resuscitative Interventions" (1995) 153 C.M.A.J. 1652A-C, at 1652A.

[101] J. Gilmour, *Study Paper on Assisted Suicide, Euthanasia and Foregoing Treatment* (Toronto: Ontario Law Reform Commission, 1996) at 57-60. The claim that DNR orders are not "treatment" was rejected by the President's Commission for the Study of Ethical Problems in Medicine and Biomedical and Behavioral Research, *Deciding to Forego Life-Sustaining Treatment* (Washington, D.C.: U.S. Government Printing Office, 1983) at 241, note 39, and the New York State Task Force on Life and the Law (see R. Baker, "The Legitimation and Regulation of DNR Orders", in R. Baker, M. Strosberg & J. Bynum, eds., *Legislating Medical Ethics: A Study of the New York State Do-Not-Resuscitate Law* (Dordrecht: Kluwer Academic Publishers, 1995) at 50-51. See also J. Downie, "Unilateral Withholding and Withdrawal of Potentially Life-Sustaining Treatment: A Violation of Dignity Under the Law in Canada" (2004) 20 J. Palliative Care 143. Requirement for consent is grounded not only on the law regarding liability for battery, but also on respect for capacity for self-determination. Barney Sneiderman, "Decision-Making at the End of Life" in Jocelyn Downie, Timothy Caulfield & Colleen Flood, eds., *Canadian Health Law and Policy*, 2nd ed. (Markham, ON: LexisNexis Butterworths, 2002) at 517, suggests that whether one agrees with the reasoning in *Lavallee* or not, it reflects reality for many incompetent patients, because families typically accept the judgment and recommendations of the attending physician.

artificial distinction between the positive and negative aspects of the plan. Consequently, it should be considered "treatment", and subject to the generally applicable provisions regarding substitute decision-making. In some provinces, "treatment" is defined to include a "treatment plan", which in turn includes withholding and withdrawing treatment.[102] There is an important role for a substitute decision-maker in determining whether such an order is appropriate for the person concerned; this is not purely a medical decision.

The argument that competent patients and substitute decision-makers have a role in decision-making about a DNR order finds indirect support in one of the few other Canadian decisions involving a dispute about the futility of treatment. In *Sawatzky v. Riverview Health Centre Inc.*, a Manitoba physician had entered a DNR order in the case of an elderly patient (a man for whom he considered CPR futile), first without the knowledge of the patient's wife, and then in the face of her opposition.[103] The Public Trustee had earlier been appointed the patient's guardian, but, relying on *Lavallee*, had refused to take any position with respect to the DNR order. On application by the patient and his wife, an interlocutory injunction was issued withdrawing the DNR order pending receipt of medical reports respecting the patient's condition. The presiding judge urged that the matter be resolved out of court if possible. She also ordered the Public Trustee to represent the interests of the patient on the application, strongly criticizing her "complete abdication of her responsibility to Mr. Sawatzky, for whom she is responsible".[104] Mediation involving all parties ensued but without a final resolution; Mr. Sawatzky died several months following the initial decision.[105]

Health care providers' associations have developed policy statements to guide decision-making on this issue. The Canadian Medical Association, Canadian Nurses Association, Canadian Healthcare Association and the Catholic Healthcare Association of Canada issued a Joint Statement on Resuscitative Interventions.[106] Relative to CPR, it distinguishes between treatment that is medically futile or non-beneficial, and instances where the benefit of treatment can only be determined "with reference to the person's subjective judgment about his or her overall wellbeing". Although the policy states that physicians determine questions of medical futility, and that there is no obligation to offer futile or non-beneficial treatment, it adds that "As a general rule, a person should be involved in determining futility in his or her own case".

Shortly after *Sawatzky* was decided, the same organizations released a "Joint Statement on Preventing and Resolving Ethical Conflicts Involving Health Care Providers and Persons Receiving Care".[107] It provides that the primary goal of care is benefit to the recipient, and that persons who are competent have the right to determine what constitutes a benefit. However, it also affirms that health

---

[102] See, *e.g.*, *Health Care Consent Act, 1996*, S.O. 1996, c. 2, Sch. A.
[103] [1998] M.J. No. 506, 167 D.L.R. (4th) 359, [1999] 6 W.W.R. 298 (Man. Q.B.).
[104] *Ibid.*, at para. 52.
[105] N. Moharib, "Victor in Resuscitation — Issue Case Dies, Wife Had Battled Successfully for Court Decision", *Winnipeg Sun* (October 28, 1999) at 6.
[106] (1995) 153 C.M.A.J. 1652 A-C.
[107] (1999) 160(12) C.M.A.J. 1757.

care providers should not be required to participate in procedures contrary to their professional judgment or values, or those of the treating facility (referencing the earlier Joint Statement on Resuscitative Interventions and futility).[108] The potential for conflict between the two approaches (patient and provider autonomy) is apparent. The College of Physicians and Surgeons of Ontario approved a policy on "Decision-Making for the End of Life" in 2002 (updated 2006).[109] It states that patients have the right to receive life-sustaining treatment that may be of benefit to them, but that physicians are not obliged to provide treatment that almost certainly will not benefit the patient, and should not begin or maintain treatment that will almost certainly not be of benefit or may be harmful to a patient. If conflicts about treatment cannot be resolved, the physician may offer to transfer care. If the patient is incapable, the policy refers physicians to the "structure for managing conflicts" set out in the *Health Care Consent Act, 1996*. Under the statute, application can be made to a tribunal to resolve disputes about substitute decision-making. While these policy statements do not have legal force, courts do rely on and defer to institutional policies and standards of practice. It is difficult to know what message they should or would draw from these; the concepts of benefit and futility remain contested, and the division of power among patients, families, physicians and health care providers remains unclear.

Concerns about continuing treatment that is in fact harmful to a patient, and about allocating scarce resources to costly therapies that are ineffective are legitimate. However, using the language of futility without addressing the assumptions underlying that terminology can give the illusion that the characterization of futility is not and cannot be contested.[110] There are two different emphases in definition among the many writers on this topic. One focuses on probability of success of the treatment in order to divide decision-making power between physicians and patients or substitute decision-makers; the other focuses on the overarching decision-making model in health care (which in this context becomes the stronger claim of patient or substitute decision-maker choice of or demand for treatment, rather than simply informed consent to treatment proposed).[111] Still others meld the two, proposing that questions of physiologic futility (treatment cannot achieve the goal) be determined by physicians and qualitative futility (goal is evaluated) be determined by patients or their representatives.[112] Arguments for physician determination of futility rest on unproven assumptions of unanimity (at least,

---

[108] (1995) 153 C.M.A.J. 1652 A-C.

[109] Online: <http://www.cpso.on.ca/Policies/endoflife2.htm>.

[110] M.Z. Solomon, "How Physicians Talk About Futility" (1993) 21 J. Law Med. & Ethics 231 at 235, suggesting "the tendency to cloak value judgments in technical, medical jargon may serve a psycho-social function: the terms used may allow all involved to avoid discussing difficult value questions".

[111] Contrast N. Jecker & L. Schneiderman, "Medical Futility: The Duty Not to Treat" (1993) 2 Cambridge Q. Healthcare Ethics 151, and R.D. Truog, A.S. Brett & J. Frader, "The Problem with Futility" (1992) 326 N.E.J.M. 1560.

[112] See, *e.g.*, K. Christiansen, "Applying the Concept of Futility at the Bedside" (1992) 1 Cambridge Q. Healthcare Ethics 242 at 244.

among physicians): first, about the goals of treatment, and second, about the likelihood of achieving those goals. It is also important to recognize that unilateral physician decision-making about questions of futility is a departure from the model of shared decision-making in consent to health care, which assumes that patients and substitute decision-makers are capable of making reasonable choices with good information. That model originated, at least in part, to address the power imbalance that exists between doctors and patients, which remains an ongoing concern. The tension between the two has not yet been resolved.

Perhaps because it is the only jurisdiction in Canada in which the issue of decision-making about futile treatment has been judicially considered (with all the attendant publicity), Manitoba has continued to give this issue careful attention at the policy level, first in a 2003 Report by the Manitoba Law Reform Commission, and more recently, in a draft policy established by that province's College of Physicians and Surgeons.[113] The Law Reform Commission distinguished between the well-recognized right of a competent patient to refuse treatment, and the question of whether patients have a positive right to require life-sustaining or life-prolonging treatment, concluding that although there are no Canadian cases on point, and that a variety of potential arguments may be raised based on constitutional grounds and federal and provincial legislation, "as a general proposition ... the physician has the ultimate power to withhold or withdraw life sustaining treatment *without the consent of the patient*".[114] Recognizing the contentious nature of the issue, it proposed policies and principles to guide decision-making. They are meant to ensure fairness to the patient and family and encourage consensus, but at the same time, to affirm the physician's right to withhold or withdraw life-sustaining treatment where such treatment would be "medically inappropriate or professionally unethical".[115] Despite the importance of autonomous decision-making and personal control in health care, it rejected the idea of a "right to indefinite life sustaining medical treatment", because of concern that it could result in unreasonable demands for unlimited and inappropriate treatment, and that such demands could and would be extended well beyond end of life care.[116]

Following the Law Commission's lead, and beginning from the premise that in Manitoba, the law regarding who has legal authority to decide these matters is "ambiguous", in 2006 the provincial College of Physicians and Surgeons proposed a process for physicians to follow when considering withholding or withdrawing life-sustaining treatment.[117] In addition to situations where a patient refuses treatment or there is consensus, it provides that a physician can withhold

---

[113] Manitoba Law Reform Commission, *Withholding or Withdrawing Life Sustaining Medical Treatment*, Report #109 (Winnipeg: Manitoba Law Reform Commission, 2003); College of Physicians and Surgeons of Manitoba, "Statement: Withholding and Withdrawing Life-Sustaining Treatment" (proposed June 2006), online: <http://www.cpsm.mb.ca/about/news/2006/10/16/38189_0610160758-046?pageNumber=1>.
[114] *Ibid.*, at 4.
[115] *Ibid.*, at 12.
[116] *Ibid.*, at 13.
[117] Online: <http://www.cpsm.mb.ca/about/news/2006/10/16/38189_0610160758-046?pageNumber=1>.

or withdraw treatment that is not medically indicated (no realistic chance of achieving the minimum goal) or not medically appropriate (chance of achieving the minimum goal poor and/or significant negative effects on patient, or expected duration of effective treatment short) without consensus, if the processes it outlines have been followed, and notice of intent to do so has been given. The proposed processes include assisting in transferring care to another physician where possible, obtaining a second opinion, and attempting to reach consensus about appropriate treatment.

Recent writing on this subject in Canada avoids using the language of "futility" in an attempt to avoid becoming mired in intractable disputes. The Manitoba Law Reform Commission eschewed the term because of both its "pejorative connotation", and its undue emphasis on evaluating the life of the person concerned. Jocelyn Downie, too, has suggested that because there is so little agreement about what "futility" means, different terminology should be employed:[118] unilateral withholding and withdrawal of potentially life-sustaining treatment. Both are deliberate efforts to distance their proposals from the unproductive and circular arguments that have typically marked discussion of the issue, in effect concluding that the language of futility has itself become futile, at least as a basis for policy development. Unlike the Manitoba Law Reform Commission, however, Downie argues that in cases of irreconcilable disagreement between health care providers and the patient or surrogate, the matter must be resolved by a court, rather than through unilateral physician action if informal dispute resolution has been unsuccessful. In her view, there is no room for a health care provider to unilaterally withhold treatment outside clear cases where the treatment demanded cannot succeed at any level. The two are at opposite poles on this issue.

There are no Canadian cases addressing the question of boundaries on either the decision-making authority of patients and substitute decision-makers to require treatment, or on the power of health care providers, institutions and health insurance plans to deny it when it is claimed that treatment is futile. While there have been a few lawsuits about access to health care, they are of limited assistance.[119] The legality of denying access to publicly funded treatment to particular individuals because of a judgment that it cannot assist, given the gravity of their underlying disease or disability, has rarely been

---

[118] Manitoba Law Reform Commission, *Withholding or Withdrawing Life Sustaining Medical Treatment*, Report #109 (Winnipeg: Manitoba Law Reform Commission, 2003) at 12; J. Downie, "Unilateral Withholding and Withdrawal of Potentially Life-Sustaining Treatment: A Violation of Dignity Under the Law in Canada" (2004) 20 J. Palliative Care 143.

[119] See, *e.g.*, *Auton (Guardian ad litem of) v. British Columbia (Attorney General)*, [2004] S.C.J. No. 71, 2004 SCC 78 (S.C.C.), *Cameron v. Nova Scotia (Attorney General)*, [1999] N.S.J. No. 297 (N.S.C.A.) (unsuccessful claims to have state fund treatment (for autism and IVF respectively) that is not included in the public health plan); *Chaoulli v. Quebec (Attorney General)*, [2005] S.C.J. No. 33, 1 S.C.R. 791 (S.C.C.) (successful constitutional challenge to prohibition on purchasing private health insurance if services cannot be accessed in a timely manner in the publicly funded system); *Eldridge v. British Columbia (Attorney General)*, [1997] S.C.J. No. 86, 3 S.C.R. 624 (S.C.C.) (successful claim that the support (sign language interpreters) needed to extend the benefit of publicly funded health services to people not able to access them because of disability (hearing impairment) must be provided).

judicially considered.[120] The issue has ramifications under the *Canadian Charter of Rights and Freedoms*, as well as human rights legislation, the *Canada Health Act*, and other federal and provincial legislation. It raises societal concerns, not just medical considerations, and entails questions about the designation of decision-makers, boundaries on their authority, resource allocation and access that would better be addressed at the level of policy, and not just in individual cases.

V. SUBSTITUTE DECISION-MAKING AND ORGAN DONATION AFTER CARDIAC DEATH

Consent to organ donation when a patient has died has not been controversial in Canada for years. Following the lead of the 1968 Report of the Ad Hoc Committee of the Harvard Medical School to Examine the Definition of Brain Death, Canadian organizations such as the Canadian Medical Association and others have clearly accepted the concept of brain death as a valid basis for determining death.[121] Legislation governing organ and tissue transplantation for the most part does not define death, but rather, accepts medical determination of death as authoritative, typically providing that for the purposes of post-mortem transplant, death must be determined by at least two physicians "in accordance with accepted medical practice".[122] Until recently in Canada, post mortem organ donations were only considered when individuals met the criteria for brain death (donation after brain death, or DBD).[123] However, changing practices in the United States and a number of European countries led the Canadian Council for Donation and Transplantation to sponsor a national forum in 2005 to consider

---

[120] See now *Flora v. Ontario (Health Insurance Plan, General Manager)*, [2007] O.J. No. 91 (Ont. Div. Ct.).

[121] "Report of the Ad Hoc Committee of the Harvard Medical School to Examine the Definition of Brain Death" (1968) 205 J.A.M.A. 85; Canadian Medical Association, "A C.M.A. Position – Guidelines for the Definition of Brain Death" (1987) 136 C.M.A.J. 200A-B; S.D. Shemie, C. Doig, E.B. Dickens *et al.*, "Severe brain injury to neurological determination of death: Canadian forum recommendations" (2006) 174(6) C.M.A.J. S1-S12. Definitions of death may vary depending on the context — for instance, medicine and the civil law may differ from the criminal law — *R. v. Green*, [1988] B.C.J. No. 1807, 43 C.C.C. (3d) 413 (B.C.S.C.). On developments in the legal definition of death generally, see J. Gilmour, *Study Paper on Assisted Suicide, Euthanasia and Foregoing Treatment* (Toronto: Ontario Law Reform Commission, 1996) at 35-40, and note 69, at paras. 8.5-8.11.

[122] For example, *Trillium Gift of Life Network Act*, R.S.O. 1990, c. H.20, s. 7(1). Of all the provinces and territories, only Manitoba specifically recognizes brain death — *Vital Statistics Act*, R.S.M. 1987, c. V60, s. 2. In *Criteria for the Determination of Death* (Report No. 15) (Ottawa: Supply and Services Canada, 1981) at 25, the Law Reform Commission of Canada recommended legislation recognizing that a person is dead when an irreversible cessation of all that person's brain function occurs, determined on the basis of prolonged absence of spontaneous circulatory and respiratory functions, or when this is impossible because of the use of artificial means of support, by any means recognized by the ordinary standards of current medical practice.

[123] C. Doig, "Is the Canadian health care system ready for donation after cardiac death? A note of caution" (2006) 175(8) C.M.A.J. 905.

proceeding with organ donation after cardiac death (DCD, also known as non-heart-beating organ donation). The report of its Forum Recommendations Group was published in 2006.[124] It proposed principles, procedures and practice related to DCD, and recommended that individual programs be developed beginning with controlled DCD (*i.e.*, in circumstances where death is anticipated but has not yet occurred) within the intensive care unit, after a consensual decision to withdraw life-sustaining therapies.[125] In June 2006, the Ottawa Hospital announced organ donation from a patient following cardiac arrest, and the Ontario agency responsible for organ and tissue donation announced it would accept donations after cardiocirculatory death.[126] With these developments, an area that had been settled is becoming newly contentious, and raises new questions for substitute decision-makers.

One of the key differences between controlled donation after cardiac death and donation after brain death is that with DCD, once a decision has been made to withdraw life support, the option of donation is presented at that point, and if accepted, then life-sustaining therapies are withdrawn, death is diagnosed using cardiac criteria, and the organs are procured. This differs from common practice with neurological determination of death, where death is first diagnosed using neurologic criteria, then the option of donation is presented, and if consent is obtained, then the organs are procured. In some DCD programs, it is permissible to perform interventions on the patient prior to death to maximize the potential for usable organs or improve the function of organs once transplanted.[127] While the Forum Report identifies optimal end of life care for the dying patient as the primary responsibility of health care providers, and support for family and loved ones about to be bereaved as a core value, it envisages interventions prior to death that may include vessel cannulation, as well as administration of vasodilators, anticoagulants and thrombolytic agents, and other procedures, raising the prospect that quality end of life care will be compromised by interventions performed not for the benefit of the dying patient, but in order to preserve organs for transplantation.[128]

As Robert Truog points out, there are concerns about conflicts of interest both when decisions are made about whether to withdraw life support, and when counselling families about DCD.[129] Delaying the withdrawal of life support may

---

[124] S. Shemie, A. Baker, G. Knoll *et al.*, "Donation after cardiocirculatory death in Canada" (2006) 175(8) C.M.A.J. S1-S23 (hereafter, "DCD in Canada"). See also Gouvernement du Québec, *Rapport de consultation sur les enjeux éthiques du don et de la transplantation d'organes: résultats des entrevues de groupes et du mini-sondage réalisé dans le cadre de l'Enquête Stat-média du printemps 2004* (Sainte-Foy, Que.: Commission de l'éthique de la science et de la technologie, 2004).

[125] "Consensual decision to withdraw life-sustaining therapies" is defined as "a decision that has been agreed to by the patient, family and the treating health care team": DCD in Canada, *ibid.*, at S4.

[126] U. Gandhi, "With death, the saving of two lives", *Globe and Mail* (June 28, 2006) at A21 (the deceased, a 32-year-old woman, had clearly indicated to her parents that she wanted to be an organ donor if she died).

[127] S. Shemie *et al.*, "DCD in Canada", at S12.

[128] *Ibid.*, at S3, S12. R. Truog, "Donation After Cardiac Death: The Next Great Advance in Organ Transplantation" (Toronto) Hospital for Sick Children (November 8, 2006).

[129] R. Truog, *ibid.*

enhance prognostic certainty for the patient concerned, but damage the quality of the organs. Difficulties in decision-making are exacerbated because there is often not consensus among physicians about end-of-life practices, including predicting outcome.[130] The risk that public trust and confidence will be eroded is real.

Interventions to facilitate donation that occur before death, such as vessel cannulation or the administration of medication, require consent — either that of the patient, if competent, or, more likely, that of the substitute decision-maker.[131] This can raise questions about whether substitute decision-makers are even entitled to make such determinations, particularly if there is no indication that the person concerned wanted to be an organ donor. First, absent prior capable wishes or directions, decisions are to be made in the best interests of the patient, and it is difficult to argue that these procedures are meant to benefit this patient; indeed, the "benefit" the Forum Report identifies is to the eventual recipient of the organs.[132] Second, substitute decision-makers are authorized to consent to or refuse "treatment", a term that may be defined in terms focused on measures taken for the good of that patient, raising questions about whether these procedures fall within the definition of "treatment" at all.[133] While some statutes include an exception from the requirement to obtain consent when the treatment poses little or no risk of harm to the patient, and the Forum Recommendations state that interventions undertaken before death to facilitate DCD should pose "no more than minimal risk", it is not clear that the two concepts of minimal risk are the same.[134]

Statutes governing organ donation may authorize substitute consent to post mortem donation when a patient is decisionally incapable and death is imminent.[135] However, they do not address substitute consent to invasive procedures performed on the patient prior to his death; they were not drafted with that possibility in mind. To confuse matters further, the substitute decision-maker identified in human tissue legislation may not be the same as the substitute decision-maker authorized to consent to or refuse treatment while the patient is alive.

DCD raises significant legal and ethical issues. They are of concern to the wider community and engage more than just medical considerations. Broader consideration before policy is finalized would be beneficial.

---

[130] C. Doig, "Is the Canadian health care system ready for donation after cardiac death? A note of caution" (2006) 175 (8) C.M.A.J. 905, citing D.J. Cook, G. Guyatt & R. Jaeschke *et al.*, "Determinants in Canadian health care workers of the decision to withdraw life support from the critically ill. Canadian Critical Care Trials Group" (1995) 273 J.A.M.A. 703-708. (Doig was a member of the Forum Recommendation Group and the CCDT but resigned, believing these issues so significant that he did not endorse the report or support proceeding with DCD based solely on one forum.)

[131] Doig notes, *ibid.*, that the patients primarily considered for DCD are patients with severe brain injury.

[132] S. Shemie *et al.*, "DCD in Canada" at S12.

[133] In Ontario, for instance, the *Health Care Consent Act, 1996*, S.O. 1996, c. 2, Sch. A, s. 2(1) defines "treatment" as "anything done for a therapeutic, preventive, palliative, diagnostic, cosmetic or other health-related purpose".

[134] S. Shemie *et al.*, "DCD in Canada" at S12.

[135] See, *e.g.*, *Trillium Gift of Life Network Act*, R.S.O. 1990, c. H.20, s. 5(2).

VI. CRIMINAL LAW

The *Criminal Code* prohibits assisted suicide and euthanasia.[136] It includes a number of other provisions that can impact on medical treatment, failure to treat or cessation of treatment as well. For the most part, they are of general application and were not framed with a view to modern medical realities.[137] Consequently, determining when and how they apply to health care is not always straightforward, nor are the standards that govern decision-making about life-sustaining treatment always clear or uncontentious.[138] Decisions about enforcement are also significant. Administration of the criminal justice system falls within provincial jurisdiction; this includes formulating policies about charging decisions.[139] One would expect accepted medical practice to be very influential in deciding whether to lay criminal charges, particularly in cases involving health care providers. However, medical norms will not always be sufficient to resolve issues that arise. Physicians have serious disagreements among themselves about many of these issues. More importantly, decisions about the provision of life-sustaining treatment are not entirely medical; they engage broader values and ethical concerns as well, and these are not areas in which doctors have special expertise.

With increasing challenges to medical authority, there is less certainty about what norms will prevail; this in turn can affect practice. Concerns over potential criminal liability underlay the refusal of the hospital and treating physician in *B. (N.) v. Hôtel-Dieu de Québec* to accede to her demand that she be removed from the ventilator that sustained her life.[140] Such hesitation is not an isolated occurrence; it arises in other areas as well, such as ensuring patients receive adequate pain management. Legal commentators and the Law Reform Commission of Canada have stressed that criminal proceedings arising out of end of life care are unlikely.[141] They point out that there have been very few criminal prosecutions for assisted suicide or euthanasia, and even fewer arising from the medical treatment involved. Further, where charges have been laid against medical personnel, there has historically been a high acquittal rate.

---

[136] R.S.C. 1985, c. C-46, ss. 241, 222.

[137] Law Reform Commission of Canada, "Euthanasia, Aiding Suicide and Cessation of Treatment", Working Paper 28 (Ottawa: Department of Supply and Services, 1982).

[138] For a more extensive discussion of the ways in which provisions in the Criminal Code could affect end-of-life decision-making and care, see J. Gilmour, *Study Paper on Assisted Suicide, Euthanasia and Foregoing Treatment* (Toronto: Ontario Law Reform Commission, 1996) at chapters 5, 6 and 12, and J. Gilmour, "Death and Dying" in M.J. Dykeman, J. Morris, L. Bayne & J. Barry, eds., *Canadian Health Law Practice Manual* (Markham, ON: LexisNexis Butterworths, 2000) at paras. 8.66-8.102.

[139] See, *e.g.*, B.C. Crown Counsel Policy Guidelines with respect to active euthanasia and assisted suicide, Policy 11-3-93, File No. 56880-01 Eut 1), reproduced in Senate Special Committee, *Of Life and Death* (Ottawa: Minister of Supply and Services Canada, 1995) at A-59.

[140] [1992] Q.J. No. 1, 86 D.L.R. (4th) 385 (Que. S.C.).

[141] Law Reform Commission of Canada, "Euthanasia, Aiding Suicide and Cessation of Treatment" Working Paper 28 (Ottawa: Department of Supply and Services, 1982) at 8, 20; J. Gilmour, "Death and Dying" in *Canadian Health Law Practice Manual* (Markham, ON: LexisNexis Butterworths, 2000) at paras. 8.62-8.66.

Nonetheless, as the circumstances of particular cases capture public attention and highlight the splintered and fluid nature of societal perceptions and expectations not only about the use of life-sustaining medical technologies, but also about appropriate decision-making processes and standards, concern about what is and is not permitted in decision-making about end of life care intensifies.

A. ASSISTED SUICIDE

Assisted suicide is "the act of intentionally killing oneself with the assistance of another who provides the knowledge, means or both".[142] The *Criminal Code* makes counselling, aiding or abetting suicide an offence, punishable by up to 14 years' imprisonment.[143] In *Rodriguez v. British Columbia (Attorney General)*, the Supreme Court of Canada considered a constitutional challenge to the prohibition on assisted suicide brought by Sue Rodriguez, a 42-year-old woman who suffered from amyotrophic lateral sclerosis, who claimed that it violated her right to liberty and security of the person under section 7 of the *Canadian Charter of Rights and Freedoms*, to equality under section 15, and to be free from cruel and unusual treatment or punishment under section 12.[144] A narrow majority of the Court rejected her challenge and upheld the law. It held that the law did not breach section 7, and that even if one assumed a breach of section 15 (a point it did not decide), the provision would be saved under section 1 of the Charter, since it was a reasonable limit demonstrably justified in a free and democratic society.[145]

While prosecutions for assisted suicide are infrequent, they do occur. Family members have been convicted of assisting suicide.[146] In Quebec, for instance, Marielle Houle was charged with assisting suicide when she helped her 36-year-old son to kill himself in 2004. He suffered from multiple sclerosis and as his

---

[142] Special Senate Committee, *Of Life and Death* (Ottawa: Minister of Supply and Services, 1995) at 14.

[143] R.S.C. 1985, c. C-46, s. 241. Attempted suicide itself was decriminalized in 1972; J. Gilmour, *Study Paper on Assisted Suicide, Euthanasia and Foregoing Treatment* (Toronto: Ontario Law Reform Commission, 1996), at 91, note 13.

[144] [1993] S.C.J. No. 94, [1993] 3 S.C.R. 519 (S.C.C.).

[145] A later attempt to revisit the issue after the Senate Committee released *Of Life and Death* in 1995, because of the Report's findings about both the inadequacy of palliative care available in Canada and a lack of societal consensus on the issue of assisted suicide, was rejected: *Wakeford v. Canada (Attorney General)*, [2001] O.J. No. 390 (Ont. S.C.J.).

[146] Earlier cases involving charges of assisted suicide and their disposition are summarized in J. Gilmour, "Death and Dying" in M.J. Dykeman, J. Morris, L. Bayne & J. Barry, eds., *Canadian Health Law Practice Manual* (Markham, ON: LexisNexis Butterworths, 2000) at para. 8.72. See also A. Mullens, *Timely Death: Considering Our Last Rights* (Toronto: Knopf, 1996) at 52; J. Downie, *Dying Justice* (Toronto: University of Toronto Press, 2004) at 34-35. See also G. Oakes, "B.C.'s top court upheld a conviction for counselling or aiding a person to commit suicide", *Lawyers Weekly* (November 5, 2004) at 2, reporting that the British Columbia Court of Appeal upheld a nine-month conditional sentence and 18 months' probation in the case of Juliana Zsiros, found guilty of aiding suicide by a jury after the body of Linda Whetung was found in her car, which had been left with the motor running and a hose leading from the exhaust pipe into the car; *R. v. Zsiros*, [2004] B.C.J. No. 2099, 203 B.C.A.C. 298 (B.C.C.A.).

condition deteriorated, had repeatedly asked her for help in taking his own life.[147] She pleaded guilty and was sentenced to three years, probation. Evidence before the court on sentencing was that the 60-year-old Houle, who was in ill health herself, had lived as a virtual recluse in a nursing home since her son's death. In passing sentence, Laramée J. emphasized that Houle was not able to judge her son's competence, and that considering the sacred nature of life and the possible abuses and lack of proper safeguards to protect the vulnerable, the prohibition on assisted suicide was neither arbitrary nor unreasonable. However, he concluded that although her actions "remained reprehensive and unlawful ... Considering the life Ms. Houle now leads ... punitive conditions are pointless", adding that what she experienced as she helped her son die was enough of a punishment.[148]

Others have sought help in ending their lives from non-family members, especially right to die organizations, and this, too, has led to criminal charges being laid for assisting suicide. Evelyn Martens, a 71-year-old member of the Canadian Right to Die Society, was charged with assisting suicide in the deaths of two British Columbia women. The women, aged 64 and 57, both ended their own lives in 2002. They were reported to have been terminally ill and to have requested Marten's assistance in dying. It was alleged that she provided them with "exit bags", helium and sleep-inducing drugs.[149] Following a jury trial, Martens was found not guilty of the charges.[150]

Health care providers have rarely been prosecuted for assisting suicide.[151] In 1996, Dr. Maurice Genereux, a Toronto physician, pleaded guilty to aiding and

---

[147] T. Thanh Ha, "Mother charged in son's death", (Toronto) *Globe and Mail*, (September 28, 2004) at A9; I. Peritz, "Assisting in her son's suicide was final act of compassion, court told", (Toronto) *Globe and Mail*, (January 24, 2006) at A24.

[148] *R. c. Houle*, [2006] J.Q. no 481, 38 C.R. (6th) 242 (Que. C.S.); T. Thanh Ha, "Mother spared jail in son's assisted suicide", (Toronto) *Globe and Mail* (January 28, 2006) at A5.

[149] D. Meissner, "Woman present at death, trial hears", (Toronto) *Globe and Mail* (October 13, 2004) at A14; D. Girard, "Suicide debate back in spotlight", *Toronto Star* (October 12, 2004) at A8.

[150] CTV.ca News Staff, "Martens not guilty in assisted suicide case" (November 5, 2004), online: <http://www.ctv.ca/servlet/ArticleNews/story/CTVNews/1099621315012_6/?hub=Canada%20>. See also R. Avery, "Jury finds son not guilty of aiding father's suicide", *Toronto Star* (April 27, 2000), online: <http://www.thestar.com>: the jury acquitted a man charged with assisting his elderly father's suicide. The father was reported to have told friends he would kill himself rather than live in a nursing home; his son was alleged to have test-fired the gun his father later used to take his own life.

[151] Professional discipline proceedings are also rare. See generally J. Gilmour, "Death and Dying" in M.J. Dykeman, J. Morris, L. Bayne & J. Barry, eds., *Canadian Health Law Practice Manual* (Markham, ON: LexisNexis Butterworths, 2000) at paras. 8.103-8.108. In an unusual turn of events, a member of the Ontario College of Psychologists complained that another psychologist had contravened its standards of practice by conspiring with a right to die organization, Dignitas, to violate the *Criminal Code* prohibition on assisting suicide, by accompanying a seriously ill friend to Switzerland (where assisted suicide without self-interest is legal), where a Dignitas representative assisted her to take her own life. The complaint was triggered when the psychologist wrote a letter to a newspaper about the experience. The College rejected the complaint, as did the Health Professions Appeal and Review Board: H. Levy, "Doctor's role in assisted suicide probed", *Toronto Star* (May 16, 2006) at A1; H. Levy, "One complains about role of other in assisted suicide", *Toronto Star* (May 17, 2006) at A4, online: <http://www.thestar.com>.

abetting suicide after prescribing lethal doses of barbiturates to two suicidal patients who were HIV-positive (but not suffering from AIDS). He knew neither was terminally ill, and that treatment could have helped both. One patient did take his own life with the medication, while the other failed in the attempt. The sentence imposed — two years less a day's imprisonment, and three years' probation — was affirmed on appeal.[152]

The infrequency of prosecution does not mean that assisted suicides are not happening. The Special Senate Committee on Assisted Suicide and Euthanasia concluded that while it could not ascertain how often assisted suicide is requested or is occurring, or under what conditions, it had "heard sufficient evidence to suspect it is being requested and provided".[153] The most well-known case is that of Sue Rodriguez. She ultimately ended her own life, reportedly with medical assistance.[154] A special prosecutor appointed to determine whether charges should be laid against a Member of Parliament present at her death concluded that charges were not warranted under British Columbia's charge approval process, as conviction was unlikely in the circumstances, given that others, reportedly including a physician, were present at the time of her death as well.[155] On the other hand, it should not be thought that suicide assistance is freely available despite the law. The Special Senate Committee heard moving testimony from surviving family members of a number of individuals whose last illnesses were pain-wracked, who had endured great suffering, and who had attempted to find a health care practitioner who would help them to die but were unable to do so.[156]

A review of developments in the law governing assisted suicide outside Canada is beyond the scope of this chapter. It is of note, however, that in the last several years, a number of jurisdictions have legalized some forms of assisted suicide in restricted circumstances. In the United States, the *Oregon Death with Dignity Act* was passed in 1994, and implemented in 1998. It protects physicians

---

[152] *R. v. Genereux*, [1999] O.J. No. 1387, 44 O.R. (3d) 339 (Ont. C.A.). Charges of assisting a patient to attempt suicide were laid against a B.C. doctor, Ramesh Sharma, in July 2006. Police said the attempted suicide was interrupted by a staff member at the care facility where the patient was a resident: G. Preston, "Doctor charged in attempted suicide", *Vancouver Sun* (August 2, 2006), online: <http://www.canada.com/vancouversun/news/westcoastnews/story.html?id=c626 f282-dd8>. The physician pleaded guilty to assisting suicide — CanWest News Service, "Doctor Who Offered to Assist in Suicide Accepts Suspension", *National Post*, April 3, 2007 at A8.

[153] *Of Life and Death* (Ottawa: Minister of Supply and Services Canada, 1995) at 55. See also R. Ogden, *Euthanasia, Assisted Suicide and AIDS* (Pitt Meadows, B.C.: Perreault/Goedmann Publishing, 1994); Proceedings of the Special Senate Committee on Euthanasia and Assisted Suicide, Testimony of Dr. Ted Boadway, Director of Health Policy, Ontario Medical Association, (October 17, 1994) at 20, 82-83.

[154] D. Wilson, D. Downey, "Patient fought to die on her own terms", (Toronto) *Globe and Mail* (February 14, 1994) at A4.

[155] Canadian Press, "Role of MP in Rodriguez suicide to be probed", *Toronto Star* (January 11, 1995) at A2; T. Harper, "MP not charged in aided suicide", *Toronto Star* (June 29, 1995) at A2.

[156] *Of Life and Death* (Ottawa: Minister of Supply and Services Canada, 1995) at 65. The stories of many of these families are expanded on in A. Mullens, *Timely Death: Considering Our Last Rights* (Toronto: Knopf, 1996).

in that state from civil or criminal liability when they dispense or prescribe a lethal dose of drugs on the request of a terminally ill patient, provided certain safeguards and conditions are met.[157] Oregon is the only state that has legalized assisted suicide. By mid-2006, 172 Oregonians had died from ingesting medications their physicians had prescribed in lethal doses.[158] The law has withstood numerous court challenges, including most recently, an attempt by the U.S. Attorney-General to interpret federal legislation regulating controlled substances so as to effectively criminalize physician-assisted suicide under federal law. *Gonzalez v. Oregon* largely bypassed the debate about "the legality and morality and practicality of physician-assisted suicide" and turned instead on administrative law questions, and an analysis of the division of powers between the federal government and states. The United States Supreme Court held that the federal legislation would not bear the interpretation for which the federal Attorney-General argued.[159] In 2002, the Netherlands became the first country to pass a law decriminalizing voluntary euthanasia, giving statutory force to an accommodation that had prevailed in that country for a number of years, which allowed voluntary euthanasia under certain conditions.[160] Belgium decriminalized assisted suicide and euthanasia in limited circumstances in 2002.[161] In Switzerland, suicide assistance has not been legally penalized for almost 100 years, provided it is without self-interest.[162] Of the jurisdictions that allow the practice, it appears to be the least restrictive in the conditions imposed.[163] In most countries, however, assisted suicide remains illegal.[164]

---

[157] B. Bostrom, "Gonzales v. Oregon" (2006) 21 Issues L. & Med. 203.

[158] D. Sclar, "U.S. Supreme Court Ruling in Gonzales v. Oregon Upholds the Oregon Death with Dignity Act" (2006) 34 J.L.M.E. 639.

[159] *Oregon v. Ashcroft*, 126 S. Ct. 904 (2006), affg 368 F.3d 1118 (9th Cir. 2004), affg 192 F.Supp.2d 1077 (D. Or. 2002); Kennedy J. was citing *Washington v. Glucksberg*, 521 U.S. 702, 735 (1997).

[160] T. Sheldon, "Holland decriminalises voluntary euthanasia" (2001) 322 B.M.J. 322, online: <http://www.bmj.com>; J. De Haan, "The New Dutch Law on Euthanasia" (2002) 10 Med. L. Rev. 57; A. Janssen, "The New Regulation of Voluntary Euthanasia and Medically Assisted Suicide in the Netherlands" (2002) Int. J. L. Policy and the Family 260.

[161] E. Vermeersch, "The Belgian Law on Euthanasia. The Historical and Ethical Background" (2002) 102 Acta chir. belg. 394. One year after euthanasia was legalized, the Belgian government reported that 203 such deaths had been officially recorded — "In Belgium, 203 chose euthanasia", *Medical Post* (December 9, 2003) at 58.

[162] G. Bosshard, D. Jermini, D. Eisenhart & W. Bar, "Assisted suicide bordering on active euthanasia" (2002) 117 Int. J. Legal Med. 106 (commenting on the expansive understanding of assisted suicide employed in Switzerland).

[163] G. Bosshard, L. Fischer & W. Bar, "How Switzerland compares with the Netherlands and Oregon" (2002) 132 Swiss Med. Wkly. 527; A. Frei, T. Schenker, A. Finzen, K. Krauchi, V. Dittmann & U. Hoffmann-Richter, "Assisted suicide as conducted by a 'Right-to-Die' society in Switzerland: A descriptive analysis of 43 consecutive cases" (2001) 131 Swiss Med. Wkly 375; S. Hurst & A. Mauron, "Assisted suicide and euthanasia in Switzerland: allowing a role for non-physicians" (2003) 326 B.M.J. 271.

[164] C. MacKellar, "Laws and Practices Relating to Euthanasia and Assisted Suicide in 34 Countries of the Council of Europe and the USA" (2003) 10 Eur. J. Health L. 63.

B. EUTHANASIA

The *Criminal Code* provides that a person commits homicide when he or she causes the death of another human being by any means, whether directly or indirectly.[165] Not all homicides are culpable, and only culpable homicides are criminal offences. Culpable homicide is murder, manslaughter or infanticide, and includes causing death by means of an unlawful act, or by criminal negligence.[166] Culpable homicide is murder, *inter alia,* where the person meant to cause the death or to cause bodily harm that he or she knows is likely to result in death, and is reckless as to whether death ensues or not.[167] Culpable homicide that is not murder — that is, where the agent lacks the necessary subjective mental element (degree of intent) — is manslaughter.[168] The penalties for each differ greatly. Manslaughter is subject to a maximum of life imprisonment, but no mandatory minimum sentence.[169] A conviction for murder carries a mandatory life sentence with a minimum period prior to parole eligibility of 25 years for first degree murder, and 10 years (or such greater time as may be imposed) for second degree murder.[170]

Clearly, euthanasia that involves the deliberate taking of a life can constitute murder. The most well known case in Canada is that of Robert Latimer. He was charged with first degree murder and convicted of second degree murder when he intentionally asphyxiated his severely disabled young daughter.[171] He was sentenced to life imprisonment, with a minimum period of parole ineligibility of 10 years. The case created a furor, for some because they believed the application of the mandatory minimum sentencing law for murder to be unjust in the circumstances, and for others, because both the crime and the public support for Latimer were seen as not only an affront to the equality and dignity of people with disabilities, but a real threat to their lives.

In one of the few cases in which criminal charges have been laid against a health professional, Dr. Nancy Morrison was charged with first degree murder in connection with the death of one of her patients, a 65-year-old terminally ill man suffering from cancer. His family had consented to the withdrawal of all life support. The charge was based on her intravenous administration of potassium chloride to him after all attempts to relieve the significant pain he was suffering had proved ineffective. She was discharged following a preliminary inquiry. The presiding judge concluded that no properly instructed jury could convict her, since credible evidence established that the intravenous tip may have been dislodged and the patient may not have received the lethal medication at all, given the massive amount of pain medication that had previously been delivered intravenously, with no effect.[172] The Nova Scotia College of

---

[165] R.S.C. 1985, c. C-46, s. 222.
[166] *Ibid.*
[167] *Ibid.*, s. 229.
[168] *Ibid.*, s. 234.
[169] *Ibid.*, s. 236.
[170] *Ibid.*, ss. 235, 742.
[171] *R. v. Latimer*, [1997] 1 S.C.R. 417 (S.C.C.).
[172] *R. v. Morrison*, [1998] N.S.J. No. 75 (N.S. Prov. Ct.). The Crown's application for *certiorari*

Physicians and Surgeons conducted its own investigation of the events; it issued a letter of reprimand to Dr. Morrison, which she signed, acknowledging that she gave the injection.[173]

Crown Attorneys have reduced charges of murder to manslaughter or some other lesser offence because of the accused's compassionate motive. Difficulties in proof can also play a role in decisions to reduce charges. The most recent example is that of André Bergeron in Quebec. He was charged with attempted murder in 2005 in the death of his 44-year-old wife, Marielle Houle.[174] She suffered from Friedrich's ataxia, a progressively degenerative neurological disorder that caused her intense pain; she had repeatedly asked to die. Bergeron had been her primary caregiver for more than two decades. He was deeply depressed at the time of her death. Members of her family were quoted as saying that he was mentally and physically exhausted, having done everything for her for many years, and that, while the family did not condone his actions, "we cannot hold it against him".[175] He pleaded guilty to a reduced charge of aggravated assault, and was sentenced to three years' probation.[176] In imposing this sentence, Côté J. said that she would have ordered a jail term, but for "the exceptional and particular tragic circumstances in his case, such as the devotion André Bergeron displayed throughout his shared life with Marielle Houle ... His act was taken not because the accused had come to consider his duty a burden but as a gesture of love for the victim, to free her of her sufferings and preserve her dignity".[177]

C. PRINCIPLE OF DOUBLE EFFECT

In Canadian criminal law, the deceased's consent to his or her own death is not a defence to criminal liability.[178] Nor is motive a constituent of the *mens rea* or *actus reus* of an offence, although it can be relevant to both.[179] However, in a departure from the general rules governing criminal liability, health care providers' motives are taken into account in certain instances. The principle of double effect, a longstanding feature of moral argument, has been incorporated into the law when analyzing the actions of health care professionals treating patients. Courts are prepared to accept the legality in medical practice of taking actions with good and bad effects, as long as the actor intended only the good effects. Providing large doses of pain medication to relieve suffering, but with the known likelihood of hastening death, is a good example of this, and one the Supreme Court of Canada explicitly accepted as appropriate in *Rodriguez v.*

---

failed — affd [1998] N.S.J. No. 41 (N.S.S.C.).

[173] J. Downie, *Dying Justice* (Toronto: University of Toronto Press, 2004) at 42-43.

[174] R. Marowits, "Case spurs debate on assisted suicide", *Toronto Star* (July 12, 2005) at A11.

[175] T. Thanh Ha, "A death that 'had to happen'", *Globe and Mail* (July 15, 2005) at A1, A7.

[176] *R. c. Bergeron*, [2006] J.Q. no 11329, 43 C.R. (6th) 148 (C.Q.); T. Thanh Ha, "Husband avoids jail in assisted-suicide case", *Globe and Mail* (October 20, 2006) at A9.

[177] T. Thanh Ha, *ibid.*

[178] *Criminal Code*, R.S.C. 1985, c. C-46, s. 14.

[179] See generally *Lewis v. R.*, [1979] S.C.J. No. 73, [1979] 2 S.C.R. 821, at 833 (S.C.C.).

British Columbia (Attorney General).[180] Although both legal scholars and philosophers have criticized reliance on the principle of double effect,[181] it does function as a limited exception to the refusal to take motive into account that otherwise prevails in criminal law.

D. PROSECUTORIAL DISCRETION

Both ending treatment and administering it can come under one or more additional intersecting and overlapping provisions of the criminal law, including causing bodily harm by criminal negligence, failing to provide the necessaries of life to someone under one's charge, administering a noxious thing, failing to use reasonable knowledge, care and skill in administering surgical or medical treatment, causing bodily harm to another person, and others.[182] Prosecutions, however, remain very rare, particularly for the most serious offences. Part of the explanation for this lies in the exercise of prosecutorial discretion. Such discretion is important and properly allows extenuating circumstances to be taken into account. However, the lack of predictability and certainty in the charging process is particularly problematic in this context, because characterizations of conduct and circumstances can and do vary so widely, and are sometimes diametrically opposed. Testifying before the Special Senate Committee on Euthanasia and Assisted Suicide, Dr. James Cairns, then Deputy Chief Coroner for Ontario, recounted that 60 senior Crown attorneys attending an educational session sponsored by the Ontario Coroner's office in the aftermath of several criminal prosecutions involving end of life care and assisted deaths "were as divided as anyone else" as to the appropriate charge to be laid should similar circumstances arise again.[183] Even the policy guidelines about charging issued in British Columbia in the wake of Sue Rodriguez's death are expressed at such a level of generality that they ultimately give little direction, beyond confirming what is already clearly accepted law.[184]

---

[180] [1993] S.C.J. No. 94, [1993] 3 S.C.R. 519 at 607 (S.C.C.).

[181] See, *e.g.*, J. Rachels, "From 'Letting Die' to Active Killing", in J. Arras & N. Rhoden, eds., *Ethical Issues in Modern Medicine*, 3rd ed. (Mountain View, CA: Mayfield Publishing, 1989 at 241-44; J. Fletcher, "The Courts and Euthanasia" (1987/88) 15 Law, Med. & Health Care 223; J. Gilmour, *Study Paper on Assisted Suicide, Euthanasia and Foregoing Treatment* (Toronto: Ontario Law Reform Commission, 1996) at 243-46.

[182] *Criminal Code*, R.S.C. 1985, c. C-46, ss. 215-221, 245, 269. The applicability of these provisions of the Code to these issues is examined in detail in J. Gilmour, *ibid.*, at 69.

[183] Proceedings of the Special Senate Committee on Euthanasia and Assisted Suicide, testimony of Dr. James Cairns (October 17, 1994) at 20:8, referenced in J. Gilmour, *Study Paper on Assisted Suicide, Euthanasia and Foregoing Treatment* (Toronto: Ontario Law Reform Commission, 1996) at para. 8.97.

[184] B.C. Crown Counsel Policy Guidelines, Policy 11-3-93, File No. 56880-01 (Eut 1), reproduced in Senate Special Committee, *Of Life and Death* (Ottawa: Minister of Supply and Services Canada, 1995), at A-59.

E. EVALUATING THE LIKELIHOOD OF CRIMINAL PROSECUTION

That said, the reality is that no charges have gone forward in Canada for withholding or withdrawing treatment. Courts have consistently drawn a distinction between allowing a patient to die from an underlying disease or condition, and causing that death. The former is non-culpable; the latter is culpable conduct. It has also been accepted that where the patient's condition requires it, a physician can prescribe medication in doses sufficient to ensure the patient's comfort, even where such doses may have the secondary effect of shortening the patient's life.[185] Courts have accorded a determinative role to health care providers' primary motivation. Against this background, the likelihood of criminal liability following on decisions made in good faith to withhold or withdraw treatment or to provide needed pain medication is small indeed. Nonetheless, the lack of clear guidelines continues to give rise to concerns about potential criminal liability. Whether warranted or not, this uncertainty can impede health care providers and families acting as substitute decision makers in their efforts to ensure that the best care possible is provided at the end of a patient's life.

VII. CONCLUSION

Canada has seen a transformation in the paradigm governing decision-making about health care in the last several decades, accomplished in large part with little litigation, and limited legislative activity. Patient autonomy and self-determination are now key in treatment decisions. That transformation has marked our thinking about care at the end of life as well. Thus, it is now clear that a decisionally capable individual can forego life-sustaining treatment, including nutrition and hydration.[186] The right to refuse treatment is rooted in the common law as well as the Constitution.[187] People can make advance directives setting out their instructions about health care decision-making, to be followed in a later period of incompetence. These, too, are recognized at common law; most provinces and territories have adopted statutory regimes to govern them as well.[188] There is also general recognition that, in the event a person is not competent to make his or her own decisions about health care and there are no known wishes or instructions that are applicable in the circumstances, then health care decisions must be made in the person's best interests.[189]

---

[185] *Rodriguez v. British Columbia (Attorney General)*, [1993] S.C.J. No. 94, [1993] 3 S.C.R. 519 (S.C.C.).

[186] *Ibid.*; *B. (N.) v. Hôtel-Dieu de Québec*, [1992] Q.J. No. 1, 86 D.L.R. (4th) 385 (Que. S.C.); *Manoir de la Pointe Bleue (1978) Inc. c. Corbeil*, [1992] J.Q. No. 98, [1992] R.J.Q. 712 (Que. C.S.).

[187] *Fleming v. Reid*, [1991] O.J. No. 1083, 4 O.R. (3d) 74 (Ont. C.A.); *Conway v. Jacques*, [2002] O.J. No. 2333, 59 O.R. (3d) 735 (Ont. C.A.).

[188] *Malette v. Shulman*, [1990] O.J. No. 450, 72 O.R. (2d) 417 (Ont. C.A.), affg [1987] O.J. No. 1180, 63 O.R. (2d) 243 (Ont. H.C.J.); *Fleming v. Reid, ibid.*

[189] *B. (R.) v. Children's Aid Society of Metropolitan Toronto*, [1994] S.C.J. No. 24, [1995] 1 S.C.R. 315 (S.C.C.).

Many difficult issues remain, however. The *Schiavo* case in the United States raised concerns about substitute decision-makers (for some, that their decisions would, and for others, that they would not be honoured) and about whether advance instructions should be binding.[190] Turning to the best interests test, when a patient's prior wishes are unknown or inapplicable, it can be difficult to determine where a patient's best interests lie or how that should be decided, especially when the burdens and benefits of treatment, and even of continued life, are contested or unclear. Questions about whether and when further treatment is futile, and who should make such decisions, complicate matters still further. There may be disagreements among family members, or among family members and health care providers and institutions, or among all those involved and the courts. Uncertainties about the application of the criminal law add to the difficulty of decision-making, and may increase instances where pain is undertreated or patients receive less than adequate care at the end of life. While there are many areas of consensus about end of life decision-making, we are sharply divided on other questions. Recent criminal prosecutions for assisted suicide and euthanasia, as well as changes in the law in some other countries to allow both in limited circumstances have led to renewed calls for legislative reform to decriminalize one or both in Canada.[191] Others, however, argue that sympathy for the accused in these cases is misplaced, and that regardless of personal tragedies and pressures, such conduct cannot be tolerated; the accused took the life of someone immensely vulnerable, or set the stage for that to occur.[192] They urge that strong legal prohibitions be maintained, in order to protect those who are vulnerable because of illness, disability or age.

Despite greater certainty in some areas of the law, more needs to be done. The present state of the law regarding end of life care can impede proper care in dying, as well as efforts to ensure that people can live their lives to the fullest. It is time for a careful examination of current practices and law, as well as proposals for reform, disengaged from the focus on the compelling circumstances of an individual case characteristic of the adversarial process and judicial decision-making. While there is no great political will for such an undertaking, it would allow consideration of both the extent to which the principles that guide decision-making accord with and assist us in realizing our

---

[190] Contrast, *e.g.*, C. Levine, "The President's Commission on Autonomy: Never Mind!" (2006) 36 Hastings Center Report 46, and R. Dresser, "Schiavo's Legacy: The Need for an Objective Standard" (2005) 35 Hastings Center Report 20.

[191] B. Jang, "B.C. charges renew debate on euthanasia", *Globe and Mail* (July 3, 2002) at A7; M. Gordon, "Physician-assisted suicide: Is it time to reconsider?", *Medical Post* (February 14, 2006); Editorial, "For assisted suicide", *Globe and Mail* (July 12, 2005) at A12; Editorial, *Globe and Mail* (August 15, 2005) at A12.

[192] See, *e.g.*, R. Matas, "Couple kill disabled son, themselves", *Globe and Mail* (January 4, 2002) at A1; R. Matas, "Sympathy misplaced, advocates say", *Globe and Mail* (January 5, 2002) at A4 (recounting both the public dismay and response of disability advocates after a couple in their mid-50s took their own lives and that of their 34-year-old developmentally disabled son. They died of carbon monoxide poisoning. The couple, who were reported to have pressed the government unsuccessfully for years to help them care for their son at home, left a note referring to their financial and health problems, and saying they did not trust anyone else to care for their son, who lived with them).

goals and values as a society, where there are gaps and deficiencies, and what reforms are needed to better achieve those ends.

Chapter 12

PUBLIC HEALTH

Barbara von Tigerstrom

I. INTRODUCTION

Public health law is a rapidly growing area of research and practice. Events like the 2003 SARS outbreak and current fears of an impending influenza pandemic have focused public attention on public health powers and responsibilities and the legal framework within which they are exercised. Less dramatic but equally deadly threats like tobacco consumption and obesity have provoked debate about legal strategies to promote public health. Underlying many issues in public health law are central questions about the limits of personal freedom and responsibility, the role of government, and collective decisions about confronting the risks of contemporary society.

II. PUBLIC HEALTH AND PUBLIC HEALTH LAW

A much-quoted definition states that public health is "what we, as a society, do collectively to assure the conditions for people to be healthy".[1] It is "public" in the sense both of collective action (primarily, though not exclusively, government action) and of concern with the health of a population rather than specific individuals.[2] Contemporary public health practice is characterized by an approach that is preventive, evidence-based and holistic. It aims to use evidence about the risk factors, determinants and incidence of disease, generated from surveillance and epidemiological analysis, to design interventions that will promote population health and prevent disease.

Public health law has been defined as the "study of legal powers and duties of the state to promote the conditions for people to be healthy ... and the limitations on the power of the state to constrain the autonomy, privacy, liberty, proprietary, or other legally protected interests of individuals for the protection

---

[1] Institute of Medicine, *The Future of Public Health* (Washington, D.C.: National Academies Press, 1988) at 1.

[2] Lawrence O. Gostin, "Health of the People: The Highest Law?" (2004) 32 J. L. Med. & Ethics 509 at 510.

or promotion of community health".[3] The legal issues arising in public health tend to differ from those most prominent in the context of medical treatment, because of the population focus of public health interventions. Whereas medical law is chiefly concerned with rights and obligations in the relationship between health care provider and patient, in public health many questions involve the powers and duties of government to protect the health of its population. The law is often called on to resolve the tensions that may arise between individual rights and interests, on the one hand, and the common interest of the community, on the other.

Public health and public health law cover a broad range of subjects. Most people associate public health with infectious disease control and sanitation, but its scope extends to such diverse matters as environmental hazards, chronic diseases and injuries.[4] An even broader conception of public health law would encompass the role of law in relation to determinants of health and the causes of disparities in health status, such as poverty and discrimination. Without discounting the importance of these matters, this chapter will focus on a narrower set of issues as an introduction to the field. It will provide an overview of the legal framework for public health in Canada, and then discuss the law relating to infectious disease control and surveillance, chronic diseases and tobacco control.

III. THE LEGAL FRAMEWORK FOR PUBLIC HEALTH IN CANADA

Health or public health is not assigned as a single subject matter under the Canadian Constitution but is spread among several heads of power, both federal and provincial.[5] Relevant federal heads of power include trade and commerce, quarantine and marine hospitals, criminal law, and the peace, order and good government (POGG) power;[6] provincial heads of power include hospitals, municipal institutions, property and civil rights, and local and private matters.[7] The federal government has enacted legislation to deal with potentially hazardous consumer products,[8] food and drug safety,[9] and quarantine of goods and

---

[3]   *Ibid.*, at 509-10.

[4]   For further details and discussion on many of these topics, see Tracey M. Bailey, Timothy Caulfield & Nola Ries, eds., *Public Health Law and Policy in Canada* (Markham, ON: LexisNexis Butterworths, 2005).

[5]   For general discussion, see, *e.g.*, Martha Jackman, "Constitutional Jurisdiction Over Health in Canada" (2000) 8 Health L.J. 95; regarding jurisdiction over public health matters see, *e.g.*, Nola M. Ries, "Legal Foundations of Public Health Law in Canada" in *ibid.*, at 11*ff*; National Advisory Committee on SARS and Public Health, *Learning from SARS: Renewal of Public Health in Canada* (Ottawa: Health Canada, 2003) at 166*ff*.

[6]   *Constitution Act, 1867* (U.K.), 30 & 31 Vict., c. 3, reprinted in R.S.C. 1985, App. II, No. 5, s. 91(2), (11), (27).

[7]   *Ibid.*, s. 92(7), (8), (13), (16).

[8]   *Hazardous Products Act*, R.S.C. 1985, c. H-3.

[9]   *Food and Drugs Act*, R.S.C. 1985, c. F-27.

persons at border crossings.[10] Both levels of government have legislation relating to emergency management,[11] tobacco control,[12] and environmental hazards.[13] Provincial legislation covers most aspects of infectious disease surveillance and control,[14] other health surveillance (such as vital statistics and cancer surveillance), and provincial health care systems.

Among the federal institutions, the Public Health Agency of Canada (PHAC) has primary responsibility for most public health matters, including chronic and infectious disease surveillance and control, injury prevention and health promotion.[15] Health Canada also plays a role in the areas of food and drug safety, consumer product safety, First Nations and Inuit health, and environmental health issues. Federal responsibility to deal with a public health emergency is shared between PHAC, Health Canada, and Public Safety and Emergency Preparedness Canada. Provincial and territorial ministries of health are responsible for administering legislation and programs, with some responsibilities being delegated to regional or local authorities.

The overlapping responsibilities of various levels of government in public health have sometimes led to difficulties. In some cases, parties adversely affected by public health legislation have challenged their provisions on the basis that the government lacked jurisdiction to enact them. This has occurred particularly with tobacco control legislation, but the courts have confirmed the concurrent jurisdiction of federal and provincial governments to legislate in this area.[16] The courts have also upheld municipal bylaws regulating pesticides as potential public health hazards.[17]

All legislation in Canada must be consistent with the *Canadian Charter of Rights and Freedoms*,[18] and may be challenged if affected persons believe their

---

[10] *Quarantine Act*, R.S.C. 1985, c. Q-1 [repealed S.C. 2005, c. 20, s. 82]; *Quarantine Act*, S.C. 2005, c. 20.

[11] See, *e.g.*, *Emergencies Act*, R.S.C. 1985, c. 22 (4th Supp.); *Emergency Management and Civil Protection Act*, R.S.O. 1990, c. E.9; *Emergency Measures Act*, S.N.B. 1978, c. E-7.1; *Emergency Planning Act*, S.S. 1989-90, c. E-8.1.

[12] See, *e.g.*, *Tobacco Act*, S.C. 1997, c. 13; *Tobacco Act*, R.S.Q., c. T-0.01; *Tobacco Control Act*, S.S. 2001, c. T-14.1; *Smoke-Free Ontario Act*, S.O. 1994, c. 10 (formerly the *Tobacco Control Act*).

[13] See, *e.g.*, *Canadian Environmental Protection Act, 1999*, S.C. 1999, c. 33; *Environmental Protection and Enhancement Act*, R.S.A. 2000, c. E-12; *Environmental Management Act*, S.B.C. 2003, c. 53.

[14] See, *e.g.*, *Health Act*, R.S.B.C. 1996, c. 179; *Public Health Act*, R.S.A. 2000, c. P-37; *Communicable Diseases Act*, R.S.N.L. 1990, c. C-26.

[15] Legislation formally establishing PHAC, the *Public Health Agency of Canada Act*, Bill C-5 (39th Parl., 1st Sess.), was introduced on April 24, 2006 and came into force December 15, 2006 (S.C. 2006, c. 5).

[16] *RJR-MacDonald Inc. v. Canada (Attorney General)*, [1995] S.C.J. No. 68, [1995] 3 S.C.R. 199 (S.C.C.); *Rothmans, Benson & Hedges Inc. v. Saskatchewan*, [2005] S.C.J. No. 1, [2005] 1 S.C.R. 188 (S.C.C.). See also *Siemens v. Manitoba (Attorney General)*, [2003] S.C.J. No. 69, [2003] 1 S.C.R. 6 (S.C.C.) (regulation of gambling).

[17] *114957 Canada Ltée (Spraytech, Société d'arrosage) v. Hudson (Town)*, [2001] S.C.J. No. 42, [2001] 2 S.C.R. 241 (S.C.C.).

[18] *Canadian Charter of Rights and Freedoms*, Part I of the *Constitution Act, 1982*, being Schedule B to the *Canada Act 1982* (U.K.), 1982, c. 11 [Charter].

Charter rights have been violated. For example, the tobacco industry has been partly successful in challenging legislation that restricts the marketing of tobacco products.[19] Restrictions on personal liberty, such as quarantine or detention for public health reasons, and intrusions into personal privacy, such as mandatory reporting of diseases, may also be challenged under the Charter.[20] However, decisions of Canadian courts to date suggest that the public health objectives of these provisions will be given considerable weight.[21] The government will be permitted to infringe rights and freedoms protected under the Charter where it can demonstrate that the limit is one which is "reasonable", "prescribed by law" and "demonstrably justified in a free and democratic society".[22] Decisions of public health authorities may also be challenged on the basis that they breached statutory or common law duties owed to affected persons.[23]

Finally, a range of international legal obligations are relevant to Canadian public health law. These include human rights treaties that guarantee the right to health,[24] as well as rights to liberty, personal security, freedom of movement, privacy and freedom of expression that must be respected in public health interventions.[25] International trade agreements may also need to be taken into account: for example the General Agreement on Tariffs and Trade prohibits various types of trade barriers, subject to an exception for measures that are "necessary to protect human ... life or health",[26] and the Agreement on Sanitary and Phytosanitary Measures sets out substantive and procedural requirements for measures relating to food safety and health risks from plant or animal pests and diseases.[27] The recently revised *International Health Regulations* provide a

---

[19]   *RJR-MacDonald Inc. v. Canada (Attorney General)*, [1995] S.C.J. No. 68, [1995] 3 S.C.R. 199 (S.C.C.); *J.T.I.-MacDonald Corp. v. Canada (Procureure générale)*, [2005] J.Q. No. 10915, 260 D.L.R. (4th) 224 at 389, 2005 QCCA 726 (Que. C.A.), leave to appeal to S.C.C. granted, Supreme Court of Canada Bulletin of Proceedings, (March 24, 2006).

[20]   *Toronto (City, Medical Officer of Health) v. Deakin*, [2002] O.J. No. 2777 (Ont. C.J.); *Canadian AIDS Society v. Ontario*, [1995] O.J. No. 2361, 25 O.R. (3d) 388 (Ont. Gen. Div.).

[21]   See, *e.g.*, *Canadian AIDS Society v. Ontario*, *ibid.*

[22]   Charter, s. 1. The framework for evaluating whether this s. 1 test has been met was set out in the case of *R. v. Oakes*, [1986] S.C.J. No. 7, 1 S.C.R. 103 (S.C.C.).

[23]   See, *e.g.*, *Jamal Estate v. Scarborough Hospital – Grace Division*, [2005] O.J. No. 3506, 34 C.C.L.T. (3d) 271 (Ont. S.C.J.); *Henry Estate v. Scarborough Hospital – Grace Division*, [2005] O.J. No. 3505, 34 C.C.L.T. (3d) 278 (Ont. S.C.J.); *Abarquez v. Ontario* (2005), 34 C.C.L.T. (3d) 249 (Ont. S.C.J.); *Laroza Estate v. Ontario*, [2005] O.J. No. 3504, 34 C.C.L.T. (3d) 264 (Ont. S.C.J.). The scope for such claims was at issue in the recent decision of the Ontario Court of Appeal in *Eliopoulos v. Ontario*, [2006] O.J. No. 4400 (Ont. C.A.), striking the plaintiff's statement of claim against Ontario for alleged negligence in failing to prevent an outbreak of West Nile Virus on the grounds that Ontario did not owe a private law duty of care to individuals in this respect.

[24]   *International Covenant on Economic, Social and Cultural Rights*, December 16, 1966, 993 U.N.T.S. 3, art. 12; *Convention on the Rights of the Child*, November 20, 1989, G.A. Res. 44/25, art. 24.

[25]   *International Covenant on Civil and Political Rights*, December 16, 1966, 999 U.N.T.S. 171, arts. 9, 12, 19, 17.

[26]   *General Agreement on Tariffs and Trade*, October 30, 1947, 58 U.N.T.S. 187, art. XX(b).

[27]   *Agreement on the Application of Sanitary and Phytosanitary Measures*, Annex 1A to the

framework for responses by states and the World Health Organization (WHO) to outbreaks of disease.[28] States are required to develop and maintain certain capacities for disease surveillance and response,[29] and must notify the WHO of any potential "public health emergency of international concern".[30] If such an emergency is found to exist, the WHO will issue temporary recommendations for measures to deal it. A range of measures that states can use to prevent the spread of disease are set out in the regulations, and states can only exceed these and the recommended measures if certain conditions are met.[31] Another landmark international instrument in public health law, the *Framework Convention on Tobacco Control* (FCTC), was negotiated under the auspices of the WHO and adopted by the World Health Assembly on May 21, 2003.[32] Canada signed the FCTC on July 15, 2003 and ratified it on November 26, 2004. The Convention came into force in 2005 and as of September 2006 had 140 parties.[33] The FCTC commits state parties to a comprehensive range of tobacco control measures, including smoking bans, marketing restrictions and preventing sales to minors.

IV. INFECTIOUS DISEASE SURVEILLANCE AND CONTROL

Public health authorities work to prevent and contain infectious diseases through surveillance and control activities that are supported by a legal framework, typically a provincial public health statute and associated regulations. Surveillance and control are closely related, since surveillance — the systematic collection and analysis of data about the incidence of disease in the population — allows the authorities to prevent and respond to outbreaks through an understanding of patterns and determinants of disease. Mandatory reporting of infectious diseases is used to facilitate comprehensive and timely collection of information. Disease control is achieved through a range of measures including testing and treatment of affected individuals and where necessary, isolation. Public health authorities also possess a range of coercive powers to respond to a disease outbreak or public health emergency.

Marrakesh Agreement Establishing the World Trade Organization, April 15, 1994, 1867 U.N.T.S. 3.

[28] *International Health Regulations (2005)*, WHA Res. 58.3, May 23, 2005 [in force 2007]. See Lawrence O. Gostin, "International Infectious Disease Law: Revision of the World Health Organization's International Health Regulations" (2004) 291 J.A.M.A. 2623.

[29] *Ibid.*, Annex 1.

[30] *Ibid.*, art. 6. A public health emergency of international concern is determined in accordance with the criteria in Annex 2.

[31] *Ibid.*, art. 43. For discussion of this issue, see Barbara von Tigerstrom, "The Revised International Health Regulations and Restraint of National Health Measures" (2005) 13 Health L. J. 35.

[32] *WHO Framework Convention on Tobacco Control*, WHA Res. 56.1, Annex (opened for signature June 16, 2003), online: WHO <http://www.who.int/tobacco/framework/en/fctc_booklet_english.pdf>.

[33] WHO, "Updated Status of the WHO Framework Convention on Tobacco Control" (2006), online: WHO <http://www.who.int/tobacco/framework/countrylist/en/index.html>.

A. MANDATORY REPORTING

Public health legislation requires designated persons to report cases of certain diseases. The list of notifiable or reportable diseases is usually prescribed by regulation, but there may also be a general requirement to report any case of a disease that is unusual or part of a suspected outbreak,[34] or provision for the medical officer to require reporting of any other disease that needs to be kept under surveillance.[35] The duty to report is imposed on physicians and other health care practitioners,[36] and may also extend to others such as school teachers or principals,[37] persons in charge of a laboratory or hospital,[38] or any individual who is aware of a case of a notifiable disease.[39] The report must be made within a specified time limit, and must include prescribed information such as the individual's name and contact information, the name of the disease, known risk factors or other information relevant to the disease, and the results of laboratory tests.[40] This is a mandatory requirement that will override any legal or ethical obligations of confidentiality that health care providers would otherwise owe to their patients. Public health legislation may include specific provisions to protect the information from further disclosure.[41]

Although mandatory reporting is important to enable public health authorities to track and respond to cases of infectious disease, there is a risk that individuals may be deterred from seeking testing and treatment if they know that their personal health information will be reported. This concern has been especially important in the case of HIV/AIDS, because of the serious consequences and social stigma attached to a positive HIV diagnosis. As a result, many jurisdictions have special provisions that allow anonymous or non-nominal testing for HIV/AIDS.[42] Under these provisions, cases must still be reported but the individual's name and contact information will not be included in the report unless the individual voluntarily agrees to this disclosure. More limited personal information such as the individual's initials, gender and/or birth date will be

---

[34] See, *e.g.*, *Diseases and Dead Bodies Regulation*, Man. Reg. 338/88 R, s. 5; *Public Health Act*, R.S.A. 2000, c. P-37, s. 26; *Health Protection Act*, S.N.S. 2004, c. 4, s. 31(5).

[35] See, *e.g.*, *Public Health Act*, R.S.A. 2000, c. P-37, s. 15.

[36] See, *e.g.*, *Health Protection and Promotion Act*, R.S.O. 1990, c. H.7, s. 25; *Communicable Diseases Act*, R.S.N.L. 1990, c. C-26, s. 4; *Public Health Act*, R.S.Q. c. S-2.2, s. 82(1).

[37] See, *e.g.*, *Public Health Act, 1994*, S.S. 1994, c. P-37.1, s. 32(1)(*c*); *Health Protection and Promotion Act*, R.S.O. 1990, c. H.7, s. 28; *Health Protection Act*, S.N.S. 2004, c. 4, s. 31(2).

[38] See, *e.g.*, *Communicable Disease Regulation*, B.C. Reg. 4/83, ss. 2(3), 3; *Public Health Act, 1994*, S.S. 1994, c. P-37.1, s. 32(1)(*b*); *Public Health Act*, R.S.A. 2000, c. P-37, ss. 22(1), 23; *Public Health Act*, R.S.Q. c. S-2.2, s. 82(2).

[39] See, *e.g.*, *Communicable Disease Regulation*, B.C. Reg. 4/83, s. 2(1).

[40] See, *e.g.*, *Communicable Disease Regulation*, *ibid.*, s. 4; *Disease Control Regulations*, R.R.S. 2000, c. P-37.1, Reg. 11, s. 14.

[41] See, *e.g.*, *Public Health Act*, R.S.A. 2000, c. P-37, s. 53. Where specific provision is not made, the information may nevertheless be protected by provincial privacy or health information legislation.

[42] Mary Anne Bobinski, "HIV/AIDS and Public Health Law" in Tracey M. Bailey, Timothy Caulfield & Nola M. Ries, *Public Health Law and Policy in Canada* (Markham, ON: LexisNexis Butterworths, 2005) at 186-87, 198-200.

required.[43] These requirements represent a compromise between protecting confidentiality and minimizing the chance of duplicate reports which would compromise the accuracy of surveillance data. In some circumstances, the medical or public health officer may be able to compel disclosure of the name of an HIV-positive individual notwithstanding provisions for anonymous reporting.[44]

The mandatory reporting provisions in the Ontario public health legislation were challenged in *Canadian AIDS Society v. Ontario* as being contrary to sections 7 (life, liberty and security of the person) and 8 (freedom from unreasonable search and seizure) of the Charter.[45] The case involved the HIV testing of blood that had been donated up to 10 years previously. The testing identified 22 HIV-positive donors, of whom 13 had not previously been identified as being HIV-positive; the issue was whether the positive tests had to be reported to public health authorities as provided under the *Health Protection and Promotion Act*,[46] and the donors contacted to notify them of the test results.[47] The applicant Canadian AIDS Society argued that under these circumstances the mandatory reporting requirements infringed sections 7 and 8 of the Charter. The Court found that the psychological stress caused by reporting could infringe donors' rights to security of the person but that this did not amount to a violation of section 7 because it was in accordance with principles of fundamental justice. The legislation struck an appropriate balance between individual rights and important public health objectives, and it incorporated protections for individuals such as a requirement that information reported under the Act be kept confidential.[48] In coming to this conclusion, Wilson J. stated that in this context, "although due consideration will be given to the privacy rights of individuals, the state objective of promoting public health for the safety of all will be given great weight".[49] The challenge based on section 8 also failed, since

---

[43]   See, *e.g., Disease Control Regulations*, R.R.S. 2000, c. P-37.1, Reg. 11, ss. 14(3), 15; *Communicable Disease Regulation*, B.C. Reg. 4/83, s. 4(5); *Reporting Requirements for HIV Positive Persons Regulations*, N.S. Reg. 197/2005, s. 9.

[44]   See, *e.g., Reporting Requirements for HIV Positive Persons Regulations*, N.S. Reg. 197/2005, s. 10; *Disease Control Regulations*, R.R.S. 2000, c. P-37.1, Reg. 11, s. 16. This will not be possible where the testing was truly anonymous in the sense that only the individual being tested has the code which links his or her identity with the test result, but will be possible under non-nominal testing where the physician or other health care provider knows the individual's identity and result. See Mary Anne Bobinski, "HIV/AIDS and Public Health Law" in Tracey M. Bailey, Timothy Caulfield & Nola M. Ries, *Public Health Law and Policy in Canada* (Markham, ON: LexisNexis Butterworths, 2005) at 186-87.

[45]   *Canadian AIDS Society v. Ontario*, [1995] O.J. No. 2361, 25 O.R. (3d) 388 (Ont. Gen. Div.); affd, [1996] O.J. No. 4184, 31 O.R. (3d) 798 (Ont. C.A.), leave to appeal dismissed, [1991] S.C.C.A. No. 33 (S.C.C.).

[46]   *Health Protection and Promotion Act*, R.S.O. 1990, c. H.7, s. 29.

[47]   It was agreed that the Red Cross was entitled to test the samples for the purpose of tracing recipients of blood from infected donors: *Canadian AIDS Society v. Ontario*, [1995] O.J. No. 2361, 25 O.R. (3d) 388 (Ont. Gen. Div.) at para. 59; affd, [1996] O.J. No. 4184, 31 O.R. (3d) 798 (Ont. C.A.); leave to appeal dismissed, [1997] S.C.C.A. No. 33 (S.C.C.).

[48]   *Ibid.*, at paras. 131-32.

[49]   *Ibid.*, at para. 133.

although there was a "seizure" of information, it was not unreasonable, again taking into account the public health purpose of the reporting requirement.[50]

B. CONTACT TRACING

Once a case of an infectious disease has been identified and reported, one way of preventing the further spread of the disease is to contact other individuals who may have been exposed to the disease, so that they can be tested and treatment or containment measures carried out if necessary. This is referred to as contact tracing, or alternatively, especially in the case of sexually transmitted diseases (STDs), partner notification. It may be done on a voluntary basis but is also provided for by statute in some jurisdictions and may be mandatory, at least for certain diseases, most commonly STDs.[51] Public health legislation may require individuals who are infected with designated diseases to provide a list of names and contact information for individuals with whom they have been in contact.[52] The individual him- or herself, health care provider or medical officer will then communicate with these contacts to inform them that they have been exposed and should be tested and take precautions against further transmission.[53]

Contact tracing is an intrusion into the privacy of the index individual whose contacts are disclosed and communicated with, and therefore mandatory contact tracing has been somewhat controversial, particularly in the case of HIV infection. The infringement of the index individual's privacy can be minimized by not disclosing his or her identity when a health care provider or medical officer communicates with contacts, although this will not necessarily prevent contacts from identifying the source of their potential infection. However, the index individual's right to privacy has to be weighed against the compelling interest in enabling contacts to be tested and treated to protect their own health and that of others to whom they might spread the infection. In addition to any statutory obligation to carry out contact tracing, health care providers may have legal and ethical duties to warn contacts of their exposure to an infectious disease, particularly if they also have a therapeutic relationship with those individuals.

C. INDIVIDUAL OBLIGATIONS

Public health legislation, as well as empowering public health authorities to take certain measures, may explicitly impose specific obligations on individuals who are or may be infected. These obligations, where they are provided for in legislation, exist independently of any order that may be made by public health

---

[50] *Ibid.*, at para. 159.
[51] For a useful summary of the variation among Canadian jurisdictions, see Elaine Gibson, "Public Health Information Privacy and Confidentiality" in Tracey M. Bailey, Timothy Caulfield & Nola M. Ries, *Public Health Law and Policy in Canada* (Markham, ON: LexisNexis Butterworths 2005) at 116-18.
[52] See, *e.g.*, *Public Health Act*, R.S.A. 2000, c. P-37, s. 56(1); *Public Health Act, 1994*, S.S. 1994, c. P-37.1, s. 33(4)(*b*); *Communicable Disease Regulations*, N.S. Reg. 196/2005, s. 11.
[53] See, *e.g.*, *Public Health Act, 1994*, S.S. 1994, c. P-37.1, ss. 33, 34, 35; *Disease Control Regulations*, R.R.S. 2000, c. P-37.1, Reg. 11, ss. 6, 7, 8.

authorities (see below). The diseases to which these obligations apply may include all communicable or infectious diseases covered by the legislation, or some subset of them, such as STDs.[54] An individual who suspects that she or he is infected with one of the prescribed diseases has an obligation to seek medical advice and/or testing, and if the test is positive, to submit to prescribed treatment until no longer infectious and take measures to prevent transmission of the disease.[55] If an infected individual refuses or neglects to submit to treatment, the physician may be required to report this to the medical officer,[56] and compulsory orders may be issued.[57] The new federal quarantine legislation requires travellers to answer questions and provide information upon request from screening officers, comply with "reasonable measures" ordered by those officers, and notify screening or quarantine officers if they suspect that they have or have come into contact with one of the designated communicable diseases.[58]

Apart from these legislative provisions, it is possible that an individual with an infectious disease who puts others at risk of infection may be liable in tort, for example for negligence or battery. Though there has apparently been few cases litigated on this basis in Canada,[59] there have been some successful actions in the United States.[60] The Supreme Court of Canada has also held that an individual who does not disclose his or her HIV-positive status and exposes another person to a significant risk of infection (for example, through unprotected sexual contact) may be convicted of aggravated assault.[61] Even if the complainant is not actually infected with the virus, her or his life is put at

---

[54] See, *e.g.*, *Public Health Act*, R.S.A. 2000, c. P-37, s. 20 (prescribed communicable diseases and prescribed STDs); *Minister's Regulation under the Public Health Act*, R.Q. c. S-2.2, r. 2, s. 9 (tuberculosis prescribed as disease for which treatment is mandatory); *Disease Control Regulations*, R.R.S. 2000, c. P-37.1, Reg. 11, Table 2 (category II diseases to which obligations apply, including HIV, hepatitis, STDs and tuberculosis); *Venereal Disease Act*, R.S.B.C. 1996, c. 475, s. 3.

[55] See, *e.g.*, *Public Health Act*, R.S.A. 2000, c. P-37, s. 20; *Public Health Act, 1994*, S.S. 1994, c. P-37.1, s. 33; *Venereal Disease Act*, R.S.B.C. 1996, c. 475, s. 3.

[56] *Communicable Disease Regulations*, N.S. Reg. 196/2005, s. 10(1); *Diseases and Dead Bodies Regulation*, Man. Reg. 338/88 R, s. 44; *Health Protection and Promotion Act*, R.S.O. 1990, c. H.7, s. 34; *Public Health Act*, R.S.Q. c. S-2.2, s. 86 (this applies only for prescribed diseases for which treatment is compulsory).

[57] *Public Health Act*, R.S.A. 2000, c. P-37, ss. 39-52. See also the discussion of coercive powers below.

[58] *Quarantine Act*, S.C. 2005, c. 20, s. 15.

[59] See, *e.g.*, *Fitzgerald v. Tin*, [2003] B.C.J. No. 203 (B.C.S.C.), though this case dealt with liability of a taxi company for a needle stick injury, rather than liability of the infected individual himself or herself.

[60] See the brief discussion in Mary Anne Bobinski, "HIV/AIDS and Public Health Law" in Tracey M. Bailey, Timothy Caulfield & Nola M. Ries, *Public Health Law and Policy in Canada* (Markham, ON: LexisNexis Butterworths, 2005) at 207-208. The decision in *Fitzgerald v. Tin*, [2003] B.C.J. No. 203 at paras. 46-50 (B.C.S.C.) discusses approaches to damages assessment in such cases in the United States jurisprudence.

[61] *R. v. Cuerrier*, [1998] S.C.J. No. 64, 2 S.C.R. 371 (S.C.C.). Subsequently, in *R. v. Williams*, [2003] S.C.J. No. 41, 2 S.C.R. 134 (S.C.C.), the Court held that the accused could only be convicted of attempted aggravated assault where it could not be established that he infected his partner after he learned of his HIV-positive status.

significant risk through the possibility of infection and this establishes the first element of aggravated assault, endangering the life of the complainant.[62] The majority also held that the second element, the application of force without consent, was established since withholding information about one's HIV status from a potential sexual partner amounts to fraud which vitiates their consent.[63] Interveners in the case had argued that criminal law is not an effective or appropriate way of addressing the risk of HIV transmission, which should be dealt with through public health statutes; they also argued that criminalization could deter people from seeking HIV testing and further stigmatize HIV-positive individuals.[64] However, these arguments were rejected by Cory J. (writing for the majority of the Court), who noted that public education about the risk of HIV transmission did not appear to be effective in all cases and thus argued that the criminal law could have an important supplementary role in deterring particularly risky conduct and thereby providing some protection.[65] Since this decision, a number of individuals have been prosecuted and convicted for concealing their HIV status (or other disease, for example, hepatitis C) and exposing others to a risk of infection.[66]

D. COERCIVE POWERS

Public health legislation also confers on public authorities, such as the medical officer and/or the Minister of Health, a range of powers to prevent and contain the spread of infectious diseases and to deal with other public health threats. These include, for example, the authority to require individuals to submit to testing or treatment, to order the quarantine or isolation of individuals, to inspect premises and order them to be closed or disinfected, to require the production of information, or to require persons to take measures to prevent transmission.[67] Additional powers may be exercised during an epidemic or public health emergency including the power to limit travel, to close public places, to procure or confiscate essential supplies, take possession of premises, or any other necessary measure.[68] Federal quarantine officers may require travellers to undergo a health assessment or medical examination if there are reasonable grounds to believe that they have or may have, or have been in contact with, a

---

[62] *R. v. Cuerrier, ibid.*, at para. 95 (*per* Cory J., for the majority).

[63] *Ibid.*, at paras. 125-39 (*per* Cory J., for the majority).

[64] *Ibid.*, at paras. 140-45.

[65] *Ibid.*, at paras. 146-47.

[66] See, *e.g.*, "Criminal Law and HIV Transmission/Exposure: Two New Cases" (2005) 10(1) HIV/AIDS Pol'y & L. Rev.; "Criminal Law and HIV Transmission/Exposure: More New Cases" (2002) 7(2/3) HIV/AIDS Pol'y & L. Rev.; "Criminal Law and HIV/AIDS: Update V" (2001) 6(1/2) HIV/AIDS Pol'y & L. Rev.

[67] See, *e.g.*, *Health Protection Act*, S.N.S. 2004, c. 4, s. 32; *Health Protection and Promotion Act*, R.S.O. 1990, c. H.7, ss. 22, 41; *Public Health Act*, R.S.A. 2000, c. P-37, ss. 29-52; *Public Health Act, 1994*, S.S. 1994, c. P-37.1, s. 38; *Health Act*, R.S.B.C. 1996, c. 179, ss. 8, 11.

[68] See, *e.g.*, *Health Protection Act*, S.N.S. 2004, c. 4, s. 53(2); *Public Health Act*, R.S.A. 2000, c. P-37, ss. 29(2.1), 52.6; *Public Health Act, 1994*, S.S. 1994, c. P-37.1, s. 45; *Health Act*, R.S.B.C. 1996, c. 179, s. 16.

communicable disease.[69] They may also order travellers to comply with treatment "or any other measure" to prevent the spread of disease.[70] Failure to comply may result in detention.[71]

Although provincial legislation provides for mandatory immunization to be ordered as well as testing and treatment, individuals may be permitted to refuse immunization on conscientious grounds.[72] However, legislation may also provide that children can be excluded from school or day care facilities if they have not been immunized against designated diseases,[73] and a few jurisdictions specifically provide for mandatory immunization of school children against specified diseases.[74] There have been a number of recent instances in which students have been suspended from Canadian schools, amid growing concerns about low rates of immunization and the resurgence of previously dormant diseases such as pertussis (whooping cough).[75]

An order for detention and treatment under Ontario public health legislation was unsuccessfully challenged in *Toronto (City, Medical Officer of Health) v. Deakin*.[76] Mr. Deakin, a "recalcitrant" tuberculosis patient, had consented to an order of detention but objected to treatment and to restraints that had been used to prevent his escape from detention. When the medical officer sought to extend the order, Deakin challenged it on the basis that it infringed his rights under sections 7 and 9 of the *Canadian Charter of Rights and Freedoms*. The Court accepted that the Charter applied to the actions of the medical centre and the doctor, who were acting under statutory authority, but held that any infringement of the patient's rights was justified under section 1 of the Charter.

In addition to the powers provided for in public health legislation, as noted above, both federal and provincial/territorial levels of government have legislation relating to emergency management, which could apply to a public health emergency. Provincial legislation allows provincial ministers and municipal authorities to declare provincial or local states of emergency,[77] and to

---

[69] *Quarantine Act*, S.C. 2005, c. 20, ss. 20, 22.
[70] *Ibid.*, s. 26.
[71] *Ibid.*, s. 28.
[72] See, *e.g.*, *Health Act*, R.S.B.C. 1996, c. 179, s. 13; *Public Health Act*, R.S.A. 2000, c. P-37, s. 38(3); *Public Health Act, 1994*, S.S. 1994, c. P-37.1, s. 64; *Immunization of School Pupils Act*, R.S.O. 1990, c. I.1, s. 3. On the controversy surrounding mandatory immunization, see Patricia Peppin, "Vaccines and Emerging Challenges for Public Health Law" in Tracey M. Bailey, Timothy Caulfield & Nola Ries, eds., *Public Health Law and Policy in Canada* (Markham, ON: LexisNexis Butterworths, 2005) at 148-56.
[73] *Public Health Act, 1994*, S.S. 1994, c. P-37.1, s. 45(2)(*d*)(ii) (in the case of a serious public health threat); *Communicable Diseases Act*, R.S.N.L. 1990, c. C-26, s. 25; *General Regulation — Health Act*, N.B. Reg. 88-200, s. 285.
[74] *Immunization of School Pupils Act*, R.S.O. 1990, c. I.1, s. 6; *General Regulation — Health Act*, N.B. Reg. 88-200, s. 284. Note, however, that these are subject to medical or conscientious objection exceptions.
[75] "Kingston students suspended until immunized" (September 25, 2006), online: CBC News <http://www.cbc.ca/health/story/2006/09/25/immunizations.html>; "More than 1,000 Waterloo students suspended from school" (May 4, 2006), online: CBC News <http://www.cbc.ca/canada/toronto/story/2006/05/04/immunization-schools20060504.html>.
[76] [2002] O.J. No. 2777 (Ont. C.J.).
[77] See, *e.g.*, *Emergency Management Act*, S.N.S. 1990, c. 8, s. 12; *Civil Emergency Measures Act*,

exercise broad powers to protect public health and safety in an emergency, including implementation of emergency plans, restrictions on movement, and regulation of essential goods and services.[78] Emergency powers may include the power to require qualified persons to provide assistance,[79] which would allow provincial or local authorities to compel medical or other health care professionals to provide services in a public health emergency.

Under the federal *Emergencies Act*, a "public welfare emergency" may include an emergency caused by an actual or imminent disease that "results or may result in a danger to life or property, social disruption or a breakdown in the flow of essential goods, services or resources, so serious as to be a national emergency".[80] A "national emergency" is defined as "an urgent and critical situation of a temporary nature" that, among other things, "seriously endangers the lives, health or safety of Canadians", if it exceeds the capacity or authority of a province and "cannot effectively be dealt with under any other law of Canada".[81] A serious epidemic of infectious disease could fall within this definition. A public welfare emergency may be declared by the Governor in Council to exist in all or part of Canada.[82] While the declaration of emergency is in effect, the Governor in Council has the authority to make orders and regulations reasonably believed to be necessary to deal with it, including, for example, restricting travel, regulating essential goods or services, or establishing emergency hospitals.[83] Another federal statute, the *Emergency Preparedness Act*, requires the responsible Minister (currently the Minister of Public Safety) to coordinate and support the development of civil emergency plans and to advance emergency preparedness, and in the case of an emergency, to monitor and coordinate the implementation of civil emergency plans.[84] Other Ministers are responsible for emergency planning within their areas of accountability.[85]

R.S.N.W.T. 1988, c. C-9, ss. 11, 14; *Emergency Measures Act*, C.C.S.M. c. E80, ss. 10-11; *Emergency Planning Act*, S.S. 1989-90, c. E-8.1, ss. 17, 20; *Emergency Management and Civil Protection Act*, R.S.O. 1990, c. E.9, ss. 4, 7.0.1.

[78] See, *e.g.*, *Emergency Management Act*, S.N.S. 1990, c. 8, s. 14; *Civil Emergency Measures Act*, R.S.N.W.T. 1988, c. C-9, ss. 12, 17; *Emergency Measures Act*, C.C.S.M. c. E80, s. 12; *Emergency Planning Act*, S.S. 1989-90, c. E-8.1, ss. 18, 21; *Emergency Management and Civil Protection Act*, R.S.O. 1990, c. E.9, s. 7.0.2(4).

[79] See, *e.g.*, *Emergency Management Act*, S.N.S. 1990, c. 8, s. 14(*c*); *Civil Emergency Measures Act*, R.S.N.W.T. 1988, c. C-9, s. 12(*d*); *Emergency Measures Act*, C.C.S.M. c. E80, s. 12(*c*); *Emergency Planning Act*, S.S. 1989-90, c. E-8.1, s. 18(1)(*m*). Compare the *Emergency Management and Civil Protection Act*, R.S.O. 1990, c. E.9, s. 7.0.2(4)12, which provides for orders authorizing, but not requiring, qualified persons to render services.

[80] *Emergencies Act*, R.S.C. 1985, c. 22 (4th Supp.), s. 5.

[81] *Ibid.*, s. 3.

[82] *Ibid.*, s. 6.

[83] *Ibid.*, s. 8(1).

[84] *Emergency Preparedness Act*, R.S.C. 1985, c. 6 (4th Supp.), ss. 4-5. This statute is to be replaced by the *Emergency Management Act*, Bill C-12 (39th Parl., 1st Sess.) (the Bill received its Second Reading in the House of Commons on September 22, 2006 and was referred to Senate Committee March 28, 2007).

[85] *Emergency Preparedness Act*, *ibid.*, s. 7.

The Centre for Emergency Preparedness and Response is responsible for emergency planning for PHAC and Health Canada.[86]

One of the key challenges in this area is striking the right balance between respect for provincial and local jurisdiction and ensuring coordinated, timely and effective action in an emergency situation. In most situations, measures at the local level will be of primary importance and broader action can be achieved through cooperation. The emergency powers of the Governor in Council under the federal *Emergencies Act* are to be used in a way that does not interfere with provincial emergency measures and "with a view to achieving, to the extent possible, concerted action" with affected provinces.[87] The Governor in Council is required to consult with affected provinces and is not to declare a public welfare emergency where the direct effects of the emergency are limited to a single province unless that province's lieutenant governor in council has indicated that the emergency exceeds the province's capacity or authority.[88] Civil emergency plans developed under the *Emergency Preparedness Act* are not to be implemented in response to a provincial emergency except at the province's request or by agreement with the province.[89] The limits established by these provisions are designed to avoid federal encroachments on provincial jurisdiction, but might prove to be unduly restrictive in a public health emergency if an affected province resists federal involvement. Coordination between jurisdictions may also be complicated by variations in emergency legislation between jurisdictions. Among the concerns raised in inquiries following the SARS outbreak were questions about the consistency and interoperability of federal, provincial and territorial legislative frameworks for emergency response and lack of clarity about the allocation of jurisdiction in emergencies.[90]

V. CHRONIC DISEASE SURVEILLANCE, PREVENTION AND CONTROL

While infectious diseases have received a great deal of recent attention, chronic diseases account for the majority of deaths and of the burden of disease in Canada and worldwide.[91] Chronic diseases are non-communicable diseases

---

[86] Public Health Agency of Canada, "Centre for Emergency Preparedness and Response", online: <http://www.phac-aspc.gc.ca/cepr-cmiu/index.html>.

[87] *Emergencies Act*, R.S.C. 1985, c. 22 (4th Supp.), s. 8(3).

[88] *Ibid.*, s. 14.

[89] *Ibid.*, s. 7(3). A "provincial emergency" is defined in s. 2 as "an emergency occurring in a province if the province or a local authority in the province has the primary responsibility for dealing with the emergency".

[90] National Advisory Committee on SARS and Public Health, *Learning from SARS: Renewal of Public Health in Canada* (Ottawa: Health Canada, 2003) at 6-7, 98-102, 108.

[91] Centre for Chronic Disease Prevention and Control, "Integrated Approach to Chronic Disease" (2003), online: Public Health Agency of Canada <http://www.phac-aspc.gc.ca/ccdpc-cpcmc/topics/integrated_e.html>; WHO, *Preventing Chronic Diseases: A Vital Investment* (Geneva: WHO, 2005) at 37 (chronic disease accounts for 60 per cent of global deaths and is the

(although infectious agents may play a role in their development) which develop and cause disability over an extended time period.[92] They include heart disease, stroke, cancer and diabetes. Prevention and control of chronic disease present some distinct challenges as compared to infectious diseases. Because these diseases may take years and even decades to develop and may have multiple causes, long-term, multi-faceted prevention strategies are required. The risk factors associated with a large proportion of the chronic disease burden are common and easily recognized — unhealthy diet, insufficient physical activity and smoking — but the interventions required to change them are challenging. Common risk factors and higher incidence of chronic disease tend to be correlated with low socio-economic status. The diseases also impose a heavy economic burden, leading to a vicious cycle of chronic disease and poverty.[93]

In part due to these challenges, the legal framework relating to chronic disease is more fragmented and difficult to analyze than that of infectious diseases. This section will focus on two main aspects: surveillance of chronic disease and cancer screening programs as a form of prevention. The following section will explore in some detail the range of legal interventions to reduce tobacco as a major cause of chronic disease.

A. REGISTRIES AND OTHER SURVEILLANCE MECHANISMS

In some provinces, compulsory reporting under public health legislation, as discussed above, may also apply to prescribed non-communicable diseases.[94] Obligations to report work-related diseases and conditions may also exist under occupational health and safety legislation. However, the most common type of formal surveillance program for chronic diseases is mandatory reporting of disease to a registry, in particular for cancer. Every Canadian province and territory has a cancer registry, and these all report to the Canadian Cancer Registry (CCR), which is maintained by Statistics Canada.[95] The operations of Statistics Canada, including the CCR, are governed by the *Statistics Act*.[96] Sharing of information between the CCR and registries throughout the country

---

       leading cause of death and burden of disease in all regions except Africa).

[92]   *Ibid.*, at 35.

[93]   *Ibid.*, at 61*ff.*

[94]   See, *e.g.*, *Public Health Act, 1994*, S.S. 1994, c. P-37.1, s. 31. No non-communicable diseases have yet been prescribed by regulation for the purpose of this section. However, s. 31.1 also requires physicians and others to report any serious illness which "is occurring at a high rate". See also *Health Protection Act*, S.N.S. 2004, c. 4, s. 4(*m*): notifiable diseases and conditions are any that are prescribed by regulation, and are not restricted to communicable diseases. To date only "vaccine associated adverse events" have been prescribed as notifiable non-communicable diseases or conditions: *Reporting of Notifiable Diseases and Conditions Regulations*, N.S. Reg. 195/2005, Schedule A, Part II.

[95]   Statistics Canada, "Canadian Cancer Registry: Detailed Information for 2004" (July 11, 2005), online: <http://www.statcan.ca/cgi-bin/imdb/p2SV.pl?Function=getSurvey&SDDS=3207&lang= en&db=IMDB&dbg=f&adm=8&dis=2>.

[96]   *Statistics Act*, R.S.C. 1985, c. S-19.

takes place under agreements between the federal government and the respective provincial or territorial government.[97]

Most, but not all, provinces and territories have legislation authorizing and governing the operation of the cancer registry, including cancer-specific legislation and/or public health legislation.[98] This legislation typically requires reporting of prescribed information, either automatically or upon request.[99] Those responsible for reporting information include physicians, hospitals and laboratories; the reportable conditions and events are defined in various ways, including a diagnosis of cancer or patient with cancer.[100] Where reporting is compulsory, the obligation to report will override legal or ethical duties of confidentiality, just as for reporting of notifiable infectious diseases. Once information is collected in the registry, it will be governed by freedom of information and protection of privacy legislation applicable to public bodies, health information legislation, and/or confidentiality provisions in the legislation governing the registry. These will allow the information to be used or disclosed only for certain purposes, such as for research, compilation of statistics, designing prevention programs and treatment or care of the individual who is the subject of the information.[101]

The variation between legislative frameworks for cancer surveillance in Canadian jurisdictions has been recognized as a problem and several groups have been working toward greater integration and development of the registries.[102] With some jurisdictions having mandatory reporting and others relying on voluntary reports, and differences in the definition of what must be reported, the data collected cannot be easily compiled and compared. In order to serve its purposes most effectively, the collection of information must be standardized. To some extent, this will require harmonization of the relevant legislation.[103] Cancer registries would also be more useful if they could be expanded to include more information (*e.g.*, information about treatment and care) and linked to other data (*e.g.*, risk factor data or other health information),

---

[97] Barbara von Tigerstrom, Mylène Deschênes, Bartha Maria Knoppers & Timothy A. Caulfield, *Use of Cancer Patient Information for Surveillance Purposes: A Systematic Review of Legislation, Regulations, Policies and Guidelines* (Ottawa: Canadian Coalition on Cancer Surveillance, March 2000) at 38-39.

[98] *Ibid.*, at 24*ff* and Appendix A.

[99] *Ibid.*, at 39.

[100] *Ibid.*, at 40.

[101] *Ibid.*, at 42-43.

[102] *Ibid.*, at 77-78; Canadian Strategy for Cancer Control, "Surveillance Action Group: Terms of Reference" (February 20, 2004), online: <http://www.cancercontrol.org/cscc/pdf/priorities_pdf/Surveillance_TOR.PDF>; Barbara Foster & Anna Maria Boscaino, "Status Report: Canadian Coalition on Cancer Surveillance" (2000) 21 Chronic Diseases in Canada 26.

[103] *Ibid.*, at 77. This report notes that some standardization can take place through guidelines, codes of practice, or other standards; however, some matters such as the definition of a reportable disease or reportable event would require legislative changes (usually changes to regulations). See also Canadian Strategy for Cancer Control, "Cancer Surveillance in Canada" (Surveillance Working Group Final Report) (January 2002), online: <http://www.cancercontrol.org/cscc/pdf/finalsurveillanceJan2002.PDF> at 11.

however expansion and integration of surveillance activities may heighten privacy concerns.[104]

B. SCREENING PROGRAMS

Screening involves testing asymptomatic members of a population or, more commonly, a target sub-population, for a disease or condition (or some precursor, risk factor, or indictor of a disease or condition). Because screening programs mean that many people will be tested who show no symptoms of a disease and may never develop it, the benefits of implementing a screening program must be carefully weighed against its costs and possible risks. The financial cost of testing, the risks it may present to individuals, rates of morbidity and mortality associated with the disease, the availability of effective preventive measures when cases are identified, and the reliability of screening results must all be considered. This decision may be controversial; for example, there are differing opinions and guidelines on the utility of screening for prostate cancer, and a recent study indicates that many men are requesting and receiving the screening test even where national guidelines have recommended against widespread use because its utility is not well established.[105] Identification of the target population may also be a matter of debate, such as in defining the age groups that should be included for prostate cancer screening (if it is implemented at all), or breast cancer screening.[106] Furthermore, our growing knowledge about the relationship between genetics and risks of disease raises the prospect of genetic screening as a public health strategy, carrying with it concerns about protection of genetic information and the use of racial categories to identify at-risk populations.[107]

The most common chronic disease screening programs in Canada are for cervical cancer and breast cancer. These programs are found in all provinces and territories, and are administered by the health department or provincial cancer agency, which may have a statutory mandate to carry out such activities.[108] The

---

[104] *Ibid.*, at 11-12; Barbara von Tigerstrom, Mylène Deschênes, Bartha Maria Knoppers & Timothy A. Caulfield, *Use of Cancer Patient Information for Surveillance Purposes: A Systematic Review of Legislation, Regulations, Policies and Guidelines* (Ottawa: Canadian Coalition on Cancer Surveillance, March 2000) at 78.

[105] Jennifer A. Beaulac, Richard N. Fry & Jay Onysko, "Lifetime and Recent Prostate Specific Antigen (PSA) Screening of Men for Prostate Cancer in Canada" (2006) 97 Can. J. Public Health 171.

[106] Richard M. Hoffman, "Viewpoint: Limiting Prostate Cancer Screening" (2006) 144 Annals of Internal Medicine 438; William J. Catalona, Stacey Loeb & Misop Han, "Viewpoint: Expanding Prostate Cancer Screening" (2006) 144 Annals of Internal Medicine 441; Linda L. Humphrey *et al.*, "Breast Cancer Screening: A Summary of the Evidence for the U.S. Preventive Services Task Force" (2002) 137 Annals of Internal Medicine 347 at 355-56.

[107] Muin J. Khoury, "From Genes to Public Health: The Applications of Genetic Technology in Disease Prevention" (1996) 86 Am. J. Public Health 1717; Michael J. Fine, Said A. Ibrahim & Stephen B. Thomas, "The Role of Race and Genetics in Health Disparities Research" (2005) 95 Am. J. Public Health 2125; Sandra Soo-Jin Lee, "Racializing Drug Design: Implications of Pharmacogenomics for Health Disparities" (2005) 95 Am. J. Public Health 2133.

[108] See, *e.g.*, *Cancer Act*, R.S.O. 2000, c. C.1, s. 5; *Cancer Programs Act*, R.S.A. 2000, c. C-2, s. 8(*d*).

programs involve the provision of screening tests to individuals in the identified target population, collection of the results in a centralized database, communication of results to the individual and her physician, and other communications with participants, for example to remind them when they are due for a test. Although the aim of screening is detection and prevention of disease rather than surveillance, organized screening programs typically also engage in systematic collection and analysis of the information generated through screening. Although the screening tests themselves are not usually mandatory,[109] the information sharing for the administration of the program may be. Personal information such as name, age, gender and contact information may be transmitted from the provincial health department to identify members of the target group, test results sent to the program, and reminders or other correspondence sent to physicians and individuals. This has raised privacy concerns, especially in the context of cervical cancer which is perceived to be more sensitive due to its association with sexually transmitted infections.

The cervical cancer screening programs in Saskatchewan and Alberta have both recently been investigated by the respective provincial Information and Privacy Commissioners following complaints from women about privacy concerns associated with the programs.[110] Both investigations found that the collection, use and disclosure of information in the screening programs were consistent with provincial health information legislation, but raised concerns about the mandatory nature of the programs and the lack of an opt-out for women who did not wish to participate. The programs allowed women to opt out of receiving reminder letters as part of the program but did not permit them to withdraw from the program entirely. The Alberta report found that the lack of a full opt-out meant that the Alberta Cancer Board "did not implement a program that complied with the duty to consider an expressed wish as an important factor in deciding how much 'health information' to disclose".[111] Prior to the report being released, the Alberta Cancer Board decided to implement a full opt-out.[112] There is no equivalent provision in the Saskatchewan health information legislation,[113] and the Commissioner there found that the legislation had been complied with; he nevertheless recommended that a full opt-out be available as a matter of policy and best practice.[114] He also found that greater transparency was

---

[109] Screening programs for newborns, most commonly for metabolic diseases, may be mandatory in some jurisdictions: see Sheila Wildeman & Jocelyn Downie, "Genetic and Metabolic Screening of Newborns: Must Health Care Providers Seek Explicit Parental Consent?" (2001) 9 Health L.J. 61.

[110] Saskatchewan Office of the Information and Privacy Commissioner, *Prevention Program for Cervical Cancer* (April 27, 2005), Investigation Report H-2005-002, online: <http://www.oipc.sk.ca/Reports/H-2005-002.pdf>; Alberta Information and Privacy Commissioner, *Report on the Collection, Use and Disclosure of Health Information for the Alberta Cervical Cancer Screening Program* (December 12, 2005), Investigation Report H2005-IR-002, online: <http://www.oipc.ab.ca/ims/client/upload/H2005_IR_002.pdf>.

[111] *Ibid.*, at para. 78. This duty is found in s. 58(2) of the *Health Information Act*, R.S.A. 2000, c. H-5.

[112] *Ibid.*, at para. 86-87.

[113] *Health Information Protection Act*, S.S. 1999, c. H-0.021.

[114] Saskatchewan Office of the Information and Privacy Commissioner, *Prevention Program for*

required and that neither the Saskatchewan Cancer Agency nor many physicians in the province had taken adequate steps to inform women about the operation of the program.[115]

VI. TOBACCO CONTROL

Tobacco-related disease is the leading cause of preventable death in Canada and in the world.[116] Half of all habitual smokers will die of tobacco-related causes such as cardiovascular disease, respiratory diseases, strokes and cancer, losing an estimated average of 15 to 25 years of life expectancy.[117] Approximately 19 per cent of Canadians aged 15 or older are current smokers.[118] According to a recent study based on 1998 data, "smoking attributable mortality" accounted for more than 47,000 deaths in Canada, representing 22 per cent of all deaths and six times the number of deaths from car accidents, alcohol, murder and suicides combined.[119]

Given the serious impact of tobacco consumption on public health, many governments have designed and implemented a broad range of measures to reduce this consumption and the harm it causes. Comprehensive tobacco control policies pursue a number of intermediate goals with the ultimate aim of reducing the human and economic cost of tobacco consumption. Common strategies include: reducing demand through marketing restrictions and price increases; restricting the supply of tobacco products, particularly to young people; and smoking bans to minimize harm from environmental tobacco smoke (ETS). Finally, judicial and other measures can be used to impose accountability, deter harmful conduct and recover costs associated with tobacco consumption.

A. REDUCING DEMAND

One of the objectives of tobacco control is to prevent people from taking up smoking, since the addictive properties of tobacco make it difficult for most people to quit.[120] Many of the same interventions also aim to encourage existing

Cervical Cancer (April 27, 2005), Investigation Report H-2005-002, online: <http://www.oipc.sk.ca/Reports/H-2005-002.pdf> at 12, 159*ff*, 180.

[115] *Ibid.*, at 10-11.

[116] Eva M. Makomaski Illing & Murray J. Kaiserman, "Mortality Attributable to Tobacco Use in Canada and its Regions, 1998" (2004) 95 Can. J. Public Health 38 at 42-43; WHO, *The World Health Report 2003* (Geneva: WHO, 2003) at 91.

[117] International Agency for Research on Cancer, Press Release No. 141 (June 19, 2002), online: <http://www.iarc.fr/ENG/Press_Releases/archives/pr141a.html>.

[118] Health Canada, "Canadian Tobacco Use Monitoring Survey 2005: Summary of Annual Results for 2005" (2006), online: <http://www.hc-sc.gc.ca/hl-vs/tobac-tabac/research-recherche/stat/ctums-esutc/2005/ann_summary-sommaire_e.html>.

[119] Eva M. Makomaski Illing & Murray J. Kaiserman, "Mortality Attributable to Tobacco Use in Canada and its Regions, 1998" (2004) 95 Can. J. Public Health 38 at 42-43.

[120] U.S. Department of Health and Human Services, *Reducing Tobacco Use: A Report of the Surgeon General* (Georgia: U.S. Department of Health and Human Services, Centers for Disease Control and Prevention, National Center for Chronic Disease Prevention and Health Promotion,

smokers to reduce (and hopefully eliminate) their consumption. The most
common legal strategies include marketing restrictions, control over packaging
and labelling of tobacco products, and increasing the price of tobacco products
through taxation. These are implemented alongside other interventions such as
public education and "countermarketing" to reduce demand.

1. Marketing Restrictions

The marketing of tobacco, like other consumer products, is subject to rules such
as the prohibition on misleading advertising, and these have been the subject of
some of the litigation against the tobacco industry, as will be seen below. In
addition, governments increasingly restrict the ability of tobacco companies to
market their products with the aim of preventing advertising and other marketing activities from increasing demand for these harmful products. In particular,
they seek to eliminate marketing that is likely to influence young people; since
most smokers become addicted before the age of 18 tobacco marketing campaigns directed at children and youth are a particular concern.[121]

In Canada, both federal and some provincial legislation restricts tobacco
marketing in a variety of ways. Part IV of the federal *Tobacco Act*[122] sets out
restrictions on promotion, which is broadly defined to include any direct or
indirect "representation about a product or service by any means, ... including
any communication of information about a product or service and its price or
distribution, that is likely to influence and shape attitudes, beliefs and
behaviours about the product or service".[123] The Act prohibits the promotion of
tobacco products or related brand elements except as authorized by the Act and
regulations, and proscribes the publication, broadcasting, or other dissemination
of prohibited promotions.[124] In addition, certain forms of promotion are
specifically prohibited, including promotion by any means that are "false,
misleading or deceptive or that are likely to create a false impression about the
characteristics, health effects or health hazards of the tobacco product or its
emissions", testimonials or endorsements (including by fictional characters), or
the use of tobacco manufacturer names or brand elements in sponsorship or in
naming of sports or cultural events or facilities.[125] Sales promotions such as gifts
with purchase, cash rebates, games and contests, and the distribution of free
tobacco products or accessories are prohibited.[126] Advertisements depicting or

---

Office on Smoking and Health, 2000), online: Centers for Disease Control and Prevention
<http://www.cdc.gov/tobacco/data-statistics/srg/srg_2000/srg_tobacco_chap_htm> at 97, 129.

[121] See, *e.g.*, Paul J. Chung *et al.*, "Youth targeting by tobacco manufacturers since the master
settlement agreement" (2002) 21 Health Affairs 254.

[122] *Tobacco Act*, S.C. 1997, c. 13.

[123] *Ibid.*, s. 18(1). Section 18(2) exempts certain activities from the operation of Part IV, such as
literary, artistic or scientific works or reports, commentaries or opinions depicting or referring to
tobacco products or brands, provided that no consideration is given by a tobacco retailer or
manufacturer for these works.

[124] *Ibid.*, ss. 19, 31(1).

[125] *Ibid.*, ss. 20, 21, 24, 25.

[126] *Ibid.*, s. 29.

evoking tobacco products, packages or brand elements are prohibited.[127] An exception is made for informational and brand preference advertising in adult direct mail, magazines or places, provided that it is not "lifestyle advertising" or reasonably interpreted as appealing to young people.[128] "Lifestyle advertising" is advertising that "associates a product with, or evokes a positive or negative emotion about or image of, a way of life such as one that includes glamour, recreation, excitement, vitality, risk or daring".[129] The sale and promotion of non-tobacco products displaying a tobacco brand element is also prohibited if they have similar "lifestyle" associations or are associated with or appealing to young persons.[130]

These provisions represent the federal government's attempt to tailor marketing restrictions in a way that would avoid unjustifiable infringements of the right to freedom of expression as interpreted by the Supreme Court of Canada in the 1995 decision of *RJR-MacDonald*.[131] In that case the former federal tobacco legislation, the *Tobacco Products Control Act*[132] was challenged as being outside Parliament's jurisdiction and a violation of the *Canadian Charter of Rights and Freedoms*. The Supreme Court found the legislation to be a valid exercise of the federal government's criminal law power,[133] but some of the provisions were struck down as contrary to the Charter. The Attorney General conceded that the prohibition on tobacco advertising and promotion infringed section 2(*b*) of the Charter, and the majority also found that the requirement of unattributed health warnings infringed this section.[134] By a narrow majority, the Court decided that some of the provisions could not be justified as reasonable limits under section 1 of the Charter. The Act's prohibition on tobacco advertising, ban on the use of tobacco trademarks on non-tobacco products and requirement of unattributed health warnings on tobacco packages were struck down (along with several other sections that could not be severed from these provisions). Despite a strong dissenting judgment by La Forest J. (with whom three other members of the Court concurred), the majority concluded that these provisions were not a minimal impairment of freedom of expression since the government had not demonstrated that less stringent measures would not be just as effective. Although both the majority and dissent stated that the necessity of such measures need not be established by definitive, scientific proof but could be supported by logic or common sense, they applied this test quite differently and thereby came to opposite conclusions

---

[127] *Ibid.*, s. 22(1).

[128] *Ibid.*, s. 22(2), (3).

[129] *Ibid.*, s. 22(4).

[130] *Ibid.*, s. 27.

[131] *RJR-MacDonald v. Canada (Attorney General)*, [1995] S.C.J. No. 68, [1995] 3 S.C.R. 199 (S.C.C.).

[132] *Tobacco Products Control Act*, S.C. 1988, c. 20 [repealed by S.C. 1997, c. 13, s. 64].

[133] All members of the Court agreed that the provisions requiring health warnings were valid criminal law, all but Major and Sopinka JJ. held that advertising bans could also fall within the criminal law power, and the majority held that the entire Act was validly enacted as criminal law.

[134] *RJR-MacDonald v. Canada (Attorney General)*, [1995] S.C.J. No. 68, 3 S.C.R. 199 at para. 124 (S.C.C.).

on these provisions.[135] The new provisions of the *Tobacco Act* will soon be considered by the Supreme Court in an appeal from the decision of the Quebec Court of Appeal in *J.T.I. MacDonald Corp. v. Canada (Attorney General)*, another challenge on constitutional grounds.[136]

Provincial legislation also restricts tobacco marketing in various ways. Some restrictions duplicate the federal *Tobacco Act* provisions, such as prohibiting sponsorship and endorsements.[137] However, in some cases provincial restrictions may be more stringent than the federal provisions. For example, several provinces prohibit or significantly restrict retail displays of tobacco products,[138] although retail display is specifically permitted by the federal legislation.[139] In *Rothmans, Benson & Hedges Inc. v. Saskatchewan*,[140] a challenge was brought against the retail display prohibition in Saskatchewan on the grounds that it was inoperative because of the doctrine of federal legislative paramountcy.[141] The Saskatchewan *Tobacco Control Act* prohibits the advertisement, promotion or display of tobacco products in premises where minors are permitted, including retail displays (the so-called "shower curtain law").[142] The Court upheld the provincial legislation, noting that a retailer could comply with both federal and provincial provisions, and the federal provisions did not create an *entitlement* to display tobacco products, but merely defined the scope of its promotion prohibition.[143] Both the federal and provincial statutes have the same purposes, so there is no inconsistency between their provisions merely because one is stricter.[144]

2. Packaging, Labelling and Warnings

Legal requirements with respect to the packaging of tobacco products aim to ensure that consumers are adequately informed about the health risks of these products. The federal *Tobacco Act* requires packages to display warnings as

[135] For discussion, see Barbara von Tigerstrom, "Healthy Communities: Public Health Law at the Supreme Court of Canada" in Jocelyn Downie & Elaine Gibson, eds., *Health Law at the Supreme Court of Canada* (Toronto: Irwin Law, forthcoming 2007).

[136] *J.T.I. MacDonald Corp. v. Canada (Attorney General)*, [2005] Q.J. No. 10915, 260 D.L.R. (4th) 224 (Que. C.A.).

[137] *Tobacco Act*, R.S.Q. c. T-0.01, ss. 22, 24(4).

[138] See, *e.g.*, *Tobacco Control Act*, S.S. 2001, c. T-14.1, s. 6; *Non-Smokers Health Protection Act*, C.C.S.M., c. N92, ss. 7.2, 7.3; *Tobacco Sales Act*, S.N.B. 1993, c. T-6.1, s. 6.21; *Tobacco Access Act*, S.N.S. 1993, c. 14, s. 9A. A recent amendment to the Quebec *Tobacco Act*, which will come into force on May 31, 2008, also prohibits retail display of tobacco products or packaging: *Tobacco Act*, R.S.Q. c. T-0.01, s. 20.2 (S.Q. 2005, c. 29, s. 24).

[139] *Tobacco Act*, S.C. 1997, c. 13, s. 30.

[140] *Rothmans, Benson & Hedges Inc. v. Saskatchewan*, [2005] S.C.J. No. 1, [2005] 1 S.C.R. 188 (S.C.C.).

[141] The legislation was also challenged on Charter grounds but the paramountcy issue was considered first by way of an application for summary determination; as of the date of writing, the Charter challenge had not yet proceeded to trial.

[142] *Tobacco Control Act*, S.S. 2001, c. T-14.1, s. 6.

[143] *Rothmans, Benson & Hedges Inc. v. Saskatchewan*, [2005] S.C.J. No. 1, [2005] 1 S.C.R. 188 at paras. 17-18 (S.C.C.).

[144] *Ibid.*, at paras. 25-26.

prescribed by the *Tobacco Products Information Regulation*.[145] The prescribed warnings contain short statements in bold lettering about the health effects of tobacco products and full-colour graphic images, and must cover at least 50 per cent of the principal display surfaces of the package.[146] The regulations also require prescribed health information to be printed on leaflet inserts or on another part of the package, covering 60 per cent to 70 per cent of the surface area in each case,[147] and the amounts of toxic emissions or constituents to be displayed on the package.[148] Some provincial statutes also enable regulations to be adopted prescribing warnings to be carried on tobacco packages.[149] Both federal and provincial legislation require health warnings to be displayed where tobacco products are sold.[150]

3. Taxation

The taxation of tobacco products is an important part of tobacco control, because raising the price of tobacco has been shown to reduce consumption, especially by young people.[151] In Canada, both the federal and provincial governments impose duties and taxes on tobacco products.[152] Federal duties are payable by the manufacturer or importer, while provincial taxes are payable at the point of sale (or upon import, if tobacco products are brought into the province by consumers). Federal and provincial legislation controls the manufacture, sale and import or export of tobacco products, and requires that these products be stamped to indicate that the duty has been paid.[153] Such measures aim to curtail smuggling of tobacco products, which has been an ongoing problem especially where there is significant variation in taxation rates between

---

[145] *Tobacco Act*, S.C. 1997, c. 13, s. 15(1); *Tobacco Products Information Regulation*, SOR/2000-272.
[146] *Ibid.*, s. 5(2).
[147] *Ibid.*, s. 7.
[148] *Ibid.*, ss. 9-11.
[149] See, *e.g.*, *Smoke-Free Ontario Act*, S.O. 1994, c. 10, ss. 5(1), 19(1)(*d*); *Tobacco Sales Act*, R.S.B.C. 1996, c. 451, s. 11(2)(*a*); *Tobacco Act*, R.S.Q. c. T-0.01, s. 28; *Non-Smokers Health Protection Act*, C.C.S.M., c. N92, s. 9(1)(*e*). Ontario has adopted regulations which require packages to carry the warnings prescribed by federal legislation: *General*, O. Reg. 48/06, s. 9.
[150] *Tobacco Act*, S.C. 1997, c. 13, s. 9 and see *e.g.*, *Smoke-Free Ontario Act*, S.O. 1994, c. 10, s. 6; *Tobacco Sales Regulation*, B.C. Reg. 216/94, s. 3; *Tobacco Access Regulations*, N.S. Reg. 9/96, s. 3, Schedules A-E; *Tobacco Act*, R.S.Q. c. T-0.01, s. 20.4.
[151] U.S. Department of Health and Human Services, *Reducing Tobacco Use: A Report of the Surgeon General* (Georgia: U.S. Department of Health and Human Services, Centers for Disease Control and Prevention, National Center for Chronic Disease Prevention and Health Promotion, Office on Smoking and Health, 2000), online: Centers for Disease Control and Prevention <http://www.cdc.gov/tobacco/sgr/sgr_2000/sgr_tobacco_chap.htm> at 337; Frank J. Chaloupka, Melanie Wakefield & Christina Czart, "Taxing Tobacco: The Impact of Tobacco Taxes on Cigarette Smoking and Other Tobacco Use" in Robert L. Rabin & Stephen Sugarman, eds., *Regulating Tobacco* (Oxford: Oxford University Press, 2001) at 39.
[152] See, *e.g.*, *Excise Act, 2001*, S.C. 2002, c. 22, ss. 42-48; *Tobacco Tax Act*, R.S.O. 1990, c. T.10; *Tobacco Tax Act*, R.S.A. 2000, c. T-4; *Tobacco Tax Act*, R.S.B.C. 1996, c. 452.
[153] See, *e.g.*, *Excise Act, 2001*, S.C. 2002, c. 22, ss. 25-41; *Tobacco Tax Act*, R.S.B.C. 1996, c. 452; *Tobacco Tax Act Regulation*, B.C. Reg. 66/2002.

jurisdictions. Lawsuits in several jurisdictions including Canada have accused major tobacco companies of collusion with smuggling.[154]

B. RESTRICTIONS ON SUPPLY

In some jurisdictions, sales of tobacco products are prohibited in certain specified locations, such as schools, child care and health care facilities, and pharmacies.[155] Vending machines selling cigarettes may be prohibited or limited to certain locations.[156]

The federal legislation and provincial legislation everywhere except Alberta prohibits the supply of tobacco products to persons under a prescribed age (18 or 19). The provisions prohibit both direct sales to minors and other forms of supply, such as purchasing tobacco on behalf of a minor (or selling to someone for this purpose).[157] A supplier will have a defence to a charge under these provisions if he or she attempted to verify the minor's age, was shown proof of age and reasonably believed that the minor was of age.[158] However, the mere fact that a minor appeared to be over the prescribed age is not a defence.[159] Retailers are required by federal and provincial legislation to post signs with the prescribed form and content stating that it is prohibited to sell tobacco products to minors.[160]

The broad prohibitions, including supply as well as sale and sales to someone buying on behalf of a minor, attempt to cover non-commercial sources such as friends and family members who give or sell cigarettes to minors, which are an increasingly important source of supply to young people.[161] However, a few jurisdictions exempt private supply by parents or legal guardians from the prohibition.[162] Several statutes also exempt gifts of tobacco for cultural or

---

[154] See the discussion in the section on tobacco litigation below.

[155] See, *e.g.*, *Tobacco Access Act*, S.N.S. 1993, c. 14, s. 9B; *Smoke-Free Ontario Act*, S.O. 1994, c. 10, s. 4; *Tobacco Act*, R.S.Q. c. T-0.01, ss. 17, 18; *Tobacco Control Act*, S.S. 2001, c. T-14.1, s. 8.

[156] See, *e.g.*, *Smoke-Free Ontario Act*, S.O. 1994, c. 10, s. 7; *Tobacco Act*, R.S.Q. c. T-0.01, s. 16; *Tobacco Act*, S.C. 1997, c. 13, s. 12.

[157] See, *e.g.*, *Tobacco Act*, S.C. 1997, c. 13, s. 8(1); *Tobacco Act*, R.S.Q. c. T-0.01, ss. 13, 14.3; *Smoke-Free Ontario Act*, S.O. 1994, c. 10, s. 3; *Tobacco Sales Act*, R.S.B.C. 1996, c. 451, s. 2(2); *Tobacco Access Act*, S.N.S. 1993, c. 14, s. 5.

[158] See, *e.g.*, *Tobacco Act*, S.C. 1997, c. 13, s. 8(2); *Tobacco Sales Act*, R.S.B.C. 1996, c. 451, s. 12(6); *Non-Smokers Health Protection Act*, C.C.S.M., c. N92, s. 7(3). The maritime provinces take a slightly different approach and provide that where a purchaser appears to be under-age, proof of age in a prescribed form must be provided before the product can be sold: see, *e.g.*, *Tobacco Sales Act*, S.N.B. 1993, c. T-6.1, s. 5(2).

[159] See, *e.g.*, *Tobacco Access Act*, S.N.S. 1993, c. 14, s. 5(3).

[160] See, *e.g.*, *Tobacco Act*, S.C. 1997, c. 13, s. 9; *Tobacco Control Act*, S.S. 2001, c. T-14.1, s. 7.

[161] Nancy A. Rigotti, "Reducing the Supply of Tobacco to Youths" in Robert L. Rabin & Stephen Sugarman, eds., *Regulating Tobacco* (Oxford: Oxford University Press, 2001) at 146-47; J. Forster *et al.*, "Social exchange of cigarettes by youth" (2003) 12 Tobacco Control 148.

[162] *Non-Smokers Health Protection Act*, C.C.S.M., c. N92, s. 7(2)(*a*); *Tobacco Control Act*, S.S. 2001, c. T-14.1, s. 4(4).

spiritual use, to accommodate traditional uses of tobacco by aboriginal peoples.[163]

Alberta and Nova Scotia prohibit the possession (and consumption, in Alberta) of tobacco products by minors.[164] In both jurisdictions, tobacco found in possession of a minor by a police officer may be confiscated; in Alberta, the minor may also be found guilty of an offence and fined up to $100.[165]

C. PROTECTION FROM ENVIRONMENTAL TOBACCO SMOKE

Environmental tobacco smoke (ETS, also known as second-hand smoke, passive smoking or involuntary smoking) has been found to cause lung cancer and cardiovascular disease, and to have serious health effects on children; a recent report of the U.S. Surgeon General concluded that there is no "safe level" of exposure to second-hand smoke.[166] As awareness has spread that ETS is not just a nuisance but a serious health hazard, jurisdictions have implemented stricter legislation on smoking in public places. These restrictions are found at local, provincial and federal levels. The federal *Non-smokers' Health Act* restricts smoking in workplaces within the jurisdiction of the federal government, which include government offices and federally-regulated industries.[167] Smoking is prohibited and employers must ensure that persons refrain from smoking in enclosed work spaces except in designated areas.[168]

The provinces and territories have imposed a range of restrictions on smoking in workplaces and public places, as have many municipalities.[169] Some have enacted comprehensive bans on smoking in public places and workplaces.[170] Others have bans applying to specific categories of places (such as schools, hospitals, or public transport).[171] It is the range of places which are covered that is most important, rather than the structure of the prohibition: a comprehensive

---

[163] See *Smoke-Free Ontario Act*, S.O. 1994, c. 10, s. 13(2); *Non-Smokers Health Protection Act*, C.C.S.M. c. N92, s. 7(2)(*b*); *Tobacco Control Act*, S.S. 2001, c. T-14.1, s. 4(5); *Smoke-free Places Act*, S.N.B. 2004, c. S-9.5, s. 2(3).

[164] *Prevention of Youth Tobacco Use Act*, R.S.A. 2000, c. P-22, s. 2; *Smoke-Free Places Act*, S.N.S. 2002, c. 12, s. 11(1).

[165] *Prevention of Youth Tobacco Use Act*, R.S.A. 2000, c. P-22, ss. 3, 4; *Smoke-Free Places Act*, S.N.S. 2002, c. 12, s. 11(2).

[166] U.S. Department of Health and Human Services, *The Health Consequences of Involuntary Exposure to Tobacco Smoke: A Report of the Surgeon General* (Atlanta, Georgia: U.S. Department of Health and Human Services, Centers for Disease Control and Prevention, Coordinating Center for Health Promotion, National Center for Chronic Disease Prevention and Health Promotion, Office on Smoking and Health, 2006) at 11.

[167] *Non-smokers' Health Act*, R.S.C. 1985 (4th Supp.), c. 15.

[168] *Ibid.*, ss. 3, 4.

[169] For an overview of municipal bylaws, see Non-Smokers' Rights Association, "Compendium of 100% Smoke-free Public Place Municipal By-laws" (August 2006), online: <http://www.nsra-adnf.ca/cms/file/pdf/compendium_Aug_4_2006.pdf>.

[170] See, *e.g.*, *Tobacco Control Act*, S.S. 2001, c. T-14.1, s. 11; *Non-Smokers Health Protection Act*, C.C.S.M. c. N92, s. 2; *Smoke-Free Environment Act, 2005*, S.N.L. 2005, c. S-16.2, s. 4; *Tobacco Control Act*, S.Nu. 2003, c. 13, ss. 13 (workplaces), 14 (public places); *Smoke-free Places Act*, S.N.B. 2004, c. S-9.5, s. 3.

[171] See, *e.g.*, *Tobacco Act*, R.S.Q., c. T-0.01, s. 2; *Smoke-free Places Act*, S.N.S. 2002, c. 12, s. 5.

list may have a similar scope to a ban on smoking in public places depending on how "public places" are defined. There is a clear trend toward more comprehensive smoking bans.[172] For example, in 2005 Ontario added a comprehensive ban covering all enclosed public places to a limited ban covering listed places,[173] and Quebec extended its list to include, most notably, restaurants and bars.[174] Such bans have been most contentious, with some restaurant and bar owners (in some cases supported by tobacco companies) opposing them on the grounds that they are harmful to their businesses, though the evidence supporting such claims is at best equivocal.[175] Several lawsuits have tried unsuccessfully to challenge municipal bylaws.[176] Comprehensive bans covering most public places including bars and restaurants now apply in a substantial number of provinces and municipalities. Some provincial statutes explicitly provide that where there are overlapping provincial and municipals laws, the stricter of these laws will prevail.[177]

Even the most comprehensive smoking bans provide for some exemptions, though increasingly only in designated areas that are limited in size, enclosed and have separate ventilation. Common exemptions include outdoor areas of bars and restaurants, private clubs, residential care facilities, and hotels or other lodgings. Several statutes exempt traditional uses of tobacco by aboriginal peoples from smoking bans.[178] The Manitoba *Non-Smokers Health Protection Act* also excludes its application to reserve lands.[179] This exemption was recently challenged by the owner of a tavern outside a reserve who argued that the differential application of the ban on and off reserve was discriminatory. Mr.

---

[172] This is true internationally, as well as in Canada: see Barbara Sibbald, "Number of countries with nationwide smoking restrictions growing" (2003) 168 C.M.A.J. 1459.

[173] Compare *Tobacco Control Act, 1994*, S.O. 1994, c. 10, s. 9 and *Smoke-Free Ontario Act*, S.O. 1994, c. 10, s. 9. The *Tobacco Control Statute Amendment Act*, S.O. 2005, c. 18 amended and renamed the legislation.

[174] *Tobacco Act*, R.S.Q., c. T-0.01, s. 2(8.1), (8.2).

[175] M. Scollo *et al.*, "Review of the quality of studies on the economic effects of smoke-free policies on the hospitality industry" (2003) 12 Tobacco Control 13; Rita Luk, Roberta Ferrence & Gerhard Gmel, "The economic impact of a smoke-free bylaw on restaurant and bar sales in Ottawa, Canada" (2006) 101 Addiction 738.

[176] See, *e.g.*, *Restaurant and Food Services Assn. of British Columbia v. Vancouver (City)*, [1998] B.C.J. No. 53, 155 D.L.R. (4th) 587 (B.C.C.A.); *Albertos Restaurant v. Saskatoon (City)*, [2000] S.J. No. 725, 2000 SKCA 135 (Sask. C.A.); *Pub and Bar Coalition of Ontario v. Ottawa (City)*, [2001] O.J. No. 3496 (Ont. S.C.J.).

[177] See, *e.g.*, *Smoke-free Places Act*, S.A. 2005, c. S-9.5, s. 10(2); *Non-Smokers Health Protection Act*, C.C.S.M., c. N92, s. 6; *Smoke-free Places Act*, S.N.S. 2002, c. 12, s. 16(2); *Tobacco Control Act*, S.Nu. 2003, c. 13, s. 15.

[178] *Smoke-Free Ontario Act*, S.O. 1994, c. 10, s. 13(3), (4); *Non-Smokers Health Protection Act*, C.C.S.M. c. N92, 2004, c. 17, s. 5.1; *Tobacco Control Act*, S.S. 2001, c. T-14.1, s. 11(3)(*c*); *Smoke-free Places Act*, S.A. 2005, c. S-9.5, s. 2(1); *Smoke-free Places Act*, S.N.B. 2004, c. S-9.5, s. 2(2).

[179] *Non-Smokers Health Protection Act*, C.C.S.M. c. N92, s. 9.4, which provides that the Act does not apply to "penitentiaries, federally regulated airports, Canadian Forces bases or to any other place or premises occupied by a federal work, undertaking or business, or on lands reserved for Indians". The New Brunswick legislation has a similar provision except that it does not mention reserve lands: *Smoke-free Places Act*, S.N.B. 2004, c. S-9.5, s. 2(3).

Jenkinson and his company (Creekside Hideaway Motel Ltd.) appealed convictions for multiple breaches of the Act on the basis that they violated the Charter.[180] Somewhat surprisingly, Clearwater J. found that section 15 had indeed been violated and that the infringement could not be saved by section 1. He assumed that there was a detrimental impact on the appellants' business from the smoking ban,[181] and found that they had therefore "been subjected to differential treatment in the conduct of their business and with respect to their right to work and earn their livelihood ... on the analogous ground of aboriginality-residence" and that this differential treatment detrimentally affected the "dignity and self-worth" of the appellant because he was "not allowed to compete in the marketplace in the same manner as aboriginal businesses".[182] The government's argument that the reason for the exemption was the province's lack of jurisdiction to regulate smoking on reserves was dismissed as "incorrect".[183] Having received no evidence or submissions to justify the provision under section 1 of the Charter, Clearwater J. struck down the exemption (section 9.4) and directed an acquittal.[184] The Manitoba government has announced its intention to appeal but in the meantime to apply the smoking ban to reserves.[185]

D. TOBACCO LITIGATION

One way of trying to hold the tobacco industry accountable for the harms caused by tobacco products and deter the most harmful marketing behaviours is through the use of litigation. Though the value of litigation in this context has been a matter of debate,[186] it has been pursued by governments as well as consumers with the aim of seeking compensation for past harms and furthering public health goals. Proponents have argued that litigation has also contributed indirectly to tobacco control efforts by increasing access to industry information, influencing public opinion, and providing funds for research and control

---

[180] *R. v. Jenkinson*, [2006] M.J. No. 250, 2006 MBQB 185 (Man. Q.B.). In the Provincial Court they had also argued that the provisions were *ultra vires* the province but this point was not pursued on appeal to the Court of Queen's Bench.

[181] As noted above, the evidence on this point is in fact quite contentious and unclear; however, Clearwater J.'s judgment takes for granted a significant economic impact apparently without examining any evidence.

[182] *R. v. Jenkinson*, [2006] M.J. No. 250, 2006 MBQB 185 (Man. Q.B.) at paras. 14, 19.

[183] *Ibid.*, at para. 19.

[184] *Ibid.*, at para. 25. The provision struck down was not the provision under which the appellants had been convicted but Clearwater J. held that they should not be convicted of charges "laid in the face of the discriminatory exemption section".

[185] Government of Manitoba, News Release: Province to Extend Smoking Ban to First Nations (September 13, 2006), online: <http://www.gov.mb.ca/chc/press/top/2006/09/2006-09-13-04.html>.

[186] See, *e.g.*, Peter D. Jacobson & Soheil Soliman, "Litigation as Public Health Policy: Theory or Reality?" (2002) 30 J. L. Med. & Ethics 224; Benedickt Fischer & Jurgen Rehm, "Some Reflections on the Relationship of Risk, Harm and Responsibility in Recent Tobacco Lawsuits, and Implications for Public Health" (2001) 92 Can. J. Public Health 7; Roberta Ferrence *et al.*, "Tobacco Industry Litigation and the Role of Government: A Public Health Perspective" (2001) 92 Can. J. Public Health 89.

efforts.[187] By far the most litigation has taken place in the United States,[188] but actions have also been attempted in other jurisdictions including Canada.[189] This litigation includes individual actions, class actions and suits by government.

Individual and class actions have used various claims and theories to recover for damage caused to the plaintiffs by tobacco products. Possible claims include negligence (failure to warn and/or negligent product design), misrepresentation, fraud, product liability, express or implied warranty, unjust enrichment or deceptive advertising (under consumer protection or advertising statutes).[190] Usually, this involves the health consequences of smoking, though an action has been brought in Ontario against Imperial Tobacco Canada for negligence and product liability in relation to fires caused by cigarettes.[191] A few individual claims have been attempted in Canada, so far without success and facing numerous procedural challenges.[192]

Class actions have been initiated both in Canada and elsewhere in an attempt to improve the prospects of plaintiffs taking on large corporate defendants which are typically able and willing to devote large resources to fighting litigation.[193] Many such actions have been attempted in the United States, although few have been successful;[194] certification of the class often presents difficulties in tobacco litigation due to the potential size and diversity of the class of individuals

---

[187] Roberta Ferrence *et al.*, *ibid.*; R. Daynard, "Why tobacco litigation? Just how important is litigation in achieving the goals of the tobacco control community?" (2003) 12 Tobacco Control 1; Robert L. Rabin, "The Third Wave of Tobacco Tort Litigation" in Robert L. Rabin & Stephen Sugarman, eds., *Regulating Tobacco* (Oxford: Oxford University Press, 2001) at 198-203.

[188] For useful overviews of tobacco litigation in the United States, see Robert L. Rabin, "The Third Wave of Tobacco Tort Litigation" in Robert L. Rabin & Stephen Sugarman, eds., *ibid.*, at 176.

[189] For a recent overview of Canadian litigation, see Smoking and Health Action Foundation & Non-Smokers' Rights Association, "Tobacco-related Litigation in Canada" (March 2006), online: Non-Smokers' Rights Association, <http://www.nsra-adnf.ca/cms/file/pdf/Tobacco_related%20Litigation%20in%20Canada%202006.pdf>. For overviews of litigation in other countries, see D. Douglas Blanke, *Towards health with justice: Litigation and public inquiries as tools for tobacco control* (Geneva: World Health Organization, 2002) at 33-43; Richard A. Daynard, Clive Bates & Neil Francey, "Tobacco litigation worldwide" (2000) 320 British Med. J. 111.

[190] D. Douglas Blanke, *Towards health with justice: Litigation and public inquiries as tools for tobacco control*, *ibid.*, at 55-56.

[191] *Ragoonanan v. Imperial Tobacco Canada Ltd.*, [2000] O.J. No. 4597 (Ont. S.C.J.) (dismissing defendant's application to strike out the plaintiff's pleadings); [2005] O.J. No. 867 (Ont. S.C.J.) (dismissing defendant's application for summary judgment); [2005] O.J. No. 4697 (Ont. S.C.J.) (refusing certification of class for class action).

[192] *Perron v. RJR Macdonald Inc.*, [1996] B.C.J. No. 2093 (B.C.C.A.); *Battaglia v. Imperial Tobacco*, [2001] O.J. No. 5541 (Ont. S.C.J.); [2002] O.J. No. 5074 (Ont. S.C.J.); [2003] O.J. No. 4360 (Ont. S.C.J.); *Spasic Estate v. Imperial Tobacco Ltd.*, [2003] O.J. No. 1797 (Ont. S.C.J.); [2003] O.J. No. 824 (Ont. S.C.J.); [2002] O.J. No. 2152 (Ont. S.C.J.); [2001] O.J. No. 4985 (Ont. S.C.J.); [2000] O.J. No. 2690, 188 D.L.R. (4th) 577 (Ont. C.A.); [2000] S.C.C.A. No. 547 (S.C.C.); [1998] O.J. No. 4906 (Ont. Gen. Div.); [1998] O.J. 6529 (Ont. Gen. Div.); [1998] O.J. No. 125 (Ont. Gen. Div.).

[193] D. Douglas Blanke, *Towards health with justice: Litigation and public inquiries as tools for tobacco control* (Geneva: World Health Organization, 2002) at 18, 30.

[194] Stephen D. Sugarman, "Mixed Results from Recent United States Tobacco Litigation" (2002) 10 Tort L. Rev. 94 at 105-10.

involved.[195] The first major tobacco class action to be filed in Canada was recently discontinued after an Ontario court refused to certify the class in 2004.[196] Class proceedings have also been ongoing in Quebec since 1998, and two classes were certified in 2005.[197] A class action against Imperial Tobacco for false and misleading marketing of "light" and "mild" cigarettes was commenced in British Columbia in 2003 and certified in 2005.[198] An appeal challenging the certification was allowed in part, allowing the action to proceed but limiting the class to those whose claims arose in May 1997 or later due to limitations issues.[199] A similar proceeding was commenced in Newfoundland in 2004 but has yet to be certified.[200]

Governments in Canada and other countries have also brought actions against tobacco companies on several grounds. In 1999 the United States government filed proceedings against tobacco companies under the *Racketeer Influenced and Corrupt Organizations Act* (RICO).[201] In August 2006 a federal court found that the companies knowingly deceived the public about the risks and addictiveness of smoking, and ordered them to publish corrective statements and to stop using terms such as "light" and "low tar" because they mislead consumers.[202] Criminal and civil proceedings have also been brought on the basis of tobacco companies' alleged participation or collusion in cigarette smuggling.[203] In the United States,[204] and more recently in Canada, governments have brought claims against tobacco companies to recover health care costs alleged to be attributable to tobacco consumption. In Canada, the province of British Columbia has been at the forefront of these efforts. It enacted specific legislation to address this issue, the *Tobacco Damages and Health Care Costs Recovery Act*,[205] and has brought an action under the Act against a group of Canadian and related foreign companies and the Canadian Tobacco Manufacturers' Council.[206] The legislation

---

195　*Ibid.*, at 106.
196　*Caputo v. Imperial Tobacco Ltd.*, [2004] O.J. No. 299, 236 D.L.R. (4th) 348 (Ont. S.C.J.); [2005] O.J. No. 842, 250 D.L.R. (4th) 756 (Ont. S.C.J.); [2006] O.J. No. 537 (Ont. S.C.J.).
197　*Conseil québécois sur le tabac et la santé c. JTI-MacDonald Corp.*, [2005] J.Q. No. 4161 (C.S.). One class is to be represented by the Conseil (at para. 128) and the second, by Cécilia Létourneau (at para. 138).
198　*Knight v. Imperial Tobacco*, [2005] B.C.J. No. 216, 250 D.L.R. (4th) 347 (B.C.S.C.).
199　*Knight v. Imperial Tobacco*, [2006] B.C.J. No. 1056, 2006 BCCA 235 (B.C.C.A.).
200　*Sparkes v. Imperial Tobacco Canada Ltd.*; the statement of claim is available online: Ches Crombie Barristers <http://www.chescrosbie.com/pdf/lc_claim.pdf>.
201　18 U.S.C. 1961-1968.
202　*United States v. Philip Morris USA Inc.*, 2006 U.S. Dist. LEXIS 61412.
203　Smoking and Health Action Foundation & Non-Smokers' Rights Association, "Tobacco-related Litigation in Canada" (March 2006), online: Non-Smokers' Rights Association <http://www.nsra-adnf.ca/cms/file/pdf/Tobacco_related%20Litigation%20in%20Canada%202006.pdf> at 7-9.
204　See Robert L. Rabin, "The Third Wave of Tobacco Tort Litigation" in Robert L. Rabin & Stephen Sugarman, eds., *Regulating Tobacco* (Oxford: Oxford University Press, 2001) at 190-93.
205　*Tobacco Damages and Health Care Costs Recovery Act*, S.B.C. 2000, c. 30 (formerly Tobacco *Damages Recovery Act*, S.B.C. 1997, c. 41).
206　This statement of claim is available online: British Columbia Ministry of Health Services <http://www.healthservices.gov.bc.ca/tobacco/litigation/pdf/agbc22.pdf>.

establishes a direct action by the government "against a [tobacco] manufacturer to recover the cost of health care benefits caused or contributed to by a tobacco related wrong", on an individual or aggregate basis.[207] It also provides for certain presumptions of causation, the use of statistical evidence to establish causation and damages, the assignment and apportionment of liability according to each defendant's contribution to risk, based on market share and other considerations, and retroactive application of the Act's provisions.[208] This legislation was unsuccessfully challenged by tobacco manufacturers, who argued that several of its provisions have extraterritorial application, and that the provisions on presumptions and retroactive application undermine judicial independence and the rule of law. The Supreme Court of Canada in 2005 rejected these arguments and upheld the legislation.[209] The British Columbia claim has proceeded following this decision,[210] and several other provinces have now enacted similar legislation.[211]

VII. CONCLUSION

Public health law is a rapidly evolving area that continues to face new challenges. The legislative frameworks that have existed for many years to address the threat of infectious diseases are under review as countries and provinces attempt to deal with the impact of globalization on the emergence and spread of infectious disease. Both within Canada and internationally, we have also seen the reemergence of disease threats that were once thought to have been rendered obsolete by modern medical science. At the same time, the burden of disease attributable to chronic diseases continues to grow and present new challenges for the law. Addressing multiple and complex causes of ill-health like diet and environmental factors requires public health lawyers to reexamine and adapt legal strategies that have been used to deal with other threats to health. For example, tobacco litigation has been used as a model for lawsuits involving other threats to health,[212] and strategies borrowed from tobacco control are being

---

[207] *Tobacco Damages and Health Care Costs Recovery Act*, S.B.C. 2000, c. 30, s. 2. A "tobacco related wrong" is defined in s. 1(1) as "a breach of a common law, equitable or statutory duty or obligation owed by a manufacturer to persons in British Columbia who have been exposed or might become exposed to a tobacco product".

[208] *Ibid.*, ss. 3(2)-(4), 5, 7-8, 10.

[209] *British Columbia v. Imperial Tobacco Canada Ltd.*, [2005] S.C.J. No. 50, 2005 SCC 49 (S.C.C.).

[210] See *British Columbia v. Imperial Tobacco Canada Ltd.*, [2006] B.C.J. No. 2080, 2006 BCCA 398 (B.C.C.A.) (rejecting a further challenge by foreign defendants on the basis of extraterritoriality).

[211] The first of these was the *Tobacco Health Care Costs Recovery Act*, S.N.L. 2001, c. T-4.2 (awaiting proclamation) but others have recently followed: see Smoking and Health Action Foundation & Non-Smokers' Rights Association, "Tobacco-related Litigation in Canada" (March 2006), online: Non-Smokers' Rights Association <http://www.nsra-adnf.ca/cms/file/pdf/Tobacco_related%20Litigation%20in%20Canada%202006.pdf> at 11.

[212] Andrew M. Dansicker, "The Next Big Thing for Litigators" (2004) 37 Maryland Bar J. 12; Brooke Courtney, "Is Obesity Really the Next Tobacco? Lessons Learned from Tobacco for Obesity Litigation" (2006) 15 Annals of Health L. 61; Jess Alderman & Richard A. Daynard,

applied to other public health concerns like obesity.[213] However, these analogies have been controversial and the expansion of regulatory strategies to new areas has even raised more fundamental questions about the proper role and scope for public health law.[214] All of these developments are taking place within a context of public debate about the rights and responsibilities of governments, corporations and individuals, and shifting perceptions and attitudes about risks to health. These challenges assure that public health will continue to be a dynamic and growing area of health law.

"Applying Lessons from Tobacco Litigation to Obesity Lawsuits" (2006) 30 Am. J. Preventive Medicine 82.

[213] Allen & Clarke (Policy and Regulatory Specialists), "Tobacco Control: What Can Be Learnt and Applied to Nutrition Policy?" (Report Commissioned by Diabetes New Zealand) (November 2004), online: Diabetes New Zealand <http://www.diabetes.org.nz/resources/files/Diabetes TobPolicy.doc>; Mickey Chopra & Ian Darnton-Hill, "Tobacco and Obesity Epidemics: Not So Different After All?" (2004) 328 British Med. J. 1558; Derek Yach *et al.*, "Improving Diet and Physical Activity: 12 Lessons from Controlling Tobacco Smoking" (2005) 330 British Med. J. 898.

[214] Richard A. Epstein, "In Defense of the 'Old' Public Health: The Legal Framework for the Regulation of Public Health" (2004) 69 Brooklyn L. Rev. 1421.

Chapter 13

EMERGING HEALTH TECHNOLOGIES*

Ian Kerr and Timothy Caulfield

I. THE ELIXIR OF THEUTH

It is not uncommon for a given society to perceive of itself as perched on the cusp of radical transformation in the fields of health and medicine. Steeped in mathematics and the natural sciences, the ancient Pythagoreans developed a careful and rigorous diet with the belief that, by understanding the four archetypal elements and keeping the body free of its base "Titanic" nature, they could achieve immortality.[1] Several centuries later, following numerous advances in the science of chemistry, Paracelsus radically transformed medicine[2] by advancing the theory that illness was not caused by an imbalance in the composition of natural elements or the four humours (as the ancients had believed), but that disease must be understood in terms of chemical causes that could be treated with chemical cures. He and other alchemists believed that the principles behind the transmutation of base metals into gold and silver might furnish a similar technique to create an "elixir of life".

---

* Research support for this chapter was provided by Angela Long through funding from the Canada Research Chairs program. The authors wish to express their deepest gratitude to Angela for lending her writing skills, excellent command of the subject matter, her superb judgment, her highly valued critical feedback and her general ability to find anything under the sun. The authors also wish to thank Alethea Adair for her excellent, careful and thorough editing.

[1] BBC, "Pythagoras, c. 580 — c. 500 BC", Historic Figures, online: <http://www.bbc.co.uk/history/historic_figures/pythagoras.shtml>.

[2] Debates raged in Paris in the mid to late 16th century over the place of alchemy within the field of medicine. As Moran notes in Bruce T. Moran, *Distilling Knowledge: Alchemy, Chemistry, and the Scientific Revolution* (Cambridge: Harvard University Press, 2005) at 74-75

> The real question being asked in the Parisian debate was this: Should alchemy be accepted as an independent discipline, which, because of its powers of understanding the operations of nature and the body, was not merely a part of medicine but *reigned over* medicine and provided medicine with a new, chemical, rationality?... The real problem was whether alchemy provided a better overall understanding of the workings of the body and better ways to maintain health than other, more ancient forms of medical wisdom.

With increasing optimism in the wake of a new millennium, the medical community continues today in its quest for a universal panacea. Articulating its vision of the 21st Century, the *World Health Organization* has proclaimed that:

> Now, as we near the end of one century and enter the next, our past achievements and technological advances make us more optimistic about our future than perhaps at any stage in recent history.[3]

Canadian health agencies have expressed similar optimism. Consider the following remarks made by Dr. Alan Bernstein[4] in an address to the Senate Standing Committee on Social Affairs, Science and Technology:

> It would not be an understatement to state that the current revolution in health research will be one of the drivers, if not the single largest driver, of change in the health care system in the next 10 to 20 years. This scientific revolution is being fueled by our rapidly emerging understanding of the molecular basis of life, of human biology and human disease, and the recent and ongoing advances in genetics and genomics, together with an appreciation that our health and susceptibility to disease is really the summation of a complex interplay between environmental factors, genetics and social factors. That appreciate [sic] will transform our health care system in the next 10 to 20 years.[5]

In light of the optimism that is practically embedded into the design of emerging health technologies, it is perhaps instructive to commence this chapter with a brief retelling of an ancient myth about an inventor and the King of Egypt.

As the story goes,[6] King Thamus was once visited by an inventor named Theuth. Seeking fame and fortune, Theuth hoped that the king would make his inventions widely available to the people of Egypt. In reference to one of his very best discoveries, Theuth promised the king that his new technology "will make the Egyptians wiser and will improve their memories; for it is an *elixir* of memory and wisdom that I have discovered".[7] Much to his chagrin, rather than praising him for the elixir, the king chided the inventor:

> Theuth, my paragon of inventors, the discoverer of an art is not the best judge of the good or harm which will accrue to those who practice it. So it is in this; you ... have out of fondness for your off-spring attributed to it quite the opposite of its real function. Those who acquire it will cease to exercise their memory and become forgetful; they will rely on [the elixir] to bring things to their remembrance by external signs instead of by their own internal resources. What you have discovered is a receipt for recollection, not for memory. And as for wisdom, your pupils will have the reputation for it without the reality: they will receive a quantity of information without proper instruction, and in consequence be thought very knowledgeable when they are for the most part quite ignorant.

[3]   World Health Organization, *The World Health Report 1998 — Life in the 21st Century: A Vision For All* (Geneva: World Health Organization, 1998) at v.
[4]   President of the Canadian Institutes of Health Research.
[5]   Standing Senate Committee on Social Affairs, Science and Technology, *The State of the Health Care System in Canada*, 1st Sess., 37th Parl., Issue 9 (April 26, 2001).
[6]   The most famous retelling of the myth of Theuth is found in Plato's *Phaedrus*.
[7]   Plato, *Phaedrus*, R. Hackforth, trans. (Cambridge: Cambridge University Press, 1972) at para. 274e.

And because they are filled with the conceit of wisdom instead of real wisdom they will be a burden to society.[8]

So, what are we to learn from this exchange?

On one level, the myth of Theuth's elixir provides a succinct articulation of the two sides in the debate about memory enhancers. Although an ancient debate, it is one that recurs in modern times.[9] The judgment of King Thamus also reminds us that we are often not well suited to evaluate emerging technologies because their future use may be subject to unintended consequences. A technology created for one purpose can be used for another: the stethoscope can be used to monitor a beating heart in crisis or to crack a safe.

But the story of Theuth's elixir is not just about opposing views on the social value of particular technological artifacts or their potential for misuse; it is not just about whether Theuth's memory elixir is good *or* bad for society. Carefully crafted by Plato,[10] the moral of the story hinges on the indeterminacy of the word "elixir". Like the Greek word *pharmakon,* from which it derives, the notion of an "elixir" carries a duality of meaning. As Jacques Derrida points out in an essay titled "Plato's Pharmacy",[11] the word *pharmakon* refers to an undulating word-play in the practically invisible quantum between "poison" and "cure". In this sense, the story of Theuth's elixir challenges us to consider what happens when a technology is both good *and* bad; when it is at one and the same time the solution and the problem.

As the philosopher of technology, Langdon Winner, once warned:

> [i]n our accustomed way of thinking technologies are seen as neutral tools that can be used well or poorly, for good, evil, or something in between. But we usually do not stop to inquire whether a given device might have been designed and built in such a way that it produces a set of consequences logically and temporally *prior to any of its professed uses.* ... technologies, however, encompass purposes far beyond their immediate use. If our moral and political language for evaluating technology includes only categories having to do with tools and uses, if it does not include attention to the meaning of the designs and arrangements of our artifacts, then we will be blinded to much that is intellectually and practically crucial.[12]

---

[8] Plato, *Phaedrus and Letters VII and VIII* (New York: Penguin Books, 1973) at 96.

[9] One might just as easily replace Theuth's elixir with modern cogniceuticals such as Prozac, Ritalin or other nootropic drugs and then imagine a reply by Francis Fukuyama not dissimilar to the judgment of King Thamus. See Francis Fukuyama, *Our Posthuman Future* (New York: Farrar, Straus and Giroux, 2002); and Ronald Bailey, "The Battle for Your Brain", Reasononline, February 2003, online: <http://www.reason.com/0302/fe.rb.the.shtml>.

[10] Plato's presentation of the myth of Theuth's elixir is rich in irony. It is told through the voice of Socrates, the philosopher most famous for never having written anything. Plato used the character of Socrates in Plato's own writing as the vehicle for the delivery of Plato's own philosophy, written in prose so intriguing and influential that it has been said that "[t]he safest general characterization of the European philosophical tradition is that it consists of a series of footnotes to Plato". Alfred North Whitehead, *Process and Reality* (New York: Free Press, 1979) at 39.

[11] Jacques Derrida, "Plato's Pharmacy", in *Dissemination,* Barbara Johnson, trans. (Chicago: University of Chicago Press, 1981).

[12] Langdon Winner, *The Whale and the Reactor: The Search for Limits in an Age of High*

In this chapter, we briefly survey four emerging technologies that are likely to have a significant impact on Canadian health law and policy in the coming years as both problems *and* solutions, as political artifacts that draw our attention to the meaning of their designs and arrangements. Our aim is not so much to prioritize or predict as it is to offer a new lens through which to consider various fundamental legal and ethical principles and their application to health law and policy in novel situations. Rather than providing comprehensive coverage of all known technologies or every issue that might possibly arise, we have chosen to sample a particular array of current and future technologies, presenting each alongside a core health law precept or principle.

We commence with a consideration of the Human Genome Project and how social policy might contend with the possibility of genetic discrimination. Then, we examine Radio Frequency Identification (RFID) technology as a means of linking an unconscious or disoriented patient to an electronic health record and the potential privacy implications of doing so. Next, we investigate stem cell research and the questions it raises about the challenges associated with making policy in a morally contested area. Finally, we contemplate issues not yet articulated in a field not yet defined: nanotechnology and how to regulate against potentially catastrophic harms that are not yet understood. After surveying these four emerging technologies and the issues they raise, we end the chapter with a brief consideration of issues associated with how science and technology are transferred from the laboratory to the community through the process of commercialization.

II. EMERGING TECHNOLOGIES

A. HUMAN GENETICS

The Human Genome Project (HGP), the international effort to map the entire human genome, was completed just a few years ago.[13] This research initiative is one of the largest and most significant research efforts in human history. It has already generated a tremendous amount of new scientific knowledge[14] and has laid the foundation for the development of new health care technologies and therapies, including genetic tests to assist in the diagnosis and prevention of disease and drugs that are tailor-made to the genetic characteristics of individual patients, thus maximizing the benefits while, at the same time, minimizing the side effects.[15] While we need to be careful not to succumb to the hype that has surrounded genetics (in fact, many of the promised breakthroughs have been

---

Technology (Chicago: University of Chicago Press, 1988) at 25.

[13] The official website for the Human Genome Project declares: "The Human Genome Project was completed in 2003". Despite this pronouncement, much of the detail work continues. See: Human Genome Project Information, Post-Human Genome Project Progress & Resources, online: <http://www.ornl.gov/sci/techresources/Human_Genome/project/progress.shtml>.

[14] Francis Collins, "The Heritage of Humanity" (2006) S1, Nature 9.

[15] For a useful overview of the uses of genetic testing technologies see Government of Canada BioPortal, "Genetic Testing", online: <http://biobasics.gc.ca/english/View.asp?x=780>.

slow to materialize),[16] there is little doubt that this is an area of research that will, one day, have a significant impact on our health care system.

However, the advances in the area of human genetics have also generated a variety of concerns.[17] Indeed, almost from the start of the HGP there has been concern that the scientific revolution in human genetics would result in new forms of genetic discrimination and the stigmatization of certain communities.[18] In particular, there was concern that the information would be used in the context of employment decisions, health care and life insurance.[19] Shortly after the start of the HGP, Professor O'Hara summarized the concerns as follows:

> The use of genetic testing or test results has many adverse social and ethical problems leading to social stigmatization as well as a potential for creating an entire population of uninsurable individuals. In addition, genetic testing by insurers can lead to serious psychological damage to those who test positive.[20]

As a result of these issues, many jurisdictions throughout the world have legislated prohibitions against the use of genetic information for anything other than health reasons and research.[21] In the U.S., for example, most states have

---

[16] Timothy Caulfield, "Popular Media, Biotechnology and the 'Cycle of Hype'" (2005) 5 J. Health L. & Pol'y 213. See also Collins, "The Heritage of Humanity" (2006) S1, Nature 9 at 12, where the author suggests that the research has been clouded by hype but: "Now, in 2006, when we consider the ultimate impact of the study of the genome on medicine and society, it is clear that, as long as we are patient, we are indeed in for some profound transformations".

[17] There is a vast literature on the ethical, legal and social issues associated with human genetics, including work on the issues associated with the patenting process, concerns about potential eugenic applications, and its impact on health care systems. For example, see Tom Murray, Mark Rothstein & R. Murray, eds., *The Human Genome and the Future of Health Care* (Bloomington: Indiana University Press, 1997); Glenn McGee, *The Perfect Baby: A Pragmatic Approach to Genetics* (New York: Rowman and Littlefield, 1997); Therese Marteau & Marin Richards, eds., *The Troubled Helix* (Cambridge: Cambridge University Press, 1996); Phillip Kitcher, *The Lives to Come: The Genetic Revolution and Human Possibilities* (Toronto: Simon and Schuster, 1996); Lori B. Andrews *et al.*, *Assessing Genetic Risks: Implications for Health and Social Policy* (Washington D.C.: National Academic Press, 1994); R. Hubbard & E. Wald, *Exploding the Gene Myth* (Boston: Beacon Press, 1993); Tom Wilkie, *Perilous Knowledge: The Human Genome Project and Its Implications* (Boston: Faber and Faber, 1993); George Annas & Susan Elias, eds., *Gene Mapping: Using Law and Ethics* (Oxford: Oxford University Press, 1992); Richard C. Lewontin, *Biology as Ideology: The Doctrine of DNA* (New York: Harpers Perennial, 1992); Danial Kevles & L. Hood, *The Code of Codes* (Cambridge: Harvard University Press, 1992).

[18] For example, see C. Lee, "Creating a Genetic Underclass: The Potential for Genetic Discrimination by the Health Insurance Industry" (1993) 13 Pace L. Rev. 227: "The single most effective way to prevent abuse is a ban on the use of genetic information in health insurance underwriting".

[19] Trudo Lemmens, "Selective Justice, Genetic Discrimination, and Insurance: Should We Single Out Genes in Our Laws?" (2000) 45 McGill L.J. 347-412.

[20] S. O'Hara, "The Use of Genetic Testing in the Health Insurance Industry: The Creation of a 'Biologic Underclass'" (1993) 22 Cambridge SW. U. L. Rev. 1227. See also P. Billings, *et al.*, "Discrimination as a Consequence of Genetic Testing" (1992) 50 Am. J. Hum. Genet. 476.

[21] Bartha Knoppers & Yann Joly, "Physicians, Genetics and Life Insurance" (2004) 170 C.M.A.J. 1421: "In Europe, the Convention on Human Rights and Biomedicine ratified by 17 countries unambiguously states that genetic testing can be used only for health reasons and for research". For an example of relevant legislation see also P. Kossiem, M. Letendre & B. Knoppers,

enacted some form of "anti-genetic discrimination" law.[22] The laws differ greatly in the types of discrimination that they protect against. Some, for example, prohibit discrimination against individuals with specific genetic traits or disorders while others "regulate both the use of genetic testing in employment decisions and the disclosure of genetic test results".[23] All, however, were enacted as a result of the concerns over genetic discrimination.

No province in Canada has enacted a specific anti-genetic discrimination law. Because of our publicly funded health care system, there is less concern about the impact of genetic testing on health care insurance and access to the health care system than in the U.S. Nevertheless, many policymaking entities have recommended some policy reforms,[24] including limiting the use of genetic information in the context of insurance and employment, strengthening privacy laws and mandating an entitlement to a minimum amount of life, disability and health insurance.[25]

The concern of and regulatory responses to genetic discrimination raise some interesting policy questions. First, to what degree is genetic discrimination really a social problem worthy of a legislative action?[26] The public certainly seems worried about it, particularly in the U.S., where access to health insurance is a profound issue.[27] In fact, there is some evidence that the concerns about discrimination may deter participation in research and therapy and "influence access to care".[28] In one study it was found that 52.4 per cent of U.S. clinicians

"Protecting Genetic Information: A Comparison of Normative Approaches" (2000) 2 GenEdit, online: <www.humgen.umontreal.ca/en/GenEdit.cfm>.

[22] Human Genome Project Information, "Genetics Privacy and Legislation", online: <http://www.ornl.gov/sci/techresources/Human_Genome/elsi/legislat.shtml#II>. See also National Conference of State Legislatures, "State Genetic Privacy Laws", State Genetic Table on Privacy Law, online: <http://www.ncsl.org/programs/health/genetics/prt.htm>:

> The majority of state legislatures have taken steps to safeguard genetic information beyond the protections provided for other types of health information. This approach to genetics policy is known as genetic exceptionalism, which calls for special legal protections for genetic information as a result of its predictive, personal and familial nature and other unique characteristics.

[23] Human Genome Project Information, "Genetics Privacy and Legislation", online: <http://www.ornl.gov/sci/techresources/Human_Genome/elsi/legislat.shtml#II>.

[24] Ontario Law Reform Commission, *Report on Genetic Testing* (Ontario, 1996); Privacy Commissioner of Canada, *Genetic Testing and Privacy* (Ottawa, 1992).

[25] For a review of possible policy options, see Bartha Knoppers *et al.*, "Genetics and Life Insurance in Canada: Points to Consider" (2002) 170 C.M.A.J. Online 2.

[26] See, for example, T. Lemmens, "Selective Justice, Genetic Discrimination, and Insurance: Should We Single Out Genes in Our Laws?" (2000) 45 McGill L.J. 347. The author provides an interesting critique of the anti-discrimination legislation, arguing that it does not address the underlying inequities associated with health disparities and access to health care.

[27] April Lynch, "Patients Fear Insurance Hikes and Hide Genetic Conditions", Knight Ridder News (December 29, 2004), online: <http://www.BillingsGazette.com>: "Afraid that they will be denied care in an increasingly cutthroat health-care market if insurers know too much about them, patients are getting genetic tests without telling insurers, or even their doctors".

[28] R. Nedelcu *et al.*, "Genetic Discrimination: The Clinician Perspective" (2004) 66 Clin. Gen. 311. See also Steve Mitchell, "Public Fears Genetic Discrimination", American Assoc. of People with Disabilities (May 26, 2005), online: <http://www.aapd-dc.org/News/disability/fearsgenetic.html>.

believed that mutation carriers have difficulty obtaining health insurance and "13% would not encourage genetic testing, despite a family history of cancer".[29] Another study of almost 90,000 patients in the U.S. and Canada found that 40 per cent agreed with the statement: "genetic testing is not a good idea because you might have trouble getting or keeping your insurance".[30]

Despite these perceptions, some commentators have questioned the existence of the genetic discrimination problem — or, at least, its magnitude. Hank Greely, for example, has suggested that: "studies have shown that although there is widespread concern about genetic discrimination, there are few examples of it — and no evidence that it is common".[31] Others note that the current value of genetic information to insurers is likely fairly limited — largely because the meaning and predictive value of genetic data remains complex and unclear. As stated by Knoppers *et al.*: "Understanding the significance and impact of genetic testing results is difficult, and therefore, at the present time, genetic information can rarely be effectively used in risk assessment".[32] Unless this information has real actuarial value, it seems unlikely that it will be widely used, at least by insurers. And if others such as employers use it to draw scientifically inappropriate conclusions about individual risk, then education about the complex nature of genetic information, rather than prohibitions on its use, may be the more appropriate policy response.

Second, this controversy provides the opportunity to ask whether genetic information is truly special. In other words, should the law be treating genetic information as distinct from other forms of health information? Survey research has shown that Canadians do, rightly or not, think that genetic information is worthy of special protection.[33] Such views accord with a number of international

---

[29] *Ibid.*

[30] Mark Hall *et al.*, "Concerns in a Primary Care Population about Genetic Discrimination by Insurers" (2005) 7 Genet Med 311; see also Peter Neuman, James Hammitt, Curt Mueller *et al.*, "Public Attitudes about Genetic Testing for Alzheimer's Disease" (2001) 20 Health Affairs 252.

[31] Hank Greely, "Banning Genetic Discrimination" (2005) 353 N.E.J.M. 865. However, see Peter Aldous, "Victims of Genetic Discrimination Speak Up", NewScientist.com (November 5, 2005) online: <http://www.newscientist.com/channel/life/genetics/mg18825244.300-victims-of-genetic-discrimination-speak-up.html>: "Evidence is growing that employers and insurers are discriminating against people whose genes make them susceptible to serious diseases. In the most complete survey yet of possible discrimination, around 1 in 12 people who have taken a genetic test said they had been disadvantaged as a result — for example, by being denied appropriate life insurance".

[32] Knoppers *et al.*, "Genetics and Life Insurance in Canada: Points to Consider" (2002) 170 C.M.A.J. Online 2. See also Trudo Lemmens *et al.*, "Genetics and Life Insurance: A Comparative Analysis" (2004) GenEdit 2: "Only a limited number of predictive tests are sufficiently reliable to be of real use to the insurers"; and Nick Raithatha and Richard Smith, "Disclosure of Genetic Tests for Health Insurance: Is It Ethical Not To?" (2004) 363 The Lancet 396: "[D]espite the introduction of innumerable screening, diagnostic, and therapeutic technologies over the past century, the percentage of people who have been able to obtain life insurance has in fact risen". The authors go on to argue that the "biggest obstacle remains public perception of genetic testing".

[33] Pollara & Earnscliffe, "Public Opinion Research into Biotechnology Issues: Presented to the Biotechnology Assistant Deputy Minister Coordinating Committee (BACC), Government of Canada" (Ottawa: Earnscliffe Research & Communications, December 2000).

policy documents, such as Article 4 of UNESCO's 2003 *International Declaration on Human Genetic Data* that declares that human genetic information *is* special because it can be used to predict genetic predispositions, has relevance to biological relatives and may have cultural significance for persons or groups. As a result, the Declaration recommends that "[d]ue consideration should be given, and where appropriate special protection should be afforded to human genetic data and to the biological samples".[34]

However, in many ways, even the genetic information that is relatively predictive has similarities to other forms of health information (information that is not afforded special legislative treatment). For example, a cholesterol test provides predictive information (that is, information about risks for cardio-vascular disease) and has relevance to one's biological relatives (cholesterol levels have a strong genetic component). Likewise, HIV status, a non-genetic condition, is also highly sensitive and predictive of future health concerns.

This line of reasoning has led some groups, such as the Nuffield Council on Bioethics, to conclude that genetic information is not significantly different from other forms of sensitive health information.[35] The Council goes on to recommend that given the "similarities between genetic and other forms of personal information, it would be a mistake to assume that genetic information is qualitatively different in some way".

The debate around genetic discrimination is far from over. With new applications on the horizon,[36] such as nutrigenomics and the profiling of athletes,[37] it seems likely that genetic testing technologies will continue to generate regulatory challenges. Genetic information can be used to individuate, providing natural identifiers that could become a basis for discrimination. Should we treat genetic information as special, and worthy of unique regulatory protection? Or, should we treat it as simply another form of sensitive health information? For the purposes of this chapter, the concerns raised about genetic discrimination stand as an example of how uncertainty and social angst about an emerging technology can trigger legal reform, such as the anti-discrimination laws in the U.S., before it is clear what the best long term regulatory response might be.

---

[34]   United Nations Educational, Scientific and Cultural Organization (UNESCO), "International Declaration on Human Genetic Data", 32nd Session, Official Records (Paris: UNESCO, 2004).

[35]   Nuffield Council on Bioethics, *Pharmacogenetics: Ethical Issues* (London: Nuffield Council on Bioethics, 2003) at 6. See also Caulfield, "Popular Media, Biotechnology and the 'Cycle of Hype'" at 232.

[36]   Carolyn Abraham, "Would you Gaze into a Genetic Crystal Ball?" *Globe & Mail* (December 31 2005) at A1.

[37]   Regarding controversy over a genetic test for athletic ability, see Steven E. Humphries, "Genetic Testing for Cardiovascular Disease Risk: Fact or Fiction?" BioNews.org.uk (December 23, 2004) online: <http://www.bionews.org.uk/commentary.lasso?storyid=2392>: "An Australian company is offering a genetic test it claims can identify children who have the potential to excel at either sprinting and 'power' sports or endurance events". Regarding nutrigenomics, an emerging field that involves the tailoring of nutrition to meet individual genetic characteristics, see Nola Ries & Timothy Caulfield, "First Pharmacogenomics, Next Nutrigenomics: Genohype or Genohealthy?" (2006) 46 Jurimetrics 281.

In the section that follows, we turn our investigation to another technology that has the ability to individuate, an identification technology that some hope will provide an access-control mechanism for the electronic health record.

B. RADIO FREQUENCY IDENTIFICATION (RFID)

Radio Frequency Identification (RFID) connotes a set of information technologies that enable the remote and automatic identification of physical entities by way of radio signals. Although best known for its ability to manage product inventory through a supply-chain,[38] RFID has many valuable applications in health care delivery. For example, RFID can be used to track the whereabouts of a mobile cardiac unit or other life-saving emergency care equipment in real-time.[39] It can be used to help prevent child abduction in neonatal units.[40] And, as we shall see, it can be used to identify unconscious patients in emergency medicine.[41]

Unlike the larger and more costly anti-theft devices that we regularly encounter in clothing and department stores, the signals generated by an RFID tag not only announce their presence, they also announce themselves as uniquely individuated identities. Using radio waves that operate in the unlicensed part of the broadcast spectrum, RFID signals can pass through clothing, knapsacks, body parts and even buildings to communicate with reader devices some distance away. When associated with a database, RFID systems allow computers to recognize and distinguish between physical objects that have been tagged and

---

[38] AME Info, "How RFID Can Optimize Supply Chain Management" (August 21, 2005), online: <http://www.ameinfo.com/66090.html>.

[39] For example, three hospitals in Virginia have committed 3.9 million USD to the implementation of RFID technology into the management of medical equipment. See Jonathan Collins, "Hospitals Get Healthy Dose of RFID", RFID J. (April 27, 2004), online: <http://www.rfidjournal.com/article/view/920>. RFID systems that track equipment are said to improve the quality of health care, as locating equipment, especially in emergency situations, is made easier. In addition, such technology saves money, as less equipment is lost. See California Healthcare Foundation, "Brigham and Women's Hospital Uses RFID to Track Medical Equipment", iHealthBeat (January 20, 2006), online: <http://www.ihealthbeat.org/index.cfm?Action=dspItem&itemID=118196>; and Les Chappell, "RFID Can be a Matter of Life and Death in the Medical World", Wisconsin Technology Network (October 19, 2005), online: <http://wistechnology.com/article.php?id=2383>.

[40] The VeriChip Corporation has developed the Hugs and HALO systems for tracking infants in hospitals. See VeriChip, Solutions: Infant Protection, online: <http://www.verichipcorp.com/content/solutions/infant_protection>. RFID tags that are attached to the infants track their whereabouts and match them with their mothers. The technology was recently heralded worldwide as a bastion of security when the Hugs system foiled the abduction of an infant in a North Carolina hospital. See John Leyden, "Security Bracelet Foils Child Abduction". *The Register*, July 21, 2005, online: <http://www.theregister.co.uk/2005/07/21/child_abduction_foiled/>.

[41] The VeriMed system from VeriChip Corporation is the first to implant RFID chips into human beings for this purpose. See VeriChip Corporation, online: <http://www.verichipcorp.com/content/solutions/verimed>.

to collect and integrate a myriad of information about those objects and the people using them.[42]

An RFID system is comprised of two main components: (i) the tag, which emits a signal that carries a unique identifier through radio waves;[43] and (ii) the reader, which receives the signal and identifies the object. The tag component is itself comprised of an antenna and an integrated circuit. Tags are usually classified as either passive or active. Passive tags do not require a power source. They remain dormant until they come in proximity with an incoming signal from an RFID reader that powers the tag, enabling it to send a radio signal of its own. Passive tags typically have a relatively short radio range, can be made to be very small and are the least expensive to produce. Active tags, by contrast, usually include a battery to power the antenna.[44] Active tags are more reliable and can broadcast at a longer range, but are significantly larger, more expensive and have a shorter shelf life.[45] The "killer-app" of the future — item-level tagging[46] — is based on speculation that the price of tags will continue to diminish to a fraction of current costs.

Information on RFID tags is stored as strings of memory that can be either burned into the chip in advance (read-only) or assigned later as read/write memory using a reader.[47] Tags can be "promiscuous",[48] that is, their signals will easily interact and be understood by *any* RFID scanner in its proximity. Secure tags,[49] on the other hand, send signals that incorporate authentication and encryption elements that prevent them from being read without a key.[50] Some tags also feature a kill switch, providing a means of deactivating the tag and preventing future communications.[51]

---

[42] There is a significant difference between objects that merely announce their presence and objects that can also identify themselves in the process. For example, consider the difference between knowing that: (1) there is "a tagged object" hidden in that knapsack, and (2) there is "a 1 kg bag of fertilizer EPC no. 016 37221 654321 2003004000, which was bought at the Home Depot Store on Merivale Road in Ottawa on February 26, 2006 at 09:06:17 by CIBC credit card holder no. 4408 0412 3456 XXXX and is hidden in the knapsack beside Ottawa Library book call no. 662.2014 B679 (titled: *Explosives*) signed out by library cardholder no. 11840003708286 on February 20, 2006 along with call no. 921 H6755 (*Mein Kampf*), call no. 320.533 H878 (*Les skinheads et l'extrême droite*), and call no. 296.6509 D288 (*Synagogue Architecture*).

[43] Also known as a "transponder".

[44] Klaus Finkenzeller, *RFID-Handbook*, 2nd ed.,. Rachel Waddington trans (Chichester: Wiley & Sons, Ltd., 2003), at 8.

[45] Simson Garfinkel & Henry Holtzman, "Understanding RFID Technology", in *RFID: Applications, Security, and Privacy*, Simson Garfinkel & Beth Rosenberg, eds. (Upper Saddle River: Addison-Wesley, 2005), at 17.

[46] That is, tagging every single item in inventory (as opposed to merely tracking crates or cartons). Item-level tagging could have incredible implications, creating what some have called "the internet of things". See Bruce Sterling, "The Internet of Things" (keynote address, O'Reilly Emerging Technology Conference, March 2006), online: <http://www.oreillynet.com/pub/a/network/2006/03/20/distributing-the-future.html>.

[47] Garfinkel & Holtzman, "Understanding RFID Technology" at 18.

[48] Sometimes referred to as "dumb".

[49] Sometimes referred to as "smart".

[50] Garfinkel & Holtzman, "Understanding RFID Technology" at 18.

[51] From a privacy perspective, this is an important feature. It allows RFID to assist in the supply-

RFID readers operate by constantly emitting radio waves until a tag is detected. When a tag comes within range, its antenna amplifies the signal and sends the information stored on the chip back to the reader. The reader usually links the information stored on the tag to a database, thus correlating potentially scads of information about the object identified by the tag. The read range depends on the power, efficiency, and data integrity requirements of both the tag and the reader.[52] The radio frequency employed resides within the unlicensed portion of the broadcast spectrum and will be further determined by industry standards. For example, the FDA has assigned high-frequency bands for prescription drug identification while animal tagging uses the low-frequency range.[53]

For present purposes, we will limit our attention to the VeriChip: a passive, proprietary promiscuous, short-range RFID that is embedded in a glass capsule and covered with a coating called biobond.[54] When an implanted individual comes in proximity with a VeriChip reader, the tag emits a unique subscriber number corresponding to its own proprietary patient registry database. This number can then be used by health care providers as a password to gain access to the online Verimed Patient Registry, linking patients and their electronic health record. Because the passive RFID inside the VeriChip is always on, it will "speak on the patient's behalf" — even if the patient is unconscious or otherwise incapacitated — enabling access to vital health information in emergency situations.

To some, the idea of an implantable microchip wirelessly connecting our unconscious bodies to computer databases filled with the most intricate and intimate details of personal health information smacks of science fiction. And, yet, from an information technology perspective, VeriChip is in fact quite primitive. It is unencrypted, which means that the information transmitted from the chip can be easily intercepted, read and understood by any interoperable reader. Its signal can also be easily "cloned" with inexpensive, everyday equipment purchased at any electronics store.[55] This means that another person can cause a device to imitate the signal emitted by the chip, thus "spoofing" its identity and enabling unauthorized access to the patient's health care record.[56] Though it may seem odd, these are not bugs in the system but are in fact design features.[57]

---

chain without interfering with consumer rights after the point of sale.

[52] Garfinkel & Holtzman, "Understanding RFID Technology" at 24.

[53] *Ibid.*, at 21.

[54] This polymer substance encourages tissue growth around the chip, preventing migration of the chip once it is implanted into the triceps. See Michael Kanellos, "RFID Tags May Be Implanted in Patients' Arms", ZDNetUK (July 28, 2004), online: <http://news.zdnet.co.uk/communications/wireless/0,39020348,39161907,00.htm>.

[55] Jonathan Westhues recently cloned a VeriChip and posted his method on his website. See Jonathan Westhues, "Demo: Cloning a Verichip", online: <http://cq.cx/verichip.pl>. See also Annalee Newitz, "RFID Hacking Underground" Wired Magazine 14 no. 5 (May 2006), online: <http://www.wired.com/wired/archive/14.05/rfid.html?pg=1&topic=rfid&topic_set=>.

[56] Or whatever privileges or permissions are assigned to the *no-longer-unique* subscriber identification number.

[57] From a design perspective, it is believed that VeriChip should be easy to clone so that an attacker

VeriChip raises a number of important issues for health law and policy. We will briefly canvass three: (i) regulating it as a medical device; (ii) informational privacy and security; and (iii) the broader implications of ICT-based medicine.[58]

On October 12, 2004, the U.S. Food and Drug Administration (FDA) approved the VeriChip as a Class II medical device. Given that VeriChip has recently opened offices in Ottawa and Vancouver, our Therapeutic Products Directorate (TPD) will likely be asked to determine whether VeriChip can be sold as a "medical device" in Canada.[59] Like that of the FDA, the role of the TPD is to ensure that all medical devices offered for sale meet basic safety and efficacy requirements. It does so by ensuring that no apparatus that falls within the definition of a "medical device" under the *Food and Drugs Act* can be sold in Canada without prior approval and a corresponding licence based on the classification of the device.

However, prior to reaching the classification stage, VeriChip must first be able to demonstrate that its devices fall within the definition of a "medical device". For this determination, it is useful to turn to the description of the device in the original FDA application:

> An implantable radiofrequency transponder system for patient identification and health information is a device intended to enable access to secure patient identification and corresponding health information. This system may include a passive implanted transponder, inserter, and scanner. The implanted transponder is used only to store a unique electronic identification code that is read by the scanner. The identification code is used to access patient identity and corresponding health information stored in a database.[60]

Notice that VeriChip is not designed to serve a therapeutic purpose. Rather, it is a general purpose device that uses radio frequencies solely as a means of linking an entity to a unique identifier. Although one potential application of implantable RFID is to use it to link a patient to an electronic health record, it is unclear whether this makes the VeriChip a "medical device".

It is instructive to look at the definition set out in section 2 of the *Food and Drug Act*:

> "device" means any article, instrument, apparatus or contrivance, including any component, part or accessory thereof, manufactured, sold or represented for use in

---

then has less incentive to coerce victims or extract VeriChips from victims' bodies: John Halamka *et al.*, "The Security Implications of VeriChip Cloning", Privacy and Security in RFID Systems, (March 10, 2006), online: <http://lasecwww.epfl.ch/~gavoine/rfid/>.

[58]   ICT is a well known acronym for "Information and Communication Technology", a term used to capture the convergence of information technology, telecommunications and data networking into a single technology.

[59]   Pursuant to a licence under the *Medical Devices Regulation*, SOR/98-282 established pursuant to s. 30(a)(iii) of the *Food and Drugs Act*, R.S.C. 1985, c. F-27.

[60]   U.S. Department of Health and Human Services, Food and Drug Administration, 21 CFR Part 880 (Docket No. 2004N-0477) "Medical Devices; Classification of Implantable Radiofrequency Transponder System for Patient Identification and Health Information" (December 10, 2004), online: <http://www.fda.gov/ohrms/dockets/98fr/04-27077.htm> (FDA Classification).

(a) the diagnosis, treatment, mitigation or prevention of a disease, disorder or abnormal physical state, or its symptoms, in human beings or animals,
(b) restoring, correcting or modifying a body function or the body structure of human beings or animals,
(c) the diagnosis of pregnancy in human beings or animals, or
(d) the care of human beings or animals during pregnancy and at and after birth of the offspring, including care of the offspring,

and includes a contraceptive device but does not include a drug;[61]

It is clear that VeriChip falls within the first part of the definition of a "device". However, it is less clear that it satisfies any of the second part of the definition's four disjuncts. First, VeriChip is not an instrument of diagnosis or treatment, nor does it mitigate or prevent diseases and the like. Second, VeriChip plays no role in restoring, correcting or modifying body function or structure. Likewise, it has no diagnostic value in pregnancy and does not facilitate care during pregnancy or after. Given that it is devoid of therapeutic value or purpose, one would think that VeriChip is an unlikely candidate for TPD approval. And yet the FDA, governed by similar legislative provisions, has approved VeriChip as a medical device. Should the TPD do the same? Who should be allowed to perform implantation procedures?[62] Is the current regulatory regime sufficient to accommodate the merger of ICT and medicine? As we shall see, such questions will gain increasing significance as future chip-enabled devices are developed that, unlike VeriChip, actually do achieve therapeutic ends.

Since the central purpose of the current VeriChip is limited to the non-therapeutic aim of automated identification, of central concern will be its privacy implications. Because the current proposals for its use are limited to those who consent to implantation, we will focus on informational privacy rather

---

[61] A similar approach has been adopted in 21 U.S.C. 201(*h*):

> The term "device" ... means an instrument, apparatus, implement, machine, contrivance, implant, in vitro reagent, or similar related article, including any component, part, or accessory, which is —
> (1) recognized in the official National Formulary, or in the United States Pharmacopeia, or any supplement to them,
> (2) intended for use in the diagnosis of disease or other conditions, or in the cure, mitigation, treatment, or prevention of disease, in man or other animals, or
> (3) intended to affect the structure or any function of the body of man or other animals, and which does not achieve its primary intended purposes through chemical action within or on the body of man or other animals and which is not dependent upon being metabolized for the achievement of its primary intended purposes.

[62] For example, body piercers in Ontario have gained some notoriety for implanting chips similar to the VeriChip. See Anna Bahny, "High Tech Under the Skin", *New York Times*, (February 2, 2006), online: <http://www.nytimes.com/2006/02/02/fashion/thursdaystyles/02tags.html?ex=1296536400&en=de01f3be5ea7ce56&ei=5088&partner=rssnyt&emc=rss>. However, it is questionable whether this practice would be considered legal, at least in Ontario. See *Regulated Health Professions Act, 1991*, S.O. 1991, c. 18, s. 27(2), which governs "controlled acts", including "[p]erforming a procedure on tissue below the dermis" and "putting an instrument, hand or finger ... into an artificial opening into the body". Exceptions to s. 27(2) have been made in the *Controlled Acts Regulation* (O. Reg. 107/96, s. 8), but only for piercing the body with jewellery.

than the bodily privacy issues raised by the invasive implantation procedure. Informational privacy is concerned with "the claim of individuals ... to determine for themselves when, how, and to what extent information about them is communicated to others".[63] While an implanted patient has voluntarily chosen to enable the chip to "communicate" information about them with emergency care workers, as described above, a passive, unencrypted chip that is easily read by inexpensive and commercially available scanners undermines the implanted individual's ability to control the collection, use or disclosure of identifiable information. With the strategic placement of RFID readers in door portals and other locations, this could not only allow locational tracking of implanted individuals in real-time, but also the ability to collect associated information that would allow aggregated profiling and surveillance.[64]

While it is tempting to think that obtaining an initial consent to implantation would suffice, the fair information practices[65] underlying federal and provincial privacy legislation generally require those who collect information about an identifiable individual to specify before or at the time of collection the purpose for doing so, and that the information collected cannot be disclosed to or otherwise used by others without fresh consent from the data subject.[66] Fair information practice principles also require that personal data be protected by reasonable security safeguards against unauthorized access or disclosure of data. VeriChip's current model for patient identification is not in accord with either of these core privacy principles.

The privacy discussion thus far has focused on the automated disclosure of the unique identifier, which is broadcast each time that a chip comes in proximity of a reader. Security concerns also arise when an unauthorized disclosure of that identifier leads to unauthorized access to an associated health record. Recall that the VeriChip subscriber number is the key that unlocks the patient's electronic health record, making VeriChip insecure by design. From an information security perspective, it is therefore not well suited as an "access control" device.[67] For some reason, this has not stopped more than 100 American hospitals and several hundred American physicians from implementing programs that use it for such purposes.[68]

---

[63] Alan F. Westin, *Privacy and Freedom* (New York: Atheneum, 1967), at 7.

[64] See generally, Katherine Albrecht & Liz McIntyre, *Spychips: How Major Corporations and Government Plan to Track your Every Move with RFID* (Nashville: Nelson Current, 2005).

[65] OECD, *Guidelines on the Protection of Privacy and Transborder Flows of Personal Data* (1980); *Personal Information Protection and Electronic Documents Act*, S.C. 2000, c. 5, Sch. 1 (PIPEDA).

[66] PIPEDA, Principle 3.1.

[67] Halamka *et al.*, "The Security Implications of VeriChip Cloning", online: <http://lasecwww. epfl.ch/~gavoine/rfid/>.

[68] The latest data from VeriChip Corporation shows that 110 hospitals have committed to implement the VeriMed system, see VeriChip Corporation, "VeriChip Corporation Announces First Emergency Room Use of VeriMed Microchip," News Release (July 27, 2006). In addition, on its website, VeriChip Corporation states that 280 physicians have elected to offer the VeriMed chip to their patients. See VeriChip Corporation, online: <http://www.verimedinfo.com/>.

The use of implantable microchips in medicine is nascent but sure to result in therapeutic innovations that will repair and perhaps even enhance bodily function. For example, cochlear implants are gaining in popularity among those with hearing impairments, and it is not difficult to imagine that they will one day enhance rather than merely restore human hearing.[69] For example, while repairing hearing function, why not include within such devices the capability to stream voice transmissions wirelessly so that one does not have to carry or wear phones or portable music players? Living in a surveillance society that will soon require all telecommunications service providers to build a global intercept capability into all communications devices[70] (so that law enforcement can "listen in" under certain circumstances), the myriad of issues that arise transcend health law and policy. As we continue to experiment with totally implantable devices such as artificial hearts,[71] and as medicine becomes more and more dependent on wireless and network technologies to manage these devices, there will be an increasing need to understand the human-machine merger, the question of technological enhancement and all of the ethical and legal issues that are bound to ensue as a result of implantable radio frequency microchips.

In the section that follows, we turn our focus to a very different technology that also strikes at the core of what it means to be human, one that has stirred much controversy while, at the same time, generating tremendous potential for treating many serious illnesses.

C. EMBRYONIC STEM CELLS

Few areas of research have generated as much controversy as embryonic stem cell research. It is a topic that has received an incredible amount of media attention and policy analysis. It has been the subject of legislative debates throughout the world and it has divided the United Nations.[72] But despite almost a decade of intense policy deliberations, there remains little international consensus about how this area should be regulated.[73]

---

[69] One of the better currently available products is in fact marketed as "HiResolution Bionic Ear System". See online: <http://www.bionicear.com/>.

[70] Though it died on the Order Page with the fall of the Liberal government in 2005, Bill C-74, *An Act regulating telecommunications facilities to facilitate the lawful interception of information transmitted by means of those facilities and respecting the provision of telecommunications subscriber information*, 1st Sess., 38th Parl., 2005 (not passed) is sure to be resurrected in a substantially similar form, given the political pressure on Canada to ratify the *European Convention on Cybercrime* (Council of Europe, *European Convention on Cybercrime*, E.T.S., No. 185 (2001)).

[71] For example, see the AbioCor, a fully implantable replacement heart manufactured by AbioMed, online: <http://www.abiomed.com/products/heart_replacement.cfm>.

[72] CBS News, "UN gives up cloning ban", (November 19, 2004), online: <http://www.cbsnews.com/stories/2005/02/18/tech/main675124.shtml>.

[73] For two excellent reviews of the regulatory variation, see Lori P. Knowles, "A Regulatory Patchwork — Human ES Cell Research Oversight" (2004) 22 Nature Biotech. 157; and Rosario Isasi & Bartha Knoppers, "Mind the Gap: Policy Approaches to Embryonic Stem Cell and Cloning Research in 50 Countries" (2006) 13 Euro. J. Health L. 9-26. See also Shaun Pattinson & Timothy Caulfield, "Variations and Voids: The Regulation of Human Cloning Around the

Why has stem cell research caused so much controversy? The focal issue is clearly the moral status of the embryo. While there are a variety of complex issues associated with this field of study — including concern about the consent processes used to obtain embryos for research[74] and the patenting of embryonic stem cell lines[75] — there seems to be little doubt that the issues related to the moral status of the embryo have been the dominant cause of controversy and the primary source of the "regulatory patchwork" that now exists throughout the world.[76]

Since 1998, when the first human embryonic stem cell lines (hESC) were created,[77] there has been a great deal of excitement about the scientific and therapeutic potential of stem cells. Embryonic stem cells, unlike stem cells derived from other sources (such as cord blood),[78] have the unique capacity to form almost any tissue in the body (and are, therefore, known as "pluripotent"). It is hoped that scientists will one day be able to coax them into becoming tissues that could be used to treat a wide variety of serious illnesses, including Parkinson's, diabetes, and heart disease. The speculation about prospective benefits has, no doubt, been fueled by the large degree of hype that has surrounded the entire area.[79] Nevertheless, few would disagree with the suggestion that the therapeutic potential is real, albeit uncertain and, perhaps, a long way off.

However, for those who believe that a human embryo has full moral status, regardless of how early its stage of biological development,[80] no amount of therapeutic potential will justify its destruction — a necessary step in the derivation of a stem cell line.[81] As such, they remain steadfastly opposed to

---

World" (2004) 5 B.M.C. Medical Ethics 9.

[74] See Bernard Lo *et al.*, "Informed Consent in Human Oocyte, Embryo, and Embryonic Stem Cell Research" (2004) 82 Fertility and Sterility 559; Henry Greely, "Moving Human Embryonic Stem Cells from Legislature to Lab: Remaining Legal and Ethical Questions" (2006) Public Library of Science Medicine e143 and Margaret Munro, "Ethicist Repeats Call to Halt Embryo Donations", *National Post* (June 28, 2006) at A7.

[75] Timothy Caulfield, "Stem Cell Patents and Social Controversy: A Speculative View From Canada" (2006) 7 Medical L. Int'l 219-32.

[76] Knowles, "A Regulatory Patchwork", at 157.

[77] James Thomson *et al.*, "Embryonic Stem Cell Lines Derived from Human Blastocysts" (1998) 282 Science 1145; Abdallah S. Daar & Lorraine Sheremeta, "The Science of Stem Cells: Some Implications for Law and Policy" (2002) 11 Health L. Rev. 5.

[78] See Oonagh Corrigan *et al.*, *Ethical Legal and Social Issues in Stem Cell Research and Therapy* (briefing paper, Cambridge Genetics Knowledge Park, March 2006) at 1: "Stem cells are cells that have the potential both for self-renewal and to differentiate into specialized cell types. Stem cells found in the early mammalian embryo, at around 5-7 days after fertilisation, are able to give rise to all the different cell types of the organism. These embryonic stem (ES) cells are said to be 'pluripotent'".

[79] See, *e.g.*, N. Theise, "Stem Cell Research: Elephants in the Room" (2003) 78 Mayo Clinic Proceedings 1004-1009.

[80] Stem cells are generally removed from the embryo at a very early stage of development, when the embryo is at only a cluster of cells called a "blastocyst".

[81] However, scientists continue to strive to develop techniques that would allow the production of a stem cell line without the destruction of the embryos. See, *e.g.*, Nicholas Wade, "Stem Cell News Could Intensify Debate", *New York Times* (August 24, 2006).

embryonic stem cell research. To cite just one example, the Catholic Church has taken a consistent position against this work. Indeed, recently, a prominent Cardinal suggested: "Destroying an embryo is equivalent to abortion. ... Excommunication is valid for the women, the doctors and researchers who destroy embryos".[82]

Despite the enduring presence of such sentiments, they seem to represent a minority position — at least in Canada. Most research has shown that the Canadian public supports embryonic stem cell research.[83] Recent studies have shown that Canadians tend to view stem cell research as one of a range of associated areas of biotechnology.[84] More significantly, a majority approve of stem cell research *under any circumstance*, as long as it is appropriately regulated.[85] Nevertheless, it seems likely that there will always remain a sector of society that will not endorse the use of human embryos for research purposes, thus making it impossible to craft policy that will be entirely satisfactory to all.

---

[82] News, "Prominent Cardinal Attacks Science Behind Stem Cell Research", *New Scientist* (July 14, 2006) at 5. See also Elisabeth Rosenthal, "Excommunication is Sought for Stem Cell Researchers", *New York Times* (July 1, 2006), online: <http://www.nytimes.com/2006/07/01/world/europe/01vatican.html?ex=1309406400&en=0e0de4c51c312ccb&ei=5088&partner=rssnyt&emc=rss>.

[83] For a list of relevant surveys, see Health Law Institute, online: <http://www.law.ualberta.ca/centres/hli/hlicando.html#>.

[84] This is in contrast to the situation in the United States, where media hype, politicization of the issue and public support by high-profile celebrities have contributed to making stem cell research "the 'poster' child of biotechnology". Government of Canada BioPortal, "A Canada-US Public Opinion Research Study on Emerging Technologies — Report of Findings" (Ottawa: Decima Research Inc. for The Canadian Biotechnology Secretariat, Industry Canada (March 31, 2005)), online: <http://www.biostrategy.gc.ca/english/view.asp?x=721&all=true#470>. See also Norma Greenway, "Canadians Embrace Stem Cell Research", *The Ottawa Citizen* (October 14, 2003).

[85] Greenway, "Canadians Embrace Stem Cell Research". See also Jeff Walker, "Report on a Study of Emerging Technologies in Canada and the U.S. 'Prevailing Views, Awareness and Familiarity", in *First Impressions: Understanding Public Views on Emerging Technologies* (Genome Prairie, September 2005) at 6-19. This finding is consistent with U.S. data. See *e.g.*, Kathy L. Hudson, Joan Scott & Ruth Faden, *Values in Conflict: Public Attitudes on Embryonic Stem Cell Research* (Genetics and Public Policy Center, October 2005). The emphasis on tighter regulations is attributed to concerns over the efficacy of existing regulatory agencies and processes, and the potential influence of corporate interests. For an interesting comparison of Canadian and US views, see Edna Einsiedel, *First Impressions: Understanding Public Views on Emerging Technologies* (Genome Alberta, Prepared for the Canadian Biotechnology Secretariat, 2005) at 12:

> Focus groups and survey research reveal that there are subtle but important differences of opinion on the morality of stem cell research. Twice as many Americans (12%) as Canadians (6%) find it flat-out morally unacceptable, more Canadians (38%) than Americans (31%) find it morally questionable — the mid-point on the five-point scale — while the same numbers (32%) in each country say it is acceptable and 17% and 18% say it is somewhat acceptable. US focus groups revealed that there is a larger core of individuals who adamantly oppose stem cell research on ethical grounds.

For a comprehensive review of European public opinion, see George Gaskell *et al.*, "Europeans and Biotechnology in 2005: Patterns and Trends" (May 2006) 64.3 Eurobarometer (A report to the European Commission's Directorate-General for Research).

Indeed, it has been noted that individuals with extreme positions at either end of the continuum have done their best to try to portray the debate in terms that will help their cause.[86] For those who favour the work, this means emphasizing the potential scientific and health benefits. For those who oppose the work, the moral issues have remained the focus of debate. In the U.S., for example, some have speculated that a religious agenda has played a role in the tone of the national bioethics discourse, skewing it toward a neo-conservative ethos.[87] Though not as dominant as in the U.S., religion has also played a role in the direction of policy development in Canada and the United Kingdom.[88] We are left, then, with a seemingly irreconcilable polarity of positions.

This division has led to a diversity of regulatory approaches.[89] For example, some countries, such as Ireland, Italy, Germany and Austria, do not allow the use of human embryos for the purpose of stem cell research.[90] Other jurisdictions, such as the U.K., Sweden, California and Israel have a more permissive environment, allowing a wide range of research activities, including the creation of embryos for research purposes and "therapeutic cloning".[91]

Where does Canada sit on the spectrum of regulatory responses? In 2004, the Canadian Parliament passed the *Assisted Human Reproduction Act*.[92] This piece of legislation, which covers a broad range of activities associated with human reproductive material, sets the parameters under which embryonic stem cell research can occur in Canada. In some respects, Canada has taken a cautious middle ground approach by allowing research on embryos that have already been created for the purposes of reproduction through *in vitro* fertilization

---

[86] Matthew Nisbet, "The Competition for Worldviews: Values, Information, and Public Support for Stem Cell Research" (2005) 17 Int'l J. Public Opinion Research 92:

> [A] scientifically literate public is assumed [to] be more appreciative of science and technology, and more supportive of science as an institution. In contrast, religious research opponents have sought to mobilize the public by attempting to define stem cell research in the media coverage as a moral issue, emphasizing certain considerations that are likely to promote public opposition to research.

[87] R.A. Charo, "Passing on the Right: Conservative Bioethics is Closer Than It Appears" (2004) 2 J.L. Med. & Ethics 307-14.

[88] A. Plomer, "Beyond the HFE Act 1990: The Regulation of Stem Cell Research in the U.K." (2002) 10 Med. L. Rev. 132-63.

[89] "[T]he determination of the moral status of the human embryo influences possible responses to questions of the permissibility of, restrictions on, and prohibitions on embryonic research". Isasi & Knoppers, "Mind the Gap: Policy Approaches to Embryonic Stem Cell and Cloning Research in 50 Countries" at 24.

[90] Many of these countries have a religious or historical precedent that, in part, informed the adoption of a more restrictive research environment — such as the role of the Catholic Church in Ireland and Italy. See, *e.g.*, Pattinson & Caulfield, "Variations and Voids: The Regulation of Human Cloning Around the World" at 9.

[91] For a detailed description of regulatory positions throughout the world see generally Isasi & Knoppers, "Mind the Gap: Policy Approaches to Embryonic Stem Cell and Cloning Research in 50 Countries" at 13; Knowles, "A Regulatory Patchwork" at 157; and Pattinson & Caulfield, "Variations and Voids: The Regulation of Human Cloning Around the World" at 9.

[92] *Assisted Human Reproduction Act*, S.C. 2004, c. 2.

(IVF).[93] So long as the regulatory requirements have been satisfied, which include approval by several research ethics boards and compliance with specific consent guidelines,[94] research on these human embryos can occur. However, the law also provides significant criminal sanctions against a number of related scientific activities that are permitted in some jurisdictions, including the creation of embryos specifically for research purposes and "therapeutic cloning".[95]

But even this middle ground approach is, for some, less than satisfactory. When immutable moral convictions are engaged, compromise is not always an option. The scientific advances that have occurred in the area of stem cell research force us to confront the question of what type of consensus is required as a prerequisite to the development of social policy.[96] To what degree should a particular view of the moral status of embryonic life dictate national policy on the use of stem cells?[97] When is it appropriate for the government to pass laws that may restrict academic research?[98]

In the section that follows we will investigate the law and policy implications of scientific rather than moral uncertainty. What are the appropriate regulatory responses to the development of technologies so powerful that we are not currently in a position to predict or evaluate their potential danger?

D. NANOMEDICINE

What would happen if modern science were capable of healing the body at the molecular level, one atom at a time? When Nobel physicist Richard Feynman first posed a generalized version of this question to the American Physical Society in a famous 1959 address,[99] he dreamed of "the great future" challenging his colleagues to think big by thinking small:

---

[93] *Ibid.*, s. 40 [not yet in force].
[94] See *ibid.*, s. 40(3.1) [not yet in force]: "The Agency shall not issue a licence under subsection (1) for embryonic stem cell research unless it has received the written consent of the original gamete providers and the embryo provider in accordance with the *Human Pluripotent Stem Cell Research Guidelines* released by the Canadian Institutes of Health Research in March, 2002, as specified in the regulations".
[95] *Ibid.*, s. 5.
[96] See Isasi & Knoppers, "Mind the Gap: Policy Approaches to Embryonic Stem Cell and Cloning Research in 50 Countries" at 25: "Can we address such divisive issues while holding intact our democratic principles and socio-cultural values?"
[97] See, *e.g.*, Norma Greenway, "Jewish, Islamic Faiths Support Controversial Stem Cell Research" (February 29, 2003) at A3.
[98] For an interesting debate about academic freedom in the context of "therapeutic cloning", see Jocelyn Downie, Jennifer Llewellyn & Françoise Baylis, "A Constitutional Defence of the Federal Ban on Human Cloning for Research Purposes" (2005) 31 Queen's L.J. 353; and Barbara Billingsley & Timothy Caulfield, "The Regulation of Science and the Charter of Rights: Would a Ban on Non-Reproductive Human Cloning Unjustifiably Violate Freedom of Expression?" (2004) 29 Queen's L.J. 647-79.
[99] Richard Feynman, "There's Plenty of Room at the Bottom: An Invitation to Enter a New Field of Physics" (lecture, American Physical Society, California Institute of Technology, December 29, 1959) (1960) Engineering and Science 22, online: <http://www.zyvex.com/nanotech/feynman.html>.

The principles of physics, as far as I can see, do not speak against the possibility of maneuvering things atom by atom. [I]t would be, in principle, possible (I think) for a physicist to synthesize any chemical substance that a chemist writes down. How? Put the atoms down where the chemist says, and so you make the substance.[100]

Feynman's vision inspired in the subsequent five decades theoretical, experimental, and applied scientists from various disciplines to conduct research collectively known today as *nanotechnology*.

Although Feynman's bottom-up approach, subsequently elaborated by Drexler and others,[101] focuses on developing an ability to program and manipulate matter with molecular precision, the term "nanotechnology" has broadened to include top-down[102] technologies that operate on the nano-scale.[103] Debates concerning the feasibility of the bottom-up approach linger.[104] If achievable,

[f]ull fledged nanotechnology promises nothing less than complete control over the physical structure of matter — the same kind of control over the molecular and structural make-up of physical objects that a word processor provides over the content and form of a text. The implications of such capabilities are significant: to dramatize only slightly, they are comparable to producing a 747 or an ocean liner from the mechanical equivalent of a single fertilized egg.[105]

However, most publicly funded nanotechnology research is a much less grandiose, much more traditional, top-down model of science (only done on the nano-scale). Even if the "assembler breakthrough" never occurs, many governments are investing heavily in nanotechnology,[106] expecting that it will address a

---

[100] *Ibid.*

[101] See, *e.g.*, K. Eric Drexler, *Engines of Creation: The Coming Era of Nanotechnology* (New York: Anchor Press/Doubleday, 1986); Eric Drexler, Chris Peterson & Gayle Pergamit, *Unbounding the Future: The Nanotechnology Revolution* (New York: William Morrow and Co. Inc., 1991).

[102] A top-down approach builds things by taking existing matter and reducing or removing unwanted material, *e.g.*, sawing a piece of wood or using a chemical reagent. A bottom-up approach would build matter atom by atom, or cell by cell. According to Drexler's vision, nano-machines known as "assemblers" would be programmed to build larger, more complex materials similar to the manner in which a human being results from a single cell. See Drexler, *Engines of Creation: The Coming Era of Nanotechnology* (New York: Anchor Press/Doubleday, 1986) at 14.

[103] Which is an order of magnitude smaller than microtechnology. A nanometer (nm) is one-billionth of a meter, which is about 3 to 6 atoms in length; the thickness of a human hair is said to be 50,000 to 100,000 nm. See Center for Responsible Nanotechnology, "Nanotechnology Glossary", online: <http://www.crnano.org/crnglossary.htm>.

[104] See, *e.g.*, Ian Kerr & Goldie Bassi, "Not Much Room? Nanotechnology, Networks and the Politics of Dancing" (2004) 12 Health L.J. 103.

[105] Glen Harlan Reynolds, "Forward to the Future: Nanotechnology and Regulatory Policy" (November 2002) Pacific Research 6, online: <http://www.pacificresearch.org/pub/sab/techno/forward_to_nanotech.pdf>.

[106] It is estimated that, as of 2005, there is approximately 9.6 billion USD in nanotechnology R&D funding worldwide. Governments are some of the heaviest investors, accounting for almost half of the money. See The Nanoethics Group, "The Nanotech Market", online: <http://www.nanoethics.org/investments.html>. In 2005, the U.S. provided approximately $1 billion in funding. See Robert F. Service, "Calls Rise for More Research on Toxicology of Nanomaterials"

broad range of environmental issues, drastically reduce energy consumption, increase food production, create new and better information technologies and consumer products, amplify the precision and efficacy of military devices and weapons, and dramatically advance medicine's ability to cure and prevent diseases.[107] Already, there have been significant advancements in fields such as microscopy and materials science.[108] But the most prolific and high profile uses of nanotechnology to date are in the field of medicine.

Nanomedicine, as it is sometimes called,[109] aims to develop molecular tools that will diagnose, treat and prevent diseases or traumatic injuries. With significantly enhanced levels of control, it promises to eclipse the profit potential of modern pharmaceuticals. Imagine, for example, nano-sized sensors able to detect and diagnose cancer in the early stages when there are only a few thousand cancerous cells in the body.[110] Now imagine firing metal-coated nanoshells[111] with precision into the cracks of the tumour cells and no others, frying the cancer by using an external infrared light to heat the metal coating and thereby burn only tumour cells. In addition to the use of these sorts of nanomaterials and devices, research and development will also focus on other novel forms of therapy, new methods of drug delivery,[112] and techniques for improving imaging and other medical diagnostics.[113]

Like the elixir of Theuth, nanomedicine offers much promise but also potential peril. The unpredictability of nano-scale products and applications raise numerous health and safety issues. As we have seen with other emerging

---

(2005) 310 Science 1609. The European Commission earmarked 1.3 billion euros for nanotechnology research between 2003 and 2006. See Robert A. Freitas Jr., "What is Nanomedicine" (2005) 51 Disease a Month 325. In Canada, the Federal government, in partnership with the government of Alberta, have guaranteed $120 million of funding for the new National Institute of Nanotechnology (NINT) from 2001 until 2007, in addition to the $100 million required to build the facility at the University of Alberta. See National Research Council of Canada, "Flagship Nanotechnology Institute's New Home Features Canada's Quietest Space", online: <http://www.nrc-cnrc.gc.ca/newsroom/news/2006/nint06-nr_e.html>.

[107] See, *e.g.*, Freitas Jr., "What is Nanomedicine?" (2005) 51 Disease a Month 325; The Nanoethics Group, "The Good", online: <http://www.nanoethics.org/good.html>.

[108] See, *e.g.*, Robert A. Wolkow, "The Ruse and Reality of Nanotechnology" (2004) 12 Health L. Rev. 14.

[109] For a comprehensive introduction to various applications in nanomedicine, see Freitas Jr. "What is Nanomedicine?" (2005) 51 Disease a Month 325.

[110] James R. Heath, Michael E. Phelps & Leroy Hood, "NanoSystems Biology" (2003) 5 Molecular Imaging & Biology 312.

[111] A nanoshell is a 100 nm spherical shell containing a coat of metal around a core of silicon dioxide atoms. Preliminary experiments for the scenario presented above have already been published. See C. Loo *et al.*, "Nanoshell-enabled Photonics-based Imaging and Therapy of Cancer" (2004) 3 Cancer Res. Treat 33; Freitas Jr., "What is Nanomedicine?" (2005) 51 Disease a Month 325.

[112] Methods that have the ability to target selected cells or receptors within the body. U. Pison *et al.*, "Nanomedicine for Respiratory Diseases" (2006) 533 Eur. J. Pharmacology 343-44.

[113] European Science Foundation (ESF), *Nanomedicine: An ESF European Medical Research Councils (EMRC) Forward Look Report* (ESF, 2005) at 7, online: <www.esf.org/publication/214/Nanomedicine.pdf>. For a discussion of nano-diagnostics in a respiratory context, see Pison, "Nanomedicine for Respiratory Diseases" (2006) 533 Eur. J. Pharmacology 342-43.

health technologies discussed in this chapter, this is not uncommon since, by definition, new technologies have not been subject to long term clinical trials. But there seems to be a crucial distinction between nano and other new technologies. Given their size, nanomaterials are governed not by the laws of gravity but the laws of quantum mechanics.[114] Quantum mechanics in some cases requires a non-intuitive understanding of various scientific relationships:

> Some of these dependencies are scientifically intuitive such as the relationship between properties of nanomaterials and their size, composition, impurities (both internally and superficially), the surface chemistry (including passivating agents) and degree of agglomeration. Other dependencies such as shape, change, zeta potential and phase seem less intuitive. And this is just the tip of the iceberg. To complicate matters further, many of the dependencies are intrinsically linked.[115]

One therefore cannot always extrapolate from existing knowledge about the behaviour of material properties on a macroscale. For example, some materials that are inert at the macroscale are reactive at the nanoscale.[116] A similar difficulty exists when it comes to the relationship between size and phase.

> Macroscopically the rutile phase is stable and the anatase phase is metastable, but when the particle size is under ~20nm this situation is reversed. ... This is of critical importance, because rutile and anatase react very differently when exposed to light. ... Both technologies are currently in use around the world without discernible risk, but a phase transition in either case would do more than reduce the efficiency of these respective products, it could also be damaging to the substrate — which in the case of rutile-based sunscreen, is us.[117]

Here, nanotechnology is *pharmakon* in the Derridean sense: the remedy becomes the poison. The inability to accurately predict what will transpire at the nanoscale can be further exacerbated by changes in temperature, pressure, humidity and the like.

Given its currently unpredictable nature, there is a budding debate about the need for a unique regulatory scheme for nanotechnology. In the U.S. context, some have argued that the Food and Drug Administration (FDA) is not particularly well-equipped to deal with many of the forthcoming challenges of nanotechnology. In addition to lacking the necessary complement of FDA scientists with sufficient expertise to evaluate new products, many nano-applications do not easily fit within existing FDA categories.[118] Others, however, see no need for a new regulatory schema. They point out that, despite the recent buzz, research in nanomedicine is not new. Various such applications have obtained FDA approval for more than a decade.[119]

---

[114] Mutaz B. Habal, "Nanosize, Mega-Impact, Potential for Medical Applications of Nanotechnology" (2006) 17 J. Craniofacial Surgery 3.

[115] Amanda S. Barnard, "Nanohazards: Knowledge is our First Defence" (2006) 5 Nature Materials 245.

[116] *Ibid.*, at 246.

[117] *Ibid.*

[118] See, *e.g.*, John Miller, "Beyond Biotechnology: FDA Regulation of Nanomedicine" (2003) 4 Columbia Sci. & Tech. L. Rev. 1.

[119] See, *e.g.*, Nuala Moran, "Nanomedicine Lacks Recogniton in Europe" (2006) 24 Nature Biotech.

The same debate would, of course, apply to Canada. In fact, such debates are themselves not new. With practically each new round of so-called "disruptive" technologies,[120] law makers toil over whether regulation should be novel and unique or whether it should comport with the principle of technological neutrality. According to this principle, new laws or regulations should not depend upon a specific development or state of technology, but ought instead to be based on core principles that can be adapted to changing technologies.[121] Since technological change is continuous, standards created in light of particular technologies are likely to become outdated with the rapid shift in technological paradigms.[122]

It is perhaps too early to tell whether nanomedicine will be evolutionary or revolutionary. However, given its nascent state of development, its inherent unpredictability and the potential risks attendant in more general uses of nanotechnology,[123] it is difficult to imagine a completely unregulated program of research and development. Like genetically modified foods in the U.K., the likely impetus of such regulation will be the precautionary principle, an approach to managing threats of serious or irreversible harm in situations of scientific uncertainty.

121, where she quotes Mike Eaton of UCB Celltech as stating, "I'm not sure you need new regulation. Nanomedicines are not new; they have been getting regulatory approval for ten years".

[120] A technology is described as disruptive when it overthrows the existing dominant technology or product in a market. Typical examples include the steam engine (replacing human-power); the automobile (displacing horse and buggy); the integrated circuit (replacing the transistor). See generally, Clayton M. Christensen, *The Innovator's Dilemma: When New Technologies Cause Great Firms to Fall* (Boston: Harvard Business School Press, 1997).

[121] One example of such an approach would be the fair information practice principles that form the basis of health privacy and other data protection regimes. See *e.g.*, Organisation for Economic Co-operation and Development (OECD), *Guidelines on the Protection of Privacy and Transborder Flows of Personal Data* (OECD, 1980); *Personal Information Protection and Electronic Documents Act*, S.C. 2000, c. 5.

[122] Michael Geist, "Is There a There There? Toward Greater Certainty for Internet Jurisdiction" (2002) 16 Berkeley Tech. L.J. 1345. For further discussion of the principle of technological neutrality, see Ian Kerr, Alanna Maurushat & Christian Tacit, "Technical Protection Measures: Part II, The Legal Protection of TPMs" (Study prepared for the Department of Canadian Heritage, April 2002) at 43, online: <http://www.patrimoinecanadien.gc.ca/progs/ac-ca/progs/pda-cpb/pubs/index_e.cfm>.

[123] To mention a few, these risks include: (i) catastrophic environmental damage due to unanticipated or uncontrollable consequences of its use; (ii) economic oppression by patent owners that would deny those in need of otherwise cheap lifesaving technologies; (iii) an unstable arms race as nanotechnology applications are developed for military or terrorist ends; (iv) ubiquitous surveillance of citizens by corporations and governments with the further miniaturization of devices. See generally David Williams, "The Risks of Nanotechnology" (2005) 16 Med. Device Tech. 6; The Nanoethics Group, "The Bad", online: <http://www.nanoethics.org/bad.html>; European Commission, *Nanotechnologies: A Preliminary Risk Analysis, on the Basis of a Workshop Organized in Brussels on 1-2 March 2004 by the Health and Consumer Protectorate General of the European Commission* (European Commission, March 2004), online: <http://www.ec.europa.eu/health/ph_risk/documents/ev_20040301_en.pdf>.

Although referred to as though it were a singular, unified and coherent concept, the precautionary principle has in fact seen many different formulations ranging from Hippocrates' "First, do no harm"[124] to the 1992 Rio Declaration on Environment and Development statement that, "[w]here there are threats of serious or irreversible damage, lack of full scientific certainty shall not be used as a reason for postponing cost-effective measures to prevent ... degradation".[125] Though there are divergent views, core elements of the precautionary approach are usually thought to entail that: (i) there exists a duty to take anticipatory action to prevent harm; (ii) the burden of proof of harmlessness for an unproven technology lies with its proponents, not the general public; (iii) prior to its adoption, there exists an obligation to examine a full range of alternatives (including the alternative of doing nothing); and (iv) applying the precautionary principle requires a process that is open, informed, democratic and inclusive of all affected parties.[126]

In September 2001, the government of Canada announced its view that "the precautionary approach is a legitimate and distinctive decision-making tool within risk management".[127] In a series of documents aiming to develop "A Canadian Perspective on the Precautionary Approach/Principle", the government enumerated a set of guiding principles aimed at supporting "consistent, credible and predictable policy and regulatory decision making when applying the precautionary principle".[128]

How ought the precautionary principle apply to nanomedicine?

There are divergent views on this. For example, the Action Group on Erosion, Technology and Concentration (ETC), has recommended that:

[g]iven the concerns raised over nanoparticle contamination in living organisms ... governments [must] declare an immediate moratorium on commercial production of new nanomaterials and launch a transparent global process for evaluating the socioeconomic, health and environmental implications of the technology.[129]

---

[124] While not part of the Hippocratic Oath itself, the maxim "First, do no harm" was reflected within Hippocrates' Corpus at *Epidemics*, Bk. I, Sect. V., where he states, "to help, or at least to do no harm".

[125] United Nations Environment Programme, *Rio Declaration on Environment and Development* (1992), Principle 15, online: <http://www.unep.org/Documents.multilingual/Default.asp?DocumentID=78&ArticleID=1163>. This approach was subsequently particularized to include health concerns in the *Wingspread Statement on the Precautionary Principle*: "When an activity raises threats of harm to human health or the environment, precautionary measures should be taken even if some cause-and-effect relationships are not fully established scientifically". Global Development Research Center, *Wingspread Statement on the Precautionary Principle* (January 1998), online: <http://www.gdrc.org/u-gov/precaution-3.html>.

[126] See Joel Tickner, Carolyn Raffensperger & Nancy Myers, *The Precautionary Principle in Action: A Handbook* (AG BioTech InfoNet), online: <http://www.rachel.org/bulletin/index.cfm?issue_ID=532>.

[127] Environment Canada, *A Canadian Perspective on the Precautionary Approach/Principle* (Privy Council Office, September 2001), Principle 1, online: <www.pco-bcp.gc.ca/raoics-srdc/docs/Precaution/Discussion/discussion_e.pdf> at Executive Summary.

[128] *Ibid.*, Foreword.

[129] ETC Group, *The Big Down: Atomtech — Technologies Converging at the Nano-scale* (January 30, 2003) at 73, online: <www.etcgroup.org/documents/TheBigDown.pdf>. ETC Group's call for a moratorium on the use of nanotechnology was recently renewed. See ETC Group,

Others, including the Center For Responsible Nanotechnology, offer a different perspective, drawing an important distinction between the "strict form" of precaution, which calls for inaction (usually by banning, prohibiting, or restricting scientific research and development), and an "active form" of precaution, which requires that we choose "less risky alternatives when they are available ... taking responsibility for potential risks".[130] Concerned that a moratorium would simply result in inaction on the part of responsible and law-abiding people/institutions while the development and use of dangerous nanotechnologies would continue underground or offshore by less responsible people/institutions, their interpretation of the precautionary principle "does not automatically forbid risky activities; instead it calls for an appropriate effort to mitigate the risk — which may well involve finding and choosing a different activity".[131] On this approach, it is "imperative to find and implement the least risky plan that is realistically feasible".[132] These authors further suggest that the safest option is to create a single research and development program for nanotechnology with widespread, though regulated use of its outputs.[133]

The government of Canada has not yet articulated how the precautionary principle might be applied to nanotechnology. Nor has it proposed any specific regulatory regimes for nanotechnology. The future abounds with question marks.

III. THE CHALLENGE OF COMMERCIALIZATION

When contemplating the appropriate regulatory responses to emerging health technologies, an important factor to remember is that the research environment is becoming ever more closely tied to private industry. Biomedical researchers are increasingly expected to obtain research funding from private sources and justify research goals in terms of economic development. Even the Canadian Institutes of Health Research (CIHR), the primary public funding agency for health research, has a mandate, explicitly stated in the CIHR enabling legislation, to "encourag[e] innovation, facilitat[e] the commercialization of health research in Canada and promot[e] economic development through health research in Canada".[134] Other funding agencies, such as Genome Canada, are charged with similar commercial goals.[135]

There are, of course, numerous benefits to working with industry, including increasing the funds available for research and providing an essential knowledge

---

"Nanotech Product Recall Underscores the Need for Nanotech Moratorium: Is the Magic Gone?" (April 1, 2006), online: <www.etcgroup.org/en/materials/publications.html?pub_id=14>.

[130] Chris Phoenix & Mike Treder, "Applying the Precautionary Principle to Nanotechnology" (Center for Responsible Nanotechnology, January 2003; revised December 2003, January 2004), online: <http://www.crnano.org/precautionary.htm>.

[131] *Ibid.*

[132] *Ibid.*

[133] *Ibid.*

[134] *Canadian Institutes of Health Research Act*, S.C. 2000, c. 6.

[135] See Genome Canada, online: <http://www.genomecanada.ca>.

translation function. Arguably, many of the therapeutic benefits associated with emerging technologies could not be realized in our society without a partnership between academic researchers and industry. For example, new drug therapies or diagnostic technologies can cost hundreds of millions of dollars to produce and disseminate. The infrastructure and funding for this aspect of the research development process must come largely from industry, as universities and other public research institutions do not have the requisite public funding or support to do it on their own. As noted by DeAngelis:

> The discovery of new medications, devices, and techniques is funded primarily by for-profit companies; testing new modalities of treatment is funded primarily by for-profit companies; and the manufacture and the profitable marketing aspects of these modalities appropriately falls in the purview of this industry.[136]

That said, there are also profound concerns that flow from the commercialization of biomedical research. Indeed, some of the greatest challenges associated with the use and integration of emerging technologies can be traced to the influence and role of commercial forces.[137] Here, we will briefly consider the role of patents.[138]

Patents provide the inventor with an exclusive, 20-year monopoly over new inventions. Patents are meant to encourage innovation by providing a clear incentive. The patenting of biomedical inventions, however, has long been a source of social concern — particularly when the "invention" involves human biological substances, such as genetic material and human embryonic stem cell lines.[139] For example, there are those who believe that such patents are unethical or contrary to notions of human dignity.[140] On a practical level, it has been suggested that the push toward patents skews the direction of research away from needed basic science toward research that focuses on commercializable products. There is also speculation that patenting pressure leads to a more secretive research environment, thus inhibiting collaborations and the free flow of valuable research data.[141] Finally, and perhaps most importantly, there is

---

[136] Catherine D. DeAngelis, "The Influence of Money on Medical Science" (2006) 296 J.A.M.A. 996.

[137] See, *e.g.*, D. Chalmers & D. Nicol, "Commercialisation of Biotechnology: Public Trust in Research" (2004) 6 Int'l J. Biotech. 116-33.

[138] There are, of course, many other important social issues associated with commercialization and the involvement of industry not covered in this chapter. For example, see J. Thompson, P. Baird & J. Downie, *Report of the Committee of Inquiry on the Case Involving Dr. Nancy Olivieri, the Hospital for Sick Children, the University of Toronto and Apotex Inc.* (Toronto: James Lorimer & Co. Ltd., 2001).

[139] See, *e.g.*, Gina Kolata, "Who Owns your Genes?", New York Times (May 15, 2000) at A-1 and Timothy Caulfield, Richard Gold & Mildred Cho, "Patenting Human Genetic Material: Refocusing the Debate" (2000) 1 Nature Rev. Genetics 227-31. See also Mark Lemley, "Patenting Nanotechnology" (2005) 58 Stanford L. Rev. 601.

[140] For a critique of this view, see D.B. Resnik, "DNA Patents and Human Dignity" (2001) 29 J.L. Med. & Ethics 152.

[141] P.A. David, "Can 'Open Science' be Protected from the Evolving Regime of IPR Protections?" (2004) 160 Journal of Theoretical and Institutional Economics 1-26; David Blumenthal, "Withholding Research Results in Academic Life Science: Evidence From a National Survey of Faculty" (1997) 277 J.A.M.A. 1224.

concern that patents will drive up the cost of emerging technologies adding to the overall costs of our health care system.[142]

This latter concern received considerable attention in the summer of 2001 when Myriad Genetics attempted to enforce its patents over the BRCA1/2 mutations (genetic mutations that, if present, increase the likelihood an individual will get breast or ovarian cancer).[143] Through cease and desist letters sent to most provincial health ministries, Myriad Genetics tried to force all testing to be done through the Myriad laboratory in Utah, at a cost of approximately $3,800, considerably more than the cost of doing the test through available processes at existing provincial laboratories. Though no patent litigation has emerged from the Myriad controversy, it was a catalyst of considerable policy debate and was considered by some as a "harbinger" of things to come.[144]

Despite such issues, the patenting of biomedical inventions, including human genes, has continued, relatively unfettered, for decades. In general, so long as an invention meets the basic statutory requirements for a patent — it must be new, useful and have a clear utility — it can be patented.[145] Indeed, it has been estimated that over 20 per cent of all human genes are associated with at least one patent.[146] That said, the concerns associated with biotechnology patents, particularly those regarding the impact of patents on access, continue to stir debate and have led to a variety of policy recommendations from provincial governments,[147] bioethics and science policy entities,[148] and international organizations.[149] Recommendations

---

[142] See Jon Merz *et al.*, "Diagnostic Testing Fails the Test" (2002) 415 Nature 577-79; and Timothy Caulfield, "Policy Conflicts: Gene Patents and Health Care in Canada" (2005) 8 Community Gen. 223-27.

[143] Bryn Williams-Jones, "History of a Gene Patent: Tracing the Development and Application of Commercial BRCA Testing" (2002) 10 Health L.J. 123-46. For a discussion of the role of these mutations in the development of cancer see M.C. King, J. Marks & J. Mandell, "Breast and Ovarian Cancer Risk Due to Inherited Mutations in BRCA1 and BRCA2" (2003) 302 Science 643-46.

[144] Bryn Williams-Jones, "History of a Gene Patent: Tracing the Development and Application of Commercial BRCA Testing" (2002) 10 Health L.J. 123-46; and Richard Gold, "From Theory to Practice: Health Care and the Patent System" (2003) Health Law Journal Special Edition 21-39.

[145] See, generally, *Diamond v. Chakrabarty*, 447 U.S. 303 (1980). Since this landmark decision by the United States Supreme Court, there have been few legal obstacles to the patenting of biologically based "inventions". It should be noted, however, that Canada is the only country with a high court decision that explicit rejects the patenting of "higher life forms" (*Harvard College v. Canada (Commissioner of Patents)*, [2002] S.C.C. No. 77, [2002] 4 S.C.R. 45, 219 D.L.R. (4th) 577 (S.C.C.)).

[146] K. Jensen and F. Murray, "Enhanced: Intellectual Property Landscape of the Human Genome" (2005) 310 Science 239-40.

[147] Ontario Ministry of Health, *Genetics, Testing and Gene Patenting: Charting New Territory in Healthcare* (Toronto: Government of Ontario, 2002).

[148] See Danish Council of Ethics, *Patenting Human Genes and Stem Cells* (Copenhagen: Danish Council of Ethics, 2004); and The Nuffield Council on Bioethics, *The Ethics of Patenting DNA: A Discussion Paper* (London: Nuffield Council of Bioethics, 2002); and National Academy of Sciences, *Reaping the Benefits of Genomic and Proteomic Research: Intellectual Property Rights, Innovation, and Public Health* (Washington, D.C.: National Academies Press, 2005).

[149] Organisation for Economic Cooperation and Development (OECD), "Genetic Inventions,

have ranged from clarifying the research exemptions (so researchers can access patented inventions without fear of infringing a patent) to a consideration of compulsory licensing (so provincial health care systems can control the cost of patented inventions).[150]

To date, there have been no major reforms to the Canadian patent system, and the degree to which the available empirical data supports or denies the existence of the noted concerns remains a subject of considerable debate.[151] Nevertheless, there is some evidence that the public is becoming increasingly uncomfortable with biotechnology patents[152] and that the patenting of controversial emerging technologies, including embryonic stem cell lines and nanotechnologies, might stir more interest in policy reform.[153] For example, because the source of embryonic stem cell lines remains controversial, there may be those who believe that the patenting of stem cell lines is morally inappropriate.

Another major concern associated with the commercialization process is that marketing pressure, inextricably tied with the involvement of industry, will lead to an inappropriate increase in the utilization of a given technology.[154] There is evidence that this is already happening in a variety of domains, such as with imaging technologies,[155] genetic testing[156] and, of course, pharmaceuticals.[157] Industry has a natural and understandable desire to increase profits by increasing demand. But this inclination may result in marketing strategies that create inappropriate expectations, patient anxiety and more utilization than what might be considered ideal. In order to counter such pressures, regulatory strategies have been proposed, including independent technology assessment and controls on marketing approaches.[158]

Intellectual Property Rights and Licensing Practices: Evidence and Policies" (2002), online: <http://www.oecd.org/dataoecd/42/21/2491084.pdf>.

[150] Ontario Ministry of Health, *Genetics, Testing and Gene Patenting* (Toronto: Government of Ontario, 2002).

[151] Timothy Caulfield, Bob Cook-Deegan, Scott Kieff & John Walsh, "Evidence and Anecdotes: An Analysis of Human Gene Patenting Controversies" (2006) 24 Nature Biotechnology 1091-94.

[152] E. Einsiedel & J. Smith, "Canadian Views on Patenting Biotechnology" (Canadian Biotechnology Advisory Committee, June 2005), online: <http://www.cbac-cccb.ca/epic/internet/incbac-cccb.nsf/vwapj/FINAL_inseidel_e.pdf/$FILE/FINAL_inseidel_e.pdf>.

[153] See, for example, Timothy Caulfield, "Stem Cell Patents and Social Controversy: A Speculative View From Canada" at 219-32; and Mark Lemley, "Patenting Nanotechnology" (2005) 58 Stanford L. Rev. 601.

[154] See, *e.g.*, Patti Peppin, "The Power of Illusion and the Illusion of Power", in Colleen Flood, ed., *Just Medicare: What's In, What's Out, How We Decide* (Toronto: University of Toronto Press, 2005) at 355.

[155] Richard Smith, "The Screening Industry" (2003) 326 B.M.J.: "Simple minded enthusiasm for screening, combined with the industrial opportunity to make fat profits, may mean that soon none of us will be normal".

[156] Stacy Gray & Olufunmilayo I. Olopade, "Direct-to-Consumer Marketing of Genetic Tests for Cancer: Buyer Beware" (2003) 21 J. Clin. Oncology 3191-93.

[157] See Steven Woloshin & Lisa Schwartz, "Giving Legs to Restless Legs: A Case Study of How the Media Makes People Sick" (2006) 3 PloS Med. 452; and Trudo Lemmens & Ron A. Bouchard, Chapter 8 in this volume.

[158] Barbara Mintzes, "Disease Mongering in Drug Promotion: Do Governments Have a Regulatory Role?" (2006) 3 PLoS Med. 461. An additional concern, not considered in this brief overview, is

Finally, the impact of commercialization on that most valuable of assets, public trust, should be considered. Indeed, many scholars have noted that public trust is an essential element of the research infrastructure and, if lost, is tremendously difficult to regain.[159] There is at least some evidence that close ties with industry have the potential to compromise public trust. For example, university researchers funded by public sources are one of the most trusted voices in the area of biotechnology. However, those funded by industry are among the least trusted.[160] The source of funding, and its perceived impact on the impartiality of researchers, seems to be the critical element. And, given the evidence that industry funding impacts the nature and tone of research findings, the public's skepticism is not without foundation.[161] In areas like stem cell research, nanotechnology and human genetics, where the public may already have concerns about the use and implications of the technology,[162] a loss of public trust could be particularly damaging.

If industry is going to continue to play an ever-increasing role in the funding of biomedical research, policies must be developed to ensure that the integrity of the research enterprise is maintained and that public trust is respected and engaged.[163]

---

the impact that commercialization pressure will have on the direction of research — skewing it toward commercializable objectives and away from basic research and less profitable public health initiatives. Caulfield has explored this issue elsewhere. See, *e.g.*, Timothy Caulfield, "Sustainability and the Balancing of the Health Care and Innovation Agendas: The Commercialization of Genetic Research" (2003) 66 Sask L. Rev. 629. See also Paul Nightingale & Paul Martin, "The Myth of the Biotech Revolution" (2004) 565 Trends in Biotech 566-67.

[159] Marcia Angel, "Is Academic Medicine for Sale?" (2000) 342, N.E.J.M. 1516-18.

[160] Government of Canada BioPortal, "A Canada-US Public Opinion Research Study on Emerging Technologies" at 55 (see slide no. 110).

[161] Council on Scientific Affairs, American Medical Association, *Influence of Funding Source on Outcome, Validity, and Reliability of Pharmaceutical Research* (C.S.A. Report 10, 2004 A.M.A. Annual Meeting, June 2004) where the authors summarize the research in the area:

> Studies with positive findings are more likely to be published than studies with negative or null results and an association exists between pharmaceutical industry sponsorship of clinical research and publication of results favoring the sponsor's products. Additionally, the publication of negative results may be delayed compared with the time to publication of studies with positive results.

[162] In a 2005 study only 49 per cent of Canadians surveyed (compared with 57 per cent of Americans), thought that biotechnology was being developed with consideration to their interests, values and beliefs, Government of Canada BioPortal, "A Canada-US Public Opinion Research Study on Emerging Technologies".

[163] See, *e.g.*, Timothy Caulfield, Edna Einsiedel, Jon Merz & Dianne Nicol, "Trust, Patents and Public Perceptions: The Governance of Controversial Biotechnology Research" (2006) 24 Nature Biotechnology 1352-54, where the use of patent pools is recommended as a way of managing the commercialization.

IV. CONCLUSION

In this chapter, we have examined four emerging health technologies. We have seen that each has significant potential health benefits to offer. Each also has various ethical and legal dimensions associated with its proposed use. In this chapter, we have limited our brief survey to a single health law and policy precept for each: genetics requires us to think about equality and equal treatment; radio frequency identification poses new challenges for informational privacy and security; embryonic stem cell techniques revive debates about the moral limits of human experimentation; nanotechnology raises questions about the practice of precaution. We also considered how scientific research is transformed into technological applications through the process of commercialization.

As we continue to think about these new elixirs, it is instructive to recall King Thamus and his admonition to the inventor: "Theuth, my paragon of inventors, the discoverer of an art is not the best judge of the good or harm which will accrue to those who practice it".

When we consider the governance of science and the proper place of technology in our health care system, it is important to recognize that the technologies that science enables are not neutral and that it is therefore not always appropriate to leave science to its own devices. As one team of scholars recently put it:

> values; science alone cannot answer them. The public expect and want science and technology to solve problems, but they also want a say in deciding which problems are worth solving. This is not a matter of attracting public support for an agenda already established by science and scientists, but rather of seeing the public as participants in science policy with whom a shared vision of socially viable science and technological innovation can be achieved.[164]

Likewise, bioethicists, lawyers, policy makers and other relevant experts all have a crucial role to play in determining the best way to harness emerging technologies that are both good *and* bad; at one and the same time the solution and the problem.

---

[164] George Gaskell *et al.*, "Social Values and the Governance of Science" (2005) 310 Science 1909.

Chapter 14

CHARTER CHALLENGES

Nola M. Ries

"As we enter the 21st century, health care is a constant concern. The public health care system, once a source of national pride, has become the subject of frequent and sometimes bitter criticism."

Deschamps J., Supreme Court of Canada decision in
Chaoulli v. Quebec (Attorney General) (2005)

I. INTRODUCTION

This chapter discusses ways in which the *Canadian Charter of Rights and Freedoms*[1] may be used to challenge various aspects of health care delivery and regulation in Canada. The Charter is relevant in a wide range of health law topics — reproduction, mental health, public health, and end of life decisions, to name just a few — and may be used to challenge various laws or government powers that impact individual rights and freedoms; indeed, many laws that aim to achieve some health goal have been challenged under the Charter. Examples of the types of laws that may implicate Charter rights include mental health laws and public health laws that authorize involuntary treatment of patients,[2] laws restricting activities of health care professionals,[3] and laws that regulate foods, drugs and tobacco.[4] Many of these topics are discussed in detail elsewhere in this text, so this chapter focuses primarily on the use of Charter challenges to

---

[1] *Canadian Charter of Rights and Freedoms*, Part I of the *Constitution Act, 1982*, being Schedule B to the *Canada Act 1982* (U.K.), 1982, c. 11.

[2] See, *e.g.*, *Fleming v. Reid*, [1991] O.J. No. 1083, 4. O.R. (3d) 74 (Ont. C.A.) (challenge to involuntary treatment of psychiatric patients) and *Toronto (City, Medical Officer of Health) v. Deakin*, [2002] O.J. No. 2777 (Ont. C.J.) (challenge to mandatory detention and treatment of a person with tuberculosis).

[3] See, *e.g.*, *Waldman v. British Columbia (Medical Services Commission)*, [1999] B.C.J. No. 2014, 1999 BCCA 508 (B.C.C.A.) (billing restrictions for new physicians held to violate mobility rights under s. 6 of the Charter) and *Rombaut v. New Brunswick (Minister of Health and Community Services)*, [2001] N.B.J. No. 243, 2001 NBCA 75 (N.B.C.A.) (physician resource management plan held not to violate s. 6 mobility rights).

[4] See, *e.g.*, *RJR -MacDonald v. Canada (Attorney General)*, [1995] S.C.J. No. 68, [1995] 3 S.C.R. 199 (S.C.C.).

influence the allocation of health care resources and the structure of our system of publicly insured health services.

This chapter begins with a brief overview of the Canadian health care system and an explanation of Charter provisions that are most often argued in health care cases — namely, section 7 rights to life, liberty and personal security and section 15 equality rights. It traces an evolution in the types of claims made under these sections of the Charter in regard to health care, beginning with cases that assert negative conceptions of rights — the freedom to make health decisions without unwarranted state intrusion — and then turning to cases involving positive claims in which litigants ask courts to compel governments to provide specific health care services.

The chapter next analyzes the contest between dollars and rights: when can fiscal constraints justify limits on constitutionally protected rights and freedoms and when should courts defer to government policy choices? The Supreme Court of Canada's guidance on these questions is examined and problems in evaluating costs and benefits of health care services are highlighted. Finally, the chapter concludes with a discussion of approaches to improve transparency and accountability in health policy choices, since more open and participatory decision-making models may mitigate costly, time-consuming and divisive legal challenges.

II. THE CANADIAN HEALTH CARE SYSTEM

Chapter 1 in this volume explains in detail the structure and governance of the Canadian health care system, so just a brief overview is provided here. Under the terms of the *Canada Health Act*,[5] the Canadian health care system provides universal public insurance for medically necessary physician and hospital services. Because the provision of health care is primarily an area of provincial authority under the Canadian Constitution,[6] each province operates a public health insurance plan in which patients and care providers participate. As there is no uniform definition of what constitutes a "medically necessary" health care service,[7] there is some variation across the country regarding the types of services that are publicly insured and the circumstances under which patients and providers can opt out of the public system.

Much contemporary debate focuses on the sustainability of the publicly funded health care system in Canada. While the public system generally

---

[5] R.S.C. 1985, c. C-6.

[6] *Constitution Act, 1982*, being Schedule B of the *Canada Act 1982* (U.K.), 1982, c. 11. For further discussion, see, *e.g.*, Martha Jackman, "Constitutional Jurisdiction Over Health in Canada" (2000) 8 Health Law Journal 95.

[7] For analysis of the challenges of defining the concept of medical necessity, see, *e.g.*, Cathy Charles *et al.*, "Medical Necessity in Canadian Health Policy: Four Meanings and ... a Funeral?" (1997) 75:3 Millbank Q. 365, Timothy A. Caulfield, "Wishful Thinking: Defining 'Medically Necessary' in Canada" (1996) 4 Health L.J. 63 and Glenn Griener, "Defining Medical Necessity: Challenges and Implications" (2002) 10 Health L. Rev. 6.

performs well in providing timely and satisfactory access to needed services,[8] numerous factors put pressure on the system. Spending on health care is an expanding proportion of government budgets, with some estimating that health care costs will consume over 50 per cent of provincial/territorial revenues by 2020.[9] Exogenous factors that drive health care spending include population growth and aging, growing incidence of chronic diseases, and increasing demand for services. Costs of new health care technologies and pharmaceuticals will escalate costs, along with health human resource spending.

Despite Canada's reputation for having a comprehensive, universal public health care system, private sources (out-of-pocket payments and private insurance) account for around 30 per cent of health care expenditures, primarily for dental and vision care and prescription drugs.[10] Out of pocket costs have been increasing by about six per cent per year since the late 1990s. Private health care clinics offer access to non-insured services, but some include a mix of non-insured and insured services, leading to concerns about user fees and extra billing.[11]

A publicly funded health care system cannot provide all services to all people so rationing is inevitable. Rationing may occur in various ways, such as excluding a service from the public system entirely, providing access only to limited populations (generally based on predicted benefit from receiving the service), or imposing waits for access to publicly insured treatment. All forms of rationing may be subject to Charter challenges. Indeed, frustration over lack of public coverage for specific services or wait lists to access insured services has motivated important Charter challenges in recent years.

III. APPLICATION OF THE CHARTER

The Charter was enacted as part of Canada's Constitution in 1982 and protects various rights and freedoms against unjustified governmental intrusion. Importantly, the Charter applies only to government[12] so, in the health context, it

---

[8] See Karen E. Lasser, David U. Himmelstein & Steffie Woolhandler, "Access to Care, Health Status, and Health Disparities in the United States and Canada: Results of a Cross-National Population-Based Survey" (2006) 96:7 American Journal of Public Health 1300. This study reports that "long waiting times led to an unmet health need for only a small percentage (3.5%) of Canadians" (at 1305) and concludes that "[u]niversal coverage attenuates inequities in health care" (at 1306).

[9] Conference Board of Canada, *Understanding Health Care Cost Drivers and Escalators* (March 2004) at i.

[10] Canadian Institute for Health Information, *Exploring the 70/30 Split: How Canada's Health Care System is Financed* (Ottawa: Canadian Institute for Health Information, 2006) at 37.

[11] For discussion of controversy over a Vancouver based private, primary care clinic, see Claudia Cornwall, "Wealth Care" *BC Business* (August 2006) at 30.

[12] Section 32(1) of the Charter is the application provision and states: "This Charter applies (a) to the Parliament and government of Canada in respect of all matters within the authority of Parliament including all matters relating to the Yukon Territory and Northwest Territories; and (b) to the legislature and government of each province in respect of all matters within the authority of the legislature of each province." For background on judicial interpretation of the

may be used to challenge health-related laws and actions of governmental bodies such as federal or provincial/territorial health departments or local health authorities. Publicly funded hospitals are only subject to the Charter in their application of government laws or policies.[13] In their general daily operations, for example with respect to employment issues, hospitals are not subject to the Charter.[14]

Unlike constitutions in some other countries, the Canadian Constitution does not explicitly protect a right to health care in the Charter. However, the Supreme Court of Canada has instructed that "where the government puts in place a scheme to provide health care, that scheme must comply with the *Charter*".[15] In the health care context, sections 7 and 15(1) of the Charter are most often relied on to bring legal challenges to government action. These sections state:

> 7 Everyone has the right to life, liberty and security of the person and the right not to be deprived thereof except in accordance with the principles of fundamental justice.
>
> .....
>
> 15(1) Every individual is equal before and under the law and has the right to the equal protection and equal benefit of the law without discrimination and, in particular, without discrimination based on race, national or ethnic origin, colour, religion, sex, age or mental or physical disability.

These rights are not absolute and infringements of them may be justified under section 1 of the Charter if the State has legitimate and compelling reasons. Section 1 states:

> The *Canadian Charter of Rights and Freedoms* guarantees the rights and freedoms set out in it subject only to such reasonable limits prescribed by law as can be demonstrably justified in a free and democratic society.

In its 1986 decision in *R. v. Oakes*,[16] the Supreme Court of Canada set out the framework for analyzing whether a limitation on a Charter right is justified under section 1. In accordance with the so-called *Oakes* test, the following questions must be addressed:

(1) Is the objective of the law or government action based on concerns that are sufficiently pressing and substantial to warrant overriding a Charter right?

(2) Is there a rational connection between the limit on the Charter right and the governmental objective?

(3) Does the limitation constitute a minimum impairment of the Charter right?

---

scope of "government", see Robert J. Sharpe, Katherine E. Swinton & Kent Roach, *The Charter of Rights and Freedoms*, 2nd ed. (Toronto: Irwin Law, 2002) at 85-96.

[13] See *Eldridge v. British Columbia (Attorney General)*, [1997] S.C.J. No. 86, [1997] 3 S.C.R. 624 (S.C.C.).

[14] For discussion of the Charter's application to hospitals, see *Stoffman v. Vancouver General Hospital*, [1990] S.C.J. No. 125, [1990] 3 S.C.R. 483 (S.C.C.).

[15] *Chaoulli v. Quebec (Attorney General)*, [2005] S.C.J. No. 33, 1 S.C.R. 791 (S.C.C.) at para. 104 *per* McLachlin C.J.C. and Major J.

[16] [1986] S.C.J. No. 7, [1986] 1 S.C.R. 103 (S.C.C.).

(4) Is there proportionality between the benefits of the limitation and its harmful impact?

The principle challenge under section 1 is to balance the rights of individuals with the competing interests of society as expressed through government action.[17] As Dickson C.J.C. (as he then was) stated in *Oakes*, "[i]t may become necessary to limit rights and freedoms in circumstances where their exercise would be inimical to the realization of collective goals of fundamental importance".[18] It is important to note that section 7 has its own internal balancing test: a limit on life, liberty or security of the person will not offend section 7 unless the limit violates principles of fundamental justice. A limitation may be fundamentally unjust on procedural or substantive grounds if it violates basic tenets of our justice system that stress "dignity and worth of the human person and the rule of law".[19] If government action affects section 7 rights but still respects principles of fundamental justice, there is no Charter violation and, consequently, no need to evaluate the impugned action under the section 1 *Oakes* test.

The following section discusses key cases in Canadian health law jurisprudence that apply these sections of the Charter in the health care context.

IV. SECTION 7 OF THE CHARTER

One important category of Charter claims in health care addresses freedom to make decisions about one's health and medical treatment without unwarranted state-imposed restrictions. In early cases, Charter challenges attacked criminalization of certain conduct related to health care choices. More recently, as the scope of section 7 has expanded through judicial interpretation, courts are now willing to apply section 7 in situations where government action outside the realm of criminal regulation has the effect of diminishing rights to life, liberty and personal security. However, as I will discuss below, the controversial 2005 Supreme Court of Canada decision in *Chaoulli v. Quebec (Attorney General)*[20] raises many questions about the appropriate scope of section 7 in health care.

R. v. Morgentaler[21] involved a section 7 challenge to the *Criminal Code* provisions that criminalized abortion unless the patient obtained a certificate of permission from a hospital therapeutic abortion committee. Many women with unwanted pregnancies experienced barriers in obtaining access to an abortion

---

[17] As Joseph E. Magnet notes in *Constitutional Law of Canada*, 8th ed. (Edmonton: Juriliber, 2001) at 225, there is "a tension inherent in s. 1: the Court must strike a balance between the collective interests of the community as expressed by representative legislatures and the rights of individuals. It is not surprising that there is, so far, no quick and easy method, that flows from constitutional doctrine, to deal with this tension".

[18] *R. v. Oakes*, [1986] S.C.J. No. 7, [1986] 1 S.C.R. 103 at 136 (S.C.C.).

[19] *Reference re s. 94(2) of the Motor Vehicle Act (British Columbia)*, [1985] S.C.J. No. 73, [1985] 2 S.C.R. 486 (S.C.C.) at para. 61, *per* Lamer J.

[20] [2000] J.Q. no 479 (C.S.Q.), affd [2002] J.Q. no 759 (Q.C.A.), revd [2005] S.C.J. No. 33, [2005] 1 S.C.R. 791 (S.C.C.).

[21] [1988] S.C.J. No. 1, [1988] 1 S.C.R. 30 (S.C.C.); R.S.C. 1985, c. C-46.

committee, especially if they lived outside major urban centres. Moreover, the requirement to seek approval from a committee of at least three medical practitioners removed a highly personal decision from the woman and placed it in the hands of third parties.

The majority of the Supreme Court of Canada[22] held the *Criminal Code* provision violated section 7 of the Charter and could not be justified under section 1. The judges who found a breach of section 7 held that the right to security of the person protected a woman's physical and mental integrity from serious state interference in the criminal law context. As Beetz J. expressed it, "security of the person must include a right of access to medical treatment for a condition representing a danger to life or health without fear of criminal sanction".[23] Although this case involved a criminal prohibition, the court did not foreclose a wider application of section 7.

Rodriguez v. British Columbia[24] also involved a section 7 challenge in the health care context. Sue Rodriguez, who had the fatal, progressive condition amyotrophic lateral sclerosis (commonly known as ALS or Lou Gehrig's disease), challenged the constitutionality of the *Criminal Code* prohibition against assisted suicide. Ms. Rodriguez wanted to have the ability to end her life when her suffering became intolerable. However, when that time came, she would physically be unable to commit suicide without assistance and wanted a physician to help her to die, but any physician who aided her risked criminal sanction.

Ms. Rodriguez sought an order, based on sections 7, 12 and 15 of the Charter, declaring unconstitutional the *Criminal Code* prohibition against assisted suicide.[25] She argued the impugned law deprived her of the right to live the last of her life in dignity and the right to be free from state interference in making fundamental personal decisions. In a closely divided decision, the Supreme Court of Canada dismissed her claim.[26] Justice Sopinka, writing for the majority of the Court, held that though the *Criminal Code* prohibition abridged Ms. Rodriguez's right to security of the person under section 7, that infringement accorded with principles of fundamental justice. With regard to the nature of the interest captured by the right to security of the person under section 7, Sopinka J. stated:

> There is no question then, that personal autonomy, at least with respect to the right to make choices concerning one's own body, control over one's physical and psychological integrity, and basic human dignity are encompassed within security of the person, at least to the extent of freedom from criminal prohibitions which interfere with these.[27]

---

[22] Chief Justice Dickson, Lamer, Beetz, Estey and Wilson JJ. all found an unjustifiable s. 7 violation. Justices McIntyre and LaForest dissented and found no breach of s. 7.

[23] *R. v. Morgentaler*, [1988] S.C.J. No. 1, [1988] 1 S.C.R. 30 at 428 (S.C.C.).

[24] [1993] S.C.J. No. 94, [1993] 3 S.C.R. 519 (S.C.C.).

[25] Section 12 of the Charter is the prohibition against cruel and unusual punishment.

[26] Justices Sopinka, LaForest, Gonthier, Iacobucci and Major constituted the majority. Chief Justice Lamer, L'Heureux-Dubé, Cory, and McLachin JJ. dissented.

[27] *Rodriguez v. British Columbia (Attorney General)*, [1993] S.C.J. No. 94, [1993] 3 S.C.R. 519 at 588 (S.C.C.). As in the *Morgentaler* decision, Sopinka J.'s reference to criminal prohibitions limits the scope of the s. 7 right.

Although Sopinka J. found Ms. Rodriguez's interests under section 7 were engaged, he held she was not deprived of her rights contrary to the principles of fundamental justice, so she could not establish a section 7 violation. He held that the state's interest in protecting vulnerable individuals and safeguarding human life justified the prohibition on assisted suicide.

In her dissent, McLachlin J. (as she then was) held the impugned law violated Ms. Rodriguez's right to security of the person in a manner inconsistent with principles of fundamental justice. Justice McLachlin stated that security of the person "has an element of personal autonomy, protecting the dignity and privacy of individuals with respect to decisions concerning their own body".[28] She further stated that the prohibition against assisted suicide was marked by arbitrariness and lack of respect for individual choice and, in her view, this violation could not be justified under section 1 of the Charter.

A more recent Charter case, *R. v. Parker*,[29] involved a challenge to provisions of the federal *Controlled Drugs and Substances Act* (formerly the *Narcotic Control Act*) prohibiting possession of marijuana. Mr. Parker suffered from a severe form of epilepsy and grew marijuana for his own use to control his seizures. Upon being charged with possession of marijuana, an offence punishable by imprisonment, Mr. Parker argued the offence provisions violated his rights under section 7 of the Charter because he faced criminal sanction for using marijuana to meet a medical need.

The trial court agreed with Mr. Parker and granted a stay of the possession charge.[30] On appeal, the Ontario Court of Appeal agreed Mr. Parker's rights to liberty and personal security were violated by the untenable choice between protecting his health and risking imprisonment. With respect to the scope of section 7, the Court of Appeal stated that the threat of prosecution and imprisonment engaged Mr. Parker's liberty interests. In the circumstances of this case, the Court held the risk of deprivation of liberty did not accord with principles of fundamental justice, nor could it be justified under section 1 of the Charter. Regarding the right to security of the person, the Court reiterated the *Morgentaler* reasoning that state interference with an individual's physical and psychological integrity violates personal security. Further, the Court emphasized that "[d]eprivation by means of a criminal sanction of access to medication reasonably required for the treatment of a medical condition that threatens life or health also constitutes a deprivation of security of the person".[31]

Charter challenges like *Morgentaler*, *Rodriguez* and *Parker* assert the right to be free from state interference that criminalizes conduct regarding one's own body and health. While these cases all involved the threat of criminal sanction, the Supreme Court of Canada has since interpreted section 7 as having application outside the criminal justice system, but debate persists over the extent to which section 7 can apply outside adjudicative proceedings.[32]

---

28 *Ibid.*, at 415-16.
29 [2000] O.J. No. 2787, 49 O.R. (3d) 481 (Ont. C.A.); S.C. 1996, c. 19.
30 *R. v. Parker*, [1997] O.J. No. 4550 (Ont. Ct. Prov. Div.).
31 *R. v. Parker*, [2000] O.J. No. 2787, 49 O.R. (3d) 481 (Ont. C.A.) at para. 97.
32 See, *e.g.*, *New Brunswick (Minister of Health and Community Services) v. G. (J.)*, [1993] S.C.J. No. 47, [1993] 3 S.C.R. 46 (S.C.C.); *Blencoe v. British Columbia (Human Rights Commission)*,

The most recent application of section 7 in the health care context is in the highly contentious case of *Chaoulli v. Quebec (Attorney General)*. In that case, Dr. Chaoulli, a physician, and George Zéliotis, a retiree awaiting hip replacement surgery, challenged the provisions of Quebec's health care and hospital insurance legislation that prohibit physicians from delivering private care in publicly funded hospitals and also prevents patients from purchasing insurance privately to pay for health care services otherwise covered through the public system. Mr. Zéliotis waited for almost a year on a wait list and argued that but for the ban on private health insurance he would have purchased private insurance to cover the cost of the surgery in the private sector. He asserted the legal prohibition violated his rights to liberty and personal security under section 7 of the Charter.

In a month-long hearing that involved testimony from numerous expert witnesses, the claimants in *Chaoulli* sought a ruling that would permit a second tier of private health care insurance and delivery for services covered through the public system. (As Mr. Zéliotis' counsel stated, "I argue for the right of wealthier individuals to have access to a parallel system of health care services".[33]) The government respondents and interveners argued that such a ruling would have detrimental impacts on accessibility and cost of health care.

At trial, Madam Justice Piché ruled the prohibition against private insurance infringed rights protected under section 7 of the Charter. In her view: "If access to the health care system is not possible, it is illusory to think rights to life and security are respected".[34] Nonetheless, she concluded that the infringement accorded with principles of fundamental justice, stating that the purpose of the provincial health care and hospital insurance legislation is to create a system of health care that is equally available to all individuals in Quebec regardless of ability to pay. She also cited the extensive evidence led during the trial describing the likelihood that a second tier of private health care would increase wait times for services and drive up total health costs. Ultimately, she stated the government was justified in adopting a legislative scheme that benefited the population as a whole even if it limited the freedom of some individuals.

The Quebec Court of Appeal dismissed the *Chaoulli* appeal but with differing reasons from each of the three justices. With respect to section 7 of the Charter, Delisle J.A. held that the interests involved in the claim amounted to economic rights (the right to enter into a private contract of health insurance) that are not protected by the constitutional rights to life, liberty and security of the person. In contrast, Forget J.A. agreed with the trial judge's reasoning regarding section 7 while Brossard J.A. suggested section 7 would have application in the circumstances of the case, but declined to opine definitively on this issue since he agreed the appeal ought to be dismissed.

The Supreme Court of Canada released a divided judgment in *Chaoulli* in June 2005 that instigated a storm of controversy over the implications of the

---

[2000] S.C.J. No. 43, [2000] 2 S.C.R. 307 (S.C.C.) and *Gosselin v. Quebec (Attorney General)*, [2002] S.C.J. No. 85, [2002] 4 S.C.R. 429 (S.C.C.).

[33] *Chaoulli v. Quebec (Attorney General)*, [2000] J.Q. No 479 at para. 8 (C.S.Q.) (translated by author).

[34] *Ibid.*, at para. 223 (translated by author).

Court's ruling. Of the seven judges who heard the appeal, three[35] ruled the legislative prohibition was an unjustifiable violation of the Charter as well as Quebec's *Charter of Human Rights and Freedoms*, three[36] ruled it did not violate the Charter, and the remaining judge[37] restricted her analysis to the Quebec Charter and found it unnecessary to consider the Canadian Charter. Due to this judicial division, the end result is a ruling that Quebec's prohibition on private health insurance violates Quebec's Charter but the Court was split on the issue of whether the legislative regime violated section 7 rights under the Canadian Charter. As a result, *Chaoulli*'s implications for health insurance legislation in other provinces, as well as its implications for interpretation of section 7 of the Charter remain unclear.

The three judges who found that lengthy wait lists violate section 7 of the Charter likened the situation to that in *Morgentaler*. In their view, when the government establishes a monopolistic public health care system, it must ensure that system provides timely access to care; failure to do so will trigger section 7 rights. Although the *Chaoulli* circumstances do not involve the criminal justice system, the judges assert they are not expanding the scope of section 7 rights: "That the sanction in *Morgentaler* was criminal prosecution while the sanction here is administrative prohibition and penalties is irrelevant. The important point is that in both cases, care outside the legislatively provided system is effectively prohibited".[38] The judges conclude that the prohibition on private medical insurance is arbitrary and cannot be justified in circumstances where the public system fails to provide quality care in a timely manner.

In contrast, the three judges who dismissed the section 7 challenge argued the case revolves around matters of "complex fact-laden policy"[39] that are for governments to address, not matters of constitutional law that are within the institutional competence of the judiciary. They show great reticence to apply the Charter in a manner that would precipitate a "seismic shift"[40] in health care policy by permitting a second tier of private health care. They are less willing to broaden the scope of section 7, noting that "[i]t will likely be a rare case where section 7 will apply in circumstances entirely unrelated to adjudicative or administrative proceedings"[41] and conclude that waiting list delays do not violate legal principles of fundamental justice under section 7.

What are the implications of *Chaoulli* for Charter challenges in health care?[42] First, the case highlights division at the Supreme Court on the proper interpretation of section 7 outside cases involving the administration of justice.

---

[35] Chief Justice McLachlin, Major and Bastarache JJ.

[36] Justices Binnie, LeBel and Fish.

[37] Justice Deschamps.

[38] *Chaoulli v. Quebec (Attorney General)*, [2005] S.C.J. No. 33, [2005] 1 S.C.R. 791 (S.C.C.) at para. 119. Interestingly, this comment appears in the judgment in parentheses: is a parenthetical statement sufficient to address what others may argue *is* a significant expansion of s. 7?

[39] *Ibid.*, at para. 164.

[40] *Ibid.*, at para. 176.

[41] *Ibid.*, at para. 196.

[42] For extensive analysis of *Chaoulli* and its implications, see Colleen M. Flood, Kent Roach & Lorne Sossin, eds., *Access to Care, Access to Justice: The Legal Debate Over Private Health Insurance in Canada* (Toronto: University of Toronto Press, 2005).

However, even the justices who read section 7 more liberally emphasize that the Charter does not constitutionalize a *positive* right to health care.[43] Future litigation will be needed to resolve the parameters of section 7, especially as it relates to non-criminal regulation that impacts individual autonomy and access to care.

In addition to its impact on constitutional law, *Chaoulli* also has uncertain repercussions for the Canadian health care system. The case highlights the lack of legislative uniformity across Canada in regard to the public-private mix in health care; some provinces have legislative regimes like the impugned Quebec law that prohibit private insurance contracts to cover publicly insured services; other provinces do not ban private insurance but use other rules to discourage the flourishing of a private sector on the basis that it will draw resources from the public health care system.[44] Provincial statutory prohibitions that impede private access to care remain vulnerable to constitutional attack and a September 2006 class action lawsuit filed in Alberta challenges that province's restrictions on private insurance.[45] If governments abandon legislative restrictions on private health care, supporters of Medicare fear the ruling will undermine the universal health care system and exacerbate inequalities in access to care. However, the judges in *Chaoulli* agreed that if the public system offers reasonable access to care and wait lists do not jeopardize health, then a prohibition on private insurance would be constitutional. The *Chaoulli* decision has instigated political efforts to address wait list delays with the Prime Minister and federal Minister of Health going so far as to promise care guarantees for timely access to specified services.[46]

Finally, the case highlights disagreement over the appropriate role of courts in adjudicating matters involving complex policy choices and resource allocation. As the federal Minister of Health warned at the 2006 annual meeting of the Canadian Medical Association, "[i]f we don't get our act together [to provide timely access to care] there will be litigation-based prescriptions … a process that is slow, adversarial and expensive".[47] The problems of litigating complex health policy problems are revisited later in this chapter.

---

[43] For discussion, see Lorne Sossin, "Towards a Two-Tier Constitution? The Poverty of Health Rights" in Colleen M. Flood, Kent Roach & Lorne Sossin, eds., *Access to Care, Access to Justice: The Legal Debate Over Private Health Insurance in Canada* (Toronto: University of Toronto Press, 2005).

[44] For instance, Manitoba, Ontario and Nova Scotia stipulate that physicians who do not participate in the public health insurance scheme may not charge patients more than the applicable fee under the public plan.

[45] Michelle Lang, "Class action challenges public health-care system" CanWest News Service (September 7, 2006).

[46] Prime Minister Stephen Harper identified care guarantees to address wait lists as a national priority, though somewhat inconsistently. For commentary, see *e.g.*, Paul Wells, "Stephen Harper's New Game: Hide the Priority — What happened to establishing a wait-times guarantee?" *Macleans Magazine* (July 13, 2006). By autumn 2006, Health Minister Tony Clement confirmed the federal government's commitment to care guarantees, asking the provinces to establish wait-time benchmarks, but refusing to provide additional funding transfers to support implementation of care guarantees.

[47] Health Minister Tony Clement's comments to the CMA in Charlottetown, P.E.I., August 21,

V. SECTION 15 AND HEALTH CARE

Section 15(1) of the Charter provides a constitutional guarantee of equality and prohibits discrimination on grounds such as race, sex and disability.[48] The Supreme Court of Canada has emphasized that discrimination refers to distinctions based on personal characteristics that impose burdens or disadvantages that others do not suffer.[49] The Court emphasizes that not all distinctions amount to unconstitutional discrimination:

> It is not every distinction or differentiation in treatment at law which will transgress the equality guarantees of s. 15 of the Charter. It is, of course, obvious that legislatures may — and to govern effectively — must treat different individuals and groups in different ways. Indeed, such distinctions are one of the main preoccupations of legislatures. The classifying of individuals and groups, the making of different provisions respecting such groups, the application of different rules, regulations, requirements and qualifications to different persons is necessary for the governance of modern society.[50]

The discrimination analysis under section 15(1) of the Charter requires an assessment of the situation of the claimant(s) in relation to an appropriate comparator group. For example, a person with a disability who does not enjoy similar access to health care compared to persons without that disability may argue this denial of access amounts to discrimination. To substantiate this assertion, the claimant must demonstrate that the denial compromises their human dignity, by "perpetuating or promoting the view that the individual is less capable or worthy of recognition or value as a human being or as a member of Canadian society, equally deserving of concern, respect and consideration".[51] It is rarely obvious when denial of public funding for health care violates fundamental human dignity and contravenes equality rights. As a result, section 15(1) cases have often been litigated through many levels of appeal, with rare judicial unanimity.

To date, Canadian courts have had several opportunities to consider Charter cases in which litigants challenged government decisions not to fund specific services in the health care context. While the initial trend suggested section 15 could be used to claim a right to public funding for health care, that trend has now been reversed, but questions remain regarding the application of constitutionally protected equality rights in the health care context.

2006, are reported by Barbara Sibbald in "Clement: Set wait-times or the courts will" (2006) 175:6 Canadian Medical Association Journal 567.

[48] The Charter also prohibits discrimination on grounds that are analogous to those listed. The Supreme Court of Canada has defined analogous grounds as "characteristics that we cannot change or that the government has no legitimate interest in expecting us to change to receive equal treatment under the law". *Corbiere v. Canada (Minister of Indian and Northern Affairs)*, [1999] S.C.J. No. 24, [1999] 2 S.C.R. 203 (S.C.C.) at para. 13.

[49] See *Andrews v. Law Society of British Columbia*, [1989] S.C.J. No. 6, [1989] 1 S.C.R. 143 (S.C.C.).

[50] *Ibid.*, at 168.

[51] *Law v. Canada (Minister of Employment and Immigration)*, [1999] S.C.J. No. 12, [1999] 1 S.C.R. 497 (S.C.C.) at para. 88.

Eldridge v. British Columbia (Attorney General)[52] was an early success —
from the perspective of Charter claimants — in using section 15 to challenge
health care resource allocation. In *Eldridge*, three deaf individuals challenged
the decision of the government of British Columbia not to fund sign language
interpreters as an insured benefit under the B.C. Medical Services Plan. The
claimants argued that, without publicly funded interpreter services, they did not
have equal access to the health care system as compared to non-deaf individuals.
The claim was dismissed at trial and on appeal but in a unanimous decision, the
Supreme Court of Canada agreed with the claimants and held the government's
failure to fund sign language interpreters, when necessary for effective
communication in the health care context, violated the claimants' rights under
section 15(1) of the Charter.[53]

The Court of Appeal ruling reveals a strong reticence to interfere with
government resource allocation decisions. Justice Lambert found that the
funding decision violated section 15(1) but was justified under section 1.[54] In his
reasoning, he elaborated on the daunting task of choosing among competing
demands for health care dollars:

> In the allocation of scarce financial resources each Province will be required to
> make choices about spending priorities. Will medical equipment be bought for city
> hospitals or for small rural hospitals? Will the health care services in remote
> communities or in First Nations communities be improved? Is the best form of
> expenditure to raise the scale of payment for doctors and other health care
> workers? Should improved public facilities be provided for detection of cervical
> cancer, prostate cancer or breast tumours?
>
> Some of the limits imposed [by] ... financial allocation choices ... will result
> in adverse effects discrimination against people suffering from disabilities,
> including serious illness itself. ... How can we say, in those circumstances, that
> expenditure of scarce resources on services that remedy infringed constitutional
> rights under s. 15, on the one hand, are more desirable than expenditures of scarce
> resources on things that cure people without affecting constitutional rights, on the
> other? And, indeed, how can we prefer the allocation of scarce resources to
> services that remedy the infringed constitutional rights of one disadvantaged group
> over the allocation of scarce resources to services that remedy the infringed
> constitutional rights of a different disadvantaged group.
>
> In my opinion the kind of adverse effects discrimination which I consider has
> occurred in this case should be rectified, if at all, by legislative or administrative
> action and not by judicial action. ...I have concluded that this is a case for judicial

---

[52]   [1992] B.C.J. No. 2229, 75 B.C.L.R. (2d) 68 (B.C.S.C.), affd [1995] B.C.J. No. 1168, 125
        D.L.R. (4th) 323 (B.C.C.A.), revd [1997] S.C.J. No. 86, [1997] 3 S.C.R. 624 (S.C.C.).

[53]   Access to publicly funded sign language interpretation services was litigated in *Canadian Assn.
        of the Deaf v. Canada*, [2006] F.C.J. No. 1228, 2006 FC 971 (F.C.). The Federal Court ruled that
        the government of Canada violated s. 15 of the Charter by not providing sign language
        interpretation services on request when a deaf person attempted to access federal government
        services. The Court did not address justification arguments because the government did not see
        "fit to submit evidence or submissions that the failure to provide accommodation is justified
        under section 1 of the *Charter*" (at para. 116).

[54]   Justices Hollinrake and Cumming found there was no s. 15(1) violation.

restraint and for deference under the Constitution and under s. 1 of the Charter to legislative and administrative expertise.[55]

The Supreme Court of Canada was not so convinced and ruled the government's funding decision discriminated against deaf patients and could not be justified under section 1. Writing for a unanimous Court, La Forest J. disagreed with the government's characterization of sign language interpretation as a "non-medical 'ancillary' service"[56] that was outside the scope of public funding. Rather, the Court viewed the service as essential for ensuring adequate access to the health care system for deaf persons. In the immediate wake of *Eldridge*, some viewed the Court's decision as a precedent for using section 15 Charter claims to expand the scope of public funding for health care services.[57] However, the decision is much narrower; it imposes an obligation on governments to fund a service to ensure deaf patients have the means to access the same basket of publicly insured services available to all, but does not require governments to add to that basket. An analogy to a public library helps explain this principle: the *Eldridge* claim is like a wheelchair user asking a library to build a ramp so she may gain access to the books in the library that are available to patrons who can walk up the stairs. In contrast, *Eldridge* is not like the disabled patron asking the library to purchase new books to put on the shelves.

The next case to raise similar issues was *Cameron v. Nova Scotia (Attorney General)*,[58] which involved an infertile male and his wife who argued the province of Nova Scotia discriminated against them by not funding fertility treatments, *in vitro* fertilization (IVF) and intra-cytoplasmic sperm injection (ICSI), that could assist infertile couples (suffering from male-factor infertility) to have a biologically related child. They argued fertile people have access to publicly funded health care services, such as prenatal and childbirth care, to assist them in having children, but the infertile are denied the chance of having a child because they are denied funding for IVF and ICSI.

The trial judge dismissed the claim on the grounds that infertility treatments are not medically necessary since infertile people have other options for becoming parents (such as adoption), the success rate of having a child through IVF and ICSI is low (around 15 per cent to 20 per cent), and there are health risks associated with the procedures.[59] On appeal, the majority found the

---

[55] *Eldridge v. British Columbia*, [1995] B.C.J. No. 1168, 125 D.L.R. (4th) 323 (B.C.C.A.) at paras. 57-59.

[56] *Eldridge v. British Columbia*, [1997] S.C.J. No. 86, 3 S.C.R. 624 (S.C.C.) at para. 68.

[57] In a 2005 review of S.C.C. equality rights jurisprudence, Bruce Porter comments on *Eldridge*, noting that "[t]he Court could have chosen to affirm more clearly in *Eldridge* a positive obligation on governments to provide appropriate health-care ... The right to equality could thus have been framed around a consensus in Canada that appropriate health-care is a social right, linked to equal citizenship. ... there were indications that this might be the direction that the Court was headed." Bruce Porter, "Twenty Years of Equality Rights: Reclaiming Expectations" (2005) 23 Windor YB. Access Just. 145.

[58] [1999] N.S.J. No. 297, 177 D.L.R. (4th) 611 (N.S.C.A.), affg [1999] N.S.J. No. 33, 172 N.S.R. (2d) 227 (N.S.S.C.), leave to appeal to S.C.C. refd, [1999] S.C.C.A. No. 531 (S.C.C.).

[59] *Cameron v. Nova Scotia (Attorney General)*, [1999] N.S.J. No. 33, 172 N.S.R. (2d) 227 (N.S.S.C.) at paras. 95 and 96.

government's funding decision contravened the claimants' rights under section 15(1). The justices held that IVF and ICSI are medically necessary services for infertile individuals, the denial of which offended their dignity in a manner contrary to the Charter's equality protection, but the violation was justified under section 1. The third justice ruled differently, finding that infertility does not constitute a disability for the purposes of section 15(1) but, even if it did, the denial of funding for IVF and ICSI would not demean the claimants' dignity. The Supreme Court of Canada denied leave to appeal.

The next significant section 15 Charter case is *Auton (Guardian ad litem of) v. British Columbia (Attorney General)*,[60] a case in which parents of children with autism challenged the B.C. government's refusal to fund therapy known as early intensive behavioural intervention (EIBI), which can be effective in reducing autistic behaviour in children. The parents argued that "by failing to fund effective treatment for autism, the government has misinterpreted its legislative mandate to provide health care services".[61] Further, they argued that lack of funding for autism therapy "neglects to take into account the disadvantaged position of autistic children and results in substantively different treatment, placing an additional burden on them"[62] that those without the disease do not face. The trial and appeal courts in B.C. ruled in the claimants' favour.

The trial judge adopted an expansive view of the medically necessary services that the Medicare system should cover: "Canadians are entitled to expect medical treatment for their physical and mental diseases. This is so, even when a disease cannot be 'cured'".[63] On appeal, Saunders J.A.[64] stated that the fact children with autism did not receive the health care service they most needed to address their disease constituted differential treatment in the section 15(1) analysis and she rejected the government's argument that a finding of discrimination was not warranted because the "health care system does not serve all health care needs and is not designed to do so".[65] In her view, the government discriminated against the children with autism by withholding funding for a treatment that held real promise of mitigating the effects of their devastating condition. She also noted that no alternative therapy was available and the health care system funds services to address other, less serious ailments.

In a surprisingly short and unanimous ruling (in contrast with *Chaoulli*), the Supreme Court of Canada overturned the lower court decisions. Chief Justice McLachlin explicitly stated that Canadians cannot expect the publicly funded health care system to cover every service that may be of some benefit. Rather, she emphasized the relatively narrow boundaries of the system: "In summary,

---

[60]   [2004] S.C.J. No. 71, 3 S.C.R. 657, revg [2002] B.C.J. No. 2258, 6 B.C.L.R. (4th) 201 (B.C.C.A.), related proceedings, [2000] B.C.J. No. 1547, 78 B.C.L.R. (3d) 55 (B.C.S.C.).

[61]   *Auton (Guardian ad litem of) v. British Columbia (Attorney General)*, [2000] B.C.J. No. 1547, 78 B.C.L.R. (3d) 55 (B.C.S.C.) at para 125.

[62]   *Ibid.*

[63]   *Ibid.*, at para. 109.

[64]   Justice Hall concurred. Justice Lambert agreed that s. 15(1) was violated and could not be justified under s. 1, but he dissented in part on a cross-appeal issue regarding remedy.

[65]   *Auton (Guardian ad litem of) v. British Columbia (Attorney General)*, [2002] B.C.J. No. 2258, 6 B.C.L.R. (4th) 201 (B.C.C.A.) at para. 46.

the legislative scheme does not promise that any Canadian will receive funding for all medically required treatment. All that is conferred is core funding for services provided by medical practitioners, with funding for non-core services left to the Province's discretion".[66] Provinces may choose to cover services of non-core practitioners, but have no legal obligation to do so and, further, courts have no legal jurisdiction to entertain a discrimination claim in regard to services that governments have not chosen to include in the Medicare basket. However, where the government decides to enter the field and fund a service, it must do so in a manner that does not discriminate on grounds protected under the Charter.

Auton was received with disappointment by those who shared the trial judge's view that the health care system should respond to a broader range of health needs. The Supreme Court's acceptance in *Auton* that the health care system provides "a partial health plan",[67] limited to "core physician-provided benefits plus non-core benefits at the discretion of the Province"[68] stands in contrast to the Court's earlier censure of a narrow conception of the health care system in *Eldridge*, where the government characterized sign language interpretation as an "ancillary" service. The McLachlin Court's depiction of funding for autism therapy as a discretionary policy choice that is outside Charter purview has been criticized as formalistic:

> In *Auton*, the Supreme Court claims that section 15 only protects against discrimination where a benefit has been conferred by law. Why would this be so? The *Charter* protects against discrimination by government action, and the government may confer benefits through a wide spectrum of means, including legislation, regulation, program criteria, and spending decisions. ... Should governments that wish to consign an increasing amount of decision-making over benefits to discretionary realms be able to immunize such benefits from *Charter* scrutiny as a result? In our view, such a result would be fundamentally inconsistent with the purpose of the *Charter*.[69]

As it stands, *Auton* leaves open the prospect of using the Charter to challenge alleged underinclusiveness in benefit regimes where a government provides publicly funded services but only to limited categories of beneficiaries. However, the first appeal court decision to address this issue post-*Auton* further restricts section 15's application. *Wynberg v. Ontario*[70] involved a challenge to Ontario's program for children with autism. In 2000, the Ontario government implemented early intensive behavioural therapy for children under age six but resource shortages meant that some children turned six before receiving any therapy. The *Wynberg* claim alleged that the age cut-off constituted unjustified age-based discrimination and the trial court in Ontario agreed. However, the appeal court overturned this ruling, finding that the government's autism

[66] *Auton (Guardian ad litem of) v. British Columbia (Attorney General)*, [2004] S.C.J. No. 71, [2004] 3 S.C.R. 657 (S.C.C.) at para. 35.
[67] *Ibid.*, at para. 43.
[68] *Ibid.*, at para. 44.
[69] Laura Pottie & Lorne Sossin, "Demystifying the Boundaries of Public Law: Policy, Discretion, and Social Welfare" (2005) 38 U.B.C.L. Rev. 147 at para. 56.
[70] [2006] O.J. No. 2732 (C.A.), revg [2005] O.J. No. 1228, 252 D.L.R. (4th) 10 (Ont. S.C.J.).

program is a targeted, ameliorative program designed to meet the needs and circumstances of pre-school age children who are most likely to benefit from intensive autism therapy and exclusion of children aged six and older "does not deny their human dignity or devalue their worth as members of Canadian society".[71] As a result, the government's implementation of an age cut-off for access to publicly funded autism therapy did not violate the children's constitutional rights to equality. This decision is a further retreat from the early prospect that *Eldridge* would open the door for successful Charter challenges to denials of public funding for health care services. Porter argues that "in *Auton*, we see worrying signs that the McLachlin Court may [be] closing the door that was quite explicitly left open to a more positive rights approach to equality in *Eldridge*".[72]

Section 15 jurisprudence regarding access to health care services now emphasizes the limits of the publicly funded health care system. Monique Bégin, who served as federal Minister of National Health and Welfare during the drafting and enactment of the *Canada Health Act*,[73] has stated that our public health care system includes more than "a basic level of care. The words of the *Canada Health Act* are generally taken to imply entitlement to a complete health care system".[74] However, judicial authority in Canada reveals a divergent conclusion: our system of publicly insured health care cannot provide funding for all services, even those that are medically indicated, and Charter claims are an increasingly unlikely means to influence government funding choices.

VI. OTHER BASES FOR LEGAL CHALLENGES

Litigants may pursue legal mechanisms other than Charter claims to assert rights of access to care. These include complaints to administrative agencies such as health service appeal boards and human rights tribunals or other types of legal claims that may be pursued through the court system. Several Canadian provinces have administrative bodies created and empowered by statute to review certain decisions regarding the provision of health care services. In Ontario, for instance, the Health Services Review and Appeal Board may hear appeals of decisions regarding health insurance benefits made by the General Manager of the Ontario Health Insurance Plan (OHIP).[75] In British Columbia, the Medical Services Commission has authority to determine insured benefits

---

[71] *Ibid.*, at para. 80.

[72] Bruce Porter, "Twenty Years of Equality Rights: Reclaiming Expectations" (2005) 23 Windor YB. Access Just. 145.

[73] For Bégin's account of the process leading to the enactment of the *Canada Health Act*, R.S.C. 1985, c. C-6, see Monique Bégin, *Medicare: Canada's Right to Health* (Montreal: Optimum Publishing International, 1988).

[74] Margaret A. Somerville, ed., *Do We Care? Renewing Canada's Commitment to Health. Proceedings of the First Directions for Canadian Health Care Conference* (Montreal: McGill-Queen's University Press, 1999) at 105.

[75] See *Health Insurance Act*, R.S.O. 1990, c. H.6 and *Ministry of Health Appeal and Review Boards Act, 1998*, S.O. 1998, c. 18, Sched. H.

under the provincial health plan.[76] The Québec Régie de l'assurance-maladie is responsible for administering and implementing the provincial health insurance plan and may control eligibility for insured services.[77] Patients in some provinces who experience barriers in accessing care in their province of residence — either because the service is not insured provincially or because of long wait lists — may seek funding (including reimbursement for privately purchased out-of-country care) through appeal to a provincial health services board or commission. These administrative bodies vary in their degree of independence, the scope of their review jurisdiction, expertise of members, and accessibility to the public.[78]

While the Charter applies only to government, provincial human rights laws apply to both public and private entities. Human rights laws across Canada prohibit discrimination in the provision of public services, including health care services, on the basis of characteristics such as disability, sex, religion and race.[79] For example, the British Columbia Human Rights Tribunal found that a physician who specialized in fertility treatments discriminated unfairly against a lesbian couple by refusing to provide artificial insemination to them on the basis of their sexual orientation.[80] Human rights tribunals have also dealt with cases

---

[76] The Medical Services Commission is composed of nine members: three government representative; three representatives from the British Columbia Medical Association (BCMA); and three public members jointly nominated by the BCMA and the government: *Medicare Protection Act*, R.S.B.C. 1996, c. 286, s. 3(1). Section 5 sets out the powers and duties of the Medical Services Commission and stipulates it must act in accordance with the principles of the *Canada Health Act*.

[77] See *An Act respecting the Régie de l'assurance-maladie du Québec*, R.S.Q., c. R-5 and the *Health Insurance Act*, R.S.Q., c. A-29.

[78] For further discussion of provincial health care appeal bodies, see, *e.g.*, Caroline Pitfield & Colleen M. Flood, "Section 7 'Safety Valves': Appealing Wait Times Within a One-Tier System" in Colleen M. Flood, Kent Roach & Lorne Sossin, eds., *Access to Care, Access to Justice: The Legal Debate Over Private Health Insurance in Canada* (Toronto: University of Toronto Press, 2005).

[79] For example, s. 1 of the Ontario *Human Rights Code*, R.S.O. 1990, c. H.19 states: "Every person has a right to equal treatment with respect to services, goods and facilities, without discrimination because of race, ancestry, place of origin, colour, ethnic origin, citizenship, creed, sex, sexual orientation, age, marital status, same-sex partnership status, family status or disability". Likewise, s. 8(1) of the British Columbia *Human Rights Code*, R.S.B.C. 1996, c. 210, states:

> A person must not, without a bona fide and reasonable justification,
> (a) deny to a person or class of persons any accommodation, service or facility customarily available to the public, or
> (b) discriminate against a person or class of persons regarding any accommodation, service or facility customarily available to the public
> because of the race, colour, ancestry, place of origin, religion, marital status, family status, physical or mental disability, sex or sexual orientation of that person or class of persons.

[80] *Korn v. Potter*, [1996] B.C.J. No. 692, 134 D.L.R. (4th) 437 (B.C.S.C.).

regarding government funding for gender reassignment surgery,[81] autism therapy[82] and funding for cancer screening.[83]

Administrative law principles, which aim to ensure decision-makers act within the bounds of their legal authority and decision-making processes are fair, may also support legal challenges to government health care decisions. For example, *Stein v. Quebec (Régie de l'Assurance-Maladie)*[84] involved judicial review of a decision to deny funding for health care services obtained outside Canada. Barry Stein was diagnosed with colon cancer that had spread to his liver. His physicians advised that the liver metastases should be removed as soon as possible but surgery was rescheduled several times and Mr. Stein ultimately sought surgery in New York to avoid further delay and to obtain a recommended surgical procedure that was considered experimental in Canada. He sought reimbursement from the Québec Régie de l'assurance-maladie for the treatment he underwent in the United States but this request was denied. Mr. Stein then appealed to the Tribunal Administratif du Québec, which upheld the Régie's decision. On review, the Quebec Superior Court ruled the Tribunal's decision was "irrational, unreasonable and contrary to the purpose of the *Health Insurance Act*"[85] and it ordered the Régie to accept the reimbursement claim.

VII. RESOURCE ALLOCATION, THE ROLE OF COURTS AND CHARTER CHALLENGES

> The fact that the matter is complex, contentious or laden with social values does not mean that the courts can abdicate the responsibility vested in them by our Constitution to review legislation for Charter compliance when citizens challenge it.

McLachlin C.J.C. and Major J. in *Chaoulli v. Quebec (Attorney General)* (para. 107)

> What, then, are constitutionally required "reasonable health services"? What is treatment "within a reasonable time"? What are the benchmarks? How short a waiting list is short enough? How many MRIs does the Constitution require?

Binnie, LeBel and Fish JJ. in *Chaoulli v. Quebec (Attorney General)* (para. 163)

---

[81] *Waters v. British Columbia (Ministry of Health Services)*, [2003] B.C.H.R.T.D. No. 11, 2003 BCHRT 13 (B.C.H.R.T.). An application for judicial review of this case was filed in the B.C. Supreme Court on June 18, 2003.

[82] *Newfoundland and Labrador v. Sparkes*, [2004] N.J. No. 34 (Nfld. S.C.).

[83] The B.C. Human Rights Tribunal heard a claim in late 2006 alleging that the provincial Ministry of Health discriminates in the provision of cancer screening services by funding mammography screening for breast cancer but does not fund prostate specific antigen (PSA) testing for prostate cancer in men. See *Armstrong v. British Columbia (Ministry of Health)*, [2006] B.C.H.R.T.D. No. 588, 2006 B.C.H.R.T. 588 (B.C.H.R.T.).

[84] [1999] Q.J. No. 2724, [1999] R.J.Q. 2416 (Que. S.C.).

[85] *Ibid.*, at para. 32.

Charter litigation that seeks to assert rights in regard to health care raises thorny legal issues regarding the appropriate scope of the Charter and the roles of courts and legislatures in policy-making and resource allocation. Charter cases can have the effect of "constitutionalizing" a right of access to services and force governments to redistribute resources to fund specific programs (with a consequent reduction in funds available for other services)[86] or change legislative regimes governing access to care.

Much constitutional law literature debates the impact of the Charter on the respective roles of courts and legislatures, with some commentators arguing the Charter allows judges to "interfere" in political matters, while others assert that judges have a legitimate role in superintending government action for compliance with the Constitution.[87] This debate has manifested itself very clearly in Charter health care litigation. This final section analyzes broader questions of judicial review in cases involving contentious health policy and resource allocation issues. It discusses how courts have weighed arguments of government financial constraint against individual claims for access to health care — what the Supreme Court of Canada has described as the "'dollars versus rights' controversy"[88] — and the degree of deference courts are willing to give governments in reviewing constitutionality of policy choices.

VIII. JUDICIAL REVIEW OF GOVERNMENT POLICY CHOICES

The Supreme Court of Canada has typically not been receptive to financial constraint arguments, and it has repeatedly warned against courts being too deferential in reviewing government action that violates Charter rights. Despite this general position, the Court has instructed that judges ought to apply a more lenient standard of review in situations where government has acted to protect a vulnerable group, where it mediates among groups with competing interests, where complex social science evidence is involved, and where it must allocate

---

[86] Joel Bakan notes the Supreme Court of Canada decisions in *Tétreault-Gadoury v. Canada (Employment and Immigration)*, [1991] S.C.J. No. 41, [1991] 2 S.C.R. 22 (S.C.C.) and *Schachter v. Canada*, [1992] S.C.J. No. 68, [1992] 2 S.C.R. 679 (S.C.C.) provide an example of governments restricting benefits levels to address a successful Charter claim. These cases required the federal government to extend unemployment insurance benefits to certain groups who had previously been ineligible. However, Bakan notes that, to comply with the Court's ruling, the federal government "raised revenue for these extensions by increasing the number of weeks that a person must work before being eligible for UI benefits, reducing the number of weeks a person can receive benefits, and stiffen[ed] penalties for workers who quit without just cause or refused to take suitable jobs or are fired for misconduct." Joel Bakan, *Just Words: Constitutional Rights and Social Wrongs* (Toronto: University of Toronto Press, 1997) at 59.

[87] For discussion of the legitimacy of the judicial role under the Charter, with a summary of key literature on point, see, *e.g.*, Robert J. Sharpe, Katherine E. Swinton & Kent Roach, *The Charter of Rights and Freedoms*, 2nd ed., Chapter 2, "The Legitimacy of Judicial Review" (Toronto: Irwin Law, 2002) at 25-44.

[88] *Newfoundland (Treasury Board) v. Newfoundland and Labrador Assn. of Public and Private Employees*, [2004] S.C.J. No. 61, [2004] 3 S.C.R. 381 (S.C.C.) at para. 65.

scarce resources.[89] Greschner points out that "[l]aws regulating the health care system usually possess all four of these characteristics".[90]

In cases where courts have found a Charter breach stemming from a government's decision not to fund a particular health care service, the government's justification argument has often rested on considerations of cost. Government respondents argue they face competing claims on public resources (and health care is just one of many), so courts must give governments latitude to establish priorities. To date, cost arguments have met with varied judicial response. The B.C. appellate court in *Eldridge* held it would be too expensive to fund sign language interpreters yet, on appeal, the Supreme Court of Canada rejected the cost justification.

In *Cameron*, the Nova Scotia Court of Appeal accepted the government's cost argument. In *Auton*, both the B.C. Supreme Court and Court of Appeal rejected cost as a factor that could justify withholding public funds for autism therapy. Since the Supreme Court of Canada dismissed *Auton* by finding no discrimination under section 15(1), it did not consider cost arguments in a section 1 justification analysis. Of course, the Court's narrow view both of the provincial health care system and section 15's application (the government funds only a partial plan and section 15 only applies to benefits provided by law) implicitly acknowledges cost constraints; government has discretion to include or exclude non-core services and cost will inevitably be a factor in those choices.

IX. DOLLARS VERSUS RIGHTS — WHERE TO DRAW THE LINE?

Although the Supreme Court of Canada has cautioned that "budgetary considerations cannot be used to justify a [Charter] violation",[91] it is clear that the state's ability to pay for an increasing array of services is a critical issue in health care litigation; financial considerations can and will be raised to justify limits on constitutionally protected rights.

Cost arguments have figured prominently in many Charter cases related to social benefit programs. For example, in *Egan v. Canada*,[92] a homosexual couple argued that the federal *Old Age Security Act* violated section 15(1) of the Charter by discriminating against same-sex partners by limiting spousal allowances to opposite-sex partners.[93] The section 1 analyses in this case

---

[89]   *Irwin Toy Ltd. v. Quebec (Attorney General)*, [1989] S.C.J. No. 36, [1989] 1 S.C.R. 927 (S.C.C.) and Peter W. Hogg, *Constitutional Law of Canada*, Stud. Ed. (Scarborough: Carswell, 2004) at 827.

[90]   Commission on the Future of Health Care in Canada, *How Will the Charter of Rights and Freedoms and Evolving Jurisprudence Affect Health Care Costs?: Discussion Paper No. 2* by Donna Greschner (Saskatoon: Commission on the Future of Health Care in Canada, 2002) at 14.

[91]   *Schachter v. Canada*, [1992] S.C.J. No. 68, [1992] 2 S.C.R. 679 at 709 (S.C.C.).

[92]   [1995] S.C.J. No. 43, [1995] 2 S.C.R. 513 (S.C.C.).

[93]   Section 19 of the *Old Age Security Act*, R.S.C. 1985, c. O-9 provided spousal allowances for spouses between 60 and 65 years of age if the family income was below a certain level. Section 2

revealed divisions in the Court as to the appropriate place of financial considerations in justifying government policy choices. The government argued that the cost of extending benefits to same-sex spouses would be prohibitive, with expert evidence estimating additional expenditures of $12 to $37 million per year.[94] However, Iacobucci J. criticized this evidence as "highly speculative and statistically weak"[95] and based on "guesswork".[96] He went on to say that even assuming the cost evidence was valid, he would still find "as a question of law, that they do not justify the denial of the appellants' right to equality".[97] Further:

> The jurisprudence of this Court reveals, as a general matter, a reluctance to accord much weight to financial considerations under a s. 1 analysis. ... This is certainly the case when the financial motivations are not, as in the case at bar, supported by more persuasive arguments as to why the infringement amounts to a reasonable limit.[98]

In contrast, Sopinka J. ruled the government was justified in limiting spousal benefits to opposite-sex couples. He remarked that "government must be accorded some flexibility in extending social benefits"[99] and

> [i]t is not realistic for the Court to assume that there are unlimited funds to address the needs of all. A judicial approach on this basis would tend to make a government reluctant to create any new social benefit schemes because their limits would depend on an accurate prediction of the outcome of court proceedings under s. 15(1) of the *Charter*.[100]

In a unanimous 2004 ruling, the Supreme Court of Canada summarized its views on cost justifications as follows:

> ... courts will continue to look with strong skepticism at attempts to justify infringements of *Charter* rights on the basis of budgetary constraints. To do otherwise would devalue the *Charter* because there are *always* budgetary constraints and there are *always* other pressing government priorities.[101]

As noted above, judicial responses to cost arguments have varied in Charter health care cases. In *Eldridge*, the Court assumed "without deciding ... that the objective of this decision – controlling health care expenditures — is 'pressing and substantial', and that this decision is rationally connected to the objective".[102] Although reiterating Sopinka J.'s statement in *Egan* that courts must afford governments latitude when making resource allocation decisions, La

---

of the legislation defined spouses as being of the opposite sex.

[94] *Egan v. Canada*, [1995] S.C.J. No. 43, 2 S.C.R. 513 (S.C.C.) at para. 193.

[95] *Ibid.*

[96] *Ibid.*

[97] *Ibid.*

[98] *Ibid.*, at para. 194.

[99] *Ibid.*, at para. 104.

[100] *Ibid.*

[101] *Newfoundland (Treasury Board) v. Newfoundland and Labrador Assn. of Public and Private Employees*, [2004] S.C.J. No. 61, [2004] 3 S.C.R. 381 (S.C.C.) at para. 72.

[102] *Eldridge v. British Columbia*, [1997] S.C.J. No. 86, [1997] 3 S.C.R. 624 (S.C.C.) at para. 84.

Forest J. concluded in *Eldridge* that even with a deferential approach to reviewing the government's decision, the choice to exclude funding for sign language interpretation failed the minimal impairment aspect of the *Oakes* test.[103] The most persuasive factor was the relatively small magnitude of the cost, since "the estimated cost of providing sign language interpretation for the whole of British Columbia was only $150,000 per annum or approximately 0.0025 percent of the provincial health care budget at the time".[104] Ultimately, the Court emphasized "the central place of good health in the quality of life of all persons in our society" and concluded that "the government has simply not demonstrated that this unpropitious state of affairs must be tolerated in order to achieve the objective of limiting health care expenditures".[105]

In *Cameron*, the Nova Scotia Court of Appeal faced the challenge of evaluating cost implications of insuring IVF and ICSI therapies. The Court considered an expert report estimating an annual expenditure of $1.6 million to insure the services, not including the cost of drugs required during the process. On cross-examination, the expert reduced this estimate in half to approximately $800,000 per year.[106] The Court also considered the evidence of an executive director with the Nova Scotia Department of Health who testified at trial that provincial health care expenditures were increasing while the federal government was reducing transfer payments for health care, leading to increased pressure on the provincial budget.[107]

In arguing that IVF and ICSI ought to be covered, the claimants pointed out that the provincial health care insurance plan covers many expensive treatments, including organ transplants that can cost the health care system close to $100,000 per surgery.[108] Their argument suggests that a simple calculation of the total annual cost of insuring a new service is relatively meaningless without comparing that expense with the cost of other services that are already publicly funded. The government's expert witness referred to a method of assessing the value of a health care service by calculating its cost in relation to years of life gained. Though the expert "had difficulty translating this [method] to fertility treatments because yet another life becomes part of the picture ... he agreed that $145.00 a year would represent the cost of IVF and ICSI",[109] much less than the cost of providing other insured services.[110] Taking only cost into account, then, a claimant could argue that funding fertility treatments would be relatively inexpensive compared to many other health care services, though certainly the

---

[103] *Ibid.* at para. 85. Although the Court canvassed arguments in support of judicial deference, it ruled (at para. 85) that it was "unnecessary to decide whether in this 'social benefits' context, where the choice is between the needs of the general population and those of a disadvantaged group, a deferential approach should be adopted".

[104] *Eldridge v. British Columbia*, [1997] S.C.J. No. 86, [1997] 3 S.C.R. 624 (S.C.C.) at para. 87.

[105] *Ibid.*, at para. 94.

[106] *Cameron v. Nova Scotia*, [1999] N.S.J. No. 297, 177 D.L.R. (4th) 611 (N.S.C.A.) at para. 227.

[107] *Ibid.*, at paras. 219-221.

[108] *Ibid.*, at para. 233.

[109] *Ibid.*, at para. 232.

[110] For example, evidence before the Court indicated that cardiac artery bypass grafts cost $50,000 per year of life saved: *Ibid.*

benefit and risks of the service — for example, whether it saves a life or addresses a non-life-threatening problem — must be part of the calculus.

In regard to the cost evidence, Chipman J.A. acknowledged that "[t]he best we can do in these circumstances ... is to arrive at an approximate figure for costs which I would estimate to be in the order of a million dollars annually".[111] This response indicates much more tolerance for the "guesswork" involved in estimating costs of insuring new health care services, a view that contrasts sharply with that of Iacobucci J. in *Egan*. Justice Chipman also took judicial notice that limited governmental resources "have been a major concern for some years"[112] and commented that such limits "have threatened, in the minds of most people, the very foundation of health care. It is the general perception that it will take a great deal of effort to make do with what we have".[113] Overall, the decision in *Cameron* seems to reveal a less exacting standard of proof on the government to present evidence regarding the cost implications of expanding public coverage for new health care services. Ultimately, Chipman J.A. adopts a deferential approach:

> The evidence makes clear the complexity of the health care system and the extremely difficult task confronting those who must allocate the resources among a vast array of competing claims.
>
> . . . . .
>
> The policy makers require latitude in balancing competing interests in the constrained financial environment. We are simply not equipped to sort out the priorities. We should not second guess them, except in clear cases of failure on their part to properly balance the *Charter* rights of individuals against the overall pressing [governmental] objective ...[114]

In *Auton*, the lower courts recognized that "[t]he Crown is entitled to judicial deference in performing its difficult task of making policy choices and allocating scarce resources among myriad vulnerable groups".[115] Yet, where the fundamental needs of disabled children are at stake, the lower courts were willing to impose a constitutional obligation to fund therapy. As Saunders J.A. commented, "the age-old reluctance of the courts to allocate the scarce resources of the taxpayer ... is not without weight. However, the principle that government monies should be allocated only by the legislature, while strong, does not always prevail when the issue is compliance with the Constitution".[116]

In *Wynberg*, the Ontario Court of Appeal addressed the section 1 analysis and concluded the trial judge erred in finding that the government did not have pressing and substantial reasons for limiting autism therapy to children under age six. The appeal court accepted the evidence of a senior government official

---

[111] *Ibid.*, at para. 228.

[112] *Ibid.*, at para. 218.

[113] *Ibid.*

[114] *Ibid.*, at paras. 234, 236.

[115] *Auton (Guardian ad litem of) v. British Columbia (Minister of Health)*, [2000] B.C.J. No. 1547, 78 B.C.L.R. (3d) 55 (B.C.S.C.) at para. 143.

[116] *Auton (Guardian ad litem of) v. British Columbia (Minister of Health)*, [2002] B.C.J. No. 2258, 6 B.C.L.R. (4th) 201 (B.C.C.A.) at paras. 56-57.

that "there is fierce competition for the resources that exist in government"[117] and noted that courts are not in a position to make difficult public policy choices that involve balancing competing demands for scarce resources. Adopting a deferential approach, the appellate justices stated that "[f]or the court to choose a different option than that selected by the legislature would be to replace one imprecise evaluation with another".[118]

X. DIFFERENT PERSPECTIVES ON COSTS AND BENEFITS

Much of the debate between claimants and the government regarding resource allocation has turned on differing conceptions of costs and benefits. Governments tend to focus on the immediate cost impacts of funding new programs, as well as the financial liability they may face by setting a precedent for other funding requests. Individuals who seek to expand health care coverage often emphasize the wider cost savings that may result from funding a service, as well as psychological and social costs incurred when some groups are excluded from accessing an important benefit. In *Eldridge*, for example, the government focused on the expense of a medical sign language interpretation program, and was particularly concerned with the possible long-term financial impact of requests for language interpretation services by other groups.[119] However, the Supreme Court criticized the government for its lack of evidence to substantiate this speculative concern.[120]

Looking at the issue through a different cost lens, the claimants focused on the broader medical, social and psychological costs that could result from a failure to ensure deaf patients could communicate effectively with their health care practitioners. These include the risk of misdiagnosis, failure to follow a prescribed treatment, and feelings of fear, anxiety and exclusion that deaf patients may experience when they are unable to communicate effectively regarding their health care needs.[121]

Similarly, in *Auton*, the claimants and the government viewed the question of costs and benefits from very different perspectives. While the government argued it could not afford the cost of funding autism therapy, the parents argued the government could not afford *not* to fund it. Without appropriate therapy, the parents argued, many children with autism are likely to "drain" public resources for their entire lives by requiring state-funded income and housing assistance as adults. The trial judge accepted this reasoning, stating that "it is apparent that the costs incurred in paying for effective treatment of autism may well be more than offset by the savings achieved by assisting autistic children to develop their educational and societal potential rather than dooming them to a life of isolation

---

[117] *Wynberg v. Ontario*, [2006] O.J. No. 2732 (Ont. C.A.) at para. 169.

[118] *Ibid.*, at para. 184.

[119] *Eldridge v. British Columbia (Attorney General)*, [1992] B.C.J. No. 2229, 75 B.C.L.R. (2d) 68 (B.C.S.C.) at para. 22.

[120] *Eldridge v. British Columbia (Attorney General)*, [1997] S.C.J. No. 86, [1997] 3 S.C.R. 624 (S.C.C.) at paras. 92 and 94.

[121] *Ibid.*, at paras. 56, 57, 69.

and institutionalization".[122] The government also contended that the lack of empirical evidence proving the effectiveness of autism therapy also justified its funding refusal, but the trial judge rejected this argument: "the fact that autism can't be 'cured' is no reason to withhold treatment. Often cancer cannot be cured but it is unthinkable that treatment designed to ameliorate or delay its effects would not be forthcoming".[123]

Governments also often emphasize the broader tradeoffs or opportunity costs that are involved in choosing to fund one service over another. Justice Lambert's comments in *Eldridge*, excerpted at length earlier, clearly demonstrate the challenge in choosing among competing health funding priorities. In *Auton*, the trial judge noted that "[t]he Crown makes the irrefragable statement that its health care resources are limited and argues that the effect of funding treatment for autistic children would direct resources away from other children with special needs".[124] On appeal, the government argued further that:

> a decision in favour of the petitioners will impel the necessarily complex administrative choices required to be made in the course of balancing the myriad and competing demands for health care, into the courts for decision on the allocation of scarce resources on a case by case basis, rather than on a comprehensive and systematic basis.[125]

The last part of this statement — the reference to a comprehensive and systematic basis for making health care funding decisions — is significant.[126] Since courts must assess the justifiability of a governmental act that violates Charter rights, governments would do well to have evidence that their choice was based on a cogent analysis of costs and benefits, including immediate and long-term financial impacts, as well as broader social impacts of their policy decisions. This will not be an easy challenge to meet as it takes substantial resources — time, money, people — and expertise to evaluate the growing number of health interventions and technologies and make decisions about funding coverage.[127] The challenge of evaluating new treatments and therapies is especially daunting when one considers the lack of evidence to substantiate the benefit of many currently insured services:

---

[122] *Auton (Guardian ad litem of) v. British Columbia (Attorney General)*, [2000] B.C.J. No. 1547, 78 B.C.L.R. (3d) 55 (B.C.S.C.) at para. 147. However, after considering an economic cost-benefit analysis of the autism therapy tendered into evidence by the claimants, the trial judge opined (at para. 145) that "it is not possible to estimate accurately either the additional immediate costs of a treatment programme or the inevitable savings in the long run".

[123] *Ibid.*, at para. 136.

[124] *Ibid.*, at para. 145.

[125] *Auton (Guardian ad litem of) v. British Columbia (Attorney General)*, [2002] B.C.J. No. 2258, 6 B.C.L.R. (4th) 201 (B.C.C.A.) at para. 56.

[126] Greschner and Lewis make this observation: see Donna Greschner & Steven Lewis, "Medicare in the Courts: *Auton* and Evidence-Based Decision-Making" (2003) 82 Can. Bar Rev. 501.

[127] For an overview of some of the challenges associated with conducting economic evaluation and technology assessment in health care, see, *e.g.*, Commission on the Future of Health Care in Canada, *Influences on the "Health Care Technology Cost-Driver" Discussion Paper No. 14* by Steve Morgan & Jeremiah Hurley (Saskatoon: Commission on the Future of Health Care in Canada, 2002).

... a large proportion of health care interventions are innocent of any formal or scientific evaluation at all, not just of efficiency, but even of efficacy. It is remarkable, and may be without parallel in human activity, that so much effort and resources are devoted through public or private channels to health care whose effectiveness has not been conclusively demonstrated, at least for the purposes claimed, either in the setting of application or at all. Odd.[128]

XI. DECISION-MAKING CHALLENGES

The assertion that courts ought to defer to the policy choices of governments rests on the principle that democratically elected legislators are in the best position to consider various options and make decisions based on their expertise and ability to respond to the needs of the public that voted them into office. This argument, however, falls down in the health care context because a full legislative process, involving opportunities for public debate, input and consultation, is usually not employed to make health care policy choices.

The *Canada Health Act* sets out a requirement for provincial governments to publicly fund medically necessary hospital and physician services on a first-dollar basis in order to attract a federal contribution. However, decisions about what services to include and exclude from the definition of "medically necessary" (and thus from the Medicare basket) have typically been made through negotiation between provincial health ministries and provincial medical associations. The shortcoming of a decision-making process that is largely limited to input from physicians and health ministry officials is that, as Colleen Flood notes, it "rel[ies] upon governments to sufficiently represent public values, and for physicians to bring their technical expertise to the determination of what is 'medically necessary'".[129]

Eldridge provides an example of the somewhat *ad hoc* and variable way in which health care funding decisions may be made. In that case, the Western Institute for the Deaf and the Hard of Hearing, an organization that provided some medical interpreting services for deaf patients in the B.C. Lower Mainland, approached the provincial government for funding in 1989 and 1990.

---

[128] Robert Evans, *Strained Mercy: The Economics of Canadian Health Care* (Toronto: Butterworths, 1984) at 267. David Eddy provides some examples:

> New studies continually reveal that practices that were once accepted without doubt can turn out to be worthless or even harmful. We were wrong about diethylstilbestrol [DES], radical mastectomies, ... hormone replacement therapy for heart disease. ... Experts from top universities with the most experience testified under oath that high-dose chemotherapy for late-stage breast cancer would produce 20 to 30 percent long-term cure rates. Randomized controlled trials later proved them wrong.

David M. Eddy, "The Use of Evidence and Cost Effectiveness by the Courts: How Can It Help Improve Health Care?" (2001) 26 J. Health Pol. 387.

[129] Colleen M. Flood, "The Anatomy of Medicare" in Jocelyn Downie, Timothy Caulfield & Colleen Flood, eds., *Canadian Health Law and Policy*, 2nd ed. (Markham, ON: LexisNexis Butterworths, 2002) 1 at 23. See also Colleen M. Flood, Mark Stabile & Carolyn Hughes Tuohy, "The Borders of Solidarity: How Countries Determine the Public/Private Mix in Spending and the Impact on Health Care" (2002) 12 Health Matrix 297 at 303.

The first request was "declined out of hand"[130] but the second request was given some consideration by Ministry of Health staff. The trial judgment notes that the executive director who initially reviewed the funding request "was sympathetic to the request because he has an understanding of many of the problems encountered by the deaf through his experience with deaf people, including his deaf nine year old daughter".[131] He recommended that the Ministry ought to fund the program but the Ministry Executive Committee decided to reject the request because "... it was felt to fund this particular request would set a precedent that might be followed up by further requests from the ethnic communities where the language barrier might also be a factor".[132] The trial decision noted that "[i]f a declined request has sufficient merit in the opinion of a Ministry of Health representative, it will be reconsidered when the budget for the next fiscal year is being formulated"[133] but the Ministry did not reconsider the funding request for medical interpretation services. The description of this process in *Eldridge* highlights a somewhat crude method of decision-making process that appears to depend largely on chance (will the bureaucrat who initially reviews the request have sympathy because of personal experience?) and speculation (if the government approves this request, will the floodgates then open?).

Over a decade ago, the Canadian Bar Association Task Force on Health Care Reform addressed concerns with the process provincial governments use to allocate funding for health care services and advocated greater room for public discussion regarding these decisions:

> The impact of provincial health care resource allocation decisions is so important for all provincial residents that it would be desirable to have public input into these decisions. Currently, these decisions are vulnerable to attack because the lack of an open and consultative process leaves the public only one option — to protest resource allocation decisions after they have been made. This can lead to public outcries which cause the government to retreat from a decision — not a desirable way to make public policy.[134]

Regrettably, these comments remain true today.

Martha Jackman has gone so far as to suggest that principles of fundamental justice under section 7 of the Charter confer a right to "participate in health policy and resource allocation decisions not only at the level of individual service delivery, but also at the broader policy-making level".[135] For example, if a patient's personal security is threatened by a government funding decision that has the effect of denying needed care, and the patient has had no opportunity to

---

[130] *Eldridge v. British Columbia (Attorney General)*, [1992] B.C.J. No. 2229, 75 B.C.L.R. (2d) 68 (B.C.S.C.) at para. 21.

[131] *Ibid.*

[132] *Ibid.*, at para. 22. This quotation comes from an internal Ministry of Health memorandum that was entered into evidence at trial.

[133] *Ibid.*

[134] Canadian Bar Association Task Force on Health Care, *What's Law Got To Do With It? Health Care Reform in Canada* (Ottawa: Canadian Bar Association, 1994) at 101 [footnote omitted].

[135] Martha Jackman, "The Right to Participate in Health Care and Health Resource Allocation Decisions under Section 7 of the *Canadian Charter*" (1995/1996) 4 Health L. Rev. 3 at 7.

participate in the decision-making process, then Jackman posits that due process rights protected under section 7 are violated. She suggests:

> In the broader policy and regulatory setting, due process requirements can be met by ensuring that generalized decisions relating to health policy and the allocation of health care resources and services are publicly discussed and debated before their implementation. ... Possible mechanisms for implementing these due process guarantees include public hearings and other forms of public consultation on such matters as the ... development of treatment criteria, the design of rationing and cost containment mechanisms ... and in relation to the listing and delisting of services under government health insurance plans.[136]

Some jurisdictions, both in Canada and abroad, have made attempts to develop health care decision-making models to address some of these concerns. In 2002, the Alberta government established The Expert Advisory Panel to Review Publicly Funded Health Services to recommend procedures to base health funding decisions on criteria of transparency, rigor, openness and timeliness.[137] The Advisory Panel recommended the creation of a provincially appointed board, composed of five to nine members (including those with health care expertise as well as representatives of the public), that would review funding for existing and new services taking into account the following factors: safety; demonstrated benefits in treating or preventing health problems; impact of the funding decision on public access to the service; ethical concerns; impact of the funding decision on the health system; availability of other health care options; and financial costs and implications.[138] This review process would involve independent assessments by individuals with expertise in health technology assessment and other relevant fields, and would include opportunities for "stakeholder participation". However, the Alberta government ultimately rejected the Advisory Panel's recommendation to create a health service review board. In a news release, the government made a fuzzy commitment to strengthen "[e]xisting processes ... to improve the rigor and timeliness of decisions on whether or not to fund new services" and, revealing obvious concern that a new board might usurp power, stated that the government "will retain its authority to make decisions on whether or not to fund new procedures".[139]

Some international jurisdictions have implemented expert advisory bodies to provide governments with guidance on health funding decisions. In the United Kingdom, the National Institute of Clinical Excellence (NICE) is an independent

---

[136] *Ibid.*

[137] Alberta, Expert Advisory Panel to Review Publicly Funded Health Services, *The Burden of Proof: An Alberta Model for Assessing Publicly Funded Health Services* (Edmonton: Alberta Health and Wellness, 2003) at 5. The report describes the role of the panel as follows: "To review and make recommendations on public funding for the current basket of health services and to recommend an appraisal process for reviewing new and existing health services on an ongoing basis. The objective is to ensure that Alberta's publicly funded health services remain comprehensive and sustainable for the future, and provide the best value" (at 1).

[138] *Ibid.*, at 1, 9.

[139] See Government of Alberta, News Release, "Government funding right health services now, focus on new process for funding future services" (July 18, 2003).

body that advises the National Health Service regarding adoption of new therapies and makes clinical practice recommendations. If, through its review process, NICE determines that a particular treatment is recommended, the National Health Service must fund the therapy; similarly, NICE may review a new therapy and find that existing evidence does not support its adoption.[140] Its decisions are sometimes controversial, particularly when it reverses or modifies earlier decisions, as it did in 2006 regarding drugs for Alzheimer's disease. In 2001, NICE recommended that specific drugs be used to treat patients with mild and moderate Alzheimer-related dementia. However, in 2006, NICE released a revised guidance document indicating that the pharmaceuticals be used only for patients at moderate stages of the disease.[141] This announcement was met with immediate appeals by the Alzheimer's Society and other advocacy groups, several drug manufacturers, and professional bodies including the British Geriatrics Society.[142] This model of independent review of health services, which permits appeals of decisions, offers an example of a decision-making process that attempts to be more evidence-based, transparent and participatory.

XII. CONCLUSION

The Charter has now been part of the Canadian legal landscape for over 20 years, but its application in many areas of governmental action — especially public benefit programs such as health care — continues to be the topic of evolution and debate. Inevitably, Charter challenges in the health care context will involve a complex balancing of fundamental individual rights against (usually) pressing governmental objectives. Early cases like *Morgentaler* and *Rodriguez* addressed very controversial social issues, but within a sphere of government activity — criminal regulation — that is clearly subject to Charter review. Subsequent cases — exemplified by *Auton* and *Chaoulli* — have delved into contentious areas of resource allocation and the structure of the overall health care system, areas which are not as susceptible to resolution through constitutional litigation.

Nonetheless, Canadians who confront barriers in accessing care will continue to turn to courts for recourse and successful challenges may have dramatic implications for the structure and operation of our health care systems. The post-*Chaoulli* challenge to Alberta's legal restrictions on private health care signals further potential for greater private sector involvement where the public system fails to meet patient needs in a timely fashion. Importantly, the Alberta litigation also alleges the provincial government had a positive duty to fund a specific

---

[140] National Institute for Health and Clinical Excellence, *About NICE guidance: what does it mean for me?*, June 6, 2006, online: <http://www.nice.org.uk/page.aspx?o=AboutGuidance>.

[141] National Institute for Health and Clinical Excellence, Press Release, "Update on NICE guidance on the use of drugs to treat Alzheimer's disease" (May 26, 2006) online: <http://www. nice.org.uk/page.aspx?o=322974>.

[142] Zosia Kmietowicz, "NICE hears appeals over dementia drugs" (2006) 333 British Medical Journal 165.

therapy for the claimant, a 57-year-old man who was denied a recommended hip surgery because the Health Ministry deemed him too old.

In *Auton* and *Wynberg*, Canadian courts show increasing reticence to accept section 15 Charter challenges regarding public funding decisions. Since *Auton* seems to preclude further litigation regarding so-called "non-core" services, future cases will likely examine the constitutionality of targeted health care programs that limit access to specific patient groups. The Supreme Court's dissension in *Chaoulli* leaves much scope for future cases to test the boundaries of section 7 rights in the context of access to health care. The Alberta case represents a critical opportunity for courts to address these issues, though protracted appeals can be anticipated, especially since the claimant is supported by the Canadian Constitution Foundation, an advocacy organization that helps "fund, co-ordinate or otherwise assist litigation necessary to protect the Constitution from existing and potential abuse".[143]

It is not just patients who initiate Charter challenges; well-resourced corporations may also litigate the constitutionality of health-related legislation. In December 2005, CanWest Mediaworks, Canada's largest media conglomerate, launched a Charter attack arguing that federal law that limits direct-to-consumer advertising of prescription drugs violates constitutional rights to free expression.[144] If advertising restrictions are struck down and direct-to-consumer marketing becomes prevalent, drug-related health care costs may balloon due to increased volume of prescribing and additional physician visits. This is but another example of how emerging Charter litigation may have dramatic influence on resource allocation within our health care system.

While "[t]here may have been a time when it was believed that a commitment to provide the best health care available at whatever cost was all that was needed to make it a reality",[145] that idealistic scenario no longer exists. Although our health care system may be comprehensive in the sense it covers more than strictly basic care, it does not promise an "unconstrained right to healthcare services, except within available resources".[146] This view is echoed in the Romanow Commission Report on the Future of Health Care in Canada where it is noted that comprehensiveness is "not so much ... a description of existing coverage [within the Medicare system], but [is] a continuing goal".[147] Indeed, the report states that the gap between services that are covered and those that could be covered to create a more comprehensive system "exists in the first place because of the impossibility of the public purse covering all health services

[143] See Canadian Constitution Foundation website, "Vision Statement", online: <http://canadianconstitutionfoundation.ca>.

[144] For commentary on the litigation, see, *e.g.*, Women and Health Protection, *Canwest's Charter Challenge on Prescription Drug Advertising: A Citizens' Guide* (June 2006) online: http://www.whp-apsf.ca/pdf/charter_challenge_en.pdf and Alicia Priest, "CanWest set to challenge ban on DTCA" (2007) 176:1 C.M.A.J.19.

[145] Rino A. Stradiotto & Jacinthe I. Boudreau, "Resource Allocation and Accountability in Health Care" (2000) 20 Health L. Can. 40 at 51.

[146] Pranlal Manga, "Medicare: ethics versus economics" (1987) 136 Can. Med. Assoc. J. 113.

[147] Commission on the Future of Health Care in Canada, *Building on Values: The Future of Health Care in Canada — Final Report* (Saskatoon: Commission on the Future of Health Care in Canada, 2002) (Commissioner: Roy J. Romanow, Q.C.) at 62.

immediately. Financial probity requires that services be added as fiscal resources permit".[148]

Canadian courts recognize the difficult task legislators face in allocating scarce resources and in regulating the health care system to safeguard the fundamental principles on which Medicare is built. Nonetheless, judges hesitate to accept cost constraints as a sole justification for limiting individual rights; as the Supreme Court of Canada did not address the section 1 analysis in *Auton*, questions remain about how significant a cost impact must be before a government is justified in limiting funding for a "core" medical service. The differing reasons in *Chaoulli* highlight enduring institutional tensions between courts and legislators over the appropriateness of judicial deference to government policy choices. Some Supreme Court rulings have been very critical of "theoretical contentions"[149] and "purely speculative"[150] arguments advanced by governments to justify limits on Charter rights. If a government finds itself in a courtroom defending health care policy choices, it would do well to have solid evidence to substantiate its position; indeed, improved decision-making processes may help avoid journeys to judges' chambers in the first place.

Where does the future of health care lie in Canada and how will the current state of Charter jurisprudence influence health policy changes? Without doubt, the Supreme Court dismissal of *Auton* led to a collective sigh of relief among Canadian health ministers and bureaucrats who are ever concerned with cost pressures and the spectre of courts instructing governments that they have a constitutional obligation to fund specific services. The *Chaoulli* result, in contrast, has instigated serious discussions about fundamental health system reforms to permit and promote greater private sector involvement. Politicians remain careful to emphasize the foundational principles of the *Canada Health Act*, but some question the sustainability of clinging to publicly funded health care as a symbol of Canadian identity.[151] Contenders vying for leadership of the federal Liberal party in late 2006 "don't appear averse to some measure of privatization, or other forms of systemic change, although they're still quick to sing from the same hymnal the Liberal choir has used for decades to cast the party as the great defender of a universal, single-payer medicare system".[152] In British Columbia, the provincial government launched a consultation exercise to solicit public views about health care via website, telephone, and community

---

[148] *Ibid.*, at 63.

[149] *Chaoulli v. Quebec (Attorney General)*, [2005] S.C.J. No. 33, [2005] 1 S.C.R. 791 (S.C.C.) at para. 149.

[150] *Eldridge v. British Columbia (Attorney General)*, [1997] S.C.J. No. 86, [1997] 3 S.C.R. 624 (S.C.C.) at para. 89.

[151] In an analysis of Canadian newspaper editorials following the *Chaoulli* decision, several commentators from McGill University found that an association between Medicare and Canadian identity "was unexpectedly used most by those who favoured private health insurance, as an example of an empty and obsolete argument that should be discounted". Amélie Quesnel-Vallée *et al.*, "In the aftermath of *Chaoulli v. Quebec*: Whose opinion prevailed?" (2006) 175:9 Canadian Medical Association Journal 1051 at 1052.

[152] Wayne Kondro, "Liberal musings on health care" (2006) 175:10 Canadian Medical Association Journal 1189.

fora. The "Conversation on Health"[153] invites citizens to comment on five health care questions raised in the provincial Throne Speech in February 2006, including: "Why are we so afraid to look at mixed health care delivery models, when other states in Europe and around the world have used them to produce better results for patients at a lower cost to taxpayers?" and "How should we define concepts like 'reasonable access' to 'medically necessary' services, so that the courts are not left to interpret them for us?"[154] These provocative questions insinuate policy directions the B.C. government may pursue. And while other provinces consider reform, Quebec's Bill 33, legislation developed in response to the *Chaoulli* decision, proposes to permit private insurance for joint replacement and cataract surgery, as well as establish care guarantees to ensure timely access to those same services in the public system.[155]

Health professional groups in Canada are divided on the course health care reform should take. At its 2006 General Council meeting, the Canadian Medical Association adopted resolutions aimed at strengthening the public system (such as articulating "pan-Canadian, medically determined wait-time benchmarks for all major diagnostic, therapeutic, surgical and emergency services") while also supporting increased private funding and service delivery (such as removing "existing bans that prevent physicians from practising in both the private and public sectors where such a restriction exists").[156] At the same time, the Canadian Federation of Nurses Unions and the Canadian Health Coalition have launched the "Medicare Works" campaign to defend the public system.[157]

Charter litigation can be a tremendously powerful force to effect changes in health law and policy in Canada. Supreme Court of Canada rulings — whether unanimous victories, defeats, or divided decisions — have reverberations through law, politics and society. If, in five years or so, some Canadians regularly obtain services in a private, parallel tier of health care (while others continue to wait in public queues), we will look back to *Chaoulli* as a key precipitator of that historic shift in the Canadian health care system, for better or for worse.

---

[153] See online: <www.bcconversationonhealth.ca> for further information. The Conversation on Health was launched on September 28, 2006.

[154] See "Conversation on Health Weekly Report, September 28, 2006 to October 9, 2006, online: <www.bcconversationonhealth.ca/media/WhatBritishColumbiansAreSayingReport228Septto9Oct.pdf>.

[155] *An Act to amend the Act respecting health services and and social services and other legislative provisions*, S.Q. 2006, c. 43, online: <http://www2.publicationsduquebec.gouv.qc.ca/home.php#>.

[156] See Barbara Sibbald, "CMA's direction on the public-private interface" (2006) 175:9 Canadian Medical Association Journal 1047.

[157] See online: <www.healthcoalition.ca/medicareworks> for more information.

INDEX

**END OF LIFE DECISION-
MAKING** — *cont'd*
• double effect principle, 474–475
• euthanasia, 473–474
• evaluation of likelihood of criminal
prosecution, 476
• generally, 468–469
• prosecutorial discretion, 475
disability equality perspective, 452
family disagreement, 449–453
futility debates
• Canada, developments in, 459–465
• England, developments in, 457–459
• generally, 456–457
• United States, developments in,
457–459
minors, 453–455
organ donation after cardiac death,
465–467
pain and symptom control in
palliative care, 455–456
refusal of treatment by substitute
decision-makers, 448–449, 456–
465
withholding and withdrawing life-
sustaining treatment
• decisionally capable patients
• • adults, 439–441
• • limitations, 445
• • mature minors, 441–445
• decisionally incapable patients
• • patients with advance directives,
445–447
• • patients without advance directives, 446–448

**ENFORCEMENT OF CANADA
HEALTH ACT**
federal enforcement, 47–49
judicial enforcement, 50–59

**ENVIRONMENTAL TOBACCO
SMOKE,** 502–504

EQUALITY RIGHTS, 428–429,
434, 549–554

ERROR OF JUDGMENT, 111–115

**ESTABLISHED PROGRAM
FINANCING (EPF) SYSTEM,**
28–29

ETHICS REVIEW, 262–264

EUROPEAN UNION, 255

EUTHANASIA, 473–474

EVERGREENING, 352–353

EXCEPTIONAL TREATMENT,
420

EXTERNAL ASSESSMENT, 76–
77

**EXTRACONTRACTUAL
RELATIONSHIP,** 145–147

FAULT, 137–140

FEDERAL GOVERNMENT
see also GOVERNMENT;
LEGISLATION
constitutional jurisdiction, 25–26
enforcement of *Canada Health Act*,
47–49
pharmaceutical regulation, 319

**FEDERATION OF MEDICAL
REGULATORY
AUTHORITIES OF CANADA
(FMRAC),** 96

**FEE-FOR-SERVICE
COMPENSATION,** 19–20, 44

FETAL PATIENTS, 106

FINANCING. *See* HEALTH CARE
FINANCING

FIRST NATIONS, 7–8

HEALTH INFORMATION — *cont'd*
• research, 251–253
oversight, 253–254
ownership, 226–227
use
• consensual, 241–242
• non-consensual, 242–253

HEALTH INFORMATION ACT (ALTA.), 233, 238–239, 254

HEALTH INFORMATION PROTECTION ACT (SASK.), 242

HEALTH INSURANCE
administrative tribunals, 40–41
private insurance, 18–20
public administration criteria, 36

HEALTH INSURANCE ACT (QUE.), 556

HEALTH PRODUCTS AND FOODS BRANCH (HPFB), 319, 320, 321, 326, 361

HEALTH PROFESSIONALS. *See* HEALTH CARE PROFESSIONALS

HEALTH PROFESSIONS ACT (ALTA.), 84, 86, 87–88, 89

HEALTH PROFESSIONS ACT (B.C.), 84–85, 89, 91, 92, 93, 98

HEALTH PROFESSIONS PROCEDURAL CODE (ONT.), 84, 86

HEALTH PROTECTION AND PROMOTION ACT, 485

HEALTH QUALITY COUNCILS, 76–77

HEALTH RECORDS. *See* HEALTH INFORMATION

HEALTH REFORM FUND, 31

HEALTH TECHNOLOGIES. *See* EMERGING HEALTH TECHNOLOGIES

HEARSAY RULE, 246

HELP-SEEKING, 333

HISTORICAL PERSPECTIVE
pharmaceutical regulation, 314–319
regulation of health professionals, 83
single-payer system, development of, 27–30

HOSPITAL INSURANCE AND DIAGNOSTIC SERVICES ACT, 27

HOSPITALS
duty of care, 105
error of judgment, 113–114
independent contractors, 130
institutional negligence
• direct liability, 130–131
• vicarious liability, 129–130
vicarious liability, 105, 129–130

HUMAN BIOMEDICAL RESEARCH
civil liability for injuries, 306–309
clinical practice, vs., 259–261
regulation
• generally, 261–262
• overview of principal regulatory instruments
• • clinical trial regulations under *Food and Drugs Act*, 264–266
• • Good Clinical Practice: Consolidated Guidelines, 264–266
• • international instruments, 267–268
• • other Canadian regulatory instruments, 268–269
• • Quebec, 266